EIGHTH
CANADIAN
EDITION

BUSINESS

RICKY W. GRIFFIN
TEXAS A & M UNIVERSITY

RONALD J. EBERT
UNIVERSITY OF MISSOURI-COLUMBIA

FREDERICK A. STARKE
UNIVERSITY OF MANITOBA

GEORGE DRACOPOULOS
VANIER COLLEGE

MELANIE D. LANG
UNIVERSITY OF GUELPH

PEARSON

Toronto

To Ann, Eric, and Grant — F. A. S.
This book is dedicated to our beautiful newborn son, Costa
Dean, from his adoring parents — G.D. and N.D.
For Paul, Hannah, and Beth — M. D. L

Vice-President, Editorial Director: Gary Bennett
Editor-in-Chief: Nicole Lukach
Acquisitions Editor: Nick Durie
Marketing Manager: Leigh-Anne Graham
Developmental Editor: Suzanne Simpson Millar
Project Manager: Jessica Hellen
Manufacturing Specialist: Jane Schell
Production Editor: GEX Publishing Services
Copy Editor: Jennifer McIntyre
Proofreader: Sally Glover
Compositor: GEX Publishing Services
Photo and Permissions Researcher: PreMediaGlobal
Art Director: Miguel Acevedo
Cover and Interior Designer: Opus House / Sonya Thursby
Cover Image: Getty Images/Gregor Schuster

Credits and acknowledgments of material borrowed from other sources and reproduced, with permission, in this textbook appear on the appropriate page within the text and on p. N-1.

If you purchased this book outside the United States or Canada, you should be aware that it has been imported without the approval of the publisher or author.

10 9 8 7 6 5 4 3 2 1   [CKV]

Library and Archives Canada Cataloguing in Publication

Business / Ricky W. Griffin ... [et al.]. – 8th Canadian ed.

Includes bibliographical references and indexes.
ISBN 978-0-13-272199-8

1. Industrial management–Textbooks. 2. Business enterprises–Textbooks. 3. Industrial management–Canada–Textbooks. 4. Business enterprises–Canada–Textbooks. I. Griffin, Ricky W

HD31.B84 2013   658   C2012-904920-4

ISBN 978-0-13-272199-8

Overview

Contents

Preface

If you're like many students, you may be starting this term with some questions about why you're here. You may be taking this course at a community college or at a university, and you may be taking it in a traditional classroom setting or online. Whatever the case, you may be wondering just what you're supposed to get from this course and how it will benefit you. In short, you may be wondering, "How will this help me?"

This is a survey course designed to introduce you to the exciting and challenging world of business, both in Canada and elsewhere. The course is designed to fit the needs of a wide variety of students. You may be taking this course as the first step toward earning a degree in business, or you may be thinking about business and want to know more about it, or you may know you want to study business but are unsure of the area you want to pursue. You may plan to major in another field but want some basic business background and are taking this course as an elective. Or you may be here because this course is required or is a prerequisite for another course. Whatever your situation, this course will be helpful to you.

If you don't have a lot of work experience, you may be uncertain as to what the business world is all about. If you have a lot of work experience, you might be a bit skeptical as to what you can actually learn about business from an introductory course. One of our biggest challenges as authors is to write a book that meets the needs of such a diverse student population, especially when we acknowledge the legitimacy of your right to ask, "How will this help me?" We also want to do our best to ensure that you find the course challenging, interesting, and useful. To achieve this goal, we think it is helpful to use the old metaphor about people wearing different "hats" as they go through life. Each individual has different roles to play in different settings. For example, your roles may include student, child, spouse, employee, friend, and/or parent. You can think of each of these roles as needing a different hat—when you play the role of a student, for example, you wear one hat, but when you leave campus and go to your part-time job, you put on a different hat. From the perspective of studying and interfacing with the world of *business*, there are at least four distinct "hats" that you might wear:

- *The Employee Hat.* One hat is "worn" as an employee working for a business. Most people wear this hat throughout their working career. To wear the hat successfully, you will need to understand your "place" in the organization—your job duties and responsibilities, how to get along with others, how to work with your boss, what your organization is all about, and so on. You'll begin to see how best to wear this hat as you learn more about organizing business enterprises in Chapter 7 and how organizations manage their human resources in Chapter 8, as well as in several other places in this book.

- *The Employer or Boss Hat.* Another business hat that many people wear is as an employer or boss. Whether you start your own business or get promoted within someone else's business, people will be working for you. You'll still need to know your job duties and responsibilities, but you'll also need to understand how to manage other people—how to motivate and reward them, how to lead them, how to deal with conflict among them, and the legal parameters that may affect how you treat them. Chapters 3, 6, 9, and 10 provide a lot of information about how you can best wear this hat, although information about the role of employer is found throughout the book.

- *The Consumer Hat.* Even if you don't work for a business, you will still wear the hat of a consumer. Whenever you fill your car with PetroCanada gasoline, bid for something on eBay, buy clothes at Urban Outfitters, or download a song from iTunes, you're consuming products or services created by businesses. To wear this hat effectively, you need to understand how to assess the value of what you're buying, your rights as a consumer, and so on. We discuss how you can best wear this hat in Chapters 2, 15, 16, and 17.

- *The Investor Hat.* The final business hat many people wear is that of an investor. You may buy your own business or work for a company that allows you to buy its stock. You may also invest in other companies through the purchase of stocks or shares of a mutual fund. In order for you to invest wisely, you must understand some basics, such as financial markets, business earnings, and the costs of investment. Chapters 4, 18, 19, 20, and Appendix B will help you learn how to best wear this hat.

Most people wear more than one of these hats at the same time. Regardless of how many hats you wear or when you may be putting them on, you will interface with many different businesses in different ways. Knowing how to best wear all of these hats is what this book is all about.

The world is populated with a breathtaking array of businesses and business opportunities. Big and small businesses, established and new businesses, broad-based and niche businesses, successful and unsuccessful businesses, global and domestic businesses—regardless of where your future plans take you, we hope that you will look back on this course as one of your positive first steps.

Keep in mind that what you get out of this course depends on at least three factors. One factor is this book and the information about business that you will acquire as a result of reading it. Another factor is your instructor, who is a dedicated professional who wants to help you grow and develop intellectually and academically. The third factor is YOU. Learning is an active process that requires you to be a major participant. Simply memorizing the key terms and concepts in this book may help you achieve an acceptable course grade, but true learning requires that you read, study, discuss, question, review, experience, evaluate—and wear the four hats—as you go along. Tests and homework are necessary, but we hope that you will finish this course with new knowledge and increased enthusiasm for the world of business. Your instructor will do his or her part to facilitate your learning. The rest, then, is up to you. We wish you success.

What's New to the Eighth Canadian Edition

In this, the eighth Canadian edition of *Business*, we continue to emphasize our long-standing principle of *"Doing the Basics Best."* Cutting-edge firsts, up-to-date issues that shape today's business world, and creative pedagogy help students build a solid foundation of business knowledge. This new edition continues with the strengths that made the first seven editions so successful—comprehensiveness, accuracy, currency, and readability.

The eighth Canadian edition of *Business* incorporates many of the changes suggested by professors and students who used the seventh edition, as well as changes suggested by reviewers. The following new material has been included:

- Many new examples of business practice have been included in each of the chapters. Some of these examples are brief and some are more detailed, but they all help students to better understand business practice. For example, in Chapter 9, several important labour-relations concepts such as mediation and arbitration are explained by describing their use in the recent labour dispute between Air Canada and its unions. In Chapter 3, the problem of counterfeit goods is described, and examples are provided to show how these goods have had a negative impact on both businesses and consumers. In Chapter 1, the debate about Canadian content in the media is noted, as well as the difficulty the CRTC has had in dealing with the regulation of internet broadcasting. These are just a few of the hundreds of examples that are included in the text.

- The impact of the aftermath of one of the most significant economic events of the past 80 years—the financial crisis of 2008—is examined in several different chapters of the text. For example, in Chapter 20, the ongoing sovereign debt crisis in Europe is examined, including the worldwide impact it is having on consumer expectations and on business activity. Concluding Case 19-2 describes the ups and downs of the world's stock markets during the past decade, and explains how this volatility has created low returns and investment dilemmas for investors. The impact of the financial crisis on business firms is also analyzed in many other places in the text.

- Two new boxed insert series are included in this eighth edition. The first—called "Managing in Turbulent Times"—describes how Canadian business firms are coping in the often volatile and uncertain economic environment that has developed during the past few years. For example, the insert in Chapter 12 describes how global supply chains were disrupted as a result of the Japanese earthquake in 2011. The second new boxed series—called "E-business and Social Media Solutions"—describes how rapidly changing technology has provided business firms with many new ways to connect with customers, and how new technologies have given customers a level of control over businesses that they did not previously have. For example, the insert in Chapter 13 describes how social media communication can help or hurt a company's reputation with customers.

- Two other boxed insert series that appeared in the seventh edition—"The Greening of Business" and "Entrepreneurship and New Ventures"—have been retained, but the material in all of these boxes is either new or updated. For example, in Chapter 3, a new "Greening of Business" box describes the difficulties consumers have in determining what product labels actually mean, and whether product claims about being environmentally friendly are really accurate. In Chapter 10, a new "Entrepreneurship and New Ventures" box describes how Netflix motivates employees by satisfying their needs.

- Approximately 90% of the opening cases, boxed inserts, end-of-chapter cases, and video cases are either new or updated. Much of this new material focuses on how the business environment is changing, and the challenges and opportunities that such change presents. For example, in Chapter 1, a new opening case describes the dramatic changes that are occurring in the mobile phone market, and how these changes have benefited some companies and presented major problems for others. In Chapter 11, Concluding Case 11-1 describes how certain changes that have occurred during the past few years (for example, the rise in the Canadian dollar) have caused problems in Canada's manufacturing sector. In Chapter 16, Concluding Case 16-1 describes how changes in requirements about information sharing regarding homes that are available for sale have shaken up the real estate industry.

- Two new video cases are included at the end of each of the five major sections of the text.

- Five comprehensive case are included in Appendix C, all of which are new to this edition. These cases are more detailed than the end-of-chapter cases, and they provide students with more extensive information to consider as they analyze the case material and make recommendations about how to resolve the problems presented in the cases.

Major Themes

Six major themes are evident in this new edition: (1) change, (2) business in a global context, (3) ethics and social responsibility, (4) small business, (5) information technology, and (6) the quality imperative. Students need to understand these themes since their careers in business will be significantly affected by them.

The Theme of Change

The dramatic changes that have been occurring in business practice during the past decade continue apace, and these changes have been complicated by the uncertain and volatile business environment that has developed during the past few years. The development of new business processes, new products, and new services all make the study of change in business exciting and necessary. New ways of doing things are replacing traditional business practices, usually with surprising speed and often with better competitive results. As authors, we have tried to communicate the theme of change by describing how real-world business firms cope with planned and unplanned events that test the mettle of managers. The boxed insert series entitled "Managing in Turbulent Times" focuses on the issue of how managers deal with change.

The Globalization of Business

The globalization of business is one of the dominant challenges of the twenty-first century. To demonstrate the salience of this challenge, we've included many examples and cases that describe the experiences of Canadian companies in the global market-place. We also describe how global companies have impacted the domestic Canadian market. In addition to these examples—which are found throughout the text—we devote an entire chapter to international business (Chapter 5, The Global Context of Business). We also examine the role of the traditional global economic powers as well as the emerging markets. A key spotlight is placed on the BRICS nations: Brazil, Russia, India, China and South Africa.

The Role of Ethics and Social Responsibility

During the past decade, the topics of business ethics and social responsibility have generated a sharply increased level of discussion and debate as a result of the often questionable behaviour of managers at companies like Livent, News Corp., and Barclay's Bank. In spite of the highly publicized misbehaviour of executives early in the twenty-first century, new cases have appeared with disturbing regularity. We therefore devote an entire chapter to the discussion of business ethics and social responsibility issues (Chapter 3, Conducting Business Ethically and Responsibly). Ethical issues are also raised in many other chapters of the text, and a team ethics exercise is found at the end of each chapter.

The Significance of Small Business

College and university graduates will develop careers in both large and small businesses. We have therefore provided coverage of both large and small companies throughout the text. For those students who are interested in a career in small business, we discuss the implications of various ideas. As well, a major section in Chapter 4 (Understanding Entrepreneurship, Small Business, and New Venture Creation) is devoted to small business and new business start-ups. The boxed series entitled "Entrepreneurship and New Ventures" gives additional information about small business activity in Canada.

Rapid Changes in Information Technology

In our information-based society, the people and organizations that learn how to obtain and use information will be the ones that succeed. The explosive growth and change in these systems is recognized as we provide a complete chapter dealing with the management of information (Chapter 13, Managing Information Systems and Communication Technology). The boxed insert series called "E-business and Social Media Solutions" also focuses on the impact of information technology on businesses and their employees.

The Quality Imperative

Because quality and productivity have become the keys to competitive success for companies in the global marketplace, we devote a full chapter to coverage of these two important topics (Chapter 12, Increasing Productivity and Quality).

Major Features of the Text

The text contains the following features to stimulate student interest in, and understanding of, the material that is presented about business.

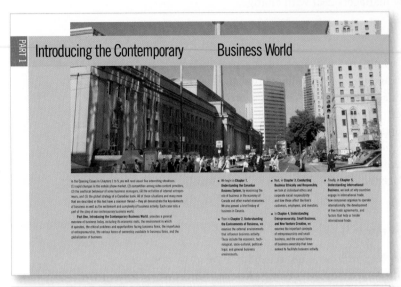

Part Opener

At the beginning of each of the five major parts of the book is a brief outline introducing the material that will be discussed in that part. These outlines give students a glimpse of the "big picture" as they start reading about a new area of the business world.

Chapter Materials

Each chapter contains several features that are designed to increase student interest in, and understanding of, the material being presented. These features are as follows:

Chapter learning objectives. A list of numbered learning objectives is presented at the beginning of each chapter. These objectives—which guide students in determining what is important in each chapter—are also referenced in the margins opposite the relevant content in the chapter.

Chapter opening case. Each chapter begins with a description of a situation that is faced by a real Canadian or international company. The subject matter of the opening case is relevant to the material presented in the chapter, and therefore helps students bridge the gap between theory and practice.

Boxed inserts. The text contains four series of boxed inserts that are positioned at strategic points in the chapters. The first series—which is brand-new to this edition—is entitled "E-business and Social Media Solutions." It describes how rapidly changing technology has provided business firms with many new ways to connect with customers, and how new technologies have given customers a level of control over businesses that they did not previously have. The second series—also brand-new to this edition—is entitled "Managing in Turbulent Times." These inserts describe how businesses in Canada and elsewhere are trying to cope with the volatility and uncertainty that exists in the aftermath of the financial crisis of 2008. The third series—entitled "Entrepreneurship and New Ventures"—provides new, real-life examples of entrepreneurs who saw an opportunity to provide a new product or service in the marketplace, and the activities they carried out in order to be successful. The fourth series—entitled "The Greening of Business"—analyzes the steps that businesses are taking to be more environmentally friendly. These inserts identify both the opportunities and challenges that businesses encounter as they try to be socially responsible.

Examples.   In addition to the boxed inserts, each chapter contains numerous examples of how businesses operate so that students can gain a better understanding of the dynamics of business practice in both Canada and elsewhere. These examples—which range in length from one sentence to several paragraphs—help students understand concepts that are discussed in the text.

Figures and tables.   The latest available data appear in tables and figures throughout the text.

End-of-Chapter Materials

Several important pedagogical features are found at the end of each chapter. These are designed to help students better understand the contents of the chapter.

Summary of learning objectives.   The material in each chapter is concisely summarized, using the learning objectives as the organizing scheme. This helps students understand the main points that were presented in the chapter.

Key terms.   In each chapter, the key terms that students should know are highlighted in the text, defined in the margin, and listed alphabetically at the end of the chapter (with page references).

Questions and exercises.   There are two types of questions here: *analysis questions* (which require students to think beyond simple factual recall and apply the concepts they have read about), and *application exercises* (which ask students to apply what they have learned). These exercises—which are designed to help students to increase their understanding of how business firms actually operate—require students to engage in practical activities such as interviewing managers about concepts and issues that are discussed in the chapter.

Building your business skills exercise. This feature asks students to examine some specific aspect of business in detail.

The exercise may ask students to work individually or in a group to gather data about an interesting business issue, and then develop a written report or a class presentation based on the information that was gathered. Each exercise begins with a list of goals, a description of the situation, a step-by-step methodology for proceeding, and follow-up questions to help students focus their responses to the challenge.

Exercising your ethics: team exercise. A team ethics exercise describes a situation that contains an ethical dilemma. Students are then asked several questions that focus on how to approach and resolve the dilemma. In the exercise, students take on the role of employee, owner, customer, or investor and examine a chapter-related business ethics dilemma through the perspective of that role. By working together as a team, students learn how to co-operate with each other, see an ethical dilemma from various points of view, and decide what outcome is ultimately best in each situation.

Concluding cases. Each chapter concludes with two case studies that focus on real Canadian or international companies. These cases are designed to help students apply the chapter material to a real company that is currently in the news. At the end of each case, several questions guide students in their analysis.

End-of-Part Material

Video cases. Two new video cases are presented at the end of each of the five major parts of the text. The instructor can show the video in class and then either conduct a class discussion using the questions at the end of the written case summary as a guide, or ask students to complete a written assignment that requires answering the questions at the end of the case. This approach to teaching adds a major new dynamic to classes because students will be able to relate text material to actual Canadian business situations. These video cases are also available on the Companion Website for *Business*, Eighth Canadian edition.

Crafting a Business Plan. The business plan project is tailor-made to match and reinforce book content. It is *software-independent* and provides students with an easy-to-understand template that they work from as they create their business plans. The business plan project is divided into logical sections, and each part (e.g., marketing, production, finance, etc.) is located at the end of the section where that material is covered. With five parts in all, students can gradually apply the concepts they've learned in the chapters to their business plans throughout the course.

Appendices

There are three appendices found at the end of the text.

Appendix A—Business Law.   The material on business law includes key topics such as contracts, the concept of agency, warranties, and bankruptcy.

Appendix B—Managing Your Personal Finances.   This feature has been overwhelmingly requested by students and instructors, and presents a down-to-earth, hands-on approach that will help students manage their personal finances. The practical information found in this feature includes a worksheet for determining net worth, insightful examples demonstrating the time value of money, a method for determining how much to invest now in order to build a future nest egg of a certain size, suggestions on how to manage credit card debt, guidelines for purchasing a house, and a personalized worksheet for setting financial goals. The information contained in this feature will be immensely useful to students.

Appendix C—Supplementary Case Studies.   Five supplementary cases are presented for student consideration. These cases are longer than the end-of-chapter cases, and they raise several issues that are important for beginning business students to consider. These cases further build students' analytical skills and help them understand the complexities of the modern business world. Specific questions are provided at the end of each case for instructors who wish to direct student attention to certain problems. Other instructors may wish to use a more general approach that simply asks students to define the problem, develop alternatives, analyze the alternatives, and choose the best one.

Supplementary Materials

MyBizLab (**www.mybizlab.com**) is an online grading, assessment, and study tool for faculty and students. It engages students and helps them focus on what they need to study. It can help students get a better grade because they are learning in an interactive and focused environment. MyBizLab delivers all classroom resources for instructors and students in one place. All resources are organized by learning objective so that lectures and studying can be customized more conveniently than ever before.

MyBizLab

For Instructors

Instructor's Resource Centre.   Instructor resources are password protected and available for download via **http://catalogue.pearsoned.ca**. For your convenience, these resources are also available online at **www.mybizlab.com** in the instructor area.

MyTest.   MyTest from Pearson Canada is a powerful online assessment-generation program that helps instructors easily create and print quizzes, tests, and exams, as well as homework or practice handouts. Questions and tests can all be authored online, allowing instructors ultimate flexibility and the ability to efficiently manage assessments at any time, from anywhere. The testbank is also available in Word format as a Test Item File that can be downloaded from the Instructor's Resource Centre.

Instructor's Resource Manual.   The Instructor's Resource Manual contains chapter synopses, detailed outlines, questions to ask students, in-class exercises, teaching tips, and suggestions on how to use the text and boxed material effectively. The manual also provides answers to the end-of-chapter questions and cases (including Questions for Analysis, Application Exercises, Building Your Business Skills, Exercising Your Ethics, Concluding Cases, and Video Cases).

PowerPoint® Presentations.   PowerPoint Presentations offer an average of about 30 PowerPoint slides per chapter, outlining the key points in the text. The slides include lecture notes that provide page references to the text, summaries, and suggestions for student activities or related questions from the text.

CBC Video Library.   The CBC Video Library for *Business,* Eighth Canadian Edition, includes 11 segments from CBC programs that accompany the video cases found at the end of each part in the text. These cases focus on Canadian companies and discuss business issues from a Canadian point of view. The cases can be viewed online at **www.pearsoned.ca/highered/videocentral**, and answers to the discussion questions are provided in the Instructor's Resource Manual. (Please contact your Pearson Canada sales representative for details.)

Pearson Custom Publishing.   Pearson Custom Publishing can provide you and your students with texts, cases, and articles to enhance your course. Choose material from Darden, Ivey, Harvard Business School Publishing, NACRA, and Thunderbird to create your own custom casebook. Contact your Pearson Canada sales representative for details.

Online Learning Solutions.   Pearson Canada supports instructors interested in using online course management systems. We provide text-related content in Blackboard/WebCT and Course Compass. To find out more about creating an online course using Pearson content in one of these platforms, contact your Pearson Canada sales representative.

Your Pearson Canada Inc. Sales Representative.   Your Pearson sales rep is always available to ensure you have everything you need to teach a winning course. Armed with experience, training, and product knowledge, your Pearson rep will support your assessment and adoption of any of the products, services, and technology outlined here to ensure our offerings are tailored to suit your individual needs and the needs of your students. Whether it's getting instructions on assessment software or specific content files for your new online course, your Pearson sales representative is there to help. Ask your Pearson sales representative for details.

Technology Specialists.   Pearson's Technology Specialists work with faculty and campus course designers to ensure that Pearson technology products, assessment tools, and online course materials are tailored to meet your specific needs. This highly qualified team is dedicated to helping schools take full advantage of a wide range of educational resources by assisting in the integration of a variety of instructional materials and media formats. Your local Pearson Canada sales representative can provide you with more details on this service program.

CourseSmart.   CourseSmart is a new way for instructors and students to access textbooks online anytime from anywhere. With thousands of titles across hundreds of courses, CourseSmart helps instructors choose the best textbook for their class and give their students a new option for buying the assigned textbook as a lower cost etextbook. For more information, visit www.coursesmart.com.

For Students

MyBizLab

MyBizLab (**www.mybizlab.com**) is an online grading, assessment, and study tool for both faculty and students. It generates a personalized study plan that focuses students on what they, individually, need to study. It engages students through and interactive and focused environment. All resources are organized by learning objective so that studying can be customized more conveniently than ever before.

Crafting a Business Plan.   A completely rewritten business plan project, tailor-made to match and reinforce book content, appears at the end of each major section of the book. This new business plan project is *software-independent* and provides students with an easy-to-understand template that they work from as they create their business plans.

ACKNOWLEDGMENTS

We owe special thanks to Jennifer McIntrye for her excellent copyediting; Sally Glover, for her careful proofreading; Melinda McLaughlin, Production Editor, for her efficient management of this project; and Kerri Wilson for her fine photo research. Thanks are also due to Nick Durie, Acquisitions Editor; Suzanne Simpson Millar, Developmental Editor; Leigh-Anne Graham, Marketing Manager, Business and Economics, and all the members of the Pearson Canada sales team.

We appreciate the insights and suggestions of the following individuals who provided feedback on the seventh edition or reviewed the manuscript for the new eighth edition:

Jane Anderson	Lethbridge College
Craig Dyer	Red River College
Dave Fleming	George Brown College
Brent Groen	Trinity Western University
Gordon Hollis	Northern Alberta Institute of Technology
Patrick C. K. Hung	University of Ontario Institute of Technology
Alan Idiens	College of New Caledonia
Michael Khan	University of Toronto
Hugh Laurence	University of Toronto
Peter Morgan	British Columbia Institute of Technology
Jennifer Percival	University of Ontario Institute of Technology
Lisa Phillips	Douglas College
Robert Riordan	Carleton University
Frank Saccucci	Grant MacEwan University
Peter Tingling	Simon Fraser University

Their comments were carefully considered and implemented wherever possible.

Frederick A. Starke
George Dracopoulos
Melanie D. Lang

About the Authors

Ronald J. Ebert is professor emeritus at the University of Missouri–Columbia where he lectures in the management department and serves as adviser to students and student organizations. Dr. Ebert draws upon more than 30 years of teaching experience at such schools as Sinclair College, University of Washington, University of Missouri, Lucian Blaga University of Sibiu (Romania), and Consortium International University (Italy). His consulting alliances include such firms as Mobay Corporation, Kraft Foods, Oscar Mayer, Atlas Powder, and John Deere. He has designed and conducted management development programs for such diverse clients as the American Public Power Association, the United States Savings and Loan League, and the Central Missouri Manufacturing Training Consortium.

His experience as a practitioner has fostered an advocacy for integrating concepts with best business practices in business education. The five business books he has written have been translated into Spanish, Chinese, Malaysian, and Romanian. Dr. Ebert has served as the editor of the *Journal of Operations Management*. He is a past president and fellow of the Decision Sciences Institute. He has served as consultant and external evaluator for *Quantitative Reasoning for Business Studies*, an introduction-to-business project sponsored by the National Science Foundation.

Ricky W. Griffin is Distinguished Professor of Management and holds the Blocker Chair in Business in the Mays School of Business at Texas A&M University. Dr. Griffin currently serves as executive associate dean. He previously served as head of the Department of Management and as director of the Center for Human Resource Management at Texas A&M. His research interests include workplace aggression and violence, executive skills and decision making, and workplace culture. Dr. Griffin's research has been published in such journals as *Academy of Management Review, Academy of Management Journal, Administrative Science Quarterly*, and *Journal of Management*. He has also served as editor of Journal of Management. Dr. Griffin has consulted with such organizations as Texas Instruments, Tenneco, Amoco, Compaq Computer, and Continental Airlines.

Dr. Griffin has served the Academy of Management as chair of the organizational behaviour division. He also has served as president of the southwest division of the Academy of Management and on the board of directors of the Southern Management Association. He is a fellow of both the Academy of Management and the Southern Management Association. He is also the author of several successful textbooks, each of which is a market leader. In addition, the books are widely used in dozens of countries and have been translated into numerous foreign languages, including Spanish, Polish, Malaysian, and Russian.

Frederick A. Starke is professor emeritus of Organizational Behaviour in the Asper School of Business at the University of Manitoba. He began his career at the University of Manitoba in 1968 and has taught courses in organizational behaviour, organization theory, decision making, and marketing. He has served in several administrative positions, including head of the Department of Business Administration from 1982–87 and from 1989–94, and as associate dean from 1996–2005.

Dr. Starke earned his BA and MBA from Southern Illinois University and his PhD in organizational behaviour from Ohio State University. He has published research articles in such scholarly journals as the *Administrative Science Quarterly, the Journal of Applied Psychology, the Academy of Management Journal, the Journal of Management Studies*, and the *Review of Religious Research*. He has also written articles for professional journals, such as the *Journal of Systems Management, Information Executive*, and the *Canadian Journal of Nursing Administration*.

Dr. Starke writes textbooks that are used by university and community college students in business programs across Canada. These titles include *Organizational Behaviour, Business Essentials, Management*, and *Business*. Dr. Starke also presents seminars on the topics of decision making and goal setting to practising managers in both the public and private sectors.

George Dracopoulos is a member of the business administration department at Vanier College. In the past, he served as chairman of the department but is now devoting considerable energy to his role as International Business Exchange Coordinator. In recent years, George has created links and built bridges with universities and businesses throughout France (and now Belgium). To date, hundreds of students have benefitted from these initiatives. George was awarded the Vanier VIP award for his dedication and devotion to the community in 2012. He is a co-organizer of the national BDC/Vanier Marketing Case Competition. George also serves as a part-time lecturer at McGill University, teaching traditional courses and building and delivering online and distance education classes. He earned his MBA at McGill, as well as a graduate diploma in education and a graduate degree in applied management. He earned his BA at Concordia University. Mr. Dracopoulos has taught a broad range of business courses and is an advocate of experiential learning. His primary interests are in the fields of marketing and management.

Outside his teaching career, Mr. Dracopoulos has worked in marketing and sales positions. He has been invited to speak and/or provide keynote addresses at events across North America. In addition to this text, he works on other publishing projects providing web content and multimedia material. While completing his university education, he spent a semester abroad studying management globalization issues in Europe. He has also spent a considerable amount of time coaching high-level sports. Recent Pearson publications include *Business in Action*, In-Class Edition, Second Canadian Edition (2009) (co-authored with Courtland L. Bovée and John V. Thill) and *Business Essentials*, Sixth Edition, (2012) (co-authored with Ronald J. Ebert, Ricky W. Griffin, and Fred Starke).

Melanie D. Lang is assistant professor at the University of Guelph and is currently director of the Centre for Business and Social Entrepreneurship (CBaSE). As director, Ms. Lang oversees the experiential learning opportunities of students working with local businesses and community-based organizations. CBaSE promotes student engagement and social responsibility while encouraging entrepreneurship in its broadest sense: the translation of ideas into action for the betterment of society.

Ms. Lang began her career at the University of Guelph in 2004 and has taught courses in marketing, consumer behaviour, and product development. One of the areas of discipline that Ms. Lang teaches includes an interdisciplinary product/business development course involving students from various academic backgrounds who work in teams to develop real products and accompanying business plans. Her research interests include the acceptance of new and emerging agri-food products into culturally dynamic consumer markets, enhancing enterprise education practices, as well as evaluating innovative teaching and learning models.

Ms. Lang earned her BComm and MSc from the University of Guelph in Marketing and Consumer Studies and has contributed to textbooks that are used by business students in commerce programs across Canada.

From the Authors

Ron Ebert, Ricky Griffin, Fred Starke, George Dracopoulos, and Melanie Lang

Businesses today face constant change—change in their competitive landscape, change in their workforce, change in government regulations, change in the economy, change in technology, change in... well, you get the idea. As we began planning this revision, we too recognized the need for change—changing demands from instructors, changing needs and preferences of students, and changing views on what material to cover in this course and how to cover it. These have all affected how we planned and revised the book.

The business world provided us with dozens of new examples, new challenges (particularly the aftermath of the financial crisis of 2008-09), new success stories, and new perspectives on what businesses must do to remain competitive. A new dedication to relevance guided our work from beginning to end. For example, we know that some business students will go to work for big companies, while others will work for small firms. Some will start

their own business, and others may join a family business. We have therefore tried to make the book as relevant and useful as possible to all students, regardless of their personal and career goals and objectives.

We have incorporated many new features in this eighth Canadian edition of *Business* (see the Preface for a description of these new features). We also carefully reviewed the existing book line by line. New material was added, and older examples were updated or replaced with newer ones. We worked extra hard to make our writing as clear and as crisp as possible. We think that these changes will help make the material even more alive and personal for you.

We believe that we have taken this book to a new, higher level of excellence. Its content is stronger, its learning framework is better, its design is more reader-friendly, and its support materials are the best on the market. We hope that you enjoy reading and learning from this book as much as we enjoyed creating it. And who knows? Perhaps one day we can tell your story of business success to other students.

Introducing the Contemporary

In the Opening Cases in Chapters 1 to 5, you will read about five interesting situations: (1) rapid changes in the mobile phone market, (2) competition among video content providers, (3) the unethical behaviour of some business managers, (4) the activities of internet entrepreneurs, and (5) the global strategy of a Canadian bank. All of these situations and many more that are described in this text have a common thread—they all demonstrate the key elements of business as well as the excitement and complexity of business activity. Each case tells a part of the story of our contemporary business world.

Part One, Introducing the Contemporary Business World, provides a general overview of business today, including its economic roots, the environment in which it operates, the ethical problems and opportunities facing business firms, the importance of entrepreneurship, the various forms of ownership available to business firms, and the globalization of business.

Business World

- We begin in **Chapter 1, Understanding the Canadian Business System,** by examining the role of business in the economy of Canada and other market economies. We also present a brief history of business in Canada.

- Then in **Chapter 2, Understanding the Environments of Business,** we examine the external environments that influence business activity. These include the economic, technological, socio-cultural, political-legal, and general business environments.

- Next, in **Chapter 3, Conducting Business Ethically and Responsibly,** we look at individual ethics and corporate social responsibility and how these affect the firm's customers, employees, and investors.

- In **Chapter 4, Understanding Entrepreneurship, Small Business, and New Venture Creation,** we examine the important concepts of entrepreneurship and small business, and the various forms of business ownership that have evolved to facilitate business activity.

- Finally, in **Chapter 5, Understanding International Business,** we look at why countries engage in international trade, how companies organize to operate internationally, the development of free trade agreements, and factors that help or hinder international trade.

Understanding the Canadian Business System

LEARNING OBJECTIVES

After reading this chapter, you should be able to:

1. Define the nature of Canadian *business* and identify its main goals.
2. Describe different types of *global economic systems* according to the means by which they control the *factors of production* through *input* and *output markets*.
3. Show how *demand* and *supply* affect resource distribution in Canada.
4. Identify the elements of *private enterprise* and explain the various *degrees of competition* in the Canadian economic system.
5. Trace the *history of business* in Canada.

The Mobile Phone Market: It's the Wild West

NOT too many years ago, no one had heard of Angry Birds, BBM, or mobile phones that could take pictures, access email, browse the web, and play music. But now consumers depend on their mobile phones for all these things, and these devices have become immensely popular. Annual sales of smartphones are expected to hit one billion units by 2015, so the market potential is huge. But competition is intense, patent infringement lawsuits are common, and shifting fortunes are evident among the companies that are competing for the consumer's dollar.

New product introductions are occurring at a rapid pace. The most publicized new product in the past few years has been Apple's iPhone, which is a strong competitor to the BlackBerry from Canada's Research In Motion (RIM). But Samsung has suddenly become a big player in this market with the introduction of its Galaxy smartphone, which presents strong competition for both Apple and RIM. Another new product is Motorola's Droid phone, which was launched by Verizon, the largest U.S. wireless

carrier (and RIM's biggest customer). A fourth entry comes from Google, which developed a touch screen mobile phone that uses Google's own Android operating system. This product may also cause problems for Apple's iPhone.

Patent infringement lawsuits abound in this rapidly changing industry, and RIM and other firms have both sued and been sued. For example, Klausner Technologies filed suit against RIM for infringing one of its visual voice mail patents. In a non-technology case, RIM was sued for patent infringement by the Canadian Bureau of Broadcast Management (BBM), a company that collects radio and TV statistics. BBM claims that it has rights to the BBM name and has used that name for decades. BBM also stands for BlackBerry Messenger, the instant messaging service that has 50 million users.

There are two industry trends that make it difficult to predict the future for any of the competitors in the smartphone industry. The first is the so-called "bring your own

device" trend, which means that companies are shifting the responsibility for having a phone onto employees. The second trend is "sandboxing," which means separating work functions from the rest of the smartphone for security reasons and allowing employees to use their own phones at work without losing access to other applications like games or social networking.

All of this uncertainty and rapid change has created problems for some companies. One of these companies is RIM, which introduced the now-famous BlackBerry in 1998. In the first quarter of 2010, RIM was one of the top five mobile phone companies in the world, but by the end of 2011 its fortunes had declined dramatically. In 2011, smartphones running on Google's Android software surpassed RIM as the king of the U.S. smartphone market. In October 2010, BlackBerry's market share was 35.8 percent, but by May 2011 it had dropped to just 9 percent. During that same period, Google's share jumped from 23.5 percent to 34.7 percent.

RIM's share price reflects its misfortunes, falling from $70 per share in 2010 to less than $10 per share in mid-2012. The late Steve Jobs (former CEO of Apple) said it would be hard for RIM to ever catch up because the leading software platforms (iOS and Android) are so popular. RIM has had problems getting its new products to the market on schedule (for example, its new BlackBerry 10 will not be available until 2013), and these delays have caused some analysts to predict that RIM will not survive.

What is happening to RIM has also happened to once-dominant Nokia. For many years, Nokia was the top producer of cellphones, but it was overtaken by Apple in 2011 and Samsung in 2012. Together, Samsung and Apple control 55 percent of the global smartphone shipments. Nokia's biggest problem is the popularity in Europe of phones that are running on the Android platform. Android phones increased their market share from 8 percent to 30 percent in just one year. During that same period, the market share of Nokia's Symbian system dropped from 40 percent to 21 percent. In 2011, Nokia announced that it would drop its Symbian platform and use Microsoft's Windows Phone 7 software. In 2012, Nokia introduced the Lumia 900 smartphone in an attempt to re-establish itself as an important player in the industry. But a software bug was found in the phone and in March 2012, Nokia said that its profits would be negatively affected by the problem.

It is difficult to predict exactly what will happen in the mobile phone industry or who will be the big winners. The only thing we can be sure of is that competition will remain fierce, new product introductions will continue at a dizzying pace, and consumers will eagerly anticipate "the next big thing." In March 2012, for example, Asian mobile phone company Huwai introduced its Ascend D smartphone, touting it as the world's fastest smartphone. ◆

HOW WILL THIS HELP ME?

All businesses are subject to the influences of economic forces. But these economic forces also provide astute managers and entrepreneurs with opportunities for profits and growth. The ideas presented in this chapter will help you to understand (1) how business *managers* deal with the challenges and opportunities resulting from economic forces, and (2) how *consumers* deal with the challenges and opportunities of price fluctuations.

The Concept of Business and Profit

The opening case illustrates the dynamic and rapidly changing nature of modern business activity, and the opportunities and challenges that are evident. It also shows how business managers must pay attention to many different factors, including the actions of competitors, rapid technological change, new product development, corporate strategy, risk management, stock prices, and a host of other variables that you will read about in this book.

Let's begin by asking what you think of when you hear the word *business*. Large corporations like Shoppers Drug Mart and Walmart? Smaller companies like your local supermarket or favourite restaurant? Successful companies like CN and Apple? Less successful companies like Nortel Networks or Yellow Media? Actually, each of these firms is a **business**—an organization that produces or sells goods or services in an effort to make a profit. **Profit** is what remains after a business's expenses have been subtracted from its revenues. Profits reward the owners of businesses for taking the risks involved in investing their time and money. In 2011, the top three companies in terms of profits were all banks (the Royal Bank, $5.2 billion in profits; the Toronto Dominion Bank, $4.6 billion; and the Bank of Nova Scotia, $4.2 billion).[1] Profits can be very large if a company produces something that consumers really like. For example, the four-part film *Hunger Games* will generate large profits for Lionsgate. The first film in the series generated box office receipts of $155 million in just its first week.

In Canada's economic system, businesses exist to earn profits for owners. But consumers also have freedom of choice, so businesses must take into account what consumers want or need. No matter how efficient a business is, it won't survive if there is no demand for its goods or services. Neither a snowblower shop in Victoria nor a beach-umbrella store in Rankin Inlet is likely to do very well. But a person who can spot a promising opportunity and then develop a good plan for capitalizing on it can

business An organization that seeks to earn profits by providing goods and services.

profit What remains (if anything) after a business's expenses have been subtracted from its revenues.

LO1 Define the nature of Canadian *business* and identify its main goals.

"Your Honor, my client pleads guilty to an overzealous but well-intentioned pursuit of the profit motive."

succeed. The opportunity always involves goods or services that consumers want or need—especially if no one else is supplying them or if existing businesses are doing so inefficiently or incompletely.

Businesses produce most of the goods and services we consume and they employ the majority of working people. They create most new innovations and provide opportunities for other businesses, which serve as their suppliers. A healthy business climate contributes directly to our quality of life and standard of living. New forms of technology, service businesses, and international opportunities promise to keep production, consumption, and employment growing indefinitely (but not always smoothly). Business profits enhance the personal incomes of owners and shareholders, and business taxes help to support governments at all levels. Many businesses also support charities and provide community leadership. A 2010 study by KPMG of the G7 industrialized countries ranked Canada as the most cost-effective place to do business, and a 2011 study by *Forbes* magazine ranked Canada the number-one country in the world (out of 134 countries) in which to do business.[2]

In addition to for-profit business firms, there are also many not-for-profit organizations in Canada. **Not-for-profit organizations** do not try to make a profit; rather, they use the funds they receive (from government or private grants or the sale of goods or services) to provide services to the public. Charities, educational institutions, churches, hospitals, labour unions, and government agencies are examples of not-for-profit organizations. Business principles are helpful to these not-for-profit organizations as they try to achieve their service goals.

> **not-for-profit organizations** Use the funds they receive (from government or private grants or the sale of goods or services) to provide services to the public.

Economic Systems Around the World

A Canadian business is different in many ways from a business in China. And both are different from businesses in Japan, France, or Peru. A major determinant of how organizations operate is the kind of economic system that characterizes the country in which they do business. An **economic system** allocates a nation's resources among its citizens. Economic systems differ in terms of who owns and controls these resources.

> Describe different types of *global economic systems* according to the means by which they control the *factors of production* through *input* and *output markets*. **LO2**

Factors of Production

The key difference among economic systems is the way in which they manage the **factors of production**—the basic resources that a country's businesses use to produce goods and services (see Figure 1.1). Traditionally, economists have focused on four factors of production: *labour, capital, entrepreneurs,* and *natural resources*. Information resources are now often included as well.[3]

> **economic system** The way in which a nation allocates its resources among its citizens.

> **factors of production** The resources used to produce goods and services: labour, capital, entrepreneurs, and natural resources.

Labour

The people who work for a company represent the first factor of production, **labour**. Sometimes called **human resources**, labour refers to the mental and physical capabilities of people. Carrying out the business of a huge company like Imperial Oil, for example, requires a labour force with a wide variety of skills ranging from managerial to geological to transportation. Employees who are well trained and knowledgeable can provide a real competitive advantage for a company.

> **labour (or human resources)** The mental and physical training and talents of people.

Capital

Obtaining and using labour and other resources requires **capital**—the financial resources needed to operate an enterprise. Capital is needed to start a new business and then to keep it running and growing. Imperial Oil needs millions of dollars in cash, and millions more in equipment and other assets, to run its operations. Capital

> **capital** The funds needed to operate an enterprise.

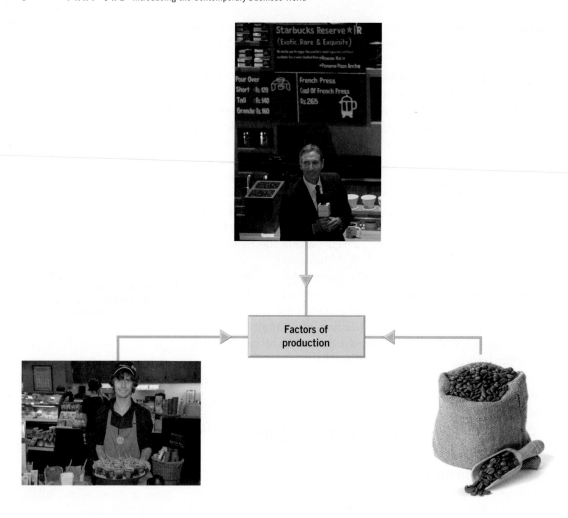

FIGURE 1.1

Starbucks uses various factors of production, including (a) labour, such as this Starbucks barrista; (b) entrepreneurs, such as CEO Howard Schultz; and (c) physical resources, including coffee beans.

can be provided by individual entrepreneurs, partners who start businesses together, or investors who buy stock in the company. Revenue from the sale of products is a key and ongoing source of capital once a business has opened its doors.[4]

Entrepreneurs

entrepreneur An individual who organizes and manages labour, capital, and natural resources to produce goods and services to earn a profit but who also runs the risk of failure.

Entrepreneurs are people who accept the opportunities and risks involved in creating and operating businesses. Sergie Brin and Larry Page (Google), Michael Dell (Dell Computer), and Mark Zuckerberg (Facebook) are well-known entrepreneurs.

Natural Resources

natural resources Items used in the production of goods and services in their natural state, including land, water, mineral deposits, and trees.

Natural resources include all physical resources such as land, water, mineral deposits, and trees. Imperial Oil makes use of a wide variety of natural resources. It processes vast quantities of crude oil each year, but it also needs the land where the oil is located, as well as land for its refineries and pipelines.

Information Resources

information resources Information such as market forecasts, economic data, and specialized knowledge of employees that is useful to a business and that helps it achieve its goals.

Information resources include the specialized knowledge and expertise of people who work in businesses, as well as information that is found in market forecasts and various other forms of economic data. Much of what businesses do results in either the creation of new information or the repackaging of existing information for new users and different audiences. Information is a key factor of production because unlike land, labour, and capital, information can be shared without it being diminished. For example, if two people exchange apples, they still each have only one apple, but if two people exchange ideas, each person now has two ideas instead of one.[5]

Types of Economic Systems

Different types of economic systems manage the factors of production in different ways. In some systems, ownership is private; in others, the government owns the factors of production. Economic systems also differ in the way that decisions are made about production and allocation. A **command economy**, for example, relies on a centralized government to control most factors of production and to make most production and allocation decisions. In **market economies**, individual producers and consumers control production and allocation decisions as they respond to changes in supply and demand.

command economy An economic system in which government controls all or most factors of production and makes all or most production decisions.

market economy An economic system in which individuals control all or most factors of production and make all or most production decisions.

Command Economies

The two most basic forms of command economies are communism and socialism. As originally proposed by the nineteenth-century German economist Karl Marx, **communism** is a system in which the government owns and operates all sources of production. Marx envisioned a society in which individuals would ultimately contribute according to their abilities and receive economic benefits according to their needs. He also expected government ownership of production factors to be only temporary. Once society had matured, government would "wither away" and the workers would gain direct ownership. But Marx's predictions were faulty, and most countries have abandoned communism in favour of a more market-based economy.

communism A type of command economy in which the government owns and operates all industries.

A GlobeScan poll of over 20 000 people in 20 different countries asked people whether they agreed with the following statement: "The free market economy is the best system." Where do you think the highest support for capitalism was found? Not in Canada, the United States, Germany, or Japan, but in *China*, where 74 percent of people polled agreed with the statement.[6] This occurred in spite of the Chinese government's strong support of the communist economic ideology. After China's constitution was amended to permit private enterprise, the private sector has become incredibly productive. It is estimated that China produces 60 percent of all the toys in the world,[7] and China's reputation for being a low-cost producer of goods is legendary. Changes are also occurring in communist Cuba: More private initiative is being encouraged, and the role of the state is being reduced in some sectors.[8]

In a less extensive command economic system called **socialism**, the government owns and operates only selected major industries. Smaller businesses such as clothing stores and restaurants may be privately owned. Although workers in socialist countries are usually allowed to choose their occupations or professions, a large proportion generally works for the government. Many government-operated enterprises are inefficient, since management positions are frequently filled based on political considerations rather than on ability. Extensive public welfare systems have also resulted in very high taxes. Because of these factors, socialism is also declining in popularity.[9]

socialism A kind of command economy in which the government owns and operates the main industries, while individuals own and operate less crucial industries.

Market Economies

A **market** is a mechanism for exchange between the buyers and sellers of a particular good or service. For example, the internet is a technologically sophisticated market

market A mechanism for exchange between the buyers and sellers of a particular good or service.

that brings buyers and sellers together through ecommerce. People usually think of ecommerce as being business-to-consumer (B2C) transactions such as buying books over the internet for personal use. But business-to-business (B2B) transactions actually far exceed B2C transactions in dollar value. B2B involves businesses joining together to create ecommerce companies that make them more efficient when they purchase the goods and services they need.

A market economy is one where B2C and B2B exchanges take place without much government involvement. To understand how a market economy works, consider what happens when a customer goes to a fruit stand to buy apples. Assume that one vendor is selling apples for $1 per kilogram and another is charging $1.50. Both vendors are free to charge what they want, and customers are free to buy what they choose. If both vendors' apples are of the same quality, the customer will likely buy the cheaper ones. But if the $1.50 apples are fresher, the customer may buy them instead. Both buyers and sellers enjoy freedom of choice.

Input and Output Markets. Figure 1.2 shows how the factors of production work in a pure market economy. Businesses and households interact in two different market relationships.[10] In the **input market**, firms buy resources from households, which are thus resource suppliers. In the **output market**, firms supply goods and services in response to demand on the part of households. (We will provide a more detailed discussion of supply and demand later in this chapter.)

As you can see, the activities of these two markets create a circular flow. GM Canada, for example, relies on various kinds of inputs. It buys labour directly from households, which may also supply capital from accumulated savings in the form of

input market Firms buy resources that they need in the production of goods and services.

output market Firms supply goods and services in response to demand on the part of consumers.

FIGURE 1.2

Circular flow in a market economy.

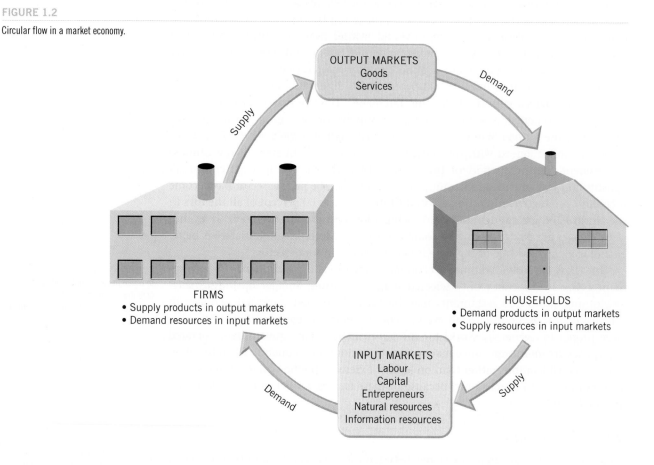

OUTPUT MARKETS
Goods
Services

Supply

Demand

FIRMS
• Supply products in output markets
• Demand resources in input markets

HOUSEHOLDS
• Demand products in output markets
• Supply resources in input markets

INPUT MARKETS
Labour
Capital
Entrepreneurs
Natural resources
Information resources

Demand

Supply

stock purchases. Consumer buying patterns provide information that helps GM decide which models to produce and which to discontinue. In turn, GM uses these inputs in various ways and becomes a supplier to households when it designs and produces various kinds of automobiles, trucks, and sports utility vehicles and offers them for sale to consumers.

Capitalism. Individuals are free to work for GM or an alternative employer and to invest in GM stock or alternative forms of saving or consumption. Similarly, GM can create whatever vehicles it chooses and price them at whatever value it chooses. But consumers are then free to buy their next car from GM or some other car company. This process contrasts markedly with that of a command economy, in which individuals may be told where they can and cannot work, companies are told what they can and cannot manufacture, and consumers may have little or no choice as to what they purchase or how much they pay for items. The political basis of market processes is called **capitalism**, which sanctions the private ownership of the factors of production and encourages entrepreneurship by offering profits as an incentive. The economic basis of market processes is the operation of supply and demand.

capitalism An economic system in which markets decide what, when, and for whom to produce.

Mixed Market Economies

Command and market economies are two extremes. In reality, most countries rely on some form of **mixed market economy**—a system featuring characteristics of both command and market economies. Beginning in the 1990s, a trend developed toward **privatization**—converting government enterprises into privately owned companies. In Canada, for example, the air traffic control system was privatized, and the federal government sold several other corporations, including Canadian National Railway and Air Canada. The Netherlands privatized its TNT Post Group N.V., and India privatized 18 different industries, including iron, steel, machinery, and telecommunications.[11] However, when a worldwide recession began in 2008, the trend slowed. Government bailouts of Chrysler and GM in both the United States and Canada meant that the government was once again a part-owner of some business firms. A few countries are even pursuing a policy of **nationalization**—converting private firms into government-owned firms. Venezuela, for example, nationalized its telecommunications industry.

mixed market economy An economic system with elements of both a command economy and a market economy; in practice, typical of most nations' economies.

privatization The transfer of activities from the government to the private sector.

nationalization The conversion of private firms into government-owned firms.

Deregulation—the reduction in the number of laws affecting business activity and in the powers of government enforcement agencies—is another trend that developed during the 1990s. Deregulation originally freed companies to do what they wanted without much government intervention, thereby simplifying the task of management. Deregulation occurred in many industries, including airlines, pipelines, banking, trucking, and communication. But this trend has also slowed (and even reversed in some cases) due to the 2008 recession. For example, there have been calls for a dramatic tightening of the laws regulating business activity, particularly in the financial sector. The British Petroleum (BP) oil spill in the Gulf of Mexico in 2010 caused the U.S. government to put pressure on BP to reimburse individuals and businesses that were harmed by the spill. Incidents like these have created a dilemma for government policy-makers because a 2009 study by the Conference Board of Canada showed that deregulation (in tandem with privatization and increased competition) had caused a sharp increase in productivity in sectors like freight and airlines.[12]

deregulation A reduction in the number of laws affecting business activity and in the powers of government enforcement agencies.

Mixed market economies are now characterized by more government involvement than was evident just a few years ago. Governments in mixed market economies have intervened in the economic system in an attempt to stabilize it, but this has led to higher budget deficits (see Chapter 2) and more control of business activity.

Many formerly planned economies have moved toward a more mixed economic model.

Interactions Between Business and Government

In Canada's mixed economic system, there are many important interactions between business and government. We look first at how government influences business and then at how business influences government.

How Government Influences Business

Government plays several different roles in the Canadian economy, and each of these roles influences business activity in some way.

Government as Customer

Government buys thousands of different products and services from business firms, including office supplies, office buildings, computers, battleships, helicopters, highways, water treatment plants, and management and engineering consulting services. The government is also the largest purchaser of advertising in Canada. Many businesses depend on government purchasing, if not for their survival, at least for a certain level of prosperity. Total government expenditures in 2011 were $267.5 billion.[13]

Government as Competitor

Government also competes with business through Crown corporations, which are accountable to a minister of parliament for their conduct. Crown corporations exist at both the provincial and federal levels and account for a significant amount of economic activity in Canada (see Table 1.1).

Government as Regulator

Federal and provincial governments in Canada regulate many aspects of business activity through administrative boards, tribunals, and commissions. For example, the **Canadian Transport Commission (CTC)** makes decisions about route and rate applications for commercial air and railway companies, and the **Canadian Radio-television and Telecommunications Commission (CRTC)** issues and renews broadcast licences. In 2011, for example, when the CRTC received thousands of complaints from consumers that TV advertisements were too loud, the agency ruled that broadcasters had to turn down the volume on TV advertisements.[14] That issue was relatively simple compared to the dispute that has arisen about the power the CRTC should have in order to police the telecommunications industry.[15] It is particularly concerned about cable and satellite providers (e.g., Shaw, Rogers, Bell Canada, etc.) buying up many of the TV channels they distribute. But these companies argue that they need more market power to compete with unregulated companies like Netflix.[16] Critics argue that the CRTC is obsolete, and that it cannot achieve its goal of a level playing field because the internet is being used to circumvent Canadian laws.[17] To further complicate matters, TV writers, directors, and actors weighed in, arguing that the survival of Canadian content would be at risk if looser regulations were enacted.[18] In February 2012, the Supreme Court of Canada ruled that internet service providers are not bound by Canada's broadcast regulations.[19]

Canadian Transport Commission (CTC) A federal regulatory agency that makes decisions about route and rate applications for commercial air and railway companies.

Canadian Radio-television and Telecommunications Commission (CRTC) A federal regulatory agency that issues and renews broadcast licences.

For many years, the **Canadian Wheat Board** regulated the price of wheat and prohibited farmers from selling their wheat directly to U.S. elevators; instead, they had to sell their wheat through the Board. When the Conservative government introduced legislation in 2011 to eliminate the Canadian Wheat Board, there was much resistance to the move.[20] Provincial boards and commissions also regulate business activity, but different situations exist in different provinces. For example, at one time the provinces of Quebec and B.C. allowed mixed martial arts events such as the UFC, but Ontario didn't. (Ontario began allowing these events in 2011.)[21]

Canadian Wheat Board A federal regulatory agency that regulates the price of wheat.

TABLE 1.1 Top 10 Crown Corporations, 2011 (ranked by sales revenue)

Company	Sales Revenue (billions of dollars)
1. Hydro-Québec	$12.3
2. Canada Mortgage and Housing Corp.	11.7
3. Canada Post	7.4
4. Ontario Lottery and Gaming Corp.	6.6
5. *Caisse de dépôt et placement du Québec*	6.5
6. Canadian Wheat Board	6.0
7. Ontario Power Generation Inc.	5.0
8. Liquor Control Board of Ontario	4.5
9. Crown Investments Corp. of Saskatchewan	4.3
10. Alberta Gaming and Liquor Commission	4.1

There are several important reasons for regulating business activity. These include promoting competition, protecting consumers, achieving social goals, and protecting the environment.

Promoting Competition. Government regulates business to ensure that healthy competition exists among business firms, because competition is crucial to a market economy. The guidelines for Canada's competition policy are contained in The Competition Act, which prohibits a variety of practices (see Table 1.2). For example, the Act prohibits agreements that are designed to reduce competition among companies. Formerly, the government had to prove that such agreements actually reduced competition, but recent changes to the legislation mean that the mere existence of a conspiracy is assumed to be proof that competition has been reduced.[22] Another big change is the dramatically increased fines for misleading marketing practices by corporations (formerly $100 000 for the first offence, but now $10 million).[23] In 2011, the makers of Nivea skin care products were fined $300 000 for making false advertising claims that My Silhouette cream could reduce fat on targeted body parts.[24]

Businesses often complain that the Competition Bureau—which investigates suspected anti-competitive behaviour—is too slow in approving or denying merger plans. For example, when Labatt Brewing wanted to take over Lakeport Brewing, it was told that the Competition Bureau would need up to six months to determine whether the takeover would lessen competition. Labatt therefore appealed to the Competition Tribunal—which hears applications relating to the Competition Act—to speed up the process. The Tribunal agreed with Labatt, and the merger went ahead sooner than it otherwise would have.[25]

Protecting Consumers. The federal government has passed various laws that are designed to protect consumers. Consumer and Corporate Affairs Canada administers most of these laws. The laws include the **Tobacco Act** (which prohibits cigarette

Tobacco Act Prohibits cigarette advertising on billboards and in stores.

TABLE 1.2   The Competition Act

Section 45	Prohibits conspiracies and combinations formed for the purpose of unduly lessening competition in the production, transportation, or storage of goods. Persons convicted may be imprisoned for up to five years or fined up to $1 million or both.
Section 50	Prohibits illegal trade practices. A company may not, for example, cut prices in one region of Canada while selling at a higher price everywhere else if this substantially lessens competition. A company may not sell at "unreasonably low prices" if this substantially lessens competition. (This section does not prohibit credit unions from returning surpluses to their members.)
Section 51	Prohibits giving allowances and rebates to buyers to cover their advertising expenses, unless these allowances are made available proportionally to other purchasers who are in competition with the buyer given the rebate.
Section 52	Prohibits marketing (promotion) activities that are false or misleading. Includes telemarketing activities.
Section 53	Prohibits the deceptive notice that a person has won a prize if the recipient is asked to pay money as a condition of winning the prize.
Section 54	Prohibits charging the higher price when two prices are shown on a product.
Section 55.1	Prohibits pyramid selling (a participant in the plan receives compensation for recruiting other individuals into the plan).
Section 61	Prohibits resale price maintenance. No person who produces or supplies a product can attempt to influence upward, or discourage reduction of, the price of the good in question. It is also illegal for the producer to refuse to supply a product to a reseller simply because the producer believes the reseller will cut the price.
Section 74	Prohibits bait-and-switch selling. No person can advertise a product at a bargain price if there is no supply of the product available to the consumer. (This tactic baits prospects into the store, where salespeople switch them to higher-priced goods.) This section also controls the use of contests to sell goods, and prohibits the sale of goods at a price higher than the advertised one.

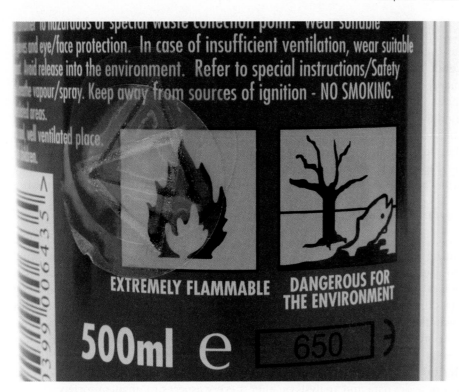

Hazardous products must have warning labels to protect consumers who use them.

advertising on billboards and in stores), the **Weights and Measures Act** (which sets standards of accuracy for weighing and measuring devices), the **Textile Labelling Act** (which regulates the labelling, sale, importation, and advertising of consumer textile articles), and the **Food and Drug Act** (which prohibits the sale of food that contains any poisonous or harmful substances). Consumers are also protected by municipal bylaws such as the "no-smoking" bylaws that are so common in Canadian cities. In 2012, the Ontario Superior Court gave the province the go-ahead to file a $50 billion dollar lawsuit against several tobacco companies in order to recover health care costs caused by smoking. [26]

On June 11, 2011, the **Canada Consumer Product Safety Act** (which replaced the former **Hazardous Products Act**) came into force. It requires poisonous, flammable, explosive, or corrosive products to be appropriately labelled. The new law applies not only to manufacturers who make potentially hazardous products, but also to retailers and to companies that import or distribute products.[27] There is concern that the new law will place additional burdens on small businesses in Canada.[28]

Achieving Social Goals. Social goals promote the well-being of our society. They include universal access to health care, safe workplaces, employment insurance, and decent pensions. All of these goals require the interaction of business firms and government. The decisions of foreign governments—as they pursue their own social goals—can also affect Canadian businesses. For example, when the U.S. government introduced legislation making it difficult for online gambling companies to operate in the United States, the stock prices of Canadian companies in that industry dropped sharply.[29]

Protecting the Environment. Key government legislation designed to protect the environment includes the **Canada Water Act**, which controls water quality in fresh and marine waters; the **Fisheries Act**, which controls the discharge of any harmful substance into water; and the **Environmental Contaminants Act**, which establishes regulations for airborne substances that are a danger to human health or the environment.

Weights and Measures Act Sets standards of accuracy for weighing and measuring devices.

Textile Labelling Act Regulates the labelling, sale, importation, and advertising of consumer textile articles.

Food and Drug Act Prohibits the sale of food that contains any poisonous or harmful substances.

Canada Consumer Product Safety Act Requires poisonous, flammable, explosive, or corrosive products to be appropriately labelled.

Canada Water Act Controls water quality in fresh and marine waters.

Fisheries Act Controls the discharge of any harmful substance into water.

Environmental Contaminants Act Establishes regulations for airborne substances that are a danger to human health or the environment.

Government as Taxation Agent

revenue taxes Taxes whose main purpose is to fund government services and programs.

Taxes are imposed and collected by federal, provincial, and local governments. **Revenue taxes** (e.g., income taxes) are levied by federal and provincial governments primarily to provide revenue to fund various services and programs. **Progressive revenue taxes** are levied at a higher rate on higher-income taxpayers and at a lower rate on lower-income taxpayers. **Regressive revenue taxes** (e.g., sales tax) are levied at the same rate regardless of a person's income. They cause poorer people to pay a higher percentage of their income for these taxes than rich people pay. **Restrictive taxes** (e.g., taxes on alcohol and tobacco) are levied partially for the revenue they provide, but also because legislators believe that the products should be controlled.

progressive revenue taxes Taxes levied at a higher rate on higher-income taxpayers and at a lower rate on lower-income taxpayers.

regressive revenue taxes Taxes that cause poorer people to pay a higher percentage of income than richer people pay.

Government as Provider of Incentives

restrictive taxes Taxes levied to control certain activities that legislators believe should be controlled.

Federal, provincial, and municipal governments offer incentive programs that help stimulate economic development. The Province of Quebec, for example, has attracted video game companies like Ubisoft by giving them multimillion-dollar subsidies if they locate in the province.[30] Governments also offer incentives through the many services they provide to business firms through government organizations. Examples include the *Export Development Corporation*, which assists Canadian exporters by offering export insurance against non-payment by foreign buyers and long-term loans to foreign buyers of Canadian products; *Natural Resources Canada*, which provides geological maps of Canada's potential mineral-producing areas; and *Statistics Canada*, which provides data and analysis on almost every aspect of Canadian society.

Industry Canada offers many different programs designed to help small businesses. The Canada Business program, for example, provides information on government programs, services, and regulations in order to improve the start-up and survival rates of small- and medium-sized businesses. It also encourages businesses to focus on sound business planning and the effective use of market research. The Department of Foreign Affairs and International Trade (DFAIT) helps Canadian companies doing business internationally by promoting Canada as a good place in which to invest and carry on business activities. It also assists in negotiating and administering trade agreements.

There are many other government incentive programs, including municipal tax rebates for companies that locate in certain areas, design assistance programs, and remission of tariffs on certain advanced technology production equipment. Government incentive programs may or may not have the desired effect of stimulating the economy. They may also cause difficulties with our trading partners, as we shall see in Chapter 5. Some critics also argue that business firms are too willing to accept government assistance—in the form of incentives or bailouts—and that managers should put more emphasis on innovation and creativity so business firms can better cope with economic difficulties when they arise, as they did during the 2008–09 recession.

Government as a Provider of Essential Services

Federal, provincial, and municipal governments facilitate business activity through the wide variety of services they supply. The federal government provides highways, the postal service, the minting of money, the armed forces, and statistical data on which to base business decisions. It also tries to maintain stability through fiscal and monetary policy. Provincial and municipal governments provide streets, sewage and sanitation systems, police and fire departments, utilities, hospitals, and education. All of these activities create the kind of stability that encourages business activity.

How Business Influences Government

lobbyist A person hired by a company or an industry to represent its interests to government officials.

While government activity influences what businesses do, businesses also try to influence the government through lobbyists, trade associations, and advertising (see Figure 1.3). A **lobbyist** is a person hired by a company or industry to represent its interests to

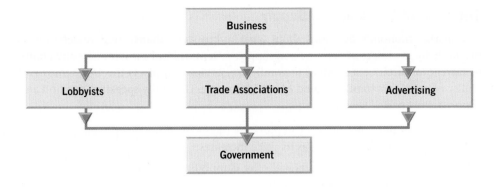

government officials. The Association of Consulting Engineers of Canada, for example, regularly lobbies the federal and provincial governments to make use of the skills possessed by private sector consulting engineers on projects like city water systems. Some business lobbyists have training in the particular industry, public relations experience, or a legal background. A few have served as legislators or government regulators.

The federal Lobbying Act requires lobbyists to register with the Commissioner of Lobbying so that it is clear which individuals are being paid for their lobbying activity. It also sets rules for accountability and transparency and requires lobbyists to report detailed information about their communications with so-called Designated Public Office Holders (DPOH).[31]

For many lobbying efforts, there are opposing points of view. The Canadian Cancer Society and the Tobacco Institute present very different points of view on cigarette smoking and cigarette advertising. Owners of small businesses who cannot afford lobbyists often join **trade associations**, which may act as an industry lobby to influence legislation. Trade associations also conduct training programs relevant to the particular industry, and they arrange trade shows at which members display their products or services to potential customers. Most publish newsletters featuring articles on new products, new companies, changes in ownership, and changes in laws affecting the industry.

trade association An organization dedicated to promoting the interests and assisting the members of a particular industry.

Corporations can influence legislation indirectly by influencing voters. A company can, for example, launch an advertising campaign designed to get Canadians to write their MPs, MPPs, or MLAs demanding passage—or rejection—of a particular bill that is before Parliament or the provincial legislature.

The Canadian Market Economy

Understanding the complex nature of the Canadian economic system is essential to understanding Canadian businesses. In the next few pages, we will examine the workings of our market economy in more detail. Specifically, we will look at demand and supply in a market economy, private enterprise, and degrees of competition.

Show how *demand* and *supply* **LO3** affect resource distribution in Canada.

Demand and Supply in a Market Economy

A market is not a specific place; it is an exchange process between buyers and sellers. A market economy consists of many different markets. In each of these markets, businesses decide what inputs to buy, what to make and in what quantities, and what prices to charge. Likewise, customers decide what to buy and how much they want to pay. Literally billions of such exchanges take place every day between businesses and individuals, between businesses, and among individuals, businesses, and governments.

The Laws of Demand and Supply

In a market economy, decisions about what to buy and what to sell are determined primarily by the forces of demand and supply.[32] **Demand** is the willingness and ability of buyers to purchase a product (a good) or a service. **Supply** is the willingness and ability of producers to offer a good or service for sale. Generally speaking, demand and supply follow basic "laws":

- The **law of demand**: Buyers will purchase (demand) more of a product as its price drops and less of a product as its price increases.

- The **law of supply**: Producers will offer (supply) more of a product for sale as its price rises and less as its price drops.

demand The willingness and ability of buyers to purchase a product or service.

supply The willingness and ability of producers to offer a good or service for sale.

law of demand The principle that buyers will purchase (demand) more of a product as its price drops.

law of supply The principle that producers will offer (supply) more of a product as its price rises.

The Demand and Supply Schedule

To appreciate these laws in action, consider the market for pizza where you live. If everyone is willing to pay $25 for a pizza (a high price), the town's only pizzeria will produce a large supply. If everyone is willing to pay only $5 (a low price), however, the restaurant will make fewer pizzas. Through careful analysis, we can determine how many pizzas will be sold at different prices. These results, called a

---

E-BUSINESS + SOCIAL MEDIA SOLUTIONS

Virtual Goods: An Emerging EMarket

Not too long ago, people doubted the commercial sales potential of bottled water because a perfectly good substitute was available for virtually no cost. At the time, many skeptics made comments like "What's next, are we going to sell air?" Today, consumers purchase approximately 200 billion litres of bottled water worldwide each year. The skeptics did not foresee an era dominated by the internet, smartphones, and social media.

At least bottled water is a physical product. But how much is an avatar worth? How much would you spend on a virtual good? If your answer is $0, you don't know what's going on in the virtual gaming world. Have you heard of Zynga? World of Warcraft? Mafia Wars? FarmVille? If you answered "no" to all these questions, you may be shocked to learn that virtual goods sales totalled US$6.1 billion in 2011 and are projected to grow to $14.2 billion by 2015. According to a report one user of a Zynga game actually spent over $75 000 to purchase virtual products in one year. While this is not common, investors are now paying attention. Under the circumstances, Zynga, with its 232 million users and a net income of $90.6 million on revenue of $597 million, decided to become a publicly traded company. Suddenly the virtual gaming world was all abuzz on Wall Street and gaming companies were in the news because of their quarterly profit numbers, rather than because of their potential and user numbers.

As we've noted, a market is an exchange process between buyers and sellers of a particular good or service.

This definition fits the evolving virtual goods world as well. Whether you are buying a potato to make french fries (to eat), or a virtual potato to plant in your own FarmVille virtual garden (for entertainment), you are involved in a market of buyers and sellers. As discussed, hard-core virtual gamers are willing to spend good money to ensure that they have the best gear available in games like Sims Social.

Facebook links people to the virtual world and has over 800 million users. The company is now trying to capitalize on its popularity by adding a new revenue stream. It is now charging companies like Zynga 30 percent on virtual game props sold on its social networking site (similar to Apple's approach to apps). It is also testing the extended use of its Facebook credits. Facebook could collect as much as $500 million over the next three years from Zynga and other gaming companies, including Electronic Arts, CrowdStar, Slide, RockYou, Digital Chocolate, and Tagged. One thing is certain: there is nothing virtual about the revenue potential.

Critical Thinking Questions

1. Have you ever purchased a virtual good? If so, describe it. Were you satisfied? If not, what do you think of the prospects for this growing market?

2. What do you think of Facebook's new revenue stream model? Will it work?

demand and supply schedule, are obtained from marketing research and other systematic studies of the market.

demand and supply schedule Assessment of the relationships among different levels of demand and supply at different price levels.

Demand and Supply Curves

The demand and supply schedule can be used to construct demand and supply curves for pizza in your town. A **demand curve** shows how many products—in this case, pizzas—will be demanded (bought) at different prices. A **supply curve** shows how many pizzas will be supplied (cooked) at different prices.

demand curve A graph showing how many units of a product will be demanded (bought) at different prices.

supply curve A graph showing how many units of a product will be supplied (offered for sale) at different prices.

Figure 1.4 shows hypothetical demand and supply curves for pizzas. Demand increases as price decreases, and supply increases as price increases. When the demand and supply curves are plotted on the same graph, the point at which they intersect is the **market price or equilibrium price**—the price at which the quantity of goods demanded and the quantity of goods supplied are equal. Note in Figure 1.4 that the equilibrium price for pizzas is $10. At this point, the quantity of pizzas demanded and the quantity of pizzas supplied are the same: 1000 pizzas per week.

market price (or equilibrium price) Profit-maximizing price at which the quantity of goods demanded and the quantity of goods supplied are equal.

Surpluses and Shortages

What would happen if the owner tried to increase profits by making more pizzas to sell? Or what if the owner wanted to reduce overhead, cut back on store hours, and reduce the number of pizzas offered for sale? In either case, the result would be an inefficient use of resources—and perhaps lower profits. For example, if the restaurant supplies 1200 pizzas and tries to sell them for $10 each, 200 pizzas will not be purchased. The demand schedule shows that only 1000 pizzas will be demanded at this price. The pizza maker will therefore have a **surplus**—a situation in which the quantity supplied exceeds the quantity demanded. The restaurant will thus lose the money it spent making those extra 200 pizzas.

surplus A situation in which quantity supplied exceeds quantity demanded.

Conversely, if the pizzeria supplies only 800 pizzas, a **shortage** will result—the quantity demanded will be greater than the quantity supplied. The pizzeria will "lose" the extra money that it could have made by producing 200 more pizzas. Even though consumers may pay more for pizzas because of the shortage, the restaurant will still earn lower profits than it would have if it had made 1000 pizzas. To optimize profits, businesses must constantly seek the right combination of the price charged and the quantity supplied. This combination is found at the equilibrium point.

shortage A situation in which quantity demanded exceeds quantity supplied.

These supply and demand ideas apply to all sorts of commodities. When demand for a commodity increases, its price goes up. But when that happens, people try to find substitutes that are cheaper. For example, when the price of oil is high, companies use palm oil to make diesel fuel (called biodiesel). But, as more producers start using palm oil, the increased demand causes the price to rise.[33] Maple syrup is a quintessential Canadian commodity (we produce 80 percent of the world's supply), but its price fluctuates because weather influences the supply. A 540 ml bottle cost $5–$6 in 2008 but rose to $8–$11 in 2009.[34]

Price increases for food put a lot of stress on the world's poorest countries, where people spend a large proportion of their income on food. The World Bank has identified 33 countries that are at risk for serious social upheaval because of high food prices.[35] Global food supplies tightened in 2011 as the result of droughts and floods in various countries, and the prices of corn, soybean, and wheat futures were up more than 50 percent.[36] To cope with potential food shortages, some countries slashed import duties and imposed export duties. This is just the reverse of what countries normally do.[37] The boxed insert entitled "The 'China Effect' on Commodity Prices" describes how demand influences prices.

Canada is the dominant supplier of maple syrup for the world market. But variable weather conditions can create conditions of either surplus or shortage.

There are usually some unanticipated outcomes when the prices of commodities rise. One of these is increased criminal activity. As the price of stainless steel and aluminum rose during the past few years, thieves began stealing items such as beer kegs, railway baggage carts, railroad tracks, light poles, and highway guard rails. These items were then sold to scrapyards for cash.[38]

FIGURE 1.4

Demand and supply.

Demand and Supply Schedules

Price	Quantity of Pizzas Demanded	Quantity of Pizzas Supplied
$2	2000	100
$4	1700	400
$6	1500	600
$8	1200	800
$10	1000	1000
$12	800	1200
$14	600	1300
$16	400	1600
$18	200	1800
$20	100	2000

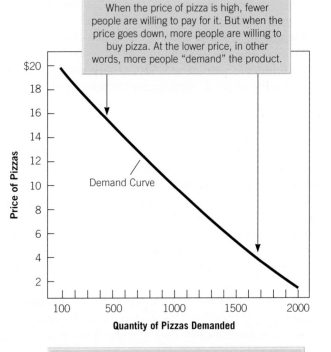

When the price of pizza is high, fewer people are willing to pay for it. But when the price goes down, more people are willing to buy pizza. At the lower price, in other words, more people "demand" the product.

When the price of pizza is low, more people are willing to buy pizza. Pizza makers, however, do not have the money to invest in making pizzas and so make fewer. Supply, therefore, is limited, and only when the price goes up will pizza makers be willing and able to increase supply.

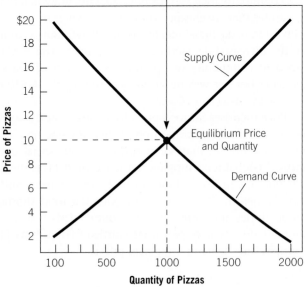

When pizza makers increase supply in order to satisfy demand, there will ultimately be a point at which the price that they can charge is the same as the price that a maximum number of customers are willing to pay. That point is the market price, or equilibrium price.

Private Enterprise and Competition in a Market Economy

Market economies rely on a **private enterprise** system—one that allows individuals to pursue their own interests with minimal government restriction. Private enterprise requires the presence of four elements: private property rights, freedom of choice, profits, and competition.

private enterprise An economic system characterized by private property rights, freedom of choice, profits, and competition.

- *Private property rights*. Ownership of the resources used to create wealth is in the hands of individuals.[39]

- *Freedom of choice*. You can sell your labour to any employer you choose. You can also choose which products to buy, and producers can usually choose whom to hire and what to produce.

- *Profits*. The lure of profits (and freedom) leads some people to abandon the security of working for someone else and to assume the risks of entrepreneurship. Anticipated profits also influence individuals' choices of which goods or services to produce.

Identify the elements of *private enterprise* and explain the various *degrees of competition* in the Canadian economic system.   **LO4**

MANAGING IN TURBULENT TIMES

The "China Effect" on Commodity Prices

During the past decade, the Chinese economy has been growing at a rapid rate, and millions of Chinese join the middle class each year. The increased demand caused by these newly affluent consumers has influenced the prices of a wide range of commodities.

One noticeable area of increased demand is in the so-called "rare earth" metals such as cerium, lanthanum, and neodymium, which are used in products like lasers, ceramics, computers, and wind turbines. China produces about 90 percent of the world's supply of these metals, but it has reduced exports because it wants to ensure a reliable supply for domestic production. This action has created concerns about supply shortages in other countries, and has motivated some of them to start developing their own rare earth mines. For example, Vancouver-based Rare Element Resources Ltd. is developing a rare earth mine in the United States. Chinese demand has also influenced the price of other metals like palladium, which is used in automobile catalytic converters to reduce toxic emissions. From 2010 to 2011, the price of palladium jumped from $400 an ounce to over $900 an ounce. High automobile sales in China are increasing demand for palladium and driving its price higher.

Chinese demand has affected other commodities besides metals. For example, China is the world's largest cotton consumer, and this high level of demand, coupled with the hoarding of supplies, has driven cotton prices to 140-year highs. Many farmers and cotton processors, as well as the Chinese government, are hoarding cotton. The total amount being hoarded is unknown, but it might equal as much as 10 percent of world's supply. Many countries don't report cotton production, so rumours abound as to how much cotton is (or isn't) available. That uncertainty drives up prices even further.

Yet another commodity that is being affected by demand from China is nuts like pistachios, almonds, walnuts, macadamias, cashews, and pecans. Prices on these commodities have risen anywhere from 40 to 70 percent in less than a year. The price of pecans, for example, has soared from $4.25 to $6.50 per pound. Mexico and the United States—the world's leading producers of pecans—now export one-quarter of their total crop to China.

Critical Thinking Questions

1. Most people find it easy to think of negative outcomes that occur because of high prices. Can you think of situations where high prices can lead to positive outcomes? Explain.

2. Consider the following statement: *The high prices of commodities like rare earth metals and palladium are not really a concern because we do not need metals to survive. But the high price of food is a concern because it threatens people's lives. The central governments of the world should therefore coordinate their efforts and put rules in place to ensure that food prices are kept low.* Do you agree or disagree with the statement? Explain your reasoning.

competition The vying among businesses in a particular market or industry to best satisfy consumer demands and earn profits.

■ *Competition.* **Competition** occurs when two or more businesses vie for the same resources or customers. While profits motivate individuals to *start* businesses, competition motivates them to *operate* their businesses efficiently. Competition forces businesses to make products better and/or cheaper. There are several degrees of competition.

Degrees of Competition

Even in a free enterprise system, not all industries are equally competitive. Economists have identified four degrees of competition in a private enterprise system: *perfect competition, monopolistic competition, oligopoly,* and *monopoly* (see Table 1.3).

perfect competition A market or industry characterized by a very large number of small firms producing an identical product so that none of the firms has any ability to influence price.

Perfect Competition. In **perfect competition**, all firms in an industry are small, the number of firms in the industry is large, and the products produced by the different firms are virtually identical. Under these conditions, no single firm is powerful enough to influence prices, so they are determined by the market forces of supply and demand. Canadian agriculture is a good example of perfect competition. The wheat produced on one farm is the same as that on another. Both producers and buyers are aware of prevailing market prices. It is relatively easy to start producing wheat and relatively easy to stop when it's no longer profitable.

monopolistic competition A market or industry characterized by a large number of firms supplying products that are similar but distinctive enough from one another to give firms some ability to influence price.

Monopolistic Competition. In **monopolistic competition**, there are fewer sellers, but still many buyers. Businesses may be large or small, and small clothing stores can compete successfully with large apparel retailers like Liz Claiborne or Limited Brands. Whatever their size, sellers try to make their products at least *seem* different from those of competitors, and this product differentiation gives sellers some control over prices. For instance, even though Sears shirts may look pretty much like Ralph Lauren Polo shirts, the latter can be priced $20 higher than the Sears shirts. Other differentiating strategies include brand names (Tide and Cheer) and advertising (Coca-Cola and Pepsi).

oligopoly A market or industry characterized by a small number of very large firms that have the power to influence the price of their product and/or resources.

Oligopoly. When an industry has only a handful of sellers, an **oligopoly** exists. These sellers are usually quite large, and it is difficult for new competitors to enter the industry because large capital investment is needed. For example, two companies dominate the large commercial aircraft market: Boeing (a U.S. company) and Airbus (a European consortium). The actions of any one firm in an oligopolistic market can significantly affect the sales of all other firms. For example, when one company raises its prices, the others generally follow suit. As a result, the prices of comparable products are usually quite similar. Since substantial price competition would reduce

TABLE 1.3 Degrees of Competition

Characteristic	Perfect Competition	Monopolistic Competition	Oligopoly	Monopoly
Example	Local farmer	Stationery store	Steel industry	Public utility
Number of competitors	Many	Many, but fewer than in perfect competition	Few	None
Ease of entry into industry	Relatively easy	Fairly easy	Difficult	Regulated by government
Similarity of goods or services offered by competing firms	Identical	Similar	Can be similar or different	No directly competing goods or services
Level of control over price by individual firms	None	Some	Some	Considerable

Consumers often buy products under conditions of monopolistic competition. For example, there are few differences among various brands of toothpaste, cold tablets, detergents, canned goods, and soft drinks.

every seller's profits, most oligopolistic firms use product differentiation to attract customers. The four major cereal makers (Kellogg, General Mills, General Foods, and Quaker Oats) control almost all of the cereal market, and each charges roughly the same price for its cereal. But each also advertises that its cereals are better tasting or more nutritious than the others. Competition within an oligopolistic market is often fierce.[40]

Monopoly. When an industry or market has only one producer, a **monopoly** exists. Being the only supplier gives a firm complete control over the price of its product. Its only constraint is how much consumer demand will fall as its price rises. For centuries, wine bottles were sealed using natural cork made from tree bark. But a new technology allows wine bottles to be sealed with plastic corks that are cheaper and work just as well. The natural wine cork industry has lost its monopoly.[41]

Natural monopolies are found in industries in which one company can most efficiently supply all the product or service that is needed. For example, a single provincial electric company can supply all the power (product) needed in an area. Duplicate facilities—such as two nuclear power plants, two sets of power lines, and so forth—would be wasteful. In Canada, laws such as the Competition Act forbid many monopolies, and the prices charged by so-called "natural monopolies" are closely watched by provincial utilities boards.

The assumption that certain activities qualify as natural monopolies is increasingly being challenged. For example, the Royal Mail Group's 350-year monopoly of the British postal service ended in 2006 and rival companies are now allowed to compete with Royal Mail.[42] India Post had a monopoly on mail delivery for several hundred years, but now private couriers like FedEx and United Parcel Service provide more than half the delivery business in India.[43] Between 2005 and 2009, the volume of mail that Canada Post handled declined by 13 percent.[44] There have been repeated calls to end Canada Post's monopoly on letters weighing less than 500 grams (competition from companies like FedEx and UPS is allowed for parcels and express mail). During the 10 years after it became a Crown corporation, Canada Post raised its rates by 41 percent. By contrast, postal rates have dropped in countries where the post office has been privatized (e.g., Germany and the Netherlands).[45]

monopoly A market or industry with only one producer, who can set the price of its product and/or resources.

natural monopoly A market or industry in which having only one producer is most efficient because it can meet all consumer demand for the product.

A Brief History of Business in Canada

L05 Trace the *history of business* in Canada.

A look at the history of business in Canada shows a steady development from sole proprietorships to the complex corporate structures of today. In this section, we will trace the broad outlines of the development of business in Canada. Table 1.4 highlights some of the specific events in Canadian business history.

The Early Years

Business activity and profit from commercial fishing were the motivation for the first European involvement in Canada. In the late 1400s, ships financed by English entrepreneurs came to the coast of Newfoundland to fish for profit. By the late 1500s, the Newfoundland coast was being visited by hundreds of fishing vessels each year.

Beginning in the 1500s, French and British adventurers began trading with the Aboriginal peoples. Items such as cooking utensils and knives were exchanged for beaver and other furs. One trading syndicate made over 1000 percent profit on beaver

TABLE 1.4 Some Important Dates in Canadian Business History

Date	Event	Date	Event
1490	English fishermen active off the coast of Newfoundland	1927	Armand Bombardier sells first "auto-neige" (forerunner of the snowmobile)
1534	Account of first trading with Aboriginal peoples written by Jacques Cartier	1929	Great stock market crash
		1929–33	Great Depression
1670	Hudson's Bay Company founded	1930	Canadian Airways Limited formed
1779	North West Company forms		
1785	Molson brewery opens	1932	Canadian Radio Broadcasting Corporation formed (it became the CBC in 1936)
1805	First Canadian paper mill built at St. Andrew's, Quebec	1935	Bank of Canada begins operations
1809	First steamboat (the *Accommodation*) put into service on the St. Lawrence River by John Molson	1947–51	Early computer built at the University of Toronto
		1947	Leduc Number 1 oil well drilled in Alberta
1817	Bank of Montreal chartered	1949	A.V. Roe (Avro) makes Canada's first commercial jetliner
1821	Hudson's Bay Company and North West Company merge	1965	Auto Pact signed with the United States
1830–50	Era of canal building	1969	Canada becomes world's largest potash producer
1850–60	First era of railroad building		
1855	John Redpath opens first Canadian sugar refinery in Montreal	1989	Free trade agreement with United States comes into effect
1857–58	First oil well in Canada drilled near Sarnia, Ontario	1993	North American Free Trade Agreement comes into effect
1861	Toronto Stock Exchange opens	2000	Tech bubble bursts; stock prices drop sharply
1869	Eaton's opens for business in Toronto	2003	Canadian internet pharmacies begin selling prescription drugs to United States citizens
1880–90	First western land boom		
1885	Last spike driven to complete the Canadian Pacific Railroad	2006	Softwood lumber dispute with United States settled
		2007	Canadian dollar reaches par with United States dollar
1897–99	Klondike gold rush	2008	Oil prices reach record high of $147 per barrel
1917–22	Creation of Canadian National Railways	2008–09	Worldwide recession occurs; stock markets drop sharply
1926	United States replaces Great Britain as Canada's largest trading partner	2011–12	European sovereign debt crisis; world economies are fragile

skins sold to a Paris furrier. Trading was aggressive and, over time, the price of furs rose as more and more Europeans bid for them. Originally the fur trade was restricted to eastern Canada, but by the late 1600s, *coureurs de bois* were travelling far to the west in search of new sources of furs.

European settlers who arrived in Canada in the sixteenth and seventeenth centuries initially had to farm or starve. Gradually, however, they began to produce more than they needed for their own survival. The governments of the countries from which the settlers came (notably England and France) were strong supporters of the mercantilist philosophy. Under *mercantilism*, colonists were expected to export raw materials like beaver pelts and lumber at low prices to the mother country. These raw materials were then used to produce finished goods such as fur coats, which were sold at high prices to settlers in Canada. Attempts to develop industry in Canada were thwarted by England and France, who enjoyed large profits from mercantilism. As a result, Canadian manufacturing was slow to develop.

The Factory System and the Industrial Revolution

British manufacturing took a great leap forward around 1750 with the coming of the **Industrial Revolution**. A new level of production was made possible by advances in technology and by the development of the **factory system**. Instead of hundreds of workers turning out items one at a time in their cottages, the factory system brought together in one place all of the materials and workers required to produce items in large quantities, along with newly created machines capable of **mass production**.

Mass production offered savings in several areas. It avoided unnecessary duplication of equipment. It allowed firms to purchase raw materials at better prices by buying large lots. And most important, it encouraged **specialization** of labour. No longer did production require highly skilled craftspeople who could do all the different tasks required to make an item. A series of semi-skilled workers, each trained to perform only one task and supported by specialized machines and tools, greatly increased output.

In spite of British laws against the export of technology and against manufacturing in North America, Canadian manufacturing existed almost from the beginning of European settlement. Modest manufacturing operations were evident in sawmills, breweries, gristmills, tanneries, woollen mills, shoemakers' shops, and tailors' shops. These operations were so successful that, by 1800, exports of manufactured goods were more important than exports of fur.

With the advent of steam power in the early 1800s, manufacturing activity began to increase rapidly. By 1850, more than 30 factories—employing more than 2000 people—lined the Lachine Canal in Montreal alone. Exports of timber to England in 1850 were 70 times greater than what they had been in 1800. The demand for reliable transportation was the impetus for canal building in the mid-1800s and then the railroad-building boom in the mid-and late 1800s.

The Entrepreneurial Era

One of the most significant features of the last half of the nineteenth century was the emergence of entrepreneurs willing to take risks in the hope of earning huge profits. Adam Smith, in his book *The Wealth of Nations*, argued that the government should not interfere in the economy but rather should let businesses function without regulation or restriction. The Canadian government often adopted this laissez-faire attitude. As a result, during the **entrepreneurial era** some individuals became immensely wealthy through their aggressive business dealings. Some railway, bank, and

Industrial Revolution A major change in goods production that began in England in the mid-eighteenth century and was characterized by a shift to the factory system, mass production, and specialization of labour.

factory system A process in which all the machinery, materials, and workers required to produce a good in large quantities are brought together in one place.

mass production The manufacture of products of uniform quality in large quantities.

specialization The breaking down of complex operations into simple tasks that are easily learned and performed.

In the production era, the emphasis was on finding the most efficient ways to produce products. These textile workers in the early 20th century worked long hours performing highly repetitive, specialized activities that resulted in dramatic increases in output compared to the "cottage" industries of earlier times.

entrepreneurial era Individuals became immensely wealthy through their aggressive business dealings.

insurance executives made over $25 000 per year in the late 1800s, and their purchasing power was immense because prices then were just a fraction of what they are now. Entrepreneurs such as Joseph Flavelle, Henry Pellatt, and John MacDonald lived in ostentatious mansions.

The size and economic power of some firms meant that other businesses had difficulty competing against them. At the same time, some business executives decided that it was more profitable to collude than to compete. They decided among themselves to fix prices and divide up markets. Hurt by these actions, Canadian consumers called for more regulation of business. In 1889, the first anti-combines legislation was passed in Canada, and legislation regulating business has increased ever since.

The Production Era

The concepts of specialization and mass production that originated in the Industrial Revolution were more fully refined as Canada entered the twentieth century. The Scientific Management Movement focused management's attention on production. Increased efficiency via the "one best way" to accomplish tasks became the major management goal.

production era The period during the early twentieth century when businesses focused almost exclusively on improving productivity and manufacturing methods.

In the United States, Henry Ford's introduction of the moving assembly line in 1913 ushered in the **production era**. During the production era, less attention was paid to selling and marketing than to technical efficiency when producing goods. By using fixed workstations, increasing task specialization, and moving the work to the worker, the assembly line increased productivity and lowered prices, making all kinds of products affordable for the average person. It also increased the available labour pool because many people could be trained to carry out assembly line tasks. Formerly, the labour pool was limited because relatively few people had the high skill levels of craftspeople.

During the production era, large businesses began selling stock—making shareholders the owners—and relying on professional managers. The growth of corporations and improved production output that resulted from assembly lines came at the expense of worker freedom. The dominance of big firms made it harder

Most of these software developers are among the 65,000 engineers that the Indian State of Andhra Pradesh graduates every year—up from 7,500 just 10 years ago. Microsoft operates an R&D center in the capital city of Hyderabad, where Oracle, computer Associates, and IBM also have facilities. The city is prospering as a hub not only for software programming, but for telephone call centres and pharmaceuticals as well.

for individuals to go into business for themselves. Company towns run by the railroads, mining corporations, and forest products firms gave individuals little freedom of choice over whom to work for and what to buy. To restore some balance within the overall system, both government and labour had to develop and grow. Thus, this period saw the rise of labour unions and collective bargaining (more detail is provided in Chapter 9). The Great Depression of the 1930s and the Second World War caused the federal government to intervene in the economic system on a previously unimaginable scale.

Business, government, and labour are the three *countervailing powers* in our society. All are big. All are strong. Yet none totally dominates the others.

The Sales and Marketing Eras

By the 1930s, businesses' focus on production had resulted in spectacular increases in the amount of goods and services for sale. As a result, buyers had more choices and producers faced greater competition in selling their wares. Thus began the so-called **sales era**. According to the ideas of that time, a business's profits and success depended on hiring the right salespeople, advertising heavily, and making sure products were readily available. Business firms were essentially production- and sales-oriented, and they produced what they thought customers wanted or simply what the company was good at producing. This approach is still used by firms that find themselves with surplus goods that they want to sell (e.g., used-car dealerships).

> **sales era** The period during the 1930s and 1940s when businesses focused on sales forces, advertising, and keeping products readily available.

Following the Second World War, pent-up demand for consumer goods kept the economy rolling. While brief recessions did occur periodically, the 1950s and 1960s were prosperous times. Production increased, technology advanced, and the standard of living rose. During the **marketing era**, business adopted a new philosophy of how to do business—use market research to determine what customers want, and then make it for them. Firms like Procter & Gamble and Molson were very effective during the marketing era and continue to be profitable today. Each offers an array of products within a particular field (toothpaste or beer, for example) and gives customers a chance to pick what best suits their needs.

> **marketing era** The period during the 1950s and 1960s when businesses began to identify and meet consumer wants in order to make a profit.

The Finance Era

In the 1980s, emphasis shifted to finance. In the **finance era** there was a sharp increase in mergers and in the buying and selling of business enterprises. Some people now call it the "decade of greed." As we will see in Chapter 2, during the finance era there were many hostile takeovers and a great deal of financial manipulation of corporate assets by so-called corporate raiders. Critics charged that these raiders were simply enriching themselves and weren't creating anything of tangible value by their activity. They also charged that raiders were distracting business managers from their main goals of running the business. The raiders responded that they were making organizations more efficient by streamlining, merging, and reorganizing them.

> **finance era** The period during the 1980s when there were many mergers and much buying and selling of business enterprises.

The Global Era

The past few years have seen the continuation of technological advances in production, computer technology, information systems, and communication capabilities. A truly global economy has also emerged. Canadians drive cars made in Japan, wear sweaters made in Italy, drink beer brewed in Mexico, and listen to stereos made in Taiwan. But we're not alone in this. People around the world buy products and services from foreign companies.

Many Canadian businesses have been hurt by foreign imports, but numerous others have profited by exploring new foreign markets. Domestic competition has forced many businesses to work harder than ever to cut costs, increase efficiency, and improve product and service quality. We will explore a variety of important trends, opportunities, and challenges of the **global era** throughout this book.

global era The emergence of a truly global economy, facilitated by advances in production, computer technology, and communication systems.

The Internet Era

internet era The rapid growth of the internet has opened up new growth possibilities for both small and large businesses.

The turn of the century has been accompanied by what many experts are calling the **internet era** of business. The growth of the internet affects business in at least three different ways:

1. The internet gives a dramatic boost to trade in all sectors of the economy, especially services. If the internet makes it easier for all trade to grow, this is particularly true for trade in services on an international scale.

2. The internet levels the playing field, at least to some extent, between larger and smaller enterprises, regardless of what products or services they sell. In the past, a substantial investment was typically needed to enter some industries and to enter foreign markets. Now, however, a small business based in central Alberta, southern Italy, eastern Malaysia, or northern Brazil can set up a website and compete quite effectively with much larger businesses located around the world.

3. The internet holds considerable potential as an effective and efficient networking mechanism among businesses. Business-to-business (B2B) networks can link firms with all of their suppliers, business customers, and strategic partners in ways that make it faster and easier for them to do business together.

MyBizLab

Capture more moments of true understanding. MyBizLab provides you with interactive study and practice tools directly related to this chapter's content. The new MyBizLab Study Plan Learning Path is designed to measure a full range of skills and provide remediation to give you what you need to master key chapter concepts. MyBizLab flexes to your unique learning needs. The result? Inspired learning, more success.

SUMMARY OF LEARNING OBJECTIVES

1. **Define the nature of Canadian *business* and identify its main goals.** *Businesses* are organizations that produce or sell goods or services to make a profit. *Profits* are the difference between the revenues and expenses of a business. The prospect of earning profits encourages individuals and organizations to open and expand businesses. The benefits of business activities also extend to wages paid to workers and to taxes that support government functions.

2. **Describe different types of *global economic systems* according to the means by which they control the *factors of production* through *input* and *output markets*.** An *economic system* is a nation's system for allocating its resources among its citizens. Economic systems differ in terms of who owns or controls the basic *factors of production*: labour, capital, entrepreneurs, natural resources, and information resources. In command economies, the government controls all or most of these factors. In *market economies*,

which are based on the principles of capitalism, individuals and businesses control the factors of production and exchange them through input and output markets. Most countries today have mixed market economies that are dominated by one of these systems but include elements of the other. The process of *privatization* is an important means by which many of the world's planned economies moved toward mixed market systems.

3. **Show how *demand* and *supply* affect resource distribution in Canada.** The Canadian economy is strongly influenced by markets, demand, and supply. *Demand* is the willingness and ability of buyers to purchase a good or service. *Supply* is the willingness and ability of producers to offer goods or services for sale. Demand and supply work together to set a *market* or *equilibrium price*—the price at which the quantity of goods demanded and the quantity of goods supplied are equal.

4. **Identify the elements of *private enterprise* and explain the various *degrees of competition* in the Canadian economic system.** The Canadian economy is founded on the principles of *private enterprise*: private property rights, freedom of choice, profits, and competition. *Degrees of competition* vary because not all industries are equally competitive. Under conditions of *perfect competition*, numerous small firms compete in a market governed entirely by demand and supply. In *monopolistic competition*, there are a smaller number of sellers, and each one tries to make its product seem different than the products of competitors. An *oligopoly* involves only a handful of sellers who fiercely compete with each other. A *monopoly* involves only one seller.

5. **Trace the *history of business* in Canada.** Modern business structures reflect a pattern of development over centuries. Throughout much of the colonial period, sole proprietors supplied raw materials to English manufacturers. The rise of the factory system during the *Industrial Revolution* brought with it mass production and specialization of labour. During the *entrepreneurial era* in the nineteenth century, large corporations—and monopolies—emerged. During the *production era* of the early twentieth century, companies grew by emphasizing output and production. During the *sales and marketing eras* of the 1950s and 1960s, business began focusing on sales staff, advertising, and the need to produce what consumers wanted. In the 1980s—the *finance era*—there was increased buying and selling of businesses, and in the 1990s—the *global era*—a significant global economy emerged. Many Canadian companies have profited from exporting their goods to foreign markets. The most recent development—the *internet era*—is the use of the internet to conduct business. To some extent, the internet should level the playing field between large and small companies.

KEY TERMS

business (p. 6)
Canada Consumer Product Safety Act (p. 15)
Canada Water Act (p. 15)
Canadian Radio-television and Telecommunications Commission (CRTC) (p. 13)
Canadian Transport Commission (CTC) (p. 13)
Canadian Wheat Board (p. 14)
capital (p. 7)
capitalism (p. 11)
command economy (p. 9)
communism (p. 9)
competition (p. 21)
demand (p. 18)
demand and supply schedule (p. 19)
demand curve (p. 19)
deregulation (p. 11)
economic system (p. 7)
entrepreneur (p. 8)
entrepreneurial era (p. 25)
Environmental Contaminants Act (p. 16)

factors of production (p. 7)
factory system (p. 25)
finance era (p. 27)
Fisheries Act (p. 15)
Food and Drug Act (p. 15)
global era (p. 28)
Industrial Revolution (p. 25)
information resources (p. 9)
input market (p. 10)
internet era (p. 28)
labour (or human resources) (p. 7)
law of demand (p. 18)
law of supply (p. 18)
lobbyist (p. 16)
market (p. 9)
market economy (p. 9)
market price (or equilibrium price) (p. 19)
marketing era (p. 28)
mass production (p. 25)
mixed market economy (p. 11)
monopolistic competition (p. 22)
monopoly (p. 23)
nationalization (p. 11)
natural monopoly (p. 23)

natural resources (p. 8)
not-for-profit organizations (p. 7)
oligopoly (p. 22)
output market (p. 10)
perfect competition (p. 22)
private enterprise (p. 21)
privatization (p. 11)
production era (p. 26)
profit (p. 6)
progressive revenue taxes (p. 16)
regressive revenue taxes (p. 16)
restrictive taxes (p. 16)
revenue taxes (p. 16)
sales era (p. 27)
shortage (p. 19)
socialism (p. 9)
specialization (p. 25)
supply (p. 18)
supply curve (p. 19)
surplus (p. 19)
Textile Labelling Act (p. 15)
Tobacco Act (p. 14)
trade association (p. 17)
Weights and Measures Act (p. 15)

QUESTIONS FOR ANALYSIS

1. Is one factor of production more important than the others? If so, which one? Why?

2. Government occasionally provides financial incentives to business firms. For example, the Canadian government provided expert assistance to Bombardier Inc. with its Technology Transfer Program. Is this consistent with a basically free market system? Explain how this might distort the system.

3. In recent years, many countries have moved from planned economies to market economies. Why do you think this has occurred? What recent events might cause a resurgence of planned economies? Explain.

4. Familiarize yourself with a product or service that is sold under conditions of perfect competition. Explain why it is an example of perfect competition and identify the factors that make it so. Then do the same for a product in each of the other three competitive situations described in the chapter (monopolistic competition, oligopoly, and monopoly).

5. Government plays a variety of roles in the Canadian mixed economy. Consider each of the roles discussed in the text and state the criteria you would use to decide whether government involvement in each role is excessive, insufficient, or about right. What criteria did you use to make your assessments?

6. Pick a specific product that you use. Explain how the factors of production work together to make that product available.

APPLICATION EXERCISES

1. Choose a locally owned business. Interview the owner to find out (1) how demand and supply affect the business, (2) how the business uses the factors of production, and (3) how the owner acquires them.

2. Visit a local shopping mall or shopping area. List each store that you see and determine what degree of competition it faces in its *immediate environment*. For example, if there is only one store in the mall that sells shoes, that store represents a monopoly. Note those businesses with direct competitors (e.g., two jewellery stores) and show how they compete with one another.

3. Go to the library or log onto the internet and research five different industries. Classify each according to the degree of competition they face.

4. Find an instance where a surplus led to decreased prices for a product not discussed in this chapter. Then find an example where a shortage led to increased prices. What eventually happened in each case? Why? Is what happened consistent with what economic theory predicts?

BUILDING YOUR BUSINESS SKILLS

Analyzing the Price of Doing eBusiness

The Purpose of the Assignment

To encourage students to understand how the competitive environment affects a product's price.

The Situation

Assume that you own a local business that provides internet access to individuals and businesses. (This kind of business is called an ISP or internet service provider.) Yours is one of four such businesses in the local market. Each of the four companies charges the same price: $20 per month for unlimited service. Your business also provides users with email service; two of your competitors also offer email service. One of these same two competitors, plus the third, also provides the individual user with a free, basic personal webpage. One competitor just dropped its price to $14 per month, and the other two have announced their intentions to follow suit. Your break-even price is $10 per customer; that is, you must charge $10 for your service package to cover your costs (but not earn any profit). You are concerned about getting into a price war that may destroy your business.

Method

Divide into groups of four or five people. Each group is to develop a general strategy for handling competitors' price changes. In your discussion, take the following factors into account:

■ how the demand for your product is affected by price changes

■ the number of competitors selling the same or a similar product

■ the methods—other than price—you can use to attract new customers and/or retain current customers

Analysis

Develop specific pricing strategies based on each of the following situations:

■ Within a month after dropping the price to $14, one of your competitors raises its price back to $18.

- Two of your competitors drop their prices further—to $12 per month. As a result, your business falls off by 25 percent.
- One of your competitors that has provided customers with a free webpage has indicated that it will start charging an extra $4 per month for this optional service.
- Two of your competitors have announced that they will charge individual users $12 per month but will charge businesses a higher price (not yet announced).
- All four providers (including you) are charging $11 per month. One goes out of business, and you know that another is in poor financial health.

Questions for Discussion

1. Discuss the role that various inducements other than price might play in affecting demand and supply in the market for internet service.
2. Is it always in a company's best interest to offer the lowest prices?
3. Eventually, what form of competition is likely to characterize the market for internet service?

EXERCISING YOUR ETHICS: TEAM EXERCISE

Making the Right Decision

The Situation

Hotel S is a large hotel in a Maritime city. The hotel is a franchise operation run by an international hotel chain. The primary source of revenue for the hotel is convention business. A major tropical storm is working its way up the east coast and is about to hit the city. When that happens, heavy flooding is likely.

The Dilemma

Because Hotel S is a licensed operation, it must maintain numerous quality standards in order to keep its licence. This licence is important because the international management company handles advertising, reservations, and so on. If it were to lose its licence, the hotel would almost certainly have to reduce its staff.

For the past few years, members of the Hotel S team have been lobbying the investors who own the hotel to undertake a major renovation. They fear that without such a renovation, the hotel will lose its licence when it comes up for renewal in a few months. The owners, however, have balked at investing more of their funds in the hotel itself but have indicated that hotel management can use revenues earned above a specified level for upgrades.

The approaching storm has cut off most major transportation avenues, and land lines and cellphone service are also down. The Hotel S staff are unable to reach the general manager, who has been travelling on business. Because the city is full of conventioneers, hotel rooms are in high demand. Unfortunately, because of the disrepair at the hotel, it has only about 50 percent occupancy. Hotel S staff have been discussing what to do and have identified three options:

1. The hotel can reduce room rates in order to help local citizens as well as out-of-town visitors. The hotel can also provide meals at reduced rates. A few other hotels are also doing this.
2. The hotel can maintain its present pricing policies. Most of the city's hotels are adopting this course of action.

3. The hotel can raise its rates by approximately 15 percent without attracting too much attention. It can also start charging for certain things it has been providing for free, such as parking and morning coffee. The staff members see this option as one way to generate extra profits for the renovation and thus protect jobs.

Team Activity

Assemble a group of four students and assign each group member to one of the following roles:

- a member of the hotel staff
- the Hotel S manager
- a customer at the hotel
- a Hotel S investor

Action Steps

1. Before discussing the situation with your group, and from the perspective of your assigned role, which of the three options do you think is the best choice? Write down the reasons for your position.
2. Before discussing the situation with your group, and from the perspective of your assigned role, what are the underlying ethical issues, if any, in this situation? Write down the issues.
3. Gather your group together and reveal, in turn, each member's comments on the best choice of the three options. Next, reveal the ethical issues listed by each member.
4. Appoint someone to record the main points of agreement and disagreement within the group. How do you explain the results? What accounts for any disagreement?
5. From an ethical standpoint, what does your group conclude is the most appropriate action that should be taken by the hotel in this situation?
6. Develop a group response to the following question: Can your team identify other solutions that might help satisfy both extreme views?

Go to MyBizLab for additional cases and exercise material.

CONCLUDING CASE 1-1

Are We Headed for Shortages?

During the past few years, much concern has been expressed by government officials and the media about looming shortages of commodities such as oil, rare earth metals, and food. Some of the reports sound alarming, and they suggest that we are entering a period when increasing demand and decreasing supply are going to cause prices to skyrocket. Some pessimists argue that we are going to run out of certain commodities (for example, oil), and this will cause a crisis in the world economy and cause a major decline in our standard of living. Are these predictions accurate? Or are they just another doomsday prediction that won't come true?

Let's look at the situation for oil to get an understanding of how debates about natural resources unfold. A few years ago, the so-called "peak oil" theory was very popular. It said that world oil production had peaked and was going to rapidly decline and cause a major crisis in the world. Supporters of this idea presented certain facts to show that peak oil was imminent:

- Output from existing oil fields around the world is declining, and that means that three to four million barrels a day of new oil will have to be found for global oil production just to remain steady.
- Top-level executives in the oil industry say that there is a limit to how much oil can be produced each year (about 100 million barrels per day), and that ceiling may be reached within the next few years.
- Oil production will peak because of factors such as restricted access to oil fields, shortages of oil field workers, rapidly increasing costs, political crises, and complex oil field geology.
- New oil discoveries have declined sharply. For example, new discoveries in the Middle East during 1963–72 totalled 187 billion barrels, but new discoveries during 1993–2002 totalled only 16 billion barrels.

Opponents of peak oil theory accepted these facts, but rejected the idea that a crisis was coming. They argued that other important facts had been ignored by peak oil supporters:

- The world's "ultimate recoverable reserves" (URR) are growing at an increasing rate. For example, during the period 1957–2006, URR grew at an annual rate of 2.4 percent, but during 2000–07 it grew at an annual rate of 6 percent. New oil discoveries were made in 2010 and 2011 off the coast of Brazil and in the Gulf of Mexico, and North American oil production is once again climbing because of the Alberta oil sands and the Bakken oil field in North Dakota.
- The U.S. Geological Services (USGS) predicts that URR will grow by about 2.4 percent annually for the next few years. The URR was 1.6 trillion barrels in 1995 and was predicted to rise to 3.3 trillion barrels in 2025, but it had already reached 3.2 trillion barrels in 2006, years ahead of schedule.
- In 1979, the "life index" of oil was estimated to be about 35 years (at 1979 consumption rates). That meant that we would experience an oil crisis early in the twenty-first century. But by 2003, the life index had actually risen to 40 years, and by 2007 it had risen to 45 years. These increases have occurred even though oil consumption rates now far exceed those of 1979.
- The global supply of proved economically accessible fossil fuels (oil, natural gas, and coal) is 5.7 trillion barrels of oil equivalent. Not included in this estimate are non-fossil fuels like hydroelectric power, hard-to-get coal deposits in Alaska (which may hold 3.2 trillion tons of coal), shale gas deposits (1.3 trillion oil equivalent barrels), or methane hydrates under the ocean (85 trillion cubic feet). If all of these are included, our supply of fossil fuels will last hundreds of years.

- As oil prices increase, greater amounts of oil will be economically extracted from formations such as the Alberta oil sands, alternate sources of fuel will be developed, and new technologies for extracting oil will be developed.
- For the first time in decades, oil production in the United States is actually increasing.

Although only a few short years have passed since the peak oil debate began, the predictions of peak oil supporters are already looking very questionable. One reason is the dramatic change that has occurred during the past few years with respect to another fossil fuel: natural gas. As recently as 2008, natural gas reserves didn't seem to be very large. But then a new technology was developed to tap "shale gas" (natural gas that is trapped in sedimentary rocks). The new technology involves pumping water, sand, and chemicals into the ground under high pressure to fracture the rock and release the natural gas (the process is called "fracking"). In 2011, the U.S.-based Energy Information Administration (EIA) released a report stating that total recoverable natural gas (including conventional natural gas and shale gas) was 4.244 quadrillion cubic feet. At present consumption rates, the supply will last 575 years. There are many other shale formations around the world, so the actual supply of shale gas may be immense. Because natural gas is relatively cheap, the dramatic increase in the supply is likely to suppress the development of other forms of power (nuclear, wind, and solar).

In the future, even more dramatic gains may be made. For example, a successful field trial was announced in 2012 using a technology to extract natural gas from methane hydrates (chunks of ice that trap natural gas). This type of natural gas is the most abundant fossil fuel, and the numbers are staggering. For example, the United States currently produces 21 trillion cubic feet (tcf) of natural gas and shale gas annually. But it is estimated that there are *330 000* tcf of methane hydrates in the United States, which is enough to last for 3000 years.

So, let's return to the original question: Are we running out of natural resources? Brian Crowley, the managing director of the Macdonald-Laurier Institute, says that we must look at both the supply and demand side before giving an answer. The "supply" of a natural resource like oil doesn't simply mean the physical amount of oil that is found in the earth; it also includes the application of human ingenuity in finding better ways to use the natural resource. So, while it is true that there is a finite quantity of natural resources (fossil fuels, oil, coal, etc.), we will not run out of them because we are becoming more and more efficient at using these natural resources. For example, we now require less land to feed people, less steel to make a car, and less gasoline to travel a given distance than we used to. Consider a specific example: Years ago, there were miles of overhead copper telephone wires along roadways, but with the development of fibre optics, the demand for copper declined. The development of wireless technology has therefore increased the reach of the telephone without any increase in the need for copper.

Questions for Discussion

1. After considering the arguments in support of peak oil theory and the arguments against it, draw a graph that shows your predictions of world oil production from now until the year 2100 (measure annual world oil production in billions of barrels on the vertical axis and time on the horizontal axis). Defend your predictions.
2. It appears that the supply of fossil fuels is very large. Discuss some potential problems that might arise, even with such a large supply.
3. Consider the following statement: *There are so many uncertainties that must be taken into account when trying to predict the supply of, and demand for, natural resources that it is impossible to have any confidence in anyone's predictions.* Do you agree or disagree with the statement? Explain your reasoning.

CONCLUDING CASE 1-2

Are Government Bailouts a Good Idea?

On May 30, 2011, at a ceremony at Chrysler's Etobicoke Casting Plant in Toronto, Finance Minister Jim Flaherty announced that the automaker was repaying $1.7 billion of the $2.9 billion in bailout loans that the Canadian government had given to Chrysler. Approximately $1.2 billion is still owed to the government, but only about $110 million is likely to be recovered when the government sells its equity stake in Chrysler. General Motors also received a bailout ($10.8 billion), but it had only repaid $1.5 billion as of May 2011.

Supporters of the bailouts said the partial repayment demonstrated that the bailouts were necessary, and that they were a good idea. Critics immediately pointed out that the payments to date have been only partial, and that the two automakers still owe billions to the Canadian government. They also said that the cost of maintaining 52 000 jobs in the Canadian automobile industry has been very high (one calculation showed that each job that was saved cost $80 000).

The partial bailout repayments are the latest event in the saga of government bailouts of the Canadian automobile industry. For the past decade or so, Chrysler and General Motors (GM) have been experiencing increasing difficulties. Their market shares have declined because they did not produce cars that captured the interest of enough consumers. Chrysler's market share, for example, dropped from about 17 percent in 1998 to 8.5 percent in 2009, and its workforce dropped from 17 000 in 2000 to 8200 in 2009. With the decline in market share came rapidly increasing financial problems, and in April 2009 Chrysler filed for Chapter 11 bankruptcy in the United States. During the six weeks Chrysler spent in bankruptcy protection, it shut down its production facilities. It reopened its manufacturing plants in Brampton and Windsor in late June 2009.

GM filed for bankruptcy in June 2009. Its biggest problem was a $7-billion shortfall in its pension plan. There is only one active GM worker for every six retired workers (at Chrysler, there is one active worker for every two retired workers). GM plans to produce the Volt (a "green" electric car), but doesn't know when it will be profitable.

The U.S. and Canadian governments required GM and Chrysler to come up with a restructuring plan before they would receive any bailout money. In the United States, GM reached an agreement with the United Auto Workers union on a new contract that reduced its costs; however, this put pressure on the Canadian Auto Workers union to also reach a new agreement. If they hadn't, GM Canada might have ceased to exist because the Government of Canada wouldn't give GM the bailout money it needed to survive. The Canadian government said it had no choice but to get involved in a bailout once the U.S. government decided to give money to GM and Chrysler. The U.S. government essentially told Canada that if we didn't help out, GM and Chrysler would leave Canada and all those auto jobs would be lost.

Back in 2008, the federal ministry of Industry said that the Government of Canada would not provide bailouts to auto companies. But in the end, the Canadian government agreed to give GM about $10 billion (the United States gave GM about $50 billion). At least for the moment, both governments own a percentage of GM (the United States owns 72 percent of the company and Canada owns 13 percent). As part of the deal, debt holders will trade $27 billion in debt in return for a 15 percent stake in GM. In return for the bailout money from the Canadian government, GM promised to maintain 16 percent of its North American production in Canada (that's down from 22 percent before bankruptcy was declared). GM Canada's workforce will be about 4400 (it was 20 000 in 2005). The Canadian and U.S. governments also gave bailout money to Chrysler (the United States owns a 20 percent stake in Chrysler and the Canadian government owns 2 percent).

The Views of Bailout Opponents

Critics of the auto bailouts raised several objections at the time they were being considered. The first, and most fundamental, objection was that government should not prop up businesses that are in trouble. If a company is not doing well, it should be allowed to fail. There is an old saying that goes something like this: "Governments are terrible at picking winners, but losers are great at picking governments." The government seems to have forgotten decades of hard lessons that they should not get involved in market-oriented businesses. But now they are involved in the automobile business, and the government is essentially investing money where private citizens would never be willing to put it. Most of the $10 billion bailout did not go toward rebuilding the

company, but rather to pay off GM's pension commitments to its workers. Critics said that Canadian taxpayers are obliged to cover pensions of auto workers that the union extracted from the auto companies. Many Canadians don't have much of a retirement fund, and they make a lot less than auto workers do, but they are being asked to help preserve the pensions of auto workers.

Second, critics argued that the GM bailout will cost Canadian taxpayers a large amount of money for each job that is "saved." There is also concern that GM will need more bailout money in the future, and the company is therefore a poor choice for a bailout. What's worse, bailouts won't save jobs overall. Rather, they will simply destroy jobs at companies like Toyota and Ford, which didn't get bailouts. Ford will now be saddled with more debt than GM or Chrysler—and is effectively being punished for not needing bailout money in the first place. Mark Milke, director of research at the Frontier Centre for Public Policy, says that the bailouts for GM and Chrysler are nothing more than a transfer of wealth to companies that consumers have already rejected.

Third, the bailouts in the auto industry will likely lead to companies in other industries asking for bailouts. For example, the forestry, fisheries, auto parts, and commercial airline industries are all having financial problems. The federal government has already announced $1 billion in aid for the pulp and paper industry so they can invest in technology that will make them more energy efficient and environmentally friendly.

Fourth, there was doubt that the bailout money would ever be totally repaid. If it is not, Canadians will have to bear the burden through higher taxes and/or cuts to public services. Critics are asking why the government is sinking money into two companies that have been steadily losing market share. Peter Coleman, president of the National Citizens Coalition, says that the bailout money will be useless if people don't start buying cars made by Chrysler and GM.

Fifth, the usual lender hierarchy is not being observed in the bailout plan. In the United States, for example, the Indiana State Police Pension Trust was entitled to first priority under U.S. bankruptcy law, but it was "persuaded" to accept only 30 cents on the dollar. The UAW, on the other hand, got 50 cents on the dollar even though it wasn't as high on the priority list. When things like this happen, creditors have difficulty pricing the risk of investing because the rules of the game are being changed on short notice. In the future, lenders will be more fearful that the government will intervene and not give them what they are due if a bankruptcy occurs.

The Views of Bailout Supporters

Critics of the bailouts have been very vocal, and their ideas have received a lot of publicity, but there are also defenders of the bailouts. The most fundamental argument in support of bailouts is that they are occasionally necessary when the ups and downs in the economy (oscillations) become so severe that chaos looms. Supporters of bailouts argue that during these times government needs to intervene to reduce the oscillations. They draw an analogy between the current economic gyrations and the physical gyrations that occurred when the Tacoma Narrows Bridge collapsed many years ago. High winds caused oscillations that became progressively more severe until the bridge collapsed in spectacular fashion. Supporters of bailouts argue that government must stop the oscillations in the economic system before they cause a disaster.

The defenders of bailouts also argue that they are necessary to protect jobs. The view is that it would be disastrous for all those auto workers to lose their jobs because those workers spend a lot of money on a wide variety of goods and services. If those expenditures stopped, the economy would suffer greatly. A study by the Centre for Spatial Economics found that the failure of any of the Big Three domestic car makers would throw Ontario into a deep recession, and 157 000 jobs would be lost (auto production workers, auto dealers, auto parts suppliers, and professional services that are tied to the auto industry). In addition, GM spends billions of dollars each year buying products and services from other Canadian companies, and those other companies employ thousands of additional workers. All those workers in turn spend a lot of money and boost the economy. They also pay a lot of income tax, and the government does not want to lose that revenue.

Questions for Discussion

1. Which roles is government playing when it gives bailout money to businesses?
2. Do you think that providing bailouts to businesses that are in trouble violates certain fundamental principles on which the Canadian economy is based? Explain your reasoning.
3. Supporters of bailouts argue that in crisis situations the government needs to step in and try to stabilize the economy so that chaos does not occur. Do you agree or disagree with this view? Explain your reasoning.
4. Given the information presented above, do you think that the Canadian government should have given bailout money to GM and Chrysler? Defend your answer.

Understanding the Environments of Business

LEARNING OBJECTIVES

After reading this chapter, you should be able to:

① Explain the concepts of *organizational boundaries* and multiple *organizational environments*.

② Explain the importance of the *economic environment* to business and identify the factors used to evaluate the performance of an *economic system*.

③ Describe the *technological environment* and its role in business.

④ Describe the *political-legal environment* and its role in business.

⑤ Describe the *socio-cultural environment* and its role in business.

⑥ Identify emerging challenges and opportunities in the *business environment*.

⑦ Understand recent trends in the *redrawing of corporate boundaries*.

Video Content Providers Must Evolve or Perish: Netflix and Beyond

FOR about two decades Blockbuster was the premier name in the video rental business. The announcement in 2011 that the company was going bankrupt was a clear sign of the times. Blockbuster's troubles turned into a crisis when Hollywood studios called in US$70 million worth of debt. Blockbuster had fallen from a shining star to a victim of technology; it tried to hold on to the past and was slow to evolve. The company announced that it would close its doors by the end of 2011 but there was still hope of a revival when Dish Network acquired the U.S. parent company. There was also some short-term profit potential in the Canadian retail DVD market as rentals still accounted for 94 percent of sales in Canada at the time. However, the devastating truth was that this figure had already declined to 43 percent in the United States. With the introduction of Netflix (and other services) into Canada those numbers were bound to decline rapidly here as well.

According to experts like Kaan Yigit, president of consultancy Solutions Research Group, we had entered the Netflix decade.

Netflix Models: Technological Shocks

Netflix represents the great promise of technology and yet it is also a perfect example of the challenge of doing business in a technological age. Here is a company that was created only about 15 years ago and yet it has already changed its core business model twice. The initial Netflix success story was based on DVD home delivery service in the United States, a novel idea at the time. Whereas competitors like Blockbuster were saddled with big locations and high rental space costs, Netflix was able to provide subscribers with a reliable home delivery service

at an economical price. But the initial success would have soon faded if Netflix had not evolved with the times. Netflix quickly jumped on the next game changing opportunity: the video-on-demand streaming business. By the end of 2011, using a dual strategy (online streaming and DVD rentals), they had amassed 25 million subscribers (including 1 million in Canada in the first year).

Competitive Forces

Netflix had become a poster child for online success. It was also a model that new competitors and suppliers would quickly copy and/or exploit. One of the reasons for that success was its ability to charge a low monthly flat fee of just US$7.99. As a pioneer, Netflix had negotiated favourable content-rights deals with movie studios and TV show producers. But soon problems began to

surface. Canadian customers complained about the limited selection on the Canadian site compared to the U.S. site. In addition, the TV and movie studios had started using Netflix to apply competitive pressure and increase prices charged to TV stations looking to buy content. This meant that Netflix, in turn, also had to pay more. The cost to acquire rights to stream video content for Netflix was eight times higher in 2011 than in 2010 (total cost US$804.9 million). In addition, Netflix had been unsuccessful in renewing rights agreements with Walt Disney and was set to lose distribution of this very important content as of March 2012 before signing a deal for another two years to distribute a limited number of older movies and programs. To make matters worse, new threats were coming in many forms:

- Traditional cable and satellite providers like Bell, Videotron, Shaw, and Rogers had launched their own direct video-on-demand service to subscribers.
- Astral Media Inc. possessed exclusive rights to distribute HBO programming in eastern Canada and refused to sell Netflix the rights to its popular shows like True Blood. To make matters worse, it was launching its own HBO Go streaming service.
- Amazon launched an online streaming service in the United States and by 2012 had over 5 million subscribers and growing.

- Apple TV was another important threat. The list goes on and on.

Government Regulation

Success is often based on how well a firm plays by the prescribed rules, but rules can be changed. Neflix's competitors were putting pressure on the Canadian Radio-Television Telecommunications Commission (CRTC) to create new rules to address the threat of "over-the-top" internet streaming services. The CRTC initially resisted making a ruling that would hurt the likes of Netflix. However, the CRTC also indicated that it will look at this issue on a yearly basis and evaluate its impact on Canadian television with a view to changing the rules if necessary.

External Pressures Leads to New Directions

Netflix had taken advantage of the shift in technology and carved its place in the market but threats were everywhere. The mounting pressure led company executives to make a couple of drastic moves that angered customers and confused investors. First, Netflix announced that it would split the DVD rental and online streaming services; there

was also a short-lived attempt to rebrand the DVD rental service under the name Quickster. And then, after it had implemented these policies, it quickly reversed its decision. Based on the trends, Netflix's decision seems inevitable, although admittedly premature and poorly researched. Customers were not happy: They could no longer get both services for the same price—and there was still strong demand for this. In essence, the subscription price doubled and convenience was sharply reduced, since each entity would require separate login accounts and bills. The result: within a month Netflix lost over 1 million subscribers and was forced to reverse this decision.

So where does Netflix go from here? By the beginning of 2012, the company had regained most of the customers it had lost and was clearly mending fences: Its total subscribers numbered 24.4 million at the time of writing. Netflix's initial success had been based on quick manoeuvring, but clearly the moves described above were not in its own best interests. What direction should Netflix take now? Who or what is the greatest threat to the long-term profitability of the company? Should Netflix consider new affiliations or a potential merger? These are just some of the questions that Netflix executives must answer if they are to continue to grow. One thing is certain, however: The external threats are multiplying. ◆

Organizational Boundaries and Environments

external environment Everything outside an organization's boundaries that might affect it.

As discussed in the opening case on Netflix, all businesses, regardless of their size, location, or mission, operate within a larger external environment. This **external environment**—which consists of everything outside an organization's boundaries that might affect it—plays a major role in determining the success or failure of any organization. Managers must therefore have an accurate understanding of the environment in which their company operates and then strive to operate and compete within it. While no single firm can control the environment, managers should not simply react to changes: They should also be proactive and at least try to influence their environment.

LO1 Explain the concepts of *organizational boundaries* and multiple *organizational environments.*

To better explain the environment of business, we begin by discussing *organizational boundaries* and *multiple organizational environments.*

Organizational Boundaries

organizational boundary That which separates the organization from its environment.

An **organizational boundary** separates the organization from its environment. Boundaries were once relatively easy to identify, but they are becoming increasingly complicated. Consider the simple case of a small neighbourhood grocery store that includes a retail customer area, a storage room, and an owner/manager's office. In many ways, the store's boundary coincides with its physical structure. When you walk through the door, you're crossing the boundary into the business, and when you go back onto the sidewalk, you cross the boundary back into the environment.

But even this simple example isn't as straightforward as it seems. During the course of the business day, distributors of soft drinks, beer, snack foods, ice, and bread products may enter the store, inventory the products that they distribute, and automatically refill coolers and shelves just as if they were employees. These distributors are normally considered part of the environment, rather than the organization, during the time that they're inside the store; but they are essentially part of the business. Customers may assume they are employees and ask them questions as they restock shelves. The bread distributor may even offer someone a fresh loaf instead of the one that he or she has taken from the shelf.

Now consider the case of a large domestic business (such as GM Canada) that is owned by an even larger international corporation (U.S.–based General Motors). The domestic business has a complex network of relationships with other businesses, like Magna International, that conduct research and build components for GM. GM Canada, also deals with companies that supply tires, glass, steel, and engines. But GM Canada also functions within the boundaries of its international parent, which has its own network of business relationships, some overlapping with and some distinct from GM Canada's network.

We can also examine similar complexities from the customer's perspective. McDonald's, for example, has a contract with Coca-Cola, stipulating that it will sell only Coke's soft-drink products. McDonald's also has partnerships with Walmart and Disney that allow it to open stores inside those firms' facilities. So when you buy a Coca-Cola soft drink from a McDonald's restaurant located inside a Walmart store or Disney theme park, you are essentially affecting, and being affected by, multiple businesses.

Multiple Organizational Environments

Although we tend to speak of the external environment as if it were a single entity, organizations actually have multiple environments. Some of them are relatively general. Prevailing economic conditions, for instance, will affect the performance of almost every business. But other dimensions are much more precise. Our neighbourhood grocery will be influenced not only by an increase in unemployment in the area but also by the pricing and other marketing policies of its nearest competitor. For example, as we discuss in the closing case, Air Canada is affected by competitive pressures from WestJet, by the general economic conditions (like unemployment levels and business confidence), and even by major global events like the volcanic ash from Iceland that caused 100 000 flight cancellations in Europe.[1]

Figure 2.1 shows the major dimensions and elements of the external environment as it affects most businesses. As you can see, these include economic conditions, technology, political-legal considerations, social issues, the global environment, issues of ethical and social responsibility, the business environment itself, and numerous other emerging challenges and opportunities. Because this book provides detailed coverage of global and ethical issues in Chapters 3 and 5, respectively, we will introduce them here only as they relate directly to the other areas in this chapter.

The Economic Environment

The **economic environment** refers to the conditions of the economic system in which an organization operates.[2] In recent years, the economic environment has been characterized by low growth, relatively high unemployment, and low inflation. Rising unemployment means that people are less likely to make unnecessary purchases; they may delay the purchase of a new car or new furniture. The fear of potential job loss is a very powerful enemy of the economy. It's only rational for individuals to reduce spending in tougher times, but this leads to a reduced demand for goods and services and can ultimately lead to more job losses for the economy as a whole. Conversely, in a positive economic period the momentum pushes unemployment down as consumers spend more.

Despite low overall inflation, rising fuel prices have put economic pressure on businesses in many sectors. Restaurants and grocery stores have increased prices or reduced package sizes to compete and survive. For example, Loblaws raised the price of its President's Choice Granola cereal from $4.99 to $5.79 while simultaneously shrinking the package from 800 grams to 750 grams.[3] Many companies that cater to lower-income consumers, such as Dollarama and Costco, have thrived in tough economic times as consumers hunt for cheaper prices. Dollarama, which has 680 stores across Canada, saw its sales and profit increase by 12 and 21 percent, respectively, in 2011 from the previous year.[4]

There are three key goals in the Canadian economic system: *economic growth*, *stability*, and *full employment*. We look first at the tools we use to measure economic growth, including *aggregate output*, *standard of living*, *gross domestic product*, and *productivity*. We then discuss the main threats to stability: *inflation* and *unemployment*. We conclude this section by discussing government attempts to manage the Canadian economy so that national economic goals are met.

economic environment Conditions of the economic system in which an organization operates.

Explain the importance of the *economic environment* to business and identify the factors used to evaluate the performance of an *economic system*.

Economic Growth

At one time, about half the population of Canada was involved in producing food. Today, less than 2.5 percent of the population works in agriculture. Agricultural efficiency has improved because we have devised better ways of producing agricultural commodities. We can therefore say that agricultural production has grown because we have been able to increase total output in the agricultural sector.

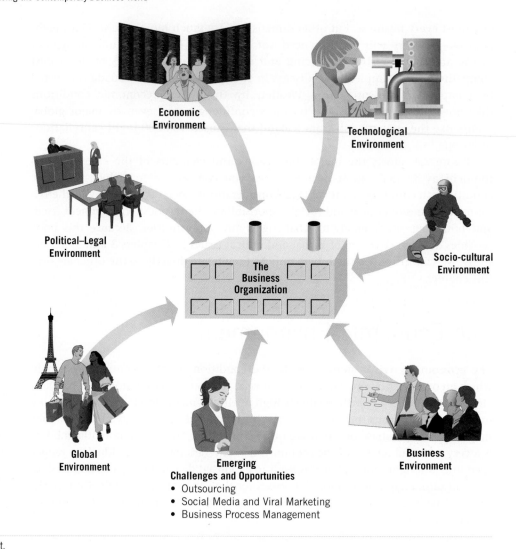

Economic Environment

Technological Environment

Political–Legal Environment

Socio-cultural Environment

The Business Organization

Global Environment

Emerging Challenges and Opportunities
- Outsourcing
- Social Media and Viral Marketing
- Business Process Management

Business Environment

FIGURE 2.1

Dimensions of the external environment.

The Business Cycle

We can apply the same concepts to a nation's economic system, but the computations are much more complex because we are dealing with many more sectors of the economy. We can tell whether or not an economic system is growing by examining the **business cycle**—the pattern of ups and downs in an economy. The business cycle has four recognizable phases: peak, recession, trough, and recovery (see Figure 2.2). A **recession** is usually defined as two consecutive quarters when the economy shrinks, but it is probably more helpful to say that a recession starts just after the peak of the business cycle is reached and ends when the trough is reached.[5] A **depression** occurs when the trough of the business cycle extends two or more years. During that period, economic activity declines, unemployment is very high, and consumer buying declines. Periods of expansion and contraction can vary from several months to several years. During the latter half of the 1990s, the Canadian economy was continuously expanding, leading some people to believe that the business cycle was a thing of the past. That belief was shattered twice in the past few years: in 2000, when the high-tech bubble burst, and in 2008, when a major financial crisis and worldwide recession occurred.

business cycle Pattern of short-term ups and downs (expansions and contractions) in an economy.

recession Period during which aggregate output, as measured by real GDP, declines.

depression Particularly severe and long-lasting recession.

The tougher economic times have led to the growth in popularity of the various dollar store retailers across the nation.

Many economists correctly predicted that the most recent recession would be long, and some even compared it to the Great Depression of the 1930s.

Aggregate Output and the Standard of Living

The main measure of growth in the business cycle is **aggregate output**—the total quantity of goods and services produced by an economic system during a given period.[6] To put it simply, an increase in aggregate output is growth (or economic growth).[7] When output grows more quickly than the population, two things usually follow: Output per capita—the quantity of goods and services per person—goes up, and the system provides relatively more of the goods and services that people want.[8] When these two things occur, people benefit from a higher **standard of living**, which refers to the total quantity and quality of goods and services that they can purchase with the currency used in their economic system.

aggregate output Total quantity of goods and services produced by an economic system during a given period.

standard of living Total quantity and quality of goods and services that a country's citizens can purchase with the currency used in their economic system.

Gross Domestic Product and Gross National Product

The term **gross domestic product (GDP)** refers to the total value of all goods and services produced within a given period by a national economy through *domestic* factors of production. Canada's GDP in 2010 was $1.65 trillion.[9] Global GDP is approximately $63 trillion, with five countries—the United States, China, Japan, Germany, and France—accounting for nearly half of the total.[10] If GDP is going up, the nation is experiencing economic growth.

gross domestic product (GDP) Total value of all goods and services produced within a given period by a national economy through domestic factors of production.

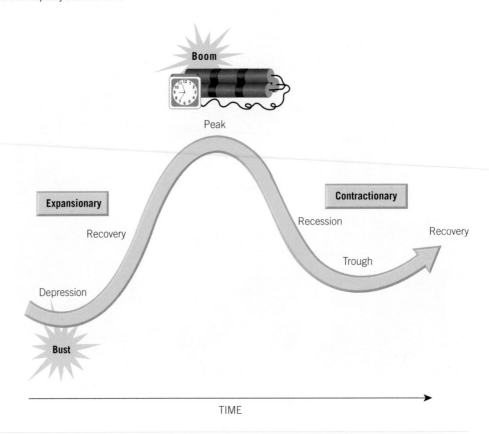

FIGURE 2.2

The business cycle.

gross national product (GNP) Total value of all goods and services produced by a national economy within a given period regardless of where the factors of production are located.

Economists also use the term **gross national product (GNP)**, which refers to the total value of all goods and services produced by a national economy within a given period *regardless of where the factors of production are located*. Thus, the profits earned by a Canadian company abroad are included in GNP but not in GDP. Conversely, profits earned by foreign firms in Canada are included in GDP. Consider the example of a Canadian-owned manufacturing plant in Brazil. The profits earned by the factory are included in Canadian GNP—but not in GDP—because its output is not produced domestically (that is, in Canada). Conversely, those profits are included in Brazil's GDP—but not its GNP—because they are produced domestically (that is, in Brazil). As you can imagine, calculations like these quickly become very complex because of different factors of production. The labour, for example, will be mostly Brazilian but the capital mostly Canadian. Thus, wages paid to Brazilian workers are part of Brazil's GNP even though profits are not.

Today, GDP is the key measure of economic growth because it tracks an economy's performance over time. However, some argue that such measures are flawed. A commission created by former French president Nicolas Sarkozy and chaired by famous economist Joseph Stiglitz declared that our obsession with GDP helped contribute to the strength of the most recent recession. According to the findings, if a bit more attention had been paid to other indicators, like rising debt, governments may have reacted more cautiously. An article in *The Economist* magazine even referred to GDP as "grossly deceptive product."[11]

Real Growth Rates. The *real growth rate of GDP* refers to the growth rate of GDP adjusted for inflation and changes in the value of the country's currency. Remember that growth depends on output increasing at a faster rate than the population. If the growth rate of GDP exceeds the rate of population growth, our standard of living should be improving.

GDP per Capita. GDP per capita is calculated by dividing total GDP by the population of a country. As a measure of economic well-being of the average person, GDP per capita is a better measure than total GDP. Luxembourg has the highest GDP per capita (approximately US$105 000), followed by Norway (US$84 000), Switzerland (US$67 000), Denmark (US$56 000), and Macao SAR China (US$51 000). Canada's per capita GDP (US$46 200) is lower than that of the United States (US$47 200).[12]

Real GDP. **Real GDP** means that GDP has been adjusted. To understand why adjustments are necessary, consider a simple example where pizza is the only product in an economy. Assume that in 2011 a pizza cost $10, and in 2012 it cost $11. In both years, exactly 1000 pizzas were produced. In 2011, the GDP was $10 000 ($10 * 1000); in 2012, the GDP was $11 000 ($11 * 1000). Has the economy grown? No. Since 1000 pizzas were produced in both years, aggregate output remained the same. The point is that we should not be misled into believing that an economy is doing better than it is. If it is not adjusted, GDP for 2012 is **nominal GDP**. Nominal GDP is measured in current dollars or with all components valued at current prices.[13]

real GDP GDP calculated to account for changes in currency values and prices.

nominal GDP GDP measured in current dollars or with all components valued at current prices.

Purchasing Power Parity. In our example, current prices would be 2012 prices. On the other hand, we calculate real GDP when we account for *changes in currency values and price changes*. When we make this adjustment, we account for both GDP and **purchasing power parity**—the principle that exchange rates are set so that the prices of similar products in different countries are about the same. Purchasing power parity gives us a much better idea of what people can actually buy with the financial resources allocated to them by their economic system. In other words, it gives us a better sense of standards of living around the world.

purchasing power parity Principle that exchange rates are set so that the prices of similar products in different countries are about the same.

Productivity

Productivity is a measure of economic growth that compares the output of an economic system with the resources that are needed to produce the output. Suppose that it takes one Canadian worker and one Canadian dollar to make 10 soccer balls in an eight-hour workday. Let's also say that it takes 1.2 Saudi workers and the equivalent of $1.20 (in riyals, the currency of Saudi Arabia) to make 10 soccer balls in the same eight-hour workday. The Canadian soccer-ball industry is said to be more *productive* than the Saudi soccer-ball industry.

productivity A measure of economic growth that compares the output of an economic system with the resources needed (input) to produce that output.

The two factors of production in this extremely simple case are labour and capital. According to the Organisation for Economic Co-operation and Development (OECD) rankings, Canada stood in seventeenth place with a productivity ratio of 76.6 percent compared to the United States. Luxembourg and Norway were the most productive nations at 127.8 percent. Ireland (107.9 percent) was also classified above the benchmark U.S. statistics.[14] If more products are being produced with fewer factors of production, the prices of these products go down. As a consumer, you would need less of your currency to purchase the same quantity of these products, so your standard of living—at least with regard to these products—has improved. If your entire economic system increases its productivity, then your overall standard of living improves. In fact, *standard of living improves only through increases in productivity*.[15] Real growth in GDP reflects growth in productivity. We examine productivity in detail in Chapter 12.

There are several factors that can help or hinder the growth of an economic system, but we'll focus on just two of them: the *balance of trade* and the *national debt*.

Balance of Trade. The **balance of trade** is the economic value of all the products that a country exports minus the economic value of those it *imports*. Canada traditionally has had a positive balance of trade. It is usually a creditor nation rather than a debtor nation. For example, Canada received $47 billion more from exports than it spent on imports in 2008, but a long trend was reversed when Canada had a trade deficit of

balance of trade The total of a country's exports (sales to other countries) minus its imports (purchases from other countries).

$4.8 billion in 2009 and $8.9 billion in 2010.[16] The United States usually has a negative balance of trade; it spends more on imports than it receives for exports.[17] It is therefore a consistent debtor nation. A trade deficit negatively affects economic growth because the money that flows out of a country can't be used to invest in productive enterprises, either at home or overseas. More information on the balance of trade is presented in Chapter 5.

national debt The total amount of money that a country owes its creditors.

National Debt. A country's **national debt** is the amount of money that the government owes its creditors. Like a business, the government has both revenues (primarily in the form of taxes) and expenses (military spending, social programs, and so on). For many years, the Government of Canada incurred annual **budget deficits**; that is, the government spent more money each year than it took in. These accumulated annual deficits created a huge national debt ($600 billion in 2010). A typical recession causes an 86 percent increase in the national debt.[18]

budget deficit The result of the government spending more in one year than it takes in during that year.

From Confederation (1867) to 1981, the *total* accumulated debt was only $85.7 billion, but in the period 1981–94, *annual deficits* were in the $20- to $40-billion range. But from 1997 to 2008, Canada was the only highly industrialized country in the world that had annual budget surpluses. That all changed in 2009 when the government announced a deficit of $46.9 billion, followed by $36.2 billion in 2010 and another $32.3 billion in 2011.[19] Big increases in annual deficits have become the norm in the United States and were made worse because of the multibillion-dollar bailouts that were given to companies in the financial and auto sectors. In spite of this, the United States is still able to borrow large amounts of money from countries like China because the United States is seen as a strong economy and a safe haven in troubled economic times.[20]

A country's national debt affects economic growth, and here's why: While taxes are the most obvious way the government raises money, it also sells *bonds*—securities through which it promises to pay buyers certain amounts of money by specified future dates. The government sells bonds to individuals, households, banks, insurance companies, industrial corporations, non-profit organizations, and government agencies, both at home and overseas.[21] These bonds are attractive investments because they are extremely safe; the Canadian government is not going to *default* on them (that is, fail to make payments when due). Even so, these bonds must offer a decent return for the buyers, so the Canadian government pays interest at a competitive rate. But when it

The Nintendo Wii is an example of a popular import. Nintendo is a very popular Japanese game console manufacturer that makes products in Japan and China.

sells bonds, the Canadian government competes with every other potential borrower—individuals, households, businesses, and other organizations—for the available supply of loanable money. The more money the government borrows, the less money is available for the private borrowing and investment that increases productivity.

Economic Stability

An important goal of an economic system is **stability**, a condition where the amount of money available and the quantity of goods and services produced are growing at about the same rate. Several factors threaten stability—namely, *inflation*, *deflation*, and *unemployment*.

stability Condition in an economic system in which the amount of money available and the quantity of goods and services produced are growing at about the same rate.

Inflation

Inflation means that widespread price increases occur throughout an economic system. Inflation occurs when the amount of money injected into an economy outstrips the increase in actual output. When this happens, people will have more money to spend, but there will still be the same quantity of products available for them to buy. As they compete with one another to buy available products, prices go up. Before long, high prices will erase the increase in the amount of money injected into the economy. Purchasing power, therefore, declines.

inflation Occurrence of widespread price increases throughout an economic system.

Inflation varies widely across countries. One of the most dramatic recent examples of inflation occurred in Zimbabwe in 2008, when inflation reached an astonishing annual rate of more than 40 million percent (most countries have rates between 2 and 15 percent). One Zimbabwean dollar from 2005 would have been worth 1 trillion Zimbabwean dollars in 2008. Many workers simply stopped going to their jobs because their pay was not enough to cover their bus fare.[22] The problem was finally solved in 2009 when the government began allowing people to pay their bills using other currencies like the U.S. dollar or the South African rand.[23]

Inflation hurts consumers because price is a primary concern when consumers are deciding whether to purchase a product. You will probably decide to make a purchase if the value of the product justifies the price that you'll have to pay. Table 2.1 reduces a hypothetical purchase decision to three bare essentials.

In which year did the cost of a hamburger go up? At first glance, you might say in both YR2 and YR3 (to $4 in YR2 and to $7.50 in YR3). In YR2, your income kept pace; although a hamburger cost twice as much, you had twice as much money to spend. In effect, the price to you was actually the same. In YR3, however, your income increased by 250 percent while the price of a hamburger increased by 275 percent. In YR3, therefore, you got hit by inflation (how hard, of course, depends on your fondness for hamburgers). Inflation, therefore, can be harmful to you as a consumer because *inflation decreases the purchasing power of your money*.

Measuring Inflation: The CPI. Remember that inflation means widespread price increases throughout an economic system. It stands to reason, therefore, that we can measure inflation by measuring price increases. To do this, we can turn to such price

TABLE 2.1 When Did the Cost of a Hamburger Go Up?				
YR1 Income	**YR2 Income**	**YR2 % Increase over YR1 Base**	**YR3 Income**	**YR3 % Increase over YR1 Base**
$5000	$10 000	100	$17 500	250
YR1 Hamburger Price	YR2 Hamburger Price	YR2 % Increase over YR1 Base	YR3 Hamburger Price	YR3 % Increase over YR1 Base
$2	$4	100	$7.50	275

indexes as the **consumer price index (CPI)**, which measures changes in the cost of a "basket" of goods and services that a typical family might buy. What is included in the basket has changed over the years as new products and services have become available and old ones have fallen out of favour. The first CPI in 1913 included items like coal, spirit vinegar, and fruit, but now the CPI includes bottom-freezer fridges, flat-screen TVs, energy-saving light bulbs, and laser eye surgery.[24] These changes in the CPI also reflect changes in consumer purchasing patterns. For example, in 1961, about 53 percent of consumer spending went to necessities like food, housing, and clothing. By the turn of the century, only 40 percent of consumer spending went to necessities.[25] Figure 2.3 shows how inflation has varied over the past 20 years in Canada.

As mentioned earlier, despite the fact that official inflation rates, as measured by the CPI, have remained low, price pressure caused by increased fuel costs is putting great strain on companies in all sectors. Food manufacturers are particularly susceptible. For example, Maple Leaf Foods announced intentions for more price increases in 2012 based on rising costs of inputs such as corn and wheat, which had risen 95 percent and 102 percent, respectively, in the previous 12 months. This announcement was similar to announcements made by Metro, George Weston Limited, and Loblaw. Inflationary forces are clear but many consumers are countering the effect by trading down to lower-cost alternatives to reduce their grocery bills.[26]

Deflation

deflation A period of generally falling prices.

When **deflation** (generally falling prices) occurs, the Bank of Canada reduces interest rates in an attempt to increase consumer demand. Prices may fall because industrial productivity is increasing and cost savings can be passed on to consumers (this is good) or because consumers have high levels of debt and are therefore unwilling to buy very much (this is bad).

FIGURE 2.3

During the past 15 years, the rate of price increases in Canada has been low and quite stable.

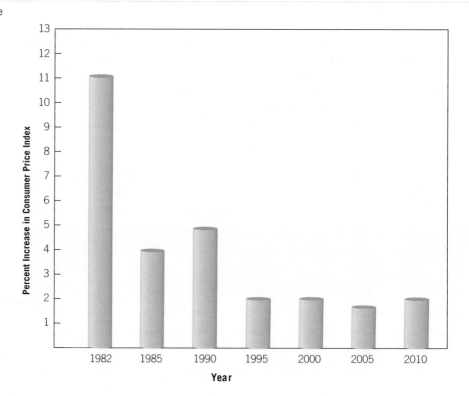

Unemployment

At the end of 2011, there were 7.85 million men and 7 million women (over age 25) working in Canada's labour force.[27] But there were many additional people who wanted a job but could not get one. **Unemployment** is the level of joblessness among people actively seeking work. There are various types of unemployment: *frictional unemployment* (people are out of work temporarily while looking for a new job); *seasonal unemployment* (people are out of work because of the seasonal nature of their jobs); *cyclical unemployment* (people are out of work because of a downturn in the business cycle); and *structural unemployment* (people are unemployed because they lack the skills needed to perform available jobs). Unemployment rates have varied greatly over the years, as Figure 2.4 shows, with the rates in recent years being higher for men than for women. At the end of 2011, the Canadian unemployment rate stood at 7.4 percent, which was better than the rate in the Unites States, which was 8.6 percent, and the depressing 21.3 percent rate found in Spain at the time.[28]

When unemployment is low, there is a shortage of labour available for businesses. As businesses compete with one another for the available supply of labour, they raise the wages that they are willing to pay. Then, because higher labour costs eat into profit margins, businesses raise the prices of their products. Thus, although consumers have more money, this increase is soon erased by higher prices. Purchasing power declines.

If wage rates get too high, businesses will respond by hiring fewer workers and unemployment will go up. But if that happens, demand may decline because unemployed workers don't purchase as much. Because of reduced sales, companies may further cut back on hiring and unemployment will go even higher. If the government tries to correct this situation by injecting more money into the economic system— by cutting taxes or spending more money—prices in general may go up because of increased consumer demand, but then inflation sets in and purchasing power declines.[29]

unemployment Level of joblessness among people actively seeking work in an economic system.

FIGURE 2.4

Historical Unemployment Rate. Historical unemployment rate. From 1970 to 1996, there was a steady upward trend in unemployment rates, but the rate began to decline in the late 1990s. The recession, which began in 2008, caused a clear increase in unemployment, as seen in the chart.

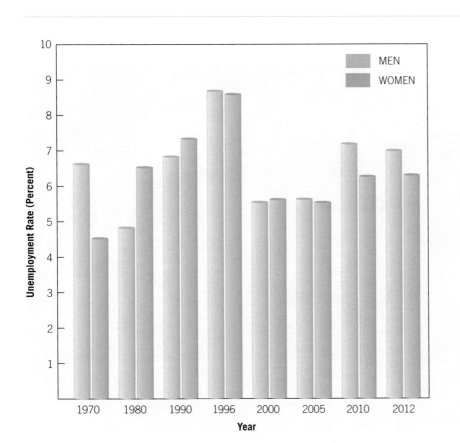

Managing the Canadian Economy

The government manages the Canadian economic system through both fiscal and monetary policies. Taken together, fiscal policy and monetary policy make up **stabilization policy**, the goal of which is to smooth out fluctuations in output and unemployment and to stabilize prices.

The Canadian government manages the collection and spending of its revenues through **fiscal policies**. Tax increases can function as fiscal policies, not only to increase revenues but also to manage the economy. For example, when the growth rate of the economy is decreasing, tax cuts will normally stimulate renewed economic growth. **Monetary policies** focus on controlling the size of the nation's money supply. Working primarily through the Bank of Canada (the nation's central bank), the government can influence the ability and willingness of banks throughout Canada to lend money. It can also influence the supply of money by prompting interest rates to go up or down. The power of the Bank of Canada to make changes in the supply of money is the centrepiece of the Canadian government's monetary policy. The principle is fairly simple:

- Higher interest rates make money more expensive to borrow and thereby reduce spending both by those who produce goods and services and by those who buy those goods and services. When the Bank of Canada restricts the money supply, we say that it is practising a *tight monetary policy*.

- Lower interest rates make money less expensive to borrow and thereby increase spending both by those who produce goods and services and by the consumers who buy those goods and services. When the Bank of Canada loosens the money supply—and thus stimulates the economy—we say that it is practising an *easy monetary policy*. When the financial crisis hit in the fall of 2008, the central banks of both Canada and the United States cut their interest rates in an attempt to stimulate their economies.

stabilization policy Government policy, embracing both fiscal and monetary policies, the goal of which is to smooth out fluctuations in output and unemployment and to stabilize prices.

fiscal policies Policies by means of which the government collects and spends revenues.

monetary policies Policies by means of which the government controls the size of the nation's money supply.

During the Depression of the 1930s, unemployment was very high, with nearly one-quarter of the population unable to find work. Lines of unemployed workers outside soup kitchens were an unfortunate reality during those difficult economic times.

The Technological Environment

Technology has a variety of meanings, but as applied to the environment of business, it generally includes all the ways firms create value for their constituents. Technology includes human knowledge, work methods, physical equipment, electronics and tele-communications, and various processing systems that are used to perform business activities. Although technology is applied within the organization, the forms and avail-ability of that technology come from the general environment. Boeing, for example, uses computer-assisted manufacturing and design techniques developed by external vendors to simulate the six kilometres of hydraulic tubing that runs through its 777 aircraft.

technology All the ways firms create value for their constituents.

Describe the *technological environment* and its role in business.

Research and Development (R&D)

Technological improvements and innovation in general are important contributors to the economic development of a country. The innovation process includes **research and development (R&D)**, which provides new ideas for products, services, and processes. (See Chapter 16 for a discussion of the importance of R&D in the marketing of products.) There are two types of R&D. **Basic (or pure) R&D** involves improving knowledge in an area without focusing on whether any discoveries will be imme-diately marketable. For example, chemists are continually experimenting with how chemical compounds behave, but this activity might or might not result in a market-able product. **Applied R&D**, on the other hand, means focusing specifically on how a technological innovation can be put to use in the making of a product or service that can be sold in the marketplace. For example, H.J. Heinz developed a tomato that is sweeter than the variety that it had previously been using in making its ketchup. This reduced the need for corn syrup, which had been rapidly increasing in price.[30]

research and development (R&D) Those activities that are necessary to provide new products, services, and processes.

basic (or pure) R&D Improving knowledge in an area without primarily focusing on whether any discoveries that might occur are immediately marketable.

applied R&D Focusing specifically on how a technological innovation can be put to use in the making of a product or service that can be sold in the marketplace.

Another example: Several Canadian companies share an office in Shanghai called the Textile Canada Business Centre. Instead of trying to sell traditional apparel fabric, they want to sell "technical textiles" for the medical, construction, and sports industries. These include heat- and flame-resistant fabric for firefighters and sheets to protect crops from sun or hail. One niche product—SilverClear—is an antibacterial liquid that is applied to bed linen. It is produced by TransTex Technologies in Saint-Hyacinthe, Quebec, and sold to Chinese companies who apply it to the sheets they make. Twenty-five years ago, only 10 percent of Canadian textiles were exported, but now well over 50 percent are.[31]

R&D spending in Canada in 2010 totalled about $14.8 billion.[32] The Canadian private sector accounts for about 55 percent of R&D, the government 10 percent, and universities 34 percent.[33] In the private sector, just 100 businesses account for over half of all R&D money that is spent.[34] The largest expenditures on R&D in Canada are concentrated in industries like computer system design, information, communications equipment, and scientific research.[35] The boxed insert entitled "What Should We Do About R&D?" describes the current issues related to research in Canada and beyond.

Canada's level of R&D lags behind that of other countries; it typically spends less than 1 percent of GDP on R&D, while Japan, Germany, and the United States, for example, spend from 1.5 to 2 percent of GDP (see Figure 2.5). This lag exists partly because many Canadian businesses are subsidiaries of large U.S. companies that carry out their R&D in the United States. When we take into account that the GDP of countries like Japan, the United States, and Germany is much larger than the GDP of Canada, it means that R&D spending in Canada (in terms of absolute dollars) is a tiny fraction of what is spent in other countries.[36]

Product and Service Technologies

Technology is used to create physical goods and services for customers. Although many people associate technology with manufacturing, it is also a significant force in the service sector. Just as an automobile is built following a predetermined pathway along an assembly line, a hamburger at McDonald's is cooked, assembled, wrapped, and bagged as it moves along a predefined path. The rapid advancement of the internet into all areas of business is also a reflection of the technological environment. For example, Starbucks Canada now offers a mobile payment program that permits consumers to use their phones as an electronic wallet through the use of an app and a QR code to pay for their grande lattes. According to a senior executive, today's customers may forget their wallet but they never forget their phones.[37] Indeed, new technologies continue to revolutionize nearly every aspect of business, ranging from the ways that customers and companies interact to where, when, and how employees perform their work and how they get their jobs. Social media and internet technology are now a major part of the job search and recruitment process.

As demonstrated in the opening case, companies must constantly be on the lookout for technological breakthroughs that might make their current products or services obsolete and thereby threaten their survival. Many of these breakthroughs do not come from direct competitors or even from the industry the company is part of. Technology is the basis of competition for some companies, especially when their goal is to be the technology leader in their industry. A company, for example, might

MANAGING IN TURBULENT TIMES

What Should We Do About R&D?

Canada has a well-educated workforce and competitive corporate tax policies, yet it lags far behind other industrialized countries when it comes to spending on research and development (R&D). Canadian spending on R&D is in the bottom third of the OECD countries, and our productivity growth rate is less than half the OECD average.

In October 2011, the Jenkins report on Canadian R&D was released. The panel—which was chaired by Tom Jenkins, an entrepreneur and the CEO of the software company Open Text Corp.—examined the structure of tax incentive programs meant to encourage R&D, the granting councils that dole out the money, and the initiatives that are in place to encourage innovation. The panel's most general finding was that the federal government spends a great deal of money each year (approximately $5 billion) trying to get businesses to boost spending on R&D, yet there has been little change in R&D spending by Canadian companies and insufficient innovation. Jenkins himself expressed dismay at how little effort has been expended figuring out how inputs (R&D expenditures) are linked to outcomes (commercial products and processes).

The current Scientific Research and Experimental Development program (SR&ED) came under criticism in a *Globe and Mail* investigation that found many dubious claims, a scatter-gun approach to funding (too many small grants), and the diversion of tax credits to high-priced consultants. A report from the Mowat Centre for Policy Innovation at the University of Toronto urged the government to reduce R&D tax breaks and instead use the money for targeted research grants (a system that is used by innovation leaders like Germany and Sweden).

The situation at Xerox Corp. illustrates the concerns. The company, which has the leading materials science lab in Canada, has developed new inks, toners, and photo receptors, and has generated more than 1500 U.S. patents. That's the good news. But Sophie Vandebroek, who runs the company's global network of research labs, says that Xerox's expertise is an underused asset in Canada, and that Xerox spends about the same amount of money on R&D in Canada as it did 10 years ago. She thinks that Canada's tax credit system for encouraging R&D is not effective.

The Jenkins report contained recommendations to make Canadian companies more globally competitive, including:

- a bigger role for business in how the government allocates its innovations budget
- the formation of an Industrial Research and Innovation Council (IRIC) that would oversee and evaluate the work of the 60 different programs that are currently run by 17 different departments
- more focused distribution of funds to high-performing organizations (turning the current R&D democracy into an R&D meritocracy)
- overhauling the SR&ED program and putting the freed-up funds into other programs, most notably direct grants to businesses and "late-stage" venture capital funding
- reducing the emphasis on tax breaks and increasing the emphasis on direct grants

Critical Thinking Questions

1. Why do you think Canada lags behind other industrialized countries in R&D?

2. Do you think increased government involvement in R&D would improve Canada's position? Explain your reasoning.

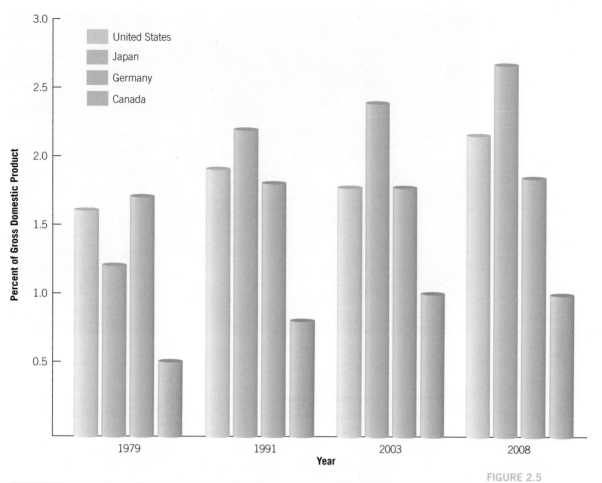

FIGURE 2.5

R&D expenditures as a proportion of GDP.

focus its efforts on having the most technologically advanced products on the market. Intel exemplifies the challenges and the risks of adopting a strategic dependence on technological leadership. Before co-founding Intel with Bob Noyce in 1968, Gordon Moore made a prediction about microprocessors (the processing components of micro-computers) that eventually became known as Moore's Law: The number of transistors in a microprocessor would double every 18 months. In effect, this rate would entail a twofold increase in processing power every 18 months—a seemingly impossible pace. Intel, however, adopted Moore's Law as a performance requirement for each new gen-eration of processor and has kept up this pace for over 45 years.[38] Because of the laws of physics and the already diminished size of microprocessors, most theorists estimate that, around 2015 to 2020, it will likely be impossible to keep up with Moore's Law.[39]

Technology is an important basis of competition for some firms. One challenge, as seen in the Intel example, is meeting constant demands to decrease *cycle time*—the time that it takes a firm to accomplish some recurring activity or function from beginning to end. Businesses are more competitive if they can decrease cycle times. Twenty years ago, it took an automaker about five years from the decision to launch a new product until it was available in dealer showrooms. Now, most companies can complete the cycle in less than two years. The speedier process allows them to respond more quickly to changing economic conditions, consumer preferences, and new competitive prod-ucts while recouping their product-development costs more quickly. The boxed insert entitled "What's the Latest on the Hydrogen Fuel Cell?" describes how time-consuming research and development can be and how hard it is to commercialize a product.

Companies must decide how much emphasis they are going to place on R&D as a competitive tool. **R&D intensity** refers to R&D spending as a percentage of a company's sales revenue. Companies with a high R&D intensity are better able to

R&D intensity R&D spending as a percentage of a company's sales revenue.

Great R&D spending and efficiency has allowed Intel to remain a leader in microprocessor development.

gain market share in global markets.[40] If a company has a strategy to be the technological leader in its industry, it will likely have a high R&D intensity. When Kenneth Frazer took over as CEO of pharmaceutical giant Merck, he immediately increased R&D spending (to 8.5 billion in 2011), placing his company on an equal footing with top research spending firm and competitor Pfizer. Mr. Frazer was particularly driven by the completion of a new blood thinner called Vorapaxar, but he was also setting a strategic tone.[41] Alternatively, if a company's strategy is to be a technology follower, it will likely have a much lower R&D intensity. Companies that have efficient **technology transfer**—the process of getting a new technology out of the lab and into the marketplace—generate more profits.

technology transfer Process of getting a new technology out of the lab and into the marketplace.

Process Technologies

Process technologies are used to improve a firm's performance of its internal operations (such as accounting, managing information flows, creating activity reports, and so on). They also help create better relationships with external constituents such as suppliers and customers. **Enterprise resource planning (ERP)** is a large-scale information system for organizing and managing a firm's processes across product lines, departments, and geographic locations. Company-wide processes—such as materials management, production planning, order management, and financial reporting—can all be managed by ERP. Figure 2.6 shows some of the areas in which ERP can be applied, including some of the common processes performed in each area.[42]

enterprise resource planning (ERP) Large-scale information system for organizing and managing a firm's processes across product lines, departments, and geographic locations.

In developing its ERP system, a firm starts by identifying the processes that need critical attention, such as supplier relationships, materials flows, or customer order fulfillment. The resulting system would thus integrate the sales process with production planning and then incorporate both of these operations into the financial accounting system. Let's say that a customer in Rome orders a product to be manufactured in Ireland. The ERP-integrated seller can schedule the order shipment via air cargo to Rome, where it can be picked up by a truck at the airport and delivered to the customer's warehouse by a specified date. All of these activities are synchronized in one massive database.

The ERP also stores updated real-time information on activities, reports recent and upcoming transactions, and posts electronic notices that certain action is required if certain schedules are to be met. It coordinates internal operations with activities by outside suppliers and notifies customers of current order status and upcoming deliveries and billings. It can integrate financial flows among the firm, its suppliers, customers, and banks and generate up-to-the-minute financial reports at a moment's notice (reduced from the traditional one-month time span).

One Canadian company that uses ERP is Crestline Coach Ltd., a relatively small company in Saskatoon that builds customized emergency vehicles and replacement parts. When problems developed with Crestline's old software—for example, customers had to wait days for parts—management decided to buy an ERP system called Business One from SAP Canada Inc. This was a scaled-down, less expensive version of the ERP systems that are usually sold to large companies. With the new ERP system, when Crestline receives an order for a replacement part, it can usually ship it the same day.[43]

THE GREENING OF BUSINESS

What's the Latest on the Hydrogen Fuel Cell?

In the 1990's, Vancouver-based Ballard Power Systems announced that the hydrogen fuel cell—which combines hydrogen with oxygen to produce pollution-free electricity—would soon be powering automobiles. Both Daimler and Ford said they were going to have fuel-cell cars on the market by 2004, but that didn't happen. Now there's a new date: 2015.

Why is the fuel cell—which looks like a fantastic product—still not widely available? There are many reasons, but two problems that have long plagued fuel cells remain. First, cars powered with this technology are expensive. Companies have provided little information on this important issue, but Toyota estimates that it will cost about $120 000 to build the fuel cell car it is planning to introduce in 2015. Second, as of 2012, there were virtually no hydrogen refuelling stations in North America (though there were a few in the Los Angeles area). General Motors recently announced the Hawaii Hydrogen Initiative (called H21), which is a partnership with several other government and private organizations. The goal is to have 20 to 25 hydrogen refuelling stations in Oahu by 2015.

Development of a commercially viable fuel cell has been frustratingly slow, but there have been some promising developments during the past couple of years:

- Daimler says it will field test fuel cells in 2012 (they are manufactured in Vancouver). Herbert Kohler, Daimler's chief environmental officer, says that fuel cell technology is already mature, and it is suitable for long-distance driving.
- Several automakers plan to introduce fuel cell cars on a commercial basis in the next few years (Nissan and Toyota by 2015, and Mercedes-Benz by 2013).

- In 2011, the B.C. government announced a $17 million program that includes cash incentives for people who purchase fuel cell vehicles.
- Daimler and Mercedes-Benz announced a $50 million investment in a new B.C. facility that will be dedicated to making fuel cell cars a reality. The goal is to achieve sales of 1000 to 10 000 units by 2015.
- In 2011, Mercedes-Benz tested a fuel cell car (the F-CELL) on a 30 000-kilometre around-the-world demonstration. The car has a range of 400 kilometres before it needs to be refilled, and at least one person who tested it had very positive things to say.
- General Motors has built more than 100 fuel cell cars in Oshawa.

Maybe the hydrogen fuel cell will eventually become popular. Keep in mind what critics said when internal combustion–powered automobiles were introduced early in the twentieth century: "They'll never become popular because there would have to be gas stations all over the place." Well, now we have gas stations all over the place.

Critical Thinking Questions

1. Have a look at the section on new product development in Chapter 16. At what stage of the new product development process is the hydrogen fuel cell?

2. Consider the following statement: "If the fuel cell had any value, it would have been fully developed by now and there would already be many cars on the road that are powered by the fuel cell." Do you agree or disagree with this statement? Explain your reasoning.

Human Resources
- Benefits
- Payroll

Data Analysis
- Product costs
- Job costs

Sales and Marketing
- Sales orders
- Pricing system

ERP System

Customer Service
- Field service
- Quality

Manufacturing
- Material requirements planning
- Scheduling

Supply-Chain Management
- Forecasting
- Purchasing
- Distribution

Accounting and Finance
- Accounts payable and receivable
- Asset management

FIGURE 2.6

ERP applications.

The Political-Legal Environment

political-legal environment
Conditions reflecting the relationship between business and government, usually in the form of government regulation.

L04 Describe the *political-legal environment* and its role in business.

The **political-legal environment** reflects the relationship between business and government, usually in the form of government regulation of business. The legal system defines in part what an organization can and can't do. Although Canada is a free market economy, it still has major regulation of business activity, as we saw in Chapter 1. At times government policy can be tremendously advantageous to businesses. The Home Renovation Tax Credit, which expired in 2010, brought a 30 percent sales increase for Winnipeg-based Acrylon Plastics (maker of window frames) and had hardware retailers smiling from coast to coast.[44] On the other hand, Shoppers Drug Mart was very vocal about its opposition to a new Ontario government regulation that would see generic drugs priced at as little as 25 percent of the original brand name product's cost—down from 50 percent. Shoppers argued that this regulation would have a tremendous impact on pharmacy profits.[45]

Pro- or anti-business sentiment can further influence business activity. During a period of anti-business sentiment, firms may find their competitive activities more restricted. For example, there may be fewer opportunities for mergers and acquisitions because of antitrust concerns. When the Royal Bank wanted to merge with the Bank of Montreal, the Canadian government blocked the merger on the grounds that it would reduce competition and harm consumers.

Political stability is also an important consideration, especially for international firms. No business wants to set up shop in another country unless trade relationships with that country are relatively well defined and stable. Thus, Canadian firms are more likely to do business with England and the United States than with Haiti and Afghanistan. For example, in 2010, mining companies were concerned about rumours that members of the South African ruling government were considering nationalization (government takeover of resources, forcing private companies to sell at a price deemed fair by the government) of up to 60 percent of the country's mining sector. This was a dangerous prospect for Vancouver-based Great Basin Gold Ltd., which was developing a $230-million gold mining operation at the time.[46] In another case, Suncor reinvested in Libya after the fall of Moammar Gadhafi; the political turmoil put a $1.4-billion project in jeopardy for a time.[47]

Relations between sovereign governments can also affect business activity. Ian Delaney, the former CEO of Toronto-based Sherritt International, struck a mining deal with Fidel Castro a couple of decades ago that helped Sherritt become one of the largest foreign investors in Cuba, but this decision also led to Mr. Delaney being blacklisted by the United States because of the American embargo against Cuba.[48] On a smaller scale, similar issues also pertain to assessments of local and provincial governments. A new mayor or provincial leader can affect many organizations, especially small firms that do business in a single location and are thus susceptible to zoning restrictions, property and school taxes, and the like.

Another aspect of the political-legal environment is described in the boxed insert entitled "The Battle of the Glen."

ENTREPRENEURSHIP AND NEW VENTURES

The Battle of the Glen

Cape Breton, Nova Scotia–based Glenora Distilleries had battled to keep its Glen Breton Rare Single Malt Whisky on store shelves. It's not that the product wasn't in demand—quite the contrary, in fact. The company distills a single-malt whisky—the only one produced in Canada—and from 2000 to 2009 Glenora Distilleries was in a court battle over the use of "Glen" in its brand name. The Scotch Whisky Association, a group representing over 50 whisky distillers in Scotland, claimed this was confusing consumers and leading them to believe that the product was distilled in Scotland.

Lauchie MacLean, Glenora's president, strongly disagreed, arguing that the name refers to Glenville, Cape Breton, which is Glenora Distillery's home community. A Canadian Federal Court of Appeal ruling in January 2009 allowed the company to continue to use the name. But the Scotch Whisky Association took the case to the Supreme Court of Canada and on June 11, 2009, the Supreme Court dismissed the application to oppose the trademark registration, ending the nine-year battle. In honour of the legal victory, Glenora released a special edition, 15-year-old single malt called The Battle of the Glen.

This clash hasn't been the only form of legal restriction imposed on Glenora Distillery and other whisky producers around the globe. Distillers based in Scotland have also set out to protect the use of the word "Scotch" on product labels. For example, an agreement signed by Canada and the European Union in 2003 prevents Canadian whisky distillers from using the word "Scotch" on their labels. This term is reserved for Scotland-based distillers only, in the sense that only true champagne comes from France's Champagne region, so real Scotch whisky is distilled only in Scotland. Not wanting to lose its brand presence and long-standing market share, the company fought back with great success. Now the future looks bright for a company that has had its fair share of challenges. Not only has it secured its most valuable possession, its brand name, it is also excited about the growing whisky market.

Because of increased demand in Europe and Asia, some single-malt whisky distillers have found their products in short supply. As a result, many distillers are pulling out of some markets and entering others. It's simple economics, according to MacLean: "They [distillers] have an asset, and they're looking at selling that asset for the most money they can get out of it." Glenora is a relatively small producer, but the company hopes to increase production at a later date to better match demand. Currently, Glenora is not "heavily into the Asian market" but expects that to change over the next few years.

Glenora's successes have partly been due to its entrepreneurial flexibility. The company experienced serious cash flow problems not long after its launch in 1991 because distilling doesn't happen overnight—it can take 10 to 12 years before a distillery will see revenues. However, some innovative approaches, which involved selling whisky futures and adding rum bottling and complementary tourism operations to the business, brought the company through the tough times. The business environment hasn't always been kind to Glenora, but in true entrepreneurial fashion, it has persevered. Sláinte!

Critical Thinking Question

1. Explain how the external environments have affected Glenora Distilleries.

The Socio-Cultural Environment

socio-cultural environment
Conditions including the customs, values, attitudes, and demographic characteristics of the society in which an organization functions.

The **socio-cultural environment** includes the customs, values, attitudes, and demographic characteristics of the society in which an organization functions. Socio-cultural processes determine the goods and services as well as the standards of business conduct that a society is likely to value and accept.

L05 Describe the *socio-cultural environment* and its role in business.

Customer Preferences and Tastes

Customer preferences and tastes vary both across and within national boundaries. In some countries, consumers are willing and able to pay premium prices for designer clothes with labels such as Armani or Calvin Klein. But the same clothes have virtually no market in other countries. While differences in tastes across national borders are sometimes clear and obvious, it is important to avoid stereotypical assumptions. Would you be surprised to hear that Canadian lingerie retailers like La Senza and La Vie en Rose have a significant presence in the Middle East? In 2012, La Senza had 96 stores and La Vie en Rose had 40 retail outlets in the region (most of them located in Saudi Arabia). Behind the conservative, strict, exterior dress code of these two countries, there is a significant market for lingerie.[49]

Product usage also varies between nations. In China, bicycles are primarily seen as a mode of transportation, but in Canada, they are marketed primarily for recreational purposes. Similarly, consumer preferences can also vary widely within the same country. Customs and product preferences in Quebec, for example, differ from those in other parts of Canada. In the United States, pre-packaged chili is more popular in the southwest states than in the northeast. McDonald's is just one company that is affected by socio-cultural factors. In response to concerns about nutrition and health, McDonald's has added salads to its menus and experimented with other low-fat foods. It was the first fast-food chain to provide customers with information about the ingredients in its products, and it attracted media attention when it announced that it would reduce the fat content in its popular french fries.

Consumer preferences and tastes also change over time. Preferences for colour, style, and so forth change from season to season. In some years, brightly coloured clothes sell best, while in other years people want more subdued colours. Some of these changes are driven by consumers, and some are driven by companies trying to convince consumers to adopt new styles. Soft drinks usually sell better during the hot summer months than in the cold winter months. Whisky, vodka, gin, and cigarettes are consumed less today than they were just a few years ago.

Socio-cultural factors influence the way workers in a society feel about their jobs and organizations. In some cultures, work carries meaningful social significance, with certain employers and job titles being highly desired by workers. But in other cultures, work is simply a means to an end, and people are concerned only with pay and job security. McDonald's has occasionally struggled with its operations in the Middle East because many people there are not interested in working in food-service operations. These and many other related issues regarding businesses and their customers are explored more fully in Chapters 15 through 17.

Ethical Compliance and Responsible Business Behaviour

Ethics and social responsibility are critical elements of the socio-cultural environment. We cover these areas in detail in Chapter 3, but a preview of them is justified here. The central issue revolves around the fact that rapid changes in business relationships, organizational structures, and financial flows pose difficulties in keeping accurate track of a company's financial position.

Keeping up with today's increasingly fast-paced business activities is putting a strain on the accounting profession's traditional methods for auditing and financial reporting, and on its time-honoured standards for professional ethics. The stakeholders of business firms—employees, stockholders, consumers, labour unions, creditors, and the government—are entitled to a fair accounting so they can make enlightened personal and business decisions, but they often get a blurred picture of a firm's competitive health. Nortel went from being the pride and joy of Canada to a historical warning after the internet bubble burst at the turn of the century. This was an external factor that had an impact on all technology companies but was not the reason Nortel failed; rather, the major reason for its bankruptcy was its failure to get its financial house in order. The company made accounting restatement after restatement of its financials throughout the last decade of its existence. Restatement is a clever way of saying that the figures that the company presented to its stakeholders were inaccurate. When this happens one time it can be seen as an error. But when it is repeated over time, it is a clear attempt to deceive the market.

In 2010, British Petroleum (BP) was in the news for all the wrong reasons after the massive Gulf of Mexico oil spill. For years, BP and other oil companies had always maintained that high-tech offshore drilling was extremely safe. But when this disaster struck, it became clear that the deep-sea environment was in fact challenging and that BP did not have an adequate solution for the spill. For months, oil spewed into the Gulf, devastating coastlines, endangering wildlife, and battering the local fishing and tourism businesses. As a result, the various stakeholders were lining up to make BP pay. Within a few days, a Facebook page promoting a BP boycott had 360 000 supporters. Advocacy groups like Public Citizen held rallies against BP. The U.S. government was publicly pushing the company for a quick solution while demanding BP halt a $10.5 billion dividend payment to shareholders. The U.S. government was also planning a legal response to make BP pay for its mistake in the court system. The future of BP was at stake, something that had been unimaginable before the crisis. In the face of all of this pressure, BP created a US$20 billion trust and escrow account to pay for legitimate claims.[50]

Appropriate standards of business conduct also vary across cultures. In Canada, accepting bribes in return for political favours is unethical and illegal. In some other countries, however, payments to local politicians are expected in return for favourable responses to such common business transactions as zoning and operating permits. The shape of the market, the ethics of political influence, and the attitudes of its workforce are only a few of the many ways in which culture can affect an organization. We examine these issues in more detail in Chapters 3 and 6.

The Business Environment

Business today is faster paced, more complex, and more demanding than ever before. As businesses aggressively try to differentiate themselves, there has been a trend toward higher-quality products, planned obsolescence, and product life cycles measured in weeks or months rather than years. This, in turn, has created customer expectations for instant gratification. Consumers and business customers want high-quality goods and services—often customized—with lower prices and immediate delivery. Sales offices, service providers, and production facilities are shifting geographically as new markets and resources emerge in other countries. Employees want flexible working hours and opportunities to work at home. Shareholder expectations also add pressure for productivity increases, growth in market share, and larger profits. At the same time, however, a more vocal public demands more honesty, fair competition, and respect for the environment.

Identify emerging challenges and opportunities in the *business environment*.

A C-Suite survey found that the three most important issues facing Canadian businesses are (1) the value of the Canadian dollar, (2) a skilled labour shortage, and (3) the environment. These three issues are all important elements of the business environment.[51]

The Industry Environment

Each business firm operates in a specific industry, and each industry has different characteristics. The intensity of the competition in an industry has a big influence on how a company operates. To be effective, managers must understand the company's competitive situation and then develop a competitive strategy to exploit opportunities in the industry.

One of the best known examples of an effective competitive strategy is Walmart's satellite-based distribution system. And WestJet has a unique management system that helps it minimize aircraft turnaround time and thus keep its costs lower than those of its competitors. Managers try hard to find a competitive strategy for their firm, because doing so will slow down new competitors or stop them from entering the industry.

One of the most popular tools to analyze competitive situations in an industry is Michael Porter's five forces model.[52] The model (see Figure 2.7) helps managers analyze five important sources of competitive pressure and then decide what their competitive strategy should be. We briefly discuss each of the elements of the model in the following paragraphs.

Rivalry Among Existing Competitors

The amount of rivalry among companies varies across industries. Rivalry can be seen in activities like intense price competition, elaborate advertising campaigns, and an increased emphasis on customer service. For many years, the rivalry among Chartered Accountants, Certified General Accountants, and Certified Management Accountants in Canada was low key, but it has recently become much more intense. These organizations are responding by trying to attain more market power, cutting costs, making pricing deals with clients, and trying to find ways to differentiate themselves from their competitors.

Threat of Potential Entrants

When new competitors enter an industry, they may cause big changes. If it is easy for new competitors to enter a market, competition will likely be intense and the industry will not be very attractive. Some industries (for example, automobile

FIGURE 2.7

Michael Porter's five forces model.

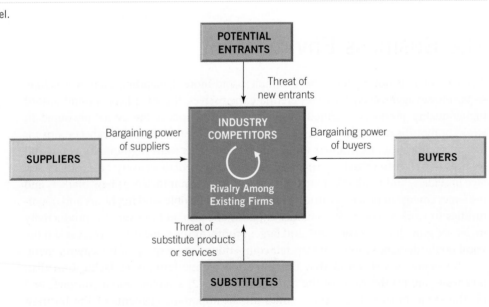

manufacturing) are very capital intensive and are therefore difficult to enter, but others (for example, home cleaning or lawn care services) are relatively easy to enter.

The entry of Target into the Canadian retail landscape is a great threat for low-cost retailers and is also a major opportunity for real estate income trust players like Primaris Retail REIT and RioCan. Target is converting approximately 135 of the 220 former Zellers stores and is making major renovations in exchange for favourable leases. It also holds options to another 85 locations and plans to sell the options to other retailers or back to the landlords. The scramble to get those prime locations was intense; Walmart secured the rights to 39 of them, and other retailers like Canadian Tire were looking at additional sites. The reallocation of 220 locations could potentially shake up the industry because one of the greatest barriers (access to prime real estate) has been temporarily weakened by the demise of Zellers. Other U.S. chains looking to further expand into Canada, like Marshalls, now have a potential opening.[53]

Suppliers

The amount of bargaining power that suppliers have in relation to buyers helps determine how competitive an industry is. When there are only a few suppliers in an industry, they tend to have great bargaining power. The power of suppliers is also influenced by the number of substitute products that are available (i.e., products that perform the same or similar functions). When there are few substitute products, suppliers obviously have more power.

Buyers

When there are only a few buyers and many suppliers, the buyers have a great deal of bargaining power. Walmart, for example, is often cited as a buyer that puts tremendous pressure on its suppliers to reduce their prices. Walmart can do this because it buys so much from these suppliers. In another example, when Canadian Tire purchased Forzani (owner of Sport Chek, Athletes World, and Hockey Experts stores) for $771 million, it was not necessarily good news for hockey equipment maker

The threat of Target's entry has materialized and the fall of Zellers is causing a shakeup in the industry as other retailers see the opportunity to enter the market or expand since prime real estate in major malls was temporarily available.

Bauer Performance Sports Ltd.: When two of your biggest customers merge it alters the power relationship somewhat. Bauer CEO Scott Davis has indicated that the Canadian Tire/Forzani merger may lead to certain price pressures on his company.[54]

Substitutes

If there are many substitute products available, the industry is more competitive. For example, various synthetic fibres can be used as substitutes for cotton.

Managers use Porter's ideas to help them decide the level of competitive intensity in an industry. A good example is the emergence of the internet in the sale of airline tickets. By making it easier for consumers to compare prices, the internet has increased the competitive intensity of the airline industry (and many other industries, for that matter) by increasing the bargaining power of ticket buyers.

Emerging Challenges and Opportunities in the Business Environment

The most successful firms are dealing with challenges and opportunities in today's business environment by focusing on their **core competencies**—the skills and resources with which they compete best and create the most value for owners. They outsource non-core business processes, paying suppliers and distributors to perform them and thereby increasing their reliance on suppliers. These new business models call for unprecedented coordination—not only among internal activities, but also among customers, suppliers, and strategic partners—and they often involve globally dispersed processes and supply chains.

In this section, we discuss some of the most publicized steps that companies have taken to respond to challenges and opportunities in the business environment. These developments include *outsourcing*, *social media* and *viral marketing*, and *business process management*.

Outsourcing

Outsourcing is the strategy of paying suppliers and distributors to perform certain business processes or to provide needed materials or services. For example, the cafeteria in a museum may be important to employees and customers, but running it is not the museum's main line of business and expertise. That's why museums usually outsource cafeteria operations to food-service management companies whose main line of business is to run cafeterias. The result is more attention to museum exhibits and better food service for customers. Firms today outsource numerous activities, including payroll, employee training, and research and development. When Levon Afeyan, CEO of Montreal-based Seatply Products Inc., searched for a solution to fight low-cost providers from China while simultaneously fending off local competitors providing premium products, he turned to an outsourcing partner in Malaysia. His seat component company now manufactures about half of its product in Malaysia; it also buys over 80 percent of its partner's output. This partnership has enabled his business to fight the competition in the new, increasingly competitive environment.[55]

Social Media and Viral Marketing

Social media sites such as Facebook are now an important part of everyday life for consumers, especially the youth market. Companies are addressing this new reality by providing content and creating links for consumers. Most organizations are careful about their online presence, preferring to be seen not as an imposition but rather as a natural extension of their real-world relationship with clients. As we discuss throughout this book, in the E-business and Social Media Solutions boxes, some companies are making strong inroads as this new model evolves and companies learn to deal with an empowered consumer base.

core competency Skills and resources with which an organization competes best and creates the most value for owners.

outsourcing Strategy of paying suppliers and distributors to perform certain business processes or to provide needed materials or services.

social media Various forms of electronic communications that allow users to form online communities and share ideas, opinions, and content.

Viral marketing predates the social media craze and first gained prominence through email; it refers to word-of-mouth that spreads information like a virus from customer to customer, and relies on the internet rather than face-to-face communication for its transmission. Messages about new cars, sports events, and numerous other goods and services travel on the internet among potential customers, who pass the information on. Using various formats—games, contests, chat rooms, and bulletin boards—marketers encourage potential customers to try out products and tell other people about them.[56] This approach has even more potential today with platforms such as Twitter providing even quicker means of distributing messages.

Viral marketing works because people increasingly rely on the internet for information that they used to get from other media such as radio and newspapers, and because the customer becomes a participant in the process of spreading the word by forwarding information to other internet users. Take a look at the E-business and Social Media Solutions box entitled "Corus Entertainment Looking for Listeners and Revenues in New Places."

viral marketing Strategy of using the internet and word-of-mouth marketing to spread product information.

Business Process Management

Every company performs numerous processes that provide goods or services for external customers or for other departments within the firm. Human resource departments perform interviewing and hiring processes, payroll departments perform the employee payment process, the purchasing department performs the process of ordering materials, accounting performs the financial reporting process, and marketing performs the process of taking orders from customers. A **process**, in short, is any activity that adds value to some input, transforming it into an output for a customer (whether external or internal).[57]

process Any activity that adds value to some input, transforming it into an output for a customer (whether external or internal).

In today's business environment, many firms are moving away from the department-oriented structures and toward process-oriented team structures that cut across old departmental boundaries. This approach is called **business process management**. Often, companies begin by asking, "What must we do well to stay in business and win new orders?" Next, they identify the major processes that must be performed well to satisfy these general goals. Then they organize resources and skills around those essential processes. By organizing according to processes rather than departments, they gain a number of benefits. Decision making is faster and more customer oriented, materials and operations are coordinated, and products get to customers more rapidly.[58]

business process management Approach by which firms move away from department-oriented organization and toward process-oriented team structures that cut across old departmental boundaries.

Redrawing Corporate Boundaries

Successful companies are responding to challenges in the environment by redrawing traditional organizational boundaries and by joining together with other companies to develop new goods and services. Some of these relationships are permanent, but others are temporary alliances formed on short notice so that, working together, partners can produce and deliver products with shorter lead times than either firm could manage alone.

Understand recent trends in the **LO7** redrawing of corporate boundaries.

Several trends in redrawing corporate boundaries have become evident in recent years. They include *acquisitions and mergers, divestitures and spinoffs, employee-owned corporations, strategic alliances,* and *subsidiary/parent corporations.*

Acquisitions and Mergers

In an **acquisition**, one firm simply buys another firm. For example, Kraft Foods Inc. recently bought British candy giant Cadbury for US$19 billion.[59] The transaction is similar to buying a car that becomes your property. In contrast, a **merger** is a

acquisition One firm buys another firm.

merger The consolidation of two firms.

consolidation of two firms, and the arrangement is more collaborative. In the third quarter of 2011, there were 251 mergers and acquisitions in Canada, with a total value of $45.5 billion, but this figure was lower than the previous quarter (292 deals worth $53.3 billion), and also lower than the same period in the previous year (278 deals worth $46.8 billion).[60]

horizontal merger A merger of companies in the same industry.

When the companies are in the same industry, as when Molson Inc. merged with Adolph Coors Co., it is called a **horizontal merger**. When one of the companies in the merger is a supplier to or customer of the other, it is called a **vertical merger**. When the companies are in unrelated businesses, it is called a **conglomerate merger**.

vertical merger A merger of companies where one is a supplier or customer of the other.

conglomerate merger A merger of companies in unrelated businesses.

E-BUSINESS + SOCIAL MEDIA SOLUTIONS

Corus Entertainment Looking For Listeners and Revenues in New Places

Do you remember when cameras were used to create photos, phones were used to make phone calls, and TVs were used to watch TV programs? Today things are different. You can watch TV on your phone, laptop, or even the LCD on your wall. Your smartphone or regular cellphone is a great tool for photos and your camera has an ever-increasing level of megapixels. As for music, it can come from your iPod, iPad, smartphone, or a satellite station, or be streamed on your laptop from the website from your favourite station in Surrey, Saskatoon, St. John's, or even South Africa. Options are limitless. Faced with this new reality, the companies that own your favourite stations are looking for new ways to attract listeners like you.

Corus Entertainment is extending its relationship with listeners and finding ways to profit from it as well. In the early days of the internet, stations were simply excited about the chance to share music and shows with anyone who would listen online. However, this also meant that their listeners could migrate to stations from anywhere—a scary prospect. Corus Entertainment has come a long way in the past decade. Visiting one of its 37 radio websites (e.g., Vancouver's 99.3 The Fox, Toronto's Edge 102.1, Calgary's Country 105, Edmonton's 92.5 Joe FM, Winnipeg's Power 97, and Hamilton's Y108) makes it clear that even if the call letters are the same, these stations are no longer simply your father's radio station (unless Dad is especially media savvy). There are links to Facebook, Flickr, MySpace, Twitter, Viigo (for BlackBerry), YouTube, and more. There are blogs and podcasts and the tools to connect, join contests, and create virtual bonds. Corus also takes it a step further; it was the first to offer an iPhone streaming app and the first to form direct links with iTunes. You can purchase, via a special version of the Apple iTunes music store linked to your station, the song that you're currently listening to. In the process, Corus stands to add a few pennies to its bottom line. The Corus App was also recently launched and has already been downloaded 400 000 times.

Here is the new math that Corus and its advertising partners are studying. In 2011, Corus achieved over 6 million online listening hours per month; one out of every 20 listeners was accessing their stations through mobile devices or online, and this figure was expected to grow. However, with all of these positive signs, Corus sold its 12 Quebec-based stations to Cogeco Cable Inc. for $81 million in 2010. Corus stated that it wanted to focus on its other key markets. Was this a sign that all was not well or was Corus simply focusing on selected stations and reinvesting its new business model in key spots? It was not clear at the time, but overall revenues and profitability increased in 2011 and the forecast was positive in 2012.

In the e-business age one thing is certain: Companies must be ready to adjust and evolve in order to be successful.

An example of a Corus Entertainment radio station website (Vancouver's 99.3 The Fox).

Critical Thinking Question

1. How do you listen to music? Have you joined or visited a social media group linked to your favourite stations? Why or why not?

A merger or acquisition can take place in one of several different ways. In a **friendly takeover**, the acquired company welcomes the acquisition, perhaps because it needs cash or sees other benefits in joining the acquiring firm. But in a **hostile takeover**, the acquiring company buys enough of the other company's stock to take control even though the other company is opposed to the takeover. Montreal-based Couche-Tard has plenty of experience in the merger and takeover game—in the past 15 years it has acquired Mac's, Dairy Mart, Circle K, and Winks; it is one of the biggest convenience store operators in North America with over 5800 stores. In 2010, it made a US$1.9 billion hostile takeover bid for Iowa-based Casey's after failing to come to a friendly agreement with the 1500-store chain.[61]

A **poison pill** is a defence that management adopts to make a firm less attractive to an actual or potential hostile suitor in a takeover attempt. The objective is to make the "pill" so distasteful that a potential acquirer will not want to swallow it. Couche-Tard was eventually unsuccessful in its hostile bid for Casey's because of a poison pill. Air Canada recently announced plans to institute a poison pill provision that would give all Class A and Class B shareholders the right to purchase stocks, at a discounted price, the moment any group or person announces the intention to buy more than 20 percent of the outstanding shares.[62]

> **friendly takeover** A merger in which the acquired company welcomes the acquisition.
>
> **hostile takeover** A merger in which one company buys enough of the other company's stock to take control even though the other company is opposed to the takeover.
>
> **poison pill** A defence adopted by management to make a firm less attractive to a hostile suitor in a takeover attempt.

Divestitures and Spinoffs

A **divestiture** occurs when a company decides to sell part of its existing business operations to another corporation. For example, Unilever—the maker of Close-Up toothpaste, Dove soap, Vaseline lotion, and Q-tips—at one time owned several specialty chemical businesses that made ingredients for its consumer products. The company decided that it had to focus more on consumer products, so it sold the chemical businesses to ICI, a European chemical company.

In other cases, a company might set up one or more corporate units as new, independent businesses because a business unit might be more valuable as a separate company. This is known as a **spinoff**. For example, PepsiCo spun off Pizza Hut, KFC, and Taco Bell into a new, separate corporation called Tricon Global Restaurants, now known as Yum! Brands Inc. Canadian Pacific spun off Canadian Pacific Railways, CP Ships, PanCanadian Petroleum, and Fording Coal.

> **divestiture** Occurs when a company decides to sell part of its existing business operations to another corporation.
>
> **spinoff** Occurs when a company sets up one or more corporate units as new, independent businesses.

Employee-Owned Corporations

Corporations are sometimes owned by the employees who work for them, and there is a growing trend today for employees to buy significant stakes of larger corporations. The current pattern is for this ownership to take the form of **employee stock ownership plans (ESOPs)**.

A corporation might decide to set up an ESOP to stimulate employee motivation or to fight a hostile takeover attempt. Here's how it works: The company first secures a loan, which it then uses to buy shares of its stock on the open market. Some of the future profits made by the corporation are used to pay off the loan. The stock, meanwhile, is controlled by a bank or other trustee. Employees gradually gain ownership of the stock, usually on the basis of seniority. But even though they might not have physical possession of the stock for a while, they control its voting rights immediately.

A survey of 471 Canadian and U.S. companies conducted by Western Compensation & Benefits Consultants of Vancouver found that three-quarters of the companies that have adopted ESOPs have experienced improvement in both sales and profits. Charlie Spiring, the CEO of Wellington West Holdings Inc., says that one of the fundamental principles of his business is employee ownership. People really have to be entrepreneurs to work well in the company.[63]

> **employee stock ownership plans (ESOPs)** Plans that allow employees to buy significant stakes of larger corporations.

Strategic Alliances

strategic alliance (or joint venture) Involves two or more enterprises co-operating in the research, development, manufacture, or marketing of a product.

A **strategic alliance**, or **joint venture**, involves two or more enterprises co-operating in the research, development, manufacture, or marketing of a product. Companies form strategic alliances for two main reasons: (1) to help spread the risk of a project, and (2) to get something of value (like technological expertise) from their strategic partner. GM and Suzuki formed a strategic alliance at the Ingersoll, Ontario, plant where Grand Vitaras are made.

Subsidiary and Parent Corporations

subsidiary corporation A company that is owned by another corporation.

parent corporation A corporation that owns subsidiary corporations.

Sometimes corporations own other corporations. A **subsidiary corporation** is one that is owned by another corporation. The corporation that owns the subsidiary is called the **parent corporation**. For example, Hudson's Bay Company (HBC) is the parent corporation of Home Outfitters.

MyBizLab

Capture more moments of true understanding. MyBizLab provides you with interactive study and practice tools directly related to this chapter's content. The new MyBizLab Study Plan Learning Path is designed to measure a full range of skills and provide remediation to give you what you need to master key chapter concepts. MyBizLab flexes to your unique learning needs. The result? Inspired learning, more success.

SUMMARY OF LEARNING OBJECTIVES

1. **Explain the concepts of *organizational boundaries* and multiple *organizational environments.*** All businesses operate within a larger external environment. An *organizational boundary* is that which separates the organization from its environment. Boundaries were once relatively easy to identify, but they are becoming harder to pin down. Organizations have *multiple environments*. Some environments are relatively general, such as prevailing economic conditions. Others are much more precise, such as the pricing policies of competitors. A full picture of a company's organizational environments would include the following elements: economic conditions, technology, political-legal considerations, social issues, the global environment, issues of ethics and social responsibility, the business environment itself, and numerous other emerging challenges and opportunities.

2. **Explain the importance of the *economic environment* to business and identify the factors used to evaluate the performance of an *economic system.*** The *economic environment* is the economic system in which business firms operate. The health of this environment affects business firms. The three key goals of the Canadian system are economic growth, economic stability, and full employment. *Economic growth* is influenced by the pattern of short-term ups and downs in an economy known as the business cycle. The main measure of growth in this cycle is aggregate output. An increase in aggregate output is growth. *Gross domestic product* (GDP) is the total value of all goods and services produced within a given period by a national economy through domestic factors of production. If GDP is going up, so is aggregate output; if aggregate output is going up, we have economic growth.

   Economic stability means that the amount of money available in an economic system and the quantity of goods and services produced in it are growing at about the same rate. There are three threats to stability: inflation, deflation, and unemployment.

   Unemployment is the level of joblessness among people actively seeking work. If people in different sectors lose their jobs at the same time, overall income and spending drop and businesses cut spending further—including spending on labour—and unemployment goes up further. Meanwhile, producers also start producing less because they can't sell as much. Aggregate output then decreases and we have a recession. A prolonged and deep recession is a depression.

   The government manages the economy through *fiscal policies* and *monetary policies*. Through the Bank of Canada, the Canadian government can influence the ability and willingness of banks to lend money. It can also influence the supply of money by prompting interest rates to go up or down.

3. **Describe the *technological environment* and its role in business.** *Technology* refers to all the ways by which firms create value for their constituents, including human knowledge, work methods, physical equipment, electronics and telecommunications, and various processing systems. There are two general categories of business-related technologies: product and service technologies and business process technologies. *Product* and *service technologies* create products—both physical goods and services—for customers. *Business process technologies* are used to improve a firm's performance of internal operations (such as accounting) and to help to create better relationships with external constituents, such as suppliers and customers. Enterprise resource planning (ERP) is a large-scale information system for organizing and managing a firm's processes across product lines, departments, and geographic locations.

4. **Describe the *political-legal environment* and its role in business.** The *political-legal environment* reflects the relationship between business and government, usually in the form of government regulation. The legal system defines in part what an organization can and can't do. Various government agencies regulate important areas such as advertising practices, safety and health considerations, and acceptable standards of business conduct. Pro- or anti-business sentiment in government can further influence business activity. During periods of pro-business sentiment, firms find it easier to compete and have fewer concerns about antitrust issues. During periods of anti-business sentiment, firms may find their competitive activities more restricted.

5. **Describe the *socio-cultural environment* and its role in business.** The *socio-cultural environment* includes the customs, values, and demographic characteristics of the society in which an organization functions. Socio-cultural processes determine the goods and services as well as the standards of business conduct that a society values and accepts. Appropriate standards of conduct also vary across cultures. The shape of the market, the ethics of political influence, and the attitudes of its workforce are only a few of the many ways in which culture can affect an organization.

6. **Identify emerging challenges and opportunities in the *business environment.*** Successful companies are responding to challenges in new ways. The innovative ways in which companies respond to emerging challenges and opportunities include outsourcing, social media and viral marketing, and business process management. *Outsourcing* is the strategy of paying suppliers and distributors to perform certain business processes or to provide needed materials or services. Social media is having an impact on various areas of business ranging from recruitment to marketing. *Viral marketing* relies on the internet to replace face-to-face communications. Many firms are moving away from the department-oriented organization and toward process-oriented team structures that cut across old departmental boundaries—an approach called *business process management*.

7. **Understand recent trends in the redrawing of** *corporate boundaries.* An *acquisition* occurs when one firm buys another outright. A *merger* occurs when two firms combine to create a new company. A *divestiture* occurs when a corporation sells a part of its existing business operations or sets it up as a new and independent corporation.

When a firm sells part of itself to raise capital, the strategy is known as a *spinoff*. The employee *stock ownership plan* (ESOP) allows employees to own a significant share of the corporation through trusts established on their behalf. In a *strategic alliance*, two or more organizations collaborate on a project for mutual gain.

KEY TERMS

acquisition (p. 61)
aggregate output (p. 41)
applied R&D (p. 49)
balance of trade (p. 43)
basic (or pure) R&D (p. 49)
budget deficit (p. 44)
business cycle (p. 40)
business process management (p. 61)
conglomerate merger (p. 62)
consumer price index (CPI) (p. 46)
core competency (p. 60)
deflation (p. 46)
depression (p. 40)
divestiture (p. 63)
economic environment (p. 39)
employee stock ownership plan (ESOP) (p. 63)
enterprise resource planning (ERP) (p. 52)

external environment (p. 38)
fiscal policies (p. 48)
friendly takeover (p. 63)
gross domestic product (GDP) (p. 41)
gross national product (GNP) (p. 42)
horizontal merger (p. 62)
hostile takeover (p. 63)
inflation (p. 45)
merger (p. 61)
monetary policies (p. 48)
national debt (p. 44)
nominal GDP (p. 43)
organizational boundary (p. 38)
outsourcing (p. 60)
parent corporation (p. 64)
poison pill (p. 63)
political-legal environment (p. 54)
process (p. 61)
productivity (p. 43)

purchasing power parity (p. 43)
R&D intensity (p. 51)
real GDP (p. 43)
recession (p. 40)
research and development (R&D) (p. 49)
socio-cultural environment (p. 56)
social media (p. 60)
spinoff (p. 63)
stability (p. 45)
stabilization policy (p. 48)
standard of living (p. 41)
strategic alliance (or joint venture) (p. 64)
subsidiary corporation (p. 64)
technology (p. 49)
technology transfer (p. 52)
unemployment (p. 47)
vertical merger (p. 62)
viral marketing (p. 61)

QUESTIONS FOR ANALYSIS

1. Why is it important for managers to understand the environment in which their businesses operate?
2. It has been argued that inflation is both good and bad. How can this be? Explain. Are government efforts to control inflation well advised? Explain.
3. What are the benefits and risks of outsourcing? What, if anything, should be done about the problem of Canadian companies outsourcing jobs to foreign countries? Defend your answer.
4. Explain how current economic indicators such as inflation and unemployment affect you personally. Explain how they might affect you as a manager.
5. At first glance, it might seem as though the goals of economic growth and stability are inconsistent with one another. How can you reconcile this apparent inconsistency?
6. What is the current climate regarding the regulation of business? How might it affect you if you were a manager today?

APPLICATION EXERCISES

1. Select two businesses with which you are familiar. Identify the major elements of their external environments that are most likely to affect them in important and meaningful ways.
2. Assume that you are the owner of an internet pharmacy that sells prescription drugs to U.S. citizens. Analyze the factors in the external environment (economic, technological, political–legal, and socio-cultural) that might facilitate your company's activities. Analyze the factors in the external environment that might threaten your company's activities.
3. Select a technology product, such as Amazon's Kindle e-reader, and research how the various environments of business (economic, technological, socio-cultural, global, political-legal, and general business) are currently impacting the sales possibilities of the product or service.
4. Interview two business owners or managers. Ask them to answer the following questions: (a) What business functions, if any, do they outsource? (b) Are they focussing more attention on business process management now than in the past? (c) How have internet applications and the growth of social media changed the way they conduct business?

BUILDING YOUR BUSINESS SKILLS

Feeling the Heat from Bad Results: Praying for Good Weather

Purpose of the Assignment

To help students identify the important role played by uncontrollable natural events on the bottom line.

The Situation

Rona Inc. is a Canadian home improvement giant with over $6 billion in annual sales coming from over 700 corporate, franchise, and affiliate stores. It is the largest Canadian retailer of hardware, home renovation, and gardening products and has a roster of over 30 000 employees. Despite its impressive growth, good strategic decisions in the past decade, and locations across the nation, Rona's results were still largely susceptible to natural weather patterns. For example, in the first quarter of 2011 the retailer lost 23 cents per share based on a 12.6 percent decline in same-store sales from the previous year. The reason, according to CEO Robert Dutton, was that "spring failed to materialize." The extra-long winter that year meant that customers did not rush out to buy things like home gardening supplies, which traditionally pad the bottom line during this sales period. Labour costs remained high while staff had fewer customers to serve. The incentive to discount to attract sales was strong, but company officials stated that they would avoid such tactics. However, the extra build-up of inventory has a direct holding cost; additionally, analysts were worried that the company would likely need to discount (and drastically slash profit margins) to rid itself of the extra stock once the shortened season arrived.[64]

Weather patterns can play an important role in the short-term success or failure of many businesses and clearly Rona was affected by this uncontrollable factor in this case.

Assignment

Divide up into groups of four or five students. Each group should begin by doing the following:

Step 1

Identify three **big companies** that might be **positively** affected by warmer-than-usual weather during a particular season.

Step 2

Identify three **big companies** that are **negatively** affected by warmer-than-usual weather patterns during a particular season. If it is appropriate, a company can appear on both lists.

Step 3

Now respond to the following items:
1. For each company that you identify, describe the specific effects on each business.
2. Describe the most logical organizational response for each company to these effects.
3. What kinds of plans, if any, should each organization develop in the event of similar future events?

Alternative Assignment

Conduct the same exercise on **small businesses** and **entrepreneurs** and highlight some of the unique challenges that they face. Then proceed with Steps 1–3 above.

Questions for Discussion

1. How could Rona better prepare for and handle negative weather patterns?
2. Are unfavourable natural weather patterns more dangerous for major retailers like Rona or for small businesses? Provide at least one argument on each side before making a choice.
3. Is it possible for a manager to spend too much time trying to anticipate future events? Why or why not?

EXERCISING YOUR ETHICS: TEAM EXERCISE

Finding the Balance

The Situation

Managers often find it necessary to find the right balance among the interests of different stakeholders. For instance, paying employees the lowest possible wages can enhance profits, but paying a living wage might better serve the interests of workers. As more businesses outsource production to other countries, these trade-offs become even more complicated.

The Dilemma

The Canadian Delta Company currently uses three different suppliers in Southeast Asia for most of its outsourced production. Due to increased demand for its products, it needs to double the amount of business it currently subcontracts to one of these suppliers. (For purposes of this exercise, assume that the company must award the new supplier contract to a single firm and that it must be one of these three. You can also assume that the quality provided is about the same for all three companies.)

Subcontractor A provides a plain but clean work environment for its workers. Even though the local weather conditions are hot and humid much of the year, the plant is not air-conditioned. Canadian Delta safety experts have verified that the conditions are not dangerous but are definitely uncomfortable at times. The firm pays its workers the same prevailing wage rate that is paid by its local competitors. While it has never had a legal issue with its workforce, Subcontractor A does push its employees to meet production quotas and it has a very tough policy regarding discipline for tardiness. For instance, an employee who is late gets put on probation; a second infraction within three months results in termination. This subcontractor provides production to Canadian Delta at a level such that it can attach a 25 percent mark-up.

Subcontractor B also provides a plain work environment. It pays its workers about 5 percent above local wage levels and hence is an attractive employer. Because of its higher pay, this firm is actually quite ruthless with some of its policies, however. For instance, any employee who reports to work more than 15 minutes late without a medical excuse is automatically terminated. This supplier's costs are such that Delta Company can achieve a 20 percent mark-up.

Subcontractor C runs a much nicer factory than either A or B, and the plant is air-conditioned. It also pays its workers about 10 percent above local wage levels. The company also operates an on-site school for the children of its employees and provides additional training for its workers so they can improve their skills. Due to its higher costs, Canadian Delta's mark-up on this firm's products is only around 15 percent.

Team Activity

Assemble a group of four students and assign each group member to one of the following roles:

- Canadian Delta executive
- Canadian Delta employee
- Canadian Delta customer
- Canadian Delta investor

Action Steps

1. Before discussing the situation with your group, and from the perspective of your assigned role, which firm do you think should get the additional business? Which firm is your second choice? Write down the reasons for your position.
2. Before discussing the situation with your group, and from the perspective of your assigned role, what are the underlying ethical issues in this situation? Write down the issues.
3. Gather your group together and reveal, in turn, each member's comments on their choices. Next, reveal the ethical issues listed by each member.
4. Appoint someone to record the main points of agreement and disagreement within the group. How do you explain the results? What accounts for any disagreement?
5. From an ethical standpoint, what does your group conclude is the most appropriate choice for the company in this situation? Why?

Go to MyBizLab for additional cases and exercise material.

CONCLUDING CASE 2-1

Air Canada's Challenging Environment: Competition, Economic Crisis, Fuel Prices, Volcanoes, and More

The name Air Canada does not always conjure up warm images for Canadian travellers. But it is the fifteenth largest airline in the world and it wins international awards. In 2010 and 2011, it was named the "best international airline in North America" by independent research firm Skytrax, which surveyed over 18.8 million worldwide travellers from 200 airlines. There have been many ups and downs for Air Canada, but the company continues to control the majority of the domestic market, with WestJet as its main competitor. Back in 2004, Air Canada used bankruptcy protection to deal with major financial problems. It may be tempting to blame that dark period on general turmoil in the travel industry following the 9/11 terrorist attacks, but placing all the blame on that significant event would be overly simplistic. The airline business has always been extremely complicated; it's a difficult business environment that is shaped by relationships with many stakeholders.

Airlines must efficiently plan their capacity. They don't buy a fleet of planes overnight; airlines make projections and try to maximize the use of planes and other resources. Some of this planning is done two to five or even seven years into the future and this sort of lengthy timeline is complicated. Air Canada must contend with the actions of competitors both at home (e.g., WestJet, Porter) and on international routes (e.g., Air France, British Airways, JAL); it must deal with government regulations (e.g., tax laws, flight restrictions, and international agreements), economic conditions (e.g., recessions, fuel/food prices), and natural weather conditions (e.g., snowstorms and even volcanic ash). Let's take a closer look at these challenges.

In recent years, a major spike in fuel costs hurt air travel and caused ticket prices to skyrocket at times. The global recession, which started in 2008, decreased tourist and business travel. In fact, in 2009 the global airline business saw its steepest decline in air traffic since the Second World War. According to the International Air Transport Association (IATA), the global industry lost $10 billion that year. While IATA predicted profit of US$4.9 billion for the industry in 2012, it was clear that the industry was struggling as a whole. Air Canada worked hard to get its finances under control by creating new agreements with suppliers and major credit providers. The company managed to increase earnings per share to 37 cents at the end of 2010, up from an 18-cent loss a year earlier.

At home, Air Canada competes with WestJet and a host of smaller players. The rivalry has pushed it to launch its lower-priced Tango fares to compete in the low-frill, budget travel segment. In addition, the company created a regional partner called Jazz mainly for short-haul flights. In order to effectively compete on the global stage, Air Canada has forged alliances to cut costs. It is a founding member of the leading airline network called Star Alliance. Its 28 members permit passengers on partner airlines to connect with over 1160 airports in 181 countries. The airlines code-share flights (e.g., booking Air Canada seats on a Lufthansa flight) and share airline lounges in airports around the world. In recent years, Air Canada also extended its partnerships with Continental, United, and Lufthansa to create Atlantic-Plus-Plus, which further enables it to integrate routes and compete in the transatlantic segment.

Governments are strongly linked to airline success or failure. Here are some key facts to consider. The government recently negotiated an agreement between Canada and the EU that creates new opportunities by reducing restrictions for Air Canada and EU airlines. So in 2010, Air Canada launched new direct services to five popular European gateway cities: Geneva, Barcelona, Brussels, Copenhagen, and Athens. A similar deal with the United States government back in 1995 was an important step in Air Canada's extensive expansion (Air Canada is the largest airline in the U.S.–Canada trans-border market, serving 60 destinations in the United States). Of course, the relationship with the government is not all rosy. Air Canada has stated that the government is making it impossible for the airline to be profitable with higher security charges, airport improvement fees, and federal and provincial fuel excise taxes. For example, the federal government collects over $300 million in rent from airports each year. This makes it much more expensive to land a plane in Canada than in the United States Air Canada pays $3400 to land an Airbus 320 in Canada's largest airports but less than half that amount ($1650) in the United States Total federal tax collected in Halifax alone amounted to $3.2 million in rent charges in one year and is expected to top $5 million by 2014. Since the airline is based in Canada, it has a tax cost disadvantage.

Weather can play a tricky role in airline operations. If you travel on a regular basis you are very familiar with airline delays. Snowstorms, severe thunder showers, icy weather, and severe winds can disrupt travel and cause delays. This results in frustrated passengers and forces airline employees and travel agents to scramble. In April 2010, a new issue hit the headlines when a volcano in Iceland halted all air travel to and from Europe for five long days, cancelling over 100 000 flights. The name of the volcano is Eyjafjallajokull (pronounced ay-yah-FYAH-lah-yer-kuhl), and customers were heard muttering similar sounds as they tried to get home. The eruption cost the airline industry huge sums of money: Air Canada lost $20 million per day; Air Transat lost approximately $750 000 per day; Air France-KLM lost an estimated $35 million per day. Airlines demanded compensation from the EU for more than $1 billion in losses. It remains to be seen what the ultimate response will be.

As you can see, airlines must create efficient strategies and plan for the unexpected. There are many elements far outside their control that impact success or failure. In addition to the issues mentioned above, there are the massive new security challenges, flu pandemics, and political conflicts (e.g., civil war) that can erupt anywhere in the world. This is why it is so hard to find an airline that is profitable on a consistent basis. This is truly a challenging industry.

Questions for Discussion

1. Identify the various environmental factors that influence Air Canada. Which of these are most important? Explain.
2. How does the multi-year planning time frame regarding the purchasing of aircraft impact management decisions?
3. How do unpredictable events impact Air Canada? Give examples.
4. What can Air Canada do to reduce the negative impact of environmental factors that complicate its activities?
5. How does government regulation of the commercial airline business affect Air Canada?

CONCLUDING CASE 2-2

Inflationary Pressure/Deflationary Pressure and the Validity of the CPI

Between 2008 and 2012, there were many contradictory signals in the economy and sustained periods of fear and confusion in financial markets. The stock market saw a major decline and a major recovery and the roller coaster ride seemed far from over. The reason was not just the credit crisis, the housing crisis, the sovereign debt crisis, or the worldwide recession. There was also uncertainty about whether inflation or deflation was going to add to the problems that already existed. On one hand, it seemed logical to predict that inflation was going to get worse because central governments around the world had cut interest rates and injected billions of dollars into their financial systems to get their economies moving again. On the other hand, the recession had become so bad that the demand for goods and services was declining, commodity prices (including oil) were falling fast, banks were not lending money (because they feared that borrowers wouldn't be able to repay their loans), consumers were reluctant to spend money, and everyone was hoarding cash. All of those factors suggested that deflation was going to occur.

To see how this complicated situation developed, we have to look back. In the first half of 2008, prices increased for many different products and services, including food, metals, energy, air transportation, gasoline, cable services, and mortgages. The Bank of Canada became concerned that inflation was becoming a real threat. The weakening of the Canadian dollar against the U.S. dollar also increased the threat since imported goods would become more expensive for Canadians. The International Monetary Fund (IMF) expressed concern that the strong demand for food and other resources in rapidly growing countries like India and China was going to cause increased inflation elsewhere in the world. The IMF's deputy managing director noted that there were about

50 countries in the world with inflation rates above 10 percent, mostly developing nations.

The interconnectedness of the global economy was also a problem. The U.S. Federal Reserve cut interest rates in an attempt to get the U.S. economy moving, but that caused the value of the U.S. dollar to decline relative to other currencies (at least for a while). That, in turn, meant that U.S. consumers would have to pay more for imported products. The rate cut also created problems for Middle Eastern and Asian countries that had pegged their dollar to the U.S. dollar in an attempt to stabilize their economies. When the United States reduced interest rates, those countries really had to follow suit; if they didn't, people would move more money into their own countries (because they could earn a higher rate of return than they could in the United States). That, in turn, would create upward pressure on the currency of those Middle Eastern and Asian countries. It would also cause increased inflation because when interest rates decline, it is easier for people to borrow money.

All of these factors suggested that inflation was going to be a problem. But economic circumstances can change very quickly. Just a few months after the Bank of Canada expressed concerns about inflation, it decided to cut interest rates, even though doing so typically increases the chance of inflation. The Bank of Canada did this because commodity prices had suddenly declined and a worldwide recession had started. In spite of the rate cut, prices soon started dropping for meat, automobiles, computers, fresh fruit, furniture, appliances, tools, hardware, and a wide range of commodities, including oil. In China, overproduction of everything from laptop computers to building materials raised fears that many products would soon be dumped on world markets at cut-rate prices. That increased the chance of deflation (negative inflation). Support for deflation fears could be found in the fact that the rate of inflation in the U.S. economy between March 2008 and March 2009 was −0.1 percent. That was the first year of negative inflation since 1955.

Fears about deflation were not without foundation. Japan experienced deflation for 15 years after its housing bubble burst in the early 1990s. Then, just when it looked like Japan would escape from that problem, the U.S. Federal Reserve cut interest rates to almost 0 percent to get the U.S. economy moving. Japan's central bank followed suit; it didn't want the yen to rise in value because that would depress Japan's exports. In 2010, matters were further complicated when the Bank of Canada announced it was raising rates and signalling that future rate hikes might be significant in the near term (partially because of fears of a potential housing bubble). In 2011, one of the major stories was the rise in food prices caused primarily by the increase in fuel prices, which was putting pressure on food retailers, restaurants, and consumers alike.

The inflation rate in May 2011 approached 4 percent, although it ended the year closer to 2 percent and stayed in that range in early 2012.

It is difficult to predict whether inflation or deflation is more likely partly because both situations are influenced by self-fulfilling prophecies. For example, if people think inflation is going to be a problem, they are motivated to buy things now in order to avoid paying the higher prices that they assume are soon to come. But buying things now creates more demand, and that causes prices to rise. Conversely, if people think deflation is going to occur, they are motivated to delay purchases until the time when the price will be lower. But putting off purchases lowers demand, and that causes prices to fall.

There is yet another angle to consider in this debate. According to statistician Phil Green, our measurement tool (CPI) is inaccurate and inflation is actually much higher than typically reported in the past 20 years. The way CPI is measured has changed, and some believe that governments are fudging the numbers. Green claims that the inflation rate in the United States was actually closer to 10 percent if measured using traditional methods. The United States is not alone in this. Governments have changed the CPI equation many times in major industrialized nations. This is no secret. But informed individuals were questioning the very integrity of this key leading indicator.

Given all this complexity, we should not be surprised if economists have trouble accurately predicting whether inflation or deflation will be the next problem we face. Inflation definitely lurks in the background. If the crisis in confidence can be overcome, people will start spending again, and with all that money that governments dished out still in the system, demand could soar and inflation could become a big problem. On the other hand, if the recession is long and deep, deflation is a distinct possibility because there will be very little demand for goods and services, and that will cause prices to fall.

Questions for Discussion

1. Based on your own observations in the marketplace, do you believe we are in an inflationary or deflationary period?
2. Go to the Bank of Canada website and find the latest inflation figures. Based on the latest statistics, is inflation or deflation a bigger problem today?
3. What do you think of Phil Green's contention that the CPI has become a deceptive tool? Do you believe that governments are purposefully massaging the numbers? If so, explain why.

Conducting Business Ethically and Responsibly

LEARNING OBJECTIVES

After reading this chapter, you should be able to:

1 Explain how individuals develop their personal *codes of ethics* and why ethics are important in the workplace.

2 Distinguish *corporate social responsibility* from *ethics*, identify *organizational stakeholders*, and characterize social consciousness today.

3 Show how the concept of social responsibility applies both to environmental issues and to a firm's relationships with customers, employees, and investors.

4 Identify four general *approaches to social responsibility* and describe the four steps a firm must take to implement a *social responsibility program*.

5 Explain how issues of social responsibility and ethics affect small businesses.

Ethical Lapses

DURING the past decade there have been several high-profile examples of ethical lapses at business firms. These include a hacking scandal at the British tabloid *News of the World*, financial misrepresentation at Livent, and fraud at Cinar. Here are the stories.

News Corp.

News Corp. is a media giant headed by Rupert Murdoch. One of its more controversial publications was a tabloid called *News of the World*, which reported on all sorts of gossip about individuals. The tabloid was Britain's bestselling Sunday paper until it was revealed that some of its reporters had hacked into the cellphones of private citizens. The public was particularly outraged about the case of a 13-year-old girl who was kidnapped and murdered. While she was missing, a reporter at *News of the World* hacked into her voice mail

and deleted messages. This led her parents to think that she was still alive. The cellphones of military personnel who had been killed in Iraq and Afghanistan were also hacked.

The scandal caused the market value of News Corp. to drop more than $5 billion. As well, a planned takeover of television network BSkyB was abandoned. Many well-known companies (Ford, Lloyd's of London, Cadbury, and Vauxhall) announced that they were pulling their advertising from *News of the World*. Two top executives also resigned: Rebekah Brooks (CEO of News International) and Les Hinton (CEO of News Corp.'s Dow Jones & Co., which publishes *The Wall Street Journal*). Shortly after the scandal broke, it was announced that *News of the World* would cease publication.

When Rupert Murdoch and his son James (the CEO) appeared before the Culture, Media, and Sport Committee of the British Parliament, they both apologized for what had

happened, but denied knowledge of the hacking. Rupert Murdoch said that his company was so big that he couldn't know about all the details of what was going on. He said that he wasn't much involved in the paper's management because it was such a small part of his media empire. He admitted that he had not looked closely enough into the activities of some of the paper's staff, but denied responsibility for what had happened because subordinates that he trusted had lied to him. The issue of how much responsibility top managers have for the actions of their subordinates was also debated in the press, with some commentators defending Murdoch and others condemning him.

In the aftermath of the scandal, allegations were made that Andy Coulson, an editor at the tabloid when the hacking took place, knew that illegal payments of CDN$185 000 had been made to police officers who provided

info the World journalists accused of illegally eavesdropping

information to reporters for stories they were writing. The story then took on strong political overtones, since Coulson had been appointed as the prime minister's communications director after he resigned from the paper. In January 2012, News Corp. settled most of the civil lawsuits it was facing by paying damages to individuals whose phones were hacked. The company agreed to pay three million pounds for hacking the phone of the kidnapped teenager; actor Jude Law received just over $200 000.

Cinar

In March 2011, four individuals were arrested and charged with multiple counts of fraud and forgery as part of a multimillion-dollar scandal at Cinar Corp., a Montreal-based animation company. The individuals were Ronald Weinberg (former co-CEO of Cinar), Hasanaim Panju (chief financial officer), Lino Matteo (former president of Mount Real, who was accused of using his company to cover up the scam), and John Xanthoudakis (the alleged mastermind behind the scheme and former CEO of Norshield Financial Group, which went bankrupt in 2005). The co-CEO of Cinar, Micheline Charest (wife of Ronald Weinberg), died in 2004. As of mid-2012, the trial had not yet taken place.

The alleged frauds took place in 2000. At that time, Cinar was an immensely successful producer of popular children's shows like *Arthur, Caillou, The Adventures of Paddington Bear,* and *Wimzie's House.* The key drivers in the company were Charest and Weinberg, who tirelessly promoted their company to the media and to financial markets. But in March 2000, they both resigned as co-chief executives of the company amid allegations that (1) over $100 million had been invested without proper approval from Cinar's board of directors, (2) Cinar had fraudulently obtained Canadian tax credits by putting the names of Canadians on television scripts actually written by Americans, and (3) Cinar had breached securities rules with its financial statements and other disclosure documents. These allegations caused the company's stock to drop sharply in value, and Cinar was eventually delisted from both NASDAQ and the Toronto Stock Exchange. In 2002, Charest and Weinberg were fined $1 million each by the Quebec Securities Commission (QSC). They were also required to resign from the board of directors, and were banned from holding directorships or voting for directors of publicly held companies in Canada. It was assumed that the QSC ruling would prevent Charest

and Weinberg from influencing who would be appointed to Cinar's board of directors. But the QSC settlement did allow them to appoint a trustee who could nominate or vote for directors, and at Cinar's next annual shareholders' meeting, trustee Robert Despres used his new-found voting clout to install directors he wanted instead of the company's proposed slate. Despres claimed that he did not represent Charest and Weinberg, and was simply interested in getting a board of directors in place that would move the company forward and increase shareholder value.

When problems originally arose at Cinar, Richard Finley, chairman of the Centre for Corporate and Public Governance, offered the view that Cinar's top management and board structure were rather peculiar and likely contributed to Cinar's difficulties. The husband–wife team of Charest and Weinberg functioned as co-CEOs and both reported to the board. The corporate governance guidelines of the Toronto Stock Exchange call for a non-executive and independent director as chairperson of the board.

The company was purchased in 2004 by a consortium headed by Nelvana co-founder Michael Hirsh and renamed Cookie Jar Entertainment.

Livent

Livent Inc., a live theatre company with outlets in Toronto, Vancouver, Chicago, and New York, was founded by Garth Drabinsky and Myron Gottlieb. In 1998, questions were raised about Livent's finances by new owners who had bought into the company. Shortly thereafter, Drabinsky and Gottlieb were fired. They were eventually charged with producing false financial statements to make the company look more profitable than it actually was. After a long delay, their trial finally started in 2008.

During the trial, prosecutors called several witnesses who admitted that they had participated in the financial manipulations, but said they had done so at the direction of Drabinsky and Gottlieb. Drabinsky and Gottlieb denied any wrongdoing and claimed that the financial manipulations were carried out by subordinates without their knowledge. Their attorneys repeatedly attacked the credibility of the witnesses and argued that accounting staff had circumvented the accounting controls that Drabinsky had put in place. The

defence presented no witnesses and Drabinsky and Gottlieb did not testify.

In 2009, Drabinsky and Gottlieb were found guilty of fraud and forgery. Drabinsky was sentenced to seven years in jail and Gottlieb to six years. In 2011, the Ontario Court of Appeals reduced their sentences by two years each. The Institute of Chartered Accountants of Ontario also found three senior Deloitte & Touche LLP auditors guilty of making errors during an audit of Livent's financial statements. The three were fined $100 000 each. ◆

HOW WILL THIS HELP ME?

There is a growing dilemma in the business world today involving the economic imperatives (real or imagined) facing managers and the pressure to function as good citizens. By understanding the material in this chapter, you'll be better able to assess the ethical and social responsibility issues that you will face as an *employee* and as a boss or business *owner*. It will also help you understand the ethical and social responsibility actions of businesses you deal with as a consumer and as an *investor*.

Ethics in the Workplace

> **LO1** Explain how individuals develop their personal *codes of ethics* and why ethics are important in the workplace.

ethics Individual standards or moral values regarding what is right and wrong or good and bad.

ethical behaviour Behaviour that conforms to individual beliefs and social norms about what is right and good.

unethical behaviour Behaviour that individual beliefs and social norms define as wrong and bad.

business ethics Ethical or unethical behaviour by a manager or employee of an organization.

Ethics are beliefs about what is right and wrong or good and bad. An individual's personal values and morals, as well as the social context in which they occur, determine whether a particular behaviour is perceived as ethical or unethical. **Ethical behaviour** is behaviour that conforms to individual beliefs and social norms about what is right and good. **Unethical behaviour** is behaviour that individual beliefs and social norms define as wrong and bad. **Business ethics** refers to ethical or unethical behaviour by a manager or employee of an organization.

Individual Ethics

Because ethics are based on both individual beliefs and social concepts, they vary from person to person, from situation to situation, and from culture to culture. But there are some commonalities. For example, most societies view stealing as wrong. But what if you happen to see someone drop a $20 bill in a store? Most people would probably say that it would be ethical to return it to the owner, but some might think it is okay to keep it. And there will be even less agreement if you find $20 and don't know who dropped it. Should you turn it in to the lost-and-found department? Or, since the rightful owner isn't likely to claim it, can you just keep it? The boxed insert entitled "Ethics in the YouTube Age" describes another common ethical issue.

Making ethical judgments is complicated by the fact that practices that are legal in one country may not be legal in another. For example, selling Nazi memorabilia online is legal in the United States, but not in Germany. There is also the complication caused by the difference between *unethical* and *illegal* behaviour. If something is illegal, most people would argue that it is also unethical. But behaviour that is legal may be either ethical or unethical. Consider the case of Netsweeper, a Canadian company that sells web-filtering products that block out pornography and computer viruses. That sounds good, but what if the products are used by repressive governments to block out information they don't want their citizens to see (e.g., information on human rights)? While it is perfectly legal for Netsweeper to sell the software, critics argue that the sales are unethical because the company knows that its products can be misused.[1]

In some cultures, ethically ambiguous practices are hallmarks of business activity. Brazilians, for example, apply the philosophy of *jeitinho*—meaning "to find a way"— by using personal connections, bending the rules, or making a "contribution."[2] For example, if you need to get an official document you might start out determined to take all the proper bureaucratic steps to get it. However, when you find yourself in a complex maze of rules and regulations and think you'll never get your document, you may resort to *jeitinho* to get the job done.

E-BUSINESS + SOCIAL MEDIA SOLUTIONS

Ethics in the YouTube Age

Technology has changed our lives in positive ways, but it has also made questionable practices easier to commit. YouTube, for example, is a great source of entertainment. Many of you spend considerable time watching comedians, actors, and consumer-generated videos. YouTube makes an effort to remove unauthorized copyright material, and even warns users that their account may be closed if they ignore such laws. YouTube also offers an authorized music library that enables content providers to insert music selections without fear of legal action. However, as you know, there is plenty of material on YouTube that does not meet legal requirements.

Most people consider themselves to be ethical individuals. Students, for example, are often very critical of unethical corporations that act solely to satisfy their own needs. However, ethical issues cannot simply be looked at through a personal or situation-specific lens. Do you consider yourself to be an ethical person? What would you tell a friend if you saw him or her shoplifting? What would you do if you caught a co-worker stealing from your company? You may have strong, clear opinions on those issues, but how many songs and movies have you illegally downloaded?

Gary Fung, the founder of the Vancouver-based internet torrent site isoHunt, believes that illegal downloading is a legitimate right. He turned this belief into a successful business with more than 100 million users who download TV shows, films, etc. Fung has clearly benefited from the work of others, without paying for the content, and yet he generates millions in advertising revenue for his website. Mr. Fung is now facing a US$150-million fine for copyright infringement and damages. His success caught the attention of the Motion Picture Association of America (MPAA), which has also pursued similar sites; for instance, TorrentSpy

(US$111-million fine). isoHunt may ultimately share the fate of Napster and Kazaa.

In 2012, the U.S. and Canadian governments were both actively pursuing new tougher legislation to deal with the problem. SOPA stands for the Stop Online Piracy Act, which is being proposed in the United States. If it becomes law, you might see popular offending domain names deleted or restricted. The government could force search sites like Google and Bing to remove them from their search engines. They could also force PayPal and Visa to stop doing business with sites that are sued by legitimate rights holders. In essence, they would have the power to shut down all the revenue sources for illegal sites. This legal battlefield may change but the ethical debate remains.

A popular argument that is often used to justify illegal downloading activity is that there are many wealthy artists who earn millions of dollars. However, for every successful star there are thousands of struggling musicians, actors, and artists trying to earn a living. They are not overnight successes. Perhaps your favourite song would have never been written if that artist was not able to make a basic living (from royalties) until that one big hit. Sites like isoHunt are far more likely to have an impact on an aspiring artist than they are on someone like Lady Gaga or Will Smith. So where do you stand?

Critical Thinking Questions

1. Do you believe that multimillion-dollar fines on isoHunt and TorrentSpy are fair?

2. What do you think of the measures that are being proposed under the SOPA legislation?

3. Do you believe ethics are a black-and-white issue or do you subscribe to a grey zone?

Ethical scandals involving business leaders have made international headlines in recent years. Bernie Madoff (shown here) cost hundreds of major investment clients their entire life savings by running a Ponzi scheme.

Individual Values and Codes

The ethical views of individuals in a business—managers, employees, agents, and other legal representatives—are determined by a combination of factors. We start to form ethical standards as children in response to our perceptions of the behaviour of parents and other adults. Soon we enter school, where peers and the entertainment media influence us, and as we grow into adulthood, experience shapes our lives and contributes to our ethical beliefs and our behaviour. We also develop values and morals that contribute to ethical standards. If you put financial gain at the top of your priority list, you may develop a code of ethics that supports the pursuit of material comfort. If you set family and friends as a priority, you'll no doubt adopt different standards.

Because ethics are both personally and culturally defined, differences of opinion can arise as to what is ethical or unethical. For example, many people who would never think of stealing a candy bar from a grocery store routinely take home pens and pads of paper from their offices. Other people who view themselves as law-abiding citizens have no qualms about using radar detectors to avoid speeding tickets. In each of the situations, people will choose different sides of the issue and argue that their actions are ethical.

Managerial Ethics

managerial ethics Standards of behaviour that guide individual managers in their work.

Managerial ethics are the standards of behaviour that guide managers in their work.[3] Although ethics can affect managerial work in any number of ways, it's helpful to classify behaviour in terms of three broad categories.

Behaviour Toward Employees

There are important questions with regard to issues like hiring and firing, wages and working conditions, and privacy. In Canada, ethical and legal guidelines state that hiring and firing decisions should be based solely on the ability to perform a job. A manager who discriminates against any ethnic minority in hiring therefore exhibits both unethical and illegal behaviour. But what about the manager who hires a friend or relative when someone else might be more qualified? Such decisions may not be illegal, but in Canada they may be seen as objectionable on ethical grounds.

Wages and working conditions are also areas for debate. Consider a manager who pays a worker less than what is deserved because she knows that the employee can't afford to quit. While some people will see that behaviour as unethical, others will see it simply as smart business.

Protecting the privacy of employees is yet another area where there are ethical implications. In Canada, the Personal Information Protection and Electronic Documents Act (PIPEDA) requires organizations to obtain consent before they collect, use, or disclose information about individuals. Many people see these guidelines as necessary and useful, but others view them as yet another example of bureaucratic red tape.

Behaviour Toward the Organization

Ethical issues also arise with respect to employee behaviour toward employers. A **conflict of interest** occurs when an activity benefits an employee at the expense of the employer. For example, suppose the shoe buyer for a large department store chain accepts a free vacation from a shoe manufacturer. If the manufacturer then asks the buyer to increase the size of an order, the buyer may feel an obligation to do so. The buyer might also conclude that more large orders will result in another vacation next year. Most companies have policies that forbid buyers from accepting gifts from suppliers. Businesses in highly competitive industries—software or fashion apparel, for example—have safeguards against designers selling company secrets to competitors. Relatively common problems in the general area of honesty include such behaviour as stealing supplies, padding expense accounts, and using a business phone to make personal long-distance calls. Most employees are honest, but organizations must be vigilant.

conflict of interest Occurs when an activity benefits an individual at the expense of the employer.

Behaviour Toward Other Economic Entities

Ethical disputes may often arise in the relationship between the firm and its customers, competitors, shareholders, suppliers, dealers, and unions. In 2012, for example, Caterpillar Inc. demanded that union workers at its London, Ontario factory take a 50 percent wage cut in order to help the company be more cost effective in its operations. When the union refused, the company closed the plant and moved the production to the United States. Is this unethical behaviour, or is it just necessary business practice? Businesses in the pharmaceuticals industry are often criticized because of the high prices

The intense competition between Air Canada and WestJet motivated a WestJet executive to access Air Canada's confidential reservations database in the hope of gaining a competitive edge for WestJet.

of drugs. The companies argue that high prices are needed to cover the cost of developing new drugs, but critics argue that the companies are engaging in *price gouging* (charging unreasonably high prices). Finding the proper balance in situations like this is difficult.[4]

After a WestJet executive accessed Air Canada's confidential reservations database, WestJet eventually admitted its actions were unethical and paid Air Canada $5 million.[5] Most people would probably see the WestJet incident as a fairly clear case of unethical behaviour. But what if a manager is given confidential information by an unhappy former employee of a competitor who wants to get revenge on his former employer? Is it acceptable in that case for the manager to use the information? Some people would say it's still unethical, but others might argue that since the manager didn't go looking for the information, it's acceptable to use it.[6]

Difficulties also arise because business practices vary globally. In some countries, bribes are a normal part of doing business, but in Canada, bribes are seen as clearly unethical and illegal. In 2011, Calgary-based Niko Resources was fined $9.5 million for bribing a Bangladeshi government official.[7] In 2012, Walmart appointed a global officer to oversee compliance with U.S. bribery laws after it became clear that its Mexican operation had paid bribes in order to get good store sites.[8] In spite of Canada's condemnation of bribery, the Organisation for Economic Co-operation and Development (OECD) has expressed concerns about loopholes in Canada's bribery laws and the lack of enforcement of bribery penalties.[9] (See Chapter 5 for more information about the issue of bribery.)

Assessing Ethical Behaviour

Given the difficulties of distinguishing ethical and unethical behaviour, how can we decide whether a particular action or decision is ethical?[10] A three-step model can be used for applying ethical judgments to situations that may arise during the course of business activities:

1. Gather the relevant factual information.
2. Determine the most appropriate moral values.
3. Make an ethical judgment based on the rightness or wrongness of the proposed activity or policy.

Let's see how this process might work for a common dilemma faced by managers involving their expense accounts. Companies routinely provide managers with accounts to cover work-related expenses when they are travelling on company business and/or entertaining clients for business purposes. Common examples of such expenses include hotel bills, meals, rental cars, and so forth. Employees are expected to claim only those expenses that are accurate and work related. If a manager takes a client to dinner while travelling on business and spends $100, submitting a receipt for that dinner and expecting to be reimbursed for $100 is clearly appropriate. Suppose, however, that the manager also has a $100 dinner the next night in that same city with a good friend for purely social purposes. Submitting that receipt for full reimbursement would be seen by most managers as unethical (although a few might rationalize that it is acceptable because they are underpaid and this is a way to increase their pay).

Other principles that come into play in a case like this include various ethical norms. Consider four such norms and the issues that they raise:

Utility: Does the act optimize what is best for those who are affected by it?
Rights: Does it respect the rights of the individuals involved?
Justice: Is it consistent with what we regard as fair?
Caring: Is it consistent with people's responsibilities to each other?

Figure 3.1 incorporates the consideration of these ethical norms.

Now, let's return to the case of the inflated expense account. The utility norm would acknowledge that the manager benefits from padding an expense account,

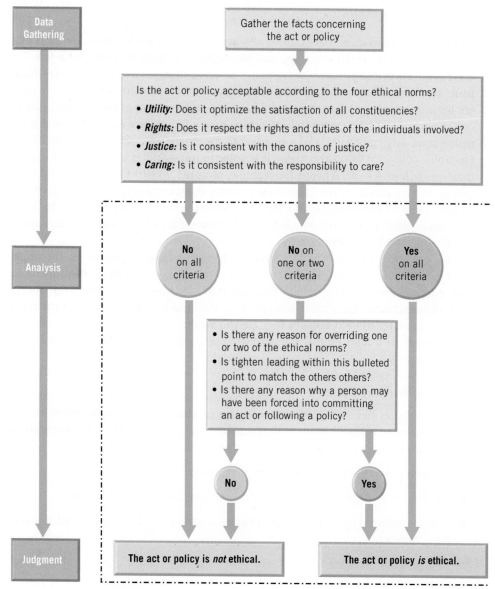

Data
Gathering

Gather the facts concerning
the act or policy

Is the act or policy acceptable according to the four ethical norms?
- *Utility:* Does it optimize the satisfaction of all constituencies?
- *Rights:* Does it respect the rights and duties of the individuals involved?
- *Justice:* Is it consistent with the canons of justice?
- *Caring:* Is it consistent with the responsibility to care?

Analysis

No
on all
criteria

No on
one or two
criteria

Yes
on all
criteria

- Is there any reason for overriding one
  or two of the ethical norms?
- Is tighten leading within this bulleted
  point to match the others others?
- Is there any reason why a person may
  have been forced into committing
  an act or following a policy?

No

Yes

Judgment

The act or policy is *not* ethical.

The act or policy *is* ethical.

FIGURE 3.1

Expanded model of ethical judgment
making.

but that others (co-workers and owners) do not. Likewise, most people would agree that this behaviour does not respect the rights of others. Moreover, it is clearly unfair and compromises the manager's responsibilities to others. This particular act, then, appears to be clearly unethical.

Figure 3.1 also provides mechanisms for considering unique circumstances—those that apply only in certain limited situations. Suppose, for example, that the manager loses the receipt for the legitimate dinner but retains the receipt for the social dinner. Would it be ethical to submit the illegitimate receipt because the manager is only doing so to be reimbursed for what he or she is entitled to? Or is submitting the other receipt unethical under any circumstance? Changes in the situation can obviously make issues more or less clear-cut.

When judging the ethics of a given behaviour, one of the simplest tests to use is the so-called "newspaper test." This means asking yourself this question: If I were to make a decision on an ethical issue and then read about it on the front page of tomorrow's paper, how would I feel? If you would feel embarrassed, you are very likely violating ethical standards and should make a different decision.

Company Practices and Business Ethics

Technological innovations have created all sorts of new ethical dilemmas: cloning, satellite reconnaissance, email snooping, and bioengineered foods, to name just a few. For every innovation that promises convenience or safety, there seems to be a related ethical issue. The internet and email, for example, are convenient and efficient, but they present business people with a variety of ethics-related problems. For example, a manager in one company sent false emails to his workers, pretending to be a recruiter from a competing firm. Any employees who responded to the emails were skipped for promotion. Electronic communication also makes it possible to run swindles with greater efficiency than ever before. A Ponzi scheme, for example, promises investors large returns on their money, but the money taken in by those running the scheme is not typically invested. Instead, money contributed by later investors is used to pay off early investors. In 2010, investment adviser Earl Jones pleaded guilty to running a Ponzi scheme that defrauded investors of over $50 million. He was sentenced to 11 years in prison.[11]

If a company wants to promote ethical behaviour among its employees, the single most effective step it can take is to demonstrate top management commitment to high ethical standards. When food products made by Maple Leaf Foods were found to be contaminated with listeria, the company took quick action to manage the crisis (see Chapter 6 for more details).[12] Two specific actions that can be taken to formalize commitment to a high ethical standard are adopting written codes and instituting ethics programs.

Adopting Written Codes

code of ethics Formal, written acknowledgment of a company's intent to do business in an ethical manner.

Many companies have adopted written **codes of ethics** that formally acknowledge their intent to do business in an ethical manner. Most codes of ethics are designed to perform one or more of the following functions:

- Increase public confidence in a firm or industry

- Stem the tide of government regulation—that is, aid in self-regulation.

- Improve internal operations by providing consistent standards of both ethical and legal conduct.

- Help managers respond to problems that arise as a result of unethical or illegal behaviour.

Figure 3.2 shows the code of ethics adopted by Mountain Equipment Co-op.

FIGURE 3.2

Mountain Equipment Co-op's statements of purpose, vision, mission, and values make up their code of ethics.

Our Purpose
To support people in achieving the benefit of wilderness-oriented recreation.

Our **purpose** is what we resolve to do.

Our Vision
Mountain Equipment Co-op is an innovative, thriving co-operative that inspires excellence in products and services, passion for wilderness experiences, leadership for a just world, and action for a healthy planet.

Our **vision** is our picture of the future and outlines where we want to go.

Our Mission
Mountain Equipment Co-op provides quality products and services for self-propelled wilderness-oriented recreation, such as hiking and mountaineering, at the lowest reasonable price in an informative, respectful manner. We are a member-owned co-operative striving for social and environmental leadership.

Our **mission** tells us what business we are in, who we serve, and how. It represents the fundamental reason for MEC's existence.

Our Values
We conduct ourselves ethically and with integrity. We show respect for others in our words and actions. We act in the spirit of community and co-operation. We respect and protect our natural environment. We strive for personal growth, continual learning, and adventure.

Our **values** influence our conduct both collectively as an organization, and individually as employees, directors and members of our community. We strive to have our actions reflect these values, demonstrate personal accountability, and be publicly defensible.

FIGURE 3.3

Core principles and organizational values.

Figure 3.3 illustrates the central role that corporate ethics and values should play in corporate policy. Strategies and practices can change frequently, and objectives can change occasionally, but an organization's core principles and values should remain steadfast.

Two-thirds of Canada's largest corporations have codes of ethics (90 percent of large U.S. firms do). More and more regulatory and professional associations in Canada are recommending that corporations adopt codes of ethics. The Canada Deposit Insurance Corp., for example, requires that all deposit-taking institutions have a code of conduct that is periodically reviewed and ratified by the board of directors. The Canadian Competition Bureau, the Canadian Institute of Chartered Accountants, and the Ontario Human Rights Commission are all pushing for the adoption of codes of ethics by corporations.[13] Many Canadian and U.S. firms are also adding a position called ethics director or ethics officer.

Instituting Ethics Programs

Can business ethics be "taught," either in the workplace or in schools? Business schools have become important players in the debate about ethics education, but most analysts agree that companies must take the lead in educating employees about ethics. In fact, more and more firms are doing so. Imperial Oil, for example, conducts workshops that help employees put Imperial's ethics statement into practice. But some firms struggle with ethical dilemmas, particularly those operating in the international business scene. In 2011, for example, allegations were made that some products sold by Victoria's Secret contained cotton that had been produced using child labour.[14] A few years earlier, a report on Nike's manufacturing partners in Asia called their practices just short of slave labour. Nike responded to the report by acknowledging its mistakes and made a commitment to improve working conditions.[15]

Social Responsibility

Corporate social responsibility (CSR) refers to the way in which a business tries to balance its commitments to **organizational stakeholders**—those groups, individuals, and organizations that are directly affected by the practices of an organization and that therefore have a stake in its performance.[16] Most companies that strive to be socially responsible concentrate on the five stakeholder groups shown in Figure 3.4. They may also select other stakeholders that are important to their particular organization and try to address their needs and expectations as well. As companies place increasing emphasis

Distinguish *corporate social responsibility* from ethics, identify *organizational stakeholders,* and characterize social consciousness today. **LO2**

corporate social responsibility (CSR) Refers to the way in which a business tries to balance its commitments to organizational stakeholders.

organizational stakeholders Groups, individuals, and organizations that are directly affected by the practices of an organization and that therefore have a stake in its performance.

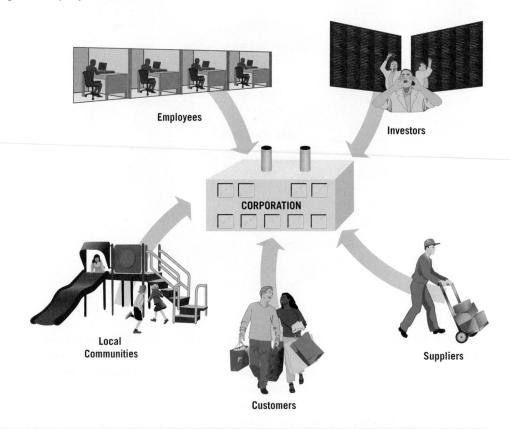

FIGURE 3.4

Major corporate stakeholders.

Starbucks helps local farmers gain access to credit, works to develop and maintain sustainability of the coffee crop, and is building farmer support centres in Costa Rica, Ethiopia, and Rwanda to provide local farmers with agricultural and technical education and support.

on their social responsibility to stakeholders, there has been a move to go beyond traditional *financial* measures of return on investment. A new measure—called the Social Return on Investment (SROI)—has been developed to help companies understand, manage, and communicate the *social* value of their activities for stakeholders.[17]

While everyone seems to accept the idea that attention must be paid to these organizational stakeholders, it is difficult to know which ones should be given the most attention. One view, called *managerial capitalism*, is that a company's only responsibility is to make as much money as possible for its shareholders, as long as the company doesn't break any laws. This view has been strongly challenged by an opposing view that says that companies must be responsible to a variety of stakeholders, including *customers, employees, investors, suppliers*, and the *local communities* in which they do business. Opponents of CSR claim that it is being imposed on businesses by a coalition of environmentalists, while supporters of CSR claim that companies have become more interested in CSR because that is what consumers prefer.[18]

Mountain Equipment Co-op (MEC) is an example of an organization with a strong sense of social responsibility. The company does not try to maximize shareholder wealth, but rather seeks a balance between financial and social/environmental goals. To demonstrate its concern for social responsibility, MEC provides a safe and healthy workplace for employees, audits suppliers who produce the products it sells, minimizes the negative impact of manufacturing and packaging on the environment, ensures that waste is disposed of in an environmentally responsible manner, treats workers with dignity, pays workers fairly, and emphasizes energy efficiency, pollution control, and recycling potential in MEC buildings.[19]

Another example of CSR in action is the **fair trade** movement, which developed because of concerns that workers in developing countries who produce commodities like coffee were not receiving fair payment for their products. Companies in developed countries that are concerned about this problem work with non-profit organizations like the Fairtrade Foundation and the Rainforest Alliance. Those non-profit organizations certify that farming co-operatives are paying workers fairly and not damaging the environment. More than 5000 companies—including Kraft Foods, Avon, and Starbucks—sell products with a Fairtrade or Rainforest Alliance logo on them.[20]

In defining their sense of social responsibility, most firms must confront four areas of concern: *responsibilities toward the environment, customers, employees,* and *investors*.

> **fair trade** A social movement designed to promote sustainability and to ensure that workers in developing countries receive fair payment for their products.

> Show how the concept of social responsibility applies both to environmental issues and to a firm's relationships with customers, employees, and investors.

Responsibility Toward the Environment

One critical area of social responsibility involves how the business relates to its physical environment. Controlling **pollution**—the injection of harmful substances into the environment—is a significant challenge for contemporary business. Air, water, and land pollution are the focus of most anti-pollution efforts by business and governments. The boxed insert entitled "Some Frustrations in the Green Movement" describes some difficulties that are evident as companies and consumers try to behave in a more environmentally friendly way.

> **pollution** The injection of harmful substances into the environment.

Air Pollution

Air pollution results when several factors converge to lower air quality. Chemicals like the carbon monoxide emitted by automobiles contribute to air pollution. So do smoke and other chemicals emitted by manufacturing plants. Air pollution is particularly bad in China, where 100 coal-fired power plants are being built each year. Each plant uses 1.3 million tonnes of coal and gives off 3.4 million tonnes of carbon dioxide. Only 5 percent of the coal-fired power plants in China are equipped with pollution control equipment.[21]

> **air pollution** When several factors converge to lower air quality.

The Kyoto Summit in 1997 was an attempt by various governments to reach an agreement on ways to reduce the threat of pollution. Australia is the world's largest greenhouse gas emitter per capita, contributing 7.3 percent of the world's total. The United States (at 6.5 percent) and Canada (at 6.4 percent) are close behind. Canada is the only one of the three leading emitters that signed the Protocol, but in 2006 the Conservative government said Canada would not be able to meet the targets for reducing pollution and that it would continue with the Protocol only if the targets were renegotiated.[22] The meetings in Copenhagen in 2009 on this issue ended with no agreement.

The United Nations has promoted a "cap and trade" system, in which companies in industrialized countries can buy carbon credits, which essentially give them the right to pollute the atmosphere with carbon dioxide. The money collected is then used to help fund clean-air projects in developing countries that would not otherwise be affordable.[23] But critics of the plan say that the scheme is an open invitation to fraudsters.[24] Suppose, for example, that an Indonesian forest operator sells a carbon permit to a German manufacturing firm that is releasing too much CO_2 into the atmosphere. That one transaction is fine, but what if the Indonesian firm sells the same carbon permit to manufacturers in other countries? That will make it appear like a lot more carbon dioxide has been reduced than is actually the case. Multibillion-dollar fraud has already occurred in the European Union's carbon trading market, and Europol's Criminal Finances and Technology section estimates that up to 90 percent of all carbon market volume in certain EU nations is fraudulent.[25]

Figure 3.5 shows atmospheric carbon dioxide (CO_2) levels for the period from 1750 to 2000, and offers three possible scenarios for future levels under different sets of conditions.

THE GREENING OF BUSINESS

Some Frustrations in the Green Movement

Consumers who are interested in buying products that are environmentally friendly face two key problems. The first problem is that companies often make misleading claims about the green characteristics of their products. A study of 5296 products by Terrachoice, an environmental marketing company, found that there was at least one misleading green claim on 95.6 percent of the products it studied. The study also found that 100 percent of toy manufacturers and 99.2 percent of baby-product makers were guilty of "greenwashing" (misleading consumers about the environmental benefits of a product). Having a product certified by a recognized, independent third party reduced the incidence of greenwashing; about one-third of certified products are free of greenwashing, compared to only about 4 percent of non-certified products. Unfortunately, fake certifications are readily available on the internet. In spite of these concerns, some progress is being made. For example, there are more and more products with accurate green claims. TerraChoice identified several green "sins," including (1) making an environmentally friendly claim but providing no proof, (2) making vague claims (e.g., saying that a product is "all natural"), (3) making a green claim for a product that is inherently harmful (e.g., cigarettes), and (4) emphasizing a product's positive attributes on a relatively unimportant environmental issue and downplaying its negative characteristics on a far more important environmental issue.

The second problem facing consumers is that green products can be very expensive. Government is subsidizing the development of electric and hybrid automobiles, but cars like Chevy's hybrid rechargeable Volt (named Car of the Year by *Motor Trend*), Nissan's all-electric Leaf, and Ford's all-electric Focus are expensive enough that many people cannot afford them. A hybrid car like the Prius, for example, costs about 30 percent more than an equivalent gasoline-powered car, and battery-powered cars cost 50 to 100 percent more. Even with fuel savings, it would take more than 10 years to recover the extra purchase price of a car like the Ford Fiesta. Gasoline-powered automobiles also outperform electric and hybrid cars in categories that are important to consumers (cost, driving range, and power). In 2010, the consulting firm J.D. Power produced a report entitled "Drive Green 2020: More Hope Than Reality," which noted that hybrid or battery vehicles constituted only 2.2 percent of global vehicle sales in 2010, and that even with healthy growth during the next few years, they will represent just over 7 percent of all vehicles sold by 2020. It's also not clear that electric-powered cars will actually mean less air pollution. Why? Because providing more electricity to recharge all the electric cars will increase demand on electrical generating plants, which typically burn fossil fuels. Manufacturing the batteries for electric cars also produces pollution. In the end, it seems likely that the application of new technologies to the traditional internal combustion engine will mean that gasoline-powered automobiles will dominate the market for years to come.

Critical Thinking Questions

1. Why are misleading green claims made for so many products?

2. What are the pros and cons of having government actively involved in subsidizing the development of green products?

FIGURE 3.5

CO$_2$ emissions, past and future.

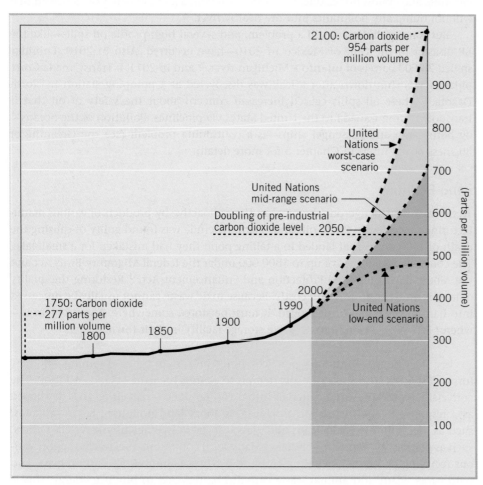

2100: Carbon dioxide 954 parts per million volume

United Nations worst-case scenario

United Nations mid-range scenario

Doubling of pre-industrial carbon dioxide level 2050

1750: Carbon dioxide 277 parts per million volume

United Nations low-end scenario

(Parts per million volume)

There is currently a great deal of discussion and debate about climate change and **global warming**—an increase in the earth's average temperature. Most people agree that global warming is happening, but there is debate about what is causing it (see Concluding Case 3-1 for more information on this issue). In difficult economic times, like those that have been evident during the past few years, people are less willing to make personal sacrifices in order to battle climate change. A poll of 12 000 people in 11 different countries showed that less than half of them were willing to make lifestyle changes to reduce carbon emissions, and only 20 percent said they would be willing to spend extra money to fight climate change.[26]

Some people think that wind power would be a good way to generate electricity while reducing air pollution. Canada is becoming a world leader in this form of power, and approximately $18 billion will be invested in wind power by 2015.[27] It is possible that 5 percent of Canada's energy needs will be supplied by wind power by 2015. However, experts note that while wind power is less polluting than coal- or gas-fired electricity generation, it is also more expensive and less reliable.

Water Pollution

For years, businesses and municipalities dumped their waste into rivers, streams, and lakes with little regard for the effects. Thanks to new legislation and increased awareness on the part of businesses, water quality is improving in many areas. For example, Millar Western Pulp Ltd. built Canada's first zero-discharge pulp mill at

global warming An increase in the earth's average temperature.

The Nature Conservancy teamed up with Indonesian logging company Sumalindo Lestari Jaya to help local villagers log a forest in a remote area of Indonesia. Why? The group believes that by working together with the company, it can better enforce sustainable practices.

Meadow Lake, Saskatchewan. There is no discharge pipe to the river, no dioxin-forming chlorine, and almost no residue. Dow Chemical built a plant at Fort Saskatchewan that will not dump any pollutants into the nearby river.[28]

But water pollution is still a problem, and several high-profile oil spills—like the BP disaster in the Gulf of Mexico in 2010—have occurred. Also in 2010, Enbridge spilled 28 000 barrels of oil into a Michigan river,[29] and in 2011, a TransCanada Corp. pipeline was shut down after a leak was discovered at a pumping station in North Dakota.[30] These oil spills caused increased concern about the safety of oil that is transported from Canada to the United States via pipelines. Pollution of the oceans—by both cargo and passenger ships—is a continuing problem (see the Greening of Business boxed insert in Chapter 5 for more detail).

Land Pollution

toxic wastes Dangerous chemical and/or radioactive by-products of various manufacturing processes.

Toxic wastes are dangerous chemical and/or radioactive by-products of various manufacturing processes. In 2010, oil sands giant Syncrude was found guilty of causing the death of 1600 ducks that landed in a tailing pond they had mistaken for a small lake. The company faced fines of up to $800 000 under the federal Migratory Birds Act and the Alberta Environmental Protection and Enhancement Act.[31] Restoring the quality of land is time consuming and costly. Because toxic waste cannot usually be processed into harmless material or destroyed, it must be stored somewhere. The problem is—where? Few people want a toxic waste storage facility in their town.

recycling The conversion of certain waste materials into useful products.

Recycling. Changes in forestry practices, limits on certain types of mining, and new forms of solid waste disposal are all attempts to address the issue of land pollution. The conversion of certain waste materials into useful products—**recycling**—has developed as a response to the increased consciousness about land pollution. Some products, such as aluminum beverage cans and glass, can be very efficiently recycled. Others, such as plastics, are more troublesome. Many local communities actively support various recycling programs, including curbside pickup of aluminum, plastics, glass, and pulp paper. Plant and animal waste can also be recycled to produce energy; this is referred to as **biomass**. Waste materials like sawdust, manure, and sludge are increasingly being turned into useful products. Ensyn Corp., for example, converts sawdust into liquid fuel by blasting wood waste with a sand-like substance that is heated. What's left is bio-oil.[32]

biomass Plant and animal waste that can be recycled to produce energy.

An interesting problem that highlights some of the complexities in recycling involves wooden pallets—those splintery wooden platforms used to store and transport consumer goods. Pallets are popular because they provide an efficient method for stacking and moving large quantities of smaller items. Pallets of merchandise can be easily and efficiently moved from factories to trucks to retail stores. Pallets are very recyclable, but since the cost of new ones is so low, many companies just toss used ones aside and get new ones. Many landfills refuse to take pallets, and others assess surcharges for recycling them. Ironically, some environmentalists argue that abandoned pallets actually serve a useful purpose because, in urban areas, they often become refuges for animals such as raccoons and abandoned pets.[33]

Many business firms are now acting to reduce various forms of land pollution. Under the Canadian and Ontario environmental protection acts, liability for a business firm can run as high as $2 million per day. To protect themselves, companies must prove that they showed diligence in avoiding an environmental disaster such as an oil or gasoline spill.[34] The Environmental Choice program, sponsored by the federal government, licenses products that meet environmental standards set by the Canadian Standards Association. Firms whose products meet these standards can put the logo—three doves intertwined to form a maple leaf—on their products.[35]

Canadian firms that do business abroad are increasingly being confronted with environmental issues. In many cases, there is opposition to a project by local residents because they fear that land pollution will result. For example, Calgary-based TVI Pacific Inc.'s planned open-pit mine and cyanide processing plant in the Philippines led to violent clashes between the company and the Subanon people. In Peru, indigenous groups threatened violence if Talisman Energy continued drilling for oil on their land.[36] At the annual meetings of Barrick Gold and Goldcorp Inc., protestors from several foreign countries alleged that the companies had acted in a socially irresponsible way. The mining companies responded that they had a major commitment to social responsibility, and they have recently aired videos showing how they helped Chilean earthquake victims and how they are rehabilitating land at former mine sites.[37]

Multinational firms have also been publicly criticized. For example, Nestlé has received negative publicity on YouTube, Facebook, and Twitter claiming that the company is contributing to the destruction of Indonesia's rainforest because it purchases palm oil from an Indonesian company that has cleared the rainforest to make way for a palm oil plantation.[38]

Responsibility Toward Customers

A company that does not act responsibly toward its customers will ultimately lose their trust and their business. As with the environment, companies differ in their level of concern about responsibility to customers. Yet unlike environmental problems, customer problems do not usually require expensive technological solutions. Most problems can be avoided if companies simply obey the laws regarding consumer rights, avoid illegal pricing practices, and behave ethically when advertising their products.

Rights of Consumers

Much of the current interest in business responsibility toward customers can be traced to the rise of **consumerism**, a form of social activism dedicated to protecting the rights of consumers in their dealings with businesses. Consumers have the following rights:

> **consumerism** A social movement that seeks to protect and expand the rights of consumers in their dealings with businesses.

1. *The right to safe products.* The right to safe products is not always honoured. In 2008, 20 people died after eating meat made by Maple Leaf Foods that was contaminated with listeria. Company sales dropped by nearly 50 percent once this became public.[39] The government of China has become concerned that negative publicity about faulty toys and contaminated pet food and toothpaste has damaged the "Made in China" label.

2. *The right to be informed about all relevant aspects of a product.* Food products must list their ingredients. Clothing must be labelled with information about its proper care. And banks must tell you exactly how much interest you are paying on a loan. Cereal companies have come under fire for some of the claims they have made about the oat bran content of their cereals, as well as its likely effects.

3. *The right to be heard.* Many companies today have offices to receive complaints. Retailers like Kmart offer a money-back guarantee if consumers aren't satisfied. Procter & Gamble puts a toll-free number on many of its products; customers can call this number if they have questions or complaints. When companies refuse to respond to consumer complaints, consumer protection agencies such as the Better Business Bureau and consumer interest groups such as the Airline Passengers Association may intervene.

4. *The right to choose what they buy.* Central to this right is free and open competition among companies. In times past, "gentlemen's agreements" were often used to avoid competition or to divide up a market so that firms did not have to truly compete against each other. Such practices are illegal today, and any attempts by business to block competition can result in fines or other penalties.

5. *The right to be educated about purchases.* All prescription drugs now come with detailed information regarding dosage, possible side effects, and potential interactions with other medications.

6. *The right to courteous service.* This right is hard to legislate, but as consumers become increasingly knowledgeable, they are more willing to complain about bad service. Consumer hotlines can also be used to voice service-related issues.

Unfair Pricing

collusion An illegal agreement among companies in an industry to "fix" prices for their products.

Interfering with competition can also mean illegal pricing practices. **Collusion** among companies—including getting together to "fix" prices—is against the law. Winnipeg-based Arctic Glacier Inc. was one of several companies served with subpoenas by the U.S. government as it investigated collusion in the U.S. market for packaged ice. One of Arctic's employees, who claimed he was fired for refusing to take part in a conspiracy to divide up markets, went to the U.S. government and helped it in its investigation.[40] Arctic eventually paid $12.5 million in fines.[41] The Canadian Competition Bureau also launched an investigation after hearing allegations from a confidential informant that Mars, Hershey, Nestlé, and Cadbury had teamed up in a candy price-fixing scheme.[42] A law firm in Toronto is organizing a class-action lawsuit against the major chocolate companies, alleging a conspiracy to fix prices.[43] In 2012, three gas companies in Kingston and Brockville—Canadian Tire, Pioneer Energy, and Mr. Gas Ltd.—were fined a total of $2 million by the Competition Bureau for fixing gas prices.[44]

In 2010, new laws came into effect that are designed to make it easier for the Competition Bureau to convict price-fixers (between 1980 and 2010, only three price-fixing convictions were secured out of the 23 cases that came before the Competition Bureau). The maximum prison sentence for price fixing has been tripled to 14 years, and the maximum fine increased from $10 million to $25 million.[45]

Ethics in Advertising

In recent years, increased attention has been given to ethics in advertising and product information. Because of controversies surrounding the potential misinterpretation of words and phrases such as *light*, *reduced calories*, *diet*, and *low fat*, food producers are now required to use a standardized format for listing ingredients on product packages. There are several key ethical issues in advertising, including truth-in-advertising claims, the advertising of counterfeit brands, the use of stealth advertising, and advertising that is morally objectionable.

Truth in Advertising. Concerns about truth in advertising are becoming more noticeable on the international scene. For example, Chinese government officials investigated Procter & Gamble's claim that its Pantene shampoo made hair "10 times stronger." Procter & Gamble also paid a $24 000 fine after one consumer complained that SK-II Skin Cream was not the "miracle water" it claimed to be and that it did not make her skin "look 12 years younger in 28 days."[46]

Advertising of Counterfeit Brands. Counterfeit goods are a problem in many different product lines, including perfume, luggage, pharmaceuticals, designer clothing, shoes, cigarettes, watches, sports memorabilia, and fine wines, to name just a few. In 2011, for example, fake jerseys of the re-born Winnipeg Jets hockey team were seized by the RCMP.[47] Canada Goose, a manufacturer of extreme weather outerwear, is battling counterfeiters who copy its bestselling products.[48] Winemakers are also coping with counterfeiting of their products because some of the top names in wine (e.g., Chateau Mouton Rothschild and Penfolds Grange) cost as much as $3000 a bottle, and this is an incentive to counterfeiters to make a lot of easy money. Wineries are fighting counterfeiting by embedding microchips in their labels that can be read with an optical scanner, and by laser-etching the wine's name and vintage year into the bottle's glass.

The International Chamber of Commerce estimates that the counterfeit goods trade may be worth as much as US$500 billion annually. According to Interpol—the International police organization in Lyon, France—organized crime groups have gotten into the business of counterfeiting products because of the high rate of return they can make (about as high as the illegal drug trade). One group in New York City, for example, imported watch components that cost them about 27 cents and then sold them to wholesalers for $12 to $20. The wholesalers then sold them to street vendors for $20 to $30 dollars and the street vendors sold them as Cartier watches for as much as $250. That was still well below the price of a real Cartier watch (about $1800).

Counterfeiting has moved beyond the manufacturing of individual products. In China and in New York City, fake Apple stores have popped up, complete with sales assistants wearing blue T-shirts with the Apple logo and signs advertising the iPad2.[50] In the Chinese city of Kunming, an Ikea knockoff store called 11 Furniture duplicates Ikea's well-known blue-and-yellow look and has essentially pirated the entire Ikea brand experience.[51]

Counterfeiting is harmful to companies that have spent a lot of time and money developing brand-name goods for sale. Every counterfeit product that is sold reduces the sales revenues of the legitimate producers. It also harms governments by denying them tax revenues (most counterfeiters do not pay taxes). While it may seem that consumers benefit because they get low prices for goods that look like the real thing, in fact consumers often pay far too much for counterfeit goods because those goods are very low quality. As well, some counterfeit goods are downright dangerous to use. While a fake handbag simply costs money, fake pharmaceuticals, electrical products, and motorcycles can kill the people who use them.[52]

One approach to reducing counterfeiting is to prosecute anyone who facilitates the sale of counterfeit products, including landlords (who own the buildings where counterfeit goods are being sold), shipping companies, credit-card companies, and others in the supply chain.[53] The argument is that these people are benefiting from the sale of knock-offs, so they should be held accountable. There is also a move in some countries to hold the consumers who buy counterfeit goods accountable. In France and Italy, for example, it is now a crime to buy counterfeit goods.

There is increasing pressure on the Canadian government to do something about counterfeit goods.[54] The Canadian Anti-Counterfeiting Network (CACN) was formed in 2005 to lobby the government for changes in laws. But changes are slow in coming, and the United States has placed Canada on its official list of countries that don't do enough to control counterfeit products (the list also includes Turkey, Belarus, Vietnam, and Uzbekistan). Canada is moving slowly toward bringing its laws into conformity with the World Intellectual Property Organization (WIPO). In 2011, an Anti-Counterfeiting Trade Agreement (ACTA) was signed by 40 countries (but not by China). The agreement is designed to fight the global trade in pirated goods.[55]

Stealth Advertising. A variation of viral advertising, **stealth advertising** (also called **undercover or guerrilla advertising**) involves companies paying individuals to extol the virtues of their products to other individuals. For example, one advertising agency hired models to pose as "tourists." These models asked real tourists to take their picture with a new Sony Ericsson camera cellphone. The models then talked up the advantages of the new product to the unsuspecting real tourists.[56] The ethics of stealth advertising are questionable if the paid individuals do not reveal that they are being paid by a company. In that case, the recipient of the advertising is not aware that it *is* advertising.

stealth advertising (undercover or guerrilla advertising) Involves companies paying individuals to extol the virtues of their products to other individuals.

Morally Objectionable Advertising. A final ethical issue concerns advertising that is morally objectionable. Benetton, for example, aired a series of commercials featuring inmates on death row. The ads, dubbed "We, on Death Row," prompted such an emotional outcry that Sears dropped the Benetton USA clothing line.[57] Other ads

Of all roadway accidents, 25 percent are distraction-related, and the biggest distractions for motorists are handheld gadgets like cell phones, pagers, and the like. In fulfilling its responsibility to consumers, some companies are conducting tests which yield important data about roadway accidents. Ford Motor Co., for example, has a Virtual Test Track Experiment simulator which determines how often drivers get distracted. Under normal circumstances, an adult driver will miss about 3 percent of the simulated "events" (like an ice patch or a deer on the road) that Ford contrives for a virtual road trip. If they're on the cell phone, they'll miss about 14 percent. Teenagers miss a scary 54 percent of the events.

receiving criticism include Victoria's Secret models in skimpy underwear, and campaigns by tobacco and alcohol companies that allegedly target young people.

Responsibility Toward Employees

Organizations also need to employ fair and equitable practices with their employees. In Chapter 8, we describe the human resource management activities essential to a smoothly functioning business—recruiting, hiring, training, promoting, and compensating. These activities are the basis for social responsibility toward employees. A company that provides its employees with equal opportunities for rewards and advancement without regard to race, sex, or other irrelevant factors is meeting its social responsibilities. Firms that ignore their responsibility to employees leave themselves open to lawsuits. They also miss the chance to hire better and more highly motivated employees.

Legal and Social Commitments

Socially responsible companies ensure that their workplaces are safe, both physically and emotionally. Such companies would no more tolerate an abusive manager or one who sexually harasses employees than they would a natural gas leak. But progressive companies go well beyond simple legal requirements. The Bank of Montreal, for example, sponsors a community college skills upgrading course for individuals with hearing impairments. The Royal Bank provides managers with discrimination awareness training. Rogers Cablesystems Ltd. provides individuals who have mobility restrictions with telephone and customer-service job opportunities.[58]

Business firms also have a responsibility to respect the privacy of their employees. Nearly everyone agrees that companies have the right to exercise some level of control over their employees, but there is controversy about exactly how much is acceptable in areas such as drug testing and computer monitoring. When Canadian National Railways instituted drug testing for train, brake, and yard employees, 12 percent failed. Trucking companies have found that nearly one-third of truckers who have been involved in accidents were on drugs.[59] It seems likely that safety will be compromised when employees in transportation companies use drugs, but there is controversy about what kind of testing is appropriate.

Differences of opinion are also evident with regard to the monitoring of employees' online activities while they are at work. New software programs allow bosses to see things like employees' Facebook comments and their opinions about pubs on Foursquare. Social Sentry, a tracking system developed by Social Logix, records employee social media activity from work or home. The program looks for workers who leak sensitive company information or who bad-mouth the company.[60] It seems reasonable to argue that workers shouldn't damage the reputation of the company they work for, but there is no consensus on what constitutes going "too far."

Whistle-Blowers. Respecting employees as people also means respecting their behaviour as ethically responsible individuals. Suppose an employee discovers that a business has been engaging in practices that are illegal, unethical, or socially irresponsible. This employee should be able to report the problem to management, but management often does not want to hear about such issues. The employee might then decide to inform a regulatory agency or perhaps the media. At this point, he or she becomes a **whistle-blower**—an employee who discovers and tries to put an end to a company's unethical, illegal, or socially irresponsible actions by publicizing them.[61]

whistle-blower An employee who discovers and tries to put an end to a company's unethical, illegal, or socially irresponsible actions by publicizing them.

John Kopchinski, a sales representative at pharmaceutical giant Pfizer, blew the whistle on the company after he learned that Pfizer was promoting certain drugs for unapproved uses. He received $5.1 million from the U.S. government for his whistle-blowing efforts.[62] In Canada, WestJet employee Melvin Crothers discovered that a fellow employee was accessing a restricted Air Canada website in order to obtain data about Air Canada's "load factor" (the proportion of seats filled) on certain flights. He felt that this was unethical, so he tried to talk to WestJet's president to tell him what was going on. But the president was out of town, so Crothers called a former WestJet president who was heading up an Air Canada discount airline. The conversation led to Air Canada discovering what WestJet was up to, and before long, Air Canada filed a lawsuit against WestJet. Crothers resigned from WestJet four days later.[63]

Whistle-blowers are often demoted—and even fired—when they make their accusations public. The boxed insert entitled "Should Whistle-Blowers Be Paid?" analyzes

MANAGING IN TURBULENT TIMES

Should Whistle-Blowers Be Paid?

In Canada, whistle-blower programs like the one established in 2009 by the Investment Industry Regulatory Organization of Canada have not paid whistle-blowers for reporting illegal acts. Rather, attention has focused on protecting whistle-blowers from retaliation by the companies they claim have behaved illegally. This contrasts with the situation in the United States, where whistle-blowers are paid a bounty of between 10 and 30 percent when more than $1 million is recovered from corporate wrongdoers.

In 2011, the Ontario Securities Commission announced that it might implement a whistle-blower program that would be more like the U.S. model. But this raises an important question: Are there unanticipated negative consequences that might arise as a result of paying whistle-blowers? There are two opposing views on this question (naturally!).

Supporters argue that paying whistle-blowers is a good idea because whistle-blowers face a great deal of hostility and harassment from their companies when they report managerial misconduct. For example, whistle-blowers are often charged with breaching confidentiality, and they then must pay legal fees as they defend themselves. Companies also try to publicly discredit the whistle-blower, and this likely reduces the person's future job prospects. The practice of "speaking truth to power" is risky for whistle-blowers, so they should be compensated for doing so. Beyond these arguments is the practical fact that the government can recover

large sums of money from companies that behave badly. The U.S. government, for example, has recovered more than $28 billion in the past 25 years from companies that made false claims for payments from government contracts.

Opponents argue that if whistle-blowers are paid, they will have an incentive to bypass existing compliance programs and go straight for the money. Undermining existing procedures is probably not a good thing. They also argue that whistle-blowers may make questionable charges as they put their own financial interests ahead of the interests of the company they work for. There may also be a "rush to judgment" about a situation, especially if a new whistle-blower law requires that quick action be taken to resolve a problem. For example, at French carmaker Renault, three high-ranking executives were fired in 2011 after an anonymous tip that they had stashed bribe money in a Swiss bank. The three executives were eventually exonerated, but they were subjected to considerable stress and the company experienced a public humiliation.

Critical Thinking Questions

1. In your own words, state the pros and cons of paying whistle-blowers for the information they provide.

2. On balance, do you think it is a good idea to pay whistle-blowers? Defend your answer.

The safety of workers is an important consideration for all organizations. The required use of protective clothing when dealing with toxic substances is just one example of precautions that companies can take to protect workers while they are on the job.

an interesting issue in whistle-blowing. Even if they retain their jobs, they may still be treated as outsiders and suffer resentment or hostility from co-workers. Many co-workers see whistle-blowers as people who simply can't be trusted. One recent study suggests that about half of all whistle-blowers eventually get fired, and about half of those who get fired subsequently lose their homes and/or families.[64]

Federal legislation to protect whistle-blowers was introduced in Canada in 2003. In 2009, the Investment Industry Regulatory Organization of Canada (IIROC) opened a whistle-blower hotline as a result of an increased incidence of securities fraud such as Ponzi schemes in both Canada and the United States. Calls regarding market fraud are forwarded to four of the top people at the IIROC so that swift action can be taken.[65]

Responsibility Toward Investors

It may sound odd to say that managers can be irresponsible toward investors, since the investors are the owners of the company. But managers behave irresponsibly when they pay themselves outlandish salaries and bonuses, or spend large amounts of company money for their own personal comfort. If managers do not use the firm's financial resources in a responsible way, the ultimate losers are the owners, since they do not receive the earnings, dividends, or capital appreciation due them. Financial mismanagement can take many forms, including *improper financial management, misrepresentation of finances, cheque kiting,* and *insider trading.*

Improper Financial Management

Improper financial management can take many forms, including executives making bad financial decisions, paying executives outlandish salaries and bonuses, or sending them on extravagant "retreats" to exotic resorts. For example, managers at American International Group became involved in very-high-risk insurance that caused the company to be on the hook for billions of dollars. The U.S. government ended up giving hundreds of billions of dollars to the company to keep it afloat. In many of these situations, creditors don't have much leverage and shareholders have few viable options. Trying to force a management changeover is not only difficult, it can also drive down the price of the company's stock, and this is a penalty shareholders are usually unwilling to assign themselves.

Misrepresentation of Finances

Occasionally, managers are guilty of financial mismanagement. In Canada, one of the most highly publicized cases involved Garth Drabinsky and Myron Gottlieb, the top managers at Livent Inc. (see the opening case). But Drabinsky and Gottlieb are not the only executives who have been charged with wrongdoing in the recent past. In 2005, Bernie Ebbers, the CEO of WorldCom, was found guilty of nine charges of securities fraud and filing false documents. He was sentenced to 25 years in prison. In 2006, Ken Lay, the CEO of Enron, was convicted of conspiracy and securities fraud, but he died before he was sentenced. In 2007, Conrad Black, CEO of Hollinger International, was convicted of fraud and obstruction of justice and was sentenced to six and a half years in prison. In December 2008, Bernie Madoff pleaded guilty to swindling investors in a $50-billion fraud. He will likely spend the rest of his life in prison.[66]

Cheque Kiting

Cheque kiting involves writing a cheque from one account, depositing it in a second account, and then immediately spending money from the second account while the money from the first account is still in transit. A cheque from the second account can also be used to replenish the money in the first account, and the process starts all over again. This practice obviously benefits the person doing the cheque kiting, but is irresponsible because it involves using innocent people's money to allow cheques that would otherwise bounce to clear.

cheque kiting Involves writing a cheque from one account, depositing it in a second account, and then immediately spending money from the second account while the money from the first account is still in transit.

"From a purely business viewpoint, taking what doesn't belong to you is usually the cheapest way to go."

Insider Trading

insider trading The use of confidential information to gain from the purchase or sale of stock.

Insider trading occurs when someone uses confidential information to gain from the purchase or sale of stock. In 2011, for example, the Alberta securities regulator charged several executives at Grand Cache Coal Corp. with insider trading for selling company stock before the company disclosed negative news about its sales.[67] Also in 2011, Raj Rajaratnam, the co-founder of Galleon Group, was sentenced to 11 years in prison for insider trading.[68]

Implementing Social Responsibility Programs

Substantial differences of opinion exist as to the appropriateness of CSR as a business goal. Supporters of CSR believe that corporations are citizens, just as individuals are, and therefore have the same social responsibilities as private citizens. Others point to the vast resources controlled by businesses and note that since businesses often create many of the problems that social programs are designed to alleviate, they should use their resources to solve those problems. Still others argue that CSR is wise because there is a payoff for the firm.

Opponents of CSR fear that if businesses become too active in social concerns, they will gain too much control over how those concerns are addressed. They point to the influence many businesses have been able to exert on the government agencies that are supposed to regulate them. Other critics of business-sponsored social programs argue that companies lack expertise in the areas they are trying to influence. For example, they believe that technical experts, not business managers, should decide how best to clean up a polluted river.

The late Max Clarkson, formerly a top-level business executive and director of the Centre for Corporate Social Performance and Ethics at the University of Toronto, designed and applied a CSR rating system for companies. He found that business firms that had a strong consciousness about ethics and CSR outperformed firms that did not.[69]

Approaches to Social Responsibility

LO4 Identify four general *approaches to social responsibility* and describe the four steps a firm must take to implement a *social responsibility program*.

Given these differences of opinion, it is little wonder that corporations have adopted a variety of approaches to social responsibility. As Figure 3.6 illustrates, the four stances an organization can take concerning its obligations to society fall along a continuum ranging from the lowest to the highest degree of CSR practices. Keep in mind that organizations do not always fit neatly into one category or another. The Ronald McDonald House program has been widely applauded, for example, but McDonald's has also come under fire for allegedly misleading consumers about the nutritional value of its food products. The Exercising Your Ethics exercise at the end of the chapter gives you an opportunity to think about the pros and cons of the various stances toward CSR.

FIGURE 3.6

Spectrum of approaches to social responsibility.

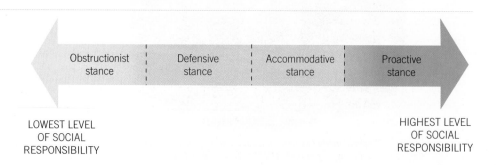

Obstructionist Stance

Businesses that have an **obstructionist stance** to social responsibility do as little as possible to solve social or environmental problems. When these businesses cross the ethical or legal line that separates acceptable from unacceptable practices, their typical response is to deny or cover up their actions. Firms that adopt this position have little regard for ethical conduct and will generally go to great lengths to hide wrongdoing.

obstructionist stance A business does as little as possible to solve social or environmental problems and denies or covers up its wrongdoings.

Defensive Stance

One step removed from the obstructionist stance is the **defensive stance**, where the organization does everything that is required of it legally but nothing more. Tobacco companies in Canada and the United States generally adopt this stance since they are legally required to include warnings to smokers on their products and to limit advertising to prescribed media. They follow these rules to the letter of the law, but they use more aggressive marketing methods in countries that have no such rules.

defensive stance An organization does only what is legally required and nothing more.

Accommodative Stance

A firm that adopts an **accommodative stance** meets its legal and ethical requirements but also goes further in certain cases. Such firms voluntarily agree to participate in social programs but only after they are convinced that these programs are worthy of their support. Many organizations respond to requests for donations to community hockey teams, Girl Guides, youth soccer programs, and so forth. The point, however, is that someone has to knock on the firm's door and ask; accommodative organizations are not generally proactively seeking avenues for contributing.

accommodative stance A company meets all of its legal and ethical requirements, and in some cases even goes beyond what is required.

Proactive Stance

The highest degree of social responsibility a firm can exhibit is the **proactive stance**. Firms that adopt this approach view themselves as citizens in a society and proactively seek opportunities to contribute. The most common—and direct—way to implement this stance is by setting up a foundation to provide direct financial support for various social programs. The boxed insert entitled "AEM Healthy Food" explains a proactive move to develop a more healthful product for consumers.

proactive stance An organization actively seeks opportunities to be socially responsible.

Corporate Charitable Donations. Donating money to different causes is one way that business firms try to show that they are socially responsible. Every four months, for example, Whole Foods (Toronto) donates 5 percent of one day's sales to a designated non-profit organization.[70] At CIBC, the Miracle Day program has raised a total of $64 million for children's charities in Canada.[71] A survey of 93 large Canadian companies found that 97 percent made a charitable contribution of some sort and that the median value of their contributions was $340 000.[72] More than 80 percent of the companies said that they made contributions because it was a good thing to do, irrespective of any financial benefits they might derive from giving.[73] Unfortunately, the difficult economic circumstances of the past few years have caused a decline in corporate donations. For example, corporate donations to the Daily Bread Food Bank in Toronto were down 40 percent in 2011. According to Statistics Canada, corporate donations to charities declined from $2.45 billion in 2008 to $2.26 billion in 2010.[74]

Businesses often help when disasters strike. When seven people died in Walkerton, Ontario, in 2000 as a result of drinking contaminated water, companies such as Petro-Canada, Shoppers Drug Mart, Sobeys, and Zellers contributed products such as bleach and bottled water. And when tens of thousands of people died in the Asian tsunamis of 2004, companies from around the world rushed aid to the stricken areas. Global *Fortune* 500 firms donated $580 million in drugs, cellphones, machinery, medical equipment, and water to the relief effort.[75]

Other types of contributions are also possible. For example, Unilever Canada gives employees four afternoons off a year to participate in community service activities.[76] Mars Canada sets aside one day each year for employees to volunteer. Tim Hortons Children's Foundation plans to open a camp for underprivileged children in 2013 at Sylvia Lake in Manitoba. The Foundation also has a youth Leadership Program that is currently offered at two sites in Ontario.[77]

Managing Social Responsibility Programs

Making a company truly socially responsible takes an organized and managed program (see Figure 3.7).

1. Top management must state strong support for CSR and be considered a factor in strategic planning. Without the support of top management, no program can succeed.

2. A committee of top managers must develop a plan detailing the level of management support. Some companies set aside percentages of profits for social programs.

ENTREPRENEURSHIP AND NEW VENTURES

AEM Healthy Food

"Do brown cows make chocolate milk?" The question most kids have posed simply expresses the growing popularity of chocolate milk beverages among consumers of all ages. In this expanding market, consumers increasingly look for more than what manufacturers are currently offering and insist on products that are good for the whole family. AEM Healthy Food is meeting the demands of health-conscious consumers in their development of a no-sodium-added, low-sugar chocolate milk, allowing consumers to reap all of the nutritional benefits of milk without the additives. This, however, is not your traditional product development success story, but rather a story that will MOOve you to understand the concept of entrepreneurship and how it can help address social issues.

An "Interdisciplinary Product Development" course at the University of Guelph in Ontario began its seventh year as it normally would, with students forming teams whose members consisted of both science and business majors. These groups were then asked to develop a new product that would help address a social, market, or consumer issue. This was a task that students Michael Lanteigne (Accounting major), Eric Martin (Agricultural Business major) and Aneta Rybak (Food Science) did not take lightly. Instead, the group of three set out to take on the challenges of developing chocolate milk with no sodium added and with less sugar.

"For many primary school students," Professor Lang explained, "chocolate milk is the only source of milk these students get and that concerns parents who worry about the amount of sugar in chocolate milk."

With this in mind and an *"udder"* dedication to the project, Lanteigne, Martin, and Rybak collaborated in developing a chocolate milk product that was well received by children and adults alike. To further test their product's market receptivity, the student team entered the chocolate milk in a number of competitions, hoping to gain feedback that would help them fine-tune their product. To their amazement, even though many of the other competitors were engineering students with very technical products, the chocolate milk product surpassed everything else.

The results spoke for themselves: People were delighted with a product that offered good taste but less sodium and sugar, and virtually everyone who sampled the chocolate milk could see themselves becoming regular consumers. Primary research also suggested that children could not detect a difference between the traditional formulation and the reformulated version. This suggests that the product could be used in school milk programs without a noticeable difference being detected.

This fourth-year interdisciplinary course allows students not only to have a positive influence on the everyday lives of consumers, but also to gain valuable experience in both entrepreneurship and product development. "It's an entrepreneurial course that pushes students outside their comfort zone. I've got accounting students working alongside science students in the lab developing new food products," says Professor Lang. The course allows students to take part in every step of the product development process, from conceptualization to commercialization. The diverse interdisciplinary strengths of students in this course, along with each enrollee's desire to become an entrepreneur, leads to endless possibilities for addressing social issues that should be milked to the fullest!

Critical Thinking Questions

1. How has AEM Healthy Food addressed the various areas of social responsibility?

2. How can educational institutions foster social responsibility?

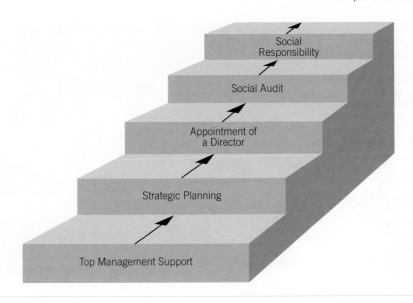

FIGURE 3.7

Establishing a social responsibility program involves four basic steps.

Mountain Equipment Co-op, for example, earmarks 1 percent of its sales revenue for charity. Managers must also set specific priorities. For instance, should the firm help with job training for the chronically unemployed or support the arts?

3. One executive must be put in charge of the firm's agenda. Whether the role is created as a separate job or added to an existing one, the selected individual must monitor the program and ensure that its implementation is consistent with the firm's policy statement and strategic plan.

4. The organization must conduct **social audits**, which are systematic analyses of its success in using funds earmarked for its CSR goals.[78] Suppose a company has a strategic plan calling for spending \$100 000 to train 200 chronically unemployed people and to place 180 of them in jobs. If the firm actually spends \$98 000, trains 210 people, and fills 175 jobs, a social audit will confirm the program's success. But if the program costs \$150 000, trains only 90 people, and places only 10 of them, the audit will reveal the program's failure. Such failure should prompt a rethinking of the program's implementation and its priorities.

social audit A systematic analysis of how a firm is using funds earmarked for social responsibility goals and how effective these expenditures have been.

An important element in a social responsibility program is the idea of **sustainable development**, which means pursuing activities that meet current needs but will not put future generations at a disadvantage when they in turn attempt to meet their own needs. When making sustainable development decisions, it is important that managers simultaneously consider economic, social, and environmental variables. Research at the London and Harvard Business Schools shows that companies that adopt mandatory sustainability reporting requirements see positive effects on corporate performance.[79]

sustainable development Pursuing activities that meet current needs but will not put future generations at a disadvantage when they in turn attempt to meet their own needs.

Canadian businesses are increasingly publishing sustainability reports that go beyond simple financial reporting and explain how the company is performing on issues such as the environment, employee relations, workplace diversity, and business ethics. For example, Artopex Inc., a furniture manufacturer in Quebec, has an active sustainability program.[80] Baxter Corp., a medical products company, publishes an annual Global Sustainability Report measuring the company's progress on nine sustainable priorities, including reductions in its carbon footprint.[81] Social audits and sustainability reports together constitute **triple bottom line reporting**—measuring the social, environmental, and economic performance of a company.[82]

triple bottom line reporting Measuring the social, environmental, and economic performance of a company.

Ronald McDonald House helps the families of children who are in hospital. It is supported by McDonald's and is an example of socially responsible behaviour by a business corporation.

The Global 100 list of the most sustainable corporations in the world is based on factors like energy productivity (the ratio of sales to energy consumption) and water productivity (sales to water usage). In the 2012 ranking, Novo Nordisk (Denmark) was first, Natura Cosmeticos (Brazil) second, and Statoil (Norway) third. Six Canadian companies made the top 100, including Suncor (#48), Enbridge (#71), and Encana Corp. (#76).[83] Each year the Corporate Knights organization publishes its Best 50 Corporate Citizens in Canada list. The rankings are based on an assessment of factors such as pension fund quality, board diversity, tax dollar generation, and Aboriginal relations. The top three companies in 2011 were The Co-operators Group Ltd., Mountain Equipment Co-op, and Domtar Corporation.[84]

Social Responsibility and the Small Business

LO5 Explain how issues of social responsibility and ethics affect small businesses.

Ethics and CSR issues must be faced by managers in all organizations, regardless of size. One key to business success is to decide in advance how to respond to these issues. As the owner of a garden supply store, how would you respond to a building inspector's suggestion that a cash payment would expedite your application for a building permit? As the manager of a nightclub, would you call the police, refuse service, or sell liquor to a customer whose ID card looks forged? As the owner of a small laboratory, would you call the board of health to make sure that it has licensed the company you want to contract to dispose of the lab's medical waste? Who will really be harmed if a small firm pads its income statement to help get a much-needed bank loan?

Can a small business afford to set CSR objectives? Should it sponsor hockey teams, make donations to the United Way, and buy light bulbs from the Lions Club? Would you join the Chamber of Commerce and support the Better Business Bureau because it is the responsible thing to do or just because it is good business?

MyBizLab

Capture more moments of true understanding. MyBizLab provides you with interactive study and practice tools directly related to this chapter's content. The new MyBizLab Study Plan Learning Path is designed to measure a full range of skills and provide remediation to give you what you need to master key chapter concepts. MyBizLab flexes to your unique learning needs. The result? Inspired learning, more success.

SUMMARY OF LEARNING OBJECTIVES

1. **Explain how individuals develop their personal *codes of ethics* and why ethics are important in the workplace.** Individual *codes of ethics* are derived from social standards of right and wrong. *Ethical behaviour* is behaviour that conforms to generally accepted social norms concerning beneficial and harmful actions. *Unethical behaviour* can result in loss of business, fines, and even imprisonment. Because ethics affect the behaviour of individuals on behalf of the companies that employ them, many firms are adopting formal statements of *ethics*.

2. **Distinguish *corporate social responsibility* from ethics, identify *organizational stakeholders*, and characterize social consciousness today.** *Corporate social responsibility* refers to the way a firm attempts to balance its commitments to organizational stakeholders. One way to understand social responsibility is to view it in terms of stakeholders—those groups, individuals, and organizations that are directly affected by the practices of an organization and that therefore have a stake in its performance. Until the second half of the nineteenth century, businesses often paid little attention to stakeholders. Since then, however, both public pressure and government regulation, especially as a result of the Great Depression of the 1930s and the social activism of the 1960s and 1970s, have forced businesses to consider public welfare, at least to some degree. A trend toward increased social consciousness, including a heightened sense of *environmental activism*, has recently emerged.

3. **Show how the concept of corporate social responsibility (CSR) applies to environmental issues and to a firm's relationships with customers, employees, and investors.** With respect to the environment, CSR requires firms to minimize pollution of air, water, and land. With respect to customers, CSR requires firms to provide products of acceptable quality, to price products fairly, and to respect consumers' rights. With respect to employees, CSR requires firms to respect workers both as resources and as people who are more productive when their needs are met. With respect to investors, CSR requires firms to manage their resources and to represent their financial status honestly.

4. **Identify four general *approaches to social responsibility* and describe the four steps a firm must take to implement a *social responsibility program*.** An *obstructionist stance* on social responsibility is taken by a firm that does as little as possible to address social or environmental problems. The *defensive stance* emphasizes compliance with minimum legal requirements. Companies adopting the *accommodative stance* go beyond minimum activities, if they are asked. The *proactive stance* commits a company to actively contribute to social projects. Implementing a *social responsibility program* entails four steps: (1) drafting a policy statement with the support of top management, (2) developing a detailed plan, (3) appointing a director to *implement* the plan, and (4) conducting social audits to monitor results.

5. **Explain how issues of social responsibility and ethics affect small businesses.** Managers and employees of small businesses face many of the same ethical questions as their counterparts at larger firms. Small businesses also face the same issues of social responsibility and the same need to decide on an approach to social responsibility. The differences are primarily differences of scale.

KEY TERMS

accommodative stance (p. 95)	defensive stance (p. 95)	proactive stance (p. 95)
air pollution (p. 83)	ethical behaviour (p. 74)	recycling (p. 86)
biomass (p. 86)	ethics (p. 74)	social audit (p. 97)
business ethics (p. 74)	fair trade (p. 83)	stealth (undercover) advertising
cheque kiting (p. 93)	global warming (p. 85)	(p. 89)
code of ethics (p. 80)	insider trading (p. 94)	sustainable development (p. 97)
collusion (p. 88)	managerial ethics (p. 76)	toxic wastes (p. 86)
conflict of interest (p. 77)	obstructionist stance (p. 95)	triple bottom line reporting (p. 97)
consumerism (p. 87)	organizational stakeholders	unethical behaviour (p. 74)
corporate social responsibility	(p. 81)	whistle-blower (p. 91)
(CSR) (p. 81)	pollution (p. 83)	

QUESTIONS FOR ANALYSIS

1. Develop an example of the way in which your personal code of ethics might clash with the operations of a specific company. How might you try to resolve these differences?

2. What kind of wrongdoing would be most likely to prompt you to be a whistle-blower? What kind of wrongdoing would be least likely? Why?

3. Which area of social responsibility is most important to you? Why? Are there areas other than those noted in the chapter that you consider important as well?

4. Identify some specific ethical or social responsibility issues that might be faced by small business managers and employees in each of the following areas: environment, customers, employees, and investors.

5. Choose a product or service and explain the social responsibility concerns that are likely to be evident in terms of the environment, customers, employees, and investors.

6. Pick one product or service that demonstrates each of the four approaches to social responsibility (obstructionist, defensive, accommodative, and proactive). What has been the impact of each stance on the company that is using it? Why did these companies adopt the particular stance they did? Have the companies that have adopted these different stances had different levels of success?

■ ■ ■ APPLICATION EXERCISES

1. Develop a list of the major stakeholders of your college or university. What priority does the school assign to these stakeholders? Do you agree or disagree with this prioritization?

2. Write a one-paragraph description of an ethical dilemma that you or someone you know faced recently. Analyze the situation using the ideas presented in the chapter. Make particular reference to the ethical norms of utility, rights, justice, and caring in terms of how they influenced the situation. What would each of these suggest about the correct decision? What was the actual outcome in the situation? Which ethical norm seems to have been most important?

3. Go to the website of the Center for Ethics and Business at Loyola Marymount University and click on "Toolbox." Then click on "Quiz: What's Your Ethical Style?" Then take the ethics quiz and analyze what your score implies about how you are likely to react when you are faced with an ethical dilemma.

4. Interview the owner of a local small business. Ask the owner to (1) give his or her views on the importance of social responsibility for small businesses, (2) describe the kinds of socially responsible activities the company is currently involved in, and (3) describe the factors that facilitate and inhibit social responsibility initiatives in small businesses.

BUILDING YOUR BUSINESS SKILLS

To Lie or Not to Lie: That Is the Question

The Purpose of This Assignment

To encourage students to apply general concepts of business ethics to specific situations.

Background

Workplace lying, it seems, has become business as usual. According to one survey, one-quarter of working adults said that they had been asked to do something illegal or unethical on the job. Four in 10 did what they were told. Another survey of more than 2000 administrative assistants showed that many employees face ethical dilemmas in their day-to-day work.

Assignment

Step 1

Working with four other students, discuss ways in which you would respond to the following ethical dilemmas. When there is a difference of opinion among group members, try to determine the specific factors that influence different responses.

■ Would you lie about your supervisor's whereabouts to someone on the phone?

■ Would you lie about who was responsible for a business decision that cost your company thousands of dollars in order to protect your own or your supervisor's job?

■ Would you inflate sales and revenue data on official company accounting statements to increase stock value?

■ Would you say that you witnessed a signature when you did not if you were acting in the role of a notary?

■ Would you keep silent if you knew that the official minutes of a corporate meeting had been changed?

■ Would you destroy or remove information that could hurt your company if it fell into the wrong hands?

Step 2

Research the commitment to business ethics at Johnson & Johnson (www.jnj.com/our_company/our_credo/index.htm) and Texas Instruments (www.ti.com/values-ethics-at-ti) by visiting their respective websites. As a group, discuss ways in which these statements are likely to affect the specific behaviours mentioned in Step 1.

Step 3

Working with group members, draft a corporate code of ethics that would discourage the specific behaviours mentioned in Step 1. Limit your code to a single typewritten page, but make it sufficiently broad to cover different ethical dilemmas.

Questions for Discussion

1. What personal, social, and cultural factors do you think contribute to lying in the workplace?
2. Do you agree or disagree with the following statement? *The term business ethics is an oxymoron.* Support your answer with examples from your own work experience or that of a family member.
3. If you were your company's director of human resources, how would you make your code of ethics a "living document"?
4. If you were faced with any of the ethical dilemmas described in Step 1, how would you handle them? How far would you go to maintain your personal ethical standards?

EXERCISING YOUR ETHICS: TEAM EXERCISE

Assessing the Ethics of Trade-Offs

The Situation

Managers must often make choices among options that are presented by environmental circumstances. This exercise will help you better appreciate the nature and complexity of the kinds of trade-offs that often result.

The Dilemma

You are the CEO of a medium-sized, unionized manufacturing corporation that is located in a town of about 15 000 people. The nearest major city is about 200 kilometres away. With about 500 workers, your company is one of the five largest employers in town. A regional recession has caused two of the other largest employers to close down (one went out of business and the other relocated to another area). A new foreign competitor has set up shop in the area, but local unemployment has still risen sharply. All in all, the regional economic climate and the new competitor are hurting your business. Your company's sales have dropped 20 percent this year, and you forecast another drop next year before things begin to turn around.

You face two unpleasant choices:

Choice 1: You can tell your employees that you need them to take cuts in pay and benefits. You know that because of the local unemployment rate, you can easily replace anyone who refuses. Unfortunately, you may need your employees to take another cut next year if your forecasts hold true. At the same time, you have reason to believe that when the economy rebounds (in about two years, according to your forecasts), you can begin reversing pay cuts. Here are the advantages of this choice: You can probably (1) preserve all 500 jobs, (2) maintain your own income, (3) restore pay cuts in the future, and (4) keep the business open indefinitely. And the disadvantages: Pay cuts will (1) pose economic hardships for your employees, and (2) create hard feelings and undercut morale.

Choice 2: You can maintain the status quo as far as your employees are concerned, but in that case, you'll be facing two problems: (1) You'll have to cut your own salary (while you can certainly afford to live on less income, doing so would be a blow to your personal finances), and (2) if economic conditions get worse and/or last longer than forecast, you *may* have to close down altogether. The firm has a cash surplus, but because you'll have to dip into that fund to maintain stable wages, it will soon run out. The advantages of this option: You can (1) avoid economic hardship for your workers, and (2) maintain good employee relations. The downside: you will reduce your own standard of living and may eventually cost everyone his or her job.

Team Activity

Assemble a group of four students and assign each group member to one of the following roles:

- CEO of the company
- the vice-president of production
- a shareholder
- an employee who is a member of the union

Action Steps

1. Before discussing the situation with your group, and from the perspective of your assigned role, which of the two options do you think is the best choice? Write down the reasons for your position.
2. Before discussing the situation with your group, and from the perspective of your assigned role, what are the underlying ethical issues in this situation? Write down the issues.
3. Gather the group together and reveal, in turn, each member's comments on the best choice of the two options. Next, reveal the ethical issues listed by each member.
4. Appoint someone to record the main points of agreement and disagreement within the group. How do you explain the results? What accounts for any disagreement?
5. From an ethical standpoint, what does your group conclude is the most appropriate action that should be taken by the company? (You may find the concepts of *utility, rights, justice,* and *caring* helpful in making your decision.)

Go to MyBizLab for additional cases and exercise material.

CONCLUDING CASE 3-1

The Problem of Consumer Skepticism

In recent years, a consensus seems to be developing that it is important to care for the environment. This "green movement" has motivated many companies to publicize what they are doing to be more eco-friendly. Coca-Cola, for example, pushed its new green image at the 2010 Winter Olympics with its "environmental call to action." Market research suggested that Coke had a lot of work to do to polish up its green image, particularly among consumers in the 13–29 age group. Critics have accused Coke of wasting water (it takes 250 litres of water to make one litre of Coca-Cola), and creating a lot of waste for landfills (75 percent of plastic bottles that contain Coca-Cola products end up in landfills). Coke therefore developed a new, eco-friendly container (called the PlantBottle) that is made partly from sugar cane and molasses. The new bottle produces 30 percent fewer emissions because less oil is used in making it.

You might think that any attempt by a company to be more eco-friendly would be viewed positively by those who are concerned about protecting the environment. But that isn't necessarily the case. Skeptics say that the new Coke bottle really doesn't accomplish much because it is still mostly plastic. They note that even though plastic bottles are recyclable, most consumers just throw them out, so simply giving consumers access to plastic bottles is a bad idea.

The criticism that Coca-Cola is getting is not unusual. The fact is that almost any proposed green idea can become caught up in controversy that inhibits the progress of green practices. For example, consider the idea of green roofs (i.e., planting vegetation on the roofs of buildings). Some companies have had green roofs for years (for example, the green roof on the Manulife Centre parkade in Toronto (see photo) has been there for 25 years, and the trees are now three storeys high), but the idea is just now starting to really catch on. In May 2009, Toronto's city council passed a bylaw that mandates green roofs on new commercial buildings and high-rise residential buildings. Starting in 2010, such buildings had to have at least part of their roof space devoted to green plantings. It is estimated that a green roof of 350 square metres with 75 percent of its area covered in greenery would reduce the "heat-island effect" by 26 percent and reduce rainwater

runoff by 38 percent. This sounds promising, but critics argue that the new bylaw may actually inhibit the progress of the green movement because it will increase building development costs and limit the options developers can choose from when they are trying to make buildings more environmentally friendly.

The bylaw is seen as one more problem that developers must solve before they can build. And during those periods when the economy is in a fragile state, that is a problem. The recession of 2008–09, for example, caused many businesses to put eco-friendly plans on hold. For example, Horizon Air, a U.S.-based airline, had planned to replace its regional jets with new Q400 turboprops made by Bombardier. The new planes burn 30 percent less fuel and therefore produce fewer emissions. But the economic slowdown forced the company to put those plans on hold. Another example: Clear Skies Solar cancelled plans to build a one-megawatt solar plant because it couldn't get enough financial backing. The plans were cancelled even though government grants are available for the development of solar power.

Consumer attitudes about eco-friendly behaviour can also limit the success of green products. A survey by the Boston Consulting Group in Toronto showed that one-third of Canadians say they often purchase environmentally friendly products, but 78 percent are unwilling to pay the higher price that is often charged for green products. Another online survey of 1000 Canadians showed that people are willing to do certain small things (for example, buying environmentally friendly light bulbs), but they are skeptical about adopting bigger measures. A third study, conducted by Procter & Gamble (P&G), showed that consumers are reluctant to spend more money just because a product is eco-friendly. Only 10 percent of consumers who were surveyed said they would pay a higher price (or accept a performance decrease) for a product that would benefit the environment. What's worse, 75 percent said they would not accept *any* trade-off. So P&G is now focusing on developing sustainable innovation products that are more eco-friendly than earlier products but cost about the same price and have the same quality.

Another survey of 10 000 people from Canada and nine other countries analyzed the willingness of consumers to pay a premium for things like improved water quality, renewable (green) energy, and organic food. Here are some illustrative results:

- For improved water quality: On average, respondents were willing to pay a 7.5 percent premium on the median amount of their water bill.
- For renewable energy: 50 percent of respondents said they weren't willing to pay *any* premium; 48 percent were willing (on average) to pay a 5-percent premium; 2 percent were willing to pay a 30-percent premium.
- For organic food: 30 percent said they weren't willing to pay *any* premium; one-third said they would pay a premium between 1 and 5 percent; 2 percent were willing to pay a 50-percent premium.

The level of acceptance of green products has also been influenced by individuals who argue that the green movement has gone too far, and that too many consumers are suffering from "eco-obsessive-compulsive disorder"—an obsession with buying only green products. Skeptics argue, for example, that the green movement negatively affects economic growth and increases unemployment. One study in Spain showed that every "green" job that was created destroyed 2.2 jobs elsewhere in the economy. The study concluded that government spending on renewable energy was only half as effective at creating new jobs as an equivalent amount of spending by the private sector.

Consumers may also be reluctant to spend money on eco-friendly products because they are confused by the green claims that are being made by various companies. The Boston Consulting Group study mentioned above also found that consumers are confused about the green options that are available because there is such a wide array of eco-labels on products. Ecolabelling.org is a Vancouver-based company that has identified 274 eco-labels, 23 of them originating in Canada. There are labels touting compostable products, fair trade products, energy efficient products, forest stewardship products, lake-friendly products, and organic products. These eco-labels are supposed to help consumers sift through environmental claims, but what do these labels actually mean? How can shoppers know which products are really eco-friendly and which ones are simply hype? The only thing that seems reasonably certain is that consumers are willing to pay a price premium in the short run if it leads to obvious long-term gains (for example, an energy-efficient refrigerator costs more than a regular one, but it saves money in the long run via lower electric bills).

There are people who are trying to help consumers sort through the maze of conflicting claims. Dara O'Rourke is a university professor who has developed a website called GoodGuide that allows consumers to identify the ingredients found in the products they buy. The website reports on both the environmental impact of products as well as their health effects. Website visitors enter a product name and get a score. The higher the score, the safer and more environmentally friendly the product is. O'Rourke's goal is to help consumers get past the green claims of companies and look at the actual facts, with a view to changing the system: Instead of having companies telling consumers what to believe about their products, the idea is to have consumers tell companies what is important to them in the products they buy.

Consumers may also become confused as they try to balance contradictory objectives about products. This problem can be clearly seen in automobile products. On the one hand, we need to sharply reduce carbon emissions by discouraging the use of gas-guzzling cars. This goal could be achieved by raising fuel-efficiency standards. But a study by the Boston Consulting Group concluded that fuel-saving improvements

that reduce emissions by 40 percent would also raise the price of the average car by $2000. On the other hand, the governments of both the United States and Canada are giving billions of dollars to Chrysler and General Motors in an attempt to save jobs at two companies that have historically produced gas-guzzling cars. These billions of dollars would move us toward the goal of reduced carbon emissions if Chrysler and GM could start producing green cars at prices consumers could afford, but industry experts say they can't (at least not in the near term). GM's all-electric car, the Volt, is too expensive to be purchased by many consumers, and GM's financial problems mean that it cannot risk the kind of money it formerly would have on a new product. It is also true that when gas prices are relatively low, consumers don't seem overly interested in green cars. Additionally, profit margins are small on green cars, and that is yet another limiting factor.

To cope with all this complexity, consumers need a good measure of ecological intelligence to help them make the distinction between style and substance in ecological claims. One proposal is for consumers to use something called life-cycle analysis, which calculates the carbon footprint of various activities (for example, a round-trip flight from Vancouver to Hong Kong, or a bouquet of flowers flown to Toronto from Kenya). But there is no guarantee that providing such detailed information would cause consumers to change their purchasing patterns. Organic foods and so-called "fair trade" products have been around for years, yet most people ignore them.

Questions for Discussion

1. Summarize in your own words the major factors that can inhibit the progress toward greener practices on the part of businesses and consumers.
2. Electric cars create far less pollution than cars powered by the internal combustion engine. In spite of this, however, it may be quite a few years before there are a lot of electric cars on the road. Why might this be so?
3. Consider the following statement: *It is not worthwhile to provide consumers with detailed information about the content of products or the carbon footprint of various activities because most consumers simply won't use the information. Consumers are struggling to get along financially from day to day, and they don't have the time or inclination to use such information.* Do you agree or disagree with the statement? Explain your reasoning.

CONCLUDING CASE 3-2

The Debate over Global Warming Is Heating Up

Until just a few years ago, there seemed to be wide acceptance of the idea that air pollution and greenhouse gases were causing the temperature of the earth to rise, that human activity was the cause, and that serious problems were going to be evident in the future unless something was done to reduce carbon dioxide emissions. This was the position of the influential United Nations Intergovernmental Panel on Climate Change (IPCC). But the global warming consensus is suddenly being vigorously challenged. In 2011, for example, research conducted at the European Organization for Nuclear Research (and published in the prestigious journal *Nature*) demonstrated the importance of the sun in global warming. A full-scale debate is now in progress, even though just a few years ago anyone who questioned whether human-caused global warming was occurring was viewed as a crackpot.

The debate has heated up (pun intended) for a variety of reasons. First, hacked emails from the Climatic Research Unit at a British university purportedly showed that researchers had manipulated data in order to support their views about human-caused global warming. After the emails were made public, charges and counter-charges flew. A British investigation of the incident—which resulted in a 160-page report entitled "The Independent Climate Change Emails Review"—concluded that the researchers were not guilty of misconduct; it did note, however, that the researchers had withheld data, provided misleading information, and were not open to the possibility that their critics' claims might have some merit. Overall, it has been difficult to determine whether unreasonable behaviour was actually evident, or whether critics were simply using the issue to argue that the supposed consensus on global warming was an illusion. One thing is clear: The incident caused both the media and the general public to start wondering whether the issue of global warming was really "settled," as many scientists had been claiming.

Second, the IPCC has made some fairly dramatic predictions during the past decade, and some of those predictions now look suspect. For example, one IPCC report predicted that the Himalayan glaciers would disappear within 30 years because of global warming. When it became

apparent that this prediction was not based on scientific research, but rather on an unsubstantiated claim made by an environmental group, the IPCC lost some credibility.

Third, several global warming "deniers" have been loudly challenging the so-called "global warming consensus." They point out, for example, that the global average temperature has stopped increasing in spite of the fact that carbon dioxide is still being released into the atmosphere. The deniers also challenge the assumption that human industrial activity is a cause of global warming. As part of their strategy, deniers carefully analyze statistics that are often cited by the media as support for the global warming consensus. For example, one research study found that 75 of 77 scientists (97 percent) supported the idea of human-caused global warming. But critics pointed out that, in fact, 10 257 scientists had been surveyed, and that reporting the views of a subset of only 77 was misleading, particularly since the views of solar scientists, cosmologists, physicists, and meteorologists were not reported. Deniers also argue that the assumptions underlying most climate models are not reasonable, and that running climate simulations based on flawed assumptions does not yield meaningful results.

Fourth, many governments are now moderating their position on global warming. The G8 meetings in 2009 were strongly in favour of actions being taken to combat global warming (for example, reducing global temperatures by two degrees), but the 2010 meetings were much more modest (for example, leaders made a commitment to "do their best" on climate change).

Fifth, more and more people are starting to think seriously about the issue of global warming. Many have concluded that it is impossible to predict what will happen in the global climate over the next 20 or 30 or 50 years because we simply do not yet have a level of understanding of climate dynamics that would allow us to make such predictions. One indication of consumer skepticism about global warming is found in answers to surveys. When asked questions such as "What do you think is the most important problem facing the country today?" very few people mention global warming.

Are there any conclusions we can reach about global warming? Let's look briefly at the two key issues in the debate: (1) Is global warming occurring?, and (2) is human activity the cause of global warming?

Is Global Warming Occurring?

A majority of scientists have concluded that global warming is real, and they point to data generated by the United Nations Intergovernmental Panel on Climate Change (IPCC), which shows that the average global temperature has risen about 0.6 degrees Celsius during the past century. Some scientists who agree that warming is occurring don't think the magnitude is as large as the IPCC claims; their main argument is that the IPCC data are contaminated and therefore exaggerate the amount of warming that has actually occurred.

To the untrained person, it might seem that measuring temperature is a pretty straightforward thing to do, but it is more complex than it appears at first glance. One problem is that the number and location of weather stations is constantly changing, so the comparability of weather data over time is not as good as scientists would like. Another problem is that the methods used to measure temperature change over time. For example, many years ago, the temperature of sea water was measured by lifting a bucket of sea water into a ship and then measuring the temperature of the water. Now, water is pumped into the engine room of a ship and then measured. But doing that might cause the reading to increase because of the warmer temperature in the engine room. Deciding *where* to measure temperature is another problem. Urban heating must be taken into account, but it is not clear what proportion of urban and rural sites should be included in temperature calculations.

Is Global Warming Caused by Human Activity?

Let us assume for the moment that global warming is a fact. The next obvious question is "What is causing global warming?" Many scientists argue that the rapid increase in carbon dioxide emissions that has occurred during the past 200 years is the cause of global warming. These emissions—which are the result of human industrial activity—trap heat in the atmosphere (the "greenhouse effect") and cause the temperature of the earth to rise. The views of scientists who hold this belief have been widely publicized, and many people accept them as fact. The IPCC has also concluded that greenhouse gases are the cause of global warming.

Other scientists have expressed skepticism about human-caused global warming. For example, Reid Bryson, emeritus professor of meteorology and one of the most-cited meteorologists in the world, says the idea that global warming is caused by the release of carbon dioxide into the atmosphere is absurd. He says that warming is occurring simply because we are still coming out of the "little ice age" of the early 1800s. More dramatically, Tad Murty, a professor in the Departments of Civil Engineering and Earth Sciences at the University of Ottawa, says that global warming is the biggest hoax ever perpetrated on humanity. He notes that there have always been cycles of warming and cooling.

Scientists who reject the idea that human activity is the cause of global warming make other, more general arguments. First, they point out that there have been variations in the earth's temperature in the distant past and that these variations couldn't possibly have been caused by human activity because there weren't any humans. Second, since the thermometer wasn't invented until 1602, we don't have a very long time period of accurate temperature records to examine as we look for warming trends. Records going back thousands of years are needed before we can say with any confidence that a warming (or cooling) trend is actually occurring. Third, research shows that changes in the earth's climate correlate better with fluctuations in the brightness of the sun than they do with fluctuations in carbon dioxide levels. Analysis of core samples from the sediment in British Columbia fjords shows a consistent 11-year cycle in marine productivity which correlates closely with the known 11-year cycle of sunspots. Scientists predict that by the year 2020 the sun will be entering a phase of weaker output, and they conclude that a period of unusually cool temperatures is likely. Several other research studies of tree rings and freshwater river levels also strongly suggest that the sun drives climate change.

What Does All This Mean?

If the scientists who say that global warming is caused by human activity are right, we had better get moving on initiatives to reduce carbon dioxide emissions. But if the scientists who say that global warming is not caused by human activity are right, there isn't much that we can do about climate change. Regardless of whether global warming is human-caused or is a natural occurrence, there will be both winners and losers if the average global temperature goes up significantly. In Greenland, for example, rising temperatures mean that more pasture area can be grazed by sheep and cows, and a greater variety of vegetables can be grown than was formerly the case; this will improve Greenland's economic performance. But rising temperatures will also undermine the seal hunting by Greenland's Inuit because of thinning ice and may also cause a decline in polar bear populations.

Questions for Discussion

1. Given the information presented above, as well as other information you have read, do you think the evidence supports the argument that global warming is occurring?
2. Given the information presented above, as well as other information you have read, do you think the evidence supports the argument that global warming is caused by human activity?
3. List some additional winners and losers that are likely as a result of global warming.
4. Consider the following statement: *While there are some uncertainties about global warming, the problem is significant enough that we need to take immediate action to reduce carbon dioxide emissions. If we don't, in 40 or 50 years it will be too late.* Do you agree or disagree with the statement? Defend your answer.

Understanding Entrepreneurship, Small Business, and New Venture Creation

Internet Entrepreneurs: Moving Products Beyond the Rack

CAN you name the fastest growing online retailer in North America? Would you be surprised to find out it is a Canadian company? According to a recent top 500 list created by *Internet Retailer* magazine, the company to watch is Montreal-based "flash sale" retailer Beyond the Rack. The company was created in 2009 by two ambitious entrepreneurs named Yona Shtern and Robert Gold, along with two full-time employees. By 2012, Beyond the Rack had 330 full-time employees, working in offices in Montreal and New York, while serving over 6 million members from across North America. Beyond the Rack has a working relationship with over 2000 consumer brands and has revenues exceeding US$120 million. Like most successful teams, the two entrepreneurs have complementary skills. Mr. Shtern is the CEO,

who spends time taking care of the marketing and merchandising and actively seeks financing, while Mr. Gold is in charge of day-to-day operations.

Business Model

The model was inspired by two highly successful European sites, Gilt and Vente Privee. Beyond the Rack obtains the rights to sell authentic designer brands at major discounted prices (up to 80 percent off retail) exclusively to its members. It is a private shopping club that hosts limited-time, limited-quantity online events. Every day, members can expect up to 15 new events, usually starting at 11 a.m. Eastern time and lasting 48 hours. Once the event is over, the merchandise is

no longer available. The whole model is built on speed. Beyond the Rack does not use a traditional retail approach: It does not buy large quantities of stock, ship it to its warehouse, and hope to sell it. At the prices they are offering, this approach would be unfeasible. Instead, they acquire the rights to sell a specific quantity of discounted products. Once the event is over and the members have committed to purchasing the units, Beyond the Rack orders the physical quantities and then ships them to members around North America. In other words, products do not come to the premises unless member orders are placed.

Beyond the Rack has created an efficient win-win-win scenario: 1) customers get designer products at great prices; 2) the designer brands have an efficient way to dispose of excess

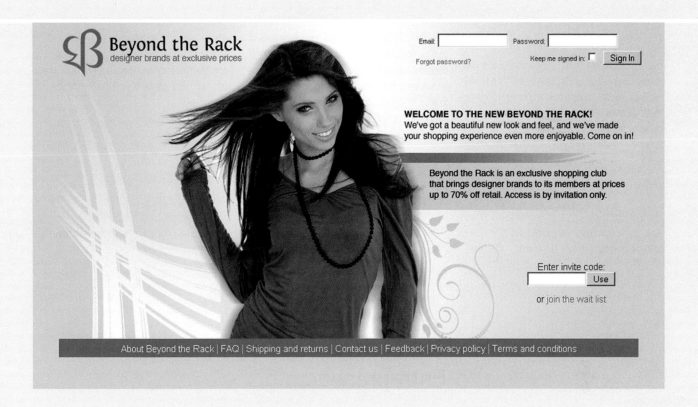

end-of-season items (from a branding point of view this approach is favourable—it's better to sell to this private club than to have expensive brands sit in cluttered racks in stores like Winners, for example); 3) Beyond the Rack earns an attractive margin as the facilitator. It's quick, it's efficient, it's online.

Financing

Successful entrepreneurs need more than a good idea; they also require the willingness to take a risk and the energy to work hard, as well as access to financing. If you are opening a small mom-and-pop store, you may need to dip into your savings or take out a loan to buy equipment and build a storefront. However, when your goals are set high, like becoming the premier online shopping club, you need to be creative and you must convince individuals and organizations to provide major financing to support growth. This is exactly what Yona Shtern and his team have done. Beyond the Rack received US$12 million financing from BDC Venture Capital Inc., a

government organization, and Highland Capital Partners LLC, a respected retail investor that has worked with many major organizations including lululemon Athletica, MapQuest, and LivePerson. Beyond the Rack raised an additional $4.5 million from Oleg Tscheltzoff and Oliver Jung (two European internet entrepreneurs), Montreal Start Up (a venture fund), and David Chamandy (an "angel investor"). A further round of financing was announced at the end of 2011 for US$36.6 million. It was led by Panorama Capital, with additional investments coming from Export Development Canada, Tandem Expansion Fund, Rho Canada, and Inovia Capital. According to Beyond the Rack CFO Michael Krebs, "Outside institutional funding is a key element to continued exponential growth; that is how Beyond the Rack generated a membership base of 6 million in three short years."

Growth and Expansion

In 2011, Beyond the Rack announced the acquisition of select assets of New York-based

BeautyStory.com. This move added to the solid base of members (a key figure for BTR's growth and bargaining power) and strengthened the already successful beauty division. This was yet another important milestone in its brief history. However, as companies grow and structures are put in place, the entrepreneurial spirit of an organization runs the risk of being smothered by bureaucracy. Its trademark creativity, flexibility, and passion will be necessary for Beyond the Rack to sustain its spirit and continue to grow in the dynamic online world. The team at Beyond the Rack is doing everything it can to ensure that employees do not forget the core mission and entrepreneurial spirit of the organization. For example, each month all employees, regardless of their official position, spend some time completing orders in the fulfilment centre. The core message of this approach: "You may be a marketer or an accountant but without these orders and the ultimate satisfaction of the end consumer, there is no business. Never forget who we are."

The Future

Over the next few years, Beyond the Rack will surely experience new challenges and will need to secure additional financing to reach its objectives. Success inevitably brings more competition. There was news that Amazon was launching MyHabit.com to compete with companies like Gilt and Beyond the Rack. What does the future hold for Beyond the Rack? That is unclear. However, the brief history of the firm is a glorious one and the company seems ready for the next challenge. For these internet entrepreneurs, the future, as is the case for more traditional companies, will be based on their ability to satisfy the needs of their brand suppliers and consumers alike, while turning a profit. ◆

HOW WILL THIS HELP ME?

By understanding the material discussed in this chapter, you'll be better prepared to (1) identify the challenges and opportunities provided in new venture start-ups, (2) assess the risks and benefits of working in a new business, and (3) evaluate the investment potential inherent in a new business.

Small Business, New Venture Creation, and Entrepreneurship

LO1 Explain the meaning of and interrelationship among the terms *small business, new venture creation*, and *entrepreneurship*.

In this chapter we examine old companies with an enduring entrepreneurial spirit (Parasuco); we look at exciting growth-oriented newcomers (Beyond the Rack and Twitter); and we examine major family organizations that have stood the test of time (McCain) and a host of small organizations with dreams and aspirations. Each of these examples gives us a glimpse of an important element of the Canadian business landscape. We begin by examining the lifeblood of an economy: small business, entrepreneurship, and new ventures.

One positive result of the recent recession was a new wave of entrepreneurial efforts. Self-employed Canadians account for 16 percent of the workforce.[1] Every day, approximately 380 businesses are started in Canada.[2] New firms create the most jobs, are noted for their entrepreneurship, and are typically small.[3] But does this mean that most small businesses are entrepreneurial? Not necessarily.

The terms *small business, new venture*, and *entrepreneurship* are closely linked terms, but each idea is distinct. In the following paragraphs we will explain these terms to help you understand these topics and how they are interrelated.

Small Business

Defining a "small" business can be tricky. Various measures might be used, including the number of people the business employs, the company's sales revenue, the size of the investment required, or the type of ownership structure the business has. Some of the difficulties in defining a small business become evident when we consider the way the Canadian government collects and reports information on small businesses.

Industry Canada relies on two distinct sources of information, both provided by Statistics Canada: the Business Register (which tracks businesses) and the Labour Force Survey (which tracks individuals). To be included in the Business Register, a business must have at least one paid employee and annual sales revenues of $30 000 or more, or be incorporated. A goods-producing business in the register is considered small if it has fewer than 100 employees, while a service-producing business is considered small if it has fewer than 50 employees.[4]

The Labour Force Survey uses information from *individuals* to make estimates of employment and unemployment levels. Individuals are classified as self-employed if they are working owners of a business that is either incorporated or unincorporated, if they work for themselves but do not have a business (some musicians, for example, would fall into this category), or if they work without pay in a family business.

In its publication *Key Small Business Statistics*, Industry Canada reports that there are 2.3 million "business establishments" in Canada and about 2.7 million people are "self-employed."[5] There is no way of identifying how much overlap there is in these two categories, but we do know that an unincorporated business operated by a self-employed person (with no employees) would *not* be counted among the 2.3 million *businesses* in the Business Register. This is an important point because the majority of businesses in Canada have no employees (just the owner), nor are they incorporated. A study conducted by members of the Entrepreneurship Research Consortium (ERC) tracked a sample of Canadian *nascent entrepreneurs*—people who were trying to start a business—over four years. Only 15 percent of those who reported establishing an operating business had incorporated their firm.[6] These facts need to be kept in mind when considering statistics or research that excludes these firms. When either of these indicators is used to find businesses to study, the number of new firms will be underestimated.

Given all this, we define a **small business** as an owner-managed business with fewer than 100 employees. We do so because it enables us to make better use of existing statistics and because you now are aware of how definitions can influence our understanding of small businesses.

Each year, the Queen's Centre for Business Venturing develops a ranking of the top 50 small- and medium-sized employers to work for. The top 10 firms in the 2011 study are shown in Table 4.1. Each of these companies exhibited superiority in employee recognition, managing performance, career opportunities, and organizational reputation.[7]

small business An owner-managed business with fewer than 100 employees.

The New Venture/Firm

Various criteria can also be used to determine when a new firm comes into existence. Three of the most common are when it was formed, whether it was incorporated, and if it sells goods and/or services.[8] A business is considered to be new if it has become

TABLE 4.1 Top 10 Small- and Medium-Sized Employers in Canada		
	Company	**Location**
1.	Imaginet	Winnipeg, MB
2.	Arrow Group of Companies	Scarborough, ON
3.	Achievers	Toronto, ON
4.	Habanero Consulting Group	Vancouver, BC
5.	Solvera Solutions	Regina, SK
6.	RL Solutions	Toronto, ON
7.	Protegra	Winnipeg, MB
8.	Vigilant Global	Montreal, QC
9.	Nurse Next Door Home Care Services	Vancouver, BC
10.	iQmetrix	Regina, SK

new venture (or new firm) A recently formed commercial organization that provides goods and/or services for sale.

operational within the previous 12 months, if it adopts any of the main organizational forms (proprietorship, partnership, corporation, or co-operative), and if it sells goods or services. Thus, we define a **new venture (or new firm)** as a recently formed commercial organization that provides goods and/or services for sale.

Entrepreneurship

entrepreneurship The process of identifying an opportunity in the marketplace and accessing the resources needed to capitalize on that opportunity.

Entrepreneurship is the process of identifying an opportunity in the marketplace and accessing the resources needed to capitalize on that opportunity.[9] **Entrepreneurs** are people who recognize and seize opportunities. For example, Mark Zuckerberg created Facebook, and in 2011 it had over 750 million active users. He is one of the richest people in the world under the age of 30. Zuckerberg worked long hours, and he is constantly tailoring the website to suit its expanding audience.[10]

entrepreneur A business person who accepts both the risks and the opportunities involved in creating and operating a new business venture.

In another example, Rahumathulla Marikkar transformed disappointment into a new business venture when he lost his job as Head of Technology and Environment of Interface Inc., the world's largest modular carpet manufacturer. In 2009, at a time when manufacturing jobs were disappearing in large volumes, Mr. Marikkar decided to use his knowledge and experience to create a company called Belletile. His company is successfully fighting the threat from offshore manufacturing by focusing on high-end niche products that low-cost producers in Asia are unable to produce.[11]

Each year, the Heritage Foundation publishes an index of economic freedom, which assesses the extent to which entrepreneurs have freedom to pursue new business opportunities. In 2011, the top three countries were Hong Kong, Singapore, and Australia, with freedom scores of 89.7, 87.2, and 82.5 respectively. Canada ranked sixth with a score of 80.8 and North Korea ranked last with a score of 1.0. Canada now ranks higher than the United States, partly due to the U.S. government's stimulus spending, which the foundation believes will hurt the U.S. economy's long-term prospects.[12]

Creativity is an important personal attribute that has come to be associated with entrepreneurs, and small businesses provide a great environment in which to unleash creativity.[13] But do not assume that only small business owners exhibit entrepreneurial characteristics. Many successful managers in large organizations in both the public and private sectors also exhibit similar characteristics.[14] Entrepreneurship is evident in a wide range of contexts: in small or new firms, in old firms, in large firms, in firms that grow slowly, in firms that grow rapidly, in non-profit organizations, and in the public sector.[15]

Historically, most innovations have come from individuals in small businesses. As businesses increase in size, however, innovation and creativity tend to become casualties in the battle for higher sales and profits. In some large companies, new ideas are even discouraged, and champions of innovation have been stalled in mid-career. But people who exhibit entrepreneurial characteristics can often create and maintain the innovation and flexibility of a small-business environment within the confines of a large, bureaucratic structure. This is known as **intrapreneuring**, and it is supported by many large firms, including Rubbermaid, 3M, and Xerox.

intrapreneuring Entrepreneurial characteristics that can create and maintain the innovation and flexibility of a small-business environment within the confines of a large, bureaucratic structure.

Mark Zuckerberg is the new-age entrepreneur who created Facebook, the wildly successful social networking site.

Compaq (which is now part of Hewlett-Packard) is an excellent example of how intrapreneuring works. The firm has one major division called the New Business Group. When a manager or engineer has an idea for a new product or product application, he or she takes it to the New Business Group and "sells" it. The managers in the group are then encouraged to help the innovator develop the idea for field testing. If the product takes off and does well, it is then spun off into its own business group or division. If it doesn't do as well as hoped, it may be maintained as part of the New Business Group or phased out.

Procter & Gamble is also known for encouraging intrapreneurship. It has earned this reputation by having divisions that focus on creating new products for specific markets.[16] The Swiffer product line is one example. Once the basic Swiffer mop was launched successfully, a whole range of products was added, such as the Swiffer WetJet and Swiffer Dusters. A key difference between intrapreneurs and entrepreneurs is that intrapreneurs typically don't have to concern themselves with getting the resources needed to bring the new product to market, since their employer provides the resources.

The Role of Small and New Businesses in the Canadian Economy

Small and new businesses play a key role in the Canadian economy, but recognition of this role is relatively recent. Prior to the 1980s, large businesses were the focus of attention in terms of economic impact within industrialized nations.

Describe the role of small and new businesses in the *Canadian economy*.   **LO2**

Small Businesses

As mentioned earlier in this chapter, there are 2.3 million business establishments in Canada. Of these, about half are classified as "employer businesses" (i.e., they have a payroll of at least one person), while the other half are classified as "indeterminate" because they have no employees registered with the Canada Revenue Agency.[17]

It may surprise you to learn that 98 percent of all employer businesses in Canada are small (they have fewer than 100 employees), and more than half of these have

A common type of small business in Canada is the convenience store. As the name suggests, it emphasizes convenience. It attracts customers from its immediate area through its long hours of operation and the product lines it carries.

fewer than five employees. Medium-sized businesses (100–499 employees) comprise just 1.8 percent of employer businesses, and large businesses (those with 500 or more employees) represent just 0.2 percent of all employer businesses.[18] This pattern is consistent across all provinces in Canada. While one large business will have many more employees than one small business, small businesses as a group provide more jobs than large businesses. Small businesses also lead the way when it comes to innovation and new technology.

Ontario and Quebec together account for the largest proportion of business establishments in Canada (about 57 percent), followed by the western provinces (37 percent) and the Atlantic provinces (6 percent). The Northwest Territories, the Yukon, and Nunavut represent just 0.3 percent of Canada's businesses.[19]

The distribution of employment by size of firm varies considerably across industries. Small businesses account for over two-thirds of employment in five industries: non-institutional health care (89 percent), forestry (77 percent), other services (75 percent), the construction industry (74 percent), and accommodation and food (66 percent).[20]

One increasingly important area is the field of green technologies and green applications for businesses of all sizes. The box entitled "Small Businesses Go Green" provides information on the growing interest around environmental concerns for small business owners.

THE GREENING OF BUSINESS

Small Businesses Go Green

A survey conducted by Ipsos Reid showed that half of Canadian small business owners currently have, or are considering implementing, a green plan for their business. Of those that already have a plan, the majority emphasize the reduction of energy costs. Actual spending on green initiatives, however, has been low (less than $500 per business during the past two years).

Many small businesses in Canada have already taken some easy-to-implement actions to become greener (e.g., changing to energy-efficient lighting, turning off photocopiers and computers overnight, using recycled paper, buying eco-friendly cleaning supplies, and using pens made of compostable material instead of plastic). Other environmentally friendly strategies have also emerged. Consider cargo bicycles, which have been popular for many years in places like China and India, but are now becoming popular in North America as environmental consciousness rises and traffic congestion in large cities increases. Here are some examples:

- Toronto-based Vert Catering uses a cargo bicycle to deliver food to its customers.

- Vancouver entrepreneurs launched SHIFT Urban Cargo Delivery, which is designed to fill the gap between bike couriers and delivery trucks. SHIFT delivers everything from office supplies to small furniture. Their cargo bicycles have an electric assist to help with heavy loads.

- Ontario-based Green Gardeners uses cargo bikes to transport garden tools to client sites.

- Featherstone Two Wheels Green Delivery in Toronto saves $7000–$9000 in insurance and maintenance costs every year by using cargo bicycles instead of cars.

Small businesses can take other actions to save money and go green at the same time. For example, The Auto West Group BMW auto dealership in Richmond, B.C., has installed a wind turbine to generate electricity. The turbine—which will reduce the company's power bill—is just the latest initiative for this company, which is committed to being green (it already has one of the greenest buildings in B.C. and has installed solar panels, geo-thermal heating and cooling technology, and a rooftop garden).

Help for small businesses that wish to "go green" is available from organizations such as Investeco Capital Corp. (a private equity group that launched a $40-million fund to help small- and medium-sized food companies to operate sustainably), Gobi Carbon Management Solutions (which developed software to help small businesses identify their emissions sources and make suggestions for saving money), and the federal government's ecoACTION program website, which contains information about programs that help organizations reduce energy costs).

Critical Thinking Questions

1. Find a small business in your area that is committed to being eco-friendly. Why did the owner decide to commit to having an eco-friendly business?

2. Consider the following statement: *Because the failure rate of small businesses is high, small business owners must focus all their energies on trying to survive. They therefore do not have the time or the money to implement green practices.* Do you agree or disagree with the statement? Explain your reasoning.

New Ventures

New ventures are important as a source of job creation and for the introduction of new products and services.[21] From 2001 to 2010, small businesses created 47 percent of all the jobs in Canada.[22] Taking into account the businesses that closed during the same time period, there were approximately 15 000 companies added per year.[23]

More and more women are starting their own small businesses; women now account for half of all new businesses that are formed. According to Statistics Canada, there are about 910 000 women entrepreneurs in Canada, and 46 percent of small- and medium-sized enterprises have some degree of female ownership.[24] Women are playing a more prominent role than ever before in starting new ventures. Kyla Eaglesham, the owner of Madeleines Cherry Pie and Ice Cream, is typical. After doing a lot of research on the ice cream and dessert industry, she left her job as a flight attendant and opened a dessert café in Toronto's trendy Annex neighbourhood. The store attracts customers who want "a little bit of cottage country in the heart of Toronto."[25] On a negative note, women lead only 12 percent of the small- and medium-sized businesses that export goods and services.[26]

Female entrepreneurs are honoured each year at the Canadian Woman Entrepreneur Awards. Previous winners included Cora Tsouflidou (Montreal-based Cora Franchise Group), Teresa Coady (Vancouver-based Bunting Coady Architects), and Yvonne Tollens (Okotoks, Alberta–based ComputerAid Professional Services).[27] Women who run businesses from their homes are sometimes called "mompreneurs."[28]

Many young entrepreneurs are also involved in creating new ventures in Canada. Consider the following examples:

- Daisy and Adam Orser were among the winners of the BDC Young Entrepreneurs Award for their Victoria, B.C.–based company called The Root Cellar Village Green Grocer. They are capitalizing on the growing demand for fresh local produce and healthier lifestyles. The company already employees 50 people and the future looks bright.[29]

- Sean McCormick is the owner of Blue Moose Clothing Company, the largest manufacturer of mukluks in Canada. McCormick employs 25 people, many of them Aboriginal. He credits Aboriginal Business Canada, which provides money to Native entrepreneurs to help them start small businesses.[30]

- Tell Us About Us (TUAU) is a Winnipeg-based company specializing in market research and customer satisfaction programs. Owners Tyler Gompf and Scott Griffith recently signed a seven-figure deal to provide mystery shopper service to Dunkin' Donuts, Baskin-Robbins, and Togo's in the United States and Canada. The mystery shoppers will note any problems at a retail sites and TUAU will then measure how quickly the problems are fixed.[31]

The Entrepreneurial Process

L03 Explain the *entrepreneurial process* and describe its three key elements.

The entrepreneurial process is like a journey. To get to the destination (the start-up of a new venture), the entrepreneur must identify a business opportunity and access the resources needed to capitalize on it. Along the way, social, economic, political, and technological factors in the broader environment will have an influence, but we will focus our attention on understanding the three key process elements—the entrepreneur, the opportunity, and the resources—and how they interact.

As these key elements interact, they may be mismatched or well matched. If elements are mismatched (a "misfit"), the journey may be abandoned before the destination is reached. For example, if an entrepreneur identifies an opportunity for a new health service but does not have the relevant background and skills to deliver

ENTREPRENEURSHIP AND NEW VENTURES

Old Traditions: New Technologies

The term *biodynamic* sounds very scientific but it is actually a very natural and holistic means of growing crops. Moray Tawse, who founded the winery that bears his family name, is a wine aficionado. After researching the potential of wine-making in Niagara, he purchased his property in 2001 and opened his showcase winery in 2005.

At its heart, the biodynamic approach to producing grapes for wine production sees the vineyard as its own ecological entity. The wines produced through biodynamic methods have stronger, purer, and more vibrant aromas and flavours. These methods lead to better balance in fruit growth, where the sugar production in the grape corresponds with its physiological ripeness. This means the wine will be better balanced in terms of flavour and alcohol content, even within the context of Ontario's ever-changing climate. Tawse unites traditional winemaking techniques with state-of-the-art technology to create wines of exceptional elegance, depth, and character.

The fruit is harvested from old-growth, low-yield vines and gently handled using natural gravity flow and geothermic energy. Rather than relying on newer and more economical approaches to winemaking, Tawse applies rigorous organic and biodynamic methods to every aspect of wine production. To showcase its efforts, Ecocert and Demeter seals, which indicate organic and biodynamic products, respectively, now appear on all Tawse vintages made by its biodynamic vineyards.

Biodynamic wines made at Tawse Winery are not inexpensive to create nor are they produced on a large scale. Given the quality of the final product and the seriousness of the global environmental situation, however, they are worth the investment. All Tawse wines are crafted using organic and biodynamic farming practices, which in turn are based on traditional agricultural methods such as planting and harvesting at certain points in the lunar calendar.

The Tawse philosophy is simple: The company believes winemaking begins in the vineyards. It uses organic and biodynamic farming techniques to ensure the health of its vines and the vitality of its soils. Grapes are harvested at optimal ripeness and are hand-picked and hand-sorted. Once the fruit arrives at the winery, a six-level gravity flow processing system is used that is based on the natural slope and contours of the property. The use of gravity as opposed to pumps allows the wine to move gently from pressing to bottling with minimum manipulation. The wine is aged in underground cellars, which keeps the ambient temperature between 10 and 16 degrees Celsius, with a natural humidity of around 85 percent. This relatively stable temperature and high humidity allows the wines to age gracefully in barrels with a minimum amount of evaporation over the 18-month cellaring period. Additionally, Tawse employs a modern geo-thermal energy system, which has reduced its use of traditional forms of energy by 80 percent. It also has a Wetland Biofilter that facilitates the complete re-use of all its sanitary and winery process water.

The wine industry has taken notice of the company's efforts; Tawse was named Canadian Winery of the Year by *Wine Access* magazine in 2010 and 2011, the first time an Ontario winery has won this distinction two years in a row. Clearly Tawse's ecologically sound business practices are driving the public's enthusiasm for its product.

Critical Thinking Questions

1. Discuss the factors of production as they apply to Tawse Winery.

2. How does Tawse's decision to craft wines using a traditional technique affect its product? When discussing your answer, consider the competitive wine industry as a whole.

TABLE 4.2 Entrepreneurial Characteristics		
Kuratko and Hodgetts (2007)	**Hornday (1982)**	**Timmons and Spinelli (2007)**
Commitment, determination, and perseverance	Self-confidence	Commitment and determination
Drive to achieve	Perseverance, determination	Leadership
Opportunity orientation	Drive to achieve	Opportunity obsession
Initiative and responsibility	Energy, diligence	Tolerance of risk, ambiguity, and uncertainty
Persistent problem solving	Resourcefulness	Creativity, self-reliance, and adaptability
Seeking feedback	Calculated risk taking	Motivation to excel
Internal locus of control	Need to achieve	Courage
Tolerance for ambiguity	Creativity	Creativity and innovativeness
Calculated risk taking	Flexibility	Energy, health, and emotional stability
Integrity and reliability	Positive responses to callenges	Values
Tolerance for failure	Independence	Intelligence
High energy level	Perceptiveness	
Creativity and innovativeness	Dynamism, leadership	
Vision	Postive attitude	
Self-confidence and optimism	Ability to get along with people	
Independence	Responsiveness to suggestions and criticism	
Team building	Profit orientation	
	Perceptiveness	

the service, the business may never get off the ground. Conversely, if the process elements are well matched (a "fit"), the new business venture will likely become operational. After start-up, the venture's next phase of development will result in one of the following outcomes: growth, stability (staying the same), decline, or demise (ceasing to exist).

The Entrepreneur

Since the entrepreneur is at the heart of the entrepreneurial process, researchers have paid considerable attention to identifying the personal characteristics of entrepreneurs. The profiles provided in Table 4.2 illustrate how wide-ranging these characteristics are.[32] Some are behavioural (for example, high energy level), others are personality traits (for example, independence), and still others are skills (for example, problem solving).

While the idea that people are "born" entrepreneurs is still quite popular, nothing could be further from the truth.[33] In fact, entrepreneurial characteristics have been found to be widely distributed in the population.[34] We also know that personal characteristics often have less impact on a person's actions than the situation a person is in.[35] In other words, the important thing is not who the person *is* but what the person *does*.[36] The two main things that entrepreneurs need to do are to identify an opportunity and to access resources.

Identifying Opportunities

Identifying opportunities involves generating ideas for new (or improved) products, processes, or services, then screening those ideas so that the one that presents the best opportunity can be developed, and then developing the opportunity.

Idea Generation

Typically, generating ideas involves abandoning traditional assumptions about how things work and how they ought to be and seeing what others do not. If the prospective new (or improved) product, process, or service can be profitably produced and is attractive relative to other potential venture ideas, it might present an opportunity.

Where do ideas come from? Most new ventures do not emerge from a deliberate search for viable business ideas but rather from events relating to work or everyday life.[37] Approximately half of all new business ideas come from insights gained or skills learned at a previous job. As employees, prospective entrepreneurs are familiar with the product or service and with the customers, suppliers, and competitors. They can relate those needs to their own personal capabilities and can determine whether they are capable of producing products or services that can fill the void.

Jay Hagan and Scott Gaidano learned how to recover data from damaged hard drives while working for a company that manufactured them. When that company went bankrupt, they started their own business and called it DriveSavers. Likewise, Gina Bianchini met Marc Andreessen while working for a company that also went bankrupt. They discovered a shared interest in the fast-growing world of social networking and together created Ning, a platform that gives users the freedom to design their own online networks.[38]

The next most frequent sources of venture ideas are a personal interest/hobby (16 percent) and a chance happening (11 percent).[39] A chance happening refers to a situation where a venture idea comes about unexpectedly. For example, while on vacation in another country you might try a new snack food that you feel would be in demand if introduced to the Canadian market.

Screening

Entrepreneurs often generate many ideas, and screening them is a key part of the entrepreneurial process. The faster you can weed out the "dead-end" venture ideas, the more time and effort you can devote to the ones that remain. The more of the following characteristics that an idea has, the greater the opportunity it presents.

The Idea Creates or Adds Value for the Customer. A product or service that creates or adds value for the customer is one that solves a significant problem or meets a significant need in new or different ways. Consider Polar Mobile, a Toronto–based developer of mobile applications that has made great strides since launching a few years ago. Polar provides a software platform called (SMART™) that makes it easy for media companies to launch apps for all types of smartphones and tablet devices. The company must be doing something right because major companies are finding value in this relatively new company. In 2011, just four years since its inception, Polar had over 300 customers in 10 countries and powered over 1000 mobile apps with its platform. Among its clients, Nokia signed a deal for Polar to build 300 mobile apps. Other notable customers include Research In Motion and Microsoft. Polar also signed a deal with Dubai-based Emitec Mobile, a large distributor of smartphones with more than 70 mobile operators from 50 countries around the Middle East, North Africa, and Central Asia. It would seem that Polar has clearly shown the capacity to add value based on this impressive list of partners.[40]

The Idea Provides a Competitive Advantage That Can Be Sustained. A competitive advantage exists when potential customers see the product or service as being better than that of competitors. Toronto-based Sentinelle Medical is counting on a very important sustainable advantage. Cameron Piron spent 10 years developing a better cancer detection technology and another two years convincing General Electric to use it in its MRI machines. He recently received the Ontario Government Innovation Award.[41] Sustaining a competitive advantage involves maintaining it in the face of competitors' actions or changes in the industry. All other things being equal, the longer markets are in a state of flux, the greater the likelihood of a company being able to sustain a competitive advantage. Lacking a competitive advantage or developing a competitive advantage that is not sustainable have been fatal flaws for many new ventures.[42]

The Idea Is Marketable and Financially Viable. While it is important to determine whether there are enough customers who are willing to buy the product or service, it is also important to determine whether sales will lead to profits.[43] Estimating market demand requires an initial understanding of who the customers are, what their needs are, and how the product or service will satisfy their needs better than competitors' products. Customers define the competition in terms of who can satisfy their needs best. However, success also requires a thorough understanding of the key competitors who can provide similar products, services, or benefits to the target customer. For example, despite some homegrown success, Vancouver-based ProSnack Natural Foods, a provider of energy bars with organic ingredients, is having difficulty accessing large retailers like MEC that would take them to the next level of sales. The problem is that the market is over-saturated, with more than 50 brands of energy bars lining the shelves of MEC; unfortunately, ProSnack is not one of them.[44]

After learning about the competition and customers, the entrepreneur must prepare a sales forecast. A **sales forecast** is an estimate of how much of a product or service will be purchased by the prospective customers for a specific period of time—typically one year. Total sales revenue is estimated by multiplying the units expected to be sold by the selling price. The sales forecast forms the foundation for determining the financial viability of the venture and the resources needed to start it.

sales forecast An estimate of how much of a product or service will be purchased by the prospective customers for a specific period of time.

Determining financial viability involves preparing financial forecasts, which are two- to three-year projections of a venture's future financial position and performance. They typically consist of an estimate of *start-up costs*, a *cash budget*, an *income statement*, and a *balance sheet* (see Chapter 14 for more detail about these financial documents). A cash budget forecasts the cash receipts and cash disbursements of the business; the income statement shows the profit or loss; and the balance sheet shows the assets (what the business owns), the liabilities (what it owes), and the owners' equity (owners' investment, including any profits that the business retains). These projections serve as the basis for decisions regarding whether to proceed with the venture, and if so, the amount and type of financing to be used in financing the new business.

The Idea Has Low Exit Costs. The final consideration is the venture's **exit costs**. Exit costs are low if a venture can be shut down without a significant loss of time, money, or reputation.[45] If a venture is not expected to make a profit for a number of years, its exit costs will be high, since the project cannot be reasonably abandoned in the short term. However, if the venture is expected to make a profit quickly, its exit costs will be lower, making the idea more attractive. For example, zero-emission car manufacturer Zenn Motors has very long-term projections: An investor in this company must understand that it will not be profitable for many years. Therefore, they must be patient and invest based on its long-term potential.

exit costs The costs in terms of time, money, and reputation that are incurred when a business shuts down.

Developing the Opportunity

As the "dead-end" venture ideas are weeded out, a clear notion of the business concept and an entry strategy for pursuing it need to be developed. As the process proceeds, the business concept often changes from what was originally envisioned. Some new ventures develop entirely new markets, products, and sources of competitive advantage once the needs of the marketplace and the economies of the business are better understood. So, while a vision of what is to be achieved is important, it is equally important to be responsive to new information and to be on the lookout for opportunities that were not originally anticipated. For example, if customers are not placing orders, it is important to find out why and to make the appropriate adjustments.

New ventures use one or more of three main entry strategies: They introduce a totally new product or service; they introduce a product or service that will compete directly with existing competitive offerings but add a new twist (such as offering the option of customizing the standard product); or they franchise.[46]

franchise An arrangement in which a buyer (franchisee) purchases the right to sell the product or service of the seller (franchiser).

A **franchise** is an arrangement in which a buyer (franchisee) purchases the right to sell the product or service of the seller (franchiser). We discuss franchising in more detail later in this chapter.

When capital requirements are high, such as when a manufacturing operation is being proposed, there is a need for considerable research and planning. Similarly, if product development or operations are fairly complex, research and analysis will be needed to ensure that the costs associated with effectively coordinating tasks will be minimized. In these circumstances, or when the aim is to attract potential investors, a comprehensive written business plan will be required. A **business plan** is a document that describes the entrepreneur's proposed business venture, explains why it is an opportunity, and outlines its marketing plan, its operational and financial details, and its managers' skills and abilities.[47] The contents of a business plan are shown in Table 4.3.

business plan A document that describes the entrepreneur's proposed business venture, explains why it is an opportunity, and outlines its marketing plan, its operational and financial details, and its managers' skills and abilities.

If market conditions are changing rapidly, the benefits gained from extensive research and planning diminish quickly. By the time the entrepreneur is ready to start, new competitors may have entered the market, prices may have changed, a location may no longer be available, and so on. Similarly, if the product is highly innovative, market research is of less value because the development of entirely new products involves *creating* needs and wants rather than simply responding to existing needs. Consequently, measuring the capacity of the product or service to fill existing customer needs or wants is less critical.

Contrary to what many people might think, planning does not have to be completed before action is taken. For example, if an electrical contracting business is being proposed in an area where there is a shortage of tradespeople, it would be important to seek out qualified employees prior to conducting other analyses that are needed to complete the business plan. Such early action also helps to build relationships that can be drawn on later. Obviously, some ventures do not lend themselves to early action, particularly those that are capital intensive, such as Zenn Motors. Since most entrepreneurs have limited resources, it is important to concentrate on the issues that can be dealt with *and* that will help determine whether to proceed and how to proceed.[48]

Accessing Resources

Typically, entrepreneurs acquire the various resources needed to make the venture a reality by **bootstrapping**, which means "doing more with less." Usually the term refers to financing techniques whereby entrepreneurs make do with as few resources as possible and use other peoples' resources wherever they can. However, bootstrapping can also refer to the acquisition of other types of resources, such as people, space, equipment, or materials that are loaned or provided free by customers or suppliers.

bootstrapping Financing techniques whereby entrepreneurs make do with as few resources as possible and use other peoples' resources whenever they can.

Financial Resources

There are two main types of financing—*debt* and *equity* (see Chapter 20 for a detailed discussion of debt and equity). Briefly, *debt financing* refers to money that is borrowed. The borrower is obliged to repay the full amount of the loan in addition to interest charges on the debt. The most common sources of debt financing are banks (which provide personal loans), trust companies, co-operatives, finance companies, equipment companies, credit unions, government agencies, and suppliers (who provide goods such as inventory to the entrepreneur with an agreement to bill the entrepreneur later).

Equity financing refers to money that the entrepreneur (or others) invests in a business in return for an ownership interest. Equity investors, as owners, are keenly interested in how any profit will be distributed. The most common sources of equity financing are personal savings (new venture founders draw heavily on their own finances to start their businesses), love money (investments from friends, relatives, and business associates), venture capitalists (who loan money to promising new

TABLE 4.3 A Business Plan

A well-written business plan is formally structured, easy to read, and avoids confusion. Information that is organized into sections is much more manageable and easier to deal with. The amount of detail and the order of presentation may vary from one venture to another and according to the person or organization for whom the plan is being prepared; for example, an investor will typically require more detail than another partner or entrepreneur. An outline for a standard business plan is provided below. While formats vary, with some better suited to the type of venture being proposed than others, most contain the following elements.

I. **Cover Page**: Name of venture and owners, date prepared, contact person, his/her address, telephone and fax numbers, email address, and the name of the organization the plan is being presented to. The easier it is for the reader to contact the entrepreneur, the more likely the contact will occur.

II. **Executive Summary**: A one- to three-page overview of the total business plan. Written after the other sections are completed, it highlights their significant points and aims to create enough excitement to motivate the reader to continue.

III. **Table of Contents**: This element lists major sections with page numbers for both the body and the appendices of the plan.

IV. **Company Description**: Explains the type of company and tells whether it is a manufacturing, retail, service, or other type of business. It also describes the proposed form of organization: sole proprietorship, partnership, corporation, or co-operative. A typical organization of this section is as follows: name and location; company objectives; nature and primary product or service of the business; and current status (start-up, buyout, or expansion) and history if applicable.

V. **Product or Service Description**: Describes the product or service and indicates what is unique about it. This section explains the value that is added for customers—why people will buy the product or service, features of the product or service providing a competitive advantage, legal protection (patents, copyrights, trademarks, if relevant), and dangers of technical or style obsolescence.

VI. **Marketing**: This section has two key parts: the market analysis and the marketing plan. The market analysis convinces the reader that the entrepreneur understands the market for the product or service and can deal effectively with the competition to achieve sales projections. The marketing plan explains the strategy for achieving sales projections.

VII. **Operating Plan**: Explains the type of manufacturing or operating system to be used. Describes the facilities, labour, raw materials, and processing requirements.

VIII. **Management**: Identifies the key players—the management team, active investors, and directors—and cites the experience and competence they possess. This section includes a description of the management team, outside investors and directors and their qualifications, outside resource people, and plans for recruiting and training employees.

IX. **Financial Plan**: Specifies financial needs and contemplated sources of financing. Presents projected financial statements, including a cash budget, a balance sheet, and an income statement.

X. **Supporting Details/Appendix**: Provides supplementary materials to the plan such as résumés and other important supporting data.

ventures in return for a share of ownership in the business), and private investors (also known as *angels*), who are financially well-off entrepreneurs who wish to recycle their wealth by investing in new businesses.

Choosing between debt and equity financing involves trade-offs with regard to potential profitability, financial risk, and control. On the one hand, borrowing money increases the potential for higher rates of return to the entrepreneur when the business is performing well. On the other hand, equity makes it possible to reduce risk by giving up some control. Since a business is at its riskiest point during the start-up phase, equity is usually more appropriate and accessible than debt. However, most new venture founders prefer debt because they are reluctant to give up any control to outsiders. To obtain debt financing the entrepreneur must have an adequate equity investment in the business—typically 20 percent of the business's value—and collateral (or security). **Collateral** refers to items (assets) owned by the business (such as a building and equipment) or by the individual (such as a house or car) that the borrower uses to secure a loan or other credit. These items can be seized by the lender if the loan isn't repaid according to the specified terms. To lenders, equity investment demonstrates the commitment of the entrepreneur, because individuals tend to be more committed to a venture if they have a substantial portion of what they own invested in it.

collateral Items (assets) owned by the business (such as a building and equipment) or by the individual (such as a house or car) that the borrower uses to secure a loan or other credit.

Entrepreneurs who want to obtain financing for a start-up business must have collateral like a house or car in order to get a loan. Would you be willing to give your house or car as collateral, knowing that if you couldn't repay the loan the bank would take them?

Besides these conventional sources of financing, the possibilities for creative boot-strap financing are almost endless. For example, an entrepreneur might require an advance payment from customers, in full or in part. Equipment can be leased rather than purchased (which reduces the risk of equipment becoming obsolete). Office furniture can be rented, premises can be shared, and the manufacture of products can be subcontracted, thereby avoiding the expense of procuring material, equipment, and facilities. All of these activities free up cash, which can then be used for other purposes. The need for cost reduction services is clear; Regus PLC, a temporary rental space company, based out of Dallas, has opened 30 office centres in Canada in the past decade. It has locations in Calgary, Montreal, Toronto, and Vancouver and is opening new locations in Fort McMurray, Halifax, Barrie, and London.[49]

Other Resources

Businesses have other resources to help them with financing and with legal, marketing, or operational advice and support. The federal and provincial governments have a wide range of financial assistance programs for small businesses. Among the various forms of assistance are low-interest loans, loan guarantees, interest-free loans, and wage subsidies. We examine three sources of information and assistance below: the Business Development Bank of Canada, business incubators, and the internet.

Business Development Bank of Canada. The Business Development Bank of Canada (BDC) has a mandate to help develop Canadian businesses, with a particular

focus on small and medium-sized companies. It provides financing, venture capital, and consulting strategies. As we saw in the opening case about online retailer Beyond the Rack, the BDC provides services to over 29 000 businesses from coast to coast and serves them through over 100 branch offices. The BDC is a financial institution wholly owned by the Government of Canada. Information can be found at www.bdc.ca or by calling 1-877-BDC-Banx.[50]

Incubators. Business **incubators** provide new businesses (newborns) with support to help nurture them into a successful future. The type of support varies but some key forms of assistance include consulting services, legal advice, accounting services, business contacts, clerical services, and office space. According to the Canadian Association of Business Incubation (CABI), business survival rates are greatly improved by getting involved with an incubator. Survival rates after five years stand at about 80 percent, which is far above the average rates for businesses that don't use incubators. You can learn more by visiting www.cabi.ca. Take a look at Table 4.4 for examples of incubators across the country.

incubators Provide new businesses with support to help nurture them into a successful future.

The Internet. There are countless resources available online that can help budding entrepreneurs gather research information, write a business plan, and access government grants. The banks all have major sites dedicated to small business and entrepreneurship resources. For example, Royal Bank of Canada (RBC) has a great site that provides checklists, business plan formats and samples, and advice on selecting business structures and more (www.rbcroyalbank.com/sme/index.html). There are also government sites, such as the Canada Business Services for Entrepreneurs, dedicated to providing information and advice on every aspect of starting a business, including accessing government grants (www.canadabusiness.ca/eng).

Businesses may be owned by one person, but entrepreneurship is not a solo process. There are various stakeholders who provide resources to the venture, including partners, employees, customers, suppliers, professionals, consultants, government agencies, lenders, shareholders, and venture capitalists. Sometimes ownership is shared with one or more of these stakeholders in order to acquire the use of their resources. When ownership is shared, decisions must be made about who to share it with, how much each stakeholder will own, at what cost, and under what conditions. The form of legal organization chosen affects whether ownership can be shared and whether resources can be accessed. We discuss this important point later in the chapter.

TABLE 4.4 Business Incubators Across Canada

Name	Location
NRC Institute for Fuel Cell Innovation	Victoria, British Columbia
Duncan McNeill Centre for Innovation	Edmonton, Alberta
Smart Virtual Incubation Winnipeg	Winnipeg, Manitoba
AgriTech Park	Truro, Nova Scotia
The Venture Centre	Pasadena, Newfoundland
NRC Institute for Information Technology	Fredericton, New Brunswick
Mississauga Technology Business Accelerator	Mississauga, Ontario
Saskatchewan Ideas Inc.	Saskatoon, Saskatchewan
J.-Armand-Bombardier Incubator	Montreal, Quebec
LaunchPad Incubator Facility in the Atlantic Technology Centre	Charlottetown, Prince Edward Island

Some small businesses are started by friends who decide to team up. For example, Candice Versace and Dolly Woo started an upscale clothing shop in Winnipeg. There were some interpersonal conflicts at first, but the partners have learned to work together. Stewart Thornhill, who teaches entrepreneurship at the Richard Ivey School of Business, says that friends who operate a business together sometimes have trouble deciding when to quit. He says they should ask themselves this question: "If the person I'm working with wasn't my friend, would I want to be in business with them?"[51]

Deciding whether to share ownership by forming a team involves considering whether having a team is desirable or necessary and whether the aim is to build a company with high growth potential. Whether a team is *necessary* depends upon certain conditions:

- *The size and scope of the venture*: How many people does the venture require? Is it a one-person operation or does it need contributions from others? Can people be hired to fill the key roles as they are required?

- *Personal competencies*: What are the talents, know-how, skills, track record, contacts, and resources that the entrepreneur brings to the venture? How do these match up with what the venture needs to succeed? If gaps are identified, the entrepreneur needs to decide what competencies are needed to complement his or her own and when they are needed.

The nature of the team depends upon the match-up between the lead entrepreneur and the opportunity and how fast and aggressively he or she plans to proceed. Most teams tend to be formed in one of two ways: (a) one person has an idea (or wants to start a business), and then several associates join the team over the first few years of the venture's operation; or (b) an entire team is formed at the outset based on such factors as a shared idea, a friendship, or an experience.

The ideal team consists of people with complementary skills covering the key success areas for the business (for example, marketing, finance, production). Small founding teams tend to work better than big ones. It is quite common for the initial team to consist of just two people—a craftsperson and a salesperson.

If the entrepreneur does not intend to establish a high-growth venture, going solo may be a realistic option. Some new venture founders bring on additional team members only as the business can afford them. Most successful solo businesses are simple types of ventures, such as small retail stores or services.[52] The odds for survival, growth, profitability, and attracting capital are increased by a team approach.[53] Read the E-business and Social Media Solutions case "New Age Entrepreneurs" to learn about the Twitter team and the challenges behind the popular site.

Assessing the "Fit" Between Elements in the Entrepreneurial Process

Assessing the "fit" between the key elements in the entrepreneurial process is an ongoing task, since the shape of the opportunity, and consequently the resources and people needed to capitalize on it, typically change as the opportunity is developed. It is the entrepreneur who stands to gain the most by attending to these "fits" and any changes they may require, although other stakeholders, such as investors, will be considering them as well.

The Entrepreneur–Opportunity Fit

The entrepreneur needs to decide whether the opportunity, as identified, is something he or she *can do* and *wants to do*. A realistic self-assessment is important. Prospective ventures that are of limited personal interest and that require skills and abilities that do not fit well with those of the entrepreneur should be quickly eliminated.

E-BUSINESS + SOCIAL MEDIA SOLUTIONS

New Age Entrepreneurs: The Rise of Twitter

Entrepreneurs have effective new promotion tools thanks to social media sites. But what about the entrepreneurs who created these new information highways? Biz Stone, Jack Dorsey, and Evan Williams created and launched Twitter, the micro-blogging site, in 2006. Before Twitter, Biz Stone helped launch Blogger, Odeo, Obvious, and Xanga. He is a blogging expert who has written two books on the subject. Jack Dorsey is the inventor on the software side of the business and Evan Williams is an entrepreneur who also built internet start-ups like Pyra Labs. A good team, a good idea, and a lot of entrepreneurial spirit, and the next thing you know "tweet" and "re-tweet" are part of our everyday lexicon.

So why is Twitter so popular? It is an instantaneous source of information (not all of it useful) delivered 140 characters at a time. As the website states, it allows you to stay informed on the issues that matter most to you. Today, Twitter is heavily promoting business applications complete with cases in a section called Twitter 101 for Businesses. You can read all about some of the showcase companies. For example, Best Buy has set up "real-time twelp" for instantaneous customer feedback from their "twelp force"; customers send queries to Best Buy's famous technical "geek squad" and receive quick answers to problems. There are also YouTube video demonstrations to provide insight on how to maximize Twitter for small business applications.

Of course, Twitter can also be used to spread negative word of mouth about organizations, so Best Buy's proactive, engaging approach is quite intelligent.

Popularity does not necessarily translate into profitability, however. Biz Stone has faced tough questions from reporters, analysts, and even comedians. When Stone appeared on the Stephen Colbert show, the host mocked him by joking that Biz is obviously not short for "business model." The crowd laughed and Stone smiled, but the issue behind the joke was very real. Popularity is great, but it does not pay the bills: You need a business model that can generate profits. In 2010, Twitter executives announced the creation of "promoted tweets," which enable companies to pay for their messages to be displayed in a more prominent manner on the site while providing Twitter with a new revenue stream. Starbucks and Red Bull were among the first companies to sign up. Even before this decision, companies were using Twitter's social power. Molson used Twitter to help launch Molson 67 and create pre-launch buzz. Authors and musicians also use the site to generate interest. Now Twitter appears ready to cash in on its success. Is this the beginning of sustainable revenues for Twitter? Will the tweeting masses object? It will be interesting to see how this business model evolves.

Critical Thinking Question

1. Are you in favour of promoted tweets? Debate Twitter's decision to implement this model.

For example, it does little good to identify an opportunity for an ecotourism business in a wilderness area if the entrepreneur is a sedentary urban dweller.

Once the entrepreneur has chosen the opportunity he or she wants to pursue, the success of the venture depends heavily upon the individual or individuals involved. No matter how good the product or service concept is, as the opportunity changes shape, it may demand skills a single entrepreneur lacks. This may prompt a decision to acquire the needed skills either by forming a team or by getting further training.

The Opportunity–Resources Fit

Assessing the opportunity–resources fit involves determining whether the resources needed to capitalize on the opportunity can be acquired. As the opportunity changes shape, so, too, will the resource requirements. When challenges or risks arise, the aim is to determine whether they can be resolved and, if so, to deal with them as quickly as possible. For example, if the venture requires a greater financial investment than originally anticipated, this does not necessarily mean that the venture should be abandoned. Other options, such as taking on partners or leasing rather than building a facility, may be viable. Of course, some ventures may not be viable regardless of the alternatives considered.

The Entrepreneur–Resources Fit

Once the resource requirements of the venture have been determined, the entrepreneur needs to assess whether he or she has the capacity to meet those requirements. For example, an entrepreneur with a strong reputation for software development will have an easier time attracting employees for a venture specializing in software development than someone with no track record. If that same entrepreneur is well connected with people in the industry, he or she will be more likely to gain commitments from customers and, in turn, investors.

After the Start-Up

LO4 Describe three *alternative strategies* for becoming a business owner—*starting a business, buying an existing business,* and *buying a franchise.*

Entrepreneurs must make the right decisions as they work toward the start-up of their new venture, but they must also pay attention to how the business will be run beyond the start-up phase. In this section, we examine three important topics that are relevant to these issues. First, we describe the three main ways that entrepreneurs start up a small business. Next, we look at the four main organizing options that are available to entrepreneurs. We conclude the chapter with a look at the reasons for success and failure in small business.

Starting Up a Small Business

In the previous section, we looked in detail at how entrepreneurs start a business from scratch. But there are two additional ways that entrepreneurs can go into business: Buy an already existing business or buy a franchise.

Buying an Already Existing Business

About one-third of all new businesses that were started in the past decade were bought from someone else. Many experts recommend buying an existing business because the odds of success are better. An existing business has already proven its ability to attract customers. It has also established relationships with lenders, suppliers, and other stakeholders. Moreover, an existing track record gives potential buyers a much clearer picture of what to expect than any estimate of a new business's prospects.

But an entrepreneur who buys someone else's business may not be able to avoid certain problems. For example, the business may have a poor reputation, its location may be poor, it may be difficult to determine an appropriate purchase price, and there may be uncertainty about the exact financial shape the business is in.

Taking Over a Family Business. A special case of buying an existing business involves family businesses. Taking over a family business poses both challenges and opportunities. On the positive side, a family business can provide otherwise unobtainable financial and management resources because of the personal sacrifices of family members. Family businesses often have a strong reputation or goodwill that can result in important community and business relationships. As well, employee loyalty is often high, and an interested, unified family management and shareholders group may emerge. Toronto-based hosiery manufacturer Phantom Industries Inc. is an example of a family-owned business that has been successful through three generations.[54]

On the other hand, major problems can arise in family businesses (see the closing case called Family Business for examples). There may be disagreements over which family members assume control. If the parent sells his or her interest in the business, the price to be paid may be an issue. The expectations of other family members may also be problematic. Some family members may feel that they have a right to a job, promotion, and impressive title simply because they are part of the family.[55]

Two other problem areas are choosing an appropriate successor and handling disagreements among family members about the future of the business. How do you fire a loved one if things are not working out?[56]

Buying a Franchise

If you drive or walk around any Canadian town, you will notice retail outlets with names like McDonald's, Pizza Pizza, RE/MAX, Canadian Tire, Chez Cora, Comfort Inn, Second Cup, and Tim Hortons. What do all these businesses have in common? They are all franchises, operating under licences issued by parent companies to local entrepreneurs who own and manage them.

Franchising became very visible in the 1950s with fast-food franchisers like McDonald's, but it actually started in the early 1800s. In the late 1800s, General Motors began franchising retail dealerships, and similar systems were created by Rexall (pharmacies) in 1902 and by Howard Johnson (restaurants and motels) in 1926. Franchising continues to increase in importance in the twenty-first century for large and small ambitions companies. For example, Doug Bourgoyne, founder of FrogBox, an eco-friendly moving box rental company, has used this approach to expand. The company was featured on *Dragons' Den* and won the support of Jim Treliving (of Boston Pizza fame) and Brett Wilson (of Canoe Financial). From this exposure, Mr. Bourgoyne received 1500 applications for franchises in Canada.[57] Depending on how it is defined, franchising now accounts for 40 percent of retail sales in Canada. There are approximately 78 000 franchise establishments in Canada that employ over 1 million people and account for over 10 percent of Canadian GDP.[58]

A franchise is an arrangement that gives franchisees (buyers) the right to sell the product of the franchiser (the seller). A **franchising agreement** outlines the duties and responsibilities of each party. For example, it stipulates the amount and type of payment that franchisees must make to the franchiser. These franchise agreements have become increasingly complicated; they are often between 60 and 100 pages long. Tim Hortons avoids this trend with a streamlined contract of about 26 pages.[59] Franchisees usually make an initial payment for the right to operate a local outlet of the franchise; they also make royalty payments to the franchiser ranging from 2 to

franchising agreement Explains in detail the duties and responsibilities of the franchiser and the franchisee.

Franchising is very popular in Canada. It offers individuals who want to run their own business an opportunity to establish themselves quickly in a local market.

30 percent of the franchisee's annual revenues or profits. The franchisee also pays an advertising fee so that the franchiser can advertise in the franchisee's local area. Franchise fees vary widely, from $23 500 for Mad Science, to over $1 million for a Burger King franchise, to hundreds of millions for a professional sports franchise.

The Advantages of Franchising. Both franchisers and franchisees benefit from the franchising way of doing business (see Table 4.5).

The Disadvantages of Franchising. There are always two sides to any story. Table 4.5 clearly outlines the obvious advantages. However, many experienced people will tell you that buying a franchise is like buying a job. The agreements are long because franchisers want to protect their image and recipes, and they want franchisees to abide by their rules. If they don't, they may be sued. If you have a great new breakfast menu idea for your outlet and have creative promotional ideas, then franchising may not be for you. If things go well it can be lucrative, but it is important to do your homework because there are many disappointed franchise owners out there. For example, you should carefully read the agreement and ensure that your territory is protected and that you have the right of first refusal on new potential stores within a certain distance (e.g., 10–15 kilometres or exclusivity of your particular town). Some franchisees have been shocked to see their franchiser place a new franchisee a few blocks away or even across the street. Franchisees can benefit from support and advertising, but that does not come for free. For example, a Harvey's franchisee pays a 5 percent royalty fee and a 4 percent advertising fee (based on gross sales), and these fees are payable each week in addition to regular operating costs and rent.[60] There are plenty of franchisees who belong to popular chains that are barely surviving and are wondering whatever happened to that promised success.

TABLE 4.5 The Benefits of Franchising

For the Franchiser

- The franchiser can attain rapid growth for the chain by signing up many franchisees in many different locations.
- Franchisees share in the cost of advertising.
- The franchiser benefits from the investment money provided by franchisees.
- Advertising money is spent more efficiently (the franchiser teams up with local franchisees to advertise only in the local area).
- The franchiser benefits because franchisees are motivated to work hard for themselves; the more revenue the franchisee generates, the more money the franchiser makes.
- The franchiser is freed from all details of a local operation, which are handled by the franchisee.

For the Franchisee

- Franchisees own a small business that has access to big business management skills.
- The franchisee does not have to build up a business from scratch.
- Franchisee failure rates are lower than rates for those who start their own business.
- A well-advertised brand name comes with the franchise and the franchisee's outlet is recognizable because it looks like all other outlets in the chain.
- The franchiser may send the franchisee to a training program run by the franchiser (e.g., the Canadian Institute of Hamburgerology run by McDonald's).
- The franchiser may visit the franchisee and provide expert advice on how to run the business.
- Economies in buying allow franchisees to get lower prices for the raw materials they must purchase.
- Financial assistance is provided by the franchiser in the form of loans; the franchiser may also help the franchisee obtain loans from local sources.
- Franchisees are their own bosses and get to keep most of the profit they make.

Is Franchising for You? Do you think you would be happy being a franchisee? The answer depends on a number of factors, including your willingness to work hard, your ability to find a good franchise to buy, and the financial resources you possess. If you are thinking seriously of going into franchising, you should consider several areas of costs that you will incur:

- the franchise sales price

- expenses that will be incurred before the business opens

- training expenses

- operational expenses for the first six months

- personal financial needs for the first six months

- emergency needs

Forms of Business Ownership

Whether they intend to run a small farm, a large factory, an online retail business, a hair salon, or any one of many other types of business, entrepreneurs must decide which form of legal ownership best suits their needs. Four options are available: the sole proprietorship, the partnership, the corporation, and the co-operative.

Describe four forms of *legal organization* for a business and discuss the advantages and disadvantages of each.

The Sole Proprietorship

The **sole proprietorship** is a business owned and operated by one person. Legally, if you set up a business as a sole proprietorship, your business is considered to be an extension of yourself (and not a separate legal entity). Though usually small, a sole proprietorship may be as large as a steel mill or as small as a lemonade stand. While the majority of businesses in Canada are sole proprietorships, this form of ownership accounts for only a small proportion of total business revenues.

sole proprietorship A business owned and operated by one person.

Advantages of a Sole Proprietorship

Freedom may be the most important benefit of a sole proprietorship. Sole proprietors answer to no one but themselves since they don't share ownership. A sole proprietorship is also easy to form. If you operate the business under your own name, with no additions, you don't even need to register your business name to start operating as a sole proprietor; you can go into business simply by putting a sign on the door. The simplicity of legal set-up procedures makes this form appealing to self-starters and independent spirits, as do low start-up costs.

Another attractive feature is tax benefits. Most businesses suffer losses in their early stages. Since the business and the proprietor are legally one and the same, these losses can be deducted from income the proprietor earns from personal sources other than the business.

Disadvantages of a Sole Proprietorship

A major drawback is **unlimited liability**. A sole proprietor is personally liable (responsible) for all debts incurred by the business. If the business fails to generate enough cash, bills must be paid out of the owner's pocket. Another disadvantage is the lack of continuity; a sole proprietorship legally dissolves when the owner dies. Finally, a sole proprietorship depends on the resources of one person, and that person's managerial and financial limitations may constrain the business. Sole proprietors often find it hard to borrow money to start up or expand. Many bankers fear that they won't be able to recover loans if the owner becomes disabled.

unlimited liability A sole proprietor is personally liable (responsible) for all debts incurred by the business.

The Partnership

partnership A form of organization established when two or more individuals agree to combine their financial, managerial, and technical abilities for the purpose of operating a business for profit.

The **partnership**, a form of organization often used by professionals like accountants and lawyers, is established when two or more individuals (partners) agree to combine their financial, managerial, and technical abilities for the purpose of operating a business for profit. Partnerships are often an extension of a business that began as a sole proprietorship. The original owner may want to expand, or the business may have grown too big for a single person to handle.

general partners Partners who are actively involved in managing the firm and have unlimited liability.

limited partners Partners who generally do not participate actively in the business, and whose liability is limited to the amount they invested in the partnership.

general partnership A type of partnership in which all partners are jointly liable for the obligations of the business.

limited partnership A type of partnership with at least one general partner (who has unlimited liability) and one or more limited partners. The limited partners cannot participate in the day-to-day management of the business or they risk the loss of their limited liability status.

There are two basic types of partners in a partnership. **General partners** are actively involved in managing the firm and have unlimited liability. **Limited partners** don't participate actively in the business, and their liability is limited to the amount they invested in the partnership. A **general partnership** is the most common type of partnership and is similar in nature to the sole proprietorship in that all the (general) partners are jointly liable for the obligations of the business. The other type of partnership—a **limited partnership**—consists of at least one general partner (who has unlimited liability) and one or more limited partners (who have limited liability). The limited partners cannot participate in the day-to-day management of the business or they risk the loss of their limited liability status.

Advantages of a Partnership

The most striking advantage of a general partnership is the ability to grow by adding talent and money. Partnerships also have a somewhat easier time borrowing funds than do sole proprietorships because banks and other lending institutions prefer to make loans to enterprises that are not dependent on a single individual. Partnerships can also invite new partners to join if they agree to invest money in the firm.

Like a sole proprietorship, a partnership is simple to organize, with few legal requirements. Even so, all partnerships must begin with an agreement of some kind. It may be written, oral, or even unspoken. Wise partners, however, insist on a written agreement to avoid trouble later. This agreement should answer several questions:

- How will disagreements be resolved?
- Who invested what sums of money in the partnership?
- Who will receive what share of the partnership's profits?
- Who does what and who reports to whom?
- How will the partnership be dissolved?
- How will leftover assets be distributed among the partners?

The partnership agreement is strictly a private document. Partners are not required by law to file an agreement with some government agency, and partnerships are not regarded as legal entities. In the eyes of the law, a partnership is nothing more than two or more persons working together. The partnership's lack of legal standing means that the partners are taxed as individuals.

Disadvantages of a Partnership

As with sole proprietorships, unlimited liability is the greatest drawback of a general partnership. By law, each general partner may be held personally liable for all debts incurred in the name of the partnership. And if any partner incurs a debt, even if the other partners know nothing about it, they are all liable if the offending partner cannot pay up. Another problem with partnerships is lack of continuity. When one partner dies or pulls out, the partnership dissolves, even if the other partners agree to stay to continue the business.

A related drawback is the difficulty of transferring ownership. No partner may sell out without the other partners' consent. Thus, the life of a partnership may depend on the ability of retiring partners to find someone compatible with the other partners to buy them out. Finally, a partnership provides little or no guidance in resolving conflict between the partners. For example, suppose one partner wants to expand the business rapidly and the other wants it to grow slowly. If under the partnership agreement the two are equal, it may be difficult for them to decide what to do.

The Corporation

When you think of corporations you probably think of giant businesses such as Air Canada, Imperial Oil, or RIM. The very word *corporation* suggests bigness and power. Yet, the tiny corner newsstand has as much right to incorporate as does a giant oil refiner. And the newsstand and oil refiner have the same basic characteristics that all corporations share: legal status as a separate entity, property rights and obligations, and an indefinite lifespan. The Top 10 corporations in Canada are listed in Table 4.6.

A **corporation** has been defined as "an artificial being, invisible, intangible, and existing only in contemplation of the law."[61] As such, corporations may sue and be sued; buy, hold, and sell property; make and sell products to consumers; and commit crimes and be tried and punished for them. Simply defined, a corporation is a business that is a separate legal entity that is liable for its own debts and whose owners' liability is limited to their investment.

corporation A business that is a separate legal entity that is liable for its own debts and whose owners' liability is limited to their investment.

Shareholders—investors who buy shares of ownership in the form of stock—are the real owners of the corporation (the different kinds of shareholders are described in Chapter 19). Profits may be distributed to shareholders in the form of dividends, although corporations are not required to pay dividends. Instead, they often reinvest any profits in the business.

shareholders Investors who buy shares of ownership in the form of stock.

The **board of directors** is the governing body of a corporation. Its basic responsibility is to ensure that the corporation is run in a way that is in the best interests of the shareholders. The board chooses the president and other officers of the business and delegates the power to run the day-to-day activities of the business to those officers. The board sets policy on paying dividends, on financing major spending, and on executive salaries and benefits. Large corporations tend to have large boards with as many as 20 or 30 directors. Smaller corporations, on the other hand, tend to have no more than five directors.

board of directors The governing body of a corporation whose basic responsibility is to ensure that the corporation is run in a way that is in the best interests of the shareholders.

TABLE 4.6 Top 10 Corporations in Canada, 2011 (Ranked by Sales Revenues)		
	Company	**Sales Revenues (billions of dollars)**
1.	Manulife Financial Corp.	50.9
2.	Suncor Energy Inc.	39.6
3.	Royal Bank of Canada	35.7
4.	Power Corp. of Canada	32.9
5.	George Weston Ltd.	32.3
6.	Imperial Oil Ltd.	30.4
7.	Magna International Inc.	28.4
8.	Toronto-Dominion Bank	27.2
9.	Bank of Nova Scotia	26.7
10.	Onex Corp.	24.3

Each year, *The Globe and Mail* analyzes the governance practices of Canadian companies in four areas: board composition, compensation, shareholder rights, and disclosure. The top-ranked companies in 2010 were Loblaw Corp., George Weston Corp., and IamGold Corp. The lowest-ranked companies were Shaw Communications and Biovail.[62]

inside directors Members of a corporation's board of directors who are employees of the company and have primary responsibility for the corporation.

Inside directors are employees of the company and have primary responsibility for the corporation. That is, they are also top managers, such as the president and executive vice-president. **Outside directors** are not employees of the corporation in the normal course of its business. Attorneys, accountants, university officials, and executives from other firms are commonly used as outside directors.

outside directors Members of a corporation's board of directors who are not employees of the corporation on a day-to-day basis.

Corporate officers are the top managers hired by the board to run the corporation on a day-to-day basis. The **chief executive officer (CEO)** is responsible for the firm's overall performance. Other corporate officers typically include the president, who is responsible for internal management, and various vice-presidents, who oversee functional areas such as marketing or operations.

chief executive officer (CEO) The person responsible for the firm's overall performance.

Types of Corporations

public corporation A business whose shares of stock are widely held and available for sale to the general public.

There are two types of private sector corporations (corporations can also be found in the municipal, provincial, federal, and non-profit sectors). The **public corporation** is a business whose shares of stock are widely held and available for sale to the general public. The shares of public corporations like Petro-Canada, Bombardier, and Air Canada are traded on securities exchanges and are widely available to the general public for purchase (see Chapter 19). By contrast, the shares of stock of a **private corporation** are held by only a few shareholders, are not widely available for purchase, and may have restrictions on their sale. For example, Kroeker Farms, a large agri-business in Manitoba, is owned by nine members of one family. Other private corporations are Para Paints of Canada, The Jim Pattison Group, and Cirque du Soleil. Most corporations are privately held.

private corporation A business whose shares of stock are held by only a few shareholders, are not widely available for purchase, and may have restrictions on their sale.

Most new corporations start out as private corporations, because few investors will buy an unknown stock. As the corporation grows and develops a record of success, it may issue shares to the public ("go public") as a way of raising additional money. This is called its **initial public offering (IPO)**. IPOs are not very attractive to investors during stock market declines, but they become more popular when stock markets recover. Market turbulence was one of the reasons Porter Aviation withdrew plans for an IPO in 2010 and again in 2011.[63] However, other companies moved forward during that same time despite turbulent markets: Capital Power Corp. raised $500 million from its IPO and retailer Dollarama raised $300 million.[64] A public corporation can also "go private," which is the reverse of going public. For example, Clearwater Seafoods Income Fund announced that it would be taken private by a consortium led by Clearwater Fine Foods.[65]

initial public offering (IPO) The sale of shares of stock in a company for the first time to the general investing public.

income trust Involves corporations distributing all or most of their earnings to investors and thereby reducing the corporation's income tax liability.

During the period from 2000 to 2005, many corporations converted to an **income trust** structure, which allowed them to avoid paying corporate income tax if they distributed all or most of their earnings to investors. For example, Bell Canada Enterprises could have avoided an $800-million tax bill in one year by becoming an income trust. The federal government estimated that it was going to lose billions of dollars of tax revenue because so many corporations were becoming income trusts. In a surprise move in 2006, the Canadian government announced that it would begin taxing income trusts more like corporations by 2011. This announcement caused a significant decline in the market value of income trusts, and ultimately meant that very few corporations chose to convert to an income trust structure.[66] By 2010, income trusts were widely being ignored in the markets; however, according to Alex Sasso of Hesperian Capital Management, there were many hidden gems in the market, such as Black Diamond Group, a provider of temporary workforce accommodation to the energy, mining, and other sectors.[67]

Formation of the Corporation

The two most widely used methods to form a corporation are federal incorporation under the Canada Business Corporations Act and provincial incorporation under any of the provincial corporations acts. The former is used if the company is going to operate in more than one province; the latter is used if the founders intend to carry on business in only one province. Except for banks and certain insurance and loan companies, any company can be federally incorporated under the Canada Business Corporations Act. To do so, it must draw up articles of incorporation. These articles include such information as the name of the corporation, the type and number of shares to be issued, the number of directors the corporation will have, and the location of the company's operations. The specific procedures and information required for provincial incorporation vary from province to province.

All corporations must attach the word *Limited* (Ltd./Ltée), *Incorporated* (Inc.), or *Corporation* (Corp.) to the company name to indicate clearly to customers and suppliers that the owners have limited liability for corporate debts. The same sorts of rules apply in other countries. British firms, for example, use PLC for "public limited company" and German companies use AG for "Aktiengesellschaft" (corporation).

Advantages of Incorporation

The biggest advantage of the corporate structure is **limited liability**, which means that the liability of investors is limited to their personal investment in the corporation. In the event of failure, the courts may seize a corporation's assets and sell them to pay debts, but the courts cannot touch the investors' personal possessions. If, for example, you invest $25 000 in a corporation that goes bankrupt, you may lose your $25 000 but no more. In other words, your liability is limited to $25 000.

> **limited liability** The liability of investors is limited to their personal investment in the corporation.

Another advantage of a corporation is continuity. Because it has a legal life independent of its founders and owners, a corporation can, in theory, continue forever. Shares of stock may be sold or passed on to heirs, and most corporations also benefit from the continuity provided by professional management. Finally, corporations have advantages in raising money. By selling shares of stock, they expand the number of investors and the amount of available funds. The term **stock** refers to a share of ownership in a corporation. Continuity and legal status tend to make lenders more willing to grant loans to corporations.

> **stock** A share of ownership in a corporation.

Disadvantages of Incorporation

One of the disadvantages for a new firm in forming a corporation is the cost (approximately $2500). Corporations also need legal help in meeting government regulations because they are far more heavily regulated than are proprietorships or partnerships. Some people say that **double taxation** is another problem with the corporate form of ownership. By this they mean that a corporation must pay corporate income taxes on its profits, and then shareholders must also pay personal income taxes on the dividends they receive from the corporation. The **dividend** a corporation pays is the amount of money, normally a portion of the profits, that is distributed to the shareholders. Since dividends paid by the corporation are not tax deductible for the corporation, this amounts to double taxation. Others point out that shareholders get a "dividend tax credit," which largely offsets the effect of double taxation.

> **double taxation** A corporation must pay corporate income taxes on its profits, and then shareholders must also pay personal income taxes on the dividends they receive from the corporation.

> **dividend** The amount of money, normally a portion of the profits, that is distributed to the shareholders by the corporation.

The Co-operative

A **co-operative** is an incorporated form of business that is organized, owned, and democratically controlled by the people who use its products and services, and whose earnings are distributed on the basis of their use of the co-operative rather than their level of investment. As such, it is formed to benefit its owners in the form of reduced

> **co-operative** An incorporated form of business that is organized, owned, and democratically controlled by the people who use its products and services, and whose earnings are distributed on the basis of their use of the co-operative rather than their level of investment.

prices and/or the distribution of surpluses at year-end. The process works like this: Suppose some farmers believe they can get cheaper fertilizer prices if they form their own company and purchase in large volumes. They might then form a co-operative, which can be either federally or provincially chartered. Prices are generally lower to buyers and, at the end of the fiscal year, any surpluses are distributed to members on the basis of how much they purchased. If Farmer Jones bought 5 percent of all co-op sales, he would receive 5 percent of the surplus.

The co-operative's start-up capital usually comes from shares purchased by the co-operative's members. Sometimes all it takes to qualify for membership in a co-operative is the purchase of one share with a fixed (and often nominal) value. Federal co-operatives, however, can raise capital by issuing investment shares to members or non-members. Co-operatives, like investor-owned corporations, have directors and appointed officers. In a co-operative, each member is entitled to one vote, regardless of how many shares he or she owns.

Types of Co-operatives

There are hundreds of different co-operatives, but they generally function in one of six main areas of business:

- *Consumer co-operatives.* These organizations sell goods to both members and the general public (e.g., Mountain Equipment Co-Op)

- *Financial co-operatives.* These organizations operate much like banks, accepting deposits from members, giving loans, and providing chequing services (e.g., Vancouver City Savings Credit Union).

- *Insurance co-operatives.* These organizations provide many types of insurance coverage, such as life, fire, and liability (e.g., the Co-operative Hail Insurance Company of Manitoba).

- *Marketing co-operatives.* These organizations sell the produce of their farm members and purchase inputs for the production process (e.g., seed and fertilizer). Some, like Federated Co-operatives, also purchase and market finished products.

- *Service co-operatives.* These organizations provide members with services, such as recreation.

- *Housing co-operatives.* These organizations provide housing for members who purchase a share in the co-operative, which holds the title to the housing complex.

In terms of numbers, co-operatives are the least important form of ownership. However, they are of significance to society and to their members since they may provide services that are not readily available or that cost more than the members would otherwise be willing to pay. Table 4.7 compares the various forms of business ownership using different characteristics.

Advantages of a Co-operative

Co-operatives have many of the same advantages of investor-owned corporations, such as limited liability of owners and continuity. A key benefit of a co-operative relates to its structure. As noted above, each member has only one vote in the affairs of the co-operative, regardless of how many shares he or she holds. This system prevents financial control of the business by a few wealthy individuals. This is particularly attractive to the less-wealthy members of the co-operative.

Unlike corporations, which are not allowed a tax deduction on dividend payments made to shareholders, co-operatives are allowed to deduct patronage refunds to members out of before-tax income. Thus, income may be taxed only at the individual member level rather than at both the co-operative and member level.[68]

Vancouver-based Mountain Equipment Co-op is one of the best-known co-operatives in Canada.

TABLE 4.7 A Comparison of Four Forms of Business Ownership

Characteristic	Sole Proprietorship	Partnership	Corporation	Co-operative
Protection against liability for bad debts	low	low	high	high
Ease of formation	high	high	medium	medium
Permanence	low	low	high	high
Ease of ownership transfer	low	low	high	high
Ease of raising money	low	medium	high	high
Freedom from regulation	high	high	low	medium
Tax advantages	high	high	low	high

Disadvantages of a Co-operative

One of the main disadvantages of co-operatives relates to attracting equity investment. Since the benefits from being a member of a co-operative arise through the level of use of the co-operative rather than the level of equity invested, members do not have an incentive to invest in equity capital of the co-operative. Another drawback is that democratic voting arrangements and dividends based purely on patronage turn off some entrepreneurs from forming or joining a co-operative.

Success and Failure in Small Business

Of every 100 small businesses that begin operation, 85 will still be operating after one year, 70 after two years, and 51 after five years.[69] A study conducted by CIBC World Markets found that small businesses with above-average revenue growth were run by owners who had more education, used professional advisers, adopted the corporate form of ownership, did outsourcing work for other companies, had a high level of internet connectivity, and used the internet to sell outside of Canada.[70]

Identify four key reasons for success **L06** in *small businesses* and four key reasons for failure.

Reasons for Success

In addition to the specific findings of the CIBC study, four general factors typically explain the success of small business owners:

1. *Hard work, drive, and dedication.* Small business owners must be committed to succeeding and be willing to put in the time and effort to make it happen. Long hours and few vacations generally characterize the first few years of new business ownership.

2. *Market demand for the product or service.* Careful analysis of market conditions can help small business owners assess the probable reception of their products. If the area around a college has only one pizza parlour, a new pizzeria is more likely to succeed than if there are already 10 in operation.

3. *Managerial competence.* Successful small business people have a solid understanding of how to manage a business. They may acquire competence through training (taking courses), experience, or by using the expertise of others. Few, however, succeed alone or straight out of university or college. Most spend time in successful companies or partner with others to bring expertise to a new business.

4. *Luck.* Luck also plays a role in the success of some firms. For example, after one entrepreneur started an environmental clean-up firm, he struggled to keep his business

afloat. Then the government committed a large sum of money for toxic waste clean-up. He was able to get several large contracts and his business is now thriving.

Reasons for Failure

Small businesses collapse for a number of reasons (see Table 4.8). Entrepreneurs may have no control over some of these factors (for example, weather, fraud, accidents), but they can influence most items on the list. Four general factors are particularly important:

1. *Managerial incompetence or inexperience.* Some entrepreneurs put their faith in common sense, overestimate their own managerial skills, or believe that hard work alone ensures success. If entrepreneurs don't know how to make basic business decisions or don't understand basic management principles, they aren't likely to succeed in the long run.

2. *Neglect.* Some entrepreneurs try to launch ventures in their spare time, and others devote only limited time to their new business. But starting a small business demands an overwhelming time commitment. If you aren't willing to put in the time and effort that a business requires, you aren't likely to survive.

3. *Weak control systems.* Effective control systems keep a business on track and alert owners to potential trouble. If your control systems don't signal impending problems, you may be in serious trouble before you spot more obvious difficulties.

4. *Insufficient capital.* Some entrepreneurs are overly optimistic about how soon they'll start earning profits. In most cases, it takes months or even years. Amazon.com didn't earn a profit for 10 years but obviously still required capital to pay employees and to cover other expenses. Experts say you need enough capital to operate at least six months without earning a profit; some recommend enough to last a year.[71]

TABLE 4.8 Causes of Small Business Failure

Poor Management Skills	Personal Reasons
■ poor delegation and organizational ability ■ lack of depth in management team ■ entrepreneurial incompetence, such as a poor understanding of finances and business markets ■ lack of experience	■ loss of interest in business ■ accident, illness ■ death ■ family problems

Inadequate Marketing Capabilities	Disasters
■ difficulty in marketing product ■ market too small, non-existent, or declining ■ too much competition ■ problems with distribution systems	■ fire ■ weather ■ strikes ■ fraud by entrepreneur or others

Inadequate Financial Capabilities	Other
■ weak skills in accounting and finance ■ lack of budgetary control ■ inadequate costing systems ■ incorrect valuation of assets ■ unable to obtain financial backing	■ mishandling of large project ■ excessive standard of living ■ lack of time to devote to business ■ difficulties with associates or partners ■ government policies change

Inadequate Production Capabilities

■ poorly designed production systems
■ old and inefficient production facilities and equipment
■ inadequate control over quality
■ problems with inventory control

MyBizLab

Capture more moments of true understanding. MyBizLab provides you with interactive study and practice tools directly related to this chapter's content. The new MyBizLab Study Plan Learning Path is designed to measure a full range of skills and provide remediation to give you what you need to master key chapter concepts. MyBizLab flexes to your unique learning needs. The result? Inspired learning, more success.

SUMMARY OF LEARNING OBJECTIVES

1. **Explain the meaning of and interrelationship among the terms** *small business*, *new venture creation*, **and** *entrepreneurship*. A *small business* has fewer than 100 employees. A *new venture* is one that has become operational within the previous 12 months, has adopted any of four main organizational forms—sole proprietorship, partnership, corporation, or co-operative—and sells goods or services. *Entrepreneurship* is the process of identifying an opportunity in the marketplace and accessing the resources needed to capitalize on it. In relation to small and/or new businesses, entrepreneurship is the process by which a small business or a new business is created.

2. **Describe the role of small and new businesses in the** *Canadian economy*. New firms create the most jobs, are noted for their entrepreneurship, and are typically small. The small business sector's capacity for entrepreneurship and innovation accounts for much of the job creation this sector contributes to the economy, with start-ups accounting for most of the growth. As the number of businesses has increased, so, too, has the number of firms led by women. About 98 percent of employer businesses in Canada are small (they have fewer than 100 employees), and the majority of those have fewer than five employees. The distribution of employment by size of firm varies considerably across industries. Small businesses account for over two-thirds of employment in five industries: non-institutional health care, forestry, other services, the construction industry, and accommodation and food. In another five industries, at least half of the workforce is employed by small businesses.

3. **Explain the** *entrepreneurial process* **and describe its three key elements.** The *entrepreneurial process* occurs within a social, political, and economic context and consists of three key elements: the *entrepreneur*, the opportunity, and resources. The entrepreneur is the driving force in identifying an opportunity and accessing the resources to capitalize on it. Opportunities don't simply materialize; entrepreneurs create them. *Opportunity* identification involves generating ideas, screening them to determine their potential, and developing the ones that remain. Entrepreneurs typically access the various resources needed by *bootstrapping*— doing more with less. These resources are both financial and non-financial. Two types of financing—debt and equity—can be accessed from a range of sources.

4. **Describe three** *alternative strategies* **for becoming a business owner**—*starting a business*, *buying an existing business*, **and** *buying a franchise*. It is necessary to work through the *entrepreneurial process when starting a business from scratch*. Whether start-up efforts will result in a new business often depends upon how well matched the entrepreneur's skills and abilities are with the opportunity and the resources required, as well as how well matched the opportunity and resources are. Of the ventures that are brought to fruition, some will grow, while others will decline, die, or remain stable.

Generally, *when buying an existing business*, the odds of success are better. An existing business has already proven its ability to attract customers. It has also established relationships with lenders, suppliers, and other stakeholders. Moreover, an existing track record gives potential buyers a much clearer picture of what to expect than any estimate of a new business's prospects. However, there are also drawbacks: There may be uncertainty about the exact financial shape the business is in, the business may have a poor reputation, the location may be poor, or it may be difficult to determine an appropriate purchase price. A special case of buying an existing business involves family businesses, which pose both opportunities and challenges.

In *buying a franchise*, the buyer (franchisee) purchases the right to sell the product or service of the seller (franchiser) according to the terms of the franchising agreement. In return the franchiser provides assistance with the business's start-up as well as with ongoing operations once the business opens its doors.

5. **Describe four forms of** *legal organization* **for a business and discuss the advantages and disadvantages of each.** A *sole proprietorship* is a business owned and operated by one person. Answering only to themselves, sole proprietors enjoy considerable freedom in running the business. The ease of setting up a sole proprietorship makes it appealing to self-starters, as do the low start-up costs and the tax benefits. A major drawback is unlimited liability. A sole proprietor is personally liable for all debts incurred by the business. Another disadvantage is lack of continuity. A sole proprietorship dissolves when the owner dies. Finally, a sole proprietorship depends on the resources of a single individual.

A *general partnership* is similar to a sole proprietorship in that all partners have unlimited liability for the obligations of the business. The biggest advantage is its ability to grow by adding new talent and money. Because banks prefer to make loans to enterprises that are not dependent on single individuals, it's easier for partnerships to borrow money. They can also invite new partners to join by investing. Although a partnership is easy to form and has few legal requirements, all partnerships should have a partnership agreement. Partners are taxed as individuals, and unlimited liability is a drawback. Each partner may be liable for all partnership debts. Partnerships may lack continuity, and transferring ownership may be hard. No partner may sell out without the consent of the others.

All *corporations* share certain characteristics. They are separate legal entities, they have property rights and obligations, and they have indefinite life spans. They may sue and be sued; buy, hold, and sell property; make and sell products; and be tried and punished for crimes committed. The biggest advantage of incorporation is limited liability; that is, investor liability is limited to one's personal investments in the corporation. If the business fails, the courts may sell a corporation's assets but cannot touch the personal possessions of investors. Another advantage is continuity—a corporation can continue forever. Shares can be sold or passed on to heirs, and most corporations benefit from the continuity of professional management. Finally, corporations have advantages in raising money. By selling stock, they expand the number of investors and the amount of available funds. Legal protections tend to make lenders more willing to grant loans. Start-up costs and complexity are among the disadvantages of incorporating. Corporations are heavily regulated and must meet complex legal requirements in the provinces in which they're chartered. A potential drawback to incorporation is *double taxation*. A corporation pays income taxes on company profits, and its shareholders pay taxes on income returned by their investments. Thus, corporate profits are taxed twice—at the corporate and at ownership levels (although the dividend tax credit given to owners may offset the effects of double taxation). Of the two types of private sector corporations—public and privately held—the vast majority are privately held. In forming a corporation, a business will incorporate federally if it is going to operate in more than one province and provincially if it is going to operate in only one province.

A *co-operative* is an organization that is formed to benefit its owners in the form of reduced prices and/or the distribution of surpluses at year-end. It is an incorporated business that is organized, owned, and democratically controlled by the people who use its products and services. The distribution of its earnings (or surpluses) is based upon the use of the co-operative rather than the level of investment. In addition to the two main advantages co-operatives share with corporations—limited liability and continuity—they also have two benefits that corporations don't have. Since all members have one vote, this democratic control means that a few people cannot dominate the decision making. Additionally, co-operatives aren't subject to double taxation, since surpluses are distributed to members from pre-tax profits. Co-operatives are not without disadvantages, however. The main drawback is that co-operatives often have difficulty raising equity, since members gain financial benefit according to their use of the co-operative, not according to the amount they have invested. While there are hundreds of different co-operatives, they usually function in one of six areas of business: consumer co-operatives, financial co-operatives, insurance co-operatives, marketing co-operatives, service co-operatives, or housing co-operatives.

6. **Identify four key reasons for success in *small businesses* and four key reasons for failure.** Four basic factors explain most small business success: (1) hard work, drive, and dedication; (2) market demand for the product or service; (3) managerial competence; and (4) luck. Four factors contribute to small business failure: (1) managerial incompetence or inexperience; (2) neglect; (3) weak control systems; and (4) insufficient capital.

KEY TERMS

board of directors   (p. 129)
bootstrapping   (p. 118)
business plan   (p. 118)
chief executive officer (CEO)   (p. 130)
collateral   (p. 119)
co-operative   (p. 131)
corporation   (p. 129)
dividend   (p. 131)
double taxation   (p. 131)
entrepreneur   (p. 110)
entrepreneurship   (p. 110)
exit costs   (p. 117)

franchise   (p. 118)
franchising agreement   (p. 125)
general partners   (p. 128)
general partnership   (p. 128)
income trust   (p. 130)
incubators   (p. 121)
initial public offering (IPO)   (p. 130)
inside directors   (p. 130)
intrapreneuring   (p. 110)
limited liability   (p. 131)
limited partners   (p. 128)
limited partnership   (p. 128)

new venture/firm   (p. 110)
outside directors   (p. 130)
partnership   (p. 128)
private corporation   (p. 130)
public corporation   (p. 130)
sales forecast   (p. 117)
small business   (p. 109)
sole proprietorship   (p. 127)
stock   (p. 131)
shareholders   (p. 129)
unlimited liability   (p. 127)

QUESTIONS FOR ANALYSIS

1. What are some of the problems that are encountered when we try to define the term *small business*?

2. Why are new ventures the main source of job creation and new product/service ideas?

3. Do you think that you would be a successful entrepreneur? Why or why not?

4. Consider a new product or service that has recently become available for purchase by consumers. To what extent did this product or service possess the "screening" characteristics that are described in the chapter (adding value, providing competitive advantage, etc.)?

5. Using the product or service you described in Question 4, analyze the extent to which there is a good "fit" among the various elements in the entrepreneurial process.

6. Why might a corporation choose to remain private? Why might it choose to "go public"?

APPLICATION EXERCISES

1. There are thousands of mobile applications on the various mobile platforms (you probably use some of them on a weekly or daily basis). Identify an idea for a new application that can serve a consumer need that is currently unmet or can be improved upon.

2. Identify three trends—in fashion, lifestyle, or something else—and describe at least five ideas for capitalizing on one of them.

3. Find a newspaper or magazine article that describes someone who is an entrepreneur. Use the information provided to explain what makes this person an entrepreneur.

4. Interview the owners of several small businesses in your area. Ask them what they have done to make their businesses more environmentally friendly. If they have not done anything, ask them what has prevented them from taking the initiative to be more environmentally friendly.

BUILDING YOUR BUSINESS SKILLS

Working the Internet

The Purpose of the Assignment

To encourage students to define opportunities and problems for small companies doing business on the internet.

The Situation

Suppose you and two partners own a gift basket store, specializing in special occasion baskets for individual and corporate clients. Your business is doing well in your community, but you believe there may be opportunity for growth through a virtual storefront on the internet.

Assignment

Step 1

Join with two other students and assume the role of business partners. Start by researching internet businesses. Look at books and articles at the library and check the following websites for help:

- Canadian Business Service Centres: www.canadabusiness.ca/eng
- U.S. Small Business Administration: www.sba.gov
- IBM Small Business Center: www.businesscenter.ibm.com
- Apple Small Business home page: www.apple.com/business

These sites may lead you to other sites, so keep an open mind.

Step 2

Based on your research, determine the importance of the following small business issues:

- an analysis of changing company finances as a result of expansion to the internet
- an analysis of your new competitive marketplace (the world) and how it affects your current marketing approach, which focusses on your local community
- identification of sources of management advice as the expansion proceeds
- the role of technology consultants in launching and maintaining the website
- customer service policies in your virtual environment

Questions for Discussion

1. Do you think your business would be successful on the internet? Why or why not?

2. Based on your analysis, how will internet expansion affect your current business practices? What specific changes are you likely to make?

3. Do you think that operating a virtual storefront will be harder or easier than doing business in your local community? Explain your answer.

EXERCISING YOUR ETHICS: TEAM EXERCISE

Public or Private? That Is the Question

The Situation

The Thomas Corporation is a very well-financed private corporation with a solid and growing product line, little debt, and a stable workforce. However, in the past few months, there has been a growing rift among the board of directors that has created considerable differences of opinion as to the future directions of the firm.

The Dilemma

Some board members believe the firm should "go public" with a stock offering. Since each board member owns a large block of corporate stock, ach would make a considerable amount of money if the company went public.

Other board members want to maintain the status quo as a private corporation. The biggest advantage of this approach is that the firm maintains its current ability to remain autonomous in its operations.

The third faction of the board also wants to remain private but clearly has a different agenda. Those board members have identified a small public corporation that is currently one of the company's key suppliers. Their idea is to buy the supplying company, shift its assets to the parent firm, sell all of its remaining operations, terminate employees, and then outsource the production of the parts it currently buys from the firm. Their logic is that the firm would gain significant assets and lower its costs.

Team Activity

Assemble a group of four students and assign each group member to one of the following roles:

- an employee at the Thomas Corporation
- a customer of the Thomas Corporation
- an investor in the Thomas Corporation
- a board member who has not yet decided which option is best

Action Steps

1. Before discussing the situation with your group, and from the perspective of your assigned role, which option do you think is best? Write down the reasons for your position.
2. Before discussing the situation with your group, and from the perspective of your assigned role, what are the underlying ethical issues, if any, in this situation? Write down the issues.
3. Gather your group together and reveal, in turn, each member's comments on the situation. Next, reveal the ethical issues listed by each member.
4. Appoint someone to record the main points of agreement and disagreement within the group. How do you explain the results? What accounts for any disagreement?
5. From an ethical standpoint, what does your group conclude is the most appropriate action that should be taken by the Thomas Corporation in this situation?
6. Develop a group response to the following question: What do you think most people would do in this situation?

Go to MyBizLab for additional cases and exercise material.

CONCLUDING CASE 4-1

Parasuco Jeans: The Story of a Born Entrepreneur

Salvatore Parasuco's company recently celebrated its thirty-fifth year of operation, so his successful denim business is definitely not a new venture, but it is a great tale of entrepreneurship. Words like *drive, determination, self-starter*, and *vision* are commonly used to describe entrepreneurs. All of these terms fit the founder of Parasuco Jeans to a T. The story begins with a budding entrepreneur whose ambition was announced at a very young age when he began selling jeans out of his high school locker in Montreal. As legend has it, he managed to convince his principal to let him sell the jeans by telling him he needed to make money to help support his family and avoid going down the wrong path. Today, Parasuco Jeans are sold in locations around the world with distribution in Canada, the United States, Europe, and Asia. The company has a particularly good presence in Italy, Hong Kong, Russia, Japan, and Korea. Celebrities such as Jessica Alba, Kate Hudson, Chris Daughtry, and many more have been photographed wearing a pair of Parasuco's trendy jeans. Yet despite the success and the longevity of the brand it does not have as much visibility across Canada as the owner thinks it deserves. He openly wonders why we Canadians (and the local media in particular) aren't as patriotic toward our homegrown brands as Americans are.

Salvatore is a Canadian whose family came here from Italy when he was just a young boy. From his humble beginnings, he learned the value of a dollar and credits his father for teaching him the art of negotiation at an early age. The rise of Parasuco Jeans is not a modern-day instant success story with a major internet IPO launch. It is a story about blood, sweat, and some tears. Before getting into the denim design business, Salvatore opened a clothing store, where he learned a lot about the business that would become his life's work. Mr. Parasuco launched Santana Jeans in 1975 and changed the name to Parasuco due to legal issues in 1988. From the early days it was clear that innovation and design would be at the foundation of the company. Parasuco was the first to launch pre-washed jeans in Canada. The company was also the first brand to introduce stretch denim to the market, a product feature that is central to the company image to this day. In a recent interview, the owner talked about how customers tend to instinctively start to stretch and pull his famous jeans. Success in business requires good vision to compete. This is even more complicated in this industry because staying ahead of the fashion trends is no easy task. The guiding mission of the company is based on eight pillars of strength: (1) respect, (2) people, (3) passion, (4) promotion of innovation, (5) performance, (6) pride, (7) pursuit of excellence, and (8) professionalism. Based on a track record that spans over 35 years, it is obvious that this company has done something right in meeting customer needs. But there are significant existing domestic and emerging international competitors; there are even other major brands based in Montreal, such as Buffalo by David Bitton (which has its own niche).

Parasuco Jeans is a brand known for its provocative ads. It has shocked and pushed boundaries for years with sexy billboards, magazine spreads, and bus shelter ads. In order to gain more attention, the company placed 25 ads in giant ice blocks around the city of Toronto to coincide with Fashion Week in 2009, with a tag line to match: "Styles so hot they will melt the ice." Like most fashion companies, Parasuco uses Twitter and Facebook to build buzz and spread the word. There is also a great deal of content on YouTube, which is a testament to the brand's cult-like following.

Even the most successful businesses have their share of disappointments and failures, but true entrepreneurs know how to overcome them, reduce their losses, and capitalize on the best available opportunity. In 2010, when Parasuco decided to close his flagship New York store, he quickly found a tenant (drugstore chain Duane Reade) that agreed to pay $1 million in rent per year, to Parasuco, who had bought the retail condominium four years earlier for about $9 million dollars. At the same time he announced intentions to build a high-end boutique hotel in Toronto. At 57 years of age, Salvatore Parasuco does not seem to be slowing down one bit; he is visibly promoting his brand and searching for new opportunities. What do you expect? Salvatore Parasuco has the DNA of a pure entrepreneur.

Questions for Discussion

1. What characteristics did Salvatore Parasuco possess that made him successful as an entrepreneur?
2. The visibility of Parasuco jeans is higher in other countries than in Canada. Why might this be so?
3. How did Salvatore Parasuco's background facilitate his success?

CONCLUDING CASE 4-2

Family Business

Family businesses are a prominent feature in many countries around the world. Most family businesses are small, but some are very large. In addition to the usual challenges facing business firms, family businesses often are threatened by disagreements between family members about how the business should be run. Here are some classic examples.

The Irving Family

The Irving family of New Brunswick is one of the great success stories of Canadian business. The company owns scores of businesses in oil refining, forestry, shipbuilding, food processing, publishing, transportation, and home improvement. The business was started in the nineteenth century by J. D. Irving and was expanded by his son K.C. The empire is now run by K.C.'s three sons, Arthur, J.K., and Jack, who are all in their seventies. Recently, it became clear that J.K.'s son Jim and Arthur's son Kenneth were competing for a chance to shape the company's fortunes, and they disagreed over the strategic direction the company should take. That disagreement drove a wedge between J.K. and his brothers.

This is a new situation for the Irving family, which has always presented a remarkably united front. The three brothers have a great deal of respect for one another, so when these succession tensions developed, they decided they would try to amicably divide the businesses. The energy business will go to Arthur's family, and the forestry business to J.K.'s family. Their approach contrasts sharply with what happened to the McCain family, another New Brunswick business dynasty.

The McCain Family

For many years, brothers Wallace and Harrison McCain were the key players at McCain Foods Ltd., the world's largest french fry producer. But in the mid-1990s, the two brothers had a falling out over the question of who would succeed Harrison as the CEO. Wallace wanted his son Michael to get the job, but Harrison wanted someone from outside the family to take over. After a nasty battle, Wallace was removed from the firm. He then took over Maple Leaf Foods and his son Michael eventually became CEO of that company.

The Mitchell Family

Mitchell's Gourmet Foods Inc. was a Saskatchewan-based family business. A family feud developed when Fred Mitchell claimed that his mother and his brother Charles were trying to take control of the business from him. Both sides in the dispute then sued each other. An accommodation of sorts was reached when the disputing parties agreed to divide up the assets of the company. Fred (and his wife, LuAn) kept Mitchell's, and Charles (and his wife, Camille) kept a beef plant the company owned.

The Antinori Family

Some family businesses manage to avoid feuds. The Antinori family business in Florence, Italy, has been making wine since 1385, and for 26 generations the family has somehow managed to pass on management of the company to the next generation without getting in a big fight. How do they do it? By going against conventional wisdom, which says that you should clearly separate the family's interest from the interest of the business, and instead blurring the two interests as much as possible. For example, the current CEO and his wife live on the top two floors of their fifteenth-century mansion, and the business operates on the bottom two floors. Perhaps more importantly, the company plans far into the future for a company the grandchildren can run.

Maybe there is something about the wine business that makes family feuds less likely. For example, Catherine and Anne Monna and their father, Bernard, run Cassis Monna & Filles near Quebec City. The sisters are the fifth generation of the family to be involved in the wine business.

Questions for Discussion

1. How is running a family business different from creating a business from scratch? What are the advantages? What are the disadvantages?
2. It seems as though the Antinori family has found a way to ensure that the entrepreneurial spirit is transferred from generation to generation in a positive manner. But this contrasts heavily with the experiences of many family businesses, even some of the biggest success stories. Are entrepreneurs born to be entrepreneurs, or can they be created?
3. How does financing a family business differ from financing a franchise or a new start-up? Outline the unique challenges in each of these situations.

The Global Context of Business

After reading this chapter, you should be able to:

1 Describe the rise of *international business* and identify the *major world marketplaces*.

2 Identify the evolving role of *emerging markets* and highlight the important role of the *BRICS nations*.

3 Explain how different forms of *competitive advantage, import–export*

balances, exchange rates, and foreign competition determine the ways in which countries and businesses respond to the *international environment*.

4 Discuss the factors involved in deciding to do business internationally and in selecting the appropriate levels of

international involvement and *international organizational structure*.

5 Describe some of the ways in which social, cultural, economic, legal, and political differences act as barriers to *international trade*.

6 Explain how free *trade agreements* assist world trade.

Scotiabank: Canadian Bank or Global Player?

IF you take a cruise to the Caribbean islands you may be surprised to see some familiar Canadian banks at the major ports and a visible presence in various towns. Scotiabank is a leader, with over 200 branches in the Caribbean including locations in Aruba, Jamaica, and Barbados. This is just a small glimpse of the international reach of this company; Scotiabank was founded in 1832 in Halifax, Nova Scotia, and now owns more than 2800 branches in 50 countries. It employs over 70 000 people (48 000 in international markets) while providing a wide range of services to over 18.6 million customers (11 million in international markets). While competitors like TD and BMO have set their sights on expanding in the more familiar U.S. market, Scotiabank took a more speculative expansion approach. It continues to build a strong presence in Central America, Mexico, Latin America, and Asia. As you will see, Scotiabank has various models around the world designed to respect local laws and adapt

to local challenges. For instance, in Mexico, the approach is direct and aggressive; Scotiabank has invested through a holding company called Grupo Financiero Scotiabank Inverlat, S de C.V., which owns two subsidiaries. Scotiabank Inverlat is Mexico's seventh-largest bank, with 558 full-service commercial branches and 1172 ATMs. The second is Scotiabank Inverlat Casa de Bolsa, an investment bank that specializes in equity trading, investment advice, and corporate financing through 45 branches in major Mexican cities. Satisfying customers from different regions of the world requires knowledge of distinct local cultures and economic systems and respect for the unique needs of each market. Managing a portfolio as wide and complicated as Scotiabank's can be extremely challenging, but the company is clearly devoted to its global mission.

Scotiabank has been conducting international business for well over 100 years and earns a great deal of its profits from

these operations. The company profile proudly states that it is the most international of the big Canadian banks. In fact, when Prime Minister Stephen Harper was looking for someone to lead a group of chief executives in a forum designed to increase international trade between Canada and Brazil, he turned to Scotiabank CEO Rick Waugh, who agreed to co-chair the forum with the Brazilian CEO of Vale SA, Murilio Ferreira. Why was Waugh chosen? The answer is experience: Scotiabank has been conducting business in Brazil for over 30 years. While some companies look at Brazil and see tough barriers and unwelcome tariffs, Scotiabank sees an established client base, a long-standing relationship, and tremendous potential. Brazil is the world's seventh-largest economy and one of the powerful emerging BRICS nations (the others are Russia, India, China, and South Africa). Scotiabank already earns over $2 billion in trade financing from its Brazilian unit. With Brazil's middle class

predicted to grow by 40 to 45 million people over the next twenty years, Scotiabank is in a good position to benefit in a major way from its early investment in this nation.

Many investments in international markets are designed for long-term gains while sacrificing profits in the short term. However, international banking is nothing new at Scotiabank, and this division is a profit driver for the firm today. At the end of 2011, the international banking business unit was a bright spot, earning profits of $350 million; this figure was up about 27 percent from the previous year. At the same time, profits from Canadian operations were up only about 4 percent. Of course, having a presence in markets around the world also means that the bank has increased exposure to risk factors from around the world. This is particularly dangerous in the unstable economic times that we have been experiencing in recent years. Fortunately, this difficult period has also created opportunities for solvent banks. According to Brian Porter, head of International Banking at Scotiabank, the company was actively seeking selective

acquisitions and was well positioned to respond in the marketplace.

Scotiabank has no intention of slowing down. In recent years its expansion plan has included 22 acquisitions in Central America and South America with a particular emphasis on Colombia and Chile. In fact, Scotiabank has set a target to capture 10 percent of the Chilean market; it recently bought Banco Sud Americano and its 142 full-service branches in that country. In 2012, Scotiabank acquired a majority stake in Banco Colpatria in a $1-billion deal in Colombia. Such acquisitions are getting more difficult to complete. As a pioneer, Scotiabank was able to make major purchases at very reasonable acquisition prices. Today more international banks are investing in this region and the prices are getting higher. Nobody ever said it was easy.

There are also tremendous prospects in Asia. Scotiabank has operations in key Asian markets including Japan, Korea, and India. Perhaps the greatest opportunities today, and probably for the next 100 years, are in China. In 2011, Scotiabank was clearly trying to deepen its roots in this nation by acquiring a

19.99 percent stake in the Bank of Guangzhou for $719 million. This bank has a network of 84 branches in China's third-largest city. (Why 19.99 percent? Because foreign companies are not allowed to own more than 19.99 percent of any Chinese bank.) This latest move follows a purchase of 14.8 percent of the Xi'an City Commercial Bank for $162 million two years earlier. All of the world's major banks are paying attention to this market for obvious reasons. However, for Scotiabank this latest move will be their last for a while because, besides the 19.99 percent rule, under current Chinese laws foreign banks are only allowed to have a stake in a maximum of two Chinese banks. This is just another example of an obstacle to conducting business abroad.

International growth must always be weighed against the specific challenges in each market (economic, legal, political, and so on). Regardless of various international obstacles, Scotiabank has shown its commitment to work with foreign companies and comply with foreign government rules in its quest to transform itself from Canada's leading international bank into "Scotiabank Global Bank." ◆

HOW WILL THIS HELP ME?

Whether you see yourself living abroad, working for a big company, or starting your own business, the global economy will affect you in some way. Exchange rates for different currencies and global markets for buying and selling are all of major importance to everyone, regardless of their role or perspective. The material in this chapter will help you to understand (1) how global forces affect you as a customer, (2) how globalization affects you as an employee, and (3) how global opportunities and challenges can affect you as a business owner and as an investor.

The Contemporary Global Economy

globalization The integration of markets globally.

imports Products that are made or grown abroad and sold in Canada.

exports Products that are made or grown in Canada and sold abroad.

The total volume of world trade today is immense—around $15 trillion each year.[1] The world economy is increasingly transforming into a single, interdependent system—a process called **globalization**. But we often take for granted the diversity of goods and services available today as a result of international trade. Your tablet, smartphone, shoes, clothing, and even the roast lamb on your dinner table may all be **imports**—that is, products made or grown abroad but sold in Canada. At the same time, the success of many Canadian firms depends on **exports**—products made or grown domestically and shipped for sale abroad. An Ontario company called 1867 Confederation Log Homes has found a way to export entire houses. It makes the homes at its factory, then dismantles them, numbers all the components, and ships them to foreign countries. When they arrive, they are easily reassembled by the buyer using only basic construction skills. Confederation exports 40 percent of its output.[2]

Back in 2010, China officially passed Germany as the world's top merchandise exporter; this was a clear sign of the importance of international trade and the ever-evolving relationships.[3] Trade between nations can be traced back at least as far as 2000 BCE, when North African tribes took dates and clothing to Assyria and Babylonia in the Middle East and traded them for olive oil and spices. In other words, international business is nothing new. In fact, MIT professor Paul Krugman argues that what we now regard as an extremely active "global economy" is not as big a change as you might imagine. He points out that imports now represent only a slightly higher proportion of GDP than they did 100 years ago, and that capital mobility (the movement of money from country to country) is about the same as it was in 1914.

Even so, international trade is becoming increasingly central to the fortunes of most nations of the world, as well as to their largest businesses. Whereas in the past many nations followed strict policies to protect domestic businesses, today more and more countries are aggressively encouraging international trade. They are opening their borders to foreign businesses, offering incentives for their own domestic businesses to expand internationally, and making it easier for foreign firms to partner with local firms through various alliances. Today, it is not simply a question of western nations pushing trade abroad. China is making major inroads and increasing its economic and political influence in Africa with major deals with Nigeria, South Africa, Ethiopia, and Zambia. China is now the largest trading partner in the region with trade totalling more than $114 billion, just ahead of the United States.[4]

Several forces have combined to spark and sustain globalization. For one thing, governments and businesses have simply become more aware of the benefits of globalization to their countries and shareholders. For another, new technologies have made international travel, communication, and commerce easier, faster, and cheaper than ever before. Overseas phone calls and seaborne shipping costs per tonne have both declined sharply over the past several decades. Likewise, transatlantic travel that once required several days aboard a ship now takes only a few hours by air. The internet has also torn down barriers for large and small companies. Finally, there are competitive pressures: Sometimes, a firm simply must enter foreign markets just to keep up with its competitors.

Advocates of globalization argue that increased international commerce benefits all sectors of society and should be actively encouraged. But critics, like these protestors, argue that globalization benefits only big business and is eroding distinctive national cultures.

Globalization is not without its critics, who charge that it allows businesses to exploit workers in less developed countries and bypass domestic environmental and tax regulations. They also charge that globalization leads to the loss of cultural heritages and often benefits the rich more than the poor. As a result, many international gatherings of global economic leaders—including the G8 and G20 meetings in Toronto in 2010—have been marked by protests and demonstrations. But despite fears and apprehensions, globalization is part of our existence and there are some interesting trends emerging. A *Globe and Mail* article listed five key trends based on a report from McKinsey: (1) the shift of the economic centre of gravity away from North America/Europe/Japan to Asia and Latin America, (2) the productivity imperative (improved productivity is essential to effectively compete), (3) the global grid (complex global networks of people and capital), (4) environmental sustainability, and (5) increased controls on businesses and markets as governments try to cope with financial crises.[5]

The Major World Marketplaces

The World Bank, an agency of the United Nations, uses **per capita income**—the average income per person in a country—as a measure to divide countries into one of four groups.[6]

1. *High-income countries* have an annual per capita income greater than US$12 276. They include Canada, the United States, most countries in Europe, Australia, Japan, South Korea, Israel, Kuwait, Cyprus, the United Arab Emirates, and Oman.

2. *Upper middle-income countries* have an annual per capita income between US$3976 and US$12 275. This group includes China, Colombia, Lebanon, Turkey, Argentina, and South Africa.

3. *Low middle-income countries* have an annual per capita income between US$1006 and US$3975. This group includes: Armenia, Morocco, Guatemala, and Vietnam.

4. *Low-income countries* (often called *developing countries*) have an annual per capita income of US$1005 or less. Bangladesh, Ethiopia, Haiti, and Afghanistan are among the countries in this group. Due to low literacy rates, weak infrastructures, unstable governments, and related problems, these countries are less attractive for international business.

Describe the rise of *international business* and identify the *major world marketplaces.*

per capita income The average income per person in a country.

Geographic Clusters

The world economy is evolving, with emerging markets playing an ever-increasing role. However, it still revolves around three major marketplaces: North America, Europe, and Asia-Pacific. In general, these clusters include relatively more of the upper-middle– and high-income nations, but relatively few low- and low-middle–income countries. For instance, because Africa consists primarily of low- and low-middle–income countries, it is not generally seen as a major marketplace. The three geographic regions that do warrant this designation are home to most of the world's largest economies, biggest corporations, most influential financial markets, and highest-income consumers.

North America. The United States dominates the North American business region. It is the single largest marketplace and has been the most stable economy in the world for decades, but the United States is encountering major problems due to various forces, most notably a large increase in the nation's debt load. Canada also plays a major role in the global economy. Moreover, the United States and Canada are each other's largest trading partner. Many U.S. firms, such as General Motors, Warner Brothers, and Procter & Gamble, have maintained successful Canadian operations for years, and many Canadian firms, such as Research In Motion and Scotiabank, are also major global competitors.

Mexico has also become a major manufacturing centre, especially along its border with the southern United States, where cheap labour and low transportation costs have encouraged many firms, from the United States and other countries, to build manufacturing plants. The auto industry has been especially active with Daimler General Motors, Volkswagen, Nissan, and Ford all running assembly plants in this region. Several major suppliers have also built facilities in the area. But Mexico's role as a low-cost manufacturing centre may have peaked, with many companies shifting production from Mexico to China.[7]

Europe. Europe is still often seen as two regions—Western and Eastern. Western Europe, dominated by Germany, the United Kingdom, France, Spain, and Italy, has long been a mature but fragmented marketplace. But the transformation of this region via the European Union (discussed later) into an integrated economic system has further increased its importance. Major international firms, such as Unilever, Renault, Royal Dutch/Shell, Michelin, Siemens, and Nestlé, are all headquartered in Western Europe.

Ecommerce and technology have also become increasingly important in this region. There has been a surge in internet start-ups in southeastern England, the Netherlands, and the Scandinavian countries, and Ireland is now one of the world's largest exporters of software. Strasbourg, France, is a major centre for biotech start-ups; Barcelona, Spain, has many flourishing software and internet companies; and the Frankfurt region of Germany is dotted with both software and biotech start-ups.

Eastern Europe, once primarily communist, has also gained importance, both as a marketplace and as a producer. Multinational corporations such as Nestlé, General Motors, and ABB Asea Brown Boveri have all set up operations in Poland. Ford, General Motors, Suzuki, and Volkswagen have all built new factories in Hungary. On the other hand, governmental instability has hampered development in Bulgaria, Albania, Romania, and other countries.

Asia-Pacific. Asia-Pacific consists of Japan, China, Thailand, Malaysia, Singapore, Indonesia, South Korea, Taiwan, the Philippines, and Australia (which technically is not in Asia, but is included because of proximity). Some experts still distinguish Hong Kong, though now part of China, as a part of the region, and others include Vietnam. Fuelled by strong entries in the automobile, electronics, and banking industries, the economies of these countries grew rapidly in the past three decades. A currency crisis in

The growth in international commerce has led to the emergence of several major marketplaces. Much of the international commerce in these marketplaces, in turn, is managed from major cities. Traditional centres of international commerce include New York, London, Paris, and Tokyo, but in recent years, cities like Shanghai, Beijing, Hong Kong, Dubai, Vancouver, Bangalore, and Kuala Lumpur have taken on increased importance. For example, international business now defines the glittering skyline of Shanghai.

the late 1990s slowed growth in virtually every country of the region, but that crisis ran its course, and most of these countries, especially Japan and China, have flourished.

As the trends indicate, Asia Pacific is a growing force in the world economy and a major source of competition for North American companies. The Japanese dominate the region, led by firms like Toyota, Toshiba, and Nippon Steel. However, South Korea (e.g., Samsung and Hyundai), Taiwan (e.g., Chinese Petroleum and manufacturing for foreign firms), and Hong Kong (a major financial centre) are also successful players in the global economy. China, the world's most densely populated country, has emerged as an important market and now boasts the world's second-largest economy behind that of the United States, after recently passing Japan.[8] As in North America and Western Europe, technology promises to play an increasingly important role in this region.

The Rising Power of Emerging Markets: From BRIC to BRICS and Beyond

BRIC is a term that has been used for over a decade, in international trade magazines and newspapers, to describe the increasing importance of four specific nations in global trade: *B*razil, *R*ussia, *I*ndia and *C*hina. The BRIC concept was first used by Goldman Sachs in 2001; since that time BRIC investment funds have become an important group for money managers and international analysts. These four nations even began to act like a unit, holding unofficial summits and discussing common strategies.

The status of these four nations has risen in international trade for different reasons. Brazil is strong in commodities and agriculture, Russia is a powerful energy supplier, and China is a major hub of manufacturing activity. India has become a leading service provider at various levels ranging from basic customer service call centres to engineering solutions providers. The growth and quick market development of the consumer market in these four nations is also providing tremendous sales opportunities for foreign companies in many different industries, including car manufacturing and high-end clothing brands.[9]

The old international trading patterns and activities are changing. Once upon a time, Western companies used less developed markets to acquire natural resources supplies and to carry out simple assembly tasks. But these four nations now demonstrate relationships that are much more complex. A clear signal of this shift was evident a few years ago, when Indian car maker Tata acquired Jaguar and Land Rover from Ford. Earlier that year Tata Steel bought the Anglo Dutch steel maker Corus Group LLC for US$12.1 billion. This was not quite business in the traditional sense.[10]

Identify the evolving role of **L02** *emerging markets* and highlight the important role of the *BRICS nations*.

BRIC A term that has been used for over a decade, in international trade magazines and newspapers, to describe the increasing importance of four specific nations in global trade: *B*razil, *R*ussia, *I*ndia and *C*hina.

Of the four countries, Russia has encountered the most profound troubles in recent years. Some analysts have even called for the exclusion of Russia from this super-group. Among the reasons cited were corruption and excessive levels of bureaucratic red tape. For example, during 10 years in the Russian market, IKEA was able to open only 11 stores despite major efforts to expand. Frustrated by the red tape, IKEA put further investment in Russia on hold.[11]

While China, India, and Russia have had most of the attention, it is Brazil that is now at the front of the pack in terms of optimism and opportunity. In 2010, Brazil's economic growth rate averaged 10 percent. While this pace slowed in 2011, the potential was evident. It was based on positive domestic demand and high levels of investment. According to Transparency International, Brazil is the least corrupt of the BRIC nations. Brazil's rich natural resources, combined with the momentum from World Cup 2014 and the Olympics in 2016, should help propel it for years to come.[12] For example, Brookfield Asset Management is positioned to reap huge rewards by building major shopping centres to meet the demand of the 30 to 40 million people who have joined the ranks of the middle class in the past decade. It is estimated that another 40 to 45 million Brazilians will achieve middle class status over the next 20 years.[13]

In 2011, the initial group of four extended an invitation to South Africa and transformed into **BRICS**. The move was surprising to many analysts because there seemed to better candidates for admission. However, it was clear that the informal group was developing into an important political club with its own goals and aspirations. South Africa is rich in mineral resources, something that these emerging markets need to sustain growth. In addition, the country serves as a gateway to the African continent, which has more than one billion potential consumers.[14]

In yet another sign of the changing times, a formal BRICS meeting was held in Washington, D.C., in late 2011 to discuss how these developing nations could help bail out Europe from the deep financial crisis. Part of the plan called for the purchase of a significant share of euro-denominated bonds. Emerging economies bailing out "old world" economies is a real eye-opener.[15]

While the BRICS nations have received a lot of publicity, there are tremendous opportunities and stories of development in other emerging nations, including Thailand, Indonesia, South Korea, and Ukraine, to name just a few. A new world order is evolving and "old" economic powers like the United States, Japan, Germany, and even Canada are going to need to adapt.

BRICS The initial group of four with the addition of South Africa.

Forms of Competitive Advantage

L03 Explain how different forms of *competitive advantage, import–export balances, exchange rates,* and *foreign competition* determine the ways in which countries and businesses respond to the *international environment.*

High levels of importing, exporting, and other forms of international business activity exist simply because no country can produce all the goods and services that its people need. Countries tend to export products that they can produce better or less expensively than other countries and then use the proceeds to import products that they cannot produce as effectively.

But this general idea does not explain why various nations export and import specific products and services. Such decisions hinge partly on the kind of advantages a particular country may enjoy regarding its ability to create and/or sell various products and resources.[16] Traditionally, economists assessed *absolute* and *comparative advantage* to explain international trade. But because this approach focuses narrowly on such factors as natural resources and labour costs, a perspective has emerged that emphasizes the more complex idea of *national competitive advantage.*

Absolute Advantage

absolute advantage A nation's ability to produce something more cheaply or better than any other country.

An **absolute advantage** exists when a country can produce something more efficiently than any other country. In other words, a country can produce a larger output of goods or services using the same or fewer input resources. This concept was first proposed by economist Adam Smith back in 1776. Saudi oil, Brazilian coffee beans, and Canadian timber approximate absolute advantage. The theory is simple: Countries should focus on producing goods and services in which they have an absolute advantage and buy products that they do not produce more efficiently than other nations in the world.[17] Canada exports timber because of its natural strengths and imports bananas because the climate here does not permit farmers to grow bananas efficiently. If trade were limited to two countries, they could negotiate which nation should produce which items for the greater good. However, the global economy is a complex network and most decisions are not quite that easy. In addition, true absolute advantages are very rare; the vast majority are actually relative. For example, when you think of good wine you might instantly think of France. Most experts say that the French vineyards produce the finest wines in the world. But the growing wine industry in California, British Columbia, and Ontario attests to the fact that winemakers in those regions can also produce very good values in wine—wines that can compete with French wines and that are available in more varieties and at lower prices.

Comparative Advantage

A country has a **comparative advantage** in goods that it can produce more efficiently or better than other goods. For example, if businesses in a given country can make computers more efficiently than they can make automobiles, that nation's firms have a comparative advantage in computer manufacturing. Canada has a comparative advantage in farming (because of capital-intensive and efficient land use), while South Korea has a comparative advantage in electronics manufacturing (because of efficient operations and cheap labour). As a result, Canadian firms export grain to South Korea and import electronic equipment from South Korea.

comparative advantage A nation's ability to produce some products more cheaply or better than it can others.

Almost all countries have a comparative advantage in *some* products, but no country has a comparative advantage in *all* products. Developed countries tend to have a comparative advantage in making high-tech products, while developing countries tend to have a comparative advantage in making products that require a lot of low-cost labour.

National Competitive Advantage

In recent years, a theory of **national competitive advantage** has become a more widely accepted model of why nations engage in international trade.[18] Basically, national competitive advantage derives from four conditions:

1. *Factor conditions* are the factors of production that we identified in Chapter 1.

2. *Demand conditions* reflect a large domestic consumer base that promotes strong demand for innovative products.

3. *Related and supporting industries* include strong local or regional suppliers and/or industrial customers.

4. *Strategies, structures, and rivalries* refer to firms and industries that stress cost reduction, product quality, higher productivity, and innovative new products.

national competitive advantage A country will be inclined to engage in international trade when factor conditions, demand conditions, related and supporting industries, and strategies/structures/rivalries are favourable.

Figure 5.1 shows why these four attributes are referred to as a national diamond. The interaction of the four elements determines the environment in which a nation's firms compete. When all of these conditions exist, a nation will naturally be inclined to engage in international business. Japan, for instance, has strong domestic demand for automobiles. Its automobile producers have well-oiled supplier networks, and its domestic firms have competed intensely with one another for decades. This set of circumstances explains why Japanese automobile companies such as Toyota, Honda, Nissan, and Mazda are generally successful in foreign markets.

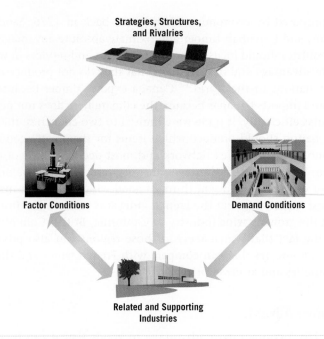

Strategies, Structures,
and Rivalries

Factor Conditions

Demand Conditions

Related and Supporting
Industries

FIGURE 5.1

Attributes of National Competitive Advantage.

international competitiveness The ability of a country to generate more wealth than its competitors in world markets.

International competitiveness refers to the ability of a country to generate more wealth than its competitors in world markets. Each year, the World Economic Forum publishes a global competitiveness ranking based on both economic data and a poll of business leaders in many countries. In the 2011–12 report, the top three countries on the list were Switzerland, Singapore, and Sweden. Canada dropped from tenth to sixteenth place. Canada's high taxes, regulated industries, relatively large bureaucracy, and overly conservative capital market structure were listed as reasons for a lower rating. The U.S. declined for the third year in a row and now ranks fifth.[19]

Import–Export Balances

Although international trade offers many potential advantages, trading with other nations can pose problems if a country's imports and exports are not balanced. In deciding whether an overall balance exists, economists use two measures: *balance of trade* and *balance of payments*.

Balance of Trade

balance of trade The difference in value between a nation's total exports and its total imports.

trade surplus Occurs when a country exports more than it imports.

trade deficit Occurs when a country imports more than it exports.

A nation's **balance of trade** is the difference in value between its total exports and its total imports. A country that exports more than it imports has a favourable balance of trade, or a **trade surplus**. A country that imports more than it exports has an unfavourable balance of trade, or a **trade deficit**. Canada's most important exports are energy products ($152 billion), industrial goods ($134.4 billion), agriculture and fish ($102.4 billion), and machinery and equipment ($94.6 billion). Our most important imports are energy products ($166.8 billion), industrial goods ($108.2 billion), agriculture and fish products ($104.7 billion), and motor vehicles ($84.8 billion).[20]

Canada had enjoyed a favourable balance of merchandise trade for many years, but in 2010 the country had a trade deficit of $8.9 billion. The United States is by far the largest trading partner Canada has, and our overall trade balance has been generally favourable only because Canada exports so much more to the United States than it imports from it. But this is changing partly due to the higher Canadian dollar. For years, economists had warned against Canada's dependence on the United States. Canada's

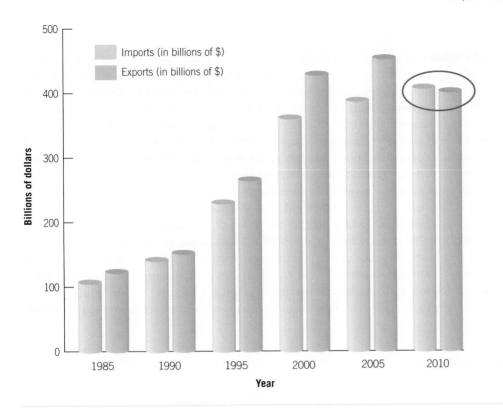

FIGURE 5.2

Canadian imports and exports
of merchandise.

nearly $47-billion surplus in 2008 turned into a deficit the following year in large part due to a major decline in exports to the States. In addition, we import more from the countries of the European Union and Japan than we export to those countries, and we import more than we export from all other countries as well (see Table 5.1).[21]

Balance of Payments

The **balance of payments** refers to the flow of money into or out of a country. The money a nation pays for imports and receives for exports—that is, its balance of trade—comprises much of its balance of payments, but other financial exchanges are also factors. For example, money spent by tourists, money spent on foreign aid programs, and money spent and received in the buying and selling of currency on international money markets all affect the balance of payments.

An unfavourable balance means that more money is flowing out than in. For Canada to have a favourable balance of payments for a given year, the total of (1) our exports, (2) foreign tourist spending in this country, (3) foreign investments here, and (4) earnings from overseas investments must be greater than the total of (1) our imports, (2) Canadian tourist spending overseas, (3) our foreign aid grants, (4) our military spending abroad, (5) the investments made by Canadian firms abroad, and (6) the earnings of foreigners from their investments in Canada. These relationships are summarized in Figure 5.3. Canada has had an unfavourable balance of payments for the past two decades. In 2009, for example, $103 billion more flowed out of Canada than flowed in.[23]

balance of payments The difference between money flowing into and out of a country as a result of trade and other transactions.

TABLE 5.1 Canadian Exports to and Imports from Selected Countries, 2010[22]		
Country	**Exports to (in $billion)**	**Imports from (in $billion)**
United States	$296.7	$259.9
European Union	36.4	40.4
Japan	9.7	10.1
All others	61.9	103.5

Exchange Rates

exchange rate The rate at which the currency of one nation can be exchanged for that of another.

The balance of imports and exports between two countries is affected by the rate of exchange between their currencies. An **exchange rate** is the rate at which the currency of one nation can be exchanged for that of another.[24] For example, if the exchange rate between Canadian dollars and British pounds is 1 to 1.55, this means that it costs $1.55 in Canadian dollars to "buy" one British pound. Alternatively, it would cost only 0.65 of a British pound to "buy" one Canadian dollar. This exchange rate means that 0.65 of a British pound and one Canadian dollar should have exactly the same purchasing power. A currency is said to be "strong" when demand for it is high and when there is high demand for the goods manufactured by using that currency.

At the end of the Second World War, the major nations of the world agreed to establish *fixed exchange rates* so that the value of any country's currency relative to that of another country remained constant. Today, however, *floating exchange rates* are the norm, and the value of one country's currency relative to that of another country varies with market conditions. The Canadian dollar, for example, fluctuates in value compared to the U.S. dollar. Exchange rates typically fluctuate by very small amounts on a daily basis, with more significant variations occurring over greater spans of time.

FIGURE 5.3

Requirements for Canada to have a favourable balance of payments.

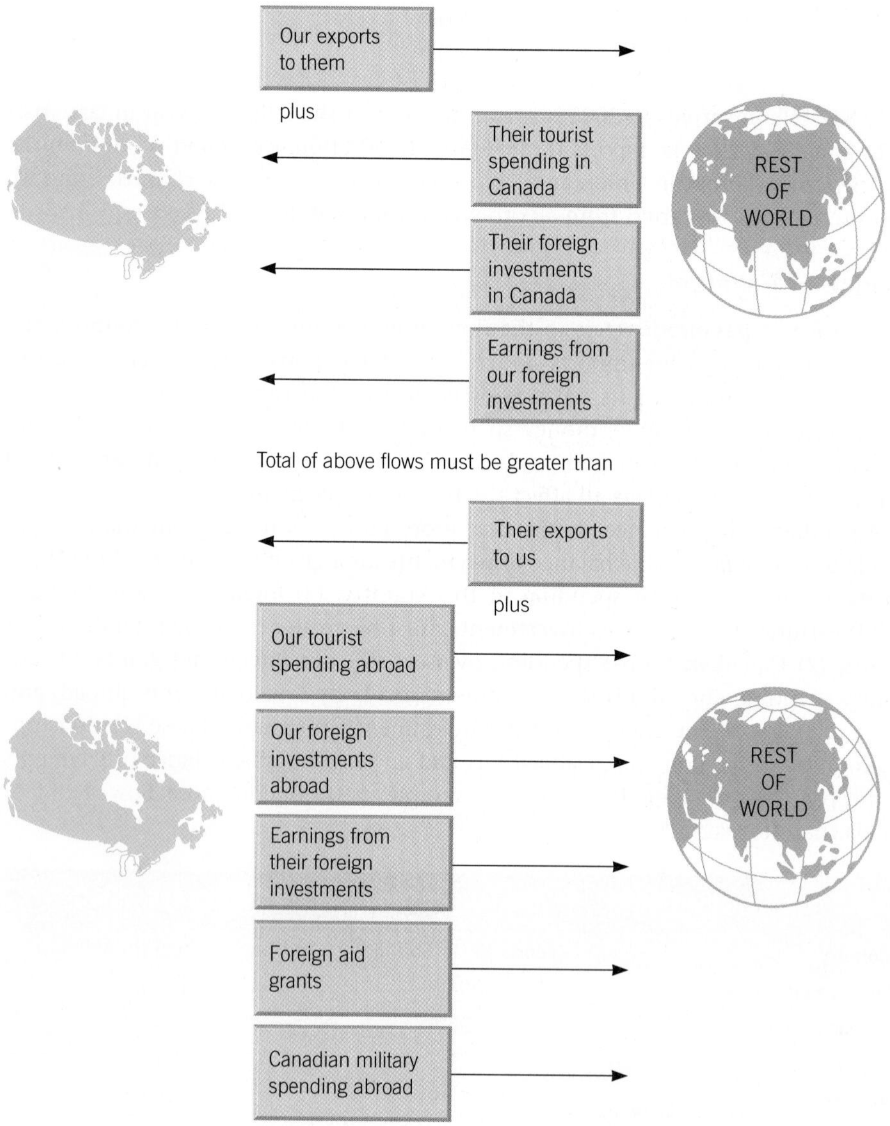

Fluctuation in exchange rates can have an important impact on the balance of trade. Suppose, for example, that you wanted to buy some English tea for 10 British pounds per box. At an exchange rate of 1.55 Canadian dollars to the British pound, a box will cost you $15.50 (10 pounds * 1.55 = 15.50). But what if the pound gets stronger? At an exchange rate of, say, 2.1 dollars to the pound, the same box of tea would cost you $21.00 (10 pounds * 2.1 = $21.00).

Of course, changes in the exchange rate would affect more than just the price of tea. If instead the Canadian dollar gets stronger in relation to the British pound, the prices of all Canadian-made products would rise in England and the prices of all English-made products would fall in Canada. As a result, the English would buy fewer Canadian-made products, and Canadians would spend more on English-made products. The result could conceivably be a Canadian trade deficit with England. This is why the recent increase in the value of the Canadian dollar has exporters very concerned. It is no coincidence that Canada is experiencing trade deficits at a time when its dollar is near parity (one for one) with the U.S. dollar. According to Export Development Canada (EDC) chief economist Peter Hall, the trade slump is directly linked to the strong dollar and exporters are running out of coping mechanisms.[25]

One of the most significant developments in foreign exchange has been the introduction of the **euro**, the common currency among 17 members of the European Union (Denmark, Sweden, and the United Kingdom do not participate). The euro was officially introduced back in 2002 and has quickly become as important as the U.S. dollar and the Japanese yen in international commerce. By 2008 the euro had risen in value against the U.S. and Canadian dollars and stood as high as $1.73 against the latter. There was a sharp drop, however, when the European economic crisis began in 2010: The euro dropped to a low of $1.25 before rising a bit in 2011, and stood at the $1.30 range in mid-2012. The primary reason for this drop is the economic instability, which has raised some concerns about the long-term survival of the currency. The southern nations Portugal, Italy, Greece, and Spain (and Ireland in the north) have struggled with various economic hardships including massive debt loads and insolvency (most notably Greece), high unemployment (25.3 percent in Spain), and high borrowing costs. The media has even coined a derogative acronym for the group of five: PIIGS.

On the other side of the continent, however, Germany's economy was still booming. In 2012 the country had its lowest level of unemployment in more than two decades.[26] This contrast was a testament to a resilient economy in Germany but was also due in large part to a lower euro; this essentially meant that German exports were now a worldwide bargain, leading to more export sales. Each nation had its own interests and its own issues, but the instability was clearly putting downward pressure on the shared currency.

euro A common currency shared among most of the members of the European Union (excluding Denmark, Sweden, and the United Kingdom).

Exchange Rates and Competition

Companies with international operations must watch exchange rate fluctuations closely because these changes affect overseas demand for their products and can be a major factor in international competition. In general, when the value of a country's domestic currency rises—becomes "stronger"—companies based there find it harder to export products to foreign markets and it is easier for foreign companies to enter local markets. It also makes it more cost efficient for domestic companies to move production operations to lower-cost sites in foreign countries.

When the value of a country's currency declines—becomes "weaker"—just the opposite patterns occur. As the value of a country's currency falls, its balance of trade should improve because domestic companies should experience a boost in exports. There should also be a corresponding decrease in the incentives for foreign companies to ship products into the domestic market. (For more detailed information on the effect of exchange rates, see Chapter 18.)

Adding to the complexity of currency and competition is the weakening of some of the world's power currencies and the evident rise of others. For decades, the U.S. dollar has been seen as the rock of the financial currency market. It remains a powerful force, but the United States's ever-increasing debt and other financial problems led Standard and Poor's to downgrade the U.S. dollar in 2011 from AAA to AA+; in particular, it cited the lack of government spending cuts for this decision. In other words, the U.S. dollar no longer merited the highest credit rating. A few weeks later Moody's rating agency downgraded the Japanese yen yet again to the AA- rating, citing the instability of Japan's political leadership.[27] At the same time, China was slowly moving toward the internationalization of the yuan. This currency is not widely available and its value is currently tightly controlled (i.e., kept artificially low) by the Chinese government. However, according to Li Daoukui, an adviser of the People's Republic of China, the yuan will be a fully international currency within the next decade.[28] This would have major effects on the world currency market, especially if the Chinese start to sell significant amounts of their large reserves of U.S. dollars.

International Business Management

L04 Discuss the factors involved in deciding to do business internationally and in selecting the appropriate levels of *international involvement* and *international organizational structure*.

Wherever a firm is located, its success depends largely on how well it is managed. International business is particularly challenging because the basic functions of management—planning, organizing, directing, and controlling—are much more difficult to carry out when a business operates in several markets scattered around the globe. (We discuss the functions of management in Chapter 6.)

Managing means making decisions, and in this section we examine the three most basic decisions a company's management must make when faced with the prospect of globalization. The first decision is whether or not to "go international." Once that decision has been made, managers must decide on the company's level of international involvement and on the organizational structure that will best meet its global needs.

"Going International"

"Going international" isn't for everyone. For example, if you buy and sell fresh fish, you'll probably find it more profitable to confine your activities to a limited geographic area in order to minimize storage and transportation costs. As Figure 5.4 shows, several factors enter into the decision to go international.

Gauging International Demand

In considering international expansion, a company must determine whether there is demand for its products abroad. Products that are successful in one country may be useless in another. Snowmobiles are popular for transportation and recreation in Canada, and they have actually revolutionized reindeer herding in Lapland, but there's no demand for them in Central America. Even when there is demand, advertising may still need to be adjusted. For instance, in Canada bicycles and small motorcycles are mainly used for recreation, but in many parts of Asia they are seen as transportation. Market research and/or the prior market entry of competitors may indicate whether there's an international demand for a firm's products.

Adapting to Customer Needs

If there is international demand for its product, a firm must consider whether and how to adapt that product to meet the special demands and expectations of foreign customers. For example, New Brunswick-based McCain Foods Limited has worked

FIGURE 5.4

The decision to go international.

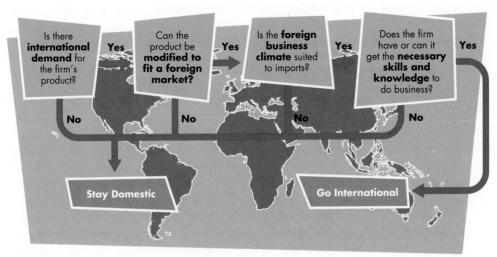

Is there **international demand** for the firm's product? — Yes →
Can the product be **modified to fit a foreign market?** — Yes →
Is the **foreign business climate** suited to imports? — Yes →
Does the firm have or can it get the **necessary skills and knowledge** to do business? — Yes →

No · No · No · No

Stay Domestic

Go International

hard to build market share in South Africa. It even developed single-sized portions of frozen vegetables to serve customers who do not have proper refrigeration.[29] KFC's dishes in China come with a side order of rice and hot soy milk.[30] Likewise, McDonald's restaurants sell wine in France, beer in Germany, and meatless sandwiches in India to accommodate local tastes and preferences. Ford products must have their steering wheels mounted on the right if they are to be sold in England and Japan. When Toyota launches upscale cars at home, they retain the Toyota nameplate; those same cars are sold under the Lexus nameplate in Canada, however, because the firm has concluded that Canadian consumers will not pay a premium price for a Toyota. BlackBerry smartphones may originate in Waterloo, Ontario, but Research In Motion has sold over 1.2 million smartphones in Indonesia; in Jakarta, a BlackBerry is an important symbol of success. To succeed in this market, RIM created prepaid scratch cards that allow customers to pay a set amount for data and email service each week or month.[31]

In addition to these issues of demand and the need to adapt products, consideration must also be given to the business climate that exists in the foreign market (these issues are discussed in detail later in this chapter). The company must also assess the specific business skills that will be needed to be successful in the foreign country. Businesses can deal with this issue by adopting various levels of involvement in international business. The boxed insert entitled "Connection that Matters: My World, My Choice" describes one organization's experience in going international.

While Toyota markets five different sport-utility vehicles in Canada (manufacturing the RAV4 in Woodstock, Ontario, and exporting the other models to Canada), it sells only its two smallest ones at home in Japan, where crowded roads, narrow driveways, and scarce parking spaces make larger vehicles impractical.

Levels of Involvement in International Business

Several different levels of involvement in international business are possible. A firm may act as an *exporter* or *importer*, organize as an *international firm*, or operate as a *multinational firm*. Most of the world's largest industrial firms are multinationals.

Exporters and Importers

exporter A firm that makes products in one country and then distributes and sells them in others.

importer A firm that buys products in foreign markets and then imports them for resale in its home country.

An **exporter** is a firm that makes products in one country and then distributes and sells them in other countries. An **importer** buys products in foreign markets and then imports them for resale in its home country. These approaches represent the lowest level of involvement in international operations and are excellent ways to learn the fine points of global business. Exporters and importers tend to conduct most of their business in their home nations. It is not just large companies that are exporting; small firms also export products and services.

Canada ranks first among the G8 countries in the proportion of its production that is exported (almost 40 percent).[32] Both large and small Canadian firms export products and services. For example, McCain Foods is a formidable presence in Europe, where it holds a 75 percent share of the market for "oven fries" in Germany; Sabian Cymbals sells 90 percent of its products in 80 different countries; Electrovert Ltd. does 95 percent of its business outside Canada; and Lingo Media Inc. is the largest supplier

ENTREPRENEURSHIP AND NEW VENTURES

Connection that Matters: My World, My Choice!

Whether you live in Bangalore, India, or Calgary, Alberta, there are countless cultural and demographic differences that affect the choices consumers make. For example, you can choose to only buy fish from sustainably sourced waters or support companies that have a strong sustainability program embedded within their company culture. According to the founders of My World, My Choice! (MWMC), making responsible choices can make all the difference in the world.

MWMC is an educational program whose mission is to encourage students from elementary to secondary school age, and from different regions of the world, to make sustainable choices, while empowering them to become leaders within their own communities. These choices range from daily tasks like packing bottle-free lunches and composting to building community gardens. Lianne Foti, director and co-founder of MWMC, says, "We want to show students that the choices they make have a lasting impact on our world, [and to understand] that the environmental, economic, and social well-being of our planet are tied together through the choices our community makes every day. [This] is the first step moving forward." This ideology is the motivating factor behind the MWMC program, which has become part of numerous schools' curricula and is making a profound impact on the minds of younger generations—the adults of tomorrow.

MWMC began as many entrepreneurial projects do, with friends and co-workers Lianne Foti and co-founder Kurt Archer sharing a conversation and a shared vision

to help make a difference in the choices that impact our world and our future. The adventure began in 2008 in Bangalore, India, where Foti and Archer tested their program on a group of several hundred students. Its success inspired the pair to bring their program back to Canada, where hundreds of students from Calgary, Alberta, to Guelph, Ontario, now participate, and to branch out farther into Pakistan and Kenya.

MWMC is used not only as a successful in-class educational tool, but also as a resource to develop leadership skills among young professionals. Participants' sensitivity to cultural differences and the program's focus on providing a simple and universal goals have contributed to MWMC's success.

Says Foti, "We have seen many insightful ideas result from these projects, and we will continue to challenge students to become the forward-thinking leaders of their generation." Her words are a testament to the impact that entrepreneurship can have on curriculum development and education around the world.

Critical Thinking Questions

1. The decision to go international requires a high degree of analysis and examination of factors both internal and external to the business. Assess MWMC's form of competitive advantage and level of involvement in international education.

2. What are some potential barriers to this initiative?

of English-language textbooks in China's primary school system and recently created speak2me.cn, a learning solution website that uses voice recognition. The site was created to solve a major problem in China: the shortage of teachers who speak English properly. The company registered one million users on the site in the first year alone.[33]

Exporting is also important to many other countries. Perhaps the most obvious examples are countries like Venezuela, Saudi Arabia, and Nigeria, which rely heavily on revenues generated from oil exports. But there are other not-so-obvious exports that are also important; for example, movies from Hollywood. During the past decade, box office sales have increased by about 33 percent in North America but have more than doubled in international markets. The ultimate success or failure of a film is increasingly being decided by youngsters in countries like China and Brazil. *Avatar* earned an astonishing $2 billion outside North America. *Gulliver's Travels*, starring Jack Black, was a disappointment in North America, with a box office take of just $42 million, but turned a profit overall because strong turnout in Russia and South Korea helped it reach sales of $150 million in international markets.[34]

International Firms

As firms gain experience and success as exporters and importers, they may move to the next level of involvement. An **international firm** conducts a substantial portion of its business abroad, and it may have some manufacturing facilities in foreign countries. Hershey, for example, sells its products in 90 foreign countries and buys ingredients for its chocolates from several foreign suppliers. But it manufactures the vast majority of its products in the United States (there is one plant in Mexico). In fact, most of that manufacturing occurs in Pennsylvania.[35] So an international firm may be large and influential in the global economy but remain basically a domestic firm with international operations. Its central concern is its own domestic market.

international firm A company that conducts a significant portion of its business abroad and maintains manufacturing facilities overseas.

Multinational Firms

Most **multinational firms** ordinarily do not think of themselves as having domestic and international divisions. Instead, planning and decision making are geared toward global markets.[36] The locations of headquarters are almost irrelevant. Royal Dutch Shell, Nestlé, IBM, and Ford are well-known multinationals.

multinational firm Controls assets, factories, mines, sales offices, and affiliates in two or more foreign countries.

The economic importance of multinational firms should not be underestimated. Consider, for example, the economic impact of the 500 largest multinational corporations. In 2011, Walmart ranked number one in the Fortune Global 500 rankings, with over $421 billion in sales and 2.1 million employees (including 700 000 international employees in its 4000 international outlets); Royal Dutch Shell ranked second with $378 billion in sales and 93 000 employees; and Exxon was third with over $354 billion in sales and 105 000 employees. Multinationals employ millions of people; buy supplies, parts, equipment, and materials from thousands of other firms; and pay billions of dollars in taxes. Moreover, their activities and products affect the lives of hundreds of millions of consumers, competitors, and investors (sometimes not in a very positive way).[37] Organized protests against the activities of multinational corporations have become quite common.

International Organizational Structures

Different levels of involvement in international business require different kinds of organizational structure. For example, a structure that would help coordinate an exporter's activities would be inadequate for the activities of a multinational firm. In this section, we briefly consider the spectrum of international organizational strategies, including *independent agents*, *licensing arrangements*, *branch offices*, *strategic alliances*, and *foreign direct investment*.

Independent Agents

independent agent A foreign individual, or organization, who agrees to represent an exporter's interests in foreign markets.

An **independent agent** is a foreign individual or organization that agrees to represent an exporter's interests in foreign markets. Independent agents often act as sales representatives as well—they sell the exporter's products, collect payment, and ensure that customers are satisfied. Independent agents often represent several firms at once and usually do not specialize in a particular product or market. Levi Strauss uses agents to market clothing products in many small countries in Africa, Asia, and South America.

Licensing Arrangements

licensing arrangement An arrangement by an owner of a process or product to allow another business to produce, distribute, or market it for a fee or royalty.

royalties Ongoing payments paid by a licence holder to the exporting firm calculated as a percentage of the licence holder's sales.

Canadian companies seeking more substantial involvement in international business may opt for **licensing arrangements**, in which the exporting firm gives individuals or companies in a foreign country the exclusive right to manufacture or market their products in that market. In return, the exporting firm typically receives a fee plus ongoing payments called **royalties**.[38] Royalties are usually calculated as a percentage of the licence holder's sales. For example, Can-Eng Manufacturing, Canada's largest supplier of industrial furnaces, exports its furnaces under licensing arrangements with businesses in Japan, Brazil, Germany, Korea, Taiwan, and Mexico.

Franchising is a special form of licensing that is also very popular.[39] McDonald's and Pizza Hut franchise locations around the world. Similarly, Accor SA, a French hotel chain, franchises its Ibis, Sofitel, and Novotel hotels. As we saw in the opening/closing case, transferring a successful model to another nation is not always easy.

Branch Offices

branch office A location that an exporting firm establishes in a foreign country in order to sell its products more effectively.

Instead of developing relationships with foreign companies or independent agents, a firm may simply send some of its own managers to overseas **branch offices**, over which it has more direct control than it does over agents or licence holders. Branch offices also give a company a more visible public presence in foreign countries. Potential customers tend to feel more secure when a business has branch offices in their country. When a business operates branches, plants, or subsidiaries in several countries, it may assign to one plant or subsidiary the responsibility for researching, developing, manufacturing, and marketing one product or line of products. This is known as **world product mandating**.

world product mandating When a business operates branches, plants, or subsidiaries in several countries, it may assign to one plant or subsidiary the responsibility for researching, developing, manufacturing, and marketing one product or line of products.

Strategic Alliances

The concept of a strategic alliance was introduced in Chapter 2. In international business, it means that a company finds a partner in a foreign country where it would like to conduct business. Each party agrees to invest resources and capital in a new business or else to co-operate in some way for mutual benefit. This new business—the alliance—is then owned by the partners, who divide its profits. For example, Manulife Financial Corp. entered the Chinese market through a strategic alliance with Sinochem, a state-owned trading company. Manulife prepares raw recruits by emphasizing training and team-building so that its sales agents can provide good service to customers. The venture now has 8 percent of the Chinese market and Manulife is the second-ranking foreign insurance firm in China.[40]

The number of strategic alliances among major companies has increased significantly over the past decade and is likely to grow even more. In many countries, including Mexico, India, and China, laws make alliances virtually the only way to do international business within their borders. In addition to easing the way into new markets, strategic alliances give firms greater control over their foreign activities than independent agents and licensing arrangements. All partners in an alliance retain some say in its decisions. Perhaps most important, alliances allow firms to benefit from the knowledge and expertise of their foreign partners. In India, Walmart partnered with Bharti Enterprises to build 10 to 15 large cash-and-carry stores. Walmart wanted to capture a share of the booming retail market without angering the local mom-and-pop merchants and middlemen that dominate the industry.[41]

There are clear advantages to forming strategic alliance but there are many obstacles as well. Groupon, the successful online coupon company, faced major problems after it formed a joint venture with GaoPeng in China. After a promising start, many offices were shut down in 2011 and approximately 400 former employees and their lawyers took legal action. One problem was that Groupon/GaoPeng faced strong competition; another obstacle was that another competitor had already acquired the right to use the groupon.cn domain name.[42] In another example, a proposed alliance between Suzuki and Volkswagen to develop and build hybrid electric cars that would be sold under both brand names turned ugly when Volkswagen described Suzuki as an associate in its annual report. VW also indicated that it would have major influence on Suzuki's operational decisions and financial operations. This was seen as an insult by Suzuki executives; the end result was a war of words and the two companies ultimately cut off all communications.[43]

Foreign Direct Investment

The term **foreign direct investment (FDI)** means buying or establishing tangible assets in another country.[44] As we've seen, many Canadian firms export goods and services to foreign countries, and they also set up manufacturing operations in other countries. For example, Bombardier recently landed a US$4-billion deal with China for the sale of 80 high-speed trains. This deal was made possible because of years of direct investments and a Bombardier/China joint venture group called Bombardier Sifang (Qingdao).[45] More recently, Bombardier has been looking at Morocco as a possible location for a new low-cost plant.[46] In another example, the Bank of Montreal recently purchased the Milwaukee-based Marshall and Ilsley bank branches (374 in all) and nearly doubled its presence in the United States. At a time of financial upheaval, BMO saw an opportunity to invest directly and did not hesitate to put this bank under its BMO Harris banner.[47] However, despite such moves, a debate has been going on for many years about how FDI by foreign firms in Canada affects Canadians. The Foreign Investment Review Agency was established in 1973 to ensure that FDI benefited Canadians. In 1985, FIRA became **Investment Canada** and the mandate was changed to focus on attracting foreign investment. Since the late 1980s, foreign ownership of Canadian industry has again been on the rise and now stands at approximately 30 percent

Recently, foreign buyouts of major firms like Inco, Four Seasons Hotels, and Alcan have caused some Canadian business leaders to express renewed fears about FDI in Canada. A study by Secor Consulting concluded that Canada is the easiest country in the world for foreigners to enter and take over a business. It also found that only three countries in the world were net sellers of their companies: Canada, the United States, and Great Britain.[48] The most general concern is that foreign buyouts of Canadian firms will damage the economy because the head offices will move abroad and major decisions will be made overseas rather than in Canada. For a recent examination of the issues, read the Managing in Turbulent Times boxed feature entitled "Saskatchewan's PotashCorp."

Another concern is that foreign takeovers will mean large job losses. However, the statistics seem to indicate that foreign investment is a key driver for growth and job creation. For example, Google recently announced the creation of new

foreign direct investment (FDI) Buying or establishing tangible assets in another country.

Investment Canada Replaced FIRA in 1985; designed primarily to attract and facilitate foreign investment in Canada.

34 000-square-foot facility in Kitchener, Ontario. In a survey of 150 senior Canadian executives, the issue of foreign ownership ranked low on their list of perceived economic challenges.[49] Many experts argue that placing limitations on foreign investment in Canada essentially shields companies from competition and makes them less efficient.[50] Table 5.2 lists the Top 10 foreign-owned companies in Canada.

TABLE 5.2 Top 10 Foreign-Controlled Companies in Canada, 2011 (Ranked by Sales Revenue)	
Company	Sales Revenue (billions of dollars)
1. Imperial Oil Ltd.	$30.7
2. Walmart Canada Corp.	23.4
3. Husky Energy Inc.	23.3
4. Costco Wholesale Canada Ltd.	13.2
5. Rio Tinto Alcan Inc.	12.0
6. Ultramar Ltd.	11.4
7. Novelis Inc.	10.7
8. Toyota Motor Manufacturing Canada Inc.	9.9
9. Direct Energy Marketing Ltd.	9.6
10. Ford Motor Co. of Canada Ltd.	9.4

MANAGING IN TURBULENT TIMES

Saskatchewan's PotashCorp

In August 2010, Australian-based BHP Billiton made a $38.6-billion takeover bid for PotashCorp of Saskatchewan (PCS). BHP's offer of US$130 per share was immediately rejected by PCS as insufficient, and the CEO of PCS, Bill Doyle, said that other investors were likely to make better offers. By mid-September, PCS shares were selling for $147 in New York. This suggested that investors thought a higher offer was eventually going to be made.

The potential sale of PCS was a big issue in Saskatchewan because the province gets large royalty revenues and income tax payments from PCS (between $200 million and $1.36 billion). One concern was BHP's stated intention that it planned to operate the potash mines at full capacity. That would increase supply and likely drive prices down; that, in turn, would reduce the royalty payments that Saskatchewan receives.

Marius Kloppers, the CEO of BHP, said that running the potash mines at full capacity would mean more jobs for Saskatchewan workers and more cash flowing into the local economy. The PCS mines have been running at just over 50 percent of capacity in recent years, and union leaders liked the idea of more employment. But they were concerned that increasing output could force potash prices lower and hurt workers at other potash production companies, like Agrium and Mosaic, that also have mines in Saskatchewan. BHP said that going to full production would likely drive some marginal foreign competitors out of the market and lead to more stable prices in the long run.

The province of Saskatchewan couldn't veto the deal on its own, but it did recommend to Ottawa that the federal government reject the deal on the grounds that it did not provide a "net benefit" to Canada. The takeover had to be approved by Industry Canada (through the Investment Canada Act, which says a foreign takeover must provide a net benefit to Canada). The federal government launched a review of the proposed takeover, and Saskatchewan hired the Conference Board of Canada to do an analysis of the proposed takeover.

On November 4, 2010, Industry Minister Tony Clement announced that the federal government was rejecting BHP's offer on the grounds that it did not provide a net benefit to Canada. The CEO of BHP, Marius Kloppers, was said to be shocked at the decision.

Critical Thinking Questions

1. What is the difference between a merger and an acquisition? A hostile takeover and a friendly takeover? A strategic alliance and a merger? How do these terms apply in the potash case?

2. Consider the following statement: *The federal government of Canada should not intervene when foreign companies attempt to buy out Canadian companies. This type of action by government interferes with normal free enterprise activity and leads to various problems, including inefficiencies in the way companies are run.* Do you agree or disagree with this statement? Defend your answer.

Barriers to International Trade

Success in foreign markets depends largely on the way businesses respond to the social, economic, legal, and political barriers that exist in international trade.

Describe some of the ways in which **L05** social, cultural, economic, legal, and political differences act as barriers to *international trade*.

Social and Cultural Differences

Any firm involved in international business needs to understand something about the society and culture of the countries in which it plans to operate. Unless a firm understands these cultural differences—either on its own or through acquiring a partner that does—it will probably not be successful in its international business activities. A French lingerie company called Jours Après Lunes recently got into trouble when it launched a new line of products aimed at children aged four to twelve. The line, along with an ad campaign that featured young girls posing in a sexually provocative manner, received little attention in France; however, it was widely criticized as inappropriate and creepy outside of Europe.[51]

Some differences are relatively obvious. For example, language barriers can cause inappropriate naming of products (see Chapter 16 for examples). The physical stature of people in different countries can also be an issue. For example, the Japanese and French are slimmer and shorter on average than Canadians, and this is an important consideration for firms that intend to sell clothes in these markets. Differences in the average age of the local population can also impact product development decision and marketing. Countries with growing populations tend to have a high percentage of young people, meaning that electronics and fashionable clothing would likely do well. Countries with stable or declining populations, on the other hand, tend to have more old people, and generic pharmaceuticals might be more successful in these markets. In addition to such obvious differences, a wide range of subtle value differences can have an important impact on international business. For example, many Europeans shop daily. To Canadians used to weekly trips to the supermarket, the European pattern may seem like a waste of time. But for Europeans, shopping is not just "buying food." It is also about meeting friends, exchanging political views, gossiping, and socializing.

Another important consideration is the subtle behavioural differences that can have an enormous influence on business activity. For example, crossing your legs in a business meeting in Saudi Arabia is inappropriate because showing the sole of your foot is viewed as an insult to the other people in the room. In Portugal, it is considered rude to discuss business during dinner, and in Taiwan, tapping your fingers on the table is a sign of appreciation for a meal. In China, it is not advisable to give a businessman a green hat or to wrap a gift in white or black: A green hat on a Chinese man is said to indicate that his wife is unfaithful, and black and white are associated with death.[52] In Japan, the word *yes* is often used to mean "I understand." So, if a Canadian businesswoman asks a Japanese business supplier to lower prices, and he says "yes," he may simply mean "I understand that you want me to lower prices." But that doesn't mean he will actually lower prices. These kinds of subtleties (and thousands of others) demonstrate that knowledge of local culture and local dos and don'ts is crucial in international business activity.

Jonathan Fischer, the president of Georgetown, Ontario–based Mold-Masters Ltd., discovered how different cultures can be when he went to Shanghai to visit some of his firm's customers. At one meeting he attended, he was dismayed to hear Chinese buyers yelling at his salespeople. When he asked his Chinese managers what was wrong, they explained that the buyers were simply demanding lower prices and faster delivery times and that the shouting was typical of negotiations in China. Fischer learned that the Chinese negotiating style is tough, focuses on price, appears theatrical, and emphasizes hierarchy, but it also requires giving the other side the opportunity to "save face" somewhere in the negotiations.[53]

Jours Apres Lunes upset many people with a series of controversial ads depicting children in images that appear beyond their age.

Economic Differences

Although cultural differences are often subtle, economic differences can be fairly pronounced. In dealing with economies like those of France and Sweden, for example, firms must be aware of when—and to what extent—the government is involved in a given industry. For example, the French government is heavily involved in all aspects of airplane design and manufacturing.

Similarly, a foreign firm doing business in a command economy must understand the unfamiliar relationship of government to business, including a host of idiosyncratic practices. General Motors, which entered a $100-million joint venture to build pickup trucks in China, found itself faced with an economic system that favoured state-owned companies over foreign investors. So, while its Chinese suppliers passed on inflation-based price increases for steel and energy, GM could not in turn pass increases on to Chinese consumers. With subsidized state-owned automakers charging considerably less per truck, GM had no choice but to hold its own prices—and lose money on each sale.

Despite such problems, however, not all companies have had negative experiences. For example, when Motorola opened a factory in China to manufacture communication devices, it involved Chinese technicians in the production process. Chinese designers and engineers played key roles in creating an operation that integrated manufacturing, sales, research, and development.

Navigating the economic differences and identifying the global opportunities is a major challenge for today's corporations. Growth is quite often fuelled by nations around the globe. For instance, luxury goods manufacturers saw an overall increase in sales of 8 percent in 2011 to US$274 billion. LVMH Moet Hennessey Louis Vuitton SA saw an increase of 17 percent in that period, due largely to a tremendous increase in sales in China.[54]

Legal and Political Differences

Legal and political differences are often closely linked to the structure of the economic systems in different countries. These issues include *tariffs* and *quotas, local-content laws,* and *business-practice laws.*

Quotas, Tariffs, and Subsidies

quota A restriction by one nation on the total number of products of a certain type that can be imported from another nation.

embargo A government order forbidding exportation and/or importation of a particular product—or even all products—of a particular country.

tariff A tax charged on imported products.

Even free market economies often use some form of quota and/or tariff that affects the prices and quantities of foreign-made products in those nations. A **quota** restricts the total number of certain products that can be imported into a country. It indirectly raises the prices of those imports by reducing their supply. The ultimate form of quota is an **embargo**: a government order forbidding exportation and/or importation of a particular product—or even all products—of a particular country. For example, Cuban products cannot be legally sold in the United States because there is a long-standing embargo on all Cuban products. Many other countries also impose quotas and embargoes.

A **tariff** is a tax charged on imported products. Tariffs raise the price of imports to consumers, who must pay not only for the products but also for the tariff. A *revenue tariff* is imposed strictly to raise money for the government. But most tariffs in effect today are *protectionist tariffs,* which are meant to discourage the importation of a particular product. A few years ago, the Canadian government placed a 34.6 percent tariff on barbecues made in China after complaints were received that Chinese companies were unfairly subsidizing the production of barbecues.[55]

In a famous case, about a decade ago, the U.S. Commerce Department imposed a 29 percent tariff on softwood lumber exported from Canada to the United States (84 percent of Canadian lumber is exported to the United States). Ottawa immediately

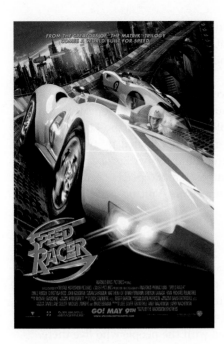

Subsidies are designed to support domestic companies. In this era of free trade, however, governments are increasingly generous with foreign firms that can help develop local industries and provide local jobs. Warner Bros. is opening a new studio to develop high-end video games in Montreal. Local talent, reputation, and knowledge were key factors but government funding helped close the deal. The Quebec government provided $7.5 million to get the studio off the ground. Speed Racer is one of the games produced by Warner Bros. Interactive Unit.

appealed the decision under the provisions of both the North American Free Trade Agreement (NAFTA) and the World Trade Organization (WTO). Both the WTO and NAFTA ruled against the United States on various points in the appeal and said that duties on Canadian lumber must be cut drastically. In spite of these rulings, the United States continued to impose the duties. After they were imposed, the Canadian lumber industry paid over $5 billion in duties to the United States.[56] An agreement that resolved the dispute was eventually reached a few years later after a lot of debate and finger-pointing.[57]

A **subsidy** is a government payment given to a domestic business to help it compete with foreign firms. Bombardier has received subsidies—funds and low-interest loans—from both federal and provincial governments that have helped the company compete and develop its major projects. Bombardier and its main rival, Brazilian-based Embraer, have accused each other of receiving excessive unfair government support, which has led to disputes at the WTO. Concluding Case 5-2 provides information on this issue.

When the government of a country pays subsidies to one of its domestic companies or industries, there can be a negative effect on producers in other countries. For example, the WTO ruled that the U.S. government's subsidies to its cotton growers broke trade rules, depressed world cotton prices, and hurt Brazilian cotton producers.[58] These subsidies also hurt small cotton farmers in Africa because they caused highly productive U.S. farmers to produce a lot of cotton, which drove down the price African farmers received.[59] Canada's supply management system, which restricts imports and guarantees markets for producers of chickens, turkeys, eggs, and milk, could also come under fire since the WTO views the system as an unfair subsidy to producers.[60] More information about the WTO is provided later in the chapter.

Protectionism—the practice of protecting domestic business at the expense of free market competition—has both advocates and critics. Supporters argue that tariffs and quotas protect domestic firms and jobs. In particular, they protect new industries until they are truly able to compete internationally. Some claim they are necessary because other nations have such measures. Still others justify protectionism in the name of national security and argue that advanced technology should not be sold to potential enemies. But opponents of protectionism are equally vocal. They note

subsidy A government payment to help domestic business compete with foreign firms.

protectionism Protecting domestic business at the expense of free market competition.

that protectionism reduces competition and drives up prices. They cite it as a cause of friction between nations. They maintain that while jobs in some industries would be lost if protectionism ceased, jobs in other industries would expand if all countries abolished tariffs and quotas.

Protectionism sometimes takes on almost comic proportions. Neither the United States nor European countries grow bananas, but American and European firms both buy and sell bananas in foreign markets. Problems arose when the EU put a quota on bananas imported from Latin America—a market dominated by two U.S. firms, Chiquita and Dole—to help firms based in current and former European colonies in the Caribbean. To retaliate, the United States imposed a 100 percent tariff on certain luxury products imported from Europe, including Louis Vuitton handbags, Scottish cashmere sweaters, and Parma ham.[61]

Local-Content Laws

local-content laws Laws requiring that products sold in a particular country be at least partly made in that country.

A country can affect how a foreign firm does business there by enacting **local-content laws** that require products sold in a particular country to be at least partly made in that country. These laws typically mean that firms seeking to do business in a country must either invest directly or have a local joint-venture partner. In this way, some of the profits earned in a foreign country are shared with the people who live there.

Many countries have local-content laws. In a fairly extreme case, Venezuela forbids the import of any product if a similar product is made in Venezuela. In 2005, in a move designed to protect its many small, local miners, Venezuela's president said he would cancel all mining licences and stop issuing new ones to foreign companies. Oil and gas licences held by foreign companies had already been cancelled. These actions make foreign companies more reluctant to invest in Venezuela.[62] In a recent case in Canada, Public Mobile challenged a government ruling that cleared Globalive's Wind Mobile and declared it a Canadian company in compliance with telecommunications rules. This industry is still highly regulated and Public Mobile is fighting the ruling concerning a direct competitor because it was heavily financed by Orascom Telecom, a Cairo-based corporation.[63]

Local-content laws may even exist within a country; when they do, they act just like trade barriers. In Canada, for example, a low bid on a bridge construction contract in British Columbia was rejected because the company that made the bid was from Alberta. The job was given to a B.C. company. A New Brunswick window manufacturer lost a contract in Nova Scotia despite having made the lowest bid; the job went to a company in Nova Scotia.

The Agreement on Internal Trade (AIT) requires all 10 Canadian provinces to remove barriers to agricultural trade. But when Quebec—which has a strong dairy lobby—prohibited margarine coloured to look like butter, it was in violation of the agreement.[64] Unilever Canada Ltd. challenged the legality of the ban on coloured margarine in 2002, but it was not until 2008 that Quebec repealed the law.[65] In another case, Prince Edward Island ignored a dispute panel ruling that PEI's milk import restrictions violated the AIT.[66] A third case involves the question of who is allowed to audit the financial statements of public companies. At present, only Chartered Accountants (CAs) are allowed to do this in Quebec. This rule is being challenged by the Certified General Accountants (CGAs), who have auditing rights in most other provinces.[67] If provincial governments do not honour their obligations, the AIT will become meaningless.

Business-Practice Laws

business-practice laws Law or regulation passed by host countries to regulate business practices within their jurisdictions.

Many businesses entering new markets encounter problems in complying with tough regulations and bureaucratic obstacles. Such **business-practice laws** are passed by host countries to regulate business practices within their jurisdictions. Walmart left Germany and South Korea because it did not effectively adapt to local tastes and was unable to achieve economies of scale.[68] In Germany, for example, Walmart had to stop refunding price differences on items sold for less by other stores because the practice is illegal in Germany. In an example closer to home, mixed martial arts UFC events were being held in Montreal, Vancouver, and the United States, but they were banned in Ontario until 2010.[69] In another case, Google agreed to pay $500 million in 2011 to settle a case with the U.S. government over advertising revenue earned from Canadian online pharmacies. The government accused Google of enabling the illegal importation of drugs.[70]

Sometimes what is legal (and even accepted) business practice in one country is illegal in another. For example, a U.S. government crackdown on internet gambling has led to the arrests of Canadian entrepreneurs. U.S. authorities have vowed to prosecute online gambling companies even when their executives are outside the United States. In 2012, Calvin Ayre, who runs the gambling site Bodog.com, was indicted along with three other entrepreneurs and faces a possible sentence of 25 years. However, Mr. Ayre is not in custody and he continues to operate the site in Canada and internationally.[71]

The boxed insert entitled "Controlling Pollution in International Waters" describes another complicated issue in international law and practice.

Paying bribes to government officials to get business is another problem area. The Canadian Corruption of Foreign Public Officials Act prohibits bribery of foreign

THE GREENING OF BUSINESS

Controlling Pollution in International Waters

Ships that carry cargo produce more sulfur dioxide than all of the world's cars, trucks, and buses combined, and they produce about one-quarter of the entire world's output of nitrogen oxide emissions (the ones that cause smog). Bunker fuel—a tar-like sludge that is left over from the process of refining petroleum—is used by cargo shippers because it is cheap, but it also releases more pollutants than high-grade fuel. Ships that carry people are also a problem. A modern cruise ship generates a lot of waste—on a typical day, a ship will produce seven tons of solid garbage, 30 000 gallons of sewage, 7000 gallons of bilge water containing oil, and 225 000 gallons of "grey" water from sinks and laundries. Multiply these numbers by more than 167 ships worldwide, cruising 50 weeks per year, and the scope of the environmental damage is substantial.

While increasing concerns about ocean pollution are evident, the International Maritime Organization—which is the United Nations agency that regulates shipping—has had extreme difficulty agreeing on what to do about it. For example, it took the group 17 years to agree that the sulfur content in marine fuel should not exceed 4.5 percent. But the sulfur content in bunker fuel had already been reduced to half that level by the time the regulation was passed. A more promising approach is for ports to set emission rules, since cargo ships obviously have to unload their cargo somewhere. Certain ports have already passed laws that prohibit ships from docking unless they use cleaner-burning fuels. California, for example, does not allow ships that use low-grade fuel to sail within 24 miles of its shores. Ports in Germany, Sweden, and Canada have also set targets to reduce air pollution from ships. But this patchwork of regulations has caused ship owners big problems, because it means that ships need to switch from low- to high-grade fuel as they sail to different locations. Because this process is complicated and dangerous, the International Association of Independent Tanker Owners and the Hong Kong Shipowners Association both think the UN should simply require ships to stop using bunker fuel.

Laws regulating ocean pollution for both cargo and cruise ships vary considerably across nations, and even when laws are strict, enforcement may be limited. You would think that cruise ships would be very concerned about clean seas for their own economic well-being, but this is often not the case. Over the past decade, as enforcement has tightened, 10 cruise lines have collectively paid US$48.5 million in fines related to illegal dumping. Critics are speaking out, but they note that that the companies won't stop as long as the profits continue. Technology exists to make the waste safe, but industry experts estimate that dumping can save a firm millions of dollars annually.

Critical Thinking Questions

1. What are the various factors that make solution to the ocean pollution problem so difficult?

2. Aside from carelessness, what factors might lead a cruise line to illegally dump waste into the ocean? What factors might cause cargo ships to use low-grade fuel?

officials, but as more Canadian companies do business abroad, they find themselves competing against companies that are not reluctant to pay bribes to get business. As a result, some Canadian companies are losing business.[72] In an attempt to create fairer competition among multinational companies, ministers from the Organisation for Economic Co-operation and Development (OECD) agreed in 1997 to criminalize bribery of foreign public officials.[73] Recently, four employees of the mining giant Rio Tinto admitted to bribery charges in China. Mr. Stern Hu, a top executive in charge of iron ore, was sentenced to 10 years for accepting a bribe of US$146 000.[74]

Transparency International (TI), an organization devoted to stamping out global corruption, says that companies from Belgium and Canada are least likely to pay bribes to win business in foreign countries; Russian firms are most likely to pay bribes.[75] TI publishes a "Corruption Perceptions Index," which ranks countries according to the amount of corruption that is perceived to exist, based on ratings by business people, academics, and risk analysts. The index shows that the least corrupt countries are Denmark, New Zealand, and Singapore, while the most corrupt countries are Myanmar, Afghanistan, and Somalia. Canada is ranked sixth and the United States is the twenty-second nation on the list.[76]

cartel Any association of producers whose purpose is to control supply of and prices for a given product.

Cartels and Dumping. A **cartel** is an association of producers whose purpose is to control the supply and price of a commodity. The most famous cartel is the Organization of Petroleum Exporting Countries (OPEC), which has given oil-producing countries considerable power in the past 25 years. At various times, other cartels have been evident in diamonds, shipping, and coffee. While nothing much can be done when governments form a cartel like OPEC, private sector businesses can be prosecuted for doing so. For example, the European Union imposed fines on importers of Dole and Del Monte bananas (fined $95.5 million), on makers of car glass (fined $2 billion), and on makers of paraffin wax used in paper plates and cups (fined $1 billion).[77] Canada is involved in a potash cartel with Belarus and Russia; these three nations account for almost 80 percent of production, and the price has quadrupled in just a few years.[78]

dumping Selling a product for less abroad than in the producing nation; illegal in Canada.

Many countries forbid **dumping**—selling a product abroad for less than the comparable price charged at home. Anti-dumping legislation typically views dumping as occurring if products are being sold at prices less than "fair value," or if the result unfairly harms domestic industry. Recently, the United States imposed duties of 10.36 to 15.78 percent on steel pipes produced in China, which denounced the move.[79] However, the United States is not alone in its concerns; India has accused China of dumping products on the Indian market that it can't sell elsewhere.[80]

Overcoming Barriers to Trade

L06 Explain how free *trade agreements* assist world trade.

Despite the barriers to trade described so far, international trade is flourishing. This is because both organizations and free trade treaties exist to promote international trade. The most significant of these are the General Agreement on Tariffs and Trade (GATT), the World Trade Organization (WTO), the European Union (EU), and the North American Free Trade Agreement (NAFTA).

General Agreement on Tariffs and Trade

General Agreement on Tariffs and Trade (GATT) International trade agreement to encourage the multilateral reduction or elimination of trade barriers.

The **General Agreement on Tariffs and Trade (GATT)**, which has often been humorously referred to as the General Agreement to Talk and Talk, was signed after the Second World War. Its purpose was to reduce or eliminate trade barriers, such as tariffs and quotas. It did so by encouraging nations to protect domestic industries within agreed-upon limits and to engage in multilateral negotiations. While 92 countries signed GATT, not all complied with its rules. The United States was one of the worst offenders. A revision of GATT went into effect in 1994, but many issues remained unresolved—for example, the opening of foreign markets to most financial services.

The World Trade Organization

On January 1, 1995, the **World Trade Organization (WTO)** came into existence as the successor to GATT. The 153 member countries are required to open markets to international trade, and the WTO is empowered to pursue three goals:

1. Promote trade by encouraging members to adopt fair trade practices

2. Reduce trade barriers by promoting multilateral negotiations

3. Establish fair procedures for resolving disputes among members

The WTO is overseeing reductions in import duties on thousands of products that are traded between countries. Canada, the United States, and the European Union are founding members of the WTO.[81] Unlike GATT, the WTO's decisions are binding, and many people feared that it would make sweeping decisions and boss countries around. These fears were a bit overstated. The WTO has served in its role as a ruling body but appeals can often drag on for years. For example, in 2010 Boeing won a ruling against Airbus because it received $4.1 billion in loans from European governments while developing its A380 jets. Despite the ruling, there appears to be even more money being given to Airbus for development of the new A350. It has been five years since the case was first presented and it could be years before Boeing sees any rewards from the ruling.[82] The WTO also recently ruled against China and its practice of controlling access to distribution of films in China. China only allows 70 foreign films to be distributed in that country per year. The WTO ordered China to open its distribution channels; this is seen as a big win for North American movie, music and print distributors.[83]

The WTO has had significant trouble dealing with the issue of agricultural subsidies. Many attempts have been made during the past few years to resolve this problem (the so-called Doha Round of trade talks). The general idea was that developing countries would lower their tariffs on industrial goods and European and American governments would lower subsidies on agricultural products. The process has dragged on, however, and was still unresolved at the end of 2011.

In addition, WTO talks on trade liberalization have often been disrupted by protestors who resent the power of the WTO and who are concerned about what world trade is doing to both the environment and the developing countries.[84] Protestors include labour unions (who regard Third World imports as unfair), environmentalists (who are concerned about business activity harming the environment), social activists (who are concerned about poor working conditions in developing countries), and farmers (who are concerned about the effect of free trade on grain prices).

The European Union (EU)

Originally called the Common Market, the **European Union (EU)** initially included only the principal Western European nations like Italy, Germany, France, and the United Kingdom. But by 2011, 27 countries belonged to the EU (see Figure 5.5). Other countries are in the process of applying for membership, notably Croatia and Turkey. The EU has eliminated most quotas and set uniform tariff levels on products imported and exported within their group. The EU is the largest free marketplace in the world, and produces nearly one-quarter of total global wealth.[85]

The North American Free Trade Agreement

The **North American Free Trade Agreement (NAFTA)** came into effect in 1994. It removes tariffs and other trade barriers among Canada, the United States, and Mexico. An earlier agreement, the Canada–U.S. Free Trade Agreement (FTA), took effect in 1989. Its goal was to achieve freer trade between Canada and the United States. Surveys conducted prior to the introduction of the FTA showed that the majority of Canadians were opposed to free trade. They feared that (1) jobs would be lost to other countries, (2) Canada would be flooded with products manufactured in lower-wage countries

World Trade Organization (WTO) Organization through which member nations negotiate trading agreements and resolve disputes about trade policies and practices.

European Union (EU) Agreement among major Western European nations to eliminate or make uniform most trade barriers affecting group members.

North American Free Trade Agreement (NAFTA) Agreement to gradually eliminate tariffs and other trade barriers among the United States, Canada, and Mexico.

FIGURE 5.5

The nations of the European Union.

such as Mexico, (3) Canada would lose the right to control its own environmental standards, (4) the United States might take our natural resources, and (5) Canadian cultural sovereignty would be lost.

Supporters of free trade, by contrast, argued that (1) access to U.S. markets would be guaranteed by free trade, and this would protect Canadian employment; (2) Canadian exports would increase because of free trade; (3) the environment was not covered in free trade agreements; (4) there was nothing in the free trade agreement that threatened Canada's control over its energy resources; and (5) the free trade agreement was about trade and tariffs, not cultural sovereignty.

What has actually happened since NAFTA took effect? A few years ago, a group of economists at the Canadian Economics Association concluded that free trade has been neither as good for Canada as its supporters predicted it would be, nor as bad for Canada as its detractors predicted.[86] Several specific effects are noticeable:

- NAFTA has created a much more active North American market

- Direct foreign investment has increased in Canada

- U.S. imports from (and exports to) Mexico have increased

- Canada has become an exporting powerhouse

- Trade between the United States and Canada has risen sharply, and Canada enjoys a large trade surplus with the United States

In the past few years, however, there is evidence that the benefits of NAFTA are slowly being eroded by ever-increasing delays at border crossings, caused mostly by heavy U.S. border security as a result of the terrorist attacks in 2001. Studies by the Conference Board of Canada and Canadian and U.S. chambers of commerce show that companies are not able to take advantage of the efficiencies of integrated supply chains because there are so many cross-border delays. Those delays are forcing companies to spend extra time and money just trying to ensure that their deliveries will get through to customers on time.[87] However, on the positive side, there is now an extensive Canadian presence in Mexico in everything from mining to auto parts to banking. For example, as we saw in the opening case, Scotiabank, the most international Canadian bank, has made great inroads in Mexico with over two million Mexican clients.[88] There is also a renewed effort to increase direct trade between Mexico and Canada. In 2010, Mexico eliminated nearly 14 000 rules and regulations to improve trade competitiveness. At the time, trade minister Bruno Ferrari was calling on Canada to increase its trading relationship with Mexico and help ensure that trade between the nations (now at $20 billion per year) continues to increase over the next decade.

Other Free Trade Agreements in the Americas

NAFTA is the most publicized trade agreement in the Americas, but there has been a flurry of activity among other countries as well. On January 1, 1995, a free trade agreement known as Mercosur went into effect among Argentina, Brazil, Uruguay, and Paraguay. Venezuela became the fifth member of the bloc in 2012. Within the first decade of Mercosur's existence, tariffs were eliminated on 80 percent of the goods traded among the original members. Brazil has proposed enlarging Mercosur into a South American Free Trade Area (SAFTA), which might eventually negotiate with NAFTA to form an Americas Free Trade Area (AFTA).

There are several other free trade areas in existence in the Americas as well: the Andean Pact (Bolivia, Ecuador, Colombia, and Peru), the Central American Common Market (Costa Rica, El Salvador, Guatemala, Honduras, and Nicaragua), the G-3 group (Colombia, Mexico, and Venezuela), and the Caribbean Common Market (many of the island nations of the Caribbean).[89] The populations of the various free trade areas of the Americas total nearly 900 million. The economies of many of these nations are growing rapidly, and they will become increasingly important to Canada during the next decade.

Free Trade Agreements Elsewhere

Free trade agreements are not restricted to the Americas. A high level of activity is evident around the world as groups of nations band together to form regional trade associations for their own benefit. Here are some examples:

- the Association of Southeast Asian Nations (ASEAN) (see Figure 5.6)

- the Asia-Pacific Economic Cooperation (many nations of the Pacific Rim, as well as the United States, Canada, and Mexico)

- the Economic Community of Central African States (many nations in equatorial Africa)

- the Gulf Cooperation Council (Bahrain, Kuwait, Oman, Qatar, Saudi Arabia, and the United Arab Emirates)

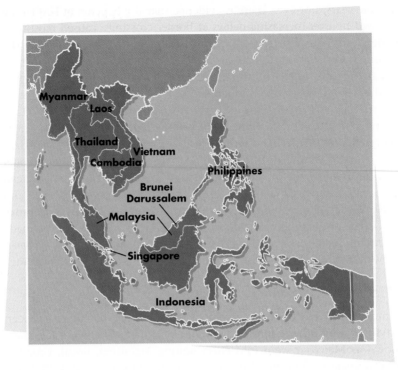

FIGURE 5.6

The nations of ASEAN.

MyBizLab

Capture more moments of true understanding. MyBizLab provides you with interactive study and practice tools directly related to this chapter's content. The new MyBizLab Study Plan Learning Path is designed to measure a full range of skills and provide remediation to give you what you need to master key chapter concepts. MyBizLab flexes to your unique learning needs. The result? Inspired learning, more success.

SUMMARY OF LEARNING OBJECTIVES

1. **Describe the rise of *international business* and identify the *major world marketplaces*.** More and more business firms are engaged in international business. *Globalization* refers to the process by which the world economy is quickly becoming a single interdependent entity. The global economy is characterized by a rapid growth in the exchange of information and trade in services. The three major marketplaces for international business are North America (the United States, Canada, and Mexico), Western Europe (which is dominated by Germany, the United Kingdom, France, and Italy), and Asia-Pacific (where the dominant country, Japan, is surrounded by such rapidly advancing nations as South Korea, Taiwan, Hong Kong, and China).

2. **Identify the evolving role of *emerging markets* and highlight the important role of the *BRICS nations*.** The old international trading patterns and activities are changing. In the past, Western companies used less

developed markets to acquire natural resources and to carry out simple assembly tasks. While this is still evident in international trade, the relationships have become much more complex and many former have-nots are now exploiting relationships for their own gain. There are great opportunities in places like Thailand, Indonesia, South Korea, and Ukraine. However, the BRICS nations are getting the most attention (and for good reason). BRICS stands for *Brazil, Russia, India, China,* and *South Africa* (which was invited to join in 2011).

3. **Explain how different forms of *competitive advantage, import–export balances, exchange rates,* and *foreign competition* determine the ways in which countries and businesses respond to the *international environment*.** With an *absolute advantage*, a country engages in international trade because it can produce a good or service more cheaply and/or of higher quality than any other country. But more

often, countries trade because they enjoy *comparative advantages*. That is, they can produce some products more efficiently or better than other products. A country that exports more than it imports has a favourable balance of trade, while a country that imports more than it exports has an unfavourable balance of trade. If the *exchange rate* decreases (i.e., if the value of the Canadian dollar falls), our exports become less expensive for other countries so they will buy more of what we produce. The reverse happens if the value of the Canadian dollar increases. Changes in the exchange rate therefore have a strong impact on our international competitiveness.

4. **Discuss the factors involved in deciding to do business internationally and in selecting the appropriate levels of *international involvement* and *international organizational structure*.** In deciding whether to do business internationally, a firm must determine whether a market for its product exists abroad and, if so, whether the firm has the skills and knowledge to manage such a business. It must assess the business climates of other nations to ensure that they are conducive to international operations. A firm must also decide on its level of international involvement. It can choose to be an exporter or importer, to organize as an *international firm*, or to operate as a *multinational firm*. The choice will influence the organizational structure of its international operations—specifically, its use of *independent agents, licensing arrangements, branch offices, strategic alliances,* and *direct investment.*

5. **Describe some of the ways in which social, cultural, economic, legal, and political differences act as barriers to *international trade*.** *Social and cultural differences* that can serve as barriers to trade include language, social values, and traditional buying patterns. Differences in economic systems may force businesses to establish close relationships with foreign governments before they are permitted to do business abroad. *Quotas, tariffs, subsidies,* and *local-content laws* offer protection to local industries. Differences in *business-practice laws* mean that standard business practices in one nation may be illegal in another.

6. **Explain how *free trade agreements* assist world trade.** Several trade agreements have attempted to eliminate restrictions on free trade internationally. The *General Agreement on Tariffs and Trade (GATT)* was instituted to eliminate tariffs and other trade barriers among participating nations. The *European Union (EU)* has eliminated virtually all trade barriers among its 27 member nations. The *North American Free Trade Agreement (NAFTA)* eliminates many of the barriers to free trade that existed among the United States, Canada, and Mexico.

KEY TERMS

absolute advantage (p. 146)
balance of payments (p. 149)
balance of trade (p. 148)
branch office (p. 156)
BRIC (p. 145)
BRICS (p. 146)
business-practice laws (p. 162)
cartel (p. 164)
comparative advantage (p. 147)
dumping (p. 164)
embargo (p. 160)
euro (p. 151)
European Union (EU) (p. 165)
exchange rate (p. 150)
exporter (p. 154)

exports (p. 142)
foreign direct investment (FDI) (p. 157)
General Agreement on Tariffs and Trade (GATT) (p. 164)
globalization (p. 142)
importer (p. 153)
imports (p. 142)
independent agent (p. 156)
international competitiveness (p. 148)
international firm (p. 155)
Investment Canada (p. 157)
licensing arrangement (p. 156)
local-content laws (p. 162)
multinational firm (p. 155)

national competitive advantage (p. 147)
North American Free Trade Agreement (NAFTA) (p. 165)
per capita income (p. 143)
protectionism (p. 161)
quota (p. 160)
royalties (p. 156)
subsidy (p. 161)
tariff (p. 160)
trade deficit (p. 148)
trade surplus (p. 148)
world product mandating (p. 156)
World Trade Organization (WTO) (p. 165)

QUESTIONS FOR ANALYSIS

1. Make a list of all the major items in your bedroom. Identify the country in which each item was made. Give possible reasons why that nation might have a comparative advantage in producing this good.

2. Assume that you are the manager of a small firm seeking to enter the international arena. What information would you need about the market that you're thinking of entering?

3. Do you think that a firm that is operating internationally is better to adopt a single standard of ethical conduct or to adapt to local conditions? Under what kinds of conditions might each approach be preferable?

4. Do you support protectionist tariffs for Canada? If so, in what instances and for what reasons? If not, why not?

5. Explain how it is possible for a country to have a positive balance of trade and a negative balance of payments.

6. The EU includes most of the Western European countries, but some (such as Switzerland) have chosen not to join. Why might that be? What are the implications for countries that do not join?

APPLICATION EXERCISES

1. Interview the manager of a local firm that does at least some business internationally. Identify reasons why the company decided to "go international," as well as the level of the firm's international involvement and the organizational structure it uses for its international operations.

2. Select a product familiar to you. Using library references and the internet, learn something about the culture of India and identify the problems that might arise in trying to market this product to India's citizens.

3. What attributes of your province or region (cultural, geographical, economic, etc.) would be of interest to a foreign firm thinking about locating there? Visit provincial government sites and find resources that are available for businesses to help them invest in your province. Identify a company that has recently invested in your province. What reasons did it give for its decision?

4. Visit the website of a major global company such as Coca-Cola and enter some of its international sites. Make sure to choose countries from different parts of the world. What are some of the differences that you see in the websites? Identify some of the similar themes and report your findings.

BUILDING YOUR BUSINESS SKILLS

Putting Yourself in Your Place

Goal

To encourage students to apply global business strategies to a small-business situation.

Situation

Some people might say that Yolanda Lang is a bit too confident. Others might say that she needs confidence—and more—to succeed in the business she's chosen. But one thing is certain: Lang is determined to grow INDE, her handbag design company, into a global enterprise. At only 28 years of age, she has time on her side—if she makes the right business moves now.

These days, Lang spends most of her time in Milan, Italy. Backed by $50 000 of her parents' personal savings, she is trying to compete with Gucci, Fendi, and other high-end handbag makers. Her target market is women willing to spend $400 on a purse. Ironically, Lang was forced to set up shop in Italy because of the snobbishness of these customers, who buy high-end bags only if they're European made. "Strangely enough," she muses, "I need to be in Europe to sell in North America."

To succeed, she must first find ways to keep production costs down—a tough task for a woman in a male-dominated business culture. Her fluent Italian is an advantage, but she's often forced to turn down inappropriate dinner invitations. She also has to figure out how to get her 22-bag collection into stores worldwide. Retailers are showing her bags in Italy and Japan, but she's had little luck in the United States. "I intend to be a global company," says Lang. The question is how to succeed first as a small business.

Method

Step 1

Join together with three or four other students to discuss the steps that Lang has taken so far to break into the U.S. retail market. These steps include:

- buying a mailing list of 5000 shoppers from high-end department store Neiman Marcus and selling directly to these customers; and

- linking with a manufacturer's representative to sell her line in major U.S. cities while she herself concentrates on Europe.

Step 2

Based on what you learned in this chapter, suggest other strategies that might help Lang grow her business. Working with group members, consider whether the following options would help or hurt Lang's business. Explain why a strategy is likely to work or likely to fail.

- Lang could relocate to the United States and sell abroad through an independent agent.
- Lang could relocate to the United States and set up a branch office in Italy.
- Lang could find a partner in Italy and form a strategic alliance that would allow her to build her business on both continents.

Step 3

Working alone, create a written marketing plan for INDE. What steps would you recommend that Lang take to reach her goal of becoming a global company? Compare your written response with those of other group members.

Questions for Discussion

1. What are the most promising steps that Lang can take to grow her business? What are the least promising?

2. Lang thinks that her trouble breaking into the U.S. retail market stems from the fact that her company is unknown. How would this circumstance affect the strategies suggested in Steps 1 and 2?

3. When Lang deals with Italian manufacturers, she is a young, attractive woman in a man's world. Often, she must convince men that her purpose is business and nothing else. How should Lang handle personal invitations that get in the way of business? How can she say no while still maintaining business relationships? Why is it often difficult for women to do business in male-dominated cultures?

4. The American consulate has given Lang little business help because her products are made in Italy. Do you think the consulate's treatment of an American businessperson is fair or unfair? Explain your answer.

5. Do you think Lang's relocation to Italy will pay off? Why or why not?

6. With Lang's goals of creating a global company, can INDE continue to be a one-person operation?

EXERCISING YOUR ETHICS: TEAM EXERCISE

Weighing the Trade-offs

The Situation

There is a small bank that is headquartered in western Canada. The firm is privately owned and all the managers own stock in the bank. The company's senior managers (and majority owners) have decided to sell the bank to a major international banking company within the next two to three years. First, though, the bank corporation needs to trim its expenses in order to make it more attractive to a potential buyer.

The Dilemma

Because the bank corporation has been a locally owned and operated enterprise, it has maintained a full slate of operations within the local market. For instance, its corporate offices, many banking outlets, and all of its support activities are housed locally. The latter category includes a large call centre—a staff of 30 people who handle most customer calls involving questions about their accounts.

There has been a growing trend in banking, though, to outsource call centres to foreign countries, most notably India. Such markets have an abundance of potential English-speaking employees and excellent technology, as well as low wages. One senior manager has argued that the bank corporation should outsource its call centre immediately. This would enable the firm to lower its costs, thus making it even more attractive to a potential buyer. When confronted with the prospect of cutting 30 jobs, the manager acknowledges that that will be tough, but he is certain that any buyer will eventually do the same anyway.

Another vocal senior manager, though, is opposed to this idea. This person argues that because the bank corporation was started locally and has strong ties to the local community, it should maintain its current operations until

the bank is sold. Then, this manager argues, if a new owner decides to cut jobs, "it will be on their conscience, not ours."

Team Activity

Assemble a group of four students and assign each group member to one of the following roles:

- senior manager (majority owner) of the bank
- call centre employee
- bank customer
- bank corporation investor

Action Steps

1. Before discussing the situation with your group, and from the perspective of your assigned role, do you think that the call centre should be outsourced immediately? Write down the reasons for your position.

2. Before discussing the situation with your group, and from the perspective of your assigned role, what are the underlying ethical issues, if any, in this situation? Write down the issues.

3. Gather your group together and reveal, in turn, each member's comments on whether the call centre should be outsourced immediately. Next, reveal the ethical issues listed by each member.

4. Appoint someone to record the main points of agreement and disagreement within the group. How do you explain the results? What accounts for any disagreement?

5. From an ethical standpoint, what does your group conclude is the most appropriate action for the bank to take in this situation?

6. Develop a group response to the following question: Can your team identify other solutions that might help satisfy both senior managers' views?

Go to MyBizLab for additional cases and exercise material.

CONCLUDING CASE 5-1

Tim Hortons USA: Exporting a Strategic Model Is No Easy Task

When you think of Tim Hortons, what images come to mind? Students typically use the following words: hockey, Timbits, maple, Canada, doughnuts, coffee, Sidney Crosby, inexpensive. Tim Hortons is very successful in Canada, and its doughnuts have become the Canadian equivalent of American apple pie or the Big Mac. The company has worked hard to create a warm, homegrown image in the minds of the Canadian consumer. Its low-cost/high-volume approach, its tremendous channel domination, and its unapologetic links to Canadian symbols are all sources of competitive advantage for Tim Hortons in Canada. According to the website, Tim Hortons is the fourth largest quick-service restaurant chain in North America, and the largest in Canada with over 3000 stores. (To put this figure into perspective, McDonald's has approximately 1400 stores in Canada.) But can Tim Hortons successfully export its business model to the United States?

The Challenge

The first U.S. Tim Hortons opened in Buffalo, New York, in 1984, and in 2012 there were 645 stores in 12 northern U.S. states. Recently the company announced plans to open 300 new U.S. stores, and it now seems ready for a more concentrated push into the United States. But what approach should be used? Should the same standardized approach that has worked in Canada be used or will the model have to be adapted for the U.S. market?

For obvious reasons, Tim Hortons has not focused on hockey and Canadian symbols to sell its doughnuts and coffee in the United States. It might try to replace hockey with baseball, but Dunkin' Donuts already has strong grassroots links to that sport. It could wrap itself in the U.S. flag, but that would leave it open to charges of being fake, and that approach might also confuse or upset Canadians who visit the States. Another problem: Tim Hortons cannot rely on a large marketing channel advantage in the United States. In Canada, there is one Tim Hortons for every 11 000 consumers, but this is not the case across the border. In the United States, there are thousands of local coffee shops in addition to major players like Dunkin' Donuts, Starbucks, and even McDonald's (especially with its recent McCafé push). In the States, these companies have the sort of market penetration that Tim Hortons enjoys in Canada.

So what can be done? Until now, Tim Hortons's central message in the United States has focused on value and freshness. This was not a very original idea, but at least it was an honest approach. Unfortunately, this hasn't differentiated Tim Hortons from its competitors. Something else

is needed. But what? The company is now pursuing several strategies, including the acquisition of prime locations, co-branding, and going upscale.

Acquiring Prime Locations

In 2009, Tim Hortons opened its first outlets in New York City after reaching an agreement with a former Dunkin' Donuts franchisee who owned 12 prime locations in Manhattan and Brooklyn. This gave Tim Hortons a great opportunity to develop its brand and gain exposure in this key market because prime locations are difficult to find, especially in New York City. The fact that people were already accustomed to going to these particular locations for their coffee fix should also help. As a result of this deal, Tim Hortons has some much-needed exposure, including a location in Madison Square Garden.

Co-Branding

A few years ago, Tim Hortons and Kahala Corporation, owner of the Cold Stone Creamery—an ice cream parlour franchise—announced a co-branding agreement that would see the development of up to 100 combined stores in the United States. At the same time, approximately 60 outlets across Canada were converted to test this new co-branded format. This should help Tim Hortons to get noticed and to improve its competitive position in the U.S. market.

Going Upscale

In 2010, Tim Hortons announced that it was planning to create upscale café/bake shops with a different menu that would include pastries baked onsite. These new stores were scheduled to open in existing markets such as New York and Michigan. The announcement raised several new questions: Could a high-end Tim Hortons work? How would the company manage the traditional stores alongside the new outlets? Would there be a sub-brand created or would it eventually transform all U.S. locations? This strategy should help relieve some of the stress of the rising food costs that have recently been squeezing low-cost food providers like Tim Hortons. But can the company manage the brand and not confuse consumers? Time will tell.

Breaking New Ground

Tim Hortons is taking a concept that has worked in Canada and trying to make it work in a foreign market. In order to succeed, Tim Hortons must develop a clear strategy that U.S. consumers can identify with. That approach is what made the company successful in Canada. Succeeding in new markets is not easy and the American expansion is still a work in progress. However, despite the challenges in a similar market down south, Tim Hortons made a bold announcement in 2011 when it decided to open a location in the United Arab Emirates and announced intentions to open 120 new outlets in the Gulf region (Kuwait, Bahrain, Saudi Arabia, and Oman were identified). Clearly this would present a whole new set of challenges but it was also an indication that Tim Hortons was serious about expansion. With the Canadian market already developed, growth will need to come from outside the borders. Only time will tell if the concept will work, but one thing is clear: They won't be selling Timbits by using images of Sidney Crosby in Dubai.

Questions for Discussion

1. Can the same business model that has been so successful in Canada work in the United States?
2. Tim Hortons has focused on hockey and Canadian symbols in Canada. What might replace hockey as an emphasis in the U.S. market?
3. How will Tim Hortons compete with the myriad small local coffee shops in the United States?
4. Tim Hortons's strategy is to acquire prime locations, engage in co-branding, and go upscale in an attempt to penetrate the U.S. market. What are the advantages and disadvantages of this strategy?
5. Do you believe that Tim Hortons will be successful if it follows through with its expansion into the Gulf region? Explain. Should Tim Hortons use a standardized or adapted approach (provide specific examples to support your choice)?

CONCLUDING CASE 5-2

After getting an initial order from Lufthansa, Bombardier began the process of producing its long-awaited CSeries plane.

Bombardier: The CSeries and Global Competition

Montreal-based Bombardier Inc. is a diversified Canadian company that specializes in transportation solutions, from commercial and business jets to rail transportation equipment and services. Bombardier was founded in 1942 to manufacture a now-classic Canadian product—tracked vehicles for transportation across snow-covered terrain. Many of the Bombardier snowmobiles that were manufactured decades ago can still be seen in various areas of Canada. One such half-track sits on the windswept shores of Yathkyed Lake in Nunavut, hundreds of kilometres from any town. It is a mute reminder of the important role Bombardier played in opening up Canada's remote North.

Bombardier's headquarters are in Montreal, but its employees also work in the United States, Mexico, Europe, and the Middle East. More than 90 percent of company revenues come from outside Canada. Bombardier's strategy is to achieve accelerated growth in foreign markets, so it is continually refining its strategy to find new business opportunities in global markets.

Bombardier has historically been very successful in the commercial airplane market with its regional jets, which seat 50–90 passengers. But competition is fierce. In the mid-1990s, Bombardier held two-thirds of the market; then Brazilian rival Embraer entered the market and became a strong competitor. In 2007, Embraer overtook Bombardier to become the market leader in regional jets. Along the way, Bombardier had

complained to the World Trade Organization that the Brazilian government was unfairly subsidizing Embraer by giving it large sums of money. But the Canadian government was also giving loans to Bombardier's customers to help them purchase Bombardier's planes.

Irrespective of how the competitive wars in the regional jet market turn out, an inescapable fact is that the regional jet market is declining because airline companies want jets with longer ranges, lower operating costs, and wider cabins. Bombardier planners reasoned that if they did not develop a new jet, they would gradually be forced out of the commercial airplane business. In 2008, at the famous Farnborough International Airshow near London, England, the company announced that it would go ahead with its new transcontinental CSeries commercial jet, a plane that will seat 110–130 passengers and is designed for transcontinental flights. The plane will be more fuel efficient than current models and much quieter due to technological improvements in the new engines. Bombardier also announced that Deutsche Lufthansa AG had signed a letter of intent (LOI) for 30 of the planes, as well as an option for 30 more. At the end of 2011, Bombardier had only recorded firm orders for 153 CSeries aircraft and options from Lufthansa, Braathens Aviation, Atlasjet Havacilik AS, Lease Corporation International Group, and Republic Airways. Qatar Airways has also expressed strong interest in the plane and the company was positioning itself to land a deal for 50 planes from this company.

The introduction of the CSeries aircraft means Bombardier will be going head to head with global giants Airbus and Boeing. That strategy is risky, but if it succeeds, it will mean huge sales revenues and profits for Bombardier. It will also mean that Canada will be one of only three countries in the world that produce intercontinental commercial jet aircraft. Market research suggests that the market for commercial jets like the CSeries will be 5000–6000 units over the next 20 years, and Bombardier hopes to get 50 percent of that market. The price of each plane is about $59 million, so if the company achieves its market share goal, it could receive approximately $190 billion in revenues over the next 20 years.

That sounds impressive, but there are three areas of risk associated with Bombardier's strategy. First, there may (or may not) be competing products from other airplane manufacturers. Here, Bombardier may get lucky. Instead of creating new airplanes to compete, Airbus and Boeing are revamping their bestselling models with new engines to cut fuel costs and somewhat address the Bombardier threat. The airlines will ultimately decide whether Bombardier's new plane is in fact a better product. If the market makes that conclusion, it will take a few years before Airbus and Boeing can create a new competing product from scratch. The two giants took this approach because there are large order backlogs (four to five years) for both the Airbus A320 and the Boeing 737, and the companies are fully engaged trying to fill those orders. In addition, they are betting that airlines are unlikely to buy Bombardier's CSeries unless there is a clear improvement in terms of fuel efficiency because the airlines have mechanics, technicians, and pilots who are accustomed to Airbus or Boeing planes. For many airlines, adding a fleet of CSeries planes would mean adding a level of complexity that ultimately may cancel out any minor gains from the CSeries's fuel efficiency. However, in addition to the barriers of the existing players, Embraer may be developing a jet to compete with the CSeries aircraft.

Second, there is some risk associated with Bombardier's alleged "cozy" relationship with the Canadian government. In the past, the federal government has loaned money to Bombardier's customers so they can purchase the planes and trains the company manufactures. But will the government decide to stop handing out money? When he was Opposition leader, Stephen Harper said he wanted to end this type of support to private-sector companies, but as prime minister he reversed his position. Given the uncertain economic times, it appears that government loans are likely to continue.

Third, there is a risk that Boeing, Airbus, and Embraer will argue at the World Trade Organization that Canada is illegally subsidizing Bombardier. There is a long and contentious history between Bombardier and Embraer about government subsidies, and each company has claimed at various times in the past that the other is being illegally subsidized by its government. The outcome of any legal action by other airplane manufacturers against Bombardier is very uncertain.

Bombardier's strategy also includes shifting some of the risk of the CSeries aircraft to suppliers and to government. The overall development cost and capital investment of the CSeries aircraft program are projected to total $3.4 billion, of which Bombardier is providing $2 billion, including $700 million in capital expenditures and $1.3 billion in non-recurring costs. The remaining $1.4 billion in CSeries aircraft program costs will be split among the government of Canada, the province of Quebec, the government of the United Kingdom (where the wings of the CSeries aircraft will be built), and suppliers. The various governments will be paid a royalty on each plane that is sold. The project will create 3500 high-paying jobs in Quebec and about 800 jobs in the United Kingdom.

Questions for Discussion

1. How does Bombardier's development of the CSeries aircraft highlight the challenges and opportunities of globalization?
2. What role will governments play in the success or failure of the CSeries aircraft? Identify the role of subsidies and debate the concepts of free trade and protectionism as they relate to this case.
3. How does this case help demonstrate the important role of the WTO in the international business arena?
4. Do you think that Bombardier will be successful in its move to capture a share of this new growing market? Explain your answer. If yes, what are some of the long-term obstacles?

VIDEO CASE 1–1
Posilight

THE COMPANY

Energy efficiency and cost-saving solutions are increasingly important in today's society. It is not often that both are able to come together in one product and be successful. But Posilight, a lighting product for grocery and variety stores, provides both cost-saving and energy-efficient solutions for retailers' refrigerators and freezer cases, and can save up to 65 percent on energy costs. Posilight is able to fit in existing refrigerator cases, and this creates additional savings because replacement display cases are not necessary. President and founder Robert Simoneau developed the Posilight idea after he decided to enter the $1.5-billion lighting industry.

Posilight differs from other light solutions in that it is an LED bulb that creates rays from the front of the glass door of a freezer to the back of the merchandise. An even amount of light is cast, with no light bands or shadows. This so-called "positional lighting" is based on the same concept as that of a spotlight on stage, where focused light is provided to attract the audience's attention. "If the light is not on the merchandise you want people to see, then it's useless and you're consuming energy for nothing," says Simoneau.

THE PITCH

In his appearance on Dragon's Den, Simoneau asked for $75 000 in return for giving the dragons 10 percent ownership of his company (valued at $750 000). This investment would help Simoneau get his product into more test stores, and give him some of the dragons' expertise in marketing.

THE DRAGONS' POINT OF VIEW

Initially, the dragons seemed interested in Simoneau's proposal. One asked about how many sales he had thus far, but interest waned when Simoneau said that he hasn't seen much sales interest after showing the product in two test stores. "It is hard to impress financial investors unless you improve sales," said Arlene Dickinson. Simoneau expressed a desire to increase the company's sales revenue and then sell the patent to a manufacturer. The dragons did not agree with this idea. "It is easier to go to a manufacturing company and say, 'Buy the license to make this product,' so why not get the money from them? It is just easier," said one dragon. Based on this concern, one dragon declined the investment opportunity, saying "There is a gap in the logic for me. I don't see the business. I'm out."

When Kevin O'Leary asked fellow dragon Jim whether or not he thought there was something to this idea, Jim said he thought there was: "We go through $75 000 worth of bulbs every year; there is money to be made here for sure."

THE OUTCOME

After a request to get participation from the dragons, and with an interest in taking advantage of Arlene Dickinson's marketing expertise, Simoneau once again began stirring up the dragons' interest. He was eventually able to convince four of the dragons to invest in his product idea after they concluded that it would be a unique product and might be a huge success in the market. The final investment deal included $75 000, with Simoneau paying an initial 11.5 percent royalty fee for every dollar of sales revenue he generated; the fee would then drop (permanently) to 5 percent after the $75 000 had been recovered. Simoneau was able to leave still owning 99 percent of the company. The dragons own just 1 percent, but will be able to say that they are partners when Posilight becomes a huge success.

Questions for discussion

1. What is quality? What quality attributes does Posilight possess?

2. The dragons thought that it was a better idea to license the product than to sell the patent to a manufacturer. Why do you think they took that position?

3. Why did the dragons conclude that Posilight had good market potential?

Source: Video Resource: "Posilight", *Dragon's Den, Season 4, episode 16* (February 3, 2010). www.Posilight.com.

VIDEO CASE 1–2
Making Money by Going Green?

As concern for the environment increases, more and more Canadian businesses are going green (and trying to make a profit by doing so). Here are three examples.

MARITIME GEOTHERMAL LTD.

Glen Kaye, of Maritime Geothermal Ltd., says that Canadians are starting to become interested in geothermal heat, which is a clean alternative to fossil fuels. Linda Naccarato, a Burlington, Ontario homeowner, is drilling for this heat in her yard. With it, she can heat her home, swimming pool, and driveway (to melt snow in the winter). This "energy from the ground" produces only one-quarter of the greenhouse gas emissions produced by fossil fuels. The initial installation cost of the system is pretty high, but the system pays for itself within 5–7 years. After that, the homeowner gets cheap heat. Electricity is needed to run the heat pump, but the cost of that is only one-quarter of the cost of a traditional furnace burning fossil fuels. Customers using geothermal heat have the added advantage of not having to worry about changes in the price of fossil fuels.

Geothermal heating works because (1) heat travels from something warm to something colder, and (2) a great deal of heat is retained in the ground as a result of the radioactive decay of minerals and solar energy falling on the planet. There are two main ways to capture geothermal heat. The most efficient method is used in areas where very hot groundwater is available (usually where tectonic plates come together). This water is pumped directly into radiators to heat homes and offices. This type of heat has been used for many years in Iceland. Thermal water is also used in Boise, Idaho and Squamish, B.C. Hot water can also be used to run turbines to generate electricity.

The second method involves getting heat from the ground. This is possible because the temperature of the ground three meters below the surface has a fairly stable temperature of about 10 degrees Celsius. Here's how it works: holes are drilled in the ground and small-diameter pipes filled with a mix of water and ethanol are installed in the holes. In the winter, the liquid is colder than the soil, so it absorbs heat from the ground. A heat pump brings the heat to the surface, and fans blow it around. The pipes are connected to a heat exchanger in the home, so no furnace is needed. Once the liquid cools off, it is then pumped back into the ground and the process starts all over again. In summer, when above-ground temperatures exceed 10 degrees, the system is reversed (i.e., the heat pump moves heat from the home or office into the ground where the liquid in the pipes is cooled by the earth and then transported back into the building to cool it).

Worldwide, less than one percent of the world's total energy needs are provided by geothermal heat. In Canada, about one percent of Canadian homes are heated this way.

THE ZENN ELECTRIC CAR

The eco-friendly Zenn electric car (*Zero Emissions, No Noise*) was designed for use in low-speed urban areas (less than 50 km/h), but the company had trouble getting the car certified as roadworthy. The car was made in St. Jérôme, Quebec and sold in the U.S. and other foreign countries, but Transport Canada was reluctant to certify the vehicle on safety grounds. Specifically, the concern was that low-speed vehicles (LSVs) are not required to meet the same safety standards as other cars, so safety is compromised when these cars share the road with faster, heavier vehicles. Frustration with the federal government led Zenn to cease production in 2010. Another company (Dynasty Electric Car Co.) also gave up and stopped producing its electric car.

MINAS BASIS PULP & POWER

Nova Scotia-based Minas Basis Pulp & Power paper mill doesn't use any trees; instead, it uses 100 percent recycled cardboard. Like other mills, it uses hydro power, but it recaptures heat and reuses it, not once but several times. Therefore, less fuel is used, which means fewer emissions. The mill also recycles all of the water it uses. As a result of these conservation measures, 1.5 million trees are spared and 270 000 tonnes of greenhouse gases are not emitted, and enough electricity to power 38 000 homes is saved each year. The company is also looking at generating energy by harnessing the power of the tides. The nearby Bay of Fundy has the world's highest tides, and clean, renewable energy can be generated by placing turbines underwater to extract energy from tidal movements.

Minas wants become the greenest paper mill in North America. If it succeeds, it will be doing its part to help save the planet and become a profitable company in the process. Minas hopes it can charge a premium price for its paper because buyers will want to buy products from a green paper mill.

Questions for Discussion

1. What kind of challenges and opportunities are evident when a company decides to go green?

2. What is social responsibility? To what extent does "going green" qualify as socially responsible behaviour by a company? Explain your reasoning.

3. Consider the following statement: *Geothermal heating is environmentally friendly and also provides cheap power, so in the next few years Canadians are going to rapidly adopt this method of heating their homes.* Do you agree or disagree with the statement? Explain your reasoning.

Sources: *CBC News in Review*, "Making Money by Going Green," May 2008; www.en.wikipedia.org/wiki/Geothermal_heating.

CRAFTING A BUSINESS PLAN
Part 1: The Contemporary Business Environment

Goal of the Exercise

In Chapter 4 we discussed how the starting point for virtually every new business is a *business plan*. Business plans describe the business strategy for any new business and demonstrate how that strategy will be implemented. One benefit of a business plan is that, in preparing it, would-be entrepreneurs are forced to develop their idea on paper and firm up their thinking about how to launch their business before investing time and money in it. In this exercise, you'll get started on creating your own business plan.

EXERCISE BACKGROUND

Part 1 of the Business Plan

The starting point for any business plan is coming up with a great idea. This might be a business that you've already considered setting up. If you don't have ideas for a business already, look around. What are some businesses that you come into contact with on a regular basis? Restaurants, childcare services, and specialty stores are a few examples you might consider. You may also wish to create a business that is connected with a talent or interest you have, such as crafts, cooking, or car repair. It's important that you create a company "from scratch" rather than using a company that already exists. You'll learn more if you use your own ideas.

Once you have your business idea, your next step is to create an "identity" for your business. This includes determining a name for your business and an idea of what your business will do. It also includes identifying the type of ownership your business will take, topics we discussed in Chapter 4. The first part of the plan also briefly looks at who your ideal customers are and at how your business will stand out from the crowd. It also looks at how the business will interact with the community and demonstrate social responsibility, topics we discussed in Chapter 3. Finally, almost all business plans today include a perspective on the impact of global business, which we discussed in Chapter 5.

YOUR ASSIGNMENT

Step 1

To complete this assignment, you first need to download the *Business Plan Student Template* file from this book's Companion Website at www.prenhall.com/griffin. This is a Microsoft Word file you can use to complete your business plan. For this assignment, you will fill in Part 1 of the plan.

Step 2

Once you have the *Business Plan Student Template* file, you can begin to answer the following questions in Part 1: The Contemporary Business Environment.

1. What is the name of your business?

   Hint: When you think of the name of your business, make sure that it captures the spirit of the business you're creating.

2. What will your business do?

   Hint: Imagine that you are explaining your idea to a family member or a friend. Keep your description to 30 words or less.

3. What form of business ownership (sole proprietorship, partnership, or corporation) will your business take? Why did you choose this form?

   Hint: For more information on types of business ownership, refer to the discussion in Chapter 4.

4. Briefly describe your ideal customers. What are they like in terms of age, income level, and so on?

   Hint: You don't have to give too much detail in this part of the plan; you'll provide more details about customers and marketing in later parts.

5. Why will customers choose to buy from your business instead of your competition?

   Hint: In this section, describe what will be unique about your business. For example, is the product special or will you offer the product at a lower price?

6. All businesses have to deal with ethical issues. One way to address these issues is to create a code of ethics. List three core principles your business will follow.

   Hint: To help you consider the ethical issues that your business might face, refer to the discussion in Chapter 3.

7. A business shows social responsibility by respecting all of its stakeholders. What steps will you take to create a socially responsible business?

   Hint: Refer to the discussion of social responsibility in Chapter 3. What steps can you take to be a "good citizen" in the community? Consider also how you may need to be socially responsible toward your customers and, if applicable, your investors, employees, and suppliers.

8. Will you sell your product in another country? If so, what countries and why? What challenges will you face?

   Hint: To help you consider issues of global business, refer to Chapter 5. Consider how you will expand internationally (i.e., independent agent, licensing, etc.). Do you expect global competition for your product? What advantages will foreign competitors have?

   Note: Once you have answere the questions, save your Word document. You'll be answering additional questions in later chapters.

The Business of Managing

Crisis management at BP, the organizational structure of the Occupy Wall Street movement, the impact of millenials on organizations, labour-management disputes in professional sports, and motivation and satisfaction in the workplace are five current issues you will read about in Chapters 6 through 10. These and many other issues must be effectively managed if companies hope to grow and prosper. Managers in all business firms—indeed, in any kind of organization—must carry out the basic management functions of planning, organizing, leading, and controlling. These important functions are the basis for this section of the text.

Part Two, The Business of Managing, provides an overview of business management today. It includes a look at the importance of managers in business firms, how businesses are structured to achieve their goals, the management of the firm's human resources, labour–management relations, and the importance of motivating and leading employees.

- We begin in **Chapter 6, Managing the Business Enterprise,** by describing the basic functions of management—planning, organizing, leading, and controlling. We also look at the different types and levels of managers, the skills that managers must possess, the importance of goal setting and strategic management, and the idea of corporate culture.

- In **Chapter 7, Organizing the Business Enterprise,** we look at the basic organizational structures that companies have adopted and

the different kinds of authority that managers have. The impact of the informal organization is also analyzed.

- In **Chapter 8, Managing Human Resources,** we explore the activities that are necessary to effectively manage employees, including assessing employee needs and training, promoting, and compensating employees.

- In **Chapter 9, Understanding Labour–Management Relations,** we look at the development of the

union movement in Canada, why and how workers organize, and how government legislation has affected workers' rights to organize into unions.

- Finally, in **Chapter 10, Motivating and Leading Employees,** we examine the important issues of motivation and leadership. We look at the reasons managers should establish good relationships with their employees, strategies for enhancing employee job satisfaction, and the various approaches to leadership that have been evident over time.

06

Managing the Business Enterprise

LEARNING OBJECTIVES

After reading this chapter, you should be able to:

1. Describe the four basic functions that constitute the *management process*.
2. Identify *types of managers* by level and area.
3. Describe the five basic *management skills*.
4. Explain the importance of *setting goals* and *formulating strategies*.
5. Discuss *contingency planning* and *crisis management*.
6. Explain the idea of *corporate culture* and why it is important.

Crisis Management at BP

A report released in June 2011 by Transocean Ltd.—the owner of the drilling rig that exploded and sank in the Gulf of Mexico in 2010—blamed BP for a series of decisions that led to the disaster. Ironically, on the day the well blew out, BP and Transocean officials were on the rig to celebrate seven years without a lost-time accident. The Transocean report was just one element in what is expected to be a long series of charges against BP. Here is the story:

Crisis in the Gulf of Mexico

On April 20, 2010, a drilling pipe snapped in two during deepwater drilling by BP in the Gulf of Mexico. A blowout preventer (BOP) was supposed to shear off the broken pipe and seal the well to prevent oil leakage or an explosion, but the BOP failed. An explosion then rocked the Deepwater Horizon drilling rig, and in the ensuing fire, 11 workers were killed and large volumes of crude oil began spewing into the Gulf of Mexico from 1600 metres below the surface. BP suddenly had a major crisis on its hands.

Management of the Crisis

In the days immediately following the accident, Tony Hayward, the CEO of BP, was calm and relaxed as he dealt with reporters' questions about the oil spill. He assured them that BP had great technical expertise in this area and large financial resources to fix the problem. He set up a special headquarters in a Ramada Inn in Louisiana to manage the crisis, he took full responsibility for the spill, and he brought in technicians and engineers to work on the problem. He also kept the U.S. government informed about progress. But after several failed attempts to stop the flow of oil, things started to go downhill for Hayward. The major television networks gave the spill prominent coverage night after night on their evening news programs. Viewers regularly saw dramatic images of animals and birds covered, and shorelines, beaches, and marshes fouled. Reporters also interviewed politicians, ecologists, commercial fishermen, and tourists, all of whom expressed poignant concerns about lost jobs, the damage to the tourist industry along the Gulf Coast, and BP's inability to stop the flow of oil.

As the negative publicity about the spill increased, Hayward began to realize that BP was facing not only a technical problem in stopping the flow of oil, but a huge public relations problem as well. The situation was worsened because Hayward made several major gaffes and strategic communication errors during the next few months. For example, he said the spill wasn't BP's fault; instead, he blamed Transocean, the company that operated the drilling rig. He also said the dangers of the spill were being exaggerated. In its press releases, BP consistently underestimated the amount of oil that was leaking. His most unfortunate (and widely quoted) remark was that the spill had caused him a lot of stress and that "he wanted his life back." Someone then observed that the wives of the men who were killed in the blast wanted their husbands back. Michael Gordon, of Group Gordon Strategic Communications, a crisis public relations firm, says that

BP's communications lacked transparency, the company didn't talk straight, and it wasn't sensitive to those who were negatively affected by the spill.

In late July 2010, BP fired Hayward as its CEO and Bob Dudley, the first non-Briton to head BP, was announced as Hayward's replacement. BP promised to become a company that was much more focused on safety. Dudley's job was to restore BP's credibility and reputation, and one of his top priorities was safety. But critics said an outsider should have been appointed if the company really wanted to change its culture. In commenting on his dismissal, Hayward said that he had been demonized by the media, and he realized that BP could not move forward until a new CEO was appointed.

As days and weeks passed and the oil continued to escape into the Gulf of Mexico, more unfavourable information came out about the spill. A *Wall Street Journal* investigation found that several questionable decisions had been made that contributed to the blowout of the well: (1) BP cut short a procedure that was designed to detect gas in the well and remove it; (2) a quality test was skipped that would have shown whether cement that had been placed around the drilling pipe had been properly poured to prevent a blowout; (3) workers prematurely removed heavy drilling fluid (called "mud"), which keeps volatile gas from escaping from the well; (4) the BP manager overseeing the well didn't have much experience in deepwater drilling; and (5) in an attempt to reduce drilling costs, BP installed only six centring devices instead of the 21 that had been recommended (centring devices reduce the risk of gas escaping from the well and exploding). One employee of Transocean also claimed that an alarm system that would have warned workers of impending danger had been disabled before the blowout. Transocean denied the allegation, and there has been some inconsistency in witness testimony about this claim.

All of this negative publicity caused BP's share price to drop by one-third and its market capitalization to drop by $100 billion as investors began to realize that BP would likely face many class-action lawsuits over the spill. These lawsuits and other fines may total $40 billion or more. BP's credit rating was cut to just above "junk" level by Fitch Ratings because of the possibility of long-term liabilities associated with the cleanup. By the end of June 2010, BP's stock price had dropped to a 14-year low. Its second-quarter loss was $17.1 billion.

As part of the negotiations with the U.S. government, BP agreed to set up a $20-billion cleanup fund. It also suspended dividend payments to shareholders. But Gulf Coast residents complained that BP's process for paying damage claims was too long and complicated, and argued that the company was paying out too little. Many spill-related lawsuits will be heard in U.S. court during 2012.

Implications for the Canadian Oil Industry

When the drilling rig Ocean Ranger sank in 1984 off the coast of Newfoundland during a major storm, 84 people died. Mark Turner has the job of reviewing oil drilling off Newfoundland's coast to determine whether a blowout like BP's in the Gulf of Mexico might occur in Canada, but it is difficult to know how much risk should be accepted in offshore drilling. The Canada-Newfoundland and Labrador Offshore Petroleum Board (C-NLOPB) has two priorities: to monitor the safety and environmental impact of the offshore oil industry, and to ensure that the maximum benefit will accrue from such drilling. But these two priorities can obviously be in conflict. The C-NLOPB has also been accused of moving too slowly on safety and environmental concerns.

Alberta oil sands companies may benefit from the BP spill because land-based oil wells are seen as safer than deepwater wells. MEG Energy Corp., for example, did a $1.25-billion initial public offering (IPO) of stock in the summer of 2010, and Athabasca Oil Sands Corp. had a $1.35-billion IPO in the spring of 2010. Global energy companies are also acquiring Canadian oil sands properties. ◆

HOW WILL THIS HELP ME?

After reading this chapter, you will have a clearer understanding of how to effectively carry out various management responsibilities. From the perspective of a *consumer* or *investor*, you'll be better able to assess and appreciate the quality of management in various companies.

Who Are Managers?

L01 Describe the four basic functions that constitute the *management process*.

managers The people who plan, organize, lead, and control the operations of an organization.

Managers are the people who plan, organize, lead, and control the operations of an organization. Although our focus is on managers in business settings, the principles of management apply to all kinds of organizations, including charities, churches, social organizations, educational institutions, labour unions, and government agencies. The prime minister of Canada, the president of the University of Toronto, the executive director of the United Way, the dean of your business school, and the chief administrator of your local hospital are all managers. Regardless of the nature and size of an organization, managers are among its most important resources.

Top managers such as (a) Marjorie Scardino (CEO of Pearson PLC), (b) Calin Rovinescu (president and CEO of Air Canada, and (c) James Sinegal (co-founder and CEO of Costco) are important resources for their companies. They set the strategic direction and provide leadership to other managers. They are also accountable to shareholders, employees, customers, and other key constituents for the performance and effectiveness of their businesses.

The Management Process

management The process of planning, organizing, leading, and controlling an enterprise's financial, physical, human, and information resources to achieve the organization's goals of supplying various products and services.

Management is the process of planning, organizing, leading, and controlling an enterprise's financial, physical, human, and information resources to achieve the organization's goals of supplying various products and services. Thus, the CEO of Walt Disney Productions is a manager because these four functions are performed as films are being made. Actors such as Julia Roberts or Tom Cruise are the stars of a movie, but they are not managers because they don't carry out the functions of management.

There are two important points to keep in mind when thinking about the management process. First, the planning, organizing, leading, and controlling aspects of a manager's job are interrelated. Sometimes they follow one another in a logical sequence, and sometimes they don't. Managers are likely to be engaged in all these activities during the course of a business day. Second, it is important to make the distinction between management effectiveness and management efficiency. **Efficiency** means achieving the greatest level of output with a given amount of input. **Effectiveness**, on the other hand, means achieving the organizational goals that have been set. Put another way, efficiency means doing things right, while effectiveness means doing the right things. A manager who focuses on being effective will likely also be efficient, but a manager who focuses on being efficient may or may not be effective.

efficiency Achieving the greatest level of output with a given amount of input.

effectiveness Achieving the organizational goals that have been set.

Planning

Planning is the process of determining the firm's goals and developing a strategy for achieving them. The planning process involves five steps:

- In *step 1*, goals are established for the organization. WestJet, for example, may set a goal to fill 90 percent of the seats on every flight.

- In *step 2*, managers identify whether a gap exists between the company's desired and actual positions. Examination of the load factor data may show that the load factor is only 73 percent.

- In *step 3*, managers develop plans to achieve the desired goal. For example, the airline may reduce fares on heavily travelled routes in order to increase the load factor to 90 percent.

- In *step 4*, the plans that have been decided upon are implemented. This involves actually charging the new reduced fare. This is the point in the planning process where thinking is converted into action.

- In *step 5*, the effectiveness of the plan is assessed. Actual results are compared with planned performance—that is, the load factor data are analyzed to determine whether the 90-percent goal has been achieved. Plans may then have to be modified and a different goal may have to be set.

McDonald's experience in Canada over the past decade demonstrates the importance of planning. Until 2002, McDonald's was the largest fast-food chain in Canada. But then it was overtaken by Tim Hortons. In response to this development, McDonald's set a goal to reinvent itself and begin to grow again (step 1). The gap between where McDonald's was and where it wanted to be (step 2) was obvious, so McDonald's top managers developed a strategic plan (called "Plan to Win") in order to achieve the new objective (step 3). This involved developing many new menu items (like the Angus Burger, new salads, and snack wraps), renovating restaurants to look more like contemporary cafés or bistros (with polished stone tabletops and fireplaces), letting franchisees target local tastes with their menus (like the McLobster sandwich in the Maritimes), and staying open longer (60 percent of McDonald's restaurants are now open 24 hours a day). These plans were implemented beginning in 2003 and 2004 (step 4). The effectiveness of the plan has now been assessed (step 5). Sales were $2.9 billion in 2008 (a record) and $3 billion in 2009 (another record).[1] These sales levels were achieved in spite of the recession of 2008–2009. In 2011, McDonald's announced that it planned to spend $1 billion on further interior and exterior renovations to its restaurants.[2]

A Hierarchy of Plans

Plans can be made on three general levels, with each level reflecting plans for which managers at that level are responsible. **Strategic plans**, which are set by top management, reflect decisions about resource allocations, company priorities, and the steps needed to meet strategic goals (we look at strategic planning later in this chapter). In 2010, Maple Leaf Foods developed a five-year strategic plan that was designed to increase its earnings by more than 75 percent by 2015.[3] **Tactical plans**, which are developed by upper and middle managers, are shorter-range plans concerned with implementing specific aspects of the company's strategic plans. Coca-Cola's plan to increase sales in Europe by building European bottling facilities is an example of a tactical plan. **Operational plans**, which are developed by middle and lower-level managers, set short-term targets for daily, weekly, or monthly performance. McDonald's, for example, establishes operational plans when it stipulates precisely how Big Macs are to be cooked and served.

Organizing

organizing Mobilizing the resources that are required to complete a particular task.

Organizing involves mobilizing the resources that are required to complete a particular task (this topic is examined in detail in Chapter 7). The importance and complexity of the organizing function can be seen by considering the restructuring that has taken place at Hewlett-Packard in recent years. HP had long prided itself on being a corporate confederation of individual businesses. Each business made its own decisions quickly and efficiently, and the competition kept each unit on its toes. This structure served the firm well for many years.[4] But as time passed, HP somehow lost its competitive edge. The decision was then made to centralize company activities and develop an integrated, organization-wide internet strategy. A reorganized HP then bounced back, at least for a few years. But when HP began to again experience profitability problems in its PC division in 2005, then-CEO Carly Fiorina decided to combine the PC and printing divisions in order to increase hardware sales to customers. When Fiorina left HP shortly thereafter, her successor (Mark Hurd) undid her changes. When Hurd left the firm a few years later, the new CEO, Meg Whitman, once again combined the two divisions.[5]

Leading

leading (or directing) Involves the interactions between managers and their subordinates as they both work to meet the firm's objectives.

Leading (or directing) involves the interactions between managers and their subordinates as they both work to meet the firm's objectives. Legendary leaders like Sam Walton (Walmart), Clive Beddoe (WestJet), and Steve Jobs (Apple) were able to unite their employees in a clear and targeted manner, and motivate them to work in the best interests of the company. While managers have the power to give orders and demand results, leading goes beyond merely giving orders. Leaders must also have the ability to motivate their employees to set challenging goals and to work hard to achieve them. This means that employees will respect their leaders, trust them, and believe that by working together, both the company and its employees will benefit. We discuss leadership in more detail in Chapter 10.

Controlling

controlling The process of monitoring a firm's performance to make sure that it is meeting its goals.

Controlling is the process of monitoring a firm's performance to make sure that it is meeting its goals. Managers at WestJet and Air Canada, for example, focus relentlessly on indicators of performance like on-time arrivals, baggage-handling errors, the number of empty seats on an airplane, and results of surveys of employees and customers. If, say, on-time arrivals start to slip, managers focus on the problem and get it fixed. No single element of the firm's performance can slip too far before it is noticed and fixed.

Figure 6.1 illustrates the control process, which begins when management establishes standards, often for financial performance. If, for example, a company wants to increase sales by 20 percent over the next 10 years, then an appropriate standard might be an increase of about 2 percent a year. Managers then measure actual performance against standards. If the two amounts agree, the organization continues along its present course. If they vary significantly, however, one or the other needs adjustment.

Consider how controlling applies to the courses that you are now taking. The instructor first indicates the knowledge areas where you must show competence, and the level of competence you must show. Next, the instructor measures your performance, usually through assignments and exams. The instructor then determines whether your performance meets the standard. If your performance is satisfactory (or unsatisfactory), you receive feedback in the form of a passing (or failing) grade in the course.

Control can also show where performance is better (or worse) than expected, and can serve as a basis for providing rewards or reducing costs. For example, when

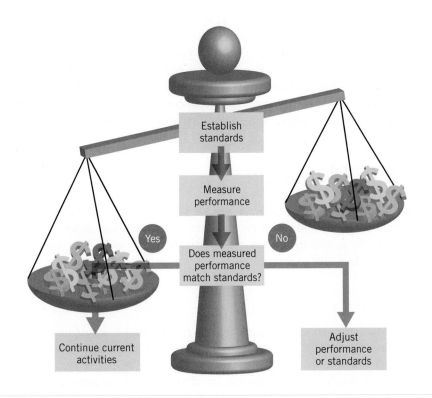

FIGURE 6.1

The control process.

the distributor of the surprise hit movie *The March of the Penguins* saw how popular the movie was becoming, the firm was able to increase advertising and distribution, making the niche movie into a major commercial success. In contrast, when the sales of the Chevrolet Super Sport Roadster (a classic, late-1940s pickup-style vehicle with a two-seat roadster design) were much lower than expected, production of the vehicle was suspended.

Management Roles vs. Management Functions

Describing managers' jobs by referring to functions like planning, organizing, leading, and controlling gives us a good *general* picture of what managers do, but it may not give a clear idea of the *specific* activities that managers are involved in. The answer to the question "What do managers actually do?" is that they play a variety of roles in organizations. The work of Henry Mintzberg of McGill University illustrates the roles approach to management. In a now-classic work, Mintzberg conducted a detailed study of the work of five chief executive officers and found that (1) they worked at an unrelenting pace; (2) their activities were characterized by brevity, variety, and fragmentation; (3) they preferred "live" action and emphasized work activities that were current, specific, and well defined; and (4) they were attracted to verbal media.[6]

Mintzberg believes that a manager's job can be described as 10 roles (in three general categories) that must be performed. The manager's formal authority and status give rise to three *interpersonal roles*: (1) figurehead (duties of a ceremonial nature, such as attending a subordinate's wedding); (2) leader (being responsible for the work of the unit); and (3) liaison (making contact outside the vertical chain of command). These interpersonal roles give rise to three *informational roles*: (1) monitor (scanning the environment for relevant information); (2) disseminator (passing information to subordinates); and (3) spokesperson (sending information to people outside the unit).

Managers are needed in all kinds of business firms, including professional sports teams. As the head coach of the Toronto Argonauts, Jim Barker is a first-line manager who is responsible for the day-to-day success of the team. Managers are necessary in all kinds of organizations, including government agencies, labour unions, charities, and the military.

The interpersonal and informational roles allow the manager to carry out four *decision-making roles*: (1) entrepreneur (improving the performance of the unit); (2) disturbance handler (responding to high-pressure disturbances, such as a strike at a supplier); (3) resource allocator (deciding who will get what in the unit); and (4) negotiator (working out agreements on a wide variety of issues, such as the amount of authority an individual will be given). The disturbance handler role, for example, is played when a manager helps resolve a conflict between two subordinates.

Types of Managers

LO2 Identify *types of managers* by level and area.

Although all managers plan, organize, lead, and control, not all managers have the same degree of responsibility for each activity. Managers also differ in the specific application of these activities. Thus, we can divide managers by their *level* of responsibility and by their *area* of responsibility.

Levels of Management

The three basic levels of management are top, middle, and first-line management. As shown in Figure 6.2, in most firms there are more middle managers than top managers and more first-line managers than middle managers. As the categories imply, the authority of managers and the complexity of their duties increase as we move up the pyramid.

Top Managers

top managers Those managers responsible for a firm's overall performance and effectiveness and for developing long-range plans for the company.

The executives who guide the fortunes of companies are **top managers**. Common titles for top managers include president, vice-president, chief operating officer (COO), chief executive officer (CEO), and chief financial officer (CFO). Top managers are

FIGURE 6.2

Organizations have three basic levels of management.

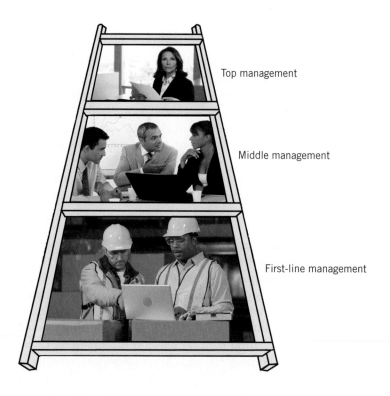

Top management

Middle management

First-line management

responsible to the board of directors and shareholders of the firm for its overall performance and effectiveness. They set general policies, formulate strategies, oversee significant decisions, and represent the company in its dealings with other businesses and government.[7] While top managers have a lot of authority, they also have something of an image problem. A 2012 study ranked CEOs very low on the "trust" dimension, and this means that some of Canada's most successful people have low credibility.[8]

Middle Managers

Middle managers occupy positions between top and first-line managers. Titles such as plant manager, operations manager, and division manager are typical of middle-management jobs. The producer of a major film like Lionsgate's *Precious* is also a middle manager. In general, middle managers are responsible for implementing the strategies, policies, and decisions made by top managers. For example, if top management decides to bring out a new product in 12 months or to cut costs by 5 percent in the next year, middle management will have to decide whether to increase the pace of new product development or to reduce the plant's workforce. With companies increasingly seeking ways to cut costs, the job of middle manager has lately become somewhat precarious in many large companies.

middle managers Those managers responsible for implementing the decisions made by top managers.

First-Line Managers

First-line managers spend most of their time working with and supervising the employees who report to them. Common titles include supervisor, office manager, and group leader. A transit supervisor who monitors bus schedules, passenger safety, and the behaviour of bus drivers is a first-line supervisor. So is the flight-services manager for a specific Air Canada flight. Table 6.1 summarizes the duties of the three basic levels of management.

first-line managers Those managers responsible for supervising the work of employees.

Areas of Management

Within any large company, the top, middle, and first-line managers work in a variety of areas, including human resources, operations, information, marketing, and finance.

TABLE 6.1 The Three Levels of Management		
Level	**Examples**	**Responsibilities**
Top managers	President, vice-president, treasurer, chief executive officer (CEO), chief financial officer (CFO)	• Responsible for the overall performance and effectiveness of the firm • Set general policies, formulate strategies, and approve all significant decisions • Represent the company in dealings with other firms and with government bodies
Middle managers	Plant manager, operations manager, division manager, regional sales manager	• Responsible for implementing the strategies and working toward goals set by top managers
First-line managers	Supervisor, office manager, project manager, group leader, sales manager	• Responsible for supervising the work of employees who report to them • Ensure employees understand and are properly trained in company policies and procedures

Human Resource Managers

Human resource managers provide assistance to other managers when they are hiring employees, training them, evaluating their performance, and determining their compensation level. In unionized companies, human resource managers are also involved in negotiations with the union. A large company like Imperial Oil has separate departments to deal with recruiting and hiring, wage and salary levels, and labour relations. A smaller firm may have just one department, while very small organizations may have only a single person responsible for human resource activities. Chapters 8 to 10 examine human resource management in detail.

Operations Managers

Operations managers are responsible for the production systems that create goods and services. These include production control, inventory control, and quality control, among others. Manufacturing companies like Steelcase, Bristol Aerospace, and Sony need operations managers at many levels. Such firms typically have a vice-president for operations (top manager), plant managers (middle managers), and foremen or supervisors (first-line managers). In recent years, operations management practices have been receiving increasing attention in service organizations, hospitals, universities, and the government. Operations management is the subject of Chapters 11 and 12.

Information Managers

Information managers are responsible for designing and implementing systems that gather, process, and disseminate information. Dramatic increases in both the amount of information available to managers and the ability to manage it have led to the emergence of this important function. Many firms, including FedEx, have a chief information officer (CIO). Middle managers engaged in information management help design information systems for divisions or plants. Computer systems managers within smaller businesses are first-line managers. Information management is discussed in Chapter 13.

Marketing Managers

Marketing managers are responsible for getting products and services to buyers. Consumer product firms like Procter & Gamble and Coca-Cola often have large numbers of marketing managers at various levels. A large firm will have a vice-president of marketing (top manager), regional marketing managers (middle managers), and several district sales managers (first-line managers). Firms that produce industrial products such as machinery and janitorial supplies tend to put less emphasis on marketing and to have fewer marketing managers. We look at marketing in detail in Chapters 15 to 17.

Financial Managers

Management of a firm's finances, including its investments and accounting functions, is extremely important to its survival. Nearly every company has *financial managers* to plan and oversee its financial resources. Levels of financial management may include a vice-president for finance (top manager), division controllers (middle managers), and accounting supervisors (first-line managers). Financial management is covered in Chapters 14 and 18 to 20.

Basic Management Skills

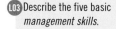
LO3 Describe the five basic *management skills.*

The degree of success that managers enjoy is determined by the skills and abilities they possess. Effective managers must have five key skills: *technical, human relations, conceptual, time management,* and *decision-making skills.*

Technical Skills

Technical skills allow managers to perform specialized tasks. An administrative assistant's ability to type, an animator's ability to draw a cartoon, and an accountant's ability to audit a company's records are all technical skills. People develop their technical skills through education and experience. The administrative assistant, for example, probably took a keyboarding course and has had many hours of practice both on and off the job. The animator may have received training in an art school and probably learned a great deal from experienced animators on the job. The accountant earned a university degree and a professional certification.

As Figure 6.3 shows, technical skills are especially important for first-line managers. Most first-line managers spend considerable time helping employees solve work-related problems, monitoring their performance, and training them in more efficient work procedures. Such managers need a basic understanding of the jobs they supervise. As a manager moves up the corporate ladder, however, technical skills become less and less important. Top managers, for example, often have only a cursory familiarity with the mechanics of basic tasks performed by their subordinates. The CEO of Disney, for example, probably can't draw Mickey Mouse or build a ride for Disney World.

> **technical skills** Skills associated with performing specialized tasks within a company.

Human Relations Skills

Human relations skills enable managers to understand and get along with other people. A manager with poor human relations skills will have trouble getting along with subordinates, which will, in turn, cause valuable employees to quit or transfer, and contribute to poor morale. When Development Dimensions International (DDI) asked 944 human resource professionals to state the reasons why newly promoted managers fail, 53 percent said it was because of poor people skills.[9] A study by Google found that technical expertise ranked last among a list of eight "Habits of Highly Effective Google Managers." At the top of the list were even-tempered bosses who made time for one-on-one meetings and who helped subordinates work through problems.[10] Human relations skills are important at all levels, but they are probably most important for middle managers, who must often act as bridges between top managers, first-line managers, and managers from other areas of the organization.

To improve their insights into employee needs and company operations, some managers work alongside lower-level employees on a temporary basis. For example, the CEO of ING Direct sits beside call centre agents and personally answers caller

> **human relations skills** Skills that enable managers to understand and get along with other people.

FIGURE 6.3

Different levels in an organization require different combinations of managerial skills.

TOP MANAGEMENT: Technical, Human Relations, Conceptual

MIDDLE MANAGEMENT: Technical, Human Relations, Conceptual

FIRST-LINE MANAGEMENT: Technical, Human Relations, Conceptual

inquiries.[11] When the CEO of 7-Eleven, Joseph De Pinto, worked undercover at a 7-Eleven outlet, he discovered how hard the people worked and why the location was selling so much coffee. Larry O'Donnell, the CEO of Waste Management, did jobs like sorting trash, picking up paper at a landfill, and cleaning portable toilets. The experience taught him the pressure for production that employees had to cope with, and he introduced changes based on what he had learned on the job.[12]

Conceptual Skills

conceptual skills A person's ability to think in the abstract, to diagnose and analyze different situations, and to see beyond the present situation.

Conceptual skills refer to a person's ability to think in the abstract, to diagnose and analyze different situations, and to see beyond the present situation. Conceptual skills help managers recognize new market opportunities (and threats). They can also help managers analyze the probable outcomes of their decisions. Top managers depend most on conceptual skills and first-line managers least, although *some* level of conceptual skill is needed at every level of management.

Time Management Skills

time management skills The productive use that managers make of their time.

Time management skills refer to the productive use that managers make of their time. Effective time management is particularly important for highly paid top managers. For example, in 2010 Aaron Regent, CEO of Barrick Resources, was paid a total of \$24 217 040.[13] Assuming that he worked 50 hours a week and took two weeks' vacation, Regent earned about \$9686 per hour, or about \$161 per minute. Any time that Regent wastes represents a large cost to Barrick and its shareholders.

To manage time effectively, managers must address the four leading causes of wasted time:

- *Paperwork.* Some managers spend too much time deciding what to do with letters and reports. Most documents of this sort are routine and can be handled quickly. Managers must learn to recognize those documents that require more attention.

- *The telephone.* Experts estimate that managers are interrupted by the telephone every five minutes. To manage time more effectively, they suggest having an administrative assistant screen all calls and setting aside a certain block of time each day to return the important ones.

- *Meetings.* Many managers spend as much as four hours per day in meetings. To help keep this time productive, the person handling the meeting should specify a clear agenda, start on time, keep everyone focused on the agenda, and end on time.

- *Email.* Many email messages are not particularly important, and some are trivial. As a result, time is wasted when managers have to sort through a variety of electronic folders, inboxes, and archives. As the average number of electronic messages grows, the potential time wasted also increases.

Decision-Making Skills

decision making Choosing one alternative from among several options.

decision-making skills Skills in defining problems and selecting the best courses of action.

Decision making means choosing one alternative from among several options. **Decision-making skills** are critical for managers because decision making affects all the functions of management. Managers can improve their decision-making effectiveness by following a rational decision-making process.

The Rational Decision-Making Process

Figure 6.4 shows the steps in the rational decision-making process. The key elements of each step are briefly described below.

Step	Detail	Example
1. Recognizing and defining the decision situation	Some stimulus indicates that a decision must be made. The stimulus may be positive or negative.	The plant manager sees that employee turnover has increased by 5 percent.
2. Identifying alternatives	Both obvious and creative alternatives are desired. In general, the more important the decision, the more alternatives should be generated.	The plant manager can increase wages, increase benefits, or change hiring standards.
3. Evaluating alternatives	Each alternative is evaluated to determine its feasibility, its satisfactoriness, and its consequences.	Increasing benefits may not be feasible. Increasing wages and changing hiring standards may satisfy all conditions.
4. Selecting the best alternative	Consider all situational factors and choose the alternative that best fits the manager's situation.	Changing hiring standards will take an extended period of time to cut turnover, so increase wages.
5. Implementing the chosen alternative	The chosen alternative is implemented into the organizational system.	The plant manager may need permission from corporate headquarters. The human resource department establishes a new wage structure.
6. Following up and evaluating the results	At some time in the future, the manager should ascertain the extent to which the alternative chosen in step 4 and implemented in step 5 has worked.	The plant manager notes that six months later, turnover dropped to its previous level.

FIGURE 6.4

Steps in the rational decision-making process.

Recognizing and Defining the Decision Situation. The first step in rational decision making is recognizing that a decision is necessary. There must be some stimulus or spark to initiate this process. For example, when equipment malfunctions, managers must decide whether to repair it or to replace it. The stimulus for a decision may be either a problem or an opportunity. A manager facing cost overruns on a project is faced with a **problem decision**, while a manager who is trying to decide how to invest surplus funds is faced with an **opportunity decision**. Managers also need to understand precisely what the problem or opportunity is. This understanding comes from careful analysis and thoughtful consideration of the situation.

Consider the situation in the international air travel industry. Because of the growth of international travel related to business, education, and tourism, global carriers such as Singapore Airlines, KLM, Japan Air Lines, British Airways, and American Airlines need to increase their capacity for international travel. Because most major international airports are already operating at or near capacity, adding new flights to existing schedules is not feasible. Rather, the most logical alternative is to increase capacity on existing flights. Thus, Boeing and Airbus recognized an important opportunity and defined their decision situation as how best to respond to the need for increased global travel capacity.[14]

Identifying Alternatives. Once the need for a decision is recognized, the second step is to identify possible alternative courses of action. In general, the more important the decision, the more attention is directed to developing alternatives. If the decision

problem decision A decision that is necessary when actual results do not conform to those expected.

opportunity decision Taking new initiatives or doing a current activity more effectively even if no problem exists.

involves a multimillion-dollar relocation, a great deal of time and expertise should be devoted to identifying alternatives, but if the decision involves choosing a name for the company softball team, much fewer resources should be devoted to the task (although it may be difficult to keep the players from arguing about what the team's name should be!).

Factors such as legal restrictions, moral and ethical norms, and available technology can limit alternatives. After assessing the question of how to increase international airline capacity, Boeing and Airbus identified three different alternatives. They could independently develop new large planes, they could collaborate in a joint venture to create a single new large plane, or they could modify their largest existing planes to increase their capacity.

Evaluating Alternatives. Once alternatives have been identified, they must be carefully evaluated. During its analysis of alternatives, Airbus concluded that it would be at a disadvantage if it tried to simply enlarge its existing planes because the competitive Boeing 747 is already the largest aircraft being made and could readily be expanded. Boeing, meanwhile, was seriously concerned about the risk inherent in building a new and even larger plane, even if it shared the risk with Airbus as a joint venture.

Selecting the Best Alternative. Choosing the best available alternative is the real crux of decision making. Many situations do not lend themselves to objective mathematical analysis, but managers and leaders can often develop subjective estimates for choosing an alternative. Decision makers should also remember that finding multiple acceptable alternatives may be possible, so selecting just one alternative and rejecting all the others might not be a good decision. Airbus proposed a joint venture with Boeing, but Boeing decided that its best course of action was to modify its existing 747 to increase its capacity. Airbus then decided to proceed on its own to develop and manufacture a new jumbo jet called the A380. Meanwhile, Boeing decided that in addition to modifying its 747, it would also develop a new fuel-efficient plane (the 787).

Implementing the Chosen Alternative. After an alternative has been selected, managers must implement it. In some situations implementation is fairly easy, but in others it is very difficult. In the case of an acquisition, for example, managers must decide how to integrate all the activities of the new business into the firm's existing organizational framework.

One of the key things that managers must deal with during implementation is employee resistance to change. The reasons for such resistance include insecurity,

After a long decision-making process, Airbus decided to design its own jumbo jet. The Airbus A380's design allows seating for up to 850 people, and major airports around the world have been building new runways and terminal areas to accommodate the behemoth. Boeing, meanwhile, went through a similar decision-making process but concluded that the risks were too great to gamble on such an enormous project. Instead, the firm decided to modify its existing 747 design and develop a new fuel-efficient aircraft, the 787.

inconvenience, and fear of the unknown. Managers must also recognize that even when all alternatives have been evaluated as precisely as possible and the consequences of each alternative have been weighed, unanticipated consequences may still occur.

Following Up and Evaluating the Results. The final step in the decision-making process requires managers to evaluate the effectiveness of their decision—that is, they should make sure that the chosen alternative has served its original purpose. If an implemented alternative appears not to be working, managers can respond in several ways. One possibility is to adopt an alternative that had previously been discarded. Or they might recognize that the situation was not correctly defined to begin with and start the process all over again. In the Boeing/Airbus case, both companies are getting feedback that they made a good decision because they have large order backlogs. But both companies are experiencing delays in meeting their new product development schedules.

Behavioural Aspects of Decision Making

Many managers make decisions with too little consideration for logic and rationality. Peter Tingling, a professor at the Segal School of Business at Simon Fraser University, says that managers too often decide what they want to have happen and then later conduct analyses to support their decision. In his words, instead of using "evidence-based decision making," managers often use "decision-based evidence making."[15] Even when managers try to be logical, they sometimes fail. When Starbucks opened its first coffee shops in New York, it relied on scientific marketing research, taste tests, and rational deliberation in making a decision to emphasize drip over espresso coffee. However, that decision proved wrong when it became clear that New Yorkers strongly preferred the same espresso-style coffees that were Starbucks's mainstays on the west coast. Hence, the firm had to reconfigure its stores hastily to meet customer preferences.

Non-logical and emotional factors often influence managerial decision making. These factors include *organizational politics*, *intuition*, *escalation of commitment*, and *risk propensity*.

Organizational Politics. The term **organizational politics** refers to the actions that people take in organizations as they try to get what they want. These actions may or may not be beneficial to the organization, but they do influence decision making, particularly if the person taking the action is powerful and can get his or her way. A study of 293 Canadian office workers found that 71 percent believed that office politics was at least somewhat necessary in order to get ahead in their organization.[16]

organizational politics The actions that people take as they try to get what they want.

Intuition. Managers sometimes decide to do something because it "feels right" or because they have a "hunch." **Intuition** is usually based on years of experience and practice in making decisions in similar situations. Such an inner sense may actually help managers make an occasional decision without going through a rational sequence of steps. For example, the New York Yankees once contacted three major sneaker manufacturers—Nike, Reebok, and Adidas—and informed them that they were looking to make a sponsorship deal. While Nike and Reebok were carefully and rationally assessing the possibilities, managers at Adidas quickly responded to the idea and ended up hammering out a contract while their competitors were still analyzing details.[17] These occasional successes can be very dramatic, but they should not cause managers to rely too heavily on intuition.

intuition An "inner sense" or "hunch" usually based on years of experience and practice in making decisions in similar situations.

Escalation of Commitment. When a manager makes a decision and then remains committed to its implementation in spite of clear evidence that it was a bad decision, **escalation of commitment** has occurred. A good example of this is Expo 86, the world's

escalation of commitment When a manager makes a decision and then remains committed to its implementation in spite of clear evidence that it was a bad decision.

fair that was held in Vancouver. When the project was first conceived, the deficit was projected at about $56 million. Over the next few years, the projected deficit kept rising until it was over $300 million. In spite of that, the project went forward. Managers can avoid over-commitment by setting specific goals ahead of time that deal with how much time and money they are willing to spend on a given project. These goals make it harder for managers to interpret unfavourable news in a positive light.[18]

risk propensity How much a manager is willing to gamble when making decisions.

Risk Propensity.   **Risk propensity** refers to how much a manager is willing to gamble when making decisions. Managers who are very cautious when making decisions are more likely to avoid mistakes, and they are unlikely to make decisions that lead to big losses (or big gains). Other managers are extremely aggressive in making decisions and are willing to take big risks.[19] They rely heavily on intuition, reach decisions quickly, and often risk big money on their decisions. These managers are more likely than their conservative counterparts to achieve big successes with their decisions, but they are also more likely to incur greater losses.[20] The organization's culture is an important factor in fostering different levels of risk propensity.

Strategic Management: Setting Goals and Formulating Strategy

L04 Explain the importance of *setting goals* and *formulating strategies*.

strategic management The process of aligning the organization with its external environment.

strategic goals The overall objectives that a business wants to achieve.

strategy The broad set of organizational plans for implementing the decisions made for achieving organizational goals.

Strategic management is the process of aligning the organization with its external environment. The starting point in effective strategic management is setting **strategic goals**—the overall objectives that a business wants to achieve. Remember, however, that deciding what it intends to do is only the first step for an organization. Managers must also make decisions about what actions will and will not achieve company goals. Decisions cannot be made on a problem-by-problem basis or merely to meet needs as they arise. In most companies, a broad program underlies those decisions. That program is called a **strategy**—the broad set of organizational plans for implementing the decisions made for achieving organizational goals. In recent years, more emphasis has been placed on sustainability as part of corporate strategy. Andrew Pelletier, vice-president of corporate affairs and sustainability at Walmart Canada, says that a green strategy means cost savings, less energy use, and improved employee engagement. This can lead to a competitive advantage.[21]

Setting Goals

goals Performance targets, the means by which organizations and their managers measure success or failure at every level.

Goals are performance targets, the means by which organizations and their managers measure success or failure at every level. Goals indicate *what* results are desired, while plans indicate *how* these goals are to be achieved. In this section, we identify the main purposes for which organizations establish goals, classify the basic levels of business goals, and describe the process that is commonly used to set goals.

The Purposes of Goal Setting

There are four main purposes in organizational goal setting:

1. *Goal setting provides direction, guidance, and motivation for all managers.* Toyota set a goal to sell 200 000 vehicles in Canada in 2012. That was a 25 percent increase over actual sales in 2011.[22] WestJet's goal is to challenge Air Canada for the top spot in domestic air travel by 2016.[23]

2. *Goal setting helps firms allocate resources.* Areas that are expected to grow will get first priority. Thus, 3M allocates more resources to new projects with large sales potential than it allocates to mature products with low growth potential.

3. *Goal setting helps to define corporate culture.* General Electric's goal is to have each of its divisions be number one or number two in its industry. The result is a competitive, often stressful, environment and a culture that rewards success and has little tolerance for failure.

4. *Goal setting helps managers assess performance.* At Port Metro Vancouver, the goal for container "dwell time"—the time containers sit on the dock—is three days (the North American standard). In January 2010, the dwell time was 3.7 days, but by November 2011, it had been reduced to 2.5 days. Setting specific goals like this helps managers assess their performance.[24]

Goal setting is effective for individuals as well as organizations. When students set goals, they achieve higher grades, lower their chances of dropping out of school, and experience greater well-being as adults. Unfortunately, a poll of U.S. students revealed that less than half of students aged 10–18 are aggressively pursuing goals.[25]

Kinds of Goals

Goals differ from company to company, depending on the firm's vision and mission. Every enterprise has a **vision** (or **purpose**)—its reason for being. The most fundamental purpose may be to make a profit (business firms), discover and transmit new knowledge (universities), or provide service to the public (government agencies). Most organizations also have a **mission statement** that indicates *how* the vision will be achieved. Bell Canada's mission, for example, is to be a world leader in helping communicate and manage information. Chrysler's mission is to have "delighted customers." Atco Ltd.'s mission is to provide products and

vision The reason for a company's existence.

mission statement An organization's statement of how it will achieve its purpose in the environment in which it conducts its business.

ENTREPRENEURSHIP AND NEW VENTURES

Planet Bean Coffee

Planet Bean began roasting coffee in 1997 in Guelph, Ontario, and now operates two coffee bars as well as a booming wholesale business supplying other companies with premium roasts and "spreading the flavour of excellent coffee to the waiting taste buds of the world." The company is dedicated to providing consumers with organic, fair trade coffee while ensuring that all practices in the supply chain are sustainable. Operating a business model such as this is no easy task, but for Planet Bean Coffee, finding the secret in every bean is the first step in unleashing the potential of a co-operative business model. With earth, fire, and water as key elements in telling their story, it is sure to be a success from the soil up.

On its website, Planet Bean says that its vision is to create "an innovative business model that is fair, sustainable and passionate." Its mission is to create "the best-tasting coffee and through fair trade, link producers and consumers in a meaningful way." The company has adopted specific principles that include being ethical, passionate, respectful, ecologically sustainable, co-operatively driven, and connecting all involved stakeholders (producers, consumers, employees, and so on). The company wants to protect the tropical forests where coffee is grown, and it works exclusively with Fair Trade Certified small family farmers and producers from around the world.

People are at the centre of all decisions at Planet Bean Coffee. After a certain period of time, employees at Planet Bean become members of SUMAC—a worker-owned, worker-operated co-operative that provides fair trade and organic products around the world. Founded in 2005, SUMAC operates under the guiding principles of integration and provides positive alternatives such as fair trade to businesses in order to reduce the negative effects of globalization. Providing such options is a requirement. According to Planet Bean, "It's not enough to be 'anti.' What is required is an integrated response: it's not only being against globalization under the control of and benefit for a few corporate giants, but also working to build positive alternatives." Providing options, inspiring changes in business structures, and putting people at the centre of all that they do is why SUMAC is also part of the global co-operative business network. Business activity isn't just about global control and profit maximization, but is about people and their relationships with each other, with the planet, and with future generations.

Critical Thinking Question

1. Explain the difference between a "vision" and a "mission."

2. Is Planet Bean Coffee's use of the terms "vision" and "mission" consistent with the way the terms are used in this textbook? Explain.

services to the energy and resource industries. The mission of Investors Group is to satisfy clients who need general and comprehensive financial planning. The boxed insert entitled "Planet Bean Coffee" explains how vision and mission can influence company activity.

Two business firms may have the same *purpose*—for example, to sell watches at a profit—but they pursue very different *missions* as they try to fulfill their purpose. Timex, for example, sells low-cost, reliable watches in outlets ranging from department stores to corner drugstores. Rolex, on the other hand, sells high-quality, high-priced fashion watches through selected jewellery stores. Regardless of a company's purpose and mission, every firm needs to set long-term, intermediate, and short-term goals:

long-term goals Goals set for extended periods of time, typically five years or more into the future.

intermediate goals Goals set for a period of one to five years.

- **Long-term goals** relate to extended periods of time—typically five years or more into the future. MasterCard, for example, might set a long-term goal of doubling the number of participating merchants during the next 10 years.

- **Intermediate goals** are set for a period of one to five years into the future. When Kazuo Hirai became CEO of Sony Corp. in 2012, he was determined to improve the performance of the consumer electronics company. He therefore set a sales target of US$105 billion for the division that makes medical equipment and electric car batteries. The goal is to be achieved in two years. He also set a goal to triple revenue in the mobile phone division.[26]

THE GREENING OF BUSINESS

Extending the Logic of Goal Setting

The logic of goal setting is being extended to make businesses greener. Green goals may be developed by managers, or they may be imposed on companies by external groups. Consider the following:

- Scotiabank set a goal to be in the top 10 percent of the companies listed on the Dow Jones Sustainability Index (DJSI).

- Employees on different floors of the Air Miles building in Toronto compete to see who can reduce energy usage the most in a specific month.

- Ford Motor Co. has set a goal of tripling its production of electric vehicles and hybrids by 2013.

- Co-operators Life Insurance Co. has set a goal to reduce emissions from business travel and climate control by 50 percent by 2014.

- Dillon Consulting Ltd. (Toronto) has a goal to invest 1 percent of revenue into social, environmental, and community initiatives.

- DuPont Canada has a goal to double investment in research and development programs with quantifiable environmental benefits.

For some organizations, their entire mission is being green. For example, the mission of B.C.–based Greener Footprints (a non-profit organization) is to reduce the use of plastic bags in Canada. For other organizations, the setting of green goals is closely tied to the success of their business.

For example, the CEO of Honda, Takeo Fukui, recognized that Toyota's popular Prius hybrid automobile had outsold Honda's hybrid car by a wide margin during the past decade, so he set a goal to make Honda the greenest company in the automobile industry. Honda has set a goal to sell 500 000 hybrid automobiles each year (Toyota's goal is one million). In 2008, Honda introduced its Clarity FCX, which is powered by a hydrogen fuel cell that generates no pollution at all. Honda also launched a new gas-electric hybrid in 2009, and plans to launch several other hybrids by 2015.

Rona Inc., the home renovation chain, has set a goal of doing business only with suppliers who address environmental sustainability and who do not contribute to deforestation. The goal for 2009 was to have all the plywood panels Rona sells made only from lumber that comes from forests that have been certified as sustainable. By 2010, the same goal applied to spruce, pine, and fir. By 2012, Rona's goal was to have 25 percent of its total wood sales come from forests that are certified by the Forest Stewardship Council.

Critical Thinking Questions

1. What are the advantages of setting green goals? Are there disadvantages? Explain.

2. What difficulties might Rona encounter as it tries to reach the goal of having 25 percent of its total wood sales come from forests that are certified by the Forest Stewardship Council?

- **Short-term goals** are set for one year or less. For example, Four Seasons Hotels and Resorts may set a goal to increase the revenue generated by each hotel room by 10 percent over the next six months. Or WestJet may set a goal to increase the proportion of occupied seats on the average flight by 8 percent over the next three months.

Whatever the time frame of the goals that are set, research shows that managers who set **SMART goals** (*S*pecific, *M*easurable, *A*chievable, *R*elevant, and *T*ime-framed) have higher performance than managers who don't. The boxed insert entitled "Extending the Logic of Goal Setting" describes the importance of setting goals that take the environment into account.

short-term goals Goals set for the very near future, typically less than one year.

SMART goals Goals that are specific, measurable, achievable, relevant, and time-framed.

Formulating Strategy

After a firm has set its goals, it must develop a strategy for achieving them. In contrast to planning, strategy is wider in scope and is a broad program that describes how a business intends to meet its goals, how it will respond to new challenges, and how it will meet new needs. For example, Brookfield Asset Management's strategy is to buy high quality assets at less than replacement cost. Developing a new strategy may not be easy (see the boxed insert entitled "Print Media").

Strategy formulation involves three basic steps: (1) setting strategic goals, (2) analyzing the organization and its environment, and (3) matching the organization and its environment (see Figure 6.5).

strategy formulation Creation of a broad program for defining and meeting an organization's goals.

E-BUSINESS + SOCIAL MEDIA SOLUTIONS

Print Media: Are e-Readers the Solution or a New Problem?

The publishing business is dealing with significant changes that will require serious strategic thinking. Consider these facts:

- According to the Newspaper Association of America, readership has fallen by more than 700 000 per year since 2000. Classified ad revenue was down 40 percent in the past decade because of online competitors like craigslist, Monster, and AutoTrader. Rupert Murdoch recently declared that news aggregator sites like Google and Digg.com are kleptomaniacs that steal content. As the owner of NewsCorp, a major media giant, his intention is to erect pay walls around his media sites.

- Book publishers and bookstore owners are also under pressure. According to Heather Reisman of Indigo Books, the e-reader threat may cause a 15 percent decline in book sales over the next five years. Others predict digital sales will comprise 25 percent of the market in three years and as high as 80 percent in 10 years.

There are several electronic devices that are having a big impact on the publishing industry, including the Kindle and the new Kindle Fire, Kobo, the Sony Reader, and of course the popular iPad. Imagine reading the newspaper on the bus without elbowing the person next to you each time you flip a page. You don't have to imagine it anymore: Look around you and you will see why these devices are transforming the print industry.

The online world has been having a negative impact on print media for some time, but the introduction of e-readers was a new tipping point. How will the print media providers and the technology device creators develop a strategic, sustainable model to satisfy the needs of consumers, columnists, authors, and technology companies alike? Developing such a strategy is not easy. Major publishers like Macmillan used the iPad launch to negotiate higher prices on e-books than had previously been dictated by Amazon (because of the virtual monopoly it once held with the Kindle). Five top publishers—including Penguin and HarperCollins—were on board for the launch of the iPad. Newspapers and magazine companies were even keener to form partnerships, since the iPad was seen as a way to display content in a new, exciting, and accessible fashion. Early results from Apple's Newsstand feature (which lets users download and display digital versions of newspapers and magazines) showed evidence of the renewed hope as app-based subscriptions for many publications rose sharply; however, approximately half the publishers surveyed in 2011 said they needed alternatives to Apple to secure their future.

Critical Thinking Questions

1. How do you think e-readers will impact the print industry in the short term? In the long term?

2. Which print media source (newspapers, magazines, or books) is more likely to benefit from the widespread adoption of e-readers? Why?

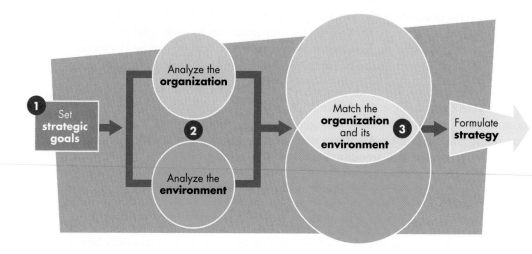

FIGURE 6.5

Strategy Formulation

Setting Strategic Goals

Strategic goals are long-term goals derived directly from the firm's mission statement. General Electric, for example, is pursuing four strategic goals to ensure continued success for the company: an emphasis on quality control, an emphasis on selling services and not just products, a concentration on niche acquisitions, and global expansion.

Analyzing the Organization and Its Environment

SWOT analysis Identification and analysis of organizational strengths and weaknesses and environmental opportunities and threats as part of strategy formulation.

organizational analysis The process of analyzing a firm's strengths and weaknesses.

environmental analysis The process of scanning the environment for threats and opportunities.

After strategic goals have been set, managers assess both their organization and its environment using a **SWOT analysis**. This involves identifying organizational **S**trengths and **W**eaknesses, and identifying environmental **O**pportunities and **T**hreats. Strengths and weaknesses are factors *internal* to the firm and are assessed using **organizational analysis**. Strengths might include surplus cash, a dedicated workforce, an ample supply of managerial talent, or technical expertise. For example, Pepsi's strength in beverage distribution through its network of soft drink distributors was successfully extended to distribution of its Aquafina brand of bottled water. Weaknesses might include a cash shortage, aging factories, and a poor public image. Garden.com's total reliance on the emerging internet-based retailing model became its downfall when the dot-com bubble burst.

Opportunities and threats are factors *external* to the firm and are assessed using **environmental analysis**. Opportunities include things like market demand for new products, favourable government legislation, weak competitors, or shortages of raw materials that the company is good at producing. For example, when Pepsi managers recognized a market opportunity for bottled water, they moved quickly to launch their Aquafina brand and to position it for rapid growth. Threats include new products and processes developed by competitors, changes in government regulations, and shifting consumer tastes. For example, in 2010, the province of Ontario proposed new legislation that sharply reduced the revenue that pharmacies would receive for dispensing prescription drugs. Some external threats are unpredictable, like the volcanic eruption in Iceland in 2010 that halted air travel in Europe for a week. Commercial airlines lost hundreds of millions of dollars of revenue, while alternative service providers like trains saw demand for their services soar.

Matching the Organization and Its Environment

The final step in strategy formulation is matching environmental threats and opportunities with corporate strengths and weaknesses. This matching process is the heart of strategy formulation. Over the long term, this process may also determine whether a firm typically takes risks or behaves more conservatively. Just because two companies are in the same industry does not mean that they will use the same strategies. The Toronto-Dominion Bank, for example, has been aggressively expanding into the U.S. retail banking industry by acquiring U.S. banks, but the Royal Bank of Canada has been much less aggressive in this area.[27]

Levels of Strategies

There are three levels of strategy in a business firm (see Figure 6.6). A **corporate-level strategy** identifies the various businesses that a company will be in and how these businesses will relate to each other. A **business-level (competitive) strategy** identifies the ways a business will compete in its chosen line of products or services. **Functional strategies** identify the basic courses of action that each department in the firm will pursue so that it contributes to the attainment of the business's overall goals.

corporate-level strategy Identifies the various businesses that a company will be in and how these businesses will relate to each other.

business-level (competitive) strategy Identifies the ways a business will compete in its chosen line of products or services.

functional strategies Identify the basic courses of action that each department in the firm will pursue so that it contributes to the attainment of the business's overall goals.

Corporate-Level Strategies

There are several different corporate-level strategies that a company might pursue, including *concentration, growth, integration, diversification,* and *investment reduction.*

Concentration. A **concentration strategy** involves focusing on one product or product line. Organizations that have successfully pursued a concentration strategy include McDonald's and Canadian National Railway. Brookfield Asset Management (formerly known as Brascan Ltd.) used to own companies in many different industries, but now the firm concentrates on just three: real estate, power generation, and infrastructure.[28] The main advantage of a concentration strategy is that the company can focus its strengths on the one business it knows well. The main disadvantage is the

concentration strategy Focusing the company on one product or product line.

FIGURE 6.6

Hierarchy of strategy.

In the wake of an industry-wide slump a few years ago, Cisco Systems, a giant maker of communications equipment, radically revised its strategic plans. Where engineers once pursued their own pet projects, engineering is now centralized under a group of top managers. Where individual units once chose their own suppliers, a committee now oversees all partnerships. Where the product line once consisted solely of networking apparatus, the company has branched out into a variety of new high-tech markets.

risk inherent in putting all of one's eggs in one basket. These risks can be overcome to some extent by adhering to the following principle: "If you put all your eggs in one basket, watch the basket!"

market penetration Boosting sales of present products through more aggressive selling in the firm's current markets.

product development Developing improved products for current markets.

geographic expansion Expanding operations in new geographic areas or countries.

horizontal integration Acquiring control of competitors in the same or similar markets with the same or similar products.

vertical integration Owning or controlling the inputs to the firm's processes and/or the channels through which the products or services are distributed.

diversification Expanding into related or unrelated products or market segments.

Growth. Several growth strategies are available, all of which focus on *internal* activities that will result in growth. These strategies include **market penetration** (boosting sales of present products through more aggressive selling in the firm's current markets), **product development** (developing improved products for current markets), and **geographic expansion** (expanding operations in new geographic areas). WestJet, for example, has used a geographic expansion strategy; it started by offering service in western Canada but has now added flights to various other cities.

Integration. Integration strategies focus on *external* activities that will result in growth. **Horizontal integration** means acquiring control of competitors in the same or similar markets with the same or similar products. For example, Hudson's Bay owns Home Outfitters (Deco Decouverte in Quebec), and U.S.-based Target acquired many Zellers stores as it prepared to enter the Canadian market. **Vertical integration** means owning or controlling the inputs to the firm's processes and/or the channels through which the products or services are distributed. Thus, major oil companies like Shell not only produce their own oil, but also refine the oil into different products and then sell those products through company-controlled outlets across Canada.

Diversification. **Diversification** means expanding into related or unrelated products or market segments. Diversification helps the firm avoid the problem of having all of its eggs in one basket by spreading risk among several products or markets. *Related diversification* means adding new, but related, products or services to an existing business. For example, CN diversified into trucking, an activity that is clearly related to railway operations. Maple Leaf Gardens Ltd., which already owned the Toronto Maple Leafs, also acquired the Toronto Raptors basketball team. *Conglomerate diversification* means diversifying into products or markets that are not related to the firm's present businesses. Eastman Kodak was the leader for many years in the film-based photography business, but it fell on hard times when digital cameras were introduced. (Oddly, Kodak invented the digital camera in the 1970s but somehow never capitalized on the idea.) Kodak then adopted a diversification strategy in an attempt to survive (and tried to reinvent itself as a printing and graphics company), but it fell into bankruptcy anyway.[29]

Target used a horizontal integration strategy when it entered the Canadian market. It purchased over 200 Zellers stores and then remade them in the Target style.

MANAGING IN TURBULENT TIMES

Will This Strategy Fly?

Montreal-based Bombardier is a world leader in the production of commercial jets, business jets, and trains. Bombardier's fortunes are often influenced by political decisions made by governments, so developing corporate strategy is difficult. For example, Bombardier and Brazil-based Embraer have repeatedly charged each other with violating World Trade Organization rules about receiving government subsidies from their home governments.

Bombardier's corporate strategy involves aggressively pursuing customers in two distinct markets: business jets and commercial jets. In the *business jet* market, Bombardier's current product offering is the Global Express XRS high-end jet. But in order to compete with U.S. rival Gulfstream Aerospace, Bombardier is planning to spend more than $1 billion to develop two new ultra-luxurious, long-range business jets that are derivatives of the Global Express. The Global 7000, which is slated for delivery in 2016, will be 20 percent wider than Gulfstream's G650 (but the G650 will come on the market in 2012). The Global 8000 is designed to compete on distance, and will fly slightly faster than the G650. In the *commercial jet* market, Bombardier is developing the CSeries jet, which is designed to compete in the 100- to 150-seat segment of the market. The new jet will have advanced avionics, new wings made of composite materials, and a fuselage made of a lithium-aluminum alloy. There are actually two planes in the series: the CS100 (which seats 100–124 people) and the CS300 (which seats 120–145 people). With its new entries, Bombardier feels that it can successfully compete against planes made by Airbus and Boeing, the two giants in

the industry. But developing a new product is risky because of the complexity of the product, the long time frame needed for its development, and the high cost of each unit (for example, the new CSeries jets will sell for about $65 million each).

At the 2011 Paris Air Show, executives of both Boeing and Airbus conceded that aircraft manufacturers in Canada, Russia, Brazil, and China are going be competitive with Boeing and Airbus. AirInsight, an aviation consultancy company, released a report showing that the CSeries aircraft will have advantages over both the Airbus A319neo and the Boeing 737. But Boeing and Airbus could also respond to the CSeries threat by lowering prices on their planes. Since they are much larger companies, Bombardier could probably not meet their prices.

If Bombardier's strategy succeeds, it will mean huge sales revenues and profits for the company, but Bombardier also has to worry about other competition, for instance from China's C919 aircraft, which is being developed by Commercial Aircraft Corp. of China (also known as Comac). Ryanair, Europe's biggest discount carrier, is working with Comac, which could make it difficult for Bombardier to sell any planes to Ryanair. New planes are also being developed by Embraer (Brazil) and Sukhoi (Russia).

Critical Thinking Questions

1. What are the various levels of strategy that exist in a business firm?

2. What corporate-level strategy is Bombardier pursuing? Explain your reasoning.

investment reduction Reducing the company's investment in one or more of its lines of business.

Investment Reduction. Investment reduction means reducing the company's investment in one or more of its lines of business. One investment-reduction strategy is *retrenchment*, which means the reduction of activity or operations. For example, Federal Industries was formerly a conglomerate with interests in trucking, railways, metals, and other product lines, but it retrenched and now focuses on a more limited set of customers and products. *Divestment* is another investment-reduction strategy; it involves selling or liquidating one or more of a firm's businesses. For example, BCE sold its *Yellow Pages* and *White Pages* businesses.

The boxed insert entitled "Will This Strategy Fly?" describes corporate-level strategic thinking at Bombardier.

Business-Level (Competitive) Strategies

cost leadership Becoming the low-cost leader in an industry.

Whatever corporate-level strategy a firm decides on, it must also have a competitive strategy. A *competitive strategy* is a plan to establish a profitable and sustainable competitive position.[30] Michael Porter identifies three competitive strategies. **Cost leadership** means becoming *the* low-cost leader in an industry. Walmart is the best-known industry cost leader. Montreal-based Gildan Activewear is dedicated to achieving the lowest possible costs in producing its T-shirts. The company has captured 29 percent of the U.S. imprinted T-shirt market with this strategy.[31] A firm using a **differentiation strategy** tries to be unique in its industry along some dimension that is valued by buyers. For example, Caterpillar Tractor emphasizes durability, Volvo stresses safety, Apple Computer stresses user-friendly products, and Mercedes-Benz emphasizes quality. A **focus strategy** means selecting a market segment and serving the customers in that market niche better than competitors. Before it was acquired by Nexfor, Fraser Inc. focused on producing high-quality, durable, lightweight paper that is used in bibles. While it still has a good reputation in the production of bible paper, Nexfor Fraser Papers is now more diversified and produces papers for a variety of uses, including dog food bags and doughnut boxes.

differentiation strategy A firm seeks to be unique in its industry along some dimension that is valued by buyers.

focus strategy Selecting a market segment and serving the customers in that market niche better than competitors.

Functional Strategies

Each business's choice of a competitive strategy (cost leadership, differentiation, or focus) is translated into supporting functional strategies for each of its departments to pursue. A functional strategy is the basic course of action that each department follows so that the business accomplishes its overall goals. To implement its cost-leadership strategy, for example, Walmart's distribution department pursued a functional strategy of satellite-based warehousing that ultimately drove down distribution costs.

Contingency Planning and Crisis Management

L05 Discuss *contingency planning* and *crisis management*.

Business environments are often difficult to predict because unexpected events may occur. Two common methods of dealing with the unforeseen are *contingency planning* and *crisis management*.

Contingency Planning

contingency planning Identifying aspects of a business or its environment that might entail changes in strategy.

Contingency planning attempts to (1) identify in advance the important aspects of a business or its market that might change, and (2) identify the ways in which a company will respond to such changes. Consider a shutdown caused by a snowstorm at Toronto's Pearson International Airport. Airlines know that this

Commercial airlines have contingency plans to deal with problems like major snowstorms. These contingency plans involve making sure that planes are not stranded at airports that are experiencing snow delays.

can happen, so they develop contingency plans for coping with that eventuality. These plans typically involve rescheduling flights into neighbouring airports and providing passengers with ground transportation into Toronto. Assessing the costs and benefits of these and other options ahead of time helps managers cope with problems when they arise.

In 2008, a strike at PotashCorp of Saskatchewan created a shortage of potassium acetate, which is the key ingredient in runway de-icer that airports use to prevent airplanes from sliding off runways in sub-freezing weather. The strike ended in November 2008, but by then airports were having trouble obtaining potassium acetate. The U.S. Federal Aviation Administration informed all airports that they should develop contingency plans to get their potassium acetate from alternate sources. Cryotech Technologies, the biggest supplier of potassium acetate to airports, responded by getting supplies of a corn-based de-icer instead.[32]

Crisis Management

Crisis management requires that an organization plan for dealing with emergencies that demand an immediate response. Business crises are more common than you might think. For example, as we saw in the opening case, BP faced a crisis when an explosion and fire at a drilling rig in the Gulf of Mexico resulted in the deaths of 11 workers and a huge oil spill. In 2010, Toyota faced a crisis when consumers began claiming that some models of its cars were accelerating out of control. And in 2011, automobile production was disrupted in Japan (by a devastating earthquake) and in Thailand (as a result of flooding).

When Maple Leaf Foods was confronted with a listeria (tainted meat) problem, it quickly recalled 686 000 kilograms of meat (which cost the company $19 million). CEO Michael McCain publicly apologized at news conferences and in television commercials and assured consumers that the company would solve the problem.[33] A few months later, a survey revealed that 78 percent of respondents had recently purchased a Maple Leaf product (that was up from only 20 percent right after the crisis occurred).[34]

crisis management An organization's plan for dealing with emergencies that require an immediate response.

Crisis management plans help organizations deal with emergencies of various kinds. Here, Red Cross volunteers organize and file paperwork submitted by hurricane Katrina victims.

LO6 Explain the idea of *corporate culture* and why it is important.

corporate culture The shared experiences, stories, beliefs, norms, and ethical stance that characterize an organization.

Management and the Corporate Culture

Just as every individual has a unique personality, every company has a unique identity, called its **corporate culture**—the shared experiences, stories, beliefs, norms, and ethical stance that characterize an organization. This culture helps define the work and business climate that exists in an organization. It is important for managers to understand the concept of corporate culture because culture influences the behaviour of employees. Managers can use that knowledge to be more effective in leading and motivating employees. Consider these examples of corporate culture:

- At ING Direct, the culture encourages employees to challenge the status quo, within both the company and the banking industry.[35]

- The culture of the Toronto Blue Jays organization is designed to make employees feel like they are part of a family. To facilitate the culture, employees have "snacks with the president" so they can talk about how the organization is operating.

- Google creates a culture of "yes" in order to encourage innovation. Employees focus on what is right with a new idea rather than what is wrong with it.[36]

- Magna International, a large Canadian producer of auto parts, is a firm with a strong culture. Its founder, Frank Stronach, is well known for his views about employees, working conditions, daycare centres, unions, the free enterprise system, and profit distribution.[37]

- Four Seasons Hotels and Resorts has a different, but equally strong, culture. Managers are judged by deeds, not words, and act as role models; employees take their cues from the managers.[38]

Companies that focus largely on one type of product (for example, Starbucks Coffee Company) may have a fairly homogeneous culture throughout the organization. But companies with many different divisions and many different types of customers (for example, the Royal Bank of Canada) are likely to have several different subcultures because the various divisions pursue different goals and because different types of people are found in the different divisions.

A strong corporate culture guides everyone to work toward the same goals and helps newcomers learn accepted behaviours. For example, in a strong culture where financial success is the key issue, newcomers quickly learn that they are expected to work long, hard hours and that the "winner" is the one who brings in the most revenue. But if quality of life is more fundamental to the culture, newcomers learn that it's more acceptable to spend less time at work and that balancing work and non-work is encouraged. Cameron Herold, a Vancouver entrepreneur who has had a string of successes in franchising, including College Pro Painters, Boyd Autobody, and 1-800-GOT-JUNK, says that culture should be "more than a business and slightly less than a religion."[39]

Each year, Waterstone Human Capital conducts in-depth interviews with senior managers at many different Canadian companies and asks them which corporate cultures they admire most. The 2011 winners included Agrium Inc., CIBC, Coast Capital Savings Credit Union, and ING Direct Canada.[40] Although many companies do not systematically monitor their corporate cultures, Starbucks is one company that does. Once every 18 months employees fill out a Partner View Survey, which contains questions that are designed to help the company determine whether it is making progress toward one of its key values—providing a work environment where people treat one another with respect and dignity. The survey is voluntary, but about 90 percent of employees fill it out (on company time). One reason the participation rate is so high is that the company actually pays attention to what employees say in the survey. For example, when one survey showed that employees were not clear about career progression possibilities in the company, Starbucks held career fairs in several Canadian cities, where company managers spoke with employees about management opportunities at Starbucks.[41]

Some culture surveys assess the business culture of countries rather than individual businesses. In summarizing the perceptions of 4875 people from 22 countries, the 2010 Edelman Trust Barometer ranked Canada and Sweden as the most trusted business cultures, and Russia and China as the least trusted cultures. Survey respondents said that trust—being able to count on business to do the right thing—was more important than the quality of goods that companies produce.[42]

Forces Shaping Corporate Culture

A number of forces shape corporate cultures. First, the values held by top management help set the tone of the organization and influence its business goals and strategies. Frank Stronach (Magna International), Timothy Eaton (Eaton's), Max Ward (Wardair), Larry Clark (Spar Aerospace), and Jean de Grandpré (BCE) are just a few of the leaders who have had a profound impact on the culture of their respective organizations. Even a large, long-time firm like Ford still bears the traces of founder Henry Ford.

The firm's history also helps shape its culture. The championship banners that line the arena where the Montreal Canadiens play signify that they are winners. Maintaining a corporate culture draws on many dimensions of business life. Shared experiences resulting from norms sustain culture. Thus, working long hours on a special project becomes a shared experience for many employees. They remember it, talk about it among themselves, and wear it as a badge of their contribution to the company.

Stories and legends are also important. Walt Disney has been dead for many years now, but his spirit lives on in the businesses he left behind. Quotations from Disney are affixed to portraits of him throughout the company's studios. And Disney's emphasis on family is still visible in corporate benefits such as paying for spouses to accompany employees on extended business trips. In fact, employees are often called "the Disney family."

Finally, strong behavioural norms help define and sustain corporate cultures. For example, a strong part of the culture at Hewlett-Packard Canada is that everyone wears a name tag and that everyone is called by his or her first name. And at Sony Corporation every employee wears a corporate smock.

A business's founder or CEO plays a major role in shaping the company's culture. For example, the late Steve Jobs, co-founder and former CEO of Apple, helped establish an informal and laid back culture at the company, which featured casual business attire and an open door policy. That culture helps Apple continue to attract and retain talented people.

Communicating the Culture and Managing Change

Managers must carefully consider the kind of culture they want for their organization, then work to nourish that culture by communicating with everyone who works there. Walmart, for example, assigns veteran managers to lead employees in new territories. Royal Bank of Canada and Four Seasons Hotels and Resorts also survey their employees to determine how well they are progressing toward their corporate culture goals.[43]

Managing Change

Organizations must sometimes change their cultures. Ontario Hydro, for example, had an "engineering" culture for many years. That meant that everything was planned and analyzed down to the last detail before any action was taken. But Ontario Hydro's culture has changed to a more consumer-oriented, risk-taking culture as it tries to cope with large debt and changes in its markets. When cultural change is required, the process usually goes through three stages:

1. At the highest level, analysis of the company's environment highlights extensive change as the most effective response to its problems. Conflict and resistance typically characterize this period.

2. Top management begins to formulate a new vision and culture for the company. Whatever that vision is, it must include a renewed focus on the activities of competitors and the needs of customers.

3. The firm sets up new systems for appraising and compensating employees: systems that enforce its new values. The purpose is to give the new culture solid shape from within the firm.

Changing an organization's culture can be difficult, so just because someone recognizes the need for cultural change does not mean that it will actually be implemented. For example, when several RCMP officers alleged that there were problems with senior management, lawyer David Brown was appointed by the government to look into the matter. His report concluded that the Commissioner had exercised absolute power, that no one questioned his management style, and that there was a "tone" at the top of the organization that resulted in little respect for employees. The report also said that whistle-blowers within the RCMP were punished when they pointed out that there were problems. The report concluded that the culture and management structure at the RCMP were "horribly broken."[44] These developments are discouraging because just a few years earlier the RCMP had completed a "visioning" process that resulted in a new mission statement, a new set of core values, and a commitment to the communities where it worked. At that time, it was reported that the culture of the RCMP was quite different than it had been in the days when military tradition dominated the organization, but subsequent events suggested that the culture had not actually changed much.

MyBizLab

Capture more moments of true understanding. MyBizLab provides you with interactive study and practice tools directly related to this chapter's content. The new MyBizLab Study Plan Learning Path is designed to measure a full range of skills and provide remediation to give you what you need to master key chapter concepts. MyBizLab flexes to your unique learning needs. The result? Inspired learning, more success.

SUMMARY OF LEARNING OBJECTIVES

1. **Describe the four basic functions that constitute the *management process*.** *Management* is the process of planning, organizing, leading, and controlling an organization's financial, physical, human, and information resources to achieve the organization's goals. *Planning* means determining what the company needs to do and how best to get it done. *Organizing* means determining how best to arrange a business's resources and the necessary jobs into an overall structure. *Leading* means guiding and motivating employees to meet the firm's objectives. *Controlling* means monitoring the firm's performance to ensure that it is meeting its goals.

2. **Identify *types of managers* by level and area.** Managers can be differentiated in two ways: by level and by area. By *level: Top managers* set policies, formulate strategies, and approve decisions; *middle managers* implement policies, strategies, and decisions; and *first-line managers* work with and supervise employees. By *area:* Managers work in areas like marketing, finance, operations, human resources, and information. Managers at all levels may be found in every area of a company.

3. **Describe the five basic *management skills*.** Most managers agree that five basic management skills are necessary for success. *Technical skills* are associated with performing specialized tasks ranging from typing to auditing. *Human relations skills* are associated with understanding and getting along with other people. *Conceptual skills* refer to the ability to think in the abstract, to diagnose and analyze different situations, and to see beyond present circumstances. *Time management skills* refer to managers' ability to make productive use of the time available to them. *Decision-making skills* allow managers to define problems and to select the best course of action.

4. **Explain the importance of *setting goals* and *formulating strategies*.** *Goals*—the performance targets of an organization—can be long term, intermediate, and short term. They provide direction for managers, they help managers decide how to allocate limited resources, they define the *corporate culture*, and they help managers assess performance. *Strategies*—the methods that a company uses to meet its stated goals—involve three major activities: setting *strategic goals*, analyzing the organization and its environment, and matching the organization and its environment. These strategies are translated into *strategic, tactical*, and *operational plans*.

5. **Discuss *contingency planning* and *crisis management*.** To deal with crises or major environmental changes, companies develop contingency plans and plans for crisis management. *Contingency planning* means identifying in advance certain key aspects of a business or its market that might change and thereby affect the operation of the business. This type of planning also identifies the ways the business will respond if the changes actually occur. *Crisis management* means developing methods and actions for dealing with an emergency that requires an immediate response. To prepare for such emergencies, organizations develop crisis plans.

6. **Explain the idea of *corporate culture* and why it is important.** *Corporate culture* is the shared experiences, stories, beliefs, norms, and ethical stance that characterize an organization. A strong, well-defined culture can help a business reach its goals and can influence management styles. Culture is determined by several factors, including top management; the organization's history, stories, and legends; and behavioural norms. If carefully communicated and flexible enough to accommodate change, corporate culture can be managed for the betterment of the organization.

KEY TERMS

business-level (competitive) strategy (p. 199)
concentration strategy (p. 199)
conceptual skills (p. 190)
contingency planning (p. 202)
controlling (p. 184)
corporate culture (p. 204)
corporate-level strategy (p. 199)
cost leadership (p. 202)
crisis management (p. 203)
decision making (p. 190)
decision-making skills (p. 190)
differentiation strategy (p. 202)
diversification (p. 200)
effectiveness (p. 182)
efficiency (p. 182)
escalation of commitment (p. 193)
environmental analysis (p. 198)
first-line managers (p. 187)
focus strategy (p. 202)

functional strategies (p. 199)
geographic expansion (p. 200)
goals (p. 194)
horizontal integration (p. 200)
human relations skills (p. 189)
intermediate goals (p. 196)
intuition (p. 193)
investment reduction (p. 202)
leading (or directing) (p. 184)
long-term goals (p. 196)
management (p. 182)
managers (p. 182)
market penetration (p. 200)
middle managers (p. 187)
mission statement (p. 195)
operational plans (p. 183)
opportunity decision (p. 191)
organizational analysis (p. 198)
organizational politics (p. 193)
organizing (p. 184)

planning (p. 183)
problem decision (p. 191)
product development (p. 200)
risk propensity (p. 194)
short-term goals (p. 197)
SMART goals (p. 197)
strategic goals (p. 194)
strategic management (p. 194)
strategic plans (p. 183)
strategy (p. 194)
strategy formulation (p. 197)
SWOT analysis (p. 198)
tactical plans (p. 183)
technical skills (p. 189)
time management skills (p. 190)
top managers (p. 186)
vertical integration (p. 200)
vision (or purpose) (p. 195)

QUESTIONS FOR ANALYSIS

1. How are the four *functions* of management related to the five *skills* of management? Use examples to clarify your answer.
2. What is the relationship between Mintzberg's *roles* of management and the *functions* of management? Use examples to clarify your answer.
3. Identify managers by level and area at your school, college, or university.

4. In what kind of company would the technical skills of top managers be more important than human relations or conceptual skills? Are there organizations in which conceptual skills are not important?
5. What differences in corporate culture might you expect to find between a 100-year-old Winnipeg manufacturing firm and a five-year-old ecommerce firm in Ottawa?

6. Consider the various corporate-level strategies discussed in the text (concentration, growth, integration, diversification, investment reduction). What is the relationship among these various strategies? Are they mutually exclusive? Are they complementary? Explain.

APPLICATION EXERCISES

1. Interview a manager at any level of a local company. Identify the manager's job according to level and area. Explain what planning, organizing, directing, and controlling mean in terms of the manager's job. Give examples. Also indicate which management skills are most important for the manager's job.
2. Review the example of the decisions made by Airbus and Boeing regarding new large aircraft. Then research the most current information on the status of the two planes. Which company seems to have made the better decision?

3. Select any group of which you are a member (your company, your family, or a club or organization, for example). Explain how planning, organizing, directing, and controlling are practised in the group.
4. Interview an administrator at your college or university. Ask the administrator to give his or her views on the school's strengths and weaknesses, and on the threats and opportunities the school is facing. Then use this information to write up a SWOT analysis for the school.

BUILDING YOUR BUSINESS SKILLS

Speaking with Power

The Purpose of This Assignment

To encourage students to appreciate effective speaking as a critical human relations skill.

Background

A manager's ability to understand and get along with supervisors, peers, and subordinates is a critical human relations skill. At the heart of this skill, says Harvard University professor of education Sarah McGinty, is the ability to speak with power and control. McGinty defines "powerful speech" in terms of the following characteristics:

- the ability to speak at length and in complete sentences
- the ability to set a conversational agenda
- the ability to deter interruption
- the ability to argue openly and to express strong opinions about ideas, not people
- the ability to make statements that offer solutions rather than pose questions
- the ability to express humour

Taken together, says McGinty, "all this creates a sense of confidence in listeners."

Assignment

Step 1

Working alone, compare your own personal speaking style with McGinty's description of powerful speech by taping yourself as you speak during a meeting with classmates or during a phone conversation. (Tape both sides of the conversation only if the person to whom you are speaking gives permission.) Listen for the following problems:

- unfinished sentences
- an absence of solutions
- too many disclaimers ("I'm not sure I have enough information to say this, but...")
- the habit of seeking support from others instead of making definitive statements of personal conviction

(saying, "As Emily has stated in her report, I also recommend consolidating the medical and fitness functions," instead of "I recommend consolidating the medical and fitness functions")
- language fillers (saying, "you know," "like," and "um" when you are unsure of your facts or uneasy about expressing your opinion)

Step 2

Join with three or four other classmates to evaluate each other's speaking styles.

- Have a 10-minute group discussion on the importance of human relations skills in business.
- Listen to other group members, and take notes on the "power" content of what you hear.
- Offer constructive criticism by focusing on what speakers say rather than on personal characteristics (Say, "Bob, you sympathized with Paul's position, but I still don't know what you think," instead of "Bob, you sounded like a weakling").

Questions for Discussion

1. How do you think the power content of speech affects a manager's ability to communicate? Evaluate some of the ways in which effects may differ among supervisors, peers, and subordinates.
2. How do you evaluate yourself and group members in terms of powerful and powerless speech? List the strengths and weaknesses of the group.
3. Do you agree or disagree with McGinty that business success depends on gaining insight into your own language habits? Explain your answer.
4. In our age of computers and email, why do you think personal presentation continues to be important in management?
5. McGinty believes that power language differs from company to company and that it is linked to the corporate culture. Do you agree, or do you believe that people express themselves in similar ways no matter where they are?

EXERCISING YOUR ETHICS: TEAM EXERCISE

Clean Up Now, or Clean Up Later?

The Situation

The top management team of a medium-sized manufacturing company is on a strategic planning "retreat," and the members are formulating ideas and plans for spurring new growth in the company. As one part of this activity, the

team, working with the assistance of a consultant, has conducted a SWOT analysis. During this activity, an interesting and complex situation has been identified. Next year, the federal government will be issuing new—and much more stringent—pollution standards for the company's industry. The management team sees this as a potential "threat" in that the company will have to buy new equipment and change some of its manufacturing methods in order to comply with the new standards.

The Dilemma

One member of the team, James Smith, has posed an interesting option: not complying. His logic can be summarized as follows:

1. The firm has already developed its capital budgets for the next two years. Any additional capital expenditures will cause major problems with the company's cash flow and budget allocations.
2. The company has a large uncommitted capital budget entry available in three years; those funds could be used to upgrade pollution control systems at that time.
3. Because the company has a spotless environmental record so far, Smith argues that if the company does not buy the equipment for three years, the most likely outcomes will be (a) a warning in year one, (b) a small fine in year two, and (c) a substantial fine in year three. However, the total amounts of the fines in years two and three will be much lower than the cost of redoing the company budgets and complying with the new law next year.

Team Activity

Assemble a group of four students and assign each group member to one of the following roles:

- management team member
- lower-level employee at the company
- company customer
- company investor

Action Steps

1. Before discussing the situation with your group, and from the perspective of your assigned role, do you think that James Smith's suggestion regarding ignoring pollution standards is a good one? Write down the reasons for your position.
2. Before discussing the situation with your group, and from the perspective of your assigned role, what are the underlying ethical issues in this situation? Write down the issues.
3. Gather your group together and reveal, in turn, each member's comments on James Smith's suggestion. Next, reveal the ethical issues listed by each member.
4. Appoint someone to record the main points of agreement and disagreement within the group. How do you explain the results? What accounts for any disagreement?
5. From an ethical standpoint, what does your group conclude is the most appropriate action that should be taken by the company in this situation?
6. Develop a group response to the following questions: (a) What are the respective roles of profits, obligations to customers, and obligations to the community for a firm in this situation? (b) Is it possible to simultaneously make an ethical decision and maximize company revenue?

Go to MyBizLab for additional cases and exercise material.

CONCLUDING CASE 6-1

The Overtime Pay Controversy

Under the terms of the Canada Labour Code, individuals in supervisory roles are not entitled to overtime pay for work beyond 40 hours per week. But this provision is now being challenged. It all started in 2003 when Sharon Michalowski, a manager at Nygard International Ltd., filed a complaint with the Manitoba Labour Board arguing that she should have been paid overtime for the extra hours that she was required to work. Nygard took the position that since Michalowski was a manager, she was required to work whatever hours were required to do the job. But the Board ruled in Michalowski's favour and awarded her $10 000 in overtime pay. Nygard appealed the case to the Supreme Court of Canada but lost. Soon after, the province of Manitoba fell into line with other provinces and passed legislation that exempted managers from overtime pay rules in its labour laws. But that didn't end the debate.

In 2010, a $250-million overtime class-action lawsuit was launched by 1500 first-line supervisors at Canadian National Railway who oversee the movement of trains and the maintenance of track. The supervisors said they had to work 50 hours a week on average, and sometimes as much as 90 hours per week. The lawsuit was certified (approved to go to trial) by the Ontario Superior Court. An important issue in this case will be whether a person who is designated as a "supervisor" can claim overtime; that is, the case will examine whether first-line supervisors at CN are properly classified as "managers" and whether they actually have managerial duties. If the judge hearing the case decides that the supervisors are *not* actually managers, CN could owe millions of dollars in overtime.

It is not just groups of employees who are filing lawsuits. Massimo Sanago, the executive chef at the Glendale Golf and Country Club in Hamilton, had the responsibility of managing kitchen operations. But because of staff shortages, he spent over half his time cooking. He also had to work long hours to finish all his work. Glendale gave him a $5000 bonus in recognition of his efforts, but he felt that was insufficient, so he filed a claim for overtime pay with the Ministry of Labour. Glendale disputed the claim, arguing that Sanago's core job was managerial in nature, that he performed cooking duties only on an emergency basis, and that he therefore did not qualify for overtime pay. But the Ontario Labour Relations Board ruled that the company had to pay him overtime.

Cases like those above should not be confused with overtime-related class-action lawsuits that have been filed by *non-management* workers. In 2008, a $360-million class-action lawsuit was filed against CIBC World Markets Inc. by salaried stock analysts, financial advisors, and investment bankers who claimed they had not been compensated for overtime work they had done. (In 2012, a judge quashed the lawsuit, saying that some employees who are classified as "analysts" are actually managers and do not qualify for overtime.) A similar class-action overtime lawsuit was filed by bank tellers at CIBC. The latter case was not allowed to go forward when the Ontario Divisional Court ruled that CIBC's overtime policy didn't violate the law. The Court also ruled that there were not enough common issues among the 31 000 tellers at CIBC to warrant a class-action lawsuit.

In 2010, non-management workers at the Scotiabank also filed a class-action lawsuit claiming that they were not paid for overtime that they had worked. The bank appealed a judge's ruling that the case could go to trial, but in 2011 the Ontario Divisional Court rejected the bank's appeal and concluded that there was evidence of systemic wrongs in Scotiabank's overtime policy. Appeals have been filed in both the CIBC and Scotiabank cases, and the issue of overtime pay for non-management workers may not be settled until the Supreme Court of Canada rules on the matter.

The threat of lawsuits has influenced other companies to take action. For example, KMPG was sued by employees who claimed that the company forced them to work as much as 90 hours a week in order to complete their work. While the lawsuit was still before the courts, KPMG agreed to fix the problem, and it may have to spend up to $10 million to do so.

Class-action suits against employers are partly the result of the way labour laws are written. For example, unless a person's occupation is specifically excluded by legislation, that person is entitled to overtime pay for each hour they work beyond the provincial maximum (in Ontario, that is 44 hours per week). In Ontario, occupations such as lawyers, accountants, dentists, veterinarians, farmers, salespeople, gardeners, janitors, taxi drivers, and IT professionals are excluded. Critics of the legislation argue that the first five make some sense because those occupations require independent work, but it makes little sense to exclude the latter four occupations.

Questions for Discussion

1. Identify the positive and negative implications of not paying managers for overtime.
2. Consider the following statement: *Managers should not expect to be paid overtime. They are highly paid, and they should focus on getting the job done rather than on how many hours it takes to complete the job. People who don't have a "get-the-job-done" attitude shouldn't be managers.* Do you agree or disagree with the statement? Defend your answer.

CONCLUDING CASE 6-2

Culture Clash

Introductory textbooks in management, introduction to business, and organizational behaviour introduce the concept of organizational culture and note its importance for both organizations and the people who work in them. Culture is usually defined something like this: the shared assumptions, experiences, stories, beliefs, norms, and ethical stance that characterize an organization and collectively influence the organization's style and how employees act. A brief summary definition might be this: "It's the way we do things around here."

There are many interesting questions that arise regarding organizational culture, three of which are as follows: (1) What happens if two companies with widely differing cultures merge? (2) Do mergers get called off because of concerns about differences in organizational cultures? (3) What if the top management of a given company disagrees with lower-level employees about the kind of culture the organization should have? These three situations are analyzed below.

Vale and Inco

When two companies with different cultures merge, a culture clash may result. Consider the case of Vale, the Brazilian mining company that bought the Canadian iron ore giant Inco for $17.6 billion. Shortly after the purchase, there was a meeting of executives of both companies, but the meeting ended suddenly when one of the Brazilian managers lost his temper. That was the first sign that the cultures of the two companies were different enough that problems were going to be evident. Over the next few months, many Canadian managers, engineers, and operating staff left the company. For example, of 29 managers who were involved in a strategy session shortly after the merger, only six were still there a few months later.

In retrospect, it is clear that the cultures of the two companies were quite different prior to the takeover. At Inco, there was a constant exchange of ideas, and decentralized decision making was encouraged by top management. But at Vale, top managers gave orders and expected them to be followed. Not surprisingly, Vale experienced resistance from Inco executives who did not agree with that approach. Some observers think that since Canadian companies were used to taking over Brazilian companies, not the other way around, Canadian executives had trouble doing what their new bosses wanted.

But even beyond that possible explanation, there might have been difficulties because of differences in the products the two companies focused on before Vale bought Inco. Vale's focus was on iron ore, a basic commodity that is mined using a relatively simple technology. But the underground mining of nickel, which is a key ingredient in stainless steel, is a more complex undertaking. One Inco manager likened nickel mining to having a Ph.D, while iron ore mining was like having a high school diploma. Canadian managers obviously felt some disdain for their new Brazilian bosses.

The cultural differences between the two companies were not limited to the top level of management. In the 1980s, the miners' union had given up annual wage increases in return for a bonus based on the price of nickel. When the price of nickel soared, workers received large bonuses. Vale now wants to raise the threshold at which the bonus kicks in, and also wants to convert the defined benefit pension plan to a defined contribution plan. The union is strongly resisting. Vale is seen as a company with an "attitude," and Vale's management has been very aggressive in dealing with the Canadian workers it inherited from Inco.

One of the most visible signs of the culture difference is the lengthy strike by the United Steelworkers union that began in July 2009. In March 2010, workers rejected an offer to settle by a wide margin, saying that Vale's offer was far short of what the union members expected. Vale then took legal action against the union, accusing it of vandalism, assaults, and death threats. It also laid off many employees and shut down various projects because of the uncertain economic environment. In mid-April 2010, Vale announced that it was going to bring in replacement workers in order to get two of the nickel mines back up to full production. On July 13, 2010—one year to the day after the strike began—the Ontario Labour Board heard presentations from the steelworkers union that Vale was bargaining in bad faith. The federal government has not gotten involved in the dispute in spite of claims by the union that Vale is a foreign company that is trying to change the culture of Canadian union–management relations.

Roger Agnelli, Vale's CEO, said that the cultures of the two companies would simply have to adjust. But Vale also removed the name "Inco" from its nickel business. (Note: The Vale takeover of Inco has not gone nearly as smoothly as the Xstrata takeover of Falconbridge, the other large Canadian nickel miner. Xstrata gave Canadian managers a lot more say in changes that were made after the takeover.)

The Role of Organizational Culture in Thwarting Mergers

Some planned mergers never happen because concerns about a culture clash inhibit negotiations. For example, in 2009 two Japanese companies (Kirin Holdings Co. and Suntory Holdings Ltd.) announced plans to merge in order to create one of the world's largest beverage companies. It was thought that a merger would create a company that could break out of the domestic Japanese market and become a major player on the international scene. But the merger never took place, partly because of differences in the management styles of the two companies. Kirin (a member of the Mitsubishi group) has solid, traditional management, but Suntory has a unique management style that is influenced by the fact that families own about 90 percent of the company's shares. During negotiations, the two companies simply could not reconcile the differences in their two corporate cultures and the merger was called off.

A planned acquisition of Sun Microsystems by IBM also failed to occur. When rumours of the takeover started circulating, James Gosling, Sun's executive vice-president, warned that there would be a culture clash if the acquisition occurred. He said that the developer staff at Sun were "weirder" than those at IBM. In fact, Sun does have a somewhat radical corporate culture because it has been pushing open systems like Unix. This contrasts with IBM's more proprietary approach. In April 2010, the merger talks broke off because the two companies could not agree on terms.

A similar-looking situation was evident when Kraft Foods tried to acquire Cadbury in 2009. Andrew Bonfield, the finance director at Cadbury (the maker of such well-known brands as Caramilk candy bars and Bubblicious gum), warned that Cadbury's unique corporate culture would be lost if Kraft acquired it. He said that the Cadbury "magic" was important for the brands it markets. The company's CEO, Todd Stitzer, also weighed in, saying that Cadbury's culture of "principled capitalism" is what makes Cadbury great. The British public was concerned about losing one of its icons, and Warren Buffett sold off almost one-quarter of his Kraft stock when he heard about the plan. The two companies do, in fact, have quite different histories and cultures. Cadbury has tried to build a socially benign business and recently launched a fair trade

initiative with its Dairy Milk brand. By contrast, Kraft has been a much more traditional multinational business firm. In spite of these concerns about differing cultures, Kraft did acquire Cadbury early in 2010 after protracted negotiations. Any problems that might arise as a result of combining two different cultures have yet to be determined.

Culture Clashes Within Organizations

Culture clashes don't just happen when two independent companies try to merge. They can also occur when a top manager's vision for a culture comes into conflict with the culture that lower-level employees prefer. Consider the situation that has arisen at the DeGroote School of Business at McMaster University. In 2004, Paul Bates, a Bay Street brokerage executive who was one of the pioneers of the discount brokerage business, was hired as dean of the business school. When he sought reappointment for a second term as dean in 2008, he was opposed by 80 percent of the faculty, but the views of faculty members were overruled by the board of governors and Bates was reappointed for another term. Many professors are unhappy with Bates's corporate management style; they accuse him of bullying and intimidation, and of not understanding the academic culture of the school. Those who support the dean say that he has done good things for the school, and that the faculty members are biased against anyone who isn't "academic" enough. A report issued by the McMaster Office of Human Rights and Equity Services concluded that the business school has a dysfunctional work environment, and that immediate action should be taken to resolve the problem. The report also noted that the school has a history of conflict between deans and faculty members.

Sometimes a new top executive is brought in to change the corporate culture in response to a crisis the company is facing. Edward Whitacre, the CEO of General Motors, was one such person. He was recruited in 2009 and given the mandate to turn the company around and change GM's plodding culture. But Whitacre did not have an easy job because GM had to introduce massive changes in order to dig itself out of the financial hole it was in. He wanted to reduce bureaucracy and push decision-making authority down into GM's many management layers so that decisions were made more quickly and the company became more responsive to changes in the marketplace. And he realized that the culture needed to change quickly or the company might not survive. Prior to Whitacre's arrival, decisions were not made until they were approved by many different committees. A few years ago, the company introduced a program to stamp out bureaucracy, but the committee that was guiding the effort had trouble deciding how many committee meetings were necessary to achieve the goal. That kind of dithering was not what Whitacre has in mind.

One of the things Whitacre did to change the culture of the company was to be more hands-on and accessible than his predecessors (who spent most of their time in the executive suite). He had some success with that strategy because GM employees talked about "Ed sightings" in the hallways and cafeteria. He also visited GM manufacturing plants to talk to workers. At the Lansing, Michigan, plant, Whitacre (dressed in jeans and a T-shirt) talked directly to workers, and at a GM plant in Fairfax, Kansas, Whitacre told workers he had taken the CEO job because he thought that GM was an American institution that the country couldn't afford to lose. Whether Whitacre changed GM's culture enough to make it a success remains to be seen. (Whitacre was replaced as CEO by Dan Akerson, who is also trying to reduce the bureaucracy at GM.)

Questions for Discussion

1. What is corporate culture? Compare and contrast the companies described in this case in terms of their corporate culture.
2. Can the CEO of a company really influence the culture of an organization in a substantial way?
3. Consider the following statement: *The idea that a culture clash is important is overstated. People generally are so focused on doing their own jobs that abstract issues like "culture" don't influence their behaviour very much.* Do you agree or disagree with the statement? Defend your answer.

Organizing the Business Enterprise

LEARNING OBJECTIVES

After reading this chapter, you should be able to:

1 Discuss the elements that influence a firm's *organizational structure*.

2 Explain how *specialization* and *departmentalization* are the building blocks of organizational structure.

3 Distinguish between *responsibility* and *authority* and explain the differences

in decision making in *centralized* and *decentralized* organizations.

4 Explain the differences among *functional*, *divisional*, *project*, and *international organizational structures*.

5 Describe the most popular new forms of *organizational design*.

6 Explain the idea of the *informal organization*.

The Organizational Structure of the "Occupy Wall Street" Movement

THERE is quite a contrast between the hierarchical structures of Canadian business firms and the Occupy Wall Street movement that received so much publicity in 2011. The movement started at Vancouver-based Adbusters, which publishes a magazine that is critical of excessive consumer consumption. Inspired by the so-called "Arab Spring" in the Middle East earlier in 2011, the staff at Adbusters got together for a brainstorming session, and came up with the image of a ballerina balanced on top of Wall Street's iconic charging bull sculpture. A simple Twitter hashtag was chosen: #OccupyWallStreet. Thousands of people became excited about the idea and before long a big protest demonstration was planned for New York City. By mid-October, protests were also taking place in major Canadian and European cities. Protest groups set up camps in many places, including city parks, the Vancouver Art Gallery, Zuccotti

Park in New York City, and the Toronto Stock Exchange. Protesters met together in large and small groups, played drums, and sang together. Unions and community groups also joined the movement, and a website called "Occupy Together" was started. The movement appeared leaderless, and stood for open, participatory, non-hierarchical decision making, with everyone entitled to provide input and push their own ideas. As one protester said, "No one is a leader because everyone is a leader."

The Occupy Wall Street movement struck a respondent chord in both Canadians and Americans who were frustrated with a political/economic system they saw as favouring corporations and rich individuals. The movement made many demands, the most general one being an end to economic inequality. The central message was "we are the 99 percent," but that message was combined with a dizzying

array of other demands: raise taxes on corporations, offer free college education, stop climate change, stop unfair treatment of Muslims, stop home foreclosures, reduce high unemployment, and nationalize the banks. While the situation seemed rather chaotic, there actually was *some* structure in the movement. For example, daily meetings (called assemblies) were held, in which participants planned the occupation, decided where marches would be held, planned communication with the media, and organized the supplies that had been donated. Anyone could participate in the assemblies, and minutes of assemblies were posted online. Since a New York bylaw prevents use of bullhorns without a permit, protesters adopted "the people's microphone" system: someone would shout a message a few words at a time to the crowd and then people who heard that message would repeat it for others who were further away.

Opposition to the camps soon developed. City officials, for example, became frustrated by the movement's occupation of public spaces. As police moved protesters out of public parks, and as winter approached, the movement started to fizzle out. A few camps were still occupied in January 2012, and a few others reappeared in May 2012, but the movement had lost a great deal of momentum.

There were plenty of explanations offered for the decline of the Occupy Wall Street movement. Observers said that the movement did not succeed because (1) it was not as egalitarian as generally assumed (the camps exhibited a hierarchy, and a few people dominated the many), (2) it had no central message and no clear goal, (3) assemblies were very inefficient and time-consuming, (3) the movement lacked an endgame

(under what conditions would protesters end their protest?), (3) it had a culture of entitlement (the protests were dominated by the younger generation, who expected to be handed the wealth of their parents), (4) it cost money (city officials wanted the encampments dismantled because costs were being incurred to control the protesters), and (5) it ignored basic human nature (internal dissension developed as the tent camps became havens for the disenfranchised of society).

However, supporters and organizers insisted that the anti-hierarchical nature of the Occupy Wall Street movement was supposed to help it succeed. Kalle Lasn, one of the founders of Adbusters, said that critics didn't understand that the Occupy movement was a new-style revolution. It was egalitarian, not vertical, and it didn't have (or want) a designated

leader. Instead, it was horizontal because it grew out of the culture of the internet. When asked about the future of the movement, Lasn said that it would adopt a different strategy for 2012, one that would involve "surprise attacks" in diverse settings like university economics departments and banks, rather than continuous occupations of city parks.

As interest in the Occupy Wall Street movement declined, attention turned to a website called leadnow.ca, which some thought would become the focal point for a leaderless organization. During 2011, leadnow.ca organized "vote mobs" on university and community college campuses, and in just a few months it attracted 60 000 members. Its goal is to have half a million members before the next federal election in Canada. ◆

HOW WILL THIS HELP ME?

Companies frequently introduce changes that are designed to improve their organization's structures. When this happens, people have to understand their "place" in the organization. By understanding the material in this chapter, as an *employee* you will also be prepared to understand your "place" in the organization that employs you. Similarly, as a *boss or owner*, you'll be better equipped to create the optimal structure for your own organization.

What Is Organizational Structure?

organizational structure The specification of the jobs to be done within a business and how those jobs relate to one another.

Organizational structure is the specification of the jobs to be done within a business and how those jobs relate to one another. To understand what organizational structure is all about, consider an analogy: a business is like an automobile. All automobiles have an engine, four wheels, fenders and other structural components, an interior compartment for passengers, and various operating systems including those for fuel, brakes, and climate control. Each component has a distinct purpose but must also work in harmony with all the others. Automobiles made by competing firms all have the same basic components, although the way they look and fit together may vary. Similarly, all businesses have common structural and operating components, each of which has a specific purpose. Each component must fulfill its own purpose while simultaneously fitting in with the others. And, just like automobiles made by different companies, how these components look and fit together varies from company to company.

Every institution—be it a for-profit company like Frantic Films, a not-for-profit organization like the University of Saskatchewan, or a government agency like The Competition Bureau—must develop a structure that is appropriate for its own unique situation. What works for Air Canada will not work for the Canada Revenue Agency. Likewise, the structure of the Red Cross will not work for the University of Toronto.

Determinants of Organizational Structure

How is an organization's structure determined? Does it happen by chance or is there some strategy that managers use to create structure? Or is it a combination of the two? Ideally, managers should assess a variety of factors as they plan for and then create a structure that will make their organization effective. But with the busyness that is evident in most organizations, structure may often develop without much planning.

Many elements work together to determine an organization's structure. Chief among these are the organization's purpose, mission, and strategy. A dynamic and rapidly growing enterprise, for example, achieved that position because of its purpose and successful strategies for achieving it. Such a firm will need a structure that contributes to flexibility and growth. A stable organization with only modest growth will function best with a different structure.

Size, technology, and changes in environmental circumstances also affect structure. A large manufacturer operating in a strongly competitive environment requires a different structure than a local barbershop or video store. Moreover, even after a structure has been created, it is rarely free from tinkering—or even outright re-creation. Indeed, most organizations change their structures almost continually.

Since it was first incorporated in 1903, for example, Ford Motor Co. has undergone literally dozens of major structural changes, hundreds of moderate changes, and thousands of minor changes. In just the last 15 years, Ford has initiated several major structural changes that were designed to eliminate corporate bureaucracy, speed up decision making, and improve communication and working relationships among people at different levels of the organization. The boxed insert entitled "Reorganizing the Irving Empire" describes structural changes at a large Canadian firm.

The Chain of Command

organization chart Illustrates the company's structure and show employees where they fit into the firm's operations.

chain of command The reporting relationships within the company.

Most businesses prepare an **organization chart** that illustrates the company's structure and show employees where they fit into the firm's operations. Figure 7.1 shows the organization chart for a hypothetical company. Each box represents a job within the company. The solid lines that connect the boxes define the **chain of command**—the reporting

MANAGING IN TURBULENT TIMES

Reorganizing the Irving Empire

The Irving family of New Brunswick owns nearly 300 businesses in areas as diverse as oil refining, forestry, shipbuilding, food processing, publishing, transportation, and home improvement. The company was founded by J.D. Irving in 1882 when he opened a sawmill in Bouctouche, New Brunswick. The business expanded dramatically under his son K.C. Irving, who then passed it on to his three sons—J.K., Arthur, and Jack. These brothers then had five sons, the two most active being Ken (Arthur's son), who headed the oil and gas operation until 2010, and Jim (J.K.'s son), who oversees the forestry operations. Over time, tensions developed between Ken and Jim regarding the strategic direction of the company because each wanted more control over the business.

Originally, K.C. Irving set up a structure that saw J.K. (and later his son Jim) running the forestry empire, trucking, food processing, and newspapers. Arthur (and later his son Ken) was in charge of oil refineries and service stations. Jack's responsibilities were in construction, steel, and real estate. The grand plan began to fall apart when Jim began to feel restricted by the structure because it tied his strategy to Ken's. As well, the third brother—Jack—began to feel like an also-ran in the company. As a result, a coalition—composed of Arthur and Jack and their families—developed and began to oppose Jim and his family.

The brothers wanted to avoid a bitter family feud, so they restructured the company and let the two main parts go their separate ways. Jim and his relatives took control of the forestry end of the business, and Ken and his relatives took over the oil and gas business. The restructuring was complicated because the various businesses in the family empire are controlled by trusts that were set up by K.C. Irving many years ago. In order to divide up the company, the dozens of family members who had an interest had to agree on what the restructuring would look like. Irving descendants will likely be offered cash or business interests in return for the original trusts being phased out. An additional complication was the unexpected resignation of Kenneth Irving in 2010. Mike Ashtar is now the president of Irving, the first non-family member to hold that position.

Critical Thinking Questions

1. What are the four basic organizational structures? Which one is evident at Irving?

2. What corporate-level strategy has Irving used over the years? (Consult the discussion in Chapter 6 before answering this question.) Explain your reasoning.

FIGURE 7.1

An organization chart shows key positions in the organization and interrelationships among them.

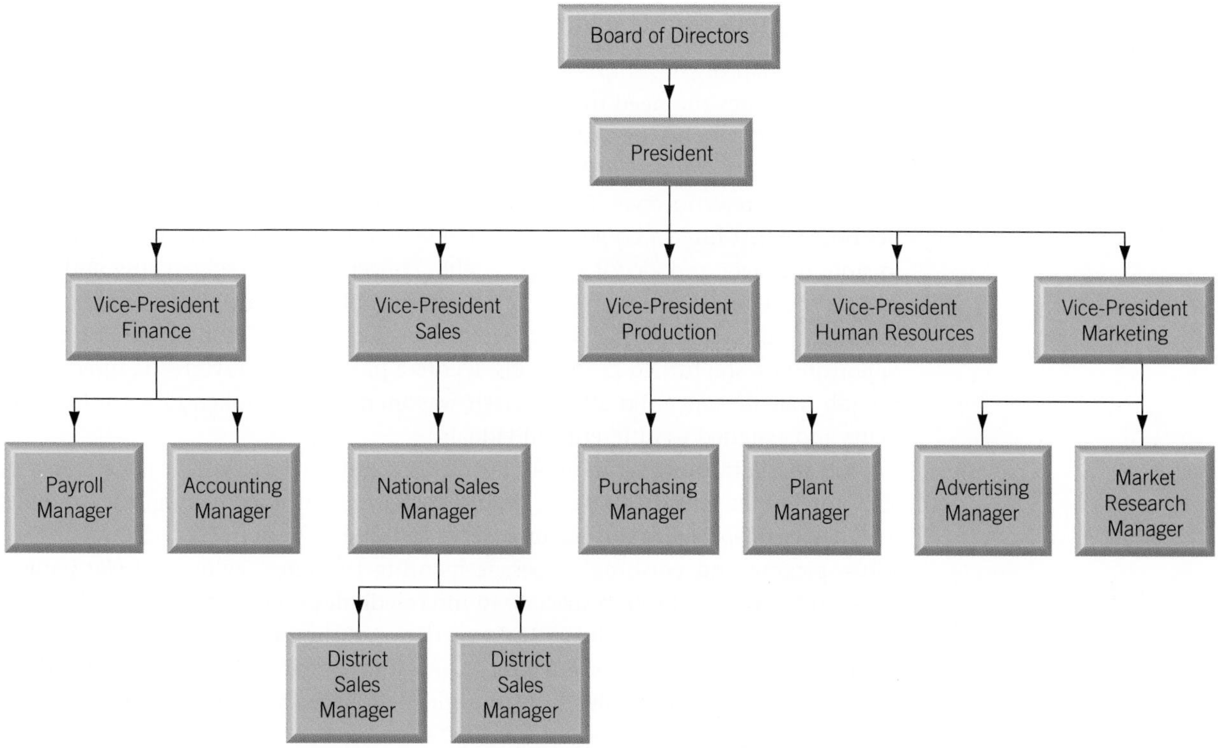

relationships within a company. For example, the plant manager reports directly to the vice-president of production, who, in turn, reports to the president. When the chain of command is not clear, many different kinds of problems can result.

An actual organization chart would, of course, be far more complex and include individuals at many more levels. Large firms cannot easily draw an organization chart with everyone on it. The chart might also show some unusual features. For example, until recently the organization chart of Research in Motion showed two CEOs and two chairpersons of the board. But in 2011, investor pressure caused the company to change the structure so that just one person did each job.[1]

The Building Blocks of Organizational Structure

The most fundamental building blocks of organizational structure are *specialization* (determining who will do what), and *departmentalization* (determining how people performing certain tasks can best be grouped together).

Specialization

Job specialization is the process of identifying the specific jobs that need to be done and designating the people who will perform them. In a sense, all businesses have only one major "job"—making a profit by selling products or services to consumers. But this overall job needs to be broken down into smaller components which are then assigned to individuals. Consider the manufacture of men's shirts. Because several steps are required to produce a shirt, each job is broken down into its component parts—that is, into a set of tasks to be completed by a series of individuals or machines. One person, for example, cuts material for the shirt body, another cuts material for the sleeves, and a third cuts material for the collar. Components are then shipped to a sewing room, where a fourth person assembles the shirt. In the final stage, a fifth person sews on the buttons.[2]

Specialization and Growth

In a very small organization, the owner may perform every job. As the firm grows, however, so does the need to specialize jobs so that others can perform them. When Mrs. Fields Cookies began, Debbi Fields did everything herself: bought the equipment, negotiated the lease, baked the cookies, operated the store, and kept the records. As the business grew, however, Fields found that her job was becoming too much for one person. She first hired a bookkeeper to handle her financial records. She then hired an in-store manager and a cookie baker. Debbi concentrated on advertising and promotions. Her second store required another set of employees—another manager, another baker, and some salespeople. While Fields focussed her attention on other expansion opportunities, she turned promotions over to a professional advertising director. Thus the job that she once did all by herself was increasingly broken down into components and assigned to different individuals.

Job specialization is a natural part of organizational growth. It is neither a new idea nor limited to factory work. In the ancient art of winemaking, for example, a high degree of specialization has existed for centuries. The activities necessary to make wine—picking and crushing grapes, fermenting the juice, aging and clarifying the wine, and selling it through specialized intermediaries—are performed by individuals who can draw on the knowledge and experience of their predecessors.

Job specialization has certain advantages—individual jobs can be performed more efficiently, the jobs are easier to learn, and it is easier to replace people who leave

LO2 Explain how *specialization* and *departmentalization* are the building blocks of organizational structure.

job specialization The process of identifying the specific jobs that need to be done and designating the people who will perform them.

When Walt Disney was just starting out, he did most of the work on his animated features all by himself. But today's features like Disney's 2011 hit *Cars II* require the work of hundreds of people.

the organization. On the other hand, if job specialization is carried too far and jobs become too narrowly defined, people get bored, derive less satisfaction from their jobs, and often lose sight of how their contributions fit into the overall organization.

Departmentalization

Departmentalization is the process of grouping specialized jobs into logical units. Departmentalization improves control and coordination because managers can see more easily how various units are performing. Departmentalization allows the firm to treat a department as a **profit centre**—a separate unit responsible for its own costs and profits. Thus, by assessing profits from sales in a particular area—for example, men's clothing—Sears can decide whether to expand or curtail promotions in that area. Departmentalization may occur along *functional, customer, product, geographic,* or *process* lines (or some combination of these).

departmentalization The process of grouping jobs into logical units.

profit centre A separate company unit responsible for its own costs and profits.

Functional Departmentalization

Functional departmentalization means organizing departments according to the function they perform—marketing, finance, production, human resources, etc. Each of these departments may be further subdivided; for example, the marketing department might be divided geographically or into separate staffs for market research and advertising.

functional departmentalization Departmentalization according to functions or activities.

Customer Departmentalization

Customer departmentalization involves setting up departments or divisions that focus on meeting the needs of specific customers. Some retail stores actually derive their generic name—department stores—from the manner in which they are structured. For example, stores like HMV are divided into departments—a classical music department, an R&B department, a pop department, and so on. Each department targets a specific customer category (people who want to buy different genres of music). Customer departmentalization makes the store more efficient and customers get better service, in part because salespeople tend to specialize and gain expertise in their departments.[3]

customer departmentalization Departmentalization according to the types of customers likely to buy a given product.

Nissan has developed an assembly process that is so efficient that it can turn out a vehicle in 10 fewer hours than Ford can. The key is the organization of the workstations. At this station, workers install just about everything that the driver touches inside the truck cab. Other stations take care of the whole vehicle frame, the entire electrical system, or completed doors.

Product Departmentalization

product departmentalization Dividing an organization according to the specific product or service being created.

Product departmentalization means dividing an organization according to the specific products or services that are being created. 3M Corp., which makes both consumer and industrial products, operates different divisions for Post-it brand tape flags, Scotch-Brite scrub sponges, and the Sarns 9000 perfusion system for open-heart surgery. In 2011, home improvement giant Lowe's reorganized its merchandising operations into two product divisions: (1) building and outdoor products, and (2) kitchen, bath, and home décor products.[4]

Geographic Departmentalization

geographic departmentalization Departmentalization according to the area of the country or world supplied.

Geographic departmentalization means creating departments based on the area of the country—or even the world—they serve. In 2011, Lowe's also created three divisions: north, south, and west.[5] In 2009, Nike introduced a new structure that was organized around six geographic regions: North America, Western Europe, Eastern/Central Europe, Greater China, Japan, and emerging markets.[6]

Choosing between product and geographic departmentalization. It may be difficult to decide whether to use geographic or product departmentalization. Geographic departmentalization ensures quick, responsive reaction to the needs of the company's

Many department stores are departmentalized by product. Concentrating different products in different areas of the store makes shopping easier for customers.

customers in specific geographic areas, but it may also lead to duplicate production and other facilities, and compartmentalization of knowledge in those same geographic areas. Many years ago, when relatively limited communications made it difficult to take the pulse of consumer needs or monitor operations abroad, it made sense to let local managers in foreign countries run their regional or country businesses as more or less autonomous companies. However, in today's global economy, competition is so intense that firms can't afford to miss an opportunity to quickly transfer product improvements from one region to another. So, some firms are switching from geographic to product departmentalization. For example, PepsiCo was formerly organized around geographic areas: North America and International. When Indra Nooyi became CEO, she reorganized the company into three divisions: Americas Foods, Americas Beverages, and International. The new structure—which is actually a combination of product and geographic departmentalization—better reflects PepsiCo's focus on snack foods (which account for nearly half its total revenue).

Process Departmentalization

Process departmentalization means creating departments according to the production processes that are used. For example, Vlasic has separate departments to transform cucumbers into fresh-packed pickles, pickles cured in brine, and relishes. Each process requires different equipment and worker skills.

> **process departmentalization**
> Departmentalization according to the production process used to create a good or service.

Large companies tend to use different types of departmentalization at different levels. The company illustrated in Figure 7.2 uses functional departmentalization at the top level, geographic departmentalization at the middle level, and product departmentalization at the lower level.

Establishing the Decision-Making Hierarchy

After jobs have been specialized and grouped into appropriate departments, the next step is to establish a decision-making hierarchy; that is, managers must define reporting relationships among positions so that everyone will know who has responsibility

FIGURE 7.2

Most organizations use multiple bases of departmentalization. This organization, for example, is using functional, geographic, and product departmentalization.

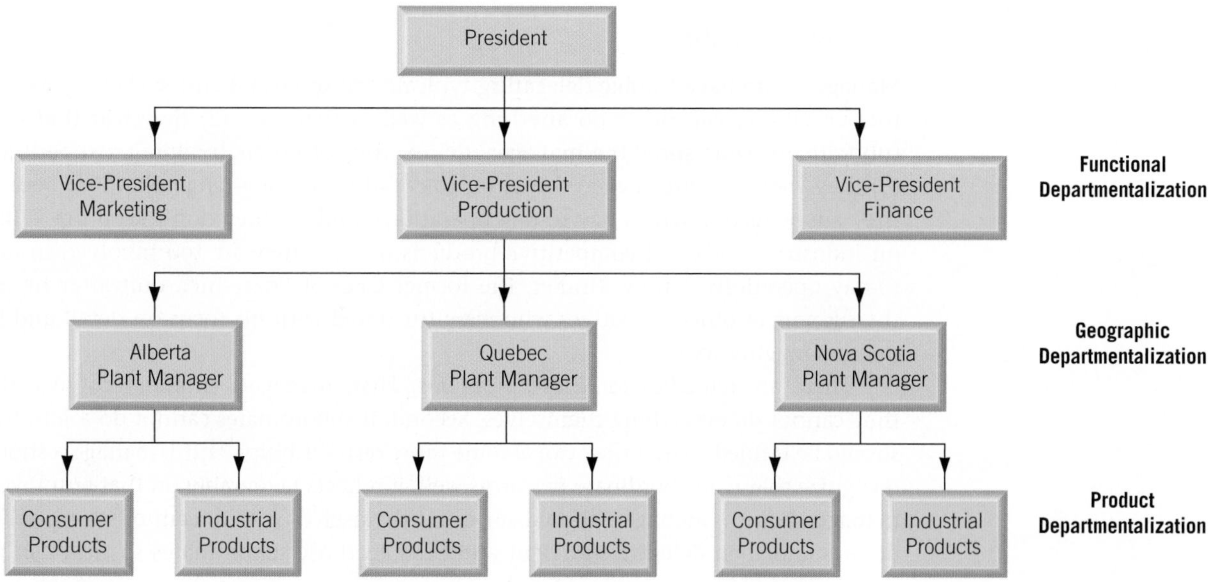

for various decisions and operations. The development of this hierarchy generally involves a three-step process:

1. **Assigning tasks:** determining who can make decisions and specifying how they should be made

2. **Performing tasks:** implementing decisions that have been made

3. **Distributing authority:** determining whether the organization is to be centralized or decentralized

Assigning Tasks

(L03) Distinguish between *responsibility* and *authority* and explain the differences in decision making in *centralized* and *decentralized* organizations.

authority The power to make the decisions necessary to complete the task.

responsibility The duty to perform an assigned task.

Authority is the power to make the decisions necessary to complete a task. **Responsibility** is the duty to perform an assigned task. These ideas may seem simple, but two distinct problems may arise when they are applied in practice. First, authority and responsibility may not be balanced. For example, suppose a buyer for a department store has an unexpected opportunity to make a large purchase at an extremely good price but does not have the authority to make the purchase without confirmation from above. The company's policies on authority and responsibility are inconsistent because the buyer is responsible for purchasing the clothes that will be sold in the store but lacks the authority to make the needed purchases. Second, when things go wrong, there is often debate about who is responsible. As we saw in the opening case in Chapter 3, for example, *News of the World* owner Rupert Murdoch said he wasn't responsible for the phone hacking that some of his reporters engaged in. But observers say that top managers *were* responsible because they put pressure on reporters to get "scoops" so the paper's circulation would increase, and this drove the reporters to take extreme measures to get stories.[7]

Performing Tasks

delegation Assignment of a task, a responsibility, or authority by a manager to a subordinate.

accountability Liability of subordinates for accomplishing tasks assigned by managers.

Delegation means assigning a task to a subordinate. Once authority has been delegated, **accountability** falls to the subordinate, who must then complete the task. When Winnipeg-based Frantic Films first began operations, the principal shareholders made all the decisions. But the CEO, Jamie Brown, thought that it was important to delegate more authority to lower-level workers so they would gain experience in making decisions that affected the company. So, he gave lower-level managers the authority to spend up to $5000 without having to get the approval of top management. This change was also made because the top managers were spending too much time dealing with requests for small amounts of money.[8]

Fear of Delegating

Managers who have trouble delegating typically make several errors: (1) they assume that employees can never do anything as well as they can; (2) they fear that their subordinates will "show the manager up" in front of others by doing a superb job; (3) they want to control everything; (4) they fail to do long-range planning because they are bogged down in day-to-day operations; and (5) they don't keep up to date on industry trends and competitive products because they are too involved in day-to-day operations. Jeffrey Kindler, the former CEO of Pfizer Inc., quit after he lost the support of other executives who were frustrated with his focus on detail and his micromanaging style.[9]

There are remedies for these problems. First, managers should recognize that they cannot do everything themselves. Second, if subordinates cannot do a job, they should be trained so that they can assume more responsibility. Third, managers should recognize that if a subordinate performs well, it reflects favourably on that employee's manager. Fourth, managers should surround themselves with a team of strong subordinates and then delegate sufficient authority to those subordinates so they can get the job done. Barry Salzberg, the global CEO for Deloitte Touche Tohmatsu Ltd., says that senior management exists to help their staff become more successful, not the other way around.[10]

There are four things to keep in mind when delegating:

- Decide on the nature of the work to be done

- Match the job with the skills of subordinates

- Make sure the person chosen understands the objectives he or she is supposed to achieve

- Make sure subordinates have the time and training necessary to do the task

Distributing Authority

Businesses must make decisions about general patterns of authority throughout the company. These patterns may be largely *centralized* or *decentralized*.

Centralized Organizations

In a **centralized organization**, top management retains the right to make most decisions, and top management must approve most lower-level decisions before they can be implemented.[11] McDonald's practises centralization as a way to maintain standardization. All restaurants must follow precise steps in buying products and making and packaging burgers and other menu items. Most advertising is handled at the corporate level, and a regional manager must approve any local advertising. Restaurants even have to follow prescribed schedules for maintenance and upgrades like floor polishing and parking lot cleaning.[12]

centralized organization Top managers retain most decision-making rights for themselves.

Decentralized Organizations

In a **decentralized organization**, much of the decision-making authority is delegated to levels of management at various points below the top level. The purpose of decentralization is to make a company more responsive to its environment by giving lower-level managers more autonomy. Reducing top-heavy bureaucracies is also a common goal of decentralization. At FedEx, for example, the commitment to decentralization promotes innovation (see the boxed insert entitled "Making the Grade").

decentralized organization Lower- and middle-level managers are allowed to make significant decisions.

McDonald's emphasis on centralization ensures standardization in its product offerings. Customers will have a consistent dining experience whenever and wherever they eat at a McDonald's restaurant.

There are advantages and disadvantages of decentralization, and they can clearly be seen in the long history of General Motors. In the 1920s, GM's legendary president, Alfred Sloan, introduced a decentralized structure that gave each car division considerable autonomy to produce cars that would attract whatever market segment the division was pursuing. It worked so well that GM had become the largest automobile manufacturer in the world by the middle of the twentieth century. But all this autonomy resulted in widely differing car designs that were very expensive to produce. As decades passed, costs soared and competition from cost-conscious Japanese automakers became ferocious. GM's sales and overall profitability plummeted. In response, GM then took away much of the autonomy that managers in various international divisions had and instituted a requirement that its worldwide units work much more closely together to design cars that could be sold (with modest variations) worldwide. A "Global Council" in Detroit made key decisions about how much would be spent on new car development. When GM engineers at its Daewoo joint venture with South Korea wanted to develop a sport utility vehicle especially suited for the South Korean market, the request was denied.[13] But even these actions were not sufficient to stem GM's decline, and in 2008 the company was bailed out by the U.S. and Canadian governments and entered bankruptcy protection as it tried to recover. By 2011, the company's performance had once again improved.

Tall and Flat Organizations

flat organizational structure An organization with relatively few layers of management.

tall organizational structure An organization with many layers of management.

Decentralized firms *tend* to have a **flat organizational structure** such as the one shown in Figure 7.3. In contrast, companies with centralized authority systems typically require multiple layers of management and thus have a **tall organizational structure**. The Canadian Forces is an example of a tall organization. Because

ENTREPRENEURSHIP AND NEW VENTURES

Making the Grade

In 1965, undistinguished Yale undergrad Fred Smith wrote a paper describing how automated technology necessitated quicker, more reliable transportation. According to legend, the paper received a poor grade. But Smith himself debunks this myth. "It's become a well-known story because everybody likes to flout authority. But to be honest, I don't really remember what grade I got."

Whatever the grade, the idea was a winner. After serving in Vietnam, Smith invested his own money to start the air transport business Federal Express. FedEx, as the firm is now named, was revolutionary in pioneering the hub-and-spoke distribution system and using bar codes, handheld PDAs, and package tracking to compete with the monopolistic U.S. Postal Service.

When rival UPS entered the air freight segment in 2000, FedEx acquired several key players in the ground transportation industry. "The economics of airplanes are such that we couldn't just keep taking prices down," Smith says. "We finally realized that if we wanted to grow, we had to get into surface transportation." FedEx's new fleet capitalized on the brand's reputation for speed and reliability: "People say

'FedEx this' when they mean 'Get it someplace fast'," says investor Timothy M. Ghriskey. "No one says 'UPS this.'"

Although standardization is important, FedEx's commitment to decentralization breeds innovation. Managers are encouraged and rewarded for questioning, challenging, and developing new ideas, which are always given serious consideration. Developments have included teaming up with Motorola and Microsoft to create a proprietary pocket-size PC, sending package information to customers' and delivery staff cellphones, and creating software products for small business logistics. "Engage in constant change" is a mantra for CEO Smith, who adds, "Companies that don't take risks—some of which are going to work and some of which aren't—are going to end up getting punched up by the marketplace."

Critical Thinking Question

1. Consider the following statement: *A company can't really emphasize standardization and decentralization at the same time because these terms are contradictory.* Do you agree with the statement? Defend your answer.

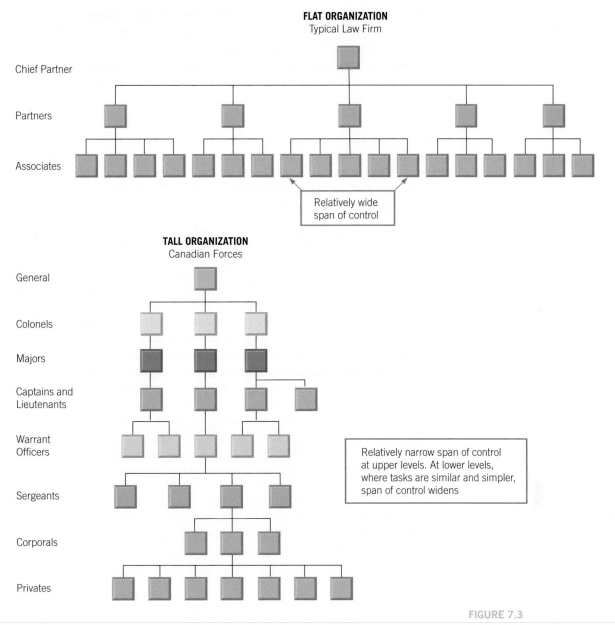

FLAT ORGANIZATION
Typical Law Firm

Chief Partner

Partners

Associates

Relatively wide
span of control

TALL ORGANIZATION
Canadian Forces

General

Colonels

Majors

Captains and
Lieutenants

Warrant
Officers

Relatively narrow span of control
at upper levels. At lower levels,
where tasks are similar and simpler,
span of control widens

Sergeants

Corporals

Privates

FIGURE 7.3

Organizational structure and span
of control.

information, whether upward or downward bound, must pass through so many organizational layers, tall structures are prone to delays in information flow. But an organization with a flat structure isn't automatically decentralized. When Steve McMillan became CEO at Sara Lee, he flattened the organization's structure by abolishing several layers of corporate hierarchy. The flatter organizational structure led to improved accountability and more centralized control over Sara Lee's far-flung operations.[14]

Span of Control

Span of control refers to the number of people who report to an individual manager. As shown in Figure 7.3, in a flat organizational structure, the span of control is typically wider than in a tall structure. The span of control is affected by many factors, including *employee skill levels* (the higher the skills, the greater the span of control that is possible), *the nature of the tasks being performed* (the simpler the tasks, the wider the

span of control The number of people
managed by one manager.

downsizing The planned reduction in the scope of an organization's activity.

span of control), **downsizing** (when entire layers of management of removed, the remaining managers end up with larger spans of control), *the amount of decentralization* (when lower-level employees are given more decision-making authority, their supervisors can have larger spans of control), and *the rate of organizational change* (the more rapid the rate of change, the narrower the span of control).

Three Forms of Authority

In an organization, it must be clear who will have authority over whom. As individuals are delegated authority and given responsibility, a complex web of interactions develops. These interactions may result in one of three forms of authority: line, staff, or committee and team. Like departmentalization, all three forms may be found in a given company, especially a large one.

line authority Authority that flows up and down the chain of command.

line departments Departments directly linked to the production and sales of specific products.

Line Authority. **Line authority** flows up and down the chain of command (refer back to Figure 7.1). Most companies rely heavily on **line departments**—departments directly linked to the production and sales of specific products. For example, Clark Equipment Corp. has a division that produces forklifts and small earth movers (see Figure 7.4). In this division, line departments include purchasing, materials handling, fabrication, painting, and assembly (all of which are directly linked to production), along with sales and distribution (both of which are directly linked to sales).

Each line department is essential to an organization's success. Line employees are the "doers" and producers in a company. If any line department fails to complete its task, the company cannot sell and deliver finished goods. Thus, the authority delegated to line departments is important. A bad decision by the manager in one department can hold up production for an entire plant. For example, say that the painting department manager at Clark Equipment changes a paint application on a batch of forklifts, which then show signs of peeling paint. The batch will have to be repainted (and perhaps partially reassembled) before the machines can be shipped.

staff authority Based on technical expertise and involves advising line managers about decisions.

Staff Authority. Most companies also rely on **staff authority**, which is based on technical expertise possessed by specialists such as lawyers, engineers, accountants, marketing researchers, and human resource managers who work in the company. Staff experts advise line managers when decisions are made, but the staff experts do not generally have the authority to make final decisions (they do, of course, have

FIGURE 7.4

Line and staff organization: Clark Equipment Corp.

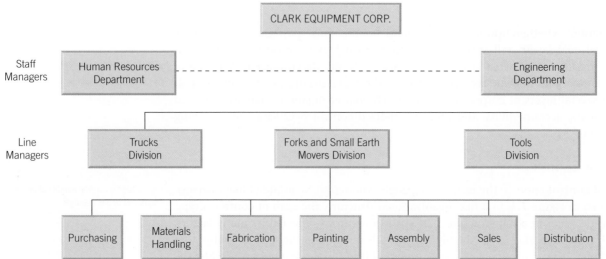

authority over members of their own staff departments). For example, if the fabrication department at Clark Equipment has an employee with a drinking problem, the manager of the department could consult a human resource staff expert for advice on handling the situation. The staff expert might suggest that the worker stay on the job but enter a counselling program. But if the line manager decides that the job is too dangerous to be handled by a person whose judgment is impaired by alcohol, the line manager's decision will most likely prevail.

Typically, the separation between line authority and staff responsibility is clearly delineated. As Figure 7.4 shows, this separation is usually shown in organization charts by solid lines (line authority) and dotted lines (staff responsibility). Remember this: the goals of the organization influence the distinction between line and staff authority. At Aluminum Company of Canada, for example, the director of personnel has staff authority because the personnel department supports the primary function of the company (the production and marketing of aluminum). But at Office Overload, the director of personnel has line authority because the primary goal of that firm is to provide personnel to other firms.

Committee and Team Authority. More and more organizations have started to use **committee and team authority**—authority granted to committees or work teams that play central roles in the firm's daily operations. A committee, for example, may consist of top managers from several areas of the firm. If the work of the committee is especially important, and if the committee will be working together for an extended time, the organization may even grant it special authority as a decision-making body that goes beyond the individual authority possessed by each of its members.

Firms are also increasingly using work teams at the operating level. These teams are made up of workers (not managers), and are empowered to plan, organize, and perform their work with a minimum of supervision. Organizations usually find it beneficial to grant special authority to work teams so that they will function more effectively.[15] More information about teams is presented in Chapter 10.

committee and team authority Authority granted to committees or work teams that play central roles in the firm's daily operations.

Basic Organizational Structures

A glance at the organization charts of many organizations reveals what appears to be an almost infinite variety of structures. However, closer examination shows that there are four basic forms: functional, divisional, project, and international.

L04 Explain the differences among *functional, divisional, project,* and *international organizational structures.*

Business firms are increasingly using work teams and allowing groups of employees to plan and organize their own work with a minimum of supervision. This contributes to employee empowerment.

The Functional Structure

functional structure The various units in the organization are formed based on the functions that must be carried out to reach organizational goals.

In the **functional structure**, the various units in the organization are formed based on the functions that must be carried out to reach organizational goals. The functional structure makes use of departmentalization by function (refer back to Figure 7.1 for an example of a functional structure). The advantages and disadvantages of the functional structure are summarized in Table 7.1. To overcome one of the disadvantages of the functional structure—poor interdepartmental communication—some companies have established *customer innovation centres* that have expertise on product development, brand management, and sales. At these centres, key customers provide feedback on product performance and brainstorm new ideas for products that will better satisfy customers.[16]

The Divisional Structure

divisional structure Divides the organization into several divisions, each of which operates as a semi-autonomous unit and profit centre.

The **divisional structure** divides the organization into several divisions, each of which operates as a semi-autonomous unit and profit centre (see Figure 7.5). Divisions in organizations can be based on products, customers, or geography. For example, Winnipeg-based Frantic Films has three product divisions: live action (which produces programs like *Pioneer Quest* and *'Til Debt Do Us Part*), TV commercials (which produces television commercials for national and international clients), and software (which creates new, stand-alone software to enhance certain visual effects).[17] Bell Canada created three customer-based divisions: consumers, small- and medium-sized businesses, and large corporations. This structure replaced the former divisional structure that was geographically based.[18] Sometimes a company reorganizes divisions in order to be more effective. In 2012, Yahoo Inc. established three divisions—consumers, regions, and technology—in order to focus its activities and to increase growth prospects.[19]

Whatever basis is used, divisional performance can be assessed because each division operates almost as a separate company. Divisionalized companies can buy, sell, create, and disband divisions without disrupting the rest of their operations. Different divisions can sponsor separate advertising campaigns and foster different corporate identities. They can also share certain corporate-level resources (such as market research data). Sometimes unhealthy competition develops between divisions, or the efforts of one division may be duplicated by those of another. At PepsiCo, for example, each of the company's three major beverage brands—Pepsi, Gatorade, and Tropicana—formerly operated as independent divisions. But this independence became a problem because the three brands were competing for the same resources and there was very little coordination and sharing of information between the divisions. Now, all three brands are in one division so that a unified approach to brand management is achieved. The advantages and disadvantages of the divisional structure are summarized in Table 7.2.

TABLE 7.1 Advantages and Disadvantages of a Functional Structure

Advantages	Disadvantages
1. It focuses attention on the key activities that must be performed.	1. Conflicts may arise among the functional areas.
2. Expertise develops within each function.	2. No single function is responsible for overall organizational performance.
3. Employees have clearly defined career paths.	3. Employees in each functional area have a narrow view of the organization.
4. The structure is simple and easy to understand.	4. Decision making is slowed because functional areas must get approval from top management for a variety of decisions.
5. It eliminates duplication of activities.	5. Coordinating highly specialized functions may be difficult.

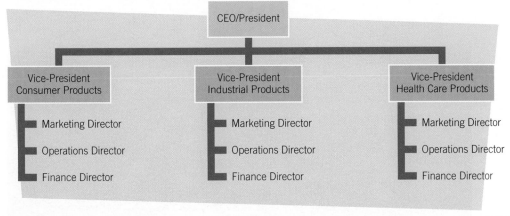

CEO/President

Vice-President
Consumer Products

Vice-President
Industrial Products

Vice-President
Health Care Products

Marketing Director

Operations Director

Finance Director

Marketing Director

Operations Director

Finance Director

Marketing Director

Operations Director

Finance Director

FIGURE 7.5

Divisional structure.

Project Organization

Most organizations are characterized by unchanging vertical authority relationships because such a set-up facilitates the production of a product in a routine and repetitive way. Procter & Gamble, for example, produces millions of tubes of Crest toothpaste each year using standardized production methods. The company has done this for years and intends to do so indefinitely.

But some organizations find themselves faced with projects that have a definite starting and ending point. These organizations often use a project structure to deal with the uncertainty encountered in new situations. **Project organization** involves forming a team of specialists from different functional areas of the organization to work on a specific project.[20] A project structure may be temporary or permanent; if it is temporary, the project team disbands once the project is completed and team members return to their regular functional area or are assigned to a new project.

Project organization is used extensively by Canadian firms, for example, in the construction of hydroelectric generating stations like those developed by Hydro-Québec on La Grande River and by Manitoba Hydro on the Nelson River. Once the generating station is complete, it becomes part of the traditional structure of the utility. Project organization is also used at shipyards. Each ship that is built is treated as a project and supervised by a project manager. The project manager for a given ship is responsible for ensuring that the ship is completed on time and within budget.[21] Project organization has proven useful for coordinating the many elements needed to extract oil from the tar sands. Project management is also used in other kinds of tasks, including construction, military weapons, aerospace, and health-care delivery.[22]

A **matrix organization** is a variation of project structure in which the project manager and the regular line managers share authority. Ford, for example, used a matrix organization to redesign the Ford Thunderbird. A design team composed of

project organization Involves forming a team of specialists from different functional areas of the organization to work on a specific project.

matrix organization A variation of project structure in which the project manager and the regular line managers share authority.

TABLE 7.2 Advantages and Disadvantages of a Divisional Structure	
Advantages	**Disadvantages**
1. It accommodates change and expansion.	1. Activities may be duplicated across divisions.
2. It increases accountability.	2. A lack of communication among divisions may occur.
3. It develops expertise in the various divisions.	3. Adding diverse divisions may blur the focus of the organization.
4. It encourages training for top management.	4. Company politics may affect the allocation of resources.

The project organization structure is very useful for construction projects like this hydroelectric generating station on the La Grande River in Quebec. Installations like this have a specific beginning and ending point. Once the construction is completed, the generating station becomes part of the traditional organizational structure of the provincial utility.

people from engineering, marketing, operations, and finance was created to design the new car. During the time the team was working on the Thunderbird project, the engineering, marketing, operations, and finance experts reported primarily to the project manager, but the line managers of the departments they came from also had some say about what work they did. After the team's work was done, team members moved back to their permanent functional jobs.

In other companies, the matrix organization is a semi-permanent fixture. Martha Stewart Living Omnimedia Inc. has created a permanent matrix organization for its burgeoning lifestyle business. The company is organized broadly into media and merchandising groups, each of which has specific product and product groups. Layered on top of this structure are teams of lifestyle experts organized into groups such as cooking, crafts, weddings, and so forth. Although each group targets specific customer needs, they all work across all product groups. A wedding expert, for example, might contribute to an article on wedding planning for a Martha Stewart magazine, contribute a story idea for a Martha Stewart cable television program, and supply content for a Martha Stewart website. This same individual might also help select fabrics suitable for wedding gowns that are to be retailed.[23]

International Organization

Because many businesses manufacture, purchase, and sell in the global market, several different **international organizational structures** have emerged. As global competition becomes more intense, companies must experiment with the ways in which they respond. For example, when Walmart opened its first store outside the U.S. back in 1992, it set up a special projects team to handle the logistics. As the years passed and more stores were opened abroad, the firm created a small international department to handle overseas expansion. But when international sales became a major part of Walmart's operations, the firm created a separate international division headed up

international organizational structures Organizational structures that are designed to help a company succeed in international markets. International departments, international divisions, or an integrated global organization are all variations of the international organizational structure.

All the signs at this 85 000-square-foot store in Numazu identify it as a Seiyu outlet run by Japan's fifth-largest supermarket chain. However, Walmart owns 38 percent of Seiyu, and this giant store is part of Walmart's effort to enter the world's second-largest retail market.

by a senior vice-president. As international operations became even more important, the international division was further divided into geographic areas where the firm does business, such as Mexico and Europe. Walmart typifies the form of organization outlined in Figure 7.6.

Other firms have also developed different approaches to international organization structure. The French food giant Danone Group, for instance, has three major product groups: dairy products (Danone yogurt), bottled water (Evian), and cookies (Pim's). Danone's structure does not differentiate internationally, but rather integrates global operations within each product group.[24] In contrast, U.S. entertainment companies are finding it advantageous to create a more local identity when they enter foreign markets. For instance, Columbia TriStar launched *Chinese Restaurant*, a sitcom filmed and shown only in China. Universal and HBO also got in on the act by setting up new television production businesses in Germany and Japan.[25]

Finally, some companies adopt a truly global structure in which they acquire resources (including capital), produce goods and services, engage in research and development, and sell products in whatever local market is appropriate, without any

FIGURE 7.6

International division structure.

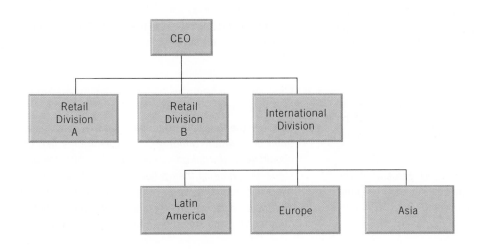

consideration of national boundaries. For example, General Electric functions as one integrated global organization. GE businesses around the world connect and interact with each other constantly, and managers freely move back and forth among them.[26]

Another kind of "structure" is described in the boxed insert entitled "Green Structures."

Organizational Design for the Twenty-First Century

As the world grows increasingly complex and fast-paced, companies adopt new forms of organization that permit them to compete effectively. Among the most popular of these new forms are the *boundaryless organization*, the *team organization*, the *virtual organization*, and the *learning organization*.

THE GREENING OF BUSINESS

Green Structures

The term "organizational structure" is commonly used to explain *theoretical* concepts like departmentalization, authority, responsibility, and the hierarchical patterns within organizations. But organizations also need *physical* structures like office buildings and factories to do their work, and managers in both the public and private sector are beginning to realize that their physical structures present significant opportunities to be eco-friendly. Sustainable buildings make sense because they reduce energy costs, attract more tenants, improve a company's image, and are a hedge against future changes in municipal building regulations. They also attract prospective employees who are concerned that the company they work for is environmentally conscious. Consider these examples:

- Winnipeg's new airport (which opened in October 2011) may be the most energy-efficient building of its size in the world. It is designed to achieve Leadership in Energy and Environmental Design (LEED) certification.

- On the 20th floor of the LEED-certified offices of Ontario Realty Corp. (ORC) the emphasis is on natural light (and smart motion-sensor lights), with heating and cooling provided by clean energy systems.

- In the Fremont Village Shopping Centre in Port Coquitlam, BC, the roofs of Walmart and Canadian Tire are covered with thousands of plants that provide insulation (which reduces energy costs), and also reduce storm water runoff and the "heat-island" effect.

- At the University of Toronto, over 90 percent of the heating requirements for the engineering and computer science building are being recovered from a nearby boiler plant.

- In October 2011, the Toronto-Dominion Bank opened a renovated branch in London, Ontario that will produce as much energy as it uses.

- In 2012, construction began on the GreenLife Business Centre in Milton, Ontario. The building will produce more energy than it consumes with its huge solar panel array.

Some architects think that over the next decade it may be possible to have buildings that require no energy at all from public utilities. Gerrit de Boer, president of Toronto-based Idomo Furniture Company, says that his firm will be "off the grid" in less than 10 years as a result of the geothermal heating system and the photovoltaic solar array that are being installed in the company's 200 000-square-foot building.

The physical advantages of green structures are only part of the story. Employees may feel more pride in their company when working in a green building, and they may also be more engaged in their work because the surroundings are so pleasant. A survey showed that ORC employees had a 96 percent satisfaction rate with their new offices (compared to 43 percent in their old offices).

Critical Thinking Questions

1. What are the advantages of "green" buildings? Are there any disadvantages? Explain.

2. Consider the following statement: *It is very expensive to build eco-friendly buildings, so expenditures like these should generally not be made. Rather, companies should focus on upgrading their production facilities so they can make higher quality, lower-priced products for consumers and more profits for their shareholders.* Do you agree or disagree with the statement? Explain your reasoning.

Boundaryless Organization

The **boundaryless organization** is one in which traditional boundaries and structures are minimized or eliminated altogether. For example, General Electric's fluid organization structure, in which people, ideas, and information flow freely between businesses and business groups, approximates this concept. Similarly, as firms partner with their suppliers in more efficient ways, external boundaries disappear. Some of Walmart's key suppliers are tied directly into the retailer's vaunted information system. As a result, when Walmart distribution centres start running low on, say, Wrangler blue jeans, the manufacturer receives the information as soon as the retailer does. Wrangler proceeds to manufacture new inventory and restock the distribution centre without Walmart having to place a new order.

boundaryless organization Traditional boundaries and structures are minimized or eliminated altogether.

Team Organization

Team organization relies almost exclusively on project-type teams, with little or no underlying functional hierarchy. People "float" from project to project as dictated by their skills and the demands of those projects. At Cypress Semiconductor, units or groups that become large are simply split into smaller units, so the organization is composed entirely of small units. This strategy allows each unit to change direction, explore new ideas, and try new methods without having to deal with a rigid bureaucratic superstructure. Although few large organizations have actually reached this level of adaptability, Apple Computer and Xerox are among those moving toward it.

team organization Relies almost exclusively on project-type teams, with little or no underlying functional hierarchy.

Virtual Organization

A **virtual organization** has little or no formal structure. Typically, it has only a handful of permanent employees, a very small staff, and a modest administrative facility. As the needs of the organization change, managers bring in temporary workers, lease facilities, and outsource basic support services to meet the demands of each unique situation. Facilities and subcontracted services also change. In other words, the virtual organization exists only in response to its own needs.

virtual organization A company with little or no formal structure, which exists only in response to its own needs.

Global Research Consortium (GRC) is a virtual organization that offers research and consulting services to firms doing business in Asia. As clients request various services, GRC's staff of three permanent employees subcontracts the work to an appropriate set of several dozen independent consultants and/or researchers with whom it has relationships. At any given time, therefore, GRC may have several projects underway and 20 or 30 people working on various projects. As the projects change, so too does the composition of the organization. Figure 7.7 illustrates the basic structure of a virtual organization.

FIGURE 7.7

A virtual organization.

Learning Organization

The **learning organization** integrates continuous improvement with continuous employee learning and development. Specifically, a learning organization facilitates the lifelong learning and personal development of all of its employees while continually transforming itself to respond to changing demands and needs.

The most frequent goals of a learning organization are improved quality, continuous improvement, and performance measurement. The idea is that the most consistent and logical strategy for achieving continuous improvement is constantly upgrading employee talent, skill, and knowledge. For example, if each employee in an organization learns one new thing each day and can translate that knowledge into work-related practice, continuous improvement will logically follow. Organizations that embrace this approach believe that only through constant employee learning can continuous improvement really occur.

In recent years, many different organizations have implemented this approach on various levels. For example, Shell Oil's executive conference centre (called the Shell Learning Center) boasts state-of-the-art classrooms and instructional technology, lodging facilities, a restaurant, and recreational amenities such as a golf course, swimming pool, and tennis courts. Line managers at the firm rotate through the centre and serve as teaching faculty. All Shell employees routinely attend various training programs and seminars, all the while gathering the latest information they need to contribute more effectively to the firm.

The Informal Organization

L05 Explain the idea of the *informal organization.*

informal organization The everyday social interactions among employees that transcend formal jobs and job interrelationships.

The formal organization of a business is the part that can be seen and represented on the organization chart. The structure of a company, however, is not limited to the organization chart and the formal assignment of authority. Frequently, the **informal organization**—the everyday social interactions among employees that transcend formal jobs and job interrelationships—effectively alters a company's formal structure. Indeed, this level of organization is sometimes more powerful than the formal structure. The power of the informal organization was evident in the highly publicized rescue of the Chilean miners in 2010. In the underground cavern where they were trapped, there were no top managers, so much of what the miners did was informal (dividing up chores, singing, providing mutual support, etc.) These activities kept the miners' hopes alive until they were rescued.[27] The Exercising Your Ethics feature at the end of the chapter presents another interesting situation that illustrates the informal organization.

Is the informal organization good or bad? On the positive side, the informal organization helps employees feel that they "belong," and it gives them an outlet for "letting off steam" in a safe environment. It also provides information that employees are interested in hearing. On the negative side, the informal organization can reinforce organizational politics that put the interests of individuals ahead of those of the firm. Likewise, a great deal of harm can be caused by distorted or inaccurate information that is communicated without management input or review. For example, if the informal organization is generating false information about impending layoffs, valuable employees may act quickly (and unnecessarily) to seek other employment. Among the more important elements of the informal organization are *informal groups* and the *organizational grapevine.*

Informal Groups

Informal groups are simply groups of people who decide to interact among themselves even though they may not be required to do so by the formal organization. They may be people who work together or who simply get together for lunch, during breaks, or after work. They may talk about business, the boss, or non-work-related topics such as families, movies, or sports. For example, at the New York Metropolitan Opera, musicians and singers play poker during the intermissions. Most pots are in the $30 to $40 range. The late Luciano Pavarotti, the famed tenor, once played and lost big.

The grapevine is a powerful informal communications network. These workers may be talking work or non-work topics—an upcoming deadline on an important project, tonight's football game, the stock market, rumours about an impending takeover, gossip about forthcoming promotions, or the weather.

The impact of informal groups on the organization may be positive (if they work together to support the organization), negative (if they work together in ways that run counter to the organization's interests), or neutral (if what they do is unrelated to the organization's interests).

Organizational Grapevine

The **grapevine** is the informal communication network that runs through the entire organization.[28] It is found in all organizations except the very smallest, and it does not always follow the same patterns as formal channels of authority and communication. Because the grapevine typically passes information orally, messages often become distorted in the process, but most office gossip has at least some kernel of truth to it. Those passing on news may deliberately alter it, either to advance their own goals or to sabotage someone else's chances. Listening to and passing on information damaging to someone's reputation can backfire, harming your credibility and making you a target for similar gossip.

grapevine The informal communication network that runs through the entire organization.

In general, the more detailed the information, the less likely it is to be true. Likewise, beware the hush-hush "don't quote me on this" type of rumour. (Cynics also claim that the better the news, the less likely it is to be true.) The higher the source, the greater the likelihood that the grapevine has the real story. Don't reject information from "lower" sources, however. Many an executive assistant can provide valuable insights into a corporation's plans.

Attempts to eliminate the grapevine are fruitless, so managers should not waste their time trying to do so. Rather, they should maintain open channels of communication and respond vigorously to inaccurate information, because this will minimize the damage the grapevine can do. In fact, the grapevine can actually be an asset. By getting to know the key people in the grapevine, for example, the manager can partially control the information received and use the grapevine to determine employee reactions to new ideas (e.g., a change in human resource policies or benefit packages). The manager can also receive valuable information from the grapevine and use it to improve decision making. Wise managers will tune in to the grapevine's message because it is often a corporate early warning system. Ignoring this valuable source of information can cause managers to be the last to know that they are about to get a new boss or that they have a potentially fatal image problem.

MyBizLab

Capture more moments of true understanding. MyBizLab provides you with interactive study and practice tools directly related to this chapter's content. The new MyBizLab Study Plan Learning Path is designed to measure a full range of skills and provide remediation to give you what you need to master key chapter concepts. MyBizLab flexes to your unique learning needs. The result? Inspired learning, more success.

SUMMARY OF LEARNING OBJECTIVES

1. **Discuss the elements that influence a firm's** *organizational structure.* Every business needs structure to operate. *Organizational structure* varies according to a firm's mission, purpose, and strategy. Size, technology, and changes in environmental circumstances also influence structure. In general, while all organizations have the same basic elements, each develops the structure that contributes to the most efficient operations.

2. **Explain how** *specialization* **and** *departmentalization* **are the building blocks of organizational structure.** The building blocks of organizational structure are job *specialization* and *departmentalization*. As a firm grows, it usually has a greater need for people to perform specialized tasks (specialization). It also has a greater need to group types of work into logical units (departmentalization). Common forms of departmentalization are *customer, product, process, geographic,* and *functional*. Large businesses often use more than one form of departmentalization.

3. **Distinguish between** *responsibility* **and** *authority* **and explain the differences in decision making in** *centralized* **and** *decentralized* **organizations.** *Responsibility* is the duty to perform a task; *authority* is the power to make the decisions necessary to complete tasks. *Delegation* begins when a manager assigns a task to a subordinate; *accountability* means that the subordinate must complete the task. *Span of control* refers to the number of people who work for any individual manager. The more people supervised by a manager, the wider his or her span of control. Wide spans are usually desirable when *employees* perform simple or unrelated tasks. When jobs are diversified or prone to change, a narrower span is generally preferable.

   In a centralized organization, only a few individuals in top management have real decision-making authority. In a decentralized organization, much authority is delegated to lower-level management. Where both line and line-and-staff systems are involved, line departments generally have authority to make decisions while staff departments have a responsibility to advise. A relatively new concept, committee and team authority, empowers committees or work teams involved in a firm's daily operations.

4. **Explain the differences among** *functional, divisional, project,* **and** *international organizational structures.* In a *functional organization*, authority is usually distributed among such basic functions as marketing and finance. In a *divisional organization*, the various divisions of a larger company, which may be related or unrelated, operate in a relatively autonomous fashion. In *project organization*, in which individuals report to more than one manager, a company creates teams to address specific problems or to conduct specific projects. A company that has divisions in many countries may require an additional level of *international organization* to coordinate those operations.

5. **Describe the most popular new forms of** *organizational design.* Four of the most popular new forms of organizational design are (1) *boundaryless organizations* (traditional boundaries and structures are minimized or eliminated), (2) *team organizations* (rely on project-type teams, with little or no functional hierarchy), (3) *virtual organizations* (have little formal structure and only a handful of permanent employees, a small staff, and a modest administrative facility), and (4) *learning organizations* (work to facilitate employees' lifelong learning and personal development while transforming the organization to meet changing demands and needs).

6. **Explain the idea of the** *informal organization.* The *informal organization* consists of the everyday social interactions among employees that transcend formal jobs and job interrelationships. The informal organization exists within the formal structure of every organization and cannot be suppressed. Effective managers work with the informal organization and try to harness it for the good of the formal organization.

KEY TERMS

accountability (p. 222)
authority (p. 222)
boundaryless organization (p. 233)
centralized organization (p. 223)
chain of command (p. 216)
committee and team authority (p. 227)
customer departmentalization (p. 219)
decentralized organization (p. 224)
delegation (p. 222)
departmentalization (p. 219)
divisional structure (p. 228)
downsizing (p. 226)
flat organizational structure (p. 224)

functional departmentalization (p. 219)
functional structure (p. 228)
geographic departmentalization (p. 220)
grapevine (p. 235)
informal organization (p. 234)
international organizational structure (p. 230)
job specialization (p. 218)
learning organization (p. 234)
line authority (p. 226)
line departments (p. 226)
matrix organization (p. 229)
organization chart (p. 216)

organizational structure (p. 216)
process departmentalization (p. 221)
product departmentalization (p. 220)
profit centre (p. 219)
project organization (p. 229)
responsibility (p. 222)
span of control (p. 225)
staff authority (p. 226)
tall organizational structure (p. 224)
team organization (p. 233)
virtual organization (p. 233)

QUESTIONS FOR ANALYSIS

1. Explain the significance of size as it relates to organizational structure. Describe the changes that are likely to occur as an organization grows.
2. Why do some managers have difficulties in delegating authority? Why do you think this problem might be more pronounced in small businesses?
3. Describe a hypothetical organizational structure for a small printing firm. Describe changes that might be necessary as the business grows.
4. Compare and contrast the matrix and divisional approaches to organizational structure. How would you feel about working in a matrix organization in which you were assigned simultaneously to multiple units and had multiple bosses?
5. If a company has a formal organizational structure, why should managers pay attention to the informal organization?
6. The argument has been made that, compared to the functional organization structure, the divisional structure does a better job of training managers for top-level positions. Do you agree or disagree with this argument? Explain your reasoning.

APPLICATION EXERCISES

1. Draw up an organization chart for your college or university.
2. Think about the organization where you currently work (or one where you have previously worked). Which of the four basic structural types was it most consistent with? What was the basis of departmentalization in the company? Why was that particular basis of departmentalization used? In what ways did the organization's structure impact your specific job?
3. Interview the manager of a local service business—a fast-food restaurant, for example. What types of tasks does this manager typically delegate? Is the appropriate authority also delegated in each case? What problems occur when authority is not delegated appropriately?
4. Interview a manager and ask about the informal organization in his or her place of business. What advantages and disadvantages does the manager see with respect to the informal organization? What is the manager's strategy for dealing with the informal organization?

BUILDING YOUR BUSINESS SKILLS

Getting with the Program

The Purpose of This Assignment

To encourage students to understand the relationship between organizational structure and a company's ability to attract and keep valued employees.

The Situation

You are the founder of a small but growing high-technology company that develops new computer software. With your current workload and new contracts in the pipeline, your business is thriving except for one problem: You cannot find computer programmers for product development. Worse yet, current staff members are being lured away by other high-tech firms. After suffering a particularly discouraging personnel raid in which competitors captured three of your most valued employees, you schedule a meeting with your director of human resources to plan organizational changes designed to encourage worker loyalty. You already pay top dollar, but the continuing exodus tells you that programmers are looking for something more.

Method

Working with three or four classmates, identify some ways in which specific organizational changes might improve the working environment and encourage employee loyalty. As you analyze the following factors, ask yourself the obvious question: If I were a programmer, what organizational changes would encourage me to stay?

- Level of job specialization. With many programmers describing their jobs as tedious because of the focus on detail in a narrow work area, what changes, if any, would you make in job specialization? Right now, for instance, few of your programmers have any say in product design.

- Decision-making hierarchy. What decision-making authority would encourage people to stay? Is expanding employee authority likely to work better in a centralized or decentralized organization?

- Team authority. Can team empowerment make a difference? Taking the point of view of the worker, describe the ideal team.

- Intrapreneuring. What can your company do to encourage and reward innovation? (Review the material in Chapter 4 on intrapreneuring before analyzing this factor.)

Questions for Discussion

1. With the average computer programmer earning nearly $70 000 per year and with all competitive firms paying top dollar, why might organizational issues be critical in determining employee loyalty?

2. If you were a programmer, what organizational factors would make a difference to you? Why?

3. As the company founder, how willing would you be to make major organizational changes in light of the shortage of qualified programmers?

EXERCISING YOUR ETHICS: TEAM EXERCISE

To Poach or Not to Poach

The Situation

The Hails Corporation, a manufacturing firm, has recently moved toward a team-based organization structure. Each team has the autonomy to divide up the work assigned to it among its individual members. In addition, each team handles its own scheduling of members' vacations and other time off. The teams also handle the interviews and hiring of new team members when the need arises. Team A has just lost one of its members, who moved to another city to be closer to his ailing parents.

The Dilemma

Since the move to the team structure, every time a team has needed new members, it has advertised in the local newspaper and hired someone from outside the company. However, Team A is considering a different approach to fill its opening. Specifically, a key member of another team (Team B) has made it known that she would like to join Team A. She likes the team members, sees the team's work as being enjoyable, and is somewhat bored with her team's current assignment.

The concern is that if Team A chooses this individual to join the team, several problems may occur. For one thing, her current team will clearly be angry with the members of Team A. Further, "poaching" new team members from other teams inside the plant is likely to become a common occurrence. On the other hand, it seems reasonable that she should have the same opportunity to join Team A as an outsider would. Team A needs to decide how to proceed.

Team Activity

Assemble a group of four students and assign each group member to one of the following roles:

- member of Team A
- member of Team B
- manager of both teams
- investor in Hails Corporation

Action Steps

1. Before discussing the situation with your group, and from the perspective of your assigned role, decide whether you think that the member of Team B should be allowed to join Team A. Write down the reasons for your position.

2. Before discussing the situation with your group, and from the perspective of your assigned role, decide what are the underlying ethical issues, if any, in this situation. Write down the issues.

3. Gather your group together and reveal, in turn, each member's comments on the situation. Next, reveal the ethical issues listed by each member.

4. Appoint someone to record the main points of agreement and disagreement within the group. How do you explain the results? What accounts for any disagreement?

5. From an ethical standpoint, what does your group conclude is the most appropriate action that should be taken by Hails in this situation? Should Team B's member be allowed to join Team A?

6. Develop a group response to the following questions: Assuming Team A asks the Team B member to join its team, how might it go about minimizing repercussions? Assuming Team A does not ask the Team B member to join its team, how might it go about minimizing repercussions?

Go to MyBizLab for additional cases and exercise material.

CONCLUDING CASE 7-1

Kodak's Troubling Moment

If you ask anyone who was born before 1990 what comes to mind when they hear the word "Kodak," they will likely respond by saying "Kodak moment" (referring to a famous Kodak advertising campaign from yesteryear). When Eastman Kodak filed for bankruptcy in January 2012, it joined the list of companies whose brands had once dominated their markets, but who had failed to adapt to changing conditions. What happened to Kodak? Here's the story.

In 1885, George Eastman invented roll film. Within three years, the first Kodak camera was produced. The company prospered by making it easy for consumers to take pictures (prior to that time, the process was very cumbersome). In 1900, the now-legendary Brownie camera was marketed, and in 1935 the first colour film—called Kodachrome—was made available to consumers. By the mid-1970s, Kodak controlled 90 percent of the market for photographic film. At that time, Fujifilm began to aggressively compete with Kodak and gradually took away some of Kodak's market share. But the most significant development was the invention of the digital camera by an engineer at Kodak in 1975. The company developed a variety of digital cameras over the next few years, but top managers apparently had difficulty envisioning a world without film. In spite of Kodak's less-than-aggressive digital strategy, it was actually No. 1 in digital camera sales in the U.S. in 2005. But things went downhill fast after that because (1) Kodak was unable to compete with lower-priced digital cameras offered by Asian competitors, and (2) Kodak failed to anticipate that many photos would eventually be taken by smartphones rather than by cameras. By 2010, Kodak was in seventh place behind companies like Nikon, Canon, and Sony.

Kodak responded to its declining fortunes by cutting costs through outsourcing many of its production activities and by drastically cutting its workforce. In the 1980s, the company employed 145 000 people worldwide, but by 2012 that number had dropped to just 17 000. The company stopped selling film cameras (2004), Kodachrome film (2009), digital cameras (2012), pocket video cameras (2012), and digital picture frames (2012). It also restructured from three business units (commercial film, consumer film, and printing) into just two (commercial and consumer printing). The new structure is expected to reduce costs and increase productivity. Kodak's new strategy is to focus on commercial and consumer inkjet printing, workflow software, and packaging. It hopes the new businesses will become profitable by 2013. In printing, Kodak currently ranks fifth worldwide, with a 2.6 percent market share.

All of these difficulties have led to a drastic decline in the price of Kodak stock. During 2011, for example, the share price declined 88 percent, and by early 2012, it was selling for just 36 cents per share. The share price improved somewhat when it was announced that the board of directors had appointed Laura Quatela, the company's general counsel, as a co-president to serve with Philip Faraci. They will both report to the CEO, Antonio Perez.

Kodak also has a lot of patents that it may be able to sell for billions of dollars, just like Nortel Networks did a few years ago. In an attempt to generate much-needed cash, Kodak filed lawsuits against Apple, RIM, and HTC, claiming that those companies violated patents that Kodak held on processes like sending photos from mobile devices and previewing images with an electronic camera.

Some observers think that there was nothing Kodak could have done to avoid its bankruptcy. But consider Fujifilm, which used to be a small company that played catch-up with Kodak for many years. When digital photography burst upon the scene, Fujifilm diversified into other areas. The restructuring meant cutting billions from its photographic businesses and spending large amounts of money getting into new businesses like cosmetics and electronics. Fujifilm is now a very profitable company.

Kodak's bankruptcy filing marks an astonishing fall from prominence for a company that had dominated the photography business for well over 100 years. The company hopes to emerge from bankruptcy as a smaller company that has very little involvement in photography. But it remains to be seen whether it can effectively compete with its new product lines.

Questions for Discussion

1. What are the key differences between the functional and divisional organizational structures? Which type is Kodak using? Explain.
2. What corporate-level strategy did Kodak pursue in the twentieth century? What are the advantages and disadvantages of such a strategy? What corporate-level strategy is Kodak pursuing in the twenty-first century? (Review the discussion on corporate-level strategy in Chapter 6 before answering this question.)
3. It is ironic that Kodak invented the digital camera, yet was unable to capitalize on that invention. Why do you think Kodak was unable to compete in the digital camera market?

CONCLUDING CASE 7-2

Restructuring Dilemmas

Companies sometimes face dilemmas when deciding how to structure their activities. Two common dilemmas are (1) whether to split a single company into two (or more) companies, and (2) whether to use geographical or product departmentalization within a single company.

Splitting a Single Company into Two (or More) Companies

In 2011, Kraft Foods decided to split into two distinct companies, one focusing on worldwide snacks (including brand names like Oreo and Lu cookies, Cadbury chocolate, and Trident gum), and the other focusing on the North American grocery business (including brands like Velveeta cheese and Maxwell House coffee). The North American grocery business will be launched as a publicly traded company, but both companies will retain the Kraft Foods name. One reason for the restructuring was the realization that sales revenue in the grocery business was growing relatively slowly compared to the snacks business. The decision to split into two companies comes only two years after Kraft's epic battle to take over Cadbury PLC. The decision to create two companies required Kraft managers to make some interesting decisions about which products would go where. It was decided, for example, that Planters Peanuts would go with the grocery company and move from its current home in snack foods. But for Philadelphia Cream Cheese—whose sales revenue is about evenly split between North America and the rest of the world—one company may have to license the brand from the other. Other decisions were made as well. Distribution for products to grocery stores will be outsourced to Acosta Sale and Marketing, while Crossmark will distribute products to convenience stores.

PepsiCo (which has been falling behind Coca-Cola) has also been under pressure from investors to split into two companies, with one focusing on snacks and the other on beverages. But to date the company has not done so.

Tyco International is another company that split up. It will now focus on selling security and fire-suppression systems to businesses. Tyco's two other divisions, which sold ADT residential alarms and industrial valves and pipes, will be spun off. It is thought that this restructuring will allow all three units to be more easily acquired by other companies, or for them to pursue other takeovers on their own.

Sometimes a company will split into two parts, but both parts will continue to operate under the umbrella of a single company.

For example, in 2011, grocery chain Sobeys split into two units. The IGA Operations unit will include IGA, IGA Extra, Les Marches Tradition, Marche Bonichoix, and Rachelle-Bery in Quebec. The Multi-Format Operations will include Sobeys, Thrifty Foods, Sobeys Urban Fresh, Foodland, FreshCo, Needs, Fast Fuel, Sobeys liquor operations, and IGA stores in western Canada.

Geographic vs. Product Departmentalization

During the past decade, many firms have switched from geographic to product departmentalization. This change has been driven by increased global competition and by reduced impediments to cross-border communication. Consider these examples:

- Food company Heinz abandoned geographical departmentalization and is now organized by products. Managers in the U.S. work with those in Europe, Asia, and other regions to apply the best ideas from one region to all the others.
- The Canadian Imperial Bank of Commerce (CIBC) also reorganized to break down the walls between the conservative retail/commercial banking side and the more volatile investment banking side. The company is now organized around product lines.
- Exide Corp.'s structure formerly consisted of several "country organizations" that had considerable latitude to make decisions that were best for that country. But it adopted a new product structure with global business units to oversee the company's various product lines such as car and industrial batteries.

Either type of departmentalization—products or geography—can cause problems if taken to an extreme. If a company organizes by products, it can standardize manufacturing, introduce new products around the world faster, and eliminate overlapping activities. But if too much emphasis is placed on product and not enough on geography, a company is likely to find that local decision making is slowed and products are not tailored to meet the needs of a specific country's customers. When Ford Motor Co. moved to product departmentalization, the reorganization saved the company $5 billion in its first few years of operation, but Ford's market share declined during the same period. Ford responded to this drop in market share by giving executives in various regions more authority to decide what types of vehicles were best for their local market. In other words, it moved back a bit toward the geographical model.

Procter & Gamble also encountered problems after it replaced country organizations with global business units in an attempt to globalize P&G brands like Tide, Pampers, and Crest. The reorganization caused great upheaval within the company as thousands of employees shifted into new jobs. As many as half of all company executives took on new roles. The CEO who ordered the change left the company just 17 months into his job.

Questions for Discussion

1. Why would a company decide to split up into two (or more) companies?
2. In your own words, explain the dilemma that managers face when they are trying to decide between product and geographic departmentalization.
3. How does the notion of managerial accountability enter into the "product vs. geographic departmentalization" decision?

Managing Human Resources

LEARNING OBJECTIVES

After reading this chapter, you should be able to:

1. Define *human resource management*, discuss its strategic significance, and explain how managers plan for human resources.

2. Identify the issues involved in *staffing* a company, including *internal* and *external recruiting and selection*.

3. Discuss different ways in which organizations go about developing the capabilities of employees and managers.

4. Explain ways in which organizations evaluate employee performance.

5. Discuss the importance of *wages* and *salaries*, *incentives*, and *benefit programs* in attracting and keeping skilled workers.

6. Describe some of the key legal issues involved in *hiring*, *compensating*, and *managing* workers.

7. Discuss *workforce diversity*, the management of *knowledge workers*, and the use of *contingent* and *temporary workers* as important changes in the contemporary workplace.

Millennials on the March

GENERATIONAL differences are evident in many aspects of social interaction. The biggest, many would argue, centre on the preferred working environments and career motivation of people born in different eras. Currently, employers are dealing with three different generations—baby boomers, Gen X, and Millennials (also known as Generation Y)—as they attempt to cater to the various characteristics and demands of each while also creating a harmonious and effective work environment.

Baby boomers (born in the "baby boom" of 1947–66) are the oldest group in the workforce and are now considering retirement options. They are often in senior management positions, and therefore manage and interact with Millennials and Generation X employees.

Generation X workers (born between 1965 and 1980) are often characterized as being independent and entrepreneurial, while "seeking emotional maturity." They desire growth in terms of experience and the ability to see their careers evolving. They value family life, which contributes to their desire for work–life balance.

Millennials (also referred to as *Generation Y*, born between 1980 and 2000) are the most recent generation to join the workforce. They are often characterized as enjoying structured lives and valuing interaction with diverse groups of people. They work well with others and often seek to make friends at work, which contributes to their desire to work in teams and groups.

As Millennials enter the work force, employers need to understand and adapt to their demands and characteristics. One difficult issue is trying to keep them around. "Things aren't always what they seem with Millennial employees," says Cam Marston from About.com. "Their definitions of loyalty, time, and success are often quite different from yours. Rest assured they do recognize all of these concepts and value them in very important ways." It is through understanding how this new generation of workers thinks and views the world that employers can truly motivate them. Marston suggests that managers "meet them where they are and they will achieve your underlying goals; try to force them to fit your definitions and they will run for the door every time." Millennials tend to have a self-centred work ethic, but they are dedicated to completing tasks well and finding the most efficient ways to work.

Younger Millennials sometimes seem to view their jobs as "something to do between the weekends." Their motivation is different from the traditional desire to climb the corporate ladder, in that they value other incentives such as paid time off as rewards.

Another predominant characteristic for Millennials is the desire for flexible working environments and putting in less "face time." "Gen Xers and Millennials view time as a currency," says Marston. "While Baby boomers tend to see time as something to invest, the younger generations view it as a valuable currency not to be wasted." The desire for work–life balance is even stronger for the Millennials than it was for previous generations. While boomers would typically accommodate their lives to their jobs and their employers, Millennials expect their employers to accommodate to their lives.

When employers don't do that, Millennials will look for an employer who will. According to Jennifer Deal, at the Center for Creative Leadership in San Diego, there is some truth to some of the common myths regarding Millennials, such as their unwillingness to comply with authority and lack of organization loyalty. Millennials do agree, however, that they should do what managers outline for them to do, and should share the same degree of loyalty to the organization as other generations.

Generational gaps have become increasingly challenging as the effects of the economic downturn are being felt. Many boomers feel that they are financially unable to retire, so they must continue working with both Generation Xers and Millennials. The effective management of Millennials is important, and managers

are seeking ways to do this. According to Susan M. Heathfield of About.com, strategies include encouraging the "can do" attitude and positive self-image possessed by Millennials, taking advantage of their desire for teamwork and group dynamics, providing a work environment that is centred around people, listening to their opinions, and supporting their desire for networking using the technological tools that are available. Perhaps the most important strategy for dealing with Millennial employees is the provision of a good work–life balance, where support is provided for multiple tasks and endeavours, including family and social lives. In North America, there are over 75 000 000 Millennials preparing to join the workforce. A group this large cannot be ignored.◆

HOW WILL THIS HELP ME?

Effectively managing human resources is critical to the success of organizations. A firm that handles this activity well has a much better chance for success than does a firm that simply goes through the motions. After reading the material in this chapter, you'll be better able to understand—from the perspective of a *manager*—the importance of properly managing human resources in a department you supervise or in a business you own. You'll also understand—from the perspective of an *employee*—why your employer has adopted certain approaches to dealing with issues like hiring, training, compensation, and benefits.

The Foundations of Human Resource Management

LO1 Define *human resource management*, discuss its strategic significance, and explain how managers plan for human resources.

human resource management (HRM)
Set of organizational activities directed at attracting, developing, and maintaining an effective workforce.

Human resource management (HRM) is the set of organizational activities directed at attracting, developing, and maintaining an effective workforce. Human resource management takes place within a complex and ever-changing environmental context and is increasingly being recognized for its strategic importance.[1]

The Strategic Importance of HRM

Human resources are critical for effective organizational functioning. HRM (or personnel, as it is sometimes called) was once relegated to second-class status in many organizations, but its importance has grown dramatically in the past two decades. This new importance stems from increased legal complexities, the recognition that human resources are a valuable means for improving productivity, and the awareness of the costs associated with poor human resource management.

Managers realize that the effectiveness of their HR function has a substantial impact on a firm's bottom-line performance. Poor human resource planning can result in spurts of hiring followed by layoffs—costly in terms of unemployment compensation payments, training expenses, and morale. Haphazard compensation systems do not attract, keep, and motivate good employees, and outmoded recruitment practices can expose the firm to expensive and embarrassing legal action. Consequently, the chief human resource executive of most large businesses is a vice-president directly accountable to the CEO, and many firms are developing strategic HR plans that are integrated with other strategic planning activities.

Human Resource Planning

Planning is the starting point in attracting qualified human resources. Human resource (HR) planning involves job analysis, forecasting the demand for and supply of labour, and matching supply and demand (see Figure 8.1).

Job Analysis

job analysis A detailed study of the specific duties in a particular job and the human qualities required for that job.

job description The duties of a job, its working conditions, and the tools, materials, and equipment used to perform it.

job specification The skills, abilities, and other credentials needed to do the job.

As the term implies, **job analysis** means analyzing the nature of jobs. It requires assessment of two items: the *job description* and the *job specification*.

- The **job description** lists the duties of a job, its working conditions, and the tools, materials, and equipment used to perform it.

- The **job specification** lists the skills, abilities, and other credentials needed to do the job.

Job analysis information is used in many HR activities. For instance, knowing about job content and job requirements is necessary to develop appropriate selection methods and job-relevant performance appraisal systems and to set equitable compensation rates.

Forecasting HR Demand and Supply

After managers have analyzed the jobs that must be performed within an organization, they can start planning for the organization's future HR needs. The manager starts by assessing trends in past HR usage, future organizational plans, and general economic trends. A good sales forecast is often the foundation, especially for smaller organizations. Historical data can then be used to predict demand for different types of

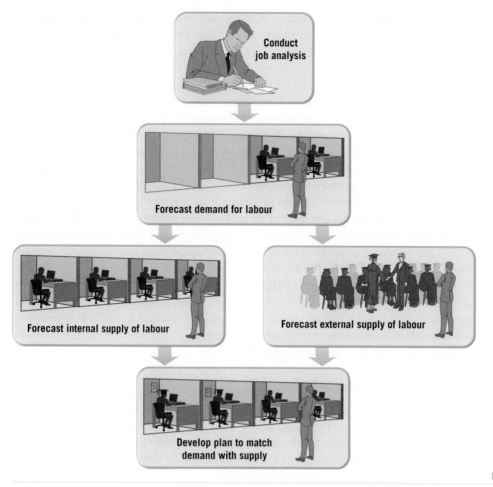

FIGURE 8.1

Planning for human resources.

employees, such as operating employees and sales representatives. Large organizations use more complicated models to predict HR needs.

Forecasting the supply of labour involves two tasks:

- forecasting internal supply—the number and type of employees who will be in the firm at some future date

- forecasting external supply—the number and type of people who will be available for hiring from the labour market at large

The simplest approach merely adjusts present staffing levels for anticipated turnover and promotions. Large organizations use sophisticated models to keep track of the present and future distributions of professionals and managers. This allows them to spot areas where there will eventually be too many qualified professionals competing for too few promotions or, conversely, too few good people available to fill important positions. Research In Motion and about 550 other high-tech companies are located in Canada's "technology triangle" (Kitchener, Waterloo, and Cambridge, Ontario). In 2010, unemployment was fairly high in Canada, but there were about 1500–2000 high-tech, high-paying jobs open in the region. Why? These jobs are highly specialized and require experienced workers, so there was a mismatch in supply and demand at the time.[2] Mismatches are also evident in other industries. A 2012 report from the Canadian Chamber of Commerce predicted shortages in a variety of industries, including construction, nursing, and trucking.[3]

Replacement Charts. At higher levels of the organization, managers make plans for specific people and positions. The technique most commonly used is the **replacement chart**, which lists each important managerial position, who occupies it, how long he

replacement chart An HR technique that lists each important managerial position, who occupies it, how long he or she will probably stay in it before moving on, and who (by name) is now qualified or soon will be qualified to move into it.

or she will probably stay in it before moving on, and who (by name) is now qualified or soon will be qualified to move into it. This technique allows ample time to plan developmental experiences for people identified as potential successors to critical managerial jobs.

Skills Inventories. To facilitate both planning and identifying people for transfer or promotion, some organizations also have **employee information systems**, or **skills inventories**. These systems are usually computerized and contain information on each employee's education, skills, work experience, and career aspirations. Such a system can quickly locate every employee who is qualified to fill a position requiring, say, a degree in chemical engineering, three years of experience in an oil refinery, and fluency in French.

Forecasting the external supply of labour is a different problem altogether. For example, how does a manager predict how many electrical engineers will be seeking work in Ontario or British Columbia three years from now? To get an idea of the future availability of labour, planners must rely on information from outside sources, such as government reports and figures supplied by colleges and universities on the number of students in major fields. These statistics show that Canada is likely to face a severe labour shortage within the next 10 years. The problem is already evident in Alberta, but labour shortages are likely to appear in almost all provinces over the next few years as thousands of baby boomers approach retirement age.[4] The worst shortages are in the construction, retail, and transportation industries.[5]

Matching HR Supply and Demand

After comparing future demand and internal supply, managers can make plans to manage predicted shortfalls or overstaffing. If a shortfall is predicted, new employees can be hired, present employees can be retrained and transferred into understaffed areas, individuals approaching retirement can be convinced to stay on, or labour-saving or productivity-enhancing systems can be installed.

If the organization needs to hire, the external labour-supply forecast helps managers plan how to recruit according to whether the type of person needed is readily available or scarce in the labour market. The use of temporary workers also helps managers in staffing by giving them extra flexibility. If overstaffing is expected to be a problem, the main options are transferring the extra employees, not replacing individuals who quit, encouraging early retirement, and laying people off.

Staffing the Organization

Once managers have decided what positions they need to fill, they must find and hire individuals who meet the job requirements. A study by the Canadian Federation of Independent Business found that the top three characteristics employers are looking for when they hire people are a good work ethic, reliability, and willingness to stay on the job.[6] Staffing of the business is one of the most complex and important aspects of good human resource management. The top 10 employers by number of employees in Canada are listed in Table 8.1.

In this section, we will describe both the process of acquiring staff from outside the company (external staffing) and the process of promoting staff from within (internal staffing). Both external and internal staffing start with effective recruiting.

Recruiting Human Resources

Recruiting is the process of attracting qualified persons to apply for the jobs that are open. Some recruits are found internally while others come from outside the organization.

---

employee information systems (or skills inventories) Computerized systems that contain information on each employee's education, skills, work experience, and career aspirations.

LO2 Identify the issues involved in *staffing* a company, including *internal* and *external recruiting and selection*.

recruiting The process of attracting qualified persons to apply for the jobs that are open.

TABLE 8.1 Top 10 Employers by Number of Employees			
Rank	Company	Head Office	Number of Employees
1	Loblaw Companies	Toronto, ON	122 000
2	Onex Corp.	Toronto, ON	98 000
3	Bombardier Inc.	Montreal, QC	80 000
4	Magna International	Aurora, ON	70 800
5	Hudson's Bay Co.	Toronto, ON	70 678
6	BCE Inc.	Montreal, QC	66 266
7	Royal Bank of Canada	Toronto, ON	59 770
8	Bell Canada	Montreal, QC	54 258
9	Alcan Inc.	Montreal, QC	48 100
10	Canadian Tire Corp.	Toronto, ON	45 000

Internal Recruiting

Internal recruiting means considering present employees as candidates for openings. Promotion from within can help build morale and keep high-quality employees from leaving. In unionized firms, the procedures for notifying employees of internal job-change opportunities are usually spelled out in the union contract. For higher-level positions, a skills inventory system may be used to identify internal candidates, or managers may be asked to recommend individuals who should be considered.

internal recruiting Considering present employees as candidates for openings.

External Recruiting

External recruiting involves attracting people outside the organization to apply for jobs. External recruiting methods include newspaper and internet advertising, campus interviews, employment agencies, executive search firms, union hiring halls, referrals by present employees, and hiring "walk-ins" (people who show up without being solicited). Private employment agencies can be a good source of clerical and technical employees, and executive search firms specialize in locating top-management talent. Newspaper and internet ads reach a wide audience and thus give minorities an equal opportunity to learn about and apply for job openings.

external recruiting Attracting people outside the organization to apply for jobs.

The boxed insert entitled "Green Recruiting" illustrates the increasing importance of environmental considerations in recruiting.

At a job fair, candidates browse through the positions available and talk face to face with recruiters. For organizations, participating in job fairs is cheaper than posting jobs with an employment agency. In 2011, more than 10 000 people signed up for a *virtual job fair* that was run by Monster.ca. Unlike campus job fairs, these events attract individuals from all career stages. Participants click on the virtual booths of employers they are interested in, and employers interview candidates via video.[7]

Internships are short-term paid positions where students focus on a specific project. Hari Pemasani, who came to Canada from India, completed a pharmacy program at the University of Toronto and then had an internship with Loblaw Cos. Ltd. He was then hired for a full-time position and soon became the pharmacy manager for the store where he worked.[8] The Canadian Undergraduate Survey Consortium found that 55 percent of graduating students had completed an internship.[9]

internships Short-term paid positions where students focus on a specific project.

The biggest change in recent years has been the advent of online recruiting. Companies post positions on websites like Monster, Workopolis, or LinkedIn, and interested applicants respond. Internet recruiting gives employers and those seeking employment a fast, easy, and inexpensive way of interacting. But there are drawbacks. Employers receive huge numbers of applications, and many are from unqualified people. Starbucks, for example, received 7.6 million applications during 2011. To cope with this situation, many companies now use résumé-filtering software that searches out key words

THE GREENING OF BUSINESS

Green Recruiting

After Chad Hunt graduated from university, he took a job with Husky Injection Molding because of the company's emphasis on protecting the environment. The vice-president of corporate affairs for Husky says that when prospective hires are asked during job interviews why they want to work for Husky, they often mention the company's environmental responsibility program. Current employees who fill out the employee satisfaction survey also give high marks to the company on questions relating to the environmental responsibility program.

Sara Wong said it was the zero waste program at Hudson's Bay Co. (HBC) that caught her attention when she was job hunting. She was concerned about the environment, and she liked the focus that HBC placed on recycling office waste. The senior vice-president for human resources at HBC says that when prospective employees visit the company's website, they often click on the corporate social responsibility report.

In a survey conducted by Monster.ca, 78 percent of respondents said they would quit their current job if they could get one at a company that had an environmentally friendly focus. In a second survey, 81 percent of the respondents said that their current employer was not environmentally friendly. Only 18 percent said the employer was "extremely green."

In recent years, Canadians have become more concerned about the environment, and many people say they want to work for companies that share their concerns. An environmentally friendly workplace is important to both current and prospective employees. Aon Hewitt's annual "Green 30" list is based on employee perceptions of their companies' environmental efforts. The 2011 list included Lush Fresh Handmade Cosmetics, ISL Engineering and Land Services, and Nexen. In these and other companies, employees are often the ones who push for green initiatives. For example, David Huang saved his company (BLJC) $400 000 by suggesting a variety of energy-saving actions. At VanCity Credit Union, Maureen Cureton encouraged other employees to buy from green and socially conscious retailers. That evolved into the Beehive, which is a searchable database that lists sustainable retailers.

Over half a million Canadians are now employed in environmentally related jobs (e.g., consultants who assess homes to see how energy efficient they are). Many of these jobs didn't even exist a generation ago. According to the Environmental Careers Organization of Canada, the top five green careers are environmental engineer, environmental technologist, conservation biologist, geographic information system analyst, and environmental communications officer.

Critical Thinking Questions

1. What are the advantages of working for an environmentally friendly company? Are there any disadvantages?

2. Consider the following statement: *All the publicity about graduates looking for jobs at environmentally friendly companies is exaggerated. Many graduates are merely claiming they want to work for an environmentally friendly company, even though most of them really don't care that much about the environment.* Do you agree or disagree with the statement? Explain your reasoning.

At job fairs, students and recruiters can talk face to face about jobs that are available.

on applications. If the key words aren't there, the applicant is not contacted.[10] IGN Entertainment, a gaming and media company, doesn't even ask for a résumé. Instead, candidates respond to challenges on IGN's website that are designed to gauge applicants' thought processes.[11] The boxed insert entitled "Job Recruitment in the Social Media Era" provides more information about the importance of social media in recruiting.

Selecting Human Resources

Once the recruiting process has attracted a pool of applicants, the next step is to select someone to hire. The intent of the selection process is to gather information from applicants that will predict their job performance and job success and then to hire the candidates likely to be most successful. The process of determining the predictive value of information is called **validation**.

validation The process of determining the predictive value of information.

E-BUSINESS + SOCIAL MEDIA SOLUTIONS

Job Recruitment in the Social Media Era

The internet has transformed the job recruitment process. Online recruitment sites like Monster.ca and Workopolis revolutionized the traditional job-hunting process a few years ago. However, the best way to find a job is still through a personal contact. Since social media plays a big role in the private lives of job hunters and HR officers, it is likely that social networking will be used more widely in the job-search process. However, a 2011 survey of 400 people (by Randstad Canada) showed that only about half of the respondents used their accounts for business purposes. Some sites like LinkedIn were designed with business networking in mind; others like Facebook and Twitter are still evolving. Here are some examples.

- Before launching a new campaign on its website and on social media sites, PepsiCo invested tens of thousands of dollars to create just the right video profiles, since effective recruitment of Gen Y candidates (its target group) requires a modern social media presence. This approach helped PepsiCo attract top candidates to fill various openings (e.g., chemists).
- Razor Suleman runs I Love Rewards Inc., a Toronto-based company that consults with companies on employee incentives and recognition programs. When the company needed to hire 17 people, Suleman did not place ads in a national paper (approximate cost $5000) or use an internet job site (approximate cost $700). Instead, he asked employees to put job postings on Facebook, share them with their LinkedIn networks, and tweet them to friends. He expects this approach to yield 1000 applicants at a minimal cost. It costs on average $2000 to fill a clerical job and $35 000 to fill an executive position using traditional means.
- Mark Buell got a job as a social media communications officer in Ottawa after reading a tweet from one

of his contacts. He wasn't actually looking for a job at the time, but used this inside track to apply for the job before it was posted. After his initial interview, he sent the company a link to his Twitter account to help demonstrate who he is. It worked. Bottom line: His tweets helped him secure the job.

- Future Shop turned to social media to help attract 5000 workers for the holiday season. The company has over 17 000 followers on its Facebook page.
- Shannon Yelland found a job at Vancouver-based ActiveState Software Inc. by using her Twitter account proactively. She updated her profile and let people know that she was looking for an online marketing position in Vancouver. She conducted a search on Twitter and Twitter-directory sites Twellow and Tweepsearch. She quickly received tips from her 4000 Twitter followers, including some recruiters.

The online options are numerous and are increasingly tailored to people's needs. For example, TheLadders.com and BlueSteps.com are sites dedicated to helping people find executive-level jobs (paying $100 000+). Social media sites are increasingly being used by job seekers, but recruiters are also using sites to discover who candidates really are. You might keep that in mind before posting material online that may hurt your future prospects.

Critical Thinking Questions

1. Have you ever used a social media or online recruiting site to find a job? In your opinion, how effective are these tools?

2. Should recruiters be legally permitted to conduct background checks on candidates based on publicly available information on social media sites? Does this prospect worry you?

To reduce the element of uncertainty, managers use a variety of selection techniques, the most common of which are shown in Figure 8.2. Each organization develops its own mix of selection techniques and may use them in almost any order.

Application Forms

The first step in selection is usually asking the candidate to fill out an application form, which is an efficient method of gathering information about the applicant's previous work history, educational background, and other information not related to the job, such as gender or national origin. Application-form data are generally used informally to decide whether a candidate merits further evaluation, and interviewers use application forms to familiarize themselves with candidates before interviewing them.

Tests

Employers sometimes ask candidates to take tests during the selection process. Tests of ability, skill, aptitude, or knowledge relevant to a particular job are usually the best predictors of job success, although tests of general intelligence or personality are occasionally useful as well. Some companies administer tests to determine how well applicants score on the "big five" personality dimensions (see Chapter 10). These scores are used to help make hiring decisions. In addition to being validated, tests should be administered and scored consistently. All candidates should be given the same directions, allowed the same amount of time, and offered the same testing environment, including temperature, lighting, and distractions.

An **assessment centre** is a location in which candidates perform realistic management tasks under the watchful eye of expert appraisers. A typical assessment centre might be set up in a large conference room and go on for two or three days. During this time, potential managers might take selection tests, engage in management simulations, make individual presentations, and conduct group discussions. Assessors check to see how each participant reacts to stress or to criticism by colleagues. A relatively new type of test that has evolved from assessment centres is **video assessment**, which involves showing potential hires videos of realistic work situations and asking them to choose a course of action to deal with the situation.

assessment centre A location in which candidates perform realistic management tasks under the watchful eye of expert appraisers.

video assessment Potential hires are shown videos of realistic work situations and are then asked to choose a course of action to deal with the situation.

FIGURE 8.2

General steps in the selection process.

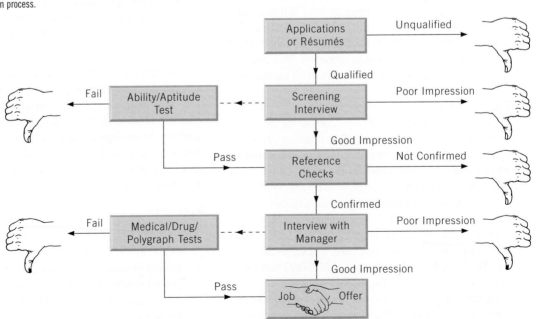

Interviews

The interview is a popular selection device, but it is sometimes a poor predictor of job success because biases that are inherent in the way people perceive and judge others on first meeting affect subsequent evaluations. Many companies are placing more emphasis on testing and less emphasis on interviewing because job candidates are becoming clever at giving all the "right" answers during interviews. Interview validity can be improved by training interviewers to be aware of potential biases, and by writing out questions in advance and asking all interviewees the same set of questions.

Interviewers can also increase interview validity by asking "curveball" questions— that is, questions that job applicants would never expect to be asked—to see how well they think on their feet. Questions such as "How would you move Mount Fuji?" or "How would you sell me a glass of water?" are examples of curveball questions.[12]

Another approach to improving interview validity is **behaviour-based interviewing**. Instead of asking a traditional interview question like "Do you often take the initiative?" behaviour-based interviewing asks "Tell me about a situation where you became aware of a problem. What did you *do*?" This approach puts a spotlight on behaviour rather than on what a person says. It can be used to test for technical skills (e.g., accounting, welding, or computer programming), management skills (e.g., organizing, motivating others, or communicating), and individual skills (e.g., dependability, discipline, or the ability to work on a team). Behaviour-based interviewing is becoming more common because companies are facing increasingly competitive environments.

> **behaviour-based interviewing** An approach to improving interview validity by asking questions that focus the interview much more on behaviour than on what a person says.

Other Techniques

Organizations also use other selection techniques that vary with the circumstances. A manufacturer afraid of injuries to workers on the job might require new employees to have a physical examination. This gives the company some information about whether the potential employee is physically able to do the work and what (if any) pre-existing injuries the person might have.

According to the Canadian Human Rights Commission policy, pre-employment drug testing and random drug testing are not permitted. However, recent legal decisions make this anything but a black-and-white issue. Rulings related to the Greater Toronto Airport Authority (GTAA) and Goodyear Canada are open to other interpretations. The decisions upheld the rights of these organizations to use drug and alcohol testing for safety-sensitive positions and as a post-treatment check for employees with a history of drug abuse. However, it was also deemed unreasonable to deny selection because of a positive pre-employment drug test. This is an area of law that will continue to evolve and be debated.[13]

Reference checks with previous employers are also used but may be of limited value because individuals are likely to provide the names of only those references who will give them positive recommendations. It is also getting harder to get good reference information because many HR people are worried about legal rulings south of the border as high as $1.4 million. Many legal experts say that the fear is unwarranted; the law protects them in giving honest, even if negative, information.[14]

Developing Human Resources

Regardless of how effective a selection system is, most employees need additional training if they are to grow and develop in their jobs. This process begins with orientation and then proceeds to the assessment of training and development needs (including the performance of a needs analysis) and the selection of the best training techniques and methods.

> Discuss different ways in which organizations go about developing the capabilities of employees and managers.

New Employee Orientation

An Ipsos Reid survey of over 1000 workers revealed that 50 percent of them felt that they didn't always fit in well at work.[15] Jennifer Cayer, a partner with the HR consulting firm PeopleSavvy, says that a new employee's first 30 days on the job have a big influence on whether the person will stay with the company.[16] Both these findings suggest that orientation of new workers is a very important activity. **Orientation** is the process of introducing new employees to the company's policies and programs, the co-workers and supervisors they will interact with, and the nature of their job. Orientation allows new employees to feel like part of a team and to become effective contributors to the organization more rapidly. It also plays a key role in job satisfaction, performance, and retention. Overall, orientation eases the transition from outsider to insider. Poor orientation, on the other hand, can result in disenchantment, dissatisfaction, anxiety, and turnover. For example, the dating website Plentyoffish is dedicated to keeping their employees happy by listening to what they have to say and by providing an open-concept office. The company also treated more than 40 employees to a two-day-long retreat at a top hotel in Whistler where they had fun taking part in a variety of training activities. Plentyoffish also uses its matchmaking techniques to find appropriate employees where, just as a friend would recommend a potential partner, employees are encouraged to refer people they may know who would be a great fit to the company as well.[17]

orientation The process of introducing new employees to the company's policies and programs, the co-workers and supervisors they will interact with, and the nature of their job.

Training and Development

Beyond orientation, employees must be continually trained and developed to improve the quality of the contributions they make to the organization. The starting point in assessing training and development needs is conducting a needs analysis—determining the organization's true needs and the training programs necessary to meet them. This analysis generally focuses on two things: the organization's job-related needs and the capabilities of the current workforce. The organization's needs are determined by the nature of the work that the organization needs to have done. That is, what knowledge, skills, and abilities does the organization need in order to compete? What skills must its workforce possess to perform the organization's work effectively?

Depending on both the content of the program and the instructors selected to present it, a number of techniques and methods can be used for the actual delivery of information. Some of the more popular techniques and methods are described below.

Work-Based Programs (On-the-Job Training)

Work-based programs tie training and development activities directly to task performance. The most common method of work-based training is **on-the-job training**. The employee is placed in the actual work situation and is shown how to perform a task by a supervisor or an experienced employee. Much on-the-job training is informal, as when one employee shows another how to operate the photocopy machine.

Another method of work-based training is **systematic job rotations and transfers**. This method is most likely to be used for lower-level managers or for operating employees being groomed for promotions to supervisory management positions. As the term suggests, the employee is systematically rotated or transferred from one job to another. The employee thus learns a wider array of tasks, acquires more abilities, and develops a more comprehensive view of the work of an organization or a particular sub-unit.

work-based program A technique that ties training and development activities directly to task performance.

on-the-job training Those development programs in which employees gain new skills while performing them at work.

systematic job rotations and transfers A technique in which an employee is systematically rotated or transferred from one job to another.

off-the-job training Those development programs in which employees learn new skills at a location away from the normal work site.

vestibule training A work simulation in which the job is performed under conditions closely simulating the actual work environment.

Instructional-Based Programs (Off-the-Job Training)

Off-the-job training is performed at a location away from the work site. It may be at a classroom within the same facility or at a different location altogether. For example, **vestibule training** involves employees performing work under conditions closely simulating the actual work environment. Montreal-based CAE is famous for building flight simulators that enable airline pilots to learn how to fly a new jet without ever leaving the ground. CAE also develops mock-up operating rooms where medical students can learn in a simulated environment.[18]

Management development programs try to enhance conceptual, analytical, and problem-solving skills. In these programs, the **lecture or discussion approach** is normally used. A company trainer presents material to attendees just as a professor would lecture to students. Depending on the situation and the size of the training class, the trainer may opt for a pure lecture method or may include discussion with trainees. Sometimes lectures are on video or audio tapes so that various individuals in the organization can receive the same training at different times and/or at different locations.

Most large companies run formal in-house management development programs or send managers to programs on university campuses. In the Build for the Future program at TD Bank, top managers meet once a month to plan leadership training and coaching of subordinates.[19] But in many companies, training for managers is not so systematic. In one survey of over 1000 managers, 57 percent said they had to learn how to manage by trial and error, and 89 percent said they had not been groomed to be a leader.[20]

Some management development does takes place informally, often through processes such as networking and mentoring. **Networking** refers to informal interactions among managers for the purpose of discussing mutual problems, solutions, and opportunities. Networking takes place in a variety of settings, both inside and outside the office. **Mentoring** means having a more experienced manager sponsor and teach a less experienced manager. Men still occupy the majority of top management positions, and they are important in mentoring women who aspire to top management jobs.[21] For both men and women, *reverse mentoring* is becoming common—younger, more tech-savvy employees mentor senior staff members on everything from viral marketing to blogging to the use of Facebook and YouTube.[22]

management development programs Programs that try to enhance conceptual, analytical, and problem-solving skills.

lecture or discussion approach An instructional-based program in which a trainer presents material in a descriptive fashion to those attending a trainee program.

networking Informal interactions among managers for the purpose of discussing mutual problems, solutions, and opportunities.

mentoring Having a more experienced manager sponsor and teach a less experienced manager.

Team Building and Group-Based Training

Since more and more organizations are using teams as a basis for doing their jobs, it should not be surprising that many of the same companies are developing training programs specifically designed to facilitate co-operation among team members.

Video conferencing has become an important part of the training function. Travel costs are reduced, and interactions between the trainer and the trainees are facilitated.

For example, Eagle's Flight is an innovative leader in the development and delivery of practical training programs for the global business community. Its offering of training programs includes team and training experiences as well as leadership development and learning.[23]

Evaluating Employee Performance

LO4 Explain ways in which organizations evaluate employee performance.

performance appraisal The specific and formal evaluation of employees to determine whether they are performing effectively.

360-degree feedback Gathering information from a manager's subordinates, peers, and superiors when assessing the manager's performance.

Performance appraisals are designed to show how well workers are doing their jobs. Typically, the appraisal process involves a written assessment issued on a regular basis. As a rule, however, the written evaluation is only one part of a multi-step process. The appraisal process begins when a manager defines performance standards for an employee. The manager observes the employee's performance and then meets with the employee to discuss the appraisal.

It is best to rely on several information sources when conducting appraisals. A system called **360-degree feedback** gathers information from supervisors, subordinates, and co-workers. The most accurate information comes from individuals who have known the person being appraised for one to three years. Ideally, eight or ten individuals should take part in the evaluation.[24] The use of social media in appraisal is increasing. When Facebook decided that traditional appraisals were not suited to its employees, it turned to Toronto-based Rypple, a company that specializes in software tools to provide real-time feedback using a Facebook-style interface. Managers can "like" tasks, ask for feedback, and monitor employee progress toward goals.[25]

Many managers are not effective when providing performance feedback, partly because they don't understand how to do it properly and partly because they don't enjoy it. As a result, managers may have a tendency to avoid giving negative feedback because they know that an employee who receives it may be angry, hurt, discouraged, or argumentative. But if employees are not told about their shortcomings, they will have no concrete reason to try to improve and will receive no guidance as to how to improve. Because of the problems with performance appraisal, some companies have abandoned them. Australian-based Atlassian Inc, for example, replaced annual appraisals with weekly one-on-one meetings between managers and workers. Discussions focus on goals and performance.[26]

Methods for Appraising Performance

Because of the nature of many jobs today, especially managerial work, most methods for appraising performance rely on judgments and ratings. A great deal of effort has been expended on trying to make relatively subjective evaluations as meaningful and useful as they can be. Both ranking and rating methods are popular.

Ranking Methods

simple ranking method A method of performance appraisal that requires a manager to rank-order, from top to bottom or from best to worst, each member of a particular work group or department.

forced distribution method A method of performance appraisal that involves grouping employees into predefined frequencies of performance ratings.

The **simple ranking method** requires a manager to rank-order, from top to bottom or from best to worst, each member of a particular work group or department. The individual ranked first is the top performer, the individual ranked second is the second-best performer, and so forth. The basis for the ranking is generally global or overall performance. Another ranking method, the **forced distribution method**, involves grouping employees into predefined frequencies of performance ratings. Those frequencies are determined in advance and are imposed on the rater. A decision might be made, for instance, that 10 percent of the employees in a work group will be grouped as "outstanding," 20 percent as "very good," 40 percent as "average," 20 percent as "below average," and the remaining 10 percent as "poor."

Rating Methods

One of the most popular and widely used methods is the **graphic rating scale**, which consists of a statement or question about some aspect of an individual's job performance. Following the statement or question is a series of answers or possible responses from which the rater must select the one that fits best. For example, one common set of responses to a graphic rating scale with five possible alternatives is strongly agree, agree, neither agree nor disagree, disagree, and strongly disagree. These responses, or "descriptors," are usually arrayed along a bar, line, or similar visual representation marked with numbers or letters corresponding to each descriptor. Figure 8.3 shows a sample graphic rating scale.

graphic rating scale A method of performance appraisal that involves a statement or question about some aspect of an individual's job performance for which the rater must select the response that fits best.

The **critical incident method** requires the employee to give an example of especially good or poor performance. Organizations that rely on this method often require raters to recall such instances and then describe what the employee did (or did not do) that led to success or failure. This technique not only provides information for feedback but also defines performance in clear behavioural terms.

critical incident method A technique of performance appraisal in which raters recall examples of especially good or poor performance by an employee and then describe what the employee did (or did not do) that led to success or failure.

FIGURE 8.3

Performance rating scale.

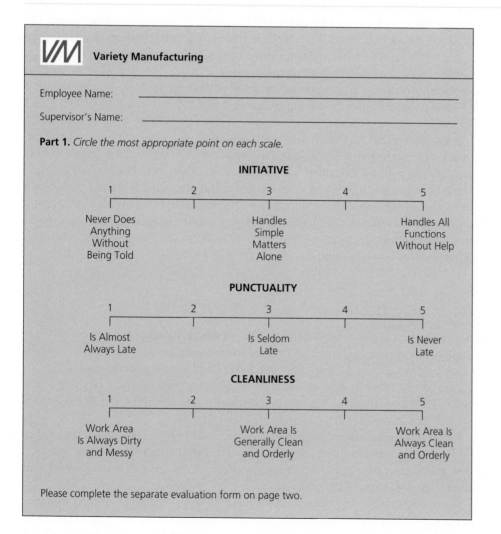

Providing Compensation and Benefits

L05 Discuss the importance of *wages* and *salaries*, *incentives*, and *benefit programs* in attracting and keeping skilled workers.

compensation The set of rewards that organizations provide to individuals in return for their willingness to perform various jobs and tasks within the organization.

Compensation refers to the set of rewards that organizations provide to individuals in return for their willingness to perform various jobs and tasks within the organization. Compensation includes a number of different elements, including base salary, incentives, bonuses, benefits, and other rewards. Compensation amounts paid to employees should be the result of a careful and systematic strategic process.

The compensation received by CEOs can be extremely large, especially when bonuses and options are included. The top 100 Canadian CEOs were paid an average of $8.4 million in 2010, a 27 percent increase over the previous year.[27] In comparison, the average Canadian earned $44 366, or 1.1 percent more than in 2009.[28] Hugh MacKenzie, an economist with the Ottawa-based non-profit research organization Hugh Mackenzie & Associates, says: "The conclusion from these data is inescapable. Soaring executive salaries have played a significant role in driving the growth in income inequality in Canada." The mostly highly paid CEOs in Canada in 2011 were all employed at Magna International Inc. Frank Stronach earned a total of $61.8 million, co-CEO Donald Walker earned $16.7 million, and former co-CEO Siegfried Wolf received $16.5 million. Only one woman made the list—Nancy Southern (who works with both Atco Ltd. and Canadian Utilities Ltd.); she ranked eighty-fifth with a total compensation package worth nearly $4.8 million. CEOs in the United States are paid even more: For example, John Hammergren (McKesson Corp.) received just over $145 million.[29] Critics have frequently questioned the wisdom of giving executives such large amounts of money, but most attempts to rein in executive salaries have failed. Until recently, income equality was improving. But since 1987, one-third of all income gains went to the richest 1 percent of Canadians, reversing a 30-year trend toward greater equality. Canada's highest-paid CEOs now earn 189 times the average wage, up from 105 times in 1998 and 85 times in 1995.[30]

In an attempt to introduce some accountability into executive compensation, Aflac Inc. (the company with the quacking duck on TV commercials) gives investors a non-binding vote on executive compensation. In 2009, shareholders at CIBC and the Royal Bank of Canada passed motions demanding that the companies give them a voice in executive compensation through non-binding shareholder votes.[31] In Sweden, Norway, and the Netherlands, shareholders have a binding vote on executive pay packages. Whether binding or non-binding, investor feedback may help boards of directors rein in executive compensation that is perceived as too high.[32]

Determining Basic Compensation

wages Hourly compensation paid to operating employees.

Basic compensation means the base level of wages or salary paid to an employee. **Wages** generally refer to hourly compensation paid to operating employees. Most of the jobs that are paid on an hourly wage basis are lower-level and/or operating-level jobs. In 2012, the average hourly wage in manufacturing was $19.76, while in retailing it was only $15.73. The manufacturing sector is shrinking, and retailers are now the biggest employers in Canada.[33]

salary Dollars paid at regular intervals in return for doing a job, regardless of the amount of time or output involved.

Rather than expressing compensation on an hourly basis, the organization may instead state compensation on an annual or monthly basis. Many college and university graduates, for example, compare job offers on the basis of annual **salary** (for example, $38 000 versus $40 000 a year).

merit pay plans Compensation plans that formally base some portion of compensation on merit.

Merit pay plans are compensation plans that base a portion of compensation on merit. Employees who make greater contributions receive higher pay than those who make lesser contributions. The most general form of a merit pay plan is the raise—a salary increase granted to employees because of their relative merit. Merit is usually defined in terms of individual performance and contribution to the organization.

Pay Surveys in Compensation

One common source of information that many organizations use to determine base compensation is **pay surveys**—surveys of compensation paid to employees by other employers in a particular geographic area, an industry, or an occupational group. Pay surveys provide the information that an organization needs to avoid an imbalance between its own pay scale and those of comparable organizations. Some pay surveys are conducted by professional associations. For example, the Canadian Federation of Business School Deans publishes an annual summary of salaries for professors teaching in business schools in Canadian universities.

pay survey A survey of compensation paid to employees by other employers in a particular geographic area, an industry, or an occupational group.

In general, a pay survey simply asks other organizations what they pay people to perform various jobs. Most organizations participate in such surveys because they will have access to the resulting data. There is, for example, a consortium of eight large electronics companies in the United States that routinely survey one another to determine what each pays new engineers and other professional employees who are hired directly out of college or university. The companies alternate the responsibility for conducting surveys from year to year, with the responsible organization sharing its results with the other members.

Job Evaluation

Another means of determining basic compensation is job evaluation, which should not be confused with job analysis. Recall that managers use job analysis to understand the requirements and nature of a job and its performance so that appropriate individuals can be recruited and selected. **Job evaluation** is a method for determining the relative value or worth of a job to the organization so that individuals who perform it can be appropriately compensated. It is mostly concerned with establishing internal pay equity.

job evaluation A method for determining the relative value or worth of a job to the organization so that individuals who perform it can be appropriately compensated.

Establishing a Pay Structure

A third method for determining basic compensation is establishing a pay structure. Compensation for different jobs is based on the organization's assessment of the relative value to the organization of each job class. Thus, there should be a logical ranking of compensation levels from the most valuable to the least valuable jobs throughout the organization. In addition, the organization decides on minimum and maximum pay ranges for each job or job class. These ranges may be decided on the basis of job performance, seniority, or a combination of the two to determine how much a person can be paid within the pay range for doing a particular job.

The internet allows job seekers and current employees to get a sense of what their true market value is more easily. If they can document the claim that their value is higher than what their current employer now pays, they may be in a position to demand higher salaries. One manager who met with a subordinate to discuss her raise was surprised when she produced data from five different websites to support her request for a bigger raise than he had intended to offer.

Incentive Programs

Employees feel better about themselves and their company when they believe that they are being fairly compensated. Money generally motivates employees if it is tied directly to performance, and the most common method of establishing this link is

incentive programs Special pay programs designed to motivate high performance.

the use of **incentive programs**—special pay programs designed to motivate high performance. These programs can be applied to individuals or teams. A survey by the Conference Board of Canada found that while 80 percent of Canadian companies offer incentive programs, 69 percent of them don't measure the effectiveness of those programs.[34]

Individual Incentives

individual incentive plans Compensation systems in which an employer gives an individual a salary increase or some other financial reward for outstanding performance immediately or shortly after the performance occurs.

piece-rate incentive plan A compensation system in which an organization pays an employee a certain amount of money for every unit produced.

sales commission Payment to salespeople based on the number of units they sell or the dollar value of sales they generate for the company.

bonuses Cash payments given to employees who exceed a certain level of performance.

pay-for-knowledge Systems that encourage individual workers to learn new skills and to become proficient at different jobs.

pay-for-performance (or variable pay) Rewards paid to managers for especially productive output—for producing earnings that significantly exceed the cost of bonuses.

Individual incentive plans reward individual performance on a real-time basis. That is, rather than increasing a person's base salary at the end of the year, an employer gives an individual a salary increase or some other financial reward for outstanding performance immediately or shortly after the performance occurs. Individual incentive systems are most common where performance can be assessed objectively (for example, by the number of units of output) rather than subjectively.

Under a **piece-rate incentive plan**, an employee receives a certain amount of money for every unit produced. An assembly-line worker, for example, might be paid 10 cents for every unit produced. Critics of piece-rate pay systems argue that piece-rate systems rely on two questionable assumptions: (1) that performance is totally under an individual's control, and (2) that the individual employee does a single task continuously during the course of his or her work time. Today, therefore, incentive compensation systems tend to be much more sophisticated.

Sales employees are often paid a **sales commission** based on the number of units they sell or the dollar value of sales they generate for the company. **Bonuses**—cash payments—may also be given to employees who exceed a certain level of performance. For example, many baseball players have contract clauses that pay them bonuses for hitting over .300, making the All-Star team, or being named Most Valuable Player.

Pay-for-knowledge systems encourage individual workers to learn new skills and to become proficient at different jobs. Workers receive additional pay for each new skill or job that they master.

With **pay-for-performance** (or **variable pay**) schemes, managers are rewarded for especially productive output—for producing earnings that significantly exceed the cost of bonuses. Such incentives go to middle managers on the basis of companywide performance, business unit performance, personal record, or all three factors. Eligible managers must often forgo merit or entitlement raises (increases for staying on and reporting to work every day), but many firms say that variable pay is a better motivator because the range between generous and mediocre merit raises is usually quite small anyway.

workforce management systems Systems whereby the most productive retail staff are scheduled to work at the store's busiest times.

Other forms of individual incentives are also used; these include additional time off or special recognition in the form of points that are awarded on the recommendation of a supervisor. Recipients can convert their points into money or they can use them to buy merchandise or trips from a special online catalogue.[35] Retailers are beginning to adopt **workforce management systems**, which schedule the most productive staff to work at the store's busiest times. When employees type their code into the cash register, it displays their "performance metrics" such as average sales per hour and dollars per transaction. Less productive employees are given fewer hours or less desirable hours.[36] Not surprisingly, this system is disliked by many workers. At one store where it was implemented, the atmosphere changed from collegial to competitive.

Team and Group Incentives

profit-sharing plans System whereby some portion of the company's profit is paid into a profit-sharing pool that is then distributed to all employees.

Some incentive programs apply to all the employees in a firm. Under **profit-sharing plans**, profits earned above a certain level are distributed to employees. At the Great Little Box Company in Richmond, BC, 15 percent of company profits are split evenly

Individual incentive plans have been a big part of professional sports for many years. Players receive multimillion-dollar annual compensation for outstanding individual performance.

among staff. The company also has an "open book" policy of providing financial information to employees so they can relate financial performance of the company to their share of the profits.[37]

Gain-sharing plans distribute bonuses to employees when a company's costs are reduced through greater work efficiency. Palliser Furniture Ltd., for example, introduced a gain-sharing plan that rewarded employees for increasing production. Any profit resulting from production above a certain level is split 50–50 between the company and the employees.[38] The underlying assumption is that employees and the employer have the same goals and should therefore share in incremental economic gains.

gain-sharing plans Plans that distribute bonuses to employees when a company's costs are reduced through greater work efficiency.

Benefits

Benefits are rewards, incentives, and other things of value that an organization gives to employees in addition to wages, salaries, and other forms of direct financial compensation. Because these benefits have tangible value, they represent a meaningful form of compensation even though they are not generally expressed in financial terms. According to a PricewaterhouseCoopers survey, some of the top benefits sought, other than money, were gift cards, extra vacation days, and being fast-tracked for promotion.[39]

benefits What a firm offers its workers other than wages and salaries in return for their labour.

Mandated Protection Plans

protection plans Plans that protect employees when their income is threatened or reduced by illness, disability, death, unemployment, or retirement.

employment insurance Provides a basic subsistence payment to employees who are between jobs.

Protection plans protect employees when their income is threatened or reduced by illness, disability, death, unemployment, or retirement. A number of these plans are required by law, but others are optional. One mandated benefit is **employment insurance**, which provides a basic subsistence payment to employees who are between jobs. It is intended for people who have stopped working for one organization but who are assumed to be actively seeking employment with another. Both employers and employees pay premiums to an employment insurance fund. The reduction in the maximum annual change permitted for the 2012 premium rate announced on November 8, 2011, meant that the 2012 premium rate cannot exceed $1.83 per $100 of insurable earnings, near its lowest level since 1982. This change is expected to save employers and employees $600 million in 2012.[40]

MANAGING IN TURBULENT TIMES

Defined Benefit vs. Defined Contribution Pension Plans

There are two basic types of pension plans offered by Canadian public- and private-sector organizations. *Defined benefit* (DB) pension plans guarantee employees a certain annual income when they retire. Employees like DB plans because they get a guaranteed income, and because they don't have to make investment decisions during retirement. But employers don't like DB plans because they are forced to make guaranteed payments to retirees even if the company runs into financial difficulties.

In contrast, *defined contribution* (DC) pension plans require companies to contribute a certain amount of money each year for employee pensions. The value of the pension upon the employee's retirement depends on how much the pension fund has earned over the years. Employers like DC plans because they put a ceiling on how much money the company must pay out. But employees don't like DC plans because they do not know how much income they will get when they retire, and because they must make decisions about their investments during retirement.

Because of low investment returns and increasing life expectancy, many companies have been replacing DB plans with DC plans. In 2012, for example, the Royal Bank of Canada stopped offering a DB plan to new hires. In 2011, Air Canada decided to offer only a DC plan to new employees, while its union (the Canadian Auto Workers [CAW]) wanted to continue with the DB plan (plus a DC top-up). Also in 2011, after being locked out for 11 months, the United Steelworkers Union in Hamilton agreed to allow U.S. Steel to implement a DC plan for new employees.

Supporters of DB plans argue that they should not be replaced. They point to the experience of countries like Australia, which abandoned DB plans but are now having problems (e.g., increased senior poverty rates). Financial expert Charles Ellis says that DB plans were one of the greatest financial services ever offered to employees, and their loss is a "social tragedy." He argues that retirees don't realize how much money they will need in retirement. For example, if a person has $150 000 in a retirement fund, that amount will only earn $6000 at a 4 percent withdrawal rate.

A hybrid DB/DC model has been proposed to resolve the tension between DB and DC pension plans. In the CAW/Air Canada dispute, for example, a Target Benefit Pension Plan (TBPP) was proposed. Under this system, an expected (target) benefit is defined and the contribution that is necessary to get such a benefit is calculated. Since the investment environment regularly changes, each year a "new" expected benefit is communicated to workers. The benefit is not guaranteed, but rather rises and falls depending on returns that can be earned in financial markets.

Critical Thinking Questions

1. In your own words, explain the advantages and disadvantages of DB and DC pension plans.

2. Consider the following statement: *Given low investment returns and increased life expectancy, a defined contribution plan is really the only type of pension that is financially feasible for companies.* Do you agree or disagree with the statement? Defend your reasoning.

The **Canada Pension Plan** provides income to retired individuals to help them supplement personal savings, private pensions, part-time work, and so forth. It is funded through employee and employer taxes that are withheld from payroll. In 2012, the Canada Pension Plan surplus rose to $152.8 billion.[41] Many companies also provide pensions for employees, but there is a lot of debate about the form that pensions should take (see the boxed insert entitled "Defined Benefit vs. Defined Contribution Pension Plans").

Workers' compensation covers individuals who suffer a job-related illness or accident. Employers bear the cost of workers' compensation insurance. The exact premium is related to each employer's past experience with job-related accidents and illnesses. For example, a steel company might pay $20 per $100 of wages, while an accounting firm might pay only 10 cents per $100 of wages.

Optional Protection Plans

Another major category of employee benefits consists of various optional protection plans. Health insurance has become the most important type of coverage and has expanded in recent years to include vision care, mental health services, dental care, and prescription drugs. Employee prescription drug plan costs are doubling about every five years, and companies are increasingly concerned about their ability to offer this kind of coverage.[42] Pension liabilities are also a problem.

Paid Time Off

Paid vacations are usually periods of one, two, or more weeks during which an employee can take time off from work and continue to be paid. Most organizations vary the amount of paid vacation with an individual's seniority, but some companies are reducing the time required to qualify for paid vacations. At Carlson Wagonlit Travel Canada, employees get four weeks of paid vacation after working at the company for just five years. Formerly, 10 years of service was required.[43]

Another common paid time off plan is sick leave. This benefit is provided when an individual is sick or otherwise physically unable to perform his or her job. Most organizations allow an individual to accumulate sick time according to a schedule, such as one sick day per month. Sometimes an organization will allow an employee to take off a small number of days simply for "personal business." This benefit is usually called personal leave. Occasions might include funerals, religious observances, weddings, birthdays, or simply personal holidays. The Catholic Children's Aid Society, for example, provides its child protection workers with time off when they need it because the workers face high-stress situations.[44] Some companies go even further and offer their employees paid or unpaid sabbaticals to help them rejuvenate themselves and increase their enthusiasm for their job.

Other Types of Benefits

There are many other benefits (often called perquisites, or perks) that companies can offer to employees.

Cafeteria-Style Benefit Plans

Most benefit programs are designed for all employees in an organization. Although the exact benefits may vary according to the employee's level in the organization, within those levels plans are generally "one size fits all." In contrast, **cafeteria-style benefit plans** allow employees to choose the benefits they really want. Under these plans, the organization typically establishes a budget, indicating how much it is willing to spend, per employee, on benefits. Employees are then presented with a list of possible benefits and the cost of each. They are free to put the benefits together in any combination they wish. Employees at Toyota's Cambridge, Ontario, plant are given the

Canada Pension Plan Provides income to retired individuals to help them supplement personal savings, private pensions, part-time work, and so forth.

workers' compensation Mandated insurance that covers individuals who suffer a job-related illness or accident.

cafeteria-style benefit plans A flexible approach to providing benefits in which employees are allocated a certain sum to cover benefits and can "spend" this allocation on the specific benefits they prefer.

opportunity once each year to restructure their benefit packages. They can give more weight to dental coverage if they have young children, or to life insurance or disability coverage, depending on their circumstances.[45]

The Legal Context of HRM

L06 Describe some of the key legal issues involved in *hiring*, *compensating*, and *managing* workers.

HRM is heavily influenced by federal and provincial law, and managers must be aware the most important and far-reaching areas of HR regulation. These include equal employment opportunity, comparable worth, sexual harassment, employee safety and health, and retirement.

Equal Employment Opportunity

equal employment opportunity regulations Regulations to protect people from unfair or inappropriate discrimination in the workplace.

The basic goal of all **equal employment opportunity regulations** is to protect people from unfair or inappropriate discrimination in the workplace. Note that discrimination in itself is not illegal. Whenever one person is given a pay raise and another is not, or when one person is hired and another is not, the organization has made a decision to discriminate. As long as the basis for this discrimination is purely job related (made, for instance, on the basis of performance or qualifications) and is applied objectively and consistently, the action is legal and appropriate. Problems arise when distinctions among people are not job related. In such cases, the resulting discrimination is illegal.

Anti-Discrimination Laws

Canadian Human Rights Act Ensures that any individual who wishes to obtain a job has an equal opportunity to apply for it.

When recruiting, firms must be careful not to violate anti-discrimination laws. The key federal anti-discrimination legislation is the **Canadian Human Rights Act** of 1977. The goal of this act is to ensure that any individual who wishes to obtain a job has an equal opportunity to compete for it. The act applies to all federal agencies, federal Crown corporations, any employee of the federal government, and business firms that do business interprovincially.

The Canadian Human Rights Act prohibits a wide variety of practices in recruiting, selecting, promoting, and dismissing personnel. The act specifically prohibits discrimination on the basis of age, race and colour, national and ethnic origin, physical handicap, religion, gender, marital status, or prison record (if pardoned). Some exceptions to these blanket prohibitions are permitted. For example, discrimination will not be charged if a blind person is refused a position as a train engineer, bus driver, or crane operator. Likewise, a firm will not be charged with discrimination if it does not hire a deaf person as a telephone operator or as an audio engineer.

bona fide occupational requirement When an employer may choose one applicant over another based on overriding characteristics of the job.

These situations are clear cut, but many others are not. For example, is it discriminatory to refuse women employment in a job that routinely requires carrying objects that weigh more than 50 kilograms? Difficulties in determining whether discrimination has occurred are sometimes dealt with by using the concept of **bona fide occupational requirement**. This means that an employer may choose one person over another based on overriding characteristics of the job in question. If a fitness centre wants to hire only women to supervise its women's locker room and sauna, it can do so without being discriminatory because it has established a bona fide occupational requirement.

The Canadian Human Rights Commission carries out enforcement of the federal act. The commission can either respond to complaints from individuals who believe they have been discriminated against, or it can launch an investigation on its own if it has reason to believe that discrimination has occurred. During an investigation, data is gathered about the alleged discriminatory behaviour, and if the claim of discrimination is substantiated, the offending organization or individual may be ordered to compensate the victim.

Each province has also enacted human rights legislation to regulate organizations and businesses operating in that province. These provincial regulations are similar in spirit to the federal legislation, but there are many minor variations from province to province. All provinces prohibit discrimination on the basis of race, national or ethnic origin, colour, religion, sex, and marital status, but some do not address such issues as physical handicaps, criminal record, or age. Provincial human rights commissions enforce provincial legislation.

The **Employment Equity Act** of 1986 addresses the issue of discrimination in employment by designating four groups as employment disadvantaged—women, visible minorities, Aboriginal people, and people with disabilities. These four groups contain six of every 10 individuals in the Canadian workforce, and it is estimated that their underemployment costs the Canadian economy around $50 billion each year.[46] Companies covered by the Employment Equity Act are required to publish statistics on their employment of people in the four designated groups.

Employment Equity Act
Federal legislation that designates four groups as employment disadvantaged—women, visible minorities, Aboriginal people, and people with disabilities.

In 2010, the Royal Bank of Canada received an award from Catalyst recognizing the bank's success in promoting diversity. For example, women at RBC now occupy nearly 40 percent of executive roles in the company, and this figure is growing.[47] Companies are increasingly making provisions for disabled employees. At Rogers Cablevision, a large workplace area was completely redesigned to accommodate workers who were either visually disabled or in wheelchairs. Special equipment was also installed—a large-print computer for workers with partial sight, and a device that allows blind workers to read printed materials.[48]

Comparable Worth

Comparable worth is a legal concept that means paying equal wages for jobs that are of comparable value to the employer. This might mean comparing dissimilar jobs, such as those of nurses and mechanics or secretaries and electricians. Proponents of comparable worth say that all the jobs in a company must be evaluated and then rated in terms of basic dimensions such as the level of skill they require. All jobs could then be compared based on a common index. People in different jobs that rate the same on this index would be paid the same. Experts hope that this will help to reduce the gap

comparable worth A legal concept that aims to pay equal wages for work of equal value.

The idea behind the concept of comparable worth is to pay equal wages for jobs that are of comparable value to the employer. This may require a comparison of jobs that are quite different.

between men's and women's pay. In a long-standing comparable worth dispute, the Supreme Court of Canada ruled that flight attendants at Air Canada—who had been trying for years to achieve pay equity with male-dominated groups of employees—could compare their pay with the pay of ground crews and pilots because all these employees work for the same company.[49]

Critics of comparable worth object on the grounds that it ignores the supply and demand aspects of labour. They say, for example, that legislation forcing a company to pay people more than the open market price for their labour (which may happen in jobs where there is a surplus of workers) is another example of unreasonable government interference in business activities. They also say that implementing comparable worth will cost business firms too much money. A study prepared for the Ontario Ministry of Labour estimated that it would cost approximately $10 billion for the public and private sectors in Ontario to establish equitable payment for jobs of equal value.

Sexual Harassment

sexual harassment Requests for sexual favours, unwelcome sexual advances, or verbal or physical conduct of a sexual nature that creates an intimidating or hostile environment for a given employee.

quid pro quo harassment Form of sexual harassment in which sexual favours are requested in return for job-related benefits.

hostile work environment Form of sexual harassment deriving from off-colour jokes, lewd comments, and so forth.

Within the job context, **sexual harassment** refers to requests for sexual favours, unwelcome sexual advances, or verbal or physical conduct of a sexual nature that creates an intimidating or hostile environment for a given employee. The Canadian Human Rights Act takes precedence over any policies that a company might have developed on its own to deal with sexual harassment problems.

Quid pro quo harassment is the most blatant form of sexual harassment. It occurs when the harasser offers to exchange something of value for sexual favours. A male supervisor, for example, might tell a female subordinate that he will recommend her for promotion or give her a raise in exchange for sexual favours. The creation of a **hostile work environment** is a subtler form of sexual harassment. A group of male employees who continually make off-colour jokes and lewd comments and perhaps decorate the work environment with questionable photographs may create a hostile work environment for a female colleague. Regardless of the pattern, the same rules apply: Sexual harassment is illegal, and the organization is responsible for controlling it. If a manager is found guilty of sexual harassment, the company is also liable because the manager is an agent of the company.

Verbal comments by prominent managers can be problematic. For example, when Neil French, a legendary advertising executive and the creative director of WPP Group PLC, gave a speech in Toronto, he was asked why there were so few women who were creative advertising directors. He replied that women focus too much on their family duties and this usually prevents them from succeeding in management. His comments caused quite a stir, and French soon resigned from his position. It is interesting to note that at that time the Toronto office of Ogilvy & Mather (a subsidiary of WPP) was headed by two creative directors, both of whom were women.[50]

Employee Safety and Health

Employee safety and health programs help to reduce absenteeism and turnover, raise productivity, and boost morale by making jobs safer and more healthful. Each province has developed its own workplace safety and health regulations, and in most of them, the Ministry of Labour appoints inspectors to enforce health and safety regulations. If the inspector finds a sufficient hazard, he or she has the authority to clear the workplace. Inspectors can usually arrive at a firm unannounced to conduct an inspection.

The Ontario Occupational Health and Safety Act illustrates current legislation in Canada. It requires all employers to ensure that equipment and safety devices are used properly. Employers must also show workers the proper way to operate machinery. At the job site, supervisors are charged with the responsibility of ensuring that workers use equipment properly. The Act also requires workers to behave appropriately on the job. Employees have the right to refuse to work on a job if they believe it is unsafe; a legal procedure exists for resolving any disputes in this area.

Some industrial work—for example, logging, construction, fishing, and mining—can put workers at risk of injury in obvious ways. But other types of work—such as typing or lifting—can also cause painful injuries. **Repetitive strain injuries (RSIs)** occur when workers perform the same functions over and over again. These injuries disable more than 200 000 Canadians each year and account for nearly half of all work-related time-loss claims.

repetitive strain injuries (RSIs) Injuries that occur when workers perform the same functions over and over again.

Retirement

Until the 1990s, Canadian courts generally upheld 65 as the mandatory retirement age, but most Canadian provinces have now abolished mandatory retirement. New rules took effect in December 2012, abolishing mandatory retirement at federally regulated employers like Air Canada.[51] Interestingly, workers are actually retiring *earlier* than they used to. In the late 1970s, the average retirement age in Canada was 65, but by 2009 it had dropped to 62.[52] A Statistics Canada study showed that "boomer" couples are unlikely to retire at the same time, with the woman often staying in the workforce longer than her husband.[53] Some managers fear that the abolition of mandatory retirement will result in less productive employees remaining at work after age 65, but research shows that employees who stay on the job past 65 are usually the most productive ones. However, workers over age 65 are nearly four times as likely to die from work-related causes as younger workers, and the health-care costs for older workers are double those for workers in their forties.[54]

New Challenges in the Changing Workplace

As we have seen throughout this chapter, HR managers face ongoing challenges in their efforts to keep their organizations staffed with effective workers. To complicate matters, new challenges arise as the economic and social environments of business change. We conclude this chapter with a discussion of several of the most important HRM issues facing business today: managing workforce diversity, managing knowledge workers, and managing contingent and temporary workers.

Discuss *workforce diversity*, the **L07** management of *knowledge workers*, and the use of *contingent* and *temporary workers* as important changes in the contemporary workplace.

Managing Workforce Diversity

One extremely important human resource challenge is the management of **workforce diversity**—the range of workers' attitudes, values, beliefs, and behaviours that differ by gender, race, age, ethnicity, physical ability, and other relevant characteristics. The situation for visible minorities is currently one of the most publicized aspects of diversity. Consider these facts:

workforce diversity The range of workers' attitudes, values, beliefs, and behaviours that differ by gender, race, age, ethnicity, physical ability, and other relevant characteristics.

- Seventy-three percent of the people who immigrated to Canada during the 1990s were visible minorities.

- By 2015, 20 percent of Saskatchewan's population will be Aboriginal.

- In 2001, approximately four million Canadians were visible minorities; by 2017, that number could increase to as much as 8.5 million.

- Visible minorities currently make up more than 40 percent of the population of Vancouver.

- By 2017, visible minorities will form more than 50 percent of the populations of Toronto and Vancouver.

- By 2017, 22 percent of the total Canadian population will be visible minorities.[55]

Many Canadian companies are actively pursuing the management of diversity. At Procter & Gamble Canada, employees come from 40 different countries and speak at least 30 different languages. Diversity is recognized through "affinity groups" such as the Women's Leadership Council, the French Canadian Network, the Asian Professional Network, the Christian Network, and the Jewish Network. The goal of these networks is to help employees feel comfortable about participating in corporate life and to act as a resource for employees who want insights about how to target specific markets.[56]

Western Union hires people who speak the language of their target market (individuals who want to send money back to relatives in their home country), and who know what it feels like to be an immigrant in Canada. This approach has yielded some interesting activities. In one area of Toronto, for example, customers who wanted to transfer money back to their family in the Philippines got a free loaf of Pan de Sal bread from a local Filipino baker.[57]

At the Royal Bank of Canada, the Diversity Leadership Council (DLC)—which is chaired by CEO Gordon Nixon—developed the RBC Diversity Blueprint, a three-year plan to support diversity within the company and in the external marketplace and community it serves.[58]

Organizations are increasingly recognizing that diversity can be a competitive advantage. By hiring the best people available from every group—rather than hiring from just one or a few groups—a firm can develop a higher-quality workforce. A diverse workforce can bring a wider array of information to bear on problems and can provide insights on marketing products to a wider range of consumers.

Managing Knowledge Workers

knowledge workers Workers who are experts in specific fields like computer technology and engineering and who add value because of what they know, rather than how long they have worked or the job they do.

Traditionally, employees added value to organizations because of what they did or because of their experience. In the "information age," however, many employees add value because of what they know.[59] These employees are usually called **knowledge workers**, and the skill with which they are managed is a major factor in determining which firms will be successful in the future. Knowledge workers, including computer scientists, engineers, and physical scientists, provide special challenges for the HR manager. They tend to work for high-tech firms and are usually experts in some abstract knowledge base. They often prefer to work independently and tend to identify more strongly with their profession than with the organization that pays them—even to the extent of defining performance in terms recognized by other members of their profession.

As the importance of information-driven jobs grows, the need for knowledge workers increases. But these employees require extensive and highly specialized training, and not every organization is willing to make the human capital investments necessary to take advantage of these employees. Even after knowledge workers are on the job, training updates are critical to prevent their skills from becoming obsolete. The failure to update such skills not only results in the loss of competitive advantage, it also increases the likelihood that knowledge workers will move to another firm that is more committed to updating their knowledge.

Knowledge Worker Management and Labour Markets

Because the demand for knowledge workers has been growing, organizations that need these workers must provide regular upward market adjustments to keep them. This is especially critical in areas in which demand is growing, as even entry-level salaries for these employees are skyrocketing. Once an employee accepts a job with a firm, the employer faces yet another dilemma. Once hired, workers are subject to the company's internal labour market, which is not likely to be growing as quickly as the external market for knowledge workers as a whole. Consequently, the longer an employee remains with a firm, the further behind the market his or her pay falls—unless, of course, it is regularly adjusted upward.

Prior to the start of the worldwide recession in 2008, some companies had to take extreme measures to attract and keep knowledge workers.[60] BP, for example, was paying starting petroleum engineers with undersea platform-drilling knowledge—not experience, just knowledge—salaries in the six figures, plus sign-on bonuses of over US $50 000. Even with these incentives, HR managers complained that they could not retain specialists because young engineers soon left to accept sign-on bonuses from competitors. The recession has reduced these extremes, but growth in demand for knowledge workers will continue.

Managing Contingent Workers

A **contingent worker** is a person who works for an organization on something other than a permanent or full-time basis. Categories of contingent workers include part-time workers, independent contractors (freelancers), on-call workers, temporary employees (usually hired through outside "temp" agencies), contract workers, and guest workers (foreigners who work in Canada for a limited time period).

> **contingent worker** A person who works for an organization on something other than a permanent or full-time basis.

Trends in Contingent Employment

Contingent employment is on the rise in Canada. Part-time employment in all categories was 7.75 percent higher in 2011 than in 2007.[61] In Canada, there is increasing demand for temporary workers in top management because the economic downturn has created a lot of turnover in top management. These "temps at the top" usually stay for a year or less until a permanent person is found.[62]

Throughout many organizations, the number of temporary or contingent workers is increasing. This allows human resource managers both scheduling flexibility and the opportunity to try potential permanent employees.

Management of Contingent Workers

The effective management of contingent workers requires consideration of three issues. First, careful planning must be done so that the organization brings in contingent workers only when they are actually needed and only in the quantity they are needed to complete necessary tasks. Second, the costs and benefits of using contingent workers must be understood. Many firms bring in contingent workers in order to reduce labour costs, but if contingent workers are less productive than permanent workers, there may be no gain for the organization. Third, contingent workers should be integrated into the mainstream activities of the organization as much as possible. This involves deciding how contingent workers will be treated relative to permanent workers. For example, should contingent workers be invited to the company holiday party? Should they have the same access to employee benefits as full-time workers do? Managers must develop a strategy for integrating contingent workers according to some sound logic and then follow that strategy consistently over time.[63]

MyBizLab

Capture more moments of true understanding. MyBizLab provides you with interactive study and practice tools directly related to this chapter's content. The new MyBizLab Study Plan Learning Path is designed to measure a full range of skills and provide remediation to give you what you need to master key chapter concepts. MyBizLab flexes to your unique learning needs. The result? Inspired learning, more success.

SUMMARY OF LEARNING OBJECTIVES

1. **Define *human resource management*, discuss its strategic significance, and explain how managers plan for human resources.** *Human resource management,* or *HRM,* is the set of organizational activities directed at attracting, developing, and maintaining an effective workforce. HRM plays a key strategic role in organizational performance. Planning for human resource needs entails several steps. Conducting a *job analysis* enables managers to create detailed, accurate *job descriptions* and *specifications*. After the analysis is complete, managers must forecast demand and supply for both the numbers and types of workers they will need. Then they consider steps to match supply with demand.

2. **Identify the issues involved in *staffing* a company, including *internal* and *external recruiting and selection*.** *Recruiting* is the process of attracting qualified persons to apply for jobs that an organization has open. *Internal recruiting* involves considering present employees for new jobs. This approach helps build morale and rewards an organization's best employees. *External recruiting* means attracting people from outside the organization to apply for openings. When organizations are actually selecting people for jobs, they generally use such selection techniques as application forms, tests, interviews, and other techniques. Regardless of what selection techniques are used, they must be valid predictors of an individual's expected performance on the job.

3. **Discuss different ways in which organizations go about developing the capabilities of employees and managers.** If a company is to get the most out of its workers, it must develop both those workers and their skills. Nearly all employees undergo some initial *orientation* process that introduces them to the company and to their new jobs. Many employees are given the opportunity to acquire new skills through various work-based and/or instructional-based programs.

4. **Explain ways in which organizations evaluate employee performance.** *Performance appraisals* help managers decide who needs training and who should be promoted. Appraisals also tell employees how well they are meeting expectations. Although a variety of alternatives are available for appraising performance, supervisors are most commonly involved. No matter who does the evaluation, however, feedback to the employee is very important. Managers can select from a variety of ranking and rating methods for use in performance appraisal.

5. **Discuss the importance of *wages* and *salaries*, *incentives*, and *benefit programs* in attracting and keeping skilled workers.** *Wages* and *salaries*, *incentives*, and *benefit packages* may all be parts of a company's *compensation* program. By paying its workers as well as or better than competitors, a business can attract and keep qualified personnel. *Incentive programs* can also motivate people to work more productively. Indirect

compensation also plays a major role in effective and well-designed compensation systems.

6. **Describe some of the key legal issues involved in** *hiring*, *compensating*, **and** *managing* **workers.** In hiring, compensating, and managing workers, managers must obey a variety of federal and provincial laws. *Equal employment opportunity* and equal pay laws forbid discrimination other than action based on legitimate job requirements. The concept of *comparable worth* states that equal wages should be paid for jobs that are of comparable value to the employer. Firms are also required to provide employees with safe working environments, as set down by the guidelines of provincial occupational health and safety acts. *Sexual harassment* is another key contemporary legal issue in business.

7. **Discuss** *workforce diversity*, **the management of** *knowledge workers*, **and the use of** *contingent* **and** *temporary workers* **as important changes in the contemporary workplace.** *Workforce diversity* refers to the range of workers' attitudes, values, beliefs, and behaviours that differ by gender, race, ethnicity, age, physical ability, and other relevant characteristics. Many firms think that having a diverse workforce creates a competitive advantage, so they have set a goal to have a workforce that reflects the growing diversity of the population as it enters the labour pool.

KEY TERMS

360-degree feedback (p. 254)
assessment centre (p. 250)
behaviour-based interviewing (p. 251)
benefits (p. 259)
bona fide occupational requirement (p. 262)
bonuses (p. 258)
cafeteria-style benefit plans (p. 261)
Canada Pension Plan (p. 261)
Canadian Human Rights Act (p. 262)
comparable worth (p. 263)
compensation (p. 256)
contingent worker (p. 267)
critical incident method (p. 257)
employee information systems (or skills inventories) (p. 246)
Employment Equity Act (1986) (p. 263)
employment insurance (p. 260)
equal employment opportunity regulations (p. 262)
external recruiting (p. 247)
forced distribution method (p. 254)
gain-sharing plans (p. 259)

graphic rating scale (p. 255)
hostile work environment (p. 264)
human resource management (HRM) (p. 244)
incentive programs (p. 258)
individual incentive plans (p. 258)
internal recruiting (p. 247)
internships (p. 247)
job analysis (p. 244)
job description (p. 244)
job evaluation (p. 257)
job specification (p. 244)
knowledge workers (p. 266)
lecture or discussion approach (p. 253)
management development programs (p. 253)
mentoring (p. 253)
merit pay plans (p. 256)
networking (p. 253)
off-the-job training (p. 252)
on-the-job training (p. 252)
orientation (p. 252)
pay survey (p. 257)
pay-for-knowledge (variable pay) (p. 258)

pay-for-performance (or variable pay) (p. 258)
performance appraisal (p. 254)
piece-rate incentive plan (p. 258)
profit-sharing plans (p. 258)
protection plans (p. 260)
quid pro quo harassment (p. 264)
recruiting (p. 246)
repetitive strain injuries (RSIs) (p. 265)
replacement chart (p. 245)
salary (p. 256)
sales commission (p. 258)
sexual harassment (p. 264)
simple ranking method (p. 254)
systematic job rotations and transfers (p. 252)
validation (p. 249)
vestibule training (p. 252)
video assessment (p. 250)
wages (p. 256)
work-based program (p. 252)
workers' compensation (p. 261)
workforce diversity (p. 265)
workforce management systems (p. 258)

QUESTIONS FOR ANALYSIS

1. Why is a good employee–job match important? Who benefits more: the organization or the employee? Explain.

2. Why is the formal training of workers so important to most employers? Why don't employers simply let people learn about their jobs as they perform them?

3. What are your views on drug testing in the workplace? What would you do if your employer asked you to submit to a drug test?

4. Have you or anyone you know ever suffered discrimination in a hiring decision? Did you or the person you know do anything about it?

5. What additional training do you think you are most likely to need when you finish school and start your career?

6. How is it possible for unemployment to be high while at the same time companies are complaining that they are having trouble hiring people?

APPLICATION EXERCISES

1. Interview an HR manager at a local company. Focus on a position for which the firm is currently recruiting applicants and identify the steps in the selection process. Do the steps match those shown in Figure 8.2? Why or why not?

2. Obtain a copy of an employment application. Examine it carefully and identify its strengths and weaknesses in terms of how useful it might be in making a hiring decision.

3. Survey 10 of your acquaintances and determine (a) how important benefits are to them as opposed to salary, (b) the benefits that are the least and most important in attracting and keeping workers, and (c) the extent to which their opinions about benefits versus salary will influence their choice of an employer after graduation.

4. Select a job currently held by you or a friend. Draw up a job description and job specification for the position.

BUILDING YOUR BUSINESS SKILLS

Getting Online for a Job

The Purpose of the Assignment

To introduce students to career-search resources available on the internet.

The Situation

If companies are on one side of the external staffing process, people looking for work are on the other. Companies need qualified candidates to fill job openings and candidates need jobs that are right for them. The challenge, of course, is to make successful matches. Increasingly, this matchmaking is being conducted on the internet. Companies are posting jobs in cyberspace, and job seekers are posting résumés in response. The number of job postings has grown dramatically in recent years. On a typical Sunday, you might find as many as 50 000 postings on the Monster board, a leading job site. With so many companies looking for qualified candidates online, it makes good business sense to learn how to use the system.

Assignment

Using internet career resources means locating job databases and preparing and posting a résumé. (You will therefore need access to the internet to complete this exercise.)

Step 1

Team up with three classmates to investigate and analyze specific job databases. In each case, write a short report describing the database (which you and other group members may use during an actual job search). Summarize the site and its features as well as its advantages, disadvantages, and costs. Start with the following sites and add others you may find on your own:

- Monster, www.monster.ca
- Careerbuilder.com, www.careerbuilder.ca
- CollegeGrad.com, www.collegegrad.com

Step 2

Investigate the job opportunities listed on the home pages of various companies. Consider trying the following:

- Air Canada, www.aircanada.com
- Dofasco, www.dofasco.ca
- Royal Bank, www.rbcroyalbank.com
- IBM, www.ibm.com/ca
- Walmart, www.walmart.ca
- McDonald's, www.mcdonalds.ca
- Bombardier, www.bombardier.ca

Write a summary of the specific career-related information you find on each site.

Step 3

Working with group members, research strategies for composing effective cyber résumés. The following websites provide some helpful information on formats and personal and job-related information that should be included in your résumé. They also offer hints on the art of creating a scannable résumé:

- Workopolis, www.workopolis.com
- CareerMag.com, www.careermag.com
- Two books by Joyce Lain Kennedy, *Electronic Job Search Revolution* and *Electronic Résumé Revolution*, also contain valuable information.

Step 4

Working as a group, create an effective electronic résumé for a fictitious college or university graduate looking for a first job. Pay attention to format, language, style, and the effective communication of background and goals.

Step 5

Working as a group, learn how to post your résumé online. (Do not submit the résumé you created for this exercise—it is, after all, fictitious!) The databases provided will guide you in this process.

Questions for Discussion

1. Why is it necessary to learn how to conduct an electronic job search? Do you think it will be more or less necessary in the years ahead?

2. Why do you think more computer-related jobs than non-technical jobs are posted online? Do you think this situation will change?

3. Why is it a waste of time to stylize your résumé with different fonts, point sizes, and centred headings?

4. What is the advantage of emailing your résumé directly to a company rather than applying for the same job through an online databank?

EXERCISING YOUR ETHICS: TEAM EXERCISE

Handling the Layoffs

The Situation

The CEO of a moderate-sized company is developing a plan to lay off some members of the company's workforce. He wants each manager to rank his or her employees according to the order in which they should be laid off, from first to last.

The Dilemma

One manager has just asked for help. He is new to his position and has little experience to draw from. The members of the manager's team are as follows:

- Tony Jones: white male, 10 years with the company, average performer, reportedly drinks a lot after work
- Amanda Wiggens: white female, very ambitious, three years with company, above-average performer, puts in extra time at work, is known to be abrasive when dealing with others
- George Sinclair: Aboriginal, 20 years with the company, average performer, was previously laid off but called back when business picked up
- Dorothy Henderson: white female, 25 years with company, below-average performer, has filed five sexual harassment complaints in last 10 years
- Wanda Jackson: black female, eight years with company, outstanding performer, is rumoured to be looking for another job

- Jerry Loudder: white male, single parent, five years with company, average performer
- Martha Strawser: white female, six years with company, excellent performer but spotty attendance, is putting husband through university

Team Activity

Assemble a group of four students. Your group has agreed to provide the manager with a suggested rank ordering of the manager's employees.

Action Steps

1. Working together, prepare this list, ranking the manager's employees according to the order in which they should be laid off, from first to last. Identify any disagreements that occurred along the way and indicate how they were resolved.
2. As a group, discuss the underlying ethical issues in this situation and write them down.
3. As a group, brainstorm any legal issues involved in this situation and write them down.
4. Do the ethical and legal implications of your choices always align?
5. Do the ethical and performance implications of your choices always align?

Go to MyBizLab for additional cases and exercise material.

CONCLUDING CASE 8-1

Behaviour-Based Interviewing

Interviewing job candidates is a long-standing practice in companies, but it is clear that interviewing often does not yield critical information that recruiters need to make good hiring decisions. One of the key problems is the types of questions that are asked in interviews. Often they take the form of "What are your strengths and weaknesses?" or "What kind of communication skills do you have?" Candidates who are good talkers (but maybe not such good performers) can do well in interviews but not perform well on the job. Dissatisfaction with traditional interview questions has led to the development of behaviour-based interviewing, which emphasizes action-oriented questions that require interviewees to describe what they have actually done when confronted with certain situations.

Behaviour-based interviewing assumes that a person's past behaviour is a good predictor of their future behaviour. It therefore assesses the behaviours of individuals as they have dealt with difficult and/ or important job situations in the past, and then assumes that these behaviours are a good indicator of how the person will react to similar job situations in the future. As noted in the chapter, this approach can be used to test for technical skills, management skills, and individual

characteristics. Typical questions that interviewers ask in behaviour-based interviewing are as follows:

- Think of a time when you had to deal with a customer who you thought was being unreasonable. How did you deal with that person?
- Tell me about the most unpopular decision you have ever made. What did you do when you found out that your decision was unpopular?
- Think of a time when you had to cope with a major change in your job. What did you do?
- Think of a time when you had to work with a person who was not "pulling their weight." What did you do?
- Tell me about a time when you worked effectively under pressure.
- Think of a time when you had to achieve consensus on a work team but encountered unexpected resistance. What did you do to facilitate the reaching of consensus?

Inexperienced candidates may not be able to adequately answer these questions because they haven't yet dealt with these situations in their career. Further behaviour-based questions—such as "Think about a time when you were in over your head on a job and tell me what you did to resolve that problem"—can be asked to determine whether the person is creative and has good problem-solving abilities. But an experienced person who cannot answer these questions is another story entirely; in those cases, the interviewer is likely to make a "no hire" decision.

Behaviour-based interviewing requires the interviewer to first identify the characteristics, skills, and behaviours that are important in the job that needs to be filled. This can be done by carefully observing current employees who excel in their jobs, and then identifying the key behaviours that are necessary for effectiveness. The interviewer then constructs open-ended questions that will determine if the interviewee possesses those characteristics, skills, and behaviours. The overall goal is to find out what it would be like working with the candidate on a daily basis.

Behaviour-based interviewing is becoming more common because companies are facing increasingly competitive environments. Since these competitive environments often lead to downsizing, it is important to determine which individuals are capable of high performance. There is also more emphasis on working in teams, and that means increased importance for interpersonal skills. These changing work situations have motivated companies to be much more focused in their hiring because they want workers who are more skilled and motivated than previously.

The increasing use of behaviour-based interviewing means that you are likely to be exposed to it at some point in your job search. What should you do to prepare for a behaviour-based interview? The main thing is to think about the job you are interviewing for and the skills that will be required to do it. Try to tell an interesting story (from a previous paid or volunteer position) that succinctly describes a situation you faced, the actions you took, and the outcome that resulted from your actions. If the outcome was good, the interviewer will likely be favourably impressed with your logical thinking and actions. If the outcome wasn't so good, you can indicate what you learned from the experience and how that experience will benefit your new employer.

Be sure to outline the specifics of the situation, how you dealt with it, what happened as a result of your decision, and what you learned from it. It is important to be able to communicate things about *you*. The best way to answer the interviewer's questions is to use the *SAB* acronym: describe the situation (S), the actions you took that made a difference (A), and how the situation benefited from your actions (B).

Also, reviewing the job posting and job description before your interview will help you develop a list of skills that are required for the job; you can then match them to your own when speaking with the interviewer.

Questions for Discussion

1. There seem to be many advantages to behaviour-based interviewing. Are there disadvantages as well? Explain.
2. Why is behaviour-based interviewing becoming so common?
3. Consider the following statement: *Behaviour-based interviewing sounds like a good idea because it forces interviewees to describe their actual behaviour. Realistically, however, it probably won't work as well as expected because people who are good talkers will always be able to present themselves well, even if they are not very good performers.* Do you agree or disagree with the statement? Explain your reasoning.

CONCLUDING CASE 8-2

Employee Recruiting and Networking Online

A major shift in the way businesses operate has been evident since the inception of the internet. Perhaps the largest shift has been seen in the way human resource issues are approached. Countless social networking sites, such as Facebook, LinkedIn, and Twitter, have been developed for interaction and networking; even Monster and Workopolis are climbing aboard. This has ultimately changed the way prospective employees and employers job- and people-search. Whether you are a company seeking the right employee to fit into your corporate culture or an employee looking for the right position, knowing how to navigate the various human resource sites can make all the difference.

"It's not enough anymore just to post a job vacancy on Monster.com, CareerBuilder.com, Craigslist.com, or other online job boards. Employers are bombarded with thousands of résumés from unqualified applicants when they post on big boards. As the online social networking world is expanding, there are better ways to recruit superior employees," says Susan Heathfield of About.com.

Active engagement in social media networking is a key part of any emerging human resource strategy. Many sites offer different tools and benefits that cater to specific industries, topics, regions, and countries. Companies that are hiring and prospective employees will reap benefits from having a presence in social media sites. As a prospective employee, it is important to establish your online brand and let others understand who you are, what expertise you have, and other relevant information, because such information can be used to establish your career path.

For employers, social media goals should be an integral part of developing and implementing a business strategy. According to Heathfield. these goals include (but are not limited to) building, expressing, and strengthening the company's brand; networking with those interested in your business (e.g., customers and suppliers), building community, developing connections over time, and establishing "a company presence on significant social media sites."

With these goals, however, comes the need to implement policies that businesses may find challenging, but that are critical nonetheless. These typically include such things as monitoring all employee interactions, blogs, and posts, as well as time spent on such sites. The benefits of developing such policies outweigh the cost.

In the end, social media tools make HRM processes more efficient and effective because employers and job seekers alike can do advanced and distinctive searches in terms of positions, skills, location, education, and so on. Perhaps the days of piled-high résumés and applications are a thing of the past!

Questions for Discussion

1. What are the advantages and disadvantages of using online recruitment tools? Address the issue of online recruitment from the perspective of both managers and prospective employees.

2. What are the costs businesses might incur when relying on online recruitment? Are there ways that organizations can avoid these costs?

3. Refer to the chapter opening case ("Millennials on the March") and explain how different workers (Gen Xers, baby boomers, and Millennials) might react to online recruitment sites.

Understanding Labour–Management Relations

After reading this chapter, you should be able to:

1. Trace the *evolution of unions* and discuss *trends in unionism* in Canada.

2. Describe the *major laws governing labour–management relations*.

3. Describe union *certification and decertification processes*.

4. Identify the steps in the *collective bargaining process*.

5. Explain what happens when bargaining fails.

Hard Hits in Professional Sports

WHEN people think of labour disputes, they often think of modestly paid production workers going on strike at a factory as they attempt to improve their economic situation. But labour disputes also occur in situations where workers are highly paid. The most obvious example of this is professional sports. The average working person can only dream of getting paid as much as a professional athlete, yet all professional athletes in the four major professional sports in North America—hockey, baseball, football, and basketball—belong to unions. This is interesting, given that only 16 percent of private sector workers in Canada belong to unions, and only 8 percent in the United States.

Professional athletes go on strike just like other private-sector workers do. In hockey, for example, the National Hockey League Players Association (NHLPA) went on strike in 1992, and players were locked out in 1994 and again in 2004. The latter lockout lasted from September 2004 to April 2005 and was the first time that an entire season was lost in

a major professional sport. In baseball, the Major League Baseball Players Association (MLBPA) went on strike from August 1994 to April 1995 after failing to negotiate a new collective agreement with team owners. As a result, post-season play, including the World Series, was cancelled. Many businesses that count on baseball—including broadcasters, advertisers, retailers, and restaurants—suffered economic losses when games were not played. In basketball, the National Basketball Players Association (NBPA) was locked out from July 1998 to January 1999 and the season was shortened by 50 games. There were also shorter lockouts in 1995 and 1996. In 2011, the season began two months late due to another labour dispute, and a full schedule was not played.

In football, the National Football League Players Association (NFLPA) went on strike in 1982 and 1987. During the 1987 strike, team owners hired replacement players for a few games until the dispute was settled. In 2011, another strike/lockout threat loomed. Problems

began in September 2010, when NFLPA representative DeMaurice Smith warned that a lockout was likely coming in March 2011. The main area of dispute was how to divide up the $9.4 billion in annual revenue that the league takes in. The NFL wanted to cap 2011 salaries for each of the 32 teams at $141 million (for a total of $4.51 billion), while players wanted the cap set at $151 million (for a total of $4.83 billion). There were also other issues in dispute, including the league's personal conduct policy, drug testing policy, pension funds, and disability plans.

On March 11, 2011, the players decertified their union and then filed an antitrust suit against the NFL. The suit asked for an injunction to prevent the owners from locking out the players. For its part, the NFL filed a complaint with the National Labor Relations Board claiming that the union was not bargaining in good faith and that the decertification was an attempt by the NFLPA to avoid its bargaining responsibilities. NFL officials then released details of the negotiations, which included a

financial analysis claiming that the union leaders had sacrificed millions of dollars of pay for players when the parties were actually pretty close to agreement. NFLPA representatives countered that the two sides weren't as close as the NFL claimed.

On March 12, 2011, the owners locked out the players after the collective agreement had expired. All off-season workouts and off-season pay ended, and the two sides dug in to prepare for a lengthy battle. NFL team owners said they had set aside money in case the 2011 season was cancelled, but that comment led the NFLPA to claim that the NFL owners had a premeditated plan to lock out the players. On April 25, a circuit court judge ruled that the lockout should be lifted to protect the players from damages. On May 16, however, a federal appeals court ruled that the lockout could remain in force because it did not grow out of a labour dispute (since the players

were no longer represented by a union). The players were not impressed with this logic. During this period, multiple days of court-ordered mediation also took place as owners and players continued to negotiate in an attempt to reach a new agreement. But no significant progress was evident.

As negotiations wore on, more than 100 non-playing staff members at seven NFL clubs had their salaries cut or were laid off until the labour dispute was settled. For example, the Buffalo Bills made across-the-board cuts for salaried employees ranging from 20 to 25 percent. As the weeks passed, pressure to reach an agreement increased. Then suddenly events began moving rapidly. The first positive news came on July 20, when rumours began circulating that the players might give tentative approval to the most recent proposal made by the NFL owners. The players' group executive committee and team reps met for 10 hours

one day to carefully look over the proposal. The NFL owners group also met to see if all owners were in agreement with the proposed terms. The owners approved the proposal on July 21. On July 25, the players voted to approve the owners' proposal.

The new 10-year agreement gave owners 53 percent of league revenues and players 47 percent (the old agreement had a 50–50 split). A $120 million cap was set for 2011. The agreement meant that NFL clubs could start signing 2011 draft picks and free agents, and that training camps could start. But some players worried that the short time available before pre-season games began would mean that players would not be in shape, and that the product the NFL provided for customers might not be up to its normal standards, at least for a while. ◆

HOW WILL THIS HELP ME?

By reading and understanding the material in this chapter, you'll gain insights into why employees at some companies decide to join a union, why conflict sometimes exists between managers and unions, and the influence that unions have on the operations of unionized companies. As an *employee*, you'll find useful information that will help you decide whether or not you wish to join a union, and as a *manager* you'll understand your responsibilities in dealing with unionized employees.

The Development of Canadian Labour Unions

LO1 Trace the *evolution of unions* and discuss *trends in unionism* in Canada.

labour union A group of individuals working together to achieve shared job-related goals, such as higher pay, shorter working hours, more job security, greater benefits, or better working conditions.

labour relations The overall process of dealing with employees who are represented by a union.

collective bargaining The process by which union leaders and managers negotiate specific terms and conditions of employment for workers who are represented by unions.

Over 2000 years ago, the Greek poet Homer wrote, "There is a strength in the union even of very sorry men." There were no labour unions in Homer's time, but his comment is an effective expression of the rationale for unions. A **labour union** is a group of individuals working together to achieve shared job-related goals, such as higher pay, shorter working hours, more job security, greater benefits, or better working conditions.[1] **Labour relations** refers to the overall process of dealing with employees who are represented by a union. **Collective bargaining** is the process by which union leaders and managers negotiate specific terms and conditions of employment for workers who are represented by unions.

The labour movement was born with the Industrial Revolution, which also gave birth to a factory-based production system that carried with it enormous economic benefits. Job specialization and mass production allowed businesses to create ever-greater quantities of goods at ever-lower costs. But there was also a dark side, as some owners treated their workers as simply resources to be deployed, with little or no regard for their well-being. Employees often worked 60 hour weeks, pay was minimal, there was no job security, workers received few benefits, and safety standards were virtually non-existent. Mining and textile companies employed large numbers of children at poverty wages, and if people complained, they were fired. Unions developed because they forced management to listen to the complaints of all their workers rather than just those of the few who were brave enough to speak out.

The earliest evidence of labour unions in Canada comes from the Maritime provinces early in the nineteenth century. These unions typically included individuals with a specific craft (e.g., printers, shoemakers, barrel makers). Most of these unions were small and had only limited success. However, they laid the foundation for the rapid increase in union activity that occurred during the late nineteenth and early twentieth centuries.

A succession of labour organizations sprang up and just as quickly faded away during the years 1840–70. In 1873, the first national labour organization was formed—the Canadian Labour Union. By 1886, the Knights of Labour (a U.S.-based union) had over 10 000 members in Canada. The Canadian labour movement began to mature with the formation of the Trades and Labour Congress (TLC) in 1886. The TLC's purpose was to unite all labour organizations and to work for the passage of laws that would ensure the well-being of the working class.

The growth of labour unions began in earnest early in the twentieth century, but sometimes disputes arose within the ranks of labour. For example, there was concern that U.S.-based unions would have a detrimental effect on Canadian unions, so the Canadian Federation of Labour was formed in 1908 to promote national (Canadian)

The Canadian Labour Congress (CLC), which was formed in 1956, brought the majority of unionized workers in Canada into one organization.

unions over U.S. unions. These and other disputes—such as how communists in the movement should be handled—often led to the creation of rival union organizations that competed for membership. By 1956, these disputes had been largely resolved, and the two largest congresses of affiliated unions—the Trades and Labour Congress and the Canadian Congress of Labour—merged to form the Canadian Labour Congress. This amalgamation brought approximately 80 percent of all unionized workers into one organization. Table 9.1 highlights some of the important events in Canadian labour history.

TABLE 9.1 Some Important Dates in Canadian Labour History

1827	First union formed: boot- and shoemakers in Quebec City	1940	ACCL and the Canadian CIO Committee unite to form the Canadian Congress of Labour (CCL)
1873	Canadian Labour Union formed; objective was to unite unions across Canada	1956	TLC and CCL merge to form the Canadian Labour Congress (CLC)
1879	First coal miners union in North America formed in Nova Scotia	1982	Founding convention of Canadian Federation of Labour (CFL)
1902	Formation of the National Trades and Labour Congress (became the Canadian Federation of Labour [CFL] in 1908); purpose was to promote national unions instead of international ones	1985	Formation of United Auto Workers of Canada; formerly part of international UAW
		1997	Strike of primary and secondary school teachers in Ontario
1919	Winnipeg General Strike	2004–05	National Hockey League players locked out; entire season lost
1921	Confédération des Travailleurs Catholiques du Canada (CTCC) organized by the Roman Catholic clergy in Quebec; goal was to keep French-Canadian workers from being unduly influenced by English-speaking and American trade unions	2005–09	United Food and Commercial Workers union tries to organize workers at various Walmart locations across Canada; Walmart aggressively resists; each group wins some battles and loses others
1927	All-Canadian Congress of Labour (ACCL) formed; objective was to achieve independence of the Canadian labour movement from foreign control	2009	Members of the Canadian Auto Workers union agree to significant wages cuts as part of a package designed to keep Chrysler and General Motors in business
1939	TLC expels industrial unions; Canadian Congress of Industrial Organization (CIO) Committee formed	2011	National Football League players locked out
		2012	Federal government prohibits strike by Air Canada pilots

Unionism Today

Unions in Canada today face both opportunities and potentially serious threats. This is evident when we look at trends in union membership, trends in union-management relations, and the future of unions.

Trends in Union Membership

Although 4.3 million Canadian workers were members of unions in 2011, union membership as a proportion of the non-agricultural workforce (called *union density*) has stagnated. Less than one-third of workers in Canada belong to unions (see Figure 9.1).[2] The highest rate of unionization is found in Newfoundland and Labrador (38.1 percent), and the lowest rate in Alberta (22.0 percent). The public sector is heavily unionized (71.1 percent), but the private sector is not (16.0 percent).[3] Rates of unionization also vary across occupations. In education, for example, over 70 percent of workers belong to unions, but in food services only 8.1 percent of workers are unionized.[4] Unionization rates also vary widely across countries. In France, only 9 percent of workers are unionized, but in Sweden 82 percent belong to unions.[5]

Many years ago, unions routinely won certification votes. But in recent years, they have experienced less success. Union members used to be predominantly white males in blue-collar jobs, but today's workforce is increasingly composed of women and ethnic minorities, and because these two groups have a weaker tradition of union affiliation, their members are less likely to join unions when they enter the workforce. The workforce is also increasingly employed in the service sector, which traditionally has been less heavily unionized. Employers have also become more aggressive in pursuing anti-unionization activities. For example, Japanese auto manufacturers that have set up shop in Canada have avoided unionization efforts by the Canadian Auto Workers (CAW) by providing a work environment in which employees are allowed to participate and be actively involved in plant management.

FIGURE 9.1

Union members as a proportion of the non-agricultural workforce.

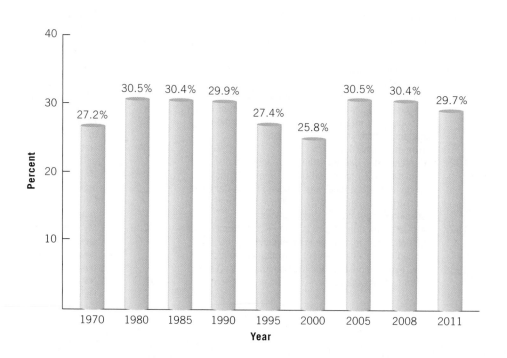

Trends in Union–Management Relations

The problems that have been experienced by unions have caused some significant changes in union–management relations. Not so long ago, most union–management bargaining was very adversarial, with unions making demands for dramatic improvements in wages, benefits, and job security. But with organizational downsizing, a decade of low inflation, and uncertainties that have persisted since the recession of 2008, unions are now able to achieve only modest improvements in wages and benefits. A common goal of union strategy is therefore to preserve what has already been won. For example, unions know that companies have an incentive to relocate jobs to lower-wage foreign countries, so unions have to work hard to keep jobs in Canada and thus maintain job security for their members. The boxed insert entitled "Public Sector Unions" describes some interesting developments in public sector unionism.

MANAGING IN TURBULENT TIMES

Public Sector Unions

In 2011, there was a showdown between public-sector unions and the state of Wisconsin when governor Scott Walker introduced a bill that proposed to end collective bargaining for state workers (except for base wage rates), required unions to hold recertification votes annually, and curtailed the practice of withholding union dues from employee paycheques. Despite noisy protests by state workers, the bill passed. Other U.S. states—Ohio, Michigan, and Indiana—were also considering changes to their labour legislation.

Are these developments relevant for Canadian labour unions? Some observers say "no," because Canadian society has a more favourable view of unions (for example, 71 percent of public-sector workers are unionized in Canada, but only 37 percent are in the U.S.). They note that when the province of B.C. tried to throw out a collective agreement with health care workers in order to save money, the Supreme Court of Canada ruled that collective bargaining in the public sector is a constitutional right. But other experts say the U.S. developments are relevant, and point out that unionization rates in northern U.S. states are similar to those in Ontario, and much lower in the southern states. In other words, the real dividing line is not the Canadian–U.S. border, but the Mason-Dixon line (the line often viewed as separating the "northern" and "southern" cultures in the U.S.). Even some union officials are concerned. For example, Mark Ferguson, president of a Toronto branch of the Canadian Union of Public Employees, says that the public hates unions. And Ken Georgetti, president of the Canadian Labour Congress, says that unions are increasingly seen as "out for themselves" and no longer have the respect of the general public in Canada.

Critics of unions say that taxpayers are increasingly unhappy with what they perceive to be the "rich" compensation and benefits that are available to public sector workers. For example, federal workers usually have a defined benefit pension that, after 35 years, pays 70 percent of the worker's highest five-year earning average. By contrast, in the private sector, two-thirds of workers don't even have a pension. Pressure is already being put on Canadian public sector unions. In Toronto, garbage collection has been privatized to reduce costs and to avoid problems like the 39-day strike of garbage collectors a few years ago. Also, the provincial premier is trying to push through legislation that takes away the right to strike from Toronto transit workers. Attempts are being made in Saskatchewan to "rebalance" the ratio of unionized to non-unionized government workers, and Quebec wants to reduce pension payments to public-sector retirees.

Critical Thinking Questions

1. Will the pressures that are being put on public-sector unions in the United States also develop in Canada? Support your conclusion.

2. Consider the following statement: *The rich benefits that members of public-sector unions receive must be reduced. It is not fair that public sector workers are given pensions that are so much better than private-sector workers.* Do you agree or disagree with the statement? Defend your answer.

Today, unions must co-operate with employers if both companies and unions are to survive and prosper. The goal is to create win-win partnerships in which managers and workers share the same goals: profitability, growth, and equitable rewards for everyone. Even in those sectors of the economy where unions remain quite strong—most notably in the automobile and steel industries—unions have changed their tactics. In the automobile industry, Buzz Hargrove, former president of the Canadian Auto Workers, urged members of the union bargaining team to come up with new ideas for improving quality and productivity so that Canadian factories will be more attractive for new investment.[6]

The Future of Unions

Unions will face some serious challenges in the next few years. In the *private sector*, companies have become much more aggressive when negotiating with unions. For example, in 2012, Electro-Motive Canada threatened to move production from its London, Ontario plant to the United States if workers didn't agree to a 50 percent wage cut.[7] The company said its Canadian workers had become too expensive, and it had to keep its labour costs down in order to compete in global markets. More generally, the high value of the Canadian dollar has made the wages of all Canadian workers rise relative to those in other countries.

In the *public sector*, the federal and provincial governments are looking for ways to save money because of large budget deficits, so there will likely be disputes between public sector unions and governments regarding changes to wages and pensions that will reduce budget deficits. Critics claim that public-sector union workers receive better wages and richer pension plans than private-sector workers, and that taxpayers are stuck paying the bill for excessive public-sector labour costs.[8]

Unions are facing other challenges as well: the decline of the so-called "smoke-stack industries" (where union power was formerly very strong), the globalization of business (which has caused the movement of jobs to areas of the world with lower labour costs), and technological change (which often reduces the number of workers that are needed). Unions are responding to these challenges in a variety of ways. For example, in 2012 two of Canada's largest unions—the Canadian Auto Workers and the Communications, Energy and Paperworkers—held merger talks.[9]

The Legal Environment for Unions in Canada

LO2 Describe the *major laws governing labour–management* relations.

In the early twentieth century, there were many political and legal barriers to unionism, and the balance of bargaining power was very much in favour of the employer. Courts often ruled that unions were conspiring to restrain business activities, and employers viewed their employees' efforts to unionize as attempts to deprive the employers of their private property. Employers also felt that the employment contract should be between individual workers and the employer—not between the employer and employees as a group. As firms grew in size, the employer–employee relationship became much less direct and communication among owners, managers, and workers became more distant and formalized. These trends, together with mounting public concern about worker safety and health issues, resulted in several laws being passed that were designed to place workers on a more even footing with employers (see Table 9.2).

Constitution Act Divided authority over labour regulations between the federal and provincial governments.

The **Constitution Act** (originally the BNA Act), passed in 1867, has also affected labour legislation. This act allocates certain activities to the federal government (e.g., labour legislation for companies operating interprovincially) and other activities to individual provinces (labour relations regulations in general).

TABLE 9.2 History of Canadian Labour Legislation

Date	Legislation	Accomplishments/Goals
1900	Conciliation Act	• designed to help settle labour disputes through voluntary conciliation • first step in creating more favourable labour conditions
1907	Industrial Disputes Investigation Act	• compulsory investigation of labour disputes by a government-appointed board before any strike action (found to violate a provision of the British North America (BNA) Act)
1943	Privy Council Order 1003	• recognized the right of employees to bargain collectively • prohibited unfair management labour practices • established a labour board to certify bargaining authority • prohibited strikes and lockouts except in collective bargaining agreements (CBAs)

While unionized workers generally have the right to bargain collectively with management, there are some interesting exceptions. For example, the Ontario Agricultural Employees' Protection Act allows agricultural workers to join an association, but does not require employers to collectively bargain with the workers. In 2011, the Supreme Court of Canada ruled that the Act was valid.[10] Union leaders responded by saying they would ask the Ontario provincial government to give agricultural workers more protection, such as that mandated in the Ontario Labour Relations Act.[11]

Federal Legislation: The Canada Labour Code

The **Canada Labour Code**, which regulates the labour practices of firms operating under the legislative authority of parliament, has four main sections: fair employment practices; standard hours, wages, vacations, and holidays; safety of employees; and Canada industrial relations regulations.

Canada Labour Code Legislation that applies to the labour practices of firms operating under the legislative authority of parliament.

Fair Employment Practices. This section prohibits an employer from either refusing employment on the basis of a person's race or religion or using an employment agency that discriminates against people on the basis of their race or religion. These prohibitions apply to trade unions as well, but not to non-profit, charitable, and philanthropic organizations. Any individual who believes a violation has occurred may make a complaint in writing to Labour Canada. The allegation will then be investigated and, if necessary, an Industrial Inquiry Commission will be appointed to make a recommendation in the case. Since 1982, fair employment practices have been covered by the Canadian Human Rights Act; they are also covered by the Canadian Charter of Rights and Freedoms.

Standard Hours, Wages, Vacations, and Holidays. This section deals with a wide variety of mechanical issues such as standard hours of work (8-hour day and 40-hour week), maximum hours of work per week (48), overtime pay (at least one-and-a-half times the regular pay), minimum wages, equal wages for men and women doing the same jobs, vacations, general holidays, and parental leave. The specific provisions are changed frequently to take into account changes in the economic and social structure of Canada, but their basic goal is to ensure consistent treatment of employees in these areas.

Safety of Employees. This section requires that every person running a federal work project do so in a way that will not endanger the health or safety of any employee. It also requires that safety procedures and techniques be implemented to reduce the risk of employment injury. This section requires employees to exercise care to ensure their own safety; however, even if it can be shown that the employee did not exercise proper care, compensation must still be paid. This section also makes provisions for a safety officer whose duty is to assure that the provisions of the code are fulfilled. The safety officer has the right to enter any federal project "at any reasonable time."

Canada Industrial Relations Regulations.   The final major section of the Canada Labour Code deals with all matters related to collective bargaining.

Provincial Labour Legislation

Each province has enacted legislation to deal with the personnel practices covered in the Canada Labour Code. These laws vary across provinces and are frequently revised; however, their basic approach and substance is the same as that of the Canada Labour Code. Certain provinces may exceed the minimum code requirements on some issues (e.g., minimum wage). Each province also has a labour relations act. To give an indication of what these acts cover, the key provisions of the Ontario Labour Relations Act are briefly summarized below.

The Ontario Labour Relations Act

The Ontario Labour Relations Act is a comprehensive document dealing with the conduct of labour relations in that province.

- A trade union may apply at any time to the Ontario Labour Relations Board (OLRB) for certification as the sole bargaining agent for employees in a company.

- The OLRB has the right to call for a certification vote. If more than 50 percent of those voting are in favour of the trade union, the board certifies the union as the bargaining agent.

- Following certification, the union gives the employer written notification of its desire to bargain, with the goal being the signing of a collective agreement. The parties are required to begin bargaining within 15 days of the written notice.

- On request by either party, the minister of labour appoints a conciliation officer to confer with the parties and to help achieve a collective agreement. On joint request, the minister of labour can appoint a mediator.

- The parties may jointly agree to submit unresolved differences to voluntary binding arbitration. The decision of the arbitrator is final.

- Employers are required to deduct union dues from the union members and remit these dues directly to the union.

- Every agreement must include a mechanism for settling grievances—differences between the parties arising from interpretation, application, or administration of the collective agreement.

- If a person objects to belonging to a labour union because of religious beliefs, he or she is allowed to make a contribution equal to the amount of the union dues to a charitable organization.

- If a trade union is not able to negotiate a collective agreement with management within one year of being certified, any of the employees in the union can apply to the OLRB for decertification of the union.

- No employer can interfere with the formation of a union. The employer is, however, free to express an opinion about the matter.

- No employer shall refuse to employ an individual because he or she is a member of a trade union.

Union Organizing Strategy

Describe the union *certification and decertification* processes. **LO3**

A union might try to organize workers when a firm is trying to move into a new geographical area, or when some workers in a firm are members and the union wants to represent other workers, or when it is attempting to outdo a rival union, or when it wants to increase the number of workers who belong to the union. For example, the United Auto Workers has seen its membership drop sharply in recent years due to layoffs at companies like General Motors and Chrysler. In response, the UAW launched a campaign to unionize workers of foreign auto manufacturers like Toyota, Honda, Nissan, Hyundai, and Volkswagen. Whether this will be successful remains to be seen, but in the past, these efforts have failed.[12]

Over the past decade, one of the most visible organizing efforts has been conducted by the United Food and Commercial Workers (UFCW) at Walmart, but Walmart has aggressively fought every UFCW attempt. Until the mid-1990s, Walmart had never had a union in any of its stores in the United States, Canada, Puerto Rico, Argentina, Brazil, or Mexico. In 1996, management first began hearing rumours that the Canadian Auto Workers (CAW) union was approaching employees at the Windsor, Ontario, store about unionizing. During the organizing drive, there was much squabbling among employees, and when the certification vote was held, the workers voted 151–43 against joining the union. In spite of this, the Ontario Labour Relations Board (OLRB) certified the union as the employees' bargaining agent on the grounds that the company had intimidated employees during the membership drive. A first collective agreement was approved, but in April 2000, the union was officially decertified.[13]

More recently, each side has had both victories and defeats. In 2009, for example, the UFCW failed in its attempt to be certified as the bargaining agent for Walmart employees in Saguenay, Quebec, but in 2008, the Quebec Labour Relations Board certified the UFCW as the sole bargaining agent for about 150 workers at a Walmart store in Gatineau. That required Walmart to negotiate with the union regarding a collective agreement. In 2005, the UFCW was certified as the sole bargaining agent for nine tire and lubrication workers at another Walmart store in Gatineau. When the UFCW and Walmart failed to negotiate a collective agreement, an arbitrator imposed an agreement that raised workers' wages. But in 2008, Walmart closed the shop.[14]

Management often becomes aware of a union organizing effort through gossip from the company grapevine. For example, WestJet became aware of union plans to unionize its workers.[15] When management discovers that an organizing drive is underway, it may try to counteract it. However, management must know what it can legally do to discourage the union. In Quebec, McDonald's has been the target of union organizing drives at several of its restaurants. After a McDonald's restaurant in Saint-Hubert closed (when it appeared that the Teamsters union might be successful in getting certified as the bargaining agent for the employees), critics called for a government investigation into the possibility of unfair labour practices on the part of the company.[16]

Some creative (and controversial) tactics are being used by unions in the United States as they attempt to cope with declining membership. Two large unions—the Service Employees International Union and Unite Here—signed deals with several large employers giving those employers the right to designate which of their locations they will allow the unions to try to organize. If enough workers sign cards indicating a desire to join the union, the union will be certified as the bargaining agent. There are no secret-ballot elections as there normally are during an organizing campaign. The unions agree that if they are certified, they will not go on strike at these locations, and they will not make derogatory comments about the company. The company sites where these arrangements will be put in place are selected jointly by union and management. Union members have not been allowed to see the details of these agreements.[17]

Certifying a Union: An Example

Suppose that a union is trying to organize employees of a Manitoba company. If the union can show that at least 50 percent of the employees are members of the union, it can apply to the Manitoba Labour Board (MLB) for certification as the sole bargaining agent for the employees. During the process, there may be an issue regarding the right of different types of workers to join or not join the union. For example, supervisors may or may not be included in a bargaining unit along with non-management workers. The **bargaining unit** includes those individuals deemed appropriate by the province, and the MLB has final authority in determining the appropriateness of the bargaining unit. Professional and non-professional employees are generally not included in the same bargaining unit unless a majority of the professional employees wish to be included. Once the MLB has determined that the unit is appropriate, it may order a **certification vote**. If a majority of those voting are in favour of the union, it is certified as the sole bargaining agent for the unit.

The same law that grants employees the right to unionize also allows them to cease being represented by a union. **Decertification** is the process by which employees legally terminate their union's right to represent them. This happened during a labour dispute over job security and safety that arose at Goldcorp Inc.'s gold mine near Red Lake, Ontario, which led to a strike involving 100 workers. The strike was settled when workers agreed to decertify their union in return for severance pay that was four times the rate mandated by Ontario law.[18] In another case, the Manitoba Labour Board decertified Local 832 of the United Food and Commercial Workers for workers at the Hampton Inn & Suites in Winnipeg. The workers said they weren't getting value for the dues they were paying to the union.[19]

Types of Unions

There are two basic types of unions: craft and industrial. **Craft unions** are organized by crafts or trades—plumbers, barbers, airline pilots, and so forth. Craft unions restrict membership to workers with specific skills. In many cases, members of craft unions

bargaining unit Individuals grouped together for purposes of collective bargaining.

certification vote A vote supervised by a government representative to determine whether a union will be certified as the sole bargaining agent for the unit.

decertification The process by which employees legally terminate their union's right to represent them.

craft unions Unions organized by trades; usually composed of skilled workers.

This outcome of this certification vote will determine whether these workers at Michelin will be represented by the CAW.

work for several different employers during the course of a year. For example, many construction workers are hired by their employers at union hiring halls. When the particular job for which they are hired is finished, these workers return to the hall to be hired by another employer. Craft unions have a lot of power over the supply of skilled workers because a person who wants to become a member of a plumbers union, for example, must go through a training (apprenticeship) program. After sufficient training, the apprentice is qualified as a journeyman plumber.

Industrial unions are organized according to industries, for example, steel, auto, and clothing. Industrial unions include semi-skilled and unskilled workers and were originally started because industrial workers were not eligible to join craft unions. Industrial union members typically work for a particular employer for a much longer period of time than do craft union members. An industrial union has a lot of say regarding pay and human resource practices within unionized firms.

> **industrial unions** Unions organized by industry; usually composed of semi-skilled and unskilled workers.

The **local union** (or **local**) is the basic unit of union organization in a specific geographical area. A local of a craft union is made up of artisans in the same craft, whereas a local of an industrial union is made up of workers in a given industry or manufacturing plant. Thus, plumbers may be members of the local plumbers (a craft union), while truck drivers in that same area may be members of the Teamsters (an industrial union).

> **local union (or local)** The basic unit of union organization.

An **independent local union** is one that is not formally affiliated with any labour organization. It conducts negotiations with management only at a local level, and the collective agreement is binding at that location only. The University of Manitoba Faculty Association is an example of an independent local union. Table 9.3 lists the 10 largest unions in Canada.

> **independent local union** One not formally affiliated with any labour organization.

A **national union** has members across Canada, while an **international union** has members in more than one country. There are many national unions in Canada, including the Canadian Union of Public Employees, the National Railway Union, and the Canadian Airline Pilots Union. The United Steelworkers of America is an international union made up of locals in the United States and Canada. National unions represent about two-thirds of unionized Canadian workers and international unions about one-third.[20]

> **national union** A union with members across Canada.
>
> **international union** A union with members in more than one country.

TABLE 9.3 The Top 10 Unions in Canada, 2011

	Union	Membership
1.	Canadian Union of Public Employees (CLC)	611 827
2.	National Union of Public and General Employees (CLC)	340 000
3.	United Food and Commercial Workers Canada (CtW/CLC)	245 327
4.	United Steel, Paper and Forestry, Rubber, Manufacturing, Energy, Allied Industrial and Service Workers International Union (AFL-CIO/CLC)	230 700
5.	Public Service Alliance of Canada (CLC)	192 080
6.	National Automobile, Aerospace, Transportation and General Workers Union of Canada (CAW Canada) (CLC)	191 500
7.	Fédération de la santé et des services sociaux (CSN)	122 193
8.	Communications, Energy, and Paperworkers Union of Canada (CLC)	114 893
9.	Teamsters Canada (CtW/CLC)	113 851
10.	Service Employees International Union (CtW/CLC)	92 781

Union Security

The greatest **union security** exists in the **closed shop**, where an employer can hire only union members. For example, a plumbing or electrical contractor who hires workers through a union hiring hall can hire only union members. In a **union shop**, an employer may hire non-union workers even if the employer's current employees are unionized. When new workers are hired, however, they must join the union within a stipulated period of time (usually 30 days). In an **agency shop**, all employees for whom the union bargains must pay union dues, but they need not join the union. This compromise between the union shop and the open shop is called the Rand formula after the judge who proposed it. In an **open shop**, an employer may hire union and/or non-union labour. Employees need not join a union nor pay dues to a union.

Collective Bargaining

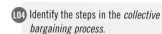 Identify the steps in the *collective bargaining process.*

When people think about collective bargaining, they usually think about the point at which a formal contract is signed between a union and a company. But collective bargaining is an ongoing process, and includes all of the time that is spent developing the agreement *before* it is signed, as well as all the time required to administer the contract *after* it has been signed.

Reaching Agreement on the Contract's Terms

The bargaining cycle begins when union leaders meet with management representatives to negotiate the terms of a new collective agreement. By law, both parties must negotiate "in good faith," but as we saw in the opening case, it can be difficult to determine exactly what that means. When each side has presented its demands, the focus is on identifying the *bargaining zone*. This concept is shown in Figure 9.2. For example, although an employer may initially offer no pay raise, it may expect to grant a raise of up to 6 percent. Likewise, the union may initially demand a 10 percent pay raise while expecting to accept a raise as low as 4 percent. The bargaining zone, then, is the region between 4 and 6 percent. Some compromise is usually reached between these levels, and the new agreement is submitted for a ratification vote by union membership.

FIGURE 9.2

The bargaining zone.

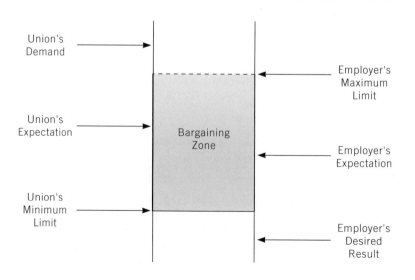

Representatives of labour and management negotiate as they attempt to reach an agreement on a labour contract. Here, members of the UAW and managers representing Ford are negotiating the terms of a collective agreement. Negotiations have become more difficult in many industries in recent years as the economy has struggled to recover from the recession of 2008.

Sometimes this process goes quite smoothly. At other times, however, the two sides have difficulty reaching agreement. For example, in 2011, members of the Air Canada Pilots Association voted to reject a tentative offer for a new collective agreement with Air Canada. They didn't like Air Canada's plan for starting a new low-cost airline that would pay lower wages than union members were currently getting. Union and management bargainers then had to return to the bargaining table and come up with a new collective agreement that the pilots would approve.[21] Air Canada also got involved in a dispute during bargaining with its sales and service agents when it wanted to increase the minimum retirement age by five years, and wanted to give new hires a defined contribution pension instead of a defined benefit pension.[22]

Very fundamental differences may be evident when labour and management try to develop a new collective agreement. At the Great Blue Heron Charity Casino in Port Perry, Ontario (which is operated by the Mississaugas of Scugog Island First Nation), a collective agreement was in place with the Canadian Auto Workers union that covered 1000 casino workers (very few of whom were band members). The band wanted to replace the collective agreement with its own labour agreement, which would have denied employees the right to strike. The band felt that it could drop the collective agreement with the CAW because it had Aboriginal treaty and self-government rights. When it tried to implement the new labour agreement, the CAW filed a grievance. Eventually, the Ontario Court of Appeal rejected the band's arguments on the grounds that the band had not proven that a labour code was part of its tradition, nor that it was integral to its ancestral culture.[23]

Contract Issues

The labour contract can address an array of different issues. *Mandatory items* are matters over which both parties must negotiate if either requests changes. This category includes wages, working hours, and benefits. *Permissive items* may be negotiated if both parties agree. For example, a union demand for veto power over the promotion of managerial personnel would be a permissive bargaining item. Most contract issues arise from demands that unions make on behalf of their members. The main issues that typically are evident during labour–management negotiations are compensation, benefits, and job security.

Compensation

Historically, the most common issue has been compensation (although recently job security has become very important). Unions generally want their employees to earn higher wages, so the union tries to negotiate increases in hourly wages for all members during subsequent years of the contract. One tool for securing wage increases is a **cost-of-living adjustment (COLA)**. Most COLA clauses tie future raises to the *consumer price index* (CPI), a government statistic that reflects changes in consumer purchasing power. The premise is that as the CPI increases by a specified amount during a given period of time, wages will automatically increase. COLA clauses are not as common as they used to be. **Wage reopener clauses** allow wage rates to be renegotiated at certain times during the life of the contract. A long-term agreement will be more acceptable to a union if management agrees to renegotiate the wage component every two years.

Benefits

Unions typically want employers to pay all or most of the costs of various kinds of insurance for employees. Other benefits commonly addressed during negotiations include retirement benefits, pensions, working conditions, and the cost of supplementary health care (prescription drugs, eye care, dental care, etc.). Pension benefits have become particularly controversial in recent years (see Chapter 8). Health-care benefits are also an issue since the cost of health care is rapidly increasing.

Job Security

Job security is an important agenda item in bargaining sessions. In some cases, demands for job security result in a promise by the company that it will not move to another location. In others, a contract may dictate that if the workforce is reduced, seniority will be used to determine which employees keep their jobs. The recession that started in 2008 meant that unions had to pay more attention to job security than to getting big wage increases. But private-sector unions have had limited success in preserving jobs, partly because so many businesses are outsourcing production to countries where labour costs are cheaper. For example, Gildan Activewear outsources much of its production to low-wage countries in the Caribbean.

Other Issues

Other possible issues might include such things as working hours, overtime policies, rest periods, differential pay plans for shift employees, the use of temporary workers, grievance procedures, and allowable union activities (dues collection, union bulletin boards, and so forth).

When Bargaining Fails

An **impasse** occurs when, after a series of bargaining sessions, management and labour are unable to agree on a first-time contract or a contract to replace an agreement that is about to expire. Both union and management may try various tactics to support their demands until the impasse is resolved.

Union Tactics

Possible union actions include *strikes*, *picketing*, *boycotts*, and *work slowdowns*.

Strikes. A **strike** occurs when employees temporarily walk off the job and refuse to work. Strikes triggered by impasses over mandatory bargaining items are called *economic strikes*, even if they occur over non-economic issues such as working hours.

cost-of-living adjustment (COLA) A contract clause specifying that wages will increase automatically with the rate of inflation.

wage reopener clause A contract clause that allows wage rates to be renegotiated at preset times during the life of the contract.

impasse Occurs when, after a series of bargaining sessions, management and labour are unable to agree on a first-time contract or a contract to replace an agreement that is about to expire.

strike Employees temporarily walk off the job and refuse to work.

Most strikes in Canada are economic strikes. During a strike, workers are not paid by the company (but they do receive some strike pay from the union), and the company is often unable to produce its normal range of products and services. In 2011, postal workers went on strike until they were forced back to work by government legislation. At Montreal-based Tembec Holdings, workers were on strike for three months before management and union negotiators were able to fashion a new collective agreement.[24]

Sometimes a union is not permitted to strike. In 2011, for example, Air Canada flight attendants were not allowed to go on strike after the Labour Minister referred the dispute to the Labour Board.[25] The Province of Nova Scotia passed a law that forbids strikes by health care workers in that province.[26] Hospital workers cannot strike in Alberta, PEI or Ontario, either. Strikes may also be illegal if the union does not go through certain necessary steps before striking.

E-BUSINESS + SOCIAL MEDIA SOLUTIONS

Tweet, Post: You're Fired

Today we are dealing with an unprecedented generational gap. Historically there has always been some tension as the next generation enters the workplace in mass numbers. However, the gap between Generation Y (Millennials) and their Baby Boomer and Generation X bosses and experienced colleagues has been heightened by a technology gap. Employee–manager relationships can be complicated at times but when you add the additional element of social media tools like Facebook and Twitter, you inevitably have a new outlet for potential misunderstandings and incidents. While the dangers are particularly clear for younger workers who have embraced this technology, there is a cautionary note for all workers looking for a new powerful outlet for their complaints.

There have been many legal cases involving the use of social media and the termination of employees in the past few years. Let's take a look at a few of them.

- Two employees at a car dealership near Vancouver, BC, were fired after they posted extremely negative comments about their employer and the managers at the location. The two workers complained about the legitimacy of the decision but the British Columbia Labour Relations Board supported the dismissal.
- An employee at Chrysler, who was hired as a social media consultant, was fired after he used the F-word in one of his official company tweets when describing how people drive in the motor city. The account had 8000 followers. Although the offensive words were quickly removed by officials, the message was quickly "retweeted" across the site and ultimately the employee paid for it with a work termination.

- In another famous case, Canadian broadcaster Damian Goddard was fired after he made a negative comment about same-sex marriage on his Twitter account. He says he was shocked when he was called in to the office and was informed that he was being fired for a tweet sent from his private account, on his own time. He has since filed a human rights complaint and says that the firing was unjust on the grounds that the action goes against freedom of religion and freedom of speech.

Employer interests seem to be well protected in such cases in Canada. Up to this point the labour tribunals have supported the management position and indicated that such acts violate the legal "duty of loyalty." Of course, this is a new and quickly evolving frontier in labour relations that is complicated by union-management contracts, outdated legislation, and inevitable groundbreaking new rulings. In addition, Canadian employers appear to be in a much stronger position than their American counterparts that have already seen decisions overturned due to stronger "freedom of speech" legislation down south.

So pay attention to what you write in your social media posts because your employer may already be doing so.

Critical Thinking Questions

1. Do you believe that employers should have the right to terminate an employee based on tweets and Facebook posts?

2. Consider the following statement: *Canadian legislation is hurting the right to freedom of speech of its citizens with these types of rulings.* Do you agree with the statement? Defend your answer.

sympathy strikes (also called secondary strikes) Strikes initiated by another labour organization.

wildcat strikes Strikes that are not authorized by the union and that occur during the life of a contract.

Sympathy strikes (also called **secondary strikes**) occur when one union strikes in sympathy with a strike initiated by another union. **Wildcat strikes**—those that are not authorized by the union and that occur during the life of a contract—deprive strikers of their status as employees and thus of the protection of labour laws. Air Canada ground crews engaged in a wildcat strike in 2012 that caused hundreds of flights to be delayed or cancelled.[27]

Unions are more reluctant to use the strike weapon than they used to be. One reason is that more and more workers are in profit-sharing plans, meaning that they receive a portion of company profits. Going on strike has a negative effect on profits, so workers are hurting themselves if they go on strike. Other reasons are the decline in union power, the bad publicity generated by strikes, and the fact that technology and globalization mean that companies can easily replace highly paid but low-skilled workers.[28]

picketing A tactic of labour unions in which members march at the entrance to the company with signs explaining their reasons for striking.

Picketing. As part of (or instead of) a strike, unions faced with an impasse may picket their employer. **Picketing** involves having workers march at the entrance to the company with signs explaining their reasons for striking. During the labour dispute between the Telecommunications Workers Union (TWU) and Telus Corp., for example, union workers picketed the company. Telus responded by getting an injunction to prevent picketers from blocking access to the property.[29]

boycott Union members agree not to buy the product of the firm that employs them.

Boycotts. A **boycott** occurs when union members agree not to buy the products of the firm that employs them. Workers may also urge other consumers to shun their firm's products.

work slowdown Workers perform their jobs at a much slower pace than normal.

Work Slowdowns. In a **work slowdown**, workers perform their jobs at a much slower pace than normal. A variation is the "sickout," during which large numbers of workers call in sick. In 2012, a large number of Air Canada pilots called in sick, and this disrupted 70 flights. The Canada Industrial Relations Board ruled that the pilots' behaviour was illegal and ordered the pilots to resume working. Individual pilots who ignored the ruling were subject to fines of $1000 per day.[30]

Members of the Association of Flight Attendants - CWA picket outside Northwest Arilines (NWA) during a strike.

Management Tactics

Management can respond to an impasse using a variety of tactics, including *lockouts, strikebreakers, plant closures, contracting out,* and forming *employers' associations.*

Lockouts. **Lockouts** occur when employers physically deny employees access to the workplace. Management might lock workers out, for example, if they fear that workers will damage expensive equipment. A lockout is illegal if it is used as a weapon to give the firm an economic advantage in the bargaining process (for example, if sales are poor and management simply wants to avoid a buildup of inventory). But it may be difficult to prove the company is using the lockout as a weapon. In 2011, workers at United States Steel's Hamilton plant were locked out for 11 months before finally ratifying a new collective agreement.[31] In 2012, Electro-Motive Canada (London, Ontario) and Rio Tinto (Alma, Quebec) locked out their workers after collective bargaining agreements expired and the parties were unable to reach agreement on a new contract. The Electro-Motive plant was eventually closed and production was moved elsewhere, causing 400 workers to lose their jobs.[32] More workers are now being locked out during collective bargaining because times are tough and companies know that workers want to keep their jobs, even if it means having to agree to accept reduced wages and benefits.

Strikebreakers. Firms faced with a strike can hire temporary or permanent replacements (**strikebreakers**) to replace the striking employees. In 2011, Air Canada planned to use non-unionized employees to fill in for union workers if they went on strike.[33] The National Football League used replacement players during a strike back in 1987.

Plant Closures. In extreme cases, management may simply close down a plant if they cannot reach agreement with the union. After a long strike at a Versatile tractor plant in Winnipeg, the Manitoba Labour Relations Board fined the company $6 million for bargaining in bad faith. But management then closed the plant and all the workers lost their jobs.[34] Magna International also shut down one of its plants when a deal could not be reached with its union.[35]

Contracting Out. Some firms *contract out* work as a way to blunt the effect of the union. Instead of doing all the assembly work they used to do themselves, many firms now contract out work to non-union contractors. This lessens the impact the unions can have because it results in fewer union workers.

Employers' Associations. **Employers' associations** are groups of companies that get together to plan strategies and exchange information about how to manage their relations with unions. They are especially important in industries that have many small firms and one large union that represents all workers. Member firms sometimes contribute to a strike insurance fund. Such a fund can be used to help members whose workers have struck. They are similar in purpose to strike funds that are built up by unions. The British Columbia Maritime Employers Association—which includes 67 companies that employ longshoremen in Vancouver and other seaports in BC—is an example of an employers' association.

Conciliation, Mediation, and Arbitration

Rather than using their "weapons" on one another, labour and management can agree to call in a third party to help resolve the dispute. In **conciliation**, a neutral third party (the conciliator) helps the two sides clarify the issues that are separating them. The conciliator cannot impose a settlement on the disputing parties. In 2012,

lockout A tactic of management in which the firm physically denies employees access to the workplace to pressure workers to agree to the company's latest contract offer.

strikebreakers Individuals hired by a firm to replace workers on strike.

employers' associations Groups of companies that get together to plan strategies and exchange information about how to manage their relations with unions.

conciliation A neutral third party (the conciliator) helps the two sides clarify the issues that are separating them.

the Canadian Press asked the federal government to appoint a conciliator to help with negotiations with the Canadian Media Guild, whose contract expired at the end of 2011.[36] Also in 2012, Canadian Pacific Railway asked that a conciliator be assigned to help in the company's negotiations with its union regarding pension reform.[37]

mediation A method of settling a contract dispute in which a neutral third party is asked to hear arguments from both the union and management and to offer a suggested resolution.

In **mediation**, the neutral third party (a mediator) goes beyond conciliation and advises the disputing parties about specific steps they might take to reach a settlement. The mediator, however, cannot impose a settlement. In 2012, when the Air Canada Pilots Association received support from its members for a strike, a mediator was appointed to assist in the negotiations between Air Canada and the union in the hope of reaching a negotiated settlement without a strike occurring.[38]

voluntary arbitration A method of settling a contract dispute in which the union and management ask a neutral third party to hear their arguments and to issue a binding resolution.

In **voluntary arbitration**, the neutral third party (an arbitrator) imposes a settlement on disputing parties that have agreed to submit to outside judgment. In 2011, for example, a pension dispute between Air Canada and the Canadian Auto Workers was sent to an arbitrator for resolution. The arbitrator ruled in favour of the union's proposal for a hybrid pension plan that included elements of both defined benefit and defined contribution pension plans.[39] In some cases, arbitration is legally required to settle bargaining disputes. Such **compulsory arbitration** is typically used to settle disputes between government and public employees such as firefighters and police officers.

compulsory arbitration A method of settling a contract dispute in which the union and management are forced to explain their positions to a neutral third party, who issues a binding resolution.

Administering a Labour Agreement

Once a labour agreement has been reached, its details are written down in the form of a contract that is legally enforceable in the courts. Some issues are quite clear. For example, if the two sides agree that the company will increase wages by 2 percent per year over the next three years according to a prescribed schedule, then there is little opportunity for disagreement because wage increases can be mathematically calculated and union members will see the effects in their paycheques. However, other provisions may be much more prone to misinterpretation and conflicting perceptions.

Suppose, for example, that a labour contract specifies the process for allocating overtime assignments. Such strategies are often complex, and the employer may have to take into account a variety of factors, such as seniority, previous overtime allocations, the hours or days in which the overtime work is needed, and so forth. Now suppose that a factory supervisor is trying to follow the labour contract and offers overtime to a certain employee. This employee, however, indicates that before he or she can accept the overtime, it may be necessary to check with the individual's spouse or partner about other obligations and commitments. The supervisor may feel the pressure of a deadline and instead award the overtime opportunity to someone else. If the first employee objects to this course of action, he or she may file a complaint with the union.

shop steward A regular employee who acts as a liaison between union members and supervisors.

When such differences of opinion arise, the union member takes the complaint to the **shop steward** (a regular employee who acts as a liaison between union members and supervisors). The shop steward may advise the employee that the supervisor handled things properly, or the shop steward may agree with the employee. In the latter case, prescribed methods for pursuing the complaint are followed. These methods might include talking with the supervisor to hear the other side of the story and then providing for an appeal further up the hierarchy of both the union and the company. In some cases, mediation or arbitration may be tried. The overtime, for example, may be reassigned to the employee to whom it was first offered. Or the overtime may remain with the second employee while the first employee is also paid.

grievance A complaint by a worker that a manager is violating the terms of the collective agreement.

A **grievance** is a complaint by a worker that a manager has violated the terms of the collective agreement. Figure 9.3 shows a typical grievance procedure. The union generally promises not to strike over disputes about contract interpretation. In return, unions get the right to file grievances in a formal procedure that culminates in binding

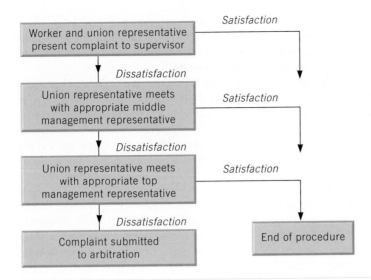

FIGURE 9.3

A typical grievance procedure.

arbitration. Most grievance arbitrations are about disputes regarding the discipline or discharge of employees, but safety issues are also a cause for arbitration in some industries.

Grievance situations can become very controversial. In 2008, members of the International Association of Machinists and Aerospace Workers (IAMAW) began wearing buttons with the message "Prepare to walk the line in '09" as the expiry date of their collective agreement neared. Air Canada management ordered workers to stop wearing the buttons when they were in view of Air Canada's customers. The union then filed a grievance, saying that the buttons were simply an attempt to promote solidarity among union members. The union also created a combative song, which was sung to the tune of Johnny Cash's famous hit "I Walk the Line."[40]

MyBizLab

Capture more moments of true understanding. MyBizLab provides you with interactive study and practice tools directly related to this chapter's content. The new MyBizLab Study Plan Learning Path is designed to measure a full range of skills and provide remediation to give you what you need to master key chapter concepts. MyBizLab flexes to your unique learning needs. The result? Inspired learning, more success.

SUMMARY OF LEARNING OBJECTIVES

1. **Explain why workers organize into *labour unions.*** The Industrial Revolution and the emergence of a factory-based production system made many workers dependent on continuing factory employment, where abuses such as minimal pay, long workdays and workweeks, unsafe working conditions, and even child labour were common. Individuals had little recourse in rectifying problems. By organizing into *labour unions,* however, workers were able to act collectively to improve work conditions. Most importantly, acting as a group, they can engage in *collective bargaining* for higher wages, greater benefits, or better working conditions.

2. **Trace the evolution of unions and discuss *trends in unionism in Canada.*** The first unions in Canada were formed in the early nineteenth century in the Maritime provinces. Many labour organizations sprang up and then faded away during the nineteenth century. In the twentieth century, unions began to develop in earnest. In 1943, *Privy Council Order 1003* gave unions the right to bargain collectively with employers.

    Since the mid-1970s, labour unions in Canada have experienced increasing difficulties in attracting new members. While millions of workers still belong to labour unions, union membership as a percentage of the total workforce has been stagnant for many years. Unions recognize that they do not have as much power as they once held and that it is in their own best interests, as well as the best interests of the workers they represent, to work with management instead of against it. Bargaining perspectives have also altered in recent years.

3. **Describe the** *major laws governing labour–management relations.* Privy Council Order 1003 gave unions the right to collectively bargain in Canada. The *Constitution Act of 1867* allows the federal government to pass labour legislation (such as the *Canada Labour Code*) for companies that operate interprovincially and allows the provincial governments to pass legislation (such as the Ontario Labour Relations Act) for companies that operate in only one province.

4. **Describe the union** *certification and decertification processes.* If a union can show that a certain percentage (usually 50 percent) of employees of a company are members of the union, it can apply to a provincial labour relations board for *certification* as the sole bargaining agent for the

employees. A certification vote is then held. If a majority of the employees are in favour of the union, it is certified. In order for a union to be decertified, employees must vote to do so.

5. **Identify the steps in the** *collective bargaining process.* Once certified, the union engages in *collective bargaining* with the organization. The initial step in collective bargaining is reaching agreement on a *labour contract.* Contract demands usually involve wages, job security, or management rights.

Both labour and management have several tactics that can be used against the other if negotiations break down. Unions may attempt a strike or a boycott of the firm or may engage in a work slowdown. Companies may hire replacement workers (strikebreakers) or lock out all workers. In extreme cases, mediation or arbitration may be used to settle disputes. Once a contract has been agreed upon, union and management representatives continue to interact to settle worker grievances and interpret the contract.

KEY TERMS

agency shop (p. 286)
bargaining unit (p. 284)
boycott (p. 290)
Canada Labour Code (p. 281)
certification vote (p. 284)
closed shop (p. 286)
collective bargaining (p. 276)
compulsory arbitration (p. 292)
conciliation (p. 291)
Constitution Act (p. 280)
cost-of-living adjustment (COLA) (p. 288)
craft unions (p. 284)

decertification (p. 284)
employers' associations (p. 291)
grievance (p. 292)
impasse (p. 288)
independent local union (p. 285)
industrial unions (p. 285)
international union (p. 285)
labour relations (p. 276)
labour union (p. 276)
local union (or local) (p. 285)
lockout (p. 291)
mediation (p. 292)
national union (p. 285)

open shop (p. 286)
picketing (p. 290)
shop steward (p. 292)
strike (p. 288)
strikebreakers (p. 291)
sympathy strikes (or secondary strikes) (p. 290)
union security (p. 286)
union shop (p. 286)
voluntary arbitration (p. 292)
wage reopener clause (p. 288)
wildcat strikes (p. 290)
work slowdown (p. 290)

QUESTIONS FOR ANALYSIS

1. Why did it take so many years for the union movement to mature in Canada?

2. Why do you think the unionization rate in the public sector is so much higher than it is in the private sector? Do you think this will change in the foreseeable future? Explain your reasoning.

3. The proportion of the Canadian workforce that is unionized has been nearly constant for many years. Why hasn't the proportion increased or decreased?

4. Workers at Ford, General Motors, and Chrysler are represented by the Canadian Auto Workers. Why are automobile workers at Toyota and

Honda—who are doing exactly the same kind of work—not unionized?

5. What are the implications for management of a closed shop, a union shop, and an agency shop?

6. What impact will intense global competition and low wage rates in some foreign countries have on the future viability of unions in Canada?

APPLICATION EXERCISES

1. Interview the managers of two local companies, one unionized and one non-unionized. Compare the wage and salary levels, benefits, and working conditions of workers at the two firms.

2. With your instructor playing the role of management and a student playing the role of a union organizer, role-play the processes involved in trying to form a union.

3. Consider the following statement: *In a union shop, newly hired employees must join the union within 30 days of starting work. Forcing workers to join a union in order to keep their job is unreasonable and violates their freedom of choice. Workers should be allowed to decide whether they want to join a union or not. Union shops should therefore not be allowed.* Do you agree or disagree with this statement? Explain your reasoning.

4. Suppose that you are a manager in a non-unionized company. You have just heard a rumour that some of your workers are discussing forming a union. What would you do? Be specific.

BUILDING YOUR BUSINESS SKILLS

A Little Collective Bargaining

The Purpose of the Assignment

To encourage students to understand why some companies unionize and others do not.

The Situation

You've been working for the same non-union company for five years. Although there are problems in the company, you like your job and have confidence in your ability to get ahead. Recently, you've heard rumblings that a large group of workers want to call for a union election. You're not sure how you feel about this, because none of your friends or family members are union members.

Assignment

Step 1

Come together with three other "co-workers" who have the same questions as you do. Each person should target four companies to learn their union status. Avoid small businesses; instead, choose large corporations such as Canadian National Railways, General Motors, and Walmart. As you investigate, answer the following questions:

- Is the company unionized?
- Is every worker in the company unionized or only selected groups of workers? Describe the groups.
- If a company is unionized, what is the union's history in that company?
- If a company is unionized, what are the main labour–management issues?

- If a company is unionized, how would you describe the current status of labour–management relations? For example, is it cordial or strained?
- If a company is not unionized, what factors are responsible for its non-union status?

To learn the answers to these questions, contact the company, read corporate annual reports, search the company's website, contact union representatives, or do research on a computerized database.

Step 2

Go to the website of CUPE (www.cupe.ca) to learn more about the current status of the union movement. Then, with your co-workers, write a short report about the advantages of union membership.

Step 3

Research the disadvantages of unionization. A key issue to address is whether unions make it harder for companies to compete in the global marketplace.

Questions for Discussion

1. Based on everything you have learned, are you sympathetic to the union movement? Would you want to be a union member?

2. Are the union members you spoke with satisfied or dissatisfied with their union's efforts to achieve better working conditions, higher wages, and improved benefits?

3. What is the union's role when layoffs occur?

4. Based on what you have learned, do you think the union movement in Canada will stagnate or thrive in the years ahead?

EXERCISING YOUR ETHICS: TEAM EXERCISE

What Should We Do?

The Situation

Danielle Yu works for a manager at a medium-sized, non-union company that is facing a serious union organizing campaign. Her boss, Curt Yaeger, who is determined to keep the union out, has just given Yu a list of things to do to thwart the efforts of the organizers. For example, he has strongly suggested that Yu do the following:

- Whenever Yu learns about a scheduled union meeting, she should schedule a "worker appreciation" event at the same time. He wants Yu to offer free pizza and hold a barbecue and to give cash prizes (winners have to be present to receive the prize).
- Look at the most recent performance evaluations of the key union organizers and terminate any of them who may have a low performance evaluation.
- Make an announcement that the firm is seriously considering new benefits such as on-site childcare, flexible work schedules, telecommuting options, and exercise facilities. Yu knows that the firm is indeed looking into these benefits, but she also knows that the boss is really not that enthusiastic about these ideas.

The Dilemma

When Yu questioned the ethics—and even the legality—of some of these tactics, Yaeger responded by saying, "Look, this is war." He went on to explain that he was seriously concerned that a union victory might lead to increased wages for employees that would, in turn, increase the company's costs and reduce its competitiveness. That could force the company to outsource production activities and, in the extreme, lead to a shutdown of the company's entire Canadian operation. He noted that a number of Canadian companies have been outsourcing significant amounts of work in the past few years. Yaeger concluded by saying that he was really looking out for the employees, even if he had to play hardball to help them. Yu realizes that there is some truth to what Yaeger says about job losses, but she is not convinced that this is the way to proceed.

Team Activity

Assemble a group of four students and assign each group member to one of the following roles:

- Danielle Yu
- Curt Yaeger
- a worker who is thinking about joining the union
- a shareholder of the company

Action Steps

1. Before discussing the situation with your group, and from the perspective of your assigned role, what do you think should be done in this situation?
2. Before discussing the situation with your group, and from the perspective of your assigned role, what are the underlying ethical issues in this situation? Write down the issues.
3. Gather the group together and reveal, in turn, each member's ideas regarding the situation.
4. Appoint someone to record the main points of agreement and disagreement within the group. How do you explain the results? What accounts for the disagreements?
5. From an ethical standpoint, what does your group conclude is the most appropriate action that should be taken? (Note: You may find that the concepts of utility, rights, justice, and caring that were discussed in Chapter 3 are helpful in making your decision.)

Go to MyBizLab for additional cases and exercise material.

CONCLUDING CASE 9-1

Unions and the Right to Work

There has been a debate for many years about the pros and cons of unionization, and how unionization affects companies and the individual workers in those companies. Here is a brief summary of the key points in the debate:

ARGUMENTS IN FAVOUR OF UNIONS	ARGUMENTS AGAINST UNIONS
In a democracy, the majority rules. If the majority of workers want a union, the union should represent all workers. Workers who don't pay union dues are "free-riding" on the backs of workers who do pay dues.	Individual workers should not be forced to join a union just because a majority of their work colleagues have voted for a union. Individuals should have freedom of choice.
Management of a company must be responsible for collecting dues from union members and remitting them to the union. If the union had to spend a lot of time keeping track of who had paid their dues and who hadn't, and then had to chase down those who hadn't, the union would not have time to represent its members.	Management should not have to spend time and money deducting union dues from employees and remitting those dues to the union. This is essentially guaranteeing revenue to the union. The company has no such guarantee of revenue, and neither should the union. The union should be responsible for collecting dues from its members.
Management has too much power—i.e., they can lay off large numbers of employees or shut down operations at certain locations in order to intimidate union members who are worried about job security.	Unions have too much power—i.e., they can shut down the operations of an entire company just by going on strike.
If we do away with unions, it will not take long before management once again starts taking advantage of its employees.	Given the variety of government support programs that exist (for example, employment insurance, pensions, safety laws, etc.), unions are no longer necessary to protect workers' rights.
If union members are unhappy with their union, they can decertify it.	If union members feel that the union is not doing much for them, they have to just keep on paying union dues anyway.

Critics of unions have recently been promoting something called worker-choice laws (called "right-to-work" laws in the United States). These laws allow each individual worker to decide whether they want to join a union, *even if a majority of their fellow workers have voted in favour of having a union*. In the United States, 23 states have right-to-work laws (Indiana passed such a law in 2012), and nine other states are considering right-to-work legislation.

No Canadian province currently has a right-to-work law, and union membership is mandatory if the majority of workers in a company vote to join a union. Six provinces and the federal government have adopted something called the Rand formula, which requires all employees at unionized companies to pay union dues (although they are not required to formally join the union). The Rand formula prevents "free-riding" by employees who do not want to join the union and pay dues, but who presumably will gain when the union collectively bargains for employees. Four provinces

(including Alberta) have not adopted the Rand formula. In provinces where the Rand formula is law, workers at a company that is unionized must either become members of the union or pay union dues, even if they don't want to. The Rand formula means that joining the union (or paying union dues) is a condition of employment in a unionized workplace. In the United States, it is illegal to require union membership as a condition of employment.

In 2009, the United Food and Commercial Workers (UFCW) union took Alberta-based Old Dutch Foods before the Alberta Labour Relations Board (ALRB). Old Dutch was an "open shop"; that is, workers did not have to join the union or pay union dues. The union wanted the ALRB to rule that Alberta's lack of a Rand formula constituted a violation of the "freedom of association" guarantee in the Canadian Charter of Rights and Freedoms. The ALRB ruled in favour of the union. After that ruling was handed down, 29 Old Dutch employees sought "party status" to comment on the ruling, but the UFCW opposed granting the workers that status. The workers thus came into conflict with their own union at their workplace. They felt that the union was not representing their interests, and the union was unhappy that the workers took that position.

In cases that are similar to the Alberta case, the Supreme Court of Canada has ruled that freedom of association includes the freedom to *not* associate. Critics of unions argue that the ALRB was essentially saying that the constitution *forced* individual employees to either join a union or to pay union dues. This view contrasts sharply with the view in Europe, where the European Court of Human Rights has said that mandatory union membership violates the freedom of association that is guaranteed by the European Convention on Human Rights (47 European countries no longer have "closed shops").

There are practical implications to the debate about right-to-work laws, since Canada has lost thousands of manufacturing jobs to various

U.S. states with such laws. In 2010, for example, Swedish appliance maker Electrolux announced that it was closing its manufacturing plant in a Montreal suburb and moving it to Memphis, Tennessee. The move meant that 1200 jobs were lost in Canada and gained in Memphis. Southern U.S. states have generally been very aggressive in persuading companies to move to the South. The publisher of the Randle Report says that right-to-work laws in the South will appeal to companies operating in a high-cost union environment. Industry analysts note that companies like Kia, Boeing, and Volkswagen have located new facilities in Southern states because of their right-to-work laws (wages are usually lower in right-to-work states).

Right-to-work laws shift power away from unions and toward individual workers; they also reduce unionization rates. Overall, the unionization rate in Canada is about 30 percent. It is 15 percent in U.S. states without worker-choice laws, and just 8 percent in states with worker-choice laws. But beyond these rather simple facts, there is much controversy about the impact of right-to-work laws. Supporters point to various research studies that show, for example, that during the past decade (1) five million workers moved out of states without worker-choice laws and into states with worker-choice laws, (2) states with worker-choice laws had lower unemployment rates and higher rates of economic growth, and (3) between 2001 and 2006, the economies of states with right-to-work laws grew by 3.4 percent on average, compared to 2.6 percent growth for states that did not have such laws. As well, the number of jobs grew by 1.2 percent in states with worker-choice laws and 0.6 percent in states without worker-choice laws. Opponents of right-to-work laws argue that levels of economic growth and unemployment rates are affected by a complex set of factors, and that attributing changes in those numbers to right-to-work laws is not defensible.

The experience of the state of Oklahoma illustrates the competing arguments. Since passing right-to-work legislation in 2001, the unionization rate has fallen and the state has consistently had unemployment rates that are lower than the national average. This is in line with predictions made by right-to-work supporters. But opponents point out that Oklahoma's unemployment rate is low because the oil boom in Oklahoma has created many new jobs. As well, no one seems to be able to identify any companies that moved to Oklahoma to take advantage of its new right-to-work law. Supporters respond by saying that companies wouldn't be willing to admit that was the reason they moved because they don't want to anger unions. The best estimate seems to be that the right-to-work law has not had as much of a positive effect as supporters expected, nor has it had as much of a negative effect as opponents expected. The situation for the entire United States is complicated, as well. Some right-to-work states (e.g., Nebraska and North Dakota) have very low unemployment rates, but other right-to-work states (e.g., North Carolina, Nevada) have very high unemployment rates.

Questions for Discussion

1. Consider the arguments and counter-arguments regarding unions. Overall, which position do you think has the stronger arguments? Explain your reasoning.
2. Consider the following statement: *Canada should adopt right-to-work laws in order to attract more business investment and jobs. Unless the present laws are changed, Canadian businesses will be tempted to move their operations to jurisdictions where right-to-work laws exist. This will have a negative impact on Canada's economic growth prospects.* Do you agree or disagree with the statement? Explain your reasoning.

CONCLUDING CASE 9-2

Challenges for Unions

These are tough times for unions. Consider one surprising development: Some companies are simply putting collective bargaining negotiations on hold and letting current contracts expire. Stewart Saxe, a labour lawyer at Blake & McKenzie LLP, says he hasn't seen anything like this in the 30 years he has been in the business. Sometimes unions agree to put bargaining on hold because they realize that their current contract is probably better than any new one they could negotiate in tough economic times. Work stoppages and lost work days have dropped sharply in recent years, and this also indicates union weakness, says Larry Savage, an associate professor at Brock University. Employers recognize this and have been able to get unions to agree to multi-year wage freezes. Ken Neumann, who was responsible for getting a new collective agreement for workers at Vale Inco, said it was the worst bargaining climate he had seen in 30 years.

Unions have always been reluctant to scale back their demands for increases in wages and fringe benefits, but when the economy is in trouble, failing to do so threatens the very existence of the companies who employ the unionized workers. If a company fails, the workers obviously lose their jobs. An interdependent global economy means that companies in other countries who have more flexible pay and labour conditions are strong competitors of Canadian companies that are inflexible. A report produced by the Ottawa-based Centre for the Study

of Living Standards offers the view that unions used to create value for Canadian workers because the Canadian economy was relatively protected, and this allowed unions to get a share of company profits for their workers. But now, the report says, unions have less ability to do this in the globally competitive and deregulated environment. So unions are under pressure to accept market conditions or face plant closures that will result in workers losing their jobs.

Jim Stafford, the chief economist for the Canadian Auto Workers (CAW) union, says that unions are more flexible than stereotypes suggest. For example, as part of the conditions of the government bailout of GM and Chrysler, the CAW accepted an agreement that froze wages until 2012 and prohibits strikes until 2015 (workers at Ford can strike if they choose, since Ford did not receive a government bailout). Also, new hires are paid only about $14 an hour, which is half of what longer-term workers are paid. All of these concessions would have been unthinkable just a few years ago. Things have also become a lot more complicated since a union-controlled trust now owns an equity stake in both GM and Chrysler. That means that worker welfare is going to be influenced by the financial performance of the automobile companies (other things being equal, the lower a company's wage costs, the higher its financial performance will be).

Top management is also taking some actions that affect unions. For example, Magna International, the big Canadian auto parts maker, agreed to unionization of its production workers as long as the union agreed to a no-strike clause. (Since that agreement, only 4 of 43 Magna plants have actually been unionized.) In the United States in 2011, the negotiations between the United Auto Workers (UAW) and the car companies included a discussion of merit pay for hourly production workers; the car companies want workers to have an incentive to be more productive.

The challenges facing unions are particularly evident in the automobile manufacturing business because GM and Chrysler had major financial problems. As part of the bailout discussions, the federal government and the government of Ontario wanted the auto companies to drastically reduce labour costs (at the Oshawa, St. Catharines, and Windsor auto plants) to those paid at non-union Toyota, and they wanted pension costs reduced, as well. That meant a $19-an-hour wage cut. The CAW eventually agreed to those cuts, but complained that Ottawa and Ontario were interfering in collective bargaining and were blackmailing the CAW to sign new agreements. Critics of government bailouts also weighed in on this issue. They said that the plan wouldn't work, at least not in the long term. Supporters argued that 100 000 jobs would be saved by the bailouts (the money will come from the pockets of Canadian taxpayers), but critics said there is no way that 100 000 jobs could be saved because there were only 100 000 jobs in the whole industry.

Ken Lewenza, the president of the CAW, says the threats to workers' jobs are unprecedented. The future of employment in the auto industry does not look good, and Lewenza accepts the fact that the auto industry is going to be smaller and employ fewer people. This is particularly true for Ford, GM, and Chrysler (where the CAW is strong).

In 2009, negotiators for Ford and the CAW met to discuss ways to cut costs. Ford initiated these talks after the CAW gave concessions to Chrysler and GM that reduced the labour costs at those companies by $19/hour. The CAW made these concessions to Chrysler and GM after receiving assurances that GM and Chrysler would preserve their manufacturing "footprint" in Canada. The CAW wanted Ford to maintain its manufacturing presence in Canada, particularly at the St. Thomas, Ontario, plant. But Ford said it had no cars to produce at that plant after 2011 (the plant makes cars like the Ford Crown Victoria and the Mercury Grand Marquis,

but those gas guzzlers are not so popular anymore). Ford threatened to pull out of Canada entirely if the CAW didn't agree to wage and benefit cuts. Ford and the CAW finally reached a new collective agreement, which included the closing of the St. Thomas assembly plant in the third quarter of 2011 (which put 1500 workers out of a job). As part of the deal, Ford also agreed to invest $2 billion in its Oakville plant, and to produce 10 percent of its total North American production in Canada (down from the former 13 percent). Ford also agreed that it would produce more cars in Canada than it sells here. Chrysler and GM had earlier agreed to this latter provision for their operations, but since Ford did not receive a government bailout, it was not required to maintain its Canadian footprint.

The difficult environment for unions is not limited to automobile manufacturing. In 2009, three unions at Air Canada (AC), which represent about 60 percent of AC's unionized workers, agreed to extend their current labour agreements with no wage increases and to allow the company to put less money into its pension plans. AC said it simply could not meet its pension contribution responsibilities because of its multi-billion-dollar pension deficit. This agreement was reached after AC opened its books to show everyone what bad financial shape it was in. The unions also agreed to a no-strike, no-lockout provision. Air Canada hoped the deal would allow the company to avoid a second bankruptcy filing. As part of the deal, the unions got a 10 percent equity stake in AC. Foreign airlines are also facing difficulties and are taking actions that threaten unions. For example, Aer Lingus, the Irish airline, announced that it was planning to lay off one-fifth of its workers and would cut salaries for those who remained. The airline did this in spite of the threat of strikes by unionized employees. British Airways PLC also planned to cut thousands of jobs in spite of strike threats by its unions.

In spite of all the challenges, the difficult economic times of the past few years may present an opportunity to union organizers. That's because many people who formerly wouldn't have considered joining a union have now experienced layoffs and they may be more interested in having a union represent their interests. The UAW is also planning to renew its efforts to unionize the workforces at Japanese, Korean, and German carmakers that have production facilities in the United States.

Questions for Discussion

1. Explain in your own words how the interdependent, global economy of the twenty-first century has caused major problems for unionized Canadian automobile manufacturers. Do non-union automobile manufacturers have the same problem?

2. What are the pros and cons of union members having an equity stake in the company they work for?

3. Consider the following statement: *Unions have historically been very successful at getting increased wages and benefits from employers, but this success will be the downfall of unions because the cost structure of unionized Canadian companies has increased to the point where they cannot price their products competitively. Once that happens, the companies will go out of business and the workers will lose their jobs.* Do you agree or disagree with the statement? Explain your reasoning.

Motivating and Leading Employees

LEARNING OBJECTIVES

After reading this chapter, you should be able to:

1 Identify and discuss the basic *forms of behaviour* that employees exhibit in organizations.

2 Describe the nature and importance of *individual differences* among employees.

3 Explain the meaning and importance of *psychological contracts* and the person–job fit in the workplace.

4 Identify and summarize the most important *models of employee motivation.*

5 Describe the *strategies* used by organizations to improve job satisfaction and employee motivation.

6 Define *leadership* and distinguish it from *management.*

7 Summarize the *approaches to leadership* that developed in the twentieth century.

8 Describe the most recent ideas about effective leadership.

Happiness and Satisfaction in the Workplace

A 2011 survey of 30 000 workers from 17 countries (including 2000 Canadians) was conducted by Mercer, a global consulting firm. Its *What's Working* survey showed that 36 percent of Canadian respondents were so unhappy with their jobs that they were considering quitting (26 percent held this view in the 2006 Mercer survey). The deterioration in happiness was influenced by the poor economic climate of the past few years, which led to wage freezes, smaller merit increases, and fewer promotion opportunities. Employees in the 16–24 and 25–34 age brackets were the most likely to be thinking about leaving their job. Compared to workers who were not considering leaving their job, those that were considering leaving were consistently less satisfied, felt less fairly treated by their employer, were less proud to work for their organization, got less of a feeling of accomplishment from their work, and were less likely to recommend their organization to others as a good place to work.

Several of the concerns in the *What's Working* survey flow from employee concerns about money. But what role does money play in happiness? A study in the Proceedings of the National Academy of Sciences reported that beyond an annual income of about $75 000, more money does not increase happiness. Lack of money does make people unhappy, but having a lot of money does not guarantee happiness. Some people have a strong drive to make a lot of money. Undergraduates who set a goal of making a lot of money generally achieve their goal. Students who want to make a lot of money generally major in areas like business, engineering, and economics. People who don't care as much about money are more likely to be in liberal arts and the social sciences. (Note: Achieving a feeling of happiness may not be as important as having a sense of purpose in life. Studies show that people with a sense of purpose are more likely to remain cognitively

intact as they age, and even live longer than people who simply focus on being happy.)

Happiness with money is not the only consideration in employee satisfaction. Another survey—this one of 3000 Canadians—revealed some interesting things about what people value in their work lives. The views of four age groups were examined:

■ "Matures" (born before 1947)
■ "Baby Boomers" (born between 1947 and 1966)
■ "Gen Xers" (born between 1967 and 1979)
■ "Millennials," also called "Generation Y" (born in 1980 or later)

Individuals in these four groups value similar things, but their priorities differ. For example, Gen Xers put the highest value on achieving a balance between work and home life, while Baby Boomers value continuing to grow and using their skills. Surprisingly,

Matures value advancement more than either Baby Boomers or Gen Xers. Other findings: Millennials change jobs three times as often as Baby Boomers formerly did, apparently moving around looking for jobs that will satisfy their needs. Millennials also have very high expectations and assume that their pay will increase rather rapidly within five years (likely a naive hope). Matures place less emphasis on fun at work than Baby Boomers, who in turn place less emphasis on fun than Gen Xers.

Gen Xers are most disappointed with how their careers have unfolded. They report the lowest level of satisfaction of all four groups, the lowest levels of met expectations, and the greatest level of conflict between work and family life. Part of the problem seems to be that Gen Xers are caught between Millennials and Baby Boomers, who are generally seen as more influential in society. One important implication of the findings is this: As the Baby Boomers retire in the next few years, the Gen Xers are going to become important to the success of the companies they work for. But if Gen Xers are unhappy with their work and career situation, this could cause problems.

How can managers address the problems that are evident in these surveys? The easy answer is to give employees what they want. *But what do employees want?* Managers often *assume* they know the answer to this question, but consider the results of a survey by the Canadian Payroll Association, which analyzed the frequency with which 39 specific benefits were provided by companies to their employees. The top five items were term life insurance, car allowances, tuition fees, disability-related employment benefits, and professional membership dues. But a survey of *worker* opinions found that they rated flexible working hours, casual dress, unlimited internet access, opportunities to telecommute, and nap time as the most desirable. There are obviously major differences in these two lists, so managers are having some difficulty assessing what employees want.

Managers can improve this unfortunate situation by gaining a greater understanding of employee needs. They can do this by asking the following questions:

- What do employees expect from their role? Employee satisfaction increases when their role provides adequate challenge and fits well with their personal purpose.
- What motivates my employees? Answering this question yields information about employee needs, which are important in job satisfaction.
- What kind of work environment do employees want? If employees want a meritocracy, they are not going to be happy if everyone receives equal rewards. If they want a lot of autonomy, they are not going to be happy with a rigidly structured job. In other words, the work environment must be structured to emphasize the things that employees value.
- What career development help do they want? Employees want to improve their skills and learning, and they want to feel that management is investing in their careers.

Beyond these specific issues, managers should also ask a very general question: Under what circumstances will employees feel happy and be willing to work enthusiastically for the company? The answer may be evident in yet another survey, this one based on responses by 8000 Canadians. The survey found that the three most important things (for employees of *all* ages) were (1) to be treated with respect, (2) to be dealt with fairly, and (3) to feel a sense of "connection" with the organization they worked for. Managers can have a very positive influence on all of these things. ◆

HOW WILL THIS HELP ME?

Some people love their jobs, while others hate them. Most people, however, fall somewhere in between. Some of these feelings are caused by the type of leadership employees are experiencing, and some are caused by the type of work that the employees do. After studying the information in this chapter, you'll be better able to understand (1) your own feelings toward your work from the perspective of an *employee*, (2) the feelings of others toward their work from the perspective of a *boss or owner*, (3) how you can function more effectively as a leader, and (4) how your manager or boss strives to motivate you through his or her leadership style.

Forms of Employee Behaviour

LO1 Identify and discuss the basic *forms of behaviour* that employees exhibit in organizations.

employee behaviour The pattern of actions by the members of an organization that directly or indirectly influence the organization's effectiveness.

performance behaviours The behaviours directly targeted at performing a job.

organizational citizenship Behaviours that provide positive benefits to the organization in indirect ways.

counterproductive behaviours Behaviours that detract from organizational performance.

absenteeism Occurs when an employee does not show up for work.

turnover The percentage of an organization's workforce that leaves and must be replaced.

Employee behaviour is the pattern of actions by the members of an organization that directly or indirectly influences the organization's effectiveness. **Performance behaviours** are the behaviours directly targeted at performing a job. An assembly line worker who sits by a moving conveyor and attaches parts to a product as it passes by has relatively simple performance behaviours. By contrast, a research-and-development scientist who works in a lab trying to find new scientific breakthroughs that have commercial potential has much more complex performance behaviours.

Other behaviours—called **organizational citizenship**—provide positive benefits to the organization but in more indirect ways. An employee who does satisfactory work in terms of quantity and quality but refuses to work overtime, won't help newcomers learn the ropes, and is generally unwilling to make any contribution beyond the strict performance requirements of the job is not a good organizational citizen. By contrast, an employee with a satisfactory level of performance who works late when the boss asks and takes time to help newcomers learn their way around is a good organizational citizen.

Counterproductive behaviours are those that detract from organizational performance. **Absenteeism** occurs when an employee does not show up for work. When an employee is absent, that person's work does not get done and a substitute must be hired to do it, or others in the organization must pick up the slack. Tardiness is also a counterproductive behaviour. A survey conducted by CareerBuilder.com revealed that 19 percent of workers admitted being late for work at least once a week.[1]

Turnover refers to the percentage of an organization's workforce that leaves and must be replaced. Some turnover is natural and healthy, but high turnover has many negative consequences, including disruption in production, decreased productivity, and increased retraining costs. Turnover results from a number of factors, including the nature of the job, the nature of supervision, a poor person–job fit, the external labour market, and family influences. One survey of 660 workers showed that 84 percent who worked for a "kind" manager planned to stay with their company a long time, while only 47 percent of those who worked for a "bully" said they planned to stay.[2]

Other forms of counterproductive behaviour may be even more costly for an organization. *Theft and sabotage*, for example, result in direct financial costs for an organization. *Sexual and racial harassment* also cost an organization, both directly (through financial liability if the organization responds inappropriately) and indirectly (by lowering morale, producing fear, and driving off valuable employees). *Workplace aggression and violence* are also counterproductive.

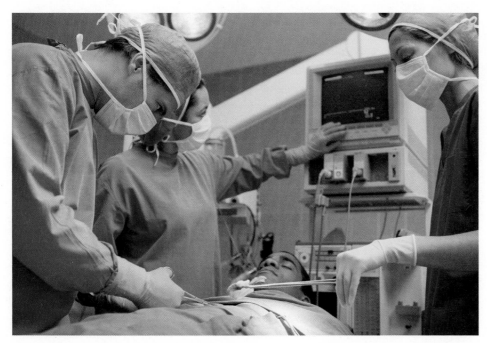

For some jobs, performance behaviours can be narrowly defined and easily measured. But for many other jobs, such as those held by scientists or doctors, performance behaviours are less objective, more diverse, and more difficult to assess.

Individual Differences Among Employees

Individual differences are physical, psychological, and emotional attributes that vary from one person to another. The individual differences that characterize a specific person make that person unique. *Personality* and *attitudes* are two main categories of individual differences.

Personality

Personality is the relatively stable set of psychological attributes that distinguishes one person from another. Researchers have identified five fundamental traits (the "big five") that are especially relevant to organizations (see Figure 10.1).

- *Agreeableness* is a person's ability to get along with others. A person with a *high* level of agreeableness is gentle, co-operative, forgiving, understanding, and good-natured in their dealings with others. A person with a *low* level of agreeableness is often irritable, short-tempered, unco-operative, and generally antagonistic toward other people. Highly agreeable people are better at developing good working relationships with co-workers, whereas less agreeable people are not likely to have particularly good working relationships.

- *Conscientiousness* refers to the number of things a person tries to accomplish. *Highly conscientious* people tend to focus on relatively few tasks at one time; as a result, they are likely to be organized, systematic, careful, thorough, responsible, and self-disciplined. *Less conscientious* people tend to pursue a wider array of tasks; as a result, they are often more disorganized and irresponsible, as well as less thorough and self-disciplined. Highly conscientious people tend to be relatively higher performers in a variety of different jobs.

- *Emotionality* refers to the degree to which people tend to be positive or negative in their outlook and behaviours toward others. People with *positive* emotionality are relatively poised, calm, resilient, and secure; people with *negative* emotionality are more excitable, insecure, reactive, and subject to mood swings. People with

Describe the nature and importance **L02** of *individual differences* among employees.

individual differences Physical, psychological, and emotional attributes that vary from one person to another and that make each person unique.

personality The relatively stable set of psychological attributes that distinguishes one person from another.

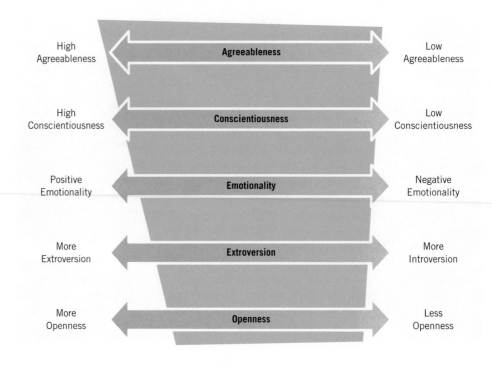

FIGURE 10.1

The "big five" personality traits.

positive emotionality are better able to handle job stress, pressure, and tension. Their stability might also cause them to be seen as more reliable than their less stable counterparts.

■ *Extroversion* refers to a person's comfort level with relationships. *Extroverts* are sociable, talkative, assertive, and open to establishing new relationships, while *introverts* are much less sociable, less talkative, less assertive, and more reluctant to begin new relationships. Extroverts tend to be higher overall job performers than introverts and are more likely to be attracted to jobs based on personal relationships, such as sales and marketing positions.

■ *Openness* reflects how open or rigid a person is in terms of his or her beliefs. People with *high* levels of openness are curious and willing to listen to new ideas and to change their own ideas, beliefs, and attitudes in response to new information. People with *low* levels of openness tend to be less receptive to new ideas and less willing to change their minds. People with more openness are often better performers due to their flexibility and the likelihood that they will be better accepted by others in the organization.

Emotional Intelligence

emotional intelligence (or emotional quotient [EQ]) The extent to which people possess social skills, are self-aware, can manage their emotions, can motivate themselves, and can express empathy for others.

Emotional intelligence, or emotional quotient (EQ), refers to the extent to which people possess social skills, are self-aware, can manage their emotions, can motivate themselves, and can express empathy for others.[3] Research suggests that people with high EQs may perform better than others, especially in jobs that require a high degree of interpersonal interaction and that involve influencing or directing the work of others. EQ appears to be something that isn't biologically based but that can be developed.[4] A survey of 2660 managers conducted by CareerBuilder.com found that 34 percent of hiring managers put a high priority on emotional intelligence when making hiring decisions. Seventy-one percent of the respondents placed a higher priority on emotional intelligence than on mental intelligence when making hiring decisions.[5]

Attitudes

Attitudes reflect our beliefs and feelings about specific ideas, situations, or other people. People in organizations have attitudes about many different things: their salary, their promotion possibilities, their boss, their employee benefits, and so on. People's attitudes also affect their behaviour in organizations. Especially important attitudes are *job satisfaction* and *organizational commitment*.

> **attitude** A reflection of our beliefs and feelings about specific ideas, situations, or other people.

- **Job satisfaction** is the degree of enjoyment that people derive from performing their jobs. (A related concept—*morale*—refers to the overall attitude people have toward their workplace.) A Workopolis survey of 577 Canadians showed that 53 percent loved their jobs, 16 percent kept their job simply because it helped pay the bills, and 14 percent felt that their current job had the potential to lead to something better.[6] A 2010 survey of workers in 23 countries found that workers in Norway, Denmark, and Canada were the most satisfied with their current employer.[7] Satisfied employees tend to be absent less often, to be good organizational citizens, and to stay with the organization. Dissatisfied employees tend to be absent more often, may experience stress that disrupts co-workers, and may be continually looking for another job. But a word of caution: Contrary to what a lot of managers believe, high levels of job satisfaction do not *automatically* lead to higher levels of productivity.

> **job satisfaction** The degree of enjoyment that people derive from performing their jobs.

- **Organizational commitment** (sometimes called *job commitment*) reflects an individual's identification with the organization and its mission. Highly committed employees see themselves as true members of the firm, overlook minor sources of dissatisfaction, and see themselves remaining as members of the organization. Less committed employees are more likely to see themselves as outsiders, to express more dissatisfaction about the work situation, and to not see themselves as long-term members of the organization. One way to increase employee commitment is to give employees a voice. Infosys Technologies in Bangalore, India, started a Voice of Youth program, which gives top-performing young employees a seat on its management council.[8]

> **organizational commitment** An individual's identification with the organization and its mission.

Matching People and Jobs

It is important to have a good match between people and the jobs they are performing. Two key concepts for facilitating this match are *psychological contracts* and the *person–job fit*.

> **L03** Explain the meaning and importance of *psychological contracts* and the person–job fit in the workplace.

Psychological Contracts

A **psychological contract** is the set of expectations held by an employee concerning what he or she will contribute to an organization (referred to as *contributions*) and what the organization will provide to the employee in return (referred to as *inducements*). If either party perceives an inequity in the contract, that party may seek a change. The employee, for example, might ask for a pay raise, promotion, or bigger office, or might put forth less effort or look for a better job elsewhere. The organization can also initiate change by training workers to improve their skills, transferring them to new jobs, or terminating them. Unlike a business contract, a psychological contract is not written on paper, nor are all of its terms explicitly negotiated. Figure 10.2 illustrates the essential features of a psychological contract.

> **psychological contract** The set of expectations held by an employee concerning what he or she will contribute to an organization (referred to as contributions) and what the organization will provide the employee in return (referred to as inducements).

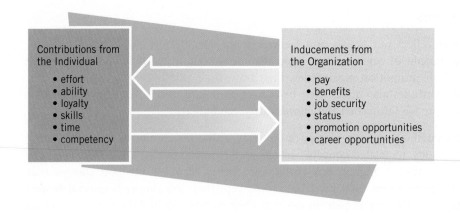

FIGURE 10.2

The psychological contract.

The Person-Job Fit

person–job fit The extent to which a person's contributions and the organization's inducements match one another.

The **person–job fit** refers to the extent to which a person's contributions and the organization's inducements match one another. Each employee has a specific set of needs that he or she wants fulfilled and a set of job-related behaviours and abilities to contribute. If the organization can take perfect advantage of those behaviours and abilities and exactly fulfill those needs, it will have achieved a perfect person–job fit. A good person–job fit, in turn, can result in higher performance and more positive attitudes. A poor person–job fit can have just the opposite effect.

Motivation in the Workplace

LO4 Identify and summarize the most important *models of employee motivation*.

motivation The set of forces that cause, focus, and sustain workers' behaviour.

Motivation is the set of forces that cause, focus, and sustain workers' behaviour. One worker may be motivated to work hard to produce as much as possible, while another may be motivated to do just enough to get by. As we saw in the opening case, effective managers recognize that because today's workers have diverse and complex needs, they must be motivated in increasingly complex ways. As well, the varying lifestyles of a diverse workforce mean that managers must pay close attention to what their employees expect to receive for their efforts and then try to link rewards with job performance.

Over the years, three major approaches to motivation in the workplace have been evident: *classical theory and scientific management, behaviour theory,* and *contemporary motivation theories.* These approaches reflect a chronology of thinking about motivation.

Classical Theory and Scientific Management

classical theory of motivation Workers are motivated solely by money.

According to the **classical theory of motivation**, workers are motivated solely by money. In his book *The Principles of Scientific Management* (1911), industrial engineer Frederick Taylor proposed a way for both companies and workers to benefit from this widely accepted view.[9] If workers are motivated by money, Taylor reasoned, then paying them more will prompt them to produce more. Meanwhile, the firm that analyzes jobs and finds better ways to have employees perform them will be able to produce goods more cheaply, make higher profits, and thus pay—and motivate—workers better than its competitors.

scientific management Analyzing jobs in order to find better, more efficient ways to perform them.

Taylor's approach—known as **scientific management**—captured the imagination of many managers in the early twentieth century. Companies across Canada

The ideas of Frederick Taylor, the founder of scientific management, had a profound impact on the way manufacturing activities were carried out in the early twentieth century. His basic ideas are still used today.

and the United States hired experts to perform *time-and-motion studies*—pioneered by Frank and Lillian Gilbreth—in order to discover the "one best way" of doing a job. Industrial-engineering techniques were applied to each facet of a job to determine how to perform it most efficiently. These studies were the first "scientific" attempts to break down jobs into easily repeated components and to devise more efficient tools and machines for performing them.[10] The results were impressive. For example, studies of workers loading iron on rail cars showed that productivity tripled when scientific management principles were used.

Early Behavioural Theory

In 1925, a group of Harvard researchers began a study at the Hawthorne Works of the Western Electric Company. Their intent was to examine the relationship between changes in the physical environment and worker output, with an eye to increasing productivity. The results of the experiment at first confused, then amazed, the scientists. Increasing lighting levels improved productivity, but so did lowering lighting levels. And against all expectations, raising the pay of workers failed to increase their productivity. Gradually they pieced together the puzzle. The explanation for the lighting phenomenon lay in workers' response to the attention they were receiving. In essence, they determined that almost any action on the part of management that made workers believe they were receiving special attention caused worker productivity to rise. This result, known as the **Hawthorne effect**, convinced many managers that paying attention to employees is indeed good for business.

Following the Hawthorne studies, managers and researchers alike focused more attention on how good **human relations**—the interactions between employers and employees and their attitudes toward one another—helped in motivating employees. Researchers eventually developed several now-classic motivation theories, including the *human resources model*, the *hierarchy of needs model*, and the *two-factor theory*.

Hawthorne effect The tendency for workers' productivity to increase when they feel they are receiving special attention from management.

human relations The interactions between employers and employees and their attitudes toward one another.

The Hawthorne studies were an important step in developing an appreciation for the human factor at work. These women worked under different lighting conditions as researchers monitored their productivity. The researchers were amazed to find that productivity increased regardless of whether lighting levels increased or decreased.

The Human-Resources Model: Theories X and Y

Behavioural scientist Douglas McGregor found that managers had radically different beliefs about how best to use the human resources at a firm's disposal. He classified these beliefs into sets of assumptions that he labelled "Theory X" and "Theory Y."[11] Managers who subscribe to **Theory X** tend to believe that people are naturally lazy and unco-operative and must therefore be either punished or rewarded to be made productive. By contrast, managers who subscribe to **Theory Y** tend to believe that people are naturally energetic, growth oriented, self-motivated, and interested in being productive.

McGregor generally favoured Theory Y beliefs, and he argued that Theory Y managers are more likely to have satisfied, motivated employees. Of course, the Theory X and Theory Y distinctions are somewhat simplistic and offer little concrete basis for action. Their value lies primarily in their ability to highlight and analyze the behaviour of managers as a result of their attitudes toward employees.

Maslow's Hierarchy of Needs Model

Psychologist Abraham Maslow's **hierarchy of human needs model** proposed that people have five basic needs, which are arranged in a hierarchy of importance (see Figure 10.3). According to Maslow, lower-level needs must be largely satisfied before a person will be motivated to satisfy higher-level needs.[12]

- *Physiological needs* are survival oriented; they include food, water, shelter, and sleep. Businesses address these needs by providing both comfortable working environments and salaries sufficient to buy food and shelter.

- *Security needs* include the needs for stability and protection from the unknown. These needs are satisfied when employers offer pension plans and job security.

- *Social needs* include the needs for friendship and companionship. Making friends at work can help to satisfy social needs, as can the feeling that you "belong" in a company.

Theory X A management approach based on the belief that people must be forced to be productive because they are naturally lazy, irresponsible, and unco-operative.

Theory Y A management approach based on the belief that people want to be productive because they are naturally energetic, responsible, and co-operative.

hierarchy of human needs model Theory of motivation describing five levels of human needs and arguing that basic needs must be fulfilled before people will work to satisfy higher-level needs.

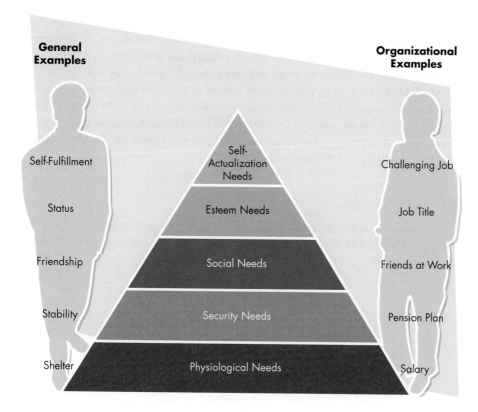

General Examples

Self-Fulfillment

Status

Friendship

Stability

Shelter

Organizational Examples

Challenging Job

Job Title

Friends at Work

Pension Plan

Salary

Self-Actualization Needs

Esteem Needs

Social Needs

Security Needs

Physiological Needs

FIGURE 10.3

Maslow's hierarchy of human needs provides a useful categorization of the different needs people have.

- *Esteem needs* include the need for status and recognition as well as the need for self-respect. Job titles and large offices are among the things that businesses can provide to address these needs.

- Finally, *self-actualization needs* are needs for self-fulfillment. They include the needs to grow and develop one's capabilities and to achieve new and meaningful goals. Challenging job assignments can help satisfy these needs.

According to Maslow, once one set of needs has been satisfied, it ceases to motivate behaviour. For example, if you feel secure in your job, a new pension plan will probably be less important to you than the chance to make new friends and join an informal network among your co-workers. If, however, a lower-level need suddenly becomes unfulfilled, most people immediately refocus on that lower level. Suppose, for example, that you are seeking to meet your esteem needs by working as a divisional manager at a major company. If you learn that your division—and consequently your job—may be eliminated, you might very well find the promise of job security at a new firm as motivating as a promotion once would have been in your old company. The boxed insert entitled "Moving People to Move Movies" describes how one company focuses on employee needs.

Two-Factor (Motivation-Hygiene) Theory

After studying a group of accountants and engineers, psychologist Frederick Herzberg proposed the **two-factor theory**, which says that job satisfaction and dissatisfaction depend on two distinct factors: *motivating factors* (such as recognition, responsibility, advancement, and achievement), and *hygiene factors* (such as working conditions, quality of supervision, interpersonal relations, pay, and job security).[13] Motivating factors cause movement along a continuum from *no satisfaction* to *satisfaction*. For example, if workers receive no recognition for successful work, they may not be satisfied, but neither will they be dissatisfied. If recognition is provided, they will likely

two-factor theory A theory of human relations developed by Frederick Herzberg that identifies factors that must be present for employees to be satisfied with their jobs and factors that, if increased, lead employees to work harder.

become more satisfied. By contrast, hygiene factors cause movement along a different continuum, one from *no dissatisfaction* to *dissatisfaction*. For example, workers will be dissatisfied if they feel that working conditions are poor, but if working conditions are improved, workers will not become *satisfied*; rather, they will no longer be *dissatisfied*. Motivating factors are directly related to the *work* that employees actually perform, while hygiene factors refer to the *environment* in which they perform it (see Figure 10.4). This theory suggests that managers must first ensure that hygiene factors are acceptable (to avoid worker dissatisfaction) and then offer motivating factors (to improve satisfaction and motivation).

Contemporary Motivation Theory

Recently, more complex models of employee behaviour and motivation have been developed. Two of the most interesting and useful ones are *expectancy theory* and *equity theory*.

ENTREPRENEURSHIP AND NEW VENTURES

Moving People to Move Movies

Selling movies to consumers is a dynamic and challenging industry today. The market is evolving so rapidly that even the basic business model, product, and technology are unresolved. In order to cope with the many complex issues the company faces, Netflix CEO and founder Reed Hastings recruited a team of top performers in fields as diverse as marketing, content management, and website operations. But he then had to find a way to motivate these stars to fulfill their potential. Netflix uses monetary rewards as a motivator. "We're unafraid to pay high," says Hastings. However, the company achieves its greatest results by focusing on employee needs.

One important set of needs that Netflix fulfills is the desire to work with friends, be part of a team, and belong. Employees recommend people they've enjoyed working with at other jobs. The atmosphere is casual and collaborative, but as Michelle Conlin of *BusinessWeek* puts it, "Netflix is no frat party with beer bashes and foosball tables." The Netflix values statement says, "The benefit of a high-performance culture is that you work with consistently outstanding colleagues, which is exhilarating. We're a high-performance team, not a family. A strong family is together forever, no matter what. A strong company, on the other hand, is more like a professional sports team, which is built to win."

Netflix works to fulfill employees' needs for esteem by being an employer that is well liked. The job pages of the company's website say, "It is satisfying to work at a company that people love. We're ranked number one in customer satisfaction across the entire Internet, narrowly besting such great companies as Apple and Amazon."

Another set of fulfilled needs is related to employees' passion to achieve. The "best in class" personnel at this firm of just 400 workers are attracted by the opportunity to have a significant impact on a successful and ever-changing company. Before founding Netflix, Hastings started Pure Software. At first, the start-up was an exciting place to work, but it became more humdrum and bureaucratic as it grew. When Pure was sold to IBM, Hastings vowed never to repeat that mistake. The Netflix values statement summarizes Hastings's viewpoint as follows: "Rules inhibit creativity and entrepreneurship, leading to a lack of innovation. Our solution to increased complexity is to increase talent density. Great people make great judgment calls, despite ambiguity. We believe in freedom and responsibility, not rules."

The Netflix motivation scheme is not for everyone. "At most companies, average performers get an average raise," says Hastings. "At Netflix, they get a generous severance package." However, the company is doing a good job of motivating stellar workers. Netflix is getting maximum performance from its workers in order to gain a competitive advantage over its key competitors.

Critical Thinking Questions

1. Why do you think the Netflix motivation scheme is not for everyone?

2. Consider the following statement: *Trying to motivate employees by focusing on their needs is not a good idea because it is hard to find out just what employee needs are, and even if you find out, that doesn't tell a manager specifically what to do to satisfy the needs.* Do you agree or disagree with the statement? Defend your answer.

Satisfaction	No Satisfaction

Motivation factors
• achievement
• recognition
• the work itself
• responsibility
• advancement and growth

Dissatisfaction	No Dissatisfaction

Hygiene factors
• supervisors
• working conditions
• interpersonal relations
• pay and security
• company policies and administration

FIGURE 10.4

According to two-factor theory, job satisfaction depends on two factors.

Expectancy Theory

Expectancy theory suggests that people are motivated to work toward rewards that they want *and* that they believe they have a reasonable chance of obtaining.[14] A reward that seems out of reach, for example, is not likely to be motivating even if it is very desirable. Figure 10.5 illustrates expectancy theory in terms of issues that are likely to be considered by an individual employee. Consider the case of an assistant department manager who learns that her firm needs to replace a retiring division manager two levels above her in the organization. Even though she wants that job, she does not apply because she doubts that she will be selected. In this case, she is being influenced by the *performance–reward link*. For whatever reason, she believes that her performance will not get her the position. Note that she may think that her performance merits the new job but that performance alone will not be enough. Perhaps she assumes that the reward will go to someone with more seniority.

Now assume that our employee learns that the firm is looking for a production manager on a later shift. She thinks that she could get this job but does not apply for this one either, because she does not want to change shifts. In this instance, she is being influenced by the *rewards–personal goals link*. Finally, she learns of an opening one level higher—department manager—in her own division. She applies for this job because she wants it *and* because she thinks she has a good chance of getting it. In this case, her consideration of all the links has led to an expectation that she can reach a desirable outcome.

Expectancy theory helps explain why some people do not work as hard as they can when their salaries are based purely on seniority. Paying employees the same whether they work very hard or just hard enough to get by removes the financial

expectancy theory The theory that people are motivated to work toward rewards that they want and that they believe they have a reasonable chance of obtaining.

FIGURE 10.5

Expectancy theory model.

Individual Effort → Individual Performance → Organizational Rewards → Personal Goals

Effort–Performance Issue   Performance–Reward Issue   Rewards–Personal Goals Issue

incentive for them to work harder. In other words, they ask themselves, "If I work harder, will I get a pay raise?" and conclude that the answer is no. Similarly, if hard work will result in one or more *undesirable* outcomes—say, a transfer to another location or a promotion to a job that requires unpleasant travel—employees will not be motivated to work hard.

Equity Theory

equity theory The theory that people compare (1) what they contribute to their job with what they get in return, and (2) their input/output ratio with that of other employees.

Equity theory focuses on social comparisons and assumes that people evaluate their treatment in an organization relative to the treatment that others receive. This approach says that people begin by analyzing *inputs* (what they contribute to their jobs in terms of time, effort, education, experience, and so on) relative to *outputs* (what they receive in return in terms of salary, benefits, recognition, security, and so on). The result is a ratio of contribution to return. Then they compare their own ratios with those of other comparable employees and ask whether their ratios are *equal to, greater than,* or *less than* those of the people with whom they are comparing themselves. Depending on the outcome of their assessments, they experience feelings of equity or inequity.[15]

Suppose that a new graduate gets a starting job at a large manufacturing firm. His starting salary is $30 000 per year, he gets a compact company car, and he shares an office with another employee. If he later learns that another new employee has received the same salary, car, and office arrangement, he will feel equitably treated. If the other newcomer, however, received $35 000, a full-size company car, and a private office, he is likely to experience feelings of inequity.

Note that the two ratios do not have to be equal—they only need to be *equitable*. Let's assume, for instance, that our new employee has a bachelor's degree and two years of work experience. Perhaps he learns subsequently that the other new employee has an advanced degree and 10 years of work experience. After first feeling inequity, our new employee may now conclude that his comparison person is actually contributing more to the organization and is therefore entitled to receive more.

When people feel that they are being inequitably treated, they are motivated to do something to restore equity. For example, they may ask for a raise, reduce their effort, work shorter hours, or just complain to their bosses. They may also rationalize their situation, find different people with whom to compare themselves, or leave their jobs altogether.

Strategies for Enhancing Motivation

(LO5) Describe the *strategies* used by organizations to improve job satisfaction and employee motivation.

Deciding what motivates workers and provides job satisfaction is only part of the manager's challenge. The other part is to apply that knowledge. Experts have suggested—and many companies have instituted—a wide range of programs designed to make jobs more interesting and rewarding and the work environment more pleasant. Six of the most popular types of programs are *reinforcement/behaviour modification theory, goal setting theory, participative management, team management, job enrichment and job redesign,* and *modified work schedules.*

Reinforcement/Behaviour Modification Theory

Reinforcement is a two-step process. The first step is to define the specific behaviours that managers want their employees to exhibit (working hard, being courteous to customers, stressing quality) and the specific behaviours they want to eliminate (wasting time, being rude to customers, ignoring quality). The second step is to "shape" employee behaviour by using reinforcement.

Reinforcement means applying (or withholding) positive (or negative) consequences in an attempt to motivate employees to exhibit behaviour the manager wants.
A manager has four basic reinforcement options: (1) *positive reinforcement* (apply positive consequences when employees exhibit desired behaviours), (2) *punishment* (apply
negative consequences when employees exhibit undesirable behaviours), (3) *omission*
(withhold positive consequences when employees exhibit undesirable behaviours),
and (4) *negative reinforcement* (withhold negative consequences when employees
exhibit desired behaviours).

Positive reinforcement is an effective approach. Most people think of monetary rewards when they think of positive reinforcement, but one of the simplest
ways for managers to motivate workers is to praise them. Yet this occurs far less
often than it should. A *Globe and Mail* web poll showed that 27 percent of the
2331 respondents had *never* received a compliment from their boss. Another
10 percent had not received a compliment in the last year, and 18 percent had not
received a compliment in the last month.[16] Other non-monetary rewards are also
useful. Calgary-based Pacesetter Directional and Performance Drilling rewards top
employees with time off from work, and Markham, Ontario–based Nobis, a manufacturer of hats and apparel, rewards employees by allowing them to name hats
after family and friends.[17]

> **reinforcement** Controlling and
> modifying employee behaviour through
> the use of systematic rewards and
> punishments for specific behaviours.

Goal Setting Theory

Goal setting theory focuses on setting goals in order to motivate employees. Research
has shown that **SMART goals** (*Specific, Measurable, Achievable, Relevant,* and *Time
framed*) are most likely to result in increased employee performance. On occasion, goal
setting may lead to bad behaviour on the part of managers. For example, if managers
are told they will receive a bonus if they achieve a certain level of sales revenue, they
may focus all their attention on generating sales *revenue* and not pay any attention
to *profits*.

One of the most popular methods for setting performance goals is called
management by objectives (MBO), which involves managers and subordinates in
setting goals and evaluating progress (see Figure 10.6). It is an effort to apply goal setting
theory throughout the organization. The motivational impact is perhaps the biggest

> **goal setting theory** The theory that
> people perform better when they set
> specific, quantified, time-framed goals.
>
> **SMART goals** Goals that are specific,
> measurable, achievable, relevant, and
> time framed and are most likely to result
> in increased employee performance.
>
> **management by objectives (MBO)** A
> system of collaborative goal setting that
> extends from the top of an organization
> to its bottom.

Research has shown that goals
that are specific, measurable,
achievable, relevant, and time
framed are most likely to
result in increased employee
performance.

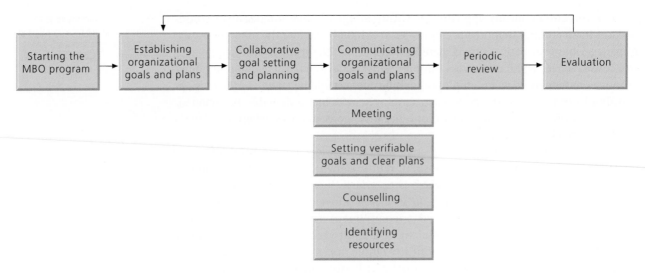

FIGURE 10.6

Management by objectives.

advantage of MBO. When employees meet with managers to set goals, they learn more about company-wide objectives, feel that they are an important part of a team, and see how they can improve company-wide performance by achieving their own goals.

Investors Group Financial Services has used MBO for many years to motivate its sales force in selling financial services. The MBO process begins when the vice-president of sales develops general goals for the entire sales force. This sets the stage for Planning Week, which is held annually in various regional centres across Canada. Sales reps review their financial accomplishments and think through their personal and financial goals for the coming year. During Planning Week, they meet with their division managers and reach a consensus about the specific goals the sales reps will pursue during the next year. Each division manager then forwards the proposed objectives for his or her division to the appropriate regional manager. This process continues all the way up to the vice-president of sales, who gives final approval to the overall sales objectives of the company for the coming year.[18]

Participative Management and Empowerment

participative management and empowerment A method of increasing employees' job satisfaction by giving them a voice in how they do their jobs and how the company is managed.

Participative management and empowerment involves tapping in to workers' knowledge about the job, encouraging them to make suggestions for improvements, and giving them more authority and responsibility so that they feel they are a real

Participative management gets employees involved in analyzing problems and suggesting solutions. This increases employee satisfaction with, and commitment to, decisions that are made.

part of the company's success. In 2009, Texas-based WorldBlu published a list of the 100 most democratic workplaces in the world. Seven Canadian companies made the list, including 1-800-GOT-JUNK?, I Love Rewards, and TakingITGlobal.[19] Some companies try to operate without the usual hierarchy and give workers a large amount of discretion. For example, at Morning Star Company—the world's largest tomato processor—workers write up a mission statement that describes how they will contribute to the overall goals of the company. Employees are expected to propose the hiring of new people if they are overloaded or if they see a need that should be met. Each employee also develops a "Colleague Letter of Understanding" with other employees who are affected by his or her work. At the end of the year, employees receive feedback on their performance from colleagues with whom they have a Letter of Understanding. Pay is determined by a committee that is elected. All business units are ranked (based on performance), and those that rank poorly have to explain what happened. One employee said that nobody is your boss, everyone is.[20]

Other illustrative examples of empowerment include the following:

- At ING Direct Canada, a webpage has been set up that allows employees to submit ideas for peers to vote on. An innovation team then evaluates the ideas.[21]

- At Toronto's Delta Chelsea Hotel, employees noticed that in the summer months there were fewer business guests and more vacationers' children in the hotel. As a result of employee suggestions, the hotel installed a waterslide, appointed a "kids' concierge," and set up a game room for teens to better serve this market segment.[22]

- AES Corporation is a large energy company where multifunctional teams manage themselves without the assistance of any legal, human resources, or other functional department or any written policies or procedures. No one person is in charge of the teams. As a result of this structure (some call it "empowerment gone mad"), employees exhibit flexibility and continuous learning.[23]

To enhance employee productivity, some companies are now using **wikis**—websites that allow employees to add content whenever they want on issues that are of interest to the business.[24] This is part of a move to "mass collaboration" that is going on in business. Another technique to encourage participative management is the **quality circle**, a group of employees who meet regularly to consider solutions for problems in their work area. The Great-West Life Assurance Company, for example, has reported success with its quality circle program.

wikis Websites that allow employees to add content whenever they want on issues that are of interest to the business.

quality circle A technique used to encourage participative management, whereby a group of employees meet regularly to consider solutions for problems in their work area.

Empowerment is not desired by all employees. Some will be frustrated by responsibilities they are not equipped to handle, and others will be dissatisfied if they see the invitation to participate as more symbolic than real. A good approach is to invite participation if employees want to have input, and if participation will have real value for an organization.

Team Management

In the past, companies usually gave individual employees the responsibility to complete certain tasks, but in recent years, an emphasis on teams has become increasingly common. These teams take a variety of forms. **Problem-solving teams** focus on developing solutions to specific problems. They are based on the idea that the best solutions to problems are likely to come from the employees who actually do the work. For example, at the Bowmanville, Ontario, plant of St. Mary's Cement Inc., members of various departments joined a problem-solving team whose goal was to find ways to reduce the company's energy bills. After analyzing the situation, the committee developed a list of energy-saving initiatives and created plans to implement them. Over a recent three-year period, the initiatives saved the company $800 000.[25] Many companies use problem-solving teams to develop "green" initiatives. For example, at

problem-solving teams Groups that focus on developing solutions to specific problems.

This team of workers at Germany's Apollo car production plant work together to design and manufacture the Apollo sports car. Such teams often help firms make decisions more effectively, enhance communication, and lead to increased employee motivation and satisfaction.

self-managed teams Groups that set their own goals, select their own team members, evaluate their own performance, and generally manage themselves.

project teams (also called **venture teams**) Groups that work on specific projects like developing new processes, new products, or new businesses.

transitional teams Groups that are composed of members from many different countries.

virtual teams Groups of geographically dispersed co-workers that are assembled to accomplish a specific task, using a combination of telecommunications and information technologies.

First Calgary Financial, an Environmental Advocacy Team develops ways to reduce water and energy use. Bentall Kennedy LP, Celestica, and Delta Hotels and Resorts also have such teams.[26]

The problem-solving idea is developed even further in **self-managed teams**, which set their own goals, select their own team members, evaluate their own performance, and generally manage themselves. At Johnsonville Foods, self-managing teams recruit, hire, evaluate, and terminate low performers on their own.[27]

Project teams (also called **venture teams**) work on specific projects like developing new processes, new products, or new businesses. The classic example of a project team is the one that developed IBM's first personal computer many years ago. **Transnational teams**, which are composed of members from many different countries, have also become common. For example, Fuji-Xerox sent 15 engineers from Tokyo to New York to work with U.S. engineers as they developed a "world copier," a product that became a big success.[28] **Virtual teams** are groups of geographically dispersed co-workers that are assembled to accomplish a specific task, using a combination of telecommunications and information technologies. These teams are becoming increasingly popular because of globalization.

Teams provide monetary benefits for companies that use them, but they can also provide non-monetary benefits such as increasing motivation and job satisfaction for employees, enhancing companywide communication, and making members feel like they are an integral part of the organization.[29] Teams work best when successful task completion requires input from several people, when there is interdependence between tasks (as in team sports), and when working together can accomplish tasks that an individual could not do alone (as in a hospital surgical team).[30]

As with participative management, managers must remember that teams are not for everyone, nor are they effective in every situation.[31] At Levi Strauss, for example, individual workers who performed repetitive tasks like sewing zippers into jeans had always been paid according to the number of jobs they completed each day. In an attempt to boost productivity, company management reorganized everyone into teams of 10 to 35 workers and assigned tasks to the entire team. Each team member's pay was determined by the team's level of productivity. But faster workers became resentful of slower workers because they reduced the group's total output. Slower workers, meanwhile, resented the pressure put on them by faster-working coworkers. As a result, motivation, satisfaction, and morale all dropped, and Levi Strauss eventually abandoned the teamwork plan altogether.[32]

Job Enrichment and Job Redesign

Job enrichment and job redesign programs are generally used to increase satisfaction in jobs that are significantly lacking in motivating factors.[33]

Job Enrichment Programs

Job enrichment means adding one or more motivating factors to a job. At one company, a group of eight typists worked in separate cubicles. Their job involved taking calls from dozens of field sales representatives and typing up service orders. They had no client contact; if they had a question about the order, they had to call the sales representative. They also received little performance feedback. Interviews with these workers suggested that they were bored with their jobs and did not feel valued. As part of a job enrichment program, each typist was paired with a small group of designated sales representatives and became a part of their team. Typists were also given permission to call clients directly if they had questions about the order. Finally, a new feedback system was installed to give the typists more information about their performance. As a result, their performance improved and absenteeism decreased markedly.[34]

> **job enrichment** A method of increasing employees' job satisfaction by extending or adding motivating factors such as responsibility or growth.

Job Redesign Programs

Job redesign involves restructuring work to achieve a more satisfactory fit between workers and their jobs. It is usually implemented in one of three ways: through *combining tasks, forming natural work groups,* or *establishing client relationships.*

> **job redesign** A method of increasing employees' job satisfaction by improving the worker–job fit through combining tasks, creating natural work groups, and/or establishing client relationships.

Combining Tasks. The job of combining tasks involves enlarging jobs and increasing their variety to make employees feel that their work is more meaningful. In turn, employees become more motivated. For example, the job done by a programmer who maintains computer systems might be redesigned to include some system design and system development work. While developing additional skills, the programmer also becomes involved in the overall system package.

Forming Natural Work Groups. People who do different jobs on the same projects are candidates for natural work groups. These groups are formed to help employees see the place and importance of their jobs in the total structure of the firm. Such groups are valuable to management because the people working on a project are usually the most knowledgeable about it and thus the most capable problem solvers. To see how natural workgroups affect motivation, consider a group where each employee does a small part of the job of assembling radios. One person attaches red wires, while another attaches control knobs. The jobs could be redesigned to allow the group to decide who does what and in what order. The workers can exchange jobs and plan their work schedules. Now they all see themselves as part of a team that assembles radios.

Establishing Client Relationships. A third way of redesigning a job is to establish client relationships by letting employees interact with customers. This approach increases the variety of a job. It also gives workers greater feelings of control over their jobs and more feedback about their performance. Lotus Software uses this approach as a means of giving necessary independence to creative employees. Instead of responding to instructions from marketing managers on how to develop new products, software writers are encouraged to work directly with customers. Similarly, software writers at Microsoft observe how test users work with programs and discuss problems with them directly rather than receiving feedback from third-party researchers.

Modified Work Schedules

Several types of modified work schedules have been developed to increase job satisfaction, including *flextime,* the *compressed workweek, telecommuting,* and *workshare programs.*

Flextime

Flextime allows people to pick their working hours. Figure 10.7 illustrates how a flextime system might be arranged and how different people might use it. The office is open from 6 a.m. until 7 p.m. Each employee works for eight hours each day. Core time is 9 a.m. until 11 a.m. and 1 p.m. until 3 p.m. Joe, being an early riser, comes in at 6 a.m., takes an hour lunch between 11 a.m. and noon, and finishes his day by 3 p.m. Sue, on the other hand, prefers a later day. She comes in at 9 a.m., takes a long lunch from 11 a.m. to 1 p.m., and then works until 7 p.m. Pat works a more traditional day, from 8 a.m. until 5 p.m.

One survey found that 88 percent of Canadian businesses offer some form of flexible work arrangements (although many businesses offer them to only the most senior employees).[35] Since many employees work more than 40 hours per week, more and more companies are offering flexible working schedules to help them cope.[36] Flextime options are provided at organizations like Next Level Games Inc. (Vancouver), the National Energy Board (Calgary), and the Office of the Auditor General (Ottawa).[37] Alexandra Jacobs, a single mother who works for the Royal Bank of Canada, works three days a week from home. Jacobs manages a staff of five, and each of those people also has a flexible work schedule.[38]

In a survey of 16 000 senior business managers, three-quarters of respondents said that flexible work programs led to increases in productivity, and two-thirds said it led to increases in revenue. The managers also noted that flexible work programs were a way to reward employees and to improve morale. Employees were more motivated when they were allowed to set their own hours.[39] But managers themselves may be under stress because technology infringes on their off-hours work time.[40]

The Compressed Workweek

In the **compressed workweek**, employees work fewer days per week but more hours on the days they do work. The most popular compressed workweek is four days, 10 hours per day, which is used in many companies and municipalities. Companies providing a compressed workweek option include Chubb Insurance Company of

Flextime schedules include core time, when everyone must be at work, and flexible time, during which employees can set their own working hours.

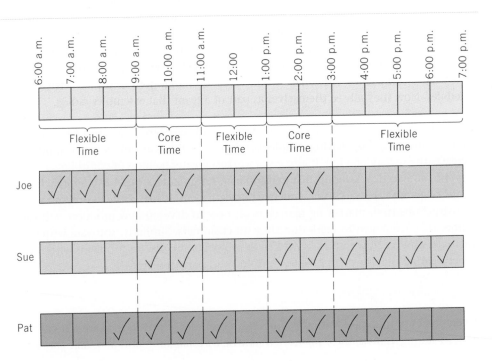

Best Buy is taking modified schedules and alternative workplaces to new extremes with its corporate "results-only-work environment" or ROWE. Under ROWE, Best Buy employees can work anytime, anywhere, as long as they achieve results. The program has been so successful that Best Buy has begun introducing the program into its retail stores.

Canada (Toronto), Next Level Games Inc. (Vancouver), and Cameco Corp. (Saskatoon).[41] The Catholic Children's Aid Society of Toronto has introduced the compressed workweek to help staff cope with long, unpredictable hours.[42]

Telecommuting

A third variation in work design is **telecommuting**, which allows people to do some or all of their work away from their office. The availability of networked computers, fax machines, smartphones, tablets, email, and overnight delivery services makes it possible for many independent professionals to work at home or while travelling. About one-third of the world's labour force now works wherever they are, not just in the office.[43] Many Canadian organizations offer telecommuting as an option. At BC Biomedical Laboratories, 15 percent of the administrative staff work from home, and at LoyaltyOne, 50 percent of call centre representatives don't commute.[44] At Cisco Systems, 90 percent of internal meetings are conducted using virtual meeting software. While 500 people work out of the downtown Toronto office, there are only 200 desks there.[45] In some business functions like customer service and telemarketing, most employees are telecommuters.[46] More information about telecommuting and the compressed workweek is presented in Concluding Case 10-2 and in the boxed insert entitled "The Four Day Workweek and Telecommuting."

telecommuting Allowing employees to do all or some of their work away from the office.

Workshare Programs

A fourth type of modified work schedule, **worksharing** (also called **job sharing**), benefits both employee and employer. This approach allows two (or more) people to share one full-time job. For example, two people might share a position advising the human resources department. One person works Mondays through Wednesdays, and the other works Wednesdays through Fridays. Or five people might share one reservationist's job at Air Canada, with each working one day a week. Each person earns some money, remains in the job market, and enjoys some travel benefits. Worksharing programs can also help ease experienced workers into retirement while their replacements are trained, and they allow co-op students to combine academic learning with practical experience. The worksharing option is used in organizations as diverse as the Ontario Public Service and the National Hockey League (where two goalies often share duties during the high-stress playoffs).[47]

worksharing (or job sharing) A method of increasing employee job satisfaction by allowing two people to share one job.

The Four-Day Workweek and Telecommuting: Are They Really Green?

The four-day workweek has been touted as good not only for employee morale and satisfaction, but also for the environment. There are two main points that are usually made in support of the argument. First, since workers will be driving to work only four days each week instead of five, they will be using less gas and therefore reducing the amount of greenhouse gases that they put into the atmosphere. But whether the four-day workweek really saves gas depends on what workers do on the fifth day. If they drive their SUV 400 kilometres to go visit relatives, they will burn more gas than they would have by simply driving to and from work. On the other hand, maybe they would have taken such a trip on the weekend if they had to work a traditional five-day workweek.

Second, a four-day workweek should mean that less electricity will be used by businesses because machines, computers, and heating systems will be running at very low levels on the fifth day. While it is true that factory machines will not be running on the fifth day, there may be no actual savings because those machines have already run for 40 hours as a result of the four previous days at 10 hours. Other electricity savings may also be elusive unless the company is committed to turning down the heat and turning off the lights on the fifth day. But that may be impossible, because there always seems to be people that need to be at work on the fifth day. Even if workers do stay at home on the fifth day, they may do other tasks that require the equivalent amount of electricity or gas that they would have consumed at work (e.g., renovating their home).

Thus, it may be difficult to determine whether the four-day workweek is better for the environment than the five-day workweek. Telecommuting may indeed be a more effective strategy because workers who telecommute don't come in to the office very much. If they are at home working, they will not be driving their car, so that should save gas. As well, companies that encourage telecommuting may save considerable money on real estate and other operating costs. But even here, we need to analyze what individual workers do as alternate activities before we can conclude that telecommuting is good for the environment.

Critical Thinking Questions

1. Using material contained in this insert as well as other material that you find, develop a list of arguments supporting the idea that the four-day workweek is better for the environment than the five-day workweek. Then develop a list of arguments that the four-day workweek is no better for the environment than the five-day workweek. Which list is most persuasive?

2. Using material contained in this insert as well as other material you can find, develop a list of arguments that telecommuting is better for the environment than the four-day workweek. Then develop a list of arguments that telecommuting is not better than the four-day workweek. Which list is most persuasive?

Leadership and Motivation

LO6 Define *leadership* and distinguish it from management.

leadership The processes and behaviours used by managers to motivate, inspire, and influence subordinates to work toward certain goals.

Leadership refers to the processes and behaviours used by managers to motivate, inspire, and influence subordinates to work toward certain goals. People often assume that "leadership" and "management" mean the same thing, but there are important differences. A person can be a manager, a leader, or both.[48] Consider a hospital setting. The chief of staff (chief physician) of a large hospital is clearly a manager by virtue of the position he or she occupies. But this individual may or may not be respected or trusted by others and may have to rely solely on the authority vested in the position to get people to do things. Thus, being a manager does not ensure that a person is also a leader. By contrast, an emergency-room nurse with no formal authority may be quite effective at taking charge of a chaotic situation and directing others in how to deal with specific patient problems. Others in the emergency room may respond because they trust the nurse's judgment and have confidence in his or her decision-making skills. In this case, the emergency-room nurse is a leader but not a manager. Finally, the head of pediatrics, supervising a staff of 20 other doctors, nurses, and attendants, may also enjoy the staff's complete respect, confidence, and trust. The staff readily take the head's advice, follow directives without question, and often go far beyond what is necessary to help carry out the unit's mission. Thus, the head of pediatrics is both a manager and a leader. The key distinctions between leadership and management are summarized in Table 10.1.

Organizations need both management *and* leadership if they are to be effective. Leadership is necessary to create and direct change and to help the organization get through tough times, and management is necessary to achieve coordination and to complete administrative activities during times of stability and predictability.[49] Management—in conjunction with leadership—can help achieve planned orderly change. Leadership—in conjunction with management—keeps the organization properly aligned with its environment. In addition, managers and leaders also play a major role in establishing the moral climate of the organization and in determining the role of ethics in its culture.[50]

Approaches to Leadership

Political, religious, and business leaders have profoundly influenced the course of human events throughout history, but careful scientific study of leadership began only about a century ago. In the following paragraphs, we briefly summarize the development of this research.

Summarize the *approaches to leadership* that developed in the twentieth century. **LO7**

The Trait Approach

The **trait approach**—which was emphasized by researchers in the first two decades of the twentieth century—was based on the idea that leaders had unique traits that distinguished them from non-leaders. Many traits were thought to be important, including intelligence, dominance, self-confidence, energy, height, and knowledge about the job. As time passed, the list became so long that it lost any practical value. The trait approach was all but abandoned by the middle of the twentieth century, but in recent years it has resurfaced once again. Some researchers now argue that certain traits (for example, intelligence, drive, motivation, honesty, integrity, and self-confidence) provide the *potential* for effective leadership, but only if the person is really motivated to be a leader. The implication is that people without these traits are not likely to be successful leaders even if they try.

trait approach An approach that focuses on identifying the traits that would differentiate leaders from non-leaders.

TABLE 10.1 Kotter's Distinctions between Management and Leadership

Activity	Management	Leadership
Creating an agenda	Planning and budgeting. Establishing detailed steps and timetables for achieving needed results; allocating the resources necessary to make those needed results happen.	Establishing direction. Developing a vision of the future, often the distant future, and strategies for producing the changes needed to achieve that vision.
Developing a human network for achieving the agenda	Organizing and staffing. Establishing some structure for accomplishing plan requirements, staffing that structure with individuals, delegating responsibility and authority for carrying out the plan, providing policies and procedures to help guide people, and creating methods or systems to monitor implementation.	Aligning people. Communicating the direction by words and deeds to all those whose co-operation may be needed to influence the creation of teams and coalition that understand the vision and strategies and accept their validity.
Executing plans	Controlling and problem solving. Monitoring results vs. plan in some detail, identifying deviations, and then planning and organizing to solve these problems.	Motivating and inspiring. Energizing people to overcome major political, bureaucratic, and resource barriers to change by satisfying very basic, but often unfulfilled, human needs.
Outcomes	Produces a degree of predictability and order and has the potential to consistently produce major results expected by various stakeholders (e.g., for customers, always being on time; for stockholders, being on budget).	Produces change, often to a dramatic degree, and has the potential to produce extremely useful change (e.g., new products that customers want, new approaches to labour relations that help make a firm more competive).

The Behavioural Approach

behavioural approach Determines how the behaviours of effective leaders differ from the behaviours of less effective leaders.

Because the trait approach was a poor predictor of leadership success, attention shifted from managers' *traits* to their *behaviours*. The goal of the **behavioural approach** was to determine how the behaviours of effective leaders differed from the behaviours of less effective leaders. This research led to the identification of two basic forms of leader behaviour: **task-oriented** (the manager focuses on how tasks should be performed in order to achieve important goals) and **employee-oriented** (the manager focuses on the satisfaction, motivation, and well-being of employees). Task-oriented managers tend to have higher-performing subordinates, but employee-oriented managers have more satisfied subordinates. Researchers have also identified three main leadership styles: the **autocratic style** (the manager issues orders and expects them to be obeyed without question), the **democratic style** (the manager requests input from subordinates before making decisions but retains final decision-making power), and the **free-rein style** (the manager serves as an adviser to subordinates who are given a lot of discretion when making decisions).

task-oriented A form of leader behaviour in which the manager focuses on how tasks should be performed in order to achieve important goals.

employee-oriented A form of leader behaviour in which the manager focuses on the satisfaction, motivation, and well-being of employees.

autocratic style A form of leader behaviour in which the manager issues orders and expects them to be obeyed without question.

democratic style A form of leader behaviour in which the manager requests input from subordinates before making decisions but retains final decision-making power.

Most leaders tend to regularly use one style and may in fact find it difficult to change from one style to another. But some leaders do manage to change their style. For example, Andrall (Andy) Pearson was abrasive, numbers-oriented, and hard to please when he was president and COO of PepsiCo. But as director of Yum Brands, he softened and transformed and truly cared about employees.[51]

free-rein style A form of leader behaviour in which the manager serves as an adviser to subordinates who are given a lot of discretion when making decisions.

The Situational (Contingency) Approach

As time passed, researchers began to realize that different situations demanded different leader behaviours. For instance, suppose a new manager takes over a work site where workers are satisfied but not very motivated to work hard. The leader should most likely exhibit task-oriented behaviours in order to improve productivity. But suppose a new manager faces a situation where productivity is high but workers are stressed out about their jobs and therefore have low levels of job satisfaction. In this instance, the manager should most likely exhibit employee-oriented behaviours to help improve job satisfaction. This line of thinking led to the development of the *situational approach to leadership*.

situational (contingency) approach An approach that emerged during the 1960s and assumed that appropriate leader behaviour varied from one situation to another.

The **situational (or contingency) approach** was first proposed as a continuum of leadership behaviour (see Figure 10.8). At one extreme, the leader makes decisions alone; at the other extreme, the leader has employees make decisions with only minimal guidance from the leader. Each point on the continuum is influenced by *characteristics of the leader* (including the leader's value system, confidence in subordinates, personal inclinations, and feelings of security), *characteristics of the subordinates* (including the subordinates' need for independence, readiness to assume responsibility, tolerance for ambiguity, interest in the problem, understanding of goals, knowledge,

"I like to think of myself as a nice guy. Naturally, sometimes you have to step on a few faces."

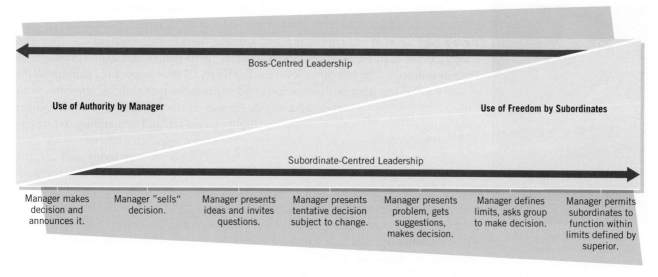

Boss-Centred Leadership

Use of Authority by Manager

Use of Freedom by Subordinates

Subordinate-Centred Leadership

| Manager makes decision and announces it. | Manager "sells" decision. | Manager presents ideas and invites questions. | Manager presents tentative decision subject to change. | Manager presents problem, gets suggestions, makes decision. | Manager defines limits, asks group to make decision. | Manager permits subordinates to function within limits defined by superior. |

FIGURE 10.8

The leadership continuum.

experience, and expectations), and the *characteristics of the situation* (including the type of organization, group effectiveness, the problem itself, and time pressures).

The leadership continuum focused attention on leader behaviours as part of a continuum rather than two simple alternatives and pointed out that various elements of any given situation affect the success of any given leadership style. Although this framework proposed the importance of certain situational factors, it was only speculative. Later models have developed more detailed and specific predictions of how different forms of leader behaviour influence subordinates' satisfaction and productivity.

Recent Trends in Leadership

During the past couple of decades, many new ideas about leadership have been developed. We conclude this chapter with a brief discussion of several of these ideas.

Describe the most recent ideas **LO8** about effective leadership.

Transformational Leadership

Transformational leadership refers to the set of abilities that allows a leader to recognize the need for change, to create a vision to guide that change, and to execute the change effectively. By contrast, **transactional leadership** involves routine, regimented activities that focus on maintaining stability of operations.

transformational leadership The set of abilities that allows a leader to recognize the need for change, to create a vision to guide that change, and to execute the change effectively.

Many leaders may find it difficult to exercise both types of leadership. For example, when Michael Eisner took over the Walt Disney organization, the company was stagnant and was heading into decline. Relying on his transformational skills, Eisner turned things around in dramatic fashion. He expanded the company's theme parks, built new hotels, improved Disney's movie business, created a successful Disney cruise line, launched several other major initiatives, and changed the company into a global media powerhouse. But when the firm began to plateau and needed some time to let the changes all settle in, Eisner was unsuccessful at changing his own approach from transformational leadership to transactional leadership and was pressured into retiring.

transactional leadership Routine, regimented activities that focus on maintaining stability of operations.

Charismatic Leadership

Charismatic leadership is a type of influence based on the leader's personal charisma. Figure 10.9 portrays the three key elements of charismatic leadership that most experts acknowledge today.[52]

charismatic leadership A type of influence based on the leader's personal charisma.

The late Steve Jobs, CEO of Apple, was a prime example of a charismatic leader.

A highly charismatic supervisor will generally be more successful in influencing a subordinate's behaviour than a supervisor who lacks charisma. Charismatic leaders have a high level of self-confidence and a strong need to influence others. They also communicate high expectations about follower performance and express confidence in their followers. The late Steve Jobs, the legendary CEO of Apple Inc., commanded a cult-like following from both employees and consumers. He exhibited charisma, confidence, originality, brilliance, and vision. He was clearly a leader who could deliver success in businesses that were evolving, highly technical, and demanding. Yet he has also been portrayed as an intimidating, power-hungry, aggressive egotist.[53]

Charismatic leadership ideas are popular among managers today and are the subject of numerous books and articles.[54] One concern is that some charismatic leaders will inspire such blind faith in their followers that the followers may engage in inappropriate, unethical, or even illegal behaviours simply because the leader instructs them to do so. This tendency likely played a role in the collapse of both Enron and Arthur Andersen, as people followed orders from their charismatic bosses to hide information, shred documents, and mislead investigators. The film *Enron: The Smartest Guys in the Room* documents this problem.

Leaders as Coaches

Many organizations are now attempting to become less hierarchical and to eliminate the old-fashioned command-and-control mentality that is often inherent in bureaucratic organizations. This change—which will motivate and empower individuals to work independently—also changes the role of leaders. Whereas leaders were once expected to control situations, direct work, supervise people, closely monitor performance, make decisions, and structure activities, many leaders today are being asked to become a *coach* instead of an *overseer*.[55]

Consider the parallel with an athletic team. The coach selects the players for the team and decides on the general direction to take (such as emphasizing offence versus defence). The coach also helps develop player talent and teaches team members how to execute specific plays. But at game time, it's up to the players to execute plays and get the job done. While the coach may get some of the credit for the victory, he or she didn't actually score any of the points.

For business leaders, a coaching perspective calls for the leader to help select team members and other new employees, to provide some general direction, to help train and develop the team and the skills of its members, and to help the team get the information and other resources it needs. The leader may also have to help resolve conflict among team members and mediate other disputes that arise. And coaches from different teams need to link the activities and functions of their respective teams. Beyond these activities, the leader is expected to keep a low profile and let the group get its work done, with little or no direct oversight from the leader.

FIGURE 10.9

Charismatic leadership.

The Charismatic Leader

Envisioning
- articulating a compelling vision
- setting high expectations
- modelling consistent behaviours

Energizing
- demonstrating personal excitement
- expressing personal confidence
- seeking, finding, and using success

Enabling
- expressing personal support
- empathizing
- expressing confidence in people

Elyse Allan, President and CEO of GE Canada reads a report in her Mississauga office, April 19, 2006 (left). In this Wednesday, March 28, 2012 photo, Bonnie Brooks, president and CEO of The Bay and president of Lord & Taylor, speaks during an interview prior to the presentation of the Ivanka Trump Ready-to-Wear Collection at the Lord and Taylor flagship store in New York (right).

Gender and Leadership

Another factor that is altering the face of leadership is the growing number of women advancing to the highest levels in organizations. Given that most leadership theories and research studies have focused on male leaders, developing a better understanding of how women lead is clearly an important next step. The key question is this: Do women and men lead differently? Some early observers predicted that (consistent with prevailing stereotypes) female leaders would be relatively warm, supportive, and nurturing compared to their male counterparts. But in reality, research suggests that female leaders are not necessarily more nurturing or supportive than male leaders. Likewise, male leaders are not systematically more harsh, controlling, or task focused than female leaders. Women do seem to have a tendency to be more democratic when making decisions, whereas men have a tendency to be somewhat more autocratic.[56]

Cross-Cultural Leadership

Culture is a broad concept that encompasses both international differences and diversity-based differences within one culture. For instance, when a Japanese firm sends an executive to head up the firm's operation in Canada, that person will need to be sensitive to the cultural differences that exist between the two countries and consider changing his or her leadership style accordingly. Japan is generally characterized by *collectivism* (group before individual), whereas Canada is based more on *individualism* (individual before group). The Japanese executive, then, will find it necessary to recognize the importance of individual contributions and rewards and the differences in individual and group roles that exist in Japanese and Canadian businesses.

Cross-cultural factors also play a growing role in organizations as their workforces become more diverse. Most leadership research has analyzed white male leaders, because those individuals have historically dominated leadership positions in North America. But as Asians, blacks, Aboriginals, and Hispanics achieve leadership positions, it will be necessary to reassess how applicable current models of leadership are when applied to the increasingly diverse pool of leaders. (For more information on diversity, see Chapter 8.)

Canadian Versus American Management Styles. The management style of Canadian managers might look a lot like that of Americans, but there are several notable differences. Most fundamentally, Canadian managers are more subtle and subdued than American managers. Canadian managers also seem more committed to their companies, less willing to mindlessly follow the latest management fad, and more open to different cultures because of the multicultural nature of Canada.[57] All of these characteristics are advantageous for Canadian companies that will increasingly be competing in global markets. The Global Leadership and Organizational Behavior Effectiveness study found that Canadian managers are very oriented toward fairness, are less likely to protect their own interests above those of their teams, and put more emphasis on long-term goals rather than short-term gratification.[58]

During the past decade, many Canadian-born managers have achieved significant success in companies that operate outside of Canada. These include Bob Kelly (CEO of the Bank of New York Mellon Corp.), Henry McKinnell (former CEO of Pfizer), Steven McArthur (president of Expedia), Patricia Arnold (vice-president of Credit Suisse First Boston), Clara Furse (CEO of the London Stock Exchange), Simon Cooper (CEO of The Ritz-Carlton Hotel Company), and Dominic Barton (chair of McKinsey & Company's Asia Region).[59]

Strategic Leadership

strategic leadership A leader's ability to understand the complexities of both the organization and its environment in order to lead change in the organization, which will enhance its competitiveness.

Strategic leadership—which focuses on leadership in top management—is a leader's ability to understand the complexities of both the organization and its environment in order to lead change in the organization, which will enhance its competitiveness. The late Steve Jobs, former CEO of Apple Inc., was an effective strategic leader who recognized the potential growth of MP3 players and the fact that those devices used technology that is similar to that found in computers. He therefore directed the development of the Apple iPod, which has become an enormously successful and profitable product.

Ethical Leadership

ethical leadership Leader behaviours that reflect high ethical standards.

In the wake of corporate scandals at firms like AIG, Enron, and WorldCom, faith in business leaders has been shaken. Business leaders are now being called on to maintain high ethical standards for their own conduct, to unfailingly exhibit ethical behaviour, and to hold others in their organizations to the same standards—in short, to practise **ethical leadership**. Those responsible for hiring new leaders are looking more closely at the backgrounds of candidates. The emerging pressure for stronger corporate governance models is likely to further increase the commitment to select for leadership positions only those individuals with high ethical standards and to hold them more accountable for both their actions and the consequences of those actions.

Virtual Leadership

virtual leadership The carrying out of leadership activities when the leader does not have regular personal contact with followers.

Virtual leadership involves carrying out leadership activities when the leader does not have regular personal contact with followers. This contrasts with earlier times, when leaders and their employees worked together in the same physical location and engaged in personal (i.e., face-to-face) interactions on a regular basis. The challenges of virtual leadership have confronted Alexey Saltykov, the CEO of InsureEye Inc., a company that helps consumers understand their insurance costs. Alexey is located in Toronto, but he has two employees in Russia, one in Montreal, and a business adviser in Australia. The company uses Skype and web-based collaboration software, but neither approach works as well as Alexey would like. He wants more in-person communication with all the people in one room.[60]

Under virtual leadership, communication between leaders and their subordinates still occurs, but it may be largely by videoconferencing, telephone, and email. In these situations, leaders have to work harder at creating and maintaining relationships with their employees. Nonverbal communication is not possible with email, for example, so managers have to make a special effort to convey appreciation, reinforcement, and constructive feedback to subordinates.

MyBizLab

Capture more moments of true understanding. MyBizLab provides you with interactive study and practice tools directly related to this chapter's content. The new MyBizLab Study Plan Learning Path is designed to measure a full range of skills and provide remediation to give you what you need to master key chapter concepts. MyBizLab flexes to your unique learning needs. The result? Inspired learning, more success.

SUMMARY OF LEARNING OBJECTIVES

1. **Identify and discuss the basic *forms of behaviour* that employees exhibit in organizations.** *Employee behaviour* is the pattern of actions by the members of an organization that directly or indirectly influences the organization's effectiveness. *Performance behaviours* are the total set of work-related behaviours that the organization expects employees to display. *Organizational citizenship* refers to the behaviour of individuals who make a positive overall contribution to the organization. *Counterproductive behaviours* are those that detract from, rather than contribute to, organizational performance.

2. **Describe the nature and importance of *individual differences* among employees.** Individual differences are personal attributes that vary from one person to another. *Personality* is the relatively stable set of psychological attributes that distinguish one person from another. The "big five" personality traits are agreeableness, conscientiousness, emotionality, extraversion, and openness. *Emotional intelligence, or emotional quotient (EQ),* refers to the extent to which people are self-aware, can manage their emotions, can motivate themselves, express empathy for others, and possess social skills. *Attitudes* reflect our beliefs and feelings about specific ideas, situations, or other people. Especially important attitudes are *job satisfaction* and *organizational commitment*.

3. **Explain the meaning and importance of *psychological contracts* and the person–job fit in the workplace.** A *psychological contract* is the overall set of expectations held by employees and the organization regarding what employees will contribute to the organization and what the organization will provide in return. A good *person–job fit* is achieved when the employee's contributions match the inducements the organization offers. Having a good match between people and their jobs can help enhance performance, job satisfaction, and motivation.

4. **Identify and summarize the most important *models of employee motivation*.** *Motivation* is the set of forces that causes people to behave in certain ways. Early approaches to motivation were based first on the assumption that people work only for money and then on the assumption that social needs are the primary way to motivate people. The *hierarchy of human needs model* holds that people at work try to satisfy one or more of five different needs. The *two-factor theory* argues that satisfaction and dissatisfaction depend on hygiene factors, such as working conditions, and motivation factors, such as recognition for a job well done. *Expectancy theory* suggests that people are motivated to work toward

rewards that they have a reasonable expectancy of obtaining. *Equity theory* focuses on social comparisons—people evaluating their treatment by the organization relative to the treatment of others.

5. **Describe the *strategies* used by organizations to improve employee motivation.** There are several major strategies and techniques often used to make jobs more interesting and rewarding. When using *reinforcement* theory, a manager has four basic strategies: (1) positive reinforcement (apply desirable consequences when employees exhibit positive behaviour), (2) punishment (apply undesirable consequences when employees exhibit negative behaviour), (3) omission (withhold desirable consequences when employees exhibit undesirable behaviour), and (4) negative reinforcement (withhold undesirable consequences when employees exhibit positive behaviour).

   Management by objectives (MBO) is a system of collaborative goal setting that extends from the top of an organization to the bottom. In participative management and empowerment, employees are given a voice in how they do their jobs and in how the company is managed. Using teams can also enhance motivation. Job enrichment adds motivating factors to job activities. Job redesign is a method of increasing job satisfaction by designing a more satisfactory fit between workers and their jobs. Some companies also use modified work schedules—different approaches to working hours. Common options include worksharing (job sharing), flextime programs, and telecommuting.

6. **Define *leadership* and distinguish it from *management*.** *Leadership* refers to the processes and behaviours used by someone to motivate, inspire, and influence the behaviours of others. While leadership and management are related concepts, they are not the same thing. Leadership involves such things as developing a vision, communicating that vision, and directing change. Management, meanwhile, focuses more on outlining procedures, monitoring results, and working toward outcomes.

7. **Summarize the *approaches to leadership* that developed in the twentieth century.** The *trait approach* to leadership focused on identifying the traits of successful leaders. The earliest researchers believed that important leadership traits included intelligence, dominance, self-confidence, energy, activity (versus passivity), and knowledge about the job. More recent researchers have started to focus on traits such as emotional intelligence, drive, honesty and integrity, self-confidence, and charisma. The *behavioural approach* identified two basic and common leader

behaviours: *task-focused* and *employee-focused* behaviours. The *situational approach* to leadership proposes that there is no single best approach to leadership. Instead, situational factors influence the approach to leadership that is most effective. This approach was proposed as a continuum of leadership behaviour, ranging from having the leader make decisions alone to having employees make decisions with minimal guidance from the leader. Each point on the continuum is influenced by characteristics of the leader, his or her subordinates, and the situation.

8. **Describe the most recent ideas about effective leadership.** *Transformational leadership* (as distinguished from *transactional leadership*) focuses on the set of abilities that allows a leader to recognize the need for change, to create a vision to guide that change, and to execute the change effectively. *Charismatic leadership* is influence based on the leader's personal charisma. The basic concept of charisma suggests that charismatic leaders are likely to have self-confidence, confidence in their beliefs and ideals, and a need to influence people. They also tend to communicate high expectations about follower performance and to express confidence in their followers.

Many organizations expect their leaders to play the role of coach—to select team members, to provide direction, and to train and develop, but otherwise to allow the group to function autonomously. Another factor that is altering the face of leadership is the number of women advancing to higher levels. While there appear to be few differences between men and women in terms of leadership style, the growing number of women leaders suggests a need for more study. Another changing perspective on leadership relates to cross-cultural issues. In this context, culture encompasses international differences and diversity-based differences within one culture.

Strategic leadership is the leader's ability to lead change in the organization so as to enhance its competitiveness. Business leaders are also being called on to practise ethical leadership—that is, to maintain high ethical standards for their own conduct and to hold others in their organizations to the same standards. As more leaders and employees work in different settings, a better understanding of virtual leadership is also becoming more important.

KEY TERMS

absenteeism (p. 302)
attitude (p. 305)
autocratic style (p. 322)
behavioural approach (p. 322)
charismatic leadership (p. 323)
classical theory of motivation (p. 306)
compressed workweek (p. 318)
counterproductive behaviours (p. 302)
democratic style (p. 322)
emotional intelligence
    (emotional quotient [EQ]) (p. 304)
employee behaviour (p. 302)
employee-oriented (p. 322)
equity theory (p. 311)
ethical leadership (p. 326)
expectancy theory (p. 311)
flextime (p. 318)
free-rein style (p. 322)
goal setting theory (p. 313)
Hawthorne effect (p. 307)
hierarchy of human needs model
    (p. 308)

human relations (p. 307)
individual differences (p. 303)
job enrichment (p. 317)
job redesign (p. 317)
job satisfaction (p. 305)
leadership (p. 320)
management by objectives (MBO)
    (p. 313)
motivation (p. 306)
organizational citizenship (p. 302)
organizational commitment (p. 305)
participative management and
    empowerment (p. 314)
performance behaviours (p. 302)
personality (p. 303)
person–job fit (p. 306)
problem-solving teams (p. 315)
project teams (p. 316)
psychological contract (p. 305)
quality circle (p. 315)
reinforcement (p. 313)

scientific management (p. 306)
self-managed teams (p. 316)
situational (contingency) approach
    (p. 322)
SMART goals (p. 313)
strategic leadership (p. 326)
task-oriented (p. 322)
telecommuting (p. 319)
Theory X (p. 308)
Theory Y (p. 308)
trait approach (p. 321)
transactional leadership (p. 323)
transformational leadership (p. 323)
transnational teams (p. 316)
turnover (p. 303)
two-factor theory (p. 309)
virtual leadership (p. 326)
virtual teams (p. 316)
wikis (p. 315)
worksharing (job sharing) (p. 319)

QUESTIONS FOR ANALYSIS

1. Describe the psychological contract you currently have or have had in the past with an employer. If you have never worked, describe the psychological contract that you have with the instructor in this class.
2. Explain how each of the "big five" personality traits influence leadership effectiveness.
3. Compare and contrast the needs-based theories of Maslow and

Herzberg with expectancy theory and equity theory.
4. How can participative management programs enhance employee satisfaction and motivation? Why do some employees not want to get involved in participative management?
5. What is the relationship between performance behaviours and organizational citizenship behaviours?

Which are more important to an organization?
6. As a manager, under what sort of circumstances might you apply each of the theories of motivation discussed in this chapter? Which would be easiest to use? Which would be hardest? Why?

APPLICATION EXERCISES

1. Interview a manager and ask what traits the manager thinks are necessary for success. How does the manager's list compare with the "big five" list in this chapter? How many differences are there? Why do you think these differences exist?
2. Interview the manager of a local company and ask what strategies the company uses to increase employee job satisfaction.
3. Interview a manager and ask whether the manager believes that leadership can be taught. What are the implications of the manager's answer?
4. Identify two Canadian and two U.S. managers who you think would also qualify as great leaders. Explain your choices.

BUILDING YOUR BUSINESS SKILLS

Too Much of a Good Thing

The Purpose of the Assignment

To encourage students to apply different motivational theories to a workplace problem involving poor productivity.

The Situation

Consider a small company that makes its employees feel as if they are members of a large family. Unfortunately, this company is going broke because too few members are working hard enough to make money for it. They are happy, comfortable, complacent—and lazy. With sales dropping, the company brings in management consultants to analyze the situation and make recommendations. The outsiders quickly identify a motivational problem affecting the sales force: Sales reps are paid a handsome salary and receive automatic year-end bonuses regardless of performance. They are also treated to bagels every Friday and regular group birthday lunches that cost as much as $200 each. Employees feel satisfied but have little incentive to work very hard. Eager to return to profitability, the company's owners wait to hear your recommendations.

Assignment

Step 1

In groups of four, step into the role of management consultants. Start by analyzing your client's workforce motivation problems from the following perspectives (the questions focus on key motivational issues):

■ **Job satisfaction and morale.** As part of a long-standing family-owned business, employees are happy and loyal, in part because they are treated so well. Can high morale have a downside? How can it breed stagnation, and what can managers do to prevent stagnation from taking hold?

■ **Theory X vs. Theory Y.** Although the behaviour of these workers seems to make a case for Theory X, why is it difficult to draw this conclusion about a company that focuses more on satisfaction than on sales and profits?

■ **Two-factor theory.** Analyze the various ways in which improving such motivational factors as recognition, added responsibility, advancement, and growth might reduce the importance of hygiene factors, including pay and security.

■ **Expectancy theory.** Analyze the effect on productivity of redesigning the company's sales force compensation structure—namely, by paying lower base salaries while offering greater earnings potential through a sales-based incentive system. How would linking performance with increased pay that is achievable through hard work motivate employees? How would the threat of job loss motivate greater effort?

Step 2

Write a short report based on your analysis and make recommendations to the company's owners. The goal of your report is to change the working environment in ways that will motivate greater effort and generate greater productivity.

Questions for Discussion

1. What is your group's most important recommendation? Why do you think it is likely to succeed?
2. Changing the corporate culture to make it less paternalistic may reduce employees' sense of belonging to a family. If you were an employee, would you consider a greater focus on profits to be an improvement or a problem? How would it affect your motivation and productivity?
3. What steps would you take to improve the attitude and productivity of long-time employees who resist change?

EXERCISING YOUR ETHICS: TEAM EXERCISE

Taking One for the Team

The Situation

You are a skilled technician who has worked for a major electronics firm for the past 10 years. You love your job—it is interesting, stimulating, and enjoyable, and you are well paid for what you do. The plant where you work is one of five manufacturing centres your firm operates in a major metropolitan area. The firm is currently developing a new prototype for one of its next-generation products. To ensure that all perspectives are reflected, the company has identified a set of technicians from each plant who will work together as a team for the next two months.

The Dilemma

You have just met with your new teammates and are quite confused about what you might do next. As it turns out, the technicians from two of the manufacturing centres have heard rumours that your company is planning to close at least three of the centres and move production to a lower-cost factory in another country. These individuals are very upset. Moreover, they have made it clear that they (1) do not intend to put forth much extra effort on this project, and (2) are all looking for new jobs. You and the other technicians, though, have heard none of these rumours. Moreover, these individuals seem as excited as you are about their jobs.

Team Activity

First, working alone, write a brief summary of how you would handle this situation. For instance, would you seek more information or just go about your work? Would you start looking for another job, would you try to form a subgroup with just those technicians who share your views, or would you try to work with everyone?

Second, form a small group with some of your classmates. Share with one another the various ideas you each identified. Then, formulate a group description of what you think most people in your situation would do and share your description with the rest of the class.

Go to MyBizLab for additional cases and exercise material.

CONCLUDING CASE 10-1

Getting Employees Involved

In a 2011 Psychometrics Canada poll of 368 Canadian HR managers, 69 percent of respondents said that low employee engagement was a problem in their organization, and 82 percent felt that company management should be doing more to increase employee engagement. The HR managers didn't think that employee motivation was low; rather, they felt that managers were not creating the working conditions that would make employees feel engaged. The respondents also expressed the opinion that managers should give employees more recognition and praise (58 percent), should listen more to employee opinions (71 percent), and should provide employees with more learning and development opportunities (57 percent).

Another 2011 survey—this one involving 30 000 workers in 17 different countries—also found reason for concern about employee engagement. The survey was conducted by the global consulting firm Mercer and defined employee engagement as a situation where employees have a vested interest in a company's success and are motivated to perform at levels that exceed stated job requirements. The survey found that one-third of workers are seriously considering leaving their current employer, and that there has been a decline in employee engagement since 2005 when a similar survey was conducted. Specifically, declines were evident in (1) the sense of commitment employees felt to their organization, (2) the pride they had in their organization, (3) employee willingness to go beyond stated job requirements, and (4) the feeling of accomplishment that employees got from their job.

One hint that employee engagement is not what it should be is when employees say things like "They have just announced that there will be no pay raises this year." In this statement, the problem is not really the lack of a pay raise, but use of the word "they." When employees use the "they" word (instead of the "we" word), this often implies a lack of employee identification and engagement with the company. In these cases, employees are really "on the outside looking in."

A lack of employee engagement is a serious problem because employees are a great source of ideas for improving company operations. Consider these examples:

- At Algoma Steel, a shop floor employee came up with a more efficient process for producing heat-treated steel plates that resulted in $90 million in additional revenue for the company.
- At ISL Engineering and Land Services, a senior urban designer was interested in making the company "greener," but he didn't want to force the idea on employees from the top down. Rather, he wanted them to help develop ideas. So, 25 employees who were known to be particularly keen about sustainability were named "green champions." They were encouraged to spend up to 10 percent of their time each day working on environmental issues. Project manager

Jason Kopman, one of the champions, is analyzing energy-efficient upgrades for the ISL building.

- When Razor Suleman, the CEO of I Love Rewards, noticed employee morale and motivation issues in his company, he decided to directly involve 10 to 12 current employees in interviewing prospective new employees. The process means that employees essentially "sell" the company to applicants, and by having staff members directly involved in hiring, it helps ensure that new hires will be a "fit" with the company culture. Employee involvement also extends to participation in objective setting, reinforced by an employee-share ownership program. Employees are also privy to the company's financial statements and can query management on any budget line expense.

One promising way to increase employee engagement is to use social media. When social media first came on the scene, businesses saw it as a tool for marketing the company's products and services to external groups like customers. But now managers are realizing that social media can be helpful in connecting workers with one another. A survey by the International Association of Business Communicators found that 70 percent of companies use social media for internal communications (up from 45 percent the previous year).

About 75 percent of Canadian workers now use social networking sites while on the job. A poll conducted by Robert Half Technology of Canada asked information officers at 270 companies about their company's policy on the use of social media at work. Forty-four percent of the companies allowed employees to use social media sites such as Twitter, Facebook, and LinkedIn for business purposes (that was up from only 22 percent a year earlier). About one-third of the companies still prohibit the use of social media in the office (that is down from 58 percent a year earlier).

Many companies are taking very specific actions to capitalize on the employee engagement characteristics of social media. At Toronto-Dominion bank, the company's internal website has been made into a social media platform that includes blogs, chat forums, surveys, and a feature that allows employees to leave comments on blog pages, news items, and memos. Wendy Arnott, the vice president of social media and digital communications, says that social media is a great way to increase employee engagement.

Sun Life Financial Inc. also uses social media—blogs, online communities, and wikis—to get ideas from employees, and the company has pilot-tested a social media feature that allows employees to respond to the ideas of colleagues. Bill McCollam, the vice president of digital

strategy, said the company got a lot of good ideas as a result of the pilot test. Sun's social media site also allows each employee to develop a personal profile, and this helps managers find people with certain skills that are needed for specific projects. Managers have also noticed that the more casual nature of social media encourages timid employees to speak up and become engaged, whereas they often wouldn't do so in formal meetings.

The push in recent years to make management greener is another area that offers many specific opportunities to increase employee engagement. Jeremy Osborn is the founder of Good Energy, a company that helps other companies get their employees engaged in thinking about sustainability. He says that innovation has to come from employees, and that increasing employee engagement contributes positively to increased social responsibility.

While employees often come up with good ideas for improvement in work processes and methods, getting them to actually share such improvements with management can be tricky, particularly when employees do not trust management. There are several reasons why workers do not share ideas for improvement. First, some workers fear that such sharing will allow others to take credit for their hard-earned knowledge, or that sharing their knowledge will weaken their position in the company. For example, a long-time employee at a small Canadian manufacturing plant taught a younger replacement worker how to run a complicated machine. Shortly thereafter, the older worker became ill and was off work for several weeks. When he returned, he found that the younger worker had essentially taken over his job. The older worker had this to say: "To pass on your experience or your knowledge to others, or to pass on to your fellow workers your secrets, how you assemble it faster, better, or more efficiently for the company, be careful; tomorrow you might have lost your job."

Second, there is a lot of "informal learning" that goes on in companies, but it is not generally recognized or rewarded in Canadian workplaces. Robin Miller, the executive director of the Winnipeg-based Centre for Education and Work, observes that if informal learning is not rewarded, we should not be surprised if employees do not share with management the efficient short-cuts they have discovered that allow them to work faster.

Third, employees fear that if they share their knowledge, management will use that knowledge to increase output. That's okay in the abstract, but if increased output leads management to conclude that they can get by with fewer workers, then layoffs will occur and employees will conclude that sharing ideas helps the company and hurts workers. Many workers have developed extra-fast ways of doing their work, but are reluctant to share those ideas with management. Since managers are always under pressure to improve productivity, the refusal of these workers to share information is frustrating.

Fourth, employees may be afraid of how they will be viewed by the boss if they suggest changes. One study of 400 employees in four different industries found that "social concerns" prevented employees from suggesting changes (they feared that bosses and co-workers would be unhappy with suggested changes to the status quo). One way to overcome this problem is to have each employee's job description include a statement to the effect that everyone in the company is responsible for suggesting improvements in the way work is done.

Fifth, employees may be intimidated by the power differences that exist between them and their managers. It is easy to say that managers should listen to employees, but that may not result in much useful information because employees are hesitant to speak their mind.

A better strategy is for managers to ask employees what they need to do their jobs better. This strategy moves the focus away from the power difference between the employee and the manager, and instead puts the focus on improving the way work is done.

Sixth, workers often don't share their knowledge because they have become convinced that management doesn't think they have anything to contribute. At one manufacturing plant, a new plant manager was trying to resolve some production problems that had developed under his predecessor. He asked for worker participation so that he could understand what was wrong in the plant and how things might be improved. Workers were surprised they were being asked for their ideas, because previous management had not solicited worker input. But in this case the workers agreed to help, and the story eventually had a happy ending.

Questions for Discussion

1. Consider the following statement: *The use of social media by employees is harmful to productivity because employees are distracted from their work and spend time on personal matters instead.* Do you agree or disagree with the statement? Support your position.
2. Why do some workers refuse to share their job knowledge with either their co-workers or with management? What can management do to encourage workers to share their job knowledge?
3. Many managers feel that since companies provide jobs for people, the company has every right to expect that employees will do things like sharing their job knowledge with their co-workers because this will make the company more successful and allow it to continue to provide jobs. Do you agree or disagree with this viewpoint? Explain your reasoning.

CONCLUDING CASE 10-2

What About Telecommuting?

On any given day, many business offices are vacant because employees are at off-site meetings, travelling, on vacation, out sick, or attending training sessions. Many companies now recognize that there are advantages for both employees and the company if they allow employees to work from home and "telecommute." Consider four fairly typical stories.

- Mary Keating, who leads the 15-person technology practice team for Hill & Knowlton, has a two-and-a-half hour commute from her home in Fonthill to Toronto. But she comes into the office only on Tuesdays and Thursdays and works from home the rest of the week. She works with clients and colleagues by using various electronic communications (conference calls, email, and instant messaging).
- Edward Moffat works for Sun Microsystems of Canada. He signed up for the company's "open work" program, which allowed him to work largely from home (or anywhere, for that matter). Before this, he wasn't in the office much anyway because he travelled a lot. Now Ed works out of his Brampton, Ontario, home 9 days out of 10. He doesn't have to pay $300 per month in highway tolls, his gas costs and car maintenance costs have gone way down, and he spends less on lunch. He thinks all those things combined save him about $50 per day.

- Sylvie Bolduc decided to take advantage of Bell Canada's telework option, partly because she was sick of the 90-minute drive to work every day. She says she is a disciplined person and doesn't feel the need to constantly interact with co-workers. She has online meetings with staff on a regular basis and makes trips to the office every two weeks to catch up on other developments.
- Deborah Corber started telecommuting to her job when her family relocated to her hometown of Montreal. Later, she worked out of her home after she started her own consulting firm. She says the biggest challenge was isolation, because she likes bouncing ideas off colleagues. She also had trouble separating her personal and professional life and felt that she was spending way too much time in her office in her home. She eventually decided to stop working at home and now shares space with several colleagues in an office close to where she lives.

These stories show how varied employee experiences are with the idea of telecommuting. They also show that there are advantages and disadvantages associated with telecommuting. Think about these:

Advantages for Employees

- health benefits (for example, lower stress levels; a survey at IBM found that workers experienced conflict between work and home life after 38 hours of traditional work, but no conflict until 57 hours if they worked at home)
- lower costs (reduced car expenses)
- better use of time (no commuting long distances, no interruptions)
- higher productivity (42 percent of workers who were surveyed felt that working remotely helped them get more work done)

Disadvantages for Employees

- lack of understanding of the corporate culture and its values, and feeling "out of the loop"; 29 percent of workers who were surveyed felt that working remotely negatively affects morale and erodes team spirit

- having difficulty separating personal and professional life (work intrudes at home)
- feeling ill-suited for telework (lack of discipline and feeling lonely)
- having difficulty interacting with colleagues and exchanging ideas (because meetings are not attended)
- underutilization of the telecommuter (because managers don't assign telecommuters enough work)
- lack of personal interaction with supervisor
- pressure to work longer hours (43 percent of workers who were surveyed felt pressure to work longer hours when working at home)

Advantages for the Employer

- increased productivity (a survey by the Computing Technology Industry Association found that two-thirds of employers felt that telecommuting boosted employee productivity and saved the company money)
- cost savings (fewer offices and office supplies are needed; Bell Canada reduced its real estate expenses by having 2000 of its workers work at home)
- lower electric bills (fewer lights and computers are turned on in offices)
- access to qualified staff (who otherwise wouldn't be available because they don't live in the area or don't want to drive so far to work)
- lower travel expenses (teleconferencing, email, networking systems take the place of travel)
- lower employee turnover

Disadvantages for the Employer

- may threaten the control of bosses who are used to having employees in sight (requires a change in management thinking, and forces managers to adopt an attitude of trust regarding employees)
- bosses have to spend more time with subordinates on the phone or other media (but the boss may prefer face-to-face communication)
- the telecommuter may not be self-motivated (when Ikon Office Solutions Inc. implemented a telecommuting program for 250 of its sales staff, there were some initial concerns that telecommuters might not work as hard when they were at home, but they were actually very productive)
- telecommuting may not work well for companies where customers must be dealt with in the office

- telecommuting may not work well if colleagues need intense face-to-face collaboration to complete jobs on time
- the telecommuter may be difficult to reach and may not respond quickly to requests from the supervisor
- the telecommuter may work for other employers at the same time, or run a personal business while claiming to be telecommuting
- concern about security of corporate data (companies are concerned about teleworkers accessing sensitive company data from their personal devices such as smartphones; these devices have been subject to increasing cyberattacks)

These advantages and disadvantages mean that telecommuting must be carefully thought through so that it is beneficial both to employees and to the company. From the company's perspective, it does not mean simply telling workers that they can now work at home. Rather, there must be a clear understanding between the bosses and workers about things like the nature of the arrangement, the types of tasks that can be completed away from the office, maintaining safety and confidentiality in the employee's home office, what telecommuting might mean for the employee's career path, and so on. Howard Levitt, an employment law practitioner, recommends that telecommuting be approved only for employees whose performance can be objectively determined (for example, individuals who work on commission or are paid on a piecework basis). He also recommends that a telecommuting contract be drawn up that requires telecommuters to return to a traditional work arrangement if the employer prefers it.

From the worker's perspective, it is important that would-be telecommuters ask themselves several important questions: Can I meet deadlines even when I'm not being closely supervised? What will it be like to be away from the social context of the office five days a week? Can I renegotiate family rules so my spouse doesn't come home expecting to see dinner on the table just because I've been home all day?

Questions for Discussion

1. How is telecommuting different from other forms of modified work schedules? How is it similar?
2. Do you think that telecommuting will become more prominent in the future? Explain the reasons for your position.
3. Interview a friend or relative who telecommutes to their job. What advantages and disadvantages do they see in such an arrangement? Compare their responses with the advantages and disadvantages listed above. If there are major differences, try to explain them.

VIDEO CASE 2–1
Nail Salons

In city centres and malls, sushi restaurants and coffee shops are just two symbols of the diversity of Canada. Another feature of Canadian society is immigrant groups who tend to cluster in certain occupations—Italians in construction, Koreans in convenience stores, and Filipinos in child care, for example. But no immigrant group has transformed its industry like the Vietnamese immigrants who own and operate nail salons. The salons are everywhere now, and they cater to women who want to pamper themselves by having their nails done. In past years, nail salons were of interest mostly to wealthy women, or to women who wanted their nails done for a special occasion like a wedding. Now, however, the cost of a nail job is low enough ($7–$15) that most women can afford it. These salons are like social clubs because there are so many repeat customers who get to know each other.

The growth of nail salons in Canada and the U.S. has been driven by global immigration from Asia and by help from a Hollywood actress. When the Vietnam War ended in 1975, one million Vietnamese fled the country to escape the "reunification" of Vietnam under communist rule. About 100 000 of these "boat people" came to Canada. Tippi Hedren, an American actress who achieved some fame as a result of her appearance in Alfred Hitchcock's movie *The Birds*, heard about the plight of the Vietnamese boat people and wanted to help Vietnamese women find jobs. The women admired her manicured fingernails, so she brought in a manicurist to teach them how to do their own nails. The women became interested in this activity and, being entrepreneurial, started opening up their own nail salons in the U.S. Over the next few years, the movement gradually spread across the U.S. from west to east, and eventually to Canada.

One of the original boat people was 11 when his family escaped. He spent two years in a refugee camp in Cambodia, then came to Canada and opened a Vietnamese restaurant in Vancouver. His wife eventually took a manicurist course and then she and her sister opened a nail salon. Some other relatives also work in the salon. The man sold his restaurant and now works in the salon as well. The tight-knit nature of families has helped the Vietnamese gain success; they want to be their own bosses and do things their way.

Like all businesses, nail salons must deal with both challenges and opportunities. First, early in the history of the nail salon business, there was some concern that Vietnamese women were being exploited because they worked long hours for low wages. But now these women can often make $1000 per week or more. Second, the pioneering wave of boat people has long since dried up, and people from other countries are now entering the industry. For example, one woman from Kazakhstan went from working in a bakery to working in a Vietnamese nail salon.

Third, the reputation of Vietnamese nail salons has been tarnished a bit in recent years because of reports of a lack of sanitation, inadequate sterilization of equipment, and the use of certain harmful chemicals. Most nail salons also do pedicures, and the water used in pedicure chairs poses a potential problem. It must be regularly filtered or the customer's feet are sitting in water that may be contaminated with fungus or warts. New pedicure chairs solve this problem by having water come out the top and drain out the bottom, but these chairs are expensive. Overall, what is needed is a nationwide system of licensing to reassure customers.

On the positive side, however, new products such as elaborate nail designs provide immense revenue potential for nail salons.

All things considered, the domination of the nail salon business by Vietnamese immigrants should serve as an inspiration for other entrepreneurs. These immigrants created a new industry and have managed to prosper with no government subsidies. And the nail industry has boomed even during the tough economic times of the last few years.

Questions for Discussion

1. What does the term "workforce diversity" mean? What are the advantages of a diverse work force? How diverse is the nail salon business?
2. What is meant by the term "motivation"? To what extent are motivational factors different for immigrants than for individuals who were born in Canada? To what extent are they similar?
3. Consider the following statement: *The concentration of certain immigrant groups in certain industries is not a good thing because these immigrants become isolated from the broader Canadian society. As a result, their loyalty to Canada is not very high.* Do you agree or disagree with the statement? Explain your reasoning.

Source: *The National*, "Hands-Down Success," May 5, 2011.

VIDEO CASE 2–2
Clash of the Co-Workers

Venture conducted a survey to determine workers' perceptions of the main causes of conflict in the workplace. Respondents were presented with a list of 10 common worker complaints and asked to list their top three. The top three vote-getters were: (1) people who talk too loudly on the phone, (2) office gossip, and (3) co-workers who waste your time. *Venture* further examined the impact of office gossip, and also looked at the issues of co-workers who don't pull their weight, and clashes between older and younger workers.

OFFICE GOSSIP

Office gossip can poison a workplace. A tanning salon owner who had worked hard to build her company encountered big problems when employees starting spreading rumours about each other. After one salon manager disciplined a worker, other workers began spreading rumours that the salon manager was incompetent. When the owner became aware of the large amount of gossip that was evident at the company, she called all employees into the head office and asked them to sign a contract that prohibited gossip—for example, talking about a co-worker when that co-worker isn't present. A year after introducing the contract idea, the salon owner is getting calls from other companies asking about the policy.

Bob Summerhurst, an HR specialist, says that gossip occurs when bosses play favourites or when they don't communicate properly. Any information void will be filled with gossip, and that gossip is often negative. His solution is not a ban on gossip, but rather regular meetings of managers and employees.

CO-WORKERS WHO DON'T PULL THEIR WEIGHT

Jerry Steinberg, a Vancouver teacher, says that workers with children are often treated as "special" and he thinks it's not fair. He says an extra burden is being borne by people like him when they are asked to work a few extra hours a week to cover for parents who are tending to their children. The problem is worst during the holiday season because people with no children are asked to work holidays so that workers with children can spend time with their kids.

Steinberg is speaking up about his concerns. He has started a website called "No Kidding" where child-free members can vent their frustrations about the unfair treatment they are receiving at their place of work. But Steinberg says it is hard to stand up for yourself because you don't want to rock the boat or be a whiner. He recognizes that it sounds heartless to be unsympathetic to parents' wishes to spend time with their children. But he also observes that these people made a choice to have children, and they shouldn't expect to have an advantage because they made that choice. He is also unhappy about the extra benefits that parents get. He has a simple solution for that problem: give each employee a certain dollar amount that they can spend on whatever benefits they want.

THE GENERATION GAP

Young people in their 20s have generally grown up in an environment where their baby boomer parents gave them lots of things. Now those young people are entering the work force, and they want more things: benefits, money, authority, and free time. And they want them right now.

Consider John and Ryan, who are recent college grads. They are part of a generation that is a problem for business. They feel that they work very hard, but they don't necessarily want to do what their predecessors did (like wearing a suit and tie to work, or working from 9 to 5). Mike Farrell, who researches attitudes of young people, notes that most young people are plugged in and well informed, and these are qualities that employers crave. Theresa Williams, who hires workers for the *Halifax Chronicle-Herald*, recognizes that young people today are different from their predecessors. For example, they don't seem grateful to be offered a job like people in her generation were. She tries to overcome the difficulties in recruiting young people by emphasizing the good working conditions at the *Chronicle-Herald*.

The way students look for jobs is also changing. The job fair approach is still used, but some companies find it doesn't attract the kind of employees they want. One company therefore came up with a gimmick: they posted a job competition on the internet, with the prize being a job for a year, a free apartment, and a trip home for the holidays. The two winners—John and Ryan—moved to Halifax. A year later, they moved out of their free apartment, but stayed on with the company. Now they are helping to design this year's job competition, and they're on board with "the old guys."

Questions for Discussion

1. What are the various forms of employee behaviour that can be observed in organizations, and what is the impact of the various forms on organizations? Identify the forms of employee behaviour evident in each of the three situations described above, and how they affected the organization in which they occurred.
2. What is the difference between "management" and "leadership"? What is the relevance of management and leadership in each of the situations described above?
3. What is the difference between the formal organization and the informal organization? How is the distinction relevant for each of the three situations described above?
4. Consider the following statement with respect to the first incident described above (office gossip): *The grapevine carries a lot of inaccurate information that prevents employees from doing their jobs well. To overcome this problem, managers should provide accurate information through formal communication channels, and that will negate the need for the grapevine.* Do you agree or disagree with the statement? Explain your reasoning.

Source: CBC's *Venture*, "Clash of the Co-Workers," March 26, 2006.

CRAFTING A BUSINESS PLAN
Part 2(a): The Business of Managing

Goal of the Exercise

In Part 1 of the business plan project, you formulated a basic identity for your business. Part 2(a) of the business plan project asks you to think about the goals of your business, some internal and external factors affecting the business, and the organizational structure of the business.

EXERCISE BACKGROUND

Part 2(a) of the Business Plan

As you learned in Chapter 6, every business sets goals. In this part of the plan, you'll define some of the goals for your business. Part 2(a) of the business plan also asks you to perform a basic SWOT analysis for your business. As you'll recall from Chapter 6, a SWOT analysis looks at the business's *strengths*, *weaknesses*, *opportunities*, and *threats*. The strengths and weaknesses are internal factors—things that the business can control. The opportunities and threats are generally external factors that affect the business, such as the following:

- Socio-cultural forces—Will changes in population or culture help your business or hurt it?
- Economic forces—Will changes in the economy help your business or hurt it?
- Technological forces—Will changes in technology help your business or hurt it?
- Competitive forces—Does your business face much competition or very little?
- Political-legal forces—Will changes in laws help your business or hurt it?

Each of these forces will affect different businesses in different ways, and some of these may not apply to your business at all.

Part 2(a) of the business plan also asks you to determine how the business is to be run. One thing you'll need to do is create an organizational chart to get you thinking about the different tasks needed for a successful business.

YOUR ASSIGNMENT

Step 1

Open the saved *Business Plan* file you began working on in Part 1. You will continue to work from the same file you started working on in Part 1.

Step 2

For the purposes of this assignment, you will answer the questions in "Part 2(a): The Business of Managing."

1. Provide a brief mission statement for your business.
   Hint: Refer to the discussion of mission statements in Chapter 6. Be sure to include the name of your business, how you will stand out from your competition, and why a customer will buy from you.

2. Consider the goals for your business. What are three of your business goals for the first year? What are two intermediate to long-term goals?
   Hint: Refer to the discussion of goal setting in Chapter 6. Be as specific and realistic as possible with the goals you set. For example, if you plan on selling a service, how many customers do you want by the end of the first year, and how much do you want each customer to spend?

3. Perform a basic SWOT analysis for your business, listing its main strengths, weaknesses, opportunities, and threats.
   Hint: We explained previously what factors you should consider in your basic SWOT analysis. Look around at your world, talk to classmates, or talk to your instructor for other ideas in performing your SWOT analysis.

4. Who will manage the business?
   Hint: Refer to the discussion of managers in Chapter 6. Think about how many levels of management as well as what kinds of managers your business needs.

5. Show how the "team" fits together by creating a simple organizational chart for your business. Your chart should indicate who will work for each manager as well as each person's job title.
   Hint: As you create your organizational chart, consider the different tasks involved in the business. To whom will each person report? Refer to the discussion of organizational structure in Chapter 7 for information to get you started.

Note: Once you have answered the questions, save your Word document. You'll be answering additional questions in later chapters.

CRAFTING A BUSINESS PLAN
Part 2(b): The Business of Managing

Goal of the Exercise

At this point, your business has an identity and you've described the factors that will affect your business and how you will operate it. Part 2(b) of the business plan project asks you to think about your employees, the jobs they will be performing, and the ways in which you can lead and motivate them.

EXERCISE BACKGROUND

Part 2(b) of the Business Plan

To complete this part of the plan, you need to refer back to the organizational chart that you created in Part 2(a). In this part of the business plan exercise, you'll take the different job titles you created in the organizational chart and give thought to the *skills* that employees will need to bring to the job *before* they begin. You'll also consider the *training* you'll need to provide *after* they are hired, as well as how you'll compensate your employees. Part 2(b) of the business plan also asks you to consider how you'll lead your employees and keep them happy and motivated.

YOUR ASSIGNMENT

Step 1

Open the *Business Plan* file you have been working on.

Step 2

For the purposes of this assignment, you will answer the questions in "Part 2(b): The Business of Managing."

1. What do you see as the "corporate culture" of your business? What types of employee behaviours, such as organizational citizenship, will you expect?
   Hint: Will your business demand a casual environment or a more professional environment? Refer to the discussion on employee behaviour in Chapter 10 for information on organizational citizenship and other employee behaviours.

2. What is your philosophy on leadership? How will you manage your employees day to day?
   Hint: Refer to the discussion on leadership in Chapter 10 to help you formulate your thoughts.

3. Looking back at your organizational chart in Part 2(a), briefly create a job description for each team member.
   Hint: As you learned in Chapter 8, a job description lists the duties and responsibilities of a job, its working conditions, and the tools, materials, equipment, and information used to perform it. Imagine your business on a typical day. Who is working and what are each person's responsibilities?

4. Next, create a job specification for each job, listing the skills and other credentials and qualifications needed to perform the job effectively.
   Hint: As you write your job specifications, consider what you would write if you were making an ad for the position. What would the new employee need to bring to the job in order to qualify for the position?

5. What sort of training, if any, will your employees need once they are hired? How will you provide this training?
   Hint: Refer to the discussion of training in Chapter 8. Will you offer your employees on-the-job training? Off-the-job training? Vestibule training?

6. A major factor in retaining skilled workers is a company's compensation system—the total package of rewards that it offers employees in return for their labour. Part of this compensation system includes wages/salaries. What wages or salaries will you offer for each job? Why did you decide on that pay rate?
   Hint: Refer to Chapter 8 for more information on forms of compensation.

7. As you learned in Chapter 8, incentive programs are special programs designed to motivate high performance. What incentives will you use to motivate your workforce?
   Hint: Be creative and look beyond a simple answer, such as giving pay increases. Ask yourself "Who are my employees and what is important to them?" Refer to Chapter 8 for more information on the types of incentives you may want to consider.

Note: Once you have answered the questions, save your Word document. You'll be answering additional questions in later chapters.

Managing Operations and

To be effective, Canadian business firms must produce high-quality goods and services. They must also have good information on which to base business decisions. The opening cases in the chapters in this section show how business firms do this.

Part Three, Managing Operations and Information, provides an overview of four aspects of business that are important to a firm's survival: efficiently producing goods and services, increasing productivity and quality, managing information systems, and understanding principles of accounting.

Information

- We begin in **Chapter 11, Producing Goods and Services,** by examining how firms manage the production of goods and services and how they control both the cost and the quality of their output.

- Then, in **Chapter 12, Increasing Productivity and Quality,** we consider the various approaches companies take to improve the productivity and the quality of their output and thus their competitive position.

- Next, in **Chapter 13, Managing Information Systems and Communication Technology,** we describe the concept of management information systems and how modern electronic technologies have revolutionized the work of managers.

- Finally, in **Chapter 14, Understanding Accounting Issues,** we examine the role of accountants in gathering, assembling, and presenting financial information about a firm. We also look at the tools accountants use and the statements they prepare to report a firm's financial standing.

Producing Goods and Services

After reading this chapter, you should be able to:

1 Explain the meaning of the terms *production* and *operations*.

2 Describe the four kinds of *utility* provided by production and explain the two classifications of *operations processes*.

3 Identify the characteristics that distinguish *service operations* from *goods production* and explain the main differences in the service focus.

4 Describe the factors involved in *operations planning*.

5 Explain some factors in *operations scheduling* and describe some activities involved in *operations control*, including materials management and the use of certain operations control tools.

Options for Homes: A Unique Business Model

FOUNDED in 1994 by Michael Labbe, Options for Homes is a non-profit organization that is dedicated to providing affordable housing solutions for people with various income levels. The organization acts as a consultant to homeowners and builders to help build communities. Since its inception, Options for Homes has facilitated home ownership for over 3700 families and has worked together with other organizations and builders to create quality homes and communities. Central to the organization's value system is the belief that everyone has the right to be a homeowner, and that homeowning households make for stronger communities. "Part of our vision is that if people have an opportunity to get into homeownership, they'll start to build up some equity," says Joe Deschenes Smith, Vice-President of Partnership at Options for Homes.

Options for Homes values suggestions and feedback, so it organizes monthly meetings for homeowners before they move in. This allows clients to have a voice in how they would like to see their community develop. "We were able to meet all the people who were going to be our neighbours at the Options meetings and we were able to decide what our building was going to be like," says Dennis Bartels, a homeowner in the Distillery District in Toronto. Building a sense of togetherness was seen as an important for Options for Homes buyers. In addition to condominiums being sold at cost, prior to actual construction, Options for Homes offers unique mortgage paying options. It provides financing for second mortgages, which don't need to be paid back until the property is sold; increase a client's down payment to 25 percent; and make the first mortgage more manageable—what it calls the "Social Equity" mortgage concept. "Options provides a loan for up to 15 percent of the cost of the unit. ... The mortgage is

repayable along with a pro-rated share of any price appreciation," says Jane Gadd, reporter for the *Globe and Mail*.

Success for Options for Homes (providing affordable housing) is largely due to its business model, which emphasizes quality and competitive prices. The organization does not try to profit from its activities, and prices are kept down by eliminating the amenities that usually contribute to costly charges (for example, pools and exercise rooms). Expenditures on marketing are limited, with word-of-mouth being the primary strategy. Options for Homes even invites its own purchasers to become its sales force, helping other buyers with their purchase decisions as well as working out of rented venues such as church basements. By eliminating the three key factors that increase home prices (amenities, marketing costs, and profit margin), Options for Homes is able to save buyers $40 000 to

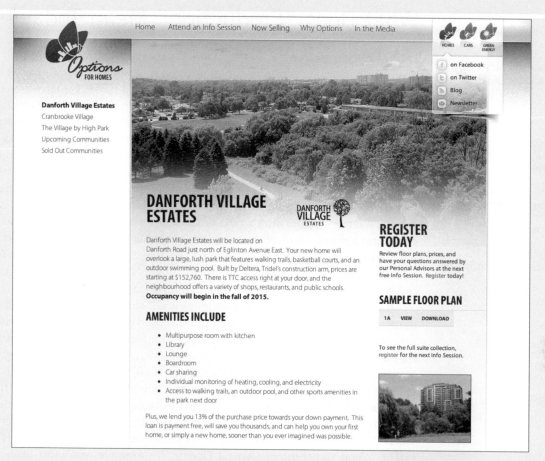

$50 000 off the normal purchase price. While costly amenities are eliminated, however, important things like green technology are retained. These include solar hot water heating, heat recovery ventilation systems, and timed lighting. There is even an Options for Cars program which allows homeowners to reserve a neighbourhood car ahead of time; this saves them the costs of owning a car. The neighbourhood shares the cost of the vehicle and each resident has equal time allocated to use it. With such green features, Options for Homes was recognized by the City of Pickering for one of its developments and was awarded the Civic Award for Sustainability in 2009. In 2011, the organization received the Tarion Award of Excellence, and it was also a finalist for the Climate Spark Social Venture Challenge in 2012. Options for Homes is also developing a new Low Carbon Condo that includes all of these green features plus many more (e.g., no private parking in order to reduce the carbon footprint).

Options for Homes does not want to compromise its goal of offering high-quality, lower-priced homes, so it has limited its activity to the Toronto area. They do, however, train and monitor other organizations across Canada, such as those in Vancouver, Montreal, Ottawa, Waterloo, and Collingwood that implement similar business models. Its unique business model has been made possible due to its purchasers forming co-operative housing corporations that retain Options for Homes as their development and marketing consultant. Options then coordinates the development of town homes and apartment condominiums for them to own. Because of the wide spectrum of sizes and the fact that prospective owners have the option of upgrading their respective suites, Options buildings are attractive to a cross-section of residents. ◆

HOW WILL THIS HELP ME?

By reading and understanding methods that managers use for producing goods and services, you will benefit in two ways: (1) As an *employee*, you'll have a clearer picture of who your customers are, what they want, and how your job depends on the goods and services your company provides, and (2) as a *manager*, you'll better understand that companies remain competitive by continually analyzing their production methods so they can efficiently produce high-quality products and services that consumers will want.

What Does "Production" Mean Today?

L01 Explain the meaning of the terms *production* and *operations*.

service operations Production activities that yield tangible and intangible service products.

goods production Production activities that yield tangible products.

operations (or production) management The systematic direction and control of the processes that transform resources into finished goods.

Everywhere you go today, you encounter business activities that provide both physical goods and intangible services to consumers. You wake up in the morning, for example, to the sound of your favourite radio station. You stop at the corner newsstand for a newspaper on your way to the bus stop, where you catch the bus to work or school. Your instructors, the bus driver, the clerk at the corner store, and the morning radio announcer are all examples of people who work in **service operations**. Firms that make tangible products like radios, newspapers, buses, and textbooks are engaged in **goods production**.

Because the term *production* has historically been associated largely with manufacturing, it has been replaced in recent years by *operations*, a term that reflects both services and goods production. **Operations (or production) management** is the systematic direction and control of the processes that transform resources into finished goods and services. Many of the things that we need or want, from health care to fast food, are produced by service operations. As a rule, service sector managers focus less on equipment and technology than on the human element in operations because success or failure may depend on the quality of provider–customer contact.

It's also true, however, that customers are increasingly involved in all kinds of production because electronic communications have become key components in winning and keeping customers in a huge range of competitive industries. Orders are placed faster, schedules are accelerated, and delivery times are shrinking. Internet buyers can be linked to the production floor itself, where their orders for products ranging from cellphones to automobiles are launched and filled in real time. B2B (business to business) customers also expect real-time response and online delivery.

While companies are typically classified as either goods producers or service providers, the distinction is often blurred. All businesses are service operations to some extent. When you think of General Electric, for example, you most likely think of appliances and jet engines. However, GE is not just a goods producer. According to its annual report, GE's "growth engines"—its most vibrant business activities—are service operations, including media and entertainment (NBC–Universal), consumer and commercial finance, investment, transportation services, health-care information, and real estate, which account for over 80 percent of the company's revenues.[1]

Changes in Production Operations

Over the past 300 years, there have been several industrial revolutions. The first occurred in Britain in the 1800s, and the second in the United States in the early 1900s. Now, a third industrial revolution is underway, based on new technologies,

General Electric (GE) can be classified as both a goods producer (for example, the GE Wind Turbine) and a service provider (for example, media and entertainment shows such as *Saturday Night Live*).

software, robots, and miniaturization.[2] For example, 3D Systems has pioneered three-dimensional printing that produces goods like car parts and dresses using successive layers of plastic ink. New technologies allow machines to run more cleanly, quickly, and safely, and to operate on a global scale. In a modern factory with online manufacturing, machines can log on to the internet, adjust their own settings, and make minor decisions without human help. They can communicate with other machines in the company (via an intranet) and with other companies' machines (via the internet). So-called "smart" equipment stores performance data that become available on desktops around the world, where designers can click on machine data, simulate machine action, and evaluate performance before the machines themselves ever swing into action. With the internet, producers of both services and goods are integrating their production activities with those of far-off suppliers and customers.

Although the factory remains the centrepiece for manufacturing, it bears little resemblance to its counterpart of a decade ago. The smoke, grease, and danger have been replaced in many companies by glistening high-tech machines, computers, and "clean rooms" that are contaminant-free and climate controlled. Production operations have also become much more environmentally friendly. Interface Inc., a Belleville, Ontario, carpet manufacturer, used to produce 500 000 litres of

ENTREPRENEURSHIP AND NEW VENTURES

The Unicycle Motorbike

Well, this vehicle may not be able to fly, but it sure looks like it could. The Uno, touted as the world's first unicycle motorbike, was invented by Ben Gulak, a then–19-year-old MIT student from Milton, Ontario. Eye-catching because of its space-age design and reminiscent of something you may have seen on the once-popular TV cartoon show *The Jetsons*, the Uno is an electric-powered motorcycle that uses gyroscope technology. It's kind of like the Segway (an electric scooter) in that it's controlled completely through body movements.

Gulak made a conscious decision to ensure that his invention provided more than just transportation; it had to possess the cool factor because "… if something doesn't look cool, people just won't be interested." Gulak got the idea for the bike during a family vacation in China in 2006. Struck by the unbelievable pollution, he saw the need to come up with a clean, environmentally friendly, alternative vehicle for densely populated urban centres. He believed a small, easily transported electric motorcycle could be the answer, but it also needed to have the right look. Back home in Milton, Gulak went to work on developing a prototype.

His first test run resulted in a chipped kneecap, but he didn't let that slow him down. The gyro control system needed some fine-tuning so the machine would move more smoothly. He also had a custom motorcycle manufacturer build the body parts out of foam and fibreglass, based on his drawings. The Uno can travel up to 24 kilometres per hour, but Gulak is aiming to reach 60 kilometres per hour. It also can run for about 2.5 hours on a single charge. So far, his parents have bankrolled his research efforts

to the tune of $50 000. But that money is now gone and the bike is not quite ready for production yet. So how does a 19-year-old fellow get the money to advance his prototype development?

He applies to CBC's *Dragon's Den*, of course! In November 2008, Gulak wowed the Dragons with his Uno prototype and landed a $1.25-million investment to be used for research purposes. In exchange, the Dragons demanded a 20 percent stake in his business. Since the show, however, four of the Dragons have reneged on their offers and Dragon Brett Wilson is the only investor remaining. According to Wilson, "Now it's just me and I'm in for $250 000." However, Gulak has not let this setback dampen his enthusiasm. "I really believe in this product and would really like to see it to production," he says.

His ultramodern design is garnering attention and raising eyebrows in media circles. *Popular Science* magazine listed the Uno among the top 10 inventions for 2008. And a profile on the Discovery Channel and a request to do an appearance on the *Tonight Show*, with motorcycle fan and host Jay Leno, haven't been bad for publicity, either. Who knows? With the right combination of engineering and business skills, Gulak just might be able to make this machine fly someday!

Critical Thinking Question

1. Explore and discuss the concepts of production value, transformation, and operations planning as they apply now, or may in the future, to the production of Gulak's Uno. Could any of these factors be reasons why the Dragons backed out of the deal?

waste water every month. It solved that problem by eliminating a printing process that used a lot of water—and saved $15 000 a month as an added benefit. It also reduced carpet remnant waste from 474 tonnes per year to 39 tonnes by making some design changes in the product.[3] The boxed insert entitled "The Unicycle Motorbike" describes one entrepreneur's efforts to build an environmentally friendly product.

Creating Value Through Production

LO2 Describe the four kinds of *utility* provided by production and explain the two classifications of *operations processes*.

utility The power of a product to satisfy a human want; something of value.

time utility That quality of a product satisfying a human want because of the time at which it is made available.

place utility That quality of a product satisfying a human want because of where it is made available.

ownership (possession) utility That quality of a product satisfying a human want during its consumption or use.

form utility That quality of a product satisfying a human want because of its form; requires raw materials to be transformed into a finished product.

production managers Managers responsible for ensuring that operations processes create value and provide benefits.

To understand the production processes of a firm, you need to understand the importance of products—both goods and services. Products provide businesses with profits, wages, goods purchased from other companies, new technology, innovations, and pollution. And they provide consumers with what economists call **utility**—the power of a product to satisfy a human want.

Four basic kinds of utility would not be possible without production. By making a product available at a time when consumers want it, production creates **time utility**, as when a company turns out ornaments in time for Christmas. By making a product available in a place convenient for consumers, production creates **place utility**, as when a local department store creates a "Trim-a-Tree" section. By making a product that consumers can take pleasure in owning, production creates **ownership (possession) utility**, as when you take a box of ornaments home and decorate your tree. But above all, production makes products available in the first place. By turning raw materials into finished goods, production creates **form utility**, as when an ornament maker combines glass, plastic, and other materials to create tree decorations.

As Figure 11.1 shows, **production managers** must bring raw materials, equipment, and labour together under a production plan that effectively uses all the resources available in the production facility. As demand for a good increases, they must schedule and control work to produce the amount required. Meanwhile, they must control costs, quality levels, inventory, and plant and equipment. The impact of production activity on the environment must also be considered. The boxed insert entitled "Producing Green Energy" describes the dilemma that exists in the production of energy.

Not all production managers work in factories. Farmers are also production managers. They create form utility by converting soil, seeds, sweat, gas, and other inputs into beef cattle, tobacco, heat, milk, cash, and other outputs. As production managers, farmers have the option of employing many workers to plant and harvest

FIGURE 11.1

The transformation system.

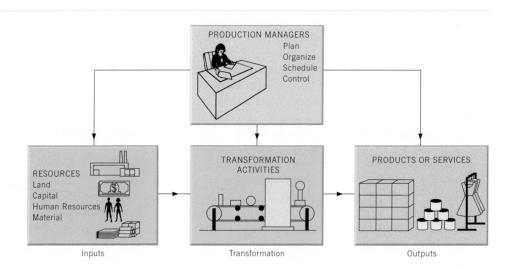

Inputs | Transformation | Outputs

THE GREENING OF BUSINESS

Producing Green Energy

When people think about the production of goods, they usually think of products like automobiles, home appliances, computers, toothpaste, and so forth. But the production of energy is also a crucial activity in our society, and in recent years, there has been a big push to produce "greener" forms of energy like wind and solar. But it is also becoming clear that making green decisions about energy is very complicated because each of the main types of energy (oil, coal, gas, nuclear, hydroelectric, wind, solar, and biofuels) has both advantages and disadvantages.

The dilemma is very clear: The most abundant and cheapest sources of energy (coal, oil, and natural gas) create significant environmental pollution when they are burned, while the least available and most expensive sources of energy (wind, solar, and nuclear) create very little pollution. The fact that consumers want to pay the lowest price possible for energy likely means that there will continue to be a reliance on coal, oil, and natural gas for most of our energy needs.

There are several other factors that complicate decisions about the production of energy. First, some scientists are now questioning whether carbon dioxide is really the driver of global warming. If their views become dominant, that will reduce the push for "greener" energy sources like wind and solar. Second, critics have noted that without large government subsidies, wind and solar power are not competitive with coal and oil, and as a result, wind and solar will not constitute a significant proportion of total energy produced for many years. Third, technological advances in the extraction of traditional fossil fuels have increased the supply of those fuels, which in turn lowers their price and makes them more attractive than wind and solar power.

Biofuels—the production of energy from sources like corn (used to make ethanol) and palm oil (used to make biodiesel)—looked promising at one time, but several unanticipated problems have arisen with this idea. For example, the increased demand for corn to make ethanol drove up corn prices and increased the costs for all businesses that use corn. That, in turn, resulted in higher prices paid by consumers. Poor people were hurt the most, because they spend a larger proportion of their total income on food.

It seems that every way we turn there are problems.

Critical Thinking Questions

1. Consult the sources listed for this boxed insert (found at the end of the book), and then develop a list of the advantages and disadvantages of each type of energy. Based on the list, which source of energy do you think is best? What problems did you encounter as you tried to make your decision about which form is best?

2. Consider the following statement: *It is unwise to continue spending large amounts of money to develop wind and solar power because these sources are too unreliable and too expensive. Instead, more emphasis should be placed on developing technologies to make traditional fossil fuels less polluting.* Do you agree or disagree with the statement? Defend your reasoning.

their crops. Or they may decide to use automated machinery or some combination of workers and machinery. These decisions affect farmers' costs, the buildings and equipment they own, and the quality and quantity of goods they produce. Table 11.1 shows examples of different types of production management.

TABLE 11.1 Inputs, Transformation, and Outputs in Production Systems			
Production System	**Inputs**	**Transformation**	**Outputs**
Farm	Land, tractors and equipment, labour, buildings, fertilizer, farmer's management skills	Cultivation of plants and livestock	Food products, profit for owner, jobs for farmer's family
Jewellery store	Fashion-conscious customers, merchandise, sales clerks, showroom, fixtures, and equipment	Exchange of merchandise between buyer and seller	Satisfied jewellery customers
Tire producer	Rubber and chemical compounds, blending equipment, tire moulds, factory, and human skills	Chemical reactions of raw materials	Tires for autos, airplanes, trucks, trailers, and other vehicles
Furniture manufacturer	Woodworking equipment fabrics, wood, nails and screws, factory, woodworking skills	Fabrication and assembly of materials	Furniture for homes and offices

Operations Processes

An **operations process** is a set of methods and technologies used in the production of a good or a service. We classify various types of production according to differences in their operations processes. In other words, we can describe goods according to the kind of transformation technology they require, or according to whether their operations process combines resources or breaks them into component parts. We can describe services according to the extent of customer contact required.

Goods-Producing Processes

All goods-manufacturing processes can be classified in two different ways: by the type of transformation technology that transforms raw materials into finished goods and by the analytic or synthetic nature of the transformation process.

Types of Transformation Technology. Manufacturers use the following types of transformation processes to turn raw materials into finished goods:

- In chemical processes, raw materials are chemically altered. Such techniques are common in the aluminum, steel, fertilizer, petroleum, and paint industries.

- Fabrication processes mechanically alter the basic shape or form of a product. Fabrication occurs in the metal forming, woodworking, and textile industries.

- Assembly processes put together various components. These techniques are common in the electronics, appliance, airline, and automotive industries. For example, Boeing missed its earnings projections partly because three of its ordered jetliners couldn't be delivered on time, due to unfinished interiors. Common components that cause delays are business and first-class seats and lavatories.[4]

- In transport processes, goods acquire place utility by being moved from one location to another. For example, trucks routinely move bicycles from manufacturing plants to consumers through warehouses and discount stores.

- Clerical processes transform information. Combining data on employee absences and machine breakdowns into a productivity report is a clerical process. So is compiling inventory reports at a retail outlet.

Analytic vs. Synthetic Processes. A second way of classifying production processes is by the way in which resources are converted into finished goods. An **analytic process** breaks down the basic resources into components. For example, Alcan manufactures aluminum by extracting it from an ore called bauxite. The reverse approach, a **synthetic process**, combines a number of raw materials to produce a finished product such as fertilizer or paint.

Service-Producing Processes

One way of classifying services is to ask whether a given service can be provided without the customer being part of the production system. Services are then classified according to the extent of customer contact.

High-Contact Processes. Think for a moment about the service provided by your local public transit system. When you purchase transportation, you must board a plane, train, or bus, so public transit is a **high-contact system**. For this reason, transit managers must worry about cleanliness of their conveyances and the appearance of the airports or stations. This is usually not the case in low-contact systems. Large industrial companies that ship coal in freight trains, for example, are generally not concerned with the appearance inside those trains.

Many industries use transport as their primary transformation technique.

Low-Contact Processes. Consider the cheque-processing operations at your bank. Workers sort the cheques that have been cashed that day and dispatch them to the banks on which they were drawn. This operation is a **low-contact system** because customers are not in contact with the bank while the service is performed. They receive the service—their funds are transferred to cover their cheques—without ever setting foot in the cheque-processing centre. Gas and electric utilities, auto repair shops, and lawn care services are also low-contact systems.

low-contact system A system in which the service can be provided without the customer being physically in the system (e.g., lawn care services).

Business Strategy as the Driver of Operations

There is no one standard way for doing production. Rather, it is a flexible activity that can be moulded into many shapes to give quite different production (or operations) capabilities for different purposes. How, then, do companies go about selecting the kind of production that is best for their company? Its design is best driven from above by the firm's larger business strategy.

In this section we present examples of four firms—two in goods production and two in services—that have contrasting business strategies and, as we shall see, have chosen different operations capabilities. All four firms are successful, but they've taken quite different operations paths to get there. As shown in Table 11.2, each company has identified a business strategy that it can use for attracting customers in its industry. For Toyota, quality was chosen as the strategy for competing in selling autos. No Frills grocery stores (owned by Loblaw Companies) emphasize discount prices. The flexibility strategy at 3M emphasizes new product development in an ever-changing line of products for home and office. FedEx captures the overnight delivery market by emphasizing delivery dependability.

Business Strategy Determines Operations Capabilities

Successful firms design their operations to support the company's business strategy.[5] In other words, production operations are adjusted to support the firms' target markets. Since our four firms use different business strategies, we should expect to see differences in their operations. The top-priority **operations capability (production capability)**—the activity or process that production must do especially well, with

operations capability (production capability) The activity or process that production must do especially well, with high proficiency.

TABLE 11.2 Business Strategies That Win Customers for Four Companies		
Company	Strategy for Attracting Customers	What the Company Does to Implement Its Strategy
Toyota	Quality	Cars perform reliably, have an appealing fit and finish, and consistently meet or exceed customer expectations at a competitive price
No Frills	Low Price	Foods and everyday items offered at prices significantly lower than conventional food chains
3M	Flexibility	Innovation, with more than 55 000 products in a constantly changing line of convenience items for home and office
FedEx	Dependability	Every delivery is fast and on time, as promised

high proficiency—is listed for each firm in Table 11.3, along with key operations characteristics for implementing that capability. Each company's operations capability matches up with its business strategy so that the firm's activities—from top to bottom—are focused in a particular direction.

As you can see in Table 11.3, Toyota's top priority focuses on quality, so its operations—inputs, transformation activities, and outputs—are devoted first and foremost to quality. Its car designs emphasize appearance, reliable performance, and desirable features at a reasonable price. All production processes, equipment, and training are designed to build better cars. The entire culture supports a quality emphasis among employees, suppliers, and dealerships. Had Toyota instead chosen to compete as the low-price car in the industry, as some successful car companies do, then a cost-minimization focus would have been appropriate, giving Toyota's operations an altogether different form. Toyota's operations support its chosen business strategy, and do it successfully.

TABLE 11.3 Operations Capabilities and Characteristics for Four Companies	
Operations Capability	Key Operations Characteristics
Quality (Toyota)	• High-quality standards for materials suppliers • Just-in-time materials flow for lean manufacturing • Specialized, automated equipment for consistent product build up • Operations personnel are experts on continuous improvement of product, work methods, and materials
Low Cost (No Frills)	• Avoids excessive overhead and costly inventory (no floral departments, sushi bars, or banks that drive up costs) • Originally provided a limited assortment of "No Name" products and only the most basic customer service (more recently, stores have expanded both products and customer services) • Customers are required to pack their own groceries and provide their own bags • Low labour costs are achieved by minimum staffing • Labour and shelving costs are reduced by selling merchandise out of custom shipping cartons (in recent years, more conventional product displays have been introduced)
Flexibility (3M)	• Maintains some excess (expensive) production capacity available for fast start-up on new products • Adaptable equipment/facilities for production changeovers from old to new products • Hires operations personnel who thrive on change • Many medium- to small-sized facilities in diverse locations, which enhances creativity
Dependability (FedEx)	• Customer automation: uses electronic and online tools with customers to shorten shipping time • Wireless information system for package scanning by courier, updating of package movement, and package tracking by customer • Maintains a company air force, global weather forecasting centre, and ground transportation for pickup and delivery, with backup vehicles for emergencies • Each of 30 automated regional distribution hubs processes up to 45 000 packages per hour for next-day deliveries

Expanding into Additional Capabilities

Over time, excellent firms learn how to achieve more than just one competence. Our four example firms eventually became excellent in several capabilities. FedEx, in addition to dependability, is noted for world-class service quality and cost containment. But in its earlier years, its primary and distinguishing capability—that set it apart from the competition—was dependability, the foundation upon which future success was built.

Differences Between Service and Manufacturing Operations

Service and manufacturing operations both transform raw materials into finished products. In service production, however, the raw materials, or inputs, are not glass or steel. Rather, they are people who choose among sellers because they have either unsatisfied needs or possessions for which they require some form of care or alteration. In service operations, then, "finished products" or "outputs" are people with needs met and possessions serviced. There are several key areas where service operations differ from production operations.

Identify the characteristics that **L03** distinguish *service operations* from *goods production* and explain the main differences in the service focus.

Focus on Performance

One very obvious difference exists between service and manufacturing operations: Whereas goods are produced, services are performed. Therefore, customer-oriented performance is a key factor in measuring the effectiveness of a service company. Walmart, for example, sells to millions of people from California to China to Canada to Chile. Its superstar status stems from an obsession with speedy product delivery that it measures not in days, or even in hours, but in minutes and seconds. Walmart's keen customer focus emphasizes avoiding unnecessary inventories, getting fast responses from suppliers, streamlining transaction processes, and knowing accurately the sales and restocking requirements for keeping the right merchandise moving from warehouses to store shelves. To implement this strategy, Walmart has made technology—namely, its vaunted computer and telecommunications system—a core competency.[6]

In many ways, the focus of service operations is more complex than that of goods production. First, service operations feature a unique link between production and consumption—between process and outcome. Second, services are more intangible and more customized and less storable than most products. Finally, quality considerations must be defined and managed differently in the service sector than in manufacturing operations.

Focus on Process and Outcome

Manufacturing operations emphasize outcomes in terms of physical goods—for example, a new jacket. But the products of most service operations are really combinations of goods and services—both making a pizza and delivering (serving) it. Service operations thus require different skills from manufacturing operations. For example, local gas company employees may need the interpersonal skills necessary to calm and reassure frightened customers who have reported gas leaks. The job, therefore, can mean more than just repairing defective pipes. Factory workers who install gas pipes while assembling mobile homes are far less likely to need such skills.

Focus on Service Characteristics

Service products are characterized by three key qualities: intangibility, customization, and unstorability.

Intangibility. Often services cannot be touched, tasted, smelled, or seen. An important value, therefore, is the intangible value that the customer experiences in the form of pleasure, satisfaction, or a feeling of safety. For example, when you hire an attorney to resolve a problem, you purchase not only the intangible quality of legal expertise but also the equally intangible reassurance that help is at hand. Although all services have some degree of intangibility, some provide tangible elements as well. Your attorney, for example, can draw up a living will for your significant other or Power of Attorney to have on hand in case of emergency.

Customization. When you visit a physician, you expect to be examined for your specific symptoms. Likewise, when you purchase insurance, have your pet groomed, or have your hair cut, you expect these services to be customized to meet your specific needs.

Unstorability. Services such as rubbish collection, transportation, childcare, and house cleaning cannot be produced ahead of time and then stored. If a service is not used when it is available, it is usually wasted. Services, then, are typically characterized by a high degree of unstorability. Airline companies try to cope with unstorability by scheduling more aircraft maintenance and cabin renovations during the slower winter months, when consumer demand for seats is lower.[7]

Focus on the Customer-Service Link

Because service operations transform customers or their possessions, the customer is often present in the operations process. To get a haircut, for example, most of us have to go to the barbershop or hair salon. As physical participants in the operations process, consumers can affect it. As a customer, you expect the salon to be conveniently located (place utility), to be open for business at convenient times (time utility), to provide safe and comfortable facilities, and to offer quality grooming (form utility) at reasonable prices (value for money spent). Accordingly, the manager sets hours of operation, available services, and an appropriate number of employees to meet customer requirements. But what happens if a customer scheduled to receive a haircut also asks for additional services, such as highlights or a shave, when they arrive? In this case, the service provider must balance customer satisfaction with a tight schedule. High customer contact has the potential to significantly affect the process.

Ecommerce: The "Virtual Presence" of the Customer. The growth of ecommerce has introduced a "virtual presence," as opposed to a physical presence, of customers in the service system. Consumers interact electronically, in real time, with sellers, collecting

The hairstyling service being provided to this customer illustrates the three key features of services operations: intangibility (customer pleasure or satisfaction with the service), customization (the service each person gets is customized for them), and unstorability (the service cannot be produced ahead of time).

information about product features, delivery availability, and after-sales service. They have around-the-clock access to information via automated call centres, and those who want human interaction can talk with live respondents or enter chat rooms. Many companies have invited "the virtual customer" into their service systems by building customer-communications relationships. The online travel agency Expedia.ca responds to your personalized profile with a welcome email letter, presents you with a tailor-made webpage the next time you sign in, offers chat rooms in which you can compare notes with other customers, and notifies you of upcoming special travel opportunities.

Internet technology also enables firms to build relationships with industrial customers. Electronic Data Systems (EDS), for example, helps client firms develop networks among their many desktop computers. In managing more than 700 000 desktops for clients throughout the world, EDS has created a special service called Renascence, which links clients, suppliers, and employees in a private, 500 000-computer electronic marketplace. Some 2000 software products can be viewed, purchased, tracked, and delivered if you are a member of the network.[8]

Focus on Service Quality Considerations

Consumers use different criteria to judge services and goods. Service managers understand that the quality of work and the quality of service are not necessarily synonymous. For example, although your car may have been flawlessly repaired, you might feel dissatisfied with the service if you were forced to pick it up a day later than promised.

Operations Planning

Now that we've contrasted goods and services we can return to a more general consideration of production that encompasses both goods and services. Like all good managers, we start with planning. Managers from many departments contribute to the firm's decisions about operations management. As Figure 11.2 shows, however, no matter how many decision makers are involved, the process can be described as a series of logical steps. The success of any firm depends on the final result of this logical sequence of decisions.

Describe the factors involved in *operations planning.*

FIGURE 11.2

Operations planning and control.

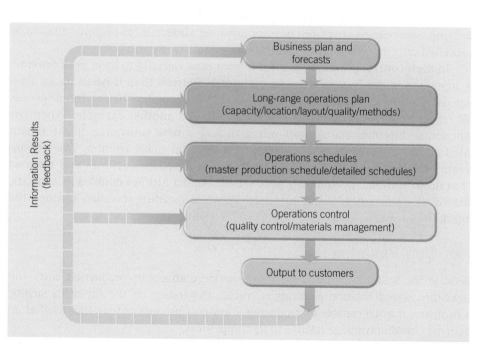

forecast Estimate of future demand for both new and existing products.

The business plan and **forecasts** developed by top managers guide operations planning. The business plan outlines goals and objectives, including the specific goods and services that the firm will offer. Managers also develop a long-range production plan through forecasts of future demand for both new and existing products. Covering a two- to five-year period, the production plan specifies the number of plants or service facilities and the amount of labour, equipment, transportation, and storage that will be needed to meet demand. It also specifies how resources will be obtained.

In the following section, we survey the main elements of operations planning, discussing the planning activities that fall into one of five categories: *capacity*, *location*, *layout*, *quality*, and *methods planning*.

Capacity Planning

capacity The amount of a good that a firm can produce under normal working conditions.

The amount of a product that a company can produce under normal working conditions is its **capacity**. The capacity of a goods or service firm depends on how many people it employs and the number and size of its facilities. Long-range planning must take into account both current and future capacity.

Capacity Planning for Producing Goods

Capacity planning for goods means ensuring that a manufacturing firm's capacity slightly exceeds the normal demand for its product. To see why this policy is best, consider the alternatives. If capacity is too small to meet demand, the company must turn away customers—a situation that not only cuts into profits but also alienates both customers and salespeople. If capacity greatly exceeds demand, the firm is wasting money by maintaining a plant that is too large, by keeping excess machinery online, or by employing too many workers. The stakes are high in the company's capacity decisions. While expanding fast enough to meet future demand and to protect market share from competitors, it must also weigh the increased costs of expanding.

Capacity Planning for Producing Services

In low-contact processes, maintaining inventory allows managers to set capacity at the level of average demand. For example, a catalogue sales warehouse may hire enough order fillers to handle 1000 orders per day. When daily orders exceed this average demand, some orders are placed in inventory—set aside in a "to-be-done" file—to be processed on a day when fewer than 1000 orders are received.

In high-contact processes, managers must plan capacity to meet peak demand. A supermarket, for instance, has far more cash registers than it needs on an average day; but on a Saturday morning or during the three days before Thanksgiving, all registers will be running at full speed. Here is another example: When the Anchorage International Airport was planning a new concourse, prime tenant Alaska Airlines insisted on not having a traditional ticket counter. This unconventional, yet tested, approach uses self-service check-in machines and manned "bag drop" stations. Even during peak season, Alaska Airlines doubled its capacity, halved its staffing needs, and cut costs, all while speeding travellers through the check-in process.[9]

Location Planning

Because the location of a factory, office, or store affects its production costs and flexibility, sound location planning is crucial. Depending on the site of its facility, a company may be capable of producing a low-cost product or may find itself at an extreme cost disadvantage relative to its competitors.

Location Planning for Producing Goods

In goods-producing operations, location decisions are influenced by proximity to raw materials and markets, availability of labour, energy and transportation costs, local and provincial regulations and taxes, and community living conditions. Slovakia, for example, is fast becoming the "Detroit" of Europe. With an existing Volkswagen plant producing 850 000 cars a year, two more giant carmakers—Peugeot Citroën (French) and Hyundai Motor Company (Korean)—opened new plants in 2006. Skilled workers, a good work ethic, and wages below those of the surrounding countries aren't the only reasons. Located in Central Europe, Slovakia has a good railroad system and nearby access to the Danube River, meaning economical transportation for incoming materials and outgoing cars.[10]

Some location decisions are now being simplified by the rise of industrial parks. Created by cities interested in attracting new industry, these planned sites come with necessary zoning, land, shipping facilities, utilities, and waste disposal outlets already in place. Such sites offer flexibility, often allowing firms to open new facilities before competitors can get started in the same area. The ready-made site also provides faster construction start-up because it entails no lead time in preparing the chosen site.

Location Planning for Producing Services

In planning low-contact services, companies have some options. Services can be located near resource supplies, labour, customers, or transportation outlets. For example, the typical Walmart distribution centre is located near the hundreds of Walmart stores it supplies, not near the companies that supply the distribution centre. Distribution managers regard Walmart stores as their customers. To better serve them, distribution centres are located so that truckloads of merchandise flow quickly to the stores.

On the other hand, high-contact services are more restricted, because they must locate near the customers who are a part of the system. Accordingly, fast-food restaurants such as Taco Bell, McDonald's, and Burger King have begun moving into non-traditional locations with high traffic—dormitories, hospital cafeterias, museums, and shopping malls.

Layout Planning

Once a site has been selected, managers must decide on plant layout. Layout of machinery, equipment, and supplies determines whether a company can respond quickly and efficiently to customer requests for more and different products or finds itself unable to match competitors' production speed or convenience of service.

Layout Planning for Producing Goods

In facilities that produce goods, layout must be planned for three different types of space:

- Productive facilities: workstations and equipment for transforming raw materials, for example

- Non-productive facilities: storage and maintenance areas

- Support facilities: offices, restrooms, parking lots, cafeterias, and so forth

In this section, we focus on productive facilities. Alternatives for layout planning include process, cellular, and product layouts.

Process Layouts. In a **process layout**, which is well suited to job shops specializing in custom work, equipment and people are grouped according to function. In a woodworking shop, for example, machines cut the wood in an area devoted to sawing, sanding occurs in a dedicated area, and jobs that need painting are taken to a dust-free

process layout A way of organizing production activities such that equipment and people are grouped together according to their function.

area where all the painting equipment is located. The various tasks are each performed in specialized locations.

The job shop produces many one-of-a-kind products, and each product, as you can see in Figure 11.3(a), requires different kinds of work. Whereas Product X needs only three production steps prior to packaging, Product Y needs four. When there is a large variety of products, there will be many flow paths through the shop and potentially much congestion. Machine shops, custom bakeries, and dry cleaning shops often feature process layouts.

cellular layout A layout used to produce goods when families of products can follow similar flow paths.

Cellular Layouts. Another workplace arrangement for some applications is called the **cellular layout**, which is used when a family of products (a group of similar products) follows a fixed flow path. A clothing manufacturer, for example, may establish a cell, or designated area, dedicated to making a family of pockets—for example, pockets for shirts, coats, blouses, trousers, and slacks. Although each type of pocket is unique in shape, size, and style, all go through the same production steps. Within the cell, therefore, various types of equipment (for cutting, trimming, and sewing) are arranged close together in the appropriate sequence. All pockets pass stage by stage through the cell from beginning to end, in a nearly continuous flow.

In plants that produce a variety of products, there may be one or two high-volume products that justify separate manufacturing cells. Figure 11.3(b) shows two production cells, one each for Products X and Y, while all other smaller-volume products are produced elsewhere in the plant.

Cellular layouts have several advantages. Because similar products require less machine adjustment, equipment set-up time in the cell is reduced as compared with set-up times in process layouts. Because flow distances are usually shorter, there is less material handling and transit time. Finally, inventories of goods in progress are lower and paperwork is simpler because material flows are more orderly. A disadvantage of cells is the duplication of equipment. Note, for example, in Figure 11.3(b) that two saws are needed (one in each cell) as well as two paint areas, but only one of each is needed in the process layout (see Figure 11.3(a)).

product layout A way of organizing production activities such that equipment and people are set up to produce only one type of good.

assembly line A type of product layout in which a partially finished product moves through a plant on a conveyor belt or other equipment.

Product Layouts. In a **product layout**, equipment and people are set up to produce one type of product in a fixed sequence of steps and are arranged according to its production requirements. Product layouts are efficient for producing large volumes of product quickly and often use **assembly lines**. A partially finished product moves step by step through the plant on conveyor belts or other equipment, often in a straight line, until the product is completed. Figure 11.3(c), for example, shows the sequence of production steps performed identically, from start to finish, on all units of Product Z as they move through the line. Automotive, food processing, and television assembly plants use product layouts.

industrial robots Computer-controlled machines like spot welders that perform repetitive operations quickly and accurately.

Many assembly lines use **industrial robots**—computer-controlled machines like spot welders that perform repetitive operations quickly and accurately. At Amazon.com, robots are used to locate items in customers' orders and to move products around the warehouse.[11] In agriculture, robots are used to pick fruit and to milk cows,[12] and hospitals use "service robots" to carry trays of medication or loads of laundry.[13]

lean manufacturing Manufacturing that involves getting rid of traditional assembly lines altogether. Suppliers pre-assemble many specific parts into modules, and then production workers combine the various modules to make the finished product.

Product layouts are efficient because the work skill is built in to the equipment; simplified work tasks can then use unskilled labour. However, product layouts tend to be inflexible because, traditionally, they have required heavy investment in specialized equipment that is hard to rearrange for new applications. In addition, workers are subject to boredom, and when someone is absent or overworked, those further down the line cannot help out. In an attempt to improve productivity even more, many companies are now emphasizing **lean manufacturing**, which involves getting rid of traditional assembly lines altogether. Suppliers pre-assemble many specific parts into modules, and then production workers combine the various modules to make the finished product. This requires fewer production workers, less factory space,

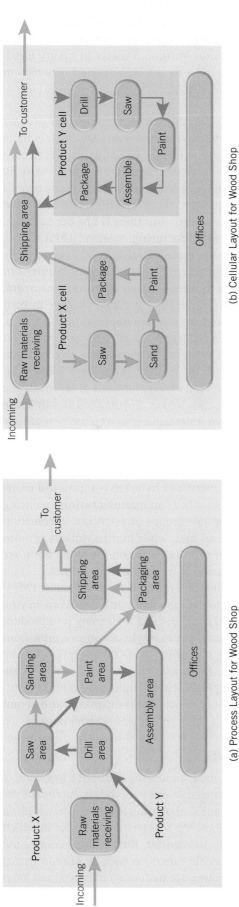

(a) Process Layout for Wood Shop

Arrows indicate unique path of workflow for each product.
Orange = Product X; Blue = Product Y

(b) Cellular Layout for Wood Shop

Arrows indicate unique path of workflow for each product.
Orange = Product X; Blue = Product Y

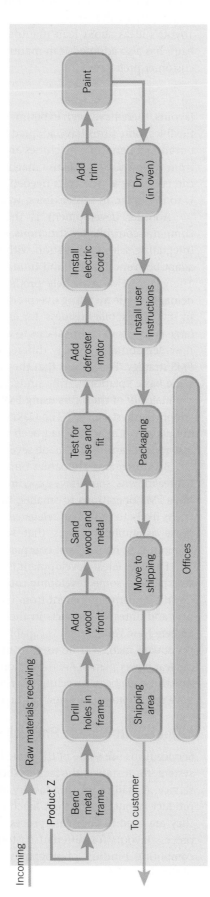

(c) Product Layout—Assembly Line

Arrows indicate the fixed path of workflow for all units of Product Z

FIGURE 11.3

Layouts for producing goods.

and less investment in equipment. In spite of its recent quality problems, Toyota is the recognized leader in lean manufacturing. Bombardier Aerospace (Montreal) and St. Joseph's Healthcare (Hamilton) are two Canadian organizations that have adopted Toyota's ideas about lean manufacturing.[14] Louis Vuitton, a maker of luxury handbags, has also adopted lean manufacturing in order to quickly respond to changes in customer preferences.[15]

Other Developments in Layout Flexibility. In addition to variations on product layouts, there have been experiments in ways to make standard production lines more flexible. Some firms have adopted **U-shaped production lines**. Rather than stretching out in a straight line, machines are placed in a narrow U shape, with workers working from within the U. Because machines are close together, one worker in slow periods can complete all the tasks needed to make a product by moving from one side of the U to the other. In busier times, workers can be added until there is one per machine.

U-shaped production line Production layout in which machines are placed in a narrow U shape rather than a straight line.

Another development is the **flexible manufacturing system (FMS)**. Using computer-controlled instructions, one factory can make a wide variety of products. By integrating sales information with factory production activities, a manufacturer can adapt both mechanical and human resources to meet changes in customer demand. The goal of FMS is to help produce sufficient numbers of products that are in high demand, while avoiding overproduction of products that are not in as high demand. In the automobile business, for example, mass production used to mean turning out large numbers of identical cars to achieve high levels of efficiency. But with consumers now demanding so many different models of cars, manufacturers have adopted an FMS strategy. This means that they can build several different models of cars using the same basic "platform" (the underbody of the car). Nissan, Toyota, and Honda make the majority of their cars using FMS, and North American car makers are now rapidly adopting the strategy.[16] The Oakville, Ontario, Ford plant was the first flexible assembly plant in Canada. It had been making minivans on a single platform, but flexible assembly meant that it made several models on a single platform.[17]

flexible manufacturing system (FMS) A production system that allows a single factory to produce small batches of different goods on the same production line.

Because many companies find large FMS operations to be too complex and prone to breakdowns, some have experimented with so-called **soft manufacturing**—reducing huge FMS operations to smaller, more manageable groups of machines. Automation is less likely to fail when relegated to jobs it does best, while human workers perform those assembly-line jobs that require dexterity and decision making. Both are supported by networks of computers programmed to assist in all sorts of tasks.

soft manufacturing Reducing huge FMS operations to smaller, more manageable groups of machines.

The very latest development is the disposable and movable factory. Because FMS is so expensive, some developing countries with lots of labour but little capital are buying up still-modern equipment from industrialized countries and then using it to produce new and untested products in their own country. For example, an unused press from upstate New York, which is capable of shaping steel with its 14 000 tonnes of pressure per square inch, will be used to manufacture the internal workings of new Chinese nuclear power plants. Areas with long-standing history in the industrial sector in North America have been recycling their old machinery to overseas companies that may not have the capital to buy new or the time to wait while equipment is being made.[18]

Layout Planning for Producing Services

Service firms use some of the same layouts as goods-producing firms. In a low-contact system, for instance, the facility should be arranged to enhance the production of the service. A mail-processing facility at UPS or FedEX, therefore, looks very much like a product layout in a factory: Machines and people are arranged in the order in which they are used in the mass processing of mail. In contrast, Kinko's copy centres use process layouts for different custom jobs: Specific functions such as photocopying, computing, binding, photography, and laminating are performed in specialized areas of the store.

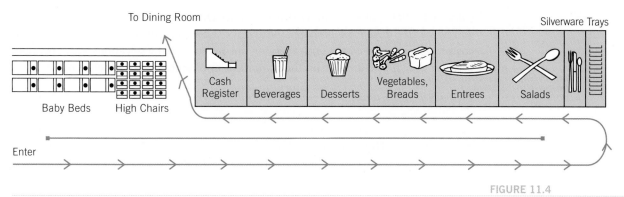

FIGURE 11.4

Layout of a typical Piccadilly cafeteria.

High-contact systems should be arranged to meet customer needs and expectations. For example, Piccadilly Restaurants in the United States focuses both layout and services on the groups that constitute its primary market: families and elderly people. As you can see in Figure 11.4, families enter to find an array of high chairs and rolling

MANAGING IN TURBULENT TIMES

What Happened to the Nano?

In 2008, Tata Motors of India made headlines around the world when it launched a new car that was designed to bring the comfort and safety of an automobile within the reach of thousands of low-income families in India (the selling price was just $2500). The Nano has a rear-mounted, 33-horsepower, twin-cylinder engine; no air bags; no air conditioning; no radio; and no power steering. But it is very roomy, fuel efficient, and easy to steer. People who have driven the car say it doesn't feel like the world's cheapest car.

To make the Nano, Tata Motors used the concept of "frugal engineering," which means making a low-cost product by reducing the manufacturing process to its component parts and then doing each part as cheaply and simply as possible. The company also plans to eventually produce a ready-to-build version of the car that could be delivered in kits. With proper training, people in India could buy the kits, assemble the cars themselves, and sell to their local market.

Surely this car would be a big success. But the initial hype has given way to a sobering reality: The Nano is not selling well. The company originally predicted sales of 25 000 cars per month, but in September 2011 just 2936 units were sold. What happened? Although the car is an engineering triumph, and is sound from a technical point of view, there are several major problems. First, it appears that low-income customers have high aspirations, and they aren't very interested in a car that is seen as a "poor people's car" and isn't much different from a motorcycle. Vinay Sharma, a professor of marketing and strategic management at the Indian Institute of Technology, thinks this issue of aspirations is a fundamental problem for the Nano. Second, very little advertising was done in support of the new car, so it hasn't developed a

strong brand identity. Third, the Nano was marketed primarily through showrooms in large cities, but this meant that many people in potential markets (small cities and towns in India) never saw the car. Fourth, even though the car was cheap, Tata Motors did not make it easy for low-income customers to finance the purchase of the car. Fifth, the world's fragile economic situation depressed sales of all cars, including the Nano (and low-income consumers were particularly hard-hit).

Critical Thinking Questions

1. What are the advantages of a car like the Nano? What are the disadvantages? Explain.

2. What lessons can be learned from the Nano with regard to the relationship of production to the other functional areas of business such as marketing and finance?

3. Do you think the Nano would satisfy consumers in countries outside of India? Explain your reasoning.

baby beds that make it convenient to wheel children through the lineup. Servers willingly carry trays for elderly people and for those pushing strollers. Note, too, that customers must pass by the entire serving line before making selections. Not only does this layout help them make up their minds, it also tempts them to select more.

Quality Planning

In planning production systems and facilities, managers must keep in mind the firm's quality goals.[19] Thus, any complete production plan includes systems for ensuring that goods are produced to meet the firm's quality standards. The issue of quality is discussed in detail in Chapter 12.

Methods Planning

In designing operations systems, managers must clearly identify every production step and the specific methods for performing them. They can then work to reduce waste, inefficiency, and poor performance by examining procedures on a step-by-step basis—an approach sometimes called methods improvement.

Methods Improvement in Goods

Improvement of production for goods begins when a manager documents the current method. A detailed description, often using a diagram called the *process flow chart*, is usually helpful for organizing and recording all information. The process flow chart identifies the sequence of production activities, movements of materials, and work performed at each stage as the product flows through production. The flow can then be analyzed to identify wasteful activities, sources of delay in production flows, and other inefficiencies. The final step is implementing improvements.

Mercury Marine, for example, used methods improvement to streamline the production of stern-drive units for powerboats. Examination of the process flow from raw materials to assembly (the final production step) revealed numerous instances of waste and inefficiency. Each product passed through 122 steps, travelled nearly seven kilometres in the factory, and was handled by 106 people. Analysis revealed that only 27 steps actually added value to the product (for example, drilling and painting). Work

Employees at the Toyota manufacturing plant in Cambridge, Ontario, discuss a production problem. At this plant, employees are responsible not only for making auRtomobiles but also for monitoring quality control and for maintaining a clean work area.

Sometimes, a conventional method of constructing car bodies from steel weakens aluminum. In those circumstances, engineers build an assembly line of robots equipped with the necessary tools to complete the task.

methods were revised to eliminate non-productive activities. Mercury ultimately identified potential savings in labour, inventory, paperwork, and space requirements. Because production lead time was also reduced, customer orders were filled more quickly.

Methods Improvement in Services

In a low-contact process, managers can use methods improvements to speed services ranging from mowing lawns to filling prescriptions and drawing up legal documents. At a bank, for example, the cash-management unit collects accounts receivable for corporate clients; the sooner cheques are collected and deposited, the sooner the client begins collecting interest.

In high-contact services, the demands of systems analysis are somewhat different. Here, for example, the steps to be analyzed include such operations as exchanging information or money, delivering and receiving materials, and even making physical contact.

Service Flow Analysis. By showing the flow of processes that make up a given service, **service flow analysis** helps managers decide whether all those processes are necessary. Moreover, because each process is a potential contributor to good or bad service, analysis also helps identify and isolate potential problems (known as fail points). Consider the traditional checkout method at hotels. The process flowchart in Figure 11.5 shows five stages of customer activities. A more efficient checkout method eliminates steps 1, 2, 3A, and 5. Customers now scan their bills on the TV in their rooms before departure. If the bill is correct, no further checkout is required, and the hotel submits the charges against the credit card the customer showed at check-in.

service flow analysis An analysis that shows the process flows that are necessary to provide a service to customers; it allows managers to determine which processes are necessary.

Designing to Control Employee Discretion in Services. Thus far, we have stressed the importance of the human factor in service activities—that is, the direct contact of server and customer. In some cases, however, the purpose of service design is to limit the range of activities of both employees and customers. By careful planning—and sometimes even by automating to control human discretion—managers can make services more customer-oriented because they can ensure product consistency.

McDonald's, for example, has done an outstanding job of designing the fast-food business as a mass-production system. By automating processes that would otherwise

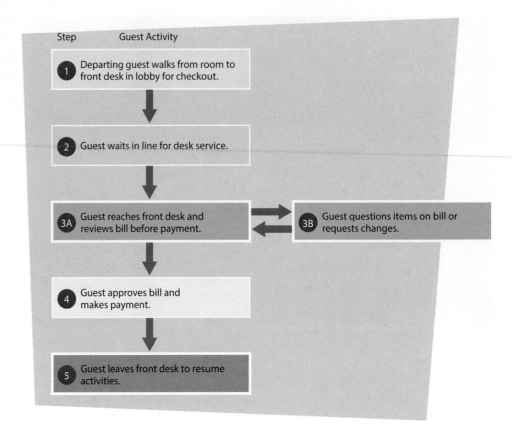

FIGURE 11.5

Service flow analysis.

rely on judgment, McDonald's has been able to provide consistent service from a staff with little specialized training. At a central supply house, for instance, hamburger patties are automatically measured and packed. Specially designed scoops measure the same amount of french fries and other items into standard-sized containers. In addition, all drawers, shelves, and bins are designed to hold the ingredients for McDonald's standard product mixes only.

Design for Customer Contact in Services. In a high-contact service, the demands on system designs are somewhat different. Here, managers must develop procedures that clearly spell out the ways in which workers interact with customers. These procedures must cover such activities as exchanging information or money, delivering and receiving materials, and even making physical contact. The next time you visit your dentist's office, for instance, notice the way dental hygienists scrub up and wear disposable gloves. They also scrub after patient contact, even if they intend to work on equipment or do paperwork, and they rescrub before working on the next patient. The high-contact system in a dental office consists of very strict procedures designed to avoid contact that can transmit disease.

L05 Explain some factors in *operations scheduling* and describe some activities involved in *operations control*, including materials management and the use of certain operations control tools.

Operations Scheduling

Once plans identify needed resources and how they will be used to reach a firm's goals, managers must develop timetables for acquiring resources for production. This aspect of operations is called *scheduling*.

Scheduling Goods Operations

Scheduling of goods production occurs on different levels within the firm. First, a top-level or **master production schedule** shows which products will be produced, when production will occur, and what resources will be used during specified time periods.

master production schedule Schedule showing which products will be produced, when production will take place, and what resources will be used.

Consider the case of Logan Aluminum Inc., for example. Logan produces coils of aluminum that its main customers, Atlantic Richfield and Alcan Aluminum, use to produce aluminum cans. Logan's master schedule extends out to 60 weeks and shows how many coils will be made during each week. For various types of coils, the master schedule specifies how many of each will be produced. This type of planning and scheduling system is required to determine how much of each product is needed.

This information, however, is not complete. For example, manufacturing personnel must also know the location of all coils on the plant floor and their various stages of production. Start and stop times must be assigned, and employees must be given scheduled work assignments. Short-term detailed schedules fill in these blanks on a daily or weekly basis. These schedules use incoming customer orders and information about current machine conditions to update the sizes and variety of coils to make within a specific time period. A classic dilemma in production scheduling is described in "Exercising Your Ethics: Team Exercise" at the end of the chapter.

Scheduling Service Operations

Service scheduling may involve both work and workers. In a low-contact service, work scheduling may be based either on desired completion dates or on the time of order arrivals. For example, several cars may be scheduled for repairs at a local garage. Thus, if your car is not scheduled for work until 3:30 p.m., it may sit idle for several hours even if it was the first to be dropped off. In such businesses, reservations and appointments systems can help smooth ups and downs in demand.

In contrast, if a hospital emergency room is overloaded, patients cannot be asked to make appointments and come back later. As we have seen, in high-contact services, the customer is part of the system and must be accommodated. Thus, precise scheduling of services may not be possible in high-contact systems. A 24-hour-a-day service operation, such as a hospital, can be an even greater scheduling challenge. Nurses, for example, must be on duty around the clock, seven days a week. Few nurses, however, want to work on weekends or during the early hours of the morning. Similarly, although enough nurses must be scheduled to meet emergencies, most hospitals are on tight budgets and cannot afford to have too many on-duty nurses. Thus, incentives are often used to entice nurses to work at times they might not otherwise choose. For example, would you choose to work 12 hours per day, seven days a week? Probably not, but what if you were entitled to have every other week off in exchange for working such a schedule? A number of hospitals use just such a plan to attract nurses.

In scheduling workers, managers must also consider efficiency and costs. McDonald's, for example, guarantees workers that they will be scheduled for at least four hours at a time. To accomplish this goal without having workers be idle, McDonald's uses overlapping shifts—the ending hours for some employees overlap the beginning hours for others. The overlap provides maximum coverage during peak periods. McDonald's also trains employees to put off minor tasks, such as refilling napkin dispensers, until slow periods.

Tools for Scheduling

Special projects, such as plant renovations or relocations, often require close coordination and precise timing. In these cases, special tools, such as Gantt and PERT charts, facilitate scheduling.

Gantt chart Scheduling tool that diagrams steps to be performed and specifies the time required to complete each step.

Gantt Charts. A **Gantt chart** diagrams steps to be performed and specifies the time required to complete each step. The manager lists all activities needed to complete the work, estimates the time required for each step, and checks the progress of the project against the chart. If it's ahead of schedule, some workers may be shifted to another project. If it's behind schedule, workers may be added or completion delayed.[20]

Figure 11.6 shows a Gantt chart for the renovation of a college classroom. It shows progress to date and schedules for the remaining work. The current date is 5/11. Note that workers are about half a week behind in removing old floor tiles and reworking tables and chairs.

PERT chart Production schedule specifying the sequence and critical path for performing the steps in a project.

PERT Charts. PERT—short for Program Evaluation and Review Technique—is useful for customized projects in which numerous activities must be coordinated. Like Gantt charts, **PERT charts** break down large projects into steps and specify the time required to perform each one. Unlike Gantt charts, however, PERT charts not only show the necessary sequence of activities but also identify the critical path for meeting project goals.[21]

Figure 11.7 shows a PERT chart for the classroom renovation that we visited above. The critical path consists of activities A, B, D, G, H, and I. It's critical because any delay in completing any activity will cause workers to miss the completion deadline (nine and one-half weeks after start-up). No activity along the critical path can be started until all preceding activities are done. Chairs and tables can't be returned to the classroom (H) until after they've been reworked (G) and after new tiles are installed (F). The chart also identifies activities that will cause delays unless special action is taken at the right time. By reassigning workers and equipment, managers can speed up potentially late activities and keep on schedule.

Operations Control

operations control Managers monitor production performance by comparing results with plans and schedules.

Once long-range plans have been put into action and schedules have been drawn up, **operations control** requires production managers to monitor production performance by comparing results with detailed plans and schedules. If schedules

FIGURE 11.6

Gantt chart.

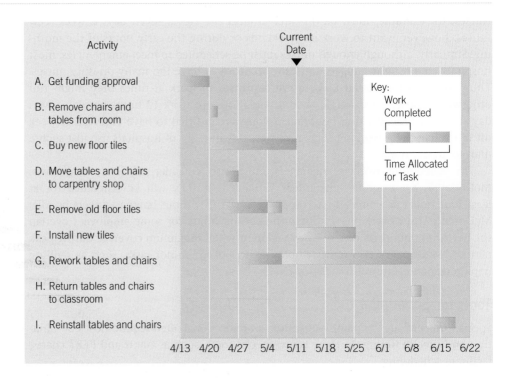

Activity	
A. Get funding approval	
B. Remove chairs and tables from room	
C. Buy new floor tiles	
D. Move tables and chairs to carpentry shop	
E. Remove old floor tiles	
F. Install new tiles	
G. Rework tables and chairs	
H. Return tables and chairs to classroom	
I. Reinstall tables and chairs	

Current Date

Key:
Work Completed

Time Allocated for Task

4/13 4/20 4/27 5/4 5/11 5/18 5/25 6/1 6/8 6/15 6/22

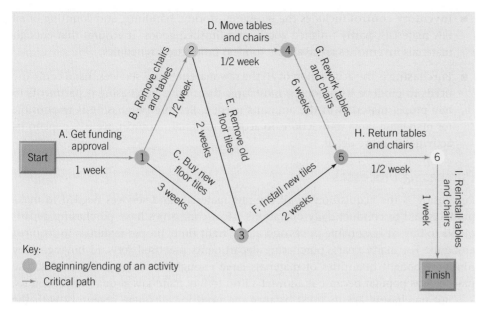

FIGURE 11.7

PERT chart.

or quality standards are not met, these managers must take corrective action. **Follow-up**—checking to ensure that production decisions are being implemented—is an essential and ongoing facet of operations control.

Operations control features materials management and production process control. Both activities ensure that schedules are met and that production goals are fulfilled, in terms of both quantity and quality. In this section, we consider the nature of materials management and look at some important methods of process control.

follow-up Checking to ensure that production decisions are being implemented.

Materials Management

Both goods-producing and service companies use materials. For many manufacturing firms, material costs account for 50 to 75 percent of total product costs. For goods whose production uses little labour, such as petroleum refining, this percentage is even higher. Thus, companies have good reasons to emphasize materials management.

The process of **materials management** not only controls but also plans and organizes the flow of materials (also called logistics). Even before production starts, materials management focuses on product design by emphasizing materials **standardization**—the use of standard and uniform components rather than new or different components. Law firms, for example, maintain standardized forms and data files for estate wills, living wills, trust agreements, and various contracts that can be adjusted easily to meet your individual needs. In manufacturing, Ford's engine plant in Romeo, Michigan, uses common parts for several different kinds of engines rather than unique parts for each. Once components were standardized, the total number of different parts was reduced by 25 percent. Standardization also simplifies paperwork, reduces storage requirements, and eliminates unnecessary material flows.

materials management Planning, organizing, and controlling the flow of materials from purchase through distribution of finished goods.

standardization Using standard and uniform components in the production process.

Once the product has been designed, materials managers purchase the necessary materials and monitor the production process through the distribution of finished goods. There are four major areas in materials management:

- **Transportation** includes the means of transporting resources to the company and finished goods to buyers.

- **Warehousing** is the storage of both incoming materials for production and finished goods for physical distribution to customers.

transportation The means of transporting resources to the company and finished goods to buyers.

warehousing The storage of both incoming materials for production and finished goods for physical distribution to customers.

inventory control The receiving, storing, handling, and counting of all raw materials, partly finished goods, and finished goods.

purchasing The acquisition of all the raw materials and services that a company needs to produce its products.

- **Inventory control** includes the receiving, storing, handling, and counting of all raw materials, partly finished goods, and finished goods. It ensures that enough materials inventories are available to meet production schedules.

- **Purchasing** is the acquisition of all the raw materials and services that a company needs to produce its products; most large firms have purchasing departments to buy proper materials in the amounts needed. Because purchasing is responsible for managing large transactions to acquire material resources, we will explain its activities in more detail.

Purchasing Processes

Purchasing is the acquisition of all the raw materials and services needed to make products and to conduct daily operations. Most companies have purchasing departments to buy, at reasonable prices and at the right time, proper materials in required amounts. For many years, purchasing departments practised forward buying—they routinely bought quantities of materials large enough to fill long-term needs. The practice was popular because it allowed a firm to buy materials at quantity discounts.

holding costs Costs of keeping extra supplies or inventory on hand.

But purchasing agents must balance the need for adequate inventory with the need to avoid excess supplies, which drive up **holding costs**—the costs of keeping inventory on hand.[22] These include the real costs of storage, handling, and insurance as well as opportunity costs—additional earnings that the company must pass up because funds are tied up in inventory.

lead times In purchasing control, the gap between the customer's placement of an order and the seller's shipment of merchandise.

Today, many purchasing departments have opted for the so-called hand-to-mouth pattern—placing small orders frequently. It requires fast delivery **lead times**—the gaps between the customer's order placement and the seller's shipment and delivery reliability. A radio maker that uses thousands of standard components may significantly reduce holding costs by ordering only what it needs for a coming day or week.

supplier selection Finding and determining suppliers to buy from.

Supplier Selection. Purchasing departments also handle **supplier selection**—deciding which suppliers to buy from. The process typically has four stages:

1. Investigating possible suppliers

2. Evaluating and isolating the best candidates

3. Negotiating terms of service with a final choice

4. Maintaining a positive buyer–seller relationship

Maintaining multiple supplier relationships is expensive. It takes time to survey, contact, and evaluate potential suppliers and build good relationships. In addition, fewer suppliers means stronger, mutually dependent purchaser–supplier relationships. Today, therefore, most purchasers try to reduce their number of suppliers. In the first year of a supplier-reduction program, one 3M factory trimmed its supplier list from 2800 to 600—and then reduced it to 300 the following year. Dana Corp., one of the world's largest suppliers of automobile components, is dropping half of its 86 000 suppliers.[23]

Tools for Operations Process Control

Numerous tools assist managers in controlling operations. Chief among these are *worker training, just-in-time production systems, material requirements planning,* and *quality control.*

Worker Training

Customer satisfaction is closely linked to the employees who provide the service. Human relations skills are vital for anyone who has contact with the public. More and more human resource experts now realize that in businesses such as airlines, employment agencies, and hotels, employees without training in relationship skills can cause the company to lose customers to better-prepared competitors. The Walt Disney Co. does an excellent job of remembering that, no matter what their jobs, service employees are links to the public. For example, Disney World has a team of sweepers constantly at work picking up bits of trash as soon as they fall to the ground. When visitors have questions about directions or time, they often ask one of the sweepers. Because their responses affect visitors' overall impressions of Disney World, sweepers are trained to respond in appropriate ways. Their work is evaluated and rewarded based on strict performance appraisal standards.[24]

Just-in-Time Production Systems

To minimize manufacturing inventory costs, many companies use **just-in-time (JIT) production systems**. JIT brings together all the needed materials and parts at the precise moment they are required for each production stage, not before. All resources are continuously flowing, from their arrival as raw materials to subassembly, final completion, and shipment of finished products. JIT reduces to practically nothing the number of goods in process (that is, goods not yet finished) and saves money by replacing stop-and-go production with smooth movement. Once smooth movements become the norm, disruptions become more visible and thus are resolved more quickly. Finding and eliminating disruptions by continuous improvement of production is a major objective of JIT. Here are just two examples:

> **just-in-time (JIT) production system** A method of inventory control in which materials are acquired and put into production just as they are needed.

- Toronto's Mount Sinai Hospital uses JIT. Individual suppliers no longer go to Mount Sinai to deliver the items they have sold to the hospital. Rather, all suppliers deliver their products to Livingston Healthcare Services Inc., which stores these items and fills Mount Sinai's order once each day; therefore, Mount Sinai no longer keeps any inventory. Once the goods are delivered, they are sent directly to the various departments in the hospital; the former centralized storeroom at the hospital no longer exists. In its first year using the new system, the hospital saved about $200 000.[25]

- Sobeys, the grocery chain, has invested in more efficient inventory management that has allowed it to reduce the size of storage rooms by 10 percent because products now move more quickly to the shelves.[26]

JIT can cause some unexpected problems, however. As more and more companies adopt the philosophy that they will carry only minimal inventories, the ordering of supplies has become much more last-minute and frantic. By definition, this makes supply systems more volatile, and it has been one of the reasons why economic indicators like capital goods orders have been swinging so wildly. This, in turn, makes it hard to know what shape the overall economy is in. The more uncertainty there is about the economy, the less investor enthusiasm there is.[27]

Material Requirements Planning

Like JIT, **material requirements planning (MRP)** seeks to deliver the right amount of materials at the right place and the right time for goods production. MRP uses a **bill of materials** that is basically a recipe for the finished product. It specifies the necessary ingredients (raw materials and components), the order in which they should be combined, and the quantity of each ingredient needed to make one batch of the product (say, 2000 finished telephones). The recipe is fed in to a computer that controls inventory and schedules each stage of production. The result is fewer early arrivals, less frequent stock shortages, and lower storage costs. MRP is most popular among companies whose products require complicated assembly and fabrication activities, such as automobile manufacturers, appliance makers, and furniture companies.

> **material requirements planning (MRP)** A method of inventory control in which a computerized bill of materials is used to estimate production needs so that resources are acquired and put into production only as needed.
>
> **bill of materials** Basically a recipe for the finished product.

Manufacturing resource planning (MRP II) is an advanced version of MRP that ties all parts of the organization into the company's production activities. For example, MRP inventory and production schedules are translated into cost requirements for the

> **manufacturing resource planning (MRP II)** An advanced version of MRP that ties together all parts of the organization into the company's production activities.

financial management department and into personnel requirements for the human resources department; information about available capacity for new orders goes to the marketing department.

Quality Control

quality control The management of the production process to manufacture goods or supply services that meet specific quality standards.

Another operation control tool is **quality control**—the management of the production process to manufacture goods or supply services that meet specific quality standards. McDonald's, for example, is a pioneer in quality control in the restaurant industry. The company oversees everything from the farming of potatoes for french fries to the packing of meat for Big Macs. Quality-assurance staffers even check standards for ketchup sweetness and french fry length. We discuss quality control in more detail in the following chapter, where we focus on the connection between productivity and quality.

MyBizLab

Capture more moments of true understanding. MyBizLab provides you with interactive study and practice tools directly related to this chapter's content. The new MyBizLab Study Plan Learning Path is designed to measure a full range of skills and provide remediation to give you what you need to master key chapter concepts. MyBizLab flexes to your unique learning needs. The result? Inspired learning, more success.

SUMMARY OF LEARNING OBJECTIVES

1. **Explain the meaning of the terms *production* and *operations*.** *Service operations* provide intangible and tangible service products, such as entertainment, transportation, education, and food preparation. Firms that make tangible products—radios, newspapers, buses, and textbooks—are engaged in *goods production*. Because the term *production* is associated just with manufacturing, we now use *operations* to refer to both service and goods production. *Operations (or production) management* is the systematic direction and control of the processes that transform resources into finished services and goods that create value for and provide benefits to customers. In overseeing *production*, *inventory*, and *quality control*, operations (or production) managers are responsible for ensuring that operations processes create value and provide benefits.

2. **Describe the four kinds of *utility* provided by production and explain the two classifications of *operations processes*.** Products provide businesses with economic results—profits, wages, and goods purchased from other companies. They also provide consumers with *utility*—the ability of a product to satisfy a human want. There are four kinds of production-based utility: (1) *time utility*—production makes products available when consumers want them; (2) *place utility*—production makes products available where they are convenient for consumers; (3) *ownership (or possession) utility*—production makes products available for consumers to own and use; and (4) *form utility*—by turning raw materials into finished goods, production makes products available in the first place. An *operations process* is a set of methods and technologies used in the production of a good or a service. There are two types of operations processes for goods: (1) An *analytic process* breaks down resources into components, and (2) a *synthetic process* combines raw materials to produce a finished product. Services are classified as *high-contact processes* and *low-contact processes*, according to the extent of customer contact. To receive the service in a high-contact system, the customer must be a part of the system. In a low-contact system, customers are not in contact with the provider while the service is performed.

3. **Identify the characteristics that distinguish *service operations* from *goods production* and explain the main differences in the service focus.** Both service and manufacturing operations transform raw materials into finished products. In service production, the raw materials are people who have either unsatisfied needs or possessions needing some form of care or alteration; "finished products" are people with needs met and possessions serviced. The focus of service operations differs from that of goods production in five ways: (1) Focus on performance—because goods are produced and services performed, customer-oriented performance is crucial to a service company. (2) Focus on process and outcome—because most service products are combinations of goods and services, services focus on both the transformation process and its outcome. (3) Focus on service characteristics—service transactions reflect the three key qualities of service products: (i) Intangibility: Because services usually can't be touched, tasted, smelled, or seen, they provide intangible

value experienced as pleasure, satisfaction, or a feeling of safety. (ii) Customization: Each customer expects a service to be designed (customized) for his or her specific needs. (iii) Unstorability: Because many services can't be produced ahead of time and then stored, they have a high degree of unstorability. (4) Focus on the customer-service link—because service operations often acknowledge the customer as part of the process, consumers can directly affect that process. (5) Focus on service quality considerations—service providers know that quality of work and quality of service are not necessarily the same thing (a properly repaired car is one thing, but getting it back when you need it is another).

4. **Describe the factors involved in** *operations planning.* The operations-management process is a series of logical steps. Whereas the business plan outlines goals and objectives, managers also develop long-range production plans through forecasts of future demand for both new and existing products. Operations planning then focuses on five major categories: (1) Capacity planning—the amount of a product that a company can produce under normal working conditions is its *capacity*. The capacity of a goods or service firm depends on how many people it employs and the number and size of its facilities. (2) Location planning—in location planning, managers in goods-producing operations consider such factors as proximity to raw materials and markets, availability of labour, energy and transportation costs, regulations and taxes, and community living conditions. (3) Layout planning—layout of machinery, equipment, and supplies determines how quickly a company can respond to customer demand for more and different products. In a *process layout*, which is well suited to job shops specializing in custom work, equipment and people are grouped according to function. *Cellular layouts* take groups of similar products through fixed flow paths. Equipment set-up is easier, flow distances are shorter, and material handling and transit time are reduced. In a *product layout*, equipment and people are set up to produce one type of product in a fixed sequence.

(4) Quality planning—products must meet standards of quality. Such standards may include reasonable price and consistent performance. (5) Methods planning—when managers reduce waste and inefficiency by identifying every production stage and the specific methods for performing it, they are practising methods improvement. A process flow chart can identify the sequence of production activities, movements of materials, and work performed at each stage. The flow can then be analyzed to identify wasteful activities, sources of delay, and other inefficiencies. *Service flow analysis* helps managers decide which processes in a service are necessary. It also helps isolate potential problems known as fail points.

5. **Explain some factors in** *operations scheduling* **and describe some activities involved in** *operations control,* **including materials management and the use of certain operations control tools.** A *master production schedule* shows which products will be produced, when production will take place, and what resources will be used during specified periods. For scheduling special projects, two tools— *Gantt charts* and *PERT charts*—assist managers in maintaining close coordination and timing. *Operations control* requires managers to monitor performance by comparing results with detailed plans and schedules. If schedules or quality standards are not met, managers take corrective action. *Follow-up*—checking to ensure that decisions are being implemented—is an essential facet of operations control. There are four areas in materials management: (1) *Transportation* includes the means of transporting resources to the company and finished goods to buyers; (2) *warehousing* is the storage of incoming materials and finished goods for distribution to customers; (3) *inventory control* includes the receiving, storing, handling, and counting of all raw materials, partly finished goods, and finished goods. It ensures that enough materials inventories are available to meet production schedules; (4) *purchasing* is the acquisition of all the raw materials and services that a company needs for production.

KEY TERMS

analytic process (p. 346)
assembly line (p. 354)
bill of materials (p. 365)
capacity (p. 352)
cellular layout (p. 354)
flexible manufacturing system (FMS) (p. 356)
follow-up (p. 363)
forecast (p. 352)
form utility (p. 344)
Gantt chart (p. 362)
goods production (p. 342)
high-contact system (p. 346)
holding costs (p. 364)
industrial robots (p. 354)
inventory control (p. 374)
just-in-time (JIT) production system (p. 365)

lead times (p. 364)
lean manufacturing (p. 354)
low-contact system (p. 347)
manufacturing resource planning (MRP II) (p. 365)
master production schedule (p. 361)
material requirements planning (MRP) (p. 365)
materials management (p. 363)
operations capability (production capability) (p. 347)
operations control (p. 362)
operations process (p. 346)
operations (production) management (p. 342)
ownership (possession) utility (p. 344)
PERT chart (p. 362)
place utility (p. 344)

process layout (p. 353)
product layout (p. 354)
production managers (p. 344)
purchasing (p. 364)
quality control (p. 366)
service flow analysis (p. 359)
service operations (p. 342)
soft manufacturing (p. 356)
standardization (p. 363)
supplier selection (p. 364)
synthetic process (p. 346)
time utility (p. 344)
transportation (p. 363)
U-shaped production lines (p. 356)
utility (p. 344)
warehousing (p. 363)

QUESTIONS FOR ANALYSIS

1. What are the major differences between goods-production operations and service operations?
2. What are the major differences between high-contact and low-contact service systems?
3. What are the resources needed and the finished "products" that are produced in the following services?
   - real estate firm
   - childcare facility
   - bank
   - city water and electric department
   - hotel
4. Identify a synthetic production process and an analytic production process. Then classify each according to whether it is chemical, fabrication, assembly, transport, or clerical. Explain your reasoning.
5. Develop a service flow analysis for some service that you use frequently, such as buying lunch at a cafeteria, having your hair cut, or riding a bus. Identify areas of potential quality or productivity failures in the process.
6. Analyze the location of a firm where you do business (perhaps a restaurant, supermarket, or sports apparel store). What problems do you see with the firm's location? What recommendations would you make to management?

APPLICATION EXERCISES

1. Pick three products (not services) that you regularly use. Then do some research to determine which of the basic production processes (chemical, fabrication, assembly, transport, or clerical processes) are used to produce these products. To what extent are multiple processes used in the production of the product?
2. Pick three services (not products) that you regularly use. Explain what customization, unstorability, and intangibility mean for each of the services. How do these factors influence the way the service is delivered to customers?
3. Interview the manager of a local service business, such as a laundry or dry cleaning shop. Identify the major decisions involved in planning its service operations. Prepare a class report suggesting areas for improvement.
4. Think of an everyday activity—either personal or professional—that you would like to do more efficiently. Describe how you would use methods planning to achieve increased efficiency in that activity. Draw a process flowchart that shows the stages in the activity you chose, and then explain how you would use it.

BUILDING YOUR BUSINESS SKILLS

The One-on-One Entrepreneur

The Purpose of the Assignment

To encourage students to apply the concept of customization to an entrepreneurial idea.

The Situation

You are an entrepreneur who wants to start your own service business. You are intrigued with the idea of creating some kind of customized one-on-one service that would appeal to baby boomers, who traditionally have been pampered, and working women, who have little time to get things done.

Assignment

Step 1

Get together with three or four other students to brainstorm ideas for services that would appeal to harried working people. Here are just a few:

- a concierge service in office buildings that would handle such personal and business services as arranging children's birthday parties and booking guest speakers for business luncheons
- a personal-image consultation service aimed at helping clients improve appearance, etiquette, and presentation style
- a mobile pet-care network through which vets and groomers make house calls

Step 2

Choose one of these ideas or one that your team thinks of. Then write a memo explaining why you think your idea will succeed. Research may be necessary as you target any of the following:

- a specific demographic group or groups (Who are your customers, and why would they buy your service?)
- the features that make your service attractive to this group
- the social factors in your local community that would contribute to success

Questions for Discussion

1. Why is the customization of and easy access to personal services so desirable in the twenty-first century?
2. As services are personalized, do you think quality will become more or less important? Why?
3. Why does the trend toward personalized, one-on-one service present unique opportunities for entrepreneurs?
4. In a personal one-on-one business, how important are the human relations skills of those delivering the service? Can you make an argument that they are more important than the service itself?

EXERCISING YOUR ETHICS: TEAM EXERCISE

Promises, Promises

The Situation

Unfortunately, false promises are not uncommon when managers feel pressure to pump up profits. Many operations managers no doubt recall times when excited marketing colleagues asked for unrealistic commitments from production to get a new customer contract. This exercise will introduce you to some ethical considerations pertaining to such promises and commitments.

The Dilemma

You are the operations manager for a factory that makes replacement car mufflers and tailpipes. Your plant produces these items for all makes and models and sells them throughout Canada to muffler-repair shops that install them on used vehicles. After several years of modest but steady growth, your company has recently suffered a downturn and must shut down 5 percent of the factory's production capacity. Two supervisors and 70 production workers have been laid off. All of the company's stakeholders—employees, managers, the union, suppliers, and owners—are concerned about prospects for the immediate future.

After returning from lunch you receive a phone call from the general manager of one of the nation's top three muffler-repair chains. He says the following: "I suppose you know that we're about to sign a contract under which your firm will supply us with replacement parts in large volumes, beginning two months from now. Your sales manager has assured me that you can reliably meet my needs, and I just want to confirm that promise with you before I sign the contract."

This is the first you've heard about this contract. While your potential customer is talking, you realize that meeting his needs will involve a 20 percent increase in your current production capacity. Two months, however, isn't enough time to add more equipment, acquire tools, hire and train workers, and contract for supplies. In fact, an increase this large might even require a bigger building (which would, of course, take considerably more than two months to arrange). On the other hand, you also know how much your firm needs the business. Your thoughts are interrupted when the caller says, "So what's your production situation insofar as meeting our needs?" The caller waits in silence while you gather your thoughts.

Team Activity

Assemble a group of four students and assign each group member to one of the following roles:

- the operations manager of the factory
- the general manager of the muffler-repair chain
- the sales manager of your company
- an employee in the factory

Questions for Discussion

1. Before discussing the situation with your group, and from the perspective of your assigned role, what are the underlying ethical issues, if any, in this situation? Write down the issues.
2. Gather your group together and reveal, in turn, each member's list of ethical issues.
3. From an ethical standpoint, what does your group conclude is the most appropriate action that should be taken by the company in this situation?
4. Develop a group response to the following question: How would you handle this situation?

Go to MyBizLab for additional cases and exercise material.

CONCLUDING CASE 11-1

What's Happening to Manufacturing in Canada?

During the past decade, there have been some troubling trends in the manufacturing sector in Canada. For example, while total factory *output* is increasing, total factory *employment* is decreasing. Between 1981 and 2010, factory output increased 59 percent, but factory employment fell 16 percent. Over the past decade, 500 000 manufacturing jobs vanished, and in 2011 factory employment in Canada dropped to its lowest level on record. Manufacturing now accounts for just 10 percent of the jobs in Canada (down from 16 percent in 2000). Manufacturing was the biggest sector in the Canadian economy from 1976 to 1990, but it is now third.

The difficulties in manufacturing are most obvious in the automobile manufacturing industry. In the 1990s, the auto industry had an annual trade surplus of $20 billion, but now it has an annual deficit of $12 billion. In 2000, 198 000 people worked in the auto industry, but by the end of 2011 the number was down to 131 000. Canada produces two million cars now compared to three million in 2000. Many auto parts plants have also disappeared. (It is estimated that one well-paying job at an auto plant supports another 7.5 jobs elsewhere.) Ontario is now the world's highest-cost place to make automobiles. Both General Motors Canada and Chrysler Canada have received bailout money from the federal government, but many problems remain. During the past few years, GM has closed manufacturing plants in Toronto, Windsor, and St. Thérèse, Quebec. In 2011, GM announced that it would close its Oshawa plant in June 2013; after that closure, GM will have just 8000 workers in Canada (down from 40 000 in the early 1990s). Industry Minister Christian Paradis said that even though the government is now a shareholder in GM (as a result of the 2009 bailout), it wouldn't try to force GM to keep plants open.

The Canadian Auto Workers union (CAW) is trying very hard to get car companies to make new investments in Canada so that new jobs will be available and so that currently employed workers can receive pay increases and regain some of the benefits they lost during the recession of 2008–09. But automakers—who are determined to hold the line on labour costs—want to move away from annual pay increases in favour of profit sharing. Negotiations on new collective agreements (which began in July 2012) were expected to be very tough.

The CAW also wants the federal government to develop a national automotive policy to help Canadian automakers cope with threats from lower-cost jurisdictions like the southern United States. The Canadian Automotive Partnership Council—a joint industry–government–union group—has been working on such a policy for 10 years, but no policy has yet been developed. The CAW also wants the federal government to (1) create a Canadian-owned automaker, (2) stop free trade talks with South Korea, Japan, and the EU, and (3) put stiff tariffs on automakers that sell cars in Canada but don't actually make any cars here.

There are three key factors that explain the decline of manufacturing generally in Canada (not just automobile manufacturing). First, the application of new technology and automation has allowed companies to increase output while employing fewer workers. For example, Maple Leaf Foods announced in 2012 that it would close five old food processing factories that were inefficient and could not compete with companies in the United States. The old plants will be replaced with one new highly efficient factory in Hamilton that will produce more than the five old plants combined, but about 1500 jobs will be lost in the process. One reason for this change is the need for the company to improve its financial performance. In 2010, for example, Maple Leaf earned nearly $50 million in pre-tax profits, but that represented only 1 cent on each dollar of sales.

Second, the Canadian dollar has increased sharply against the U.S. dollar during the past decade, rising from $0.62 in 2001 to parity in 2012. This has increased the cost of Canadian-made products in foreign markets and has led to declining export sales.

Third, in addition to foreign competition being intense, other countries are very aggressive in trying to attract manufacturing plants. Some U.S. states, for example, have been giving companies millions of dollars in incentives in order to encourage them to open manufacturing facilities in their jurisdiction. For example, Volkswagen recently received more than $500 million from the state of Tennessee. And Mexico has been successful in convincing both Honda and Nissan to build new plants there (because

of relatively low wage rates). Representatives of foreign organizations also come to Canada to tout the benefits of their location. For example, Greg Wathen, the CEO of the Economic Development Coalition of Southwest Indiana, came to Canada to encourage Canadian auto parts makers to set up shop in the state of Indiana.

All of these developments sound pretty ominous, but there are some hopeful signs. Contrary to widely held perceptions, Canadians don't just drill for oil and flip burgers. While manufacturing may be facing serious problems in eastern Canada, it is booming in western Canada. Consider the Nisku industrial complex south of Edmonton, which is the second-biggest energy park in North America (the biggest one is in Houston, Texas). Pipes are the building blocks of refineries, petrochemical plants, and oil sand extraction sites, and they are fitted together at Nisku into the necessary configurations. Manufacturing here is not mass production; rather, it is engineered-to-order modules made one at a time. The oil sands boom has drastically increased the number of jobs available for welders, pipefitters, and electricians. In Edmonton, manufacturing jobs are up 50 percent since the recession ended.

Another encouraging development can be seen in Ottawa. When the tech bubble burst in 2000, several big companies sharply reduced their payrolls. For example, employment at JDS dropped from 10 000 in 2001 to 2500 in 2002. Nortel employed 17 000 people in 2000, but by 2009, there were only 3000. That's the bad news. The good news is that many new companies have started up. In 2010, there were 1944 tech companies in Ottawa, which was almost double the number a decade earlier. These are smaller, more entrepreneurial companies with highly skilled workforces that may not even own their own factories. Instead, they contract out most activities except their new product ideas and the building of prototypes. A company called eSight Corp. is typical. It makes glasses containing electronic optics that allow users to adjust the brightness and contrast of what they are looking at, and to zoom in and out and for a better view. The actual production of the glasses is done in an Ottawa-based factory that has expertise in assembling high-end electronics products.

Questions for Discussion

1. Explain in your own words the developments during the past decade that have created problems for Canadian manufacturing.
2. Should the Canadian government intervene more aggressively in the automobile industry to maintain employment? Explain your reasoning.
3. Consider the following statement: *The Alberta oil sands development has had a negative effect on manufacturing in Canada because the emphasis on oil has driven up the value of the Canadian dollar and made Canadian manufacturers less competitive in export markets.* Do you agree or disagree with the statement? Defend your reasoning.

CONCLUDING CASE 11-2

Some Glitches in the Production of Goods and Services

When consumers purchase a tangible product like a lawn mower, washing machine, or automobile, it is generally not difficult for them to tell whether the product is working as expected. But is the same

thing true for intangible services such a hair care, air travel, or legal services? That's a bit more complicated because of the nature of intangible services, but what we do know is that consumers are very vocal about expressing dissatisfaction with the intangible services they have purchased. Consider the case of air travel. While it is very popular, consumer unhappiness with this service is often in the news (think of the highly publicized cases of passengers being forced to sit in an aircraft on the tarmac for eight hours with no food, water, or air conditioning and overtaxed bathrooms).

In recent years, commercial airlines have received a lot of negative publicity about many aspects of the services they provide. The list of consumer complaints is long: higher fares, less in-flight service, extra baggage fees, lost baggage (airlines lose 26 million passengers' bags each year due to theft, mishandling, and labelling errors), cramped cabins, inconvenient scheduling, discourteous airline personnel, overbooked flights, long waits, cancelled flights, and late flights, just to name a few. All of this has led to a decline in customer satisfaction with commercial airlines. A 2010 poll showed that the majority of passengers held a negative view of airlines.

Skytrax is a U.K.-based consulting firm that conducts surveys of international travellers to determine which airlines have the best airport lounges, cabin staff, and in-flight entertainment. Skytrax also publishes the annual World Airline Star Ranking, which is based on a quality analysis system that assesses airline products and services. There are five star ranking levels in the system:

- 5-star—"high" level of quality (e.g., Singapore Airlines)
- 4-star—"good" level of quality (e.g., Air France)
- 3-star—"acceptable" level of quality (e.g., Air Canada)
- 2-star—"poor" level of quality (e.g., Air Malawi)
- 1-star—"very poor" level of quality (e.g., Air Koryo)

The star rankings are *not* based on customer feedback, but rather on a systematic audit of the activities of airline companies. Obvious factors such as on-time arrivals, cancelled flights, mishandled bags, passengers being bumped from flights, and so on are included in the assessment, but so are less obvious ones like seat comfort and seating arrangements (the complete listing of criteria is available only to airlines). Each year, Skytrax publishes a list of the Top 10 International Airlines. In 2012, Singapore Airlines placed first, followed by Cathay Pacific (second), and Qantas (third). Interestingly, almost all of the top 10 airlines operate out of Asia.

Commercial airlines constitute only one part of the travel industry. Other parts of the industry such as travel companies and booking agents have also come under fire from dissatisfied consumers in recent years. For example, when Conquest Vacations suddenly ceased operations in 2009, many Canadian travellers were stranded in hotels in Mexico, the Dominican Republic, and Cuba. Many of these travellers were told by hotel officials that they had to pay for their room because their bill had not been paid by the travel company.

The Ontario government established the Travel Industry Council of Ontario (TICO) to ensure that fair business practices and ethical behaviour are adhered to, and that Canadian travellers are not scammed or taken advantage of. But Conquest's sudden shutdown meant that TICO was not given proper notice and therefore could not provide sufficient information to travellers. The outcome left many critics questioning the usefulness of the travel council.

Customer complaints about poor service are not limited to the travel business. To observe consumer dissatisfaction in action, go to Complaints.com, a forum for people who have had bad consumer experiences. Enter "missed appointment" or "late repairman" in the search engine and you will get pages of hits. Typical is this complaint about a failed window installation: "I then made an appointment for [an] employee to come to my house the next day between 2 p.m. and 4 p.m. . . . I took a day off from work and stayed home to wait for the [company] truck. Four p.m. came and went. No one from [the company] showed up or called."

ConsumerAffairs.com, the website of an advocacy group for customers who have received poor service or purchased shoddy merchandise, also details numerous incidents in which people were left waiting helplessly for repair people who were late for scheduled appointments. Part of the problem is that the company that manufactures a product may not be the same company that provides service for that product. This is often the case with mass-produced products purchased in department stores or wholesale outlets. For example, General Electric may make a refrigerator, but a GE repair person is not located in every town where that refrigerator is sold. Outside contractors must then be hired to perform repairs, and they may lack the specific expertise required to do the job in a timely manner.

It's not only products in need of installation or repair that can cause customers frustrations over missed appointments. How many hours have you spent waiting in crowded doctors' offices, overbooked salons, and slow-service restaurants? In each case, even if the quality of the product or service turns out to be excellent, you may still feel dissatisfied with the overall experience. For service providers in particular, that failure can be as costly as producing a defective product.

Questions for Discussion

1. In your own words, explain the similarities and differences between manufacturing and service operations. How do the examples presented above illustrate your points?
2. How do the service factors of intangibility, customization, and unstorability *generally* influence the provision of services? How do these factors *specifically* impact the air travel and home repair industries?
3. Describe how process flowcharts may be helpful for methods improvement in airline service operations. What kinds of information would you hope to gain from the flowcharts?
4. Consider the following statement: *It is well known that airlines have had difficulties making profits during the past few years. Increased fees and the declines in service quality that consumers are experiencing are the direct result of airlines having to decrease their costs in order to increase their profitability.* Do you agree or disagree with the statement? Defend your answer.

Increasing Productivity and Quality

LEARNING OBJECTIVES

After reading this chapter, you should be able to:

1 Describe the connection between *productivity* and *quality*.

2 Understand the importance of increasing productivity.

3 Identify the activities involved in *total quality management* and describe six tools that companies can use to achieve it.

4 Identify three trends in productivity and quality management, including *supply chain management*.

5 Explain how a *supply chain strategy* differs from traditional strategies for coordinating operations among firms.

6 Discuss four strategies that companies use to improve productivity and quality.

Canada Goose: High Quality Outerwear

CANADA Goose (formerly called Metro Sportswear) was founded in 1957 by Sam Tick. The company—which originally manufactured shirts and jackets—is now the most recognizable worldwide brand for extreme-weather outerwear. The manufacture of down-filled garments began in 1970, and interest grew as the Canadian Rangers, the Environment Ministry, and municipal workers began to custom-order parkas. Canada Goose entered the European market in the early 1990s, and in 1997, Dani Reiss took over the family business and grew the company from a staff of 40 working primarily out of a single Toronto location to more than 700 employees spread across Canada. By 2000, sales were also being made in Japan and the Scandinavian countries. By 2009, the company was selling its products in 40 countries and was experiencing increased

demand within Canada as well. In 2011, Canada Goose acquired a new manufacturing facility in Winnipeg and opened a headquarters in Stockholm, Sweden. For his work and dedication to "Canadian-made," Dani Reiss, president and CEO of Canada Goose, earned the prestigious Ernst & Young Entrepreneur of the Year designation in 2011.

Canada Goose products are used by a diverse group of consumers. Scientists at the North and South Poles wear the Canada Goose "Expedition Parka" and law enforcement agencies around the world wear the "Constable Parka." Canada Goose outerwear is also popular with dogsledders who enter the Iditarod competition in Alaska, and with workers on movie sets in remote locations. The company's reputation for high-quality outerwear is based on the usefulness of its products in extreme climate conditions. In

addition to the extreme outerwear collection, Canada Goose also manufactures garments for more temperate weather conditions. These products include its Multi-Zone collection, which uses lighter down and its own HyBridge™ technology. Its product portfolio doesn't stop there: Accessories such as hats, mitts, scarves, and a spring collection are also available and made with the same high quality customers have come to expect.

During production of outerwear, the emphasis is on building quality into the products. Down is one of the world's best insulators, and Canada Goose has been an industry leader in understanding insulation technology. Canada Goose was a founding member of the Down Association of Canada, a non-profit organization that is dedicated to educating consumers about feather products in order to make better purchasing decisions.

The company's sole down supplier is Feather Industries Canada Limited. Strict guidelines are followed and down materials that are harvested by live-plucking are not used. All down material is a by-product of the Canadian Poultry Industry and the company does not use material in its jackets that comes from animals bred specifically for their down.

Once products are completed, the emphasis on quality continues as they are field tested by industry professionals to ensure that they can endure the extreme weather conditions that customers are exposed to. With great success, however, comes the problem of counterfeiters, who produce and sell knockoff Canada Goose outerwear. Consumers who buy these knockoffs face health and safety risks (for example, counterfeiters don't use sanitized product materials). To combat counterfeiting, Canada Goose works closely with border service agencies and anti-counterfeiting associations, and pursues counterfeiters whenever possible.

In 2012, Canada Goose filed a statement of claim asking the Federal Court to stop International Clothiers from using logos and other misleading marks on its lower-quality products that were very similar to those used by Canada Goose. The case is now before the courts. On its website, Canada Goose lists hundreds of internet addresses where counterfeit Canada Goose products are sold.

Since Canada Goose products rely heavily on fur and down, it is important to ensure that suppliers share the same passion for ethical trapping practices as the company does. One way to secure this understanding is by having strong supplier relationships. As James Gibb, a Trapper for over 30 years, explains, "We have been doing it for over 300 years and our goal is not to catch the last one but to manage a self-sustaining population so that when I finish trapping, I can pass it on to my kids. . . . . People should understand that trappers do not aim to be apart from nature, but a part of nature." Canada is a world leader

in scientific research to develop the most humane practices in trapping, and Canada Goose does not use endangered species in the making of its jackets.

Canada Goose has also developed several different partnerships and supplier relationships. The company is a Platinum sponsor of Polar Bears International, a non-profit organization dedicated to preserving polar bear habitats around the world. In 2012, Canada Goose joined The Conservation Alliance, an organization that protects threatened wild places across North America. In partnership with First Air, which provides service to remote areas of Canada's north, Canada Goose supplies free fabric and materials to seamstresses in Northern Canada to support the making of Canadian jackets and apparel for members of remote communities. Numerous other environmental initiatives and community outreach programs are also supported by Canada Goose. ◆

◼◼◼ HOW WILL THIS HELP ME?

You will benefit in three ways by reading and understanding important productivity and quality concepts: (1) As an *employee*, you'll gain a better understanding of why every employee in a business should be concerned about productivity and quality; (2) as a *manager*, you'll understand that in order to remain competitive, your business must continually analyze its production methods so that high-quality products and services are efficiently produced; and (3) as a *consumer*, you'll gain insights into how much attention companies must pay to productivity and quality issues if they hope to produce products and services that consumers will want.

It is no secret that *productivity* and *quality* are watchwords in today's business. Companies are not only measuring productivity and insisting on improvements but also insisting on quality so they can bring to market products that satisfy customers, improve sales, and boost profits. By focusing on the learning objectives of this chapter, you will better understand the increasingly important concepts of productivity and quality.

The Productivity–Quality Connection

L01 Describe the connection between *productivity* and *quality.*

productivity A measure of economic performance that measures how much is produced relative to the resources used to produce it.

quality A product's fitness for use in terms of offering the features that consumers want.

Productivity is a measure of economic performance. It measures how much is produced relative to the resources used to produce it. The more we are able to produce the right things while using fewer resources, the more productivity grows and everyone—the economy, businesses, and workers—benefits.

Productivity considers both the amounts and the quality of what is produced. By using resources more efficiently, the quantity of output will be greater. But unless the resulting goods and services are of satisfactory quality (the "right things"), consumers will not want them. **Quality**, then, means fitness for use—offering features that consumers want.

Responding to the Productivity Challenge

Productivity has both international and domestic ramifications. When one country is more productive than another, it will accumulate more wealth. Similarly, a nation whose productivity fails to increase as rapidly as that of competitor nations will see its standard of living fall.

It is important to understand the true meaning of *productivity* and to devise ways to measure it. Since *quality* must be defined in terms of value to the customer,

Workers at this call centre in Bangalore, India, operated by ICICI OneSource, field calls from the customers of multinational firms headquartered in North America and Europe. Global broadband makes this business model possible, so many of these jobs are outsourced to Indian service suppliers because workers get paid only a fraction of what Canadian workers would get.

companies must design their marketing efforts to cultivate a more customer-oriented focus. As quality-improvement practices are implemented, more and more firms will receive payoffs from these efforts. Four factors interact in this process: *customers, quality, productivity,* and *profits.*

Measuring Productivity

How do we know how productive a country is? Most countries use **labour productivity** to measure their level of productivity:

labour productivity Partial productivity ratio calculated by dividing gross domestic product by total number of workers.

$$\text{labour productivity of a country} = \frac{\text{gross domestic product}}{\text{total number of workers}}$$

This equation reflects the general idea of productivity. It compares a country's total annual output of goods and services with the resources used to produce that output. The focus on labour, rather than on other resources (such as capital or energy), is preferred because most countries keep accurate records on employment and hours worked.

A Statistics Canada report showed that foreign-controlled manufacturing plants in Canada accounted for two-thirds of the growth in labour productivity during one recent period. But the study emphasized that it wasn't the fact that the plants were foreign controlled that led to higher productivity; rather, it was the extent to which the companies had an international orientation. In other words, Canadian producers that had foreign units were just as productive as foreign-owned plants. It seems that firms that compete internationally have more incentive to be more productive.[1]

Productivity Among Global Competitors

A 2011 study by the Organisation for Economic Co-operation and Development (OECD) reported on productivity levels in selected countries (see Figure 12.1). Output per hour worked was the highest in Norway (74.9) and lowest in Mexico (20.4).

FIGURE 12.1

International productivity comparisons (selected countries, 2011).

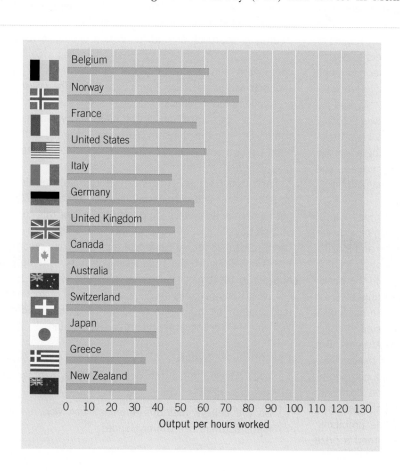

Canadian productivity (46.6) usually lags behind that of the United States (60.9), but in 2011, Canadian productivity growth outpaced the United States for the first time since 2006.[2]

Why are there such productivity differences from nation to nation? The answer lies in many factors: technologies, human skills, economic policies, natural resources, and even traditions. In Japan, for example, the food-production industry is a fragmented, highly protected one and, compared with Canadian and U.S. food production, it is extremely inefficient (the average U.S. worker produces 3.5 times as much food as a Japanese worker).[3]

According to Michael Porter, a Harvard University expert on international competitiveness, Canada's international competitiveness is a concern because we have been living off our rich diet of natural resources. In Porter's view, Canada will have to start emphasizing innovation and develop a more sophisticated mix of products if it wants to be more successful in international markets. Porter also criticizes Canadian business, government, and labour for failing to abandon outdated ways of thinking regarding productivity and innovation.[4] Many believe that Canada is stuck

E-BUSINESS + SOCIAL MEDIA SOLUTIONS

Open Source Automobile Manufacturing

In the early 1900s, Henry Ford revolutionized the automobile industry by applying the assembly-line approach to manufacturing, bringing prices down, and making cars more affordable for the masses. What would he think of the latest innovation in the industry: open-source design? Jay Rogers of Local Motors is building a community of engineers to design cars. Local Motors is a mass participation designer and niche product provider that has developed a unique solution for a very old industry. The company's mission is lofty: *"To lead the next generation of crowd-powered automotive manufacturing, design, and technology in order to enable the creation of game changing vehicles."* The company has upgraded the initial site and created an online community called "the Forge" to spread the message and work with designers, engineers, CAD modellers, and fabricators.

Open-source is usually associated with new technology; it became popular in the 1990s with the creation of software programs like Linux (computer operating system) and Mozilla (Firefox), the popular web browser. The approach is gaining popularity in various areas as companies tap into the power of the internet and social media. Crowdsourcing involves posting challenges or questions in the form of an open call. This can be accomplished in an unsophisticated manner through general sites like wikiHow and Yahoo! Answers. But companies like Toronto-based Innovations Exchange have gone a step further and created a website to link companies with a community of marketers, engineers, and designers to build customer solutions. Organizations pay to post challenges and then individuals or teams tackle the problems. For example, two New York college buddies earned a prize

of US$40 000 for creating a better yogurt container. Now yogurt containers are one thing, but can this open-source approach really work for car manufacturers?

Automobile manufacturing has traditionally been characterized by secrecy. Designs are tightly guarded until they are unveiled at major car shows. Local Motors is flipping this traditional approach around. It posts a challenge (competition rules and an ignition kit) that addresses a certain car component and invites engineering volunteers to upload sketches and ideas. Participants can submit their designs for assessment and feedback. The final designs are then posted in the "design garage" to be evaluated and voted on by the community and the company. Prizes are awarded to the winners. Once there is enough support for a model, the car is manufactured in limited batches.

According to Jay Rogers, this unique development approach reduces his break-even point to as little as 200 cars per model. Inclusiveness is part of the DNA of this company, and participation does not end with the design. Car owners can also be involved in the actual manufacturing process (up to 60 hours) under the supervision of staff. This approach appeals to the typical car enthusiast, who is likely to offer comments and opinions on the website. Local Motors aims to revolutionize the industry by using radical design, production, and engineering concepts. It's off to a good start.

Critical Thinking Questions

1. What do you think of this approach to car manufacturing and design?

2. Do you believe that this approach can work for major manufacturers like GM or Honda?

in a "productivity trap," meaning that Canadians are collectively working harder and using up more natural resources, but the benefits and outputs we receive aren't proportional. The productivity trap is also reducing Canada's ability to compete in international markets.[5]

Domestic Productivity

Nations must be concerned about domestic productivity regardless of their global standing. A country that improves its ability to make something out of its existing resources can increase the wealth of all its inhabitants. Conversely, a decline in productivity shrinks a nation's total wealth. When that happens, an increase in one person's wealth comes only at the expense of others with whom he or she shares an economic system.

For example, additional wealth from higher productivity can be shared among workers (as higher wages), investors (as higher profits), and customers (as stable prices). When productivity drops, however, wages can be increased only by reducing profits (penalizing investors) or by increasing prices (penalizing customers). It is understandable, then, that investors, suppliers, managers, and workers are all concerned about the productivity of specific industries and companies.

Manufacturing vs. Service Productivity

Manufacturing productivity is higher than service productivity. For many years, it was widely believed that the service sector suffered from "Baumol's disease," named after economist William Baumol, who argued that since the service sector focused more on hands-on activity that machines couldn't replace, it would be more difficult to increase productivity in services. Baumol noted, for example, that four musicians would always be required to play a Mozart quartet. But the Opera Company of Brooklyn is challenging Baumol's basic assumption. It now puts on Mozart's opera *The Marriage of Figaro* without the usual full orchestra. Instead, it uses just 12 musicians and a technician who oversees a computer program that plays all the other musical parts. The orchestra's productivity has increased sharply because it does not have to pay for the usual complement of musicians.[6]

Productivity gains are starting to appear among a wide array of service providers such as airlines, pet stores, package delivery companies, providers of financial services, and retail establishments. Many of these organizations have increased their productivity by becoming more like factories, and they use modern information technology to eliminate inefficiencies. Automated check-in kiosks in airports are a good example: Two-thirds of Northwest Airlines passengers now check in using the kiosks.

It is important to improve service productivity because the service sector is an important and growing part of the Canadian economy. From 1998–2008, for example, the services sector grew by 40.5 percent, compared to only 18.5 percent for the goods-producing sector. More than 75 percent of employed Canadians work in the services sector.[7]

Industry Productivity

The productivity of an industry is of interest to different groups for different reasons. For example, labour unions take it into account in negotiating contracts, since highly productive industries can give raises more easily than can less productive industries. Investors and suppliers consider industry productivity when making loans, buying securities, and planning their own future production. Productivity varies across different industries (for example, manufacturing is more productive than services). Productivity within a given industry also varies across countries (for example, Canadian agriculture is more productive than agriculture in many other nations because we use more sophisticated technology and possess superior natural resources).

Understand the importance of increasing productivity. LO2

The productivity of many industries has increased over time. In the steel industry, for example, about 10 hours of labour were required to produce a tonne of steel in the 1980s, but now only about four hours of labour are needed. The boxed insert entitled "Green Changes in Steelmaking" provides more information about productivity improvements in steelmaking that are also environmentally friendly.

Company Productivity

The productivity of individual companies is also important to investors, workers, and managers. Comparing the productivity of several companies in the same industry helps investors in buying and selling stocks. Employee profit-sharing plans are often based on the company's productivity improvements each year. And managers use information about productivity trends to plan for new products, factories, and funds to stay competitive in the years ahead.

High productivity gives a company a competitive edge because its costs are lower. As a result, it can offer its product at a lower price (and gain more customers), or it can make a greater profit on each item sold. Increased productivity also allows companies to pay workers higher wages without raising prices. To more effectively manage its forestry

THE GREENING OF BUSINESS

Green Changes in Steelmaking

The iron and steel industry has a reputation for air, water, and noise pollution. In order to be successful in today's highly competitive international business environment, the steel industry must improve its productivity, and it must demonstrate its environmental responsibility to legislators, employees, investors, and customers. Knowing that change needs to happen is one thing, but successfully implementing change is quite another. One overriding consideration in any contemplated change is cost. With the worldwide economic problems that have developed during the past few years, it's no wonder companies are now reluctant to spend money to change their business practices. But companies need to understand that having an effective environment management system in place may actually improve operational efficiency and reduce costs.

There are some promising developments. Companies in Europe, Australia, and North America have developed processes that allow them to skip a high-polluting step in the manufacturing of iron, and they are actively wooing steelmakers in Asia and Africa that are willing to gamble on the innovation. POSCO, a Korean steel giant, has focused on improving customer-related services, including product quality, prices, and on-time delivery. The company changed its production methods and developed Finex, a furnace that can prepare cheaper types of coal and iron ore to be converted into pig iron. The new manufacturing process eliminates the need for separate material processing and uses

cheaper inputs, thus increasing productivity. Chung Joon-yang, POSCO's president, said, "We could go two ways. One was to look for a totally new business. The second one was to go for new technology. We decided to look at alternative processes."

Over the years, cost pressures have grown for steelmakers as they have been forced to accept huge price increases for coal and iron inputs. These companies must keep quality high and costs down (in order to be competitive), and they must control environmental pollutants (in order to meet strict government standards designed to protect the environment). Improving energy efficiency is a basic yet significant way of addressing both energy security concerns and environmental concerns. While upgrades can be costly, particularly for old steel plants, promoters for new projects are working to initiate sweeping changes, from the initial design stage to the final stage of site selection and plant equipment. All of these drivers together are needed to increase productivity and foster green improvements.

Critical Thinking Questions

1. In addition to changing processing technologies, what are some other ways that steel manufacturers can help protect the environment?

2. Research the different ways to measure energy efficiency performance (MEEP) and discuss how each would apply to the steel industry.

On the left, workers assemble a truck the old way, manually lowering and bolting frames onto axles. On the right, the process is highly automated (and safer), with robotic grippers to flip and align the bulky frames.

operations, Canfor Corp. developed Genus, a computerized database containing geographic information and other essential data about Canfor's vast lumber and pulp operations in British Columbia and Alberta. Genus is used as a strategic planning tool to determine how the company should adjust its logging plans to reflect both market demand and logging regulations laid down by the Forest Practices Code of British Columbia Act.[8]

Improvements in company productivity can also come from more efficient work on the part of individual employees, and sometimes this occurs in unexpected ways. While managers are often concerned that certain activities (for example, web surfing, social networking, and water cooler conversations) will inhibit productivity, the reverse may actually be true.[9] When management permits or encourages these activities, employees may see the permission as a sign of trust the company has placed in them.

Total Quality Management

It is no longer enough for businesses to simply measure productivity in terms of the numbers of items produced. They must also take quality into account. In the decades after the Second World War, business consultant W. Edwards Deming tried to persuade firms in North America that they needed to improve quality at least as much as quantity. He wasn't very successful, but his arguments won over the Japanese. Through years of meticulous hard work, Japan's manufacturers have changed "Made in Japan" from a synonym for cheap, shoddy merchandise into a hallmark of reliability. In the 2012 Initial Quality Study published by J.D. Power & Associates, Toyota's Cambridge, Ontario plant won the gold medal for North American car companies. Toyota's Woodstock, Ontario plant won the bronze medal.[10]

Quality advocates such as Joseph Juran and Kaoru Ishikawa introduced methods and tools for implementing quality. Juran's "Quality Trilogy"—*quality planning, quality control*, and *quality improvement*—was the first structured process for managing quality, and it identifies several management steps. In addition to management actions, Juran, like Deming and Ishikawa, championed the idea of company-wide employee participation. These theorists also developed quality tools for day-to-day work activities because they knew that, without employee participation, real quality improvement would never happen. Ishikawa, for example, developed so-called fishbone diagrams, also known as cause-and-effect diagrams or Ishikawa diagrams, which help teams of employees investigate and track down causes of quality problems in their work areas.

Identify the activities involved in *total quality management* and describe six tools that companies can use to achieve it. **L03**

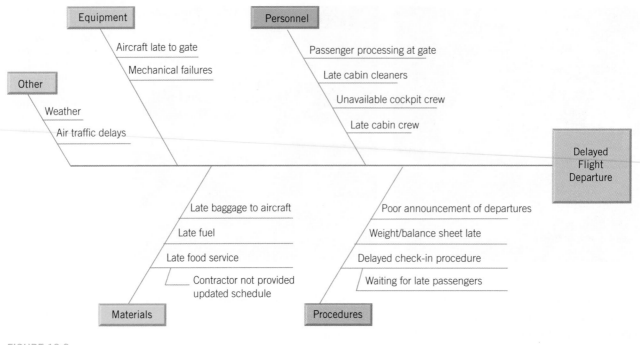

FIGURE 12.2

Fishbone or cause-and-effect diagram.

The diagram in Figure 12.2, for instance, was designed to help an airport manager find out why his facility had so many delayed departures. Focusing on five major categories of possible causes, he then noted several potential causes of the problem in each. (It turns out that there weren't enough tow trucks to handle baggage transfers.)[11]

Managing for Quality

total quality management (TQM)
All the activities necessary for getting high-quality goods and services into the marketplace.

Total quality management (TQM) (sometimes called *quality assurance*) includes all the activities necessary for getting high-quality goods and services into the marketplace. It must consider all parts of the business, including customers, suppliers, and employees. TQM emphasizes that no defects are tolerable and that employees are responsible for maintaining quality standards. At Toyota's Cambridge, Ontario plant, for example, workers can push a button or pull a rope to stop the production line when something is not up to standard.[12]

The strategic approach to TQM begins with leadership and the desire for TQM. This approach involves getting people's attention, getting them to think in an entirely new way about what they do, and then getting them to improve both processes and products.[13]

Customer focus is the starting point. Companies must develop methods for determining what customers want and then direct all their resources toward fulfillment of those needs to gain greater customer satisfaction. Total participation is mandatory. Unless all employees are working toward improved quality, the firm is wasting potential contributions from its human resources and is missing a chance to become a stronger competitor in the marketplace. TQM in today's competitive markets demands unending and continuous improvement of products; after-sales services; and all of the company's internal processes, such as accounting, delivery, billing, and information flow. To bring the interests of all these stakeholders together, TQM involves planning, organizing, directing, and controlling.

Successful use of TQM requires a high level of commitment from all members of the organization. Consider the case of Standard Aero in Winnipeg, which is in the business of aircraft overhaul. When the company instituted TQM, the process began with the formation of a "change council" consisting of the CEO and five senior managers. This council ensured that the TQM initiative received the money, equipment, and support it needed for success. Next, a nine-person task force was formed that consisted of employees who had done the full range of jobs on one of Standard's major overhaul contracts. Its first job was to find out what the customer wanted. It did this by designing a questionnaire and visiting customer plants around the world to gather information. The task force also worked within Standard Aero to determine exactly how the company did its aircraft overhaul work. After weeks of analysis, the task force was able to significantly reduce the time required for overhaul work. For example, the number of times a certain gearbox was handled as it moved through the repair process was reduced by 84 percent.[14]

Planning for Quality

Planning for quality should begin before products are designed or redesigned. Managers need to set goals for both quality levels and quality reliability in the beginning. **Performance quality** refers to the features of a product and how well it performs. For example, Maytag gets a price premium because its washers and dryers offer a high level of performance quality. Customers perceive Maytag as having more advanced features and being more durable than other brands. (Everyone knows that the Maytag repair technician is a lonely and idle person.)

performance quality The features of a product and how well it performs.

ENTREPRENEURSHIP AND NEW VENTURES

Fraberts Fresh Food: Taking Local to a New Level

Making local and fresh food choices has been something of a fad these past few years, what with globalization and its effects becoming more and more prevalent. Consumers are now looking to make "local" a primary consideration in their consumption choices, although time constraints and busy lifestyles often upstage this preference. For Chef Derek Roberts and Local Food Forager Jackie Fraser, this was an opportunity to provide consumers with exactly what they are looking for: homemade, ready-made meals using fresh local produce.

Located in Fergus, Ontario, Fraberts Fresh Food is a small family-operated market whose product offerings are far from what you would normally find at your local produce market. With its vision of "local" in mind, Fraberts offers fresh local produce, fresh bread baked daily, local meats, and even homemade meals that cater to consumers' local cravings while still acknowledging today's hectic lifestyles. Catering is also on the menu for those looking to share their experience of local and fresh food. Fraberts Fresh Food encourages consumers to "buy local and buy fresh."

Chef Derek Roberts and his wife, Jackie Fraser, started Fraberts Fresh Foods with a passion, drive, and love to make something work. While pursuing a second career as a chef, Derek's vision was to "create comfort-food meals that families can enjoy any time using local, fresh, quality ingredients." It was only a matter of time before Jackie shared in the same

vision. She is no stranger to farmers' markets as she not only grew up on a dairy farm in Huttonville, Ontario, but also worked at a local market as a teen where her passion for local and fresh produce grew. Fraberts Fresh Foods was an opportunity for both Derek and Jackie to get back to their roots and provide customers with quality local food choices.

Fraberts Fresh Foods's success comes from their determination to "provide only quality, authentic food for your family. If we wouldn't be proud to serve it to our own family, we won't sell it." The company guarantees an enjoyable shopping experience, and is dedicated to answering all customers' questions about its products. It wants to support Ontario farmers by using fresh, local, and wholesome ingredients, with no preservatives or additives.

Although Fraberts has been in business for only a few years, it has moved fast in terms of establishing solid relationships with local farmers and stakeholders. It has made its mark in the local community by supporting local food banks and by hosting numerous community events, and won the Centre Wellington Small Business of the Year Award in 2011. Now that's fresh!

Critical Thinking Question

1. Using the fishbone diagram in Figure 12.2 as a guide, analyze the various ways quality at Fraberts can be managed.

quality reliability The consistency or repeatability of performance.

Performance quality may or may not be related to quality reliability in a product. **Quality reliability** refers to the consistency or repeatability of performance. At Courtyard by Marriott hotels, for example, consistency is achieved by maintaining the same features at all of Marriott's nearly 700 locations (high-speed internet access, meeting space, access to an exercise room and swimming pool, and 24-hour access to food). Another example of quality reliability is described in the boxed insert entitled "Fraberts Fresh Food: Taking Local to a New Level."

Organizing for Quality

Perhaps most important to the quality concept is the belief that producing quality goods and services requires an effort from all parts of the organization. The old idea of a separate "quality control" department is no longer enough. Everyone—from the chairperson of the board to the part-time clerk, purchasers, engineers, janitors, marketers, machinists, and other personnel—must work to ensure quality. In Germany's Messerschmitt-Boelkow-Blohm aerospace company, for example, all employees are responsible for inspecting their own work. The overall goal is to reduce eventual problems to a minimum by making the product correctly from the beginning. The same principle extends to teamwork practice at Heinz Co., where teams of workers are assigned to inspect virtually every activity in the company. Heinz has realized substantial cost savings by eliminating waste and rework.

Although everyone in a company contributes to product quality, responsibility for specific aspects of total quality management is often assigned to specific departments and jobs. In fact, many companies have quality assurance, or quality control, departments staffed by quality experts. These people may be called in to help solve quality-related problems in any of the firm's other departments. They keep other departments informed of the latest developments in equipment and methods for maintaining quality. In addition, they monitor all quality control activities to identify areas for improvement.

Leading for Quality

Too often, firms fail to take the initiative to make quality happen. Leading for quality means that managers must inspire and motivate employees throughout the company to achieve quality goals. They need to help employees see how they affect quality and how quality affects their jobs and their company. Leaders must continually find ways to foster a quality orientation by training employees, encouraging their involvement, and tying wages to quality of work. If managers succeed, employees will ultimately accept **quality ownership**—the idea that quality belongs to each person who creates or destroys it while performing a job.

quality ownership The idea that quality belongs to each person who creates or destroys it while performing a job.

Controlling for Quality

By monitoring its products and services, a company can detect mistakes and make corrections. To do so, however, managers must first establish specific quality standards and measurements. Consider the control system for a bank's teller services: Observant supervisors periodically evaluate transactions against a checklist. Specific aspects of each teller's work—appearance, courtesy, efficiency, and so on—are recorded. The results, reviewed with employees, either confirm proper performance or indicate changes that are needed to bring performance up to standards.

Companies who pay attention to quality standards and measurements typically provide high quality products and services to customers. In 2012, Alaska Airlines and Delta Air Lines were the top-rated airlines in a study published by The Middle Seat, a company that ranks air carriers on key quality measures like on-time arrivals, cancelled flights, and mishandled bags. Both Alaska and Delta had ranked poorly in previous years, but both had instituted major operational overhauls that focused on improving quality.[15]

In the auto industry, a key measure of quality is the number of recalls. By this standard, there's room for improvement in total quality management at General Motors, which has recalled many vehicles during the last few years.

When safety and quality procedures are not regularly followed, human and environmental disasters may result. In 2010, for example, an oil-drilling rig in the Gulf of Mexico that was leased by BP exploded and killed 11 workers. Millions of litres of oil escaped into the ocean, creating an environmental catastrophe. A *Wall Street Journal* investigation found that several quality and safety checks had not been carried out at the rig, partly because the drilling was behind schedule.[16]

Tools for Total Quality Management

In managing for quality, many leading companies rely on assistance from proven tools. Often, ideas for improving both the product and the production process come from **competitive product analysis**. For example, Toshiba will take apart a Xerox photocopier and test each component. Test results help Toshiba's managers decide which Toshiba product features are satisfactory (in comparison to the competition), which product features need to be upgraded, or whether Toshiba's production processes need improvement.

competitive product analysis Process by which a company analyzes a competitor's products to identify desirable improvements.

There are many specific tools that can be used to achieve TQM. Here, we briefly describe the following: value-added analysis, statistical process control, quality/cost studies, quality improvement teams, benchmarking, getting closer to the customer, ISO 9000:2000 and ISO 14000, re-engineering, and adding value through supply chains.

Value-Added Analysis

Value-added analysis refers to the evaluation of all work activities, material flows, and paperwork to determine the value that they add for customers. It often reveals wasteful or unnecessary activities that can be eliminated without jeopardizing customer service. For example, when Hewlett-Packard reduced its customer contracts from 20 pages to as few as two, computer sales rose by more than 18 percent.

value-added analysis The evaluation of all work activities, material flows, and paperwork to determine the value that they add for customers.

Statistical Process Control

Although every company would like complete uniformity in its outputs, all firms experience unit-to-unit variations in their products. Companies can gain better control, however, by understanding the sources of variation. **Statistical process control (SPC)**

statistical process control (SPC) Statistical analysis techniques that allow managers to analyze variations in production data and to detect when adjustments are needed to create products with high-quality reliability.

methods—especially process variation studies and control charts—allow managers to analyze variations in production data.

Process Variation

process variation Any change in employees, materials, work methods, or equipment that affects output quality.

Variations in a firm's products may arise from the inputs in its production process. As people, materials, work methods, and equipment change, so do production outputs. While some amount of **process variation** is acceptable, too much can result in poor quality and excessive operating costs. Consider the box-filling operation for Honey Nuggets cereal. Each automated machine fills two 400-gram boxes per second. Even under proper conditions, slight variations in cereal weight from box to box are normal. Equipment and tools wear out, the cereal may be overly moist, and machinists make occasional adjustments. But how much variation is occurring? How much is acceptable?

Information about variation in a process can be obtained from a *process capability study*. Boxes are taken from the filling machines and weighed. The results are plotted, as in Figure 12.3, and compared with the upper and lower specification limits (quality limits) for weight. These limits define good and bad quality for box filling. Boxes with more than 410 grams are a wasteful "giveaway." Underfilling has a cost because it is unlawful.

The chart in Figure 12.3 reveals that Machine A's output is acceptable because none of its boxes violate the quality limits. Machine A, then, is fully capable of meeting the company's quality standards. Machines B and C, however, have problems. In their present condition, they are not "capable" because they cannot reliably meet Honey Nuggets' quality standards. The company must take special—and costly—actions to sort the good from the bad boxes before releasing the cereal for shipment. Unless Machines B and C are renovated, substandard production quality will plague Honey Nuggets.

Control Charts

control chart A statistical process control method in which results of test sampling of a product are plotted on a diagram that reveals when the process is beginning to depart from normal operating conditions.

Knowing that a process is capable of meeting quality standards is not enough. Managers must still monitor the process to prevent its drifting astray during production. To detect the beginning of bad conditions, managers can check production periodically and plot the results on a **control chart**. For example, several times a day a machine operator at Honey Nuggets might weigh several boxes of cereal together to ascertain the average weight.

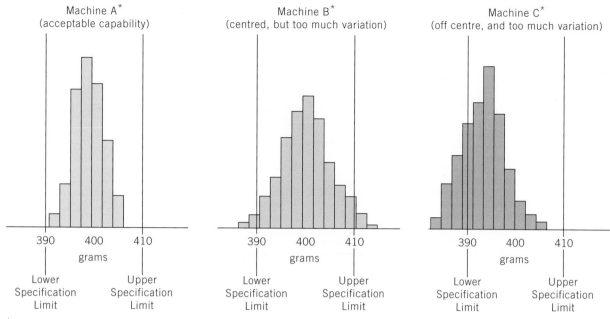

Machine A* (acceptable capability)

Machine B* (centred, but too much variation)

Machine C* (off centre, and too much variation)

*Distribution of weights for 500 boxes from each machine

FIGURE 12.3

Process variation in box filling for Honey Nuggets cereal.

Figure 12.4 shows the control chart for Machine A, in which the first five points are randomly scattered around the centre line, indicating that the machine was operating well. However, the points for samples 5 through 8 are all above the centre line, indicating that something was causing the boxes to overfill. The last point falls outside the upper *control limit*, confirming that the process is out of control.

At this point, the machine must be shut down so that a manager and/or the operator can investigate what is causing the problem—equipment, people, materials, or work methods. Control is completed by correcting the problem and restoring the process to normal.

Quality/Cost Studies

Statistical process controls help keep operations up to existing capabilities, but in today's competitive environment, firms must consistently raise quality capabilities. However, any improvement in products or production processes means additional costs, whether for new facilities, equipment, training, or other changes. Managers thus face the challenge of identifying those improvements that offer the greatest promise. **Quality/cost studies** are useful because they not only identify a firm's current costs but also reveal areas with the largest cost-savings potential.[17]

Quality costs are associated with making, finding, or repairing goods and services, or preventing defects in them. All of these costs should be analyzed in a quality/cost study. For example, Honey Nuggets must determine its costs for **internal failures**. These are expenses—including the costs of overfilling boxes and the costs of sorting out bad boxes—incurred during production and before bad products leave the plant. Studies indicate that many manufacturers incur very high costs for internal failures—up to 50 percent of total costs.

Despite quality control procedures, however, some bad boxes may get out of the factory, reach the customer, and generate complaints from grocers and cereal eaters. These are **external failures**, which occur outside the factory. The costs of correcting them—refunds to customers, transportation costs to return bad boxes to the factory, possible lawsuits, factory recalls—should also be tabulated in the quality/cost study.

quality/cost studies A method of improving product quality by assessing a firm's current quality-related costs and identifying areas with the greatest cost-saving potential.

internal failures Expenses incurred during production and before bad product leaves the plant.

external failures Expenses incurred when defective products are allowed to leave the factory and get into consumers' hands.

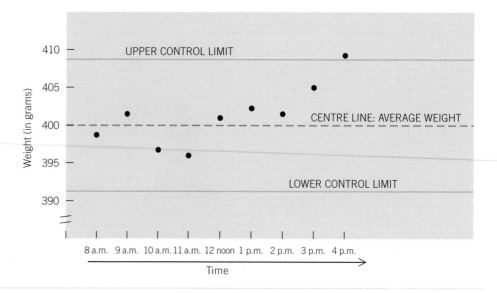

FIGURE 12.4

Honey Nuggets cereal process control chart for machine A.

Quality Improvement Teams

quality improvement (QI) teams TQM tool in which groups of employees work together to improve quality.

Quality improvement (QI) teams are groups of employees from various work areas who meet regularly to define, analyze, and solve common production problems. Their goal is to improve both their own work methods and the products they make.[18] Many QI teams organize their own work, select leaders, and address problems in the workplace. Motorola sponsors company-wide team competitions to emphasize the value of the team approach, to recognize outstanding team performance, and to reaffirm the team's role in the company's continuous-improvement culture. Teams get higher marks for dealing with projects closely tied to Motorola's key initiatives.[19]

Benchmarking

benchmarking Comparing the quality of the firm's output with the quality of the output of the industry's leaders.

A powerful TQM tool that has been effective for some firms is called **benchmarking**. To improve its own products or its business procedures, a company compares its current performance against its own past performance, or one company finds and implements the best practices of others. With *internal benchmarking*, a firm tracks its own performance over time to evaluate its progress and to set goals for further improvement. As an example, the percentage of customer phone calls with more than two minutes of response time may be 15 percent this month. Compared with past months, this percentage may be high or low. In short, past performance is the benchmark for evaluating recent results.

External benchmarking begins with a critical review of competitors (or even companies in other lines of business) to determine which goods or services perform the best; these activities and products are called *best practices*. For example, Toronto Hospital gathered performance data on 26 indicators from various Canadian hospitals so that it could determine how well it was performing compared with other organizations in the health-care industry.[20] Executives from Ford, Chrysler, and General Motors frequently tour Toyota manufacturing facilities as they try to figure out how Toyota makes cars so efficiently.

Getting Closer to the Customer

One advocate of quality improvement says that "Customers are an economic asset. They're not on the balance sheet, but they should be." Successful businesses keep close to their customers and know what they want in the products and services they consume. For example, the Coast Capital Savings Credit Union branch in Surrey, B.C., simplified the banking experience of its customers and developed an innovative new service called "You're the Boss Mortgage," which was named the Mortgage of the Year by canadianmortgagetrends.com.[21] Cornell Publishing House (CPH) uses Voice-of-the Customer (VOC) procedures to gather input from customers (e.g., compliments, product ideas, and complaints). Afterward, Product Teams analyze customer data and design products that will meet customer requirements. As a result of such dedication, CPH's Customer Call Center was ranked as a "Center of Excellence" by Purdue University from 2009 to 2011.[22] CPH also received the 2011 Malcolm Baldridge National Quality Award as a result of customer satisfaction scores of 98 percent plus.

By contrast, struggling companies often lose sight of the fact that customers must be the driving force for their business activities. As a result, they may waste resources designing products that customers do not want, ignore customer reactions to existing products, and fail to keep up with changing consumer tastes.

ISO 9000:2000 and ISO 14000

DuPont Co. had a problem: A moulding press used to make plastic connectors for computers had a 30 percent defect rate. Efforts to solve the problem went nowhere until, as part of a plant-wide quality program, press operators were asked to submit detailed written reports describing how they did their jobs. After comparing notes, operators realized that they were incorrectly measuring the temperature of the moulding press; as a result, temperature adjustments were often wrong. With the mystery solved, the defect rate dropped to 8 percent.

The quality program that led to this solution is called **ISO 9000**—a certification program attesting to the fact that a factory, a laboratory, or an office has met the rigorous quality management requirements set by the International Organization for Standardization. ISO 9000 (pronounced *ICE-o nine thousand*) originated in Europe to standardize materials received from suppliers in such high-technology industries as electronics, chemicals, and aviation. More than 160 countries have adopted ISO 9000 as a national standard and more than 800 000 certificates have been issued.[23]

The name of the latest version, ISO 9000:2000, indicates that it was revised in 2000. Revised standards allow firms to show that they follow documented procedures for testing products, training workers, keeping records, and fixing defects. To become certified, companies must document the procedures followed by workers during every stage of production. The purpose is to ensure that a manufacturer's product is exactly the same today as it was yesterday and as it will be tomorrow. Ideally, standardized processes would ensure that goods would be produced at the same level of quality even if all employees were replaced by a new set of workers.

The **ISO 14000** program certifies improvements in *environmental* performance. Extending the ISO approach into the arena of environmental protection and hazardous waste management, ISO 14000 requires a firm to develop an *environmental management system (EMS)*—a plan documenting how the company has acted to improve its performance in using resources (such as raw materials) and in managing pollution. A company must not only identify hazardous wastes that it expects to create; it must also stipulate plans for treatment and disposal. ISO 14000 covers practices in environmental labelling—the use of such terms as *energy efficient* and *recyclable*—and assesses the total environmental impact of the firm's products, not just from manufacturing, but also from use and disposal.

Process Re-engineering

Every business consists of *processes*—activities that it performs regularly and routinely in conducting business. Examples abound: receiving and storing materials from suppliers, billing patients for medical treatment, filing insurance claims for auto accidents, inspect-

Identify three trends in productivity **L04** and quality management, including *supply chain management*.

ISO 9000 A certification program attesting to the fact that a factory, a laboratory, or an office has met the rigorous quality management requirements set by the International Organization for Standardization.

ISO 14000 Certification program attesting to the fact that a factory, laboratory, or office has improved environmental performance.

ing property for termite infestation, opening chequing accounts for new customers, and filling customer orders from internet sales. Any business process can add value and customer satisfaction by performing processes well. By the same token, any business can disappoint customers and irritate business partners by managing them poorly.

business process re-engineering
Redesigning of business processes to improve performance, quality, and productivity.

Business process re-engineering focuses on improving both the productivity and quality of business processes—rethinking each step of an organization's operations by starting from scratch. *Re-engineering* is the fundamental rethinking and radical redesign of business processes to achieve dramatic improvements in measures of performance, such as cost, quality, service, and speed.[24] The example given above of the methods used by Cornell Publishing House to gather customer feedback and VOC is an example of process re-engineering. Through this process, CPH is able to improve existing products as well as use customer feedback to develop new products.

The Re-Engineering Process

Figure 12.5 shows the six steps involved in the re-engineering process. It starts with a statement of the benefits envisioned for customers and the company and then flows logically through the next five steps:

1. Identify the business activity that will be changed.

2. Evaluate information and human resources to see if they can meet the requirements for change.

3. Diagnose the current process to identify its strengths and weaknesses.

4. Create the new process design.

5. Implement the new design.

As you can see, re-engineering is a broad undertaking that requires know-how in technical matters, depends on leadership and management skills, and calls upon knowledge about customer needs and how well they are being met by the company and its competition. The bottom line in every re-engineering process is adopting a company-wide, customer-first philosophy. Redesign is guided by a desire to improve operations so that goods and services are produced at the lowest possible cost and at the highest value for the customer.

Adding Value Through Supply Chains

Managers sometimes forget that a company belongs to a network of firms that must coordinate their activities. The term *supply chain* refers to the group of companies and stream of activities that work together to create a product. A **supply chain** for any product is the flow of information, materials, and services that starts with raw-materials suppliers and continues through other stages in the operations process until the product reaches the end customer.[25]

supply chain The flow of information, materials, and services that starts with raw-materials suppliers and continues through other stages in the operations process until the product reaches the end customer.

Figure 12.6 shows the supply chain activities involved in supplying baked goods to consumers. Each stage adds value for the final customer. Although a typical beginning stage is product design, our bakery example begins with raw materials (grain harvested from the farm). It also includes additional storage and transportation activities, factory operations for baking and wrapping, and distribution to retailers. Each stage depends on the others for success in getting fresh-baked goods to consumers.

The Supply Chain Strategy

LO5 Explain how a *supply chain strategy* differs from traditional strategies for coordinating operations among firms.

Traditional strategies assume that companies are managed as individual firms rather than as members of a coordinated supply system. Supply chain strategy is based on the idea that members of the chain, working as a coordinated unit, will gain competitive

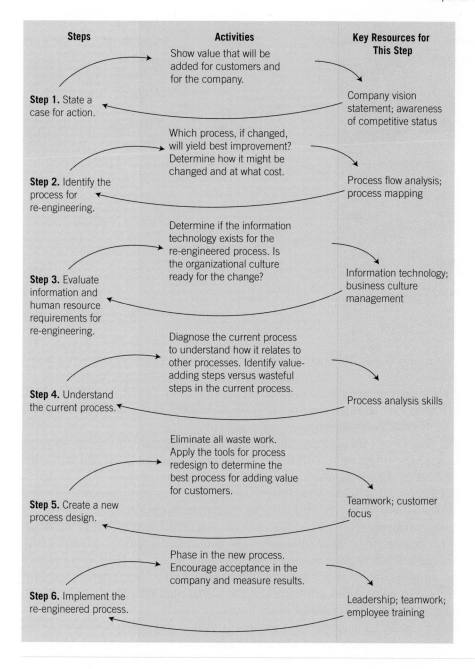

Steps	Activities	Key Resources for This Step
Step 1. State a case for action.	Show value that will be added for customers and for the company.	Company vision statement; awareness of competitive status
Step 2. Identify the process for re-engineering.	Which process, if changed, will yield best improvement? Determine how it might be changed and at what cost.	Process flow analysis; process mapping
Step 3. Evaluate information and human resource requirements for re-engineering.	Determine if the information technology exists for the re-engineered process. Is the organizational culture ready for the change?	Information technology; business culture management
Step 4. Understand the current process.	Diagnose the current process to understand how it relates to other processes. Identify value-adding steps versus wasteful steps in the current process.	Process analysis skills
Step 5. Create a new process design.	Eliminate all waste work. Apply the tools for process redesign to determine the best process for adding value for customers.	Teamwork; customer focus
Step 6. Implement the re-engineered process.	Phase in the new process. Encourage acceptance in the company and measure results.	Leadership; teamwork; employee training

FIGURE 12.5

Re-engineering process.

advantage. Although each company looks out for its own interests, it works closely with suppliers and customers throughout the chain. Everyone focuses on the entire chain of relationships rather than on just the next stage in the chain.[26]

A traditionally managed bakery, for example, would focus simply on getting production inputs from flour millers and paper suppliers and supplying baked goods to distributors. Unfortunately, this approach limits the chain's performance and doesn't allow for possible improvements when activities are more carefully coordinated. Supply chain management can improve performance and, as a result, provide higher quality at lower prices.

Supply Chain Management

Supply chain management (SCM) looks at the chain as a whole to improve the overall flow through a system composed of companies working together. The smooth flow of accurate information along the chain reduces unwanted inventories, avoids delays,

supply chain management (SCM) Principle of looking at the chain as a whole to improve the overall flow through the system.

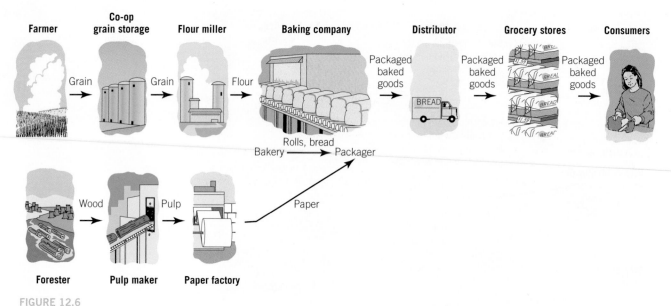

FIGURE 12.6

Supply chain for baked goods.

and cuts supply times. Materials move faster to businesses and ultimate consumers, and the efficiency of SCM means faster deliveries and lower costs than customers could get if each member acted only according to its own operations requirements. Because customers ultimately get better value, SCM gains competitive advantage for each supply chain member.[27]

Dell Computer's supply chain, for example, improves performance by allowing people to share information. Dell shares long-term production plans and up-to-the-minute sales data with suppliers via the internet. The process starts when customer orders are automatically translated into updated production schedules on the factory floor. These schedules are used not only by operations managers at Dell but also by such parts suppliers as Sony, which adjust their own production and shipping activities to better meet Dell's production needs. In turn, parts suppliers' updated schedules are transmitted to their materials suppliers, and so on. As Dell's requirements change, suppliers synchronize their schedules to produce the right materials and parts efficiently. As a result, Dell's prices are low and turnaround time for shipping PCs to customers is reduced to a matter of hours instead of days.

Supply chains are important for services as well as physical products, and they are becoming increasingly global and more sophisticated. For example, a Malaysian architect might sketch out a new office tower for the city of London, a Philippine architect develops the detailed renderings, and a Chinese engineer assesses the structural soundness of the building.[28] On occasion, problems arise in global supply chains, as the boxed insert "Supply Chain Disruptions" demonstrates.

Fashion house Louis Vuitton, which produces upscale products like the Reade tote bag, used to focus mainly on product image and product design. When an item became a hot seller, retailers often ran out of products because the company's production system and supply chain was not responsive to increased consumer demand. Vuitton has revamped its systems in order to ensure that retailers always have a supply of in-demand Vuitton products on their shelves. Other luxury-goods manufacturers, like Armani, Gucci, and Versace were doing the same thing.[29]

Supply chain management is also important in transportation. As we saw in Chapter 6, Port Metro Vancouver developed a supply-chain strategy that reduced container "dwell time"—the time containers sit on the dock—from 3.7 days to 2.5 days after managers determined that the port had to become more competitive with American ports. This reduction in dwell time also improved the port's relationships with operators like Canadian National Railway and Canadian Pacific Railway Ltd.[30]

MANAGING IN TURBULENT TIMES

Supply Chain Disruptions

On March 11, 2011 a devastating earthquake and tsunami struck north eastern Japan, killing thousands of people and destroying entire communities. The disaster also disrupted the production of automobiles, automobile parts, and electronic components like flash memory and dynamic random access memory for computing devices and smartphones. The earthquake damaged a Sony factory that produces the HDCAM-SR tapes used by movie and television producers. Since Sony is the only supplier in the world of that product, the sharply reduced supply caused prices to suddenly triple for the tapes.

When a supply chain shock occurs at one of its suppliers, a manufacturer may have to scramble to find another supplier. For example, Advanced Semiconductor Engineering Inc., a Taiwan-based chip-packaging company, had to look for new suppliers in China and South Korea after its Japanese supplier was unable to deliver supplies of plastic moulding compounds that are used to wrap semiconductors.

Just-in-time inventory systems (JIT) were negatively impacted by the Japanese earthquake. Manufacturing plants in various countries around the world had to be shut down for a period of time due to parts shortages. Ford Motor closed its manufacturing plants in South Africa, China, and Taiwan, and Toyota and Honda shut down production at Canadian assembly plants during the months of April and May 2011. In November 2011, Toyota and Honda had to again shut down assembly lines in Canada because of parts shortages caused by flooding in Thailand, and Intel also warned of shortages of hard disks because of the flooding. Companies continue to use JIT, but many of

them are starting to hold larger stocks of inventory in case of supply disruptions.

Supply chain disruptions seem to be occurring with greater frequency. Political unrest in the Middle East and China's restrictions on the export of rare earth metals are just two illustrations of how supply chains can be disrupted. But companies are planning for and reacting very quickly to disruptions. Just after the Japanese earthquake, for example, there was concern that supply chain disruptions would cause worldwide shutdowns of manufacturing plants. But that didn't happen for two reasons: First, companies had already diversified their sources of supply for critical inputs to their production processes. So, if a disruption occurred at one supplier (in this case, Japan), the company already had an alternative in place. Another (somewhat surprising) reason is that Japan is simply not a key foreign supplier for many companies. In a survey of supply chain managers, only 2 percent of respondents said that Japan was their top foreign supplier.

Critical Thinking Questions

1. What can companies do to lessen the impact of supply chain disruptions?

2. Consider the following statement: *Companies should reconsider their use of just-in-time inventory systems because if a supply disruption occurs, the manufacturing process will almost immediately have to be shut down because the company carries virtually no inventory.* Do you agree or disagree with the statement? Explain your reasoning.

Re-Engineering Supply Chains for Better Results

Process improvements and re-engineering often are applied in supply chains to lower costs, speed up services, and coordinate flows of information and materials. Because the smoother flow of accurate information along the chain reduces unwanted inventories and transportation, prevents delays, and cuts supply times, materials move faster to business customers and industrial consumers. Faster deliveries result in lower costs than customers could get if each member acted only according to its own operations requirements.

Heightened concerns about supply chain risks and costs are the result of soaring energy prices and volatile financial markets, according to a report by McKinsey & Company. Businesses are responding by managing complex products and services closer to home. The study found that 56 percent of executives at large global companies have employed centralized supply chain management over the past five years, "not only to take advantage of synergies, but also to strengthen their operational expertise."[31] As companies are increasingly going global, risks and

Before too long, you will be able to pick up an item from a Walmart shelf and scan it automatically onto your mobile phone, skipping the checkout line altogether. The same technology—called radio frequency identification (RFID)—will signal the Walmart storeroom to restock the item you bought.

hesitations about suppliers from developing countries have been reduced. Bruce Catoen, the Chief Technology Officer at Mold-Masters, says "We used to be worried about supply-chain quality from some of the developing countries, but we're finding that their quality, service and deliveries are outstanding. The capabilities in places like India and China and Eastern Europe have come up to speed very quickly." This type of international outlook is important for Canadian companies that are involved in global supply chains.[32]

Productivity and Quality as Competitive Tools

LO6 Discuss four strategies that companies use to improve productivity and quality.

A company's ability to compete by improving productivity and quality depends on participation by all parts of the firm. Total firm involvement stems from having company-wide strategies that we consider in this section: the company's willingness to invest in innovation, its long-run perspective on its goals, its concern for the quality of work life, and its improvement of service operations.

Invest in Innovation and Technology

Many firms that have continued to invest in innovative technology have enjoyed rising productivity and rising incomes. For example, while Steinway & Sons's piano factory is just as concerned as ever about maintaining the highest quality in its products, it's using newer technology to help the woodworkers do their jobs more efficiently and precisely. "It still takes us a year to craft one of these things," says Steinway president Bruce Stevens, "but technology is assisting us in making more precise parts that our people can assemble. It's helping us create a better instrument."[33]

Adopt a Long-Run Perspective

Instead of emphasizing short-run results, many quality-oriented firms are committed to a long-run perspective for **continuous improvement**—the ongoing commitment to improving products and processes, step by step, in pursuit of ever-increasing customer satisfaction. Motorola is a good example. In 1996, its Six Sigma program set a target of 3.4 defects per million parts. By 2003, the company's production-monitoring software—Manufacturing Intellitrak—had helped to reduce errors in some applications to two defects per *billion* parts.[34]

The Six Sigma program, which is used by many other companies besides Motorola, continuously captures, measures, and eliminates defects in every company-wide process, from financial transactions and accounting practices, to R&D (research and development) and production processes, to marketing and human resources activities. The earliest adopters of Six Sigma in Canada have been full-service brokerages such as Royal LePage Commercial, which have international clients.[35] A consulting firm like Global Training Systems—which prepares corporate professionals for global business success and trains employees in other companies to use Six Sigma programs—also uses the program in its own activities.[36]

continuous improvement The ongoing commitment to improving products and processes, step by step, in pursuit of ever-increasing customer satisfaction.

Emphasize Quality of Work Life

The products and services of businesses represent such a large part of total national output that the well-being and participation of their workers is central to improving national productivity. How can firms make their employees' jobs more challenging and interesting? Many companies are enhancing workers' physical and mental health through recreational facilities, counselling services, and other programs. In addition, more and more firms have started programs to empower and train employees.

Employee Empowerment

Many firms are replacing the work environments of yesterday, based on the principle of management-directed mass production, with worker-oriented environments that foster loyalty, teamwork, and commitment. Trident Precision Manufacturing has a program for full employee involvement. Over 95 percent of employee recommendations for process improvements have been accepted since the program started. As a result, employee turnover has fallen from 41 percent to less than 5 percent. Sales per employee have more than doubled.

As we saw in Chapter 10, firms using this approach have found success in the concept of *employee empowerment*—the principle that all employees are valuable contributors to a business and should be entrusted with certain decisions regarding their work. The Hampton Inns motel chain, for example, initiated a program of refunds to customers who were dissatisfied with their stays for any reason. Managers were pleased, and the refund policy created far more additional business than it cost. A surprise bonus was the increased morale when employees—everyone from front-desk personnel to cleaning staff—were empowered to grant refunds. With greater participation and job satisfaction, employee turnover was reduced to less than one-half its previous level. Such confidence in employee involvement contrasts sharply with the traditional belief that managers are the primary source of decision making and problem solving.

Employee Training

Employee involvement is effective when it is implemented with preparation and intelligence. *Training* is a key method of preparing employees for productivity-improvement programs. In fact, a recent American Management Association survey found a direct relationship between training and greater productivity and profitability. Firms that increased training activities were 66 percent more likely to report improved productivity and three times more likely to report increased profits. Moreover, after training, waste diminishes and quality increases. Finally, team training not only teaches employees to work in groups, but it also acquaints them more fully with the company's markets and operations.[37]

Improve the Service Sector

As important as employee attitudes are to goods production, they are even more crucial to service production, since employees often *are* the service. The service sector has grown rapidly, but this growth has often come at a cost of high inefficiency. Many newly created service jobs have not been streamlined. Some companies operate effectively, but many others are very inefficient, dragging down overall productivity. As new companies enter these markets, however, the increased need to compete should eventually force service producers to operate more productively.

Quality begins with listening to customers to determine what services they want. Companies in the temporary-services industry, for example, have long emphasized the needs of clients for clerical and light-industrial employees. More recently, however, temp services have realized the need for highly skilled, specialized temps such as nurses, accountants, and scientists.

In trying to offer more satisfactory services, many providers have discovered five criteria that customers use to judge service quality.[38]

- *Reliability*: Perform the service as promised, both accurately and on time.

- *Responsiveness*: Be willing to help customers promptly.

- *Assurance*: Maintain knowledgeable and courteous employees who will earn the trust and confidence of customers.

- *Empathy*: Provide caring, individualized attention to customers.

- *Tangibles*: Maintain a pleasing appearance of personnel, materials, and facilities.

MyBizLab

Capture more moments of true understanding. MyBizLab provides you with interactive study and practice tools directly related to this chapter's content. The new MyBizLab Study Plan Learning Path is designed to measure a full range of skills and provide remediation to give you what you need to master key chapter concepts. MyBizLab flexes to your unique learning needs. The result? Inspired learning, more success.

SUMMARY OF LEARNING OBJECTIVES

1. **Describe the connection between *productivity* and *quality*.** *Productivity* is a measure of economic performance; it compares how much is produced with the resources used to produce it. *Quality* is a product's fitness for use. However, an emphasis solely on productivity or solely on quality is not enough. Profitable competition in today's business world demands high levels of both productivity and quality.

2. **Understand the importance of increasing productivity.** It is important that Canadian business firms increase their

rate of productivity growth so that they can be competitive in world markets. As Canadian business firms increase productivity, they will be able to produce a greater quantity of goods without using more resources.

3. **Identify the activities involved in *total quality management*, and describe six tools that companies can use to achieve it.** *Total quality management (TQM)* (sometimes called *quality assurance*) includes all the activities necessary for getting high-quality goods and services into the marketplace. The strategic approach to TQM begins with customer focus. This includes methods for determining what customers want and then directing all the company's resources toward satisfying those wants and needs. Total participation is mandatory, and TQM is more than part-time. It demands continuous improvement of products and services, and improvement in all of the company's internal processes, such as accounting, delivery, billing, and information flows. Six tools that are used to achieve TQM: (1) *value-added analysis* (the evaluation of all work activities, material flows, and paperwork to determine the value that they add for customers); (2) *statistical process control* (SPC) (methods by which employees can gather data and analyze variations in production activities to determine when adjustments are needed); (3) *quality/cost* studies (studies that identify a firm's current costs but also reveal areas with the largest cost-savings potential); (4) *quality improvement (QI) teams* (groups of employees from various work areas who meet regularly to define, analyze, and solve common production problems); (5) *benchmarking* (improving business products or procedures by comparing them to either the firm's own past performance or the best practices of others); and (6) *getting closer to the customer* (know what customers want in the products they consume).

4. **Identify three trends in productivity and quality management, including *supply chain management*.** (1) *ISO 9000* is a certification program attesting to the fact that a factory, a laboratory, or an office has met the rigorous quality management requirements set by the International Organization for Standardization. It allows firms to show that they follow documented procedures for testing products, training workers, keeping records, and fixing product defects. *ISO 14000* certifies improvements in environmental performance. (2) *Business process re-engineering* focuses on improving both the productivity

and quality of business processes—rethinking each step of an organization's operations by starting from scratch. *Re-engineering* is the fundamental rethinking and redesign of processes to achieve dramatic improvements in measures of performance. (3) The *supply chain* refers to the group of companies and stream of activities that operate together to create a product. Traditional strategies assume that companies are managed as individual firms rather than as members of a coordinated supply chain. *Supply chain management (SCM)* looks at the chain as a whole to improve the overall flow through a system composed of companies working together. Because customers ultimately get better value, SCM gives chain members a competitive advantage.

5. **Explain how a *supply chain strategy* differs from traditional strategies for coordinating operations among firms.** The supply chain strategy is based on the idea that members of the supply chain can gain competitive advantage by working together as a coordinated system of units. For example, sharing information allows companies to reduce inventories, improve quality, and speed delivery of products to consumers. In contrast, traditional strategies assume that companies are managed as individual firms, with each one acting in its own interest.

6. **Discuss four strategies that companies use to improve productivity and quality.** (1) *Invest in innovation and technology*: Many firms that have continued to invest in innovative technology have enjoyed rising productivity and rising incomes. Increasingly, investments in the internet and information technology are rising, with new applications in every major industry. (2) *Adopt a long-run perspective*: Many quality-oriented firms are committed to long-term efforts at continuous improvement—the ongoing commitment to improving products and processes, step by step, in pursuit of ever-increasing customer satisfaction. (3) *Emphasize quality of work life*: Business products and services represent such a large part of total national output that the well-being and participation of workers is crucial to improving national productivity. (4) *Improve the service sector*: As important as employee attitude is to goods production, it is even more crucial to service production, where employees often are the service. In trying to offer more satisfactory services, many companies have discovered five criteria that customers use to judge service quality: reliability, responsiveness, assurance, empathy, and tangibles.

KEY TERMS

benchmarking (p. 386)
business process re-engineering (p. 388)
competitive product analysis (p. 383)
continuous improvement (p. 393)
control chart (p. 384)
external failures (p. 385)
internal failures (p. 385)
ISO 14000 (p. 387)

ISO 9000 (p. 387)
labour productivity (p. 375)
performance quality (p. 381)
process variation (p. 384)
productivity (p. 374)
quality (p. 374)
quality improvement (QI) teams (p. 386)
quality ownership (p. 382)
quality reliability (p. 382)

quality/cost studies (p. 385)
statistical process control (SPC) (p. 383)
supply chain (p. 388)
supply chain management (SCM) (p. 389)
total quality management (TQM) (p. 380)
value-added analysis (p. 383)

QUESTIONS FOR ANALYSIS

1. What is the relationship between productivity and quality?
2. High productivity in the service sector has historically been difficult to achieve. Why was this so? What might be changing in this area that will cause service productivity to increase during the next decade?
3. Explain how inputs and outputs relate to each other in the basic equation for measuring labour productivity.
4. What are the costs and benefits for a company that has decided to pursue quality and productivity as competitive tools?
5. Explain how the functions of management (planning, organizing, leading, and controlling) relate to one another in the pursuit of quality.
6. How might benchmarking be used to increase productivity in the service sector?

APPLICATION EXERCISES

1. Interview a production manager in a local firm and determine which of the tools for total quality management the company is currently using. Also determine why the company has chosen not to use some of the tools.
2. Using a local company as an example, show how you would conduct a quality/cost study. Identify the cost categories and give some examples of the costs in each category. Which categories do you expect to have the highest and lowest costs? Why?
3. Develop a list of internal customers and internal suppliers for the organization where you work. Identify areas of potential productivity and quality improvement in these internal customer-supplier relationships.
4. Choose a consumer item and trace its supply chain. Can you see areas where improvements might be made?

BUILDING YOUR BUSINESS SKILLS

Making Your Benchmark in the Business World

The Purpose of the Assignment

To encourage students to understand ways in which benchmarking can improve quality and productivity.

The Situation

As the director of maintenance for a regional airline, you are disturbed to learn that the cost of maintaining your 100-plane fleet is skyrocketing. A major factor is repair time; when maintenance or repairs are required, work often proceeds slowly. As a result, additional aircraft must be pressed into service to meet the schedule. To address the problem, you decide to use a powerful total quality management tool called *benchmarking*. You will approach your problem by studying ways in which other companies have successfully managed similar problems. Your goal is to apply the best practices to your own maintenance and repair operation.

Assignment

Step 1

Working with three or four other students, choose your benchmarking target from among the following choices:

- the maintenance and repair operations of a competing airline
- the pit crew operations of an Indianapolis 500 race car team
- the maintenance and repair operations of a nationwide trucking company

Write a memo explaining the reasons for your choice.

Step 2

Write a list of benchmarking questions that will help you learn the best practices of your targeted company. Your goal is to ask questions that will help you improve your own operation. These questions will be asked during on-site visits.

Step 3

As part of a benchmarking project, you will be dealing with your counterparts in other companies. You have a responsibility to prepare for these encounters, and you must remember that what you learn during the exchange process is privileged information. Given these requirements, describe the steps that you would take before your first on-site visit and outline your benchmarking code of ethics.

Questions for Discussion

1. Why is benchmarking an important method for improving quality?
2. Why did you make your benchmarking choice? Explain why the company you selected holds more promise than other companies in helping you solve your internal maintenance problems.

3. What kind of information would help you improve the efficiency of your operations? Are you interested in management information, technical information, or both?

4. In an age of heightened competition, why do you think companies are willing to benchmark with each other?

EXERCISING YOUR ETHICS: TEAM EXERCISE

Calculating the Cost of Conscience

The Situation

Product quality and cost affect every firm's reputation and profitability as well as the satisfaction of customers. This exercise will expose you to some ethical considerations that pertain to certain cost and service decisions that must be made by operations managers.

The Dilemma

As director of quality for a major appliance manufacturer, Ruth was reporting to the executive committee on the results of a recent program for correcting problems with a newly redesigned rotary compressor that the company had recently begun putting in its refrigerators. After receiving several customer complaints, the quality lab and the engineering department had determined that some of the new compressor units ran more loudly than expected. Some remedial action was needed. One option was simply waiting until customers complained and responding to each complaint as it occurred. Ruth, however, had decided that this approach was inconsistent with the company's policy of offering the highest quality in the industry. Deciding that the firm's reputation called for a proactive, "pro-quality" approach, Ruth had initiated a program for contacting all customers who had purchased refrigerators containing the new compressor.

Unfortunately, her "quality-and-customers-first" policy was expensive. Local service representatives had to phone every customer in each area of the country, make appointments for home visits, and replace original compressors with a newer model. But because replacement time was only half an hour, customers were hardly inconvenienced, and food stayed refrigerated without interruption. Customer response to the replacement program was overwhelmingly favourable.

Near the end of Ruth's report, an executive vice-president was overheard to comment, "Ruth's program has cost this company $400 million in service expenses." Two weeks later, Ruth was fired.

Team Activity

Assemble a group of four students and assign each group member to one of the following roles:

- Ruth
- Ruth's boss
- a customer
- a company investor

Action Steps

1. Before discussing the situation with your group, and from the perspective of your assigned role, do you think that Ruth's firing is consistent with the company's desire for industry leadership in quality? Write down the reasons for your position.

2. Before discussing the situation with your group, and from the perspective of your assigned role, what are the underlying ethical issues, if any, in this situation? Write down the issues.

3. Gather your group together and reveal, in turn, each member's comments on Ruth's firing. Next, reveal the ethical issues listed by each member.

4. Appoint someone to record the main points of agreement and disagreement within the group. How do you explain the results? What accounts for any disagreement?

5. From an ethical standpoint, what does your group conclude is the most appropriate action that should have been taken by the company in this situation?

6. Develop a group response to the following question: What are the respective roles of profits, obligations to customers, and employee considerations for the firm in this situation?

Go to MyBizLab for additional cases and exercise material.

CONCLUDING CASE 12-1

Keeping The Quality High At Toyota

J.D. Power & Associates is a marketing information services company that produces two annual rankings of automobile quality and reliability. The Initial Quality Study assesses consumer satisfaction with new-vehicle quality during the first 90 days of ownership, while the Vehicle Dependability Study assesses consumer satisfaction after three years of vehicle ownership. Both studies are based on feedback from thousands of car owners. In both studies, the measure is problems per 100 vehicles (PP100).

In the 2012 Initial Quality Study (IQS), the top three vehicles were the Toyota Lexus ES350 (73 PP100), Jaguar (75 PP100), and Porsche (75 PP100). The initial quality average was 102 PP100, down from

105 PP100 in 2011 (the lower the number, the higher the quality). Of the 34 *brands* that were ranked, 26 showed improved quality over 2011. Of the 185 *models* that were ranked, 65 percent improved their quality over 2011. Toyota automobile models exhibited very high quality, ranking in the top three in multiple categories, including "sub-compact car" (Toyota Yaris), "compact car" (Toyota Corolla), "large car" (Toyota Avalon), "compact MPV" (Toyota Prius), "premium car" (Lexus ES350), and "minivan" (Toyota Sienna).

In the 2012 Vehicle Dependability Study (VDS), the top three vehicles were the Toyota Lexus (86 PP100), Porsche (98 PP100), and Cadillac (104 PP100). The overall dependability average was 132 PP100, down from 151 PP100 in 2011 (again, the lower the number, the higher the dependability). Of the 32 *brands* that were ranked, 78 improved their dependability from 2011. Here again, Toyota automobile models exhibited very high dependability, ranking in the top three in multiple categories, including "sub-compact car" (Toyota Yaris), "compact car" (Toyota Prius), "large car" (Toyota Avalon), "premium car" (Lexus ES350), and "large pickup" (Toyota Tundra).

Toyota has received lots of positive publicity about "The Toyota Way," which emphasizes efficient production methods, continuous improvement, and high quality products. Toyota's production system was so impressive that executives from other automobile companies regularly toured Toyota's manufacturing plants in an attempt to discover Toyota's secret. One of the most highly publicized achievements for Toyota came in 2009, when it overtook General Motors as the largest car manufacturer in the world.

But Toyota ran into significant problems in mid-2009 when it reported the first operating loss in its history. Things got worse in November 2009, when Toyota announced that it was recalling more than five million of its cars because accelerator pedals were getting jammed in the driver's side car mat and causing the car to surge forward uncontrollably. That was bad enough, but in January 2010 Toyota announced another recall—this one involving 2.3 million vehicles (270 000 in Canada)—that also had to do with jamming accelerators. Production and sales were halted on eight of Toyota's most popular vehicles: the Corolla, RAV4, Camry, Avalon, Matrix, Highlander, Tundra, and Sequoia. These models accounted for 60 percent of Toyota sales in Canada. In February 2010, the highly publicized Prius was also recalled, and later Sienna vans.

These recalls created great concern among Toyota owners, who were suddenly scared to drive their cars. Toyota worked frantically with its supplier, CTS Corp., to figure out a way to fix the problem. The solution was to insert a steel reinforcement bar in the accelerator pedal assembly that reduced the tension that was causing the pedal to stick. CTS began producing the redesigned pedal in just a few days. Toyota admitted that the accelerator had a design flaw and that CTS was not at fault (CTS also produces accelerator pedals for Honda and Nissan and no problems were found in those cars). In an effort to reassure the public, senior executives from Toyota went on TV to tell customers that they were going to fix the problem quickly and install redesigned accelerator pedals in the recalled cars.

The recall was a public relations nightmare for Toyota because the company had always had a good reputation for producing high-quality automobiles. In the J.D. Power 2009 Initial Quality Study, Toyota had 10 cars rated as the best in 18 different vehicle categories, and many consumers in Canada and the United States did, in fact, have the perception that Toyota produced higher quality cars than those produced by Ford, Chrysler, and GM. But the recalls changed those perceptions, at least temporarily. In May 2010, a *Consumer Reports* survey found that Toyota lost the top spot in terms of customer loyalty (it was passed by both Ford and Honda). And in the 2010 Initial Quality Survey, Chrysler, Ford, and GM had fewer design-related problems and defects than their foreign competitors. That was the first time in nearly 50 years that domestic car makers had beaten foreign rivals in quality.

A Canadian class-action lawsuit against Toyota and CTS Corp. claimed that Toyota knew (or should have known) that there were also design defects in Toyota's electronic throttle control system. Toyota also faced a lawsuit in the United States because of 19 deaths caused by jammed accelerators. The law firm bringing the suit claimed that Toyota knew about the defect, but didn't do anything about it. These claims eventually led the U.S. government to ask the National Highway Traffic Safety Administration (NHTSA) to examine that possibility that there were faults in the electronic throttle system. The NHTSA then called on the Engineering and Safety Center at NASA to study Toyota vehicles. While the engineers did find a few cases where Lexus floor mats that had been installed in Toyotas caused the throttle to remain open, they could find no evidence of any electronic cause of unintended acceleration. This led many people to conclude that drivers were hitting the accelerator rather than the brake.

In the aftermath of the crisis, Toyota implemented several new quality- and safety-related changes to its operations, including a global computer data base that tracks vehicle repairs and customer complaints, and the appointment of a high-level manager to oversee safety issues. The latest J.D. Power quality and reliability ratings seem to indicate that Toyota has weathered the crisis.

Questions for Discussion

1. What is total quality management? How is it relevant for automobiles?
2. What is the difference between internal and external benchmarking? Do the J.D. Power Initial Quality and Vehicle Dependability studies facilitate benchmarking? Explain.
3. Consider the following statement: *Consumer opinions about which cars have the best quality or dependability are unreliable because people have preferences for a certain car before they buy it. They therefore are unlikely to give an objective opinion about the car's quality or dependability.* Do you agree or disagree with the statement? Defend your reasoning.

CONCLUDING CASE 12-2

Tree Planters

At Touchwood Lake, Alberta, 36 rookie tree planters (as well as a group of veteran planters) meet Cal Dyck, who has contracts to plant seven million white and black spruce seedlings in Alberta and Saskatchewan. The trees won't be ready to harvest for 90 years. The tree planting industry was born in the 1970s when the idea of sustainable forestry caught on. Originally, detention workers were used to plant the seedlings, but then forestry companies found out that there was an even cheaper demographic: hippies.

During a two-day orientation session, Cal gives the workers a lot of information about tree planting. He knows most of them want to make a lot of money in a short period of time, and he tells them they can do that if they are highly motivated and committed to working hard (planters can burn up to 7000 calories per day). Workers are paid between 10 and 25 cents per tree, depending on the terrain. For $30 per day, Cal will feed the tree planters and move them around to various planting sites. He also provides hot showers.

Among the rookies at the orientation are three friends: Misha (who is studying journalism at Concordia), Megan (a student at the Emily Carr Institute in Vancouver), and Lianne (also a student at the Emily Carr Institute). They will soon learn about the frailty of the human body in the business of tree planting (blisters, tendonitis, twisted ankles, and so on). The orientation also includes all-important demonstrations about how to properly plant a seedling. Spacing the seedlings, planting them at the right depth, choosing the right type of soil, and having the seedlings at the right temperature are all important considerations. The rookies train as a group, but then they're on their own and can work at their own pace. Their work is constantly checked for quality. If planting is not done right, it must be redone.

The rookies plant for just four hours during their first day on the job. While rookies are learning how to plant, they may plant fewer than 100 trees a day, but an experienced veteran can plant 3000 trees in a day. These high-volume planters—called "pounders" because of their intense work ethic—can earn $15 000 during the summer season. They set their own high production goals to motivate themselves to work hard.

For the rookies, the first week is already starting to blur. They eat, sleep, and plant. The work cycle is four days on and one day off. Within just a few weeks, some rookies are already starting to wonder why they

are in the bush, especially on days when the rain is pouring down and they are soaked through and through. At Kananaskis, Alberta, work slows down because the terrain is rough and steep. It's only halfway through the season, but some planters already have bad cases of tendonitis from the repeated motions of jamming their shovel into the ground as they plant seedlings. Already eight of the 36 rookies have quit.

Lianne has made $2500 so far, and she is one of the top rookie planters. By season's end, Lianne will have planted more than 98 000 trees. Megan (Lianne's school buddy) is starting to waver. She is fighting a sinus infection and is not even making minimum wage. Misha has decided to quit. A friend of hers is getting married back east and she will not return after the wedding. A week later, Megan quits as well.

At Candle Lake, Saskatchewan, the planting crews are behind schedule as the season nears its end. They still have 1.2 million trees to plant, and the ranks of rookie planters are thinning fast. Only 14 of 36 rookies are still on the job. Smaller work crews mean more work for those who are left, and the opportunity to make more money. After more than three months in the bush, each rookie who is still on the job has planted thousands of trees. Lianne has learned to stop calculating her daily earnings. Brad, a veteran planter, says that he admires the rookies who have pulled through. He says that it's amazing that people can be brought into the bush from the city to do this kind of work.

Questions for Discussion

1. Refer to the terms *productivity* and *quality* found in this chapter. How do they apply to the practice of tree planting?

2. Consider the following statement: *The productivity and quality of rookie tree planters is very low, and the turnover rate is very high. Tree planting companies should therefore hire only experienced tree planters.* Do you agree or disagree with the statement? Defend your answer. (You may need to refer to Chapter 8 for additional information to support your response).

3. Explain the various forms of employee behaviour. How does each one of these forms of behaviour influence the productivity and quality of tree planters? (Review the relevant material in Chapter 10 before answering this question.)

Understanding Information Systems and Communication Technology

LEARNING OBJECTIVES

After reading this chapter, you should be able to:

1 Explain the importance of *information management* to business firms.

2 Understand what an *information system* is, who the key users of information systems are, and the most widely used types of information systems.

3 Explain how the rapid growth of information technologies has affected *organizational processes and operations.*

4 Describe the building blocks of *information technology.*

5 Identify the *threats and risks* that are associated with the use of information technology by businesses.

6 Describe the ways in which businesses protect themselves from the threats and risks posed by information technology.

Skype: The Game Changer?

ONE of the most talked-about acquisitions in 2011 was Microsoft's purchase of Skype, an internet phone company. Microsoft paid $8.5 billion, making it the largest investment the company has ever made. Both Skype and Microsoft share similar product profiles: Microsoft's Messenger offers chat, voice, and video, as well as file transfers, with over 300 million users, and Skype, with 600 million users, offers similar services. Tony Bates, formerly the CEO of Skype, is now president of the newly formed Microsoft Skype Division.

Many in the industry questioned Microsoft's motives in the acquisition. Some believed that it was the company's attempt to gain market share from Google, Apple, and Facebook. Others believed that it made sense in terms of building the company's product portfolio, since Skype has a stronger voice platform and this gave Microsoft greater potential to penetrate into the cellphone market. Zeus Kerravala, founder and principal analyst of ZK Research, says that

"Skype does make official partnerships with a number of mobile operators who endorse the usage of Skype to make calls. This could give a boost to Microsoft's fledging mobile strategy." With Skype's technology capability, it can carry conversations from a cellphone to a TV or tablet, and Microsoft plans to integrate Skype into devices other than cellphones (for example, Xbox and Kinect, Xbox Live, the Windows Phone, Lync, and Outlook, and other non-Microsoft systems). This has potentially opened the door for Microsoft to tap into diverse product markets, thereby expanding its product profile and strategy. Microsoft's CEO Steve Ballmer expressed his excitement about the merger, saying "Skype is a phenomenal service that is loved by millions of people around the world. Together we will create the future of real-time communications so people can easily stay connected to family, friends, clients and colleagues anywhere in the world."

Critics of the deal argued that Microsoft paid too much for Skype. Others, like Norm Johnston,

Global Leader for Digital at Mindshare, thought "the deal was essential for Microsoft to acquire strategic technology it needed that they could not have developed organically to get to where they want to go." With Skype's existing platform and expertise, Microsoft was able to acquire not only the services but also Skype's brand recognition across markets and customers. Skype's offering of free internet calling had competitors on edge, and Preston Gralla, editor for *Computerworld*, noted that "when you make Skype calls, you're using your carrier's data plan, not its voice plan. Carriers charge more for voice minutes than for data, and so the more that people use Skype, the less revenue they get." Gralla believes that the investment might help the Windows Phone in its struggle to gain more market share—which was just 2 percent in the United States in May 2012—but thinks that Microsoft would need more than Skype to become successful. Gralla may be right. Microsoft and Nokia introduced their newest smartphone in May 2012 (the Lumia, powered by Windows Phone 7), but

cellphone carriers have not been eagerly picking it up. However, Larry Walsh, founder and executive director of Channel Vanguard Council, says this acquisition is typical of the technology industry as collaborations are steadily increasing (for example, Cisco with HP, IBM, and Dell, and many others on different products). Says Walsh: "Rapidly emerging technologies, as well as new and different business models, have the potential of keeping the IT marketplace unstable as vendors and service providers look for ways to replace commoditized revenue and increase their value. Caught in the crossfire will be solution providers, who will be forced to either concede pieces of the market to direct sales or get wedged between vendors in their conflicting go-to-market strategies." ◆

HOW WILL THIS HELP ME?

Services such as those offered by Skype are examples of the way the internet and related technologies are reshaping the business landscape. But even the most traditional businesses must change with the times, whether those times are defined by paper and pencil, fax machines, or digital language translators and smartphones. Indeed, it may seem like the times are changing more rapidly with each passing year, and it is in this context that our discussion of the various kinds of information technologies, their functions, and the benefits and risks associated with each assumes particular importance. By understanding the material in this chapter, you'll have a clearer picture of how technology is used by businesses, how it affects businesses, and how you can use it to your best advantage.

Information Management

The activities of business firms—for example, designing products and services, ensuring product delivery and cash flow, evaluating personnel, and creating advertising—require information. Because information is so important, companies have **information managers**, just as they have production, marketing, and finance managers. The goal of **information management** is to organize the firm's information resources to support business performance and outcomes.

Explain the importance of *information management* to business firms.

401

information manager The manager responsible for the activities needed to generate, analyze, and disseminate information that a company needs to make good decisions.

information management An internal operation that arranges the firm's information resources to support business performance and outcomes.

data Raw facts and figures.

information A meaningful, useful interpretation of data.

information system (IS) An organized method of transforming data into information that can be used for decision making.

L02 Understand what an *information system* is, who the key users of information systems are, and the most widely used types of information systems.

The question that faces so many businesses today is how to get useful information to the right people at the right time. Although managers often complain that they receive too much information, they usually mean that they get too much **data**—raw facts and figures. **Information** refers to data that have been interpreted so they are useful (see Figure 13.1). Consider the modern grocery store. The checkout scanner reads the bar code on the product you buy. Data are then transmitted to the store's inventory-control system, which updates the number of available units. If inventory falls below a given level, more product is ordered electronically. Meanwhile, the correct price is added to your bill and checkout coupons are printed automatically according to the specific product you bought. Your debit card transfers funds, sales reports are generated for the store's management, and all the while, satellite transmissions are dispatching a truck to begin loading replacement supplies for the store. This entire process extracts useful information from raw data.

Information Systems

An **information system (IS)** transforms raw data into information and transmits it for use in decision making. IS managers must first determine what information is needed, gather the relevant data, convert that data into information, and finally see that the information goes to those people who need it.[1] The information that is supplied varies according to such factors as the functional areas in which people work (say, accounting or marketing) and their management levels.

At one time, IS applications were quite narrow and technically focused—processing payroll data, simulating new engineering designs, compiling advertising expenditures. But managers now use IS not merely to solve technical problems but also to analyze management control and planning problems (e.g., applying quality control standards to production, comparing costs against budgeted amounts, keeping records on employee absences and turnover, and making decisions on a firm's products and markets for the next 5 to 10 years). There is also increased interdependence between a company's business strategy and its IS. The choice of a business strategy—say, to be the lowest-cost provider or the most flexible provider or the highest-quality provider—requires an information system that can support that strategy.

Walmart's information system gathers data on the billions of sales transactions—time, date, place—at the company's locations around the world. Keeping track of

FIGURE 13.1

From data to information and knowledge.

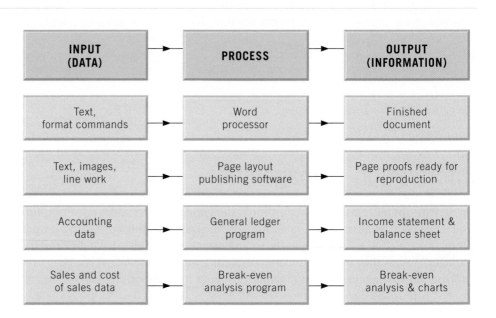

nearly 700 million stock-keeping units (SKUs) weekly, the information system enforces uniform reordering and delivery procedures—on packaging, timing, and quantities—for more than 30 000 suppliers. It also regulates the flow of the more than five billion cases through its distribution centres and deliveries by nearly 8000 Walmart truck drivers to its stores.

The top priority for Walmart's IS—improving in-stock reliability—requires integration of Walmart's and suppliers' activities with store sales. That's why Procter & Gamble, Johnson & Johnson, and other suppliers connect into Walmart's information system to observe up-to-the-minute sales data on individual items, by store. They can use the system's computer-based tools—spreadsheets, sales forecasting, weather information—to forecast sales demand and plan delivery schedules. Coordinated planning avoids excessive inventories, speeds up deliveries, and holds down costs throughout the supply chain while keeping shelves stocked for retail customers.

Key Users of Information Systems

Four different groups—top, middle, and first-line managers and knowledge workers (see Chapter 8)—have different information needs. *Top managers* need information to carry out long-range planning for the entire organization, to assess the business environment, and to improve overall company performance. *Middle managers* need summaries and analyses for setting intermediate and long-range goals for the departments or projects under their supervision. *First-line managers* need information to oversee the day-to-day details of their departments or projects. *Knowledge workers* need special information for conducting technical projects.

Consider how these different needs for information are evident in a flooring manufacturer. Knowledge workers who are developing new flooring materials need information on the chemical properties of adhesives and compression strengths for floor structures. Sales managers (first-level managers) supervise salespeople, assign territories to the sales force, and handle customer service and delivery problems; they need current information on the sales and delivery of products—lists of incoming customer orders and daily delivery schedules to customers in their territories. Regional

New tools are available to managers to help deal with the flood of data and exchanges of information. Companies are always looking for cost effective ways to manage the sharing of knowledge.

managers (middle managers) set sales quotas for each sales manager, prepare budgets, and plan staffing needs for the upcoming year; they need information on monthly sales by product and region. Finally, top managers need both internal information (e.g., sales data summarized by product, customer type, and geographic region, along with comparisons to previous years) and external information (e.g., consumer behaviour patterns, the performance of competitors, and economic forecasts).

Types of Information Systems

The term *information system* is something of a misnomer because it suggests that there is just one system. In reality, "the information system" is several systems that share information while serving different levels of the organization, different departments, and different operations. Several of the most well-known and highly developed information systems are discussed below.

Transaction Processing Systems

transaction processing systems (TPS) Applications of information processing for basic day-to-day business transactions.

Transaction processing systems (TPS) are applications of information processing for basic day-to-day business transactions. Customer order-taking by online retailers, approval of claims at insurance companies, receiving and confirming reservations by airlines, payroll processing and bill payment at almost every company—all are routine business processes. Typically, the TPS for first-level (operational) activities is well defined with predetermined data requirements and follows the same steps to complete all transactions in the system.

Systems for Knowledge Workers and Office Applications

Systems for knowledge workers and office applications support the activities of both knowledge workers and employees in clerical positions. IS knowledge workers include both systems analysts (who design systems that meet users' requirements) and systems programmers (who write the software instructions that tell computers what to do).

system operations personnel People who run a company's computer equipment.

People who run the company's computer equipment are called **system operations personnel**. They ensure that the right programs are run in the correct sequence, and they monitor equipment to ensure that it is operating properly. Many organizations also have personnel for entering data into the system for processing.

computer-aided design (CAD) Computer analysis and graphics programs that are used to create new products.

Support systems like word processing, document imaging, desktop publishing, computer-aided design, and simulation modelling have increased the productivity of both office and knowledge workers. **Computer-aided design (CAD)** assists in designing products by simulating the real product and displaying it in three-dimensional graphics. The Communitech Hub, in Kitchener, Ontario, offers its clients access to The HIVE (Hub Interactive Virtual Environment). By integrating 3D technology and user-directed displays, the HIVE provides partner companies with both promotional and research opportunities. For example, architects and engineers can upload detailed drawings of a new retail or service space and "walk around" using virtual technology. The technology allows the designers and owners a chance to see the space in a 3D scenario and make any necessary changes before construction even starts.[2] Products ranging from cellphones to auto parts are created using CAD because it creates faster designs at lower cost than manual modelling methods.

computer-aided manufacturing (CAM) Computer systems used to design and control all the equipment and tools for producing goods.

Computer-aided manufacturing (CAM) is used to design the manufacturing equipment, facilities, and plant layouts for better product flows and productivity. *Computer operations control* refers to any system for managing the day-to-day production activities for either goods or service production. Hospitals, for instance, use computer-based scheduling for preparing patients' meals, just as manufacturers do for making cars, clocks, and paper products.

Management Information Systems

Management information systems (MIS) support an organization's managers by providing reports, schedules, plans, and budgets. Each manager's information activities vary according to his or her functional area (say, accounting or marketing) and management level. Whereas mid-level managers focus mostly on internal activities and information, higher-level managers are also engaged in external activities. Middle managers, the largest MIS user group, need information to plan such upcoming activities as personnel training, materials movements, and cash flows. They also need to know the current status of the jobs and projects being carried out in their departments: What stage is it at now? When will it be finished? Is there an opening so the next job can be started? Many of a firm's management information systems—cash flow, sales, production scheduling, and shipping—are indispensable for helping managers find answers to such questions.

management information systems (MIS) Systems that support an organization's managers by providing reports, schedules, plans, and budgets.

Decision Support Systems

Middle- and top-level managers receive decision-making assistance from a **decision support system (DSS)**—an interactive system that locates and presents information needed to support the decision-making process. Whereas some DSSs are devoted to specific problems, others serve more general purposes, allowing managers to analyze different types of problems. Thus a firm that often faces decisions on plant capacity, for example, may have a *capacity DSS* in which the manager inputs data on anticipated levels of sales, working capital, and customer-delivery requirements. Then the system's built-in transaction processors manipulate the data and make recommendations on the best levels of plant capacity for each future time period.

decision support system (DSS) An interactive system that locates and presents information needed to support the decision-making process.

Executive Support Systems

An **executive support system (ESS)** is designed to assist with executive-level decisions and problems, ranging from "What lines of business should we be in five years from now?" to "Based on forecasted developments in electronic technologies, to what extent should our firm be globalized in five (or 10) years?" An ESS uses a wide range of internal information and external sources, such as industry reports, global economic forecasts, and reports on competitors.

executive support system (ESS) A quick-reference, easy-access application of information systems specially designed for upper-level managers.

The 3-D computer model of this dinosaur is constructed from digital scans of fossilized tissue.

Artificial Intelligence

artificial intelligence (AI) The development of computer systems to imitate human thought and behaviour.

Artificial intelligence (AI) refers to the development of computer systems to imitate human thought and behaviour—in other words, systems that perform physical tasks, use thought processes, and learn. For example, a credit-evaluation system may decide which loan applicants are creditworthy and which are too risky, and it may then compose acceptance and rejection letters accordingly.

Some AI systems possess sensory capabilities, such as lasers that "see," "hear," and "feel." KeyLemon is a software company that offers simple, fast, and convenient computer access solutions, based on face and speech recognition, for all internet users with a webcam. The biometric identification technology behind KeyLemon's products is the result of 10 years of research.[3]

ENTREPRENEURSHIP AND NEW VENTURES

Speaking Loud and Clear: A New Voice Technology

IT users for years have sought a natural-sounding voice interface to enhance IT systems with vocal output, beyond traditional print or visual output. Vocal technologies, however, were less than effective—that is, until 2005 when Matthew Aylett and Nick Wright formed CereProc (short for Cerebral Processing) in Edinburgh, Scotland. From the outset, the firm has been dedicated to creating better synthetic voices with character and emotion that stimulate listeners with natural-sounding messages. Before CereProc, these lofty goals were prohibitive. Speech experts couldn't create text-to-voice software that sounded realistically conversational, varying tone-of-voice and providing various vocal inflections for different situations. Previous software couldn't adapt incoming text (from word processing or from text messages) into natural voice formats. To attack these challenges, CereProc brought together a team of leading speech experts. It also partnered with leading universities and research programs in speech science technology and in developing new applications and markets for voice output.

The company's main product is CereVoice, an advanced text-to-voice technology available on mobile devices, PCs, servers, and headsets, that has applications in almost any company's products for better synthetic voices. Any computer's existing voice system can be replaced with more natural-sounding speech in a choice of accents, including British English, Scottish, and American, that can be sampled with live voice demos at the firm's website. Potential applications are endless—kitchen appliances,

alarm systems, traffic controllers, automobile appliances, radio broadcasting, telephone messaging, and movies, to name a few. Although consumers may not see the CereVoice label, they will be hearing its various voices often in their everyday lives.

CereProc's Voice Creation service can create a synthesized imitation of a person's voice, including its tones and inflections. That's how noted film critic Roger Ebert got his voice back, four years after losing the ability to speak following cancer-related surgery. CereProc's voice engineers used recordings of Ebert's voice from 40 years of past television broadcasts, capturing individual sounds and identifying various voice characteristics. With meticulous care, specialists then pieced them back together into software that mimics the Pulitzer-Prize winner's earlier voice. Ebert types his comments into a computer that, in turn, converts the text into words that are spoken in his voice. This first-of-its-kind application made a memorable public appearance on the *Oprah* show, as Roger enthusiastically demonstrated his voice coming from the computer. Beyond its technical success, this project vividly displays a compassionate side in CereProc's business.

Critical Thinking Question

1. Technological advances can provide significant advantages to individuals (like Roger Ebert) and to companies (in terms of effective information management). Can you think of disadvantages that are also evident with respect to technological advances?

Robotics is a category of artificial intelligence. Robots can "learn" repetitive tasks and "remember" the causes of past mistakes.

A special form of AI, the **expert system**, is designed to imitate the thought processes of human experts in a particular field.[4] For example, Campbell Soup Co. developed an expert system to mimic complex decision processes and save the expert knowledge that was going to be lost when a long-time expert soup maker announced his intention to retire.[5] While the benefits of an expert system infer increased output, productivity, and quality, there are some limitations. The knowledge may not be readily available, or the expertise may be hard to "extract" from humans and only work in a narrow domain of knowledge.[6]

expert system A form of artificial intelligence in which a program draws on the rules an expert in a given field has laid out to arrive at a solution for a problem.

Information Technology

No matter where we go, we can't escape the impact of **information technology (IT)**—the various devices for creating, storing, exchanging, and using information in diverse modes, including visual images, voice, multimedia, and business data. We see ads all the time for the latest cellphones, MP3 players, laptops, and software products, and most of us connect daily to the internet. Email has become a staple in business, and even such traditionally "low-tech" businesses as hair salons and garbage collection companies are becoming dependent on the internet, computers, and networks. As consumers, we interact with databases every time we withdraw money from an ATM, order food at McDonald's, or check on the status of a package at UPS or FedEx. The top 10 information technology companies in Canada are listed in Table 13.1.

information technology (IT) The various devices for creating, storing, exchanging, and using information in diverse modes, including visual images, voice, multimedia, and business data.

IT developments have also had a major impact on how individual managers do their jobs. For example, the packing list for Barry Martin's upcoming fishing trip reflects his new outlook on where, when, and how he gets his work done. It reads, in part, as follows: (1) fly rod, (2) dry-pack food, (3) tent, and (4) BlackBerry. Ten years ago, his list would have included a cellphone, road and area maps, phone directory,

TABLE 13.1 Top 10 Information Technology Companies in Canada, 2011
1. Research In Motion
2. BCE (wireless and internet)
3. Rogers Communications (wireless and internet)
4. TELUS (wireless and internet)
5. Celestica
6. CGI Group
7. Shaw Communications (internet)
8. CAE
9. Open Text
10. Softchoice

appointments calendar, office files, and client project folders, all of which are replaced now by just one item, his BlackBerry—a wireless handheld messaging device that allows him to take the office with him wherever he goes.

For a project manager like Martin, the BlackBerry is more than just a cellphone. With its continuous connection, there's no dialling in, and his email is displayed the same moment it arrives on his PC back at the office. Even in the Canadian wilderness, Martin can place phone calls and read new email messages. Along with internet browsing, there's access to desktop tools—such as an organizer and an address book—for managing work and staying in touch with customers, suppliers, and employees from any location.

The mobile messaging capabilities of devices like the BlackBerry offer businesses powerful tools that save time and travel expenses. They also mean that employees no longer work only at the office or the factory and that not all of a company's operations are performed at one place. When using such devices, offsite employees have continuous access to information instead of being forced to be at a desk to access their files and the internet. Helping to support these networks and devices is SOTI Inc., which develops world-leading technology to solve the unique challenges involved in managing, securing, supporting and tracking remote mobile and desktop devices.[7]

Information Technology and Organizational Processes

L03 Explain how the rapid growth of information technologies has affected *organizational processes and operations.*

The rapid growth of new information technologies has changed organizational processes and operations in many different ways, some of which are discussed below.

Better Service Through Coordination of Remote Deliveries

With access to the internet, company activities may be geographically scattered but remain coordinated through a networked system that provides better service for customers. Many businesses, for example, coordinate activities from one centralized location, but their deliveries flow from several remote locations, often at lower cost. When you order furniture from an internet storefront—for example, a chair, a sofa, a table, and two lamps—the chair may come from a warehouse in Toronto, the lamps from a manufacturer in China, and the sofa and table from a supplier in North Carolina. Beginning with the customer's order, activities are coordinated through the company's network, as if the whole order were being processed at one place. This avoids the expensive in-between step of first shipping all the items to a central location.

Leaner, More Efficient Organizations

Networks and technology are also leading to leaner companies with fewer employees and simpler structures. Because networks enable firms to maintain information linkages between employees and customers, more work and customer satisfaction can be accomplished with fewer people. Bank customers can access 24-hour information systems and monitor their accounts without employee assistance. Instructions that once were given to assembly workers by supervisors are now delivered to workstations electronically. Truck drivers delivering freight used to return to the trucking terminal to receive instructions from supervisors on reloading for the next delivery, but now instructions arrive on electronic screens in the trucks so drivers know in advance what will be happening next.

Increased Collaboration

Collaboration among internal units and with outside firms is greater when firms use collaboration software and other IT communications devices. Companies are learning that complex problems can be solved better through IT-supported collaboration, either with formal teams or through spontaneous interaction among people and departments. The design of new products, for example, was once largely an engineering responsibility. Now it is a shared activity using information from people in marketing, finance, production, engineering, and purchasing who collectively determine the best design. When Boeing designed its new 777 aircraft, information came not just from engineers, but also from passengers (who said they wanted electronic outlets to recharge personal electronic devices), cabin crews (who wanted more bathrooms and wider aisles), and air-traffic controllers (who wanted larger, safer airbrakes).

Improved Global Exchange

The global reach of IT is enabling business collaboration on a scale that was unheard of just a few years ago. Consider Lockheed Martin's contract for designing the Joint Strike supplying thousands of the planes in different versions for Canada, the United States, the United Kingdom, Italy, Denmark, and Norway. Lockheed can't do the job alone, so it is collaborating with the United Kingdom's BAE Systems and more than 70 U.S. and 18 international subcontractors at some 190 locations. Over the project's 20-year life, more than 1500 firms will supply everything from radar systems to engines to bolts. Collaboration on this massive scale is essential for coordinating design, testing, and construction while avoiding delays, holding down costs, and maintaining quality.[8]

Greater Independence of Company and Workplace

Many employees no longer work only at the office or the factory, and not all of a company's operations are performed at one location. The sales manager for an advertising agency may visit the company office in Toronto once every two weeks, preferring instead to work over the firm's electronic network from her home office in Montreal. A medical researcher for a Calgary clinic may work at a home office networked into the clinic's system. With new developments in IT, a company's activities may also be geographically scattered but still highly coordinated. Many ebusinesses, for example, do not conduct any activities at one centralized location; rather, all of their activities are launched instantaneously by the customer's order and coordinated through the network, just as though all of them were being processed at one location.

Improved Management Processes

IT has also changed the nature of the management process. At one time, upper-level managers didn't concern themselves with all of the detailed information filtering upward from the workplace because it was expensive to gather, slow in coming, and quick to become out of date. Now, it's easier than ever for companies to monitor what their employees are doing online, even when they do it on their own computers and on their own time. For example, Social Sentry is a tracking system offered by California-based Social Logix that records and archives social media activities by employees from any location. The purpose of the program is to guard against workers who might leak sensitive data or waste work time on Twitter. It also aims to protect a company's reputation.[9]

Improved Flexibility for Customization

IT has also created new manufacturing capabilities that enable businesses to offer customers greater variety and faster delivery cycles. Whether it's a laptop, an iPhone, or a Rawlings baseball glove, today's design-it-yourself world has become possible through fast, flexible manufacturing using IT networks. At Timbuk2's website, for example, you can "build your own" custom messenger bag at different price levels with choices of size, fabric, colour combinations, accessories, liner material, strap, and even left- or right-hand access.[10] The principle is called **mass-customization**: Although companies produce in large volumes, each unit features the unique options the customer prefers. As shown in Figure 13.2, flexible production and speedy delivery depend on an integrated network of information to coordinate all the activities among customers, manufacturers, suppliers, and shippers.

mass-customization Producing large volumes of products or services, but giving customers the choice of features and options they want.

FIGURE 13.2

Networking for mass-customization.

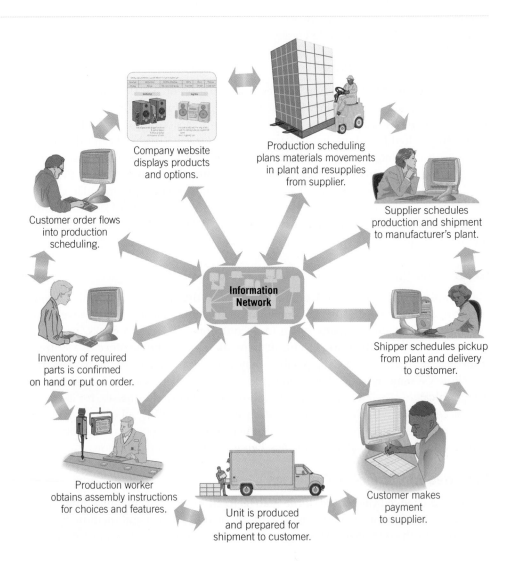

Company website displays products and options.

Production scheduling plans materials movements in plant and resupplies from supplier.

Customer order flows into production scheduling.

Supplier schedules production and shipment to manufacturer's plant.

Information Network

Inventory of required parts is confirmed on hand or put on order.

Shipper schedules pickup from plant and delivery to customer.

Production worker obtains assembly instructions for choices and features.

Unit is produced and prepared for shipment to customer.

Customer makes payment to supplier.

Providing New Business Opportunities

Not only is IT improving existing businesses, it is creating entirely new businesses where none existed before. For big businesses, this means developing new products, offering new services, and reaching new clients. Today, cloud technology allows businesses and consumers alike to share files, access servers, and share personal information. Cloud computing is a game changer because everyone has immediate access to an unlimited amount of computing resources, and, as such, technology is no longer a constraint for creativity and innovation.[11]

The IT landscape has also presented small business owners with new ebusiness opportunities. Consider Richard Smith, who began collecting stamps at age seven. Now, some 40 years later, he's turned his hobby into a profitable eBay business. Each day begins at the PC in his home office, scanning eBay's listings for items available and items wanted by sellers and buyers around the world. With more than 3000 sales transactions to date, Richard maintains a perfect customer rating and recently earned more than $4000 on a single eBay transaction.

To assist start-up businesses, eBay's services network is a ready-made online business model, not just an auction market. Services range from credit financing to protection from fraud and misrepresentation, information security, international currency exchanges, and post-sales management. These activities enable users like Richard to complete sales transactions, deliver merchandise, and get new merchandise for future resale, all from the comfort of their own homes.

Meanwhile, eBay's PayPal system—an online financial institution—processes $20 billion in transactions annually. As a seller, Richard receives payments into his PayPal account from buyers using credit cards, debit cards, bank accounts, or their own PayPal accounts. When buying merchandise, he can pay in any of six currencies, including the euro and Japanese yen, with PayPal making the conversion between Canadian dollars and the seller's currency.

Improving the World and Our Lives

Can advancements in IT really make the world a better place? Hospitals and medical equipment companies certainly think so. For example, when treating combat injuries, surgeons at Walter Reed National Military Medical Center in the United States now rely on high-tech graphics displays that are converted into three-dimensional physical models for pre-surgical planning. These 3-D mock-ups of shoulders, femurs, and facial bones give doctors the opportunity to see and feel the anatomy as it will be seen in the operating room, before they even use their scalpels.[12] Meanwhile, vitamin-sized cameras that patients swallow are providing doctors with computer images of the insides of the human body, helping them to make better diagnoses for such ailments as ulcers and cancer.[13]

After this capsule is swallowed, the camera inside it can transmit 50 000 images during its eight-hour journey through the digestive tract.

IT Building Blocks

LO4 Describe the building blocks of *information technology.*

We have already seen how dramatically IT is affecting the business landscape. The *tools* that make it work are things like the *internet, email* and other communications technologies, *networks, hardware devices,* and *software.*

The Internet and Other Communication Technologies

internet The gigantic network of networks that serves millions of computers; offers information on business, science, and government; and provides communication flows among more than 170 000 separate networks around the world.

The **internet** is a system of more than 100 million interconnected computers in over 100 countries around the world that allows for easy access to information, and transmission of that information. The **World Wide Web** is a standardized code for accessing information and transmitting data over the internet. For thousands of businesses, the internet is replacing the telephone, fax machine, and standard mail as the primary communication tool. This surge in communication has created huge demands on internet capacity, and has led to intense debates about the prices that consumers should pay for access (see Concluding Case 13-2 for more detail about this issue).

World Wide Web A standardized code for accessing information and transmitting data over the internet, which provides the common language that allows information sharing on the internet.

According to ComScore, Canadians spend more time each month on the internet (about 45 hours) than people in any other country.[14] The internet contributed $49 billion to Canada's GDP in 2011, and that figure is expected to rise to $76 billion by 2016. But the growth rate projected for Canada's internet economy lags behind that of other countries.[15]

The internet has spawned a number of other business communications technologies, including *intranets, extranets, electronic conferencing,* and *VSAT satellite communications.*

intranet A company's private network that is accessible only to employees via entry through electronic firewalls.

Intranets. Many companies maintain internal websites linked throughout the firm. These private networks, or **intranets**, are accessible only to employees. For example, Ford Motor Company's intranet connects 175 000 workstations in Asia, Europe, and North America to thousands of Ford websites containing private information on Ford's employee benefits, production management tools, and product design resources. Sharing information on engineering, distribution, and marketing has reduced the lead time for getting new models into production and has shortened customer delivery times.[16]

extranet A network that allows outsiders limited access to a firm's internal information system.

Extranets. **Extranets** allow outsiders limited access to a firm's internal information network. The most common application allows buyers to enter a system to see which products are available for sale and delivery, thus providing convenient product availability information. Industrial suppliers are often linked into customers' information networks so that they can see planned production schedules and prepare supplies for customers' upcoming operations. The extranet at lululemon, for example, lets customers shop online for clothing and merchandise and browse through their inventory of available colours and sizes.

electronic conferencing Allows people to communicate simultaneously from different locations via telephone, video, or mail group software.

Electronic Conferencing. **Electronic conferencing** allows groups of people to communicate simultaneously from various locations via email, phone, or video. One form, called *data conferencing,* allows people in remote locations to work simultaneously on one document. Working as a team, they can revise a marketing plan or draft a press release. *Video conferencing* allows participants to see one another on video screens while the conference is in progress. GoToMeeting is an example of an online conferencing service that allows businesses to collaborate with small and large working groups; it is available for meetings, Webinars, and training programs.[17]

VSAT satellite communications A transmitter-receiver (transceiver) that sits outdoors with a direct line of sight to a satellite. The hub—a ground station computer at the company's headquarters—sends signals to and receives signals from the satellite, exchanging voice, video, and data transmissions.

VSAT Satellite Communications. Another internet technology businesses use to communicate is **VSAT satellite communications**. VSAT (short for *Very Small Aperture Terminal*) systems have a transmitter-receiver (*transceiver*) that sits outdoors with a direct line of sight to a satellite. The hub—a ground station computer at the company's headquarters—sends signals to and receives signals from the satellite, exchanging voice,

Larry Page (left) and Sergey Brin started the search engine Google when both were graduate students in the mid-1990s. They originally called their program "BackRub" because it was good at analyzing the "back links" from one website to another. Raising money primarily from Silicon Valley venture capitalists, they incorporated Google in 1998. When the six-year-old company went public in 2004, its founders, each of whom held 38 million shares, cleared $3 billion apiece.

video, and data transmissions. An advantage of VSAT is privacy. A company that operates its own VSAT system has total control over its communications without dependence on other companies. A firm might use VSAT to exchange sales and inventory information, advertising messages, and visual presentations between headquarters and store managers at remote sites.

Networks: System Architecture

A **computer network** is a group of two or more computers linked together by some form of cable (fibre-optic, coaxial, or twisted wire) or by wireless technology to share data or resources, such as a printer. The most common type of network used in businesses is a client–server network. In **client–server networks**, *clients* are usually the laptop or desktop computers through which users make requests for information or resources. *Servers* are the computers that provide the services shared by users. In big organizations, servers are usually assigned a specific task. For example, in a local university or college network, an *application server* stores the word-processing, spreadsheet, and other programs used by all computers connected to the network. A *print server* controls the printer, stores printing requests from client computers, and routes jobs as the printer becomes available. An *email server* handles all incoming and outgoing email. With a client–server system, users can share resources and internet connections—and avoid costly duplication.

computer network A group of two or more computers linked together by some form of cable (fibre-optic, coaxial, or twisted wire) or by wireless technology to share data or resources.

client–server network A network composed of both clients (users) and servers that allows the clients to access various services without costly and unnecessary duplication.

Wide Area Networks (WANs). Computers that are linked over long distances—province-wide or even nationwide—through telephone lines, microwave signals, or satellite communications make up what are called **wide area networks (WANs)**. Firms can lease lines from communications vendors or maintain private WANs. Walmart, for example, depends on a private satellite network that links 5000 retail stores to its Bentonville, Arkansas headquarters.

wide area networks (WANs) Computers that are linked over long distances—province-wide or even nationwide—through telephone lines, microwave signals, or satellite communications.

Local Area Networks (LANs). In **local area networks (LANs)**, computers are linked in a smaller area, such as all of a firm's computers within a single building. On cable TV's Home Shopping Network (HSN), for example, hundreds of operators at the HSN facility are united by a LAN for entering call-in orders. The arrangement requires only one computer system with one database and one software system.

local area networks (LANs) Computers that are linked in a smaller area, such as all of a firm's computers within a single building.

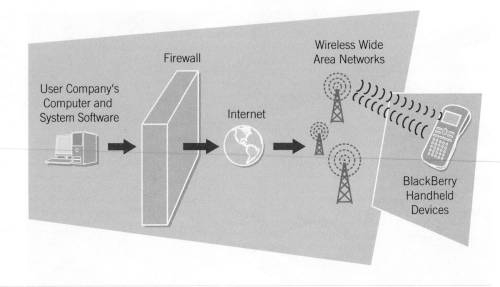

FIGURE 13.3

BlackBerry wireless internet architecture.

Wireless Networks. Wireless networks use airborne electronic signals to link network computers and devices. Like wired networks, wireless networks can reach across long distances or exist within a single building or small area. For example, the BlackBerry system shown in Figure 13.3 consists of devices that send and receive transmissions on **wireless wide area networks (WWANS)** of more than 100 service providers in over 40 countries. The wireless format that the system relies on to control wireless messaging is supplied by Research In Motion (RIM), the Canadian company that makes the BlackBerry, and is installed on the user company's computer. The *firewall* provides privacy protection (we discuss firewalls in more detail later).

Wi-Fi. Hotspots are specific locations such as coffee shops, hotels, and airport terminals that provide wireless internet connections for people on the go. Each hotspot, or **Wi-Fi** (short for wireless fidelity) access point, is actually its own small network, called a **wireless local area network (wireless LAN or WLAN).**

The benefit of Wi-Fi is that you're not tethered to a wire for accessing the internet. Employees can wait for a delayed plane in the airport and still be connected to the internet through their wireless-enabled laptop. However, as with every technology, Wi-Fi has drawbacks, most notably its limited range. This means that your laptop's internet connection can be severed if you move farther than about 90 metres from the hotspot. So, while a city may have hundreds of hotspots, your laptop must remain near one to stay connected. This distance limitation is expected to be improved soon by *WiMax* (*Worldwide Interoperability for Microwave Access*), the next step in wireless advancements, with its wireless range of 48 kilometres.

Hardware and Software

Any computer network or system needs **hardware**—the physical components, such as keyboards, monitors, system units, and printers. In addition to laptops, desktops, iPads, and BlackBerrys, handheld computers are also used in businesses. For example, Walmart employees roam store aisles using handhelds to identify, count, and order items; track deliveries; and update backup stock at distribution centres to keep store shelves replenished with merchandise. The boxed insert entitled "The Death of the PC?" describes the rapid changes that are occurring in hardware.

The other essential in any computer system is **software**—programs that tell the computer how to function. Software includes *system software*, such as Microsoft

wireless wide area networks (WWANs) Networks that use airborne electronic signals instead of wires to link computers and electronic devices over long distances.

Wi-Fi (wireless fidelity) An access point in a specific location, such as a coffee shop, hotel, or airport terminal, that provides wireless internet connections for people on the go.

wireless local area network (wireless LAN or WLAN) The individual network that provides Wi-Fi.

hardware The physical components of a computer, such as keyboards, monitors, system units, and printers.

software Programs that tell the computer how to function.

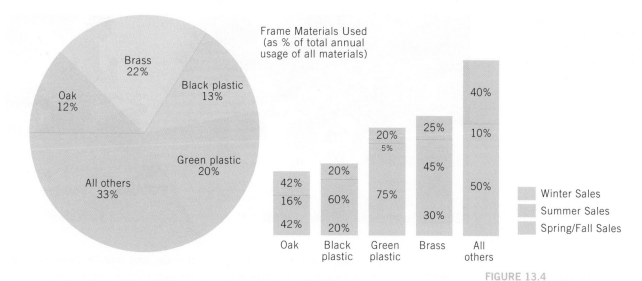

FIGURE 13.4

Both the pie chart and the bar graph show that four frame materials are the most used, but the bar graph also shows that brass and oak are the most popular materials in winter.

Windows, which tells the computer's hardware how to interact with the software. It also includes *application software* (apps), which meets the needs of specific users. Examples of application software include word-processing programs like Microsoft Word, spreadsheet programs like Excel, message centre software like Microsoft's Live Messenger, integrated programs like Quicken, and database programs like Access. Several different types of software are presented in the following paragraphs.

Computer Graphics. One example of a software program is **computer graphics**, which converts numeric and character data into pictorial information like charts and graphs. These allow managers to see relationships more easily and generate clearer and more persuasive reports and presentations. As Figure 13.4 shows, both types of graphics can convey different kinds of information—in this case, the types of materials that should be ordered by a picture framing shop like Artists' Frame Service.

IBM's Visualization Data Explorer software uses data from field samples to model the underground structure of an oil field. The imagery in Figure 13.5, for example, provides engineers with better information on oil location and reduces the risk of their hitting less productive holes.

computer graphics programs
Programs that convert numeric and character data into pictorial information like charts and graphs.

FIGURE 13.5

3-D computer modelling software gives engineers a better idea of where oil might be located.

The realism of the space creatures and alien environments in *Star Wars* is due to special effects created with computer graphics.

groupware Software that connects group members for email distribution, electronic meetings, message storing, appointments and schedules, and group writing.

Groupware. Collaboration among a firm's internal units and outside firms (remote collaboration) is made possible with **groupware**—software that connects group members for email distribution, electronic meetings, message storing, appointments and schedules, and group writing. Linked by groupware, people can collaborate from their own desktop PCs, even if they're remotely located. Groupware systems include IBM Lotus Domino 6.5, Microsoft Exchange Server 2007, and Novell GroupWise 6.5.

MANAGING IN TURBULENT TIMES

The Death of the PC?

People who started their careers in the 1960s and 1970s can easily remember a time when there were no personal computers (PCs). Their business and personal lives were revolutionized when the PC was introduced in the early 1980s. Now, just a few decades later, people are already talking about the death of the PC. If that seems impossible, consider this: At the 2011 Electronics Show in Las Vegas, the emphasis was on new tablets, smartphones, and mobile devices, not on PCs. That's a big change from years past. By 2013, the number of smartphones will surpass the number of PCs, and even today more people are accessing the internet from mobile devices than from PCs (59 percent in 2010, up from just 25 percent in 2009). More than 70 percent of the 900 technology executives surveyed by the Pew Research Center said that by 2020 most people won't work with software running on a PC. Instead, they will access the internet or cloud-based applications using other devices.

In *businesses*, the PC is being replaced by "thin clients" (also called virtual PCs). At TD Financial, for example, 250 computers were replaced with "thin clients" that have little storage capacity or processing power and contain no software. Instead, the computing work is done by a server farm, and each machine is linked to that farm by a connector box. These devices are cheaper than PCs and easier to maintain, and TD plans to install 10 000 virtual PCs over the next two years. Fewer than five million corporate computers were virtual in 2010, but by 2014, 50 million will be virtual.

A shift away from PCs is also occurring because of changes in *consumer* preferences. For example, retailers like Best Buy report that Apple's iPad—which is more portable than a laptop and is immensely popular—is cannibalizing laptop sales. There is also more specialization in the way that consumers use electronic products. They don't use their PC for everything; rather, they use a smartphone for, say, email and a tablet for reading. Sandvine Corp.'s tenth Global Internet Phoneomena Report found that 55 percent of the real-time entertainment in homes was received by devices like set-top boxes, smart TVs, tablets, and mobile devices.

Some industry analysts say that just as the PC killed the dedicated word processor late in the twentieth century, smartphones and tablets will kill the PC early in the twenty-first century. Others disagree with this prediction, and point out that companies have invested millions of dollars in their PC networks. Switching to something new will be very expensive, and companies will also have to change their software so that it can run on servers instead of locally on a PC. Additionally, for actual content creation, the PC is still seen by many people as the best option.

Critical Thinking Question

1. Do you think the PC will become obsolete soon? Explain your reasoning.

Electronic Spreadsheets. **Electronic spreadsheets** like Excel arrange data across and down the page in rows and columns. Users enter data, including formulas, at row and column intersections, and the computer automatically performs the necessary calculations. Payroll records, sales projections, and a host of other financial reports can be prepared in this manner. Spreadsheets are good planning tools because they let managers see how making a change in one item affects related items. For example, you can insert operating-cost percentages, tax rates, or sales revenues into the spreadsheet and the program will automatically recalculate all the other figures and determine net profit.

electronic spreadsheets Arrange data across and down the page in rows and columns.

IT Risks and Threats

Unfortunately, IT has attracted abusers who are intent on doing mischief, with severity ranging from mere nuisance to outright destruction. In this section, we look at various IT threats, and in the next section, we describe steps that businesses have taken to protect themselves.

Identify the *threats and risks* that are associated with the use of information technology by businesses. **L05**

Hackers

Hackers are cyber-criminals who gain unauthorized access to a computer or network, either to steal information, money, or property or to tamper with data. For example, one 16-year-old British hacker got into the U.S. Air Force's top command-and-control facility 150 different times. From there, he got into the computers of several defence contractors and the South Korean Atomic Research Institute.

hackers Cyber-criminals who gain unauthorized access to a computer or network, either to steal information, money, or property or to tamper with data.

At Equifax Canada, computer hackers breached its system and gained access to personal information on hundreds of Canadians.[18] In the United States, a computer hacker was charged with stealing more than one billion records from Acxiom, a data-selling company. The company admitted that the stolen data could include information about millions of people. It also admitted that it didn't even know its system had been hacked into until it was contacted by investigators in the case. Since then, Acxiom has beefed up its password protocols and its encryption and has also conducted many security audits.

One common reason hackers break into a computer network is to launch *denial of service (DOS) attacks*. DOS attacks flood networks or websites with bogus requests

At Acxiom, computer systems track consumer data provided by nearly every credit card issuer, bank, and insurance company in North America. The company is currently improving its computer-security models, but many people who worry about the potential for abuse point out that Acxiom itself has been successfully "hacked" more than once in the past couple of years.

for information and resources, thereby shutting down the networks or websites and making it impossible for legitimate users to access them. Such attacks cost companies millions in lost productive time and revenue.

Wireless mooching is also a growing problem. Once hackers get inside an unsecured wireless network, they use it to commit identity theft and to steal credit card numbers, among other activities. When police try to track down these criminals, they're long gone, leaving the network host exposed to criminal prosecution. The boxed insert entitled "Social Media Can Be Just as Dangerous as Hacker Attacks" describes another problem that can be as bad as a hacker attack.

Software Piracy

software piracy The unauthorized use of software such as word processing and spreadsheets.

Software piracy—the unauthorized use of software such as word processing and spreadsheets—is a worldwide problem. A 2011 study by the Business Software Alliance valued computer piracy at $1.1 billion in Canada. The study also found that nearly one third of software was unlicensed.[19] But the piracy rate in countries like Vietnam and China is over 90 percent.[20]

E-BUSINESS + SOCIAL MEDIA SOLUTIONS

Social Media Can be Just as Dangerous as Hacker Attacks

Computer hackers pose a threat because of their attacks on computer networks, but threats can also be delivered with simple words rather than malicious codes. Managers want their company to have a good reputation in the eyes of consumers, so they keep an eye on the results of "corporate reputation" surveys like "The Most Respected Corporations in Canada," published by KPMG/Ipsos-Reid.

Where companies place in these rankings is increasingly influenced by Facebook, Twitter, and YouTube. These social media sources have created a dilemma for managers. On the one hand, if they happen to generate positive "buzz," it will likely enhance the company's reputation. On the other hand, social media can rapidly disseminate negative information that can harm a company's reputation. (Note: Just as social media are facilitated by new technologies, so also is the tracking of company reputations. For example, Radian6 is a New Brunswick-based company that develops software to help companies track what is being said about them online. The company has 2200 clients, including well-known ones like Pepsi and Microsoft.)

Dave Jones, the vice-president for digital communications at Hill & Knowlton, says it can be difficult for a company to know how to respond to repeated bashing from, say, an environmentalist on a blog. Should the company respond to the charges, or just ignore them? Consider what happened to Tim Hortons, which is trying to make inroads in the U.S. market. As part of its strategy, it agreed to be one of the sponsors of a family-oriented event in the United States run by a group called The National Organization for Marriage

(NOW). When it was discovered that the event was part of NOW's opposition to the legalization of gay marriage, the story developed into an online controversy. Within a few days Tim Hortons withdrew its support, and bloggers took credit for squelching the sponsorship. But, of course, another segment of the population was unhappy that Tim Hortons withdrew its support for the event. You can't win, it seems.

In 2011, a lawsuit was filed against Taco Bell by an unhappy customer who claimed that there was more filler than beef in the company's tacos. When news of this lawsuit began spreading rapidly on the internet, the company decided it had to respond forcefully. It developed Facebook postings and a YouTube video that pointed out that the taco mixture is 88 percent beef, not the 35 percent claimed in the lawsuit. Taco Bell also took out a full-page newspaper ad that had the aggressive headline Thank You for Suing Us. Although it is too soon to tell what effect the lawsuit will have on the company, Taco Bell says that the response to its advertisements so far has been positive on both Facebook and Twitter.

One thing is clear: There is a new battlefield in the social media arena and victory or defeat in this domain is based on preparation and a clearly developed strategy of monitoring and appropriate response.

Critical Thinking Question

1. Contrast the responses of Tim Hortons and Taco Bell to the negative online publicity they received. Which response do you think was the most effective? Defend your answer.

Identity Theft

Identity theft refers to the unauthorized stealing of personal information (such as social insurance numbers and addresses) to get loans, credit cards, or other monetary benefits by impersonating the victim. Clever crooks get information on unsuspecting victims by digging in trash, luring internet users to bogus websites, and stealing mail. Some America Online customers, for example, received an email notifying them of a billing problem with their AOL accounts. The email, displaying AOL logos and legitimate-looking links, requested personal information like credit card numbers, social security numbers, and banking accounts with passwords and PINs. When the customers clicked on the AOL Billing Center link, they were transferred to a spoofed (falsified) AOL-looking webpage, where they submitted the requested information—into the hands of the thief. The accounts were soon empty. The thieves in this case used *phishing* or *pharming*—emailing a deceptive, real-looking imitation of a popular website (e.g., AOL, PayPal, or your local bank) as bait, to masses of recipients, tricking them into giving up personal information.

Identity theft is rapidly becoming a major problem. Identity thieves are not often caught, but when they are, they may receive stiff penalties. One hacker was sentenced to nine years in prison for breaking into a computer system and stealing the credit card account numbers of customers of a Lowe's home improvement store.[21]

identity theft The unauthorized stealing of personal information (such as social insurance numbers and addresses) to get loans, credit cards, or other monetary benefits by impersonating the victim.

Intellectual Property Theft

Information is so valuable that most companies enforce security precautions to protect it. Nearly every company faces the dilemma of protecting product plans, new inventions, and industrial processes. **Intellectual property** is a product of the mind—something produced by the intellect, with great expenditure of human effort—that has commercial value. Its ownership and the right to its use may be protected by patent, copyright, trademark, and other means. Hackers often break in to company networks to steal such intellectual property, but it's not just hackers who are doing the stealing. Because the chances of getting caught seem slim, home users continue, illegally, to download unpaid-for movies, music, and other resources from file-swapping networks. A study by the Institute for Policy Innovation estimates the annual harm at $12.5 billion dollars in losses to the economy as well as more than 70 000 lost jobs and $2 billion dollars in lost wages.[22]

intellectual property A product of the mind—something produced by the intellect, with great expenditure of human effort—that has commercial value.

Computer Viruses, Worms, and Trojan Horses

Another IT risk facing businesses is rogue programmers who disrupt IT operations by contaminating and destroying software, hardware, or data files. Viruses, worms, and Trojan horses are three kinds of malicious programs that, once installed, can shut down any computer system. A *computer virus* exists in a file that attaches itself to a program and migrates from computer to computer as a shared program or as an email attachment. It does not infect the system unless the user opens the contaminated file, and users typically are unaware they are spreading the virus by file-sharing. It can, for example, quickly copy itself over and over again, using up all available memory and effectively shutting down the computer.

Worms are a particular kind of virus that travels from computer to computer within networked computer systems without your needing to open any software to spread the contaminated file. In a matter of days, the notorious Blaster Worm infected some 400 000 computer networks, destroying files and even allowing outsiders to take over computers remotely. The worm replicates itself rapidly, sending out thousands of copies to other computers in the network. Travelling through internet connections and email address books in the network's computers, it absorbs system memory and shuts down network servers, web servers, and individual computers.

Unlike a virus, a *Trojan horse* does not replicate itself. Instead, it most often comes into the computer at your request, masquerading as a harmless, legitimate software product or data file. Once installed, the damage begins. For instance, it may simply redesign desktop icons or, more maliciously, delete files and destroy information.

Spyware

As if forced intrusion isn't bad enough, internet users unwittingly invite spies masquerading as a friendly file available as a "giveaway" or shared among individual users on their PCs. This so-called **spyware** is downloaded by users who are lured by "free" software. Once installed, it crawls around to monitor the host computer's activities, gathering email addresses, credit card numbers, passwords, and other inside information that it transmits back to someone outside the host system. Spyware authors assemble incoming stolen information to create their own "intellectual property" that they then sell to other parties to use for marketing or advertising purposes or for identity theft.[23]

spyware Software masquerading as a friendly file available as a "giveaway," or shared among individual users on their PCs, that monitors the host computer's activities.

Spam

Spam is junk email sent to a mailing list or a newsgroup (an online discussion group).[24] Spam is a greater nuisance than postal junk mail because the internet is open to the public, email costs are negligible, and massive mailing lists are accessible through file-sharing or by theft. Spam operators send unwanted messages ranging from explicit pornography to hate mail to advertisements and even destructive computer viruses. In addition to wasting users' time, spam also consumes a network's bandwidth, thereby reducing the amount of data that can be transmitted in a given amount of time.

spam Junk email sent to a mailing list or a newsgroup.

The fast-growing networking site, Pinterest, encountered a spam problem in the form of fake accounts that crowded out other content and yielded artificially high referral fees to the spammer.[25] The cost of spam is not easily measured, but a person who reads 10–20 emails per day may receive 160–180 spam messages along with their business correspondence. That means that they will spend five or six hours per month just deleting spam, to the detriment of their productive working time.[26]

IT Protection Measures

LO6 Describe the ways in which businesses protect themselves from the threats and risks posed by information technology.

Security measures against intrusion and viruses are a constant challenge. Businesses guard themselves against intrusion, identity theft, and viruses by using *firewalls*, *special software*, and *encryption*.

Firewalls

firewall Security system with special software or hardware devices designed to keep computers safe from hackers.

Many systems guard against unauthorized access by requiring users to have protected passwords. This helps ensure that intruders are unable to access your computer or the data on it. However, many firms rely on additional safeguards, such as **firewalls**, which are security systems with special software or hardware devices designed to keep computers safe from hackers. Figure 13.6 shows how a firewall works. The firewall is located where the two networks— the internet and the company's internal network—meet. It contains two components for filtering each incoming message:

- The company's *security policy*—Access rules that identify every type of message that the company doesn't want to have pass through the firewall.

- A *router*—A table of available routes or paths, a "traffic switch" that determines which routes or paths on the network to send each message through after it is tested against the security policy.

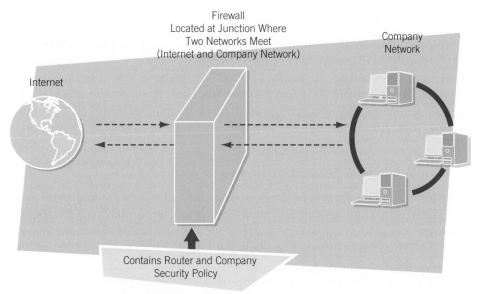

Firewall
Located at Junction Where
Two Networks Meet
(Internet and Company Network)

Company
Network

Internet

Contains Router and Company
Security Policy

What happens inside:
1. Message enters firewall.
2. Message source is compared against security policy.
3. If message passes security policy, router sends the message to the other network.
   Otherwise, router closes the gate to prevent entry.

FIGURE 13.6

How a firewall works.

Only those messages that meet the conditions of the user's security policy are routed through the firewall and permitted to flow between the two networks. Messages that fail the access test are blocked and cannot flow between the two networks. As mentioned earlier, a firewall is used for protecting the BlackBerry wireless network from intrusion.

Preventing Identity Theft

Internet privacy experts say that a completely new identity verification system is needed to stop the rising tide of internet identity theft. One possibility is an "info-card," which would act like a credit card and would allow websites to verify a customer's identity without keeping personal information on the customer.[27] While foolproof prevention is impossible, steps can be taken to reduce the chance that you will be victimized. A visit to the Identity Theft Resource Center (www.idtheftcenter.org) is a valuable first step to get information on everything from scam alerts to victim issues—including assistance on lost and stolen wallets—to media resources, current laws, and prevention of identity theft in the workplace. Identify theft affects businesses as well; according to experts, the loss or theft of just one laptop can cost a company as much as $90 000 or more in fines, credit monitoring for victims, public relations damage control, and class action litigation.[28]

Preventing Viruses: Anti-virus Software

Combatting viruses, worms, and Trojan horses has become a major industry for systems designers and software developers. Installation of **anti-virus software** products protects systems by searching incoming email and data files for "signatures" of known viruses and for virus-like characteristics. Contaminated files are discarded or placed in quarantine for safekeeping. Many viruses take advantage of weaknesses in operating systems in order to spread and propagate. Network administrators must make sure that the computers on their systems are using the most up-to-date operating system, which includes the latest security protection.

anti-virus software Products that protect systems by searching incoming email and data files for "signatures" of known viruses and for virus-like characteristics.

Encryption Software

encryption system The use of a secret numerical code to scramble characters in a message, so that the message is not understandable during transmission.

Unprotected email can be intercepted, diverted to unintended computers, and opened, revealing contents to intruders. Protective software is available to guard against those intrusions, adding a layer of security by encoding emails so that only the intended recipients can open them. The **encryption system** works by locking an email message to a unique code number (digital fingerprint) for each computer so only that computer can open and read the message.[29]

Avoiding Spam and Spyware

To help their employees avoid privacy invasion and to improve productivity, businesses often install anti-spyware and spam filtering software on their systems. Dozens of anti-spyware products provide protection—software such as Webroot's Spy Sweeper and the Microsoft AntiSpyware Beta—but they must be continually updated to keep pace with new spyware techniques.

internet service providers (ISPs) Commercial firms that maintain a permanent connection to the internet and sell temporary connections to subscribers.

While it cannot be prevented entirely, spam is abated by many **internet service providers (ISPs)** that ban the spamming of ISP subscribers. One ISP was recently awarded $1 billion in a lawsuit against 300 spammers that jammed the ISP system with an astounding 10 million emails a day. Anti-spam groups, too, promote the public's awareness of known spammers. The Spamhaus Project (www.spamhaus.org), for example, maintains a list—Register of Known Spam Operators (ROKSO)—of over 200 professional spammers who are responsible for over 80 percent of spam traffic in North America and Europe.

MyBizLab

Capture more moments of true understanding. MyBizLab provides you with interactive study and practice tools directly related to this chapter's content. The new MyBizLab Study Plan Learning Path is designed to measure a full range of skills and provide remediation to give you what you need to master key chapter concepts. MyBizLab flexes to your unique learning needs. The result? Inspired learning, more success.

SUMMARY OF LEARNING OBJECTIVES

1. **Explain the importance of *information management* to business firms.** Businesses possess a large amount of data—raw facts and figures—about their customers, competitors, and their own operations. Converting this *data* into *information*—usefully interpreted data—is necessary for business success. The activities of business firms—for example, designing products and services, ensuring product delivery and cash flow, evaluating personnel, and creating advertising—require information. Because information is so important, companies have *information managers*, just as they have production, marketing, and finance managers. The goal of *information management* is to organize the firm's information resources to support business performance and outcomes.

2. **Understand what an *information system* is, who the key users of information systems are, and the most widely used types of information systems.** *An information system (IS)* transforms raw data into information and transmits it for use in decision making. IS managers must determine what information is needed, gather data and convert it into information, and see that the information goes to those people who need it. Control is important to ensure not only that the system operates correctly but also that data and information are transmitted through secure channels to people who really need them.

The key users of information systems are top managers (who need information to carry out long-range planning for the entire organization), middle managers (who need summaries and analyses for setting intermediate and long-range goals for the departments or projects under their supervision), first-line managers (who need information to oversee the day-to-day details of their departments or projects), and knowledge workers (who need special information for conducting technical projects). Widely used types of information systems include *transaction processing systems (TPS)*, which are useful for routine transactions such as taking reservations and meeting payrolls, systems for knowledge workers, which include personal productivity tools such as word processing, document imaging, desktop publishing, and *computer-aided design (CAD)*; *management information systems (MIS)*, which support an organization's managers by providing daily reports, schedules, plans, and budgets; *decision support systems (DSSs)*, which assist the decision-making processes of middle and top-level managers; *executive support systems (ESSs)*, which are quick-reference, easy-to-access programs to assist upper-level managers; and *artificial intelligence (AI)* and *expert systems*, which are designed to imitate human thinking and behaviour and provide computer-based assistance in performing certain business activities.

3. **Explain how the rapid growth of information technologies has affected *organizational processes and operations*.** Information networks are leading to leaner organizations—businesses with fewer employees and simpler organizational structures—because networked firms can maintain electronic, rather than human, information links among employees and customers. Operations are more flexible because electronic networks allow businesses to offer greater product variety and faster delivery cycles. Aided by *intranets* and the *internet*, greater collaboration is possible, both among internal units and with outside firms. With access to the internet, company activities may be geographically scattered but remain coordinated through a networked system that provides better service for customers. Many businesses, for example, coordinate activities from one centralized location, but their deliveries flow from several remote locations, often at lower cost. The global reach of *IT* is enabling business collaboration on a scale that was unheard of just a few years ago. Separation of the workplace and the company is more common because electronic links are replacing the need for physical proximity between the company and its workstations. Improved management processes are evident because managers have rapid access to more information about the current status of company activities and easier access to electronic tools for planning and decision making. Not only is IT improving existing businesses, it is also helping to create entirely new businesses where none existed before. For existing large businesses, IT helps with the development of new products and new services and with reaching new clients.

4. **Describe the building blocks of *information technology*.** The building blocks of IT include the internet (the system of more than 100 million interconnected computers in over 100 countries around the world), the *World Wide Web* (the standardized code for accessing information and transmitting data over the internet), intranets (company-maintained internal websites linked throughout the firm), *extranets* (which allow outsiders limited access to a firm's internal information network), *electronic conferencing* (which allows groups of people to communicate simultaneously from various locations via email, phone, or video), *VSAT satellite communications* (sending and receiving signals from a satellite, exchanging voice, video, and data transmissions), *computer networks* (a group of two or more computers linked together by some form of cable or by wireless technology to share data or resources, such as a printer), *wide-area networks* (computers that are linked over long distances—province-wide or even nationwide—through telephone lines, microwave signals, or satellite communications), *local area networks* (computers that are linked in a smaller area, such as all of a firm's computers within a single building), *wireless networks* (which use airborne electronic signals to link network computers and devices), *Wi-Fi* (specific locations—called hotspots—such as coffee shops, hotels, and airport terminals that provide wireless internet connections for people on the go), *hardware* (the physical devices and components, including the computer), and *software* (the computer's operating system and application programs like computer graphics, *groupware*, spreadsheets, and word processing).

5. **Identify the *threats and risks* that are associated with the use of information technology by businesses.** The following threats and risks exist: (1) *Hackers* are cyber-criminals who gain unauthorized access to a computer or network, either to steal information, money, or property or to tamper with data. (2) *Software piracy* is the unauthorized use of software such as word processing and spreadsheets. (3) *Identity theft* refers to the unauthorized stealing of personal information (such as social insurance number and address) to get loans, credit cards, or other monetary benefits by impersonating the victim. (4) *Intellectual property* is a product of the mind—something produced by the intellect, with great expenditure of human effort—that has commercial value. Intellectual property theft includes the theft of things like a company's new product plans, new inventions, and new industrial processes, as well as illegal downloading of unpaid-for movies, music, and other resources from file-swapping networks. (5) A *computer virus* exists in a file that attaches itself to a program and migrates from computer to computer as a shared program or as an email attachment. Worms are a particular kind of virus that travels from computer to computer within networked computer systems without your needing to open any software to spread the contaminated file. (6) *Spyware* is downloaded by users who are lured by "free" software. (7) *Spam* is junk email sent to a mailing list or a newsgroup (an online discussion group).

6. **Describe the ways in which businesses protect themselves from the threats and risks posed by information technology.** Businesses guard against intrusion with a variety of tactics, including the following: (1) *Firewalls* are security systems with special software or hardware devices designed to keep computers safe from hackers. One possibility is an *"infocard,"* which acts like a credit card and allows websites to verify a customer's identity without keeping personal information on the customer. (2) Installation of *anti-virus software* products protects systems by searching incoming email and data files for "signatures" of known viruses and virus-like characteristics. Contaminated files are discarded or placed in quarantine for safekeeping. (3) An *encryption system* works by locking an email message to a unique code number (digital fingerprint) for each computer so only that computer can open and read the message. (4) To help their employees avoid privacy invasion and to improve productivity, businesses often install anti-spyware and spam filtering software on their systems. Dozens of anti-spyware products provide protection, but they must be continually updated to keep pace with new spyware techniques.

KEY TERMS

anti-virus software   (p. 421)
artificial intelligence (AI)   (p. 406)
client–server network   (p. 413)
computer graphics programs   (p. 415)
computer network   (p. 413)
computer-aided design (CAD)   (p. 404)
computer-aided manufacturing
   (CAM)   (p. 404)
data   (p. 342)
decision support system (DSS)   (p. 405)
electronic conferencing   (p. 412)
electronic spreadsheets   (p. 417)
encryption system   (p. 422)
executive support system (ESS)
   (p. 405)
expert system   (p. 407)
extranet   (p. 412)
firewall   (p. 420)

groupware   (p. 416)
hackers   (p. 417)
hardware   (p. 414)
identity theft   (p. 419)
information   (p. 342)
information management   (p. 402)
information manager   (p. 402)
information system (IS)   (p. 402)
information technology (IT)   (p. 407)
intellectual property   (p. 419)
internet   (p. 412)
internet service providers (ISPs)
   (p. 422)
intranet   (p. 412)
local area networks (LANs)   (p. 413)
management information systems
   (MIS)   (p. 405)
mass-customization   (p. 410)

software   (p. 414)
software piracy   (p. 418)
spam   (p. 420)
spyware   (p. 420)
system operations personnel   (p. 404)
transaction processing systems
   (TPS)   (p. 404)
VSAT satellite communications
   (p. 412)
wide area networks (WANs)   (p. 413)
Wi-Fi (wireless fidelity)   (p. 414)
wireless local area network (wireless
   LAN or WLAN)   (p. 414)
wireless wide area networks
   (WWANs)   (p. 414)
World Wide Web   (p. 412)

QUESTIONS FOR ANALYSIS

1. Why must business managers view information as a resource?
2. How can an electronic conferencing system increase productivity and efficiency?
3. Why do the four levels of user groups in an organization need different kinds of information from the IS?
4. In what ways are local area networks (LANs) different from, or similar to, wide area networks (WANs)?
5. Give two examples (other than those in this chapter) of each of the major types of business application programs.
6. Describe three activities in which you regularly engage that would be made easier by technology like that found in a global positioning system (GPS) or a personal digital assistant (PDA).

APPLICATION EXERCISES

1. Visit a company and interview an individual who is knowledgeable about the firm's management information system. Determine what problems and opportunities exist with the system.
2. Describe the IS at your school. Identify its components and architecture. How much attention has been paid to dealing with the threats from computer hackers, computer viruses, and spam? Explain.
3. Visit a small business in your community to investigate the ways it is using communication technologies now, and the ways it plans to use them in the future. Prepare a report for class presentation.
4. Think in general terms about the ways that IT influences your daily life. Then describe three specific activities that have been impacted by IT. Were the outcomes positive or negative? Explain.

BUILDING YOUR BUSINESS SKILLS

The Art and Science of Point-and-Click Research

The Purpose of the Assignment

To introduce students to internet search sites.

The Situation

In a recent survey of nearly 2000 web users, two-thirds said they used the web to obtain work-related information. With an estimated 320 million pages of information on the web, the challenge for business users is fairly obvious—how to find what they're looking for.

Assignment

You'll need a computer and access to the internet to complete this exercise.

Step 1

Get together with three classmates and decide on a business-related research topic. Choose a topic that interests you—for example, "Business Implications of the Most Recent Census," "Labour Disputes in Professional Sports," or "Marketing Music Lessons and Instruments to Parents of Young Children."

Step 2

Search the following sites for information on your topic, dividing them among group members to speed the process:

- Alta Vista www.altavista.com
- Ask.com www.ask.com
- Dogpile www.dogpile.com
- Excite www.excite.com
- Google www.google.ca
- Hotbot www.hotbot.com
- Go www.go.com
- Lycos www.lycos.ca
- Metacrawler www.metacrawler.com
- Northern Light www.northernlight.com
- Yahoo! www.yahoo.com

Take notes as you search so that you can explain your findings to other group members.

Step 3

Working as a group, answer the following questions about your collective search.

1. Which sites were the easiest to use?

2. Which sites offered the most helpful results? What specific factors made these sites better than the others?
3. Which sites offered the least helpful results? What were the problems?
4. Why is it important to learn the special code words or symbols—called operators—that target a search? (Operators are words like AND, OR, and NOT that narrow search queries. For example, using AND in a search tells the system that all words must appear in the results—for example, American AND Management AND Association.)

Questions for Discussion

1. Research the differences between search engines and search directories. Then place the sites listed in Step 2 in the proper category. Which did you find more helpful in this exercise, search engines or search directories?
2. Why is it important to learn how to use the search site "Help" function?
3. Based on your personal career goals, how do you think that mastering web research techniques might help you in the future?
4. How has the web changed the nature of business research?

EXERCISING YOUR ETHICS: TEAM EXERCISE

Supplying the Right Answers

The Situation

Networked systems facilitate information sharing among companies and often involve sensitive customer data. This exercise asks you to consider ethical issues that might arise when firms are developing information technologies for use in networked systems.

The Dilemma

Home Sweet Home-e (HSH-e) was an ebusiness start-up that sold virtually everything in home furnishings—from linens and towels to cleaning supplies and furniture. From home computers, HSH-e members could shop in virtual storefronts, chat online with other shoppers, talk live with virtual store clerks, and pay electronically at a one-stop website. In reality, HSH-e was a virtual store: a network of numerous suppliers located around the country, each specializing in a particular line of goods. The network was connected by a centrally controlled information technology that HSH-e developed, owned, and operated. Once a customer's order was placed, suppliers instantaneously received information on what to ship, where to ship it, and how much to charge.

HSH-e chose only suppliers that guaranteed fast, reliable deliveries and promised to supply HSH-e exclusively. The linen supplier, for example, could not supply products to other home-furnishings ebusinesses. In return, the supplier was guaranteed all HSH-e orders for linen products. As HSH-e grew, suppliers stood to gain more business and to prosper in

an expanding etail industry. As it turns out, some prospective suppliers refused to join the network and others in the network were discontinued by HSH-e for failing to expand fast enough to keep up with demand.

Team Activity

Assemble a group of four students and assign each group member to one of the following roles:

- customer of HSH-e
- employee of HSH-e
- supplier of HSH-e
- owner of HSH-e

Questions for Discussion

1. Before discussing the situation with your group, and from the perspective of your assigned role, what are the underlying ethical issues, if any, in this situation?
2. Assemble the group and have each member list the ethical issues that he or she identified. Did the different roles result in different kinds of ethical issues being identified? If so, why might role differences result in dissimilar priorities on ethical issues?
3. For the various ethical issues that were identified, decide as a group which one is most important for HSH-e to resolve. Which is second most important? Explain your group's reasoning.
4. What does your group finally recommend be done to resolve the most important ethical issue? And to resolve the second most important ethical issue?

5. Consider past suppliers that have been discontinued or have withdrawn from the HSH-e network. Do they face any ethical issues involving HSH-e customers? Involving HSH-e operations? Involving other HSH-e suppliers?

6. Suppose you work at HSH-e and discover a non-network supplier that is more attractive than one of the company's existing suppliers. What ethical considerations do you face in deciding whether or not to replace an existing supplier?

Go to MyBizLab for additional cases and exercise material.

CONCLUDING CASE 13-1

Computer Hacking

Computers, the internet, and technology in general have caused revolutionary changes in the way businesses and governments operate, and in the way that individuals interact with each other. While there are many obvious benefits to these developments, there have also been some serious problems. For example, in 2011 video gamers were shocked to hear that hackers had obtained personal information and credit card numbers by successfully breaching the security system that supposedly protected Sony's PlayStation Network. A 2011 study conducted jointly by Telus Corp. and the University of Toronto's Rotman School of Management found that information security breaches in Canadian businesses increased by 50 percent between 2010 and 2011. Many believe that Canadian businesses are not prepared for cyber attacks and that far more emphasis on precautionary measures is needed.

There are potentially serious problems with the internet, as well. The 2011 Norton Cybercrime Report found that more than seven million Canadian internet users were victims of cyber attacks of some kind in 2010. These attacks cost a total of $840 million in direct financial losses, as well as an estimated $4.7 billion in lost productivity. Worldwide, 430 million people were victimized at a cost of $US388 billion. More than three times as many people have been victims of cyber crime than of actual physical crime. Symantec, the world's largest security software maker, found that 40 percent of all cyber attacks are directed at small businesses because their computer systems are generally easier to penetrate than those of large businesses.

In 2011, Google warned people that they might be the victim of malicious software. Google then encouraged individuals to find out whether or not they were victims by using Google's services. Skeptics felt that this was just a ploy to get people to use the company's search engine, but Fabrice Jaubert, a software engineer and a member of Google's anti-malware team, argued that it would have been unethical for Google not to warn people that they might have a problem. Jaubert tried to put the situation in perspective with an analogy: "We used to live out in the country and we could leave our doors unlocked, but we are growing up into a big city and we have to get everyone to understand they need to lock their doors".

Cyber crime is an increasing threat as organizations and individuals have become increasingly reliant on computer technology. For example, criminals hack into automatic teller machines (ATMs) to steal money and collect data and personal information. Suzanne Kapner, a writer for

The Wall Street Journal, says, "An ATM is just a personal computer stored in a box that contains cash." Anti-crime efforts must therefore be intense for these devices. In response to increasing ATM fraud, Diebold Inc. is working on a machine that uses cloud computing to store information remotely, which reduces the risk of a data breach. Another technology developed by NCR Corp. allows the ATM to identify its customers by reading vein patterns in customers' hands as they make specific hand gestures without physically touching the machine. With touchless transaction capability, ATM's can also be kept behind bulletproof glass, which further reduces the likelihood of criminal activity. Another approach is to have customers download apps onto their cellphones that allow them to make transactions at an ATM by tapping their phones on the machines, eliminating the need for PINs or bankcards.

Automobiles increasingly rely on computer technology, and drivers of newer cars can now connect their mobile device with the car's onboard computer. By connecting cellphones and tablets to a car, however, users make personal information—such as banking details and email passwords—vulnerable to hackers, who could also potentially use these devices to control the car itself. Doug Cooke is director of sales engineering for McAfee Canada, a company that has been working closely with automakers to address these issues. He observes that "very sophisticated hackers can get to where they want to go. It will be only a matter of time before they get what they want."

Computer technology has great potential to move the world forward, but the dark side of human nature means that great care must be taken to avoid the downside of technology. Doug Cooke says that hackers will seize the opportunity to make everyone's life more complicated. Businesses, governments, and individuals must be constantly on guard against the threat of cyber crime.

Questions for Discussion

1. What measures are you taking to safeguard yourself from internet hacking?
2. Refer to the section on IT risks and threats in the chapter. What else can businesses do to protect themselves and their customers?
3. Should consumers be wary about adopting new technologies, given the surge and sophistication of hacking tactics? Explain your answer.

CONCLUDING CASE 13-2

Web Pricing Dispute: Free the Internet!

In 2011, the Canadian Radio-television and Telecommunications Commission (CRTC) decided that it would allow network operators like Bell, Shaw, and Rogers to apply the concept of usage-based billing (UBB) to smaller wholesale internet service providers (ISPs) like Teksavvy, Acanac, and Telnet (these ISPs lease bandwidth from the network operators). Usage-based billing for *retail* customers had been introduced some years earlier. Mirko Bibic, senior vice-president of Regulatory and Government Affairs at Bell, says "Third-party ISPs are taking advantage of Bell's network, and of Bell's customers, and they're not contributing a fraction of what Bell is to the growth of the networks required to actually deliver the internet to Canadians." Companies like Bell argue that billions of dollars have been invested in order to be able to keep up with the demands caused by internet growth. Bell's pricing change was intended to limit the impact that wholesale ISPs had as a result of their customers' increasing usage and limiting the network capabilities for others. Most customers felt that such a change in billing would personally impact their monthly bill, but the changes were likely to impact only the 2 percent of internet users serviced by the wholesale ISPs. After a consumer uproar, Bell withdrew its proposal.

When usage-based pricing for ISPs was first announced, opponents (including the ISPs) charged that Bell's decision was unfair and that it would markedly increase customers' fees. Much of the comment on social media sites had a "free the internet" flavour. These social media sites were the primary communication tool for those protesting the initiative, but critics pointed out that information shared on such sites is not always factual, and is subject to differing interpretations.

When Industry Minister Tony Clement announced that he intended to review the CRTC's decision, the controversy intensified. While government ministers can review decisions made by regulators like the CRTC, bloggers were concerned about Clement's motives, especially when talk of an election was in the air. Many people felt that a review of the CRTC's decision weakened the regulator's powers and threatened the dynamics between the government and the CRTC. Richard French, the CN-Tellier Professor at the University of Ottawa and past vice-chair of the CRTC, said, "We established independent regulators because they're supposed to have the expertise, the freedom from partisan pressures, the time, and the longer-term perspective to make the painful and complex decisions required to keep industries that are otherwise liable to market failure operating in some semblance of the public interest." French felt that intervention by the government was unnecessary and inhibited the CRTC's ability to exercise its authority.

Nevertheless, in mid-2011, the CRTC held hearings on the issue of usage-based internet pricing for ISPs. Arguments were heard from those who supported usage-based billing and those who opposed it. There were heated debates about the motivations of the network operators, the reality of the alleged limited supply of internet bandwidth, and the impact of usage-based billing on customers. After several weeks of hearings, the CRTC handed down a compromise decision by introducing a billing model that allowed ISPs to pay for the *total* capacity they needed, not the volume of data that is downloaded by *individual* users. The CRTC concluded that this approach more suitably addressed the issues of increasing demand for bandwidth, and would allow the ISPs to offer competitive pricing plans to their customers. The decision reinforced the basic idea that the smaller ISPs should not be able to offer unlimited downloading plans that made these ISPs so popular with customers. Activist groups were torn in terms of their standing on this decision. Some—like ISP TekSavvy solutions—believed it was a step backward, while others—like OpenMedia.ca—believed the compromise was a step in the right direction.

In March 2012, BCE appealed the CRTC's decision, arguing that the CRTC made mistakes in deciding on the rate ISPs would have to pay for access. Mirko Bibic, for example, expressed his concerns about the CRTC's compromise decision by comparing it to having to pay for space on a highway, "I think the philosophy is (to) put the ISP in a position of responsibility. If usage goes up, you're going to have to buy more lanes— it's the same decision that we have to make." Not to be outdone, the ISPs also appealed the decision, arguing that it would allow companies like Rogers and BCE to impose costly tariffs on the ISPs.

Questions for Discussion

1. Why do you think there was such an uproar when Bell announced that it was introducing usage-based billing?
2. Take the position of one of the network operators like Shaw or Bell and develop a list of arguments in favour of usage-based billing. Then take the position of an ISP and develop a list of arguments opposing user-based billing. Which list seems more persuasive? Why?
3. Consider the following statement: *"The proposal to introduce usage-based billing was completely fair because it was based on the idea that the average person shouldn't have to subsidize individuals who use a lot of bandwidth. People who use more bandwidth should pay more than those who use less."* Do you agree or disagree with the statement? Defend your answer.

Understanding Accounting Issues

LEARNING OBJECTIVES

After reading this chapter, you should be able to:

1 Explain the role of *accountants* and distinguish among the three types of professional accountants in Canada.

2 Describe how the *accounting equation* is used.

3 Describe three basic *financial statements* and show how they reflect the activity and financial condition of a business.

4 Explain the key standards and principles for reporting financial statements.

5 Explain how computing *financial ratios* can help in analyzing the financial strengths of a business.

6 Explain some of the special issues that arise in *international accounting*.

Untangling an Accounting Mess at Bankrupt Nortel

IN 2012, the trial of three former top executives of Nortel Networks finally began. They were charged by the RCMP with criminal fraud, and with allegedly manipulating the company's accounting system in order to inflate profits during a difficult time in Nortel's history. In more familiar terms, the executives were charged with "cooking the books." The three defendants acknowledged that there were accounting mistakes, but rejected the claim that they had engaged in fraudulent behaviour. The trial will be long and expensive.

In 1895, the Northern Electric and Manufacturing Co. was established to manufacture Bell telephones. The company eventually became Nortel Networks. By the late twentieth century, Nortel had become the "crown jewel" in Canada's high tech-sector, dominating global markets for digital telephone-switching and fibre-optic transmission systems. By 2000, Nortel employed 95 000 people, had a market value of $440 billion, and shares of stock were

priced as high as $124 per share. But over the next few years, the company experienced significant problems, and by 2009 (when the company was delisted from the Toronto Exchange), its shares sold for just 18 cents each.

What happened? Richard Powers, a professor at the Rotman School of Management at the University of Toronto, says, "Nortel rode the tech boom and became complacent." But complacency wasn't Nortel's only problem. When the tech bubble burst in 2000, Nortel could not maintain its growth trajectory. Its share price plummeted from $124 per share in August 2000 to just $7.56 in September 2001, and there were nearly 50 000 fewer employees in the company than there had been in 2000. The CEO, John Roth, left the company (and received $86 million after cashing in his stock options). He was replaced by Frank Dunn, who took various steps to turn Nortel around. After incurring massive losses in 2001 and 2002, the company reported a profit of $54 million in

2003, and Dunn was seen as having rescued the company. In 2003, Nortel reported its third consecutive quarterly profit, and these profits triggered a total of $43.6 million in bonuses for senior managers.

But dark clouds appeared on the horizon after Nortel's auditor, Deloitte & Touche, expressed concerns that the profits were not what they seemed, and that some accounting adjustments had been made that turned losses into profits. The crisis deepened when Nortel said it was going to restate about $900 million of liabilities that were on its balance sheet because it had overestimated what these liabilities would be. Nortel's audit committee then set about finding out how Nortel could have overstated liabilities by $900 million. The group concluded that there were significant accounting irregularities and a "tone at the top" that encouraged the manipulation of accounting rules in order to reach profit targets.

In 2004, Frank Dunn (CEO), Douglas Beatty (Chief Financial Officer), and Michael Gollogly (Controller) were fired after a report by a U.S. law firm concluded that the three had used financial practices that did not comply with U.S. rules. The report also noted that top managers had created an "aggressive accounting culture" in order to exploit the bonus system to their advantage. The three managers filed a wrongful dismissal lawsuit against Nortel in 2006, alleging defamation and mental stress.

Between 2003 and 2007, the release of Nortel's audited financial statements was delayed on four separate occasions as the company tried to determine its actual financial position. These delays created much uncertainty and anxiety among shareholders, and they finally ran out of patience. In 2009, Nortel filed for bankruptcy protection. Richard Powers says, "I don't think the accounting scandal destroyed the company, but it certainly contributed to it by becoming a huge distraction." ◆

HOW WILL THIS HELP ME?

By understanding the material presented in this chapter, you'll benefit in three ways: (1) If you're an *entrepreneur* thinking about starting your own business, you'll discover your obligations for reporting your firm's financial status; (2) as an *employee*, you'll learn how to evaluate your company's financial condition and its prospects for the future; and (3) as an interested *citizen*, you'll learn about accounting ethics and the regulatory requirements for maintaining the public's trust in the Canadian business system.

What is Accounting?

Accounting is a comprehensive information system for collecting, analyzing, and communicating financial information. As such, it is a system for measuring business performance and translating those measures into information for management decisions. **Bookkeeping** is just one phase of accounting—the recording of accounting transactions. Clearly, accounting is much more comprehensive than bookkeeping because accounting involves more than just the recording of information.

Accounting also uses performance measures to prepare performance reports for owners, the public, and regulatory agencies. To meet these objectives, accountants keep records of such transactions as taxes paid, income received, and expenses

accounting A comprehensive system for collecting, analyzing, and communicating financial information.

bookkeeping Recording accounting transactions.

incurred, and they analyze the effects of these transactions on particular business activities. By sorting, analyzing, and recording thousands of transactions, accountants can determine how well a business is being managed and how financially strong it is.

Because businesses engage in many thousands of transactions, ensuring consistent, dependable financial information is mandatory. This is the job of the **accounting information system (AIS)**—an organized procedure for identifying, measuring, recording, and retaining financial information so that it can be used in accounting statements and management reports. The system includes all the people, reports, computers, procedures, and resources for compiling financial transactions.[1]

There are numerous users of accounting information:

- *Business managers* use accounting information to set goals, develop plans, set budgets, and evaluate future prospects.

- *Employees and unions* use accounting information to get paid and to plan for and receive such benefits as health care, insurance, vacation time, and retirement pay.

- *Investors and creditors* use accounting information to estimate returns to shareholders, to determine a company's growth prospects, and to decide whether the company is a good credit risk before investing or lending.

- *Tax authorities* use accounting information to plan for tax inflows, to determine the tax liabilities of individuals and businesses, and to ensure that correct amounts are paid in a timely fashion.

- *Government regulatory agencies* rely on accounting information to fulfill their duties; the provincial securities commissions, for example, require firms to file financial disclosures so that potential investors have valid information about a company's financial status.

If a company does not produce accurate accounting information, all of these groups may be hurt. As we saw in the opening case, Nortel restated its accounting information on multiple occasions in the years before it eventually went bankrupt. Investors lost millions, and thousands of Nortel employees lost their jobs. More recently, reborn General Motors warned its investors that it did not yet have an effective accounting control system in place, and that it could not guarantee the reliability of its financial statements.[2] The Sarbanes-Oxley Act (passed in the U.S. in 2002) required senior managers in companies to certify that their company had an effective internal control system in place. In Canada, this idea was partially adopted in 2004 through National Instrument 52-109. Critics of this type of legislation argue that it has been very expensive to implement and has not achieved the goal of more reliable accounting information.[3]

Who Are Accountants and What Do they Do?

At the head of the AIS is the **controller**, who manages all the firm's accounting activities. As chief accounting officer, the controller ensures that the accounting system provides the reports and statements needed for planning, controlling, and decision-making activities. This broad range of activities requires different types of accounting specialists. In this section, we will begin by distinguishing between the two main fields of accounting, *financial* and *managerial*. Then we will discuss the different functions and activities of the three professional accounting groups in Canada.

accounting information system (AIS) An organized procedure for identifying, measuring, recording, and retaining financial information so that it can be used in accounting statements and management reports.

L01 Explain the role of *accountants* and distinguish among the three types of professional accountants in Canada.

controller The individual who manages all the firm's accounting activities.

Financial and Managerial Accounting

In any company, two fields of accounting—financial and managerial—can be distinguished by the different users they serve. As we have just seen, it is both convenient and accurate to classify users of accounting information as users outside the company and users inside the company. This same distinction allows us to categorize accounting systems as either *financial* or *managerial*.

Financial Accounting

A firm's **financial accounting system** is concerned with external users of information—consumer groups, unions, shareholders, and government agencies. It prepares and publishes income statements and balance sheets at regular intervals. All of these documents focus on the activities of *the company as a whole*, rather than on individual departments or divisions.

financial accounting system The process whereby interested groups are kept informed about the financial condition of a firm.

In reporting data, financial accountants must conform to standard reporting formats and procedures imposed by both the accounting profession and government regulatory agencies. This requirement helps ensure that users can clearly compare information, whether from many different companies or from the same company at different times. The information in such reports is mostly *historical;* that is, it summarizes financial transactions that have occurred during past accounting periods.

Managerial Accounting

In contrast, **managerial (or management) accounting** serves internal users. Managers at all levels need information to make decisions for their departments, to monitor current projects, and to plan for future activities. Other employees, too, need accounting information. Engineers, for instance, want to know costs for materials and production so they can make product or operations improvements. To set performance goals, salespeople need data on past sales by geographic region. Purchasing agents use information on materials costs to negotiate terms with suppliers.

managerial (or management) accounting Internal procedures that alert managers to problems and aid them in planning and decision making.

Reports to these users serve *the company's individual units*, whether departments, projects, plants, or divisions. Internal reports may be designed in any form that will assist internal users in planning, decision making, and controlling. Furthermore, as *projections* and *forecasts* of both financial data and business activities, internal reports are an extremely important part of the management accounting system: They are forward looking rather than historical in nature.

Professional Accountants

Users of financial statements want to be confident that the accountants who have prepared them have a high level of expertise and credibility. Three professional accounting organizations exist in Canada to certify accounting expertise.

Chartered Accountants

The Canadian Institute of Chartered Accountants (CICA) grants the **chartered accountant (CA)** designation. To achieve this designation, a person must earn a university degree, then complete an educational program and pass a national exam. About half of all CAs work in CA firms that offer accounting services to the public; the other half work in government or industry. CA firms typically provide audit, tax, and management services (see Table 14.1 for a list of the top 10 CA firms in Canada). CAs focus on external financial reporting; that is, certifying for various interested parties (shareholders, lenders, Canada Customs and Revenue Agency, and so on) that the financial records of a company accurately reflect the true financial condition of the firm. In 2011, about 40 percent of CAs were in public practice, while the other 60 percent were employed in industry, government, or education.[4]

chartered accountant (CA) An individual who has met certain experience and education requirements and has passed a licensing examination; acts as an outside accountant for other firms.

TABLE 14.1 Top 10 Chartered Accountant Firms in Canada, 2011		
	Company	**Annual Revenues (millions of dollars)**
1	Deloitte & Touche LLP	1505
2	PricewaterhouseCoopers LLP	1180
3	KPMG LLP	1138
4	Ernst & Young LLP	870
5	Grant Thornton Canada	515
6	BDO Dunwoody LLP	426
7	Meyers Norris Penhy LLP	374
8	Collins Barrow National Cooperative Inc.	143
9	RSM Richter LLP	84
10	Mallette	53

Certified General Accountants

certified general accountant (CGA) An individual who has completed an education program and passed a national exam; works in private industry or a CGA firm.

The Certified General Accountants Association of Canada grants the **certified general accountant (CGA)** designation. To become a CGA, a person must complete an education program and pass a national exam; to be eligible, a person must have an accounting job with a company. Formerly, CGAs were not allowed to audit the financial statements of publicly held companies, but this is rapidly changing, and now CGAs can audit corporate financial statements in most provinces. Most CGAs work in private companies, but there are a few CGA firms. Some CGAs also work in CA firms. CGAs also focus on external financial reporting and emphasize the use of the computer as a management accounting tool. From time to time, CGA Canada commissions reports on important issues such as pensions. In 2011, there were approximately 75 000 professional accountants and students in Canada and internationally with education programs, member services and products, and national and international representation.[5]

Certified Management Accountants

certified management accountant (CMA) An individual who has completed a university degree, passed a national examination, and completed a strategic leadership program; works in industry and focuses on internal management accounting.

The Society of Management Accountants of Canada grants the **certified management accountant (CMA)** designation. To achieve the designation, a person must a have university degree, pass a two-part national entrance examination, and complete a strategic leadership program while gaining practical experience in a management accounting environment. CMAs work in organizations of all sizes and focus on applying best management practices in all the operations of a business. CMAs bring a strong market focus to strategic management and resource deployment, synthesizing and analyzing financial and non-financial information to help organizations maintain a competitive advantage. CMAs emphasize the role of accountants in the planning and overall strategy of the firm in which they work. In 2011, there were about 50 000 CMAs across Canada.[6]

Accounting Services

CAs and CGAs usually perform several accounting services for their clients. The most common of these are *auditing, tax services*, and *management services*.

Auditing

In an **audit**, the accountant examines a company's AIS to determine whether the company's financial reports fairly present its financial operations. Companies normally must provide audited financial reports when applying for loans or when selling stock. The audit will determine whether the firm has controls to prevent errors or fraud from going undetected. Auditors also examine receipts such as shipping documents, cancelled cheques, payroll records, and cash receipts records. In some cases, an auditor may physically check inventories, equipment, or other assets, even if it means descending 200 metres to an underground mine or travelling to an offshore oil drilling platform. When audits are being conducted, **forensic accountants** are sometimes used to track down hidden funds (see the boxed insert entitled "Forensic Accounting: Detecting Accounting Fraud"). Because white-collar crime is on the rise, the number of forensic accountants has increased in recent years.

audit An accountant's examination of a company's financial records to determine whether it used proper procedures to prepare its financial reports.

forensic accountant An accountant who tracks down hidden funds in business firms, usually as part of a criminal investigation.

MANAGING IN TURBULENT TIMES

Forensic Accounting: Detecting Accounting Fraud

Anyone who watches television knows about the forensic investigations that police officers conduct as they try to catch the bad guys (think *CSI: Miami*). It's pretty interesting stuff. But did you know that forensics is also very relevant to the field of accounting? The numerous corporate financial scandals of the past few years have caused an increase in demand for forensic accountants—individuals who investigate the financial transactions of companies in order to determine whether something fishy is going on. According to the latest Kroll Global Fraud Report, companies lost an average of $8.2 million to fraud in the past three years, largely because of the credit crunch and tough economic climate. With the introduction in 2003 of Bill 198, the Budget Measures Act, which amended the Ontario Securities Act and other statutes, regulations similar to those in the United States became mandated in Canada, an effort widely viewed as having major implications for institutions with accounting specializations. This new act will undoubtedly contribute to an increase in demand for specific areas of emphasis within the accounting field.

Fraud examiners interview high-level executives, pursue tips from employees or outsiders, and comb through emails, searching for suspicious words and phrases. The CA designation in investigative and forensic accounting (CA IFA) provides in-depth knowledge and experience in investigative and forensic accounting. This is accomplished through a profession-endorsed certification process that has ongoing experience and education requirements. Individuals who pursue a career in IFA are well positioned to practise in areas such as fraud and economic loss quantification. Some of their responsibilities include testifying as expert witnesses, investigating and analyzing financial evidence, and getting involved in criminal investigations (especially in the rapidly evolving area of computer and internet fraud).

Most of the publicity about financial scandals focuses on large companies, but forensic investigation is needed in businesses of all shapes and sizes. The Atlantic Lottery Corporation, for example, hired a forensic accounting firm to review the operations of its small, individually owned lottery retail outlets when reported winnings were higher than statistically possible. That led to widespread concerns that some retailers were cheating by pocketing prizes won by other players who weren't properly notified of their winnings.

At the other end of the size scale, a major multinational consumer-goods producer became concerned when one of its best-known products began to lose market share in Europe because a competitor was selling its brand at a substantially lower price. Kroll was asked to determine whether the competitor's actions were legitimately supported by lower production costs or whether they reflected unfair market practices. After considerable research, Kroll discovered that the competitor had indeed found a novel means of production that sharply reduced its costs without reducing the quality of its product. Kroll recommended that the company license the technology so that it could also achieve lower costs.

Critical Thinking Questions

1. Visit the Canadian Institute of Chartered Accountants website (www.cica.ca). How much emphasis is placed on forensic accounting? How does a person become a forensic accountant?

2. Conduct online research regarding forensic accountants and answer the following questions: (a) What general approach do forensic accountants take when investigating the financial statements of companies? (b) What specific techniques are used to determine whether accounting fraud has occurred?

In recent years there has been much publicity about the alleged failure of auditors to detect financial problems in companies before they go bankrupt. In 2011, for example, a Quebec Superior Court judge ruled that auditors were negligent when they failed to correctly assess the financial condition of Montreal-based Castor Holdings Ltd., which was $1.6 billion in debt when it collapsed.[7] A British regulator opened a probe into Deloitte's auditing of the Royal Bank of Scotland, the lender that received a $70 billion bailout in 2008.[8] And Deloitte was sued in the United States for allegedly failing to detect problems in the financial records of a company that went bankrupt.[9]

For many years, auditors had the responsibility of ensuring that their clients' accounting systems adhered to **generally accepted accounting principles (GAAP)**—a body of theory and procedure developed and monitored by the CICA. At the end of an audit, the auditor certified whether the client's financial reports complied with GAAP. But in 2011, many *public* Canadian companies moved away from GAAP and adopted International Financial Reporting Standards (IFRS). This helped investors in other countries understand the financial statements of Canadian companies, thus making for improved access to global capital markets.[10] *Private* companies can choose either the IFRS or a new accounting standard for private enterprises—called private enterprise GAAP—which are both based on the former Canadian GAAP.[11] Various concerns have been raised about the adoption of IFRS guidelines (see Concluding Case 14-2 for details).

generally accepted accounting principles (GAAP) Standard rules and methods used by accountants in preparing financial reports.

Tax Services

Tax services include helping clients not only with preparing their tax returns but also with their tax planning. Tax laws are complex. A CA's advice can help a business structure (or restructure) its operations and investments and save millions of dollars in taxes. To serve their clients best, of course, accountants must stay abreast of changes in tax laws—no simple matter.

Management Consulting Services

management consulting services Specialized accounting services to help managers resolve a variety of problems in finance, production scheduling, and other areas.

Management consulting services range from personal financial planning to the planning of corporate mergers. Other services include plant layout and design, marketing studies, production scheduling, computer feasibility studies, and design and implementation of accounting systems. Some accounting firms even assist in executive recruitment. Small wonder that the staffs of accounting firms may include engineers, architects, mathematicians, and even psychologists.

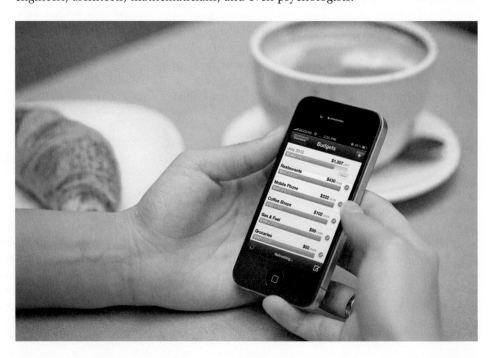

A financial report is an integral component of the financial accounting system.

Private Accountants

To ensure the fairness of their reports, CAs and CGAs must be independent of the firms they audit. They are employees of accounting firms and provide services for many clients. But businesses also hire their own **private accountants** as salaried employees to deal with the company's day-to-day accounting needs.

Private accountants perform a variety of accounting jobs. An internal auditor at Petro-Canada, for example, might fly to the Hibernia site to confirm the accuracy of oil-flow meters on the offshore drilling platform. But a supervisor responsible for $200 million in monthly accounts payable to vendors and employees may travel no further than the executive suite. The nature of the accounting job thus depends on the specific business and the activities needed to make that business a success. Large businesses employ specialized accountants in such areas as budgets, financial planning, internal auditing, payroll, and taxation. Each accounting area has its own challenges and excitement. In small businesses, a single individual may handle all accounting tasks.

private accountant An accountant hired as a salaried employee to deal with a company's day-to-day accounting needs.

The Accounting Cycle

Private accountants use a six-step process to develop and analyze a company's financial reports (see Figure 14.1). The first step is to analyze data that are generated as a result of the company's regular business operations (sales revenue, income tax payments, interest income, inventory purchases, etc.). These transactions are first entered in a *journal* (which lists them in chronological order) and then in a *ledger* (which shows the increases and decreases in the various asset, liability, and equity accounts). Then the ledger amounts for each account are listed in a *trial balance* (which assesses the accuracy of the figures). Financial statements (balance sheet, income statement, and statement of cash flows) are then prepared. The last step in the process involves analyzing the financial statements (for example, by using ratio analysis). Many years ago, these steps were done laboriously by hand, but now computers are used to help private accountants efficiently work through the six steps.

accounting equation The most basic tool of accounting, used to balance the data pertaining to financial transactions: assets = liabilities – owners' equity.

The Accounting Equation

All accountants, whether public or private, rely on record keeping. Underlying all record-keeping procedures is the most basic tool of accounting: the **accounting equation**. At various points in the year, accountants use the following equation to balance the data pertaining to financial transactions:

Describe how the *accounting equation* is used.

$$\text{Assets} = \text{Liabilities} + \text{Owners' Equity}$$

FIGURE 14.1.

The accounting cycle.

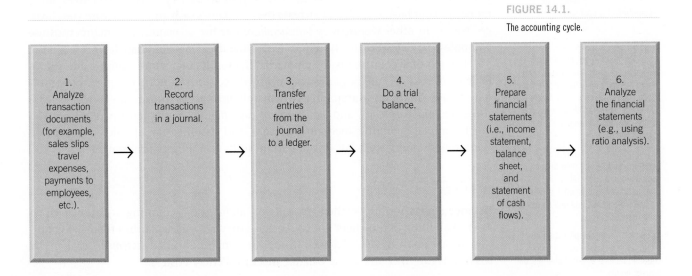

| 1. Analyze transaction documents (for example, sales slips travel expenses, payments to employees, etc.). | → | 2. Record transactions in a journal. | → | 3. Transfer entries from the journal to a ledger. | → | 4. Do a trial balance. | → | 5. Prepare financial statements (i.e., income statement, balance sheet, and statement of cash flows). | → | 6. Analyze the financial statements (e.g., using ratio analysis). |

After each transaction (e.g., payments to suppliers, sales to customers, wages to employees, and so on), the accounting equation must be in balance. To understand the importance of this equation, we must first understand the terms *assets, liabilities,* and *owners' equity*.[12]

Assets and Liabilities

asset Any economic resource that is expected to benefit a firm or an individual who owns it.

liability A debt that the firm owes to an outside party.

An **asset** is any economic resource that is expected to benefit a firm or an individual who owns it. Assets include land, buildings, equipment, inventory, and payments due the company (accounts receivable). A **liability** is a debt that the firm owes to an outside party.

Owners' Equity

owners' equity The amount of money that owners would receive if they sold all of a company's assets and paid all of its liabilities.

You may have heard of the equity that a homeowner has in a house—that is, the amount of money that could be made by selling the house and paying off the mortgage. Similarly, **owners' equity** is the amount of money that owners would receive if they sold all of a company's assets and paid all of its liabilities. We can rewrite the accounting equation to highlight this definition:

$$\text{Assets} - \text{Liabilities} = \text{Owners' equity}$$

If a company's assets exceed its liabilities, owners' equity is *positive*; if the company goes out of business, the owners will receive some cash (a gain) after selling assets and paying off liabilities. If liabilities outweigh assets, owners' equity is *negative*; assets are insufficient to pay off all debts. If the company goes out of business, the owners will get no cash and some creditors won't be paid. Owners' equity is meaningful for both investors and lenders. Before lending money to owners, for example, lenders want to know the amount of owners' equity in a business. Owners' equity consists of two sources of capital:

1. the amount that the owners originally invested; and

2. profits earned by and reinvested in the company.

When a company operates profitably, its assets increase faster than its liabilities. Owners' equity, therefore, will increase if profits are retained in the business instead of paid out as dividends to stockholders. Owners' equity also increases if owners invest more of their own money to increase assets. However, owners' equity can shrink if the company operates at a loss or if owners withdraw assets.

Financial Statements

L03 Describe three basic *financial statements* and show how they reflect the activity and financial condition of a business.

double-entry accounting system A bookkeeping system, developed in the fifteenth century and still in use, that requires every transaction to be entered in two ways—how it affects assets and how it affects liabilities and owners' equity—so that the accounting equation is always in balance.

financial statement Any of several types of broad reports regarding a company's financial status; most often used in reference to balance sheets, income statements, and/or statements of cash flows.

balance sheets Supply detailed information about the accounting equation factors: assets, liabilities, and owners' equity.

If your business purchases inventory with cash, you do two things: (1) decrease your cash and (2) increase your inventory. Similarly, if you purchase supplies on credit, you (1) increase your supplies and (2) increase your accounts payable. If you invest more money in your business, you (1) increase the company's cash and (2) increase your owners' equity. In other words, *every transaction affects two accounts.* Accountants thus use a **double-entry accounting system** to record the *dual effects* of financial transactions.

The job of accounting is to summarize the results of a firm's transactions and to issue reports to help managers make informed decisions. Among the most important reports are **financial statements**, which fall into three broad categories—*balance sheets, income statements,* and *statements of cash flows*.[13] Entrepreneurs often put too much emphasis on the income statement and assume that if sales are growing everything is going well. But it is important to look at all financial statements.[14]

Balance Sheets

Balance sheets supply detailed information about the accounting equation factors: assets, liabilities, and owners' equity. Because they also show a firm's financial condition at one point in time, balance sheets are sometimes called *statements of financial position.* Figure 14.2 shows the balance sheet for Perfect Posters.

Assets

As we have seen, an asset is any economic resource that a company owns and from which it can expect to derive some future benefit. From an accounting standpoint, most companies have three types of assets: *current*, *fixed*, and *intangible*.

Current Assets. **Current assets** include cash and assets that can be converted into cash within a year. They are normally listed in order of **liquidity**—the ease with which they can be converted into cash. Business debts, for example, can usually be satisfied only through payments of cash. A company that needs but cannot generate cash (in other words, a company that is not liquid) may thus be forced to sell assets at sacrifice prices or even go out of business.

By definition, cash is completely liquid. *Marketable securities* purchased as short-term investments are slightly less liquid but can be sold quickly if necessary. Marketable securities include stocks or bonds of other companies, government securities, and money market certificates. There are three other important non-liquid assets held by many companies: *accounts receivable*, *merchandise inventory*, and *prepaid expenses*.

Accounts receivable are amounts due from customers who have purchased goods on credit. Most businesses expect to receive payment within 30 days of a sale. In our hypothetical example, the entry labelled *Less: Allowance of doubtful accounts* in Figure 14.2 indicates $650 in receivables that Perfect Posters does not expect to collect. Total accounts receivable assets are decreased accordingly.

current assets Cash and other assets that can be converted into cash within a year.

liquidity The ease with which assets can be converted into cash.

accounts receivable Amounts due from customers who have purchased goods on credit.

FIGURE 14.2

Perfect Posters's balance sheet shows clearly that the firm's total assets equal its total liabilities and owners' equity.

🗆🗆🗆🗆🗆🗆🗆🗆 **Perfect Posters, Inc.**
555 Riverview, Toronto, Ontario

Perfect Posters, Inc.
Balance Sheet
As of December 31, 2012

Assets

Current Assets:
Cash		7050
Marketable securities. . . .		2300
Accounts receivable.	$26 210	
Less: Allowance of.		
doubtful accounts.	(650)	25 560
Merchandise inventory.		21 250
Prepaid expenses		1050
Total current assets		**$57 210**

Fixed Assets:
Land		18 000
Building	65 000	
Less: Accumulated		
depreciation	(22 500)	42 500
Equipment	72 195	
Less: Accumulated		
depreciation	(24 815)	47 380
Total fixed assets. . .		**107 880**

Intangible Assets:
Patents	7 100	
Trademarks	900	
Total intangible assets		**8 000**
Total assets		**$173 090**

Liabilities and Owners' Equity

Current Liabilities:
Accounts payable.	$16 315	
Wages payable.	3700	
Taxes payable.	1920	
Total current liabilities		**$21 935**

Long-Term Liabilities:
Notes payable, 8%		
due 2010	10 000	
Bonds payable, 9%		
due 2012	30 000	
Total long-term liabilities		**40 000**
Total liabilities		**$61 935**

Owners' Equity
Common stock, $5 par	40 000	
Additional paid-in capital	15 000	
Retained earnings	56 155	
Total owners' equity		**111 155**
Total liabilities and owners' equity . . .		**$173 090**

merchandise inventory The cost of merchandise that has been acquired for sale to customers and is still on hand.

prepaid expenses Includes supplies on hand and rent paid for the period to come.

fixed assets Assets that have long-term use or value to the firm, such as land, buildings, and machinery.

depreciation Distributing the cost of a major asset over the years in which it produces revenues; calculated by each year subtracting the asset's original value divided by the number of years in its productive life.

intangible assets Non-physical assets, such as patents, trademarks, copyrights, and franchise fees, that have economic value but the precise value of which is difficult to calculate.

goodwill The amount paid for an existing business beyond the value of its other assets.

current liabilities Debts that must be paid within one year.

accounts payable Unpaid bills to suppliers for materials, as well as wages and taxes that must be paid in the coming year.

long-term liabilities Debts that are not due for at least one year.

Following accounts receivable on the Perfect Posters balance sheet is **merchandise inventory**—the cost of merchandise that has been acquired for sale to customers and is still on hand. Accounting for the value of inventories on the balance sheet is difficult because inventories are flowing in and out throughout the year. Therefore, assumptions must be made about which ones were sold and which ones remain in storage.

Prepaid expenses include supplies on hand and rent paid for the period to come. They are assets because they have been paid for and are available to the company. In all, Perfect Posters's current assets as of December 31, 2012, totalled $57 210.

Fixed Assets. **Fixed assets** (for example, land, buildings, and equipment) have long-term use or value. But as buildings and equipment wear out or become obsolete, their value decreases. To reflect decreasing value, accountants use **depreciation** to spread the cost of an asset over the years of its useful life. Depreciation means calculating an asset's useful life in years, dividing its worth by that many years, and subtracting the resulting amount each year. Each year, therefore, the asset's remaining value decreases on the books. In Figure 14.2, Perfect Posters shows fixed assets of $107 880 after depreciation.

Intangible Assets. Although their worth is hard to set, intangible assets have monetary value. **Intangible assets** usually include the cost of obtaining rights or privileges such as patents, trademarks, copyrights, and franchise fees. **Goodwill** is the amount paid for an existing business beyond the value of its other assets. Perfect Posters has no goodwill assets; however, it does own trademarks and patents for specialized storage equipment. These are intangible assets worth $8000. Larger companies, of course, have intangible assets that are worth much more.

Liabilities

Like assets, liabilities are often separated into different categories. **Current liabilities** are debts that must be paid within one year. These include **accounts payable**—unpaid bills to suppliers for materials, as well as wages and taxes that must be paid in the coming year. Perfect Posters has current liabilities of $21 935.

Long-term liabilities are debts that are not due for at least one year. These normally represent borrowed funds on which the company must pay interest. Perfect Posters's long-term liabilities are $40 000.

The inventory at this car dealership is part of the company's assets. The cars constitute an economic resource because the firm will benefit financially as it sells them. When they are sold, at the end of the company's accounting period, the dealership will convert the cost of the cars as expenses and show them as costs of goods sold.

Owners' Equity

The final section of the balance sheet in Figure 14.2 shows owners' equity broken down into *common stock, paid-in capital,* and *retained earnings.* When Perfect Posters was formed, the declared legal value of its common stock was $5 per share. By law, this $40 000 (8000 shares) cannot be distributed as dividends. **Paid-in capital** is additional money invested in the firm by its owners. Perfect Posters has $15 000 in paid-in capital.

paid-in capital Additional money invested in the firm by its owners.

Retained earnings are net profits minus dividend payments to shareholders. Retained earnings accumulate when profits, which could have been distributed to shareholders, are kept instead for use by the company. At the close of 2012, Perfect Posters had retained earnings of $56 155.

retained earnings Net profits minus dividend payments to shareholders.

Income Statements

The **income statement** is sometimes called a **profit-and-loss statement** because its description of revenues and expenses results in a figure showing the firm's annual profit or loss. In other words,

income (profit-and-loss) statement A description of revenues and expenses in a figure showing the firm's annual profit or loss.

$$\text{Revenues} - \text{Expenses} = \text{Profit (or loss).}$$

Popularly known as "the bottom line," profit or loss is probably the most important figure in any business enterprise. The boxed insert entitled "How Will Twitter Turn Tweets into Treasure?" contains information about profit uncertainties in new startups.

ENTREPRENEURSHIP AND NEW VENTURES

How Will Twitter Turn Tweets into Treasure?

Widely accepted accounting measurements provide useful information about established firms, but are a bit foggier with start-ups. Consider the continuing questions from the investment community about Twitter's ambiguous financial status. With several firms interested in buying Twitter, how can they know its market value (estimated at $4.5 billion in 2011) without solid financial data? The real numbers are confidential and closely guarded by Twitter. As to its profitability, Twitter reports, "we spend more money than we make." Since Twitter was launched in 2006, its total losses have not been reported publicly. When (and how) will losses blossom into profitability? As stated by co-founder and former CEO Evan Williams, "We will make money, and I can't say exactly how because ... we can't predict how the business we're in will work." And until they know *how*, they don't know *when* profits will occur.

Twitter's balance sheet is another source of ambiguity. The accounting equation requires a fixed relationship among three items: Assets = Liabilities + Owners' equity. Twitter insiders have a clear accounting of its outstanding liabilities, and paid-in capital (a part of shareholders' equity) is known, too. It includes the co-founders' personal investments plus a series of venture capital infusions, bringing the suspected total to over $800 million.

But there are difficulties valuing Twitter's assets. For example, Twitter acquired the assets of a company called

Values of n to get needed technology and intellectual property into its operations. Exactly how Twitter will use them is unknown, so how should they be valued? Twitter's greatest asset is a massive loyal customer base with a phenomenal growth rate—190 million visitors per month and 65 million tweets daily—and its enormous advertising potential. Celebrities, media, politicians, and organizations such as Warner Bros Pictures, Toyota, and Papa Johns are using Twitter for sales and marketing promotions. Should this untapped advertising potential be recognized as an intangible asset? At what value? While the company's market, customer base, and products are rapidly emerging, how should its many assets—tangible and intangible—be valued? On what basis can those evaluations be justified? Clearly, these issues at Twitter are less well settled than at the more established firms.

Critical Thinking Question

1. Consider the following statement: *Accounting information is meaningful and useful for well-established companies, and is particularly helpful for individuals and organizations when making investment decisions. But accounting information is not very helpful in making investment decisions for newly established companies.* Do you agree or disagree with the statement? Defend your answer.

❏❏❏❏❏❏❏❏❏❏❏❏❏ **Perfect Posters, Inc.**
555 Riverview, Toronto, Ontario

Perfect Posters, Inc.
Income Statement
Year ended December 31, 2012

Revenues (gross sales).			**$256 425**
Costs of goods sold:			
Merchandise inventory,			
January 1, 2012	$22 380		
Merchandise purchases			
during year.	103 635		
Goods available for sale.		$126 015	
Less: Merchandise inventory,			
December 31, 2012		21 250	
Cost of goods sold			**104 765**
Gross profit			**151 660**
Operating expenses:			
Selling and repackaging expenses:			
Salaries and wages.	49 750		
Advertising.	6380		
Depreciation—warehouse and . .			
repackaging equipment.	3350		
Total selling and repackaging			
expenses.		59 480	
Administrative expenses:			
Salaries and wages.	55 100		
Supplies.	4150		
Utilities	3800		
Depreciation—office equipment .	3420		
Interest expense	2900		
Miscellaneous expenses.	1835		
Total administration expenses.		71 205	
Total operating expenses.			**130 685**
Operating income (income before taxes). . .			20 975
Income taxes.			8390
Net income.			**$12 585**

FIGURE 14.3

Perfect Posters's income statement. The final entry on the income statement, the bottom line, reports the firm's profit or loss.

Figure 14.3 shows the 2012 income statement for Perfect Posters, whose bottom line that year was $12 585. The income statement is divided into three major categories: *revenues, cost of goods sold*, and *operating expenses.*

Revenues

When a law firm receives $250 for preparing a will or when a supermarket collects $65 from a customer buying groceries, both are receiving **revenues**—the funds that flow into a business from the sale of goods or services. In 2012, Perfect Posters reported revenues of $256 425 from the sale of art prints and other posters.

revenues The funds that flow into a business from the sale of goods or services.

Cost of Goods Sold

On Perfect Posters's income statement, the **cost of goods sold** category shows the costs of obtaining materials to make the products sold during the year. Perfect Posters began 2012 with posters valued at $22 380. Over the year, it spent $103 635 to purchase posters. During 2012, then, the company had $126 015 worth of merchandise available to sell. By the end of the year, it had sold all but $21 250 of those posters, which remained as merchandise inventory. The cost of obtaining the goods sold by the firm was thus $104 765.

cost of goods sold Any expenses directly involved in producing or selling a good or service during a given time period.

Gross Profit (or Gross Margin). To calculate **gross profit (or gross margin)**, subtract the cost of goods sold from the revenues obtained from goods sold. Perfect Posters's gross profit in 2012 was $151 660 ($256 425 – $104 765). Expressed as a percentage of sales, gross profit is 59.1 percent ($151 660/$256 425).

Gross profit percentages vary widely across industries. In retailing, Home Depot reports 30 percent; in manufacturing, Harley-Davidson reports 34 percent; and in pharmaceuticals, Wyeth reports 75 percent. For companies with low gross margins, product costs are a big expense. If a company has a high gross margin, it probably has low cost-of-goods-sold but high selling and administrative expenses.

gross profit (or gross margin) A firm's revenues (gross sales) less its cost of goods sold.

Operating Expenses

In addition to costs directly related to acquiring goods, every company has general expenses ranging from erasers to the president's salary. Like cost of goods sold, **operating expenses** are resources that must flow out of a company for it to earn revenues. As you can see in Figure 14.3, Perfect Posters had operating expenses of $130 685 in 2012. This figure consists of $59 480 in selling and repackaging expenses and $71 205 in administrative expenses.

operating expenses Resources that must flow out of a company for it to earn revenues.

Selling expenses result from activities related to selling the firm's goods or services. These may include salaries for the sales force, delivery costs, and advertising expenses. General and administrative expenses, such as management salaries, insurance expenses, and maintenance costs, are expenses related to the general management of the company.

Operating Income and Net Income. Sometimes managers must determine **operating income**, which compares the gross profit from business operations against operating expenses. This calculation for Perfect Posters ($151 660 – $130 685) reveals an operating income, or income before taxes, of $20 975. Subtracting income taxes from operating income ($20 975 – $8390) reveals **net income** (also called **net profit or net earnings**). In 2012, Perfect Posters's net income was $12 585.

operating income Compares the gross profit from business operations against operating expenses.

net income (or net profit or net earnings) A firm's gross profit less its operating expenses and income taxes.

Net income can be significantly affected by the rules under which companies in different countries operate. For example, Toronto-based Manulife Financial Corp. reported a loss of $1.28 billion for the third quarter of 2011. But if Manulife was based in the United States its profit would have been $2.2 billion. How can that be? Because in Canada, assets are shown on the balance sheet at their market value, while in the United States companies show assets at their book value (what they originally paid for the asset).[15]

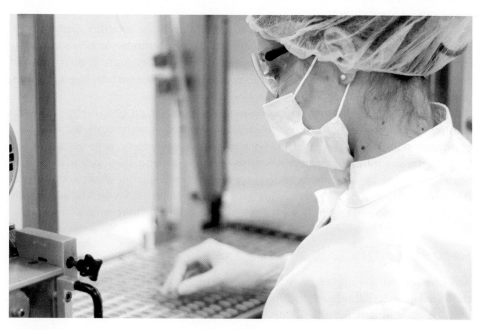

At the end of its accounting period, this pharmaceuticals company will subtract the cost of making the goods that it sold from the revenues received from sales. The difference will be its gross profit (or gross margin). Cost of goods sold does not include the firm's operating expenses, including such selling expenses as advertising and sales commissions. In part, gross margins in the pharmaceuticals industry are high because they do not account for high selling expenses.

Statement of Cash Flows

Some companies prepare only balance sheets and income statements. However, many firms also report a **statement of cash flows**. This statement describes a company's yearly cash receipts and cash payments. It shows the effects on cash of three business activities:

- *Operating cash flow.* This part of the statement is concerned with the firm's main operating activities: the cash transactions involved in buying and selling goods and services. It reveals how much of the year's profits result from the firm's main line of business (for example, Jaguar's sales of automobiles) rather than from secondary activities (for example, licensing fees a clothing firm paid to Jaguar for using the Jaguar logo on shirts).

- *Cash flows from investing.* This section reports net cash used in or provided by investing. It includes cash receipts and payments from buying and selling stocks, bonds, property, equipment, and other productive assets.

- *Cash flows from financing.* The final section reports net cash from all financing activities. It includes cash inflows from borrowing or issuing stock as well as outflows for payment of dividends and repayment of borrowed money.

Sometimes companies report "free cash flow," which is usually defined as operating cash flow minus capital expenditures. Two professors who run a blog called "Grumpy Old Accountants" praised Facebook for its cash flow reporting because the company subtracts not only the cost of capital equipment but also the payments on leases that were used to acquire the equipment. But the professors criticized Groupon for not providing a more detailed cash flow statement.[16] The overall change in cash from these three sources provides information to lenders and investors. When creditors and shareholders know how firms obtained and used their funds during the course of a year, it is easier for them to interpret the year-to-year changes in the firm's balance sheet and income statement.

The Budget: An Internal Financial Statement

For planning, controlling, and decision making, the most important internal financial statement is the **budget**—a detailed statement of estimated receipts and expenditures for a period of time in the future. Although that period is usually one year, some companies also prepare budgets for three- or five-year periods, especially when considering major capital expenditures.

Budgets are also useful for keeping track of weekly or monthly performance. Procter & Gamble, for example, evaluates all of its business units monthly by comparing actual financial results with monthly budgeted amounts. Discrepancies in "actual vs. budget" totals signal potential problems and initiate action to get financial performance back on track.

Although the accounting staff coordinates the budget process, it requires input from many people in the company regarding proposed activities, needed resources, and input sources.[17] Figure 14.4 shows a sample sales budget. In preparing such a budget, the accounting department must obtain from the sales group its projections for units to be sold and expected expenses for each quarter of the coming year. Accountants then draw up the final budget, and throughout the year, the accounting department compares the budget with actual expenditures and revenues.

Reporting Standards and Practices

Accountants follow numerous standard reporting practices and principles when they prepare external reports, including financial statements. The common language dictated by standard practices is designed to give external users confidence in the

FIGURE 14.4

Perfect Posters, Inc. sales budget, first quarter, 2013.

🞐🞐🞐🞐🞐🞐🞐🞐🞐🞐🞐🞐🞐   **Perfect Posters, Inc.**
555 Riverview, Toronto, Ontario

Perfect Posters, Inc.
Sales Budget
First Quarter, 2013

	January	February	March	Quarter
Budgeted sales (units)	7 500	6 000	6 500	20 000
Budgeted selling price per unit	$3.50	$3.50	$3.50	$3.50
Budgeted sales revenue	**$26 250**	**$21 000**	**$22 750**	**$70 000**
Expected cash receipts:				
From December sales	$26 210[a]			$26 210
From January sales	17 500[b]	$8 750		26 250
From February sales		14 000	$7 000	21 000
From March sales			15 200	15 200
Total cash receipts:	**$43 710**	**$22 750**	**$22 200**	**$88 660**

[a] This cash from December sales represents a collection of the Account Receivable appearing on the December 31, 2012 Balance Sheet.

[b] The company estimates that two-thirds of each month's sales revenues will result in cash receipts during the same month. The remaining one-third is collected during the following month.

accuracy and meaning of the information in any financial statement. These principles cover a wide range of issues, such as when to recognize revenues from operations, the so-called "matching" of revenues and expenses, and full public disclosure of financial information to the public. Without agreed-upon practices in these and many other accounting categories, users of financial statements would be unable to compare financial information from different companies and thus misunderstand—or be led to misconstrue—a given company's true financial status.

Revenue Recognition

As we noted earlier, revenues are funds that flow in to a business as a result of its operating activities during the accounting period. *Revenue recognition* is the formal recording and reporting of revenues in the financial statements. Although any firm earns revenues continuously as it makes sales, earnings are not reported until the earnings cycle is completed. This cycle is complete under two conditions:

1. The sale is complete and the product has been delivered.

2. The sale price to the customer has been collected or is collectible (accounts receivable).

The completion of the earning cycle, then, determines the timing for revenue recognition in the firm's financial statements. Revenues are recorded for the accounting period in which sales are completed and collectible (or collected). This practice assures the reader that the statement gives a fair comparison of what was gained for the resources that were given up.

Matching

Net income is calculated by subtracting expenses from revenues. The *matching principle* states that expenses will be matched with revenues to determine net income for an accounting period.[18] Why is this principle important? It permits the user of the statement to see how much net gain resulted from the assets that had to be given up to generate revenues during the period covered in the statement. Consequently, when we match revenue recognition with expense recognition, we get net income for the period.

Explain the key standards and principles for reporting financial statements.

Consider the hypothetical case of Little Red Wagon Co. Let's see what happens when the books are kept in two different ways:

1. Correct method: Revenue recognition is matched with expense recognition to determine net income when the earnings cycle is *completed*.

2. Incorrect method: Revenue recognition occurs *before* the earnings cycle is completed.

Suppose that 500 red wagons are produced and delivered to customers at a sales price of $20 each during 2011. In 2012, 600 red wagons are produced and delivered. In part (A) of Table 14.2, the correct matching method has been used: Revenues are recorded for the accounting period in which sales are completed and collectible from customers, as are the expenses of producing and delivering them. The revenues from sales are matched against the expenses of completing them. By using the matching principle, we see clearly how much better off the company is at the end of each accounting period as a result of that period's operations: It earned $2000 net income for 2011 and $3000 for 2012.

In part (B) of Table 14.2, revenue recognition and the matching principle have been violated. Certain activities of the two accounting periods are disguised and mixed together rather than separated for each period. The result is a distorted performance report that incorrectly shows that 2011 was a better year than 2012. Here's what Little Red Wagon's accountants did wrong: The sales department sold 200 red wagons (with revenues of $4000) to a customer late in 2011. Those *revenues* are included in the $14 000 for 2011. But because the 200 wagons were produced and delivered to the customer in 2012, the *expenses* are recorded, as in (A), for 2012. The result is a distorted picture of operations. It looks as if expenses for 2012 are out of line for such a low sales level, and it looks as if expenses (as compared with revenues) were kept under better control during 2011.

The firm's accountants violated the matching principle by ignoring *the period during which the earnings cycle was completed*. Although $4000 in sales of wagons occurred in 2011, the earnings cycle for those wagons was not completed until they were produced and delivered, which occurred in 2012. Accordingly, both the revenues and expenses for those 200 wagons should have been reported in the same period—namely, in 2012, as was reported in part (A). There, we can see clearly what was gained and what was lost on activities that were completed *in an accounting period*. By requiring this practice, the matching principle provides consistency in reporting and avoids financial distortions.

TABLE 14.2 Revenue Recognition and the Matching Principle

(A) The correct method reveals each accounting period's activities and results.

	Year ended December 31, 2011	Year ended December 31, 2012
Revenues	$10 000	$12 000
Expenses	8000	9000
Net income	2000	3000

(B) The incorrect method disguises each accounting period's activities and results.

	Year ended December 31, 2011	Year ended December 31, 2012
Revenues	$14 000	$8000
Expenses	8000	9000
Net income	6000	1000

Full Disclosure

Full disclosure means that financial statements should include not just numbers but also interpretations and explanations by management so that external users can better understand information contained in the statements. Because management knows more about inside events than outsiders, management prepares additional useful information that explains certain events or transactions or discloses the circumstances underlying certain financial results.

Analyzing Financial Statements

Financial statements present a great deal of information, but what does it all mean? How, for example, can statements help investors decide what stock to buy or help managers decide whether to extend credit? Statements provide data, which in turn can be applied to various ratios (comparative numbers). These ratios can then be used to analyze the financial health of one or more companies. They can also be used to check a firm's progress by comparing current and past statements.

> Explain how computing *financial ratios* can help in analyzing the financial strengths of a business. **L05**

Ratios are normally grouped into three major classifications:

- **Solvency ratios**, both short-term and long-term, estimate risk.

- **Profitability ratios** measure potential earnings.

- **Activity ratios** reflect management's use of assets.

Depending on the decisions to be made, a user may apply none, some, or all the ratios in a particular classification.

> **solvency ratios** Ratios that estimate the financial risk that is evident in a company.

> **profitability ratios** Measures of a firm's overall financial performance in terms of its likely profits; used by investors to assess their probable returns.

> **activity ratios** Measures of how efficiently a firm uses its resources; used by investors to assess their probable returns.

Solvency Ratios

What are the chances that a borrower will be able to repay a loan and the interest due? This question is first and foremost in the minds of bank lending officers, managers of pension funds and other investors, suppliers, and the borrowing company's own financial managers. Solvency ratios provide measures of the firm's ability to meet its debt obligations.

Short-Term Solvency Ratios

Short-term solvency ratios measure a company's liquidity and its ability to pay immediate debts. The most commonly used ratio is the **current ratio**, which reflects a firm's ability to generate cash to meet obligations through the normal, orderly process of selling inventories and collecting revenues from customers. It is calculated by dividing current assets by current liabilities. The higher a firm's current ratio, the lower the risk to investors. For many years, the guideline was a current ratio of 2:1 or higher— which meant that current assets were at least double current liabilities. More recently, many firms that are financially strong operate with current ratios of less than 2:1.

> **short-term solvency ratios** Measure a company's liquidity and its ability to pay immediate debts.

> **current ratio** A form of liquidity ratio calculated as current assets divided by current liabilities.

How does Perfect Posters measure up? Look again at the balance sheet in Figure 14.2. Judging from its current assets and current liabilities at the end of 2012, we see that the company looks like a good credit risk:

$$\frac{\text{Current assets}}{\text{Current liabilities}} = \frac{\$57\,210}{\$21\,935} = 2.61$$

Long-Term Solvency

Stakeholders are also concerned about long-term solvency. Has a company been over-extended by borrowing so much that it will be unable to repay debts in future years? A firm that can't meet its long-term debt obligations is in danger of collapse or takeover— a risk that makes creditors and investors quite cautious. To evaluate a company's risk of running into this problem, creditors turn to the balance sheet to see the extent to which a firm is financed through borrowed money. Long-term solvency is calculated by dividing **debt**—total liabilities—by owners' equity. The lower a firm's debt, the lower the risk to investors and creditors. Companies with **debt-to-owners'-equity ratios** above 1.0 may be relying too much on debt. In the case of Perfect Posters, we can see from the balance sheet in Figure 14.2 that the debt-to-equity ratio calculates as follows:

debt A company's total liabilities.

debt-to-owners'-equity ratio A form of debt ratio calculated as total liabilities divided by owners' equity.

$$\frac{\text{Debt}}{\text{Owners' equity}} - \frac{\$61\ 935}{\$111\ 155} = \$0.56$$

Sometimes, high debt can be not only acceptable but also desirable. Borrowing funds gives a firm **leverage**—the ability to make otherwise unaffordable investments. In *leveraged buyouts*, firms have sometimes taken on huge debt in order to get the money to buy out other companies. If owning the purchased company generates profits above the cost of borrowing the purchase price, leveraging makes sense. Unfortunately, many buyouts have caused problems because profits fell short of expectedΩ levels or because rising interest rates increased payments on the buyer's debt.

leverage Using borrowed funds to make purchases, thus increasing the user's purchasing power, potential rate of return, and risk of loss.

Profitability Ratios

Although it is important to know that a company is solvent in both the long term and the short term, safety or risk alone is not an adequate basis for investment decisions. Investors also want some measure of the returns they can expect. Return on equity and earnings per share are two commonly used profitability ratios. (Sometimes these are called *shareholder return ratios* or *performance ratios*.)

Return on Equity

Owners are interested in the net income earned by a business for each dollar invested. **Return on equity** measures this performance by dividing net income (recorded in the income statement, Figure 14.3) by total owners' equity (recorded in the balance sheet, Figure 14.2).[19] For Perfect Posters, the return-on-equity ratio in 2012 can be calculated as follows:

return on equity A form of profitability ratio calculated as net income divided by total owners' equity.

$$\frac{\text{Net income}}{\text{Total owners' equity}} - \frac{\$12\ 585}{\$111\ 155} = 11.3\%$$

Is this figure good or bad? There is no set answer. If Perfect Posters's ratio for 2012 is higher than in previous years, owners and investors should be encouraged. But if 11.3 percent is lower than the ratios of other companies in the same industry, they should be concerned.

Return on Sales

Companies want to generate as much profit as they can from each dollar of sales revenue they receive. The **return on sales** ratio is calculated by dividing net income by sales revenue (see Figure 14.3). For Perfect Posters, the return on sales ratio for 2012 is as follows:

return on sales Calculated by dividing net income by sales revenue.

$$\frac{\text{Net income}}{\text{Sales revenue}} - \frac{\$12\ 585}{\$256\ 425} \times 100 = 4.9\%$$

Is this figure good or bad? Once again, there is no set answer. If Perfect Posters's ratio for 2012 is higher than in previous years, owners and investors should be encouraged, but if 4.9 percent is lower than the ratios of other companies in the same industry, they will likely be concerned.

Earnings per Share

Defined as net income divided by the number of shares of common shares outstanding, **earnings per share** determines the size of the dividend a company can pay to its shareholders. Investors use this ratio to decide whether to buy or sell a company's

earnings per share A form of profitability ratio calculated as net income divided by the number of common shares outstanding.

stock. As the ratio gets higher, the stock value increases, because investors know that the firm can better afford to pay dividends. Naturally, stock will lose market value if the latest financial statements report a decline in earnings per share. For Perfect Posters, we can use the net income total from the income statement in Figure 14.3 to calculate earnings per share as follows:

$$\frac{\text{Net income}}{\text{Number of common shares outstanding}} = \frac{\$12\,585}{\$8\,000} = \$1.57 \text{ per share}$$

Activity Ratios

The efficiency with which a firm uses resources is linked to profitability. As a potential investor, then, you want to know which company gets more mileage from its resources. Activity ratios measure this efficiency. For example, suppose that two firms use the same amount of resources or assets. If Firm A generates greater profits or sales, it is more efficient and thus has a better activity ratio.

Inventory Turnover Ratio

Certain specific measures can be used to explain how one firm earns greater profits than another. One of the most important measures is the **inventory turnover ratio**, which calculates the average number of times that inventory is sold and restocked during the year—that is, how quickly inventory is produced and sold.[20] First, a company needs to know its average inventory—the typical amount of inventory on hand during the year. Average inventory can be calculated by adding end-of-year inventory to beginning-of-year inventory and dividing by two. The company can then calculate the inventory turnover ratio, which is expressed as the cost of goods sold divided by average inventory:

inventory turnover ratio An activity ratio that measures the average number of times inventory is sold and restocked during the year.

$$\frac{\text{Cost of goods sold}}{\text{Average inventory}} = \frac{\text{Cost of goods sold}}{\text{Beginning inventory} + \text{Ending inventory} \div 2}$$

High inventory turnover ratio means efficient operations. Because a smaller amount of investment is tied up in inventory, the company's funds can be put to work elsewhere to earn greater returns. However, inventory turnover must be compared with both prior years and industry averages. An inventory turnover rate

The inventory turnover ratio measures the average number of times that a store sells and restocks its inventory in one year. The higher the ratio, the more products that get sold and the more revenue that comes in. Supermarkets must have a higher turnover ratio than, say, auto supply or toy stores. In almost all retail stores, products with the highest ratios get the shelf spaces that generate the most customer traffic and sales.

of five, for example, might be excellent for an auto supply store, but it would be disastrous for a supermarket, where a rate of about 15 is common. Rates can also vary within a company that markets a variety of products. To calculate Perfect Posters's inventory turnover ratio for 2012, we take the merchandise inventory figures for the income statement in Figure 14.3. The ratio can be expressed as follows:

$$\frac{\$104\,765}{(\$22\,380 + \$21\,250) \div 2} = 4.8 \text{ times}$$

In other words, new merchandise replaces old merchandise every 76 days (365 days divided by 4.8). The 4.8 ratio is below the average of 7.0 for comparable wholesaling operations, indicating that the business is slightly inefficient.

International Accounting

L06 Explain some of the special issues that arise in *international accounting*.

As we saw in Chapter 5, many companies receive large portions of their operating revenues from foreign sales. Canadian companies also purchase components from foreign countries. Retailers such as Sears buy merchandise from other countries for sale in Canada. In addition, more and more companies own subsidiaries in foreign countries. With all this international activity, there is obviously a need to keep track of foreign transactions. One of the most basic accounting needs is translating the values of the currencies of different countries.

Foreign Currency Exchange

foreign currency exchange rate
What buyers are willing to pay for a given currency.

A unique consideration in international accounting is the value of currencies and their exchange rates. As we saw in Chapter 5, the value of any country's currency is subject to occasional change. Political and economic conditions, for instance, affect the stability of a nation's currency and its value relative to the currencies of other countries.

As the currency is traded around the world, market forces determine the currency's value—what buyers are willing to pay for it. The resulting values are called **foreign currency exchange rates**. When a currency becomes unstable—that is, when its value changes frequently—it is regarded as a *weak currency*. The value of the Brazilian real, for example, fluctuated between 0.601 and 0.549—a negative variation of 9 percent in Canadian dollars—during the period from 2011 to 2012. On the other hand, a *strong currency* historically rises or holds steady in comparison to other currencies.[21]

As changes in exchange rates occur, they must be considered by accountants when recording international transactions. They will affect, perhaps profoundly, the amount that a firm pays for foreign purchases and the amount it gains from sales to foreign buyers.

International Transactions

International purchases, credit sales, and accounting for foreign subsidiaries all involve transactions affected by exchange rates. When a Canadian company imports Bordeaux wine from the French company Pierre Bourgeois, the Canadian company's accountant must be sure that the company's books reflect its true costs. The amount owed to Pierre Bourgeois changes daily along with the exchange rate between euros and Canadian dollars. Thus, the accountant must identify the actual rate *on the day that payment in euros is made* so that the correct Canadian-dollar cost of the purchase is recorded.

International Accounting Standards

Professional accounting groups from about 80 countries are members of the International Accounting Standards Board (IASB), which is trying to eliminate national differences in financial reporting procedures.[22] Bankers, investors, and managers want procedures that are comparable from country to country and applicable to all firms regardless of home nation. Standardization is occurring in some areas but is far from universal. IASB financial statements include an income statement, balance sheet, and statement of cash flows similar to those issued by Canadian and U.S. accountants. International standards, however, do not require a uniform format, and variety abounds. Concluding Case 14-2 provides more information on this important topic.

"It's up to you now, Miller. The only thing that can save us is an accounting breakthrough."

THE GREENING OF BUSINESS

The Green Revolution Hits Accounting

In accounting, there is at least one important activity that impacts the environment, and that is the use of paper for all those financial statements. But the electronic revolution has provided accountants with the opportunity to reduce paper waste; to quickly respond to clients; to reduce the costs associated with storing, tracking, and accessing documents; and to work virtually anywhere in the world via the internet. Traditional accounting firms spend a lot of valuable time handling paperwork such as invoices. A paperless system eliminates the need to store paper invoices by storing their digital images and retrieving the images as needed. Firms now have easier access to more data, facilitating analyses that can save thousands of dollars.

There are real incentives for companies to embrace environmentally friendly business practices like saving paper. But careful thought has to be given to how this will be done because of the well-known tendency of human beings to resist change. To resolve any resistance that is based on *technical* concerns, management must ensure that the IT infrastructure is working properly and that there is an adequate storage and security system. To deal with resistance that is based on *emotional* concerns, management needs to provide incentives to motivate people to change to the new system. Digital files, for example, reduce the need to travel in order to share documents with clients and other associates. This also enables companies

to reduce their dependency on a traditional work environment because more employees can choose to work flexible hours and have a more balanced work and family life. Another incentive is the increased efficiency that will be evident with the use of electronic technology. Increased efficiency means that a given amount of work can be done with fewer people than were previously needed, and this will increase competitiveness.

It is anticipated that accounting firms will increasingly train their clients to perform more of the initial data entry to allow for the electronic exchange of information. Firms will no longer be limited by geographic boundaries. They can also bill for higher-level accounting tasks and be much more selective about their clients. These new methods will help eliminate the bottom 10 to 20 percent of unproductive clients and allow more time to cultivate the profitable files.

Critical Thinking Questions

1. There are clearly benefits for firms that embrace green accounting practices, but are there also benefits to clients? If so, describe them.

2. Why might there be reluctance on the part of accounting firms or their clients to embrace green initiatives like paperless systems?

MyBizLab

Capture more moments of true understanding. MyBizLab provides you with interactive study and practice tools directly related to this chapter's content. The new MyBizLab Study Plan Learning Path is designed to measure a full range of skills and provide remediation to give you what you need to master key chapter concepts. MyBizLab flexes to your unique learning needs. The result? Inspired learning, more success.

SUMMARY OF LEARNING OBJECTIVES

1. **Explain the role of *accountants* and distinguish among the three types of professional accountants in Canada.** By collecting, analyzing, and communicating financial information, accountants provide business managers and investors with an accurate picture of a firm's financial health. *Chartered accountants (CAs)* and *certified general accountants (CGAs)* provide accounting expertise for client organizations that must report their financial condition to external stakeholders. *Certified management accountants (CMAs)* provide accounting expertise for the firms that employ them.

2. **Describe how the *accounting equation* is used.** Accountants use the following equation to balance the data pertaining to financial transactions:

   Assets – Liabilities = Owners' equity.

   After each financial transaction (e.g., payments to suppliers, sales to customers, wage payments to employees), the accounting equation must be in balance. If it isn't, then an accounting error has occurred. The equation also provides an indication of the firm's financial health. If *assets* exceed *liabilities, owners' equity* is positive; if the firm goes out of business, owners will receive some cash (a gain) after selling assets and paying off liabilities. If liabilities outweigh assets, owners' equity is negative; assets aren't enough to pay off debts. If the company goes under, owners will get no cash and some creditors won't be paid, thus losing their remaining investments in the company.

3. **Describe three basic *financial statements* and show how they reflect the activity and financial condition of a business.** The *balance sheet* summarizes a company's assets, liabilities, and owners' equity at a given point in time. The *income statement* details revenues and expenses for a given period of time and identifies any profit or loss. The *statement of cash flows* reports cash receipts and payment from operating, investing, and financial activities.

4. **Explain the key standards and principles for reporting financial statements.** Accountants follow standard reporting practices and principles when they prepare financial statements. Otherwise, users wouldn't be able to compare information from different companies, and they might misunderstand—or be led to misconstrue—a company's true financial status. Revenue recognition is the formal recording and reporting of revenues in financial statements. All firms earn revenues continuously as they make sales, but earnings are not reported until

the earnings cycle is completed. This cycle is complete under two conditions: (a) The sale is complete and the product delivered, and (b) the sale price has been collected or is collectible. This practice assures interested parties that the statement gives a fair comparison of what was gained for the resources that were given up.

5. **Explain how computing *financial ratios* can help in analyzing the financial strengths of a business.** Drawing upon data from financial statements, ratios can help creditors, investors, and managers assess a firm's finances. The *current, liquidity,* and *debt-to-owners'-equity ratios* all measure solvency, a firm's ability to pay its debt in both the short and long runs. *Return on sales, return on equity,* and *earnings per share* are all ratios that measure profitability. The *inventory turnover ratio* shows how efficiently a firm is using its funds.

6. **Explain some of the special issues that arise in *international accounting.*** Accounting for foreign transactions involves special procedures, such as translating the values of different countries' currencies and accounting for the effects of exchange rates. Moreover, currencies are subject to change; as they're traded each day around the world, their values are determined by market forces— what buyers are willing to pay for them. The resulting values are *foreign currency exchange rates*, which can be fairly volatile. When a currency becomes unstable— when its value changes frequently—it is called a weak currency. The value of a strong currency historically rises or holds steady in comparison with the U.S. dollar.

   International purchases, sales on credit, and accounting for foreign subsidiaries all involve transactions affected by exchange rates. When a Canadian company imports a French product, its accountant must be sure that its books reflect its true costs. The amount owed to the French seller changes daily along with the exchange rate between euros and dollars. The Canadian accountant must therefore identify the actual rate on the day that payment in euros is made so that the correct Canadian-dollar cost of the product is recorded.

   With accounting groups from about 80 countries, the International Accounting Standards Board (IASB) is trying to eliminate national differences in financial reporting. Bankers, investors, and managers want financial reporting that is comparable from country to country and across all firms regardless of home nation. Standardization governs some areas but is far from universal.

KEY TERMS

accounting (p. 429)

accounting equation (p. 435)

accounting information system (AIS) (p. 430)

accounts payable (p. 438)

accounts receivable (p. 437)

activity ratios (p. 445)

asset (p. 436)

audit (p. 433)

balance sheets (p. 436)

bookkeeping (p. 429)

budget (p. 442)

certified general accountant (CGA) (p. 432)

certified management accountant (CMA) (p. 432)

chartered accountant (CA) (p. 431)

controller (p. 430)

cost of goods sold (p. 440)

current assets (p. 437)

current liabilities (p. 438)

current ratio (p. 445)

debt (p. 446)

debt-to-owners'-equity ratio (p. 446)

depreciation (p. 438)

double-entry accounting system (p. 436)

earnings per share (p. 446)

financial accounting system (p. 430)

financial statement (p. 436)

fixed assets (p. 438)

foreign currency exchange rate (p. 448)

forensic accountant (p. 433)

generally accepted accounting principles (GAAP) (p. 434)

goodwill (p. 438)

gross profit (gross margin) (p. 440)

income (profit-and-loss) statement (p. 439)

intangible assets (p. 438)

inventory turnover ratio (p. 447)

leverage (p. 446)

liability (p. 436)

liquidity (p. 437)

long-term liabilities (p. 438)

management consulting services (p. 434)

managerial (management) accounting (p. 431)

merchandise inventory (p. 438)

net income (net profit or net earnings) (p. 441)

operating expenses (p. 441)

operating income (p. 441)

owners' equity (p. 436)

paid-in capital (p. 439)

prepaid expenses (p. 438)

private accountant (p. 435)

profitability ratios (p. 445)

retained earnings (p. 439)

return on equity (p. 446)

return on sales (p. 446)

revenues (p. 440)

short-term solvency ratios (p. 445)

solvency ratios (p. 445)

statement of cash flows (p. 442)

QUESTIONS FOR ANALYSIS

1. Balance sheets and income statements are supposed to be objective assessments of the financial condition of a company. But the accounting scandals of the past few years show that certain pressures may be put on accountants as they audit a company's financial statements. Describe these pressures. To what extent do these pressures make the audit more subjective?

2. If you were planning to invest in a company, which of the three types of financial statements would you want most to see? Why?

3. A business hires a professional accountant like a CA or CGA to assess the financial condition of the company. Why would the business also employ a private accountant?

4. How does the double-entry system reduce the chances of mistakes or fraud in accounting?

5. Explain how financial ratios allow managers to monitor their own efficiency and effectiveness.

6. Explain the difference between financial and managerial accounting. In your answer, describe the different audiences for the two types of accounting and the various individuals who are involved in the process.

APPLICATION EXERCISES

1. Suppose that Inflatables Inc., makers of air mattresses for swimming pools, has the following transactions in one week:

   ■ sold three deluxe mattresses to Al Wett (paid cash $50, remaining $25 on credit) on 7/16

   ■ received cheque from Ima Flotein payment for mattresses bought on credit ($120) on 7/13

   ■ received new shipment of 200 mattresses from Airheads Mfg. (total cost $3000, paying 50 percent cash on delivery) on 7/17

   Construct a journal for Inflatables Inc.

2. Dasar Company reports the following data in its September 30, 2012 financial statements:

Gross sales $225 000

Current assets $50 000

Long-term assets $130 000

Current liabilities $33 000

Long-term liabilities $52 000

Net income $11 250

   a. Compute the owners' equity.

   b. Compute the current ratio.

   c. Compute the debt-to-equity ratio.

   d. Compute the return on sales.

   e. Compute the return on owners' equity.

3. Interview an accountant at a local manufacturing firm. Trace the process by which budgets are developed in

that company. How does the firm use budgets? How does budgeting help its managers plan business activities? How does budgeting help them control business activities? Give examples.

4. Interview the manager of a local retail or wholesale business about taking inventory. What is the firm's primary purpose in taking inventory? How often is it done?

BUILDING YOUR BUSINESS SKILLS

Putting the Buzz in Billing

The Purpose of the Assignment

To encourage students to think about the advantages and disadvantages of using an electronic system for handling accounts receivable and accounts payable.

Assignment

Step 1

Study Figure 14.5. The outside cycle depicts the seven steps involved in issuing paper bills to customers, payment of these bills by customers, and handling by banks of debits and credits for the two accounts. The inside cycle shows the same bill issuance and payment process handled electronically.

Step 2

As the chief financial officer of a provincial hydroelectric utility, you are analyzing the feasibility of switching from a paper to an electronic system of billing and bill payment. You decide to discuss the ramifications of the choice with three business associates (choose three classmates to take on these roles). Your discussion requires that you research electronic payment systems now being developed. Specifically, using online and library research, you must find out as much as you can about the electronic bill-paying systems being developed by Visa International, Intuit, IBM, and the Checkfree Corp. After you have researched this information, brainstorm the advantages and disadvantages of using an electronic bill-paying system in your company.

FIGURE 14.5

Managing operations and information.

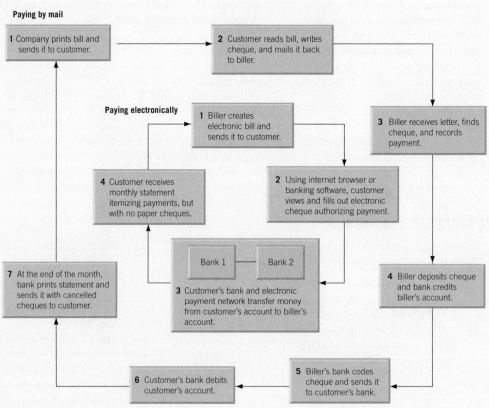

Questions for Discussion

1. What cost savings are inherent in the electronic system for both your company and its customers? In your answer, consider such costs as handling, postage, and paper.
2. What consequences would your decision to adopt an electronic system have on others with whom you do business, including manufacturers of cheque-sorting equipment, Canada Post, and banks?

3. Switching to an electronic bill-paying system would require a large capital expenditure for new computers and computer software. How could analyzing the company's income statement help you justify this expenditure?
4. How are consumers likely to respond to paying bills electronically? Are you likely to get a different response from individuals than you get from business customers?

EXERCISING YOUR ETHICS: TEAM EXERCISE

Confidentially Yours

The Situation

Accountants are often entrusted with private, sensitive information that should be used confidentially. In this exercise, you're encouraged to think about ethical considerations that might arise when an accountant's career choices come up against a professional obligation to maintain confidentiality.

The Dilemma

Assume that you're the head accountant in Turbatron, a large electronics firm that makes components for other manufacturing firms. Your responsibilities include preparing Turbatron's financial statements that are then audited for financial reporting to shareholders. In addition, you regularly prepare confidential budgets for internal use by managers responsible for planning departmental activities, including future investments in new assets. You've also worked with auditors and CA consultants who assess financial problems and suggest solutions.

Now let's suppose that you're approached by another company, Electrolast, one of the electronics industry's most successful firms, and offered a higher-level position. If you accept, your new job will include developing Electrolast's financial plans and serving on the strategic planning committee. Thus, you'd be involved not only in developing strategy but also in evaluating the competition, perhaps even using your knowledge of Turbatron's competitive strengths and weaknesses.

Your contractual commitments with Turbatron do not bar you from employment with other electronics firms.

Team Activity

Assemble a group of four to five students and assign each group member to one of the following roles:

- head accountant (leaving Turbatron)
- general manager of Turbatron
- shareholder of Turbatron
- customer of Turbatron
- general manager of Electrolast (if your team has five members)

Questions for Discussion

1. Before discussing the situation with your group, and from the perspective of your assigned role, are any ethical issues confronting the head accountant in this situation? If so, write them down.
2. Return to your group and reveal the ethical issues identified by each member. Were the issues the same among all roles or did differences in roles result in different issues?
3. Among the ethical issues that were identified, decide as a group which one is most important for the head accountant. Which is most important for Turbatron?
4. What does your group finally recommend be done to resolve the most important ethical issue(s)?
5. What steps do you think Turbatron might take in advance of such a situation to avoid any difficulties it now faces?

Go to MyBizLab for additional cases and exercise material.

CONCLUDING CASE 14-1

It's A Battle of Accounting Acronyms: The Merger of Three Canadian Accounting Groups

For many years, there have been three professional accounting groups in Canada: chartered accountants (CAs), certified management accountants (CMAs), and certified general accountants (CGAs).

In total, these three groups have about 215 000 members. On various occasions, there has been talk about merging the three groups into one since there has been some blurring of the differences among them over the years. For example, CAs used to be the only group that could perform audits on public companies, but now the other designations can often do that as well. In 2004, preliminary discussions about a merger took place between the CAs and CMAs, but members rejected the idea. In 2011, all three groups began seriously discussing the possibility of merging and creating a new designation called the chartered professional accountant (CPA). This acronym happens to be the same as the long-standing certified public accountant (CPA) designation in the United States. The CGAs initially resisted the merger discussions, but then agreed to take part once three of their own provincial groups became involved in such discussions. In 2012, Manitoba, Newfoundland and Labrador, Alberta, Saskatchewan, and British Columbia all released provincial merger proposals.

Supporters of the merger argue that there are several advantages. First, a merger would streamline the activities of the accounting profession and simplify its governance system. There are currently 36 separate provincial accounting bodies, and merging those into just one body in each province makes sense (in Quebec, the three groups have already agreed to merge). Kevin Dancey, the head of the Canadian Institute of Chartered Accountants, believes that "the current system makes for a pretty inefficient structure, particularly when the world is going global." Second, a merger should save millions of advertising dollars that the three separate groups now spend each year competing with each other. Third, a merger would provide a united voice for the Canadian accounting profession in an era of increasing foreign competition. For example, in 2012, the London-based Chartered Institute of Management Accountants (CIMA) and the U.S.-based American Institute of Certified Public Accountants (AICPA) launched a new joint venture, which yielded yet another new acronym: the chartered global management accountant (CGMA). Other competition is coming from Britain's Association of Chartered Certified Accountants (ACCA). There has been a long-running feud between the ACCA and Canada's CAs about use of the designation "CA," and this feud is seen as yet another argument for a merger of Canada's three accounting groups. A merger would also allow the Canadian accounting profession to speak with a united voice regarding the new

International Financial Accounting Standards (IFRS) that were adopted in Canada in 2011 (see Concluding Case 14-2).

Opponents of the merger argue that there are very different jobs within the accounting profession, and these different jobs require different training, designations, and experiences. Ricky Tsiu, a CA from Ontario, got 3600 signatures on an internet petition opposing the merger and asking for a binding vote on the issue. That number of signatures satisfied the rules of the Institute of Chartered Accountatns of Ontario (ICAO), but the ICAO refused to put the matter up for a vote, saying that not all the bylaw rules were followed. Opposition to the merger is evident among many CAs, who feel that their designation is "superior" to the others. But opposition is also evident among individuals in all three groups, who feel that the merger would not benefit them and would not accurately reflect the skills and level of professionalism of their current designation. Al Rosen, a Toronto-based forensic accountant, believes that the merger would create a powerful lobby group to pressure governments to lower accounting standards. He says that "the disadvantage is going to be that the one-size-fits-all shoe-store mentality will be there." Opponents also are concerned that if an account with a foreign designation behaves unethically, that person is not subject to the profession's domestic discipline procedures.

In May 2012, the merger idea suddenly looked less likely because the CGAs withdrew from the merger talks. This move followed the withdrawal of several provincial CGA groups that were concerned about member protection and minority rights.

Questions for Discussion

1. Outline the possible pros and cons of the proposed merger from the perspective of each of the Canadian accounting groups.
2. Supporters of the merger argue that it will result in marketing cost savings. Do you think there will actually be such savings? What other costs might be reduced (or increased) by the merger?
3. How might the proposed merger affect the differentiation that has historically existed in the Canadian accounting profession?

CONCLUDING CASE 14-2

International Accounting Standards

In 2011, public Canadian companies adopted the International Financial Reporting Standards (IFRS), which is a set of principles that guide accountants when they address various accounting issues. The IFRS—which is becoming the global standard for financial reporting—was created by the International Accounting Standards Board (IASB) in 2005 and has been adopted by 120 countries, including the European Union, Britain, and Australia. The purpose of the IFRS is to ensure that companies around the world operate under the same basic accounting system. The IFRS developers therefore had to create principles that were broad enough to be useful for companies operating in diverse economic, political, and cultural settings. Accounting firms and multinational companies say that IFRS will simplify accounting activities and make it easier for companies to raise funds in global financial markets.

But there are pros and cons regarding the shift from GAAP to IFRS. On the positive side, IFRS will improve comparability of financial statements worldwide, reduce the cost of sharing financial data globally, and help stakeholders make more efficient decisions. But there is a significant education cost for regulators, companies, and investors. As well, changes may come slowly without competing standards (the shift means that oversight of standards will reside in a single international body, the London-based IFRS Foundation).

The IFRS guidelines—which are more flexible than the Generally Accepted Accounting Principles (GAAP) that have been used for decades in Canada and the United States—allow managers more discretion when they are reporting financial information. For example, Canadian GAAP had strict rules about revenue recognition for goods and services, but IFRS guidelines are not as rigid. That flexibility has caused some forensic accountants to see potential problems with IFRS. Al Rosen, a Toronto-based forensic accountant, says that IFRS guidelines are a step back from Canadian GAAP because they will allow unethical managers to "massage" accounting information to make their companies look good. He calls it a "Ponzi scheme in progress," and argues that investors will be short-changed. Peter Martin, director of accounting standards at the Canadian Accounting Standards Board, does not see it that way. He says, "The long-term gain is that we're getting closer to the point where investors will be able to look at any financials, from anywhere in the world, and understand them and be able to make comparisons." Rosen disagrees, saying that loosening up standards does not improve compatibility because there are too many options available to companies using IFRS. There may be a lack of compatibility even within an industry, depending on how the different companies convert from valuing assets at book value (the GAAP approach) to valuing them at market value (the IFRS approach).

Many Canadian companies that have switched to IFRS have encountered a steep learning curve. At Toronto-based Stonegate Agricom, for example, many hours were spent getting financial statements ready using IFRS for the first time. Companies making the conversion have found that many different departments are impacted, including human resources, investor relations, and even IT. The mining industry has experienced several challenges. Ronald Gagel, chartered accountant and director at the Prospectors and Developers Association of Canada, says this: "With IFRS, there are certain areas with different possible interpretations, so the industry is looking towards standardizing practices across IFRS once we understand and work out all the wrinkles." In order to address these "wrinkles," the mining industry collaborated to work out the challenges that the IFRS posed. As part of the collaboration, companies developed separate documents for each significant issue the IFRS raised for the mining industry, and policies on how to address the issue. Kin Lo, an associate professor of accounting at the University of British Columbia, says, "There are certain requirements under IFRS that affect the dollar amounts mining companies need to report and that make record keeping more extensive. Mining firms that used the 'full cost' or aggregated method to account for exploration and development costs in multiple reserves now have to break down these numbers by individual reserve, based on the 'successful efforts' method under IFRS." The majority of Canada's mining industry has now converted to IFRS, but the switch is still a work in progress, and there are many detailed issues to consider.

While most public Canadian companies have embraced the new IFRS, some have expressed concern. Life insurance companies, for example, feel that IFRS will result in a distorted financial picture and will place Canadian life insurance companies at a competitive disadvantage compared to their U.S. rivals. David Tweedie, the chair of the International Accounting Standards Board of the IFRS, says that his group is aware of the problem and is looking for ways to alleviate it.

There has also been resistance to IFRS in the United States particularly from small companies. In February 2012, the SEC's chief accountant hinted that a middle ground was possible, where the Securities and Exchange Commission would recommend IFRS for U.S. companies, but the U.S. Financial Accounting Standards Board would retain the authority to assess future global rules and how they would be applied to U.S. companies. W. Anderson Bishop says that "U.S accounting rules are the gold standard; why would we want to lower our standards just to make the rest of the world happy?" When embracing the IFRS, companies did so in order to be able to be comparable to books around the globe, and as the United States denies these standards, comparability is threatened. Jack T. Ciesielski, head of The Analyst's Accounting Observer, says, "How global are such accounting standards anyway? With the U.S and the EU constituting 52 percent of global market capitalization, nearly half the world would be using a variation of IFRS." He believes the goal of the IFRS is unrealistic.

Questions for Discussion

1. Recognizing the benefits and costs of the IFRS on the international markets, how will this change affect provincial and national reporting standards?
2. What measures should be put in place to monitor and govern the use of the IFRS?
3. Given that some Canadian companies have embraced the new standards, what is the likelihood that others will reject it, as did the United States Securities and Exchange Commission? Do you anticipate there being options for customization standards based on company needs and business industries?

VIDEO CASE 3–1
Tickle Your Tummy Nut-Free Cookie Company

THE COMPANY

Tickle Your Tummy Nut-Free Cookie Company is an Aurora, Ontario–based company that sells all-natural, nut-free cookies made with whole ingredients. The company was established in 2003 by Jennifer Montoni, a single, stay-at-home mom with three children. Tickle Your Tummy has recently expanded its product offerings to include cupcakes, cakes, brownies, and oatmeal bars, all with a quality guarantee.

Montoni first saw the potential and market need for a nut-free cookie when one of her daughters was discovered to be allergic to peanuts and tree nuts. Mortoni then decided to create baked goods that tasted great and were safe to eat. With a limited amount of simple, quality, whole ingredients to work with, she made her first shortbread cookies with elaborate and fun designs and saw $20 000 worth of cookie sales in her first year of business. Now, her cookies are available for online purchasing and are also sold in specialty food stores across North America for $5.00/package. Sales revenue for Tickle Your Tummy Nut-Free Cookie Company was $800 000 in 2009 and the company has seen 50 to 100 percent growth per year.

The company's success is due mainly to Montoni's dedication to quality during the production of her cookies. Each step in the production process adheres to the highest quality standards of freshness. From using whole ingredients, to cutting, decorating, and packaging cookies individually, production and quality are always at the heart of it all with nut-free safety in mind. Personalized baked goods can also be ordered from the company and this contributes to the company's quality image.

THE PITCH

Montoni's desire to take her business to the next level led her to be a candidate on Dragon's Den, where she pitched her nut-free cookie business to the dragons. She asked for $300 000 in return for giving the dragons 30 percent of her company.

Montoni was hopeful that the investment would help her automate the company's current handmade cookie process, and thereby enable the company to continue its rapid growth and keep up with consumer demand. She also wanted to be able to pursue her goal to inspire others and become an allergy educator for parents through various marketing initiatives.

THE DRAGONS' POINT OF VIEW

Dragon Kevin O'Leary was skeptical of Montoni's claim that her company should be valued at $900 000. He said, "The cookie business is a low-growth business. You're making $70 000, worth $400 000, and you value your business at $900 000, and you are not worth that much."

O'Leary argued that the business was worth only about $450 000, and he wondered whether Montoni would still be motivated if he (O'Leary) invested $300 000 and therefore owned 66 percent of the business. Montoni stood her ground, saying that "there is a lot of speculation on how to value a business in the real world; you don't have the formula and neither do I, and my valuation is based on the fact that my company has seen growth from 50 to 100 percent per year."

The other dragons were impressed with the amount of cookies that were being sold each year and thought that Montoni was a great sales rep. In particular, Arlene Dickinson was impressed by the allergy educator idea as well as Montoni's credibility and knowledge.

THE OUTCOME

Once O'Leary finished debating her valuation of the business, the other dragons thought about their potential interest in the offer. One said, "You're generating $250 000 a year; if you took a smaller salary, your company would be larger in terms of the valuation that Mr. O'Leary is so worried about. I can take 50 percent of the business for $300 000."

Three of the dragons, including Arlene Dickinson, eventually decided to invest $100 000 each. They felt that Montoni had made a great presentation and had an inspiring story to tell. Robert Herjavec said, "I just don't know why she would sell that much of her business for $300 000 when she built it out of her basement." Dickinson responded by saying, "I know why: she's been on her own with three kids running a business and she is smart enough that she knows she needs people to help her along now, to help her with the next level, and she gets it."

Despite one dragon's reluctance because of the low growth rate in the cookie industry, Montoni was finally able to make a deal with three of the dragons. They are now partners, having invested $300 000 in total for a 50 percent ownership share in her company (remember that Montoni was originally offering just 30 percent ownership for $300 000).

The big lesson here is ownership and control. An entrepreneur must know when to relinquish control in order to be able to expand and grow the business.

Questions for Discussion

1. What is quality? What factors define quality for Montoni's products?
2. What lessons about valuing a business can you take away from this video?
3. What do you think of the market potential for this product? Do you think Tickle Your Tummy Nut-Free Cookie Company has a future? Explain your answer.

CBC THE NATIONAL: SELF-EMPLOYED

As a result of the latest recession felt by countries all over the world, the unemployment rate in many countries has risen to troublesome levels. In Canada, however, the unemployment rate in 2011 was at its lowest level in two years (7.4 percent). But this may simply mean that many people have given up looking for work and are therefore not counted as being unemployed. It is also possible that this reduced unemployment rate is the result of more Canadians starting their own businesses and being self-employed. For example, when Alex Hobcraft lost his job, he didn't look for another position; instead, he started his own business teaching guitar. As an entrepreneur, Hobcraft needs to find new clients, and he has been pretty successful at doing so (he now has more than 80 students). His business has grown to the point where he needs to employ other teachers and expand the type of lessons he offers to include piano, violin, vocal, and drums.

This type of entrepreneurial activity looks very positive to some people, but some economists are worried, and see this trend as evidence of a weak Canadian economy. Derek Burleton, economist at TD Bank, says that self-employed jobs are often less stable than other jobs and may not provide the benefits that traditional employment does.

While Canadian economists have expressed some concerns about Canada's current unemployment rate, it is still better than the rate in the U.S., where unemployment rose to 9 percent in 2011. Half the people out of work had been unemployed for a considerable period of time. "We are much better off than the Americans. … Today's numbers suggest that our labour market is still quite strong (and) the business confidence is high," says Burleton.

Even when unemployment is relatively high, there may still be many jobs that go unfilled. This happens for several reasons. First, many jobs that are available are located in geographical areas where unemployed people don't want to work, and they are not willing to move to those areas in order to get work. In Canada, for example, jobs in the far North may go unfilled because workers don't want to live there. Second, the high demand for jobs in certain areas (e.g., in Alberta's oil sands) causes housing shortages and workers simply cannot find a place to live. In the Bakken oil fields in North Dakota, the situation is so extreme that when a person inquires about a job, the first question they are asked is not "What are your qualifications?" but "Do you have a place to live?" Third, jobs often go unfilled because the unemployed people who are looking for work do not possess the specialized skills and training that are necessary to do the jobs that are available.

Questions for Discussion

1. What are the four basic types of unemployment? Which type is most pronounced during difficult economic times such as we have been experiencing during the last few years? Which type is most pronounced in periods of rapid technological change?

2. What are some alternative paths that people might choose when they lose their jobs?

3. What are some of the advantages of self-employment? What are the disadvantages?

4. Review current unemployment rates for Canada and two other countries of your choice. How does Canada compare? Why might differences exist? (Review the relevant material in Chapter 2 before answering this question.)

CRAFTING A BUSINESS PLAN
Part 3: Managing Operations and Information

Goal of the Exercise

This part of the business plan project asks you to think about your business in terms of operations, accounting concepts, and information technology (IT) needs and costs. (Review Chapter 13 for material on IT.)

EXERCISE BACKGROUND:

Part 3 of the Business Plan

An increasingly important part of a business plan is a consideration of how IT—computers, the internet, software, and so on—influences businesses. This part of the business plan asks you to assess how you will use technology to improve your business. Will you, for example, use a database to keep track of your customers? How will you protect your business from hackers and other IT security risks?

   This part of the business plan also asks you to consider the costs of doing business, such as salaries, rent, and utilities. You'll also be asked to complete the following financial statements:

■ *Balance sheet.* The balance sheet is a foundation for financial reporting. This report identifies the valued items of the business (its *assets*) as well as the debts that it owes (its *liabilities*). This information gives the owner and potential investors a "snapshot" view of the health of the business.

■ *Income statement* (or *profit-and-loss statement).* This is the focus of the financial plan. This document will show you what it takes to be profitable and successful as a business owner for your first year. You'll also be asked to consider various factors relating to operating your business.

YOUR ASSIGNMENT

Step 1

Open the saved *Business Plan* file you have been working on.

Step 2

For the purposes of this assignment, you will answer the following questions in "Part 3: Managing Operations and Information":

1. What kinds of IT resources will your business require?
   Hint: Think about the employees in your business and what they will need in order to do their jobs. What computer hardware and software will they need? Will your business need a network and an internet connection? What type of network? Refer to Chapter 13 for a discussion on IT resources you may want to consider.

2. How will you use IT to keep track of your customers and potential customers?
   Hint: Many businesses—even small businesses—use databases to keep track of their customers. Will your business require a database? What about other information systems? Refer to Chapter 13 for more information on these topics.

3. What are the *costs* of doing business? Equipment, supplies, salaries, rent, utilities, and insurance are just some of these expenses. Estimate what it will cost to do business for one year.
   Hint: The Business Plan Student Template provides a table for you to insert the costs associated with doing business. Note that these are just estimates—just try your best to include accurate costs for the expenses you think will be a part of doing business.

4. How much will you charge for your product? How many products do you believe you can sell in one year (or how many customers do you think your business can attract)? Multiply the price that you will charge by the number of products that you hope to sell or the amount you hope each customer will spend. This will give you an estimate of your *revenues* for one year.
   Hint: You will use the amounts you calculate in the costs and revenues questions in this part of the plan in the accounting statements, so be as realistic as you can.

5. Create a balance sheet and an income statement (profit-and-loss statement) for your business.
   Hint: You will have two options for creating these reports. The first option is to use the Microsoft Word versions that are found within the Business Plan Student Template itself. The second option is to use the specific Microsoft Excel templates created for each statement, which are found on the book's MyBusinessLab. These Excel files are handy to use because they already have the worksheet calculations preset—all you have to do is "plug in" the numbers and the calculations will be performed automatically for you. If you make adjustments to the different values in the Excel worksheets, you'll automatically see how changes to expenses—for example, how you can improve the "bottom line."

6. Create a floor plan of the business. What does it look like when you walk through the door?

   Hint: When sketching your floor plan, consider where equipment, supplies, and furniture will be located.

7. Explain what types of raw materials and supplies you will need to run your business. How will you produce your good or service? What equipment do you need? What hours will you operate?

   Hint: Refer to the discussion of operations in Chapter 11 for information to get you started.

8. What steps will you take to ensure that the quality of the product or service stays at a high level? Who will be responsible for maintaining quality standards?

   Hint: Refer to the discussion of quality improvement and TQM in Chapter 12 for information to get you started.

   Note: Once you have answered the questions, save your Word document. You'll be answering additional questions in later chapters.

Managing Marketing

What is the first thing you think of when you hear the names Coffee Crisp, Post-it, Crest, and Eno? If you grew up in Canada, you probably didn't hesitate at all before picturing candy, little slips of paper with one sticky edge, toothpaste, and something to calm your stomach. Your rapid association of company names and the goods or services they provide is a tribute to the effectiveness of the marketing managers of the firms that produce these goods. These and many other names have become household words because companies have developed the right products to meet customers' needs, have priced those products appropriately, have made prospective customers aware of the products' existence and qualities, and have made the products readily available.

Part Four, Managing Marketing, provides an overview of the many elements of marketing, including developing, pricing, promoting, and distributing various types of goods and services.

- We begin in **Chapter 15, Understanding Marketing Processes and Consumer Behaviour**, by examining the ways in which companies distinguish their products, determine customer needs, and otherwise address consumer buying preferences.

- Then, in **Chapter 16, Developing and Promoting Goods and Services**, we explore the development of different types of products, the effect of brand names and packaging, how promotion strategies help a firm meet its objectives, and the advantages and disadvantages of several promotional tools.

- Finally, in **Chapter 17, Pricing and Distributing Goods and Services**, we look at the strategies firms use to price their products. We also consider the various outlets business firms use to distribute their products, and we discuss the problems of storing goods and transporting them to distributors.

Understanding Marketing Processes and Consumer Behaviour

After reading this chapter, you should be able to:

1. Explain the concept of *marketing* and describe the five forces that constitute the *external marketing environment*.
2. Explain the purpose of a *marketing plan* and identify the four components of the *marketing mix*.
3. Explain *market segmentation* and show how it is used in *target marketing*.
4. Explain the purpose and value of *market research*.
5. Describe the key factors that influence the *consumer buying process*.
6. Discuss the three categories of *organizational markets* and explain how *organizational buying behaviour* differs from consumer buying behaviour.
7. Describe the *international* and *small business marketing mixes*.

lululemon: A Clear Marketing Strategy, Even in Trying Times

CHIP WILSON founded lululemon after taking a rejuvenating yoga class in 1998. After two decades in the ski, snowboard, and skate business, he made an abrupt change and built this yoga-inspired athletic gear retailer. The first outlet opened in Vancouver's Kitsilano area in 2000. By 2010, lululemon had well over 100 stores in Canada, the United States, Australia, and China with revenues of $453 million. At the time, CEO Christina Day was proudly pointing to a same-store sales increase of 29 percent over the previous year. She also indicated that these results reflected the strength of the brand and its mission to focus on quality, design, innovation, and unique positioning. Who could argue with her? Lululemon had carved a clearly identifiable niche and transformed people's buying behaviour while creating a lifestyle community.

Lululemon strives to be more than just a retailer. According to the company, the intent is to elevate the world from mediocrity to greatness. Strong words for a clothing retailer. Its mission is to create components for people to live longer, healthier, and more fun lives. To further distinguish itself, lululemon has developed a mantra, a manifesto, ambassadors, and a community hub to get the message out. Their values are a major stretch (no pun intended) from the tainted corporate image that defines so many firms these days.

From day one, Chip Wilson set out to provide superior products for his target consumer. It was clear to Chip that traditional sweatpants were totally unfit for the job, and an opportunity was identified. But he needed to educate consumers and offer better alternatives than the pure cotton clothing most people were wearing

in yoga studios. His previous experience in developing technical athletic fabrics led to the creation of a design studio that moonlighted as a yoga studio in the evenings. Experts were consulted; yoga instructors were given clothing and enlisted as product testers. The efforts paid off. Lululemon created a fabric called "luon," which is moisture wicking and preshrunk, has improved stretching ability, and maintains its shape. Today, lululemon makes products from Luxtreme, Coolmax, Silverscent, and Beechlu (to name a few); these fabrics are lighter weight and antibacterial.

Lululemon offers important services to supplement its goods and build its community. Every outlet offers weekly complimentary yoga classes. In addition, they offer running clinics, boot camps, and Pilates courses. Lululemon still consults yogis and elite athletes; a

continuous improvement approach is the foundation of its product development cycle. Even the brand name was developed in this manner. Before the original launch, it surveyed 100 individuals to select the name and logo from a list of 20 options. Clearly, lululemon is a firm by the people, for the people.

In terms of place or distribution, over 100 retail outlets are being supplemented by 25 new showrooms, in 2010 alone, in key locations like Florida, California, Texas, and Vancouver. These showrooms are not permanent but rather leased spaces that aim to test new market locations and create buzz. In 2009, the successful launch of lululemon's ecommerce site was another major step in improving distribution. At the same time, the expansion of its wholesale business, to more yoga studios and gyms, helped create stronger ties and increased selling avenues. Lululemon was also investing in its supply chain to ensure that popular products were kept in stock.

Lululemon uses virtually no traditional advertising, with the exception of strategically placed ads in highly targeted maga-

zines like *Yoga Journal*. The company benefited from buzz generated by the 2010 Vancouver Winter Olympic Games held in its hometown. Lululemon took advantage with two key stores located in high-traffic areas. Other promotional approaches are also being used. According to the CEO, a single email notification to clients about a new product can generate more than $6000 of sales. It has an ambassador program designed for loyal devotees who embody the lifestyle. You can go to the website and read about or get in touch with hundreds of ambassadors. In addition, there are approximately 60 "elite" ambassadors like Olympians Clara Hughes, Jennifer Heil, and Thomas Grandi. There are plenty of other ways to communicate with a yogi or fellow devotees; the website creates synergy with all modern communication tools, including basic blogging and the ever-popular social media sites Twitter, Facebook, and Flickr.

High-end quality is usually accompanied by high-end prices. Lululemon's products are expensive and the company is unapologetic;

the focus is on value, not price. Having a strategy is one thing, but sticking to it is something else. Many organizations overreact to current market circumstances and forget who they are. In the face of the most recent recession and price pressure from competitors, lululemon stood firm. Prices were kept high. Lululemon also has announced the testing of product lines including swimwear and other yoga products. "It's the right thing as a market leader to continue to innovate," says CEO Christine Day.

In the quarter ending January, 2012 the firm saw a net revenue increase of 51.4 percent, a clear indication that by continuing to look at the big picture and focusing on long-term strategy, growth will continue. According to a marketing study released by Interbrand in June 2012, lululemon was the fastest growing brand in that year. Lululemon embodies and displays the confidence that it tries to instil in its members. It will be interesting to see how this company evolves over the next decade. ◆

HOW WILL THIS HELP ME?

Marketing is a business activity that focuses on providing value to customers so they will want to purchase goods and services that companies offer for sale. If you understand the marketing methods and ideas that are presented in this chapter, you will benefit in two ways: (1) You'll be better prepared to enhance your career by using effective marketing ideas, both as an *employee* and as a *manager*; and (2) you'll be a more informed *consumer*, with greater awareness of how businesses use marketing to influence your purchases.

What Is Marketing?

LO1 Explain the concept of *marketing* and describe the five forces that constitute the *external marketing environment.*

marketing Planning and executing the development, pricing, promotion, and distribution of ideas, goods, and services to create exchanges that satisfy both buyers' and sellers' objectives.

What do you think of when you hear the word **marketing**? If you are like most people, you probably think of advertising for something like detergent or soft drinks. But marketing is more than just advertising. Marketing is the process of planning and executing the conception, pricing, promotion, and distribution of ideas, goods, and services to create exchanges that satisfy individual and organizational goals.

Because we are all consumers and because we all buy goods and services, we are influenced by the marketing activities of companies that want us to buy their products. But as consumers, we are in fact the essential ingredients in the marketing process. Every day, we express needs for such essentials as food, clothing, and shelter and wants for such non-essentials as entertainment and leisure activities. Our needs and wants are the forces that drive marketing.

marketing concept The idea that the whole firm is directed toward serving present and potential customers at a profit.

The **marketing concept** means that the whole firm is coordinated to achieve one goal—to serve its present and potential customers and to do so at a profit. This concept means that a firm must get to know what customers really want and follow closely the changes in tastes that occur. The various departments of the firm—marketing, production, finance, and human resources—must operate as a system, well coordinated and unified in the pursuit of a common goal—customer satisfaction.

We begin our study of marketing by looking at how marketing focuses on providing value and utility for consumers. We then explore the marketing environment and the development of marketing strategy. Finally, we focus on the four activities that compose the marketing mix: *developing, pricing, promoting,* and *placing products.*

Providing Value and Satisfaction

What attracts buyers to one product instead of another? While our desires for the many goods and services available to us may be unbounded, limited financial resources force most of us to be selective. Accordingly, consumers buy products that offer the best value when it comes to meeting their needs and wants.

Value and Benefits

value Relative comparison of a product's benefits vs. its costs.

Value compares a product's benefits with its costs. The benefits of a high-value product are much greater than its costs. Benefits include not only the functions of the product but also the emotional satisfactions associated with owning, experiencing, or possessing it. Every product has costs, including sales price, the expenditure of the buyer's time, and the emotional costs of making a purchase decision. The satisfied

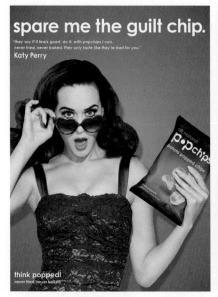  

Each of these advertisements provides information about a specific product, service, or idea. The bag of chips, for example, is a tangible consumer product. The advertisement for the fitness club promotes a service that can be enjoyed. The public service ad promotes the idea of healthy behaviour.

buyer perceives the benefits derived from the purchase to be greater than its costs. Thus the simple but important ratio for value:

$$\text{Value} = \frac{\text{Benefits}}{\text{Costs}}$$

Marketing strategies focus on increasing value for customers. Marketing resources are deployed to add value to products to satisfy customers' needs and wants. Satisfying customers may mean developing an entirely new product that performs better (provides greater benefits) than existing products. Or it may mean keeping a store open extra hours during a busy season (adding the benefit of greater shopping convenience). Some companies simply offer price reductions (the benefit of lower cost). Customers may also gain benefits from an informational promotion that explains how a product can be used in new ways.

Value and Utility

To understand how marketing creates value for customers, we need to know the kind of benefits that buyers get from a firm's goods or services. Products provide consumers with **utility**—the ability of a product to satisfy a human want or need. Marketing strives to provide four kinds of utility.

utility Ability of a product to satisfy a human want or need.

- When a company turns out ornaments in time for Christmas, it creates *time utility:* It makes products available when consumers want them.

- When a department store opens its annual Christmas department, it creates *place utility:* It makes products available where customers can conveniently purchase them.

- When the store sells ornaments, it provides *ownership utility* by conveniently transferring ownership from store to customer.

- By making products available in the first place—by turning raw materials into finished ornaments—the ornament maker creates *form utility*.

Marketing plays a role in all four areas—determining the timing, place, terms of sale, and product features that provide utility and add value for customers. Marketers, therefore, must begin with an understanding of customers' wants and needs. Their methods for creating utility are described in this and the following two chapters.

Goods, Services, and Ideas

The marketing of tangible goods is obvious in everyday life. You walk into a department store and are given a free scented paper strip as an initial product sample of a new perfume. A pharmaceutical company proclaims the virtues of its

---

E-BUSINESS + SOCIAL MEDIA SOLUTIONS

Apps, Apps, and More Apps: New Age Product Opportunities

The increased size and capabilities of devices like the iPad are opening up new opportunities for app developers. By 2012 the pace of development had accelerated and the number of Apple apps had already reached over half a million—and was growing quickly.

Apple transformed the music industry with its successful marketing of the iPod and the creation of iTunes, and recently with the launch of the iCloud music service. Within a few years, music executives went from opponents to allies with a growing reliance on Apple to propel the industry into the future. Unfortunately for them, Apple had other plans. With iPod sales projected to flatten, Apple turned its attention to its iPhone device and the huge potential of applications (apps). The iPhone's success is clear. In the fourth quarter of 2011 alone, Apple sold 21.5 million iPhone 4s devices, and new generation iPhones will keep revenues flowing for years. The launch of the iPad tablet back in 2010 provided a new and exciting outlet, but Apple also had a great opportunity on the content side. By 2012, Apple had already amassed over 5 000 000 apps to serve various client needs.

Most of you can list dozens, if not hundreds, of your favourite apps. The range is impressive. The "cigarette lighter" app is now a staple at music concerts. Dominos Pizza has an app that allows you to order pizza and have it delivered today or even a week from now. The "Shazam" app can help you download music or identify a song playing on the radio. There are sports scores, cooking tips, stock quotes, and much more. There were approximately 11 billion app downloads in 2010 and this number is projected to reach 185 billion in 2014. With over 1.2 billion apps downloaded in the last week of 2011 alone, these figures are sure to balloon.

How did Apple manage to develop so many apps so quickly? On the consumer side, people were excited by the touch screen and advanced graphics offered by the products. The gadget-loving tech generation had found a platform that fit their endless thirst for information and entertainment. It was a tool for increased social connectivity in an easily transportable format. How could this product be denied?

Apple has proven that it can identify, develop, and exploit opportunities, and it quickly seized this one. Apple created a generous profit-sharing plan that provides the developer with 70 percent of the revenue generated by its apps. This provides the profit incentive that has pushed individuals and firms to create new applications.

Who is taking advantage of this business opportunity? Like the Yukon Gold Rush of the 1890s, everyone and anyone with a dream is entering this market space. Ethan Nicolas developed a game called iShoot and quit his job after earning $37 000 in a single day. Over three million people downloaded the free version of his game and over 320 000 eventually bought an extended version at a cost of $3 each. Major gaming companies like EA Sports are providing content like NBA Live. Old technology companies, like Marvel Comics, are finding new ways to deliver their products with the help of the iPad's large, user-friendly format. Whether we are talking about individuals with a dream or organizations with problems to solve, there is a potential solution in the world of apps. Once again, Apple is leading the way.

Critical Thinking Questions

1. What are your favourite apps? List and explain what makes them effective and/or useful.

2. Form a group of three or four and come up with a new application that you believe would meet the needs of a particular target group. Explain.

new cold medicine. Your local auto dealer offers to sell you an automobile with no interest charges for four years. These products—the perfume, the cold medicine, and the car—are all **consumer goods**: products that you, the consumer, buy for personal use. Firms that sell products to consumers for personal consumption are engaged in consumer marketing.

Marketing is also important for **industrial goods**, which are products used by companies to produce other products. Surgical instruments and earth movers are industrial goods, as are such components and raw materials as integrated circuits, steel, and unformed plastic. Firms that sell products to other manufacturers are engaged in industrial marketing.

Marketing is also relevant for **services**—intangible products such as time, expertise, or some activity that you can purchase. Service marketing has become a major growth area in Canada. Insurance companies, airlines, investment counsellors, health clinics, and accountants all engage in service marketing. There are many *pure goods* (e.g., fishing reels, toothpaste, cameras, etc.) and many *pure services* (e.g., investment advice, life insurance, lawn care, etc.). But many consumer purchases involve elements of both goods and services. For example, when you eat lunch at The Olive Garden, you get a physical product (the food), but you also receive a service (the attention your waiter or waitress provides). The boxed insert entitled "Apps, Apps, and More Apps : New Age Product Opportunities" describes another popular service delivery format.

Finally, marketers also promote ideas. Television ads, for example, can remind us that teaching is an honourable profession, that drinking and driving is irresponsible, and that smoking is detrimental to our health.

consumer goods Products purchased by individuals for their personal use.

industrial goods Products purchased by companies to use directly or indirectly to produce other products.

services Intangible products, such as time, expertise, or an activity that can be purchased.

Relationship Marketing

Although marketing often focuses on single transactions for products, services, or ideas, marketers also take a longer-term perspective. Thus, **relationship marketing** emphasizes lasting relationships with customers and suppliers. Stronger relationships— including stronger economic and social ties—can result in greater long-term satisfaction and customer loyalty.[1]

Banks, for example, offer economic incentives to encourage longer-lasting relationships. Customers who purchase more of the bank's products (for example, chequing accounts, savings accounts, and loans) accumulate credits toward free or reduced-price services, such as unlimited monthly transactions. Motorcycle manufacturer Harley-Davidson offers social incentives through the Harley Owners Group (H.O.G.), which gives motorcyclists the opportunity to bond with other riders and to develop long-term friendships. For companies needing assistance and ideas, Loyalty Works designs and manages incentive and loyalty marketing programs. Their programs focus not only on building loyal customers but also on aligning channel partners and employees for an integrated approach to improving relationship marketing.

relationship marketing A type of marketing that emphasizes lasting relationships with customers and suppliers.

The Marketing Environment

Marketing plans, decisions, and strategies are not determined unilaterally by any business—not even by marketers as experienced and influential as Coca-Cola and Procter & Gamble. Rather, they are strongly influenced by powerful outside forces. As you can see in Figure 15.1, any marketing program must recognize the outside factors that compose a company's **external environment**. In this section, we will describe five of these environmental factors: the *political/legal*, *social/cultural*, *technological*, *economic*, and *competitive environments*.

external environment Outside factors that influence marketing programs by posing opportunities or threats.

FIGURE 15.1

The external marketing environment.

Political and Legal Environment

Political activities, both foreign and domestic, have profound effects on business (refer back to Chapter 1 for a discussion of how government influences business). Legislation on the use of cellphones in cars and legislation on pollution can determine the destinies of entire industries. Marketing managers therefore try to maintain favourable political/legal environments in several ways. For example, to gain public support for their products and activities, marketing uses advertising campaigns for public awareness on issues of local, regional, or national importance. They also lobby and contribute to political candidates (although there are legal restrictions on how much they can contribute). Such activities sometimes result in favourable laws and regulations and may even open up new international business opportunities. Shopper's Drug Mart, for example, was affected when the Government of Ontario changed the laws regarding the sale of generic drugs; this change negatively impacted its product offerings and sales.

Social and Cultural Environment

More people are working at home, more women are entering the workforce, the number of single-parent families is increasing, food preferences and physical activities reflect the growing concern for healthy lifestyles, and the growing recognition of cultural diversity continues. These and other issues reflect the values, beliefs, and ideas that form the fabric of Canadian society today. These broad attitudes toward issues have direct effects on business. Today, for example, as we continue to insist on a "greener" Canada, we have seen the demise of Freon in air conditioners and increased reliance on recycled materials in the goods that we consume.

Changing social values force companies to develop and promote new products for both individual consumers and industrial customers. For example, although most of us value privacy, web surfers are discovering that a loss of privacy is often a price for the convenience of internet shopping. Dot-com sites regularly collect personal information that they use for marketing purposes and that they often sell to other firms. Responding to the growing demand for better privacy protection, firms like iNetPrivacy offer such products as Anonymity 4 Proxy software, which allows you to surf the internet anonymously. Many companies have capitalized on the increasing demand for green products; for example, Canadian-based ECO-Products provides disposable dishes and cutlery for commercial and home use.

Technological Environment

New technologies affect marketing in several ways. Obviously, they create new goods (e.g., the iPad) and services (e.g., online shopping). New products make some existing products obsolete (for example, music downloads are replacing CDs), and many of them change our values and lifestyles. In turn, they often stimulate new goods and services not directly related to the new technology itself. Cellphones, for example, not only facilitate business communication but also free up time for recreation and leisure.

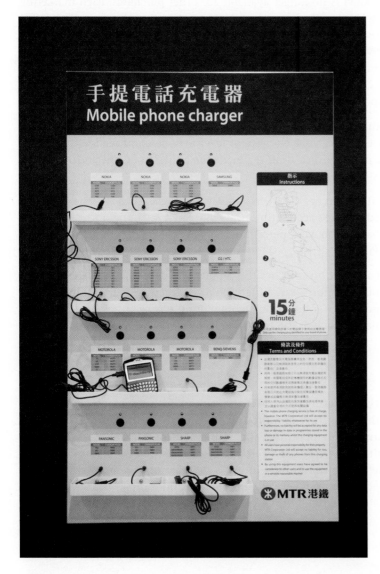

Marketing strategies are strongly influenced by powerful outside forces. For example, new technologies create new products, such as the Chinese mobile "filling station" kiosk shown here. Called shouji jiayouzhan in Chinese, these kiosks enable customers to recharge their mobile devices as they would refuel their cars.

Economic Environment

Economic conditions determine spending patterns by consumers, businesses, and governments. Thus they influence every marketer's plans for product offerings, pricing, and promotional strategies. Among the more significant economic variables, marketers are concerned with inflation, interest rates, recession, and recovery. In other words, they must monitor the general business cycle, which typically features a pattern of transition from periods of prosperity to recession to recovery (return to prosperity). Not surprisingly, consumer spending increases as consumer confidence in economic conditions grows during periods of prosperity. Conversely, spending decreases during low-growth periods, when unemployment rises and purchasing power declines.

Traditionally, analysis of economic conditions focused on the national economy and the government's policies for controlling or moderating it. Increasingly, however, as nations form more and more economic connections, the global economy is becoming more prominent in the thinking of marketers everywhere.[2]

Competitive Environment

In a competitive environment, marketers must convince buyers that they should purchase their products rather than those of some other seller. In a broad sense, because both consumers and commercial buyers have limited resources to spend, every dollar spent to buy one product is no longer available for other purchases. Each marketing program, therefore, seeks to make its product the most attractive; theoretically, a failed program loses the buyer's dollar forever (or at least until it is time for the next purchase decision). Competitive environments are everywhere in business and in all industries; for example, Apple versus PC or Canon versus Nikon

By studying the competition, marketers determine how best to position their own products for three specific types of competition:

substitute product A product that is dissimilar from those of competitors but that can fulfill the same need.

- **Substitute products** are dissimilar from those of competitors but can fulfill the same need. For example, your cholesterol level may be controlled with either a physical-fitness program or a drug regimen; the fitness program and the drugs compete as substitute products.

brand competition Competitive marketing that appeals to consumer perceptions of similar products.

- **Brand competition** occurs between similar products, such as the auditing services provided by large accounting firms like Ernst & Young and KPMG. The competition is based on buyers' perceptions of the benefits of products offered by particular companies.

international competition Competitive marketing of domestic against foreign products.

- **International competition** matches the products of domestic marketers against those of foreign competitors—say, a flight on Swiss International Air Lines vs. Air Canada. The intensity of international competition has been heightened by the formation of alliances such as the European Union and NAFTA.

LO2 Explain the purpose of a *marketing plan* and identify the four components of the *marketing mix*.

Strategy: The Marketing Mix

marketing managers Managers responsible for planning and implementing all the marketing-mix activities that result in the transfer of goods or services to customers.

As a business activity, marketing requires management. Although many individuals also contribute to the marketing of a product, a company's **marketing managers** are typically responsible for planning and implementing all the marketing-mix activities that result in the transfer of goods or services to its customers. These activities culminate in the **marketing plan**—a detailed and focused strategy for gearing marketing activities to meet consumer needs and wants. Marketing, therefore, begins when a company identifies a consumer need and develops a product to meet it.

marketing plan A detailed strategy for gearing the marketing mix to meet consumer needs and wants.

| *Product* choices determine basic design of the product offered to consumers. | + | *Price* choices determine how much consumers pay for the product. | + | *Promotion* choices determine the visibility and image of the product to consumers. | + | *Place* choices determine where and when the product is available to consumers. | = | CUSTOMER SATISFACTION and BUSINESS PROFITABILITY |

FIGURE 15.2

In planning and implementing strategies, marketing managers develop the four basic components (often called the "four Ps") of the **marketing mix** (see Figure 15.2). In this section, we briefly describe each of those components: *product, price, place,* and *promotion*.

marketing mix The combination of product, pricing, promotion, and distribution strategies used in marketing a product.

THE GREENING OF BUSINESS

Green Products and Services

During the past few years, more and more companies are responding to consumers' concerns about the environment by developing and marketing products and services that are environmentally friendly. Consider the following examples:

- In 2011, Quebec-based Cascades Inc. announced that it had developed a new technology that will make it possible to produce toilet paper from recycled paper that is as soft as toilet paper produced from new wood. Previously, toilet paper made from recycled paper had a rougher texture than toilet paper made from newly cut trees because the recycling process damages the wood fibres. Cascades's new product—called Enviro—is designed to compete with products like Charmin and Cottonelle Ultra.

- Ford Motor Co. has set a goal to make one-quarter of the vehicles it produces either electric or hybrid by 2013. The company is not just tinkering around the edges, but is investing $135 million to redesign its core models.

- PepsiCo introduced a new bottle in 2012 that is fully recyclable. It is made from switchgrass, corn husks, and pine bark; by-products left over the from the company's food business (for example, orange and potato peels) may also be used in the future. The new technology creates as molecular structure from these waste materials that is very similar to the petroleum-based plastic bottles that currently dominate the market. Coca-Cola—which introduced a plastic bottle in 2009 that was 30 percent plant-based—will also introduce a new bottle that is completely plant-based within a couple of years.

- Bridgestone, Goodyear, Michelin, and Pirelli have developed new tires that reduce fuel consumption (and therefore reduce exhaust emissions).

- Con-way Inc., a large trucking firm, has been involved in discovering new ways to increase the fuel efficiency of trucks and thereby reduce greenhouse gas emissions. The company joined with truck and engine manufacturers, transport firms, and scientists to develop regulations that are expected to save companies $50 billion in fuel costs, reduce oil consumption by 530 million barrels, and reduce greenhouse gas emissions by 270 million tonnes.

- Canadian National Railways knows that many of its customers are very conscious of their carbon footprint, so CN has made sustainability an integral part of its business. The company estimates that it can now move one tonne of freight 197 miles using only one litre of diesel fuel.

The emphasis on products and services that are environmentally friendly is welcomed by consumers who are concerned about the environment. But environmentally friendly products can be expensive. For example, electric cars like the Chevrolet Volt and Nissan Leaf produce far less air pollution than cars powered by the traditional internal combustion engine, but many consumers cannot afford these new products (the sticker price for the Volt is $41 545 and for the Leaf is $38 395). Even consumers who can afford these cars may not be willing to pay the price premium.

Critical Thinking Question

1. What other environmentally friendly products and services are you aware of from your own personal experience?

The importance of these four elements varies, depending on the product that is being sold. Price might play a large role in selling fresh meat but a smaller role in selling newspapers. Distribution might be crucial in marketing gasoline but not so important for lumber. Promotion is vital in toy marketing but of little consequence in marketing nails. The product is important in every case, but probably less so for toothpaste than for cars.

Product

product A good, service, or idea that satisfies buyers' needs and demands.

Marketing begins with a **product**—a good, a service, or an idea designed to fill a consumer need or want. Mass-customization (see Chapter 3) allows marketers to provide products that satisfy very specific needs of consumers. Conceiving and developing new products is a constant challenge for marketers, who must consider how changing technologies, consumer wants/needs, and economic conditions influence what products should be produced (the boxed insert entitled "Green Products and Services" describes one such change.)

product differentiation The creation of a product or product image that differs enough from existing products to attract consumers.

Producers often promote particular features of products to distinguish them in the marketplace. **Product differentiation** is the creation of a feature or image that makes a product differ enough from existing products to attract consumers. For example, Crest toothpaste has different products for different consumer needs. People looking for alternatives in a car might consider a hybrid; GM's EV1 used the slogan "A different driving experience," which appealed to early users looking for a unique driving technology that also helps the environment.

Price

price That part of the marketing mix concerned with choosing the appropriate price for a product to meet the firm's profit objectives and buyers' purchasing objectives.

Price refers not only to the actual amount of money that consumers must pay for a product or service but also to the total value of things that consumers are willing to give up in return for being able to have the benefits of the product or service. For example, if a person wants to own a new car, that person may have to take money out of a savings account to pay for the car. The value of the interest that would have been earned on the savings account is part of the value that the customer gives up to own the car. Car manufacturers are always looking for ways to attract consumers. For example, when BMW Canada sets prices for its 3 Series line of cars, it needs to consider the competition. Recently, the Acura TL was offering $3000 rebates and the Audi A4 was available at 2.9 percent financing.[3] Determining the best price at which to sell a product is a difficult balancing act. From a manufacturer's point of view, prices must support the organization's operating, administrative, research, and marketing costs. On the other hand, prices cannot be so high that consumers turn to competing products.

Both low- and high-price strategies can be effective, depending on the situation. For example, Canadian Tire maintained healthy sales in patio furniture and barbecues during the most recent recession by stocking more lower-priced items and scaling back more expensive items.[6] At the same time, de Grisogono was launching The Meccanico watch in style, by winning the Prix du Public at a prestigious competition in Geneva. The company proclaims that The Meccanico is the world's most complicated watch and it retails for about $200 000—roughly as much as a Ferrari. The company had expected to sell approximately 177 watches but had only managed to sell 35, with another 60 orders in place, in the first six months.[7] Low prices will generally lead to a larger volume of sales. High prices will usually limit the size of the market but will increase a firm's profits per unit. In some cases, however, high prices may actually attract customers by implying that the product is especially good or rare. We discuss pricing in more detail in Chapter 17.

Place (Distribution)

In the marketing mix, place refers to **distribution**. Placing a product in the proper outlet—say, a retail store—requires decisions about several activities, all of which are concerned with getting the product from the producer to the consumer. Decisions about warehousing and inventory control are distribution decisions, as are decisions about transportation options.

Firms must also make decisions about the channels through which they distribute products. Many manufacturers, for instance, sell goods to other companies that, in turn, distribute them to retailers. Others sell directly to major retailers such as Rona, Walmart, or Loblaws. Still others sell directly to final consumers. We explain distribution decisions further in Chapter 17.

distribution That part of the marketing mix concerned with getting products from the producer to the buyer, including physical transportation and choice of sales outlets.

Promotion

The most highly visible component of the marketing mix is **promotion**, which refers to techniques for communicating information about products. The most important promotional tools include advertising, personal selling, sales promotions, and public relations. One example of a promotional tactic used to entice consumers is the loyalty program. Shoppers Drug Mart has partnered with RBC Royal Bank to offer its customers a faster way to earn loyalty points—by opening a Shoppers Optimum Banking account. Customers will earn points each time they use their card at any store that accepts a debit card.[6] We describe promotional activities more fully in Chapter 16.

promotion Techniques for communicating information about products.

Product, price, place, and promotion focus on the seller's perspective. From the buyer's perspective, each of the four Ps provides a certain benefit. In effect, the seller's four Ps are a mirror image of the buyer's four Cs: customer solution (product), customer cost (price), customer convenience (place), and customer communication (promotion).[7]

Target Marketing and Market Segmentation

Marketing managers long ago recognized that they cannot be "all things to all people." People have different tastes, different interests, different goals, different lifestyles, and so on. The marketing concept's recognition of consumers' various needs and wants has led marketing managers to think in terms of target marketing. **Target markets** are groups of people with similar wants and needs.

Explain *market segmentation* and show how it is used in *target marketing*. **L03**

Target marketing clearly requires **market segmentation**, dividing a market into categories of customer types or "segments." For example, Mr. Big & Tall sells to men who are taller and heavier than average, while special interest magazines are oriented toward people with specific interests like fishing, cooking, and gardening (see Table 15.1). Once they have identified market segments, companies may adopt a variety of product strategies. Some firms decide to provide a range of products to the market in an attempt to market their products to more than one segment. For example, General Motors of Canada offers compact cars, vans, trucks, luxury cars, and SUVs with various features and prices. Its strategy is to provide an automobile for nearly every segment of the market.

target market Any group of people who have similar wants and needs and may be expected to show interest in the same product(s).

market segmentation Dividing a market into categories according to traits customers have in common.

TABLE 15.1 Magazines with Specific Target Audiences	
Accounting	**Fishing/Hunting**
CAmagazine	*Canadian Fly Fisher*
CGA Magazine	*Outdoor Canada*
CMA Management	*B.C. Outdoors Sport Fishing*
Agriculture	**Automotive**
Agro-Nouvelles	*Aftermarket Canada*
Meat & Poultry Magazine	*Bodyshop*
Country Life in B.C.	*World of Wheels*
Sports	**Boating**
Cycle Canada	*Boating Business*
Chalk and Cue	*Canadian Boating*
Athletics Canada	*Porthole Magazine*
Gardening	**Music**
Canadian Gardening	*CHART Magazine*
The Gardener for the Prairies	*CODA Magazine*
Gardening Life	*Opus*

In contrast, some businesses restrict production to one market segment. Rolls-Royce understands that only a relatively small number of people are willing to pay $310 000 for exclusive touring limousines. Rolls, therefore, makes no attempt to cover the entire range of possible products; instead, it markets to only a very small segment of the total automobile buyers market. In contrast, U.S. retailer Target has deals with Mossimo Giannulli and Isaac Mizrahi. Through these partnerships, says Target vice-president Trish Adams, "our guests have learned, and come to expect, that high fashion doesn't have to mean high prices." The key to luxury today lies in creating an emotional rapport between the consumer and the product.[10]

Table 15.2 shows how a marketer of home electronics equipment might segment the radio market. Note that segmentation is a strategy for analyzing consumers, not products. The analysis in Table 15.2, for example, identifies consumer users—joggers, commuters, and travellers. Only indirectly, then, does it focus on the uses of the product itself. In marketing, the process of fixing, adapting, and communicating the nature of the product itself is called positioning.

TABLE 15.2 Possible Segmentation of the Radio Market	
Segmentation	**Product/Target Market**
Age	Inexpensive, unbreakable, portable models for young children
	Inexpensive equipment—possibly portable—for teens
	Moderate-to-expensive equipment for adults
Consumer attitude	Sophisticated components for audio buffs
	All-in-one units in furniture cabinets for those concerned with room appearance
Product use	Miniature models for joggers and commuters
	"Boom box" portables for taking outdoors
	Car stereo systems for travelling
	Components and all-in-one units for home use
Location	Battery-powered models for use where electricity is unavailable
	AC current for North American users
	DC current for other users

Identifying Market Segments

The members of a market segment must share some common traits or behaviours that will affect their purchasing decisions. In identifying market segments, researchers look at geographic, demographic, psychographic, and product-use variables.

Geographic Variables

In some cases, where people live affects their buying decisions. The heavy rainfall in British Columbia prompts its inhabitants to purchase more umbrellas than does the climate in Arizona's desert. Urban residents have less demand for pickup trucks than do their rural counterparts. Sailboats sell better along both coasts than they do in the prairie provinces. **Geographic variables** are the geographical units, from countries to neighbourhoods, that may be considered in a segmentation strategy.

These patterns affect marketing decisions about what products to offer, at what price to sell them, how to promote them, and how to distribute them. For example, consider the marketing of down parkas in rural Saskatchewan. Demand will be high, price competition may be limited, local newspaper advertising may be very effective, and the best location may be one easily reached from several small towns.

Although the marketability of some products is geographically sensitive, others enjoy nearly universal acceptance. Coca-Cola, for example, gets more than 70 percent of its sales from markets outside the United States. It is the market leader in Great Britain, China, Germany, Japan, Brazil, and Spain. By contrast, Pepsi Co earns 78 percent of its income from the United States. Coke's chief competitor in most countries is not Pepsi but a local soft drink.

geographic variables Geographical units that may be considered in a segmentation strategy.

Demographic Variables

Demographic variables describe populations by identifying characteristics such as age, income, gender, ethnic background, marital status, race, religion, and social class. These are objective criteria that cannot be altered, so marketers must work with or around them. Table 15.3 lists some demographic market segments. Depending on the marketer's purpose, a segment can be a single classification (aged 20–34) or a combination of categories (aged 20–34, married with children, earning $25 000–$34 999). Foreign competitors, for example, are gaining market share in auto sales by appealing to young

demographic variables Characteristics of populations that may be considered in developing a segmentation strategy.

TABLE 15.3 Demographic Market Segmentation	
Age	Under 5; 5–11; 12–19; 20–34; 35–49; 50–64; 65+
Education	Grade school or less; some high school; graduated high school; some college or university; college diploma or university degree; advanced degree
Family life cycle	Young single; young married without children; young married with children; older married with children under 18; older married without children under 18; older single; other
Family size	1, 2–3, 4–5, 6+
Income	Under $9000; $9000–$14 999; $15 000–$25 000; over $25 000
Nationality	Including but not limited to African, Asian, British, Eastern European, French, German, Irish, Italian, Latin American, Middle Eastern, and Scandinavian
Race	Including but not limited to Asian, black, Inuit, and white
Religion	Including but not limited to Buddhist, Catholic, Hindu, Jewish, Muslim, and Protestant
Sex	Male, female
Language	Including but not limited to English, French, German, Inuktitut, Italian, and Ukrainian

buyers (under age 30) with limited incomes (under $30 000). While companies such as Hyundai, Kia, and Daewoo are winning entry-level customers with high-quality vehicles and generous warranties, Volkswagen targets under-35 buyers with its entertainment-styled VW Jetta.[10]

Demographic variables are important for companies in many different industries. For example, Campbell's Soup has discovered that Millennials are buying less soup than the population as a whole.[10] In 2011, Silicon Sisters Inc., Canada's first female-owned and -run video game studio, developed "School 26," a social mastery game for teen girls.[11] So-called "tweens" (kids aged 8 to 12) have "pester power" as they try to influence their parents to buy products like video games and cellphones.[12] And the Bank of Montreal has developed specialized products and services for the retirement needs of baby boomers, who represent approximately 40 percent of the working population.[13] The boxed insert entitled "Marketing to the Boomers" provides more information about the importance of baby boomer demographics.

multicultural marketing Marketing activities directed at various identifiable ethnic groups in Canada.

Canada's great ethnic diversity requires companies to pay close attention to ethnicity as a segmentation variable. Visible minorities in Canada control $76 billion in annual buying power, and to be effective in **multicultural marketing**, companies

MANAGING IN TURBULENT TIMES

Marketing to the Boomers

One of the important demographic variables that marketers must take into account is changes in the age distribution of the population of Canada, particularly the increasing proportion of older people. In 2011, for example, there were four million people in Canada aged 65 or over, an increase of 11.5 percent since 2001. The proportion of seniors in Canada is projected to double in the next 25 years as a result of increased life expectancy (currently 82.5 years for women and 77.7 years for men).

These numbers present both problems and opportunities. The *opportunities* include more sales of prescription drugs (because older people take more medications), more demand for financial services (because older people want advice on how to invest their pension earnings), and more demand for leisure activities like cruising (because older people have the time and money to travel). But companies have found that boomers aren't receptive to marketing that treats them as "old."

Opportunities also exist in terms of housing, where boomers have been the driving force for many years. When they were young, they demanded the traditional single-family residences, but when they retire they are more likely to demand a condominium (because they don't want the hassle of home maintenance) or assisted-living facilities (because of declining health). A study conducted by the Conference Board of Canada predicts that, by 2030, about 80 percent of new housing demand will come from seniors for condominiums or seniors' residences. Since there will be less demand for traditional homes, the price of those is likely to stagnate or decline.

But there are also *problems* with an aging population. A key one is the impact that an aging population will have on the stock market. When large numbers of baby boomers retire during the period 2015 to 2025, it will mean less investment in equity markets, and this could well mean relatively poor stock market performance. Here's the reason: Most people save the most money during middle age, but after that they save very little. These so-called "prime savers" increase demand for equity investments, and therefore drive up the price of stocks (other things being equal). The problem is that the ratio of prime savers to other consumers (seniors and younger adults) peaked in 2010. When the ratio peaked in Japan in the early 1990s, it started a two-decade long stagnation of the Japanese economy and the Japanese stock market. The same thing may happen in Canada. Boomers will likely "de-risk" their portfolios by selling stocks and buying bonds as they get older. Some analysts predict that there won't be any significant growth in the stock market until after 2025.

Things might not turn out so badly if Canadians retire later than expected (and thus have more money to invest), or if investors from developing countries (with larger proportions of younger people in their populations) make investments in Canada through sovereign wealth funds.

Critical Thinking Question

1. Develop a list of products and services for which demand will increase in the next two decades. Then develop a list of products and services for which demand will decrease. Defend your conclusions.

must understand the underlying values that ethnic minority customers hold.[14] These consumers can be precisely targeted using one of the 370 media outlets geared toward 87 ethnic groups in Canada. Ethnic TV stations include the Fairchild Network (Cantonese and Mandarin) and ATN (South Asian). There are 44 language groups represented in 228 publications ranging from Punjabi to Italian. There are 66 languages represented on 57 radio stations across the country, including CHIN in Toronto, CFMB in Montreal, and CJVB in Vancouver.[15]

Psychographic Variables

Members of a market can also be segmented according to such **psychographic variables** as lifestyle, opinions, interests, and attitudes. One company that is using psychographic variables to revive its brand is Burberry, whose plaid-lined gabardine raincoats have been a symbol of British tradition since 1856. After a recent downturn in sales, Burberry is repositioning itself as a global luxury brand, like Gucci and Louis Vuitton. The strategy calls for luring top-of-the-line, fashion-conscious customers. Burberry pictures today's luxury-product shopper as a world traveller who identifies with prestige fashion brands and monitors social and fashion trends in *Harper's Bazaar*.[16] Robert Polet, chief executive of the Gucci Group, agrees with this strategy. "We're not in the business of selling handbags. We are in the business of selling dreams."[17]

Psychographics are particularly important to marketers because, unlike demographics and geographics, they can sometimes be changed by marketing efforts. Many companies have succeeded in changing at least some consumers' opinions by running ads highlighting products that have been improved directly in response to consumer desires. For example, Las Vegas began courting the gay community a few years ago as part of a broader effort to target a range of audiences. Studies showed that the gay and lesbian travel market was among the most lucrative. According to research from Community Marketing Inc., a gay and lesbian market research company, gay and lesbian travel accounts for $55 billion of the overall U.S. travel market.[18]

> **psychographic variables** Psychological traits that a group has in common, including motives, attitudes, activities, interests, and opinions.

Product-Use Variables

The term **product-use variables** refers to the ways in which consumers use a product, the benefits they expect from it, their reasons for purchasing it, and their loyalty to it.[19] For example, a woman buying an athletic shoe may not care about its appearance but may care a great deal about arch support and traction in the sole. A woman buying a casual shoe will want it to look good and feel comfortable. A woman buying a dress shoe may require a specific colour or style and may even accept some discomfort. Speaking of shoes, when Nike—the leader in the $15.5 billion athletic footwear industry—found that women's footwear accounted for about one-third of industry sales but generated only about one-fifth of Nike's business, it changed its strategy and introduced a marketing campaign that focused on differences between the way men and women think about sports and the way they shop for clothing. According to Nike marketers, women are more interested in image trends and active lifestyles than in athletic competition and sports celebrities.

Whatever basis is used for segmenting a market, care must be taken to position the product correctly. A product's position refers to the important attributes that consumers use to assess the product. For example, a low-priced car like the Ford Focus tends to be positioned on the basis of economy, while a Porsche is positioned in terms of high performance. In Figure 15.3, the product positioning chart shows that Tim Hortons emphasizes a standardized product and provides fast service to people in a hurry, while Starbucks provides more customized products in more leisurely surroundings.

> **product-use variables** The ways in which consumers use a product, the benefits they expect from it, their reasons for purchasing it, and their loyalty to it.

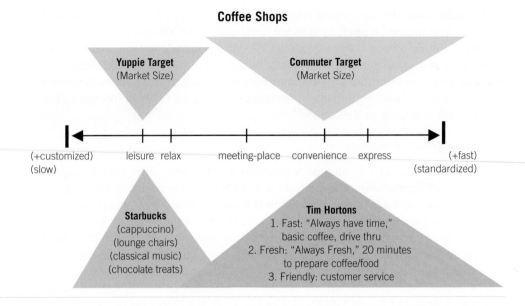

FIGURE 15.3

Product positioning.

Market Segmentation: A Caution

Segmentation must be done carefully. A group of people may share an age category, income level, or some other segmentation variable, but their spending habits may be quite different. Look at your friends in school. You may all be approximately the same age, but you have different needs and wants. Some of you may wear cashmere sweaters, while others wear sweatshirts. The same holds true for income. University professors and truck drivers frequently have about the same level of income. However, their spending patterns, values, tastes, and wants are generally quite different.

In Canada, the two dominant cultures—English and French—have historically shown significant differences in consumer attitudes and behaviour. Researchers have found, for example, that compared with English Canadians, French Canadians are more involved with home and family, attend ballet more often, travel less, eat more chocolate, and are less interested in convenience food. But this does not necessarily mean that companies must have different product offerings for Quebec. The adoption process for new products varies from one individual to another according to socio-economic and demographic characteristics.

Marketers are very interested in a person's system of values because values can have a big influence on an individual's tendency to adopt a new product. One study using business school students from France, Quebec, and the rest of North America identified three types of consumers: the conservatives, the dynamics, and the hedonists. The conservatives are typically those consumers who are least likely to adopt new products, while the hedonists (pleasure seekers) are categorized as innovators and are the most likely to adopt a new product. Those individuals in the dynamics category are somewhat likely to adopt new products, but are often seen as imitators.[19]

Market Research

L04 Explain the purpose and value of *market research*.

market research The systematic study of what buyers need and how best to meet those needs.

Market research—the study of what buyers need and how best to meet those needs—can address any element in the marketing mix. Business firms spend millions of dollars each year as they try to figure out their customers' habits and preferences. Market research can greatly improve the accuracy and effectiveness of market segmentation.[21] For example, LEGO decided to expand its market share by introducing a new line called "LEGO Friends" for "the other 50 percent of the world's children," and is aimed at girls aged five and older. The company's confidence is evident in the launch—a full line of 23 different products backed by a $40-million global marketing push. "This is the most significant strategic launch we've done in a decade," says LEGO Group Chief Executive Officer Jørgen Vig Knudstorp.[22]

The place of market research in the overall marketing process is shown in Figure 15.4. Ultimately, its role is to increase the firm's competitiveness by understanding the relationship among the firm's customers, its marketing variables, and its marketing decisions. Market researchers use a variety of methods to obtain, interpret, and use information about customers. They determine the kinds of information that are needed for decisions on marketing strategy, goal setting, and target-market selection. In doing so, they may conduct studies on how customers will respond to proposed changes in the current marketing mix. One researcher, for example, might study consumer response to a new kind of pizza (new product). Another might explore the response to a price reduction (new price) on SUVs. A third might check response to a proposed advertising campaign (new promotion). Marketers can also try to learn whether customers are more likely to purchase a given product in a specialty shop or online (new place).

Most companies will benefit from market research, but they need not do the research themselves. For example, using a new tool and a virtual store developed by Kimberly-Clark Corp., Safeway stores asked participants to walk through the "store" and shop for items. The shoppers were actually in a virtual store and were surrounded by three screens showing a typical store aisle. A retina-tracking device recorded their every glance. When Safeway tested the display inside its stores, sales of items in that section increased.[23] Recently, critics have expressed concerns about *neuromarketing*, which involves scanning people's brains to understand which stimuli they best respond to.[25]

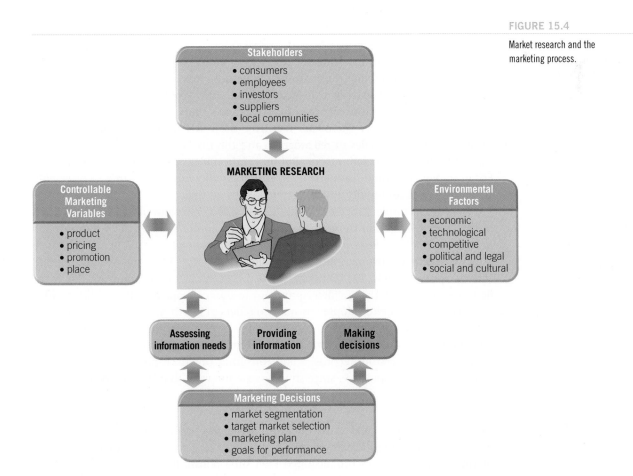

FIGURE 15.4

Market research and the marketing process.

The Research Process

Market research can occur at almost any point in a product's existence. Most commonly, however, it is used when a new or altered product is being considered. These are the five steps in performing market research:[25]

1. Study the current situation. What is the need and what is being done to meet it at this point?

2. Select a research method. In choosing a method, marketers must bear in mind the effectiveness and costs of different methods.

secondary data Information already available to market researchers as a result of previous research by the firm or other agencies.

primary data Information developed through new research by the firm or its agents.

3. Collect data. **Secondary data** is information already available as a result of previous research by the firm or other agencies. For example, Statistics Canada publishes a great deal of data that is useful for business firms. Using secondary data can save time, effort, and money. But in some cases secondary data are unavailable or inadequate, so **primary data**—new research by the firm or its agents—must be obtained. Hostess Frito-Lay, the maker of Doritos, spent a year studying how to best reach its target market—teenagers. The researchers hung around shopping malls, schools, and fast-food outlets to watch teens.[26]

4. Analyze the data. Data are not useful until they have been organized into information.

5. Prepare a report. This report should include a summary of the study's methodology and findings. It should also identify alternative solutions (where appropriate) and make recommendations for the appropriate course of action.

Research Methods

The four basic types of methods used by market researchers are *observation, surveys, focus groups*, and *experimentation*.

Observation

observation A market research technique involving viewing or otherwise monitoring consumer buying patterns.

Probably the oldest form of market research is simple **observation** of what is happening. It is also a popular research method because it is relatively low in cost, often drawing on data that must be collected for some other reason, such as reordering. In earlier times, when a store owner noticed that customers were buying red children's wagons, not green ones, the owner reordered more red wagons, the manufacturer's records showed high sales of red wagons, and the marketing department concluded that customers wanted red wagons. But observation is now much more sophisticated. For example, electronic scanners in supermarkets allow marketers to "observe" consumers' preferences rapidly and with tremendous accuracy.

Another example: Procter & Gamble sent video crews into about 80 households in the United Kingdom, Germany, and China to capture people's daily routines and product interaction. P&G uses this kind of information to develop new products to satisfy needs that consumers didn't even know they had.[27] Retail guru Paco Underhill collects approximately 50 000 hours of video every year for customers like Walmart, Best Buy, and Gap.[28] Using video equipment to observe consumer behaviour is called video mining. It is being adopted by many retailers in North America, who use hidden cameras to determine the percentage of shoppers who buy and the percentage who only browse. They do this by comparing the number of people taped with the number of transactions the store records. Some consumer organizations are raising privacy concerns about this practice, since shoppers are unaware that they are being taped.[29]

Surveys

survey A market research technique based on questioning a representative sample of consumers about purchasing attitudes and practices.

Sometimes marketers need to ask questions about new marketing ideas or about how well the firm is doing its marketing tasks. One way to get answers is by conducting a **survey**. When Sara Lee Corp. acquired Kiwi shoe polish, it surveyed 3500 people in eight countries about shoe care needs. It learned that people do not care as much about the shine on their shoes as they do about how fresh and comfortable they are on the inside. The firm has since unveiled several new products under the Kiwi name and is doing quite well.[30]

Because no firm can afford to survey everyone, marketers must be careful to get a representative group of respondents when they do surveys. They must also construct the survey questions so that they get honest answers that address the specific issue being researched. Surveys can be expensive to carry out and may vary widely in their accuracy.

In the past, surveys have been mailed to individuals for their completion, but online surveys are now gaining in popularity because the company gets immediate results and because the process is a less intrusive way of gathering data. At Hudson's Bay Co., customers can use online surveys to tell the company how happy or unhappy they are about the service they received at any of the Bay's department stores. The company can then make any changes that are needed to keep customers happy. The Bay used to hire mystery shoppers to find out how well it was serving the public, but that program ended when the online survey system was adopted.[31]

Focus Groups

Many firms also use **focus groups**, where six to 15 people are brought together to talk about a product or service. A moderator leads the group's discussion, and employees from the sponsoring company may observe the proceedings from behind a one-way mirror. The people in the focus group are not usually told which company is sponsoring the research. The comments of people in the focus group are taped, and then researchers go through the data looking for common themes.

focus group A market research technique involving a small group of people brought together and allowed to discuss selected issues in depth.

When Procter & Gamble was developing a new air freshener, it asked people in focus groups to describe their "desired scent experience." They discovered that people get used to a scent after about half an hour and no longer notice it. P&G used this information to develop Febreze Scentstories, which gives off one of five different scents every 30 minutes.[32] Focus groups at farm implement manufacturer John Deere have suggested many improvements in farm tractors, including different ways to change the oil filter and making the steps to the tractor cab wider.[33]

Consumers don't necessarily express their real feelings when participating in focus groups or when filling out surveys. This has led marketers to look at other ways of gathering information. Sensory Logic Inc., for example, studies facial expressions and eye movements to determine what consumers really think of a product.[34] Culinary Twist—a company that sells exotic sauces—interacts with shoppers who have app-enabled smartphones that allow them to give opinions about the store's products using QR (quick response) codes.[35] Developments like these are speeding up the information that a company gets from focus groups.[36]

Experimentation

The last major form of market research, **experimentation**, also tries to get answers to questions that surveys cannot address. As in science, experimentation in market research attempts to compare the responses of the same or similar individuals under different circumstances. For example, a firm trying to decide whether to include walnuts in a new candy bar probably would not learn much by asking people what they thought of the idea. But if it made some bars with nuts and some without and then asked people to try both, the responses could be very helpful.[37]

experimentation A market research technique in which the reactions of similar people are compared under different circumstances.

Data Warehousing and Data Mining

Almost everything you do leaves a trail of information about you. Your preferences in movie rentals, television viewing, internet sites, and groceries; the destinations of your phone calls, your credit-card charges, your financial status; personal information

Retailers such as Walmart rely on data warehousing and mining to keep shelves stocked with in-demand merchandise.

about age, gender, marital status, and even health—these are just some of the items in a huge cache of data that are stored about each of us. The collection, storage, and retrieval of such data in electronic files is called **data warehousing**. For marketing researchers, the data warehouse is a gold mine of clues about consumer behaviour.[38]

data warehousing Process of collecting, storing, and retrieving data in electronic form.

The Uses of Data Mining

data mining Application of electronic technologies for searching, sifting, and reorganizing data to collect marketing information and target products in the marketplace.

After collecting information, marketers use **data mining**—the application of electronic technologies for searching, sifting, and reorganizing pools of data—to uncover useful marketing information and to plan for new products that will appeal to target segments in the marketplace.[39] Using data mining, for example, the insurance company Farmers Group discovered that a sports car is not an exceptionally high insurance risk if it's not the only family car. The company thus issued more liberal policies on Corvettes and Porsches and so generated more revenue without significantly increasing payout claims. Among retailers, Walmart has long been a data-mining pioneer, maintaining perhaps the world's largest privately held data warehouse. Data include demographics, markdowns, returns, inventory, and other data for forecasting sales and the effects of marketing promotions.[40]

Understanding Consumer Behaviour

Market research in its many forms can be of great help to marketing managers in understanding how the common traits of a market segment affect consumers' purchasing decisions. Why do people buy certain products? What desire are they fulfilling? Is there a psychological or sociological explanation for why consumers purchase one product and not another? These questions and many others are addressed in the area of marketing known as **consumer behaviour**, which focuses on the decision process customers use when deciding what products to buy.

consumer behaviour The study of the process by which customers come to purchase and consume a product or service.

Influences on Consumer Behaviour

To understand consumer behaviour, marketers draw heavily on the fields of psychology and sociology. The result is a focus on four major influences on consumer behaviour: psychological, personal, social, and cultural. By identifying the four influences that are most active, marketers try to explain consumer choices and predict future purchasing behaviour.

- *Psychological influences* include an individual's motivations, perceptions, ability to learn, and attitudes.

- *Personal influences* include lifestyle, personality, economic status, and life-cycle stage.

- *Social influences* include family; opinion leaders (people whose opinions are sought by others); and reference groups such as friends, co-workers, and professional associates.

- *Cultural influences* include culture (the "way of living" that distinguishes one large group from another), subculture (smaller groups, such as ethnic groups, with shared values), and social class (the cultural ranking of groups according to criteria such as background, occupation, and income).

Although these factors can have a strong impact on a consumer's choices, their effect on actual purchases is sometimes weak or negligible. Some consumers, for example, regularly purchase certain products because they are satisfied with their performance. Such people are less subject to influence and stick with preferred brand names. On the other hand, as we saw in the opening case about lululemon, the clothes you wear often reflect social and psychological influences on your consuming behaviour.

The Consumer Buying Process

Researchers who have studied consumer behaviour have constructed models that help marketing managers understand how consumers come to purchase products. Figure 15.5 presents one such model. At the heart of this and similar models is an awareness of the psychosocial influences that lead to consumption. Ultimately, marketing managers use this information to develop marketing plans.

Describe the key factors that influence the *consumer buying process.* **LO5**

Problem/Need Recognition

The buying process begins when a consumer becomes aware of a problem or need. After strenuous exercise, you may recognize that you are thirsty and need refreshment. After the birth of twins, you may find your one-bedroom apartment too small for comfort. After standing in the rain to buy movie tickets, you may decide to buy

FIGURE 15.5

Consumer buying process.

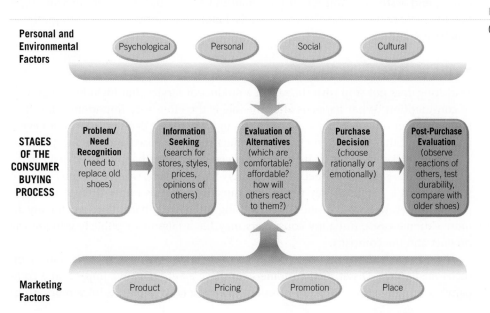

an umbrella. Need recognition also occurs when you have a chance to change your purchasing habits. For example, the income from your first job after graduation will allow you to purchase items that were too expensive when you were a student. You may also discover a need for professional clothing, apartment furnishings, and a car. Credit cards and credit issuing companies recognize this shift and market their credit cards to graduates.

Information Seeking

Having recognized a need, consumers seek information. But the search is not always extensive. If you are thirsty, you may ask where the vending machine is, but that may be the extent of your information search. Other times you simply rely on your memory for information. If you are thirsty after a workout, Gatorade probably comes to mind because of all the ads you've seen reminding you that it is great way to replenish lost fluids. Before making major purchases, most people seek information from personal sources, marketing sources, public sources, and experience. For example, if you move to a new city, you will want to find out who is the best local dentist, physician, hair stylist, or pizza maker. To get this information, you may check with personal sources such as acquaintances, co-workers, and relatives. Before buying an exercise bike, you may read the latest issue of *Consumer Reports*—a public source of consumer ratings—on such equipment. You may also ask market sources such as the sales clerk or rely on direct experience. For example, you might test ride the bike to learn more before you buy. The internet has become an important source of information, with 80 percent of Canadians relying on it to gather information.[41]

Evaluation of Alternatives

If you are in the market for a set of golf clubs, you probably have some idea of who produces clubs and how they differ. You may have accumulated some of this knowledge during the information-seeking stage and combined it with what you knew before. Based on product attributes such as colour, taste, price, prestige, quality, and service record, you will decide which product best meets your needs.

Purchase Decisions

rational motives Those reasons for purchasing a product that involve a logical evaluation of product attributes such as cost, quality, and usefulness.

emotional motives Those reasons for purchasing a product that involve non-objective factors.

Ultimately, you make a purchase decision. "Buy" decisions are based on rational and emotional motives. **Rational motives** involve a logical evaluation of a product's cost, quality, and usefulness. **Emotional motives** include fear, sociability, imitation of others, and aesthetics. You might buy mouthwash to avoid ostracism, or you might buy the same brand of jeans as your friends. Emotional motives can lead to irrational purchase decisions.

Post-Purchase Evaluations

word-of-mouth marketing (or buzz marketing) Opinions about the value of products, passed among consumers in informal discussions.

Marketing does not stop with the sale of a product or service, but includes the process of consumption. What happens after the sale is therefore very important. Marketers know that consumers do not want to go through a complex decision process for every purchase and that they often choose a product they have used and liked in the past. Therefore marketers are very motivated to keep consumers happy so they will make repeat purchases of the product. Unfortunately for marketers, when consumers are not satisfied with a purchase they typically complain to friends rather than to the company. This negative word-of-mouth advertising can be very harmful to a company. In more extreme cases, unhappy consumers may file a lawsuit or publicly criticize the product and the company.

People can complain about products or services at www.complaints.com or on social media sites. Dissatisfied customers can have a very negative impact on a company's marketing effort. **Word-of-mouth marketing** (also known as **buzz marketing**) is therefore a very powerful marketing tool. It can, however, be the most devastating, since businesses cannot control it.[42]

Companies need to be proactive to satisfy their consumers. After a very tough year full of embarrassing recalls, Toyota Canada began offering customers free maintenance for two years or 48 000 kilometres on select 2010 vehicles. This approach is often used by high-end auto manufacturers. This response could be effective for three reasons: (1) It allows Toyota to identify unsatisfied customers and fix their problems before they spread negative word of mouth, (2) it is relatively inexpensive—in essence, four oil changes, and (3) it ensures that customers will get into the habit of visiting the dealership, a behaviour that can be very lucrative after the two-year period expires.[43]

Organizational Marketing and Buying Behaviour

Buying behaviour is observable daily in the consumer market, where marketing activities, including buying and selling transactions, are visible to the public. Equally important, however, but far less visible, are organizational (or commercial) markets— organizations that buy goods and services to be used in creating and delivering consumer products. Marketing to these buyers involves different kinds of organizational markets and buying behaviours that are quite different from those found in consumer markets.

> **LO6**
> Discuss the three categories of *organizational markets* and explain how *organizational buying behaviour* differs from consumer buying behaviour.

Organizational Markets

Organizational or commercial markets fall into three categories: *industrial*, *reseller*, and *government/institutional markets*.

Industrial Market

The **industrial market** includes businesses that buy goods falling into one of two categories—goods to be converted into other products and goods that are used up during production. This market includes farmers, manufacturers, and some retailers. For example, Seth Thomas purchases electronics, metal components, and glass to make clocks for the consumer market. The company also buys office supplies, tools, and factory equipment—items never seen by clock buyers—to be used during production.

industrial market Businesses that buy goods to be converted into other products that will be sold to ultimate consumers.

Reseller Market

Before products reach consumers, they pass through a **reseller market** consisting of intermediaries, including wholesalers and retailers, who buy the finished goods and resell them (wholesalers and retailers are discussed in Chapter 17). Retailers like department stores, drugstores, and supermarkets buy clothing, appliances, foods, medicines, and other merchandise for resale to the consumer market. Retailers also buy such services as maintenance, housekeeping, and communications.

reseller market Intermediaries like wholesalers and retailers who buy finished products and resell them.

Government and Institutional Market

Federal, provincial, and municipal governments purchase millions of dollars worth of computer equipment, buildings, paper clips, and other items. The **institutional market** consists of non-governmental organizations, such as hospitals, places of worship, museums, and charitable organizations, which also compose a substantial market for goods and services. Like organizations in other commercial markets, these institutions use supplies and equipment, as well as legal, accounting, and transportation services.

institutional market Non-government organizations such as hospitals, places of worship, and schools.

Organizational Buying Behaviour

In some respects, industrial buying behaviour bears little resemblance to consumer buying practices. Differences include the buyers' purchasing skills and an emphasis on buyer–seller relationships.

Differences in Buyers

Unlike most consumers, organizational buyers are professional, specialized, and expert (or at least well-informed).

- As professionals, organizational buyers are trained in methods for negotiating purchase terms. Once buyer–seller agreements have been reached, buyers also arrange for formal contracts.

- As a rule, industrial buyers are company specialists in a line of items. As one of several buyers for a large bakery, for example, you may specialize in food ingredients. Another buyer may specialize in baking equipment (industrial ovens and mixers), while a third may buy office equipment and supplies.

- Industrial buyers are often experts about the products they buy. On a regular basis, organizational buyers study competing products and alternative suppliers by attending trade shows, by reading trade magazines, and by conducting technical discussions with sellers' representatives.

Differences in the Buyer–Seller Relationship

Consumer–seller relationships are often impersonal, short-lived, one-time interactions. In contrast, industrial situations often involve frequent and enduring buyer–seller relationships. The development of a long-term relationship provides each party with access to the technical strengths of the other as well as the security of knowing what future business to expect. Thus, a buyer and a supplier may form a design team to create products of benefit to both. Accordingly, industrial sellers emphasize personal selling by trained representatives who understand the needs of each customer.

The International Marketing Mix

LO7 Describe the *international* and *small business marketing mixes.*

Marketing products internationally means mounting a strategy to support global business operations. This is no easy task, since foreign customers may differ from domestic buyers in language, customs, business practices, and consumer behaviour. When companies decide to go global, marketers must consider how each element of the marketing mix might be affected.

International Products

Some products (e.g., Heineken and Coca-Cola) can be sold in many different countries with virtually no changes, but often only a redesigned (or completely different) product will meet the needs of foreign buyers. To sell its computers in Japan, for example, Apple had to develop a Japanese-language operating system.

Mattel, the maker of Barbie dolls, is just one company that has learned some interesting lessons about the international market. When it conducted focus groups with kids in dozens of countries, it found that worldwide demand existed for many of the same products. Mattel discovered, in essence, that children have similar tastes no matter where they live. Mattel's experience with its famous Barbie doll is illustrative. The dolls sold in Japan, for example, had always had black hair and Asian features, not the blonde, blue-eyed appearance of Barbie dolls sold in North America. This seemed to make intuitive sense, but now Mattel is finding that the original Barbie doll is selling just as well in Asia as in North America.

But there are still important differences between countries, and these cannot be ignored. For example, German children aren't attracted to action toys the way Canadian and American children are. There are also differences even within basic product lines. American kids, for example, want NASCAR toy cars, while European children want Formula One models.

International Pricing

When pricing for international markets, marketers must handle all the considerations of domestic pricing while also considering the higher costs of transporting and selling products abroad. Some products cost more overseas than in Canada because of the added costs of delivery. In contrast, products like jet airplanes are priced the same worldwide because delivery costs are incidental; the huge development and production costs are the major considerations regardless of customer location.

International Promotion

Some standard Canadian promotional techniques do not always succeed in other countries. In fact, many Europeans believe that a product must be inherently shoddy if a company does any hard-sell advertising. International marketers must also be aware that cultural differences can cause negative reactions to products that are advertised improperly. Since Europeans, for example, are offended by television commercials that show weapons or violence, Dutch commercials for toys do not feature the guns and combat scenes that are commonplace on Saturday morning television in North America. Meanwhile, cigarette commercials that are banned from Canadian and U.S. television are thriving in many Asian and European markets. Advertising practices are regulated accordingly. Quebec is the only province, and in fact the only jurisdiction in North America, in which commercial advertising to persons under 13 is generally prohibited.

Symbolism, too, is a sometimes surprising consideration. In France, for instance, yellow flowers suggest infidelity. In Mexico, they are signs of death—an association made in Brazil with the colour purple. Clearly, product promotions must be carefully matched to the customs and cultural values of each country.

International Distribution

In some industries, delays in starting new distribution networks can be costly. Therefore, companies with existing distribution systems often enjoy an advantage over new businesses. Several companies have gained advantages in time-based competition by buying existing businesses. Procter & Gamble, for example, saved three years of start-up time by buying Revlon's Max Factor and Betrix cosmetics, both of which are well established in foreign markets. P&G can thus immediately use these companies' distribution and marketing networks for selling its own brands in the United Kingdom, Germany, and Japan. On the other hand, Coca-Cola has been a major player on the international distribution scene for decades and it's a good thing. While sales have been sluggish in North America, the firm is benefiting from major growth in China and India. North American sales now account for only 18 percent of Coca-Cola's profits.[44]

Other companies contract with foreign firms or individuals to distribute and sell their products abroad. Foreign agents may perform personal selling and advertising, provide information about local markets, or serve as exporters' representatives. But having to manage interactions with foreign personnel complicates a marketing manager's responsibilities. In addition, packaging practices in Canada must sometimes be adapted to withstand the rigours of transport to foreign ports and storage under conditions that differ radically from domestic conditions.

Feathercraft is a small B.C. manufacturer that has been successful selling kayaks in the Japanese market.

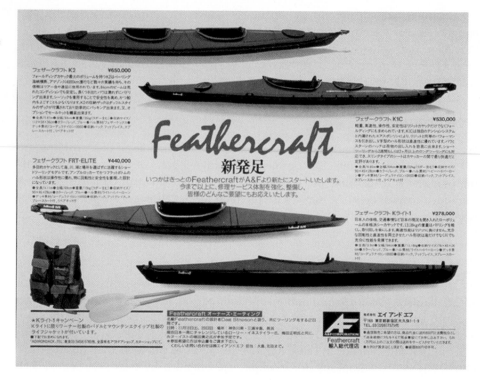

Small Business and the Marketing Mix

As we noted in Chapter 4, far more small businesses fail than succeed, yet many of today's largest firms were yesterday's small businesses. McDonald's began with one restaurant, a concept, and one individual (Ray Kroc) who had tremendous foresight. Behind the success of many small firms lies a skilful application of the marketing concept and careful consideration of each element in the marketing mix.

Small Business Products

Some new products—and firms—are doomed at the start simply because few consumers want or need what they have to offer. Too often, enthusiastic entrepreneurs introduce products that they and their friends like, but they fail to estimate realistic market potential. Other small businesses offer new products before they have clear pictures of their target segments and how to reach them. They try to be everything to everyone, and they end up serving no one well. In contrast, sound product planning has paid off for many small firms. "Keep it simple" is a familiar key to success—that is, fulfill a specific need and do it efficiently.

Small Business Pricing

Haphazard pricing that is often little more than guesswork can sink even a firm with a good product. Most often, small business pricing errors result from a failure to project operating expenses accurately. Owners of failing businesses have often been heard to utter statements like "I didn't realize how much it costs to run the business!" and "If I price the product high enough to cover my expenses, no one will buy it!" But when small businesses set prices by carefully assessing costs, many earn very satisfactory profits—sometimes enough to expand or diversify.

Small Business Promotion

Successful small businesses plan for promotional expenses as part of start-up costs. Some hold down costs by taking advantage of less expensive promotional methods. Local newspapers, for example, are sources of publicity when they publish articles about new or unique businesses. Other small businesses have succeeded by identifying themselves and their products with associated groups, organizations, and events. Thus a custom-crafts gallery might join with a local art league and local artists to organize public showings of their combined products.

Small Business Distribution

Problems in arranging distribution can make or break small businesses. Perhaps the most critical aspect of distribution is facility location, especially for new service businesses. The ability of many small businesses—retailers, veterinary clinics, and gourmet coffee shops—to attract and retain customers depends partly on the choice of location.

In distribution, as in other aspects of the marketing mix, however, smaller companies may have advantages over larger competitors, even in highly complex industries. They may be quicker, for example, in applying service technologies. Everex Systems Inc.

ENTREPRENEURSHIP AND NEW VENTURES

ModCloth: For the Love of Vintage

ModCloth is an online clothing and accessories store for all things retro and vintage. From shoes to home decor, ModCloth provides consumers with an array of indie trends and designs and one-of-a-kind items that its consumer base values. ModCloth has built its business with a passion for originality, and on empowering independent designers and suppliers around the world. ModCloth features the work of over 700 independent designers and ensures each artist full legal ownership and copyright of his or her designs.

With its non-traditional business model and a knack for style and anything vintage, ModCloth reaches its customer base through the internet and by word of mouth. From its first shop in co-founder Susan Gregg Koger's dorm room, to a growing business with over 275 employees, its marketing principles have remained the same: combining the power of personal communication and sharing with the tools of an online community.

Susan began her ModCloth adventure as a teen, spending countless hours at thrift stores shopping for items that were unique and expressed her personality. What she found rarely fit her, but with a needle and thread and a lot of imagination, she was able to make the needed alterations. Ultimately she decided to set up an online shop in her dorm room with co-founder (and eventually husband) Eric Koger.

In addition to word-of-mouth and its use of online communities, ModCloth's success is also due to its marketing efforts. Customer engagement is a powerful tool, and ModCloth has managed to create an engaging shopping atmosphere and social marketplace by running a fashion business in a democratic way. "Supplying [customers] with the opportunity to have their voices heard is what keeps our company fresh, relevant, and growing by leaps and bounds," says Koger. Such a marketplace is created by encouraging interactions among customers, designers, and suppliers through social media sites such as Twitter, Facebook, and the ModCloth blog. But it doesn't stop there. With ModCloth's "Be the Buyer" program, consumers are encouraged to act as members of the design team and vote on samples that they wish ModCloth would manufacture and sell. While shopping, customers also have the opportunity to get in touch with an online fashion consultant to get inspiration and share ideas. "We want to be the fashion company you're friends with," says Susan.

But she admits ModCloth's journey is just beginning. In a world of "designers know best," Susan wants to radically change the fashion industry, giving customers the loudest voice instead of having designers telling *them* what to wear.

"There's so much further to go," she says. "Our list of to-dos is a mile long. Stay tuned!"

Critical Thinking Questions

1. How would you describe ModCloth's segmentation strategy?
2. What elements of the four Ps apply to ModCloth's marketing strategy?
3. Using current marketing communication tools, how has ModCloth differentiated itself from its competitors?

sells personal computers to wholesalers and dealers through a system the company calls "Zero Response Time." Phone orders are reviewed every two hours so that the factory can adjust assembly to match demand.

MyBizLab

Capture more moments of true understanding. MyBizLab provides you with interactive study and practice tools directly related to this chapter's content. The new MyBizLab Study Plan Learning Path is designed to measure a full range of skills and provide remediation to give you what you need to master key chapter concepts. MyBizLab flexes to your unique learning needs. The result? Inspired learning, more success.

SUMMARY OF LEARNING OBJECTIVES

1. **Explain the concept of *marketing* and describe the five forces that constitute the *external marketing environment.*** *Marketing* is the process of planning and executing the conception, pricing, promotion, and distribution of ideas, goods, and services to create exchanges that satisfy individual and organizational goals. Products provide consumers with *utility*—the ability of a product to satisfy a human want or need. Marketing can be used to promote consumer and industrial goods and services, as well as ideas. The *external environment* consists of the outside forces that influence marketing strategy and decision making. The *political/legal environment* includes laws and regulations, both domestic and foreign, that may define or constrain business activities. The *social and cultural environment* is the context within which people's values, beliefs, and ideas affect marketing decisions. The *technological environment* includes the technological developments that affect existing and new products. The *economic environment* consists of the conditions—such as inflation, recession, and interest rates—that influence both consumer and organizational spending patterns. Finally, the *competitive environment* is the environment in which marketers must persuade buyers to purchase their product rather than that of their competitors.

2. **Explain the purpose of a *marketing plan* and identify the four components of the *marketing mix.*** Marketing managers plan and implement all the marketing activities that result in the transfer of products to customers. These activities culminate in the *marketing plan*—a detailed strategy for focusing the effort to meet consumer needs and wants. Marketing managers rely on the four Ps of marketing, or the *marketing mix:* (1) *Product:* Marketing begins with a product, a good, a service, or an idea designed to fill a consumer need or want. Product differentiation is the creation of a feature or image that makes a product differ from competitors. (2) *Pricing:* Pricing is the strategy of selecting the most appropriate price at which to sell a product. (3) *Place* (distribution): All distribution activities are concerned with getting a product from the producer to the consumer. (4) *Promotion:* Promotion refers to techniques for communicating information about products and includes advertising.

3. **Explain *market segmentation* and show how it is used in *target marketing.*** Marketers think in terms of *target markets*—groups of people who have similar wants and needs and who can be expected to show interest in the same products. Target marketing requires *market segmentation*—dividing a market into customer types or "segments." Four of the most important influences are (1) *geographic variables* (the geographical units that may be considered in developing a segmentation strategy), (2) *demographic variables* (population traits such as age, income, gender, ethnic background, marital status, race, religion, and social class), (3) *psychographic variables* (such as lifestyles, interests, and attitudes), and (4) *product-use variables* (the ways in which consumers use a product, the benefits they expect from it, their reasons for purchasing it, and their loyalty to it).

4. **Explain the purpose and value of *market research.*** *Market research* is the study of what buyers need and of the best ways to meet those needs. This process involves a study of the current situation, the selection of a research method, the collection of data, the analysis of data, and the preparation of a report that may include recommendations for action. The four most common research methods are *observation, surveys, focus groups,* and *experimentation.*

5. **Describe the key factors that influence the *consumer buying process.*** *Consumer behaviour* is the study of the process by which customers decide to purchase products. The result is a focus on four major influences on consumer behaviour: (1) *Psychological influences* include motivations, perceptions, ability to learn, and attitudes; (2) *personal influences* include lifestyle, personality, and economic status; (3) *social influences* include family, opinion leaders, and such reference groups as friends, co-workers, and professional associates; (4) *cultural influences* include culture, subculture, and social class. By identifying which influences are most active in certain circumstances, marketers try to explain consumer choices and predict future purchasing behaviour.

6. **Discuss the three categories of *organizational markets* and explain how *organizational buying behaviour* differs from *consumer buying behaviour.*** *Organizational (or commercial)* markets, in which organizations buy goods and services

to be used in creating and delivering consumer products, fall into three categories: (1) *The industrial market* consists of businesses that buy goods to be converted into other products or goods that are used during production. (2) Before products reach consumers, they pass through a *reseller market* consisting of intermediaries that buy finished goods and resell them. (3) The third category is *government and institutional markets.* Federal, provincial, and local governments buy durable and nondurable products. The institutional market consists of non-governmental buyers such as hospitals, places of worship, museums, and charities. Organizational buying behaviour differs from consumer buyer behaviour in two major ways: (1) *Differences in buyers:* Organizational buyers are professionals trained in arranging buyer–seller relationships and negotiating purchase terms. They are usually specialists in a line of items and are often experts about the products they are buying. (2) *Differences in the buyer–seller relationship:* Whereas consumer–seller relationships are often fleeting, one-time interactions, industrial situations often involve frequent, enduring buyer–seller relationships.

7. **Describe the** *international* **and** *small business marketing mixes.* When they decide to go global, marketers must reconsider each element of the marketing mix. (1) *International products:* Whereas some products can be sold abroad with virtually no changes, sometimes only a redesigned product will meet the needs of foreign buyers. (2) *International pricing:* When pricing for international markets, marketers must consider the higher costs of transporting and selling products abroad. (3) *International distribution:* In some industries, companies have gained advantages by buying businesses already established in foreign markets. (4) *International promotion:* Occasionally, a good ad campaign can be transported to another country virtually intact. Quite often, however, standard Canadian promotional tactics do not succeed in other countries.

Behind the success of many small firms lies an understanding of each element in the marketing mix. (1) *Small business products:* Understanding of what customers need and want has paid off for many small firms. (2) *Small business pricing:* Haphazard pricing can sink even a firm with a good product. Small business pricing errors usually result from failure to project operating expenses accurately. But when small businesses set prices by carefully assessing costs, many earn satisfactory profits. (3) *Small business distribution:* Perhaps the most critical aspect of distribution is facility location. The ability of many small businesses to attract and retain customers depends partly on the choice of location. (4) *Small business promotion:* Successful small businesses plan for promotional expenses as part of start-up costs. Some take advantage of less expensive promotional methods.

KEY TERMS

brand competition (p. 470)
consumer behaviour (p. 482)
consumer goods (p. 465)
data mining (p. 482)
data warehousing (p. 482)
demographic variables (p. 475)
distribution (p. 473)
emotional motives (p. 484)
experimentation (p. 481)
external environment (p. 467)
focus group (p. 481)
geographic variables (p. 474)
industrial goods (p. 465)
industrial market (p. 485)
institutional market (p. 485)

international competition (p. 470)
market research (p. 478)
market segmentation (p. 473)
marketing (p. 464)
marketing concept (p. 464)
marketing managers (p. 470)
marketing mix (p. 471)
marketing plan (p. 470)
multicultural marketing (p. 476)
observation (p. 480)
price (p. 472)
primary data (p. 480)
product (p. 470)
product differentiation (p. 472)
product-use variables (p. 477)

promotion (p. 473)
psychographic variables (p. 477)
rational motives (p. 484)
relationship marketing (p. 467)
reseller market (p. 485)
secondary data (p. 480)
services (p. 465)
substitute product (p. 470)
survey (p. 480)
target market (p. 473)
utility (p. 465)
value (p. 464)
word-of-mouth (buzz)
   marketing (p. 484)

QUESTIONS FOR ANALYSIS

1. Why and how is market segmentation used? Select an everyday product (books, CDs, skateboards, dog food, or shoes, for example) and explain how different versions of the product are aimed at different market segments.

2. Consider a service such as transportation, entertainment, or health care. What are some ways that more customer value might be added to this product? Why would your improvements add value for the buyer?

3. What is the value to consumers of loyalty cards and discount cards? Why would companies offer consumers such cards?

4. Why has the in-store use of hidden cameras become so popular? Is this "video mining" ethical? If not, how could it be made more acceptable?

5. If you were starting your own small business, what key marketing pitfalls would you try to avoid?

6. Select two products or services that you regularly use. Then explain the relative importance of each of the four elements in the marketing mix (product, price, promotion, and place) for each product. Are there differences in the relative emphasis placed on each element of the marketing mix? Why do you think these differences are evident?

APPLICATION EXERCISES

1. Interview the marketing manager of a local business. Identify the degree to which this person's job is focused on each element in the marketing mix.

2. Select a product made by a foreign company and sold in Canada. What is the product's target market? What is the basis on which the target market is segmented? Do you think that this basis is appropriate? How might another approach, if any, be beneficial? Why?

3. Interview someone who has recently purchased or is in the process of purchasing a car. Identify the actions the person took at each stage of the consumer buying process. Did the manufacturer help simplify the process? How? Is the consumer experiencing post-purchase regret?

4. Visit the websites of three major banks and identify how they help their clients gather information to ease the home-buying process (e.g., mortgage products and services).

BUILDING YOUR BUSINESS SKILLS

Dealing in Segments and Variables

The Purpose of the Assignment

To encourage students to analyze the ways in which various market segmentation variables affect business success.

The Situation

You and four partners are thinking of purchasing a heating and air conditioning (H/AC) dealership that specializes in residential applications priced between $2000 and $40 000. You are now in the process of deciding where that dealership should be. You are considering four locations: Miami, Florida; Toronto, Ontario; Vancouver, British Columbia; and Dallas, Texas.

Assignment

Step 1

Working with four classmates (your partnership group), do library research to learn how H/AC makers market their residential products. Check for articles in *The Globe and Mail*, *Canadian Business*, *The Wall Street Journal*, and other business publications.

Step 2

Continue your research. This time, focus on the specific marketing variables that define each prospective location. Check Statistics Canada data at your library and on the internet and contact local chambers of commerce (by phone and via the internet) to learn about the following factors for each location:

- geography
- demography (especially age, income, gender, family status, and social class)
- psychographic variables (lifestyles, interests, and attitudes)

Step 3

Meet with group members to analyze which location holds the greatest promise as a dealership site. Base your decision on your analysis of market segment variables and their effects on H/AC sales.

Questions for Discussion

1. Which location did you choose? Describe the market segmentation factors that influenced your decision.
2. Identify the two most important variables you believe will have the greatest impact on the dealership's success. Why are these factors so important?
3. Which factors were least important in your decision? Why?

4. When equipment manufacturers advertise residential H/AC products, they often show them in different climate situations (in winter, summer, or high-humidity conditions). Which market segments are these ads targeting? Describe these segments in terms of demographic and psychographic characteristics.

EXERCISING YOUR ETHICS: TEAM EXERCISE

A Big Push for Publicity

The Situation

Marsden Corp. is known as a "good citizen" and prides itself on the publicity it receives from sponsoring civic programs and other community projects. The company's executive vice-president, Jane Martin, has just been named chairperson of annual fundraising for the Coalition for Community Services (CCS), which is a group of community services organizations that depend on voluntary donations. In the highly visible chairperson's role, Martin has organized the support of officials at other firms to ensure that the fundraising target is met or surpassed.

The Dilemma

Martin began a meeting of 30 department managers to appeal for 100 percent employee participation in CCS giving in the fundraising drive. As follow-up the week before the drive officially started, she met with each manager, saying "I expect you to give your fair share and for you to ensure that all your employees do likewise. I don't care what it takes, just do it. Make it clear that employees will at least donate cash. Even better, get them to sign up for weekly payroll deductions to the CCS fund because it nets more money than one-time cash donations."

An hour after meeting with Martin, Nathan Smith was both surprised and confused. As a newly appointed department manager, he was unsure how to go about soliciting donations from his 25 subordinates. Remembering Martin's comment, "I don't care what it takes, just do it," Nathan wondered what to do if someone did not give. Personally, too, he was feeling uneasy. How much should he give? With his family's pressing financial needs, he would rather not give money to CCS. He began to wonder if his donation to CCS would affect his career at Marsden.

Team Activity

Assemble a group of four to five students and assign each group member to one of the following roles:

- Nathan Smith (employee)
- Jane Martin (employer)
- director of CCS (customer)
- Marsden stockholder (investor)
- Marsden CEO (use this role only if your group has five members)

Questions for Discussion

1. Before discussing the situation with your group, and from the perspective of your assigned role, do you think there are any ethical issues with Marsden's fundraising program? If so, write them down.
2. Before discussing the situation with your group, and from the perspective of your assigned role, are any problems likely to arise from Marsden's fundraising program? If so, write them down.
3. Together with your group, share the ethical issues you identified. Then share the potential problems you listed. Did the different roles you were assigned result in different ethical issues and problems?
4. For the various ethical issues that were identified, decide as a group which one is the most important for Marsden to resolve. Likewise, for potential problems that were identified, which is the most important one for Marsden?
5. From an ethical standpoint, what does your group recommend be done to resolve the most important ethical issue? How should the most important problem be resolved? Identify the advantages and drawbacks of your recommendations.

Go to MyBizLab for additional cases and exercise material.

CONCLUDING CASE 15-1

Target: Major Changes to the Canadian Market

Target, an American-based retailer, owns and operates more than 1700 stores in the United States and is the second-largest discount store in that country, following Walmart. Its product offerings include discounted clothing, accessories, housewares, and many other products. Its product portfolio, however, doesn't stop there: Target also offers a variety of "higher-end" products, tapping into more than one market segment. With the desire to expand its ability to reach multiple segments, an international move and expansion into the Canadian market was inevitable.

The first step was to take over the Zellers stores, which were owned by the Hudson's Bay Company, North America's oldest retailer. By taking over 220 Zellers leases (at a cost of $1.83 billion) Target will be able to speed up its debut in the Canadian retail market. The American retailer also plans to open 100–150 Target brand stores in Canada by 2014. These stores will be operated under the Zellers name for only a certain period of time before making the change over to the Target brand. This move is expected to yield good performance from the Canadian stores, which are similar to those in the United States. Target's revenues rose from US$65 billion in 2009 to US$69.87 billion in 2011.

As with any first entry into a market, Target had to consider several possible changes to their retail operations. New strategic moves are always challenging, especially during a weak economic period, and contingency plans are crucial. The U.S. market was hit hard by the 2008 recession, as shown by consumer spending habits. Total retail sales in the United States in 2008 were $295.65 billion, but had risen to $355.55 billion by 2011. Patty Edwards, chief investment officer of Trutina Financial, says, "I don't believe the U.S. consumer market is going to get that much better for a number of years. So you want to go where the money is, and frankly, the money's in Canada." Canada was less affected by the 2008 recession, and the value of the Canadian dollar has remained strong relative to that of the United States.

Collier International's 2011 Retail Report said that it "becomes increasingly worthwhile to sell in Canadian stores rather than to sell only to those Canadian customers who shop online or who make cross-border shopping trips." Target's chief executive, Gregg Steinhafel, says that "making the first move into Canada for Target's international expansion was a natural place to start, with 60 percent of Canadians previously being familiar with the Target brand and its logo." In addition to strong brand presence in the Canadian market prior to the opening of any location, Target Corporation also decided to capitalize on an existing Canadian retailer portfolio that was similar to its own. This expansion strategy allowed the retailer to not only avoid having to start from scratch in many instances, but also created a platform from which to market both Zellers and Target brands because they are similar in product offerings and positioning strategies. "The Zellers stores will provide a strong initial foundation for a more robust Target presence in Canada over time," says Steinhafel.

Existing competition is an important factor to consider before entering an international market. The takeover of the Zellers stores allowed Target to avoid further competition within the Canadian market, killing two birds with one stone. With Zellers under control, Target must turn its attention to industry leader Walmart, which made its move into Canada in 1994 and is now well entrenched with 323 stores. But Target is no stranger to the competition, and it embraces such natural market factors. Patty Edwards says that "while the Canadians love Walmart, they'll love Target even more, I think." With additional product offerings that include its REDcard Rewards program, as well as pursuing a credit card offering. Target actively seeks ways to not only be ahead of the competition, but also to successfully perform in an international market.

Questions for Discussion

1. What are the advantages and disadvantages of retaining the Zellers brand for a while before switching over to the Target brand?
2. To what extent does Target differ from Walmart in terms of market segmentation strategy?
3. What, if any, effect will the Target move into Canada have on cross-border shopping? Explain your answer.

CONCLUDING CASE 15-2

Why So Serious?

The five *Batman* movies released between 1989 and 2008 grossed more than $1.6 billion worldwide. It would be understandable, then, if the producers decided to skimp on the marketing budget for film number six. If ever a movie could be expected to market itself, it would be *The Dark Knight*. Instead, the producers teamed with 42 Entertainment, a California-based creator of alternate reality games, to immerse fans in one of the most elaborate viral marketing campaigns ever conceived. The fun began over a year before the movie opened, with the appearance of posters and a website "supporting" one of the film's characters, Harvey Dent, in his campaign to become district attorney of Gotham City. Visitors to the website quickly discovered a link to a similar site—www.whysoserious.com—that appeared to have been vandalized by the movie's main villain, the Joker.

The emergence of the Joker set in motion a series of games in which fans vied with one another to solve puzzles. The fastest fans received cellphones that let them access information that led them deeper into the puzzle. Meanwhile, the websites multiplied: fake newspapers with articles like "Batman Stops Mob Melee"; safety tips from the Gotham Police Department; even a link to Betty's House of Pies, a restaurant that plays a small but crucial role in the movie's plot.

The appeal of viral marketing, according to Jonathan Waite, owner of the Alternate Reality Gaming Network, is that "you're not a passive onlooker; you're taking an active role. And any time you take an active role, you're emotionally connecting." Or, as one blogger put it, "I've never been a fan of the Batman series, but this sort of thing makes me want to go see it."

The Dark Knight's innovative marketing campaign helped catapult the movie to a record-breaking box office debut, earning over $158 million in its opening weekend. Domestically and internationally, the film was a great success, earning more than $873 million worldwide. That was more than half the money earned by the previous five *Batman* movies combined. Was it the innovative marketing tactics or the captivating line-up of stars that contributed to the film's success? We may never know.

While it was not the first movie that has employed the use of viral marketing, *The Dark Knight*'s success with the tactic could arguably be seen as the launching point that has made it more commonplace, with studios continuously looking for new and unique ways to create consumer-generated "buzz" about their forthcoming movies. *Super 8*, released in 2011, made great use of viral marketing. Teaser trailers and other character-related material were slowly and steadily released for nearly a full year, through sources such as Twitter accounts and letters, before the movie hit theatres. *Inception*, released in 2010 and directed by Christopher Nolan, also the director of *The Dark Knight*, launched a viral marketing campaign that included an online game called "Mind Crime." With the sequel to *The Dark Knight*, *The Dark Knight Rises*, hitting theatres in the summer of 2012, viral marketing was again at the forefront of the movie's promotion efforts. Approximately six months before the movie's scheduled release, a "CIA Memo" presumably linked to a character was leaked online and was later followed by a website titled "Operation Early Bird," where a countdown to the release of an extended prologue was held. Viral marketing of movies has taken on a life of its own and there is now an online culture of people who enjoy and critique the campaigns as if they were movies themselves.

Questions for Discussion

1. What factors occurred in the external environment that allowed for the increase in use and success of viral marketing campaigns? Do any of these factors also pose related threats?

2. How do the decisions made by marketing managers about the marketing mix of the product (a movie like *The Dark Knight*) affect the implementation of a viral marketing campaign?

3. There are now online websites and forums that discuss, critique, and even hand out annual "awards" to viral campaigns independently of the movies that they advertise. What are the implications of this trend for the actual movies that the campaigns are meant to advertise?

4. Would viral marketing campaigns be as effective for repeat-purchase goods (for example, groceries), or are they most useful in building anticipation for future consumption of a product such as a movie? Can viral marketing be used to build relationships with customers?

Developing and Promoting Goods and Services

LEARNING OBJECTIVES

After reading this chapter, you should be able to:

1 Explain the definition of a product as a *value package*.

2 Describe the new product development process and trace the stages of the *product life cycle*.

3 Explain the importance of *branding*, *packaging*, and *labelling*.

4 Identify the important objectives of *promotion* and discuss the considerations in selecting a *promotional mix*.

5 Discuss the most important *advertising* strategies and describe the key *advertising media*.

6 Outline the tasks involved in *personal selling* and list the steps in the personal selling process.

7 Describe the various types of *sales promotions*, and distinguish between *publicity* and *public relations*.

8 Describe the development of international and small business *promotion* strategies.

New Product Development Strategies & the Importance of Brand Equity

WHAT'S in a brand name? When you choose between two items, how much of your decision is based on the brand's reputation and how much is based on the actual features? If you had to choose between two cars with identical features, how would the brand make the difference? As you will see below, you don't need to imagine this scenario. In order to reduce new product development costs, companies are using many techniques, including outsourcing and even partnerships with competing brands. This is especially true in the automobile sector, where development is long and costs are high. Recently, Toyota (which owns the Scion brand) and Subaru teamed up their engineering capabilities to create one new sports car and sell it under two different brand names: the Subaru BRZ and the Scion FRS.

Outsourcing

Outsourcing is a popular cost and time reduction technique in the auto sector; it involves farming out some or all of the development and manufacturing process to external companies. Magna International (headquartered in Aurora, Ontario) is a company that many manufacturers turn to for solutions. Magna was founded in 1957 but today has 288 manufacturing and 88 product development facilities in 26 countries. Here are just a few examples of Magna's product content solutions in the car industry:

- Dodge Caravan: door panels and transmission components
- Mercedes Benz M-Class: body structure stamping and assembly
- Lincoln MKZ: engine, underbody stamping and assembly
- BMW X3: full vehicle assembly, original engineering design

Direct Partnerships

Some companies have created joint ventures and built common manufacturing plants with competitors to assemble their vehicles (i.e., Suzuki and GM in Ontario; Toyota and Peugeot Citroen in the Czech Republic). In order to truly leverage strengths, some companies even make the ultimate commitment and merge (Renault-Nissan have had a positive union, while Daimler-Chrysler split up after a turbulent marriage). This latest "project" partnership between Subaru and Toyota (Scion)

enables these companies to share their expertise to build a better car. Scion is strong in design, geared for the Generation Y drivers, and Subaru is famous for its advanced technology and the symmetrical all-wheel drive system.

Brand Equity

Why do people pay premium prices for a Louis Vuitton purse or a Mercedes car? The material is top quality but we all know that the cost to manufacture does not fully justify the extra price. People are willing to pay extra for a brand logo, for the positive association, for the status granted, and for the image. In the case of Toyota and Subaru, the two cars are the same, so which one would you buy if you had the choice—the Subaru or the Scion? Most consumers will never know the truth about these cars, but you do. Your answer will be based on the brand you value more. There is no other rational basis for comparison in this case. However, if you did not know the truth, your perception of each brand might blur your opinions. One thing is clear: Both companies believed that they could produce a better product at a lower base cost by teaming up. In the end, the market will decide their fates. ◆

■■ HOW WILL THIS HELP ME?

By understanding the material in this chapter, you can benefit in three ways: (1) As an *employee* and as a *manager*, you'll be better able to use the concepts of developing and promoting products in your career; (2) as a *consumer*, you'll have a clearer picture of how the complex process of new product development and promotion leads to more consumer choice; and (3) as an *investor*, you'll be better prepared to evaluate a company's marketing program and its competitive potential before buying shares of the company's stock.

What Is a Product?

In developing the marketing mix for any product—whether ideas, goods, or services—marketers must consider what consumers really buy when they purchase products. Only then can they plan their strategies effectively. In this section we look first at product features and benefits, then explain the major classifications of products, and then discuss the product mix.

Explain the definition of a product as a *value package*. **L01**

Product Features and Benefits

Product **features** are the qualities—tangible and intangible—that a company builds into its products. Products are much more than just visible features. In buying a product, consumers are also buying an image and a reputation. For example, Gibson

features Qualities—tangible and intangible—that a company builds into its products.

Guitars sells more than just the sum of the features for its legendary Les Paul guitars (mahogany headstock and neck, nickel and silver frets, rosewood fingerboard, solid mahogany back and body, and a maple top); it also sells a powerful package that is linked to the very history of rock and roll. Some of the greatest legends of music have used this guitar, including Jimmy Page of Led Zeppelin.

Consumers ultimately purchase based on the benefits that are provided by those features. In the case of Gibson's Les Paul guitars, it is not simply the maple top or the fact that the Gibson carefully glues the necks of the guitars onto the main bodies (a more expensive, time-consuming process compared to simply bolting them on, as most other makers do). It is also the results and ultimate benefits that guitar enthusiasts seek; Gibson believes this approach leads to a warmer tone and a more resonant sound. According to Jimmy Vivino, the bandleader of the *Conan* show, "The mahogany-necked Gibson creates a lingering sound, with more 'fur' around the notes, and this is the sound I want."[1]

value package Product marketed as a bundle of value-adding attributes, including reasonable cost.

Today's consumers regard a product as a bundle of attributes, which, taken together, marketers call the **value package**. Increasingly, buyers expect to receive products with greater value—with more benefits at reasonable costs. For example, the possible attributes of a personal computer value package include choices of colour, attractive software packages, fast online ordering, speedy delivery, and social media connectivity. Although the products includes physical features, like processing devices and other hardware, most items in the value package are services or intangibles that, collectively, add value by providing benefits that increase the customer's satisfaction. The intangibles for Apple's computers and tablets have actually helped the company gain market share, although the products sell for a premium price. Apple tells consumers, "If you want our excellent value package, pay for it." And, judging from the line-ups for most of its product launches, consumers are voting in favour of this approach. This may change in the future for Apple, but for now the masses are running to pay more for what they *perceive* to be better quality.

Classifying Goods and Services

Buyers fall into two basic groups: consumer and industrial. Marketing products and services to consumers is vastly different from marketing them to companies.

Gibson's Les Paul guitars have been used by some of the most famous guitarists in rock and roll history. Jimmy Page of Led Zeppelin and Slash from Guns N' Roses are two iconic music figures who have enhanced the legend of this guitar.

Classifying Consumer Products

Consumer products are commonly divided into three categories that reflect buyers' behaviour: convenience, shopping, and specialty products.

- **Convenience goods** (such as milk and newspapers) and **convenience services** (such as those offered by fast-food restaurants) are consumed rapidly and regularly. They are relatively inexpensive and are purchased frequently and with little expenditure of time and effort.

- **Shopping goods** (such as HDTVs and tires) and **shopping services** (such as insurance) are more expensive and are purchased less frequently than convenience goods and services. Consumers often compare brands, sometimes in different stores. They may also evaluate alternatives in terms of style, performance, colour, price, and other criteria.

- **Specialty goods** (such as wedding gowns) and **specialty services** (such as catering for wedding receptions) are extremely important and expensive purchases. Consumers usually have strong preferences, will accept no substitutes, and will often spend a great deal of time and money to get a specific product or service.

convenience goods/services Relatively inexpensive consumer goods or services that are bought and used rapidly and regularly, causing consumers to spend little time looking for them or comparing their prices.

shopping goods/services Moderately expensive consumer goods or services that are purchased infrequently, causing consumers to spend some time comparing their prices.

specialty goods/services Very expensive consumer goods or services that are purchased rarely, causing consumers to spend a great deal of time locating the exact item desired.

Classifying Industrial Products

Industrial products are usually divided into two categories, based on how much they cost and how they will be used.

- **Expense items** are materials and services that are consumed within a year by firms producing other goods or services. The most obvious expense items are industrial goods used directly in the production process—for example, bulk loads of tea processed into tea bags.

- **Capital items** are permanent—that is, expensive and long-lasting—goods and services. All these items have expected lives of more than a year. Buildings (offices, factories), fixed equipment (water towers, baking ovens), and accessory equipment (computers, airplanes) are capital goods. **Capital services** are those for which long-term commitments are made. These may include purchases for employee food services, building and equipment maintenance, or legal services.

expense items Relatively inexpensive industrial goods that are consumed rapidly and regularly.

capital items Expensive, long-lasting industrial goods that are used in producing other goods or services and have a long life.

capital services Services for which long-term commitments are made.

Black & Decker has a wide range of product categories, but one fairly recent category has proven to be quite successful. The company now sells branded toy replicas to kids so that they can catch the do-it-yourself bug at a young age.

The Product Mix

product mix The group of products a company has available for sale.

The group of consumer or industrial products a company has available for sale is known as the firm's **product mix**. For example, Black & Decker's website is split up into the following categories: appliances, hand tools, lawn and garden, power tools, cleaning products, home and office, painting and crafts, automotive, portable lighting, storage, and protective equipment. In addition, Black & Decker has added a toys category to the mix; it's never too early to get new customers involved with the brand.[2] Bob the Builder needs tools, so why not get all his disciples to buy a Black & Decker workbench?

Product Lines

product line A group of similar products intended for a similar group of buyers who will use them in a similar fashion.

A **product line** is a group of products that are closely related because they function in a similar manner or are sold to the same customer group, who will use them in similar ways. Many companies that begin with a single product find that, over time, the initial product fails to suit every consumer shopping for the product type. To meet market demand, they introduce similar products designed to reach more customers. For example, ServiceMaster originally offered mothproofing and carpet cleaning, then subsequently expanded into other closely related services for homeowners—lawn care (TruGreen, ChemLawn), pest control (Terminix), and cleaning (Merry Maids).

Companies may also introduce multiple product lines that go well beyond their existing product line. After years of serving residential customers, ServiceMaster added business and industry services (landscaping and janitorial), education services (management of schools and institutions, including physical facilities and financial and personnel resources), and health-care services (management of support services like plant operations, asset management, and laundry/linen supply for long-term care facilities).

Developing New Products

L02 Describe the new product development process and trace the stages of the *product life cycle*.

All products and services—including once-popular TV shows like *Lost* and *One Tree Hill*—eventually fall out of favour with consumers. Firms must therefore develop and introduce new products. Levi's jeans, for example, was once one of Canada's most popular brands, but the company failed to keep pace with changing tastes and lost market share. Nintendo is hoping to avoid that fate. The launch of the Nintendo Wii was a smashing success a few years back and restored the brand to prominence. However, at the beginning of 2012 Nintendo announced losses of US$838 million, its worst loss in three decades. What was the problem? Consumers have been turning to social games and inexpensive apps like Angry Birds rather than traditional consoles. The president of Nintendo, Mr. Satoru Iwata, was counting heavily on the success of the Wii U, which was scheduled to be launched at the end of 2012.[3]

While new product development is critical, it is also very risky. Take a look at some recent and some classic product failures in Figure 16.1.

The Time Frame of New Product Development

Companies often face multi-year time horizons and high risks when developing new products. The Tesla roadster was officially approved for sale in Canada in 2010. What is it? It's an electric roadster that costs $125 000 and can go from zero to 60 mph in 3.7 seconds. Unfortunately, profits are not accelerating that quickly. Tesla sold slightly fewer than 1200 cars worldwide from 2008 to 2012. At the beginning of 2010, the company was trying to raise $100 million in an initial public offering, but it is clear that this is a long-term investment. In a statement, Tesla indicated that it does not

Famous Product and Brand Failures	Reasons for Failure
 Qwikster	Is this the biggest product failure since New Coke? When Netflix announced that it was splitting its online streaming and DVD mail service, consumers were outraged. The DVD-by-mail service was going to be called Qwikster, but the outrage over the loss of convenience and increased prices led to the loss of about 800 000 customers. Netflix ultimately reversed the decision and killed the Qwikster brand.
Pepsi Blue	Despite a good marketing campaign linked to hip-hop artists, the X-games, and the March Madness Basketball tournament, Pepsi Blue was a failure. The ultimate test for any product is consumer response; Pepsi's blue cola did not taste or look right and consumers rejected it.
 Toshiba's HD DVD	Consider the battle between Toshiba (HD DVD) and Sony (Blu-ray) for global dominance in the format of high-definition DVDs. Both companies invested millions of dollars, and experts predicted that there would be a long fight between the two companies. But in less than two years, Toshiba gave up and stopped producing its product. Why? Because Sony was successful in convincing movie studios like Warner to release movies only in Blu-ray. Major retail outlets like Walmart and Netflix also announced they would only sell Blu-ray.[4]
New Coke	This example dates back over 25 years but teaches a big lesson in marketing research. At the time, Coke reformulated its century-old flagship brand to deal with the threat of Pepsi. The new beverage tested well in research labs but consumers did not realize that Coke was going to replace its original formula. The new formula was launched, the public was outraged, and the company quickly came back with Coca-Cola Classic.
 XFL	Vince McMahon (the founder of WWE wrestling) founded the XFL to compete indirectly with the NFL. There were great gimmicks and exciting camera angles but consumers were not fooled. The league quickly folded because the ultimate product was inferior.

FIGURE 16.1

Recent and classic product and brand failures.

expect to be able to claim tax deductions it has earned in recent years before they expire in 2024. In other words, the product is evolving but its financial success is not around the corner.[5]

In another example, Bombardier expects to finally put into service the new CSeries line of passenger jets in late 2013, nearly a decade after it first announced intentions to build this new line of planes. There are still doubts but the company is doing everything it can to ensure the launch date. A rumoured delay of six to nine months would likely cost the company an estimated US$350 million. As of early 2012, Bombardier had 133 firm orders, options for another 129 planes, and 45 additional letters of intent.[6] The launch process is quite complicated in the aerospace business.

Product Mortality Rates

It takes about 50 new product ideas to generate one product that finally reaches the market. Even then, only a few of these survivors become successful products. Many seemingly great ideas have failed as products. Indeed, creating a successful new product has become increasingly difficult, even for the most experienced marketers. Why? The number of new products hitting the market each year has increased dramatically, and thousands of new household, grocery, and drugstore items are introduced

Nintendo has put a lot of time and effort into the launch of the new Wii U; it is looking to reverse a recent sales slump and regain the confidence that the original Wii brought to the company.[7]

annually. But at any given time, the average supermarket carries a total of only 20 000 to 25 000 different items. Because of lack of space and customer demand, about 9 out of 10 new products will fail. Those with the best chances are innovative and deliver unique benefits.

Speed to Market

speed to market Strategy of introducing new products to respond quickly to customer and/or market changes.

The more rapidly a product moves from the laboratory to the marketplace, the more likely it is to survive. By introducing new products ahead of competitors, companies establish market leadership and become entrenched in the market before being challenged by newer competitors. The importance of **speed to market**—a firm's success in responding to customer demand or market changes—can be seen in this statistic: A product that is only three months late to market (three months behind the leader) loses 12 percent of its lifetime profit potential. A product that is six months late will lose 33 percent.[8]

The Seven-Step Development Process

To increase their chances of developing successful new products or services, many firms use a basic seven-step process. Steps 2, 3, 4, 6, and 7 are the same for both products and services, but there are some differences in Steps 1 and 5.

service package Identification of the tangible and intangible features that define the service.

1. *Product ideas.* Product development begins with a search for ideas for new products. Product ideas can come from consumers, the sales force, research and development, or engineering. Developing services ideas includes a task called defining the **service package**, which involves identification of the tangible and intangible features that define the service and state service specifications.

2. *Screening.* This stage is an attempt to eliminate all product ideas that do not mesh with the firm's abilities, expertise, or objectives. Representatives from marketing, engineering, and production must have input at this stage.

3. *Concept testing.* Once ideas have been culled, companies use market research to solicit consumers' input. Firms can identify benefits that the product must provide as well as an appropriate price level for the product.

4. *Business analysis.* This involves developing a comparison of costs and benefits for the proposed product. Preliminary sales projections are compared with cost projections from finance and production to determine whether the product can meet minimum profitability goals.

5. *Prototype development.* Using input from the concept-testing phase, engineering and/or research and development produce a preliminary version of the product. Prototypes can be extremely expensive, often requiring extensive hand crafting, tooling, and development of components, but this phase can help identify potential production problems. **Service process design** involves selecting the process (identifying each step in the service, including the sequence and the timing), identifying worker requirements (specifying employee behaviours, skills, capabilities, and interactions with customers), and determining facilities requirements (designating all of the equipment that supports delivery of the service).

service process design Selecting the process, identifying worker requirements, and determining facilities requirements so that the service can be effectively provided.

6. *Product testing and test marketing.* The company begins limited production of the item. If the product meets performance requirements, it is made available for sale in limited areas (test markets). This stage is very costly, since promotional campaigns and distribution channels must be established. Test marketing gives a company its first information on how consumers will respond to a product under real market conditions.

7. *Commercialization.* If test-marketing results are positive, the company will begin full-scale production and marketing of the product. Gradual commercialization, with the firm providing the product to more and more areas over time, prevents undue strain on the firm's initial production capabilities, but delays in commercialization may give competitors a chance to bring out their own version.

The Product Life Cycle

The concept of the **product life cycle (PLC)** is based on the idea that products have a limited profit-producing life. This life may be a matter of months, years, or decades, depending on the ability of the product to attract customers over time. Products such as Kellogg's Corn Flakes, Coca-Cola, Ivory soap, Argo cornstarch, and Caramilk candy bars have had extremely long product life cycles.

product life cycle (PLC) The concept that the profit-producing life of any product goes through a cycle of introduction, growth, maturity (levelling off), and decline.

Stages in the Product Life Cycle

The life cycle for both goods and services is a natural process in which products are born, grow in stature, mature, and finally decline and die.[9] In Figure 16.2(a), the four phases of the PLC are applied to several products with which you are familiar.

1. *Introduction.* The introduction stage begins when the product reaches the marketplace. During this stage, marketers focus on making potential consumers aware of the product and its benefits. Because of extensive promotional and development costs, profits are non-existent. But the use of social media tools like Twitter and YouTube is providing cost-efficient alternatives for companies to generate attention and buzz.

2. *Growth.* If the new product attracts and satisfies enough consumers, sales begin to climb rapidly. During this stage, the product begins to show a profit. Other firms in the industry move speedily to introduce their own versions. Heavy promotion is often required to build brand preference over the competition.

3. *Maturity.* Sales growth begins to slow. Although the product earns its highest profit level early in this stage, increased competition eventually leads to price cutting

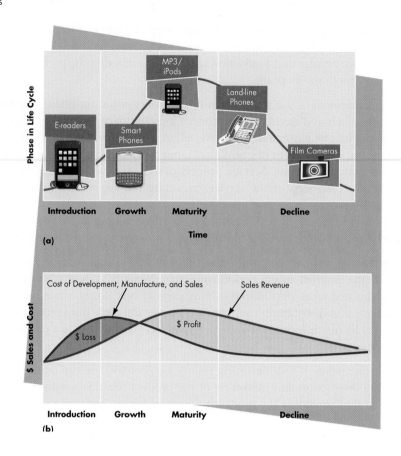

FIGURE 16.2

The Product Life Cycle

and lower profits. Marketing communications tend to focus on reminder advertising. Toward the end of the stage, sales start to fall.

4. *Decline.* During this final stage, sales and profits continue to fall. New products in the introduction stage take away sales. Companies remove or reduce promotional support (ads and salespeople) but may let the product linger to provide some profits.

Figure 16.2(b) plots the relationship of the PLC to a product's typical sales, costs, and profits. Although the early stages of the PLC often show negative cash flows, successful products usually recover those losses and, in fact, continue to generate profits until the decline stage. For most products, profitable life spans are short—thus, the importance placed by so many firms on the constant replenishment of product lines. In the pension industry, for example, "defined benefit" programs are approaching the end of their life cycle, while "defined contribution" plans are in the growth stage.

Extending Product Life: An Alternative to New Products

Companies try to keep products in the maturity stage as long as they can. Sales of TV sets, for example, have been revitalized by such feature changes as colour, portability, miniaturization, stereo capability, high definition, and 3D. Companies can extend product life through a number of creative means. Foreign markets offer three possibilities for lengthening product life cycles:

1. In **product extension**, an existing product is marketed globally; Coca-Cola is a prime example of international product extensions.

2. With **product adaptation**, the product is modified for greater appeal in different countries. In Germany, a McDonald's meal includes beer; in Japan, Ford puts the steering wheel on the right side. After Kraft Foods changed the shape of the

product extension The process of marketing an existing, unmodified product globally.

product adaptation The process of modifying a product to have greater appeal in foreign markets.

traditional round Oreo Cookie to be long and thin (and coated the cookie in chocolate), it became the bestselling cookie in China. The new shape is also sold in Canada.[10]

3. **Reintroduction** means reviving, for new markets, products that are becoming obsolete in older ones. NCR has reintroduced manually operated cash registers in Latin America.

reintroduction The process of reviving, for new markets, products that are obsolete in older ones.

Identifying Products

As we noted earlier, developing a product's features is only part of a marketer's job. Marketers must also identify products so that consumers recognize them. Three important tools for this task are branding, packaging, and labelling.

Explain the importance of *branding,* **L03** *packaging,* and *labelling.*

Branding Products

Branding is the use of symbols to communicate the qualities of a particular product made by a particular producer. In 2012, technology companies were at the top of the brand value list. According to Millward Brown Optimor, which creates the BrandZ Top 100 Global Brands Ranking, the three most successful brands in the world were Apple, Google, and IBM. Four Canadian brands made the Top 100: BlackBerry (no. 25), RBC (no. 39), TD (no. 42) and Scotiabank (no. 87). Test your brand knowledge and take a look at the branding exercise in Figure 16.3.

So how much is a successful brand worth? Kellogg's recently purchased the Pringles potato chip brand and its assets from Procter & Gamble for US$2.7 billion. Procter & Gamble is turning its focus to household goods and beauty and personal care products; Pringles was the last remaining asset in its food business. For Kellogg's,

branding The use of symbols to communicate the qualities of a particular product made by a particular producer.

FIGURE 16.3

Branding Exercise: Name that Logo

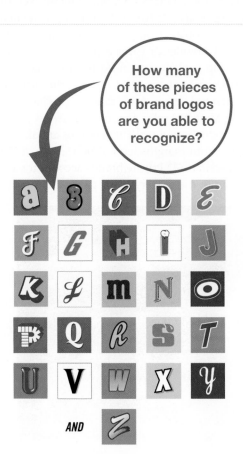

the purchase helps solidify the company as the fourth-largest maker of sweet and savoury snacks in the world. Having a powerful brand like Pringles on its roster will help as the company tries to gain more sales in international markets.[11]

Adding Value through Brand Equity

brand equity The added value a brand name provides to a product beyond its basic functional benefits.

Many companies that once measured assets in terms of cash, buildings, equipment, and inventories now realize that a strong brand is an equally important asset. Widely known and admired brands are valuable because of their power to attract customers. Those with higher **brand equity** generate greater brand awareness and loyalty on the part of consumers, have larger market shares than competing brands, and are perceived to have greater quality. As you saw on the previous page, BlackBerry is the most recognizable and highest ranked Canadian brand, but the company's overall brand equity has been declining in the past few years. Product and service failures and a reputation for launching "me-too" products (e.g., the Playbook tablet) have hurt its brand equity. Negative comments from investment firms like Jarislowsky and Fraser Ltd. have hurt public confidence in the brand, as well.[12] This is somewhat quantified by a Brand Finance survey that indicated that BlackBerry lost approximately 24 percent of its brand equity in 2011 alone.[13]

Types of Brand Names

national brands Products distributed by and carrying a name associated with the manufacturer.

licensed brands Selling the limited rights, to another company, to use a brand name on a product.

National brands are those that are produced and distributed by the manufacturer across the entire country (e.g., Chips Ahoy, Crest). When a company with a well-known brand sells another company the right to place that brand on its products, these are called **licensed brands**. Harley-Davidson's famous logo—emblazoned on boots, eyewear, gloves, purses, lighters, and watches—brings the motorcycle maker more than $210 million annually. Along with brands such as Coors and Ferrari, licensing for character-based brands like Spider-Man is equally lucrative.

private brands Products promoted by and carrying a name associated with the retailer or wholesaler, not the manufacturer.

Private brands carry the retailer's own brand name even though they are manufactured by another firm. Sears has two well-known private brands—Craftsman tools and Kenmore appliances. Loblaw Companies Ltd. created a line of upscale products under the private brand President's Choice (PC). If you want Loblaw's famous PC Decadent Chocolate Chip cookies, you need to visit a Loblaws outlet or one of its subsidiaries. Shoppers Drug Mart has tried to copy the success of President's Choice with its private label brands: Life for a wide range of products and Quo for cosmetics.[14] In fact, Shoppers Drug Mart has set a goal to increase its private-label shelf space to 25 percent of overall product offerings. These brands are often 25 percent cheaper for consumers, and yet the profit margins tend to be 15 percent higher for the company. This is a clear win-win scenario.[15] Private brands account for 19 percent of the overall market and $10.9 billion in the grocery market.[16]

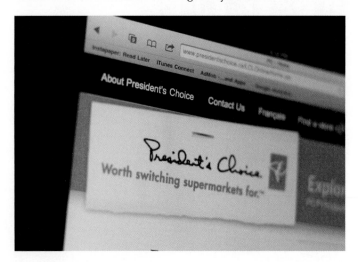

Loblaw's PC Decadent Chocolate Chip cookies have built a reputation that all private-label brands strive for. Consumers who love these cookies must go to Loblaws, or one of its subsidiaries, to buy them.

Generic brands are also gaining more shelf space; they are the products that you see in grocery stores that simply state a category name like "bacon" or "peanut butter." If you've been to Costco recently, you may have picked up its very popular generic chocolate chip cookies. Major retailers are carrying fewer national brands and more of their own private brands as well as these less-expensive, no-frills generic brands.

generic brands No-frills products sold under the general category name rather than a specific company name.

Brand Loyalty

Brand loyalty means that when customers need a particular item, they will go back and buy the same brand. Brand loyalty exists at three levels: *brand awareness* (customers recognize the brand), *brand preference* (consumers have a favourable attitude toward the brand), and *brand insistence* (consumers demand the brand and will go out of their way to get it). Brand insistence implies consumer trust in a brand. Canadians have less trust than they did 20 years ago, but some well-known brands like Kellogg's, RBC, and Apple are still viewed positively.[17]

brand loyalty Customers' recognition of, preference for, and insistence on buying a product with a certain brand name.

Brand loyalty is strong in several sports, including baseball, basketball, and soccer, and fans respond to marketing efforts by companies like Nike and Adidas. But in some other sports (e.g., skateboarding) brand loyalty is difficult to develop. Because skateboarders go through a lot of boards each year, they are reluctant to buy brand-name boards, which cost three to five times what "blank" boards cost. The International Association of Skateboard Companies estimates that 50 to 70 percent of all boards sold are blank, not branded.[18]

Brand loyalty can have a major impact on a company's profits. In the beer industry, each market share point is worth about $25 million in profit. This is why beer brands have such fierce battles.[19]

Global Branding Issues

How do you take a successful domestic brand and launch it internationally? For many companies with Canadian origins, it seems as though an infusion of cash or support from larger American or European companies is step number one. Brands like Mac, Club Monaco, and La Senza have all established a strong presence abroad after building a name as domestic Canadian brands. In these three cases, the road to stronger global presence began with takeovers by Estée Lauder, Ralph Lauren, and the Limited Brands for the respective companies. As you read in Chapter 5, Tim Hortons is having a hard time selecting the right brand image as it expands further into the United States. The large, spread-out Canadian market landscape, combined with the small relative population, makes it more difficult to gain the monetary resources to expand without support. However, there are success stories like Montreal-based Aldo group, which has stores in over 60 countries.[20]

Firms that sell products internationally also face another branding strategy issue. They must consider how product names will translate in various languages. Chevrolet learned this lesson decades ago when it entered the Latin American market with the Nova. This name was not well received simply because "no va" translates into "it does not go."[21] More recently, the Buick Lacrosse has been catching attention in Quebec for the wrong reasons: In French slang, lacrosse is a term for pleasuring yourself. What's even more surprising is that GM was aware of this unfortunate naming issue and originally released the car back in 2005 as the Buick Allure. But in an effort to cut down marketing costs, it ignored the potential embarrassment and decided to launch the Lacrosse in 2010.[22]

Trademarks, Patents, and Copyrights

Because brand development is very expensive, a company does not want another company using its name and confusing consumers. Companies can apply to the Canadian government and receive a **trademark**, the exclusive legal right to use a brand name. Trademarks are granted for 15 years and may be renewed for further periods of 15 years, but only if the company continues to protect its brand name.[23] Target Corp. had been in a decade-long dispute with a Canadian retailer, Isaac Benitah, over who owns the

trademark The exclusive legal right to use a brand name.

Target name in Canada. Just before Target (the U.S. retailer) was set to open up its new stores north of the border, the two parties agreed to a settlement. Mr. Benitah agreed to stop using the Target name as of January, 31, 2013, and in return received a sizable undisclosed settlement (estimated in the millions) and also avoided a long legal battle. Mr. Benitah had threatened to seek an injunction banning Target from selling clothing in Canada.[24] In a similar case, a Montreal-based "cheap chic" retail chain called Top Shop is fighting the British retail giant Topshop, which sold the rights to The Bay to sell its brand in Canada. The Bay is investing a lot in Topshop as it tries to rebuild its image. The case is heading to the courts.[25]

Exactly what can be trademarked is not always clear. If a company allows its name to lapse into common usage, the courts may take away protection. Common usage occurs when the company fails to use the symbol for its brand. It also occurs if the company fails to correct those who do not acknowledge the brand as a trademark. Windsurfer (a popular brand of sailboards) lost its trademark by not protecting it: Like the trampoline, yo-yo, and thermos, the brand name Windsurfer has become the common term for the product and can now be used by any sailboard company. But companies owning brands like Xerox and Coke have successfully defended their brand names.

Companies want to be sure that both product brands and new product ideas are protected. A **patent** protects an invention or idea for a period of 20 years. The cost is $1600 to $2500 and it takes from 18 months to three years to secure a patent from the Canadian Patent Office.[26] Patents can be very valuable. A few years back, Research

patent Exclusive legal right to use and license a manufactured item or substance, manufacturing process, or object design.

MANAGING IN TURBULENT TIMES

Patents Are Big Business

Patents can be very valuable, as shown by the recent auction of patents held by the now-defunct Nortel Networks. Companies therefore often sue each other to defend their patent rights. For example, Ottawa-based Wi-Lan, a company that licenses intellectual property patents, sued some of the biggest computer chip makers, alleging patent infringement by those companies on wireless and Bluetooth patents that were held by Wi-Lan. The patents in question are used in smartphones, laptops, and other mobile devices. In 2011, the dispute was settled out of court, and Wi-Lan may receive as much as $600 million in damages over the next six years or so.

Another Canadian software company, i4i, holds a patent on a technology that is used to open documents using the XML computer language. It filed a patent infringement lawsuit against Microsoft in 2007, alleging that Microsoft used i4i technology in its Word 2003 and 2007 software. In 2009, a U.S. judge ruled in favour of i4i and ordered Microsoft to pay US$290 million in damages. Microsoft appealed the ruling, but in June 2011, the U.S. Supreme Court denied Microsoft's appeal. The ruling showed that small companies could battle industry giants.

Companies that have historically not paid much attention to patents are now starting to pay attention. Oil companies, for example, are trying to develop new technologies to reach the 1.7 trillion barrels of oil that are thought to be in the Alberta oil sands, and these companies are seeking patents for their discoveries because they want to shield them from competitors. In Alberta, more than twice as many patent applications were filed between 2005 and 2010 than were filed between 2000 and 2004. These patent applications focus on processes like chemical mixes that are used to make oil flow more easily and methods for cleaning up toxic wastes. These patents could be a significant source of new revenue in the future, since competitors would have to pay licensing fees to the companies that patented the new processes. This possibility has already resulted in patent disputes. For example, a patent was granted to Cenovus in 2010 for a technique that uses high-pressure injection of steam underground to melt out oil sands bitumen. Within two months, Suncor raised a legal challenge, arguing that Cenovus had defrauded the Patent Office by trying to patent something that shouldn't be patentable.

Patent battles are not limited to high-tech industries or to big businesses. When Aldo Buccioni, who makes a hockey equipment bag called the Hockey Tower, noticed that Walmart was selling a very similar hockey bag, he sued the manufacturer (Travelway Group International) for violating his patent. Travelway said that its bag was different and that Buccioni's lawsuit had no merit.

Critical Thinking Questions

1. If Microsoft had won its appeal, do you think that would have reduced the motivation to develop innovative new ideas? Defend your reasoning.

2. To what extent are patent disputes similar to the disputes regarding the downloading of music from the internet?

In Motion (RIM), maker of BlackBerry, agreed to pay $612.5 million to NTP Inc., a U.S. firm that claimed RIM was infringing on some patents it held.[27] Patents are a big business: By the end of 2011, Google had applied for or received just over 300 patents, while Research In Motion had over 3000 and Microsoft and Nokia each owned over 2500 patents. This perceived weakness on Google's part was addressed when Google bought Motorola Mobility (and its 17 000 patents) for $12.5 billion.[28] For more information on patents, see the boxed insert called "Patents Are Big Business."

Copyrights give exclusive ownership rights to the creators of books, articles, designs, illustrations, photos, films, and music. Computer programs and even semiconductor chips are also protected. In Canada, the copyright process is relatively simple, requiring only the use of the copyright symbol © and the date. Copyrights extend to creators for their entire lives and to their estates for 50 years thereafter in Canada. Copyrights apply to the tangible expressions of an idea, not to the idea itself. For example, the idea of cloning dinosaurs from fossil DNA cannot be copyrighted, but Michael Crichton, the author of *Jurassic Park*, had a copyright for his novel (which is now held by his estate) because it is the tangible result of the basic idea.

> **copyright** Exclusive ownership rights belonging to the creators of books, articles, designs, illustrations, photos, films, and music.

There is much debate about how copyrights apply to material that appears on the internet. In 2005, the Author's Guild and several publishers sued Google, claiming that its book-scanning project was infringing on their copyrights. A few years ago, Google agreed to pay US$125 million to settle the lawsuits. Google can now make available millions of books online.[29] The issue of file sharing is making copyright a big issue these days. New laws and new interpretations of old ones will redefine the role of copyright over the next few years.

Packaging Products

Except for products like fresh fruits and vegetables and structural steel, almost all products need some form of **packaging** so they can be transported to the market. Packaging also serves several other functions: It is an in-store advertisement that makes the product attractive; it clearly displays the brand; it identifies product features and benefits; and it reduces the risk of damage, breakage, or spoilage. The package is the marketer's last chance to say "buy me" to the consumer.

> **packaging** Physical container in which a product is sold, advertised, or protected.

Companies are paying close attention to consumer concerns about packaging. Beyond concerns about product tampering, packaging must be tight enough to withstand shipping but not so tight that it frustrates consumers when they try to open the package. Nestlé—which spends more than $6 billion annually on packaging—spent nine months coming up with a new, easier-to-open lid and an easier-to-grip container for its Country Creamery ice cream. In general, companies have found that packaging costs can be as high as 15 percent of the total cost to make a product, and features like zip-lock tops can add 20 percent to the price that is charged.[30]

Labelling Products

Every product has a **label** on its package. Like packaging, labelling can help market the product. First, it identifies the product or the brand, such as the name Campbell on a can of soup or Chiquita on a banana. Labels also promote products by getting consumers' attention. Attractive colours and graphics provide visual cues to products that otherwise might be overlooked on the shelf. Finally, the label describes the product by providing information about nutritional content, directions for use, proper disposal, and safety.

> **label** That part of a product's packaging that identifies the product's name and contents and sometimes its benefits.

The federal government regulates the information on package labels. The **Consumer Packaging and Labelling Act** has two main purposes: The first is to provide a comprehensive set of rules for packaging and labelling of consumer products, and the second is to ensure that manufacturers provide full and factual information on labels. All pre-packaged products must state in French and English the quantity enclosed in metric units, as well as the name and description of the product.

> **Consumer Packaging and Labelling Act** A federal law that provides comprehensive rules for the packaging and labelling of consumer products.

Sellers are very sensitive to what is on the label of the products they sell. However, consumers can also be very sensitive and loyal to the visual presentation of a brand. In 2009, Tropicana learned that consumers were fond of the company's classic logo with the orange and straw as the centrepiece. When the company tried to replace it with a new design, consumers responded with emails, letters, and complaints. PepsiCo, which owns Tropicana, immediately reversed the decision.[31]

Promoting Products and Services

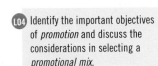
L04 Identify the important objectives of *promotion* and discuss the considerations in selecting a *promotional mix.*

promotion Any technique designed to sell a product.

As we noted in Chapter 15, **promotion** is any technique designed to sell a product. It is part of the *communication mix*—the total message a company sends to consumers about its product. Promotional techniques, especially advertising, must communicate the uses, features, and benefits of products. Sales promotions also include various programs that add value beyond the benefits inherent in the product. For example, it is nice to get a high-quality product at a reasonable price, but it is even better when the seller offers a rebate or a bonus pack with "20 percent more *free.*"

Information and Exchange Values

In free market systems, businesses use promotional methods to accomplish four objectives with potential customers:

- make them aware of products
- make them knowledgeable about products
- persuade them to like products
- persuade them to purchase products

Successful promotions provide communication about the product and create exchanges that satisfy the objectives of customers (who get a desired product) and sellers (who get sales and profits). The promotion program can determine the success or failure of any business or product, whether it is in the introduction stage (promoting for new product awareness) or the maturity stage (promoting brand benefits and customer loyalty).

Promotional Objectives

The ultimate objective of any promotion is to increase sales. However, marketers also use promotion to *communicate information, position products, add value,* and *control sales volume.*[32]

Communicating Information

Consumers cannot buy a product unless they have been informed about it. Information can advise customers about the availability of a product, educate them on the latest technological advances, or announce the candidacy of someone running for a government office. Information may be communicated in writing (newspapers and magazines), verbally (radio, in person, telephone), or visually (television, the internet, a matchbook cover, or a billboard). Today, the communication of information regarding a company's products or services is so important that marketers try to place it wherever consumers may be. The average Canadian sees about 3000 marketing messages every day, much more than the average consumer saw 30 years ago.[33] The boxed insert entitled "Promoting a Green Image" describes how companies communicate information about their green initiatives to consumers.

Positioning Products

As we saw in Chapter 15, **product positioning** establishes an easily identifiable image of a product in the minds of consumers. For many years Estée Lauder products were only sold in department stores and not in drugstores because they were positioned as a more upscale brand, meant to appeal to a specific segment of the market rather than to the market as a whole. This decision changed a few years ago after Shoppers Drug Mart and other competitors invested heavily in their cosmetics sections, in terms of both service and dedicated space, making them acceptable outlets for more upscale brands, including Estée Lauder.

product positioning The establishment of an easily identifiable image of a product in the minds of consumers.

Adding Value

Today's value-conscious customers gain benefits when the promotional mix is shifted so that it communicates value-added benefits in its products. Burger King, for instance, shifted its promotional mix by cutting back on advertising dollars and using those funds for customer discounts. Receiving the same food at a lower price is added value for Burger King's customers.

THE GREENING OF BUSINESS

Promoting a Green Image

In July 2011, the Auto West Group BMW auto dealership in Richmond, B.C., unveiled the on-site wind turbine it will use to generate electricity. The turbine is quiet (producing less noise than a passing car), it will cut the company's power bill, and it will help in promoting the company's image as a green company (Auto West occupies one of the greenest buildings in B.C., and it has already installed solar panels, geo-thermal heating and cooling technology, and a rooftop garden). This is just one example of how Canadian businesses are promoting themselves as "green" enterprises. The advertising agency Agent of Change—which provides its clients with media tools that will affect social change—develops advertising campaigns for environmental issues, animal rights, and international justice. And the Fur Council of Canada—which emphasizes its ties with Native Canadians and its made-in-Canada attributes—is promoting itself as a green industry with billboard and print advertisements that stress the sustainability of the fur industry.

But convincing customers that a business is green is increasingly difficult. The 2010 Canadian Green Gap Index survey found that an overwhelming majority of Canadians either couldn't name a green retailer or didn't think any retailer was deserving of the label. A Gandalf Group survey of 1500 Canadians found that the majority of consumers think that environmental claims by businesses are just a marketing ploy, and that labelling regulations are needed so buyers can understand what terms like "eco-friendly" actually mean.

The term "greenwashing" has been coined to describe the practice of exaggerating or making false claims about the environmental impact of a product or service. There is even a Greenwashing Index (published by EnviroMedia) that ranks the eco-friendly advertising claims of various companies. In response to concerns about greenwashing, the Canadian Competition Bureau, in co-operation with the Canadian Standards Association, has drafted industry guidelines that will require companies to back up their environmental claims with scientific evidence. The guidelines will create national definitions for terms like "recyclable" and will also prohibit vague claims about products (for example, "our product is non-toxic").

Critical Thinking Questions

1. What is your reaction to the Fur Council of Canada's green advertising campaign? What would you say to an animal rights activist who is outraged at the claims the Fur Council is making?

2. Consider the following statement: *The Competition Bureau's plan to create national guidelines to define terms like "recyclable" is well intentioned, but it will not work in practice because companies will figure out ways to get around the rules and still make unwarranted claims about how green they are.* Do you agree or disagree with the statement? Explain your reasoning.

Controlling Sales Volume

Many companies, such as Hallmark Cards, experience seasonal sales patterns. By increasing promotional activities in slow periods, these firms can achieve more stable sales volume throughout the year. They can thus keep production and distribution systems running evenly. Promotions can even turn slow seasons into peak sales periods. For example, greeting card companies and florists together have done much to create Grandparents Day. The result has been increased consumer demand for cards and flowers in the middle of what was once a slow season for both industries.

Promotional Strategies

push strategy A promotional strategy whereby a company aggressively pushes its product through wholesalers and retailers, who persuade customers to buy it.

pull strategy A promotional strategy in which a company appeals directly to customers, who demand the product from retailers, who demand the product from wholesalers.

Once a firm's promotional objectives are clear, it must develop a promotional strategy to achieve these objectives. A company using a **push strategy** will aggressively "push" its product through wholesalers and retailers, who in turn persuade customers to buy the product. In contrast, a company using a **pull strategy** appeals directly to customers, who then demand the product from retailers, who in turn demand the product from wholesalers. Makers of industrial products often use a push strategy, while makers of consumer products often use a pull strategy. Many large firms use a combination of the two strategies. For example, Coca-Cola uses advertising to create consumer demand (pull) for its various beverages—Coke, Fruitopia, Dasani, and PowerAde. It also pushes wholesalers and retailers to stock these products (push).

The Promotional Mix

promotional mix That portion of marketing concerned with choosing the best combination of advertising, personal selling, sales promotions, and publicity to sell a product.

As we noted in Chapter 15, here are four types of promotional tools: advertising, personal selling, sales promotions, and publicity/public relations. The best combination of these tools—the **promotional mix**—depends on many factors, with the most important being the target audience. In establishing a promotional mix, marketers match promotional tools with the five stages in the buyer decision process we described in Chapter 15:

1. *Buyers recognize the need to make a purchase.* At this stage, marketers must make sure that buyers are aware of their products. Advertising and publicity, which can reach many people quickly, are important.

2. *Buyers seek information about available products.* Advertising and personal selling are important because both can be used to educate consumers.

3. *Buyers compare competing products.* Personal selling can be vital. Sales representatives can demonstrate product quality and performance in comparison with competitors' products.

FIGURE 16.4

The Consumer Buying Process and the Promotional Mix

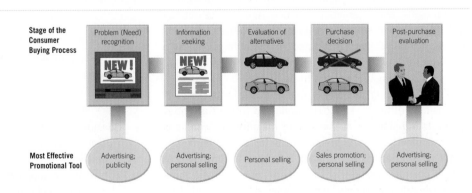

4. *Buyers purchase products*. Sales promotion is effective because it can give consumers an incentive to buy. Personal selling can help by bringing products to convenient purchase locations.

5. *Buyers evaluate products after purchase*. Advertising, or even personal selling, is sometimes used to remind consumers that they made wise purchases.[34] Figure 16.4 summarizes the effective promotional tools for each stage of the consumer buying process.

Advertising Promotions

Advertising is paid, non-personal communication by which an identified sponsor informs an audience about a product. You can probably remember many jingles and slogans from your early childhood. If a friend tells you that he or she has dandruff, you may instinctively tell them to use Head and Shoulders shampoo. Companies have been planting messages in your mind for years. Like it or not, we are all a little bit brainwashed. Consumers remember brand names more easily if the company has a catchy advertising slogan. Buckley's Cough Mixture is well known in Canada. You remember the slogan, don't you? "It tastes awful, and it works." Advertising can convince customers to try a company's product or service, but it has limits. It is the customers' experience with the product or service that determines whether they will make repeat purchases.

> Discuss the most important *advertising* strategies and describe the key *advertising media*. **L05**

> **advertising** A promotional tool consisting of paid, non-personal communication used by an identified sponsor to inform an audience about a product.

Advertising Strategies

Advertising strategies depend on the stage of the product life cycle the product is currently in. During the introduction stage, **informative advertising** can help develop an awareness of the company and its product among buyers and can establish a primary demand for the product. For example, before a new textbook is published, instructors receive email advertisements notifying them of the book's contents and availability. During the growth stage, **persuasive advertising** can influence a larger number of consumers to buy the company's products. During the maturity stage, **comparative advertising**—which involves comparing the company's brand name with a competitor's brand name in such a way that the competitor's brand looks inferior—is often used. This sort of approach is usually used by the number two brand in the market. Pepsi has used this approach for many years. The Pepsi Challenge has been replaced by hip youthful images associated with Pepsi as opposed to Coke. Coke does not engage in this fight. Like most market leaders, it does not provide Pepsi with additional free exposure (not even to put the brand down). During the latter part of the maturity stage, **reminder advertising** keeps the product's name in front of the consumer.

> **informative advertising** An advertising strategy, appropriate in the introduction stage of the product life cycle; the goal is to build awareness.

> **persuasive advertising** An advertising strategy, appropriate in the growth stage of the product life cycle; the goal is to influence the customer to buy the firm's product rather than a competitor's product.

> **comparative advertising** An advertising strategy, appropriate in the maturity stage of the product life cycle; the goal is to influence the customer to switch from a competitor's product by directly comparing the two.

> **reminder advertising** An advertising strategy, appropriate to the latter part of the maturity stage of the product life cycle, in which the goal is to keep the product's name in the minds of customers.

Advertising Media

Consumers tend to ignore the bulk of advertising messages that bombard them. Marketers must therefore find out who their customers are, which media they pay attention to, what messages appeal to them, and how to get their attention. Thus, marketers use several different **advertising media**—specific communication outlets for carrying a seller's message to potential customers. For example, IBM uses television ads to keep its name fresh in the minds of consumers, newspaper and magazine ads to educate them about product features, and trade publications to introduce new software. Often marketers turn to a multimedia company so that the seller's message is the same across the different advertising media. The combination of media through

> **advertising media** The specific communication devices—television, radio, newspapers, direct mail, magazines, billboards, the internet—used to carry a firm's advertising message to potential customers.

TABLE 16.1 Top 10 Multimedia Companies in Canada, 2011
(ranked by sales revenue)

	Company	Sales Revenue (billions of dollars)
1.	Shaw Communications	$4.7
2.	Quebecor Inc.	4.2
3.	Rogers Cable Inc.	3.7
4.	Vidéotron Ltd.	2.4
5.	Rogers Media Inc.	1.6
6.	Bell Media Inc.	1.5
7.	Cogeco Inc.	1.4
8.	Astral Media Inc.	1.0
9.	Corus Entertainment Inc.	0.8
10.	CBC/Radio-Canada	0.6

media mix The combination of media through which a company chooses to advertise its products.

which a company chooses to advertise its products is called its **media mix**. Although different industries use different mixes, most depend on multiple media to advertise their products and services. The Top 10 Multimedia companies in Canada are listed in Table 16.1.

An advertiser selects media with a number of factors in mind. The marketer must first ask, "Which medium will reach the people I want to reach?" If a tech company is trying to reach the youth market, it is more likely to use "promoted tweets" on Twitter or Facebook ads rather than an advertisement on the six o'clock news. If a firm is selling hog breeding equipment, it might choose a trade magazine read by hog farmers. If it is selling silverware, it might choose a magazine for brides. Each advertising medium has its own advantages and disadvantages. In the following paragraphs, we will examine the various media formats. In addition, Table 16.2 provides a summary of their advantages and disadvantages.

Newspapers

Newspapers are a widely used advertising medium; in 2010, Canadian advertisers spent $2.1 billion on this medium. This figure was up over 3 percent from the previous year; however, the medium lost nearly 20 percent two years earlier.[35] Newspapers offer excellent coverage, since each local market has at least one daily newspaper and many people read the paper every day. This medium offers flexible, rapid coverage, since ads can change from day to day. Newspapers also offer believable coverage, since ads are presented next to news. In addition, a larger percentage of individuals with higher education and income level tend to read newspapers on a daily basis. For example, newspapers attract a 47 percent readership from individual households with an income of $75 000 or above, as opposed to only a 5 percent readership of individual households under $20 000.[36] However, the focus in the newspaper business is definitely changing. Postmedia Network Canada has the largest roster of papers in the nation; this company has officially adopted a "digital first" strategy and saw an 8.6 percent increase in digital sales in the first half of 2011. Some papers are even trying unorthodox tricks to catch viewer attention; for example, the *Los Angeles Times* had a full front-page ad a couple of years ago.[37] This could not have been imagined decades ago, but newspapers are looking for revenues and new ways to get noticed.

TABLE 16.2 Media Strengths and Weaknesses

Advertising	Strengths	Weaknesses
Television	Program demographics allow for customized ads Large audience	Most expensive
Magazines	Often reread and shared Variety of ready market segmentation	Require advanced planning Little control over ad placement
Newspapers	Broad coverage Ads can change daily	Quickly discarded Broad readership limits ability to target specific audience
Direct mail	Targeted audience Personal messages Predictable results	Easily discarded Environmentally irresponsible
Internet	Targeted audience Measurable success	Nuisance to consumers Easy to ignore
Radio	Inexpensive Large audience Variety of ready market segmentation	Easy to ignore Message quickly disappears
Outdoor	Inexpensive Difficult to ignore Repeat exposure	Presents limited information Little control over audience

Note: A combination of additional unmeasured media—catalogues, sidewalk handouts, skywriting, telephone calls, ads on PDAs, special events, movies, and door-to-door communication—are not included.

Television

Television allows advertisers to combine sight, sound, and motion, thus appealing to almost all of the viewer's senses. (Ads can use many techniques to emphasize motion. A few years back, there was a great Cadillac ad that focused on motion by turning off the sound for seven seconds and capturing viewer attention in a unique manner.) Information on viewer demographics for a particular program allows advertisers to promote to their target audiences. National advertising is done on television because it reaches more people than any other medium. One disadvantage of television is that too many commercials cause viewers to confuse products. In addition, viewers who record programs on DVRs (digital video recorders) often fast-forward through the ads appearing on the TV shows they have recorded. This is a growing concern, since 26 percent of Canadians owned DVRs in 2012.[38] The brevity of TV ads also makes television a poor medium to educate viewers about complex products.

Spending on television advertising in Canada totalled $3.4 billion in 2010.[39] Television is the most expensive advertising medium. In 2012, a 30-second commercial on U.S. television during the NFL Super Bowl cost about $3.5 million, up from $1.3 million in 1998. A national 30-second spot in Canada during the Super Bowl costs approximately $130 000.[40] A comparable 30-second Grey Cup spot costs about $65 000.[41]

Product placement, which involves using brand-name products as part of the actual storyline of TV shows, is gaining popularity. Shows like *Survivor* and *American Idol* are noticeably full of placements. *American Idol* contestants are interviewed in the Coca-Cola room and the judges drink from prominently placed Coca-Cola glasses. The contestants film a music video featuring a Ford product each week, which is presented as part of the show. Finally, the audience is invited to vote using AT&T. In all, there were over 4100 plugs in one recent season of *American Idol*.[42] In the early days of TV, live commercials featured actors or characters like Howdy Doody selling the merits of products. Decades later, in an attempt to break through the clutter, it appears as if this old technique has been revived and updated.

Direct Mail

Direct mail involves flyers or other types of printed advertisements that are mailed directly to consumers' homes or places of business. Direct mail allows the company to select its audience and personalize its message. The goal is to generate an immediate response and to have the customer contact a firm directly. Although many people discard "junk mail," targeted recipients with stronger-than-average interest are more likely to buy. Although direct mail involves the largest advance costs of any advertising technique, it does appear to have the highest cost-effectiveness. With "fax attacks," advertisers can send their "mail" messages electronically via fax machines and get higher response rates than they would if they used Canada Post. Targeted emails are also serving this purpose. Advertisers spent $1.3 billion on direct mail promotion in 2010.[43]

Radio

According to BBM research, more than 90 percent of Canadians aged 12 years and over listen to the radio more than 19 hours a week.[44] Radio ads are fairly inexpensive and, since most radio is programmed locally, this medium gives advertisers a high degree of customer selectivity. For example, radio stations are already segmented into listening categories such as classic rock, country and western, jazz, talk, news, and religious programming. Radio only permits an audio presentation and ads are over quickly. As well, people tend to use the radio as "background" while they are doing other things, so they may pay little attention to advertisements. Spending on radio advertisements totalled $1.5 billion in Canada in 2010.[45] Subscriber-based satellite radio poses a significant long-term threat to the traditional radio model.

Magazines

The many different magazines on the market provide a high level of consumer selectivity. The person who reads *Popular Photography* is more likely to be interested in the latest specialized lenses from Canon than is a *Gourmet* magazine subscriber. Magazine advertising allows for excellent reproduction of photographs and artwork that not only grab buyers' attention but also may convince them of the product's value. Magazines also provide advertisers plenty of space for detailed product information. Magazines have a long life and tend to be passed from person to person, thus doubling and tripling the number of exposures. The Canadian magazine with the largest readership is *Reader's Digest* with 557 701 subscribers; unfortunately the magazine saw a 10 percent decrease in subscribers in 2012. *Chatelaine* has the second highest number of subscribers at 536 447 and *Canadian Living* is third with 508 479 subscribers.[46] Spending on magazine advertisements totalled $606 million in Canada in 2010. Fortunately, this figure represents a 2.7 percent increase from the previous year; however, the previous year was disastrous with a nearly 15 percent decline.[47]

Outdoor Advertising

Outdoor advertising—billboards, signs, and advertisements on buses, taxis, and subways—is relatively inexpensive, faces little competition for customers' attention, and is subject to high repeat exposure. Like many other areas of advertising, outdoor advertising has gone high-tech. Winnipeg-based Sidetrack Technologies Inc., for example, has developed a system of 360 digital strips that are placed at intervals along subway walls. When a train passes by, the strips blend together, creating the impression of an artificial video. The strips can be changed remotely, thus allowing a company like McDonald's to advertise Egg McMuffins during the morning commute and Big Macs during the afternoon commute.[48]

Titan Worldwide has developed an LED display that shows commercials on New York City buses. The display contains GPS technology, so it can target audiences based on the time of day and the postal code where the bus is located. The technology will also be introduced to Canada and Ireland.[49] A Montreal-based company called iGotcha Media has built a network of LCD screens for malls and golf courses.[50] Many billboards now feature animation and changing images, and today's billboard messages are cheaper because they can be digitally printed in colour in large quantities. On the downside, outdoor ads can present only limited information, and sellers have little control over who sees their advertisements. Outdoor advertising in Canada totalled $482 million in 2010, an increase of over 15 percent from the previous year and the highest figure in a decade.[51]

Word-of-Mouth Advertising

Word-of-mouth advertising occurs when consumers talk to each other about products they are using. According to the Word of Mouth Marketing Association, there are several varieties of word-of-mouth advertising. These include buzz marketing (using high-profile news to get consumers talking about a product), viral marketing (consumers passing product information around on the internet), product seeding (providing free product samples to influential consumers), and cause marketing (involving consumers who feel strongly about a cause such as reducing poverty).[52]

word-of-mouth advertising Opinions about the value of products passed among consumers in informal discussions.

Consumers form very strong opinions about products as a result of conversations with friends and acquaintances, so when consumers start talking about a new product or idea, the information can build momentum and spread like wildfire. This "spreading the word" can happen without any expenditure of money by the company selling the product in question. But companies do spend money developing formal word-of-mouth advertising campaigns because they recognize how powerful they are. The now-famous "Evolution" ad for Dove soap (which showed an "ordinary" girl being transformed into a goddess) was posted on YouTube instead of traditional media. It was eventually viewed by 300 million people and generated huge publicity for the brand. The only cost to the company was that incurred in making the video.[53] Toronto-based Hook Communications launched its Voice Over Internet Protocol (VOIP) service in 2010 with an incentive to spread the word. Customers are asked to provide the emails of friends and then Hook sends friendly messages on their behalf. If two people join the service, the referrer receives a year of free service and $100 in loyalty rewards.[54]

The Internet and the Power of Consumer Engagement

Online ad sales were valued at $2.3 billion in Canada in 2010, a net increase of 22.5 percent since the previous year. The growth in this area has been tremendous and the power of this medium is unquestionable as it encompasses various powerful forms including search, display, classifieds, and email.[55]

To understand the transformational power of this medium, consider the strategic fortress of TV advertising: the Super Bowl. Even this sacred advertising event has changed. Instead of tightly guarding secret campaigns for the big day, companies are now creating teaser campaigns on YouTube and Facebook to build interest weeks before the event and encouraging consumers to participate in events. In addition, the immense audience is being directed from TV to the internet during the game. For example, Budweiser Canada used the Super Bowl to drive people to its Facebook page in order to enter a live contest that concluded at the end of the game.[56] For a detailed example, take a look at the e-Business and Social Media Solutions Box entitled "The 'Gamification' of Promotions."

Internet advertising offers advantages for both buyers and sellers. For buyers, advantages include convenience, privacy, selection, easily accessible information, and control. For sellers, advantages include reach, direct distribution, reduced expenses, relationship building (with customers on interactive websites), flexibility, and feedback (sellers can measure the success of messages by counting how many people see each ad and track the number of click-throughs to their own websites).[57]

Online marketing can be profitable for companies, but what happens when consumers turn against them? With so many individuals participating in social networking sites like Facebook and keeping personal blogs, it's increasingly common for a single unhappy customer to wage war against a company for selling faulty products or providing poor service. Individuals may post negative reviews of products on blogs, upload angry videos outlining complaints on YouTube, or join public discussion forums where they can voice their opinion. While companies benefit from the viral spread of good news, they must also be on guard against an online backlash that can damage their reputation.[58]

Virtual Advertising

virtual advertising A technique that uses digital implants of brands or products onto live or taped programming, giving the illusion that the product is part of the show.

Another method of advertising, called **virtual advertising**, uses digital implants of brands or products onto live or taped programming, giving the illusion that the product is part of the show. With this technique, an advertiser's product can appear as part of the television show—when viewers are paying more attention—instead of during commercial breaks. In a televised basketball game, the digital image of a brand—for example, the round face of a Rolex watch or an Acura hubcap—can be electronically enlarged and superimposed

E-BUSINESS + SOCIAL MEDIA SOLUTIONS

The "Gamification" of Promotions

For many years, the predominant approach used by marketers was to tell customers about the benefits of using their company's products and hope that consumers would respond favourably to the promotional message. Of course, there have always been some exceptions to this approach. For example, the rock band The Grateful Dead was an early user of what we now call "social media" because it encouraged fans to tape the band's concerts. This reduced record sales, but the band developed a huge fan following because people who taped the concerts passed the tapes around to their friends. The band therefore made a lot of money from live concerts.

In recent years, the use of social media in marketing has become widespread and sophisticated, partly because of advances in technology. The term "social media" refers to many different activities, including (but not limited to) social networking (e.g., Facebook, Twitter, Orkut), blogs (e.g., Xanga, WordPress, LiveJournal), wikis (e.g., PBworks, Wetpaint), microblogging (e.g., Foursquare, Facebook places), video (e.g., YouTube), social bookmarking (e.g., Google Reader, CiteULike), and online games (e.g., Farmville).

Companies are actively using social media to promote products. Consider a few examples:

- Farmville recently incorporated Cascadian Farm, an organic food company, into the game (players can virtually plant Cascadian's blueberries). One million players got involved in the first three days of the promotion.
- In another Farmville promotion, players who purchased certain drinks at 7-Eleven received codes that could be redeemed for virtual products in the Farmville game.
- Rapper Jay-Z's autobiography was promoted by having fans log on to a dedicated page on Bing. Fans could win an autographed copy of a page of the book if they correctly decoded clues online or via a smartphone.

Traditional loyalty programs (where customers get rewards for being a frequent user) are a common marketing tactic that has also entered the realm of social media. For example, Foursquare allows users to earn free products or receive price discounts at retail stores they frequently visit. Users "check in" at a retail location (e.g., Starbucks) and let their friends know where they are. If the user is the most frequent visitor at a retail outlet, they get the title of "mayor" of that outlet and also get free or reduced-price products. Such new techniques may even threaten traditional loyalty programs for two reasons: (a) People get a kick out of playing online games; and (b) the high-tech version may be cheaper for companies because some games provide only virtual rewards to customers. The popularity of so-called "gamification" is behind the explosive growth of companies like Groupon, as well. In 2011, a Gamification Summit was held to show marketers how to use gaming effectively.

Finally, social media has influenced the way marketers assess the success of promotional efforts. Brand engagement is now an important metric to evaluate social media marketing efforts.

Questions for Discussion

1. What is promotion? What are the five specific areas within the general area of promotion? Where do social media fit within the overall area of promotion?

2. Consider the following statement: *Social media is rapidly going to become more important than traditional media in promoting the products and services of companies.* Do you agree with the statement? Defend your answer.

on centre court without physically changing the playing floor. For recorded movies, digital images can be inserted easily. For example, a Reitmans shopping bag can be digitally added to the table in a kitchen scene.[59]

Mobile and Other Advertising Media

Mobile phone ads are growing in importance for obvious reasons. There are 21.5 million Canadian wireless phone subscribers, which translates into a 67.5 percent penetration rate. In addition, with more of these users moving to smartphones, the range of ad possibilities are improving.[60] The importance of the smartphone market cannot be underestimated; it is one of the reasons Facebook paid over $US1 billion to acquire photo-based service Instagram in 2012.[61]

A combination of many additional media—including catalogues, sidewalk handouts, Yellow Pages, skywriting, special events, and door-to-door communications—make up the remaining advertisements to which Canadians are exposed. The combination of media that a company chooses for advertising is called its media mix. Although different industries use different mixes, most depend on multiple media to advertise their products and services. As you can read in the Entrepreneurship and New Ventures boxed insert, advergaming is also a major venue for advertising. There were approximately 130 million console and computer gamers in North America in 2010, with a projected 170 million expected by 2013.[62]

Types of Advertising

Regardless of the media used, advertisements fall into one of several categories. **Brand advertising** promotes a specific brand, such as Beats by Dr. Dre headphones, Air Canada, or Nike Air Jordan basketball shoes. A variation on brand advertising, **product advertising**, promotes a general type of product or service such as dental services and milk. The "Got Milk?" advertisements are an example of product advertising. **Advocacy advertising** promotes a particular candidate or viewpoint, as in ads for political candidates at election time and anti-drug commercials. **Institutional advertising** promotes a firm's long-term image rather than a specific product.

In consumer markets, local stores usually sponsor **retail advertising** to encourage consumers to visit the store and buy its products and services. Larger retailers, such as Kmart and The Bay, use retail advertising both locally and nationally. Often retail advertising is actually **co-operative advertising**, with the cost of the advertising shared by the retailer and the manufacturer.

brand advertising Advertising that promotes a specific brand-name product.

product advertising A variation on brand advertising that promotes a general type of product or service.

advocacy advertising Advertising that promotes a particular viewpoint or candidate.

institutional advertising Advertising that promotes a firm's long-term image, not a specific product.

retail advertising Advertising by retailers designed to reach end-users of a consumer product.

co-operative advertising Advertising in which a manufacturer together with a retailer or a wholesaler advertise to reach customers.

Beats by Dr. Dre headphones have built a reputation through online buzz, YouTube videos, and more traditional techniques like cinema ads.

trade advertising Advertising by manufacturers designed to reach potential wholesalers and retailers.

In industrial markets, some firms use **trade advertising** publications to communicate with companies that distribute their products. For example, a firm that makes plumbing fixtures might advertise in *Hardware Retailer* to persuade large hardware stores to carry its products. And to reach the professional purchasing agent and managers at firms buying raw materials or components, companies use **industrial advertising**.

industrial advertising Advertising by manufacturers designed to reach other manufacturers' professional purchasing agents and managers of firms buying raw materials or components.

Preparing an Advertising Campaign

advertising campaign The arrangement of ads in selected media to reach target audiences.

An **advertising campaign** is the arrangement of ads in selected media to reach target audiences. It includes several activities that, taken together, constitute a program for meeting a marketing objective, such as introducing a new product or changing a company's image in the public mind. A campaign typically includes six steps:

1. identifying the target audience

2. defining the objectives of the advertising messages

3. establishing the advertising budget

4. creating the advertising messages

5. selecting the appropriate media

6. evaluating advertising effectiveness

advertising agencies Firms that specialize in creating and placing advertisements in the media for clients.

Advertising agencies—independent companies that provide some or all of their clients' advertising needs—help in the development of advertising campaigns by providing specialized services. The agency works together with the client company to determine the campaign's central message, create detailed message content, identify advertising media, and negotiate media purchases.[63] The advantage offered by agencies is expertise in developing advertising themes, message content, and artwork, as well as in coordinating advertising production and advising on relevant legal matters. As payment for its services, the agency usually receives a percentage, traditionally 15 percent of the media purchase cost. For example, if an agency purchases a $1-million television commitment for a client's campaign, it would receive $150 000 for its services.[64]

The creative power behind a strong ad agency is key for a firm looking to generate the type of buzz that Nancy Vonk and Janet Kestin (formerly of Ogilvy Mather Toronto) are known for; two highly successful campaigns that were created under their leadership are the Dove Real Beauty campaign and the Diamond Shreddies campaign.[65]

Personal Selling

LO6 Outline the tasks involved in *personal selling* and list the steps in the personal selling process.

Virtually everyone has done some personal selling. Perhaps as a child you had a lemonade stand or sold candy for the drama club. Or you may have gone on a job interview, selling your abilities as an employee to the interviewer's company. In personal selling, a salesperson communicates one-on-one with a potential customer to identify the customer's need and match that need with the seller's product.

personal selling Promotional tool in which a salesperson communicates one-on-one with potential customers.

Personal selling—the oldest form of selling—provides the personal link between seller and buyer. It adds to a firm's credibility because it provides buyers with someone to interact with and to answer their questions. Because it involves personal interaction, personal selling requires a level of trust between the buyer and the seller. When a buyer feels cheated by the seller, that trust has been broken and a negative attitude toward salespeople in general can develop.

Personal selling is the most expensive form of promotion per contact because presentations are generally made to one or two individuals at a time. Personal selling expenses include salespeople's compensation and their overhead, usually travel, food, and lodging. The average cost of each industrial sales call has been estimated at nearly $300.[66]

Costs have prompted many companies to turn to telemarketing—using telephone solicitations to conduct the personal selling process. Telemarketing is useful in handling any stage of this process and in arranging appointments for salespeople. It cuts the cost of personal sales visits to industrial customers, each of whom requires about four visits to complete a sale. Such savings are stimulating the growth of telemarketing, which provides 150 000 jobs in Canada and generates $25 billion in annual sales. Telemarketing returns $6.25 for every dollar that is spent.[67]

Because many consumers are annoyed by telemarketing pitches, a do-not-call registry was set up in Canada in 2008, and six million people quickly registered. Heavy fines can be levied on companies that ignore the new rules. A survey by VoxPop showed that 80 percent of Canadians who registered now receive fewer telemarketing calls than they used to, but in 2009, it was discovered that some unscrupulous marketers were actually using the registry to call people.[68] Michael Geist, a Canada Research Chair in Internet and E-commerce Law at the University of Ottawa, says the government's registry is flawed.[69]

Sales Force Management

Sales force management means setting goals at top levels of the organization, setting specific objectives for individual salespeople, organizing the sales force to meet those objectives, and implementing and evaluating the success of the overall sales plan.

sales force management Setting goals at top levels of an organization; setting practical objectives for salespeople; organizing a sales force to meet those objectives; implementing and evaluating the success of a sales plan.

Personal Selling Situations

Managers of both telemarketers and traditional salespeople must consider the ways in which personal sales activities are affected by the differences between consumer and industrial products:

- **Retail selling** is selling a consumer product for the buyer's personal or household use.

- **Industrial selling** is selling products to other businesses, either for the purpose of manufacturing other products or resale.

retail selling Selling a consumer product for the buyer's own personal or household use.

industrial selling Selling products to other businesses, either for manufacturing other products or for resale.

Levi's, for instance, sells jeans to the retail clothing chain Gap Inc. (industrial selling). In turn, consumers purchase Levi's jeans at one of Gap's stores (retail selling). Each of these situations has distinct characteristics. In retail selling, the buyer usually comes to the seller, but in industrial selling, the salesperson comes to the buyer.

Personal Selling Tasks

Improving sales efficiency requires marketers to consider salespeople's tasks. Three basic tasks are generally associated with selling: order processing, creative selling, and missionary selling. Sales jobs usually require salespeople to perform all three tasks to some degree, depending on the product and the company.

Order Processing. In **order processing**, a salesperson receives an order and oversees the handling and delivery of that order. Route salespeople are often order processors. They call on regular customers to check the customer's supply of bread, milk, snack foods, or soft drinks. Then, with the customer's consent, they determine the size of the reorder, fill the order from their trucks, and stack the customer's shelves.

order processing In personal sales, the receiving and follow-through on handling and delivery of an order by a salesperson.

Creative Selling. When the benefits of a product are not clear, **creative selling** may persuade buyers that they have a need for it. Most industrial products involve creative selling because the buyer has not used the product before or may not be familiar with its features and uses. Creative selling is also crucial for high-priced consumer products, such as homes, where buyers comparison shop. Any new product can benefit from creative selling that differentiates it from other products.

creative selling In personal sales, the use of techniques designed to persuade a customer to buy a product when the benefits of the product are not readily apparent or the item is very expensive.

missionary selling In personal sales, the indirect promotion of a product by offering technical assistance and/or promoting the company's image.

Missionary Selling. The goal of **missionary selling** is to promote the company and its products over the long term, rather than to make a quick sale. Drug company representatives promote their companies' drugs to doctors who, in turn, may eventually prescribe them to their patients. The sale is actually made at the drugstore.

The Personal Selling Process

Although all three sales tasks are important to an organization using personal selling, perhaps the most complicated is creative selling. It is the creative salesperson who is responsible for most of the steps in the personal selling process described below.

prospecting In personal sales, the process of identifying potential customers.

qualifying In personal sales, the process of determining whether potential customers have the authority to buy and the ability to pay for a product.

Prospecting and Qualifying. **Prospecting** is the process of identifying potential customers. Salespeople find prospects through past company records, existing customers, friends, relatives, company personnel, and business associates. **Qualifying** means determining whether prospects have the authority to buy and the ability to pay.

Approaching. The *approach* refers to the first few minutes that a salesperson has contact with a qualified prospect. The success of later stages depends on the prospect's first impression of the salesperson, since this impression affects the salesperson's credibility. Salespeople need to present a neat, professional appearance and to greet prospects in a strong, confident manner.

Presenting and Demonstrating. Presenting involves a full explanation of the product, its features, and its uses. It links the product's benefits to the prospect's needs. A presentation may or may not include a demonstration of the product, but it is wise to demonstrate a product whenever possible, since most people have trouble visualizing what they have been told.

Handling Objections. Prospects may have objections to various aspects such as price. Objections show the salesperson that the buyer is interested in the presentation and which parts of the presentation the buyer is unsure of or has a problem with. They tell the salesperson what customers feel is important and, essentially, how to sell to them.

closing In personal sales, the process of asking the customer to buy the product.

Closing. The most critical part of the selling process is the **closing**, in which the salesperson asks the prospective customer to buy the product. Successful salespeople recognize the signs that a customer is ready to buy. For example, prospects who start to figure out monthly payments for the product are clearly indicating that they are ready to buy. Salespeople can ask directly for the sale or they can indirectly imply a close.

Following Up. The sales process does not end with the close of the sale. Sales follow-up activities include fast processing of the customer's order and on-time delivery. Training in the proper care and use of the product and speedy service if repairs are needed may also be part of the follow-up.

Sales Promotions

sales promotions Short-term promotional activities designed to stimulate consumer buying or co-operation from distributors and other members of the trade.

Sales promotions are short-term promotional activities designed to stimulate consumer buying or co-operation from distributors, sales agents, or other members of the trade. For example, soap may be bound into packages of four with the promotion "Buy three and get one free." Sales promotions are important because they enhance product recognition and increase the likelihood that buyers will try products. To be successful, sales promotions must be convenient and accessible when the decision to purchase occurs. If Harley-Davidson has a one-week motorcycle promotion and there is no dealer in your area, the promotion is neither convenient nor accessible to you. But if The Bay offers a 20-percent-off coupon that you can save for later use, the promotion is convenient and accessible.

One cautionary note: Frequent sales promotions may condition consumers to build negative habits from the retailer's perspective. If customers know that there will be a discount day every three to six weeks, they may hold off on purchases. The overuse of promotions like "Bay Days" may actually cause customers to delay purchases to maximize savings. Sales promotions must be used in moderation to avoid this scenario. Even successful promotions like Tim Hortons Roll up the Rim (which is a once-a-year event) must be carefully monitored. The result of the twenty-fifth anniversary event for Tim Hortons was the usual increase in traffic, but the firm's results were disappointing, which led to a major hit in the stock market. The company blamed higher food costs; ironically, the promotion odds fell from nine-to-one down to six-to-one, which meant more winners and higher costs. Despite the results, however, the popular promotion was back without changes in 2012.[70]

Types of Sales Promotions

The best-known sales promotions are coupons, point-of-purchase displays, purchasing incentives (such as free samples, trading stamps, and premiums), trade shows, and contests and sweepstakes.

Describe the various types of *sales promotions*, and distinguish between *publicity* and *public relations*.

■ Certificates entitling the bearer to stated savings off a product's regular price are **coupons**. Coupons may be used to encourage customers to try new products, to attract customers away from competitors, or to induce current customers to buy more of a product. These days, consumers like their coupons online and the success of sites like Coupons.ca is clear and growing annually.

coupon A method of sales promotion featuring a certificate that entitles the bearer to stated savings off a product's regular price.

■ To grab customers' attention as they walk through a store, some companies use **point-of-purchase (POP) displays**, which often coincide with a sale on the item(s) being displayed. Displays are located at the end of an aisle or near the checkout in supermarkets to make it easier for customers to find a product and easier for manufacturers to eliminate competitors from consideration.

point-of-purchase (POP) displays A method of sales promotion in which a product display is so located in a retail store as to encourage consumers to buy the product.

■ Free samples and premiums are purchasing incentives. **Free samples** allow customers to try a product for a few days at no cost. They may be given out at local retail outlets or sent by manufacturers to consumers via direct mail. **Premiums** are free or reduced-price items, such as pens, calendars, and coffee mugs, given to consumers in return for buying a specified product. Premiums may not work as well as originally hoped, since customers may switch to a new brand just to get the premiums that company is offering and then return to their customary brand.

free samples A method of sales promotion in which a small sample of product is offered free, allowing customers to try a product for a few days at no cost.

premium A method of sales promotion in which some item is offered free or at a bargain price to customers in return for buying a specified product.

■ **Trade shows** allow companies to rent booths to display and demonstrate their products to customers who have a special interest or who are ready to buy. Trade shows are relatively inexpensive and are very effective, since the buyer comes to the seller already interested in a given type of product.

trade shows A method of sales promotion in which members of a particular industry gather for displays and product demonstrations designed to sell products to customers.

■ Customers, distributors, and sales representatives may all be persuaded to increase sales of a product through the use of contests and sweepstakes. For example, distributors and sales agents may win a trip to Hawaii for selling the most pillows in the month of February, or customers may win $1 million in a magazine sweepstake.

Publicity and Public Relations

Much to the delight of marketing managers with tight budgets, **publicity** is free. Moreover, because it is presented in a news format, consumers see publicity as objective and highly believable. However, marketers often have little control over publicity, and that can have a very negative effect on the company. For example, a YouTube video showing what appeared to be a Guinness beer commercial portrayed several people in a suggestive sexual arrangement with the title "Share One with a Friend."

publicity Information about a company that is made available to consumers by the news media; it is not controlled by the company, but it does not cost the company any money.

Guinness was quick to distance itself from the fake advertisement, saying that was not how it wanted its product portrayed.[71]

public relations A company-influenced activity that attempts to establish a sense of goodwill between the company and its customers through public-service announcements that enhance the company's image.

In contrast to publicity, **public relations** is company-influenced publicity. It attempts to create goodwill between the company and its customers through public service announcements that enhance the company's image. For example, a bank may announce that senior citizens' groups can have free use of a meeting room for their social activities. As well, company executives may make appearances as guest speakers representing their companies at professional meetings and civic events. They also may serve as leaders in civic activities like the United Way campaign and university fundraising.

McDonald's has used Ronald McDonald as an ambassador for nearly 50 years, but recently a group of 600 health care professionals singled out the mascot and asked the company to retire Ronald and stop marketing to kids. The company denied the request and pointed to the great charities associated with the figure. However, it is clear that Ronald is losing some of his appeal. In a recent Omnicom survey Ronald ranked 2179th out 2800 celebrities in terms of likeability. The clown has no Facebook page, and if he does not gain more relevance in the modern age, he may be retired for other reasons.[72]

ambush marketing occurs when a company launches an advertising campaign to coincide with a major event, like the Olympics; it capitalizes on viewer interest without paying an official sponsorship fee.

Corporate sponsorships of athletic events also help promote a company's image. Roots has been successful in getting high-profile individuals to wear its products. These sponsorships rely on a positive brand association with the event; however, sometimes sponsors can be frustrated by a competitor that benefits from the same exposure without paying official sponsor fees, a practice known as **ambush marketing**. The Royal Bank was an official sponsor of the 2010 Winter Olympic Games, so when Scotiabank launched a national photo contest to display Canadian pride, cleverly timed to benefit from the exposure of the games, the Olympic organizing committee took notice.[73] Most large firms have a department to manage their relations with the public and to present a desired company image.

L08 Describe the development of international and small business *promotion* strategies.

International Promotion Strategies

As we saw in Chapter 5, recent decades have witnessed a profound shift from "home-country" marketing to "multi-country" marketing and now to "global" marketing. Nowhere is this rapidly growing global orientation more evident than in marketing promotions, especially advertising.

Ciroc Vodka is a strong beneficiary of PR and publicity; this is the reason Diageo, the world's largest producer of alcohol products, teamed up with Sean "Diddy" Combs, the entertainment artist and entrepreneur, and made him a brand ambassador. He does not miss a chance to promote this brand.[75]

Emergence of the Global Perspective

Every company that markets products in several countries faces a basic choice—use a decentralized approach (maintaining separate marketing for each country) or adopt a global perspective (directing a coordinated marketing program at one worldwide audience). The **global perspective** is a philosophy that directs marketing toward worldwide rather than local or regional markets.

global perspective A company's approach to directing its marketing toward worldwide rather than local or regional markets.

The Movement Toward Global Advertising

A truly global perspective means designing products for multinational appeal—that is, genuinely global products.[74] A few brands, such as Coca-Cola, McDonald's, Mercedes-Benz, and Rolex enjoy global recognition and have become truly global brands. One universal advertising program would obviously be more efficient and cost effective than developing different programs for each of many countries. For several reasons, however, global advertising is not feasible for many companies. Four factors make global advertising a challenging proposition:

- *Product variations.* Even if a product has universal appeal, some variations are usually preferred in different cultures. In the magazine business, *Reader's Digest* has English and French editions in Canada and overall it has 50 editions in more than 70 countries in 21 languages.[75] Many companies have found that without a local or national identity, universal ads don't cause consumers to buy. Coca-Cola's "think global, act local" strategy and Nestlé's approach to small-scale local advertising call for ads tailored to different areas. Such ads are designed to produce variations on a universal theme while appealing to local emotions, ideas, and values. Advertising agencies have set up worldwide agency networks that can coordinate a campaign's central theme while allowing regional variations.

- *Language differences.* Compared with those in other languages, ads in English require less print space and airtime because English is a more efficient and precise language than most others. But translations can be inexact and confusing. When Coke first went to China many years ago, the direct translation of *Coca-Cola* came out as "Bite the wax tadpole" in Chinese.

- *Cultural receptiveness.* There are differences across nations regarding the mass advertising of sensitive products (such as birth control or personal hygiene products), not to mention those for which advertising may be legally restricted (alcohol, cigarettes). A Canadian in Paris may be surprised to see nudity in billboard ads and even more surprised to find that France is the only country in the European Union (EU) that bans advertising or selling wine on the internet. In the EU and through much of Asia, comparative advertising is considered distasteful or even illegal.

- *Image differences.* Any company's image can vary from nation to nation, regardless of advertising appeals for universal recognition. American Express and IBM have better images in the United States than in the United Kingdom, where Heinz and Coca-Cola have better images.

Promotional Practices in Small Business

Although small businesses generally have fewer resources, cost-effective promotions can improve sales and enable small firms to compete with much larger firms.

Small Business Advertising

Few developments in history have provided more advertising opportunities than the internet. Cheaper access to computing equipment, to online services, and to website expertise puts cyberspace within the grasp of nearly every firm. Still, owners must decide which audiences to target and what messages to send. And even though the web can instantaneously reach distant customers, other methods depend on the market that the small business is trying to reach—local, national, or international.

Non-primetime ads on TV have good impact at costs within the reach of many small firms. More often, however, small firms use newspaper, radio, and, increasingly, internet and direct mail (particularly catalogues) to reach local markets. For year-round advertising, the Yellow Pages is popular for both industrial and consumer products. However, many small businesses, especially those selling to consumer markets, rely more on seasonal advertising.

The Role of Personal Selling in Small Business

As with advertising, small business personal selling strategies depend on intended markets. Some small firms maintain sales forces, especially in local markets, where clients can be quickly visited. But most small companies cannot afford to establish international offices, although some entrepreneurs do visit prospective customers in other countries. For most small businesses, even sending sales representatives abroad is too expensive. Some contract with sales agencies—companies that act on behalf of several clients. Because the costs of a national sales force are high, small companies prefer sales agencies and such methods as telemarketing. By combining telemarketing with catalogues or other print media, small businesses can sometimes compete with larger companies on a national scale. Syncsort Inc. combined a telemarketing staff with eight national sales reps to become the number-one developer of computer software for sorting data into convenient formats (IBM is number two).

Small Business Promotions

Small companies also use sales promotions to market their products. Large firms tend to rely on coupons, POP displays, and sales contests, but small firms prefer premiums and special sales because they are less expensive.[76] An automobile dealership, for example, might offer you a fishing reel if you come in to road test a new car. Service companies ranging from martial arts centres to dry cleaners frequently feature special sale prices.

MyBizLab

Capture more moments of true understanding. MyBizLab provides you with interactive study and practice tools directly related to this chapter's content. The new MyBizLab Study Plan Learning Path is designed to measure a full range of skills and provide remediation to give you what you need to master key chapter concepts. MyBizLab flexes to your unique learning needs. The result? Inspired learning, more success.

SUMMARY OF LEARNING OBJECTIVES

1. **Explain the definition of a product as a *value package.*** A product is a good, service, or idea that is marketed to satisfy consumer needs and wants. Consumers regard a product as a bundle of attributes that, taken together, constitute the *value package.* Consumers expect to receive products with greater value—that is, products with more benefits at a reasonable price. A successful product is a value package that provides the right *features* and offers

the right *benefits.* Features are the qualities, tangible and intangible, that a company builds into its products.

2. **Describe the new product development process and trace the stages of the *product life cycle.*** Many firms adopt some version of a basic seven-step new product development process: (1) *product ideas*—searching for product ideas; (2) *screening*—eliminating all ideas that do not fit the firm's abilities or objectives; (3) *concept testing*—using

market research to get consumers' input about product benefits and prices; (4) *business analysis*—comparing manufacturing costs and benefits to see whether a product meets minimum profitability goals; (5) *prototype development*—producing a preliminary version of a product; (6) *product testing and test marketing*—going into limited production, testing the product to see whether it meets performance requirements, and, if so, selling it on a limited basis; and (7) *commercialization*—beginning full-scale production and marketing.

The *product life cycle (PLC)* is a series of four stages characterizing a product's profit-producing life: (1) *Introduction*—marketers focus on making potential consumers aware of the product and its benefits; (2) *growth*—sales begin to climb and the product begins to show a profit; (3) *maturity*—although the product earns its highest profit level, increased competition eventually leads to price cutting and lower profits, and sales start to fall; and (4) *decline*—sales and profits are further lost to new products in the introduction stage.

3. **Explain the importance of *branding*, *packaging*, and *labelling*.** *Branding* is a process of using symbols to communicate the qualities of a particular product made by a particular producer. Brands are designed to signal uniform quality. *Packaging* refers to the physical container in which a product is sold, advertised, or protected. A package makes the product attractive, displays the brand name, and identifies features and benefits. It also reduces the risk of damage, breakage, or spoilage, and it lessens the likelihood of theft. Every product has a *label* on its package that identifies its name, manufacturer, and contents. Like packaging, labelling can help market a product.

4. **Identify the important objectives of *promotion* and discuss the considerations in selecting a *promotional mix*.** *Promotion* is any technique designed to sell a product. Besides the ultimate objective of increasing sales, marketers may use promotion to accomplish any of the following four goals: *(1) communicating information, (2) positioning products, (3) adding value, and (4) controlling sales volume.*

There are four types of promotional tools: *advertising, personal selling, sales promotions,* and *publicity and public relations*. The best combination of these tools—the best *promotional mix*—depends on several factors, the most important of which are the target audience and buyer decision process. Marketers try to match promotional tools with stages in the buyer decision process.

5. **Discuss the most important *advertising* strategies and describe *the key advertising media*.** The advertising strategies used for a product most often depend on the stage of the product life cycle the product is in. As products become established and competition increases, advertisers may choose one of three strategies: (1) *persuasive advertising*, (2) *comparative advertising*, and (3) *reminder advertising*.

Marketers use several different media-specific communication devices for conveying a seller's message to potential customers: (1) *television*, (2) *newspapers*, (3) *direct mail*, (4) *radio*, (5) *magazines*, (6) *outdoor advertising*, (7) *internet advertising*, and (8) *virtual advertising*.

6. **Outline the tasks involved in *personal selling* and list the steps in the personal selling process.** There are three basic tasks in personal selling: (1) *order processing*, (2) *creative selling*, and (3) *missionary selling*. The creative salesperson goes through most of the following six steps in the personal selling process: (1) *prospecting and qualifying*—identifying potential customers and determining whether they have the authority to buy and ability to pay; (2) *approaching*—the first few minutes of contact with a qualified prospect make up the approach; (3) *presenting and demonstrating*—after the approach, the salesperson makes a presentation; (4) *handling objections*—objections pinpoint the parts of the presentation with which the buyer has a problem and that the salesperson must overcome; (5) *closing*—in the closing, the salesperson asks the prospective customer to buy the product; and (6) *following up*—to cement lasting relationships with buyers, sellers supply additional after-sale services.

7. **Describe the various types of *sales promotions*, and distinguish between *publicity* and *public relations*.** Sales promotions are short-term promotional activities designed to stimulate consumer buying or co-operation from members of the trade. The following are the best-known forms of promotions: (1) *Coupons* are certificates entitling bearers to savings off regular prices. (2) *Point-of-purchase (POP)* displays are used by companies to grab customers' attention as they move through stores. (3) *Free samples* are purchasing incentives that allow customers to try products without risk. (4) *Premiums* are gifts to consumers in return for buying certain products. (5) Industries sponsor *trade shows,* at which companies rent booths to display and demonstrate products to customers with a special interest in them. (6) *Contests* are a means to persuade customers, distributors, and sales reps to increase sales.

Publicity is a promotional tool in which information about a company or product is created and transmitted by general mass media. It is free, and because it is presented in a news format, consumers often see it as objective and credible. However, marketers often have little control over it, and it can be as easily detrimental as beneficial. *Public relations* is company-influenced publicity that seeks to build good relations with the public and to deal with unfavourable events.

8. **Describe the development of international and small business *promotion* strategies.** Recent decades have witnessed a profound shift from home-country marketing to global marketing. Every company that markets its products in several countries faces a basic choice: Use a *decentralized approach,* with separate marketing management for each country, or adopt a *global perspective*, directing marketing toward a worldwide rather than a local or regional market. There are four factors that determine whether global advertising is feasible: (1) *product variations*, (2) *language differences*, (3) *cultural receptiveness*, and (4) *image differences*. In recognizing national differences, many global marketers try to build on a universal advertising theme that nevertheless allows for variations. In doing so, they rely on help from different advertising agencies in various geographic regions.

KEY TERMS

advertising (p. 513)
advertising agencies (p. 520)
advertising campaign (p. 520)
advertising media (p. 513)
advocacy advertising (p. 519)
ambush marketing (p. 524)
brand advertising (p. 519)
brand equity (p. 506)
brand loyalty (p. 507)
branding (p. 505)
capital items (p. 499)
capital services (p. 499)
closing (p. 522)
comparative advertising (p. 513)
Consumer Packaging and Labelling
    Act (p. 509)
convenience goods/services (p. 499)
co-operative advertising (p. 519)
copyright (p. 509)
coupon (p. 523)
creative selling (p. 521)
direct mail (p. 516)
expense items (p. 499)
features (p. 497)
free samples (p. 523)
generic brands (p. 507)

global perspective (p. 525)
industrial advertising (p. 520)
industrial selling (p. 521)
informative advertising (p. 513)
institutional advertising (p. 519)
label (p. 509)
licensed brands (p. 506)
media mix (p. 514)
missionary selling (p. 522)
national brands (p. 506)
order processing (p. 521)
packaging (p. 509)
patent (p. 508)
personal selling (p. 520)
persuasive advertising (p. 513)
point-of-purchase (POP) displays
    (p. 523)
premium (p. 523)
private brands (p. 506)
product adaptation (p. 504)
product advertising (p. 519)
product extension (p. 504)
product life cycle (PLC) (p. 503)
product line (p. 500)
product mix (p. 500)
product positioning (p. 511)

promotion (p. 510)
promotional mix (p. 512)
prospecting (p. 522)
publicity (p. 523)
public relations (p. 524)
pull strategy (p. 512)
push strategy (p. 512)
qualifying (p. 522)
reintroduction (p. 505)
reminder advertising (p. 513)
retail advertising (p. 519)
retail selling (p. 521)
sales force management (p. 521)
sales promotions (p. 522)
service package (p. 502)
service process design (p. 503)
shopping goods/services (p. 499)
specialty goods/services (p. 499)
speed to market (p. 502)
trade advertising (p. 520)
trademark (p. 507)
trade shows (p. 523)
value package (p. 498)
virtual advertising (p. 518)
word-of-mouth advertising (p. 517)

QUESTIONS FOR ANALYSIS

1. What does *brand equity* mean and how do companies like Apple take advantage of their strong brand equity?

2. Analyze several advertisements that use comparative advertising. Do these advertisements leave you with a positive or negative image of the company? Also, analyze differences in the comparative advertisements that are shown on U.S. and Canadian television networks. Do these differences affect your opinion of the advertiser?

3. How would you expect the branding, packaging, and labelling of convenience, shopping, and specialty goods to differ? Why? Give examples to illustrate your answers.

4. Choose two advertising campaigns that have recently been conducted by business firms in your area. Choose one that you think is effective and one that you think is ineffective. What differences in the campaigns make one better than the other?

5. Select a good or service that you have purchased recently. Try to retrace the relevant steps in the buyer decision process as you experienced it. Which steps were most important to you? Which steps were least important?

6. Why would a business use a push strategy rather than a pull strategy?

APPLICATION EXERCISES

1. Interview the manager of a local manufacturing firm. Identify the company's different products according to their positions in the product life cycle.
2. Select a product that is sold nationally. Identify as many media used in its promotion as you can. Which medium is used most often? On the whole, do you think the campaign is effective? What criteria did you use to make your judgment about effectiveness?
3. Interview the owner of a local small business. Identify the company's promotional objectives and strategies, and the elements in its promotional mix. What, if any, changes would you suggest? Why?
4. Check out your college's or university's website and determine how effective it is as a tool for promoting your school.

BUILDING YOUR BUSINESS SKILLS

Greeting Start-up Decisions

The Purpose of the Assignment

To encourage students to analyze the potential usefulness of two promotional methods—personal selling and direct mail—for a start-up greeting card company.

The Situation

You are the marketing adviser for a local start-up company that makes and sells specialty greeting cards in a city of 400 000. Last year's sales totalled 14 000 cards, including personalized holiday cards, birthday cards, and special-events cards for individuals. Although revenues increased last year, you see a way of further boosting sales by expanding into card shops, grocery stores, and gift shops. You see two alternatives for entering these outlets:

1. Use direct mail to reach more individual customers for specialty cards.
2. Use personal selling to gain display space in retail stores.

Your challenge is to convince the owner of the start-up company which alternative is the more financially sound decision.

Assignment

Step 1

Get together with four or five classmates to research the two kinds of product segments, personalized cards and retail store cards. Find out which of the two kinds of marketing promotions will be more effective for each of the two segments. What will be the reaction to each method from customers, retailers, and card company owners?

Step 2

Draft a proposal to the company owner. Leaving budget and production details to other staffers, list as many reasons as possible for adopting direct mail. Then list as many reasons as possible for adopting personal selling. Defend each reason. Consider the following reasons in your argument:

- Competitive environment: Analyze the impact of other card suppliers that offer personalized cards and cards for sale in retail stores.

- Expectations of target markets: Who buys personalized cards, and who buys ready-made cards from retail stores?

- Overall cost of the promotional effort: Which method—direct mail or personal selling—will be more costly?

- Marketing effectiveness: Which promotional method will result in greater consumer response?

Questions for Discussion

1. Why do you think some buyers want personalized cards? Why do some consumers want ready-made cards from retail stores?
2. Today's computer operating systems provide easy access to software for designing and making cards on home PCs. How does the availability of this product affect your recommendation?
3. What was your most convincing argument for using direct mail? And for using personal selling?
4. Can a start-up company compete in retail stores against industry giants such as Hallmark?

EXERCISING YOUR ETHICS: TEAM EXERCISE

Cleaning Up in Sales

The Situation

Selling a product—whether a good or a service—requires the salesperson to believe in it, to be confident of his or her sales skills, and to keep commitments made to clients. Because so many people and resources are involved in delivering a product, numerous uncertainties and problems can give rise to ethical issues. This exercise encourages you to examine some of the ethical issues that can surface in the selling process for industrial products.

The Dilemma

Cleaning Technologies Corporation (CTC) is a U.S.-based company that manufactures equipment for industrial cleaners. The Canadian division of CTC has just hired Denise Skilsel and six other new graduates, and these seven individuals have just completed the sales training program for a new line of high-tech machinery that CTC has developed. As a new salesperson, Skilsel is eager to meet potential clients, all of whom are professional buyers for companies—such as laundries and dry cleaners, carpet cleaners, and military cleaners—that use CTC products or those of competitors. Skilsel is especially enthusiastic about several facts that she learned during training: CTC's equipment is the most technically advanced in the industry, carries a 10-year performance guarantee, and is safe—both functionally and environmentally.

The first month was difficult but successful. In visits to seven firms, Skilsel successfully closed three sales, earning large commissions (pay is based on sales results) as well as praise from the sales manager. Moreover, after listening to her presentations, two more potential buyers had given verbal commitments and were about to sign for much bigger orders than any Skilsel had closed to date. As she was catching her flight to close those sales, Skilsel received two calls, one from a client and one from a competitor. The client, just getting started with CTC equipment, was having some trouble: Employees stationed nearby were getting sick when the equipment was running. The competitor told Skilsel that the U.S. Environmental Protection Agency (EPA) had received complaints from some of CTC's U.S. customers that the new technology was environmentally unsafe because of noxious emissions.

Team Activity

Assemble a group of four students and assign each group member to one of the following roles:

- Denise Skilsel: CTC salesperson (employee)
- CTC sales manager (employer)
- CTC customer
- CTC investor

Questions for Discussion

1. Before discussing the situation with your group, and from the perspective of your assigned role, what do you recommend that Skilsel say to the two client firms she is scheduled to visit? Write down your recommendation.
2. Gather your group together and reveal, in turn, each member's recommendation.
3. Appoint someone to record the main points of agreement and disagreement within the group. How do you explain the results? What accounts for any disagreement?
4. Identify any ethical issues involved in group members' recommendations. Which issues, if any, are more critical than others?
5. From an ethical standpoint, what does your group finally recommend that Skilsel say to the two client firms she is scheduled to visit? Explain your result.
6. Identify the advantages and drawbacks resulting from your recommendations.

Go to MyBizLab for additional cases and exercise material.

CONCLUDING CASE 16-1

Promoting a Successful Yogurt Craze

In recent years, there have been many product introductions in the yogurt aisles, with each one promising a unique benefit or ingredient to capture market share. However, in this competitive industry it is hard to make a real dent. With food costs rising and consumers watching their wallets, there has been a noticeable trend: Prices have increased or alternatively packages have been reduced and prices have been maintained (which essentially means that prices have been increased in a more creative manner). It seems like every year the packages get smaller and smaller and smaller. If you had collected large yogurt containers to see what you could buy for approximately $3.99 in each of the past 10 years, you would likely have the yogurt equivalent of the classic wooden Russian Matryoshka dolls—in other words, you could probably fit the successive new containers into the old containers based on the year manufactured.

Old Product, New Market

In the fight for yogurt supremacy, something interesting has been occurring and it is not exactly a new product that is leading the way (unless you believe that products that have been around for centuries are new). What's old is now new in Canadian yogurt aisles and leading the revolution is the Greek yogurt category. According to Nielsen, Greek yogurt accounted for about 6 percent of the Canadian market, by volume, in 2012, up from just a 1 percent share the previous year. This is significant traction. For example, in its first year, the President's Choice Greek brand has become the number-one selling yogurt at Loblaws. To truly appreciate the potential for growth, we need to look south of the border, where the Greek yogurt craze started two years earlier than in Canada and achieved a 13 percent market share in just three years (it took energy drinks twice as long to get an equivalent share of the beverage market). According to Consumer Edge Research, Greek yogurt could

actually capture as much as half of the U.S. market, which is expected to be worth $9 billion by 2015 (Euromonitor). These numbers are all impressive, and what is even more spectacular is that this product is usually sold in smaller packages for significantly higher prices than regular yogurt. With all of this potential, it seems like everyone is trying to take advantage of the trend. Even Ben & Jerry's has created a frozen Greek yogurt.

Product Fundamentals

The success of this sub-category is based on some very solid fundamentals. The product fits in with the increased trend toward healthy living and eating habits. People are willing to pay more for good, healthy products, and in this case the creamier taste is not created by artificial flavours or unhealthy ingredients. Rather, Greek yogurt is unique because it is strained using a filter or cheesecloth to remove the liquid. That is why it is thicker and has a different texture that consumers seem to appreciate.

Creative Marketing, Building Buzz

Like any great launch, the marketing has been a key ingredient to the product's success. In Canada, the President's Choice brand was supported by a significant marketing campaign. Liberte brand launched with an emphasis on health and conducted sampling events and taste-tests in gyms and other health-related venues. Down south, Chobani is the market leader ahead of Fage (an authentic Greek brand). Chobani spread the word using a roving truck it called the "Chomobile," which travelled around promoting the health benefits of its yogurt and supplying product samples.

These grassroots approaches built the initial buzz, but it is clear that the stakes are rising along with the popularity. Danone (the French multinational) recently invested in a mass marketing campaign and spent $3 million on a Super Bowl advertisement featuring John Stamos for its Oikos Greek yogurt brand. This was a clear signal that this niche was quickly transforming into a major segment. Who will win the battle of the Greek yogurt brands? Time will tell, but after centuries in existence this "new" segment of the North American market appears to be here to stay.

Questions for Discussion

1. What are the primary features and benefits that help explain the successful commercialization of this yogurt category in the North American market?
2. In the case, we identified both private brands and national brands. Categorize each of the brands mentioned, and explain the difference between national and private brands.
3. If you were involved in launching a new brand of Greek yogurt for a major food manufacturer, would you employ a push or a pull strategy?
4. If you were in charge of creating a new campaign for the President's Choice Greek yogurt brand, what elements of the promotional mix would you employ? How would you use social media tools to get the message out?

CONCLUDING CASE 16-2

Harnessing the Power of Word-of-Mouth Advertising

Vocalpoint is a community for women that provides valuable and interesting insights about new products, surveys, daily tips, articles, and coupons/samples. It is run by a division of Procter & Gamble.

Word of mouth is probably the oldest form of advertising, yet today more and more companies are truly embracing new tools to make this old technique work in their favour. Social networking sites like YouTube, Facebook, and personal blogs are enabling consumers to spread those messages at lightning speeds, changing the advertising landscape.

Ever since the first brand names were developed hundreds of years ago, consumers have been exchanging information about positive and negative product features. In the eighteenth and nineteenth centuries, marketing was very fragmented and most products were promoted only in local areas at retailers like the general store. Word-of-mouth advertising was therefore mostly confined to local or regional markets because existing technology did not allow consumers to be well connected. By the 1930s, the development of radio, and later television, allowed businesses to market their products nationwide. Word of mouth did not disappear, but it was overshadowed by mass marketing.

Today, word-of-mouth advertising has a great new ally: the internet. Word-of-mouth advertising is relatively cheap, and the messages that it carries are trusted by those who hear them. A Nielsen study showed that 78 percent of consumers trust word-of-mouth messages. Newspapers are trusted by 63 percent of consumers, television by 56 percent, and text ads on cellphones by only 18 percent. However, this approach is a double-edged sword. If consumers are spreading positive messages about a product, sales will likely soar. If, however, consumers are spreading negative messages, sales will suffer. For example, an advertisement by Belvedere Vodka that was posted on Twitter and Facebook drew outrage from its audience. The tag line was, "Unlike some people, Belvedere always goes down smoothly." The images associated with the ad seemed to poke fun at sexual assault. Customers were not impressed and Belvedere was forced to remove the ad after people attacked the brand and spread the negative message to their friends.

When Procter & Gamble introduced the new Venus Breeze razors, it sent samples to members of Vocalpoint (a group of 450 000 brand "evangelists" who talk up P&G products) to see whether the product indeed left their legs feeling smooth and silky. P&G is famous for traditional TV ads, yet it also has a word-of-mouth unit called Tremors, which includes over 200 000 teenagers who are active on social networks. These individuals are often early adopters of new products. P&G is planning to use Canada as a testing ground for online advertising spending, especially in light of the fact that an Ipsos-Reid survey showed that Canadian consumers spend 39 percent of their media consumption time on the internet, 26 percent on TV, and 11 percent on print media. This large percentage of time spent on the internet means great opportunities for word of mouth.

Many other companies also recognize the importance of word-of-mouth advertising:

- Google did no marketing of Gmail when it first launched; instead, it gave Gmail accounts to certain "power users" and the resulting word of mouth increased demand for the service.
- Volkswagen Canada cancelled a scheduled advertising campaign for its Eos automobile because the cars were rapidly being sold due to positive word of mouth.
- Small start-up companies like Vancouver-based The Soap Dispensary rely on the power of word of mouth because they cannot

afford large traditional campaigns. Mr. Linh Truong runs this small boutique-style refill store, which sells high-quality eco-friendly soaps, cleaners, and body care products. He is able to stretch his limited $1000 marketing budget by using social media tools like Facebook to create buzz. He praises the use of social media and says his sales have been increasing by 25 percent a month since he adopted the approach.

A group called The Influencers is Canada's first word-of-mouth community. It has created its own word-of-mouth campaign for promoting word-of-mouth advertising and cites various interesting statistics:

- The average person has 56 word-of-mouth interactions each week.
- Ninety-three percent of customers say word of mouth is the most trustworthy source of product information.
- Word of mouth is rated as the most reliable of 15 different marketing influences.

- Seventy-seven percent of word-of-mouth advertising is face to face.
- Forty-four percent of Canadians avoid buying products that overwhelm them with advertising.

Questions for Discussion

1. In your experience, is most word-of-mouth advertising positive or negative?
2. Why does word-of-mouth advertising have such an impact?
3. Why would companies like Procter & Gamble (which have historically focused on mass advertising) turn their attention to word-of-mouth advertising?
4. Do the statistics about word-of-mouth that have been cited by the group called The Influencers square with your own personal experiences?

Pricing and Distributing Goods and Services

After reading this chapter, you should be able to:

1 Identify the various *pricing objectives* that govern pricing decisions and describe the price-setting tools used in making these decisions.

2 Discuss *pricing strategies* and tactics for existing and new products.

3 Explain the *distribution mix*, the different *channels of distribution*, and different *distribution strategies*.

4 Explain the differences between *merchant wholesalers* and *agents/ brokers*, and describe the activities of e-intermediaries.

5 Identify the different types of *retailing* and *retail stores*.

6 Define *physical distribution* and describe the major activities in *warehousing* operations.

7 Compare the five basic forms of *transportation* and explain how distribution can be used as a marketing strategy.

Price-Conscious Consumers

IT is not difficult to find evidence that Canadian consumers are influenced by the prices of goods and services they purchase. Consider air travel services. Canadians living near the U.S. border (and there are lots of them) are increasingly driving to the United States and flying out of U.S. airports because the price is so much lower than flying out of Canadian airports. For example, Ontarians can fly round-trip from Buffalo to New York City for about $200 less than flying from Toronto to New York City. AirTrav Inc., a consulting firm, estimates that the loss of Canadian passengers to U.S. airports is costing Canada over $1 billion a year in economic output. Or, consider the success of so-called dollar stores—retailers like The Silver Dollar, Dollarama, and Buck or Two—that offer ultra-cheap prices on a

limited selection of goods. Sales revenues for this type of retail outlet have increased dramatically over the past decade. While dollar stores originally targeted low-income shoppers, they now are appealing to buyers at all income levels, and they are gaining the attention of companies that once ignored them. Procter & Gamble, for example, created a special version of Dawn dish soap that sells for $1, and Kraft Foods sells boxes of macaroni and cheese in dollar stores.

Canadians have expressed unhappiness that U.S. prices are often substantially lower than Canadian prices on identical products. This has occurred in spite of the fact that the Canadian dollar has recently been on par with the U.S. dollar. Because prices are so important to consumers, companies continually adjust

the prices they charge for their products. Consider these examples:

- Pizza Hut introduced new everyday low prices for its pizzas (medium pizzas are $8, large pizzas are $10, and specialty pizzas are $12). In some cases, these changes mean a reduction in price of almost 50 percent
- Quiznos promoted a value menu with sandwiches prices at $3, $4, and $5.
- Campbell Soup gave out coupons touting its Chunky soups as part of its "$4 Dinner Ideas" promotion

But companies often face a dilemma when they try to reduce prices because the prices they have to pay for the commodities that are used in their products have been increasing.

This means they cannot simply lower prices; rather, they have to keep their input prices in mind when they set retail prices. This has led many companies to adopt a strategy of keeping prices stable, while reducing the amount of product they provide in the package. This practice has become common because marketers believe that people don't notice the change in *quantity* like they do the change in *price*. For example:

- When faced with big cost increases in the price of soybean oil used in Hellmann's Mayonnaise, Unilever Canada Ltd. decided to keep the price the same, but decreased the size of the mayonnaise jar from 950 ml to 890 ml.
- Kimberly-Clark Corp. cut the price of its diapers, but cut the quantity in the package even more (this was, in effect, a 5 percent price increase).
- General Motors started charging extra for antilock brakes instead of including them at no charge as it used to.
- Juicy Fruit gum reduced the number of pieces in a pack from 17 to 15 while keeping the price the same.

- General Mills introduced smaller boxes for Cheerios and Wheaties, and Kellogg Co. did the same with many of its cereals.

The long-standing tension between consumers and retailers (consumers want the lowest price possible and retailers want to maximize their margins) continues to intensify. When the U.S. fashion chain J. Crew opened its first Canadian store in Yorkdale Mall in 2011, it charged 15 percent more for in-store items than it was charging at its U.S. stores (and some online purchasers paid as much as 50 percent more because of duties and taxes). When customers discovered this, they loudly complained on online forums. J. Crew quickly backed down and rescinded its decision to charge duties for online purchases. In a similar incident, consumers in New Zealand were outraged when they discovered that they were paying much higher prices for jerseys of New Zealand's national rugby team than consumers in other countries were paying. Then, news reports surfaced that Adidas had instructed internet sellers to remove New Zealand from its delivery options. Adidas later apologized and withdrew that instruction. In 2011,

Finance Minister Jim Flaherty challenged businesses to explain why Canadian consumers are charged higher prices (sometimes as much as 30 percent higher) than American consumers for identical products.

These disputes between consumers and companies are facilitated by technologies that allow consumers to make price comparisons much more easily than before. In a study conducted by IBM, 94 percent of the respondents said that they planned to use the internet for making price comparisons. Shoppers can now go online to decide what they want to buy and then go to the store and get it. In fact, they can now be in a store shopping and decide to use their phone to check prices in competitive stores (or make an online purchase). This capability puts downward pressure on the prices retailers can charge. Since the consumers who are most likely to use the latest technology to check prices are the youngest consumers, this has big implications for pricing in the future. The emergence of websites that offer reduced price coupons (e.g., Groupon, RedFlagDeals, WagJag, and Buytopia) is further evidence of the continuing importance of price to consumers.

535

Retailers are not simply passively watching these trends; rather, they are actively trying to figure out how to price products so they can maintain their profit margins and maximize their revenue. Two basic strategies are evident. First, retailers are trying to attract more than just the "cherry-picking" customers (those who go from store to store buying only on-sale items). For example, Walmart tries to cope with cherry-picking consumers by placing products that customers might overlook close to high-demand items (e.g., placing reduced-priced slippers next to higher-priced boots). Retailers also cope with cherry-pickers by limiting quantities (e.g., "one per customer"), advertising higher-margin items, and developing promotional programs that encourage shoppers to buy a broad range of products.

A second strategy involves conducting systematic analyses of how price increases change demand for products. Analyzing the effect of price increases is important because sales volume doesn't automatically decline if prices rise. When Stella Artois beer increased its advertising, it also increased its price. But sales volume increased in spite of the price increase. Why? Because the product is consumed mostly by males in bars and apparently they think it helps convey an image of success. Another example: When a chemical company discovered that it was the only company that could guarantee the supply of a certain product, it was able to raise its price 15 percent without any loss of sales volume.

Many companies focus on lowering the prices they charge in an attempt to keep their customers. But others have concluded that it is better to turn their back on some customers—for example, those who demand ultra-low prices or excessive amounts of service—because sales to them are not profitable. Ignoring certain demanding customers often increases a company's profitability and allows it to maintain the integrity of its pricing system. This is particularly true for industrial products, where customers and company sales representatives may engage in intensive negotiations before deals are made. ◆

HOW WILL THIS HELP ME?

By understanding the material presented in this chapter, you will benefit in three ways: (1) As a *consumer*, you will have a better understanding of how a product's development, promotion, and distribution affect its selling price; (2) as an *investor*, you'll be better prepared to evaluate a company's marketing program and its competitive potential before buying the company's stock; and (3) as an *employee* and/or *manager*, you'll be able to use your knowledge about product pricing and distribution to further your career.

Pricing Objectives and Tools

L01 Identify the various *pricing objectives* that govern pricing decisions and describe the price-setting tools used in making these decisions.

pricing Deciding what the company will receive in exchange for its product.

pricing objectives Goals that producers hope to attain in pricing products for sale.

In **pricing**, managers decide what the company will receive in exchange for its products and services. In this section, we discuss the objectives that influence a firm's pricing decisions and the major tools that companies use to achieve those objectives.

Pricing to Meet Business Objectives

Different companies have different **pricing objectives**. Some firms want to maximize profit, while others try to achieve a high market share. Pricing decisions are also influenced by other objectives (for example, survival in the marketplace, or showing consumers that the company is focusing on social and ethical concerns, or conveying a certain image to consumers).

Profit-Maximizing Objectives

Pricing to maximize profits is tricky. If prices are set too low, the company will sell a lot of units of its product, but it may miss the opportunity to make additional profit on each unit—and may in fact lose money on each exchange. Conversely, if prices are set too high, the company will make a large profit on each item but will sell fewer units, resulting in excess inventory and a need to reduce production operations. Again, the firm loses money. Some companies try to set prices in such a way as to maximize profits. For example, Coca-Cola tested a vending machine that automatically raised the price of a Coke as the temperature climbed.[1] Coke also discovered that it could

"O.K., who can put a price on love? Jim?"

charge more for a can of soda in the sportswear aisle of Walmart than in the beverage aisle near competing colas.[2] In the United Kingdom, one auto insurer charges varying premiums depending on how much, where, and when a person drives. A 40-year-old driver who is driving on a divided highway at 2 p.m. might pay only one pence per mile to drive, but a teenager driving at 1 a.m. would pay dramatically more (about one *pound* per mile).[3]

Profits are calculated by comparing revenues against costs for materials and labour that are necessary to create the product or service. But there are many other factors to consider if a firm is trying to maximize profits. These include the cost of plant and equipment, the cost of maintaining a sales staff, and the impact of context factors on sales (for example, dealing with longtime customers rather than skeptical potential customers). Consideration of all of these factors has led many firms to set prices to achieve a targeted level of return on sales or capital investment, rather than trying to maximize profit.[4]

Market Share Objectives

When companies initially set low prices on new products in order to get buyers to try them, they are using pricing to establish **market share**—a company's percentage of the total market sales for a specific product. Even with established products, market share may outweigh profits as a pricing objective. For a product like Philadelphia brand cream cheese, dominating a market means that consumers are more likely to buy it because they are familiar with a well-known, highly visible brand name.

market share A company's percentage of the total market sales for a specific product.

Retailers like Walmart are very concerned about market share. In 2010, Walmart cut prices in order to attract customers who were shopping for food at supermarkets instead of at Walmart.[5] And Toyota cut prices in 2010 in an attempt to regain its market share, which had declined after millions of its cars were recalled due to reports of uncontrolled acceleration.[6]

Other Pricing Objectives

Companies adopt various other pricing objectives beyond profit maximization or market share. For example, during difficult economic times, a company's pricing objective may be to simply survive (during the recession that began in 2008, retailers cut prices in an attempt to attract customers). Some companies improve their bottom line by emphasizing their concern for the environment. At Staples, for example, the Fifty Green program at the business-to-business division encourages customers to eliminate small orders, which reduces the number of deliveries. That, in turn, reduces Staples's costs for items like fuel and vehicle depreciation.[7] Still other companies use pricing to promote a luxury image to customers (e.g., Mont Blanc pens or Lamborghini automobiles).

Price-Setting Tools

Two basic tools are used for setting prices: *cost-oriented pricing* and *break-even analysis*. These tools are often combined to identify prices that will allow the company to reach its objectives.

Cost-Oriented Pricing

Cost-oriented pricing considers the firm's desire to make a profit and takes into account the need to cover production costs. A video store manager, for instance, would price DVDs by calculating the cost of making them available to shoppers. Included in this figure would be store rent, employee wages, utilities, product displays, insurance, and the cost of buying DVDs from the manufacturer.

Let's assume that the cost from the manufacturer is $8 per DVD. The manager must account for product and other costs in order to set a price that will result in a profit. Together, these figures constitute markup. For example, a markup of $7 over costs would result in a $15 selling price. Markup is usually stated as a percentage of selling price. Markup percentage is thus calculated as follows:

$$\text{Markup percentage} = \frac{\text{Markup}}{\text{Sales price}}$$

In the case of our DVD retailer, the markup percentage is 46.7:

$$\text{Markup percentage} = \frac{\$7}{\$15} = 46.7\%$$

In other words, out of every dollar taken in, 46.7 cents will be gross profit for the store. From this profit the store must still pay rent, utilities, insurance, and all other costs. Markup can also be expressed as a percentage of cost: The $7 markup is 87.5 percent of the $8 cost of a DVD ($7 ÷ $8).

Cost-oriented pricing is not used by some companies. When you go to a first-run movie theatre, for example, you pay the same price for each film you see. But it may cost as little as $2 million or as much as $200 million to make a film. Shouldn't the admission price be based on how much the film cost to make? After all, you pay a lot more for a Lincoln Continental than you do for a Ford because the Lincoln costs more to make. Shouldn't the same pricing system apply to Hollywood? Apparently not. Consumers are simply not willing to pay more than a certain amount to see a movie, regardless of how much it cost to make the movie.

One annoying element for consumers in cost-oriented pricing is the difficulty of determining how much it costs the seller to make the product or service available to the customer. When buying a new car, for example, price negotiation is very important, but consumers are often frustrated because they don't know the dealer's cost. To help consumers, Unhaggle.com now provides information on dealer costs for most car models.[8] The government may also force some companies to provide clear pricing information. In 2011, for example, the federal government made it mandatory for airlines to provide total ticket prices (including taxes and all fees), not just the basic air fare price.[9]

There is more subjectivity in the pricing of services than there is in the pricing of physical products because it is more difficult to place a value on an expert's time. For example, how much should a financial advisor charge for the services he or she provides? One client was surprised to discover that his fees declined 40 percent when the firm he had been dealing with was taken over by another financial institution.[10]

Break-Even Analysis: Cost–Volume–Profit Relationships

Using cost-oriented pricing, a firm will cover its **variable costs**—costs that change with the number of goods or services produced or sold. It will also make some money toward paying its **fixed costs**—costs that are unaffected by the number of goods or services produced or sold. But how many units must the company sell before all of its fixed costs are covered and it begins to make a profit? To determine this figure, it needs to do a **break-even analysis**.[11]

To continue with our video store example, suppose again that the variable cost for each DVD (in this case, the cost of buying the DVD from the producer) is $8. This means that the store's annual variable costs depend on how many DVDs are sold—the number of DVDs sold multiplied by the $8 cost per DVD. Let's assume that the fixed costs for keeping the store open for one year are $100 000. These costs are unaffected by the number of DVDs sold; costs for lighting, rent, insurance, and salaries are steady regardless of how many DVDs the store sells. How many DVDs must be sold to cover both fixed and variable costs and to start to generate some profit? The answer is the **break-even point**, which is 14 286 DVDs. We arrive at this number through the following equation:

$$\text{Break-even point (in units)} = \frac{\text{Total fixed costs}}{\text{Price} - \text{Variable cost}}$$

$$= \frac{\$100\ 000}{\$15 - \$8} = 14\ 286\ \text{DVDs}$$

Figure 17.1 shows the break-even point graphically. If the store sells fewer than 14 286 DVDs, it loses money for the year. If sales exceed 14 286 DVDs, profits grow by $7 for each DVD sold. If the store sells exactly 14 286 DVDs, it will cover all of its costs but will earn zero profit. Zero profitability at the break-even point can also be seen by using the following profit equation:

Profit = total revenue − (total fixed costs + total variable costs)
   = (14 286 DVDs × $15) − ($100 000 fixed costs + [14 286 DVDs × $8 variable costs])

The video store owner would certainly like to hit the break-even quantity as early as possible so that profits will start rolling in. So, why not charge $20 per DVD and reach the break-even point earlier? The answer lies in the downward-sloping demand curve we discussed in Chapter 1. At a price of $20 per DVD, sales at the store would drop. In setting a price, the manager must consider how much DVD buyers will pay and what the store's local competitors charge.

variable costs Those costs that change with the number of goods or services produced or sold.

fixed costs Those costs unaffected by the number of goods or services produced or sold.

break-even analysis An assessment of how many units must be sold at a given price before the company begins to make a profit.

break-even point The number of units that must be sold at a given price before the company covers all of its variable and fixed costs.

FIGURE 17.1

Break-even analysis.

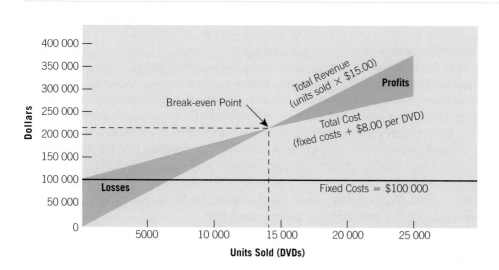

Pricing Strategies and Tactics

LO2 Discuss *pricing strategies* and tactics for existing and new products.

The pricing tools discussed in the previous section provide guidance for managers trying to set prices on specific goods. But they do not provide direction for managers who are trying to decide on an overall *pricing strategy* (a planning activity that affects the marketing mix) or on *pricing tactics* (ways in which managers implement a firm's pricing strategies).

Pricing Strategies

Here are two important questions: First, can a manager really identify a single "best" price for a product? Probably not. One study of prices for popular non-aspirin pain relievers (such as Tylenol and Advil) found variations of 100 percent.[12] Such large price differences may reflect some differences in product costs, but the bigger issue is likely differing brand images that attract different types of customers. Second, just how important is pricing as an element in the marketing mix? As we have already seen, it is a mistake to try to isolate any element in the marketing mix from the others. Nevertheless, we can say that pricing is a critical variable because it has a major impact on company revenues, and it is extremely important to consumers.

Pricing Existing Products

A firm can set prices for its existing products *above* prevailing market prices for similar products, *below* prevailing prices, or *at* prevailing prices. Companies pricing above the market play on customers' beliefs that higher prices mean higher quality. Companies such as Godiva chocolates and Rolls-Royce have succeeded with this pricing philosophy. In contrast, both Budget and Dollar car rental companies promote themselves as low-priced alternatives to Hertz and Avis. Pricing below the prevailing market price can succeed if the firm can offer a product of acceptable quality while keeping costs below those of higher-priced options.

price leadership The dominant firm in the industry establishes product prices and other companies follow suit.

In some industries, a dominant firm establishes product prices and other companies follow along. This is called **price leadership**. (Don't confuse this approach with *price fixing*, the illegal process of producers agreeing among themselves what prices will be charged.) Price leadership is often evident in products such as structural steel, gasoline, and many processed foods because these products differ little in quality from one firm to another. Companies compete through advertising, personal selling, and service, not price.

Pricing New Products

price skimming The decision to price a new product as high as possible to earn the maximum profit on each unit sold.

Companies introducing new products into the market have to consider two contrasting pricing policy options. **Price skimming**—setting an initially high price to cover costs and generate a profit—may generate a large profit on each item sold. The revenue is often needed to cover development and introduction costs. Skimming works only if marketers can convince consumers that a product is truly different from those already on the market. High-definition TVs, microwave ovens, electronic calculators, video games, and video cameras were all introduced using price skimming. In contrast, **penetration pricing**—setting an initially low price to establish a new product in the market—seeks to create consumer interest and stimulate trial purchases. When Carbonite Inc. started its online backup service, it charged "one flat low price" no matter how many computer files you needed to back up.[13] To attract customers, Apple's initial iTunes policy was to price all songs at $0.99, but now it prices older tunes at $0.69 and currently popular tunes at $1.29.

penetration pricing The decision to price a new product very low to sell the most units possible and to build customer loyalty.

Using low-cost, direct-to-consumer selling and market share pricing, Dell profitably dominated the personal computer market while its competitors—Apple, IBM, Compaq, and Hewlett-Packard—sold through traditional retailers (which added costs that prevented them from matching Dell's low prices). Competitors have switched to direct-to-consumer sales, but Dell is strongly anchored as the industry's number-two PC seller (after HP).

Fixed vs. Dynamic Pricing for eBusiness

The electronic marketplace has introduced a highly variable pricing system as an alternative to more conventional—and more stable—pricing structures for both consumer and business-to-business (B2B) products. *Dynamic pricing* works because information flows on the web notify millions of buyers of instantaneous changes in product availability. To attract sales that might be lost under traditional fixed-price structures, sellers can alter prices privately, on a one-to-one, customer-to-customer basis.[14] For example, at Priceline.com, consumers can state a price (below the published fixed price) that they are willing to pay for airfare. An airline can complete the sale by accepting the bid price. Progressive Casualty Insurance Company has introduced what is perhaps the ultimate dynamic pricing system. It sets insurance rates for drivers based on their real-time driving behaviour—information that is generated by the automobile's GPS system.[15]

Pricing Tactics

Regardless of its general pricing strategy, a company may adopt one or more specific pricing tactics, such as *price lining* or *psychological pricing*. Managers must also decide whether to use *discounting* tactics.

Price Lining

Companies selling multiple items in a product category often use **price lining**—offering all items in certain categories at a limited number of prices. Three or four *price points* are set at which a particular product will be sold. For example, all men's suits might be priced at $175, $250, or $400. The store's buyers select suits that can be purchased and sold profitably at one of these three prices.

Psychological Pricing

Psychological pricing is based on the idea that customers are not completely rational when making buying decisions. **Odd-even pricing** assumes that customers prefer prices that are not stated in even dollar amounts. Thus, customers may regard a price

price lining The practice of offering all items in certain categories at a limited number of predetermined price points.

psychological pricing The practice of setting prices to take advantage of the non-logical reactions of consumers to certain types of prices.

odd-even pricing A form of psychological pricing in which prices are not stated in even dollar amounts.

Dynamic pricing, with online bidding screens on the wall, is a mainstream feature of this salesroom for the British Car Auctions (BCA) site in Brighouse, West Yorkshire, UK.

of $99.95 as significantly lower than a price of $100.00. But Walmart sometimes goes against this trend. In an attempt to make it easier for money-conscious customers to calculate their bill before they get to the cash register, Walmart is rounding prices to the nearest dollar on many products.[16]

Discounting

discount Any price reduction offered by the seller to persuade customers to purchase a product.

cash discount A form of discount in which customers paying cash, rather than buying on credit, pay lower prices.

seasonal discount A form of discount in which lower prices are offered to customers making a purchase at a time of year when sales are traditionally slow.

trade discount A discount given to firms involved in a product's distribution.

quantity discount A form of discount in which customers buying large amounts of a product pay lower prices.

The price that is set for a product is not always the price at which all items are actually sold. Many times a company offers a price reduction—a **discount**—to stimulate sales. In recent years, **cash discounts** have become popular. A gas station, for example, may sell gas for 4 cents per litre less than the listed price if you pay cash. Stores may also offer **seasonal discounts** to stimulate the sales of products during times of the year when most customers do not normally buy the product. **Trade discounts** are available to companies or individuals in a product's distribution channel (for example, wholesalers, retailers, and interior designers pay less for fabric than the typical consumer does). **Quantity discounts** involve lower prices for purchases in large quantities. For example, if you purchase a case of soft drinks, you will pay less per can than if you buy only one can.

International Pricing

When Procter & Gamble reviewed its prospects for marketing products in new overseas markets, it encountered an unsettling fact: Because it typically priced products to cover hefty R&D costs, profitably priced items were out of reach for too many foreign consumers. The solution was, in effect, to reverse the process. Now P&G conducts research to find out what foreign buyers can afford and then develops products that can be priced at the right level. P&G penetrates markets with lower-priced items and then encourages customers to trade up as they become able to afford higher-quality products.

International pricing is complicated because more factors must be considered. Income and spending trends must be analyzed, and the number of intermediaries varies from country to country, as does their effect on a product's cost. Exchange rates change daily, there may be large shipping costs, import tariffs must be considered, and different types of pricing agreements may be permitted.

If the manufacturer says a product should retail for $349, why does every retailer sell it for, say, $229? Such discrepancies between a manufacturer's suggested retail price and the actual retail price are the norm in the electronics industry, and consumers have come to expect discounted prices. "You can't have a discount until there's a price to discount it from," explains an editor at *Consumer Reports*, but the practice raises an interesting question: If no one charges suggested retail prices, is anyone really getting a discount?

The Distribution Mix

The **distribution mix** is the combination of distribution channels a firm uses to get a product to end-users. In this section, we first explain the need for *intermediaries*, then describe several *distribution strategies*, and then consider some special issues in channel relationships.

The Need for Intermediaries

Intermediaries (formerly called middlemen) are individuals or firms that help distribute a producer's goods. **Wholesalers** are intermediaries who sell products to other businesses, which resell them to final consumers, while **retailers** are intermediaries who sell products directly to final consumers (more detail about these intermediaries later). Some firms rely on independent intermediaries, but others employ their own distribution networks and sales forces. Intermediaries have appeared in places where people might think they aren't needed. For example, a Canadian company called Imagine This Sold Ltd. provides expertise to people who are trying to sell items on eBay. It charges a percentage of the selling price for providing this service. This company exists because trading has become so competitive on eBay that more expertise is needed to succeed than a lot of people thought.[17] As another example, small business owners can now go to websites such as Fundingstore.com to find organizations that want to invest money in promising small business ventures.[18] If a deal is made, Fundingstore.com receives a fee.

Because each link in the distribution chain makes a profit by charging a markup or commission, the use of intermediaries means higher prices. Calculated as a percentage of cost, *markups* are applied each time a product is sold. They may range from 10 to 40 percent for manufacturers, from 2 to 25 percent for wholesalers, and from 5 to 100 percent for retailers. *E-intermediaries*—wholesalers and agents who use internet channels—also charge markups.

But intermediaries do provide *added value* by saving consumers both time and money. Moreover, the value accumulates with each link in the supply chain.

Explain the *distribution mix*, the different *channels of distribution*, and different *distribution strategies*. **L03**

distribution mix The combination of distribution channels a firm selects to get a product to end-users.

intermediary Any individual or firm other than the producer who participates in a product's distribution.

wholesalers Intermediaries who sell products to other businesses, which in turn resell them to end-users.

retailers Intermediaries who sell products to end-users.

"On the one hand, eliminating the middleman would result in lower costs, increased sales, and greater consumer satisfaction; on the other hand, we're the middleman."

Intermediaries provide time-saving information and make the right quantities of products available where and when consumers need them. Figure 17.2 illustrates the problem of making chili without benefit of a common intermediary—the supermarket. As a consumer/buyer, you would obviously spend a lot more time, money, and energy if you tried to gather all the ingredients from one retailer at a time.

Even if intermediaries are eliminated, the costs associated with their functions are not. Intermediaries exist because they do necessary jobs (although they may not provide a *low-cost* service when doing their jobs). More and more people are trying to save money by selling their homes without using the services of a real estate agent. Since the agent's fee is normally 5 percent of the purchase price of the house, the savings can be substantial. But a do-it-yourself seller has to do all the work that the agent would normally do to earn their fee. Detailed information on this issue is provided in Concluding Case 17-1.

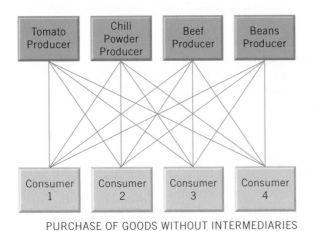

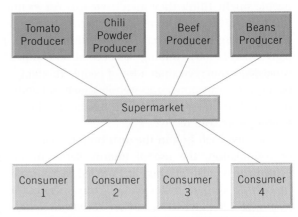

PURCHASE OF GOODS WITHOUT INTERMEDIARIES   PURCHASE OF GOODS WITH INTERMEDIARIES

FIGURE 17.2

Advantages of intermediaries.

Distribution of Consumer Products

A **distribution channel** is the path that a product follows from producer to end-user. Figure 17.3 shows eight primary distribution channels based on the kinds of channel members involved in getting products to buyers. Note that all channels must begin with a producer and end with a consumer or an industrial user.

distribution channel The path a product follows from the producer to the end-user.

Channel 1: Direct Distribution of Consumer Products. In a **direct channel**, the product travels from the producer to the consumer without intermediaries. Using their own sales forces, companies such as Avon, Fuller Brush, and Tupperware use this channel. The direct channel is also prominent on the internet, where consumers can purchase airline reservations (and thousands of other products and services) directly from internet sites.

direct channel A distribution channel in which the product travels from the producer to the consumer without passing through any intermediary.

Channel 2: Retail Distribution of Consumer Products. In channel 2, producers distribute products through retailers. Goodyear, for example, maintains its own system of retail outlets. Levi's has its own outlets but also produces jeans for other retailers such as Gap Inc.

Channel 3: Wholesale Distribution of Consumer Products. Many retailers cannot afford both retail and storage space, so wholesalers exist to provide the storage function. For example, the typical convenience store/gas station uses about 90 percent of its space used to display merchandise, so only 10 percent is left for storage and office facilities. Wholesalers therefore store merchandise and restock it frequently. Wholesalers are also prominent in ecommerce because internet stores give customers access to information and product displays 24 hours a day. Buyers can place orders electronically and confirm delivery almost instantaneously.

Channel 4: Distribution Through Sales Agents or Brokers. **Sales agents** represent producers and sell to wholesalers, retailers, or both. They receive commissions based on the prices of the goods they sell. Lafferty and Co. Food Brokers Inc. represents

sales agents (or brokers) Independent business people who represent a business and receive a commission in return, but never take legal possession of the product.

FIGURE 17.3

Channels of distribution: How the product travels from producer to consumer or user.

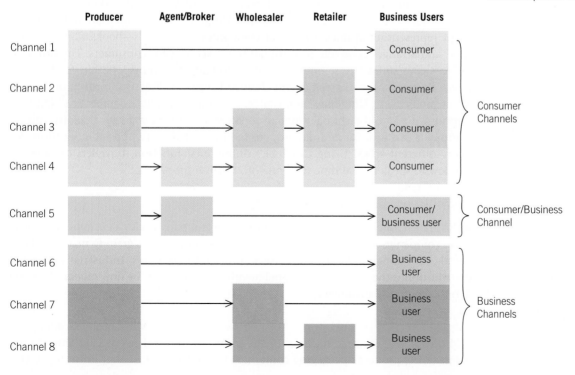

At this plant of an electrical components supplier, an employee assembles electrical systems that meet the requirements of their industrial customers. The finished assemblies are shipped from the plant to customers' facilities, illustrating a direct (producer to customer) channel of distribution.

several prominent food manufacturers—Pillsbury, Old El Paso, and Sunkist. To relieve manufacturers of sales activities, Lafferty arranges sales of their products to other companies, allowing manufacturers to do what they do best—produce food products—rather than divert resources to sales and distribution. Agents generally deal in the related product lines of a few producers and work on a long-term basis. Travel agents, for example, represent airlines, car-rental companies, and hotels. In contrast, **brokers** match sellers and buyers as needed. The real estate industry relies on brokers to match buyers and sellers of property. The boxed insert entitled "Airline Intermediaries Face Some Challenges" describes how changes in the way that airline tickets are sold to customers has upset the traditional way that travel agents do business.

Channel 5: Distribution by Agents to Consumers and Businesses. In this channel, agents function as the sole intermediary and they distribute to both consumers and business customers. Vancouver-based Uniglobe Travel International—a travel agent representing airlines, car-rental companies, and hotels—books flight reservations and arranges complete recreational travel services for consumers. The firm also services companies whose employees need lodging and transportation for business travel. Ecommerce works well in this channel because it directly informs more people about products. At Uniglobe, for instance, an online subsidiary combines a high-tech website with an old-fashioned human touch in a specialty market—booking cruises. Customers can scan for destinations, cruise lines, restaurants, and cabin locations for many different ships. Using Uniglobe's online chat function, travellers can open a window to speak in real time with one of 75 cruise specialists.[19]

Distribution of Business Products

Industrial channels are important because every company is also a customer that buys other companies' products. The Kellogg Co., for example, buys grain to make breakfast cereals, and Imperial Tobacco buys tobacco to make cigarettes. **Industrial (business) distribution** is the network of channel members involved in the flow of manufactured goods to business customers.

industrial (business) distribution The network of channel members involved in the flow of manufactured goods to business customers.

Channel 6: Direct Distribution of Business Products. Most business goods are sold directly by the manufacturer to the industrial buyer. Lawless Container Corp., for instance, produces packaging containers for direct sale to Fisher-Price (toys), Dirt

Devil (vacuum cleaners), and Mr. Coffee (coffee makers). Many manufacturers maintain **sales offices** as contact points with customers and headquarters for salespeople. Ecommerce technologies have popularized channel 6. Dell Computer Corp., a pioneer in direct internet sales, now gets about two-thirds of its sales from other businesses, governments, and schools.[20]

sales offices Offices maintained by sellers of industrial goods to provide points of contact with their customers.

Channel 7: Wholesale Distribution of Industrial Products. Channel 7 mostly handles accessory equipment (computers, fax machines, and other office equipment) and supplies (USB memory sticks, pencils, and copier paper). Manufacturers produce these items in large quantities, but companies buy them in small quantities. For example, few companies order truckloads of paper clips, so intermediaries help end-users by breaking down large quantities into smaller sales units.

Channel 8: Wholesale Distribution to Business Retailers. In the office-products industry, channel 7 is being displaced by a channel that looks very much like channel 3 for consumer products. Instead of buying office supplies from wholesalers (channel 7), many businesses are now shopping at office discount stores such as Staples, Office Depot, and Office Max. Before selling to large companies, these warehouse-like superstores originally targeted retail consumers and small businesses

MANAGING IN TURBULENT TIMES

Airline Intermediaries Face Some Challenges

A battle is shaping up over how airline tickets are sold to customers, and the outcome may affect the fortunes of online ticket sellers like Travelocity, Expedia, and Orbitz. The dominant airline ticket distribution system currently uses intermediaries known as global distribution systems (GDSs), which are organizations that summarize fares from many different airlines and make that information available to travel agents. These GDSs often own online travel agents (for example, Travelport Ltd. owns Orbitz and Sabre owns Travelocity). Travel sites typically receive a $3–$5 fee for each airline flight they book. For most airlines, the majority of their tickets are sold to customers by intermediaries like online or traditional travel agents.

But there are exceptions. JetBlue and Southwest, for example, which started out as "discount" airlines, sell most of their tickets directly to their customers. And now, another airline (American Airlines) has decided it also wants to "cut out the middleman" and sell tickets directly to consumers. As part of that strategy, in December 2010, it pulled its flights from the Orbitz website. In addition to avoiding the fee on each ticket, direct selling gives American the opportunity to establish a closer relationship with its customers. This, in turn, should allow the company to "upsell" to customers by offering special deals or upgrades when a customer purchases a ticket. American's move is consistent with a developing view among many airline companies that the services they provide are "content" that they should be paid for, not something they should have to pay others (i.e., GDS intermediaries) to display. But this strategy is now in doubt because in June 2011, a U.S. court ruled that American Airlines had to make its flights available on Orbitz's website.

GDSs naturally view the airlines' new strategy with alarm, so they are happy with the court ruling. But things are very confused at the moment. Sabre, for example, has increased the fees it charges American Airlines, and it is also displaying American fares less prominently on its website than it used to. Expedia has dropped information about American flights from its website, and has characterized American's attempts to sell directly to customers as "anti-consumer" and "anti-choice." More generally, intermediaries argue that if other airlines follow American's lead, it is going to be more difficult for consumers to comparison shop because airlines will post only their own fares and customers will not see comparison fares. Customers will therefore end up paying higher prices. Of course, if other airlines follow American's lead, online travel agents will lose revenues, so it is not surprising that they have expressed concerns about American's move. One industry analyst said, "There's going to be a shoot-out in the airline distribution corral."

Critical Thinking Question

1. Do you think consumers will be better off or worse off if airlines "cut out the middleman" and deal directly with their customers? Defend your answer.

that bought supplies at retail stores (and at retail prices). Today, however, small business buyers shop at discount stores designed for industrial users, selecting from 7000 items at prices 20 to 75 percent lower than retail.

Distribution Strategies

intensive distribution A distribution strategy in which a product is distributed in nearly every possible outlet, using many channels and channel members.

exclusive distribution A distribution strategy in which a product's distribution is limited to only one wholesaler or retailer in a given geographic area.

selective distribution A distribution strategy that falls between intensive and exclusive distribution, calling for the use of a limited number of outlets for a product.

Intensive distribution means distributing a product through as many channels and channel members (using both wholesalers and retailers) as possible. For example, as Figure 17.4 shows, Caramilk candy bars flood the market through all suitable outlets. Intensive distribution is normally used for low-cost consumer goods such as candy and magazines.

In contrast, **exclusive distribution** occurs when a manufacturer grants the exclusive right to distribute or sell a product to one wholesaler or retailer in a given geographic area. Exclusive distribution agreements are most common for high-cost prestige products. For example, Jaguar or Rolls-Royce automobiles are typically sold by only one dealer in a metropolitan area.

Selective distribution falls between intensive and exclusive distribution. A company that uses this strategy selects only wholesalers and retailers that will give special attention to the product in terms of sales efforts, display position, and so on. Para Paints uses a selective distribution policy to keep its high-end paint products out of the "big-box" stores. This strategy increases Para's margins (because big-box stores demand steep discounts); it has also increased sales because the independent stores that sell Para paint have remained loyal to Para.[21]

Channel Conflict and Channel Leadership

channel conflict Conflict arising when the members of a distribution channel disagree over the roles they should play or the rewards they should receive.

Channel conflict occurs when members of a distribution channel disagree over the roles they should play or the rewards they should receive. For example, when a manufacturer-owned factory outlet store discounts the company's apparel or housewares, it runs the risk of alienating the independent retailers that also sell the manufacturer's products. Channel conflict may also arise if one member has more power than the others, or is viewed as receiving preferential treatment. Such conflicts

FIGURE 17.4

Amounts of market exposure from the three kinds of distribution.

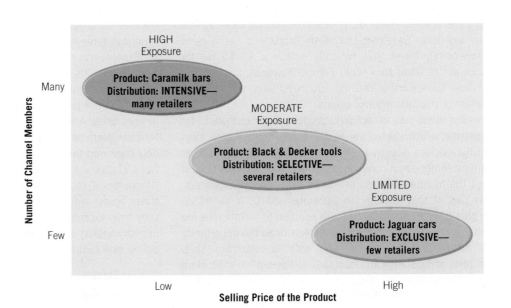

defeat the purpose of the system by disrupting the flow of goods to their destinations. Conflicts are resolved when members' efforts are coordinated by a **channel captain** who determines the roles and rewards of other members. The channel captain is often a manufacturer, particularly if the manufacturer's product is in high demand. In some industries, an influential wholesaler or a large retailer such as Walmart may emerge as the channel captain because of its large sales volumes.

The **vertical marketing system (VMS)** is designed to overcome channel conflicts. In a VMS, separate businesses join to form a unified distribution channel, with one member coordinating the activities of the whole channel. There are three main types of VMS arrangements. In a *corporate* VMS, all stages in the channel are under single ownership. The Limited, for example, owns both the production facilities that manufacture its apparel and the retail stores that sell it. In a *contractual* VMS, channel members sign contracts agreeing to specific duties and rewards. The Independent Grocers' Alliance (IGA), for example, consists of independent retail grocers joined with a wholesaler who contractually leads—but does not own—the VMS. Most franchises (see Chapter 4) are contractual VMSs. In an *administered* VMS, channel members are less formally coordinated than in a corporate or contractual VMS. Instead, one or more of the members emerge as leader(s) and maintain control as a result of power and influence. The administered VMS is more fragile than the corporate and contractual forms, but it is more unified than channels relying on independent members.

> **channel captain** The channel member that is the most powerful in determining the roles and rewards of organizations involved in a given channel of distribution.

> **vertical marketing system (VMS)** A system in which there is a high degree of coordination among all the units in the distribution channel so that a product moves efficiently from manufacturer to consumer.

Wholesaling

Now that you know something about distribution channels, we can consider the role played by specific intermediaries in those channels. Wholesalers provide a variety of functions for their customers, who are buying products for resale to consumers or to businesses. In addition to storing products and providing an assortment of products for their customers, wholesalers offer delivery, credit, and information about products. The specific services that wholesalers offer depend on what type of intermediary they are: *merchant wholesaler* or *agent/broker*.

> Explain the differences between *merchant wholesalers* and *agents/brokers*, and describe the activities of e-intermediaries. **LO4**

Merchant Wholesalers

Most wholesalers are independent operators that derive their income from sales of goods produced by a variety of manufacturers. **Merchant wholesalers** take title to merchandise; that is, they buy and own the goods they resell to other businesses. They usually provide storage and a means of delivery.

A **full-service merchant wholesaler** provides credit, marketing, and merchandising services, while **limited-function merchant wholesalers** provide only a few services, sometimes merely storage. The **drop shipper** receives orders from customers, negotiates with producers to supply goods, takes title to them, and arranges for shipment to customers. Other limited-function wholesalers, known as **rack jobbers**, market consumer goods—mostly non-food items—directly to retail stores.[22] Procter & Gamble, for example, uses rack jobbers to distribute products like Pampers diapers. After marking prices, setting up display racks, and displaying diapers in one store, the rack jobber moves on to another outlet to check inventories and shelve products.

> **merchant wholesaler** An independent wholesaler that buys and takes legal possession of goods before selling them to customers.

> **full-service merchant wholesaler** A merchant wholesaler that provides storage and delivery in addition to wholesaling services.

> **limited-function merchant wholesaler** An independent wholesaler that provides only wholesaling—not warehousing or transportation—services.

> **drop shipper** A type of wholesaler that does not carry inventory or handle the product.

> **rack jobber** A limited-function merchant wholesaler specializing in non-food merchandise that sets up and maintains display racks of some products in retail stores.

Agents and Brokers

Agents and brokers (including internet e-agents) serve as the sales and merchandising arms of manufacturers that do not have their own sales forces. They work on commissions, usually about 4 to 5 percent of net sales. Unlike merchant wholesalers, they do not take title to the merchandise they sell. The value of agents and brokers lies primarily in their knowledge of markets and their merchandising expertise. They provide a wide range of services, including shelf and display merchandising and advertising layout. They also maintain product saleability by removing open, torn, or dirty packages; arranging products neatly; and generally keeping them attractively displayed. Many supermarket products are handled through brokers.

Retailing

L05 Identify the different types of *retailing* and *retail stores*.

If you are like most Canadians, you buy nearly all the goods and services you consume from retailers. Most retailers are small operations, often consisting of just the owner and some part-time help. But there are a few very large retailers, and these account for billions of dollars of sales each year in Canada (see Table 17.1). The boxed insert entitled "Overwaitea Food Group: 'Simply the Best in the West!'" provides information on one successful Canadian retailer.

Types of Retail Outlets

There are three basic categories of retail stores: *product line retailers, bargain retailers,* and *convenience stores*.

Product Line Retailers

department stores Large retail stores that offer a wide variety of high-quality items divided into specialized departments.

supermarkets Large retail stores that offer a variety of food and food-related items divided into specialized departments.

specialty stores Small retail stores that carry one line of related products.

category killers Retailers that carry a deep selection of goods in a narrow product line.

Retailers that feature broad product lines include **department stores**, which are organized into specialized departments such as shoes, furniture, women's clothing, and so forth. These stores are usually large and handle a wide range of goods, and they offer a variety of services, such as generous return policies, credit plans, and delivery. **Supermarkets** are also divided into departments of related products—food products, household products, and so on. The emphasis is on wide selection and self-service.

In contrast, **specialty stores** are small stores that carry one line of related products. They serve specific market segments with full product lines in narrow product fields and often feature knowledgeable sales personnel. Sunglass Hut International, for instance, has 1600 outlets in Canada, the United States, Europe, and Australia that carry a deep selection of competitively priced sunglasses. Retailers like this are called **category killers**. Home Depot and Staples are also examples of category killers.

TABLE 17.1 Top 10 Retailers in Canada, 2011 (ranked by sales revenue)	
Company	**Sales Revenue (billions of dollars)**
1. Walmart Canada Corp.	$23.4
2. Costco Wholesale Canada Ltd.	13.2
3. Canadian Tire Corp. Ltd.	10.3
4. Best Buy Canada	5.6
5. Home Depot of Canada	5.2
6. Rona Inc.	4.8
7. Sears Canada Inc.	4.6
8. Liquor Control Board of Ontario	4.5
9. BC Liquor Distribution Branch	2.6
10. Societé Des Alcools Du Québec	2.6

Overwaitea Food Group: "Simply the Best in the West!"

Overwaitea Food Group (OFG) is a West Coast grocery chain that operates under six different banner names: Save-on-Foods, Overwaitea Foods, PriceSmart Foods, Cooper's Foods, Urban Fare, and Bulkley Valley Wholesale. With a mission to be "Simply the Best in the West," OFG is dedicated to providing healthy, local food and other home essentials to its niche market with a focus on sustainability and diversity. Overwaitea Food Group opened its first store way back in 1915 in New Westminster, British Columbia. The store's odd name came from its practice of selling 18 ounces of tea for the price normally charged for 16 ounces (hence the name over-weight-tea). OFG is now the largest food chain on Canada's West Coast, with more than 120 stores. New stores have recently been opened in Richmond (PriceSmart), Abbotsford (Save-on-Foods), and Sherwood Park (Save-on-Foods).

All OFG outlets address the needs of their local communities by offering consumers a unique shopping experience that includes affordable product offerings and in-store restaurants that make meals primarily with local ingredients. Stores provide eco-friendly and sustainable products, and the company demonstrates a strong concern for the environment and for sustainable practices and products. When Ipsos-Reid asked consumers to think of an environmentally friendly retailer, Save-on-Foods received the most mentions.

OFG was also ranked second in a Greenpeace study on seafood sustainability. The company has also received an energy efficiency award from BC Hydro.

OFG's pricing strategy means that stores operating under different banner names have different pricing policies. For example, Save-on-Foods and PriceSmart Foods emphasize low prices, while Urban Fare has a premium price policy and sells organic products. OFG's differentiation strategy (stores operating under various names) means that it can meet the needs of the various local communities it serves. For example, some OFG stores now offer locally produced, sustainable sushi products. Staying close to the community and providing customers with attractive local foods is the foundation that Overwaitea Food Group has been built upon; it is also the key to future growth.

Critical Thinking Questions

1. What are the three basic categories of retailers? In which category does OFG fit? Explain your reasoning.

2. What elements of consumer behaviour has Overwaitea utilized when deciding on its differentiation and pricing strategies? (Review the relevant sections of Chapter 15 before answering this question.)

Bargain Retailers

Bargain retailers carry a wide range of products and come in many forms. **Discount houses** originally sold large numbers of items (such as televisions and other appliances) at substantial price reductions. As name-brand items became more common, they offered better product assortments while still transacting cash-only sales in low-rent facilities. As they became firmly entrenched, they began moving to better locations, improving decor, and selling better-quality merchandise at higher prices. They also began offering a few department store services, such as credit plans and non-cash sales. Walmart and Target are bargain retailers. In 2011, Target announced that it would purchase 220 Zellers stores, and that it was planning to open many new stores in Canada over the next few years.[23]

Catalogue showrooms use mail catalogues to attract customers into showrooms to view display samples, place orders, and wait briefly while clerks retrieve orders from attached warehouses. **Factory outlets** are manufacturer-owned stores that avoid wholesalers and retailers by selling merchandise directly from factory to consumer. **Wholesale clubs** like Costco offer large discounts on a wide range of brand name merchandise to customers who pay annual membership fees.

Some bargain retailers open temporary outlets called *pop-up stores*. For example, Target Brands Inc. opened a pop-up store in Toronto—its first Canadian store—for

bargain retailers Retail outlets that emphasize low prices as a means of attracting consumers.

discount houses Bargain retail stores that offer major items such as televisions and large appliances at discount prices.

catalogue showroom A bargain retail store in which customers place orders for items described in a catalogue and pick up those items from an on-premises warehouse.

factory outlets Bargain retail stores that are owned by the manufacturers whose products they sell.

wholesale clubs Huge membership-only, combined retail–wholesale operations that sell brand-name merchandise.

just one day in 2012 to showcase a collection of clothes by designer Jason Wu and to introduce Target stores to Canada.[24] Well.ca launched a pop-up store featuring images of products in a Toronto commuter hub. Using a smartphone app, customers place orders by scanning quick response codes. Products are delivered the next day. The idea is to bring the store to the customer.[25]

Convenience Stores

convenience stores Retail stores that offer high accessibility, extended hours, and fast service on selected items.

Convenience stores such as 7-Eleven, Mac's, and Circle K offer ease of purchase, easily accessible locations, extended store hours, and speedy service. They differ from most bargain retailers in that they do not feature low prices. Like bargain retailers, they control prices by keeping in-store service to a minimum. In 2009, more than 2300 convenience stores closed across Canada, partly because contraband cigarettes siphoned off about $2.5 billion in sales. The Canadian Convenience Stores Association estimates that half of Ontario's cigarette sales and 40 percent of Quebec's are cheap black-market cigarettes on which no tax has been paid.[26]

Non-Store Retailing

Not all goods and services are sold in stores. In fact, some retailers sell all or most of their products without bricks-and-mortar stores. For example, consumer goods like candy, soft drinks, newspapers, and cigarettes are sold from *vending machines*. Other types of non-store retailing are *direct-response retailing*, *syndicated selling*, *shopping agents*, and *electronic retailing*.

Direct-Response Retailing

direct-response retailing A type of retailing in which firms make direct contact with customers both to inform them about products and to receive sales orders.

mail order (or catalogue marketing) A form of non-store retailing in which customers place orders for merchandise shown in catalogues and receive their orders via mail.

telemarketing Use of the telephone to sell directly to consumers.

direct selling Form of non-store retailing typified by door-to-door sales.

In **direct-response retailing**, firms contact customers directly to inform them about products and to take sales orders. **Mail order (or catalogue marketing)** is a popular form of direct-response retailing. So is **telemarketing**—the use of the telephone to sell products or services.

The oldest form of direct-response retailing is **direct selling**, which is still used by companies that sell door-to-door or through home-selling parties. Avon Products has more than four million sales reps in 100 different countries[27], and Tupperware has more than 60 000 salespeople in Russia alone.[28] L'Oreal has introduced "personal beauty advisors" in department stores in Brazil.[29]

The Fuller Brush Company, which was started in 1906 by Arthur Fuller, a self-described "country bumpkin" from Nova Scotia, used to be well known in door-to-door selling. Two of its most famous salespeople were the Reverend Billy Graham and disc jockey Dick Clark. Sweeping changes in North American society—women leaving the home to work, mass retailing, and the globalization of business—caused the company to fall on hard times, and it declared bankruptcy in 2012.[30]

e-intermediaries Internet-based distribution-channel members that collect information about sellers and present it in convenient form to consumers and/or help deliver internet products to consumers.

An increasingly important category of non-store retailing includes **e-intermediaries**—internet-based intermediaries who either collect information about sellers and provide it for consumers or help deliver internet products to buyers. This category includes *syndicated sellers*, *shopping agents*, and *electronic retailing*.

Syndicated Sellers

syndicated selling Occurs when a website offers other websites a commission for referring customers.

Syndicated selling occurs when one website offers another website a commission for referring customers. For example, Expedia's webpage shows a list of car rental companies, and when Expedia customers click on, say, the Dollar banner for a car rental, they are transferred from the Expedia site to the Dollar site. Dollar pays Expedia a fee for each booking that comes through this channel. The new intermediary increases the cost of Dollar's supply chain, but it adds value for customers because they are efficiently guided to a car-rental agency.[31]

Shopping Agents

Shopping agents (e-agents) help internet consumers by gathering and sorting information. They know which websites and stores to visit, give accurate comparison prices, identify product features, and help consumers complete transactions by presenting information in a usable format—all in a matter of seconds. PriceScan.com is a well-known shopping agent. Since e-agents have become so plentiful, unsure shoppers are turning to rating sites, such as eSmarts.com, that evaluate and compare e-agents.

Ecommerce intermediaries called *business-to-business (B2B) brokers* have also emerged for business customers. The pricing process between B2B buyers and sellers of commodities can be outsourced, for example, to an internet company like Ariba that links large-volume buyers with potential suppliers that bid to become the supplier for the buyer. Commodity buyers like Quaker Oats or Emerson Electric pay Ariba a fixed annual subscription fee and receive networking into its auction headquarters, where real-time bids come in from suppliers at remote locations. The website provides up-to-date information until the bidding ends with the low-price supplier.[32]

> **shopping agent (or e-agent)** A type of intermediary that helps internet consumers by gathering and sorting information they need to make purchases.

Electronic Retailing

Electronic retailing (also called **etailing**) allows consumers to shop from home using the internet. Etailing is made possible by communications networks that let sellers post product information on consumers' PCs. Electronic retailing is carried on through *electronic catalogues, internet-based stores, electronic storefronts and cybermalls,* and *interactive and video marketing.*

> **electronic retailing (or etailing)** Allows consumers to shop from home using the internet.

Electronic Catalogues. **Ecatalogues** use the internet to display products for both retail and business customers. Using electronic displays (instead of traditional mail catalogues), firms give millions of users instant access to pages of product information. The seller avoids mail distribution and printing costs, and once an online catalogue is in place, there is little cost in maintaining and accessing it. Popular consumer ecatalogues include JCPenney, L.L.Bean, and Victoria's Secret. Top B2B ecatalogues include Dell Computer and Office Depot.[33]

> **ecatalogues** Non-store retailing that uses the internet to display products and services for both retail shoppers and business customers.

Internet-Based Stores. Online retail sales in Canada in 2011 were approximately $18 billion, which was 3.4 percent of total retail sales. Online sales are projected to climb to $34 billion by 2016 (5.3 percent of total retail sales).[34] Ice.com, a Montreal-based

> Wolfgang Puck products are distributed through QVC and HSN television networks. The chef's name-brand kitchen appliances and cookware are also marketed through such online outlets as eBay and shopping.com.

company, is a typical internet-based store. It sells mid- and low-priced jewellery over the internet to mostly U.S. customers. The company is profitable because it deals in products that are high value, high margin, small size, and easy to ship to customers.[35] More and more online shopping is done by mobile devices and laptops.[36] For example, online sales on December 25, 2011, were 16.4 percent higher than on December 25, 2010. The use of the internet to do *comparison shopping* is increasingly common. Internet sites like Ask Jeeves Inc., Google Inc., and Yahoo! Inc. allow consumers to compare prices and products before making a purchase. Retailers are being forced to adapt to this new situation.[37] Additional information on the growth of ebusiness is presented in the boxed insert entitled "Exploiting e-Distribution Opportunities."

electronic storefront A seller's website from which consumers collect information about products and buying opportunities, place sales orders, and pay for their purchases.

Electronic Storefronts and Cybermalls. Today, a seller's website is an **electronic storefront** (or virtual storefront) from which consumers collect information about products and buying opportunities, place orders, and pay for purchases. Producers of

E-BUSINESS + SOCIAL MEDIA SOLUTIONS

Exploiting e-Distribution Opportunities

When retailers initially started selling online, they often kept their sites separate from traditional outlets. But this led to confusion when customers were unable to exchange items in stores. Similarly, today organizations are struggling with the implementation of social media strategies. Here are some recent developments in e-distribution and mobile retailing:

■ Walmart transformed the traditional retail landscape, and it is now serious about online sales as well. It has total online sales of approximately $6 billion (which is only 2% of its overall sales), and has clear intentions of growing this position. Walmart recently purchased a Chinese online merchant and created a division called @WalmartLabs which has the mandate to bring the company up to date on the latest social media applications and smartphone payment and promotional approaches. For example, @WalmartLabs analyzes the Twitter network to help find patterns of consumer interest to predict trends and fine-tune in-store and online product selection.

■ Amazon is the poster child for e-distribution success. It is the key destination for book and DVD sales and has a growing presence in everything from glassware to patio furniture. Amazon's development of the Kindle e-reader further demonstrates its willingness to embrace new distribution trends. Amazon created the Kindle even though it had no previous experience in hardware development.

■ Sears Canada has leveraged its traditional strength in catalogue sales with internet distribution. Today the company is focused on creating "an endless aisle." Sears Canada recently hired 80 ecommerce specialists, many from rivals like Indigo and Home Depot. It plans to double online sales in the next five years. Sears is taking advantage of the poor online presence of competitors like The Bay.

■ A few years ago, Procter & Gamble surprised retailers by announcing that it would sell hundreds of its brands, including Tide and Pampers, in its new estore. This places P&G in direct competition with its retailers. P&G executives argue that the site will actually provide consumer research, which could benefit loyal retailers.

■ HMV was slow to embrace digital music distribution. In Canada, HMV Digital was only launched in 2009 (iTunes.ca launched in 2004). When the music industry switched from records to CDs, HMV made a seamless transition. But it did not react quickly to this new distribution challenge and suffered accordingly. HMV is now trying to regain strength; it has an uphill battle, but it's a step in the right direction.

■ Future Shop and Best Buy were early investors and embraced the mobile retail platform. In November 2011, on Cyber Monday, 11 percent of shoppers at Future Shop made purchases online, and 8 percent of purchases were made using mobile devices. The statistics were similar for Boxing Day and, what's more, consumers were able to avoid the sometimes dangerous in-store atmosphere on that day.

New technology continues to revolutionize distribution relationships. The fastest-growing cellphone activity is shopping. Success today is measured by a company's ability to identify challenges and opportunities, and to develop solutions that satisfy consumers and the bottom line. It's not an easy task.

Critical Thinking Questions

1. What are the strengths and weaknesses of e-distribution?

2. Have you ever purchased items from any of the sites mentioned above? Were your experiences positive or negative? Explain.

large product lines, such as Dell Computer, dedicate storefronts to their own product lines. Other sites are category sellers whose storefronts feature products from many manufacturers.

Search engines like Yahoo! serve as **cybermalls**—collections of virtual storefronts representing diverse products. After entering a cybermall, shoppers can navigate by choosing from a list of stores, product listings, or departments. When your virtual shopping cart is full, you check out and pay your bill. The value-added properties of cybermalls are obvious—speed, convenience, 24-hour access, and efficient searching.

cybermalls Collections of virtual storefronts representing diverse products.

From Door-to-Door to eSales? Not surprisingly, cyberspace is encroaching on door-to-door distribution. Amway is famous for a **multilevel marketing** channel in which self-employed distributors get commissions for recruiting new customers and new Amway reps. Amway has expanded this system to the internet with a spinoff called Quixstar. With help from Quixstar, you can start your own at-home internet business. You will be paid for directing new customers to the Quixstar site and for encouraging others to become Quixstar reps. The internet's huge at-home sales potential is also luring other famous door-to-door names—for example, Tupperware, Avon, and Mary Kay. Such firms are racing to board the internet train even though they are courting potential channel conflict. Thousands of loyal door-to-door sales reps stand to lose customers to their own companies' internet outlets.[38]

multilevel marketing A system in which salespeople earn a commission on their own sales and on the sales of any other salespeople they recruit.

Interactive and Video Marketing. Both retail and B2B customers interact with multimedia sites using voice, graphics, animation, film clips, and access to live human advice. One good example of **interactive marketing** is LivePerson.com, a leading provider of real-time sales and customer service for over 3000 websites. When customers log on to the sites of Toyota, Earthlink, Hewlett-Packard, Verizon, Microsoft—all of which are LivePerson clients—they can enter a live chat room where a service operator initiates a secure one-on-one text chat. Questions and answers go back and forth to help customers get answers to specific questions before deciding on a product. Another form of interaction is the so-called banner ad that changes as the user's mouse moves about the page, revealing new drop-down, check, and search boxes.[39]

interactive marketing Selling products and services by allowing customers to interact with multimedia websites using voice, graphics, animation, film clips, and access to live human advice.

Video marketing, a long-established form of interactive marketing, lets viewers shop at home from TV screens by phoning in or emailing orders. Most cable systems offer video marketing through home-shopping channels that display and demonstrate products and allow viewers to phone in or email orders. One U.S. network, QVC, also operates in the United Kingdom, Germany, Mexico, and South America.

video marketing Selling to consumers by showing products on television that consumers can buy by telephone or mail.

Physical Distribution

Physical distribution refers to the activities needed to move products efficiently from manufacturer to consumer. The goals of physical distribution are to keep customers satisfied, to make goods available when and where consumers want them, and to keep costs low. Companies are continually experimenting with physical distribution to improve efficiency and open new markets. For example, Maersk Line and Aqualife AS have partnered to create a transport system to ship seafood from Canada's east coast aquaculture companies to customers in Europe. Specialized tanks on board the ships oxygenate water without having to use pumps. The new system will open new markets for aquaculture products grown in Canada.[40] Coca-Cola Co. decided to take over Coca-Cola Enterprises (CCE)—which focused on bottling and distribution—because Coca-Cola Co. thought it could cut distribution costs by doing so. Pepsi did the same thing with its bottlers in 2009.[41] Physical distribution includes *warehousing* and *transportation operations*, as well as *distribution for ecustomers*.

Define *physical distribution* and describe the major activities in *warehousing* operations.

physical distribution Those activities needed to move a product from the manufacturer to the end-consumer.

Warehousing Operations

warehousing That part of the distribution process concerned with storing goods.

Storing, or **warehousing**, is a major part of distribution management. In selecting a strategy, managers must keep in mind both the different characteristics and costs of warehousing operations.

Types of Warehouses

There are two basic types of warehouses—*private* and *public*. Facilities can be further divided according to use as *storage warehouses* or *distribution centres*.

public warehouse An independently owned and operated warehouse that stores the goods of many firms.

private warehouse A warehouse owned and used by just one company.

Public and Private Warehouses. **Public warehouses** are independently owned and operated. Because companies rent only the space they need, they are popular with firms needing storage only during peak periods. Manufacturers that need multiple storage locations to get products to multiple markets also use public warehouses. **Private warehouses** are owned by a single manufacturer, wholesaler, or retailer. Most are run by large firms that deal in mass quantities and need regular storage.

storage warehouse A warehouse used to provide storage of goods for extended periods of time.

distribution centre A warehouse used to provide storage of goods for only short periods before they are shipped to retail stores.

Storage Warehouses and Distribution Centres. **Storage warehouses** provide storage for extended periods. Producers of seasonal items, such as agricultural crops, use this type of warehouse. **Distribution centres** provide short-term storage of products whose demand is both constant and high. Retail chains, wholesalers, and manufacturers that need to break down large quantities of merchandise into the smaller quantities that stores or customers demand also use them. Distribution centres are common in the grocery and food industry. Kellogg's, for example, stores virtually no products at its plants. Instead, it ships cereals from factories to regional distribution centres.

Warehousing Costs

Typical warehouse costs include such obvious expenses as storage-space rental or mortgage payments (usually computed on a square-foot basis), insurance, and wages. They also include the costs of *inventory control and materials handling*.

inventory control The part of warehouse operations that keeps track of what is on hand and ensures adequate supplies of products are in stock at all times.

Inventory Control. **Inventory control** means ensuring that an adequate supply of a product is in stock at all times, while avoiding an excessive inventory of supplies.

materials handling The transportation and arrangement of goods within a warehouse and orderly retrieval of goods from inventory.

unitization Standardizing the weight and form of materials.

Materials Handling. Most warehouse personnel are involved in **materials handling**—the transportation, arrangement, and orderly retrieval of inventoried goods. Holding down materials-handling costs requires making decisions about product placement within the warehouse as well as decisions about whether to store products as individual units, in multiple packages, or in sealed containers. A **unitization** strategy calls for standardizing the weight and form of materials. A GE warehouse, for example, receives apartment-size refrigerators from Europe in containers of 56 refrigerators each. Dealing with the huge containers rather than individual boxes not only makes handling easier but also reduces theft and damage. It also optimizes shipping space and makes restocking easier.

Transportation Operations

LO7 Compare the five basic forms of *transportation* and explain how distribution can be used as a marketing strategy.

The highest cost faced by many companies is that of physically moving a product, so cost is a major consideration in managing transportation operations. In 2010, Walmart decided to take over the delivery of products to its stores from any manufacturer whose transportation costs Walmart could beat. These savings will be used to further cut prices at its retail stores.[42] Cost is a factor when a company chooses a transportation method, but companies must also consider other factors such as the nature of the product, the distance it must travel, the speed with which it must be received, and customer wants and needs. So a company shipping orchids or other perishable goods will probably use air transport, while a company shipping sand or coal will use rail or water transport.

Transportation Modes

The major transportation modes are rail, water, truck, air, and pipeline. In the early part of the twentieth century, railroads dominated the Canadian transportation system, but by the 1970s, truck and air transportation had become important as well. Using operating revenue as the criterion, the most important modes of transportation in Canada are now trucks, air, and rail. Each of the major transportation modes has advantages and disadvantages. Key differences in cost are most directly related to delivery speed.

Trucks. The advantages of trucks include flexibility, fast service, and dependability. All sections of Canada except the Far North can be reached by truck. Trucks are a particularly good choice for short-distance distribution and more expensive products. Large furniture and appliance retailers in major cities, for example, use trucks to shuttle merchandise between their stores and to make deliveries to customers. Trucks can, however, be delayed by bad weather. They also are limited in the volume they can carry in a single load.

Planes. Air is the fastest available transportation mode (but also the most expensive), and in Canada's Far North, it may be the *only* available transportation. Other advantages include greatly reduced costs in packing, handling, unpacking, and final preparations necessary for sale to the consumer. Also, eliminating the need to store certain commodities can reduce inventory-carrying costs. Fresh fish, for example, can be flown to restaurants each day, avoiding the risk of spoilage that comes with packaging and storing. Spanish apparel chain Zara is willing to pay the extra cost because it can get new merchandise to stores in Europe within 24 hours by using air freight. Because Zara minimizes the inventory it carries, it doesn't have to cut prices to move out-of-date apparel items, so it earns higher margins on the products it sells.[43]

Railroads. Railroads have been the backbone of the Canadian transportation system since the late 1800s. Until the 1960s, when trucking firms lowered their rates and attracted many customers, railroads carried a wide variety of products. Railroads are now used primarily to transport heavy, bulky items such as cars, steel, and coal, and even oil. Because of a shortage of pipeline capacity, by the end of 2013 trains may be transporting 800 000 barrels of oil a day out of the Bakken oil fields in North Dakota.[44]

Water Carriers. Of all the transportation modes, transportation by water is the least expensive. Unfortunately, it is also the slowest. Boats and barges are mainly used for extremely heavy, bulky materials and products (like sand, gravel, oil, and steel) for which transit times are relatively unimportant. The St. Lawrence Seaway is a vital link in Canada's domestic water transportation system. Water transportation is also important in Canada's Far North, where barges deliver commodities such as fuel oil to isolated hamlets along the western edge of Hudson's Bay during the summer months. In recent years, Northern Transportation Company Ltd. has received inquiries from foreign freight experts who want to move large industrial components for the Alberta oil sands from the Arctic Ocean and then up the Mackenzie River to Fort McMurray.[45] Perhaps the river will become a Canadian "Mississippi for the oil sands." In international trade, manufacturers often use water carriers for long distance ocean transportation because many ships are now specially constructed to load and store large standardized containers. But there is an oversupply of ocean-going vessels, and given the reduced demand for shipping because of the fragile world economy, it is likely that many vessels will sit idle.[46]

Modern long-haul trucks have satellite capabilities, anti-collision radar, vehicle-detection sensors, computers for shifting through 10 speeds, and roomy cabs with sleepers, refrigerators, and microwaves.

Pipelines. Pipelines provide a constant flow of liquids and gases, and they are largely unaffected by weather conditions. Like water transportation, pipelines are slow in terms of overall delivery time. They also have a lack of adaptability to other products, and limited routes make pipelines a relatively unimportant transportation method for most industries. In recent years, several oil pipeline spills have occurred, and that has increased concerns about this mode of transportation.[47] In spite of the fact that Enbridge did a good job of cleaning up an oil spill from one of its pipelines in Michigan,[48] activists object to the proposed Keystone XL pipeline, which is designed to transport Alberta crude oil to the Texas coast (see the boxed insert entitled "The Keystone XL Pipeline" for more detail).

Changes in Transportation Operations

For many years, transport companies specialized in one mode or another. With deregulation, however, this pattern has changed. New developments in cost efficiency and competitiveness include *intermodal transportation, containerization,* and *order fulfillment through ecommerce channels.*

intermodal transportation The combined use of different modes of transportation.

Intermodal Transportation. The combined use of different modes of transportation— **intermodal transportation**—has come into widespread use. For example, shipping by a combination of truck and rail ("piggyback"), water and rail ("fishyback"), or air and rail ("birdyback") has improved flexibility and reduced costs.

containerization The use of standardized heavy-duty containers in which many items are sealed at the point of shipment; they are opened only at the final destination.

Containerization. To make intermodal transport more efficient, **containerization** uses standardized heavy-duty containers into which many items are sealed at point of shipment; the containers are opened only at their final destination. Containers may be stowed on ships for ocean transit, transferred to trucks, loaded onto railcars, and delivered to final destinations by other trucks. Unloaded containers are then returned for future use.

order fulfillment All activities involved in completing a sales transaction, beginning with making the sale and ending with on-time delivery to the customer.

Order Fulfillment Through eCommerce Channels. New ecommerce companies often focus on sales, only to discover that delays in after-sale distribution cause customer dissatisfaction. **Order fulfillment** begins when the sale is made and involves getting the product to each customer in good condition and on time. But the volume

A container train negotiates Morants Curve in the Rocky Mountains of Alberta.

THE GREENING OF BUSINESS

The Keystone XL Pipeline

Oil is Canada's largest export, and it has a significant positive effect on our favourable balance of trade and on our national wealth. The United States imports more oil from Canada than from any other country, and to facilitate the exporting of even more oil, TransCanada wants to build the Keystone XL pipeline to carry oil from Alberta to Houston, Texas (where many oil refineries are located).

After studying the proposal, the U.S. State Department concluded that the pipeline would not be an environmental threat, but environmental groups in both Canada and the United States disagreed. Their concerns about pipeline safety intensified after several recent incidents where pipelines began leaking. For example, an Enbridge pipeline ruptured during July 2010 and spilled 3.8 million litres of oil into the Kalamazoo River in Michigan, and an Exxon Mobil pipeline later spilled 95 000 litres of oil into the Yellowstone River in Montana. Environmental groups also claimed that U.S. State Department officials advised TransCanada Corp. on how to build public support for the Keystone pipeline, even though the State Department was at that time in the process of deciding whether to approve the project.

Canadian activists—led by Greenpeace Canada, the Council of Canadians, and the Indigenous Environmental Network—organized a protest in Ottawa in September 2011 to raise awareness of the problem and stop approval for the pipeline. On November 7, 2011, thousands of protestors demonstrated outside the White House. Their goal was to convince U.S. President Barack Obama to deny approval

for the Keystone pipeline. After that the pipeline was put on hold. Cynics claimed that Obama was fearful that if he ignored the protestors, many people who voted for him in 2008 would not vote for him in 2012.

In a further attempt to get the pipeline approved, in April 2012 TransCanada submitted a revised proposal that avoided an environmentally sensitive area in Nebraska. If the Keystone pipeline fails to get approval, one alternative is for Canada to export more oil to the Far East, where demand is expected to be high. Enbridge, for example, is planning a Northern Gateway pipeline that would move oil across northern B.C. to Kitimat. But that idea has run into resistance from Canadian Aboriginal groups that claim it will be an environmental hazard. When opposition like this develops, and when there are many different groups with different agendas, the approval process can be very drawn out and the outcome is not certain. For example, the Mackenzie Valley pipeline, which has been discussed for 40 years, was finally cancelled in 2011.

Questions for Discussion

1. What is "the external environment of business?" How does it impact companies like TransCanada Corp. and Enbridge? (Review the material in Chapter 2 before answering this question.)

2. Do you think the Keystone XL pipeline should be approved? Defend your answer.

of a firm's transactions can be huge, and fulfillment performance—in terms of timing, content, and terms of payment—has been disappointing for many ebusinesses.

To improve on-time deliveries, many businesses, such as Amazon.com, maintain distribution centres and ship from their own warehouses. Other etailers, however, entrust order-filling to distribution specialists such as UPS. The clients of Atomic Box, a much smaller company, range from manufacturers to dot-coms that prefer to concentrate on selling while outsourcing logistics and storage activities. The company maintains 325 000 square feet of warehousing through which it annually delivers products worth more than $200 million. It handles the flow of goods and information in both B2B and business-to-consumer transactions.

Companies like Atomic Box and UPS process customer orders, ship goods, provide information about product availability, inform customers about the real-time status of their orders, and handle returns. To perform these tasks, the client's computer system must be integrated with that of the distribution specialist. In deciding whether to build their own distribution centres or to use third-party distributors, clients must consider fixed costs as well as the need for shipping expertise. Because the capital investment required for a one-million-square-foot distribution centre is $60 to $80 million, only high-volume companies can afford it. The alternative is paying a third-party distributor about 10 percent of each sale to fulfill orders.[49]

Companies Specializing in Transportation

The major modes of transportation are available from one or more of four types of transporting companies: *common carriers, freight forwarders, contract carriers,* and *private carriers.*

common carriers Transportation companies that transport goods for any firm or individual wishing to make a shipment.

Common carriers transport merchandise for any shipper—manufacturers, wholesalers, retailers, and even individual consumers. They maintain regular schedules and charge competitive prices. The best examples of common carriers are truck lines and railroads.

freight forwarders Common carriers that lease bulk space from other carriers and resell that space to firms making small shipments.

Not all transportation companies own their own vehicles. A **freight forwarder** is a common carrier that leases bulk space from other carriers, such as railroads or airlines. It then resells parts of that space to smaller shippers. Once it has enough contracts to fill the bulk space, the freight forwarder picks up whatever merchandise is to be shipped. It then transports the goods to the bulk carrier, which makes delivery to an agreed-on destination and handles billing and any inquiries concerning the shipment.

TABLE 17.2 Top 10 Transportation Companies in Canada, 2011 (ranked by sales revenue)	
Company	**Sales Revenue (billions of dollars)**
1. Air Canada	$11.6
2. Canadian National Railway Co.	9.0
3. Canadian Pacific Railway Ltd.	5.1
4. WestJet Airlines Ltd.	3.0
5. Transforce Inc.	2.6
6. Chorus Aviation Inc.	1.6
7. Purolator Holdings Ltd.	1.6
8. Nav Canada	1.1
9. Greater Toronto Airports Authority	1.1
10. Toronto Transit Commission	0.9

Some transportation companies will transport products for any firm for a contracted amount and time period. These **contract carriers** are usually self-employed operators who own the vehicle that transports the products. When they have delivered a contracted load to its destination, they generally try to locate another contract shipment (often with a different manufacturer) for the return trip.

contract carriers Independent transporters that contract to serve as transporters for industrial customers only.

A few manufacturers and retailers maintain their own transportation systems (usually a fleet of trucks) to carry their own products. The use of such **private carriers** is generally limited to very large manufacturers such as Kraft Foods and Canada Safeway.

private carriers Transportation systems owned by the shipper.

Distribution as a Marketing Strategy

Distribution is an increasingly important way of competing for sales. Instead of just offering advantages in product features and quality, price, and promotion, many firms have turned to distribution as a cornerstone of their business strategies. This approach means assessing and improving all the activities that are involved in getting products from manufacturers to customers. Consider how distribution is used as a marketing strategy at Walmart. When you purchase a product, the scanner at the checkout counter reads the bar code and tells the inventory system that a replacement product is needed. That replacement is provided from the small amount of inventory that is held in the back of the store. When that inventory declines to a certain level, it triggers an order to the manufacturer for another batch of the product. The manufacturer's suppliers are also notified and so on up the supply chain. This system means that Walmart does not have to carry a large amount of inventory in any one of its retail outlets. It also has contributed to Walmart's successful marketing strategy because it means that customers get the products they want when they want them.

MyBizLab

Capture more moments of true understanding. MyBizLab provides you with interactive study and practice tools directly related to this chapter's content. The new MyBizLab Study Plan Learning Path is designed to measure a full range of skills and provide remediation to give you what you need to master key chapter concepts. MyBizLab flexes to your unique learning needs. The result? Inspired learning, more success.

SUMMARY OF LEARNING OBJECTIVES

1. **Identify the various *pricing objectives* that govern pricing decisions and describe the price-setting tools used in making these decisions.** *Pricing objectives* are the goals that producers hope to achieve as a result of pricing decisions. These objectives may include (1) pricing to maximize profits and (2) pricing to achieve *market share* objectives. Sometimes, neither profit maximizing nor market share is the best objective. During difficult economic times, loss containment and survival may be the main objectives. Managers use two basic pricing tools, which are often combined: (1) *cost-oriented pricing* and (2) *break-even analysis*. Break-even analysis assesses total costs versus revenues for various sales volumes. It shows, at any particular sales price, the financial result—the amount of loss or profit—for each possible sales volume.

2. **Discuss *pricing strategies* and tactics for existing and new products.** There are three *strategies* for pricing existing products: (1) pricing above the market, (2) pricing below the market, (3) and pricing at or near the market. Companies pricing new products must often choose between two pricing policy options: (1) *price skimming* (setting an initially high price) or (2) *penetration pricing* (setting an initially low price).

Regardless of its pricing strategy, a company may adopt various *pricing tactics*, including *price lining* (offering all items in certain categories at a limited number of prices), *psychological pricing* (taking advantage of the fact that customers are not completely rational when making buying decisions), and using *discounts* to stimulate sales.

3. **Explain the distribution mix, the different *channels of distribution*, and different *distribution strategies*.** The *distribution mix* refers to the combination of distribution channels a firm selects to get a product to end-users. In selecting a distribution mix, a firm may use all or any of eight distribution channels. The first four are aimed at getting products to consumers, the fifth is for consumers or business customers, and the last three are aimed at getting products to business customers. There are three basic *distribution strategies:* (1) *intensive* (make products available in as many outlets as possible), (2) *selective* (make products available in a few outlets), and (3) *exclusive* (make products available in only one outlet in a geographic area).

4. **Explain the differences between *merchant wholesalers* and *agents/brokers*, and describe the activities of e-intermediaries.** *Merchant wholesalers* buy products from manufacturers (i.e., they take title to the products) and sell them to other businesses, usually providing storage and delivery. A *full-service merchant wholesaler* also provides credit, marketing, and merchandising. *Limited-function merchant wholesalers* provide only a few services, sometimes merely storage. *Agents and brokers* are independent representatives of many companies and work on commissions. They serve as sales and merchandising arms of producers that don't have sales forces.

   E-intermediaries are internet-based channel members that perform one or both of two functions: (1) They collect information about sellers and present it to consumers; (2) they help deliver internet products. There are three types of e-intermediaries: *syndicated sellers*, *shopping agents*, and *business-to-business brokers*.

5. **Identify the different types of *retailing* and *retail stores*.** Retail operations fall under three classifications. (1) *Product line retailers* feature broad product lines. Types of stores include *department stores* and *supermarkets*, which are divided into departments of related products. Small *specialty stores* serve clearly defined market segments by offering full product lines in narrow product fields. (2) *Bargain retailers* carry wide ranges of products and come in many forms, such as *discount houses, catalogue showrooms, factory outlets*, and *warehouse clubs*. (3) *Convenience stores* offer ease of purchase, easily accessible locations, extended store hours, and speedy service, but not low prices.

   Important forms of non-store retailing include *direct-response retailing, mail order (or catalogue marketing), telemarketing*, and *direct selling*. Electronic retailing uses communications networks that allow sellers to connect to consumers' computers. Sellers provide members with internet access to product displays. Buyers can examine detailed descriptions, compare brands, send for free information, or purchase by credit card. *Ecatalogues* use the internet to display products for both retail and business customers. A seller's website is an *electronic storefront* through which consumers collect information about products, place orders, and pay for purchases. Search engines such as Yahoo! serve as *cybermalls*. In a *multilevel marketing channel*, self-employed distributors get commissions for recruiting new customers and reps. Both retail and B2B customers participate in *interactive marketing*. *Video marketing* lets viewers shop at home from television screens.

6. **Define *physical distribution* and describe the major activities in *warehousing* operations.** *Physical distribution* (which includes *warehousing*) refers to the activities needed to move products from manufacturer to consumer. These activities make goods available when and where consumers want them, keep costs low, and provide customer services. There are two types of warehouses: *private warehouses* are owned and used by a single manufacturer, wholesaler, or retailer; while *public warehouses* are independently owned and operated and permit companies to rent only the space they need. *Storage warehouses* provide storage for extended periods. *Distribution centres* store products whose market demand is constant and high. Retail chains, wholesalers, and manufacturers use them to break down large quantities of merchandise into the smaller quantities that stores or customers demand. In addition to keeping track of what is on hand at any time, *inventory control* involves the balancing act of ensuring that an adequate supply of a product is in stock at all times and avoiding excessive supplies of inventory. *Materials handling* refers to the transportation, arrangement, and orderly retrieval of inventoried goods.

7. **Compare the five basic forms of *transportation* and explain how distribution can be used as a marketing strategy.** The advantages of trucks include flexibility, fast service, and dependability. Railroads are now used primarily to transport heavy, bulky items such as cars and steel. Air transport is the fastest available mode of transportation but also the most expensive. Transportation by water is the least expensive but the slowest. Pipelines are slow and inflexible, but do provide a constant flow of products and are unaffected by weather. Many firms regard distribution as a cornerstone of business strategy.

KEY TERMS

QUESTIONS FOR ANALYSIS

1. How do cost-oriented pricing and break-even analysis help managers measure the potential impact of prices?
2. What general factors motivate marketing managers to price their products at, above, or below prevailing market prices?
3. From the manufacturer's point of view, what are the advantages and disadvantages of using intermediaries to distribute products? From the end-user's point of view?
4. Explain how the activities of e-agents (internet shopping agents) or brokers differ from those of traditional agents or brokers.
5. A retailer buys a product from a manufacturer for $25 and sells it for $45. What is the markup percentage? Explain what the term *markup percentage* means.
6. Give three examples (other than those provided in the chapter) of products that use intensive distribution. Do the same for products that use exclusive distribution and selective distribution. What are the characteristics of the products in each category? For which category was it easiest to find examples? Why?

APPLICATION EXERCISES

1. Choose any consumer item at your local supermarket and trace the chain of physical distribution activities that brought it to the store shelf.
2. Suppose that a small publisher selling to book distributors has fixed operating costs of $600 000 each year and variable costs of $3 per book. How many books must the firm sell to break even if the selling price is $6? If the company expects to sell 50 000 books next year and decides on a 40 percent markup, what will the selling price be?
3. Consider the various kinds of non-store retailing. Give examples of two products that typify the kinds of products sold to at-home shoppers through each form of non-store retailing. Are different products best suited to each form of non-store retailing? Explain.
4. Identify two products that you purchased in the past six months for which price was very important. Also identify two products for which price was not very important. What characteristics of the products caused you to assign higher or lower importance to price?

BUILDING YOUR BUSINESS SKILLS

Are You Sold on the Net?

The Purpose of the Assignment

To encourage students to consider the value of online retailing as an element in a company's distribution system.

The Situation

As the distribution manager of a privately owned clothing manufacturer specializing in camping gear and outdoor clothing, you are convinced that your product line is perfect for online distribution. However, the owner of the company is reluctant to expand distribution from a successful network of retail stores and a catalogue operation. Your challenge is to convince the boss that retailing via the internet can boost sales.

Assignment

Step 1

Join together with four or five classmates to research the advantages and disadvantages of an online distribution system for your company. Among the factors to consider are the following:

- The likelihood that target consumers are internet shoppers. Young, affluent consumers who are comfortable with the web generally purchase camping gear.
- The industry trend to online distribution. Are similar

companies doing it? Have they been successful?
- The opportunity to expand inventory without increasing the cost of retail space or catalogue production and mailing charges.
- The opportunity to have a store that never closes.
- The lack of trust many people have about doing business on the web. Many consumers are reluctant to provide credit card information over the web.
- The difficulty that electronic shoppers have in finding a website when they do not know the store's name.
- The frustration and waiting time involved in web searches.
- The certainty that the site will not reach consumers who do not use computers or who are uncomfortable with the web.

Step 2

Based on your findings, write a persuasive memo to the company's owner stating your position on expanding to an online distribution system. Include information that will counter expected objections.

Questions for Discussion

1. What place does online distribution have in the distribution network of this company?
2. In your view, is online distribution the wave of the future? Is it likely to increase in importance as a distribution system for apparel companies? Why or why not?

EXERCISING YOUR ETHICS: TEAM EXERCISE

The Chain of Responsibility

The Situation

Because several stages are involved when distribution chains move products from supply sources to end-consumers, the process offers ample opportunity for ethical issues to arise. This exercise encourages you to examine some of the ethical issues that can emerge during transactions among suppliers and customers.

The Dilemma

A customer bought an expensive wedding gift at a local store and asked that it be shipped to the bride in another province. Several weeks after the wedding, the customer contacted the bride, who had not confirmed the arrival of the gift. It hadn't arrived. Charging that the merchandise had not been delivered, the customer requested a refund from the retailer. The store manager uncovered the following facts:

- All shipments from the store are handled by a well-known national delivery firm.

- The delivery firm verified that the package had been delivered to the designated address two days after the sale.
- Normally, the delivery firm does not obtain recipient signatures; deliveries are made to the address of record, regardless of the name on the package.

The gift giver argued that even though the package had been delivered to the right address, it had not been delivered to the named recipient. It turns out that, unbeknownst to the gift giver, the bride had moved. It stood to reason, then, that the gift was in the hands of the new occupant at the bride's former address. The manager informed the gift giver that the store had fulfilled its obligation. The cause of the problem, she explained, was the incorrect address given by the customer. She refused to refund the customer's money and suggested that the customer might want to recover the gift by contacting the stranger who received it at the bride's old address.

Team Activity

Assemble a group of four students and assign each group member to one of the following roles:

- customer (the person who originally purchased the gift)
- employee (of the store where the gift was purchased)
- bride (the person who was supposed to receive the gift)
- customer service manager (of the delivery company)

Questions for Discussion

1. Before discussing the situation with your group, and from the perspective of your assigned role, do you think there are any ethical issues in this situation? If so, write them down.
2. Before discussing the situation with your group, and from the perspective of your assigned role, decide how this dispute should be resolved.
3. Together with your group, share the ethical issues that were identified. What responsibilities does each party—the customer, the store, and the delivery company—have in this situation?
4. What does your group recommend be done to resolve this dispute? What are the advantages and disadvantages of your recommendations?

Go to MyBizLab for additional cases and exercise material.

CONCLUDING CASE 17-1

A New Reality for Real Estate Agents

Intermediaries like real estate agents bring buyers and sellers together. For many years, the Canadian Real Estate Association (CREA) allowed only "full service" real estate agents access to its Multiple Listing Service (MLS), the database that lists most of the houses for sale in Canada. Since 90 percent of all homes are sold through the MLS, this meant that people who were selling their home really had no alternative but to pay for the "full service" that an agent would give them, even if they didn't want all the services. These services did not come cheap. For example, a real estate agent would typically receive a $20 000

commission when selling a $400 000 house for a client (half of that amount would be shared with the buyer's agent).

While real estate agents provide an essential service, it is not necessarily a *low-cost* service. Buyers and sellers have long felt that these commissions were way too high. In recent years, e-brokers have emerged who charge a flat rate for selling a house, and their rate is far below what traditional real-estate agents charge (as little as $100). This has created competition for traditional real estate agents, and it is not surprising that they view e-brokers with alarm (even though e-brokers were not allowed access to the MLS). E-brokers began appearing on the scene in the mid-1990s. For example, Nicolas Bouchard founded Duproprio.com, which focused on private sales without an agent. At first, the site attracted mostly people who knew each other, or had seen someone's For Sale sign on their lawn. Bouchard's company developed slowly over the years, but he says it now has 1.25 million visitors each month (although this is still a lot smaller than the 12 million visits on the MLS).

Beyond the competition from e-brokers, another problem developed for CREA in 2010 when the Canadian Competition Bureau filed a complaint with the Competition Tribunal, alleging that CREA was engaging in anti-competitive restrictions that were designed to maintain high fees for traditional real estate brokers by denying e-brokers access to the MLS, and by not allowing CREA agents to provide less than full service. The outcome of the Competition Bureau's investigation of CREA was the signing of a consent agreement that allows people who are selling their home to buy whatever level of service they want from their real estate agent (anything from a cheap, flat-rate MLS listing all the way up to "full service"). The agreement essentially prohibits CREA members from discriminating against e-brokers who simply want to post homes for sale on the MLS. Sellers who buy a flat-rate listing are guaranteed that their house will appear on the MLS listing (CREA did not previously allow this). The seller must offer a finder's fee to any real estate agent who brings them a buyer for their house, but no minimum payment is required. Sellers who are willing to do most of the work of negotiating the sale of their house will therefore pay far less to an agent than they used to. Agents are required by the agreement to show their clients any listing that the client is interested in, including those that are posted by low-fee brokers.

After the consent agreement, the Competition Bureau said that it was satisfied that its anti-competitive concerns had been dealt with, but critics then began charging that the system was still rigged because CREA was trying to keep agents from doing business across provincial boundaries. After the consent agreement, e-brokers thought that they would be able to deal with clients across Canada. But real estate boards in several provinces interpreted provincial legislation in such a way as to prohibit real estate agents from other provinces to compete in their province. For example, Joe William, an Ottawa-based real estate agent who charged just $100 for putting a listing on the MLS, got multiple requests from people outside Ontario, but he was fined by the province of Quebec, which claimed he was violating provincial law. He dropped his listings in Quebec but appealed the decision. William also got an email from the Manitoba Securities Commission saying that before he could do real estate transactions in Manitoba, he had to have a Manitoba licence. He says he can't understand why he needs a licence simply to post real estate listings online. The consent agreement was supposed to allow MLS listings, but e-brokers keep getting threatened with court action when they try to list homes for sale on the MLS.

So, the situation is not as clear as it seemed right after the Competition Bureau ruling in 2010. The question is this: Are flat-fee real estate agents actually trading in real estate, or are they simply posting houses for sale online? The answer to this seemingly simple question is important because if agents *are* trading, they must have a licence in the province where they are trading. But flat-fee real estate agents say that all they are doing is newspaper or online advertising, and that homeowners are handling the actual sale.

Critics have also complained that real estate agents have a basic conflict of interest because the agent for the buyer typically receives a commission from the seller. So, a buyer's agent could inform a seller that he or she has a buyer for the house, but that the agent wants 2.5 percent of the sales price before the agent will bring the buyer to look at the house. If the seller says no, will the agent still bring the buyer to look at the house? If not, the agent is not looking out for buyer, but is instead looking out for his or her own interests (i.e., showing the buyer a house where the seller is willing to pay the agent a 2.5 percent commission). Overall, critics say that the high commissions in the industry attract too many people to the business. One industry executive says the industry is overrun with people who lack experience and knowledge.

If commissions decline under the new system, fewer people may seek employment in the industry.

Supporters of CREA responded to these complaints by noting that the consent agreement really didn't change anything because real estate agents have never been able to sell in different provinces. As well, they argue that since CREA developed the MLS, it shouldn't be forced to share it with competitors. In terms of agent knowledge and experience, they say that should be addressed by licensing and apprenticeship programs for aspiring agents.

In 2011, the Competition Bureau filed another lawsuit, this one against the Toronto Real Estate Board (TREB), arguing that its practices were still preventing brokers from sharing information over the internet. The Competition Bureau acknowledged that real estate agents were allowed to give customers information in person or via fax, but said that TREB's guidelines did not allow customers access to websites that would give them the detailed information they needed to make housing purchase decisions. TREB responded by adopting a new policy that it claimed would give consumers access to information on the Multiple Listing Service. Whether this new policy will resolve the dispute is unclear. What is clear is that the internet has already shaken up several industries (book and music sellers, travel agents, and classified ads), and is now in the process of shaking up the business of selling homes.

And change continues. Late in 2011, information that used to be impossible to get without the help of a real estate agent was posted by a listings website that was backed by Rogers Communications. It tapped private databases to give people an estimate of a property's value. And CREA also announced that it would provide extensive data that is not currently available to homebuyers. This will likely lead to the creation of websites similar to those like Zillow.com and Redfin.com in the United States. Interestingly, these sites have not weakened the position of traditional real estate agents. Instead, agents often post their offerings on the site.

Questions for Discussion

1. Do you think that changes in the way real estate agents are paid will end up saving money for people who buy a home? For people who sell their home?
2. Consider the following statement: *It is unreasonable for the Competition Bureau to force CREA to share its MLS listings with e-brokers because CREA has spent a lot of time and money developing the MLS. Why should CREA have to share information with its competitors when other companies are not forced to?* Do you agree or disagree with this statement? Defend your answer.

CONCLUDING CASE 17-2

The Continuing Revolution in Music Channels of Distribution

Some highly publicized changes have recently occurred in channels of distribution for artistic works like books, movies, and music. While it may seem that these changes are unusual, a brief look back through history shows that disruptions have been common in this industry. In the nineteenth century, for example, companies that published sheet music were the dominant force in the music industry, but they were suddenly faced with a major threat when Thomas Edison invented the phonograph. In 1881, the writer Mark Twain visited Montreal to protect his new book *The Prince and the Pauper* from copyright pirates. He did that because Canadian publishers had produced knock-offs of his previous book, *Tom Sawyer*, and were selling them in the U.S. market for one-sixth the price of his real book. Even before that, U.S. publishers were pirating books written by popular British writers because U.S. law didn't recognize copyrights from other countries. Thus, American publishing firms got free content, and consumers got books at low prices. These historical changes caused industry disruption just like the current technology-induced changes that are occurring in the music, movie, and book businesses.

Consider how the channels of distribution in the music industry have changed in the past few decades. In the 1950s, consumers visited record shops like the legendary Sam the Record Man store in downtown Toronto. They looked over the merchandise, and then decided what to buy (originally breakable records, then 45 rpm records, then vinyl LPs, then eight-track tapes, then cassettes, and finally CDs). Senior citizens fondly remember the "music store experience."

Further changes occurred in the distribution of music when internet stores began offering thousands of titles among CDs and cassettes. Customers searched the lists, placed orders electronically or over the phone, and then received their music by mail. Then an online music service called Napster appeared, which changed the game again. Customers downloaded free software onto their computers that allowed them to put their music on Napster's website and trade with anyone else who was live on the internet at the same time. Not surprisingly, recording industry executives were not impressed with this new channel of distribution. They argued that file-sharing denied music artists the royalties they were due. The threat from Napster was seen as so great that the Recording Industry Association of America (RIAA) decided to prosecute. The courts soon shut Napster down for copyright infringement, but the victory was short-lived, and other file-sharing services like Morpheus, KaZaA, and Grokster popped up. People who used those services were prosecuted as well. In 2007, for example, a U.S. mother of four children was fined $1.92 million for illegal file sharing (in 2010, her fine was reduced to $54 000, but it is not clear whether she will ever be able to pay even that reduced amount). In 2009, a Swedish court found four

men guilty of illegally posting a pirated copy of the film *X-Men Origins: Wolverine*. The men were sentenced to one year in jail and ordered to pay $3.6 million in damages to various entertainment companies. Their website—called Pirate Bay—indexed songs, movies, and TV shows and was visited by more than 22 million people each day.

In spite of these court actions, illegal downloading of music and movies continues unabated. For example, a Canadian file-sharing service called IsoHunt has become one of the world's most visited websites. Overseas programmers also offer new software to consumers and they are beyond the reach of the law in North America. According to the file-sharing blog TorrentFreak.com, the most downloaded movie of 2010 was *Avatar*, which was downloaded 16.6 million times.

As all these actions and counter-actions play out, the physical distribution of music in the form of CDs is rapidly declining in Canada (down from $572 million in 2007 to just $275 million in 2011). At the same time, digital distribution of music from sites like iTunes is rapidly increasing (from $122 million in 2007 to $366 million in 2011). Thus, the value of digital distribution now exceeds that of physical distribution. In response to the decline in traditional music formats, record stores have shifted their emphasis away from CDs and toward DVDs and video games. In 2010, worldwide digital music revenue was $US6.4 billion, but that was less than 30 percent of the music industry's total revenue. What's worse, less than 17 percent of the people online paid for digital.

In 2011, a free (and legal) service called Spotify was introduced in the United States (it is also available in several European countries). The service is supported by advertisements and is available only to current users or to consumers who request it on Twitter. Consumers are given access to catalogues of music and they can pick whatever songs interest them. It took a lot of negotiation with record companies, but they are on board with Spotify's free service because Spotify shares advertising revenues with the record companies. In 2010, Spotify paid $60 million in royalties to European record labels; that made it the second largest sourced of digital revenue for record companies after iTunes. There are some limitations in the service Spotify provides. For example, for the first six months, users are limited to 20 hours of listening per month. In 2011, a small Spanish company named 24symbols introduced a similar service for digital books.

All of these developments pose a great challenge to the music industry. Not too many years ago, the business was dominated by four major labels: EMI, Universal Music Group, Sony Music Entertainment, and Warner Music Group. They controlled channels of distribution and radio play, and had a big influence on which artists became popular. But all that has changed, and the record industry is (belatedly) realizing that it cannot stop the march of technology. So, it is trying all sorts of things to make sure that recording artists get a fair share of the action. For example, the recording industry launched two online music services—MusicNet and Pressplay. If customers used MusicNet, they paid $9.95 a month and got 100 downloads (but couldn't copy them and the deal expired at the end of the month). If they used Pressplay, they got 100 downloads for $24.95 per month (and the right to burn 20 tracks to a CD). Other similar services are offered by iTunes (the industry leader), Microsoft, Yahoo!, and a rejuvenated Napster. The industry is also trying promotions whereby fans get digital downloads for free when they buy vinyl records. Record companies have also struck deals with companies like iTunes and Spotify.

It is difficult to predict what the future holds, given the complex and rapidly changing situation. The one obvious fact is that the need for bricks-and-mortar retail outlets for movie theatres, book stores, and music stores is declining. Of course, there still are music stores, but they find themselves in an increasingly precarious position, and some industry analysts are predicting their eventual demise. To counter this perception, the Association of Independent Media Stores (AIMS) sponsors an annual International Record Store Day in Canada. The event is designed to show that record stores are still viable entities. In 2011, events were held in various cities across Canada. In Calgary, for example, The Inner Sleeve offered a 25 percent price reduction on new and used vinyl records and CDs. In Winnipeg, the Music Trader had draws for prizes and provided live music from a local band.

Other changes are also taking place. For example, some artists avoid the music industry altogether; they use new technology to make songs cheaply, and then market them on the web. Other groups make most of their money from concerts and merchandising. CD sales continue to be strong for older people who are fans of groups like the Beatles. There is also a debate about what music should cost. The traditional view is consumers should pay for music so that artists are compensated for their creative endeavours. But some argue that music should be free to everyone, just like television, where content is paid for by advertisers (this is the Spotify model). In the run-up to the 2011 federal election, a fringe political party—the Pirate Party—proposed reforming copyright laws so that the internet would be an unfettered medium for the exchange of information (including music). The party said that non-commercial file-sharing is under attack by the established powers in much the same way that the printing press was attacked in the fifteenth century. A similar argument was made in a cinematic essay/documentary entitled *RiP*. The work of digital mash-up artist Girl Talk (who remixed samples from other artists) was cited to illustrate the argument.

Questions for Discussion

1. Consider the traditional channels of distribution for music. Which channel elements are most affected by the presence of services like Spotify? Explain how those elements are affected.
2. Develop arguments opposing the legality of online downloading of music. Then take the reverse position and develop an argument in favour of these services.
3. What other products, besides music, are the most likely candidates for distribution on the internet, now and in the future?
4. Will Spotify's free service take away sales from other options like iTunes, where consumers have to pay?

VIDEO CASE 4–1
Boomer Ads

The general population is getting older and baby boomers (people born between 1947 and 1966 in Canada) continue to dominate. They have transformed major aspects of society for years. Their large numbers led to the construction of new schools and had an impact on everything from housing trends to vacation needs and pharmaceuticals. Today you may be noticing more individuals with grey hair and wrinkles in advertisements. Marketers are really starting to focus on the real needs of the 50-plus age demographic. In addition, there has clearly been a shift to a more open and frank language in ads, with terms like *menopausal skin* being employed. Marketers are creating products aimed specifically at boomers, with a focus not on age but rather on lifestyle. Louis Vuitton's "personal journey" campaign is a perfect example. The luxury brand had once been resistant to using images of older consumers, choosing instead to focus on flashier photos of youthful individuals. Now, however, Louis Vuitton caters to wealthy customers who are more often than not a bit older. The "personal journey" campaign, for example, featured many older celebrities like Sean Connery, Keith Richards, and Catherine Deneuve.

Baby boomers were the original "Pepsi Generation" and, back in the 60s, they defined what it meant to be young. Advertisers believe youth sells and constantly bombard consumers with images of youth. However, with one in three Canadians now belonging to the boomer classification, and coming face to face with the aches and pains of age, marketers are now catering to these needs. For example, *Zoomer* magazine is designed for and geared towards boomers. Instead of images of sweet grandmothers on the cover, however, *Zoomer* paints a more youthful picture using stars like Wayne Gretzky, Margaret Atwood, and Bryan Adams.

Traditionally, it was mainly financial institutions, retirement homes, and pharmaceutical companies that catered to this age group; but today it is not uncommon to see luxury brands and high-end cosmetics companies creating entire campaigns based on the boomers.

Demographer David Foot believed that this change was inevitable; however, for a time, as the first baby boomers entered their fifties, marketers were still consumed with images of youth and often ignored this massive generation. Part of the thinking was based on an assumption that boomers were very brand loyal and less likely to switch brands so there was less need to advertise to them. However, research is showing otherwise: a 55-year-old is just as likely to switch brands as a 25-year-old.

One thing is clear: the boomers are a lucrative market. Even as the economy crashed a few years ago, the boomers still had money to spend because most had paid off their mortgages and had savings to tap into. Life expectancy is going up; fifty really is the new forty. Boomers are healthy, they grew up with marketing, and they are willing to spend on themselves and their loved ones. Based on those facts, boomers will be heavily pitched to for many years to come.

Questions for Discussion

1. What do you think of the approach taken by some marketers in using very direct language (such as *menopausal skin*) in their ads?

2. Explain the basic elements of segmentation, targeting, and positioning by using the Louis Vuitton "Personal Journey" campaign as an example.

3. What forms of media would you use to capture the boomer demographic? Avoid stereotypical assumptions and think carefully about social media approaches (that fit) as well as traditional media.

4. List the various influences on consumer behaviour and identify how these influences might have a greater or a less important impact on a baby boomer as opposed to a millennial (Generation Y) consumer.

VIDEO CASE 4-2
Joe Fresh

At a recent Toronto fashion event, one brand stood out from the crowd. It was different not because of outrageous styling but because of the retailer supporting it. Joe Fresh is the brainchild of Joe Mimran, who is a legend of the Canadian fashion scene. He is the man behind famous brands like Club Monaco and Caban. What is Joe Fresh? Think fashionable merchandise at very low prices offered conveniently at your local Loblaw grocery stores. According to Joe Mimran, the challenge presented by Loblaw was to create fashions that could appeal to various tastes across the country and yet also be stylish at very low prices. Joe could provide the fashion expertise but there was also a need for a brand "that would actually resonate with the consumer." Clearly, Joe Fresh is a nice play on words that both fits consumers' constant insatiable search for new product styles and pays respect to the retail home of the brand. Although this combination is a very unlikely fit for the fashion catwalk, Joe Fresh is already making a major impression on the industry.

You may be wondering why Loblaw would go down this route and make a major stake on the clothing business (which is not part of their core strength). However, if you examine the market it is clear that there is a growing consolidation and sticking to the status quo was dangerous. At the time, Loblaw was struggling after installing a new inventory management system. Competitors like Walmart were hurting Loblaw by selling food items and providing low-cost clothing. Walmart was also planning to add new superstores. Joe Fresh was Loblaw's way of addressing this growing threat. While Walmart has strong clothing sales figures, its retail brand perception is low. If Joe Fresh can meet low price points and add cachet, there is a great opportunity for Loblaw. It is all part of the market evolution. Pharmacies (like Shoppers Drug Mart) are selling groceries, Walmart and Loblaw are now selling pharmaceuticals, and naturally Loblaw is now selling clothes.

Joe Fresh is trying to help capture some of Loblaw's previous glory. Low-cost fashion is a potential hit, especially in troubled economic times. According to the video, Joe Fresh is now the second-largest clothing line (by sales) in Canada. The company does not disclose its statistics but its goal is to reach $1 billion a year in sales. Based on its initial success, Loblaw has asked Joe Mimran to design other household goods to add unique flavour and freshness to those categories. Mr. Mimran knows a thing or two about such an expansion, as his Caban business failed after a similar attempt. But he plans to use this firsthand knowledge and the lessons learned to make Joe Fresh a success across product lines. Time will tell whether this relationship continues to bear fruit or starts to rot in the attempt to expand.

Questions for Discussion

1. How does the Joe Fresh brand of fashion products create value for consumers? What is their value equation?
2. Describe the target market for Joe Fresh fashions across various market segmentation variables.
3. Explain the concept of brand equity and link it to the growth of the Joe Fresh Brand. How does the Joe Fresh brand stack up to Walmart's low-cost fashion? How does it stack up to popular fashionable brands like Zara?
4. What do you think of the brand extension of Joe Fresh into other categories such as housewares? Do you think it is a good idea? Why or why not?
5. How can Loblaw use social media to create extra buzz for the Joe Fresh brand? Provide concrete examples and a framework of ideas (slogan, social media campaigns, advergaming, etc.)

CRAFTING A BUSINESS PLAN
Part 4: Principles of Marketing

Goal of the Exercise

So far, your business has an identity; you've described the factors that will affect your business; and you've examined your employees, the jobs they'll be performing, and the ways in which you can motivate them. Part 4 of the business plan project asks you to think about marketing's four Ps—product, price, place (distribution), and promotion—and how they apply to your business. You'll also examine how you might target your marketing toward a certain group of consumers.

EXERCISE BACKGROUND

Part 4 of the Business Plan

In Part 1, you briefly described what your business will do. The first step in Part 4 of the plan is to describe more fully the product (good or service) you are planning to sell. Once you have a clear picture of the product, you'll need to describe how this product will "stand out" in the marketplace—that is, how it will differentiate itself from other products.

In Part 1, you also briefly described who your customers would be. The first step in Part 4 of the plan is to describe your ideal buyer, or target market, in more detail, listing their income level, educational level, lifestyle, age, and so forth. This part of the business plan project also asks you to discuss the price of your products, as well as where the buyer can find your product.

Finally, you'll examine how your business will get the attention and interest of the buyer through its promotional mix—advertising, personal selling, sales promotions, and publicity and public relations.

This part of the business plan encourages you to be creative. Have fun! Provide as many details as you possibly can, as this reflects an understanding of your product and your buyer. Marketing is all about finding a need and filling it. Does your product fill a need in the marketplace?

YOUR ASSIGNMENT

Step 1

Open the saved *Business Plan* file you have been working on.

Step 2

For the purposes of this assignment, you will answer the following questions in "Part 4: Principles of Marketing":

1. Describe your target market in terms of age, education level, income, and other demographic variables.
   Hint: Refer to Chapter 15 for more information on the aspects of target marketing and market segmentation that you may want to consider. Be as detailed as possible about who you think your customers will be.

2. Describe the features and benefits of your product or service.
   Hint: As you learned in Chapter 16, a product is a bundle of attributes—features and benefits. What features does your product have—what does it look like and what does it do? How will the product benefit the buyer?

3. How will you make your product stand out in the crowd?
   Hint: There are many ways to stand out in the crowd, such as a unique product, outstanding service, or a great location. What makes your great idea special? Does it fill an unmet need in the marketplace? How will you differentiate your product to make sure that it succeeds?

4. What pricing strategy will you choose for your product, and what are the reasons for this strategy?
   Hint: Refer to this chapter for more information on pricing strategies and tactics. Since your business is new, so is the product. Therefore, you probably want to choose between price skimming and penetration pricing. Which will you choose, and why?

5. Where will customers find your product or service? (That is, what issues of the distribution mix should you consider?)
   Hint: If your business does not sell its product directly to consumers, what types of retail stores will sell your product? If your product will be sold to another business, which channel of distribution will you use? Refer to Chapter 17 for more information on aspects of distribution you may want to consider.

6. How will you advertise to your target market? Why have you chosen these forms of advertisement?
   Hint: Marketers use several different advertising media—specific communication devices for carrying a seller's message to potential customers—each having its advantages and drawbacks. Refer to Chapter 16 for a discussion of the types of advertising media you may wish to consider here.

7. What other methods of promotion will you use, and why?
   Hint: There's more to promotion than simple advertising. Other methods include personal selling, sales promotions, and publicity and public relations. Refer to the discussion of promotion in this chapter for ideas on how to promote your product that go beyond just advertising.

Note: Once you have answered the questions, save your Word document. You'll be answering additional questions in later chapters.

Managing Financial Issues

The opening cases in each of the chapters in this part of the text deal with some aspect of the critical area of financial management. Management of the financial transactions of a business firm is critical to its survival. Whether it involves raising money to start a new firm, assessing the riskiness of the firm's investments, managing the firm's cash, or monitoring the firm's activities in securities markets, financial management is a key business activity.

Part Five, Managing Financial Issues, provides an overview of business finance, including how firms raise and manage money, how they define and manage risk, and how they use Canadian and international securities markets to meet their financial needs.

■ We begin in **Chapter 18, Understanding Money and Banking**, by exploring the nature of money, its creation through the banking system, and the role of the Bank of Canada in the nation's financial system. We also describe other important financial services organizations.

■ Next, in **Chapter 19, Understanding Securities and Investments**, we consider the securities markets in which firms raise long-term funds by examining how these markets operate and how they are regulated.

■ Finally, in **Chapter 20, Financial Decisions and Risk Management**,

we look at three reasons businesses need funds and how financial managers raise both long- and short-term funds. We also examine the kinds of risks businesses encounter and the ways in which they deal with such risks.

18

Understanding Money and Banking

After reading this chapter, you should be able to:

1 Define *money* and identify the different forms it takes in the nation's money supply.

2 Understand the different kinds of *financial institutions* in the Canadian financial system, including the *Bank of Canada*.

3 Explain the role of *chartered banks* in the Canadian financial system.

4 Explain the role of *alternate banks, specialized lending and savings intermediaries,* and *investment dealers* in the Canadian financial system.

5 Understand the key concepts and activities in *international banking and finance*.

Beware of the Credit Card Trap!

AS you walk in the downtown core of any major metropolitan city, what do you see on top of the buildings? You will notice that many of them bear the names of banks and insurance companies. The financial services industry is very healthy; the top five banks in Canada earned combined profits of $22.3 billion in 2011 alone. Despite some recent missteps, the fundamental math is strong. In 2012, the Canadian banking system was ranked number one in the world for the fourth straight year. The industry is governed by the rules of the Bank Act and supported by internal company policies. In recent years, banks have expanded their services to meet a wider range of consumer investment needs, and service fees have grown and added to the bottom line. Credit cards are another major source of revenues. How many bank-issued credit cards do you possess? How responsible are you with those

credit cards? How much interest do you pay every year? Do you even know the answer to these questions?

Look around your lecture hall. Let's say there are 100 people in your class and they are all clients of your local bank. Your classmates deposit money in their accounts (thus providing funds) and receive a very low interest rate in return (in recent years it has been below the 1 percent range). You use your bank-issued credit card to charge $1000 to pay for your spring break vacation. You don't have the money to pay it back so you have contractually agreed to pay back interest of 20 percent. Most people won't think twice about how much interest they pay every year because the credit card issuers allow individuals to pay back borrowed money slowly with the help of minimum payments. If you only pay the minimum, it will take you years—and hundreds of dollars—to pay off even this minor debt.

Beware of the Minimum Payment

It may seem like you are getting a great deal by being generously allowed to make only the minimum payment of $50 (or 2 to 3 percent of the balance), but of course this deal comes with a major price. For example, if you are carrying $10 000 of credit card debt at 20 percent interest, you are paying about $2000 in interest per year. Could you think of anything else you could do with an extra $2000 (a trip, a nice music system, new furniture)? For many people the whole credit card experience is like getting onto a defective treadmill that actually starts off slowly, and then gets progressively quicker before the button gets stuck on high speed. In that situation, you would need to find an effective way to jump off or get someone to pull the plug for you. Unfortunately, many people do not know how to help themselves get out of the credit card trap.

Some people even delude themselves into thinking that their situation is better than it

actually is. They make the minimum payments and may carry a debt load of, say, $10 000 on their credit cards but in the meantime they have the same amount of money sitting in a bank account. Why would someone collect 1 percent on a $10 000 bank account balance and simultaneously pay 20 percent interest on a credit card debt? It's illogical. Under these circumstances, it is costing you $1900 (−$2000 cost of credit + $100 interest from the account) to fool yourself. Some people just never do the math. They can't be bothered or they just don't understand. (You have been warned.) Others are fearful that if they pay off their credit card bills, they will just load their cards up again. If that is the case for you, then you need to use your scissors to cut up your credit cards. Discipline is required.

If you don't have the money to pay for previous debts, you can use other sources of lower-interest borrowing to pay off the bills. Here are *some short-term options*:

- A home equity line of credit (HELOC) can be used to pay down your debt (these days you can get a rate of 4 to 5 percent (total savings: $1500–$1600 per year on the same $10 000 debt). So why not transfer the credit card debt to this lower-rate option and use the savings to pay down your debt quicker?

- Credit card issuers often offer cheque transfers at, say, 0.99 to 3.99 percent for six to nine months. For example, you can transfer your 20 percent debt on your Visa to your MasterCard that's offering a temporary 1.99 percent deal; this sort of offer can save you hundreds of dollars and gives you extra funds to pay off principal. The catch is that, at the end of the six to nine months, you will be charged a high rate again. (Remember, this is only a short-term solution. Don't add to your debt; instead, use the time to pay it off).

- If you must take on debt by credit card, there are some products that charge more reasonable rates. According to the Canadian Bankers Association (CBA), there are over 70 low-interest credit cards on the market. The CBA defines low interest as below 12 percent (which is still very high). RBC launched a credit card called the RBC My Project Credit MasterCard. It provides as much as $40 000 with zero percent interest for six months and interest of 4.99 percent above prime after that.

The real solution: Buy what you can afford and pay cash. Then there is no need for long-term calculations and financially troubling interest payments.

Benefits and the Best Advice

Credit cards are still a great way to make purchases conveniently without carrying large sums of money—if you act responsibly. They provide a 21- to 30-day interest-free loan if you pay on time. In addition, you can earn points that can lead to free travel and free products. If you are responsible, you can take advantage of the benefits without over-contributing to the construction of another high-rise building. In this chapter, we learn about the definition of money. Credit cards are not money. They can be used as a medium of exchange but they must be used wisely or they will have a very negative effect on your personal wealth. ◆

By understanding the material in this chapter, you will benefit in two ways: (1) As a *consumer*, you'll learn what money is, where it comes from, how the supply of money grows, and the kinds of services that are available to you from the financial services industry; and (2) as a *manager*, you will have a greater understanding of the various financial institutions in Canada and how the activities of these financial institutions influence business firms.

What Is Money?

L01 Define *money* and identify the different forms it takes in the nation's money supply.

When someone asks you how much money you have, what do you say? Do you count the bills and coins in your pockets? Do you include the funds in your chequing and savings accounts? What about stocks, bonds, or your car? Taken together, the value of everything you own is your personal *wealth*. Not all of it, however, is *money*. In this section, we will consider the characteristics of money, the functions of money, and the supply of money.

The Characteristics of Money

Over the years, many different objects have been used as money in different societies. Modern money usually takes the form of stamped metal or printed paper—Canadian dollars, U.S. dollars, and euros—issued by governments. The Chinese were using metal money as early as 1100 BCE to represent the objects they were exchanging (e.g., bronze spades and knives). Coins probably came into use in China sometime around 600 BCE and paper money around 1200 CE. Just about any object can serve as **money** if it is portable, divisible, durable, and stable. To understand why these qualities are important, imagine using as money something that lacks these features— a 35-kilogram salmon, for example.

money Any portable, divisible, durable, and stable object generally accepted by people as payment for goods and services.

- *Portability.* If you wanted to use the salmon to buy goods and services, you would have to lug a 35-kilogram fish from shop to shop. Modern currency, by contrast, is lightweight and easy to handle.

- *Divisibility.* Suppose you wanted to buy a hat, a book, and some milk from three different stores—all using the salmon as money. How would you divide the fish? First, out comes a cleaver at each store. Then, you would have to determine whether a kilogram of its head is worth as much as a kilogram from its middle. Modern currency is easily divisible into smaller parts with fixed values for each unit. In Canada, for example, a dollar can be exchanged for four quarters, 10 dimes, 20 nickels, 100 pennies, or any combination of these coins.

- *Durability.* Fish seriously fail the durability test. Each day, whether or not you "spend" it, the salmon will be losing value (and gaining scents). Modern currency, on the other hand, does not spoil, it does not die, and, if it wears out, it can be replaced with new coins or paper money. The Canadian government recently converted paper bills into polymer plastic bills to increase durability. However, just months after the release there were questions about the bills' ability to withstand heat after a family claimed that the bills shrivelled and melted after being placed close to a heater.[1]

- *Stability.* If salmon were in short supply, you might be able to make quite a deal for yourself. But in the middle of a salmon run, the market would be flooded with fish. Since sellers would have many opportunities to exchange their wares for salmon, they would soon have enough fish and refuse to trade for salmon. While the value of the paper money we use today has fluctuated over the years, it is considerably more stable than salmon.

The Functions of Money

Imagine a successful fisherman who needs a new sail for his boat. In a *barter economy*—one in which goods are exchanged directly for one another—he would have to find someone who not only needs fish but who is willing to exchange a sail for it. If no sail maker wants fish, the fisherman must find someone else—say, a shoemaker—who wants fish and will trade for it. Then the fisherman must hope that the sail maker will trade for his new shoes. In a *money economy*, the fisherman would simply sell his catch, receive money, and exchange the money for such goods as a new sail. Thus, the barter economy is relatively inefficient compared to the money economy. This example clearly demonstrates the three functions of money:

■ *Medium of exchange.* We use money as a way of buying and selling things. Without money, we would be bogged down in a barter system.

■ *Store of value.* Pity the fisherman who catches a fish on Monday and wants to buy a beer the following Saturday. By then, the fish would have spoiled and be of no value. By contrast, money can be used for future purchases and therefore "stores" value.

■ *Unit of account.* Money lets us measure the relative values of goods and services. It acts as a unit of account because all products can be valued and accounted for in terms of money. For example, the concepts of "$1000 worth of clothes" or "$500 in labour costs" have universal meaning because everyone deals with money every day.

The Spendable Money Supply: M-1

For money to serve as a medium of exchange, a store of value, or a unit of account, buyers and sellers must agree on its value. The value of money depends in part on its supply; how much money is in circulation. When the money supply is high, the value of money drops. When the money supply is low, the value of money increases.

It is not easy to measure the supply of money, nor is there complete agreement on exactly how it should be measured. The "narrow" definition of the money supply is called M-1. **M-1** counts only the most liquid forms of money—currency and demand deposits (chequing accounts) in banks.

M-1 Only the most liquid forms of money (currency and demand deposits).

Currency is paper money and coins issued by the government. It is widely used to pay small bills. The phrase "This note is legal tender," which appears on Canadian paper money, means that the law requires a creditor to accept it in payment of a debt. Illegal tender (counterfeiting) has been a problem for many years. It is now a worldwide problem, partly because new technologies allow counterfeiters to make real-looking bills rather easily. In 2011, there were over 1.5 billion Bank of Canada notes in circulation with over 52 000 counterfeit bills detected.[2] To reduce counterfeiting, the Bank of Canada has issued new high-tech polymer $20, $50, and $100 bills.[3]

currency Paper money and coins issued by the government.

A **cheque** is an order instructing the bank to pay a given sum to a specified person or firm. Cheques enable buyers to make large purchases without having to carry large amounts of cash. Sellers gain a measure of safety because the cheques they receive are valuable only to them and can later be exchanged for cash. Money in chequing accounts, known as **demand deposits**, is counted in M-1 because such funds may be withdrawn at any time without notice.

cheque An order instructing the bank to pay a given sum to a specified person or firm.

demand deposits Money in chequing accounts; counted as M-1 because such funds may be withdrawn at any time without notice.

M-1 Plus the Convertible Money Supply: M-2

M-2 Everything in the M-1 money supply plus savings deposits, time deposits, and money market mutual funds.

M-2 includes everything in M-1 plus items that cannot be spent directly but that are easily converted to spendable forms: *time deposits, money market mutual funds*, and *savings deposits*. M-2 accounts for nearly all of the nation's money supply. It thus measures the store of monetary value that is available for financial transactions. As this overall level of money increases, more is available for consumer purchases and business investment. When the supply is tightened, less money is available; financial transactions, spending, and business activity thus slow down. As of November 2011, M-2 totalled $1060.8 billion in Canada.[4] M2 was up about 10 percent in early 2012 from the previous year and, despite low inflation at the time, this statistic brought renewed fears of higher inflation ahead.[5]

time deposits A deposit that requires prior notice to make a withdrawal; cannot be transferred to others by cheque.

Unlike demand deposits, **time deposits** require prior notice of withdrawal and cannot be transferred by cheque. On the other hand, time deposits pay higher interest rates. The supply of money in time deposits—such as *certificates of deposit (CDs)* and *savings certificates*—grew rapidly in the 1970s and 1980s as interest rates rose to 15 percent. But when interest rates dropped in the late 1990s, consumers began putting more of their money into mutual funds.

money market mutual funds Funds operated by investment companies that bring together pools of assets from many investors.

Money market mutual funds are operated by investment companies that bring together pools of assets from many investors. The fund buys a collection of short-term, low-risk financial securities. Ownership of and profits (or losses) from the sale of these securities are shared among the fund's investors.

Credit Cards: Plastic Money?

Although not included in M-1 or M-2, credit—especially credit cards—has become a major factor in the purchase of consumer goods in Canada. The use of MasterCard, Visa, American Express, and credit cards issued by individual businesses has become so widespread that many people refer to credit cards as "plastic money." Credit cards are actually a *money substitute*; they serve as a temporary medium of exchange but are not a store of value. More detail about credit cards is provided in Appendix B.

In 2012, Canadians held 74.5 million MasterCard and Visa credit cards. The value of goods and services bought with credit cards in Canada was US$301 billion.[6] Worldwide, the total value of goods purchased with Visa cards is above over $3 trillion annually.[7]

Credit cards are big business for two reasons. First, they are quite convenient for consumers. Second, credit cards are extremely profitable for issuing companies because of the fees they collect. Some cards charge annual fees to holders, and all of them charge interest on unpaid balances. Depending on the issuer, cardholders pay interest rates ranging from 11 to 20 percent. Merchants who accept credit cards also pay fees to card issuers.

Banks like the Bank of Montreal, the Canadian Imperial Bank of Commerce, the Bank of Nova Scotia, and TD Canada Trust are the biggest issuers of Visa cards in Canada. Each time a card is used, the banks receive an "interchange" fee, which is a percentage of the purchase value of the transaction. The banks use these fees to offset costs they incur with loyalty and points programs. Despite rising fees, merchants understand the value of plastic to their businesses; there are over 1.25 million merchant outlets that accept Visa and MasterCard in Canada.[8]

Credit card fraud has been a major concern for both consumers and retailers. In 2011, criminals were responsible for over $366 million in fraudulent charges from nearly half a million Canadian customers. To deal with these problems, credit card companies have developed new chip encryption technology that requires an additional password. However, this does not mean that these new cards are totally safe, but simply safer. Just like with debit cards, there are ways for crooks to bypass the added layer of security, ranging from simple observation to hidden cameras. In addition, the

Chip encryption technology was introduced to reduce credit card fraud.

new chip cards, in Canada at least, are also equipped with the traditional magnetic stripes (which can have information skimmed from compromised terminals) because many merchants are still not equipped with the new chip terminals; merchants in the United States are also resisting this change. The credit card companies don't want to lose potential transactions so they are currently supplying cards with both features.[9] Industry sources still claim there has been a reduction of fraud with the new cards.

The Canadian Financial System

Many forms of money, especially demand deposits and time deposits, depend on the existence of financial institutions to provide a broad spectrum of services to both individuals and businesses. In the sections that follow, we describe the major types of financial institutions found in Canada, explain how they work, and describe the services they offer.

 Understand the *different kinds* of financial institutions in the Canadian financial system, including the *Bank of Canada*.

Financial Institutions

There are several different types of financial institutions in Canada, but their main function is to facilitate the flow of money from sectors with surpluses to those with deficits by attracting funds into chequing and savings accounts. Incoming funds will be loaned to individuals and businesses and perhaps invested in government securities.

For many years, the financial community in Canada was divided rather clearly into four distinct legal areas. Often called the "four financial pillars," they were (1) chartered banks; (2) alternate banks, such as trust companies and credit unions (or *caisses populaires*); (3) life insurance companies and other specialized lending and saving intermediaries, such as factors, finance companies, venture capital firms, mutual funds, and pension funds; and (4) investment dealers. We will discuss each of these financial institutions in detail a bit later in this chapter, but it is important to understand that since so many changes have taken place in the financial services industry in the past couple of decades, the differences across the four divisions have become very blurred.

Changes Affecting Financial Institutions

The crumbling of the four financial pillars began in 1980 when several changes were made to the Bank Act. Since then, additional changes have been made: (1) Banks are now permitted to own securities dealers, to establish subsidiaries to sell mutual funds, and to sell commercial paper (see Chapter 20); and (2) trust companies have declined in importance, and many trust companies have been bought by banks or insurance companies. The largest trust company—Canada Trust—merged with the Toronto-Dominion Bank and is now called TD Canada Trust. Additional changes are evident as a result of *deregulation, changing consumer demands,* and *changes in international banking.*

Deregulation

Deregulation has allowed banks to shift away from their historical role as intermediaries between depositors and borrowers. Canada's banks have been diversifying to provide a wider array of financial products to their clients. Training bankers to be effective in this environment is necessary, and over 100 executives at TD Canada Trust have attended a Harvard University course that taught them to think like investment bankers. They have learned the lessons well and have embraced their new role. In fact, the major Canadian banks recently petitioned U.S. regulators to exempt them from the Volker rule (part of the Dodd Frank Wall Street Reform Consumer Protection Act) that currently prevents them from investing in private equity funds and other speculative investments because they are deposit-taking banks.[10]

Deregulation has opened up new revenue streams for Canadian banks but, in an interesting twist, in early 2010, the "Big Six" banks actually asked the government to get tougher with mortgage rules to cool off the housing market. They called for the minimum down payment to be increased from 5 percent to 10 percent and a reduction of the maximum amortization period from 35 to 25 years.[11]

Changing Consumer Demands

Consumers are no longer content to simply keep money in a bank when they can get more for it elsewhere. They are increasingly turning to electronic banks like ING Direct and President's Choice Financial that pay higher interest on savings accounts. Such companies can pay higher interest rates because they don't incur the costs associated with having branches like traditional banks do.

Traditional banks are responding to this new competition by selling a growing array of services in their branches. For example, the Bank of Montreal recently started providing bereavement services. If a customer's mother dies, BMO offers a service that takes care of everything from the funeral planning to forwarding the deceased person's mail.[12] Banks are finding new ways to attract and serve their clientele in order to remain competitive and attract a new generation that does not have the same loyalties as previous generations. The boxed insert entitled "Online and Mobile Banking Solutions Straight to the Consumer" describes some new developments in banking.

Banks also want to get much more involved in selling insurance in their branches, but as of 2012, the Bank Act still prohibited banks from selling insurance *in their branch offices* (they are allowed to sell insurance at other locations). Canadian banks are being "creative" in keeping insurance and banking activities separate (but not too separate). In Oakville, Ontario, Royal Bank of Canada consumers who enter the branch will notice the RBC bank on the right and RBC Insurance on the left. The two operations are separated by only a glass wall. Dan Danyluk, the CEO of the Insurance Brokers Association of Canada, says that RBC's strategy is flouting the intent of the law. He argues that credit-granting institutions like banks should not be allowed to sell insurance in their branches because they may try to tie the buying of, say, car insurance to the approval of the loan to buy the car.[13] The government agrees and, in 2010, it sent a message by banning banks from selling unauthorized insurance on their websites.[14]

All of this activity is transforming the profit base of banks. In the past, they made most of their money from the spread between interest rates paid to depositors and the rates charged on loans. Investment banking, on the other hand, is fee based. Banks are making a larger proportion of their profits from fees, and this is blurring the traditional boundary between banks and securities firms.

Changes in International Banking

Because U.S. and other foreign banks are now allowed to do business in Canada, Canada's banks are going to experience increased competition. They are responding to this threat with a variety of tactics, including attempts to merge with one another so they can afford the millions of dollars in technology investment that will be needed to

E-BUSINESS + SOCIAL MEDIA SOLUTIONS

Online and Mobile Banking Solutions Straight to the Consumer

In the past decade, the banking industry has embraced technology. Why? Each time Apple launches a device, or a new generation of an old device (e.g., iPhone or iPad), people line up to buy it. Overnight campouts were once reserved for major music concerts, but today's consumers have a growing obsession with technology. Here are some key statistics to back this up. At the beginning of 2012:

- Approximately 80 percent of Canadians were using mobile devices and that number was expected to rise to 85 percent by 2014.

- About 40 percent of Canadians were already using smartphones and this figure was rising quickly.

- 65 percent of Canadians were using online banking services and about half of those customers used online banking as their main form of banking.

Only 5 percent of Canadian consumers were using mobile banking services at the beginning of 2012, but that number is expected to grow quickly. Many experts predict that mobile banking will eventually surpass online banking. So how can banks take advantage of such trends?

In the United States, some banks are enabling clients to email a photo of a cheque from their mobile devices, to be deposited without an actual visit. In Canada, CIBC was the first bank to launch a mobile banking application for the iPhone platform. And a few years back, RBC designed a peer-to-peer website for students, with a slogan to match: "Not your parents' banking site." RBC was also one of the first Canadian banks to create a Facebook group, called RBC Campus Connections. TD Canada Trust created an equivalent group called the Money Lounge, where students can win trips or discuss the merits of making their first RRSP investment. These relationships help students learn in a non-threatening manner. This sort of contact is important; according to an Ipsos-Reid poll, 44 percent of Canadians have an account at the bank where they opened their first account. For the banks themselves, opportunities to mine data are also a significant benefit of building such relationships.

The discount brokerage divisions are also trying to exploit opportunities. For example, BMO InvestorLine offers video demonstrations for clients. RBC Dominion Securities has created practice accounts where prospective investors can manage an imaginary $100 000 portfolio. Banks are also offering online seminars and webinars, as well as online tutorials. A simulation video game called Financial Football was released in New York to help students learn how to balance their chequebooks; the game uses the graphics and rules of professional football. It was sponsored by Visa but it is yet another possible tool for banks to engage consumers, drive traffic to their sites, and build brand loyalty. One thing is clear: Banks are now fighting a whole new battle for your financial loyalty.

Critical Thinking Question

1. Have you used a banking smartphone application or visited a bank-sponsored social media group? How effective do you think these tools are for the consumer? For the banks?

remain competitive. But bank mergers have been blocked by the federal government because it feared the mergers would reduce competition and harm consumers. As we saw earlier, however, the government did allow Canada Trust and Toronto-Dominion Bank to merge. Banks are also trying other things to be more competitive, like co-operating to spread their fixed costs. Syncor Services, for example, is a joint venture between three of the "Big Six" banks that provides cheque-clearing services across Canada.[15]

The Bank of Canada

Bank of Canada Canada's central bank; formed in 1935.

The **Bank of Canada**, formed in 1935, is Canada's central bank. It has a crucial role to play in managing the Canadian economy and in regulating certain aspects of chartered bank operations. The Bank of Canada is managed by a board of governors composed of a governor, a deputy governor, and 12 directors appointed from different regions of Canada. The directors, with cabinet approval, appoint the governor and deputy governor. The deputy minister of finance is also a non-voting member of the board. Between meetings of the board, normally held eight times per year, an executive committee acts for the board. This committee is composed of the governor, the deputy governor, two directors, and the deputy minister of finance. The executive committee meets at least once a week.

Operation of the Bank of Canada

The Bank of Canada plays an important role in managing the money supply in Canada (see Figure 18.1). If the Bank of Canada wants to *increase* the money supply, it can buy government securities. The people selling these bonds deposit the proceeds in their banks, and these deposits increase banks' reserves and their willingness to make loans. The Bank of Canada can also lower the bank rate; this action will cause increased demand for loans from businesses and households because these customers borrow more money when interest rates drop.

If the Bank of Canada wants to *decrease* the money supply, it can sell government securities. People spend money to buy bonds, and these withdrawals bring down banks' reserves and reduce their ability to make loans. The Bank of Canada can also raise the bank rate; this action will cause decreased demand for loans from businesses and households because these customers borrow less money when interest rates rise.

In 2012, the Canadian government and the Bank of Canada were given a strong endorsement of their management of the Canadian money supply when it was announced that Iceland was considering adopting the Canadian dollar as its official currency. It is still unclear whether Iceland will begin to take serious action in that direction, but the option is being discussed at high levels and the strong monetary and fiscal policy in recent years has made the Canadian currency an attractive stable alternative for Iceland.[16]

Will the Canadian loonie be seen swimming in Icelandic waters? As Iceland considers a move to the Canadian dollar, one thing is clear: The historically underrated currency has earned respect as a stable force backed by strong government policy.

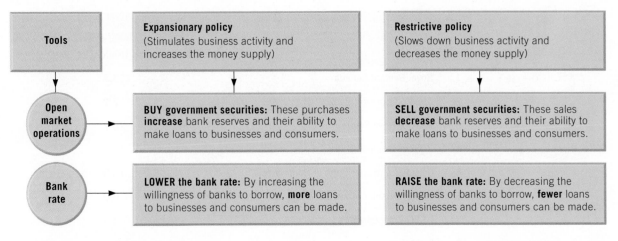

FIGURE 18.1

Bank of Canada monetary policy actions.

Member Bank Borrowing from the Bank of Canada

The Bank of Canada is the lender of last resort for chartered banks. The rate at which chartered banks can borrow from the Bank of Canada is called the **bank rate**, or **rediscount rate**. It serves as the basis for establishing the chartered banks' prime interest rates. By raising the bank rate, the Bank of Canada depresses the demand for money; by lowering it, the demand for money increases. In practice, chartered banks seldom have to borrow from the Bank of Canada. However, the bank rate is an important instrument of monetary policy as a determinant of interest rates.

bank rate (rediscount rate) The rate at which chartered banks can borrow from the Bank of Canada.

Financial Pillar #1—Chartered Banks

A **chartered bank** is a privately owned, profit-seeking firm that serves individuals, non-business organizations, and businesses as a financial intermediary. Chartered banks offer chequing and savings accounts, make loans, and provide many other services to their customers. They are the main source of short-term loans for business firms.

Explain the role of *chartered banks* in the Canadian financial system.

Chartered banks are the largest and most important financial institutions in Canada. In November 2011, Canadian chartered banks had assets totalling $2.2 trillion.[17] They offer a unique service. Their liability instruments (the claims against their assets) are generally accepted by the public and by business as money or as legal tender. As you will see in the Managing in Turbulent Times box entitled "Canadian Banks Are No. 1 Again," there is a lot of praise directed at the Canadian banking system. *The Guardian* referred to Canadian banks as the envy of the world and *The Economist* referred to them as the primary reason for Canada's economic resilience.[18]

chartered bank A privately owned, profit-seeking firm that serves individuals, non-business organizations, and businesses as a financial intermediary.

The 1980 Bank Act requires Schedule A banks to be Canadian owned and to have no more than 10 percent of their voting shares controlled by a single interest. The five largest Schedule A banks account for about 90 percent of total bank assets. There are thousands of bank branch offices in Canada, about one for every 3300 people. The Bank Act also permits Schedule B banks, which may be domestically owned banks that do not meet the 10 percent limit or may be foreign controlled. Schedule B banks are initially limited to one main office and one branch. Since the passing of the Act, several foreign banks have set up Schedule B subsidiaries. The act limits foreign-controlled banks to deposits that do not exceed 8 percent of the total domestic assets of all banks in Canada. The largest chartered banks in Canada are shown in Table 18.1.

TABLE 18.1 Top 10 Banks in Canada, 2011 (ranked by sales revenue)	
Company	**Sales Revenue (billions of dollars)**
1. Royal Bank of Canada	$35.7
2. Toronto-Dominion Bank	27.2
3. Bank of Nova Scotia	26.7
4. Bank of Montreal	17.5
5. Canadian Imperial Bank of Commerce	15.9
6. National Bank of Canada	6.0
7. HSBC Bank Canada	3.3
8. BOFA Canada Bank	1.4
9. Alberta Treasury Branches	1.3
10. ING Bank of Canada	1.2

Services Offered by Banks

The banking business today is a highly competitive industry. No longer is it enough for banks to accept deposits and make loans. Most, for example, now offer many other services, such as pension services, trust services, international services, financial advice, and electronic money transfer.

Pension Services

Most banks help customers establish savings plans for retirement. Banks serve as financial intermediaries by receiving funds and investing them as directed by customers. They also provide customers with information on investment possibilities.

Trust Services

trust services The management of funds left "in the bank's trust."

Many banks offer **trust services**—the management of funds left "in the bank's trust." In return for a fee, the trust department will perform such tasks as making your monthly bill payments and managing your investment portfolio. Trust departments also manage the estates of deceased persons.

"And, hey, don't kill yourself trying to pay it back.
You know our motto—'What the hell, it's only money.'"

International Services

The three main international services offered by banks are *currency exchange, letters of credit*, and *banker's acceptances*. Suppose, for example, that a Canadian company wants to buy a product from a French supplier. For a fee, it can use one or more of three services offered by its bank:

1. It can exchange Canadian dollars for euros at a Canadian bank and then pay the French supplier in euros.

2. It can pay its bank to issue a **letter of credit**—a promise by the bank to pay the French firm a certain amount if specified conditions are met.

3. It can pay its bank to draw up a **banker's acceptance**, which promises that the bank will pay some specified amount at a future date.

> **letter of credit** A promise by a bank to pay money to a business firm if certain conditions are met.
>
> **banker's acceptance** A promise that the bank will pay a specified amount of money at a future date.

Financial Advice

Many banks, both large and small, help their customers manage their money. Depending on the customer's situation, the bank may recommend different investment opportunities. The recommended mix might include guaranteed investment certificates, mutual funds, stocks, and bonds. Today, bank advertisements often stress the growing role of banks as financial advisers. CIBC's first-quarter profit for its wealth management division was $100 million in 2012, which was an increase of 50 percent.[19]

Electronic Funds Transfer

Electronic funds transfer (EFT) combines computer and communication technology to transfer funds or information into, from, within, and among financial institutions. Examples include the following:

> **electronic funds transfer (EFT)** Combines computer and communication technology to transfer funds or information into, from, within, and among financial institutions.

Automated Banking Machines (ABMs). **ABMs** (called automated teller machines—ATMs—in the United States), let you bank at almost any time of the day or night. There are over 17 000 ABM machines in Canada and many of them are located inside the more than 6000 Canadian bank branches. However, there are plenty of independent "white label" machines that usually charge higher fees. First Ontario Credit Union recently launched a new version it called the Personal Assistant Teller (PAT). This system provides a video link with a teller who can talk to the consumer about loans or listen to complaints in addition to offering the traditional ABM transactions.[20]

> **automated banking machines (ABMs)** Automated machines that allow bank customers to conduct account-related activities 24 hours a day, 7 days a week.

Online Payment and Pay-by-Phone. These systems let you communicate with your financial institution and pay bills or transfer funds between accounts.

Direct Deposits and Withdrawals. This system allows you to authorize in advance specific regular deposits and withdrawals. You can arrange to have paycheques and social assistance cheques automatically deposited and recurring expenses, such as insurance premiums and utility bills, automatically paid.

Point-of-Sale Transfers. These let you pay for retail purchases with your **debit card**, a type of plastic money that immediately reduces the balance in your bank account when it is used. Approximately 94 percent of Canadians have a debit card and they are accepted in over 450 000 retail establishments across the nation; over four billion transactions are completed annually using the Interac network.[21]

> **debit card** A type of plastic money that immediately on use reduces the balance in the user's bank account and transfers it to the store's account.

Smart Cards. **Smart cards**—also known as "electronic purses" or "stored-value cards"—can be programmed with "electronic money" at ABMs or, with special telephone hookups, even at home. After using your card to purchase an item, you can then check an electronic display to see how much money is left on your card. Phone callers and

> **smart card** A credit card-sized computer that can be programmed with "electronic money."

shoppers in Europe and Asia are the most avid users. In North America, smart cards are most popular in gas pump payments, followed by prepaid phone service, ABMs, self-operated checkouts, and automated banking services.[22] Analysts predict that, in the near future, smart cards will function as much more than electronic purses.

ecash Money that moves among consumers and businesses via digital electronic transmissions.

Ecash. Electronic money, known as **ecash**, is money that moves along multiple channels of consumers and businesses via digital electronic transmissions. Ecash moves outside the established network of banks, cheques, and paper currency. How does ecash work? Traditional currency is used to buy electronic funds, which are downloaded into an "electronic wallet" that can store and transmit ecash. Ecash is purchased from any company that sells it, including banks. When shopping online—say, to purchase jewellery—a shopper sends digital money to the merchant instead of using traditional cash, cheques, or credit cards. Businesses can purchase supplies and services electronically from any merchant that accepts ecash. The money flows from the buyer to the seller's ecash funds, which are instantaneously updated and stored on a microchip.

Although ecash transactions are cheaper than handling cheques and the paper records involved with conventional money, there are some potential problems. Hackers, for example, may break into ecash systems and drain them instantaneously. Moreover, if the issuer's computer system crashes, it is conceivable that money "banked" in memory may be lost forever. Finally, regulation and control of ecash systems remain largely non-existent; there is virtually none of the protection that covers government-controlled money systems.

Mobile (Digital) Wallet. Recently the country's largest banks agreed to standards, at a meeting of the Canadian Bankers Association, that will set the tone for the transition from plastic cards to mobile wallets. Financial institutions and telecommunications companies will embed credit and debit card information in smartphones, allowing you to pay for groceries and shop for clothes using your mobile device.[23] CIBC and Rogers Communications have already signed a deal; the service is launching on BlackBerry devices first and will quickly expand to include other platforms.[24]

Bank Deposits

Chartered banks provide a financial intermediary service by accepting deposits and making loans with this money. One type of deposit a customer can make in a bank is a chequable, or demand, deposit. A **chequable deposit** is a chequing account. Customers who deposit coins, paper currency, or cheques in their chequing accounts can write cheques against the balance in those accounts. Their banks must honour these cheques immediately; this is why chequing accounts are also called demand deposits.

chequable deposit A chequing account.

Technology is changing even the most basic banking functions. At the Chase Bank in New York, clients are now able to use a photo cheque cashing system. Customers can use their cellphone cameras to take a picture of a cheque and send the digital image to the bank. A few minutes later the money is in their account. No need for a visit to the bank or ATM. All of the Canadian banks are scrambling to introduce the system. Down south, over US$3 billion of the technology's existence transferred in this manner in the first two years.[25]

term deposit Money that remains with the bank for a period of time with interest paid to the depositor.

The other type of deposit a customer can make in a chartered bank is a **term deposit**, one that remains with the bank for a period of time. Interest is paid to depositors for the use of their funds. There are two types of term deposits—the regular passbook savings account (intended primarily for small individual savers and non-profit organizations) and guaranteed investment certificates (a deposit made for a specified period of time ranging from 28 days to several years that normally pays higher rates of interest than regular savings accounts).

Once your local bank adopts the photo chequing system that is already popular in the United States, there will be no need to go to the bank to cash a cheque. All you will need is your cellphone.

Bank Loans

Banks are the major source of short-term loans for business. Although banks make long-term loans to some firms, they prefer to specialize in providing short-term funds to finance inventories and accounts receivable. A *secured* loan is backed by collateral such as accounts receivable or a life insurance policy. If the borrower cannot repay the loan, the bank sells the collateral. An *unsecured* loan is backed only by the borrower's promise to repay it. Only the most creditworthy borrowers can get unsecured loans.

Borrowers pay interest on their loans. Large firms with excellent credit records pay the prime rate of interest. The **prime rate of interest** is the lowest rate charged to borrowers. This rate changes constantly owing to changes in the demand for and supply of loanable funds as well as to policies of the Bank of Canada. The so-called "Big Six" Canadian banks (Royal Bank, CIBC, Bank of Montreal, Bank of Nova Scotia, TD Canada Trust, and National Bank of Canada) typically act in concert with respect to the prime rate.

prime rate of interest The lowest rate charged to borrowers.

People who want to start their own small business but who have no real assets are typically turned away by banks. Muhammad Yunus thought that wasn't right, so he started the Grameen Bank in Bangladesh, which loans money to women who wouldn't otherwise qualify for a loan. Small loans—typically $100 to $500—have been made to thousands of women in the past few years, and they almost always pay them back. Yunus won the Nobel Peace Prize for his microfinance idea in 2006. The Grameen Bank has given women an opportunity for personal growth and business success that traditional banks will not give them. Now Yunus is making the same kinds of loans to low-income Latin American immigrants in New York.[26]

Banks as Creators of Money

In the course of their activities, banks provide a special service to the economy—they create money. This is not to say that they mint bills and coins. Rather, by taking in deposits and making loans, they expand the money supply. We will first look at how this expansion process used to work when banks had a **reserve requirement**—that is, that they had to keep a portion of their chequable deposits in vault cash or as deposits with the Bank of Canada (the reserve requirement was dropped in 1991).

reserve requirement The requirement (until 1991) that banks keep a portion of their chequable deposits in vault cash or as deposits with the Bank of Canada.

Suppose that you saved $100, took it to a bank, and opened a chequing account. Let's assume that there is a reserve requirement, and that it is 10 percent. Your bank must therefore keep $10 of your $100 deposit in reserve, so it has only $90 to lend. Now suppose that a person named Jennifer Leclerc borrows $90 from your bank. She now has $90 added to her chequing account. Assume that she writes a cheque for $90 payable to Canadian Tire. Canadian Tire's bank ends up with a $90 deposit, and that bank is also required to keep 10 percent in reserve. It therefore has $81 to lend out to someone else. This process of deposit expansion is shown in abbreviated form in Figure 18.2. As you can see, your original deposit of $100 increases the total supply of money.

What happens if there is no reserve requirement? At the extreme, it means that banks could (theoretically) create infinite amounts of money because they don't have to keep any in reserve. But banks will not do this because it is risky. So, in practice, the dropping of the reserve requirement simply means that banks will be able to create more money than they did when there was a reserve requirement.

The boxed insert entitled "Canadian Banks Are No. 1 Again" provides information on some key differences between banks in Canada and the United States.

MANAGING IN TURBULENT TIMES

Canadian Banks Are No. 1 Again

In 2012, the World Economic Forum ranked Canadian banks as the soundest in the world. It was the fourth year in a row that Canadian banks achieved the top ranking. This was particularly impressive given the uncertainty about the global economic situation, stock market volatility, and the sovereign debt crisis in Europe. Canada's strong banking system began to get a lot of publicity in 2009, when the worldwide recession occurred, and there was increasing concern that many U.S. banks were in financial trouble. The situation was much different in Canada, where the top five Canadian banks at that time earned $18.9 billion in profits, while the top five U.S. banks lost $37 billion.

Canadian banks are strictly regulated. For example, they must maintain a big cushion to absorb potential losses, and their shares must be widely held. The Office of the Superintendent of Financial Institutions (OSFI), Canada's banking regulator, is very conservative and keeps a close watch on the activities of Canadian banks. The OSFI's rules on Canadian banks are stricter than the rules that many foreign countries impose on their banks. For example, at Canada's six largest banks, levels of the most secure capital (known as Tier 1 capital) are almost double the OSFI standard (and more than three times the global standard). There is a bit of irony here, because the conservative nature of the Canadian banking system has been a source of complaints from Canadian consumers. But consumers appreciate the strength of the Canadian banking system now.

Mortgages loans are an important activity for banks, and here, too, Canadian banks have been very conservative relative to their U.S. counterparts. This conservatism can be seen in mortgage arrears statistics: Less than 1 percent of Canadian mortgage holders have gone more than three months without making a payment. By contrast, the U.S. financial system has received multibillion-dollar bailouts, and President Obama admitted that the Canadian banking system was managed much better than the U.S. system. Canadian banks in the United States—Royal Bank's RBC Bank, Bank of Montreal's Harris Bank, and Toronto Dominion's TD Bank—have all noted a surge in deposits as their U.S. rivals struggled with financial problems.

Canadian banks are also better off because they are shielded from a certain amount of foreign competition. Because of that, Canadian banks did not feel compelled to get involved in the kinds of risky mortgages that got U.S. banks into trouble. When Canadian banks did get involved (on a much smaller scale), they showed the risky mortgages on their balance sheets so the public knew exactly what their financial condition was.

Critical Thinking Questions

1. Is there a trade-off between bank responsiveness to customers and customer satisfaction with banks?

2. Consider the following statement: *Governments around the world should continuously apply very strict standards for banks, even in good economic times, so that the kinds of financial problems that developed in the United States will not happen again.* Do you agree with the statement? Explain your reasoning.

Deposit	Money Held in Reserve by Bank	Money to Lend	Total Supply
$100.00	$10.00	$90.00	**$190.00**
90.00	9.00	81.00	**271.00**
81.00	8.10	72.90	**343.90**
72.90	7.29	65.61	**409.51**
65.61	6.56	59.05	**468.56**

FIGURE 18.2

How the chartered banking system creates money.

Financial Pillar #2—Alternate Banks

Trust Companies

A **trust company** safeguards property—funds and estates—entrusted to it. For example, a corporation selling bonds to investors appoints a trustee, usually a trust company, to protect the bondholders' interests. A trust company can also serve as a transfer agent and registrar for corporations. A transfer agent records changes in ownership of a corporation's shares of stock. A registrar certifies to the investing public that stock issues are correctly stated and comply with the corporate charter. Other services include preparing and issuing dividend cheques to shareholders and serving as trustee for employee profit-sharing funds. Trust companies also accept deposits and pay interest on them. As noted previously, trust companies have declined in importance during the past couple of decades.

Credit Unions/Caisses Populaires

One in every three Canadians are members of **credit unions** (called *caisses populaires* in Quebec), with 5 million members in Quebec and 5.1 million members in the rest of Canada.[27] Credit unions and *caisses populaires* are co-operative savings and lending associations formed by a group with common interests. They are important to businesses because they lend money to consumers to buy durable goods such as cars and furniture. They lend money to businesses as well. Members (owners) can add to their savings accounts by authorizing deductions from their paycheques or by making direct deposits. They can borrow short-term, long-term, or mortgage funds from the credit union. Credit unions pay somewhat higher interest rates than chartered banks on money that is invested in financial instruments like GICs. Credit unions also invest substantial amounts of money in corporate and government securities. The largest credit unions in Canada are listed in Table 18.2.

Each year, the market research firm Synovate ranks Canadian financial institutions in 11 areas of service provided to customers. In a recent survey, credit unions ranked ahead of all banks and other financial institutions in overall customer service excellence, financial planning and advice, and branch service excellence.[28]

Explain the role of *alternate banks, specialized lending and savings intermediaries,* and *investment dealers* in the Canadian financial system. **L04**

trust company Safeguards funds and estates entrusted to it; may also serve as trustee, transfer agent, and registrar for corporations.

credit union Co-operative savings and lending association formed by a group with common interests.

TABLE 18.2 Top 10 Credit Unions in Canada, 2011 (ranked by sales revenue)	
Company	**Sales Revenue (millions of dollars)**
1. Mouvement des Caisses Desjardins	$13, 206
2. Vancouver City Savings Credit Union	718
3. Caisse Centrale Desjardins	624
4. Servus Credit Union Ltd.	527
5. Coast Capital Savings Credit Unioin	490
6. Central 1 Credit Union	438
7. First West Credit Union	323
8. Meridian Credit Union Ltd.	274
9. Concentra Financial Services Association	193
10. Conexus Credit Union	159

Financial Pillar #3—Specialized Lending and Savings Intermediaries

Life Insurance Companies

life insurance company A mutual or stock company that shares risk with its policyholders for payment of premiums.

An important source of funds for individuals, non-business organizations, and businesses alike is the life insurance company. A **life insurance company** shares risk with its policyholders in return for payment of a premium and lends some of the money it collects from premiums to borrowers. Life insurance companies are substantial investors in real estate mortgages and in corporate and government bonds. Next to chartered banks, they are the largest financial intermediaries in Canada. The industry as a whole has over $514 billion dollars invested in Canada (10 percent of all provincial and federal bonds, 15 percent of corporate bonds, and 20 percent of mutual fund assets) and employs over 135 000 people.[29] We discuss insurance companies in more detail in Chapter 20.

Factoring Companies

factoring company Buys accounts receivable from a firm for less than their face value, and then collects the face value of the receivables.

An important source of short-term funds for many firms is factoring companies. A **factoring company** (or factor) buys accounts receivable (amounts due from credit customers) from a firm. It pays less than the face value of the accounts but collects the face value of the accounts. The difference, minus the cost of doing business, is the factor's profit.

A firm that sells its accounts receivable to a factor without recourse shifts the risk of credit loss to the factor. If an account turns out to be uncollectible, the factor suffers the loss. However, a factor is a specialist in credit and collection activities. Using a factor may enable a business firm to expand sales beyond what would be practical without the factor. The firm trades accounts receivable for cash. The factor then notifies the firm's customers to make their overdue payments to the factor.

Financial Corporations

sales finance company Specializes in financing instalment purchases made by individuals or firms.

There are two types of financial corporations—sales finance companies and consumer finance companies. A **sales finance company** specializes in financing instalment purchases made by individuals and firms. When you buy durable goods from a retailer on an instalment plan with a sales finance company, the loan is made directly to you. The item you purchased serves as security for the loan. Sales finance companies enable many firms to sell on credit, even though the firms could not afford to finance credit sales on their own. General Motors Acceptance Corporation (GMAC) is a sales finance company. It is a captive company because it exists to finance instalment contracts resulting from sales made by General Motors. Industrial Acceptance Corporation is a large Canadian sales finance company.

A **consumer finance company** makes personal loans to consumers. Often the borrower pledges no security (collateral) for the loan. For larger loans, collateral may be required, such as a car or furniture.

consumer finance company Makes personal loans to consumers.

Venture Capital Firms

A **venture capital firm** provides funds for new or expanding firms that have significant potential. For example, Google started a venture capital fund to support "young companies with awesome potential."[30] Venture capital firms prefer a situation where the company they have invested in becomes very successful and experiences substantial increases in its stock price. Venture capital firms may provide either equity or debt funds to businesses, but they typically buy shares in companies they are interested in. They may demand an ownership stake of 50 percent or more before they will buy in to a company. Because financing new, untested businesses is so risky, venture capital firms want to earn a higher-than-normal return on their investment. They may insist that they be given at least one seat on the board of directors so they can observe first hand how their investment is faring.

venture capital firm Provides funds for new or expanding firms thought to have significant potential.

Venture capital firms obtain their funds from initial capital subscriptions, from loans from other financial intermediaries, and from retained earnings. The amount of venture capital that is raised varies according to economic conditions. In 2011, venture capital firms raised a total of $1.5 billion in Canada. This figure was up 34 percent from the previous year but was well shy of the $2.1 billion raised four years earlier.[31] Canada's venture capital industry has been experiencing serious problems and many Canadian entrepreneurs have turned to U.S.-based venture capital companies for funding.[32]

Pension Funds

A **pension fund** accumulates money that will be paid out to plan subscribers at some time in the future. The money collected is invested in corporate stocks and bonds, government bonds, or mortgages until it is to be paid out. Many private pension funds are being evaluated and there are great concerns about funding and management in this area. For example, the pension fund at Air Canada was estimated to have a funding deficit of $2.1 billion in 2011 (although this was an improvement of $600 million from the previous year).[33]

pension fund Accumulates money that will be paid out to plan subscribers in the future.

Financial Pillar #4—Investment Dealers

Investment dealers (called stockbrokers or underwriters) perform two important financial functions. First, they are the primary distributors of new stock and bond issues (underwriting). Second, investment dealers facilitate secondary trading of stocks and bonds, both on stock exchanges and on over-the-counter stock and bond markets (the brokerage function). These two functions are discussed in more detail in Chapter 19.

Other Sources of Funds

In Canada, a number of different government suppliers of funds are important to business. In general, they supply funds to new and/or growing companies. However, established firms can also use some of them.

The Business Development Bank of Canada (BDC) makes term loans, primarily to smaller firms judged to have growth potential but unable to secure funds with reasonable terms from traditional sources. It provides proportionally more equity financing and more management counselling services. A variety of provincial industrial development corporations also provide funds to developing business firms in the hope that they will provide jobs in the province. A number of federal and provincial programs are specifically designed to provide loans to agricultural operators. Most of these are long-term loans for land purchase.

The federal government's Export Development Corporation finances and insures export sales for Canadian companies. The Canada Mortgage and Housing Corporation (CMHC) is involved in providing and guaranteeing mortgages. The CMHC is particularly important to the construction industry.

International Banking and Finance

L05 Understand the key concepts and activities in *international banking and finance*.

International banking networks and electronic technologies now permit nearly instantaneous financial transactions around the globe. The economic importance of international finance is evident from both the presence of foreign banks in the Canadian market and the sizes of certain banks around the world. In addition, each nation tries to influence its currency exchange rates for economic advantage in international trade. The subsequent country-to-country transactions result in an *international payments process* that moves money between buyers and sellers on different continents.

Exchange Rates and International Trade

As we saw in Chapter 5, a country's currency exchange rate affects its ability to buy and sell on the global market. The value of a given currency, say, the Canadian dollar, reflects the overall supply and demand for Canadian dollars both at home and abroad. This value changes with economic conditions worldwide; therefore, firms watch for trends.

A good case in point is the fluctuation in the Canadian dollar relative to the American dollar. As we entered the new millennium, Canadians had grown accustomed to a weak dollar, in the 65- to 70-cent range against the U.S. dollar. A dollar at parity with the American dollar was almost unthinkable. Yet on November 9, 2007, the dollar reached US$1.09, a level that had not been seen for decades. That movement and strength encouraged Canadians to cross the U.S. border and purchase everything from clothing to cars. Over the next few years the dollar retreated at bit, but a new era was upon Canadians. At the end of 2012 the dollar was once again above parity and had consistently remained near the parity mark for a few years.[34]

These dollar fluctuations have also had a huge impact on businesses. Canadian companies are finding it more difficult to compete internationally since they can no longer rely on a cheap dollar to make their products more affordable across the border and abroad. But after the initial shock, companies are learning to cope. According to the chairman and CEO of Clearwater Seafoods Income Fund, "The way you deal with the stronger Canadian dollar is to increase the efficiency of your operations."[35] Other companies, like Nova Scotia-based High Liner Foods, which buys most of its raw fish on the world markets in U.S. dollars, has seen a net benefit. The rise in the Canadian dollar helped the company increase profits by 40 percent in one year.[36]

The Law of One Price

How do firms determine when exchange rates are favourable? When a country's currency becomes overvalued, its exchange rate is higher than warranted by its economic conditions. Its high costs make it less competitive. Because its products are too expensive to make and buy, fewer are purchased by other countries. The likely result is a trade deficit (see Chapter 5). In contrast, an undervalued currency means low costs and low prices. It attracts purchases by other countries, usually leading to a trade surplus.

How do we know whether a currency is overvalued or undervalued? One method involves a simple concept called the **law of one price**—the principle that identical products should sell for the same price in all countries. In other words, if the different prices of a Rolex watch in different countries were converted into a common currency, the price should be the same everywhere.

But what if prices are not equal? In theory, the pursuit of profits should equalize them. Sellers in high-priced countries will have to reduce prices if they are to compete successfully and make profits. As prices adjust, so should the exchange rates between different currencies until the Rolex can be purchased for the same price everywhere.

A simple example that illustrates over- and undervalued currencies is the Big Mac Index, published annually in *The Economist*. The index lists a variety of countries and their Big Mac prices in terms of U.S. dollars. In March 2012, a Big Mac cost $4.20 in the United States. If a Big Mac in another country costs more than $4.20, the currency is overvalued; if it costs less than $4.20, the currency is undervalued. In 2012, the most overvalued currencies were Switzerland ($6.81), Norway ($6.79), and Sweden ($5.91). Canada ranked eighth at ($4.63). The most undervalued currencies were India, Ukraine, and Hong Kong. These different values mean that, in theory, you could buy Big Macs in China and sell them in Norway at a profit. If you did that, the demand for burgers would increase in China, driving up the price to match the other countries. In other words, the law of one price would set it.[37]

law of one price The principle that identical products should sell for the same price in all countries.

Government Influence on Exchange Rates

What happens when a currency becomes overvalued or undervalued? A nation's economic authorities may take action to correct its balance-of-payments conditions. Typically, they will devalue or revalue the nation's currency. The purpose of *devaluing* is to cause a decrease in the home country's exchange value. It will then be less expensive for other countries to buy the home country's products. As more of its products are purchased, the home country's payment deficit goes down. The purpose of *revaluation* is the reverse—to increase the exchange value and reduce the home country's payment surplus.

The International Payments Process

Now we know why a nation tries to control its balance of payments and what, at least in part, it can do about an unfavourable balance. Exactly how are payments made? Transactions among buyers and sellers in different countries are simplified through the services provided by their banks. For example, payments from buyers flow through a local bank that converts them from the local currency into the foreign currency of the seller. Likewise, the local bank receives and converts incoming money from the banks of foreign buyers. The payments process (ignoring any fees charged for conversion) is shown in Figure 18.3.[38]

Step 1	A Canadian olive importer withdraws $1000 from its chequing account to buy olives from a Greek exporter. The local Canadian bank converts those dollars into euros at the current exchange rate (0.76704 euros per dollar).
Step 2	The Canadian bank sends the cheque for 767.04 euros (EUR 767.04 = 0.76704 multiplied by 1000) to the exporter in Greece.
Steps 3 and 4	The exporter sends olives to its Canadian customer and deposits the cheque in its local Greek bank. While the exporter now has euros that can be spent in Greece, the importer has olives to

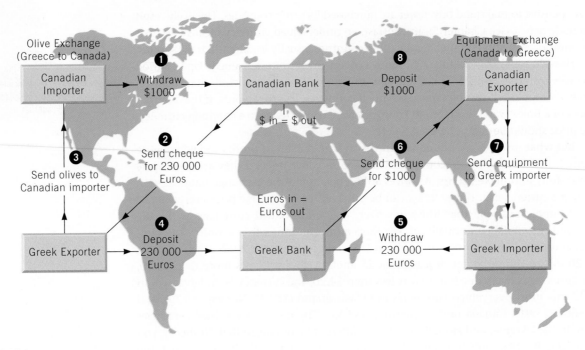

FIGURE 18.3

The international payments process.

sell in Canada. At the same time, a separate transaction is being made between a Canadian machine exporter and a Greek olive oil producer. This time, the importer/exporter roles are reversed between the two countries: The Greek firm needs to import a $1000 olive oil press from Canada.

Steps 5 and 6   EUR 767.04 withdrawn from a local Greek bank account is converted into $1000 Canadian and sent via cheque to the Canadian exporter.

Steps 7 and 8   The olive oil press is sent to the Greek importer, and the importer's cheque is deposited in the Canadian exporter's local bank account.

In this example, trade between the two countries is *in balance*: Money inflows and outflows are equal for both countries. When such a balance occurs, *money does not actually have to flow between the two countries*. Within each bank, the dollars spent by local importers offset the dollars received by local exporters. In effect, therefore, the dollars have simply flowed from Canadian importers to Canadian exporters. Likewise, the euros have moved from Greek exporters to Greek importers.

The International Bank Structure

There is no worldwide banking system that is comparable—in terms of policy-making and regulatory power—to the system of any single industrialized nation. Rather, worldwide banking stability relies on a loose structure of agreements among individual countries or groups of countries.

The World Bank and the IMF

World Bank A United Nations agency that provides a limited scope of financial services, such as funding national improvements in underdeveloped countries.

Two United Nations agencies, the World Bank and the International Monetary Fund (IMF), help to finance international trade. Unlike true banks, the **World Bank** (technically the International Bank for Reconstruction and Development) provides only a very limited scope of services. For instance, it funds national improvements by making loans to build roads, schools, power plants, and hospitals. The resulting improvements eventually enable borrowing countries to increase productive capacity and international trade.

The **International Monetary Fund** is a group of 188 nations that have combined their resources for the following purposes:

- to promote the stability of exchange rates

- to provide temporary, short-term loans to member countries

- to encourage members to co-operate on international monetary issues

- to encourage development of a system for international payments

The IMF collects money—called *quotas*—from member nations, with the amount being proportional to each country's size and strength (Canada's quota is about $10 billion).[39] The IMF then makes loans to nations suffering from temporary negative trade balances. By making it possible for these countries to continue buying products from other countries, the IMF facilitates international trade. In 2011, the IMF had about $396 billion available for loans.[40]

International Monetary Fund A United Nations agency consisting of about 188 nations that have combined resources to promote stable exchange rates and provide temporary short-term loans, among other purposes.

MyBizLab

Capture more moments of true understanding. MyBizLab provides you with interactive study and practice tools directly related to this chapter's content. The new MyBizLab Study Plan Learning Path is designed to measure a full range of skills and provide remediation to give you what you need to master key chapter concepts. MyBizLab flexes to your unique learning needs. The result? Inspired learning, more success.

SUMMARY OF LEARNING OBJECTIVES

1. **Define *money* and identify the different forms it takes in the nation's money supply.** Any item that is portable, divisible, durable, and stable satisfies the four basic characteristics of money. Money also serves three functions: As a medium of exchange, a store of value, and a unit of account. The nation's money supply is often determined by two measures. *M-1* includes liquid (or spendable) forms of money—currency (bills and coins), demand deposits, and other *"chequable" deposits* (such as chequing accounts and ABM withdrawals). *M-2* includes M-1 plus items that cannot be directly spent but that can be easily converted to spendable forms—*time deposits, money market funds,* and *savings deposits.* Credit must also be considered as a factor in the money supply.

2. **Describe the different kinds of *financial institutions* that make up the Canadian financial system, including the *Bank of Canada.*** The financial intermediaries in Canada are *chartered banks*, alternate banks, specialized lending and savings intermediaries, and investment dealers. The chartered banks are the most important source of short-term funds for business firms. The chartered banking system creates money in the form of expanding demand deposits. The four kinds of financial institutions offer services like financial advice and brokerage services,

electronic funds transfer, pension and trust services, and lending of money. They also expand the money supply by taking in deposits and making loans. The *Bank of Canada* manages the Canadian economy, controls the money supply, and regulates certain aspects of chartered banking operations. If the Bank of Canada wants to increase the money supply, it can buy government securities or lower the *bank rate*. If it wants to decrease the money supply, it can sell government securities or increase the bank rate.

3. **Explain the role of *chartered banks* in the Canadian financial system.** A chartered bank is a privately owned, profit-seeking firm that serves individuals, businesses, and non-business organizations as a financial intermediary. Chartered banks are the largest and most important financial institutions in Canada. Banks offer a wide variety of services, including chequing and savings accounts, pension services, trust services, international services, loans, financial advice, and various electronic funds transfer services. They are the main source of short-term loans for businesses.

4. **Explain the role of *alternate banks, specialized lending and savings intermediaries*, and *investment dealers* in the Canadian financial system.** *Alternate banks* include trust companies and credit unions. *Trust companies* safeguard

property that is entrusted to them. *Credit unions* are co-operative savings and lending associations formed by a group with common interests. They lend money to both businesses and consumers. *Specialized lending* and *savings intermediaries* include life insurance companies, (which share risks with their policyholders in return for payment of a premium), *factoring companies* (which buy accounts receivable from businesses at a discount and then collect the face value of the account receivable), financial corporations (which specialize in financing instalment purchases made by businesses and individuals), *venture capital* firms (which provide funds for new or expanding businesses), and *pension funds* (which accumulate and invest money that will be paid out to plan subscribers at some time in the future).

5. Understand the key concepts and activities in *international banking and finance.* Electronic technologies now permit speedy global financial transactions to support the growing importance of international finance. Country-to-country transactions are conducted according to an *international payment process* that moves money among buyers and sellers in different nations. Each nation tries to influence its currency exchange rates to gain advantage in international trade. For example, if a currency is over-valued, a higher exchange rate usually results in a trade deficit. Conversely, undervalued currencies can attract buyers and create trade surpluses. Governments may act to influence exchange rates by *devaluing* or *revaluing* their national currencies (that is, by decreasing or increasing them). Devalued currencies make it less expensive for other countries to buy the home country's products.

KEY TERMS

automated banking machines (ABMs) (p. 585)
Bank of Canada (p. 582)
bank rate (rediscount rate) (p. 583)
banker's acceptance (p. 585)
chartered bank (p. 583)
chequable deposit (p. 586)
cheque (p. 577)
consumer finance company (p. 591)
credit union (p. 589)
currency (p. 577)
debit card (p. 585)

demand deposits (p. 577)
ecash (p. 586)
electronic funds transfer (EFT) (p. 585)
factoring company (p. 590)
International Monetary Fund (p. 595)
law of one price (p. 593)
letter of credit (p. 585)
life insurance company (p. 590)
M-1 (p. 577)
M-2 (p. 578)
money (p. 576)
money market mutual funds (p. 578)

pension fund (p. 591)
prime rate of interest (p. 587)
reserve requirement (p. 587)
sales finance company (p. 590)
smart card (p. 585)
term deposit (p. 586)
time deposits (p. 578)
trust company (p. 589)
trust services (p. 584)
venture capital firm (p. 591)
World Bank (p. 594)

QUESTIONS FOR ANALYSIS

1. How are modern tools of banking revolutionizing the relationship between banks and their clientele?
2. What kinds of changes in banking are shifting banks away from their historical role?
3. Do we really need all the different types of financial institutions we have in Canada? Could we make do with just chartered banks? Why or why not?
4. Should credit cards be counted in the money supply? Why or why not? Support your view by using the definition of money.
5. If the Bank of Canada wants to increase the money supply, what options does it have? Explain how each of these options works to increase the money supply.
6. What is the logic behind the "law of one price" concept? Give an example using Switzerland and China.

APPLICATION EXERCISES

1. Start with a $1000 deposit and assume a reserve requirement of 15 percent. Now trace the amount of money created by the banking system after five lending cycles.

2. Interview several consumers to determine which banking services and products they use (debit cards, ABMs, smart cards, mobile banking, and so on). If interviewees are using these services, determine the reasons. If they are not, find out why not.

3. Interview the manager of a local chartered bank. Identify the ways in which the Bank of Canada helps the bank and the ways in which it limits the bank.

4. Interview five people and ask them how their banking habits have changed in the past few years. Ask the following questions: How many times a month do you set foot in your bank? How often do you withdraw funds from your account using an ABM? How often do you use a debit card? Are you excited about the possibility of using your smartphone as a digital wallet?

BUILDING YOUR BUSINESS SKILLS

The Risks and Rewards of Credit Cards

The Purpose of the Assignment

To help students evaluate the risks and rewards associated with excessive credit card use.

The Situation

Suppose that you've been out of school for a year and are now working in your first job. Your annual $30 000 salary is enough to support your apartment, car, and the basic necessities of life, but the luxuries are still out of reach. You pay cash for everything until one day you get a pre-approved credit card solicitation in the mail, which offers you a $1500 line of credit. You decide to take the offer and begin charging purchases. Within a year, five other credit card companies have contacted you, and you accumulate a total credit card debt of $12 000.

Assignment
Step 1

Working with three or four classmates, evaluate the advantages and dangers inherent in this situation, both to the consumer and to credit card issuers. To address this issue, research the current percentage of credit card delinquencies and rate of personal bankruptcies. Find out, for example, how these rates compare with those in previous years. In addition, research the profitability of the credit card business.

Step 2

Evaluate the different methods that credit card companies use to attract new customers. Specifically, look at the following practices:

- sending unsolicited, pre-approved credit card applications to consumers with questionable and even poor credit

- offering large credit lines to consumers who pay only monthly minimums
- lowering interest rates on accounts as a way of encouraging revolving payments
- charging penalties on accounts that are paid in full at the end of every billing cycle (research the GE Rewards MasterCard)
- sending cardholders catalogues of discounted gifts that can be purchased with their charge cards
- linking credit card use to a program of rewards—say, frequent flyer miles linked to amounts charged

Step 3

Compile your findings in the form of a set of guidelines designed for consumers receiving unsolicited credit card offers. Your guidelines should analyze the advantages and disadvantages of excessive credit card use.

Questions for Discussion

1. If you were the person in our hypothetical example, how would you handle your credit situation?
2. Why do you think credit card companies continue to offer cards to people who are financially overextended?
3. What criteria can you suggest to evaluate different credit card offers?
4. How do you know when you have enough credit?

EXERCISING YOUR ETHICS: TEAM EXERCISE

Telling the Ethical from the Strictly Legal

The Situation

When upgrading services for convenience to customers, chartered banks are concerned about setting prices that cover all costs so that, ultimately, they make a profit. This exercise challenges you to evaluate one banking service—ABM transactions—to determine if there are also ethical issues that should be considered in a bank's pricing decisions.

The Dilemma

Assume that a bank has more than 300 ABMs serving the nearly 400 000 chequing and savings accounts of its customers. Customers are not charged a fee for their 30 million ABM transactions each year, so long as they use their bank's ABMs. For issuing cash to non-customers, however, the bank charges a $2 ABM fee. The bank's officers are re-examining their policies on ABM surcharges because of public protests.

In considering its current policies, the bank's vice-president for community relations is concerned about more than mere legalities. She wants to ensure that her company is "being a good citizen and doing the right thing." Any decision on ABM fees will ultimately affect the bank's customers, its image in the community and industry, and its profitability for its owners.

Team Activity

Assemble a group of four students and assign each group member to one of the following roles:

- a bank customer
- the bank's vice-president for community relations
- a bank shareholder
- the bank's CEO

Questions for Discussion

1. Before discussing the situation with your group, and from the perspective of your assigned role, do you think there are any ethical issues in this situation? If so, write them down.
2. Before discussing the situation with your group, and from the perspective of your assigned role, decide how this dispute should be resolved.
3. For the various ethical issues that were identified, decide as a group which one is the most important for the bank to resolve. Which issue is second in importance?
4. From an ethical standpoint, what does your group recommend be done to resolve the most important ethical issue? To resolve the second most important ethical issue? What are the advantages and disadvantages of your recommendations?

Go to MyBizLab for additional cases and exercise material.

CONCLUDING CASE 18-1

Canadian Banks: On the Edge of a Mortgage Crisis?

In 2012, potential home buyers were facing a potentially worrisome question as they watched home prices continue to soar with the help of cheap mortgage rates: to buy or not to buy? For anyone considering this question in the previous decade, the correct answer was clearly to buy. But could the positive upward trend continue? We have seen a dramatic rise in home prices across the country: In early 2012 the value in Vancouver (average price $775 693), Toronto (average price $494 879), and Montreal (average price $402 455). Overall, the average price across Canada stood at $360 396; this figure had more than doubled in a decade. Some homeowners who had seen their equity rise sharply were asking the opposite question: to sell or not to sell? In the previous decade, most people sold and bought bigger homes with their newfound wealth. That strategy is beneficial if prices continue to rise and if you are not too overextended with debt.

If you examined these rising valuations and thought that this large increase could be sustained because the trend in salaries and inflation was not keeping pace with housing price increases, you had a very sound traditional argument. However, if you acted on this logic and took a conservative approach, you may have missed out on the wealth accumulation trend. The majority have bought into the following train of thought: "The prices will keep rising, and if I wait I will have to pay more. So I might as well buy as much house as I can and get the maximum loan the bank is offering." Investors who have been waiting on the sidelines for a market correction have been punished. Of course, the housing market, like other investment vehicles, goes in cycles. At times it can be flat and at others it booms. The long-term trend is up, but not at this pace. A correction will hit the housing market at some point and prices will stabilize for a period. The question really is, what should you do today? In order to answer this, you have to look at the fundamentals, despite their poor performance in predicting the market lately: the regulators, the role of the banks, the lessons from history and the U.S crisis, and, ultimately, your long-term ability to pay.

The Role of the Banks

When it comes to mortgages, banks are in the business of making money by lending to people who can pay back their loans and the interest. Canadian banks have traditionally been prudent in providing mortgage loans; however, in recent years this conservative approach has taken a dangerous turn. The big banks (with the full support of the Bank of Canada) have been severe enablers in the rise of housing prices. Low rates and great terms have made it possible for more people to buy homes and for all potential customers to buy bigger (and/or more expensive) homes than they could rationally afford. After years of low interest rates, it seemed like the housing market could not be given any additional stimulus. Or so it seemed. In 2012, the Bank of Montreal caused new waves with an unbelievably low five-year mortgage rate of 2.99 percent. The competitors quickly followed, although they offered the rate for four years rather than five. These are the types of deals that we expect from used car salespeople, not responsible banks. However, something interesting occurred: Within a few weeks, some of the other banks retreated from this overly aggressive stance; the Bank of Nova Scotia was the first to step back. There was also a bizarre plea for help as some bank executives began to ask for tighter regulations.

The Regulators

Part of Jim Flaherty's job as Finance Minister is to cool down the economy when it is too hot. However, his task is difficult because, on the one hand, we see a major bubble forming in the housing market. The appropriate response to this problem is to raise rates to dampen consumer appetite for debt. On the other hand, rates are so low worldwide that an increase in the Canadian rate would lead to a potentially damaging increase in the Canadian dollar. The U.S. Federal Reserve Chairman had already indicated that he would not increase rates until at least 2014 and that the U.S. rate would remain near zero until that time. So any increase in Canadian rates would mean that the Canadian dollar would likely soar even higher, which could further hurt exports. So what could the finance minister do?

Flaherty warned Canadians against taking on too much debt—good fatherly advice. In addition, other subtle steps were taken.

For example, Ottawa has made some adjustments through the Canadian Mortgage and Housing Corporation (CMHC), which provides mortgage insurance to financial institutions: It determines which mortgages are insurable and which are not. For years, mortgages in Canada had a maximum amortization period of 25 years, but in 2006 this policy changed; now mortgages could be granted for 40 years with very little or no down payment. This meant people's monthly payments were now much lower (pay over 40 vs. 25 years) and it also meant that people could take on much more debt. The end result: Soaring housing prices and massive accumulated debt for consumers. The average household-debt-to-disposable-income ratio reached 153 percent in Canada in 2012. The Americans and the British reached levels of 160 percent before it caught up to them in the form of a major housing market crisis. In response to this concern, Mr. Flaherty lowered the amortization maximum to 35 years and later to 30 years, and more recently back to 25 years. This move was fully supported by key industry players like Ed Clark, CEO of TD Bank.

Why Should You Care?

Many people think that the housing mortgage crisis in the United States only hurt individuals who could not pay their mortgages. Of course, many of these individuals lost their homes, but some who bought homes they could not afford actually made a lot of money by selling before the crisis hit. Probably the biggest victims of the crisis are the responsible home buyers who were forced to overpay for their homes because of a false market bubble. For example, Jane and Tom paid $550 000 for a house that was actually worth only $300 000. They saved their money, made a down payment of $150 000, and took out a mortgage for $400 000. They have very strong incomes and could afford this major mortgage even though they were very nervous about taking out such a big loan. They never missed their payments.

After the crisis, however, their property's market value dropped to $250 000 but they still owe $375 000 on their mortgage—and don't forget, they also made a down payment of $150 000. Jane and Tom are victims of a system that was out of control and now they are stuck with a mortgage that does not make sense. The consumers who put a zero down payment on a house they could not afford lived in that home for a few years and walked away from their mortgage. For Jane and Tom, however, the nightmare is just beginning.

Fundamental Math

The sustained low-interest-rate environment has encouraged people to purchase more house than they can probably afford. Some people believe that these low rates will last forever or do not understand what even a small increase can mean. Let's take a look at an example.

John and Mary buy a home for $500 000. They make a down payment of $150 000 and take out a mortgage for $350 000.

They lock in their mortgage of $350 000 for five years at a rate of 2.99 percent, with an amortization of 30 years.

Rate	**2.99**
Period	5 years
Amortization	**30 years**
Monthly Payment	$1470.25

What would that same house cost in monthly payments under traditional terms?

They lock in their mortgage rate for five years at an amortization of **25 years**.

Rate	**5.99 (historically a very good rate)**
Period	5 years
Amortization	**25 years (traditional approach)**
Monthly Payment	$2237.24

The same house costs $767 more per month and that is with a very conservative 5.99 percent figure. Nobody expects to see rates above double digits in the foreseeable future, but reasonable rates should be part of your long-term "what if" planning. If you can afford the home either way, then you are probably okay. If not, maybe you should take some time to think about it before you sign.

Conclusion

Time will tell if the market was indeed out of control in early 2012, but as investors and homeowners you should know the facts. There are great opportunities in real estate, but do your homework and understand the implications of interest rates and the functions of the banking system.

Questions for Discussion

1. How has the change in government policy with regard to amortization periods and down payments influenced the housing market?
2. Why are bank executives asking the government to increase regulations? Isn't it in the interest of all business executives to have less regulation to enable them to create profits for their shareholders?
3. Visit the TD Canada Trust website and access the Mortgage Calculator tool at www.tdcanadatrust.com. How much is the posted rate for a five-year mortgage? How much will it cost you (monthly payment) to get a mortgage of $250 000 with a 25-year amortization? What is the total cost of your interest payments over the lifetime of the loan?
4. Based on the scenario provided in the case, what should Jane and Tom do in the situation that they are facing? Should they wait for the market to improve and stay in their home? Should they walk away and buy another home? What other factors must they consider?

CONCLUDING CASE 18-2

The Logic Behind the Forms of Money

In 2012, the Canadian federal government announced that it would no longer issue pennies. The lowly penny was very durable but was seen as a nuisance by many consumers who simply stored them or outright refused to carry the coins in their wallets. The ultimate push to abolish the penny was economic; it cost the government 1.6 cents to produce each penny, and an estimated $130 million a year to keep the 30 billion estimated pennies in circulation. Ultimately, the decision to kill the penny saves the Canadian taxpayers money.

Money has been important in business (and family) transactions for thousands of years. Various objects have served as money, including pig tusks (New Guinea), whale teeth (Fiji Islands), large stones (Islands of Yap in the western Pacific Ocean), cows (Ireland), and cowrie shells (China). Objects that have been used as money typically have one (or more) of the following characteristics: They are rare (e.g., gold or silver), are hard to get (e.g., whale teeth), or have some intrinsic beauty that makes them desirable (e.g., feathers from a beautiful bird).

Some items that we would consider odd are still used for money. For example, the teeth of spinner dolphins are used as money in the Solomon Islands of the South Pacific. One dolphin tooth is equal to about two Solomon Islands dollars (a dollar was worth about US$0.137 in 2012). The governor of the Central Bank of the Solomon Islands says people keep dolphin teeth as a "store of wealth" in much the same way that people in most countries put money in the bank. A pig costs about 50 dolphin teeth, while just a handful of dolphin teeth are needed to buy some yams and cassava. Counterfeiting is an issue in the Solomon Islands just as it is in industrialized societies—for example, counterfeiters try to pass off the teeth of fruit bats as the real thing!

The demand for dolphin teeth as currency is driven by a couple of unique aspects of Solomon Island society. First, tribal disputes that result in the loss of property or human life are often settled by paying compensation in teeth rather than in dollars. Second, teeth are the currency of choice when young men choose a bride (a bride costs at least 1000 teeth). Each dolphin yields only about 20 teeth, so many dolphins are killed each year to balance supply and demand. Henry Sukufatu is a dolphin hunter who sells about 1000 teeth a month. He says he can't keep up with demand, which is why the exchange value of teeth is rising.

In most societies today, metal coins and paper money predominate. But have you ever wondered how a country decides what denominations of coins and paper money it should have? One model, called D-metric, uses the average day's net pay to make suggestions about the denomination structure of a country's currency. For example, if the average day's pay in a country is $100, the D-metric model recommends that the lowest denomination should be the nickel, and that a $500 bill should be introduced. The model also recommends introducing a $5 coin when the average day's net pay reaches $150. Another model looks at other factors, including cultural preferences, the impact of other methods of paying for things (credit and debit cards), and the average size of exchange transactions. It provides similar recommendations.

Canada's decision to eliminate the penny had been discussed for years. New Zealand stopped making the penny in 1987 and Australia in 1990. France, Norway, and Britain have also eliminated low-denomination coins. In 2008, a report from the Desjardins Group proposed eliminating the nickel, replacing the $5 bill with a coin, adding a 20-cent piece, making the 50-cent piece smaller, and introducing a $200 bill. The United States is also dealing with the question of denominations for its currency. Many people wonder why the United States is still using a $1 bill and note that it is out of step with many other industrialized countries. For example, the smallest bill used in the euro zone is the five-euro note (worth US$6.25 in 2012). In Britain, the smallest bill is the five-pound note (worth US$7.83 in 2012), and in Japan, it's the 1000-yen note (worth about US$12.55 in 2012). It is estimated that if the United States switched to a $1 coin like Canada has done, it would save taxpayers there about $522 million a year in production expenses. Each dollar bill costs about 4 cents to produce, and has a life span of only about 21 months. In contrast, a coin costs more to produce (about 20 cents), but lasts 30 years or more.

The use of coins and paper money dominates in modern society. But the barter system—exchanging goods and services instead of paying money for them—is still evident. For example, a painter might agree to paint a plumber's house if the plumber will fix the painter's leaky pipes.

Barter was common in ancient societies, and it is making something of a comeback. In the 1990s, when Russia was trying to move away from a command economy and toward a market-based economy, barter accounted for more than half of the business transactions. When the recession began in 2008, barter exchanges reported a big jump in the number of transactions that were taking place. Barter became more important even in North America because during an economic downturn participants want to conserve cash.

High-tech barter organizations like International Monetary Systems and U-Exchange.com make it possible for people from around the world to get involved in the barter economy. For example, Rich Rowley of Tacoma, Washington, offered to provide new home construction, remodelling, home repairs, home maintenance, and commercial improvements in return for things like tickets to sporting events, vacations, land, medical and dental care, a boat, and a motor home. Participants can build up credits that they can use for future transactions. The trade publication Barternew.com estimates that in the United States, bartering is worth more than $3 billion annually.

Questions for Discussion

1. Why do people in some countries keep using things other than coins or bills for money?
2. As noted in the case, a variety of items are used for money. To what extent does each item satisfy the four characteristics that money should possess?
3. Discuss the advantages and disadvantages of eliminating the penny in Canada. Why do you think the United States has resisted this move and the move to replace the U.S. $1 bill?
4. Why is the barter system generally considered to be inferior to the use of money? Are there some ways in which the barter system may be superior?

Understanding Securities and Investments

LEARNING OBJECTIVES

After reading this chapter, you should be able to:

1. Explain the difference between *primary* and *secondary securities markets*.

2. Discuss the value of *common stock* and *preferred stock* to shareholders and describe the secondary market for each type of security.

3. Distinguish among various types of *bonds* in terms of their issuers, safety, and retirement.

4. Describe the investment opportunities offered by *mutual funds* and *commodities*.

5. Explain the process by which securities are bought and sold.

6. Explain how securities markets are regulated.

Growing Up Social: Graduating to an IPO

WHAT do you get when you mix the investment banking establishment with new-age internet companies? It is not quite a marriage made in heaven, is it? For example, some traditionalists were upset at the sight of young Marc Zuckerberg showing up to important meetings sporting a "hoodie" sweatshirt despite being a wealthy businessman. (They felt it was disrespectful.) There can be some awkward moments, but the stock market is designed to raise money and support companies that have the potential to earn more of it, regardless of how their CEOs dress. In the past few years, a string of social media companies have taken the leap and matured from radical idea-seekers to publicly traded companies. The initial public offering (IPO) is a key moment in that growing process when companies launch into the public domain. Let's take a look at some notable examples.

Facebook

In May 2012, Facebook was making all the headlines with a highly anticipated IPO. Based on the initial price, the company was valued at US$104 billion, a figure 104 times higher than its profit levels from the previous year. While the market believed in Facebook's growth potential, certain fundamental rules of the IPO game had experts openly saying that its stock was overpriced. Within two weeks, Facebook shares had lost 25 percent of their value. Facebook earned $205 million in the first quarter of 2012 (a decrease of 12 percent from the previous year) despite increased revenues. The costs of running this business were a major concern for investors. In addition, with relatively low barriers to entry, new threats were emerging to current and future revenue streams.

For example, its $1-billion acquisition of Instagram was a bit of an eye-opener if you consider that Facebook has developed its own version of this app. Officially, the company was purchasing a stronger presence on the smartphone platform; however, Facebook paid a big price considering it was not acquiring the technology—it was essentially buying a threat. Instagram had 12 employees at the time, but over 50 million users: In this business, "users are king." A company's potential advertising revenues are correlated to the number of eyeballs. But if Instagram could transform into a threat after just two years in operation, what did this mean for the future of Facebook? It will be interesting to see how Facebook's stock performs in the long term, given that the initial "marriage" did not include the traditional honeymoon period.

Groupon

Groupon's IPO, six months earlier, was not exactly a mirror image of Facebook's, but there were distinct highs and lows as well. The IPO price valuation was set at about $12 billion. The online daily discount site launched its stock at a price of $20 per share and saw the market react favourably. In fact, in the first two weeks alone (the "honeymoon period"), the stock rose over 30 percent. However, problems for Groupon surfaced before the IPO ceremony; there were many legitimate questions that caused the company to restate its previous financial statements. At time of the IPO, the company had posted net operating losses of $218 million on revenue of $1.1 billion and was trying to manage growth with a salesforce of over 10 000 people. It was proving difficult. Six months after the launch of the IPO, amid a new round of financial irregularities, Groupon was trading at about half its original price (in the $10 range). The growing pains were clearly surfacing.

LinkedIn

LinkedIn can be considered the more mature version of Facebook. After all, it was designed with a business slant from day one. So you might expect this IPO to run a bit more smoothly. At the time, LinkedIn had an impressive 160 million users. Although this number paled in comparison to the 900 million users on Facebook, it was the revenue potential that the investment community was primarily concerned with. LinkedIn had a growing number of "paid subscribers" and the company was increasing revenues in the area of "hiring solutions," which enable employers to post job openings and search for candidates. The lower membership numbers also meant that there was more room for growth ahead. LinkedIn went public in 2011 and within a day the stock price had doubled from the original $45 to over $90. A year later, the stock showed strength as it stood over $100 with an average 12-month analyst projection set at $130. So the early returns from the market seemed to be a clear signal that LinkedIn was indeed more mature.

Planning IPO's

The success or failure of an IPO is based on a lot of factors, including timing. But the long-term fate of any stock is based on fundamental stock market factors such as revenue, growth, and profitability. So although some of the social media players have graduated, they must now compete in the "real world" of stock evaluations, which can be brutal. Other social media firms, such as Twitter, are still building their models before taking the IPO leap. In order to earn the respect of the market, they must show maturity and the ability to generate long-term growth and earnings. ◆

By understanding the material in this chapter, you will benefit in two ways: (1) As an *investor*, you'll be better prepared to evaluate investment opportunities that will improve your personal financial situation in both the short and long term; and (2) as a *manager*, you'll be able to more clearly understand how securities markets affect the firm you work for and the various alternative sources of funds that are available to your company.

Securities Markets

LO1 Explain the difference between *primary* and *secondary securities markets.*

securities Stocks and bonds (which represent a secured or asset-based claim on the part of investors) that can be bought and sold.

Stocks and bonds are known as **securities** because they represent *secured*, or *asset-based*, claims on the part of investors. In other words, holders of stocks and bonds have a stake in the business that issued them. As we saw in Chapter 4, shareholders have claims on some of a corporation's assets (and a say in how the company is run) because each share of stock represents part-ownership. In contrast, *bonds* represent strictly financial claims for money owed to bondholders by a company. Companies sell bonds to raise long-term funds. The markets in which stocks and bonds are sold are called *securities markets*.

Primary and Secondary Markets for Securities

primary securities market The market for the sale and purchase of newly issued stocks and bonds by firms or governments.

Primary securities markets handle the buying and selling of new stocks and bonds by firms or governments. New securities are sometimes sold to one buyer or a small group of buyers. These so-called *private placements* allow the businesses that use them to keep their plans confidential.

Investment Banking

investment banker Any financial institution engaged in purchasing and reselling new stocks and bonds.

Most new stocks and some bonds are sold to the wider public market. To bring a new security to market, the issuing corporation must obtain approval from a provincial securities commission. It also needs the services of an **investment banker**, who serves as a financial specialist in issuing new securities. Such well-known firms as RBC Dominion Securities and TD Securities provide three types of investment banking services:

1. They advise the company on the timing and financial terms for the new issue.

2. By *underwriting* (buying) the new securities, investment bankers bear some of the risk of issuing the new security.

3. They create the distribution network that moves the new securities through groups of other banks and brokers into the hands of individual investors.

secondary securities market The market for the sale and purchase of previously issued stocks and bonds.

New securities represent only a small portion of securities traded, however. The market for existing stocks and bonds, the **secondary securities market**, is handled by organizations such as the Toronto Stock Exchange. We will consider the activities of these markets in a moment.

Stocks

LO2 Discuss the value of *common stock* and *preferred stock* to shareholders and describe the secondary market for each type of security.

Each year, financial managers, along with millions of individual investors, buy and sell the stocks of thousands of companies. This widespread ownership has become possible because of the availability of different types of stocks and because markets have been established for conveniently buying and selling them. In this section, we will focus on the value of *common* and *preferred stock* as securities. We will also describe the *stock exchanges* where they are bought and sold.

Common Stock

Individuals and other companies buy a firm's common stock in the hope that the stock will increase in value, affording them a capital gain, and/or will provide dividend income. But what is the value of a common stock? Stock values are expressed in three different ways—as *par value*, as *market value*, and as *book value*.

Par Value

The face value of a share of stock—its **par value**—is set by the issuing company's board of directors. Each company must preserve the par value money in its retained earnings, and it cannot be distributed as dividends.

> **par value** The arbitrary value of a stock set by the issuing company's board of directors and stated on stock certificates; used by accountants but of little significance to investors.

Market Value

A stock's real value is its **market value**—the current price of a share on the stock market. Market value reflects buyers' willingness to invest in a company. The market price of a stock can be influenced by both objective factors (e.g., a company's profits) and subjective factors, like *rumours* (unverified information such as a claim that a company has made a big gold strike), *investor relations* (playing up the positive aspects of a company's financial condition to financial analysts and financial institutions), and *stockbroker recommendations* (a recommendation to buy a stock may increase demand for the stock and cause its price to increase, while a recommendation to sell can decrease demand and cause the price to fall).

> **market value** The current price of one share of a stock in the secondary securities market; the real value of a stock.

Book Value

Recall from Chapter 14 our definition of *owners' equity*—the sum of a company's common stock par value, retained earnings, and additional paid-in capital. The **book value** of common stock represents owners' equity divided by the number of shares. Book value is used as a comparison indicator because, for successful companies, the market value is usually greater than the book value. Thus, when market price falls to near book value, some investors buy the stock on the principle that it is underpriced and will increase in value in the future.

> **book value** Value of a common stock expressed as total shareholders' equity divided by the number of shares of stock.

Investment Traits of Common Stock

Common stocks are among the riskiest of all securities. Uncertainties about the stock market can quickly change a given stock's value. Furthermore, when companies have unprofitable years, they often cannot pay dividends. Shareholder income—and perhaps share price—may both drop as a result. At the same time, however, common stocks offer high growth potential. The prospects for growth in various industries change from time to time, but blue-chip stocks such as IBM and Imperial Oil have historically provided investors with steady income through consistent dividend payouts. A **blue-chip stock** is one that has been issued by a well-established, financially sound firm. For example, Rogers Communications is a strong stock, and it increased its dividend payout in 2012 (it had a yield of about 4.3 percent at the time).[1]

> **blue-chip stocks** Stocks from well-established, financially sound firms.

Market Capitalization. The market value of a company's stock is known as its **market capitalization**. It is computed by multiplying the number of a company's outstanding shares times the value of each share. The top 10 Canadian companies in terms of market capitalization are shown in Table 19.1. As you can see below, the Royal Bank of Canada topped the list with a market capitalization of approximately $82 billion.

> **market capitalization** The dollar value (market value) of stocks listed on a stock exchange.

TABLE 19.1 Top 10 Canadian Companies, 2011 (ranked by market capitalization)	
Company	**Market Capitalization (in billions of dollars)**
1. Royal Bank of Canada	$82.3
2. Toronto-Dominion Bank	75.6
3. Bank of Nova Scotia	62.3
4. Suncor Energy Inc.	50.8
5. Barrick Gold Corp.	39.8
6. Imperial Oil Ltd.	38.9
7. Canadian Natural Resources Ltd.	37.7
8. Bank of Montreal	37.7
9. Canadian National Railway	36.9
10. Potash Corp. of Saskatchewan Inc.	36.0

Preferred Stock

preferred stock Stock that pays dividends that are expressed as a percentage of par value.

Preferred stock is usually issued with a stated par value, such as $100. Dividends paid on preferred stock are usually expressed as a percentage of the par value. For example, if a preferred stock with a $100 par value pays a 6 percent dividend, shareholders would receive an annual dividend of $6 on each share. Some preferred stock is *callable*. The issuing firm can require the preferred shareholders to surrender their shares in exchange for a cash payment. The amount of this cash payment, known as the *call price*, is specified in the agreement between the preferred shareholders and the firm.

Investment Traits of Preferred Stock

cumulative preferred stock Preferred stock on which dividends not paid in the past must first be paid up before the firm may pay dividends to common shareholders.

Because of its preference on dividends, preferred stock is less risky than the common stock of the same company. Moreover, most preferred stock is cumulative. With **cumulative preferred stock**, any dividend payments the firm misses must be paid later, as soon as the firm is able. Typically, the firm cannot pay any dividends to its common shareholders until it has made up all late payments to preferred shareholders.

The income from cumulative preferred stock is not as certain as the corporate bonds of the same company. The company cannot pay dividends if it does not make a profit. The purchase price of the preferred stock can also fluctuate, leading to a capital gain or loss for the shareholder. And the growth potential of preferred stock is limited due to its fixed dividend.

Stock Exchanges

stock exchange An organization of individuals formed to provide an institutional setting in which shares of stock can be bought and sold.

Most of the secondary market for stocks is handled by organized stock exchanges. In addition to stock markets, a so-called "dealer," or the over-the-counter market, handles the exchange of some stocks. A **stock exchange** is an organization of individuals formed to provide an institutional setting in which shares of stock can be bought and sold. The exchange enforces certain rules to govern its members' trading activities. Most exchanges are non-profit corporations established to serve their members.

To become a member, an individual must purchase one of a limited number of memberships—called "seats"—on the exchange. Only members (or their representatives) are allowed to trade on the exchange. In this sense, because all orders to buy or sell must flow through members, they have a legal monopoly. Memberships can be bought and sold like other assets.

The Trading Floor

Each exchange regulates the places and times at which trading may occur. Trading used to take place only at an actual physical location called the *trading floor*, where specialists matched buy and sell orders they received from brokers. Over 400 traders worked on the trading floor of the Toronto Stock Exchange in the 1980s, but the floor was closed in 1997. Now, alternative trading systems (ATSs) like Pure Trading, Alpha, and Chi-X Canada use computers to match buy and sell orders. These ATSs have lowered the cost and increased the speed of stock trading.[2]

Brokers

A **broker** receives buy and sell orders from those who are not members of the exchange and executes the orders. In return, the broker earns a commission from the order placer. Brokerage assistance can be purchased at either discount or full-service prices.

broker An individual licensed to buy and sell securities for customers in the secondary market; may also provide other financial services.

Discount Brokers. Discount brokers offer well-informed individual investors a fast, low-cost way to participate in the market. For example, you can buy shares and pay brokers' fees of less than $10, depending on how often you trade, how large your account is, and which firm you use. For example, you could buy 100 shares of a $50 stock and pay just $1.00 in brokers' commissions if you use Virtual Brokers because they charge only 1 cent per share with a minimum charge of $0.99.[3] The same purchase might cost you $50 or more at a full-service brokerage firm.[4] Discount brokerage services cost less because sales personnel receive fees or salaries, not commissions. Discount brokers generally do not offer investment advice or person-to-person sales consultations. They do, however, offer automated online services, such as stock research, industry analysis, and screening for specific types of stocks.

Online trading is popular among investors because it enables fast, no-nonsense transactions and the opportunity for investors to manage their own portfolios while paying low fees for trading. But online traders must still use a broker. Using costs and fees as key criteria, a 2011 survey of online brokers rated Qtrade Investor, Virtual Brokers, and BMO Investorline as the top three online brokers.[5] The process is continuously being simplified and today the options include mobile investing, as you will see in the E-Business and Social Media Box entitled, "The Next Frontier, Mobile Investing."

Full-Service Brokers. Despite the emergence of discount brokers and online investing, there is still demand for full-service brokerages, which help both new, uninformed investors and experienced investors who don't have time to keep up with all the latest developments. Full-service brokers offer clients suggestions on investments that clients might overlook when trying to sift through an avalanche of online financial data. They also provide estate planning, tax strategies, and a wider range of investment products. Initial public offerings (IPOs) of stock, for example, are generally not available to the public through online retail brokers. But a full-service broker, who is also the investment banker who sells the IPO shares, can sell IPO shares to his or her clients.

Canadian Stock Exchanges

The *Toronto Stock Exchange (TSX)* is the largest stock exchange in Canada and consists of about 110 individual members who hold seats. The securities of most major corporations are listed here. A company must pay a fee before it can list its security on the exchange. The TSX has recently gained strength from an unexpected source: During the last economic recession, many U.S. companies looked north and listed on the TSX to take advantage of Canada's relatively strong economic climate.[6]

The stock market procedures and tools have changed in recent years but the fundamentals remain the same. The markets can be volatile and homework is required to assess the long-term trends.

E-BUSINESS + SOCIAL MEDIA SOLUTIONS

The Next Frontier, Mobile Investing

Quick—what are all the different ways you access money, make payments, or invest using electronic means? Online banking, mobile banking, ABMs, credit cards, debit cards, email money transfers, quick swipe passes, QR codes—the list goes on and the methods are quickly multiplying. Now mobile investing is emerging as an important investment tool in Canada.

Basic mobile banking has been around for a while but most Canadian institutions have been much slower to build mobile investing apps (trading platforms designed for your iPhone fingertips). TD Waterhouse experimented with the possibility a decade ago but found that the infrastructure and conditions in Canada (number of clients, high cost of data plans, and customer readiness) were not right at the time. Instead, American institutions led the way in this area. For example, mobile trades accounted for 5 percent of all transactions at TD Ameritrade Holding Corp in 2011. This figure doubled in 2012 and with the accelerated market penetration of smartphones in the consumer market, it became clear that similar services were now more necessary north of the border. In 2012, most of the major Canadian banks and discount brokerages were quickly pushing forward to build effective mobile investing apps. According to an Ipsos-Reid poll, about one in five discount brokerage customers is interested in mobile investing and, not surprisingly, the positive results are directly correlated with the age of the investor: Younger consumers are much more likely to use this approach. Another informal *Globe and Mail* poll showed similar results, with 22 percent of individuals claiming that they were either currently conducting mobile trading or were open to it.

The convenience of taking care of your investing needs from anywhere at any time on a smartphone is clear; however, there is always that lingering security issue that makes a large portion of the population hesitate when it comes to newer financial transaction tools. According to the president of TD Waterhouse, John See, its mobile investing protection is already just as secure as it is for basic online transactions.

However, there is still one very fundamental issue that exists no matter what tools you use: You still need to pick the right stocks to invest in. Before making your first mobile investing trade, make sure to do your homework. In the spirit of the times, you might want to look at some popular investment blogs, found on sites such as Canadian Capitalist (canadiancapitalist.com), Money Index (moneyindex.org/Canada), The *Wall Street Journal*'s Deal Journal (wsj.com/deals), or Tech Finance (techfinance.ca). Good luck.

Critical Thinking Questions

1. Have you ever bought or sold securities using the mobile investing platform? Are you open to this approach? Explain your response.

2. Consider the following statement: *Mobile investing is dangerous. People need to carefully analyze investment data and not make quick on-the-go decisions. This approach may cause inexperienced investors to feel a false sense of security and will lead to more foolish impulse investments.* Do you agree with the statement? Defend your answer.

Foreign Stock Exchanges

Several foreign stock exchanges—most notably those in the United States and the United Kingdom—trade far more shares each day than the TSX does.

The New York Stock Exchange. For many people, "the stock market" means the New York Stock Exchange (NYSE), which was founded in 1792 and is the largest of all U.S. exchanges. Only firms meeting certain minimum requirements—earning power, total value of outstanding stock, and number of shareholders—are eligible for listing on the NYSE.[7]

NYSE Amex Equities. The second largest U.S. exchange, **NYSE Amex Equities**— formerly known as the American Stock Exchange (AMEX)—is also located in New York City. It accounts for about 10 percent of all shares traded on U.S. exchanges. The minimum requirements for listings are less stringent.

Other Foreign Stock Exchanges. Thirty years ago, the U.S. market accounted for more than half the value of the world market in traded stocks. Market activities, however, have shifted as the value of shares listed on foreign exchanges continues to grow. The annual dollar value of trades on exchanges in London, Tokyo, and other cities is in the trillions, and there are actually more stocks listed on the London exchange than there are on the NYSE. Exchanges are also flourishing in cities from Shanghai to Warsaw, but risk levels in some markets are very high. The Chinese stock market has been compared to a casino, and it is plagued with corruption, lax government regulation, and financially troubled companies. For example, the Chinese stock market lost 19 percent of its value in just one month.[8]

The Over-the-Counter Market. The **over-the-counter (OTC) market** is so called because its original traders were somewhat like retailers. They kept supplies of shares on hand and, as opportunities arose, sold them over the office counter to interested buyers. Even today, the OTC market has no trading floor. Rather, it consists of many people in different locations who hold an inventory of securities that are not listed on any of the major exchanges. The over-the-counter market consists of independent dealers who own the securities that they buy and sell at their own risk.

over-the-counter (OTC) market Organization of securities dealers formed to trade stock outside the formal institutional setting of the organized stock exchanges.

NASDAQ. The **National Association of Securities Dealers Automated Quotation (NASDAQ)** is the world's first electronic stock market.[9] The NASDAQ telecommunications system operates the NASDAQ Stock Market by broadcasting trading information

National Association of Securities Dealers Automated Quotation (NASDAQ) A stock market implemented by NASD that operates by broadcasting trading information on an intranet to more than 350 000 terminals worldwide.

Founded in 1792 and located on the corner of Wall and Broad Streets in New York City, the NYSE sees billions of shares change hands each day.

on an intranet to over 350 000 terminals worldwide. NASDAQ orders are paired and executed on a computer network. Many newer firms are listed here when their stocks first become available in the secondary market. Highly traded listings include Apple, Microsoft, Groupon, RIM, Facebook, and Netflix.[10] The stocks of nearly 3700 companies are traded by NASDAQ; however, Apple disproportionately affects the overall index because it represents about 11 percent of the overall value. In one eight-week span in 2012, Apple's stock market value increased by more than $100 billion.[11]

Bonds

L03 Distinguish among various types of *bonds* in terms of their issuers, safety, and retirement.

bond A written promise that the borrower will pay the lender, at a stated future date, the principal plus a stated rate of interest.

A **bond** is an IOU—a written promise that the borrower will pay the lender, at some stated future date, a sum of money (the principal) plus an additional amount (the interest). Bondholders have a claim on a corporation's assets and earnings that comes before the claims of common and preferred shareholders. Bonds differ from one another in terms of maturity, tax status, and level of risk vs. potential yield. Investors must take these factors into consideration when deciding which particular bond to buy.

To help bond investors make assessments, several services rate the quality of bonds from different issuers. Table 19.2 shows ratings by two principal rating services, Moody's and Standard & Poor's. The rating measures the bond's default risk—the chance that one or more promised payments will be deferred or missed altogether. The recent financial crisis revealed some significant problems with bond rating agencies. The credibility of companies like Moody's and Standard & Poor's has declined because they gave overly favourable ratings to mortgage-backed securities that were actually very risky investments. People who made investments based on the ratings lost billions of dollars when bonds they thought were safe turned out not to be.[12] Standard & Poor's is revamping its procedures to help investors understand the difference between traditional corporate bonds and the so-called *structured securities* that turned out to be much riskier than anyone thought.[13]

Although all corporations issue common stock, not all of them issue bonds. Shareholders provide equity (ownership) capital, while bondholders are lenders (although they are also considered "investors" as far as the securities market is concerned). Stock certificates represent ownership, while bond certificates represent indebtedness.

Corporate Bonds

corporate bonds Bonds issued by a company as a source of long-term funding.

Corporate bonds are a major source of long-term financing for Canadian corporations. They have traditionally been issued with maturities ranging from 10 to 30 years. Longer-term corporate bonds are somewhat riskier than shorter-term bonds. Bond ratings of new and proposed corporate issues are published to keep investors informed of the latest risk evaluations on many bonds. Negative ratings do not preclude a bond's success, but they do raise the interest rate that issuers must offer. Corporate bonds may be categorized in one of two ways: (1) according to methods of interest payment, and (2) according to whether they are *secured* or *unsecured*.

TABLE 19.2 Bond Ratings				
	High Grade	**Medium Grade (investment Grade)**	**Speculative**	**Poor Grade**
Moody's	Aaa Aa	A Baa	Ba B	Caa to C
Standard & Poor's	AAA AA	A BBB	BB B	CCC to D

Interest Payment: Registered and Bearer Bonds

Registered bonds register the names of holders with the company, which simply mails out cheques to the bondholders. **Bearer (or coupon) bonds** require bondholders to clip coupons from certificates and send them to the issuer to receive payment. Coupons can be redeemed by anyone, regardless of ownership.

registered bonds Bonds where the names of holders are registered with the company.

bearer (or coupon) bonds Bonds that require bondholders to clip coupons from certificates and send them to the issuer to receive interest payments.

Secured and Unsecured Bonds

With **secured bonds**, borrowers can reduce the risk of their bonds by pledging assets to bondholders in the event of default. First mortgages, other mortgages, or other specific assets may back secured bonds. If the corporation does not pay interest when it is due, the firm's assets can be sold and the proceeds used to pay the bondholders.

secured bonds Bonds issued by borrowers who pledge assets as collateral in the event of non-payment.

Unsecured bonds are called **debentures**. No specific property is pledged as security for these bonds. Holders of unsecured bonds generally have claims against property not otherwise pledged in the company's other bonds. Accordingly, debentures have inferior claims on the corporation's assets. Financially strong corporations often use debentures.

debentures Unsecured bonds.

The Retirement of Bonds

Maturity dates on bonds of all kinds may be very long. Of course, all bonds must be paid off, or retired, at some point. With regard to maturity dates, there are three types of bonds: *callable*, *serial*, and *convertible*.

Callable Bonds

The issuer of **callable bonds** may call them in and pay them off at a price stipulated in the indenture, or contract, before the maturity date. Usually the issuer cannot call the bond for a certain period of time after issue, often within the first five years. Issuers usually call in existing bonds when prevailing interest rates are lower than the rate being paid on the bond. The issuer must still pay a *call* price to call in the bond. The call price usually gives a premium to the bondholder. The premium is merely the difference between the face value and call price. For example, a bond that bears a $100 face value might be callable by the firm for $108.67 any time during the first year after issue. The call price (and therefore the premium) decreases annually as the bonds approach maturity.

callable bonds Bonds that may be paid off by the issuer before the maturity date.

Sinking Funds. Callable bonds are often retired by the use of **sinking fund provisions**. The issuing company is required to put a certain amount of money into a special bank account annually. At the end of a certain number of years, the money (including interest) will be sufficient to redeem the bonds. Failure to meet the sinking fund provision places the issue in default. Such bonds are generally regarded as safer investments than many other bonds.

sinking fund provision A clause in the bond indenture (contract) that requires the issuing company to put enough money into a special bank account each year to cover the retirement of the bond issue on schedule.

Serial Bonds

Some corporations issue serial or convertible bonds. With a **serial bond**, the firm retires portions of the bond issue in a series of different preset dates. For example, a company with a $100-million issue maturing in 20 years may retire $5 million each year.

serial bond A bond issue in which redemption dates are staggered so that a firm pays off portions of the issue at different predetermined dates.

Convertible Bonds

Convertible bonds can be converted into the common stock of the issuing company. At the option of the holder, payment is made in shares of stock instead of in cash. Because holders are given such flexibility and because there are potential benefits of converting bonds into stock, firms can offer lower interest rates when the bonds are

convertible bonds Any bonds that offer bondholders the option of accepting common stock instead of cash in repayment.

issued. However, because holders cannot be forced to accept stock instead of cash, conversion works only when the bond buyer also regards the issuing corporation as a good investment.

Suppose that Bell Canada Enterprises sold a $100-million issue of 4.5 percent convertible bonds in 2010. The bonds were issued in $1000 denominations, and they mature in 2020. At any time before maturity, each debenture of $1000 is convertible into 19.125 shares of the company's common stock. Suppose that between October 2010 and March 2017, the stock price ranged from a low of $28 to a high of $67. In that time, then, 19.125 common shares had a market value ranging from $535 to $1281. The bondholder could have exchanged the $1000 bond in return for stock to be kept or sold at a possible profit (or loss).

Government Bonds

government bonds Bonds issued by the federal government.

Government bonds—for example, Canada Savings Bonds—are among the safest investments available because the Canadian government backs all federal bonds. Government securities are sold in large blocks to institutional investors who buy them to ensure desired levels of safety in portfolios. As their needs change, they may buy or sell government securities to other investors. As with corporate bonds, government bonds with longer maturities are somewhat riskier than short-term issues because their longer lives expose them to more political, social, and economic changes.

municipal bonds Bonds issued by provincial or local government.

Provincial and local governments also issue bonds (called **municipal bonds**) to finance school and transportation systems and a variety of other projects. Banks invest in bonds nearing maturity because they are relatively safe, liquid investments. Pension funds, insurance companies, and private citizens also make longer-term investments in municipal bonds.

Secondary Markets for Bonds

Nearly all secondary trading in bonds occurs in the OTC market rather than on organized exchanges. Thus, precise statistics about annual trading volumes are not recorded. As with stocks, however, market values and prices change daily. As interest rates go up, bond prices tend to go down. The prices of riskier bonds fluctuate more widely than those of higher-grade bonds.

Ethical Funds, a division of NEI Investments does not invest in companies involved primarily in tobacco, weapons, or nuclear power.

Other Investments

Stocks and bonds are very important, but they are not the only marketable securities for businesses. Financial managers are also concerned with investment opportunities in *mutual funds*, *hedge funds*, *commodities*, and *stock options*. In striking the right balance for risk among investment alternatives, financial managers use *diversification* and *asset allocation*.

 Describe the investment opportunities offered by *mutual funds* and *commodities*.

Mutual Funds

Companies called **mutual funds** pool investments from individuals and other firms to purchase a portfolio of stocks, bonds, and short-term securities. Investors are part-owners of this portfolio. For example, if you invest $1000 in a mutual fund that has a portfolio worth $100 000, you own 1 percent of the portfolio. Mutual funds usually have portfolios worth many millions of dollars. Investors in **no-load funds** are not charged a sales commission when they buy into or sell out of the mutual fund. **Load funds** levy a charge of between 2 and 8 percent of the invested funds.

Mutual funds vary by the investment goals they stress. The portfolios of mutual funds that emphasize safety include Treasury bills and other safe issues that offer immediate income (liquidity). Other funds seek higher returns and are willing to sacrifice some safety. They invest in long-term municipal bonds, corporate bonds, and in common stocks with good dividend-paying records. Mutual funds that stress growth take on even more risk and hold a mixture of bonds, preferred stocks, and common stocks. Aggressive growth mutual funds seek maximum capital appreciation. To get it, these funds sacrifice current income and safety. They invest in stocks of new companies, troubled companies, and other high-risk securities. Table 19.3 lists the top 10 mutual funds in Canada.

Mutual funds that stress socially responsible investing are called **ethical funds**. They do not invest in cigarette manufacturers or companies that make weapons, for example, and instead focus on investing in companies that produce safe and useful products and show concern for their employees, for the environment, and for human rights. While many companies offer such investments, The Socially Responsible Funds Company is dedicated to this mission.

mutual fund Any company that pools the resources of many investors and uses those funds to purchase various types of financial securities, depending on the fund's financial goals.

no-load fund A mutual fund in which investors are not charged a sales commission when they buy in to or sell out of the fund.

load fund A mutual fund in which investors are charged a sales commission when they buy in to or sell out of the fund.

ethical funds Mutual funds that focus on investing in companies that produce safe and useful products and do good in terms of employee relations, environmental practices, and human rights.

	Company	Assets (billions of dollars)
TABLE 19.3 Top 10 Mutual Funds in Canada, July 2008 (latest data available)		
1.	RBC Asset Management	$92.3
2.	IGM Financial Inc.	84.5
3.	CI Financial Corp.	64.2
4.	TD Asset Management	46.9
5.	CIBC Asset Management	41.9
6.	Fidelity Investments Canada ULC	33.6
7.	BMO Financial Group	29.5
8.	Invesco Trimark Ltd.	28.6
9.	AGF Funds Inc.	19.9
10.	Franklin Templeton	18.4

Mutual funds give small investors access to professional financial management. Their managers have up-to-date information about market conditions and the best large-scale investment opportunities. But there are no guarantees of good returns, and during difficult periods many people pull their money out of mutual funds. Some estimates indicate that up to 80 percent of mutual funds do not perform as well as the average return of the overall stock market.[14] This under-performance has resulted in the emergence of *index mutual funds*, which hold many of the same stocks as the market they track. This requires little human input and reduces management expenses.

exchange-traded fund (ETF) A bundle of stocks (or bonds) that are in an index that tracks the overall movement of a market.

Like an index mutual fund, an **exchange-traded fund (ETF)** is a bundle of stocks (or bonds) that are in an index that tracks the overall movement of a market. But ETFs can be traded throughout the day, much like a stock. Unlike mutual funds—which are priced only at the end of each day—you can buy or sell ETFs at any time during the day when the market reaches your target price. Also unlike mutual funds—which incur the costs of active management—ETFs have lower operating expenses because they are bound by rules that specify what stocks will be purchased and when. Once the rule is established, little human action is needed, and this reduces management expenses. Annual fees for mutual funds average 1.4 percent of assets, but for ETFs the rate is as low as 0.09 percent.[15]

Hedge Funds

hedge funds Private pools of money that try to give investors a positive return regardless of stock market performance.

Hedge funds are private pools of money that try to give investors a positive return regardless of stock market performance. Hedge funds often engage in risky practices like *short-selling* (essentially betting that a company's stock price will go down) and *leveraging* (borrowing money against principal). Historically, interest in hedge funds has been limited to wealthy people (called "accredited investors") who are assumed to be very knowledgeable about financial matters and are able to weigh the risks of investing. But recently, hedge funds have begun marketing their products to the average investor with something called "principal-protected notes." These guarantee that investors will get their original investment back at a certain time, but they do not guarantee that any additional returns will be forthcoming.

The number of hedge funds has increased rapidly in recent years, and the majority of money invested in hedge funds is now in the form of principal-protected notes.[16] Hedge funds are not as closely regulated as mutual funds and are not required to report management fees. But these management fees can be higher than those charged by mutual funds, so there are concerns that investors will be shortchanged. In addition, some hedge funds have been in the news for the wrong reasons. An Ontario Securities Commission panel ruled that two executives from the now-defunct Norshield Asset Management Ltd. knowingly misled their clients and investigators and failed to keep proper books. Losses are estimated at $159 million from 1900 retail investors.[17] As a result, there are now calls for increased regulation of hedge funds.[18]

Commodities

futures contract Agreement to purchase specified amounts of a commodity (or stock) at a given price on a set future date.

commodities market Market in which futures contracts are traded.

Commodities are products ranging from coffee beans and hogs to propane and platinum. **Futures contracts**—agreements to purchase specified amounts of commodities at given prices on set dates—can be bought and sold in the **commodities market**. These contracts are available not only for commodities but also for stocks. Because selling prices reflect traders' *estimates* of future events and values, futures prices are quite volatile, and trading is risky.

For example, on January 3, 2012, the price of gold was $1625 per ounce. If futures gold contracts for July 2013 were selling for $1575 per ounce, this price would reflect investors' judgment that gold prices would be slightly lower in July. Now suppose that you purchased a 100-ounce gold futures contract in January for $157 500 ($1575 × 100). If, in March 2013, the July gold futures sold for $1700, you could sell your contract for $170 000. Your profit after the two months would be $12 500. Of course, if the futures contract had been selling for less than $1575, you would have lost money.

Margins

Usually, buyers of futures contracts need not put up the full purchase amount. Rather, the buyer posts a smaller amount—the **margin**—that may be as little as $3000 for contracts up to $100 000.

margin The percentage of the total sales price that a buyer must put up to place an order for stock or a futures contract.

Let us look again at our gold futures example. If you had posted a $4250 margin for your July gold contract, you would have earned a $12 500 profit on that investment of $4250 in only two months. However, you also took a big risk involving two big ifs: If you had held on to your contract until July and if gold had dropped, say to $1525, you would have lost $5000 ($157 500 – $152 500). If you had posted a $4250 margin to buy the contract, you would have lost that entire margin and would owe an additional $750. Between 75 and 90 percent of all small-time investors lose money in the futures market. The boxed insert entitled "Does Green Trading Work?" describes a different kind of trading that is being increasingly debated.

THE GREENING OF BUSINESS

■ ■ ■

Does Green Trading Work?

Traders are accustomed to using financial markets for investing in just about everything—ranging from pork bellies to movie production—in the hope of gaining a profit. However, new financial markets for commodities known as carbon credits are driven not just by the profit motive but also by a sense of social responsibility. The economic incentives of emissions trading (ET) bring together both environmental polluters and green companies in an effort to save the planet and turn a profit.

Here's how it works. Regulators in various countries set limits on the amounts of several industrial pollutants that can be released into the atmosphere, including carbon dioxide (CO_2), sulphur dioxide, and mercury. A leading example is the European Union's Emissions Trading Scheme (ETS), which was started by the European Commission in 2005 to meet the EU's obligations for carbon reductions in accordance with the Kyoto Protocol on climate change. The ETS annually sets a cap for the total amount of CO_2 emission allowed for each EU country and for each business in that country. The country totals and the EU total cannot exceed the caps.

Individual companies are then issued a permit containing a number of credits that represent the right to emit a certain amount of CO_2. Any company producing below its CO_2 cap can sell its surplus credits to other, more pollution-prone companies that need more credits to keep operating without going over their cap (for example, a forest operator in Thailand could sell a carbon permit to a German manufacturing firm that is exceeding its cap). This is where the trading opportunities arise. It's like a stock exchange that matches up buyers and sellers, in this case buyers and sellers of emissions credits. With emissions trading, environmentally oriented companies sell unneeded emissions allowances and gain a financial return on their past investment for reducing pollution. Such companies view environmental cleanup not as an expense but as a responsible investment. Other companies that have previously avoided making such investments face higher costs as they bid for others' unused carbon credits.

This sounds pretty promising because the trading scheme creates a financial incentive for the development of cleaner industries that reduce carbon emissions and other greenhouse gases. But, as we saw in Chapter 3, the system is prone to fraud (for example, the operator in Thailand might sell the same carbon permit to manufacturers in France as well as Germany). Europol's Criminal Finances and Technology section estimates that up to 90 percent of all carbon market volume in certain EU nations is fraudulent.

Critical Thinking Questions

1. What has been the experience of the European Union to date with emissions trading?

2. Consider the following statement: *The trading of carbon emissions will not achieve any useful outcomes. It will simply attract companies that will try to "game" the system for their own benefit. The fraud that is already apparent is proof of this.* Do you agree or disagree with the statement? Explain your reasoning.

Stock Options

A **stock option** is the right to buy or sell shares of a stock. A **call option** gives its owner the right to buy shares of a particular stock at a certain price, with that right lasting until a particular date. A **put option** gives its owner the right to sell shares of a particular stock at a specified price, with that right lasting until a particular date. These options are traded on several stock exchanges.

If you thought the price of Goldcorp Inc. (which sold for $40 per share in June 2012) was going to go up, you might buy a call option giving you the right to buy 100 shares of Goldcorp any time in the next two months at a so-called strike price of $50. If the stock rose to $60 before July, you would exercise your call option. Your profit would be $10 per share ($60 − 50) less the price you paid to buy the option. However, if the stock price fell instead of rising, you would not exercise your call option because Goldcorp shares would be available on the open market for less than $50 per share. Your stock option would be "under water"; that is, it would be worthless. You would lose whatever you paid for the option. In recent years, there has been much negative publicity about stock options that are given to executives to motivate them to work hard for the company.

Making Choices for Diversification, Asset Allocation, and Risk Reduction

Investors seldom take an extreme approach—total risk-seeking or total risk avoidance—in selecting their investments. Extreme positions cause extreme results, and while most investors have a preference toward either risk or risk avoidance, they are not totally oriented to either end of the risk spectrum. Instead, they select a mixture, or *portfolio*, of investments—some riskier and some more conservative—that provides the level of risk and financial stability at which they are comfortable. They do this in two ways—through *diversification* and through *asset allocation*.

Diversification

Diversification means buying several different kinds of investments rather than just one. Diversification as applied to common stocks means, for example, that you invest in stocks of several different companies, such as lululemon, IBM, Cisco Systems, and Bombardier, rather than putting all your money into just one of them. The risk of loss is reduced by spreading the total investment across more stocks because while any one stock may tumble, there is less chance that all of them will fall, especially if the companies are from different industries. Even more diversification is gained when funds are spread across more kinds of investment alternatives—stocks, bonds, mutual funds, real estate, and so on.

But these are only general principles, and they will not always apply. This was demonstrated when the financial crisis hit in 2008 and the value of most investments dropped sharply. Think for a moment about the difference between insurance and investments. An insurance company diversifies its risks by selling, say, homeowner's insurance in different geographic areas because a house fire in Saskatoon will not spread to Toronto. But the same logic does not necessarily apply to financial investments. If a problem develops in one area (for example, subprime mortgages), investors may panic and conclude that all investments are at risk (this is called *contagion*). This contagion drives down the value of all investments, so even people who had diversified portfolios in 2008 saw the value of most of their investments decline.[19]

Asset Allocation

Asset allocation is the proportion of funds invested in each of the investment alternatives. You may decide, for example, to allocate $20 000 to common stocks, $10 000 to a money market mutual fund, and $10 000 to a Canada Savings Bond. Ten years later, you may decide on a less risky asset allocation of $10 000, $15 000, and $15 000 in the same investment categories, respectively. As your investment objectives change (in this example, from moderate risk to lower risk for capital preservation), your asset allocation must be changed accordingly.

asset allocation The relative amount of funds invested in (or allocated to) each of several investment alternatives.

Buying and Selling Securities

Explain the process by which securities are bought and sold.

The process of buying and selling stocks, bonds, and other financial instruments is complex. To start, you need to find out about possible investments and match them to your investment objectives. Then you must decide whether you want to get advice from experts or whether you want to make decisions on your own.

Using Financial Information Services

Have you ever looked at the financial section of your daily newspaper and found yourself wondering what all those tables and numbers mean? If you cannot read stock and bond quotations, you probably should not invest in these issues. Fortunately, this skill is easily mastered.

Stock Quotations

Figure 19.1 shows the type of information newspapers provide about daily market transactions of individual stocks. The corporation's name (for example, Goldcorp) is shown along with the number of shares sold, the high and low prices of the stock for that trading day, the closing price of the stock, and the change from the closing price on the previous day.

FIGURE 19.1

How to read a daily stock quotation.

Company	Volume	High	Low	Close	Change
Bombardier	5875	3.82	3.66	3.67	–0.11
Goldcorp	**6203**	**41.52**	**38.70**	**40.93**	**+3.23**
Royal Bank	3664	50.89	49.84	49.99	–1.56
Magna Intl.	892	41.30	39.14	39.50	–2.25
IAMGold	4615	12.26	11.36	12.15	+1.08
Kinross	3232	8.41	8.94	8.88	+0.59

- *Stock*
  Goldcorp Inc. (name of company).
- *Volume*
  6203 (total number of shares traded on this date [in 100s]).
- *High and Low*
  During the trading day, the highest price was $41.52 and the lowest price was $38.70.
- *Close*
  At the close of trading on this date, the last price paid per share was $40.93.
- *Net Change*
  Difference between today's closing price and the previous day's closing price. Price increased by $3.23 per share.

Bond Quotations

Bond prices also change from day to day. These changes form the *coupon rate*, which provides information for firms about the cost of borrowing funds. Prices of domestic corporation bonds, Canadian government bonds, and foreign bonds are reported separately. Bond prices are expressed in terms of 100, even though most have a face value of $1000. Thus, a quote of 85 means that the bond's price is 85 percent of its face value, or $850.

A corporation bond selling at 155¼ would cost a buyer $1552.50 ($1000 face value × 1.5525), plus commission. The interest rate on bonds is also quoted as a percentage of par, or face, value. Thus "6½ s" pays 6.5 percent of par value per year. Typically, interest is paid semi-annually at half of the stated interest or coupon rate.

The market value (selling price) of a bond at any given time depends on its stated interest rate, the "going rate" of interest in the market, and its redemption or maturity date. A bond with a higher stated interest rate than the going rate on similar quality bonds will probably sell at a premium above its face value—its selling price will be above its redemption price. A bond with a lower stated interest rate than the going rate on similar-quality bonds will probably sell at a discount—its selling price will be below its redemption price. How much the premium or discount is depends largely on how far in the future the maturity date is. The maturity date is shown after the interest rate. Figure 19.2 shows the type of information daily newspapers provide about bond transactions.

Bond Yield. Suppose you bought a $1000 par-value bond in 1999 for $650. Its stated interest rate was 6 percent, and its maturity or redemption date is 2019. You therefore received $60 per year in interest. Based on your actual investment of $650, your yield is 9.2 percent. If you held it to maturity, you would receive $1000 for a bond that originally cost you only $650. This extra $350 increased your true, or effective, yield.

FIGURE 19.2

How to read a bond quotation.

Issuer	Coupon	Maturity	Price	Yield
Government of Canada				
Canada	4.20	June 1, 18	117.45	3.57
Canada	3.5	June 1, 20	115.40	3.03
Provincials				
Hy Que	6.50	Feb. 15, 35	147.09	4.42
BC	4.7	June. 18, 37	124.83	3.76
Corporate				
Telus	**4.95**	**Mar 3, 17**	**101.92**	**4.86**
Bank of Mon.	5.10	Apr 21, 21	109.38	4.66

- *Issuer*
  Company name is Telus.
- *Coupon*
  The annual rate of interest at face value is 4.95 percent.
- *Maturity*
  The maturity date is March 3, 2017.
- *Price*
  On this date, $101.92 was the price of the last transaction.
- *Yield*
  The yield is computed by dividing the annual interest paid by the current market price.

  Note: Yield to Maturity (YTM) would also take into account duration and capital repayment.

Mutual Funds Quotations

Selling prices for mutual funds are reported daily or weekly in most newspapers. Additional investor information is also available in the financial press. Figure 19.3 shows a partial listing of T. Rowe Price funds from *Barron's Mutual Funds*, a prominent weekly financial newspaper. Three funds are listed in the figure—Balanced, Science and Technology, and Short-Term Bond—but the published list would include all of Price's more than 90 different funds.

The fund's net asset value (NAV), the current market value of one share, is perhaps the key term for understanding the quotations. The fund managers calculate NAV at day's end by taking the fund's net assets—securities it owns, plus cash and any accumulated earnings, minus liabilities—and dividing the remainder by the number of shares outstanding. Let's focus on the first fund listed, the Balanced fund:

FIGURE 19.3

How to read a mutual fund quotation.

①	②	③	④	⑤	⑥	⑦	⑧
52 Week		Fund	Close	Wk's	% Return		
High	Low	Name	NAV	Chg	1-Wk	YTD	3-Yrs
		Price Funds:					
19.04	16.51	Balanced *n*	18.37	–0.01	–0.1	+0.4	+7.8
20.00	15.03	SciTec *n*	18.29	–0.21	–1.1	–2.7	–33.4
4.90	4.75	Sht-Bd *n*	4.75	–0.01	–0.2	–0.3	+13.5

■ Column 1 shows the fund's highest net asset value (NAV)—$19.04—during the past 52 weeks.

■ Column 2 shows the 52-week low NAV ($16.51).

■ Column 3 lists the company name (Price Funds) at the top and the individual fund names beneath the company name. The "n" code indicates no front-end or back-end sales charge (a *no-load* fund)

■ Column 4 lists the NAV ($18.37) at the close of the most recent week.

■ Column 5 shows the net asset value change—that is, the dollar gain or loss based on the previous week's NAV. The Balanced fund closed $0.01 lower this week than in the previous week.

■ The next three columns report each fund's recent and longer-term performance. These numbers reflect the percentage change in NAV. These three columns show the percentage return of the fund for the most recent past week (column 6), current year to date (column 7), and the past three years (column 8).

Market Indexes

Although they do not indicate how specific securities are performing, **market indexes** provide a useful summary of trends in specific industries and the stock market as a whole. Market indexes reveal bull and bear market trends. **Bull markets** are periods of upward-moving stock prices. Periods of falling stock prices are called **bear markets**.

market index A measure of the market value of stocks; provides a summary of price trends in a specific industry or of the stock market as a whole.

bull market A period of rising stock prices; a period in which investors act on a belief that stock prices will rise.

bear market A period of falling stock prices; a period in which investors act on a belief that stock prices will fall.

Dow Jones Industrial Average (DJIA) Market index based on the prices of 30 of the largest firms listed on NYSE and NASDAQ.

The Dow Jones Industrial Average. The most widely cited market index is the **Dow Jones Industrial Average (DJIA)**, which measures the performance of U.S. financial markets by focusing on 30 blue-chip companies as reflectors of economic health. The Dow is the average of the stock prices for these 30 large firms. Because of the small number of firms it considers, however, it is a limited gauge of the overall stock market. The Dow increased sharply in the 1990s. It reached 11 000 early in 2000 but dropped to less than 8000 in 2002. By mid-2012, it stood at 12 100.

Standard & Poor's Composite Index (S&P 500) Market index based on the performance of 400 industrial firms, 40 utilities, 40 financial institutions, and 20 transportation companies.

The S&P 500. **Standard & Poor's Composite Index (S&P 500)** is a broader report than the Dow. It consists of 500 stocks, including 400 industrial firms, 40 utilities, 40 financial institutions, and 20 transportation companies. Because the index average is weighted according to market capitalization of each stock, the more highly valued companies exercise a greater influence on the index.

S&P/TSX index An average computed from 225 different large Canadian stocks from various industry groups.

The S&P/TSX Index. The **S&P/TSX index** is an average computed from 225 large Canadian stocks from various industry groups.[20] The index has also been very volatile during the past few years. It moved sharply upward during the bull market of the 1990s and topped 11 000 in the summer of 2000. It then dropped to 6500 by the end of the century. In mid-2012, it stood at 11 300.

NASDAQ Composite Index Value-weighted market index that includes all NASDAQ-listed companies, both domestic and foreign.

The NASDAQ Composite Index. Because it considers more stocks, some financial observers regard the **NASDAQ Composite Index** as the most important of all market indexes. Unlike the Dow, the S&P 500, and the S&P/TSX, all NASDAQ-listed companies are included in the index. The popularity of the NASDAQ index goes hand in hand with investors' growing interest in technology and small-company stocks. The NASDAQ index has also been very volatile. In early 2000, it reached 5000, but by 2001 it had dropped to just 1300. In mid 2012, it stood at 2700.

Buying and Selling Stocks

market order An order to a broker to buy or sell a certain security at the current market price.

limit buy order An order to a broker to buy a certain security only if its price is less than or equal to a given limit.

limit sell order An order to a broker to sell a certain security only if its price is equal to or greater than a given limit.

stop order An order to a broker to sell a certain security if its price falls to a certain level or below.

round lot The purchase or sale of stock in units of 100 shares.

odd lots The purchase or sale of stock in units other than 100 shares.

Based on your own investigations and/or recommendations from your broker, you can place many types of orders. A **market order** authorizes the broker to buy or sell shares of a certain stock at the prevailing market price. A **limit buy order** authorizes the broker to purchase shares of a stock if its price is less than or equal to a given limit. For example, a limit buy order at $80 per share means that the broker is to buy it if and only if the stock price is $80 or less. A **limit sell order** authorizes the sale of shares of a stock when its price is equal to or greater than a given limit. For example, a limit sell order at $80 per share means that the broker is to sell it if and only if the stock price is $80 or more. A **stop order** instructs the broker to sell shares of a stock if its price falls to a certain level. For example, a stop order of $80 on a particular stock means that the broker is to sell it if and only if its price falls to $80 or below.

You can also place orders of different sizes. A **round lot** order requests 100 shares or some multiple thereof. Fractions of a round lot are called **odd lots**. Trading odd lots is usually more expensive than trading round lots because an intermediary called an odd-lot broker is often involved, which increases brokerage fees.

The business of buying and selling stocks is changing rapidly. More and more individuals are buying and selling stocks on the internet and through mobile platforms. Traditional brokers are worried that before long customers will avoid using their services altogether.

Financing Securities Purchases

When you place a buy order of any kind, you must tell your broker how you will pay for the purchase. You might maintain a cash account with your broker. Then, as stocks are bought and sold, proceeds are added to the account and the broker subtracts commissions and costs of purchases. In addition, as with almost every good in today's economy, you can buy shares on credit.

Margin Trading

As with futures contracts, you can buy stocks on margin—putting down only a portion of the stock's price. You borrow the rest from your broker, who, in turn, borrows from the banks at a special rate and secures the loans with stock.

Margin trading offers several advantages. Suppose you purchased $100 000 worth of stock in WestJet. Let's also say that you paid $50 000 of your own money and borrowed the other $50 000 from your broker at 10 percent interest. Valued at its market price, your stock serves as your collateral. If shares have risen in value to $115 000 after one year, you can sell them and pay your broker $55 000 ($50 000 principal plus $5000 interest). You will have $60 000 left over. Your original investment of $50 000 will have earned a 20 percent profit of $10 000. If you had paid the entire price out of your own pocket, you would have earned only a 15 percent return.

Although investors often recognize possible profits to be made in margin trading, they sometimes fail to consider that losses, too, can be amplified. Suppose, for example, that you decided on January 4, 2013, to buy 1000 shares of Canadian Petroleum for $53 per share. You put up $26 500 of your own money and borrow $26 500 from your broker. As the stock rises, you reason, the loan will enable you to profit from twice as many shares. Now let us say that shortly after you purchase your stock, its market price begins to fall. You decide to hold on until it recovers, but by January 4, 2015, when the price has fallen to $23 per share, you give up hope and sell.

Now let us see how margin trading has amplified your losses. If you had invested your own $26 500 instead of borrowing it, you would recover $23 000 of your $53 000 investment (excluding commissions). Your loss, therefore, would be nearly 57 percent ($30 000 loss divided by $53 000 invested). By trading on margin, however, even though you still recover $23 000 of your $26 500 investment, you must repay the $26 500 that you borrowed, plus $2 650 in loan interest (at a 10 percent annual rate). In this case, your losses total $32 650 ($55 650 in outlays less $23 000 recovered). The percentage loss is 123 percent of your investment ($32 650 loss divided by $26 500 investment)—much greater than the 57 percent loss you would have suffered without margin trading.

The rising use of margin credit by investors was a growing concern during the bull market of 2004–06. Investors focused on the upside benefits but were not sensitive enough to the downside risks of margin trading. Especially at online

If you're a day trader, are volatile markets good or bad? When the market is volatile, there are often wider spreads between bid prices (what traders pay for a share of stock) and ask prices (what they charge for it). The difference isn't necessarily large, but if you can make a number of quick hits during the day, you can make a dime here and a dollar there. That strategy appeals to traders at large firms but also to individual traders working on their own.

brokerages, inexperienced traders were borrowing at an alarming rate, and some were using the borrowed funds for risky and speculative day trading. So-called *day traders* visited websites online to buy and sell a stock in the same day (so-called *intraday trades*), seeking quick in-and-out fractional gains on large volumes (many shares) of each stock. While some day traders were successful, most ended up as financial losers.

Short Sales

short sale Selling borrowed shares of stock in the expectation that their price will fall before they must be replaced, so that replacement shares can be bought for less than the original shares were sold for.

A **short sale** occurs when you borrow a security from your broker and sell it (one of the few times it is legal to sell what you do not own). At a given time in the future, you must restore an equal number of shares of that issue to the brokerage, along with a fee. For example, suppose that in June you believe the price of a certain company's stock will soon fall. You order your broker to sell short 100 shares at the market price of $38 per share. Your broker will make the sale and credit $3800 to your account. If the company's price falls to $32 per share in July, you can buy 100 shares for $3200 and give them to your broker, leaving you with a $600 profit (before commissions). The risk is that the price will not fall but will hold steady or rise, leaving you with a loss. Take a look at the Managing in Turbulent Times box called "Selling Sino-Forest Short" for a recent controversial example in the news.

MANAGING IN TURBULENT TIMES

Selling Sino-Forest Short

Muddy Waters is a research firm and a short seller. On June 3, 2011, it released a report that was critical of the accounting practices of Sino-Forest Corp., a company that owns timber lands in China. The report essentially questioned whether Sino-Forest actually owned the timber assets it claimed, and whether it was actually receiving the revenue it claimed. Muddy Waters said that readers of its report should assume that it had a short position in Sino-Forest. The report, and a review of Sino-Forest by Moody's Rating Service, had an immediate impact. On June 1, Sino-Forest shares were trading for $18.21 each, but by June 21, they were trading for just $1.29. By that time, Paulson & Co., the biggest shareholder of Sino-Forest, had sold all of the 34.7 million shares that it owned.

The incentives for short sellers are very high if they can demonstrate that there are problems in a company (or if they can convince investors that there *might* be problems). For example, if you had borrowed 1000 shares of Sino-Forest from your broker on June 1, 2011, and sold them, you would have received $18 210 (1000 x $18.21). You could then have purchased 1000 replacement shares on June 21 for just $1290.00 (1000 x $1.29). Your profit would have been $16 920 ($18 210 minus $1290).

The Muddy Waters report did not go unchallenged. On June 8, Richard Kelertas, an analyst at Dundee Capital Markets, vigorously attacked the report, saying that it was "a pile of crap." He accused Muddy Waters's founder, Carson Block, of promoting his report to hedge funds five weeks before making it public in an attempt to generate interest in short sales of Sino-Forest shares. He pointed out that Muddy Waters had used this tactic a year earlier when it targeted a company called Orient Paper Corp. The comments by Kelertas had little effect, and the market price of Sino-Forest shares continued to decline.

After the Muddy Waters report was released, investors became concerned about the complex (and hard-to-understand) business model that Sino-Forest was using. Basically, the company uses subsidiaries in the British Virgin Islands to buy trees in China. The subsidiaries hold the trees for a few years and then sell them to customers called "authorized intermediaries" (AIs). The suppliers of the trees and the buyers are supposedly distinct entities, but there is some dispute about whether this is really the case. Sino-Forest has been reluctant to disclose who the AIs are, claiming that doing so would harm its competitive position. Allen Chan, the CEO of Sino-Forest, said the AI structure was set up in the 1990s when it was the only way that Sino-Forest could do business in China. This clarification didn't stop the share decline either, and critics wonder why the company is still using that complex structure.

Critical Thinking Question

1. Consider the following statement: *Short selling should be banned because it creates instability in the price of a company's stock.* Do you agree or disagree with the statement? Defend your reasoning.

Securities Regulation

The buying and selling of securities is regulated in both Canada and the United States. There are both similarities and differences in the way the two countries regulate securities.

Explain how securities markets are regulated.

Canadian Securities Regulations

Canada, unlike the United States, does not have comprehensive federal securities legislation or a federal regulatory body. Government regulation is primarily provincial and emphasizes self-regulation through the various provincial securities exchanges. A report by a government-appointed committee that studied Canada's system of securities regulation concluded that it is in dire need of reform. The committee noted that Canada is the only country in the industrialized world with a patchwork of provincial regulations. It recommended a single regulator for Canada. The main complaints the committee noted were lack of meaningful enforcement of securities laws and unnecessary costs and time delays that make Canada's capital markets uncompetitive internationally.

In 1912, the Manitoba government pioneered in Canada laws applying mainly to the sale of new securities. Under these **blue-sky laws**, corporations issuing securities must back them up with something more than the "blue sky." Similar laws were passed in other provinces. Provincial laws also generally require that stockbrokers be licensed and securities be registered before they can be sold. In each province, issuers of proposed new securities must file a prospectus with the provincial securities exchange. The prospectus must be made available to prospective investors.

blue-sky laws Laws regulating how corporations must back up securities.

Ontario is generally regarded as having the most progressive securities legislation in Canada. The Ontario Securities Act contains disclosure provisions for new and existing issues, prevention of fraud, regulation of the Toronto Stock Exchange, and takeover bids. It also prohibits **insider trading**, which is the use of special knowledge about a firm to make a profit in the stock market. The Toronto Stock Exchange provides an example of self-regulation by the industry. The TSX has regulations concerning listing and delisting of securities, disclosure requirements, and issuing of prospectuses for new securities.

insider trading The use of special knowledge about a firm to make a profit in the stock market.

Unlike the United States with its Securities and Exchange Commission (SEC), Canada does not yet have a comprehensive federal regulatory body. In fact, Canada is the only country in the industrialized world that does not have a single regulator.[21] But in 2010, the federal government continued to move toward a new national securities act complete with a governing body called the Canadian Securities Regulatory Authority (CSRA). Reactions have been mixed, with the RCMP claiming that the Act does not go far enough to address criminal activity in securities trading. Time will tell, but it is clearly a step in the right direction.[22] As of 2012, changes had still not been made.

U.S. Securities Regulation

To protect the investing public and to maintain smoothly functioning markets, the U.S. Securities and Exchange Commission (SEC) oversees many phases of the process through which securities are issued. The SEC regulates the public offering of new securities by requiring that all companies file a prospectus before a proposed offering can go forward. A **prospectus** contains pertinent information about both the offered security and the issuing company. False statements are subject to criminal penalties.

The SEC has been criticized for failing to protect investors from various other financial manipulation schemes. The most prominent recent case is that of Bernie Madoff, who operated a Ponzi scheme that defrauded investors of

prospectus A detailed registration statement about a new stock filed with a provincial securities exchange; must include any data helpful to a potential buyer.

$50 *billion*. In spite of being warned on multiple occasions by an independent researcher that Madoff's operation was a Ponzi scheme, the SEC did nothing and investors lost everything.[23]

In addition to regulation by government agencies, both the NASD and the NYSE exercise self-regulation in an attempt to maintain the public trust and to ensure professionalism in the financial industry. A visible example is the NYSE's actions in establishing so-called *circuit breakers*—trading rules for reducing excessive market volatility and promoting investor confidence—that suspend trading for a preset length of time. For example, if the DJIA drops more than 1050 points before 2 p.m., trading is halted for an hour. The interruption provides a "cooling off" period that slows trading activity, gives investors time to reconsider their trading positions, and allows computer programs to be revised or shut down.[24] Bigger drops lead to longer "cooling off" periods.

program trading Large purchase or sale of a group of stocks, often triggered by computerized trading programs that can be launched without human supervision or control.

One oft-cited cause of sudden market fluctuations is **program trading**—the portfolio trading strategy involving the sale or purchase of a group of stocks valued at $1 million or more. It is often triggered by computerized trading programs that can be launched without human supervision or control. As market values change and economic events transpire during the course of a day, computer programs are busy recalculating the future values of stocks. Once a calculated value reaches a critical point, the program automatically signals a buy or sell order. Because electronic trading can cause the market to spiral out of control, it has led to the establishment of circuit breakers.

MyBizLab

Capture more moments of true understanding. MyBizLab provides you with interactive study and practice tools directly related to this chapter's content. The new MyBizLab Study Plan Learning Path is designed to measure a full range of skills and provide remediation to give you what you need to master key chapter concepts. MyBizLab flexes to your unique learning needs. The result? Inspired learning, more success.

SUMMARY OF LEARNING OBJECTIVES

1. **Explain the difference between *primary* and *secondary* securities markets.** *Primary securities* markets involve the buying and selling of new securities, either in public offerings or through private placements (sales to single buyers or small groups of buyers). *Investment bankers* specialize in trading securities in primary markets. *Secondary securities* markets involve the trading of existing stocks and bonds through such groups as the New York Stock Exchange and the Toronto Stock Exchange.

2. **Discuss the value of *common stock* and *preferred stock* to shareholders and describe the secondary market for each type of security.** *Common stock* affords investors the prospect of capital gains, dividend income, or both. Common stock values are expressed in three ways—as *par value* (the face value of a share when it is issued), *market value* (the current market price of a share), and *book value* (the value of shareholders' equity compared with that of other stocks). Market value is the most important value to investors. *Preferred stock* is less risky than common stock; for example, cumulative preferred stock entitles holders to receive missed dividends when the company is financially capable of paying. It also

offers the prospect of steadier income than common stock. Shareholders of preferred stock must be paid dividends before shareholders of common stock.

Both common and preferred stock are traded on *stock exchanges* (institutions formed to conduct the trading of existing securities) and in *over-the-counter (OTC)* markets (dealer organizations formed to trade securities outside stock exchange settings). "Members" who hold seats on stock exchanges act as brokers—agents who execute buy-and-sell orders—for non-members. Exchanges include the New York Stock Exchange, the Toronto Stock Exchange, and regional and foreign exchanges.

3. **Distinguish among various types of *bonds* in terms of their issuers, safety, and retirement.** The safety of bonds issued by various borrowers is rated by such services as Moody's and Standard & Poor's. *Government bonds* are the safest investment because the federal government backs them. *Municipal bonds*, which are offered by provincial and local governments to finance a variety of projects, are also usually safe. *Corporate bonds* are issued by businesses to gain long-term funding. They may be secured (backed by pledges of the issuer's assets) or unsecured

(debentures), and they offer varying degrees of safety. *Serial bonds* are retired as portions are redeemed at preset dates; *convertible bonds* may be retired by conversion into the issuer's common stock or by cash. Some government and corporate bonds are callable; that is, they can be paid off by the issuer prior to their maturity dates.

4. **Describe the investment opportunities offered by** *mutual funds* **and** *commodities.* Like stocks and bonds, *mutual funds*—companies that pool investments to purchase portfolios of financial instruments—offer investors different levels of risk and growth potential. *Load funds* require investors to pay commissions of 2 to 8 percent; *no-load* funds do not charge commissions when investors buy in or sell out. *Futures contracts*—agreements to buy specified amounts of commodities at given prices on preset dates—are traded in the *commodities market*. Commodities traders often buy on *margin*—the percentage of the total sales price that must be put up to order futures contracts.

5. **Explain the process by which securities are bought and sold.** Investors generally use such financial information services as newspaper and online stock, bond, and OTC quotations to learn about possible investments. Market indexes such as the *S&P/TSX index*, the *Dow Jones Indus-*trial *Average, Standard & Poor's Composite Index*, and the *NASDAQ Composite Index* provide useful summaries of trends, both in specific industries and in the market as a whole. Investors can then place different types of orders. *Market orders* are orders to buy or sell at current prevailing prices. Because investors do not know exactly what prices will be when market orders are executed, they may issue *limit* or *stop orders* that are to be executed only if prices rise to or fall below specified levels. *Round lots* are purchased in multiples of 100 shares. *Odd lots* are purchased in fractions of round lots. Securities can be bought on margin or as part of short sales (investors sell securities that are borrowed from brokers and returned at a later date).

6. **Explain how securities markets are regulated.** To protect investors, provincial securities commissions regulate the public offering of new securities and enforce laws against such practices as insider trading (using special knowledge about a firm for profit or gain). Many provincial governments prosecute the sale of fraudulent securities and enforce *blue-sky laws* that require corporations to back up securities with something more than the "blue sky." As well, stockbrokers must be licensed and securities must be registered before they can be sold.

KEY TERMS

asset allocation (p. 616)
bear market (p. 619)
bearer (coupon) bonds (p. 611)
blue-chip stocks (p. 605)
blue-sky laws (p. 623)
bond (p. 610)
book value (p. 605)
broker (p. 607)
bull market (p. 619)
call option (p. 616)
callable bonds (p. 611)
commodities market (p. 614)
convertible bonds (p. 611)
corporate bonds (p. 610)
cumulative preferred stock (p. 606)
debentures (p. 611)
diversification (p. 616)
Dow Jones Industrial Average (DJIA) (p. 620)
ethical funds (p. 613)
exchange-traded fund (ETF) (p. 614)

futures contract (p. 614)
government bonds (p. 612)
hedge funds (p. 614)
insider trading (p. 623)
investment banker (p. 604)
limit buy order (p. 620)
limit sell order (p. 620)
load fund (p. 613)
margin (p. 615)
market capitalization (p. 605)
market index (p. 619)
market order (p. 620)
market value (p. 605)
municipal bonds (p. 612)
mutual fund (p. 613)
NASDAQ Composite Index (p. 620)
National Association of Securities Dealers Automated Quotation (NASDAQ) (p. 609)
no-load fund (p. 613)
odd lots (p. 620)

over-the-counter (OTC) market (p. 609)
par value (p. 605)
preferred stock (p. 606)
primary securities market (p. 604)
program trading (p. 624)
prospectus (p. 623)
put option (p. 616)
registered bonds (p. 611)
round lot (p. 620)
secondary securities market (p. 604)
secured bonds (p. 611)
securities (p. 604)
serial bond (p. 611)
short sale (p. 622)
sinking fund provision (p. 611)
S&P/TSX index (p. 620)
Standard & Poor's Composite Index (S&P 500) (p. 620)
stock exchange (p. 606)
stock option (p. 616)
stop order (p. 620)

QUESTIONS FOR ANALYSIS

1. Suppose you decided to invest in common stocks as a personal investment. Which kind of broker—full-service or online discount—would you use for buying and selling stock? Why?

2. Choose a stock from the TSX and find a newspaper listing of a recent day's transactions for the stock. Explain what each element in the listing means.

3. Choose a bond from the TSX and find a newspaper listing of a recent day's transactions for the bond. Explain what each element in the listing means.

4. Which of the three measures of common stock value is most important? Why?

5. Explain how an investor might make money in a commodities trade. Then explain how an investor might lose money in a commodities trade.

6. How do the provincial securities commissions regulate securities markets? Give an example of how they are doing their job well and an example of how they failed to do their job.

APPLICATION EXERCISES

1. Interview the financial manager of a local business. What are the investment goals of the organization? What mix of securities does it use? What advantages and disadvantages do you see in its portfolio?

2. Contact a broker for information about setting up a personal account for trading securities. Prepare a report on the broker's requirements for placing buy/sell orders, credit terms, cash account requirements, services available to investors, and commissions/fees schedules.

3. Visit an online stock site such as globeinvestor.com and find the latest prices for the following stocks: Canadian Tire, Research In Motion, and Rona. What are the trends? Has the stock price risen in the past six months?

4. Find three discount online brokers and identify their billing policies. Which company offers the most attractive deals? Which company offers the most attractive investment analysis tools?

BUILDING YOUR BUSINESS SKILLS

Market Ups and Downs

The Purpose of the Assignment

To encourage students to understand the forces that cause fluctuations in stock prices.

The Situation

Investing in stocks requires an understanding of the various factors that affect stock prices. These factors may be intrinsic to the company itself or part of the external environment.

- Internal factors relate to the company itself, such as an announcement of poor or favourable earnings, earnings that are more or less than expected, major layoffs, labour problems, management issues, and mergers.

- External factors relate to world or national events, such as a threatened war in the Persian Gulf, the possibility of a bird flu epidemic, weather conditions that affect sales, the Bank of Canada's adjustment of interest rates, and employment figures that were higher or lower than expected. By analyzing these factors, you will often learn a lot about why a stock did well or why it did poorly. Being aware of these influences will help you anticipate future stock movements.

Assignment

Step 1

Working alone, choose a common stock that has experienced considerable price fluctuations in the past few years. Here are several examples (but there are many others): Research in Motion, IBM, Amazon.com, and Apple. Find the symbol for the stock and the exchange on which it is traded.

Step 2

At your library, find the *Daily Stock Price Record*, a publication that provides a historical picture of daily stock closings.

There are separate copies for the various stock exchanges. Find your stock and study its trading pattern.

Step 3

Find four or five days over a period of several months or even a year when there have been major price fluctuations in the stock. (A two- or three-point price change from one day to the next is considered major.) Then research what happened on that day that might have contributed to the fluctuation. The best place to begin is the *Globe and Mail* or *The Wall Street Journal*.

Step 4

Write a short analysis that links changes in stock price to internal and external factors. As you analyze the data, be aware that it is sometimes difficult to know why a stock price fluctuates.

Step 5

Get together with three other students who studied different stocks. As a group, discuss your findings, looking for fluctuation patterns.

Questions for Discussion

1. Do you see any similarities in the movement of the various stocks during the same period? For example, did the stocks move up or down at about the same time? If so, do you think the stocks were affected by the same factors? Explain your thinking.

2. Based on your analysis, did internal or external factors have the greater impact on stock price? Which factors had the more long-lasting effect? Which factors had the shorter effect?

3. Why do you think it is so hard to predict changes in stock price on a day-to-day basis?

EXERCISING YOUR ETHICS: TEAM EXERCISE

Serving Two Masters: Torn Between Company and Client

The Situation

Employees in financial services firms are sometimes confronted by conflicting allegiances between the company and its clients. In managing customers' stock portfolios, for example, the best timing for buy and sell decisions for clients' financial positions may not be the most profitable for the financial manager's firm. Investment managers, as a result, must choose a "right" course of action for reconciling possible conflicting interests.

The Dilemma

George Michaels is a customer portfolio manager employed by Premier Power Investments. His 35 clients—individual investors—have portfolios with market values ranging from $200 000 to $2 million in stocks, bonds, and mutual funds. Clients generally rely on George's recommendations to buy, sell, or hold each security based on his knowledge of their investment goals and risk tolerance, along with his experience in keeping up with market trends and holding down transactions costs. Premier Power Investments Company earns sales commissions ranging from 2 percent to 4 percent of market value for each buy and sell transaction.

On Monday morning, George's boss, Vicky Greene, informs George that due to Premier Power Investments Company's sagging revenues, it is to everyone's benefit to increase the number of transactions in customers' portfolios. She suggests that he find some different and attractive securities to replace existing securities for his customers. As George thinks about possible ways for accelerating his buy and sell recommendations, he has qualms about the motivation behind Vicky's comments. He is unsure what to do.

Team Activity

Assemble a group of four students and assign each group member to one of the following roles:

- George Michaels (employee)
- Vicky Greene (employer)
- portfolio owner (customer)
- owner (one of many outside shareholders of Premier Power Investments Company)

Questions for Discussion

1. Before discussing the situation with your group, and from the perspective of your assigned role, do you think there are any ethical issues in this situation? If so, write them down.
2. Return to your group and reveal any ethical issues that were identified by each member. Be especially aware of whether the different roles resulted in different kinds of ethical issues. Why might role differences result in dissimilar priorities on ethical issues?
3. For the various ethical issues that were identified, decide as a group which one is the most important for Premier Power Investments to resolve. Which issue is second in importance?
4. From an ethical standpoint, what does your group finally recommend be done to resolve the most important ethical issue? To resolve the second most important ethical issue?

Go to MyBizLab for additional cases and exercise material.

CONCLUDING CASE 19-1

Stock Market Games and the Dark Side of Financial Advising

The stock market is supposed to be a place where you can increase your assets over time if you invest wisely and have patience. But some people don't want to trust their financial situation to unpredictable markets, so they come up with creative (often illegal) ways to manipulate the market to ensure that they will get a positive outcome. Unfortunately, it only takes the bad behaviour of a few people to make it seem like the stock market is a haven for con artists. In the following paragraphs, several classic frauds are briefly described.

Manipulating Investor Funds

Vincent Lacroix (pictured), the founder of Norbourg Asset Management Inc., was found guilty of diverting $115 million from Norbourg into accounts that he and his wife controlled. Some investors lost their entire life savings. Lacroix was sentenced to 12 years in prison in 2009 and

fined $255 000, but after appealing his sentence and serving just one-sixth of the time, he was paroled and was actually living in a halfway house in 2012. Norbourg's accountant, Jean Cholette, and its director, Serge Beaugre, were also charged on 100 counts and received sentences of eight years each in 2011. The case was brought against Lacroix by the Autorité des marchés financiers (AMF), which is the securities watchdog in Quebec. The AMF itself is the target of a class action suit that claims that it didn't do enough to protect small investors.

Ponzi Schemes

Bernie Madoff confessed to running a Ponzi scheme that bilked investors out of $50 billion. A Ponzi scheme attracts investors by promising them that they will make very large returns, much larger than can normally be made. Investors who join the scheme early may indeed make large returns because they are being paid with money that is being contributed by later investors. But eventually the scheme collapses, and almost everyone loses their investment. For years, Madoff reported to investors that they were making 12 percent annually on their investment. That was about double what investors could normally be expected to make. But it is alleged that Madoff never invested anyone's money in anything. Rather, he simply falsified financial reports and told people that their "investments" were doing fine. Charitable organizations and rich individuals alike lost millions of dollars as a result of their investment with Madoff.

Earl Jones was sentenced to 11 years in prison after his scheme cost 158 Montreal investors a total of $50 million. He promised investors 12 percent returns but never invested a penny for them. Upon hearing the sentence, his own brother, Bevan Jones (who lost $1 million in this scheme), said that he thought the sentence was too lenient and that his brother should never see the light of day. Fortunately, in 2012 a class action suit against RBC Investments was settled for $17 million, which meant that defrauded investors could expect between 30 and 50 percent of their funds returned in the settlement. The plaintiffs claimed that Royal Bank turned a blind eye to Earl Jones's activities as he funnelled money from his account to buy properties in the United States and expensive cars while never investing a dime for his clients.

Insider Trading

Andrew Rankin was an investment banking star with RBC Dominion Securities when he was charged with insider trading and "tipping" his friend Daniel Duic about several big corporate deals that were about to

take place. Using the information provided by Rankin, Duic made over $4 million in profit by buying and selling the stocks of these companies at opportune times. When this was discovered, Duic made a deal with the Ontario Securities Commission to testify against his friend. Rankin was convicted of "tipping" and was sentenced to six months in jail. However, he appealed, and the Ontario Securities Commission agreed to withdraw the criminal charges and Rankin was spared jail time. Rankin was also fined $250 000 and barred for life from working in the securities industry.

In another case, Glen Harper, the president of Golden Rule Resources Ltd., was found guilty of insider trading. He had sold $4 million worth of shares in his company after he found out that its supposedly huge gold find in Ghana was in doubt. When Harper sold his shares, the price of Golden Rule's stock was about $13 per share. After the bad news became public, the stock fell to $0.10 a share. Harper was sentenced to one year in prison and fined nearly $4 million.

High-Closing

In this scheme, just before the stock exchange closes, a trader buys enough shares of a given stock that the price of that stock rises above the price of the previous trade. This makes it look as if the stock has upward momentum. The motivation to "high-close" a stock can be strong for money managers, because they are under intense pressure to increase the value of their portfolios so they can demonstrate high performance and attract more clients. The temptation is particularly strong at year-end because money managers' annual bonuses are tied to their performance.

Questions for Discussion

1. What factors determine the market price of a share of stock? Which of those factors were at work in the cases described above that dealt with the issue of stock prices?
2. What is the difference between debt and equity financing? Are the situations described above examples of debt or equity issues? Explain.
3. Consider the following statement: "*Insider trading should not be illegal. In a free-market economy, individuals who have the motivation and intelligence to gather information that allows them to make a lot of money should not be prevented from capitalizing on the information they have collected.*" Do you agree or disagree with the statement? Explain your reasoning.

CONCLUDING CASE 19-2

Bouncing Markets: Moving up, Going Down

From 2000 to 2012, stock markets in Canada and the United States were extremely volatile, with stock prices soaring during some time periods and dropping dramatically in others. What was causing this volatility? Here is the story.

In the late 1990s, thousands of Canadian and American investors became paper millionaires in a booming economy spurred by a vibrant stock market. Annual returns of 15 to 25 percent were commonplace as investors pumped money into the market at a record pace. Major market indexes—the Toronto Stock Exchange (S&P/TSX), the Dow Jones Industrial Average (DJIA), and the NASDAQ Composite—climbed to record highs. Dot-coms and other beneficiaries of the new economy led a parade toward record levels of wealth and prosperity. Government revenues grew so fast that legislators struggled to figure out how to spend the nation's newfound wealth. As investor assets rapidly accumulated, older workers began planning for early retirement.

Then something happened. A slowdown that had first surfaced in late 1999 gradually gained momentum and began to dampen stock prices in 2000. Soon the slowdown became an unmistakable retreat, particularly after it became apparent that many dot-com companies were simply grand-sounding ideas that were never going to be profitable. The stock market was also negatively affected by a series of corporate scandals involving well-known firms—Enron, Arthur Andersen, WorldCom, and a host of others—that caused both fear and anger in retirees, employees, and investors alike. The public's trust dwindled until, by the fall of 2002, the market had tumbled to its lowest level in years as wary investors pulled money out of stocks and went looking for safer investments. In 2000, the S&P/TSX was at 11 000, but it fell to 7000 by the summer of 2002. The NASDAQ Composite fell from a record high 5100 in 2000 to just above 1300 in mid-July 2002, losing 74 percent of its value. In that same period, the DJIA fell 32 percent.

To respond to the crisis of confidence and to get economies moving again, the Bank of Canada, the U.S. Federal Reserve, and other central banks around the world cut interest rates. This strategy worked. By mid-2003, markets were recovering, and there were positive economic signs—increases in sales and industrial production, low inflation, and strong consumer spending. But low interest rates eventually caused even bigger problems, especially in the United States. Why? One of the reasons was home mortgages, which could now be obtained with very low interest rates. People who had previously not been able to get a mortgage suddenly found that banks were willing to lend them money. With more people looking to buy a house, it was not surprising that house prices soared.

Another bubble was forming, this one caused not by dot-com companies but by housing. And, like all bubbles, it eventually burst. When it did (in 2006), house prices started dropping, and many people found that they owed more on their mortgage than their house was worth. This led to a wider financial crisis as banks and other financial institutions discovered that they had on their books literally trillions of dollars in mortgage loans that would likely never be repaid. Once this became clear to investors, they lost confidence in the stock prices of these (and other) companies, and stock markets plunged once again. As confidence eroded, companies began laying off employees in anticipation of tough times ahead. Consumers started spending less freely, and this worsened the problem.

The DJIA reached a peak of 14 000 in the fall of 2007, and then started dropping. In Canada, where there was no housing crisis, markets kept rising a bit longer. The S&P/TSX index reached 15 000 in June 2008, but as the problems in the U.S. economy spread around the world, all stock markets began to drop dramatically. By September 2008, the S&P/

TSX had dropped to 12 000 and by late October it was down to 9200. By February 2009, the index had dropped to 7500, meaning that it had lost half its value. Stunned investors realized that this drop was even worse than the one that had occurred in 2000–02. Stock market declines were not limited to Canada and the United States. Indexes in China, India, and Russia declined by 40 to 70 percent.

In 2009, most economists were predicting a deep and lengthy recession for the world economy. This meant that stock prices were going to be depressed for some time, perhaps years. Inevitably, there were comparisons to the great stock market crash that occurred in 1929. There is an old saying about the stock market that "there is greed on the way up and fear on the way down." And that is exactly what has been evident during the past 12 years. In both of the big run-ups, all sorts of people eagerly bought stocks in an attempt to cash in on the boom. But when the big declines started, everyone looked around in desperation for a way out.

By the summer of 2012, the S&P/TSX had stood at around 11 000 (exactly where it stood in the fall of 2009) and it continued to be quite volatile. This volatility was evidence that investors were jumpy and were responding to any data that suggested that the economic problems were (or were not) being resolved.

How long will it take the S&P/TSX to get back to 15 000? Well, after the stock market crashed in 1929, it took 25 years for the DJIA to get back to the high point it reached in 1929. Could that happen this time? Everyone hopes not, but investors now have some tough questions to answer. Should they stay in the market or get out (and take big losses if they sell)? Should they put their money in money market mutual funds? Should they gamble on further downfalls by selling short? How about buying more stock because current prices are so low?

Questions for Discussion

1. After reading this case, what have you learned or what can you say about the role of central banks (i.e., Bank of Canada, Federal Reserve) in the proper functioning of the economy and the stock market?

2. History holds many lessons for individual investors. However, quite often the enthusiasm or panic of the time takes control of the decision-making process. The present-day mood of the market often causes investors to act in irrational ways. What, if anything, can the government and securities authorities do to try to limit the damage in bad times and dampen expectations in good times?

3. Research the S&P/TSX index and chart the performance in the past three months, six months, one year, and three years. How is it performing overall? What is the level of volatility? (Find articles to support your findings.)

Financial Decisions and Risk Management

After reading this chapter, you should be able to:

1 Describe the responsibilities of a *financial manager*.

2 Distinguish between *short-term* (operating) and *long-term* (capital) expenditures.

3 Identify four sources of *short-term financing* for businesses.

4 Distinguish among the various sources of *long-term financing* and explain the risks involved in each.

5 Discuss some key issues in financial management for small businesses.

6 Explain how *risk* affects business operations and identify the five steps in the *risk management process*.

7 Explain the distinction between *insurable* and *uninsurable risks*, and distinguish among the different *types of insurance* purchased by businesses.

Hoarding Cash: Good or Bad Idea?

IN 2012, corporations in Europe, Japan, Canada, and the United States held large amounts of cash—a total of $7.75 *trillion* dollars, according to the Institute of International Finance. Canadian corporations were sitting on $475 billion in liquid assets, while U.S. corporations had almost $2 trillion. Canadian mining company Teck Resources Ltd. held $4.5 billion as a result of high prices for coal, copper, and other commodities the company mines. The company wanted to maintain a large cash balance because it expected lowered production of certain commodities and lower commodity prices in 2012 due to weaker demand. In Europe, the ratio of investment to GDP is at a 60-year low, even though companies have large amounts of cash and are maintaining so-called "fortress

balance sheets." In the United States, companies with fortress balance sheets include General Electric ($91 billion in cash), Pfizer ($36.4 billion), General Motors ($33 billion), and Coca-Cola ($13.8 billion). Technology companies hold particularly large amounts of cash (Apple, $97 billion; Microsoft, $41 billion; Cisco Systems, $40 billion; Google, $34 billion). While some Canadian companies do hold large amounts of cash, overall they are not nearly as cash-rich as U.S. companies. For example, the average cash-to-book-value of companies on the S&P 500 is 37.2 percent, but only 14.5 percent for companies on the S&P/TSX.

Hoarding of cash is viewed as a bad thing by many people. Critics say that companies made the financial crisis of 2008

worse because they hoarded cash instead of spending it on job creation. They argue that would have constituted a "second stimulus" beyond the government's stimulus spending. There were many specific critical comments. For example, a *Washington Post* columnist concluded that corporations that sit on large sums of money do not invest in any job-creating enterprises. *The Wall Street Journal* said that it would be good if cash-rich companies stepped up their hiring so that the high unemployment rate would be reduced. David Bianco, the chief equity strategist at Merrill Lynch, criticized chief financial officers of companies for holding too much cash, and said that cash hoarding was depressing share prices. He noted that shareholders were unhappy because dividend payout ratios were

near historical lows. Some critics went so far as to suggest a 2 percent tax on corporation cash balances. A study of 25 companies that had $10 billion or more cash on hand showed that their stock prices were underperforming compared to the general market, and that they had slow growth rates.

But financial managers have a different perspective on the appropriateness of holding large amounts of cash. Even though several years have passed since the economic downturn hit in 2008, financial managers are still wary. They see many possible problems on the horizon—the possibility of a "double-dip" recession, a slowdown in China's economy, volatility in commodity markets, and low consumer confidence, to name just a few. Financial managers are therefore being very conservative in how they manage cash. Cost-cutting and cash hoarding have become key strategies, and financial managers have adopted a wait-and-see attitude before spending large amounts of money on things like hiring more staff.

The view that it is bad for financial managers to hoard cash is also challenged by Alan Reynolds, a senior fellow at the U.S.-based Cato Institute. He says that such a view reveals ignorance about basic financial realities. (He analyzes data from U.S. corporations, but the same principles apply to Canadian companies.) Reynolds makes four key points. First, net worth, not the form in which assets are held (e.g., cash, accounts receivable, fixed assets, etc.), indicates the health of a corporation. The net worth of U.S. nonfinancial corporations dropped from $15.9 trillion in 2007 to $12.6 trillion in 2011. The ratio of cash to total assets rose because the value of total assets fell, not because the corporation was hoarding large amounts of cash. Second, liquid assets like cash serve as a safety cushion to deal with unexpected business difficulties. To characterize the holding of cash as "hoarding" without also considering the level of short-term debt is meaningless. U.S. corporations hold nearly $2 trillion in cash, but that is far less than the $3.67 trillion in short-term debt on their books. Third, there is a big difference between the assets a corporation owns (which are shown on the balance sheet) and the money it spends and receives (which is shown on the income statement). Companies don't draw down assets (liquid or otherwise) to meet payroll expenses; rather, they add workers when they think that they can increase their after-tax revenues by doing so. Fourth, the idea that investing in liquid assets (e.g., bonds, time deposits, and mutual funds) somehow reduces hiring is simply wrong. Corporations can, and do, make capital expenditures (e.g., in buildings and inventories) at the same time they are making investments in liquid assets. It's also true that even if cash-rich technology companies like Apple spend some of their cash, it would likely create jobs in foreign countries, not in North America. ◆

The Role of the Financial Manager

LO1 Describe the responsibilities of a *financial manager*.

financial managers Those managers responsible for planning and overseeing the financial resources of a firm.

finance (or corporate finance) The business function involving decisions about a firm's long-term investments and obtaining the funds to pay for those investments.

Financial managers plan and control the acquisition and dispersal of the company's financial assets. The business activity known as **finance (or corporate finance)** involves four responsibilities:

■ determining a firm's long-term investments

■ obtaining funds to pay for those investments

■ conducting the firm's everyday financial activities

■ helping to manage the risks that the firm takes

In recent years, more and more chief financial officers (CFOs) have been appointed as chief executives officers (CEOs). For example, at Pepsico, Indra Nooyi was promoted from CFO to CEO. About 20 percent of CEOs were formerly CFOs.[1] The skill set of CFOs is expanding because they have access to a great deal of information about the internal workings of companies, and because they are responsible for setting budgets and dealing with regulatory agencies.[2]

Objectives of the Financial Manager

A financial manager's overall objective is to increase a firm's value—and thus shareholders' wealth. To achieve this goal, financial managers collect funds, pay debts, establish trade credit, obtain loans, control cash balances, and plan for future financial needs. Whereas accountants create data to reflect a firm's financial status, financial managers make decisions for improving that status. Financial managers must ensure that a company earns a profit.

Responsibilities of the Financial Manager

The key responsibilities of the financial manager are *cash flow management*, *financial control*, and *financial planning*.

Cash Flow Management

cash flow management Managing the pattern in which cash flows into the firm in the form of revenues and out of the firm in the form of debt payments.

To increase a firm's value, financial managers must ensure that it has enough funds on hand to purchase the materials and human resources that it needs to produce goods and services. Funds that are not needed immediately must be invested to earn more money for a firm. This activity—**cash flow management**—requires careful planning. If excess cash balances are allowed to sit idle instead of being invested, a firm loses the cash returns it could have earned. By putting idle cash to work, firms not only gain additional income, they also avoid having to borrow from outside sources. These savings can be substantial.

Financial Control

Financial control is the process of checking actual performance against plans to ensure that the desired financial status occurs. For example, actual revenues usually turn out to be higher or lower than planned revenues because sales are unpredictable. Control involves monitoring revenue inflows and making appropriate financial adjustments. Excessively high revenues may be deposited in short-term interest-bearing accounts, or they may be used to pay off short-term debt. In contrast, lower-than-expected revenues may necessitate short-term borrowing to meet current debt obligations.

Budgets (see Chapter 14) are the key to financial control. The budget provides the "measuring stick" against which performance is evaluated. The cash flows, debts, and assets of each department and the whole company are compared at regular intervals against budgeted amounts. Discrepancies indicate the need for financial adjustments so that resources are used to the best advantage.

financial control The process of checking actual performance against plans to ensure that the desired financial status is achieved.

Financial Planning

A **financial plan** describes a firm's strategies for reaching a desired future financial position. In 2012, for example, Canadian Pacific Railway Ltd. announced that it would make strategic investments totalling $1.2 billion in order to improve its operating ratio (which, in 2011, was the worst among North America's Big Six railways).[3] When constructing a financial plan, several questions must be answered:

financial plan A description of how a business will reach some financial position it seeks for the future; includes projections for sources and uses of funds.

- What amount of funds does the company need to meet immediate plans?

- When will it need more funds?

- Where can it get the funds to meet both its short-term and its long-term needs?

To answer these questions, a financial manager must develop a clear picture of *why* a firm needs funds. Managers also assess the relative costs and benefits of potential funding sources. In the sections that follow, we explain why businesses need funds and identify the main sources of business funding for both the short term and the long term.

Financial managers have the responsibility of ensuring that the financial assets of a company are used effectively. This includes investments it may have in other companies in the form of shares of stock. Regular assessment of how these investments are performing is an important responsibility of financial managers.

Why Do Businesses Need Funds?

LO2 Distinguish between *short-term* (operating) and *long-term* (capital) expenditures.

Every company needs money to survive. Failure to make a contractually obligated payment can lead to bankruptcy and the dissolution of the firm. To be effective, financial managers must make a distinction between *short-term (operating) expenditures* and *long-term (capital) expenditures*.

Short-Term (Operating) Expenditures

A firm makes short-term expenditures regularly in its everyday business activities. To handle these expenditures, financial managers must pay attention to *accounts payable*, *accounts receivable*, *inventories*, and *working capital*.

Accounts Payable

As noted in Chapter 14, accounts payable are unpaid bills owed to suppliers, plus wages and taxes due within the upcoming year. For most companies, this is the largest single category of short-term debt. To plan for funding flows, financial managers want to know *in advance* the amounts of new accounts payable as well as when they must be paid. For information about such obligations and needs—for example, the quantity of supplies required by a certain department in an upcoming period—financial managers must rely on other managers. (The Exercising Your Ethics feature at the end of the chapter presents an interesting dilemma regarding accounts payable.)

Accounts Receivable

Accounts receivable consist of funds due from customers who have bought on credit. Because accounts receivable represent an investment in products for which a firm has not yet received payment, they temporarily tie up its funds. Clearly, the seller wants to receive payment as quickly as possible. A sound financial plan requires financial managers to project accurately how much credit is advanced to buyers, and when they will make payments on their accounts. For example, managers at Kraft Foods must know how many dollars' worth of cheddar cheese Safeway supermarkets will order each month, as well as Safeway's payment schedule.

credit policy Rules governing a firm's extension of credit to customers.

Credit Policies. Predicting payment schedules is a function of **credit policy**—the rules governing a firm's extension of credit to customers. This policy sets standards as to which buyers are eligible for what type of credit. Typically, credit is extended to customers who have the ability to pay and who honour their obligations. Credit is denied to firms with poor payment histories.

Credit policy also sets payment terms. For example, credit terms of "2/10, net 30" mean that the selling company offers a 2 percent discount if the customer pays within 10 days. The customer has 30 days to pay the regular price. Under these terms, the buyer would have to pay only $980 on a $1000 invoice on days 1 to 10, but $1000 on days 11 to 30. The higher the discount, the more incentive buyers have to pay early. Sellers can thus adjust credit terms to influence when customers pay their bills.

inventory Materials and goods currently held by the company that will be sold within the year.

raw materials inventory That portion of a firm's inventory consisting of basic supplies used to manufacture products for sale.

work-in-process inventory That portion of a firm's inventory consisting of goods partway through the production process.

Inventories

Between the time a firm buys raw materials and the time it sells finished products, it ties up funds in **inventory**—materials and goods that it will sell within the year. Too little inventory of any kind can cost a firm sales, while too much inventory means that funds are tied up and cannot be used elsewhere. The basic supplies a firm buys to use in its production process are its **raw materials inventory**. Levi Strauss's raw materials inventory includes huge rolls of denim. **Work-in-process inventory** consists of goods partway through the production process. Jeans that are cut out but not yet sewn are part of the work-in-process inventory. Finally, **finished goods inventory** refers to items that are ready for sale. Completed blue jeans ready for shipment to dealers are finished goods inventory.

finished goods inventory That portion of a firm's inventory consisting of completed goods ready for sale.

Working Capital

Working capital is the difference between a firm's current assets and current liabilities. It is a liquid asset out of which current debts can be paid. A company calculates its working capital by adding up the following:

- inventories—that is, raw materials, work-in-process, and finished goods on hand

- accounts receivable (minus accounts payable)

Large companies typically devote 20 cents of every sales dollar to working capital. If companies can reduce working capital, they benefit because every dollar that is not tied up in working capital becomes a dollar of more useful cash flow. Reducing working capital also raises earnings permanently because money costs money (in interest payments and the like). Reducing working capital means saving money.

Long-Term (Capital) Expenditures

Companies also need funds to cover long-term expenditures for fixed assets. *Fixed assets* are items that have a lasting use or value, such as land, buildings, and machinery. In 2012, for example, Walmart Canada spent $750 million on remodelling, expanding, or relocating 73 different retail outlets.[4] Long-term expenditures differ from short-term outlays in the following ways, all of which influence the ways that long-term outlays are funded:

- Unlike inventories and other short-term assets, they are not normally sold or converted into cash.

- Their acquisition requires a very large investment.

- They represent a binding commitment of company funds that continues long into the future.

Sources of Short-Term Funds

Firms can call on many sources for the funds they need to finance day-to-day operations and to implement short-term plans. These sources include *trade credit, secured* and *unsecured loans,* and *factoring accounts receivable.*

Identify four sources of *short-term financing* for businesses.

Trade Credit

Trade credit—the granting of credit by one firm to another—is effectively a short-term loan. The most common form is **open-book credit**, which is essentially a "gentlemen's agreement." Buyers receive merchandise along with invoices stating credit terms. Sellers ship products on faith that payment will be forthcoming on the due date. If sellers want more reassurance, they may insist that buyers sign legally binding **promissory notes** before merchandise is shipped. The agreement states when and how much money will be paid to the seller. The **trade draft** is attached to the merchandise shipment by the seller and states the promised date and amount of payment due. To take possession of the merchandise, the buyer must sign the draft. Once signed by the buyer, the document becomes a **trade acceptance**. Trade drafts and trade acceptances are useful forms of credit in international transactions.

trade credit The granting of credit by a selling firm to a buying firm.

open-book credit Form of trade credit in which sellers ship merchandise on faith that payment will be forthcoming.

promissory note Form of trade credit in which buyers sign promise-to-pay agreements before merchandise is shipped.

trade draft Form of trade credit in which buyers must sign statements of payment terms attached to merchandise by sellers.

trade acceptance Trade draft that has been signed by the buyer.

Trade credit insurance is available for sellers (particularly Canadian companies that export to the United States) who are concerned that buyers may not pay their bills. Premiums are generally 1 to 2 percent of the value of the goods that are being sold (there is a 10 percent deductible provision). Montreal-based ELPRO International Inc., an exporter of luggage and handbags, is happy it bought trade credit insurance, because one of its U.S. customers suddenly went out of business and didn't pay what it owed. ELPRO received payment for the shipment from the insurance company.[5]

Secured Short-Term Loans

secured loan A short-term loan for which the borrower is required to put up collateral.

collateral Any asset that a lender has the right to seize if a borrower does not repay a loan.

For most firms, bank loans are a vital source of short-term funding. Such loans almost always involve a promissory note in which the borrower promises to repay the loan plus interest. In **secured loans**, banks require the borrower to put up **collateral**—assets that the bank can seize if loan payments are not made as promised. Secured loans allow borrowers to get funds when they might not qualify for unsecured credit. Secured loans generally carry lower interest rates than unsecured loans. Most short-term business borrowing is secured by inventories and accounts receivable.

Inventory as Collateral

When a loan is made with inventory as collateral, the lender loans the borrower some portion of the stated value of the inventory. Inventory is attractive as collateral when it can be readily converted into cash. Boxes full of expensive, partially completed lenses for eyeglasses aren't very valuable on the open market, but a thousand crates of canned tomatoes might well be convertible into cash.

Accounts Receivable as Collateral

pledging accounts receivable Using accounts receivable as collateral for a loan.

When accounts receivable are used as collateral, the process is called **pledging accounts receivable**. In the event of nonpayment, the lender may seize the receivables—that is, funds owed the borrower by its customers. This option is especially important to service companies such as accounting firms and law offices. Because they do not maintain inventories, accounts receivable are their main source of collateral. Typically, lenders who will accept accounts receivable as collateral are financial institutions with credit departments capable of evaluating the quality of the receivables.

Factoring Accounts Receivable. A firm can raise funds by *factoring*—selling the firm's accounts receivable. The purchaser of the receivables, usually a financial institution, is known as the factor. The factor pays some percentage of the full amount of receivables. The seller gets this money immediately. For example, a factor might buy $40 000 worth of receivables for 60 percent of that sum ($24 000). The factor profits to the extent that the money it eventually collects exceeds the amount it paid. This profit depends on the quality of the receivables, the cost of collecting them, and interest rates.

Unsecured Short-Term Loans

unsecured loan A short-term loan in which the borrower is not required to put up collateral.

With an **unsecured loan**, the borrower does not have to put up collateral. In many cases, however, the bank requires the borrower to maintain a *compensating balance*—, that is, the borrower must keep a portion of the loan amount on deposit with the bank in a non-interest-bearing account.

The terms of the loan—amount, duration, interest rate, and payment schedule—are negotiated between the bank and the borrower. To receive an unsecured loan, a firm must ordinarily have a good banking relationship with the lender. Once an agreement is made, a promissory note will be executed and the funds transferred to the borrower. Although some unsecured loans are one-time-only arrangements, many take the form of *lines of credit*, *revolving credit agreements*, or *commercial paper*.

Lines of Credit

A **line of credit** is a standing agreement with a bank to lend a firm a maximum amount of funds on request (although the bank does not guarantee that the funds will always be available when requested). For example, suppose that the Bank of Montreal gives Sunshine Tanning Inc. a $100 000 line of credit for the coming year. By signing promissory notes, Sunshine's borrowings can total up to $100 000 at any time. Sunshine benefits from the arrangement by knowing that the bank regards the firm as creditworthy and will loan funds to it on short notice.

line of credit A standing agreement between a bank and a firm in which the bank specifies the maximum amount it will make available to the borrower for a short-term unsecured loan; the borrower can then draw on those funds, when available.

Revolving Credit Agreements

With a **revolving credit** agreement, a lender agrees to make a specified amount of money available on demand to a firm for continuing short-term loans. The lending institution guarantees that funds will be available when sought by the borrower. The bank charges a *commitment fee* (usually 0.5 to 1 percent of the committed amount), which is a charge for holding open a line of credit for a customer even if the customer does not borrow any funds. For example, suppose that the Bank of Montreal agrees to lend Sunshine Tanning up to $100 000 under a revolving credit agreement. If Sunshine borrows $80 000, it still has access to $20 000. If it pays off $50 000 of the debt, reducing its debt to $30 000, then it has $70 000 available to it. Sunshine pays interest on the borrowed funds and also pays a fee on the unused funds in the line of credit.

revolving credit agreement A guaranteed line of credit for which the firm pays the bank interest on funds borrowed as well as a fee for extending the line of credit.

Commercial Paper

Some large and creditworthy firms can raise short-term funds by issuing **commercial paper**. Here's how it works: A corporation issues commercial paper with a face value, but buyers pay less than that value. At the end of a specified period (usually 30 to 90 days but legally up to 270 days), the issuing company buys back the paper—*at the face value*. The difference between the price the buying company paid and the face value is the buyer's profit. For example, if CN needs to borrow $10 million for 90 days, it might issue commercial paper with a face value of $10.2 million. An insurance company with excess cash might buy the paper for $10 million. After 90 days, CN would pay $10.2 million to the insurance company. (See Concluding Case 20-1 for the story of how serious problems developed in the commercial paper market in Canada.)

commercial paper A method of short-run fundraising in which a firm sells unsecured notes for less than the face value and then repurchases them at the face value within 270 days; buyers' profits are the difference between the original price paid and the face value.

Sources of Long-Term Funds

L04 Distinguish among the various sources of *long-term financing* and explain the risks involved in each.

Firms need long-term funding to finance expenditures on fixed assets—the buildings and equipment necessary for conducting their business. They may seek long-term funds through *debt financing* (that is, from outside the firm), *equity financing* (by drawing on internal sources), or *hybrid financing* (a middle ground). In making decisions about sources of long-term funds, companies must consider the *risk–return relationship*.

Debt Financing

debt financing Raising money to meet long-term expenditures by borrowing from outside the company; usually takes the form of long-term loans or the sale of corporate bonds.

Long-term borrowing from outside the company—**debt financing**—is a major component of most firms' long-term financial planning. The two primary sources of such funding are *long-term loans* and the sale of *corporate bonds*.

Long-Term Loans

Most corporations get their long-term loans from a chartered bank, usually one with which the firm has developed a long-standing relationship. Credit companies (like Household Finance Corp.), insurance companies, and pension funds also grant long-term business loans. The interest rate the borrower must pay is negotiated between the borrower and the lender. Although some bank loans have fixed rates, others have floating rates tied to the prime rate (the rate the bank charges its most creditworthy customers). For example, a loan at 1 percent above prime is payable at one percentage point higher than the prime rate. This rate may fluctuate, or float, because the prime rate itself goes up and down as market conditions change.

Long-term loans are attractive to borrowers for several reasons:

- Because the number of parties involved is limited, loans can often be arranged very quickly.

- The firm need not make public disclosure of its business plans or the purpose for which it is acquiring the loan (in contrast, the issuance of corporate bonds requires such disclosure).

- The duration of the loan can be matched to the borrower's needs.

- If the firm's needs change, the terms of the loan can usually be changed.

Long-term loans also have some disadvantages. Large borrowers may have trouble finding lenders to supply enough funds, they may have restrictions placed on them as conditions of the loan, they may have to pledge long-term assets as collateral, and they may have to agree not to take on any more debt until the borrowed funds are repaid.

Corporate Bonds

bond indenture Statement of the terms of a corporate bond.

A corporate *bond* is a contract—a promise by the issuing company or organization to pay the holder a certain amount of money on a specified date. Most bonds pay the bondholder a stipulated sum of interest annually or semi-annually. In many cases, bonds may not be redeemed for 30 years from the time of issue. The **bond indenture** spells out the terms of a bond, including the amount to be paid, the interest rate, and the maturity (payoff) date. The indenture also identifies which of the firm's assets, if any, are pledged as collateral for the bonds. If the company fails to make a bond payment, it is in *default*.

Bonds are attractive when companies need large amounts of funds for long periods of time. The issuing company gets access to large numbers of lenders through nationwide bond markets. But bonds involve expensive administrative and selling costs. They also may require very high interest payments if the issuing company has a poor credit rating. Because of the risk of default, debt financing appeals most strongly to

BELLSOUTH TELECOMMUNICATIONS, INC.

FORTY YEAR 8¼% DEBENTURE, DUE JULY 1, 2032

This corporate bond was issued by BellSouth Telecommunications, Inc. The company will use the money to purchase items like buildings and machinery that are necessary for the production of goods.

MANAGING IN TURBULENT TIMES

The European Debt Crisis Goes On and On ... and On

Individuals and businesses must make sure that the debt they carry does not exceed their capacity to do so. The same thing is true for sovereign nations. Well, sort of. Consider the problems that Greece has experienced. In 2010, concerns arose about the country's ability to pay back investors who had purchased its government bonds. During 2010 and 2011, many meetings were held that focused on solving the problem, but no clear resolution emerged. Eventually it became apparent that some investors were going to take a "haircut" (i.e., lose part of their investment), but there was a disagreement about whether it would be public creditors like the European Central Bank (ECB) and euro zone governments, or private creditors like banks, hedge funds, and asset managers. The ECB resisted taking a haircut because that might cause people to think that the ECB would be less willing in the future to buy the bonds of other countries that were in financial trouble.

In an attempt to resolve Greece's problems, the European Central Bank (ECB) gave the country a $300-billion bailout on the condition that Greece introduce austerity measures (like cutting wages and increasing taxes). Citizens then rioted in the streets, protesting high unemployment levels, low economic growth, and business bankruptcies. In February 2012, the Greek parliament passed a new round of austerity measures that reduced pensions and the minimum wage. The measures that demanded by euro zone finance ministers as proof that Greece was *really* serious about getting its financial house in order. The austerity measures created a deep recession in Greece, driving unemployment above 20 percent (53 percent among youth).

On March 8, 2012, an agreement was reached that gave Greece a $170-billion rescue deal that allowed it to make payments on bonds that were coming due on March 20. Private investors took losses of up to 75 percent of their investment. The ECB took no losses. But in May 2012, an election in Greece resulted in even more uncertainty when no party received enough votes to form a government. The likelihood of Greece exiting from the euro increased again.

A great clash of ideologies is evident as attempts are made to solve this problem. One school of thought says that European governments should introduce big stimulus programs (like those in the United States) to increase economic growth. People who support this idea also claim that Germany is benefiting from the problem because the uncertainty has caused the euro to decline in value, and this has made German exports very attractive (Germany's level of unemployment is the lowest in 40 years). German leaders respond by saying that they are tired of bailing out countries like Greece that do not control their government spending, and that austerity is necessary to reduce government debt.

Critical Thinking Questions

1. Why was progress toward a solution to Greece's problems so slow?

2. What would happen to individual Canadian consumers or Canadian corporations who consistently spent more money than they earned?

companies that have predictable profits and cash flow patterns. For example, demand for electric power is quite steady from year to year and predictable from month to month. Thus, provincial hydroelectric utility companies enjoy steady streams of income and can carry substantial amounts of debt. With equity markets in turmoil, many companies have turned to the bond market. In 2011, Canadian companies borrowed $68.7 billion, which was 7.5 percent more than in 2010. The Royal Bank arranged $21.5 billion of the total, and has been the bond leader for many years.[6]

Debt financing is important for sovereign nations as well as for individual companies (see the insert entitled "The European Debt Crisis Goes On and On … and On").

Equity Financing

equity financing Raising money to meet long-term expenditures by issuing common stock or by retaining earnings.

Equity financing takes the form of *issuing common stock* or of *retaining the firm's earnings*. Both options involve putting the owners' capital to work.

Issuing Common Stock

By selling shares of stock, the company gets the funds it needs for buying land, buildings, and equipment. Suppose that Sunshine Tanning's founders invested $10 000 by buying the original 500 shares of common stock (at $20 per share) in 2003. If the company used these funds to buy equipment and succeeded financially, by 2012 it might need funds for expansion. A pattern of profitable operations and regularly paid dividends might allow Sunshine to raise $50 000 by selling 500 new shares of stock for $100 per share. This additional paid-in capital would increase the total shareholders' equity to $60 000, as shown in Table 20.1.

The use of equity financing via common stock can be expensive because paying dividends is more expensive than paying bond interest. This is because interest paid to bondholders is tax deductible, but dividends paid to shareholders are not. Even though equity financing is expensive, financial managers cannot rely totally on debt capital because long-term loans and bonds carry fixed interest rates and represent a promise to pay regardless of the profitability of the firm. If the firm defaults on its obligations, it may lose its assets and even go into bankruptcy. In 2012, for example, Yellow Media Inc. was trying to pay off a $1.5 billion debt it had accumulated. To get money to pay bondholders, the company cut off dividends for preferred shareholders, but that caused the value of those shares to drop by up to 55 percent. Common shares dropped in value by 97 percent.[7]

Retained Earnings

As we saw in Chapter 14, *retained earnings* are profits that have not been paid out as dividends. Using retained earnings means that the firm will not have to borrow money and pay interest on loans or bonds. When Hertz bought out the Dollar Thrifty Automotive Group for US$1.17 billion, about 80 percent of that deal was financed with cash from Hertz, with the remaining 20 percent coming in the form of Hertz stock.[8]

TABLE 20.1 Shareholders' Equity for Sunshine Tanning	
Common Shareholders' Equity, 2003	
Initial common stock (500 shares issued @ $20 per share, 2003)	$10 000
Total shareholders' equity	$10 000
Common Shareholders' Equity, 2012	
Initial common stock (500 shares issued @ $20 per share, 2003)	$10 000
Additional paid-in capital (500 shares issued @ $100 per share, 2012)	50 000
Total shareholders' equity	$60 000

There are some practical limitations in using retained earnings. For example, if Sunshine Tanning had net earnings of $50 000 in 2012, it could pay a $50-per-share dividend on its 1000 shares of common stock. But if it plans to remodel at a cost of $30 000 and therefore retains $30 000 of earnings to finance the project, only $20 000 is left to distribute for stock dividends ($20 per share).

Hybrid Financing: Preferred Stock

Preferred stock is a hybrid because it has some of the features of corporate bonds and some features of common stocks. As with bonds, payments on preferred stock are for fixed amounts, such as $6 per share per year. Unlike bonds, however, preferred stock never matures. It can be held indefinitely, like common stock. And dividends need not be paid if the company makes no profit. If dividends are paid, preferred shareholders receive them first, in preference to dividends on common stock.

A major advantage of preferred stock to the issuing corporation is its flexibility. It secures funds for the firm without relinquishing control, since preferred shareholders have no voting rights. And it does not require repayment of principal or payment of dividends in lean times.

Choosing Between Debt and Equity Financing

A key part of financial planning involves striking a balance between debt and equity financing to meet the firm's long-term need for funds. The mix of debt vs. equity is the firm's **capital structure**. Financial plans contain targets for the capital structure, such as 40 percent debt and 60 percent equity. But choosing a target is not easy. A wide range of debt-vs.-equity mixes is possible.

capital structure Relative mix of a firm's debt and equity financing.

The most conservative strategy is to use all equity financing and no debt because a company has no formal obligations for financial payouts. At the other extreme, the strategy is to use all debt financing. While less expensive than equity funding, indebtedness increases the risk that a firm will be unable to meet its obligations and will go bankrupt. Financial planners try to find a mix between these two extremes that will maximize shareholder wealth. Figure 20.1 summarizes the factors that must be taken into account when deciding between debt and equity financing.

Indexes of Financial Risk

To help understand and measure the amount of financial risk they face, financial managers often rely on published indexes for various investments. *Financial World*, for example, publishes independent appraisals of mutual funds, using risk-reward ratings of "A" (very good) to "E" (poor) to indicate each fund's riskiness in comparison with its anticipated financial returns. An A-rated fund is judged to offer very good returns relative to the amount of risk involved. An E-rated fund carries the greatest risk with smaller returns. Similarly, Standard & Poor's publishes various indexes for numerous funds and for stocks that are available for purchase by financial managers.

The Risk-Return Relationship

When developing plans for raising capital, financial managers have to take into account the different motivations of individual investors, because these motivations determine why some individuals and firms invest in stocks while others invest only in bonds.

If bond rating agencies like Moody's, Standard & Poor's, or Fitch downgrade a company's ratings to low enough levels, its bonds become junk bonds. When that happens, investors demand higher interest rates to reflect the increased risk of investing in the company.

Debt Financing

Equity Financing

When must it be repaid?

Fixed deadline	No limit

Will it make claims on income?

Yes, regular and fixed	Only residual claims

Will it have claims on assets?

In liquidation, creditors come first	In liquidation, shareholders must wait until creditors are paid, and preferred equity precedes common equity

Will it affect management control?

No	May cause challenge for corporation control

How are taxes affected?

Bond interest is deductible	Dividends are not deductible

Will it affect management flexibility?

Yes, many constraints	No, few constraints

FIGURE 20.1

Comparing debt and equity financing.

risk–return relationship Shows the amount of risk and the likely rate of return on various financial instruments.

Investors give money to firms and, in return, anticipate receiving future cash flows. But some cash flows are more certain than others. Investors generally expect to receive higher payments for higher uncertainty. Each type of investment has a risk–return relationship. Figure 20.2 shows the general **risk–return relationship** for various financial instruments. High-grade corporate bonds, for example, rate low in terms of risk on future returns but also low on the size of expected returns. The reverse is true of junk bonds, those with a higher risk of default. Over time, a company can reposition itself on the risk continuum by improving its record on dividends, interest payments, and debt repayment.

Financial Management for Small Businesses

L05 Discuss some key issues in financial management for small businesses.

One of the key problems with new businesses is inadequate funding. Why are so many start-ups underfunded? For one thing, entrepreneurs often underestimate the value of establishing *bank credit* as a source of funds and use *trade credit* ineffectively. In addition, they often fail to consider *venture capital* as a source of funding, and they are notorious for not *planning cash flow needs* properly. Many small business owners are also not aware of government programs that are avail-

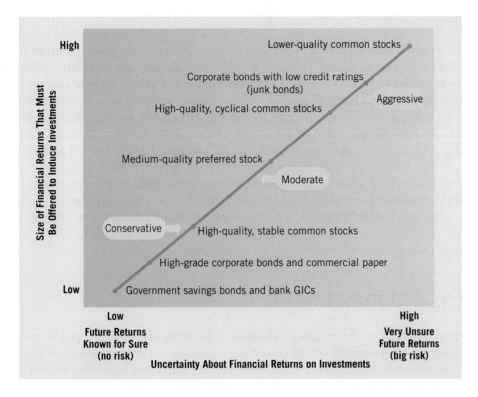

FIGURE 20.2

The risk–return relationship.

able for support. For example, programs like the Canada Small Business Funding Program enable entrepreneurs to receive up to $350 000 worth of loans and up to $500 000 for the purchase of real property. Each year the program provides approximately 10 000 loans totalling over $1 billion of financing.[9] Of course, companies that do not apply, or are unaware of the program, get nothing even if they are good potential candidates.

Establishing Bank Credit and Trade Credit

Some banks have liberal credit policies and offer financial analysis, cash flow planning, and suggestions based on experiences with other local firms. Some provide loans to small businesses in bad times and work to keep them going. Obtaining credit, therefore, begins with finding a bank that can—and will—support a small firm's financial needs. Once a line of credit is obtained, the small business can seek more liberal credit policies from other businesses. Sometimes, for instance, suppliers give customers longer credit periods—say, 45 or 60 days rather than 30 days. Liberal trade credit terms with their suppliers let firms increase short-term funds and avoid additional borrowing from banks.

Start-up firms without proven financial success usually must present a business plan to demonstrate that the firm is a good credit risk.[10] As we saw in Chapter 4, a business plan is a document that tells potential lenders why the money is needed, the amount needed, how the money will be used to improve the company, and when it will be paid back.

Venture Capital

Many newer businesses—especially those undergoing rapid growth—cannot get the funds they need through borrowing alone. They may, therefore, turn to **venture capital**—outside equity funding provided in return for part-ownership of the borrowing firm. Venture capital was discussed in Chapter 4.

venture capital Outside equity financing provided in return for part-ownership of the borrowing firm.

Planning for Cash Flow Requirements

All businesses should plan for their cash flows, but it is especially important for small businesses to do so. Success or failure may hinge on anticipating times when cash will be short and when excess cash is expected. Figure 20.3 shows possible cash inflows, cash outflows, and net cash position (inflows minus outflows) on a month-by-month basis for Slippery Fish Bait Supply. In this highly seasonal business, bait stores buy heavily from Slippery during the spring and summer months. Revenues outpace expenses, leaving surplus funds that can be invested. During the fall and winter, expenses exceed revenues. Slippery must borrow funds to keep going until sales revenues pick up again in the spring. Comparing predicted cash inflows from sales with outflows for expenses shows the firm's monthly cash flow position.

By anticipating shortfalls, a financial manager can seek funds in advance and minimize their cost. By anticipating excess cash, a manager can plan to put the funds to work in short-term, interest-earning investments.

Risk Management

Risk—uncertainty about future events—is a factor in every manager's job because nearly every managerial action creates the possibility for either positive or negative outcomes. Risk management is essential because Canadian businesses face risks in many different areas—the company's computer network may be hacked into, interest rates may change, executive talent may be raided by another company, a natural disaster or terrorist attack may occur, consumers may sue the company, or a recession may occur. Businesses cope with these risks by taking various steps, including creating a top-level executive position to oversee risk management, buying insurance to shield the company from various kinds of risks, and instituting control systems that will reduce the risk that inappropriate employee behaviour will cause financial harm to the company.

Companies have traditionally had a chief executive officer (CEO), a chief operating officer (COO), and a chief financial officer (CFO), but not too many of them have had chief risk officers (CRO). But that is rapidly changing. At Coast Capital Savings

L06 Explain how *risk* affects business operations and identify the five steps in the *risk management process.*

risk Uncertainty about future events.

FIGURE 20.3

Cash flow for Slippery Fish Bait Supply.

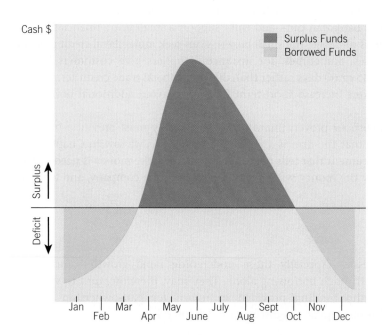

Credit Union, for example, the CRO focuses on protecting the company against online fraud, holdups, and information system failures.[11] Hydro One Inc. also has a CRO, partly because the deregulation of electricity means that it needs to manage the risk of price fluctuations in the new market-based pricing system.[12]

The financial crisis that erupted in 2008 caused many firms to take a second look at their risk management practices. For example, the Caisse de dépôt et placement du Québec incurred heavy losses in 2008 as a result of its involvement in currency- and stock-related derivatives and the commercial paper crisis.[13] The Bank of Montreal (BMO) also had problems and reported writedowns of $490 million in 2008. That was on top of the $850-million charge it incurred as the result of fraud committed by one of its traders (see Concluding Case 20-2 for details). As a result of those losses, BMO did a complete review of its risk management systems and procedures. The CEO admitted that BMO got involved in some business activities that were beyond the company's risk tolerance and strategic plan.[14]

According to a survey of 600 executives conducted by Toronto-based recruitment firm Watson Gardner Brown, the most difficult jobs to staff are in the risk management and compliance areas. Why? Because firms are increasing the size of these divisions due to the scandals and the meltdown in some securities in recent years. Institutional investors are demanding more attention to risk oversight before they will trust their funds to such organizations. Finding enough highly qualified people to fill these spots, even with generous salaries, has been a challenge.[15]

Coping with Risk

Speculative risks involve the possibility of *gain* or *loss*, while **pure risks** involve only the possibility of *loss* or *no loss*. Manufacturing and selling a new product, for example, is a speculative risk, while the chance of a warehouse fire is a pure risk. For a company to survive and prosper, it must manage both types of risk in a cost-effective manner. **Risk management** is the process of "conserving the firm's earning power and assets by reducing the threat of losses due to uncontrollable events."[16] It is the logical development and implementation of a plan to deal with chance losses. The risk management process usually involves the five steps outlined in Figure 20.4.

speculative risk An event that offers the chance for either a gain or a loss.

pure risk An event that offers no possibility of gain; it offers only the chance of a loss.

risk management Conserving a firm's (or an individual's) financial power or assets by minimizing the financial effect of accidental losses.

FIGURE 20.4

The risk management process.

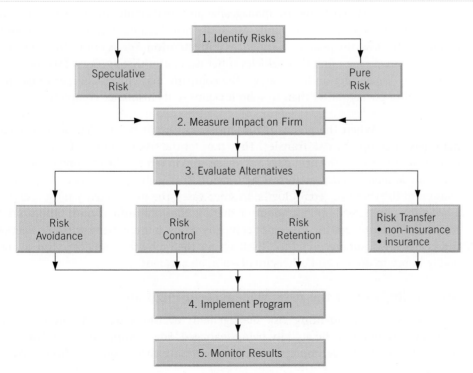

Step 1: Identify Risks and Potential Losses

Managers analyze a firm's risks to identify potential losses. For example, a firm with a fleet of delivery trucks can expect that one of them will eventually be involved in an accident. The accident may cause bodily injury to the driver or to others, may cause physical damage to the truck or other vehicles, or both.

Step 2: Measure the Frequency and Severity of Losses and Their Impact

To measure the frequency and severity of losses, managers must consider both past history and current activities. How often can the firm expect the loss to occur? What is the likely size of the loss in dollars? For example, our firm with the fleet of delivery trucks may have had two accidents per year in the past. If it adds trucks, however, it may reasonably expect the frequency of accidents to increase.

Step 3: Evaluate Alternatives and Choose the Techniques That Will Best Handle the Losses

Having identified and measured potential losses, managers are in a better position to decide how to handle them. With this third step, they generally have four choices: *risk avoidance*, *control*, *retention*, or *transfer*.

risk avoidance Stopping participation in or refusing to participate in ventures that carry any risk.

Risk Avoidance. A firm opts for **risk avoidance** by declining to enter into or by ceasing to participate in a risky activity. For example, the firm with the delivery trucks could avoid any risk of physical damage or bodily injury by closing down its delivery service. Similarly, a pharmaceutical maker may withdraw a new drug for fear of liability lawsuits.

risk control Techniques to prevent, minimize, or reduce losses or the consequences of losses.

Risk Control. When avoidance is not practical or desirable, firms can practise **risk control**—say, the use of loss-prevention techniques to minimize the frequency of losses. A delivery service, for instance, can prevent losses by training its drivers in defensive-driving techniques, mapping out safe routes, and conscientiously maintaining its trucks.

risk retention The covering of a firm's unavoidable losses with its own funds.

Risk Retention. When losses are manageable and predictable, the firm may decide to cover them out of company funds. Since the firm "assumes" the financial consequences of the loss, the practice is known as **risk retention**. For example, the firm with the fleet of trucks may find that vehicles suffer vandalism that averages $500 per year per vehicle. Depending on its coverage, the company may find it cheaper to pay for repairs out of pocket rather than to submit claims to its insurance company.

risk transfer The transfer of risk to another individual or firm, often by contract.

Risk Transfer. When the potential for large risks cannot be avoided or controlled, managers often opt for **risk transfer**. They transfer the risk to another firm—namely, an *insurance company*. The firm pays a *premium*, and in return, the insurance company issues an *insurance policy*—a formal agreement to pay the policyholder a specified amount in the event of certain losses. In some cases, the insured party must also pay a *deductible*—an agreed-upon amount of the loss that the insured must absorb prior to reimbursement from the insurance company. Thus, our company with the fleet of trucks may buy insurance to protect itself against theft, physical damage to trucks, and bodily injury to drivers and others involved in an accident.

Step 4: Implement the Risk-Management Program

The means of implementing risk management decisions depends on both the technique chosen and the activity being managed. For example, risk avoidance for certain activities can be implemented by purchasing those activities from outside providers, such as hiring delivery services instead of operating delivery vehicles. Risk control might be implemented by training employees and designing new work methods and equipment for on-the-job safety. For situations in which risk retention is preferred, reserve funds can be set aside out of revenues. When risk transfer is needed, implementation means selecting an insurance company and buying the right policies.

Step 5: Monitor Results

Because risk management is an ongoing activity, follow-up is always essential. New types of risks, for example, emerge with changes in customers, facilities, employees, and products. Insurance regulations change, and new types of insurance become available. Consequently, managers must continually monitor a company's risks, re-evaluate the methods used for handling them, and revise them as necessary.

Insurance as Risk Management

To deal with some risks, both businesses and individuals may choose to purchase one or more of the products offered by insurance companies. Buyers find insurance appealing for a very basic reason: In return for a relatively small sum of money, they are protected against specific losses, some of which are potentially devastating. With insurance, individuals and businesses share risks by contributing to a fund out of which those who suffer losses are paid. Insurance companies are willing to accept these risks for other companies because they make profits by taking in more in **premiums** than they pay out to cover policyholders' losses. Although many policyholders are paying for protection against the same type of loss, it is unlikely that all of them will suffer such a loss.

premiums Money paid to an insurance company by customers in return for being covered for certain types of losses should they occur.

Insurable vs. Uninsurable Risks

Like every other business, insurance companies must avoid certain risks. Insurers thus divide potential sources of loss into *insurable* and *uninsurable risks*. Obviously, they issue policies only for insurable risks, which must satisfy the four criteria of *predictability*, *casualty*, *unconnectedness*, and *verifiability*.

Explain the distinction between *insurable* and *uninsurable risks*, and distinguish among the different *types of insurance* purchased by businesses.   **L07**

Predictability. The insurer must be able to use statistical tools to forecast the likelihood of a loss. For example, an auto insurer needs information about the number of car accidents in the past year to estimate the expected number of accidents for the following year. With this knowledge, the insurer can translate expected numbers and types of accidents into expected dollar losses. The same forecast also helps insurers determine premiums charged to policyholders.

Losses are reduced or prevented when this security specialist uses electronic surveillance (left), when valuables are stored under lock and key (middle), and when workers are reminded to wear safety gear at this construction site (right).

Casualty. A loss must result from an accident, not from an intentional act by the policyholder. For example, an insurer does not have to cover damages if a policyholder deliberately sets fire to a business. To avoid paying in cases of fraud, insurers may refuse to cover losses when they cannot determine whether policyholders' actions contributed to them.

Unconnectedness. Potential losses must be random and must occur independently of other losses. No insurer can afford to write insurance when a large percentage of those who are exposed to a particular kind of loss are likely to suffer such a loss. One insurance company, for instance, would not want all the hail coverage in Saskatchewan or all the earthquake coverage in Vancouver. By carefully choosing the risks it will insure, an insurance company can reduce its chances of a large loss.

Verifiability. Finally, insured losses must be verifiable as to cause, time, place, and amount. Did an employee develop emphysema because of a chemical to which she was exposed or because she smoked 40 cigarettes per day for 30 years? Did the policyholder pay the renewal premium before the fire destroyed his factory? Were the goods stolen from the company's office or from the president's home? What was the insurable value of the destroyed inventory? When all these points have been verified, payment by the insurer goes more smoothly.

The Insurance Product

Some insurers offer only one area of coverage—life insurance, for example—while others offer a broad range. In this section, we briefly describe three major categories of business insurance—*liability*, *property*, and *life*.

Liability Insurance. Liability means responsibility for damages in case of accidental or deliberate harm to individuals or property. **Liability insurance** covers losses resulting from damage to people or property when the insured party is judged liable. A business is liable for any injury to an employee when the injury arises from activities related to occupation. When workers are permanently or temporarily disabled by job-related accidents or disease, employers are required by law to provide **workers' compensation coverage** for medical expenses, loss of wages, and rehabilitation services.

There is growing concern about fraudulent claims submitted by people who buy liability insurance. One popular scam is the "staged accident." The swindler purposely (but carefully) runs into, say, a telephone pole, and then everyone in the car claims that they are suffering from whiplash. After the accident is reported, the insurance company contacts the car's occupants and sends them accident benefit packages. Sometimes people who aren't even insured are paid benefits because they use counterfeit "proof of insurance" cards.

Every year in Canada, well over $1 billion is lost to insurance fraud. The insurance industry estimates that between $10 and $15 of every $1000 dollars you pay in premiums goes to cover fraud losses. The Insurance Bureau of Canada (IBC) is an industry association that represents Canadian companies that provide car, home, and business insurance. The IBC protects honest policyholders by monitoring insurance claims and determining which ones are fraudulent. Two areas of particular concern are organized crime rings and fraudulent injury claims. The IBC also lobbies the government to make legislative changes that will deter insurance fraud. Visit the IBC website at www.ibc.ca.

Property Insurance. Firms purchase **property insurance** to cover injuries resulting from physical damage to real estate or personal property. Property losses may result from fire, lightning, wind, hail, explosion, theft, vandalism, or other destructive forces, such as hurricanes. In 2005, insurance companies received claims exceeding $55 billion as a result of several hurricanes that hit the southern United States and flooded New Orleans. That figure was double the previous record (which was set in 2004). Canadian insurers were expected to pay out about $570 million of the 2005 total.

liability insurance Covers losses resulting from damage to people or property when the insured party is judged liable.

workers' compensation coverage Compensation for medical expenses, loss of wages, and rehabilitation services for injuries arising from activities related to occupation.

property insurance Covers injuries to firms resulting from physical damage to or loss of real estate or personal property.

Catastrophic losses like those caused by fire are avoided when a business buys property insurance. The cost of the rebuilding will be paid by the insurance company. But interruption of the firm's normal operations will also be harmful, so many businesses buy business interruption insurance as well.

In some cases, loss to property is minimal in comparison with loss of income. A manufacturer, for example, may have to close down for an extended time while fire damage is being repaired. During that time, the company is not generating any income, but certain expenses—such as taxes, insurance premiums, and salaries for key personnel—may continue. To cover such losses, a firm may buy *business interruption insurance*.

Life Insurance. Insurance can also protect a company's human assets. As part of their benefits packages, many businesses purchase **life insurance** for employees. Life insurance companies receive premiums in return for the promise to pay beneficiaries after the death of insured parties. As with other types of insurance, a portion of the premium is used to cover the insurer's own expenses.

life insurance Insurance that pays benefits to survivors of a policyholder.

Life insurance can, of course, also be purchased by individuals. For many years, Canadian life insurance companies have sold insurance policies to Canadians, but now they are rapidly expanding overseas, particularly in China and India. Sun Life Financial, for example, has formed a joint venture with Aditya Birla Group to sell life insurance and mutual funds in India. As a result of this partnership, Sun Life is the second largest privately owned life insurance company in India.[19] But in 2011, both Sun Life and Standard Life Assurance decided to stop selling individual life insurance policies in the United States because low interest rates and volatile stock markets made it difficult to make a profit selling such policies.[20] In some areas of the world, unstable and dangerous situations have motivated entrepreneurs to sell special kinds of insurance. For example, the al Ameen Insurance Co. pays out $3500 to beneficiaries of people who are killed as a result of insurgent activity in Iraq. The annual premium is about $35. The largest life insurance companies in Canada are shown in Table 20.2.

Most companies buy **group life insurance**, which is underwritten for groups as a whole rather than for each individual member. The insurer's assessment of potential losses and its pricing of premiums are based on the characteristics of the entire group.

group life insurance Life insurance underwritten for a group as a whole rather than for each individual member.

Special Forms of Business Insurance

Many forms of insurance are attractive to both businesses and individuals. For example, homeowners are as concerned about insuring property from fire and theft as businesses are. Businesses, however, have some special insurable concerns—the departure or death of key employees or owners.

TABLE 20.2 Top 10 Life Insurance Companies, 2011 (ranked by sales revenue)	
Company	**Sales Revenue (billions of dollars)**
1. Manulife Financial	$50.9
2. Great-West Lifeco Inc.	29.8
3. Sun Life Financial Inc.	22.5
4. Industrial Alliance Insurance and Financial Services Inc.	8.0
5. Desjardins Financial Security Life Assurance Co.	5.2
6. Standard Life Financial Inc.	3.3
7. Société d'assurance-vie inc.	2.0
8. RBC Life Insurance Co.	1.7
9. La Capitale Civil Service Mutual	1.6
10. Empire Life Insurance Co.	1.5

key person insurance Insurance that protects a company against loss of the talents and skills of key employees.

Key Person Insurance. Many businesses choose to protect themselves against loss of the talents and skills of key employees. If a salesperson who brings in $2.5 million of sales revenue dies or takes a new job, the firm will suffer loss. It will also incur recruitment costs to find a replacement and training expenses once a replacement is hired. **Key person insurance** is designed to offset both lost income and additional expenses.

business continuation agreement An agreement in which owners of a business make plans to buy the ownership interest of a deceased associate from his or her heirs.

Business Continuation Agreements. Who takes control of a business when a partner or an associate dies? Surviving partners are often faced with the possibility of having to accept an inexperienced heir as a management partner. This contingency can be handled in **business continuation agreements**, whereby owners make plans to buy the ownership interest of a deceased associate from his or her heirs. The value of the ownership interest is determined when the agreement is made. Special policies can also provide survivors with the funds needed to make the purchase.

MyBizLab

Capture more moments of true understanding. MyBizLab provides you with interactive study and practice tools directly related to this chapter's content. The new MyBizLab Study Plan Learning Path is designed to measure a full range of skills and provide remediation to give you what you need to master key chapter concepts. MyBizLab flexes to your unique learning needs. The result? Inspired learning, more success.

SUMMARY OF LEARNING OBJECTIVES

1. Describe the responsibilities of a *financial manager*. *Finance* (or corporate finance) entails four responsibilities: (1) determining long-term investments, (2) obtaining funds to pay for those investments, (3) conducting everyday financial activities, and (4) helping to manage risks. *Financial managers* plan and control the acquisition and dispersal of financial resources. But a financial manager's overall objective is to increase a firm's value and shareholders' wealth.

The specific responsibilities of the financial manager are (1) *cash flow management* (ensuring that the company

has enough funds on hand to purchase the resources that it needs to produce products); (2) *financial control* (the process of checking actual performance against plans to ensure that desired financial results occur); and (3) *financial planning* (developing a plan that describes how a firm will reach some future financial position).

2. Distinguish between *short-term* (operating) and *long-term* (capital) expenditures. *Short-term (operating)* expenditures are incurred in a firm's everyday business activities. Managers must pay special attention to three areas of financial activity: (1) *accounts payable,* (2) *accounts receivable,* and (3) *inventories.* Between the time a firm buys raw materials and the time it sells finished products, it ties up funds in *inventory*—materials and goods that it will sell within the year. Too little inventory can mean lost sales; too much inventory means tied-up funds. *Working capital* is the difference between a firm's current assets and current liabilities. It is a liquid asset from which current debts can be paid. Working capital is calculated by adding up inventories (*raw materials, work-in-process,* and *finished goods* on hand) and accounts receivable (minus accounts payable).

3. **Identify four sources of *short-term financing* for businesses.** (1) *Trade credit* is really a short-term loan from one firm to another. (2) *Secured short-term loans* like bank loans usually involve *promissory notes* in which the borrower promises to repay the loan plus interest. These loans require *collateral,* which can be seized if payments are not made as promised. (3) *Factoring accounts receivable* raises funds by selling the firm's accounts receivable. (4) *Unsecured short-term loans* are those where a borrower does not have to put up collateral. The bank may, however, require the borrower to maintain a *compensating balance*—a portion of the loan amount kept on deposit with the bank.

4. **Distinguish among the various sources of long-term financing and explain the risks involved in each.** Firms may seek long-term funds to pay for fixed assets through two channels. (1) Long-term borrowing from sources outside the company is called *debt financing.* There are two primary sources of such funding: *long-term loans* from chartered banks, or the issuance of *corporate bonds* (a promise by the issuer to pay the holder a certain amount of money on a specified date). (2) Looking inside the company for long-term funding is sometimes preferable to debt financing. *Equity financing* usually means issuing common stock or using retained earnings for expenditures. Equity financing by means of common stock can be expensive because paying dividends is more expensive than paying bond interest. A middle ground between debt financing and equity financing is the use of *preferred stock.* As with bonds, payments on preferred stock are fixed amounts. But like common stock, preferred stock can be held indefinitely.

5. **Discuss some key issues in financial management for small businesses.** Obtaining credit begins with finding a bank that will support a small firm's financial needs. Once a *line of credit* is obtained, the small business can seek more liberal *credit policies* from other businesses. Obtaining long-term loans is more difficult for new businesses than for established companies, and start-ups pay higher interest rates than older firms. To demonstrate that it's a good credit risk, a start-up must usually present a business plan—a document explaining why the money is needed, the amount, how it will be used to improve the company, and when it will be paid back.

Many newer businesses can't get needed funds through borrowing alone. They may turn to *venture capital*—outside equity funding provided in return for part-ownership. But with the high failure rates of small businesses, such investors demand high returns. Planning for cash flows is especially important for small businesses. Success or failure may hinge on anticipating those times when cash will be short or when excess cash can be expected.

6. **Explain how *risk* affects business operations and identify the five steps in the *risk management process*.** Businesses face two basic types of risk. (1) *Speculative risks,* such as financial investments, involve the possibility of gain or loss. (2) *Pure risks* (such as the chance of a warehouse fire) involve only the possibility of loss or no loss. *Risk management* means conserving earning power and assets by reducing the threat of losses due to uncontrollable events. The process has five steps: (1) identify risks and potential losses, (2) measure the frequency and severity of losses and their impact, (3) evaluate alternatives and choose the techniques that will best handle the losses (*risk avoidance, risk control, risk retention,* and *risk transfer*), (4) implement the risk management program, and (5) monitor results.

7. **Explain the distinction between *insurable* and *uninsurable* risks, and distinguish among the different *types of insurance* purchased by businesses.** In return for a relatively small sum of money, insurance buyers are protected against certain losses. Thus, *buying insurance* is a function of risk management, which is the implementation of a plan to deal with chance losses. Insurance companies make profits by taking in more *premiums* than they pay out to cover policyholders' losses. Insurers divide potential losses into *insurable* and *uninsurable risks,* and an insurable risk must meet four criteria: (1) Predictability—the insurer must be able to use statistical tools to forecast the likelihood of a loss. (2) Casualty—a loss must result from an accident, not from an intentional act. (3) Unconnectedness—potential losses must be random and occur independently of other losses. (4) Verifiability—insured losses must be verifiable as to cause, time, place, and amount.

There are three major categories of business insurance: (1) *Liability insurance*—liability means responsibility for damages in case of accidental or deliberate harm, and liability insurance covers losses resulting from damage to people or property when the insured party is held liable. The law requires most employers to provide employees injured on the job with *workers' compensation coverage* for medical expenses, loss of wages, and rehabilitation services. (2) *Property insurance*—firms purchase property insurance to cover injuries resulting from damage to or loss of real estate or personal property. A firm may buy *business interruption insurance* to cover expenses incurred when it is closed down and generating no income. (3) *Life insurance*—life insurance policies promise to pay beneficiaries after the death of insured parties. Most companies buy *group life insurance,* which is underwritten for groups as a whole rather than for each individual member.

Two forms of business insurance apply to the loss of key employees or owners: (1) Many businesses protect themselves against loss of the talents and skills of key employees by buying *key person insurance.* (2) Certain contingencies are handled in *business continuation agreements,* in which owners make plans to transfer the ownership interest of a deceased associate.

KEY TERMS

bond indenture   (p. 638)

business continuation agreement
   (p. 650)

capital structure   (p. 641)

cash flow management   (p. 632)

collateral   (p. 636)

commercial paper   (p. 637)

credit policy   (p. 634)

debt financing   (p. 638)

equity financing   (p. 640)

finance (corporate finance)   (p. 632)

financial control   (p. 633)

financial managers   (p. 632)

financial plan   (p. 633)

finished goods inventory   (p. 635)

group life insurance   (p. 649)

inventory   (p. 634)

key person insurance   (p. 650)

liability insurance   (p. 648)

life insurance   (p. 649)

line of credit   (p. 637)

open-book credit   (p. 635)

pledging accounts receivable   (p. 636)

premiums   (p. 647)

promissory note   (p. 635)

property insurance   (p. 648)

pure risk   (p. 645)

raw materials inventory   (p. 634)

revolving credit agreement   (p. 637)

risk   (p. 644)

risk avoidance   (p. 646)

risk control   (p. 646)

risk management   (p. 645)

risk retention   (p. 646)

risk transfer   (p. 646)

risk–return relationship   (p. 642)

secured loan   (p. 636)

speculative risk   (p. 645)

trade acceptance   (p. 635)

trade credit   (p. 635)

trade draft   (p. 635)

unsecured loan   (p. 636)

venture capital   (p. 643)

workers' compensation coverage
   (p. 648)

work-in-process inventory   (p. 634)

QUESTIONS FOR ANALYSIS

1. In what ways do the two sources of debt financing differ from each other? How do they differ from the two sources of equity financing?

2. What is the basic relationship between the amount of risk associated with a project and the likelihood of gains (or losses) on the project? Explain how several financial instruments (GICs, common stocks, preferred stocks, corporate bonds) illustrate this basic relationship.

3. What factors should be taken into account when deciding on the best mix of debt and equity for a company?

4. Give two examples of risks that are uninsurable. Why are they uninsurable?

5. As a risk manager of a large firm, what risks do you think your firm would face? What are the risks for a small firm? What accounts for the most important differences?

6. What are the risks and benefits associated with the sources of short-term funds (trade credit, secured and unsecured loans, and factoring accounts receivable)? How do these risk and benefits compare with those associated with sources of long-term funds (debt and equity)?

APPLICATION EXERCISES

1. Interview the owner of a small local business. Identify the types of short-term and long-term funding that this firm typically uses. Why has the company made the financial management decisions that it has?

2. Go to Sedar.com and find the balance sheets of two corporations operating in the same industry. Determine the relative emphasis each company places on raising money through debt versus equity. Why might these differences exist?

3. Interview a risk manager of a large firm and ask the following questions: What risks do you think your firm faces? How does your firm manage these risks? How have your policies changed over the years to adjust for new risk levels?

4. Interview the owner of a small local business. Ask this person to describe the risk management process that the firm follows. What role, for example, is played by risk transfer? Why has the company made the risk management decisions that it has?

BUILDING YOUR BUSINESS SKILLS

Understanding Risk-Management Issues

The Purpose of the Assignment

To encourage students to gain a better understanding of the major financial and risk management issues that face large companies.

The Situation

During the past few years, all of the following companies reported financial problems relating to risk management:

■ Air Canada

■ Bombardier

- EarthLink Inc.
- Levi Strauss & Co.
- Nortel Networks

Assignment

Step 1

Working alone, research one of the companies listed above to learn more about the financial risks that were reported in the news.

Step 2

Write a short explanation of the risks and financial management issues that were faced by the firm you researched.

Step 3

Join in teams with students who researched other companies and compare your findings.

Questions for Discussion

1. Were there common themes in the "big stories" in financial management?
2. What have the various companies done to minimize future risks and losses?

EXERCISING YOUR ETHICS: TEAM EXERCISE

Doing Your Duty When Payables Come Due

The Situation

Sarah Keats is the vice-president of finance at Multiverse, a large firm that manufactures consumer products. On December 15, 2012 (two weeks before the end of the fiscal year), she attends an executive committee meeting at which Jack Malvo, the CEO, expresses concern that the firm's year-end cash position will be less favourable than projected. The firm has exceeded analysts' performance expectations in each of his eight years at the helm and Malvo is determined that shareholders will never be disappointed as long as he is CEO. The purpose of the meeting is to find solutions to the cash problem and decide on a course of action.

The Dilemma

To open the meeting, Malvo announces, "We have just two weeks to either reduce expenses or increase revenues. We need a $100-million swing to get us where market analysts predicted we'd be on cash flows for the year. Any suggestions?"

In the discussion that ensues, it is noted that Multiverse owes $150 million to about 80 different companies that supply component parts and other operating supplies to Multiverse. The money is due before year-end. Sarah Keats says, "Our cash outflows for the year will be lower if we delay paying suppliers, which will help the bottom line. And it's like getting a free loan." The procurement director, Julie Levin, expresses the following concern: "Our agreements with suppliers call for faithful payments at designated times, and many of the smaller firms depend on receiving that cash to meet their obligations.

Also, we've worked hard for two years at improving relationships with all suppliers, and that effort could go down the drain if we don't meet our financial commitments as promised."

As the meeting draws to a close, Malvo announces, "Keep me posted on any unexpected developments, but if nothing helpful comes up in the next few days, let's go ahead and withhold supplier payments for three weeks."

Team Activity

Assemble a group of four students and assign each group member to one of the following roles:

- Jack Malvo (CEO of Multiverse)
- Sarah Keats (vice-president of finance)
- Julie Levin (procurement director)
- a shareholder of Multiverse

Questions for Discussion

1. Before discussing the situation with your group, and from the perspective of your assigned role, do you think there are any ethical issues here?
2. Before discussing the situation with your group, and from the perspective of your assigned role, what action do you think should be taken? Write down your recommended action.
3. Gather your group together and reveal, in turn, each member's comments and recommendations.
4. Appoint someone to record the main points of agreement and disagreement within the group. How do you explain the results? What accounts for any disagreements?
5. From an ethical standpoint, what does your group recommend?

Go to MyBizLab for additional cases and exercise material.

CONCLUDING CASE 20-1

The Aftermath of The Commercial Paper Crisis

In March 2012, an Ontario Superior Court judge approved the distribution of $60 million to investors who had been financially damaged by problems in the Canadian commercial paper market a few years earlier. The money came from fines levied in 2009 against CIBC, HSBC Bank of Canada, Scotia Capital, Canaccord Financial Ltd., and Credential Securities Inc. for the part they played in the crisis. In November 2011, an Ontario Securities Commission panel also fined Coventree Inc. and three of its executives a total of $2.2 million because the company failed to tell investors that the commercial paper they were buying was much riskier than investors thought. These decisions are the latest in a series of events that disrupted the commercial paper market in Canada. Here is the story.

Commercial paper is sold to investors on the promise that the issuing organization will pay back the principal (plus interest) in the near future (usually 30 or 60 days). In effect, the issuer might say something like this: If you loan my company, say, $99 dollars, in one month my company will give you $100. So, the investor earns $1 of interest in one month on a $99 loan. Both individuals and organizations buy commercial paper because they want to put their extra cash into a liquid (and safe) short-term investment that will earn interest until they need the money.

In recent years, a variation of this basic system came into being. Non-bank, asset-backed commercial paper (ABCP) is issued by companies (called conduits) that sold subprime mortgages to people with poor credit ratings. They then packaged these mortgages together with other more traditional loans (on credit cards, automobiles, and regular home mortgages) and sold them as collateralized debt obligations (CDOs) to investors. These products were much riskier than traditional commercial paper, but investors typically didn't know that.

In 2007, problems developed in the Canadian commercial paper market as a result of difficulties in the U.S. subprime mortgage market (where people who wouldn't usually qualify for mortgage money go to get money to buy a house). People who wanted to buy a home but had a poor credit rating got subprime mortgages with low interest "teaser" rates for the first two years. But those rates then rose to market rates for the remaining years of the mortgage. When people with subprime mortgages started defaulting in 2006 because they couldn't afford the higher interest rates, the subprime market collapsed. Foreclosures increased and the returns that normally would have been earned on these mortgages dropped sharply. And since these subprime mortgages were included in commercial paper that was sold to investors, the conduits couldn't pay their investors as they had promised. When word got out about this problem, investors refused to "roll over" their commercial paper (i.e., they wouldn't agree to keep their money in commercial paper for another 30 or 60 days) because they felt that it was too risky. The conduits thus experienced a sharp decline in the money they had available. They then went to their liquidity providers (Canadian banks) to get more money, but the banks argued that since the whole commercial paper market hadn't seized up (just the non-bank part of the market), they weren't obliged to provide the conduits with any money. The result was that many holders of commercial paper did not receive their principal and interest when they thought they would.

Many individuals who bought ABCP were assured by their financial advisers or by the Canadian bond rating firm DBRS that it was AAA-rated and was as safe as guaranteed investment certificates (GICs). DBRS was later criticized for giving such high ratings to such risky investments. Many *individual* investors didn't even know they owned any ABCP until they tried to get some of their money and were told it was "frozen." For example, Angela Speller, a retiree in Victoria, invested almost $1 million in ABCP and expected to be able to withdraw money as she needed it.

Baffinland Iron Mines Corp. is typical of *companies* that discovered they were not going to get their money when they wanted it. Baffinland mines iron ore deposits on Baffin Island and needs money to buy equipment of all kinds to carry on its regular operations. In July 2007, the company bought $43.8 million of ABCP to earn interest on extra cash that it had. In August 2007, some of the proceeds of the ABCP (principal plus interest) that were supposed to be paid to Baffinland, were not paid because the company Baffinland had bought the ABCP from was unable to pay. This caused a cash shortage at Baffinland, which hindered its exploration activities. Another example is Petrolifera Petroleum Ltd. of Calgary. The company invested about $37 million in ABCP, but when $31 million of the notes came due, they were not paid.

One way to solve this problem was to simply convert short-term commercial paper into longer-term debt and then gradually pay off investors. But that solution ignores the very reason that investors buy commercial paper in the first place, i.e., short-term liquidity. In 2007, a group called the Pan-Canadian Investors Committee was formed for the purpose of resolving the commercial paper mess. In April 2008, the Committee announced that noteholders had voted in favour of a plan that was designed to solve the problem. But in September 2008, the financial crisis hit and that further delayed settlement. Finally, in December 2008, the Committee announced a formal agreement to restructure $33 billion of ABCP by exchanging short-term notes for longer-term ones. Purdy Crawford, the chair of the group, said that most individuals and companies would likely get all their money back if they held the restructured notes to maturity. The agreement required the federal government and the provinces of Quebec, Ontario, and Alberta to provide over $4 billion to ensure that the $32 billion in ABCP was actually restructured.

In 2009, there were still fears that investors would incur big losses. But by 2011, it appeared that investors might recover as much as 80 percent of their original investment. The improvement came because more investors concluded that the restructured notes would increase toward par value as the maturity date (2017) approaches.

But some problems remain. For example, in 2010 the Investment Industry Regulatory Organization of Canada (IIROC) issued a warning to certain firms that still did not have the required written policies in place to indicate how they would decide whether or not to sell new financial products. The IIROC noted that even those companies that did have written policies were deficient in some other areas.

Questions for Discussion

1. Why do investors buy commercial paper? Why did some investors buy non-bank commercial paper?
2. How does the commercial paper crisis demonstrate the risk–return principle?
3. Explain how problems in the U.S. subprime mortgage market caused difficulties in the Canadian commercial paper market.
4. Should Canada's federal government become more involved in regulation of the commercial paper market so problems like the one described above won't happen again? Defend your answer.

CONCLUDING CASE 20-2

Risk and the Cost of Insurance

Business firms face risks in many different areas—the company's computer network may be hacked into, interest rates may change, executive talent may be raided by another company, consumers may sue the company, a recession may occur, or a natural disaster or terrorist attack may occur.

Risk and Insurance

One way that business firms cope with risks is to buy insurance. One particularly interesting area of insurance involves insurance for Hollywood movies, Broadway productions, and rock concerts. Fireman's Fund—which insures 80 percent of the movies that are made in Hollywood—named the Angelina Jolie movie *Salt* the riskiest movie of 2010 because Jolie opted to do risky stunts like hurling explosives and jumping off a bridge. If a star is injured, it can halt production and cost up to $250 000 a day. A Fireman's Fund representative is typically on the set on those days when risky stunts are scheduled for filming. Actors are required to get a physical exam before the film starts production, and what the doctor reports can affect the cost of policy premiums.

For the Broadway production of *Victor/Victoria*, an insurance policy was purchased on the star Julie Andrews that insured the producers of the show for up to US$2 million if she missed performances. And producers of the Broadway show *Titanic* paid about US$400 000 for insurance to cover things such as a member of the audience being hit by a flying deck chair, or a cast member being injured during the performance.

In 2009, Lloyd's of London issued a non-appearance and concert cancellation policy for Michael Jackson's comeback concert tour, but when Jackson died two months later, Lloyd's asked a judge to nullify the policy and eliminate Lloyd's liability because the promoter of the concerts hadn't informed Lloyd's of Jackson's medical history. Insurance is also purchased by music companies for top musicians. But insuring a "gangsta rap" concert is difficult given the violence that has occurred at such concerts in the past.

In business firms, risk managers must decide what kind of insurance their company needs to carry and whether it can afford to buy such insurance. Consider what happened to Kitchener, Ontario–based Kentain Products, which manufactures chemical tank liners. Its products have been very successful in Canada, so owner Glen Lippert thought it was a natural extension of the business to begin exporting the products to the United States. But he was in for a rude shock. When his insurance company found out what he was planning, it would no longer sell him liability insurance because it felt that selling to the United States was too risky. When Lippert checked around at other insurance companies, he discovered that it would cost him $50 000 in annual premiums to get liability insurance. Since that figure exceeded the profit he expected to make in the United States, he abandoned his export plans.

It's not just exporting companies that are having trouble with insurance premiums. One Waterloo, Ontario–based company that sells industrial air compressors had its premiums increased from $6500 to $40 000 in one year. A cabinetmaking firm saw its premiums double from $10 000 to $20 000 in one year, and then to $60 000 two years later. Many small businesses can't get insurance at any price. This is a big problem because banks usually demand that a company have liability insurance before they will loan it money. A survey by the Federation of Independent Business found that most small businesses have faced increases in the 30 percent range during each of the past few years. In the survey, 83 percent of the respondents said that high insurance premiums were their single biggest cost.

Insurance companies say that rates are going up because they are not getting enough revenue from premium payments and from their investments to pay all the claims that are arising. So they increase premiums and refuse to cover some high-risk activities. Insurance companies identify a number of specific reasons for rapidly escalating insurance premiums: uncertainty in the stock market (where insurance companies have much of their money invested), low interest rates, terrorist activity, liability lawsuits against companies, and natural disasters. In 2011, for example, a devastating earthquake hit Japan. In addition to the loss of human life, damage to business firms and homes was extensive (some estimates go as high as $200 billion). The earthquake was very costly for insurance companies, but they won't have to pay $200 billion because a lot of property wasn't covered by earthquake insurance. The costs of insurance payouts in other recent earthquakes include $20.6 billion (California), $3.5 billion (Japan), and $4.4 billion (New Zealand).

Life Insurance

Life insurance for individuals is an area where recent changes are creating some potential problems. There are about 757 000 individual life insurance policies sold each year in Canada, and billions of dollars in commissions are generated by these sales. Formerly, most of these policies were sold by agents who worked for the insurance companies. But now, about 70 percent of the policies are sold by independent agents. Insurance companies pay these independent agents incentives to motivate the agents to direct business to the insurance company. Critics charge that insurance premiums paid by buyers of policies are inflated because insurance companies often pay for luxury trips for independent agents in an attempt to get those agents to sell their life insurance policies. A *Globe and Mail* investigation revealed that some insurance companies spend $8000–$12 000 per agent in order to compete with other insurance companies. If they don't give these free trips to agents, they might recommend the life insurance policies of other companies to their clients. The companies and individuals who are buying life insurance are paying for these trips via higher premiums. Rather than looking for the best deal for their clients, brokers often direct almost all their business to just one or two insurance companies because those companies give them the best deal on bonuses and perks. Critics argue that agents therefore have a conflict of interest—their perks vs. their customer's best deal.

Instituting Control Systems

Insurance is useful for dealing with risks, but risk managers must also institute control systems that will reduce the chance that some employees will act in ways that are financially detrimental to their employer. Unfortunately, creative fraudsters sometimes find ways to circumvent these control systems. In 2011, for example, a trader at UBS engaged in unauthorized trades that cost the company $2 billion. Moody's put the company's credit rating under review for possible downgrade, noting that there were weaknesses in the company's risk management controls.

Or, consider the case of David Lee, a Bank of Montreal (BMO) natural gas trader who was based in New Jersey. For a while he was flying high. During the period from 2003 to 2006, his annual compensation rose from about $722 000 to $5.35 million. But in 2008, he pled guilty to charges of conspiracy, fraud, making false bank entries, and obstructing a U.S. regulatory investigation. Lee falsified records to make it look like his natural gas trades were profitable when, in fact, they were not. BMO had controls in place to prevent this sort of thing, but the system was circumvented by Lee. Here's how: BMO verified the values Lee was claiming for his portfolio by obtaining a quote from an independent brokerage firm called Optionable Inc. But that firm has now been charged with providing phony quotes to BMO. The quotes were simply made up so that they matched the numbers Lee was claiming. The fraud was discovered when BMO also got quotes from other independent brokerages that did not match the quotes that Optionable was providing. The CEO of Optionable Inc. (who had previously spent time in prison for money laundering) has also been charged with conspiracy, fraud, and making false bank entries. By the end of 2007, BMO had incurred trading losses of $850 million as the result of Lee's activities.

A more complicated case is that of Jérôme Kerviel, a trader who worked at Société Générale SA (SocGen), a large bank in France. The bank alleged that Kerviel forged trading records and circumvented the bank's control system in a fraud that eventually cost the bank over $7 billion. Kerviel says that he actually made money with his trades in 2007, and that as long as he was making money, his bosses ignored his unauthorized trades. It was only when he started losing money on his trades in 2008 that fraud was alleged by his bosses. Other traders in the industry also expressed doubt that a person like Kerviel could conceal so much unauthorized trading for so long without being detected. Some observers say that Kerviel is guilty of a breach of trust (that is, making decisions he did not have the authority to make) but not fraud. As a result of the dispute, SocGen has come under increasing pressure to explain how its risk management system failed to detect Kerviel's unauthorized trades. The president of France even called for the CEO of SocGen to step down.

These cases are just the latest in a series of situations where risk controls didn't quite work. For example, John Rusnak, a currency trader at Allfirst Financial, defrauded the company of $691 million by creating phony currency trades. Stephen Humphries, a trader at Sussex Futures Ltd. in England, engaged in so much fraudulent trading activity that he destroyed the company he worked for. Sussex Futures ceased operations, and 70 people lost their jobs. Nicholas Leeson, who worked for Barings PLC, a British merchant bank, bought and sold futures contracts, particularly investments known as derivatives. Over a three-week period, Leeson managed to incur trading losses of nearly $1 billion. When losses spiralled out of control, Leeson fled, and Barings had to declare bankruptcy. Leeson was eventually convicted and sentenced to six-and-a-half years in prison.

In all of these cases, there were control systems in place to prevent fraud, but they simply were not up to the job of detecting creative and determined individuals who were engaged in fraudulent activities. There was, in effect, a failure to properly manage risk. That failure led to massive financial losses, corporate bankruptcies, and the loss of many jobs.

Questions for Discussion

1. Briefly describe the steps in the risk management process. To what extent does the risk management process focus on detecting employee fraud?

2. Assume for a moment that Jérôme Kerviel's bosses knew what he was doing and they went along with it as long as he was making money for SocGen. Assume also that they charged him with fraud only after he started losing money. If that was really the situation, do you think Kerviel should have been charged with breach of contract (i.e., with making decisions he was not authorized to make)? Explain your reasoning.

3. Consider the following statement: *In every company, there are likely to be at least a few people who will engage in fraudulent behaviour in order to benefit themselves at the expense of others. Therefore, all companies should have a CRO in order to eliminate the possibility of employee fraud.* Do you agree with the statement? Explain your reasoning.

VIDEO CASE 5–1
Credit Card Fraud

A new trend is evident in criminal activity: smash-and-grab thieves are stealing hard drives from retail stores. When a big Canadian grocery chain hired an expert to find out why their point-of-sale (POS) terminals were being stolen, they discovered that the thieves wanted the credit and debit card information on the POS. Businesses are supposed to wipe these terminals clean at the end of each business day so that customers' credit and debit card numbers are not left on the terminals overnight, but businesses may not do this on a regular basis. The grocery chain's problem is not an isolated occurrence. Starbucks, Boston Pizza, and Husky oil have all been hit by POS terminal theft.

Thieves use the credit and debit card numbers they get from the POS terminals to make counterfeit credit cards. Blank gift cards are run through a reader, and the stolen credit or debit card numbers are put on the stripe on the back of the gift card. But crooks don't just buy stuff with the fake credit or debit cards they make: With your credit card numbers in hand, criminals can go into your bank and use the data there to impersonate you. They can even transfer your line of credit to another bank account that they have opened up in someone else's name. Criminals no longer have to rob banks because POS terminals are "open bank vaults" and they are everywhere.

Twice in one week, thieves stole POS terminals from a Sammy J. Peppers restaurant in Coquitlam, B.C. *Marketplace* brought in a security expert to look into the problem. The restaurant owner said the POS terminals were checked to see that no customer data was kept on them overnight. The computer expert removed the hard drive from the restaurant's POS terminal to see what was stored there. Fortunately, he found that the hard drive had indeed been wiped clean. So, even if thieves stole the POS terminal, they wouldn't get any of the customers' credit or debit card numbers. But other retail establishments are not doing such a good job. Husky, for example, admits it is not sure what was on the hard drives that were stolen from it.

There are 630 000 POS terminals in Canada processing thousands of transactions every day. In Abbotsford, B.C., 28 retail businesses were broken into in a short time period. An Abbotsford detective says that one company was targeted 100 times. Retailers have been keeping quiet about this problem, and although credit card companies make good on customers' losses, we all ultimately pay a price because overall costs go up.

It is not uncommon for consumers to get a notice from their credit card company saying that their card has been "compromised," but it is hard to pinpoint where the problem occurred. A representative from the Retail Council of Canada admits there is a problem, but says it is hard to keep up with the innovative activities of thieves who are always one step ahead of security measures. The representative says that customers know about the possibility that their credit or debit card could be compromised, but the people that *Marketplace* interviewed seemed oblivious to this fact. Stores should therefore tell consumers about the problem instead of keeping silent, but there is no law in Canada requiring retailers to tell you your card has been stolen. Companies are often confident that nothing is on the POS hard drives that would be helpful to thieves, but in reality there often is. Crown Prosecutor Peter Stabler says that retailers know that important information is on their POS hard drives and so do the crooks.

Questions for Discussion

1. Why aren't POS terminals wiped more often?

2. What actions can retailers take to reduce credit card fraud?

3. Consider the following statement: *Retail outlets should be required by law to put up signs warning customers that their credit and debit card numbers may be stolen.* Do you agree or disagree with the statement? Defend your position.

THE COMPANY

When Jacqueline Sava walked into the Dragon's Den, she had already amassed over a million dollars worth of sales. Soakwash is designed to clean women's delicate items such as bras and lingerie; it is formulated specifically for hand-washable items. The products are sold in yarn shops, quilting shops, lingerie shops, and apparel stores. As an added benefit, customers using Soakwash do not need to rinse out the items (a significant point of differentiation from the competition).

THE PITCH

After presenting the benefits of her product, Jacqueline requested $300 000 for a 25 percent equity stake in her company. She informed the dragon's that the funding would help her create a salesforce to garner a stronger presence in the market and hurt her competitors. According to Jacqueline, she needed to hire salespeople to take her company to the next level. Specifically, she pointed to an estimated 6000 upper-end lingerie shops in the United States. Jacqueline explained that she had a proven track record of training retail stores to up-sell the product but asserted that at present she could not reach enough retailers to convince them to carry her products.

THE DRAGON'S POINT OF VIEW

After Jacqueline's pitch, it was clear that there were many questions and more concern than enthusiasm. First, the dragons pointed to a huge well-known competitor, namely Zero fabric wash. Second, when asked about her sales figures, Jacqueline revealed that the one million dollars were actually a total that spanned more than two-and-a-half years. It also became clear that her sales were not growing and had remained at $400 000 for each of the last two years. Third, the dragons were very concerned that she had a bank loan of $300 000 in addition to the $200 000 that she had already invested out of her own pocket. When pressed about this issue, Jacqueline replied, "It's a great time to have debt." Kevin O'Leary (always the compassionate one) bluntly

told her she was wrong and said, "They are going to call your loan and squeeze your head like a pimple."

THE OUTCOME

When it was time for the dragons to make their decisions, the questions had already mounted and one by one the dragons walked away from the deal with the following comments:

- "You valued her company at more than a million dollars. I can't get near the valuation, I'm out."
- "Your sales are flat-lining. Slug it out one retailer at a time. I don't see the market. I'm out."
- "You came out asking for three times the value of the company. I think the valuation is outrageous. I'm out."
- "When you have sales of 400k and 300k of debt, it's an issue. I'm out."
- "I love you as an entrepreneur, love your product, but for 300k I'd have to own your company! I'm out."

The big lesson: the numbers… the numbers… the numbers. The panel of experts thought the numbers were out of line and that Jacqueline's request was outrageous, and every one of them backed out while giving her some stern advice.

Questions for Discussion

1. What lessons about financing a business can you take away from this video? If Jacqueline were given a second opportunity to make a pitch to the dragons, what advice would you give her?

2. What do you think of the market potential for this product? Do you think Soakwash has a bright future? Explain why or why not.

3. In your opinion, which of the dragons made the most compelling point?

CRAFTING A BUSINESS PLAN
Part 5: Financial Issues

Goal of the Exercise

In this final part of the business plan project, you'll consider how you'll finance your business as well as create an executive summary for your plan.

EXERCISE BACKGROUND:

Part 5 of the Business Plan

In the previous part of the business plan, you discussed the costs of doing business as well as how much revenue you expect to earn in one year. It's now time to think about how to finance the business. To get a "great idea" off the ground requires money. But how will you get these funds?

You'll then conclude this project by creating an executive summary. The purpose of the executive summary is to give the reader a quick snapshot of your proposed business. Although this exercise comes at the end of the project, once you're done writing it, you'll end up placing the executive summary at the beginning of your completed business plan.

YOUR ASSIGNMENT

Step 1

Open the saved *Business Plan* file you have been working on.

Step 2

For the purposes of this assignment, you will answer the following questions, based on issues discussed in "Part 5: Managing Financial Issues."

1. How much money will you need to get your business started?
   Hint: Refer back to Part 3 of the plan, where you analyzed the costs involved in running your business. Approximately how much will you need to get your business started?

2. How will you finance your business? For example, will you seek out a bank loan? Borrow from friends? Sell stocks or bonds initially or as your business grows?
   Hint: Refer to Chapter 19 for information on securities such as stocks and bonds. Refer also to Chapter 20 and Chapter 4 for more information on sources of short-term and long-term funds.

3. Now, create an executive summary for your business plan. The executive summary should be brief—no more than two pages long—and should cover the following points:

   ▨ the name of your business
   ▨ where your business will be located
   ▨ the mission of your business
   ▨ the product or service you are selling
   ▨ who your ideal customers are
   ▨ how your product or business will stand out in the crowd
   ▨ who the owners of the business are and what experience they have
   ▨ an overview of the future prospects for your business and industry

Hint: At this point, you've already answered all of these questions, so what you need to do here is put the ideas together into a "snapshot" format. The executive summary is really a sales pitch—it's the investor's first impression of your idea. Therefore, as with all parts of the plan, write in a clear and professional way.

Congratulations on completing the business plan project!

Business Law

The Role of Law in Canadian Society

Law is the set of rules and standards that a society agrees upon to govern the behaviour of its citizens. Both the British and the French influenced the development of law in Canada. In 1867, the British North America (BNA) Act created the nation of Canada. The BNA Act was "repatriated" to Canada in 1982 and is now known as the Constitution Act. This act divides legislative powers in Canada between the federal and provincial governments.

Sources of Law

The law in Canada has evolved and changed in response to our norms and values. Our laws have arisen from three sources: (1) customs and judicial precedents (the source of common law), (2) the actions of provincial and federal legislatures (the source of statutory law), and (3) rulings by administrative bodies (the source of administrative law).

Common law, sometimes referred to as case law, is the unwritten law of England, derived from ancient precedents and judges' previous legal opinions. Common law is based on the principle of equity, the provision to every person of a just and fair remedy. Canadian legal customs and traditions derive from British common law. All provinces except Quebec, which uses the French Civil Code, have laws based on British common law, and court decisions are often based on precedents from common law. That is, decisions made in earlier cases that involved the same legal point will guide the court.

Statutory law is written law developed by city councils, provincial legislatures, and parliament. Most law in Canada today is statutory law.

Administrative law is the rules and regulations that government agencies and commissions develop based on their interpretations of statutory laws. For example, Consumer and Corporate Affairs Canada develops regulations on false advertising, using federal legislation.

The Court System

In Canada, the judiciary branch of government has the responsibility of settling disputes among organizations or individuals by applying existing laws. Both provincial and federal courts exist to hear both criminal and civil cases. In all provinces there exists a court hierarchy consisting of a lower court, a superior court, and an appellate court. The Supreme Court of Canada is the highest court in Canada. It decides whether to hear appeals from lower courts.

Business Law

Business firms, like all other organizations, are affected by the laws of the country. **Business law** refers to laws that specifically affect how business firms are managed. Some laws affect all businesses, regardless of size, industry, or location. For example, the Income Tax Act requires businesses to pay income tax. Other laws may have a greater impact on one industry than on others. For example, pollution regulations are of much greater concern to Inco than they are to Carlson Wagonlit Travel.

Business managers must have at least a basic understanding of eight important concepts in business law:

- contracts
- agency
- bailment
- property
- employment or labour law
- torts
- negotiable instruments
- bankruptcy

Contracts

Agreements about transactions are common in a business's day-to-day activity. A **contract** is an agreement between two parties to act in a specified

law The set of rules and standards that a society agrees upon to govern the behaviour of its citizens.

common law The unwritten law of England, derived from precedent and legal judgments.

statutory law Written law developed by city councils, provincial legislatures, and parliament.

administrative law The rules and regulations that government agencies and commissions develop based on their interpretations of statutory laws.

business law Laws that specifically affect how business firms are managed.

contract An agreement between two parties to act in a specified way or to perform certain acts.

breach of contract When one party to an agreement fails, without legal reason, to live up to the agreement's provisions.

way or to perform certain acts. A contract might, for example, apply to a customer buying a product from a retail establishment or to two manufacturers agreeing to buy products or services from each other. A valid contract includes several elements:

- *Intent*—There must be an intention to create a legally enforceable agreement.

- *Offer and Acceptance*—All parties must consciously agree about the contract.

- *Consideration*—The parties must exchange something of value (e.g., time, products, services, money, and so on).

- *Capacity*—All parties to the contract must be legally able to enter into an agreement. Individuals who are below a certain age or who are legally insane, for example, cannot enter into legal agreements.

- *Legal purpose*—What the parties agree to do for or with each other must be legal. An agreement between two manufacturers to fix prices is not legal.

The courts will enforce a contract if it meets the criteria described above. Most parties honour their contracts, but occasionally one party does not do what it was supposed to do. **Breach of contract** occurs when one party to an agreement fails, without legal reason, to live up to the agreement's provisions. The party who has not breached the contract has three alternatives under the law in Canada: (1) discharge, (2) sue for damages, or (3) require specific performance.

An example will demonstrate these three alternatives. Suppose that Barrington Farms Inc. agrees to deliver 100 dozen long-stemmed roses to the Blue Violet Flower Shop the week before Mother's Day. One week before the agreed-upon date, Barrington informs Blue Violet that it cannot make the delivery until after Mother's Day. Under the law, the owner of Blue Violet can choose among the following actions.

Discharge

Blue Violet can consider the contract at an end due to the breach by Barrington Farms. It can then choose to contract with another supplier.

Sue for Damages

Blue Violet can legally demand payment for losses caused by Barrington's failure to deliver the promised goods. Losses might include any increased price Blue Violet would have to pay for the roses or court costs incurred in the damage suit.

Require Specific Performance

If monetary damages are not sufficient to reimburse Blue Violet, the court can force Barrington to live up to its original contract. Courts in Canada rarely rely on this equitable remedy.

Agency

agency-principal relationship Established when one party (the agent) is authorized to act on behalf of another party (the principal).

In many business situations, one person acts as an agent for another person. Well-known examples include actors and athletes represented by agents who negotiate contracts for them. An **agency-principal relationship** is established when one party (the agent) is authorized to act on behalf of another party (the principal).

The agent is under the control of the principal and must act on behalf of the principal and in the principal's best interests. The principal remains liable for the acts of the agent as long as the agent is acting within the scope of authority granted by the principal. A salesperson for IBM, for example, is an agent for IBM, the principal.

Bailment

Many business transactions are not covered by the agency-principal relationship. For example, suppose that you take your car to a mechanic to have it repaired. Because the repair shop has temporary possession of something you own, it is responsible for your car. This is a **bailor-bailee relationship**. In a bailor-bailee relationship, the bailor (the car owner) gives possession of his or her property to the bailee (the repair shop) but retains ownership of the item. A business firm that stores inventory in a public warehouse is in a bailor-bailee relationship. The business firm is the bailor and the warehouse is the bailee. The warehouse is responsible for storing the goods safely and making them available to the manufacturer upon request.

bailor-bailee relationship In a bailor-bailee relationship, the bailor (the property owner) gives possession of his or her property to the bailee (a custodian), but retains ownership of the item.

The Law of Property

Property includes anything of tangible or intangible value that the owner has the right to possess and use. **Real property** is land and any permanent buildings attached to that land. **Personal property** is tangible or intangible assets other than real property. Personal property includes cars, clothing, furniture, money in bank accounts, stock certificates, and copyrights.

property Anything of tangible or intangible value that the owner has the right to possess and use.

real property Land and any permanent buildings attached to that land.

personal property Tangible or intangible assets other than real property.

Transferring Property

From time to time, businesses and individuals need to transfer property to another person or business. A **deed** is a document that shows ownership of real property. It allows the transfer of title of real property.

A **lease** grants the use of an asset for a specified period of time in return for payment. The business or individual granting the lease is the lessor and the tenant is the lessee. For example, a business (the lessee) may rent space in a mall for one year from a real estate development firm (the lessor).

A **title** shows legal possession of personal property. It allows the transfer of title of personal property. When you buy a snowmobile, for example, the former owner signs the title over to you.

deed A document that shows ownership of real property.

lease Grants the use of an asset for a specified period of time in return for payment.

title Shows legal possession of personal property.

Warranty

When you buy a product or service, you want some assurance that it will perform satisfactorily and meet your needs. A **warranty** is a promise that the product or service will perform as the seller has promised it will.

There are two kinds of warranties—express and implied. An **express warranty** is a specific claim that the manufacturer makes about a product. For example, a warranty that a screwdriver blade is made of case-hardened steel is an express warranty. An **implied warranty** suggests that a product will perform as the manufacturer claims it will. Suppose that you buy an outboard motor for your boat and the engine burns out in one week. Because the manufacturer implies by selling the motor that it will work for a reasonable period of time, you can return it and get your money back.

Because opinions vary on what is a "reasonable" time, most manufacturers now give limited time warranties on their products. For example, they will guarantee their products against defects in materials or manufacturing for six months or one year.

warranty A promise that the product or service will perform as the seller has promised it will.

express warranty A specific claim that the manufacturer makes about a product.

implied warranty A suggestion that a product will perform as the manufacturer claims it will.

Torts

A **tort** is a wrongful civil act that one party inflicts on another and that results in injury to the person, to the person's property, or to the person's good name. An **intentional tort** is a wrongful act intentionally committed. If a security guard in a department store suspects someone of shoplifting and uses excessive force to prevent

tort A wrongful civil act that one party inflicts on another and that results in injury to the person, to the person's property, or to the person's good name.

intentional tort A wrongful act intentionally committed.

negligence A wrongful act that inadvertently causes injury to another person.

him or her from leaving the store, the guard might be guilty of an intentional tort. Other common torts are libel, embezzlement, defamation, nuisance, and trespass.

Negligence is a wrongful act that inadvertently causes injury to another person. For example, if a maintenance crew in a store mops the floors without placing warning signs in the area, a customer who slips and falls might bring a negligence suit against the store.

In recent years, the most publicized area of negligence has been product liability. **Product liability** means that businesses are liable for injuries caused to product users because of negligence in design or manufacturing. **Strict product liability** means that a business is liable for injuries caused by their products even if there is no evidence of negligence in the design or manufacture of the product.

product liability The liability of businesses for injuries caused to product users because of negligence in design or manufacturing.

strict product liability The liability of businesses for injuries caused by their products even if there is no evidence of negligence in the design or manufacture of the product.

Negotiable Instruments

negotiable instruments Types of commercial paper that can be transferred among individuals and business firms.

Negotiable instruments are types of commercial paper that can be transferred among individuals and business firms. Cheques, bank drafts, and certificates of deposit are examples of negotiable instruments.

The Bills of Exchange Act specifies that a negotiable instrument must

- be written,

- be signed by the person who puts it into circulation (the maker or drawer),

- contain an unconditional promise to pay a certain amount of money,

- be payable on demand, and

- be payable to a specific person (or to the bearer of the instrument).

endorsement Signing your name to a negotiable instrument, making it transferable to another person or organization.

Negotiable instruments are transferred from one party to another through an endorsement. An **endorsement** means signing your name to a negotiable instrument; this makes it transferable to another person or organization. If you sign only your name on the back of a cheque, you are making a *blank* endorsement. If you state that the instrument is being transferred to a specific person, you are making a *special* endorsement. A *qualified* endorsement limits your liability if the instrument is not backed up by sufficient funds. For example, if you get a cheque from a friend and want to use it to buy a new stereo, you can write "without recourse" above your name. If your friend's cheque bounces, you have no liability. A *restrictive* endorsement limits the negotiability of the instrument. For example, if you write "for deposit only" on the back of a cheque and it is later stolen, no one else can cash it.

Bankruptcy

bankruptcy The court-granted permission for organizations or individuals to not pay some or all of their debts.

At one time, individuals who could not pay their debts were jailed. Today, however, both organizations and individuals can seek relief by filing for **bankruptcy**, which is the court-granted permission to not pay some or all of their debts.

Thousands of individuals and businesses file for bankruptcy each year. They do so for various reasons, including cash flow problems, reduced demand for their products, or some other problem that makes it difficult or impossible for them to resolve their financial problems. In recent years, large businesses like Eaton's, Olympia & York, and Enron have sought the protection of bankruptcy laws. Three main factors account for the increase in bankruptcy filings:

1. The increased availability of credit

2. The "fresh-start" provisions in current bankruptcy laws

3. The growing acceptance of bankruptcy as a financial tactic

In Canada, jurisdiction over bankruptcy is provided by the Bankruptcy and Insolvency Act. An **insolvent person (or company)** is defined as one who cannot pay current obligations to creditors as they come due, or whose debts exceed their assets. A **bankrupt person (or company)** is one who has either made a voluntary application to start bankruptcy proceedings (voluntary bankruptcy) or has been forced by creditors into bankruptcy (involuntary bankruptcy) by a process referred to as a *receiving order*. A person who is insolvent may or may not be bankrupt, and a person who is bankrupt may or may not be insolvent, as there are other bases for bankruptcy under the act. Another procedure under the act is referred to as a *proposal*, which can delay or avoid liquidation by providing the debtor with time to reorganize affairs and/or propose a payment schedule to creditors.

On a practical basis, business bankruptcy under the act may be resolved or avoided by one of three methods:

- Under a *liquidation plan*, the business ceases to exist. Its assets are sold and the proceeds are used to pay creditors.

- Under a *repayment plan*, the bankrupt company works out a new payment schedule to meet its obligations. The time frame is usually extended, and payments are collected and distributed by a court-appointed trustee.

- *Reorganization* is the most complex form of business bankruptcy. The company must explain the sources of its financial difficulties and propose a new plan for remaining in business. Reorganization may include a new slate of managers and a new financial strategy. A judge may also reduce the firm's debts to ensure its survival. Although creditors naturally dislike debt reduction, they may agree to the proposal, since getting, say, 50 percent of what you are owed is better than getting nothing at all.

insolvent person (or company)
One who cannot pay current obligations to creditors as they come due, or whose debts exceed their assets.

bankrupt person (or company)
One who has either made a voluntary application to start bankruptcy proceedings (voluntary bankruptcy) or has been forced by creditors into bankruptcy (involuntary bankruptcy) by a process referred to as a receiving order.

Managing Your Personal Finances

This feature presents a down-to-earth, hands-on approach that will help you manage your personal finances. The practical information found in this feature includes a worksheet for determining net worth, insightful examples demonstrating the time value of money, a method for determining how much to invest now in order to build a future nest egg of a certain size, suggestions on how to manage credit-card debt, guidelines for purchasing a house, and a personalized worksheet for setting financial goals.

The information contained in this feature will be immensely useful to you.

Please visit MyBizLab for practical information about managing your own financial situation.

MyBizLab

Comprehensive Cases

Dynamic Designs: Proud Heritage and New Models For Survival

Origins of a Family Business

The Michaud family has been part of the Canadian furniture manufacturing industry for nearly sixty years. It all started with Phillip Michaud, an ambitious, hard-working individual, who learned everything he could about the business the old-fashioned way: he put in the hours and concentrated on the details. At the age of 35 he founded a company called Dynamic Designs and quickly built a modest but loyal following in his community. His business supplied local furniture retailers with quality sofas and reclining chairs. Philip prided himself in his end product and preached his passion for quality to all his employees. Above the manufacturing shop door he hung a sign that read "Reputation is built one chair at a time." Employees shared and respected his uncompromising approach. By the time he was 50, he had 10 full-time employees working in his shop. He began an expansion program and made substantial progress in the next few years but health problems got in the way at a fairly young age. Fortunately for Philip and his legacy, his son Martin had been trained in the "Michaud manner" and was ready to take over the reins.

Over the next 35 years, Martin Michaud and his wife Cynthia took Dynamic Designs to levels that Philip had only dreamed of. The husband and wife team were intent on expansion and used their respective expertise to build a large, well-respected company. Martin understood the intricate manufacturing processes and constantly searched for new techniques to improve efficiency while always maintaining quality. Martin was also quite the salesman. Cynthia was a strong individual who was well admired by her employees; she made sure that the company headquarters ran smoothly as Martin went on the road to drum up sales. Near the turn of the millennium, Dynamic Designs reached its peak as a manufacturer with sales across Canada and some significant exports to the United States. The organization had a good relationship with most of the major retailers in the Canadian industry, including companies like Sears Canada, Leon's, The Brick, and Brault and Martineau.

Jason Michaud: Third Generation Plans and a New Reality

Jason Michaud represented the third generation of this family business. He was well aware of the negative stereotypes about a third-generation owner. As the old saying goes, "The first generation builds, the second generation expands, and the third generation destroys or lets it all fall apart." Jason was determined to avoid such a fate, however, and planned to take Dynamic Designs to yet another level.

At the age of 33 he took control of the business from his dad and mom who were ready to enjoy their semi-retirement. They remained involved in the business and tried to pass on their advice and knowledge to Jason but they enjoyed long holidays and left the big decisions to their son. Jason had been working for the family business since he was a very young man. He had plenty of hands-on experience and he also had an MBA from McGill University. At the time, one of his friends questioned why he had earned his master's degree since his family was quite wealthy and he had a vital position and responsibilities waiting for him at Dynamic Designs. Although Jason already had so much first-hand knowledge, he never doubted the value of his education. He used those years to do more than join the local fraternity: he studied new marketing, production, and management methods and tried to apply every idea to help him with his family's business. For example, in one of his courses he spent a semester working on an advertising campaign for his company and then implemented the plan in real life. Jason was focused and he had a clear goal in mind.

The New Ever-Changing Profit Equation

Unfortunately for Jason, times had changed. The strategies that his father, mother, and grandfather had used to build the company were simply no longer feasible in an age of globalization. For a period of time, the Dynamic Designs reputation for quality helped the company keep accounts and maintain sales but it became harder and harder each year. Jason and his dad plotted and strategized but it was clear that the industry had transformed and that old successful models were not working. Dynamic Designs had fallen far from its glory days; at its peak there were over five hundred employees and two busy manufacturing plants. The company was very profitable, with quality manufacturing facilities and an unrivalled salesforce that understood what their retailers and, ultimately, their consumers wanted. The company had built a solid reputation for great workmanship at a reasonable price. However, the competitive advantage that this company established could not withstand the new environment of business. Free trade agreements and the flood of cheap products from places like China hurt the business badly. The first response was to maintain price and try to appeal to the "Made in Canada" label on the Dynamic Design logo. Unfortunately, for Jason and his family (and ultimately the Canadian employees who lost their jobs), consumers wanted the cheaper imitations. It eventually became clear that they could not compete and attempts to sell higher-end homemade product lines (with better margins) also failed.

Today, Dynamic Designs has fewer than 30 full-time employees; in effect, the company is now a design house that manufactures in China and has a local sales team. Despite its fall from glory, however, the company's very existence is a testament to its management team because most of their old Canadian rivals could not cope and shut down their businesses. After trying various approaches, Jason and his dad decided to find manufacturers in China to make their products abroad. "If you can't beat them, join them," Jason said at the time.

Jason used his considerable contacts to convince many of the retailers that had stopped doing business with Dynamic Designs (because of cost) to give the revamped company some much-needed business. Things were back on track, to some extent. Unfortunately, Jason soon learned that it is much more complicated to deal with a contract manufacturer in China rather than with employees working in your local manufacturing plant. For example, he spent last Christmas and New Year's Eve in China working with his contractor to iron out manufacturing problems. His wife was not very happy. Problems that were small and easily fixed by a trip to the local plant were now complicated by distance, language issues, and complex relationships. He had received products that were not up to par and had had some complaints from retailers, but Jason managed to keep them to a minimum because of his tireless efforts. Unfortunately, the contract manufacturer's relationship is a constant juggling act at best. Jason used different partners for his various product lines because they were not very flexible nor did they have the expertise to do a variety of jobs that once existed on his shop floor in Canada. It was clear to Jason that a change was needed, but what would be the best choice for the long-term survival of Dynamic Designs?

Making Choices: The Extended Chinese Option

Jason considered building his own small facility in China but understood that the laws were very strict and that he would need a local partner to form a joint venture. On the positive side, he could benefit from more stability and control over his workforce and could start addressing quality issues by investing in equipment and long-term quality solutions. However, such a direct approach was also very risky and meant full commitment to a location and to government legislation in China. None of his contractors in China had met his high standards so he might need to forge a new relationship to create this ideal manufacturing plant. The partner could also give him some much-needed local support in China (for example, improved knowledge of local laws and customs). On the negative side, Jason was worried that he might be creating a new competitor if the partnership did not work out. Under this scenario he would need to share his contacts and many company secrets.

Making Choices: Hello Vietnam

More recently Jason visited Vietnam after reading reports that indicated that foreign direct invest (FDI) flow into Vietnam was expected to increase by 140 percent in the next year because of favourable government policies. Jason has been speaking to Vietnamese consultants and was strongly considering FDI in Vietnam because of the more business-friendly laws, the attractive costs (which were even lower than Chinese costs), and the fact that he could have better control over his manufacturing process. In essence, he could try rebuilding a version of his old manufacturing plant abroad. He would have total control over his plant, but of course the company would still be subject to the whims of a foreign government. The Vietnamese workers in this industry could be paid approximately $100 to $150 per month compared to approximately $300 dollars in Southern China. This was a significant savings in labour costs but Vietnam's infrastructure was not as good as China's. There were more power outages and shipping delays in Vietnam's underdeveloped ports.

Making Choices: Maple Leaf Horizons

To complicate matters, one local consultant told Jason to bring the manufacturing plant back home to Canada because some very cheap manufacturing spaces were now available and skilled unemployed workers were looking for work and would take lower pay. Of course, the lower pay of a Canadian furniture manufacturing worker was still approximately 10 times higher than the average wages in China and 20 to 30 times higher than the wages in Vietnam. However, the company could also apply for and receive new grants from the federal government (for plant refurbishing costs and new equipment). The move back to Canada would also provide tremendous savings in transportation costs.

After examining all the costs and benefits, Jason estimated that it would still cost Dynamic Designs an additional 10 to 30 percent to manufacture in Canada over the next five years. However, on the positive side, the move would mean increased responsiveness and quicker delivery times. This would allow Dynamic designs to fill special orders and create niche products for the market. The "Made in Canada" label might help increase sales slightly but, as Jason had learned firsthand, most consumers look at their pocketbook ahead of their passport. Finally, if Jason could make Dynamic Designs profitable while manufacturing in Canada, it would mean less travel and a more balanced life. It was clearly the ideal solution for him, but was it realistic?

The Real Decision

There were still many other issues to consider before making the final decision. Recently, one of his employees overheard Jason muttering to himself, "Dad, life was a lot easier in your day." That is absolutely true, but the question remains: What should Jason do?[1]

Promoting the Right Person at Claremont Plastics

Michele Monroe was a well-respected sales manager at Claremont Plastics. She was the type of person who united people and created a cohesive work environment. Michele had a very open management style and was very supportive but she was no pushover. Her employees knew they could always count on her but she was quite demanding. Michele understood sales; during her 30-year career she had held practically every type of sales position. For the last 15 years she had been the sales manager at Claremont. Michele had planned to retire in three or four years' time but unfortunately an illness in her family changed everything abruptly. She walked into Claremont one Monday morning and announced to her director that she was moving to Florida as soon as possible and taking her early retirement to care for her ailing daughter. Michele knew she was leaving a void but the obligation to her family was greater. A hiring committee was created to replace this valuable employee.

The Candidates

Monique Sloan was a rising young star at Claremont Plastics. She was not the front-runner for the job, because of her limited experience, but she was very impressive in her interview. Monique only had six years of relevant experience and was by far the youngest member of the staff but her dedication and her product knowledge were exceptional. Monique had built a very good rapport with her clients and her colleagues; her reports were impeccable and (unlike some of her colleagues) she really understood and respected this aspect of the job. Monique was very meticulous and analytical but she had no previous management experience. She had worked on a few team selling account projects and had quickly earned the respect of more seasoned colleagues. For example, Tim Myers (a 30-year veteran) described her as "wise beyond her years." He even tried to set her up with his nephew. Monique confidently answered tough employee management questions during her interview. While she was definitely on the right track, there was a concern that she was not quite ready.

Andre Leclerc had earned a great reputation; he was the leading salesperson at Claremont for seven straight years. There was nothing that he enjoyed more than meeting a customer and closing a deal. He provided great after sales service and did not take any call lightly. He had a passion for his job and his customers knew it. They didn't all necessarily love his methods but they knew he was the most reliable salesperson in the industry. Unless a competitor's product was clearly superior, Andre's customers would remain loyal. This fact had not escaped upper management at Claremont. As one committee member put it, "Who better to lead the troops than our best salesperson?" Andre had been with the company for over fifteen years and had always excelled at his tasks. On the other hand, Andre did not have any previous management experience and there was concern that he might lack some of the "soft skills" needed to manage the department. His sales statistics were unquestionable but he was described by some colleagues as being overly imposing and a bit inflexible, and was often characterized as being too aggressive. One member of the hiring committee warned everybody, "We risk losing our best salesperson and gaining a lousy manager." However, Andre had a lot of friends and supporters in high places (including on the committee) and despite these objections there were plenty of positive attributes that were presented to diminish these concerns.

Phil Mead was also a front-runner for the position and six of the ten salespeople in the department were actually pulling for him to get the job: they believed he would be a more stable and fair leader. Phil had only been with Claremont for six years but his experience was extensive. He had worked at two of Claremont's major competitors over his 22-year career, and had a great understanding of various work systems. In addition, he had spent two years as a sales manager at his previous organization (when his manager left on maternity leave on two occasions). By all accounts he had done a good job at this post. His rapport with his clients had been impeccable and he quickly became the second-ranked salesperson in the organization. However, his sales territory was a bit more challenging than Andre's, and he did not have access to the top accounts. In terms of performance, Phil's results were just as impressive as Andre's, if not more so.

The Decision

After much debate, the committee decided that Monique was not quite ready but had future potential. The choice was between Phil and Andre and, after some deliberation, Andre was given the job. The committee also noted that Phil could take over some of Andre's key sales accounts without hurting the company's sales figures. Monique could also fill the void and pick up some of Andre's and Phil's smaller accounts.

Andre's Managerial Transition

Andre believed that he had earned the promotion and did not hesitate to make the leap even though he would have to give up some of his hands-on sales duties and take on what he openly called tedious managerial functions. Unfortunately, he did not get off to a good start with his new subordinates. In his first official meeting he surprised and upset his former colleagues by talking about making a major change. He presented his new vision for success but it came off a bit too strong. He left his former colleagues thinking that he disapproved of their work. It just did not feel appropriate for the situation. After all, the sales figures were quite respectable and they had increased each of the last three years. The greatest resistance stemmed from his intentions to change the territorial structure. Tim Myers openly questioned him, asking "Don't you think you should review the accounts and speak to us about our territories before announcing a major structural change?" Andre just looked at him and said, "That's up to me to decide." It was clear that Andre was not there to make friends and did not mind losing a couple of old ones in his new role. People don't like change and in a business where rapport with clients is everything, it was not the best way to start his new position with the people who held these relationships with Claremont clients. That night Andre realized that his tone may have been a bit too authoritarian, but he believed it had to be done and did not back down one bit.

As the weeks passed and Andre settled into his role, concerns began to surface from subordinates and upper management alike. Subordinates felt that Andre was stepping into their territory and spending too much time micro-managing their accounts. Phil Mead was the type of person who was open to criticism and who often asked for advice from colleagues. In fact, Phil had sought out Andre's advice when he first came to the company. However, that was a few years ago. He felt he had earned some leeway and respect but now that Andre was the sales manager Phil was getting frustrated because Andre was imposing his will on everyone. He was spending almost all of his time in meetings with his sales force taking away valuable time to service accounts. According to Phil, "It was as if Andre forgot what made him successful as a salesperson. If we are stuck in meetings with him we spend less time with our customers. That is not good for the organization." Questions were also being asked by Andre's director since sales reports were slow in surfacing and sales were down. It seemed like the paperwork, which after all was part of the sales manager's job, was very low on the priority list for Andre. Instead, he saw himself as a super sales consultant.

Minor Annoyances, Major Repercussions

As time went by, the problems became worse and Andre's direct supervisor had a little chat with him about the importance of his managerial duties. Andre was told in no uncertain terms that he needed to treat all of his duties with equal care and improve his human relations approach. But nothing changed. Two months later, three of the key salespeople (including Phil Mead) left the company and indicated that Mr. Leclerc had made their lives unbearable. He constantly questioned them and removed all their freedom to manage their respective accounts. Monique was still with the company but she too was growing weary of Andre's approach and had begun to inquire about another job. Yet despite the mounting issues, Andre seemed unfazed and blamed his subordinates for not doing the job his way. Andre took on more of their responsibilities as his key subordinates left but the results were very poor. He was overwhelmed by time pressures and his new replacements were still being trained. Sales had decreased by 12 percent at a time when the industry was up nearly 3 percent. After 8 months in his position it was clear that something had to be done.

Correcting the Problem

With results like this, Andre's director, Martin Blake, felt that action needed to be taken. But what sort of action? Should Andre be fired? Did Andre need to be re-trained for his new position and duties? Clearly he did not understand the soft skills required for his new job. Perhaps the organizations had not properly supported Andre? Should Andre be demoted back to his previous position? As Martin thought about it, he was convinced that Andre might even be a bit relieved by a demotion because he preferred the sales task and hated the managerial paperwork. In addition, Andre could actually make more money in his previous position, because of the commission structure. However, he knew Andre had tremendous pride so he would likely quit if he demoted him.

Should he bring someone in from outside the organization? Could they promote Monique before losing another potential star? Clearly a decision needed to be made and change was required. What should Martin Blake do?[2]

Questions for Discussion

1. Discuss the following statement: Promoting the most successful subordinate is not always the best move. Quite often you lose a star employee and gain a lousy manager.
2. Based on what you read in the case, who would you have hired for the job? Explain.
3. Assuming that you decided to hire Andre for the new position, what could the company have done to help improve the transition from salesperson to sales manager?
4. How would you describe Andre's technical skills, human relations skills, and time management skills?

Richard Ivey School of Business
The University of Western Ontario

Online Piracy: Jaywalking or Theft?

Alex Beamish and Professor Paul Beamish wrote this case solely to provide material for class discussion. The authors do not intend to illustrate either effective or ineffective handling of a managerial situation. The authors may have disguised certain names and other identifying information to protect confidentiality.

In September 2009, Brian Lee purchased a computer game developed by a major company and, like some other customers, was experiencing difficulty running it. The source of the problems was a highly restrictive system of digital rights management (DRM),[3] which, while more or less universally disliked, was causing serious technical problems for a minority of users. Lee began to share his experience on the company's message board and was soon engaging in a debate about online piracy with a company representative. He was curious about piracy in the file-sharing age and wondered why it would be wrong to download a pirated version of the game with the DRM circumvented.

The Dialogue

Brian: I have been a loyal supporter of your company for over a decade, but that is going to change. I pre-ordered your newest game and since it arrived a week ago, I have tried repeatedly to run it but my DVD-ROM drive will not recognize the disc.

Updating drivers at the request of technical support did not fix the problem. In fact, technical support insinuated that I must be using a pirated version, which is outrageous. Many people on this message board are experiencing problems running the game and yet for the most part our computers are perfectly capable according to the box's specifications. It seems that many of the difficulties customers are experiencing result from the new system of DRM employed by the game. When it was announced months ago that the game would use this form of DRM, some were skeptical, particularly because it entailed an installation limit of five times. Yet we all expected to play the game through at least once! The retailer from which I purchased the game will not issue a refund or allow an exchange for a different game. It did permit me to swap for another copy of the same game in case the first copy was defective, but I did so and my problems remained. Also, when I tried to sell the game, I discovered that the used computer games market is now virtually non-existent due to DRM. Thus, I am out $60 and hours of time and I will never give business to your company again.

Customer Support: Dear Brian, we regret that you are experiencing this problem. It has come to our attention that a minority of users (approximately two per cent) are having trouble running the game because of DRM conflicts. We encourage you to stay in touch with technical support until a solution is reached. We are aware of the unpopularity of what seems like a draconian anti-piracy system and can assure you that our decision to use it was not taken lightly. We deemed it necessary after our games were pirated 50,000 times in 2008. That equates to 50,000 stolen games — 50,000 lost sales! We deeply regret the problems our customers face due to DRM, but we believe their frustration is better directed at the pirates who have forced us to take these measures.

Brian: Technical support has stopped replying to my e-mails. Nonetheless, I would like to respond to one of your points; namely, where you claim you lost 50,000 sales in 2008 after your games were "stolen" 50,000 times. It is incorrect to equate an illegal game download with a game stolen off a store shelf, because in the latter instance each game stolen represents a physical and likely irretrievable loss for the company, whereas software piracy entails illegal duplication. While piracy certainly cuts into your company's profits, you cannot assume that each user of a pirated software program would have purchased the retail version if a pirated version was unavailable.

Customer Support: I acknowledge that an illegally downloaded piece of media does not equate perfectly with a lost sale. However, I will in turn point out a misconception that many piracy advocates believe — that if they are morally obligated to pay for content, it should merely be the materials cost (e.g. a couple dollars for a DVD, booklet and case). But this neglects to factor in all the labour involved in the creation of the content and it suggests that intellectual property itself is worthless. How is a record company supposed to pay salaries if it receives money for the raw materials cost of CDs but not also for the creativity on the CDs? As Mark Helprin writes in *Digital Barbarism*: "The advocates of 'music sharing' think that, because the Beatles, half of whom are dead, have hundreds of millions, or perhaps even billions of dollars, and the people who would filch a song or two may have to buy their salad one tomato at a time and use milk crates as chairs, these expropriations are somehow mathematically justified. They aren't, and not merely because their cumulative effect has destroyed the music industry.... It doesn't matter if you steal a lot or a little, or if you get away with it, or not: theft is ugly."[4] I regret your problems, but I stand firm in my belief that piracy is always wrong.

Brian: I do believe intellectual property is of monetary value, and indeed I have never used pirated content. However, this is the first time I have been unable to run purchased content. While I have been waiting (I hope not in vain) for a patch to fix the game, I have researched online piracy and have learned some surprising facts. Your assertion that "piracy is always wrong" is probably off the mark. In Free Culture, Lawrence Lessig defines four different types of file sharers: a) those who "use sharing networks as substitutes for purchasing content"; b) those who "use sharing networks to sample music before purchasing it"; c) those who "use sharing networks to get access to copyrighted material that is no longer sold or that they would not have purchased because the transaction costs off the Net are too high"; and d) those who "use sharing networks to get access to content that is not copyrighted or that the copyright owner wants to give away."[5] Of course, type A is unambiguously wrong, and type D is perfectly acceptable. The grey area falls within types B and C. Some think it not unreasonable that users illegally download and "sample" a program or album before buying it and admittedly, doing so quickly eliminates many weak, overpriced products from consideration. Also, some who sample products will then buy them and a few of these converted pirates would never have known about these products had they been unavailable in pirated form. As for acquiring content no longer manufactured or commercially available but still copyrighted, I see no harm in this. Waiting for content with a "dead copyright" to enter the public domain is increasingly unrealistic considering the average copyright term in the United States has ballooned from 32 years in 1973 to 95 years in 2003.[6] In addition, it can be next to impossible to locate copyright holders of dormant works.

By the way, are there any updates on the patch?

Customer Support: We are actively working on a patch, although if we are unsuccessful we might arrange for a refund or a coupon for our products.

As for type B file sharing, I find this sense of entitlement preposterous and I doubt there is conclusive evidence that pirates often purchase works they have illegally sampled. Type C file sharing also involves a sense of entitlement. Indeed, pirates are abetted by a sense of entitlement that coincides with the new potential for massive accumulation of content and information. This sense of entitlement, Mark Helprin believes, stems from a faulty belief in endless, ubiquitous wealth; the relative youth of the anti-copyright movement and its adherents; the view that intellectual property is not property; and the expectation of paying for media not with cash, but through subjection to nonstop commercials, banners, and other advertising intrusions.[7] It is plain to see that there is a slippery slope in both types B and C. Conscientiously sampling content with a genuine willingness to buy good content turns into carelessly "sampling" everything and buying nothing. Rigorously searching the web and store bargain bins for an old underground album before downloading a pirated version as a last resort quickly degenerates into conducting a 30-second web search, conveniently concluding the album is commercially unavailable and downloading an illegal copy. Besides, there are legal means for acquiring rare content, such as eBay. The point is that types B and C quickly become type A. Ultimately, we can fret about the details but it is fair to conclude that piracy is utterly harmful not only to content creators, but also to users. Increased piracy drives up prices and necessitates measures that occasionally cause problems for paying customers such as yourself. Nobody likes intrusive DRM, but the fact remains that a mere four per cent of video games entering production will earn a profit.[8] Worldwide, more than a third of all software used in 2007 was pirated, causing lost revenues to the software industry of approximately $48 billion,[9] and DRM is a logical response to this reality. Critics of DRM hold that because DRM is sometimes circumvented, it should cease to exist. By this logic, because locks on houses are often broken, we should not bother to lock our houses.[10] The point of DRM is deterrence, and it performs this function more or less admirably.

Brian: But at what cost? DRM can undoubtedly be expensive and tricky to maintain for companies, and the drawbacks for consumers are even worse. Much of the DRM used in games, for example, is so intrusive that it remains on a user's computer after a game is uninstalled. If it retains the potential to collect information about a user's computer after the user has removed the program, is it much better than malware?[11] Installation limits are also troubling. Users are constantly formatting their hard drives or uninstalling programs to free up space, and a limit of three or five installations is unfair. Of course, I am posting here simply because of the impasse DRM has brought me to and I sense that in time we will look back on most of these anti-piracy measures with disbelief. Remember DRM audio CDs? They suffered a quick demise after it was discovered that Sony BMG was including rootkits on their DRM CDs, causing potential security vulnerabilities for customers' computers.[12] More recently, Steve Jobs, the driving force behind Apple, has identified the folly of DRM in iTunes and has succeeded in relaying his opinion to the big four record companies, who control the distribution of 70 per cent of the world's music,[13] so that the iTunes Store is now DRM-free. Fairplay, iTunes's DRM, used to mean that only iPods could play tracks purchased from iTunes, that tracks purchased from iTunes would not play on competing music players, and that there were other limitations such as only being able to access purchased tracks on a maximum of five computers. Unsurprisingly, many other digital music players and online music stores employed their own systems of DRM. Yet the vast majority of worldwide music sales were still in the form of CDs and thus were DRM-free, so it was silly and overly complex for music distributed online, which comprised a small portion of music sales, to be saddled with these different forms of DRM. Even Bill Gates himself criticized DRM, saying it has "huge problems."[14]

Customer Support: DRM is not perfect, and the anti-piracy measures of the future will undoubtedly look different from those used now. But no good comes of piracy and necessary steps need to be taken to prevent it.

Brian: Is it entirely true that no good comes of piracy? While I recognize the harm caused by piracy, it has brought certain inadvertent benefits. Jeff Raikes, when he was president of the Microsoft Business Division, stated, "Our number one goal is that we want people to use our product. If they're going to pirate somebody, we want it to be us rather than somebody else.... What you hope to do is over time you hope to convert them to licensing the software, legally licensing it."[15] Regarding the competition in China between Microsoft Windows and Linux, a free open source operating system, Bill Gates said, "It's easier for our software to compete with Linux when there's piracy than when there's not."[16] And generally speaking, have not many of the technological and cultural milestones in the West been inextricably linked to piracy? Consider Hollywood, born of pirates evading the patent laws of Thomas Edison, the inventor of filmmaking.[17] What about the United States, which neglected to recognize foreign copyrights for the first hundred years of its existence?[18] How about extensive "borrowing" and refining by Disney?[19] It was Rupert Murdoch who said that without Napster, there was no Internet, and we can see that high-speed Internet boomed due to Napster.[20] In Canada, Bell had 51,000 high-speed Internet customers when Napster launched in June 1999. By 2002, this number had jumped to 1.1 million.[21] Consider the iPod now. Hank Berry, former Napster CEO, said, "Without Napster, there is no iPod, period.... Remember that the iPod launched two years before the iTunes store was around, so you have a two-year period where essentially the only source of music for people's iPods was people doing their own ripping from their own CD collection and getting things from Napster or some other service."[22] I could go on — YouTube, cable television, radio, VCRs, CD burners, tape recorders; all these technologies owe a debt to piracy, and many could not have thrived without it.

Customer Support: I cannot say I share your utopian vision of piracy. I will grant that much of the technology we use today is or was associated with piracy, but whether we should be proud of this is another question. You seem to champion piracy and imply that theft is a key driver of innovation. Indeed, there are many likeminded individuals on the web and you would find a better reception for your views at the Pirate Bay, the famous torrent[23] indexing site. In case you were unaware, BitTorrent has taken the baton of file sharing from the older generation of peer-to-peer (P2P) programs like Napster and while there are plenty of sites from which to download torrents, none is as famous as the Pirate Bay, which is the centre of an anti-copyright, counter-culture movement touting "freedom of information" to justify facilitating massive piracy. But if you ask me, the four men who own the Pirate Bay are just masquerading as revolutionaries and their grievances about the supposed greed of corporate America lose credibility when you consider that the site racks up millions of dollars a year in ad revenues, not to mention donations. They do not simply promote and facilitate piracy, they get rich off of it. And as a result, they have been sentenced to serve a year in jail and pay millions of dollars in fines. As a matter of fact, following their sentencing the "business" has been sold to a gaming company for nearly $8 million. The company, Global Gaming Factory X, promises that the Pirate Bay will introduce legitimate business models with which to pay content owners, but the owners of the Pirate Bay seem to tell a different story, suggesting the sale will not affect the site.[24] Only time will tell. Suffice it to say, I find it repugnant to see my company's work available on the Pirate Bay for free under the pretence of "freedom of information." The fact that the Pirate Bay has many loyal fans hardly legitimizes it — is it surprising that people flock to its banner after using it to steal thousands of dollars of free content? You even have a Norwegian socialist party launching filesharer.org, a website where users are supposed to post their mug shots to demonstrate they are "criminals" like the owners of the Pirate Bay. I doubt the pro-piracy movements, political or otherwise, offer coherent, realistic plans for intellectual property rights. What they do offer is a tired communitarian philosophy, or worse — anarchy.

Brian: Geez, why are we talking about anarchy? I'm still trying to get my computer game working.

Customer Support: Fair enough. But my little rant is due to the fact that if my company cannot generate revenues, people like me lose their job.

Brian: Nobody wants you to lose your job. But can we get back to my problem? On Google, I searched for the name of the game plus the word "torrent" and was astounded at the depth of matches. The torrent sites offer a version of the game that is complete, yet cracked, so that the DRM is removed.[25] This means that following a few hours' download time, I could install a pirated copy of your game and it would probably play successfully (since there is no potential for a DRM incompatibility), not to mention present fewer hassles than the retail version. I am somewhat confounded that BitTorrent is resilient to the legal problems that defeated Napster, but I would wager that BitTorrent survives because the standard BitTorrent client does not feature a built-in search engine for torrents (these must be downloaded from a site like the Pirate Bay) and because torrents only contain metadata and not "real data."

Companies do not seem to be giving enough thought to the future of the relationship between the Internet and intellectual property. In my view, this is where our focus should lie, so I have compiled a list of technological and other ways that content could be protected from piracy. In fact, I have created a new message board thread because this is such an important topic (see Exhibit 1).

EXHIBIT 1 A Few Ways to Reduce Piracy

The first way to reduce piracy is to launch an attack against file-sharing technologies such as BitTorrent. The idea of stifling technology in order to protect copyrights is not unprecedented in recent decades. Jack Valenti, when he was president of the Motion Picture Association of America, was virulently opposed to VCRs, calling them "tapeworms": "When there are 20, 30, 40 million of these VCRs in the land, we will be invaded by millions of 'tapeworms,' eating away at the very heart and essence of the most precious asset the copyright owner has, his copyright."[26] Quashing file-sharing technologies would be an overreaction, causing technological regression, and is impractical. Much more realistic is the prospect of Internet service providers (ISPs) blocking access to file-sharing sites like the Pirate Bay and, as I understand, that site is blocked in Denmark. One problem with this measure is that torrent indexing sites are almost ubiquitous; another is that some ISPs are reluctant to offer restrictive access to the Internet because it undermines the free, limitless nature of the technology. France just narrowly rejected legislation to enact a three-strikes policy whereby users who illegally download copyrighted content would be warned twice before their Internet was cut off. A common means by which ISPs reduce traffic is "throttling," where download speeds of BitTorrent users are mitigated, and this is inadvertently an anti-piracy measure. Finally, it is evident that monitoring piracy on the Internet and then pursuing the culprits is incredibly unpopular — witness the notorious efforts of the Recording Industry Association of America to sue casual P2P users for hundreds of thousands of dollars.

There is, of course, the DRM question. DRM has arguably proven unsuccessful with digital music but is still a factor in PC games, e-books (e.g. to control copying and printing), Blu-rays and DVDs (e.g. region codes), operating systems, and even ring tones. The very fact of my writing this post speaks to one of DRM's shortcomings — inconveniencing legitimate customers, whether through bogging down the experience or stopping it altogether. An alternative to the sort of DRM that irritates computer gamers is selling games through Steam, an online distribution system (somewhat like an iTunes for games) that requires users to log in and for some games be connected to the Internet. This could be considered "DRM-lite." Most games sold on Steam do not use a separate system of DRM; hence, most do not have installation limits or disc checks (since Steam games are all downloaded), and do not leave remnants of DRM on the computer after removal.

Bundling software with new computers is an effective method of combating software piracy. Another good method is cloud computing, in which software functionality lies on a vendor's server instead of on a local PC.[27] Another possibility is software asset management, which helps users keep track of software licenses. The potential rise of streaming media services offering a vast archive of high-quality media could mitigate the appeal of downloading media illegally (and perhaps with lower quality) through BitTorrent. Last.fm is an innovative Internet radio site that streams free music with ads, and offers a premium service for a small subscription fee. Spotify streams free ad-supported music to computer users and is experimenting with a subscription model for mobile phone users. These business models accept that the current generation, rightly or wrongly, feels entitled to music for free or for dirt cheap.

Moving on, there are ways to protect content that are rooted more in ideology than technology. Does overpriced content significantly increase piracy rates? Certainly some users engage in piracy out of a belief that big business does not need or deserve their money. However, the correlation between price and piracy rates is difficult to gauge for general Western populations. On the other hand, many users in the developing world are simply too poor to pay for content, whether it costs $2 or $20, and unsurprisingly the highest software piracy rates in the world are in Georgia (95 per cent), Bangladesh (92 per cent), Armenia (92 per cent) and Zimbabwe (92 per cent), while the lowest piracy rates are in North America (21 per cent) and Western Europe (33 per cent).[28] Finally, globalization means that emerging markets will increasingly value legitimate software, and will be more active in cracking down on intellectual property violations. This seems to be playing out in China right now.

It is plausible that some tweaking of copyright laws is in order. For example, Canada has not updated its copyright law since 1997, two years before the release of Napster.[29] As well, some argue that people need to change their perceptions about piracy — should it remain illegal to download "abandonware," that is, software no longer sold or supported and for which no one is actively asserting copyright ownership? The following system could be implemented for users who want to draw from, or publishers who want to make available, orphan works: "In the absence of a claimant, a notice could be posted on a universal copyright internet notice board. After a reasonable time and no response, a potential user or publisher could be granted permission to use or publish, with royalties held in escrow for yet another period, until they were claimed. And if they were not claimed, they could be directed to a fund of some sort, or revert to the payer. These simple steps would make orphan works available and protect the copyright holders at the same time."[30] Are copyright terms in general too long? In the United States, the only software that has entered the public domain due to copyright expiration is software published before 1964 that was not renewed in its copyright during its 28th year following publication; for unpublished software, the copyright lasts 70 years plus the life of the author, regardless of when it was written.[31] Hopefully Creative Commons[32] will grow in popularity so that content creators can conveniently permit their work to be available to others with minimal restrictions if they so desire. New possibilities for abandonware and orphan works, as well as the availability of a more flexible copyright, could reduce the scope of what is considered piracy and copyright infringement.

More sample or trial versions[33] of software, music, and movies could reduce piracy rates to a small degree. Evolving attitudes, perhaps influenced through educational initiatives, could present purchasing content as classy and pirating as reprehensible. The public should be informed that pirated content frequently comes with malware, and that unpaid taxes on pirated content can hurt communities.

To end, I would like to share a scheme proposed by Harvard law professor William Fisher to solve the problem of online piracy: "Under his plan, all content capable of digital transmission would (1) be marked with a digital watermark.... Once the content is marked, then entrepreneurs would develop (2) systems to monitor how many items of each content were distributed. On the basis of those numbers, then (3) artists would be compensated. The compensation would be paid for by (4) an appropriate tax."[34] Thus, users would simply download what they wanted and taxes would compensate content creators according to how much their work was downloaded. Lawrence Lessig has proposed a slight modification to this scheme.

At this juncture, I must say that it has been weeks since I first notified technical support of my problems and that the assistance I have received has been disappointing, if not unethical. When I first explained my problem, tech support provided me with a customer complaint number and asked a question about my computer hardware, then received a response, sent another question, received another response and stopped replying. When I e-mailed to ask why they stopped responding, they gave me a new customer complaint number, started asking the same questions as before and again stopped replying. They have issued four customer complaint numbers now and I suspect they keep placing me at the top of the queue so that I give up trying. They have never apologized or indicated a serious effort to fix my problem, and especially disconcerting is their suggestion that I am using a pirated version and that this must be the source of my difficulties (ironically, a pirated version would probably play fine). As a former part-time business student, I detect a weakness in your service recovery. In fact, in my view, it is so bad that it is bordering on immoral. I found an old ethics textbook which says that the minimal moral obligation of a business organization toward customers is "Accurately labeled, safe goods and services of good value. Adequate customer information. Respect promises on delivery and performance."[35]

Customer Support: I take issue with your claim that the company has conducted itself unethically in response to your problem. We care deeply about customers' concerns, though unfortunately technical support is overstretched and cannot always provide immediate assistance. I can assure you we are operating in accordance with ethical standards. But remember, if users object to the glitches, installation limits, and other hassles brought on by DRM in games, they should not forget that the pirates are the offending party, not us.

Brian: Whatever you say! Did you read the new thread about ways to cut down on online piracy?

Customer Support: Yes, I read it over and it's interesting stuff. At this time I regret to inform you that due to cash flow issues, we cannot issue a refund. Furthermore, we have been unsuccessful in developing a patch. Thank you for your understanding.

Richard Ivey School of Business
The University of Western Ontario

The Pepsi Ultimate Taste Challenge 2012: Social Enough?

Jawwad Khurshid, Jill Campbell, Miguel Huller, Paul Strachan, and Zoe Baldwin wrote this case under the supervision of Professor June Cotte solely to provide material for class discussion. The authors do not intend to illustrate either effective or ineffective handling of a managerial situation. The authors may have disguised certain names and other identifying information to protect confidentiality.

It was mid-April 2012 as Robb Hadley sat in his Toronto office contemplating the busy summer ahead of him. As Director of Marketing for Pepsi Beverages Canada (PBC), Hadley was responsible for the overall success of what used to be called The Pepsi Challenge. Now known as the Ultimate Taste Challenge (UTC), this year's iteration had some lofty targets.

PepsiCo's UTC participation goal was 1.5 million taste challenges designed to target segment growth in Millennials[36]—particularly those 16 to 25 years of age—in urban, lower-share markets, principally in Toronto and Vancouver.

Historically the Pepsi Challenge had played a key role in driving Pepsi brand leadership in Canada. However the last time the challenge was executed was in 2004, the same year Facebook was invented. Hadley wondered what would happen if Pepsi combined the power of one of the best grass roots marketing programs, UTC, with the power of social media?

Hadley would soon have to decide whether or not to approve the UTC marketing plan as developed by their agency, BBDO. The final proposal from the agency sat on his desk but Hadley had a few concerns. One concern was if the plan would achieve the targets set for the program. The plan was big—with 15 challenge teams attending local and national events over the course of the summer. New technologies had been incorporated to accent the UTC experience and Hadley was confident these would be a hit with participants. However, PepsiCo's competitor's plans would present a challenge, as Coca Cola would be an official sponsor of both the London Summer Olympics and the UEFA Champions League Euro Cup soccer tournament. This would undoubtedly drive Coca Cola company's image, and Coca Cola was already beginning to challenge PepsiCo's Canadian market share leadership.

Hadley was particularly concerned with the depth of the BBDO proposal in terms of social media. There was no doubt that there was tremendous potential for social media to amplify the impact of the traditional Pepsi Taste Challenge experience. As he gazed out the window on a beautiful sunny spring day he wondered, "Had BBDO properly addressed the social media component of the UTC or was there more that should be done?"

History of Pepsi in Canada and the Carbonated Soda Drink (CSD) Market

PepsiCo expanded to Canada in 1934. On June 12th of that year, the company opened their first bottling plant in Montreal, Quebec. It was currently the market leader in Canada due to its strong heritage. Seventy-eight years after opening its first plant, PepsiCo's products were in more than 10 million households across the country. The company employed 5,000 people nationwide and their main goal was to grow PepsiCo brands.

The Canadian soft drink market was very competitive. Both PepsiCo and Coca Cola (with 45.3 points and 44.2 points total market share with their combined brands, respectively) recognized their strengths and where they had opportunity to grow (see Exhibit 2).

EXHIBIT 2 Pepsico Beverages Company and Coca-Cola Enterprises Market Shares

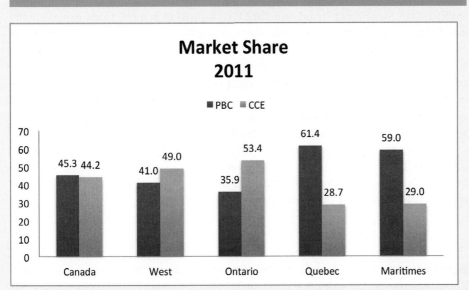

Source: Internal Company Data

PepsiCo's beverage portfolio consisted of some of the world's most popular brands: Pepsi, Diet Pepsi, Pepsi Max, Tropicana, Gatorade, 7UP, Mountain Dew, Lipton Brisk, Aquafina, Amp, SoBe, and Starbucks bottled beverages. Coca Cola's product line was similar to that of PepsiCo's—consisting of both cola and non-cola carbonated drinks. The Coca Cola brands included: Coke, Diet Coke, Coke Zero, Vitamin Water, Nestea, Dasani, Simply Orange, and PowerAde.

PBC Market Strategy

PBC's goal in 2012 was to solidify its leadership by growing its market share in Canada. In order to achieve this objective, PBC wanted to significantly increase its investment in its Pepsi brand (this included Pepsi, Diet Pepsi, Pepsi Max). This increase in spending revolved around three big initiatives:

1. "Max it with Millennials" (PBC had achieved strong sales growth with Pepsi Max—205 percent increase in the last year);
2. "Own Taste this Summer" (Ultimate Taste Challenge); and
3. "Leverage our Properties" (sponsorships of the television show X-Factor and the Canadian Football League)

With such a substantial budget increase in 2012, it was clear that these initiatives were of the utmost importance to Pepsi. In order to achieve the target growth, PBC had decided the segment that it would focus on would be Millennials—specifically those between the ages of 16 and 25 years.

Pepsi Ultimate Taste Challenge (UTC)

The UTC had been a long-standing part of Pepsi's brand advertising strategy. First launched in Canada in 1942, the 'Pepsi Taste Test' (as it was then known) aimed to highlight Pepsi's superior taste to consumers.[37] The UTC was essentially a blind taste test. Participants were given unmarked glasses of Pepsi and Coke and asked which they preferred. On average, these taste tests revealed that Canadians preferred the taste of Pepsi.[38]

2012 Ultimate Taste Challenge

Dubbed "The Summer of Firsts", the 2012 UTC aspired to achieve a new experience by using technology to revolutionize the way the event was conducted. A number of new elements had been added to make the user experience more modern, interactive, and cool. These updates included allowing customers to personalize the challenge to their particular sub-brand of Pepsi and Coke (Pepsi versus Coke, Diet Pepsi versus Diet Coke or Pepsi Max versus Coke Zero). The 2012 UTC was scheduled to run from May 17 to August 31, 2012 using a series of on-site street teams, which would be deployed at selected events across Canada (see Exhibit 3).

Hadley's objective was to drive an unprecedented 1.5 million people to experience the UTC. In particular, he wanted to ensure the campaign would resonate with Millennials. This UTC would be the first to integrate social media in order to allow customers to share their experience beyond the booth.

BBDO

Headquartered in New York City with a presence in over 80 countries worldwide, BBDO was one of the world's leading advertising agencies. For the past 6 years, the Gunn Report ranked BBDO as the world's most awarded advertising agency.[39] The agency's prestigious list of clients included Diageo, FedEx, Starbucks and PepsiCo.

EXHIBIT 3 Roll-Out Plans: 2012 Ultimate Taste Challenge

Source: Internal Company Data

PepsiCo and BBDO had collaborated on advertising since 1960 and BBDO's iconic ad campaigns for Pepsi helped transform the brand into a leading soft drink, challenging the Coca Cola company constantly for leadership in the carbonated beverage market.[40]

BBDO Proposal: Social Media and the UTC

Hadley gave BBDO the challenge of taking the UTC "to the next level" by extending the experience online using social media as a hub. This included some clear objectives for the social media campaign: drive consumers to participate in the UTC through their social networks to communicate their experiences, generate new fans, and drive consumers to participate at a live UTC event.

In response to Hadley's request, BBDO put together a social media strategy using Facebook as the central page for all activity. In order to drive customers to PepsiCo's Facebook page, BBDO planned a massive television, radio, and point of sale (POS) campaign. This landing page would be set up to promote the UTC, to host feedback and selected video/picture content from the UTC (uploaded by street teams), and to advertise locations and schedules for UTC events. An online website featuring a virtual taste challenge would be incorporated and participants would be rewarded with coupons and QR codes[41] that could be redeemed for prizes. Customers would then load these coupons/QRs on the Facebook page to win different prizes. Twitter would be used to drive traffic to the Facebook page and in-store displays and packaging would promote the UTC as well, carrying QR codes to drive customers to Facebook, as well.

The Facebook page would allow users to create an online profile and take an online taste challenge, which would pit a user against another or against a clock to score points redeemable for prizes. A leader board would update and display points leaders in real time. The agency indicated, however, that there remained some question as to whether the avatars and characteristics of user profiles would be customizable due to budgetary considerations (see Exhibit 4).

A Twitter feed had been discussed as a component of the Facebook portal, but it was described as being accessible only to street teams to tweet updates and event

EXHIBIT 4 Promotional Budget 2012 Canadian Ultimate Taste Challenge

14%

4%

8%

46%

28%

- ☐ TV
- ▨ Grassroots
- ☐ Radio
- ■ Digital
- ▨ Other

Source: Internal Company Data

notifications, rather than an interactive facility for participants to share their thoughts and experiences with the UTC. Limited video uploads would also be included, as determined by street teams and site managers.

Where to from Here?

Hadley returned his attention to the BBDO proposal sitting on his desk. Overall, he felt BBDO had done a good job revamping the booths and integrating new Microsoft surface technology[42] to enhance the "coolness" of the participants' experience. He was comfortable with the campaign, in general, as it had always been a successful formula for PepsiCo in the past; however, the new strategy relied heavily on social media to drive increased awareness of the campaign and to drive traffic to the UTC booths. Previous UTCs had attracted less than 1 million people. Had BBDO designed a social media strategy that would achieve the aggressive goals Hadley had set out? Would it appeal to Millennials? Should he proceed with the proposal as planned or were changes needed?

Hadley recognized that there were many considerations in designing a social media campaign. It was unclear if BBDO had properly incorporated it or if it had been more of a "plug-in" on the back of a traditional media effort. What would a successful social media campaign look like? Hadley summoned his marketing team and posed this very question. He asked them to conduct relevant research and to report to him in a week's time with recommendations. The timing of the UTC program would allow Hadley the opportunity to develop a social media platform for the Pepsi brand that could grow into a more permanent way to connect with the company's consumers in the future. He had to get this right.

Healthy Life Group

Richard Ivey School of Business
The University of Western Ontario

Ian Dunn wrote this case under the supervision of Elizabeth M.A. Grasby solely to provide material for class discussion. The authors do not intend to illustrate either effective or ineffective handling of a managerial situation. The authors may have disguised certain names and other identifying information to protect confidentiality.

It was early June 2010, and two months had passed since Heather Larson had been granted exclusive Canadian distribution rights to the Nutrifusion product. She had been very busy trying to develop the best strategy for this exciting new product. Nutrifusion had been sold successfully in the United States, and Larson believed it had the potential to earn strong profits and to provide her with a new career; however, as with any new venture, inherent risks were involved. Larson, in partnership with her father, Jeff Larson, was contemplating the launching of Healthy Life Group (HLG) to market Nutrifusion throughout Canada. The partners wanted to evaluate the product's financial feasibility before deciding whether to proceed with the opportunity. If they did decide to proceed, HLG would incorporate and begin operations on January 1, 2011.

Nutrifusion

Nutrifusion was an intriguing new product in the health-food industry. A patented production process used select parts of the fruits and vegetables, namely the stem and core, and protected micronutrients[43] and phytochemicals[44] to retain 99.7 per cent of their nutritional value. The end result was a tasteless powder that could be added to baked goods or to liquids to provide additional servings[45] of fruits and vegetables, thereby significantly increasing the food's nutritional value. Nutrifusion also had the benefits of high levels of antioxidants, was an excellent source of plant-derived vitamins A and C, was 100 per cent natural, and had a shelf life of 36 months. See Exhibit 5 for a comparison of the nutritional value of normal tortilla chips and tortilla chips made with Nutrifusion.

Healthy Life Group

The Partners

Heather Larson was a fourth-year student at The University of Western Ontario. She was working towards a bachelor's degree in management and organizational studies, with a double major in sociology. Larson had spent the previous summer working as an assistant product manager at Loblaws in the dairy, snack, and beverage department. She had been exposed to entrepreneurial activities most of her life since her father had founded and owned several companies. Upon graduation, Larson hoped to have a full-time job in a venture that would allow her to start up her own company.

Larson's father, Jeff Larson, was eager to support his daughter with her business venture. He offered an array of experience in the retail food industry, including a valuable network of contacts. In 1994, Jeff Larson co-founded Concepts Food and also worked for Cott Corporation. While at Cott, he worked closely with Dave Nichol, the long-time president of Loblaw who launched the "President's Choice" label. The pair was involved in the management buy-out of Destination Products, a division of Cott Corporation. Currently, Jeff Larson (no longer working for Cott Corporation) owned Innovative Food Group, a company that specialized in private-label sales and marketing.

EXHIBIT 5 Nutritional Facts and Label Claims

Organic Tortilla Chips

Compare Vitamins

Nutrition Facts

Serving Size   1 oz (28-35g)
Servings Per Container About 8

Amount per Serving		
Calories 140	Calories from fat 60	
		% Daily Values*
Total Fat	6 g	9%
Saturated Fat	0.5 g	3%
Trans Fat	0 g	
Cholesterol	0 g	0%
Sodium	100 mg	4%
Total Carbohydrates	18 g	6%
Dietary Fiber	2 g	8%
Sugars	0 g	
Protein	2 g	

Vitamin A 0%	•	Vitamin C 0%
Calcium 2%	•	Iron 2%

*Percent Daily Values are based on a 2000 calorie diet. Your daily values may be higher or lower depending on your calorie needs.

	Calories	2,000	2,500
Total Fat	Less than	65 g	80 g
Sat Fat	Less than	20 g	25 g
Cholesterol	Less than	300 mg	300 mg
Sodium	Less than	2,400 mg	2,400 mg
Total Carbohydrate		300 g	375 g
Dietary Fiber		25 g	30 g

Calories per gram:

Fat 9   •   Carbohydrates 4   •   Protein 4

INGREDIENTS: ORGANIC YELLOW CORN, EXPELLER PRESSED SAFFLOWER OIL AND/OR SUNFLOWER OIL AND/OR CANOLA OIL, SEA SALT

Nutrition Facts

Serving Size   10-12 chips (28g)
Servings Per Container 8

Amount per Serving		
Calories 140	Calories from Fat 50	
		% Daily Values*
Total Fat 6g		9%
Saturated Fat 0.5g		3%
Trans Fat 0g		
Cholesterol 0g		0%
Sodium 100mg		4%
Total Carbohydrates 18g		6%
Dietary Fiber 2g		8%
Sugars 0g		
Protein 2g		

Vitamin A 50%	•	Vitamin C 30%
Calcium 2%	•	Iron 2%
Vitamin E 2%	•	Thiamin 10%
Riboflavin 2%	•	Vitamin B12 10%

*Percent Daily Values are based on a 2000 calorie diet. Your daily values may be higher or lower depending on your calorie needs.

	Calories	2,000	2,500
Total Fat	Less than	65g	80g
Saturated Fat	Less than	20g	25g
Cholesterol	Less than	300mg	300mg
Sodium		2,400mg	2,400mg
Total Carbohydrate		300g	375mg
Dietary Fiber		25g	30g

Calories per gram:

Fat 9   •   Carbohydrates 4   •   Protein 4

INGREDIENTS: ORGANIC YELLOW CORN, EXPELLER PRESSED SAFFLOWER OIL AND/OR SUNFLOWER OIL AND/OR CANOLA OIL, NATURAL WHOLE FOOD CONCENTRATE OF (APPLES, BROCCOLI, CRANBERRIES, CARROTS, ORANGES AND TOMATOES), SEA SALT.

- High in Antioxidants
- Excellent source of Vitamin A (Beta Carotene)
- Excellent source of Vitamin C
- Each Serving contains 400mcg of Lycopene
- Each serving of chips contains a healthy source of nutritional ingredients.

Source: Company files

Objectives

Larson and her father hoped HLG could earn a profit of $50,000 in its first year of operations, with plans to grow profits by 20 per cent each subsequent year. This growth could be achieved by broadening the product line and expanding into additional stores. Another of HLG's goals was to help society move towards a healthier lifestyle: the Nutrifusion product would allow Canadians to improve their diets and overall health by supplying servings of fruits and vegetables in products like bagels, chips, and cookies, which might otherwise be considered junk food.

Investment

In order to start the business Larson and her father planned to invest $25,000 each, and, in return, each would receive 1,000 common shares. The largest portion of this capital investment would be used to obtain the Canadian patent on the Nutrifusion production process. The company's law firm, Stikeman Elliot LLP, estimated the drafting of this patent would cost $10,000, and the cost to prosecute the patent into issuance would be $12,000.[46] HLG would also incur fees, estimated to total $8,000, to incorporate the business, obtain a master business licence, and complete name registration.

The Food Industry

Food sales of Canadian supermarkets and convenience stores surpassed $75,727 million in 2007. The Province of Ontario represented 33.5 per cent of the total sales. The grocery industry typically averaged a net profit margin of six per cent. Canadians had readily supported the movement towards healthier lifestyles, as reflected in an increased demand for organic and healthy foods, as well as vitamins and supplements, over the past five years; however, these nutritional products were often more expensive than alternative food choices. Industry studies reported that high-income households most often met the recommended minimum fruit and vegetable intake; however, lower-income families and "on-the-go" individuals were less likely to consistently eat organic produce. Larson completed a survey of grocery shoppers, and her results showed a desire for higher nutritional value in bread products and snack foods. A recent study revealed that 75 per cent of U.S. residents failed to consume the minimum recommended intake of five servings of fruits and vegetables each day.[47]

In 2009, Canada was in the midst of an economic recession. In particular, Southwestern Ontario, a major automotive manufacturing centre, was hard hit, a circumstance that forced Canadian consumers to reduce their spending and to become more price-conscious. As a result, many Canadians eliminated non-staple items from their grocery lists, such as vitamins, supplements, and organic fruits and vegetables. Although the economy showed signs of improvement in 2010, economists predicted that Canadian consumers would remain price-conscious for some time.

All products sold in the food industry were subject to approval from the Canadian Food Inspection Agency (CFIA). Before distribution occurred, companies had to submit nutritional and production information to CFIA for evaluation, a process that could take up to two years to be completed.

The Competition

Nutrifusion had no direct competition in Canada. It was the only product of its kind that offered full servings of fruits and vegetables in the form of a tasteless powder that retained micronutrients and phytochemicals. Furthermore, HLG had been granted exclusive distribution rights to the Nutrifusion product for Canada. To ensure that other companies could not duplicate this product in Canada, HLG planned to obtain a patent for the ingredients, the technology and the process used to break down fruits and vegetables into the powder.

There was plenty of indirect competition facing both HLG and Nutrifusion. Consumers could readily purchase servings of fruits and vegetables and consume them on their own or use them as ingredients in various dishes; however, for the nutritional value offered by Nutrifusion, consumers would need to purchase organic fruits and vegetables for consumption. Alternatively, consumers could choose to forgo the fresh fruit and vegetable servings, instead opting to improve their diets through vitamins and supplements, which were widely marketed to provide similar benefits. Varieties of these products existed and were easily available throughout grocery stores, drug stores, and nutritional supplement specialty stores, which were growing in popularity.

Another form of indirect competition existed. If HLG chose to infuse products such as potato chips, cookies, and bagels with Nutrifusion powder, it also had to convince consumers to purchase the company's new line of these three items: potato chips, cookies, and bagels. Consequently, all other brands of potato chips, cookies and bagels would become HLG's competition. Because of their high fibre content, items such as multigrain and whole-wheat bagels had historically represented healthy-choice items to consumers, but they did not provide any fruit or vegetable servings. For potato chips, the closest competition likely came from kettle chips that were marketed as containing 65 per cent less fat than regular potato chips. Whichever product HLG chose, many competitive products existed, some made by large international companies. Corporations such as Lays and Nabisco had the resources and ability to market their snack foods as "healthy" based on a variety of parameters, and they often had eye-catching advertisements to attract buyers.

Distribution Plans

After evaluating several distribution alternatives, Larson believed a strategic alliance with Loblaw Companies (Loblaw) would be most lucrative. Loblaw showed strong interest in the Nutrifusion product and was willing to work closely with HLG since it had exclusive distribution rights to the product. The agreement would use Nutrifusion in the production of several President's Choice products. President's Choice was Loblaws' own private label brand and was distributed in over 1,700 stores throughout the provinces of Ontario and Quebec. President's Choice offered a variety of grocery products, which were marketed as equal quality to brand name merchandise but at a lower price.

In its first year, HLG planned on infusing President's Choice cookies, bagels, and potato chips with Nutrifusion powder to improve the products' nutritional values. Both Loblaw and HLG were excited to see the sales results of these test products and would consider adding Nutrifusion powder to more products if the test's sales results were successful.

Projected Sales and Costs

Sales

In its first year of operations, all HLG sales would be made to Loblaw on credit. HLG agreed to offer Loblaw credit terms of net 60. Loblaw would purchase quantities of Nutrifusion powder for use in its production of cookies, bagels, and potato chips. Although there were no guarantee of sales volumes, Loblaw and HLG estimated first-year sales based on a combination of U.S. data and Loblaw's experience in launching new products. Together, the companies estimated that first-year sales would be 36,500 packages of the Nutrifusion cookies, 50,000 bagels, and 28,000 bags of potato chips. Loblaws production requirements called for 10 grams of Nutrifusion for each package of cookies and potato chips and five grams of Nutrifusion for each bagel. HLG would sell the Nutrifusion powder in bulk to Loblaws at $19.99 per 100-gram package.

Costs

HLG purchased the Nutrifusion powder from its American distributor on account, and the American supplier extended credit terms of net 30. The powder cost amounted to 30 per cent of HLG's sales to Loblaws. HLG also planned to maintain a 15-day inventory of Nutrifusion powder at all times.

HLG planned to rent office space in close proximity to the Loblaw headquarters, in Toronto, Ontario, in order to facilitate distribution. Office rent would be $990 a month and required immediate payment of both first and last months' rent. The office space needed some furnishings and fixtures, such as desks, chairs, tables and additional lighting, so Larson budgeted $5,000 for these items. The furniture and fixtures would be amortized using the straight-line method and had an estimated useful life of five years with no salvage value. Another $4,500 would be spent on computer equipment, which would be amortized using the double declining balance method over an estimated useful life of four years, assuming a salvage value of $500.

Other anticipated annual costs are listed in Exhibit 6. All costs in Exhibit 6 would be paid in full by fiscal year-end. Any income taxes owing would have to be paid two months after the fiscal year ended, i.e., December 31.[48]

Larson would work full-time for HLG as its only employee, while her father pursued another business opportunity. Larson projected a $40,000 salary for herself in HLG's first year of operations. Larson and her father were also interested in receiving dividends from HLG, but they thought it would be wise to wait until after the first year of operations to see whether the business had sufficient cash and retained earnings to pay any dividends.

Conclusion

The partners were excited about securing the exclusive Canadian distribution rights for Nutrifusion. Before making a decision to pursue the venture, they had to assess the attractiveness of Nutrifusion to the industry, the idea's overall feasibility and the financial viability of their arrangement with Loblaw. Heather Larson wanted to project an income statement and a balance sheet for the year ending December 31, 2011, to see whether HLG could generate the profit targeted by the Larsons and, if so, whether it could pay dividends. She also wondered whether Loblaw was too optimistic in its sales projections, so she wanted to determine what effect a 20 percent decrease in Loblaw's original sales estimate would have on HLG's projected statements. Projections and profitability aside, would the Larsons' decision to distribute solely through Loblaw foster or inhibit future growth? Taking these questions into consideration, Larson hoped to make a decision quickly on whether to launch HLG so she could either begin the process of incorporating the business or move on to another new business idea.

EXHIBIT 6 Projected Annual Expenses	
Advertising	$ 3,000
Utilities	1,200
Printing	440
Travel	2,250
Insurance	800
Phone and Internet	770
Office supplies	340
Miscellaneous	500
TOTAL	$ 9,300

Source: Company files

Notes, Sources, and Credits

Reference Notes

Chapter 1

1. "2011 Rankings of Canada's Top 1000 Public Companies by Profit," *The Globe and Mail*, June 23, 2011.

2. Richard Blackwell, "Canada Ranks High in Low Business Costs," *The Globe and Mail*, March 31, 2010, p. B5; also "Best Country for Business: Canada," *The Globe and Mail*, October 5, 2011, B2.

3. See Robert A. Collinge and Ronald M. Ayers, *Economics by Design: Principles and Issues*, 2nd ed. (Upper Saddle River, NJ: Prentice Hall, 2000), 41–42; Michael J. Mandel, "The New Economy," *Business Week*, January 31, 2000, 73–77.

4. Karl E. Case and Ray C. Fair, *Principles of Economics*, 6th ed. (Upper Saddle River, NJ: Prentice Hall, 2003), 224–225.

5. Sean Wise, "Social Networks Reshaping Economics," *Winnipeg Free Press*, May 18, 2011, A11.

6. Andres Oppenheimer, "Latin America Is Skeptical," *The Orlando Sentinel*, February 20, 2006, A19.

7. James Kynge, "Private Firms' Growth in China Striking: Report," *National Post*, May 11, 2000, C14.

8. "Cuba Allows Private Ads in Phone Book," *The Globe and Mail*, December 9, 2011, p. B7.

9. Richard I. Kirkland, Jr., "The Death of Socialism," *Fortune*, January 4, 1988, 64–72.

10. See Karl E. Case and Ray C. Fair, *Principles of Economics*, 5th ed. (Upper Saddle River, NJ: Prentice Hall, 1999), 69–74; Robert A. Collinge and Ronald M. Ayers, *Economics by Design: Principles and Issues*, 2nd ed. (Upper Saddle River, NJ: Prentice Hall, 2000), 51–52.

11. Andres Oppenheimer, "While Latin America Nationalizes, India Opens Up," *Orlando Sentinel*, January 22, 2007, A11.

12. John Greenwood, "Study Cites Privatization in Productivity Gains," *National Post*, June 26, 200, p. FP1.

13. *Bank of Canada Banking and Financial Statistics*, Series G1, Government of Canada Fiscal Position, April 26, 2012, S84.

14. Barbara Shecter, "CRTC Orders Broadcasters to Quiet Down; ADS too Loud; Quebecor, CBC Given a Year to Comply," *National Post*, September 14, 2011, FP6.

15. Iain Marlow, "CRTC, Industry Canada Push for Greater Powers," *The Globe and Mail*, November 24, 2010, B5.

16. Susan Krashinsky, "CRTC Faces Confounding 'New World,'" *The Globe and Mail*, June 29, 2011, B6.

17. Terence Corcoran, "Power Grab; CRTC Uses Vertical Integration as Excuse to Expand its Authority," *National Post*, September 22, 2011, FP11. For a competing opinion, see George Burger, "Boosting Competition; Muscular New CRTC Regime Will Benefit Consumers," *National Post*, September 28, 2011, FP15.

18. Susan Krashinsky, "In the Netflix Era, Regulating TV Gets a Lot Tougher," *The Globe and Mail*, July 8, 2011, B1.

19. Steve Ladurantaye, "Internet Service Providers Not Subject To Broadcast Regulations, Supreme Court Rules," *The Globe and Mail*, February 10, 2012, B3.

20. Laura Rance, "Wheat Board's Going … Now What?" *Winnipeg Free Press*, May 7, 2011, B6.

21. "UFC May Have Long Wait to Crack Ontario Market," thestar.com, May 23, 2010, www.thestar.com/printarticle/783892.

22. Jim Middlemiss, "Don't Get Caught Offside in Rules Changes; Wrong Advice on Competition Act Could Be Costly," *National Post*, March 23, 2009, FP6. For an analysis of the current situation in the United States regarding resale price maintenance, see Joseph Pereira, "Price-Fixing Makes Comeback After Supreme Court Hearing," *The Wall Street Journal*, August 18, 2008, A1, A12.

23. Hollie Shaw, "Bogus Ads: If You Mislead the Consumer, Be Ready to Suffer the Financial Fallout," *National Post*, May 22, 2009, FP12.

24. Simon Houpt, "Fat Chance Nivea's Slimming Cream Worrks, Competition Bureau Rules," *The Globe and Mail*, September 8, 2011, B1.

25. Shirley Won and Jacquie McNish, "Antitrust Watchdog Loses Beer Battle," *The Globe and Mail*, March 29, 2007, B1, B6.

26. "Ontario to Move Ahead with $50B Lawsuit Against Tobacco Majors," *National Post*, January 7, 2012, FP6.

27. Drew Hasselback, "Scope of Safety Act is Broad; Law Applies to Retailers as Much as Manufacturers," *National Post*, February 22, 2011, FP10.

28. Karen Selick, "The C-36 Shutdown; Consumer Safety Act May Shutter Small Businesses," *National Post*, March 9, 2011, FP17.

29. John Gray, "Texas Fold 'Em," *Canadian Business*, October 9–22, 2006, 44–46.

30. "Alberta Film, TV Production Faces Decline," May 19, 2010, CBC News, www.cbc.ca/arts/film/story/2010/05/18alberta-film-production-decline.html.

31. Jennifer Allen, "New Lobby Rules Mean More Work for Lawyers," *The Globe and Mail*, August 13, 2008, B5.

32. See Karl E. Case and Ray C. Fair, *Principles of Economics*, 5th ed. (Upper Saddle River, NJ: Prentice Hall, 1999), 70–90; Robert A. Collinge and Ronald M. Ayers, *Economics by Design: Principles and Issues*, 2nd ed. (Upper Saddle River, NJ: Prentice Hall, 2000), 74–77.

33. Patrick Barta and Jane Spencer, "As Alternative Fuels Heat Up, Environmental Concerns Grow," *The Wall Street Journal*, December 5, 2006, pp. A1, A13.

34. Andy Hoffman, "Global Demand for Maple Syrup Keeps Rising. Sweet!," *The Globe and Mail*, March 12, 2009, B1.

35. Bob Davis and Douglas Belkin, "Food Inflation, Riots Spark Worries for World Leaders," *The Wall Street Journal*, April 14, 2008, p. A1.

36. Scott Kilman and Liam Pleven, "Prices Soar on Crop Woes," *The Wall Street Journal*, January 13, 2011, p. A1.

37. For a detailed analysis of the rise in food prices, see Sinclair Stewart and Paul Waldie, "The Byzantine World of Food Pricing: How Big Money is Wreaking Havoc," *The Globe and Mail*, May 31, 2008, pp. B4–B7.

38. Joel Millman, "Metal Is So Precious that ScrAP Thieves Now TAP Beer Kegs," *The Wall Street Journal*, March 14, 2006, pp. A1, A15.

39. See Paul Heyne, Peter J. Boettke, and David L. Prychitko, *The Economic Way of Thinking*, 10th ed. (Upper Saddle River, NJ: Prentice Hall, 2003), 190, 358–359.

40. Karl E. Case and Ray C. Fair, *Principles of Economics*, 6th ed. (Upper Saddle River, NJ: Prentice Hall, 2003), 300–309.

41. Timothy Aeppel, "Show Stopper: How Plastic Popped the Cork Monopoly," *The Wall Street Journal*, May 1, 2010, A1.

42. "Royal Mail's Reign Comes to an End," *The Globe and Mail*, January 2, 2006, B7.

43. Eric Bellman, "As Economy Zooms, India's Postmen Struggle to Adapt," *The Wall Street Journal*, October 3, 2006, A1, A12.

44. Barrie McKenna, "Snail Mail Corp. Tries to Break out of its Shell," *The Globe and Mail*, January 21, 2011, B1.

45. Vincent Geloso and Youri Chassin, "Postal Monopoly is Becoming a Dead Letter," *National Post*, June 2, 2011, FP11.

Chapter 2

1. Eric Reguly, "As Ash Spreads, So Does Damage," *The Globe and Mail*, April 19, 2010, B1.

2. See Jay B. Barney and William G. Ouchi, ed., *Organizational Economics* (San Francisco: Jossey-Bass, 1986) for a detailed analysis of linkages between economics and organizations.

3. Marina Strauss, "Grocers Scramble to Offset Higher Food Costs," *The Globe and Mail*, May 2, 2011, B4.

4. Simon Avery, "Great Expectations for Dollarama and Costco Reports," *The Globe and Mail*, December 5, 2011, B12.

5. Richard Blackwell, "The 'R' Word," *The Globe and Mail*, October 16, 2008, B5.

6. Karl E. Case and Ray C. Fair, *Principles of Economics*, 6th ed., updated (Upper Saddle River, NJ: Prentice Hall, 2003), 432–433.

7. Ibid., 15.

8. Ibid.

9. Bank of Canada Banking and Financial Statistics, Table H1 (November 2011): S98.

10. World Bank website, GDP statistics, http://sitesources.worldbank.org/DATASTATISTICS/Resources/GDP.pdf [accessed December 22, 2011].

11. Matthew McLearn, "Our Dangerous Addiction to GDP," *Canadian Business*, October 12, 2009, 23.

12. World Bank website, GDP statistics, http://sitesources.worldbank.org/DATASTATISTICS/Resources/GDP.pdf [accessed December 22, 2011].

13. Olivier Blanchard, *Macroeconomics*, 3rd ed. (Upper Saddle River, NJ: Prentice Hall, 2003), 24–26.

14. OECD website, http://stats.oecd.org/Index.aspx?DatasetCode=LEVEL [accessed December 21, 2011]; Kevin Lynch, "Innovation + Productivity = Global Competitiveness," *The Globe and Mail*, November 24, 2011, B2.

15. Jay Heizer and Barry Render, *Operations Management*, 6th ed. (Upper Saddle River, NJ: Prentice Hall, 2001), 15–16.

16. Statistics Canada website, www40.statcan.gc.ca/l01/cst01/gblec02a-eng.htm [accessed December 21, 2011].

17. Greg Hitt and Murray Hiebert, "U.S. Trade Deficit Ballooned to a Record in 2005," *The Wall Street Journal*, February 11–12, 2006, A1, A10.

18. Neil Reynolds, "Stimulating Our Way into a Crisis," *The Globe and Mail*, February 18, 2009, B2.

19. Canadian Federal Budget website, www.budget.gc.ca/2011/glance-apercu/brief-bref-eng.pdf [accessed December 27, 2011].

20. Neil Reynolds, "U.S. Debt: Don't Worry, Be Happy (till 2017)," *The Globe and Mail*, April 3, 2009, B2.

21. This section is based on Paul Heyne, Peter J. Boettke, and David L. Prychitko, *The Economic Way of Thinking*, 10th ed. (Upper Saddle River, NJ: Prentice Hall, 2003), 491–493.

22. Celia Dugger, "Life in Zimbabwe: Wait for Useless Money, Then Scour for Food," *The New York Times*, October 2, 2008, A1, A14.

23. Geoffrey York, "How Zimbabwe Slew the Dragon of Hyperinflation," *The Globe and Mail*, March 23, 2009, B1.

24. Tavia Grant, "A Snapshot of How We Spend," *The Globe and Mail*, April 20, 2010, B2; Tavia Grant, "Lard in 1913, Plasma TV Now: CPI Tracks Changes," *The Globe and Mail*, April 21, 2005, B1, B15.

25. Bruce Little, "There's Been a Huge Shift in How Consumers Spend," *The Globe and Mail*, July 5, 2004, B4.

26. Rita Trichur, "Maple Leaf Takes on Challenge of Food Inflation," *The Globe and Mail*, April 29, 2011, B9; Marina Strauss, "Loblaw Finds Worrisome Trends in Higher Gas Prices and Food Inflation," *The Globe and Mail*, May 5, 2011, B3.

27. *Bank of Canada Banking and Financial Statistics*, Series H5, Labour Force Status of the Population, December 2011, S103.

28. Emma Ross-Thomas, "Spanish Unemployment Rate Rises to More Than 21% as Inflation Accelerates," Bloomberg News website, April 29, 2011, www.bloomberg.com/news/2011-04-29/spanish-unemployment-rate-rises-to-more-than-21-as-inflation-accelerates.html [accessed December 27, 2011].

29. Paul Heyne, Peter J. Boettke, and David L. Prychitko, *The Economic Way of Thinking*, 10th ed. (Upper Saddle River, NJ: Prentice Hall, 2003), 403–409, 503–504.

30. Julie Jargon, "Seeking Sweet Savings," *The Wall Street Journal*, October 2, 2007, B1–B2.

31. Sarah Efron, "Miracle Fibres," *Financial Post Business*, September 2007, 46–49.

32. Statistics Canada, Industrial Research and Development: Intentions, Catalogue no. 88-202-X, Table 4, Concentration of Total Intramural Research and Development Expenditures by Companies Size (Ottawa: Minister of Industry, 2010), www.statcan.gc.ca/pub/88-202-x/88-202-x2010000-eng.pdf [accessed December 27 2011].

33. Statistics Canada, *Industrial Research and Development Intentions*, Catalogue no. 88-202-XIE2005000, (Ottawa: Minister of Industry, 2005), 10.

34. Statistics Canada, Industrial Research and Development: Intentions, Catalogue no. 88-202-X, Table 4, Concentration of Total Intramural Research and Development Expenditures by Companies Size (Ottawa: Minister of Industry, 2010), www.statcan.gc.ca/pub/88-202-x/88-202-x2010000-eng.pdf [accessed December 27 2011].

35. Invest in Ontario, "Canadian Industrial Intramural R&D Expenditures, Selected Industries," www.investinontario.com/siteselector/bcrd_508.asp.

36. Industrial Research and Development: *Intentions 2008*, Catalogue No. 88-202-XWE, Table 2, International Comparison of Business Enterprise Expenditures on Research and Development as a Percentage of Gross Domestic Product, by Selected OECD Countries (Ottawa: Minister of Industry, December 2010), http://publications.gc.ca/collections/collection_2011/statcan/88-202-X/88-202-x2010000-eng.pdf.

37. Marina Strauss, "Starbucks Rolls Out Smart Phone Payments," *The Globe and Mail*, November 11, 2011, B4.

38. Intel website, Moore's Law, www.intel.com/technology/mooreslaw [accessed June 11, 2010].

39. Timothy Taylor, "Welcome to the Machines," *The Globe and Mail Report on Business*, September 2011, P. 14.

40. Jeremy Cato, "Can Nissan Ride the Innovation Bandwagon?" *The Globe and Mail*, January 6, 2012, D6; Michael Bettencourt, "Toyota to Debut five Cars in Tokyo," *The Globe and Mail*, November 25, 2011, D19; Robert Matas, "B.C. Forecasts Boom Market for Clean-Energy Vehicles," *The Globe and Mail*, November 17, 2011, S3; Michael Vaughan, "Hydrogen Technology, Two Centuries Later," *The Globe and Mail*, May 13, 2011, D18; Jeremy Cato, "Fire and Ice," *The Globe and Mail*, March 25, 2011, D13; Jeremy Cato, "Will Fuel Cells Finally Reach the Promised Land?" *The Globe and Mail*, March 25, 2011, D12.

41. L. G. Franko, "Global Corporate Competition: Who's Winning, Who's Losing, and the R&D Factor as One Reason Why," *Strategic Management Journal* (September–October 1989): 449–474.

42. Tom Randall, "Merck's Risky Bet on Research," *Bloomberg Businessweek*, April 25–May 1, 2011, P25–26.

43. Roberta S. Russell and Bernard W. Taylor III, *Operations Management*, 4th ed. (Upper Saddle River, NJ: Prentice Hall, 2003), Chapter 12.

44. Terrence Belford, "The Little Guys Are Getting with Big Boys' Program," *The Globe and Mail*, June 2, 2005, B16.

45. Tavia Grant, "Wishful Thinking, a Tax Credit That Doesn't End," *The Globe and Mail*, January 20, 2010, B5.

46. Michael Babad, "How Ontario's Drug Reforms Could Hit Shoppers Drug Mart," *The Globe and Mail*, April 8, 2010, B1; Marina Strauss, "Cost-Lowering Drug Reform Expected to Hit Shoppers," *The Globe and Mail*, July 23, 2009, B5.

47. Geoffrey York, "Nationalization Talks Put Miners on Edge," *The Globe and Mail*, February 2, 2010, B3.

48. Carrie Tait, "Suncor Gears Up to Go Back Into Libya," *The Globe and Mail*, February 2, 2010, B3.

49. Brenda Boum, "No Regrets From the Capitalist Miner Who Built Bridges to Communist Cuba," *The Globe and Mail*, November 25, 2011, B1.

50. Angelina Chapin, "Under Cover Economy," *Canadian Business*, September 26, 2011, P 50–52.

51. David Ebner, "BP Spill Causes Transatlantic Tensions," *The Globe and Mail*, September 27, 2011, B3; Eric Reguly, "Now Come the Lawyers," *The Globe and Mail*, June 5, 2010, B1, B4; Peter Coy and Stanley Reed, "Lessons of the Spill," *Bloomberg Businessweek*, May 10–16, 2010; BP website, www.bp.com/sectiongenericarticle.do?categoryId=9036580&contentId=7067577 [accessed December 28, 2011].

52. Richard Blackwell, "The Greening of the Corner Office," *The Globe and Mail*, March 26, 2007, B1, B4.

53. Michael Porter, *Competitive Strategy: Techniques for Analyzing Industries and Competitors* (New York: The Free Press, 1980).

54. Hollie Shaw, "Target Unveils Canadian Stores," *Financial Post*, May 26, 2011; Marina Strauss, "Target's Rejected Sites In High Demand by Rivals," *The Globe and Mail*, September 24, 2011, B5.

55. "Bauer Expects Price Pressure as Big Customers Merge," *The Globe and Mail*, August 19, 2011, B5.

56. Diane Peters, "Setting the Bar High for Outsourcing," *The Globe and Mail*, November 29, 2011, B15.

57. Judy Strauss and Raymond Frost, *E-Marketing* (Upper Saddle River, NJ: Prentice Hall, 2001), 245–246.

58. Lee J. Krajewski and Larry P. Ritzman, *Operations Management: Strategy and Analysis*, 6th ed. (Upper Saddle River, NJ: Prentice Hall, 2002), 3–4.

59. Ibid., Chapter 3.

60. Gordon Pitts, "Kraft CEO Still Digesting Cadbury Takeover," *The Globe and Mail*, June 7, 2010, B8.

61. Christine Dobby, "Respectable Canadian M&A activity Comes in at 45.5 Billion ion Q3," *The Financial Post*, December 1, 2011.

62. Andrew Willis, "Couche-Tard Shows No Stomach for Casey's Fight," *The Globe and Mail*, June 9, 2010, B16.

63. Ross Marowits, "Air Canada Adopts Poison Pill," *The Globe and Mail*, March 31, 2011, B1.

64. "Culture of Fun Benefits Clients, Staff," *National Post*, October 27, 2008, FP12.

65. David Milstead, "Rona Forecast Remains Cloudy Despite Sunny Days Ahead," *The Globe and Mail*, May 24, 2011, B13.

Chapter 3

1. Chris MacDonald, "Sweeping Ethics Under the Rug," *Canadian Business*, January 23, 2012, 12.

2. Ronald Ebert and Ricky Griffin, *Business Essentials* (Upper Saddle River, NJ: Prentice Hall, 2009), 21.

3. Thomas Donaldson and Thomas W. Dunfee, "Toward a Unified Conception of Business Ethics: An Integrative Social Contracts Theory," *Academy of Management Review* 19, no. 2 (1994): 252–284.

4. "Drug Companies Face Assault on Prices," *The Wall Street Journal*, May 11, 2000, B1, B4.

5. John Saunders, "Bitter Air Carrier Dogfight Heads to Court," *The Globe and Mail*, July 8, 2004, B3.

6. Andrew Crane, "Spying Doesn't Pay; Intelligence Gathering is Still an Ethical and Legal Minefield," *National Post*, November 11, 2008, FP12.

7. "Niko Penalized $9.5 M for Bangladesh Bribe," *Winnipeg Free Press*, June 25, 2011, B5.

8. Brad Dorfman, "Wal-Mart Hires Global Anti-Bribery Watchdog; Mexico Stores Scandal," *National Post*, April 25, 2012, FP2.

9. Julian Sher, "OECD Slams Canada's Record on Prosecuting Bribery," *The Globe and Mail*, March 28, 2011, B4.

10. This section follows the logic of Gerald F. Cavanaugh, *American Business Values with International Perspectives*, 4th ed. (Upper Saddle River, NJ: Prentice Hall, 1998), Chapter 3.

11. Bertrand Marotte, "Victims Unmoved by Fraudster's Courtroom Tears," *The Globe and Mail*, January 16, 2010, A16.

12. Steve Ladurantaye, "Maple Leaf Battered by Meat Recall Costs," *The Globe and Mail*, October 30, 2008, B3; Kristine Owram, "Maple Leaf Claims 'Progress' After Recall," *The Globe and Mail*, February 25, 2009, B5.

13. Mark Schwartz, "Heat's on to Get an Effective Code," *The Globe and Mail*, November 27, 1997, B2.

14. "Parent Company of Victoria's Secret to Probe Claims of Child Labour," *National Post*, December 16, 2011, FP6.

15. Julie Schmidt, "Nike's Image Problem," *USA Today*, October 4, 1999, 1B, 2B.

16. Jeffrey S. Harrison and R. Edward Freeman, "Stakeholders, Social Responsibility, and Performance: Empirical Evidence and Theoretical Perspectives," *Academy of Management Journal* 42, no. 5 (1999): 479–485. See also David P. Baron, *Business and Its Environment*, 3rd ed. (Upper Saddle River, NJ: Prentice Hall, 2000), Chapter 17.

17. www.sroi-canada.ca/about/index.html; also www.thesroinetwork.org/publications.

18. An idea of the conflicting ideas that exist in this debate can be seen in two articles: Peter Foster, "Milton's Loophole," *National Post*, June 22, 2011, FP15; and Eleanor Vaughan, "Just What Milton Would Have Wanted?" *National Post*, June 24, 2011, FP11.

19. Laura Pratt, "Sustainability Reporting," *CGA Magazine*, September–October, 2007, 18–21; also Sharda Prashad, "Good Green Goals," *The Toronto Star*, April 27, 2007, www.thestar.com/printArticle/205855; also Ralph Shaw, "Peak Performance (Mountain Equipment Co-op)," *Alternatives Journal*, 31, No. 1 (2005), 19–20.

20. John Lyons, "Skin-Deep Gains for Amazon Tribe," *The Wall Street Journal*, May 5, 2011, A1.

21. Neil Reynolds, "The Dirty Truth of China's Energy," *The Globe and Mail*, March 28, 2007, B2.

22. Bill Curry, "Ottawa Wants Kyoto Softened," *The Globe and Mail*, May 12, 2006, A1, A7.

23. Jeffrey Ball, "U.N. Effort to Curtail Emissions in Turmoil," *The Wall Street Journal*, April 12–13, 2008, A1, A5.

24. Other potential problems with CAP and trade are discussed in Peter Foster, "CAP and Tirade," *National Post*, February 16, 2011, FP13.

25. Patricia Adams, "The Next Big Scam," *National Post*, January 13, 2010, FP15.

26. "Going Green Losing Its Shine Among World's Citizens: Poll," *Winnipeg Free Press*, November 28, 2008, A20.

27. Richard Blackwell, "Canada Becoming a Wind Powerhouse," *The Globe and Mail*, March 9, 2007, B3.

28. Catherine Collins, "The Race for Zero," *Canadian Business*, March 1991, 52–56.

29. Nathan Vanderklippe, "Aging Pipes," *The Globe and Mail*, February 19, 2011, p. B6.

30. Nathan Vanderklippe, "Spill Shuts Trans-Canada's Keystone Line," *BNN*, www.bnn.ca/News/2011/5/9.

31. "Syncrude Guilty in Duck Deaths," *Winnipeg Free Press*, June 26, 2010, A10; also Tim Shufelt, "Trial Goes Far Beyond Ducks; Syncrude Case Affects All Tailings Pond Users," *National Post*, March 19, 2010, FP1.

32. Egle Procuta, "One Man's Garbage is Another's Gold," *The Globe and Mail*, April 11, 2006, B7.

33. Daniel Machalaba, "As Old Pallets Pile Up, Critics Hammer Them as New Eco-Menace," *The Wall Street Journal*, April 1, 1998, A1.

34. Geoffrey Scotton, "Cleanups Can Hurt, Companies Warned," *Financial Post*, June 25, 1991, 4.

35. Marc Huber, "A Double-Edged Endorsement," *Canadian Business*, January 1990, 69–71.

36. Claudia Cattaneo, "Talisman Braces for Jungle Standoff: Threats of Violence," *National Post*, November 14, 2008, FP1.

37. Barry Critchley, "Gold Industry Eager to Send CSR Message," *National Post*, May 25, 2010, FP2.

38. Emily Steel, "Nestlé Takes a Beating on Social Media Sites," *The Wall Street Journal*, March 29, 2010, B5.

39. Steve Ladurantaye, "Maple Leaf Battered by Meat Recall Costs," *The Globe and Mail*, October 30, 2008, B3.

40. John Wilke, "U.S. Probes Ice Makers Collusion Case," *The Wall Street Journal*, August 7, 2008, B1, B10.

41. Martin Cash, "Icemaker Facing Heat Over Finances," *Winnipeg Free Press*, July 20, 2011, p. B5.

42. Paul Waldie, "Chocolate Bar Makers Probe Over Prices," *The Globe and Mail*, November 28, 2007, B1, B10.

43. "Chocolate Makers Face Legal Challenges," *The Globe and Mail*, February 20, 2008, B9.

44. Christine Dobby, "Three Gas Retailers Fined in Price Fixing," *National Post*, March 22, 2012, FP4.

45. Jacquie McNish and Jeff Gray, "'Quaint' Canada Called No Match for Price-Fixers," *The Globe and Mail*, January 27, 2010, B11.

46. Jonathan Cheng, "False Ads: Chinese Consumers Awaken to a Western Problem," *The Wall Street Journal*, July 8, 2005, B9.

47. "These Just Won't Fly," *Winnipeg Free Press*, September 1, 2011, p. B1.

48. "Canada Goose vs. Counterfeiters," *National Post*, July 19, 2011, p. FP16; also "Down With Counterfeits," *National Post*, November 7, 2011, FP8.

49. Stacy Meichtry, "Swell or Swill?" *The Wall Street Journal*, August 10, 2006, B1-B2.

50. Louise Watt, "Fake Apple Stores Pop Up In China," *Winnipeg Free Press*, July 22, 2011, p. B11; also "Apple Hits New York's Fake Stores With Lawsuit," *The Globe and Mail*, August 6, 2011, p. B2.

51. Melanie Lee, "Blue, Yellow and Fake; China's Penchant for Fake Products Expands to the Whole Brand Experience," *National Post*, August 2, 2011, p. FP3.

52. Daryl-Lynn Carlson, "The Costly Reality of Fakes," *National Post*, December 5, 2007.

53. Shawn McCarthy, "Crackdown on New York's Canal Street," *The Globe and Mail*, August 30, 2004, pp. B1, B11

54. Daryl-Lynn Carlson, "Canada's IP Protection Laws Soft," *National Post*, December 5, 2007

55. Gabriel Madway, "Countries Vow to Fight Trade in Pirated Goods; Pact Nearly Done; China Not a Party to Negotiations," *National Post*, October 7, 2010, FP9.

56. Tim Barker, "Word-of-Mouth Advertising Grows in Influence, Concern," *Orlando Sentinel*, March 17, 2006, A1, A19.

57. Michael McCarthy and Lorrie Grant, "Sears Drops Benetton After Controversial Death Row Ads," *USA Today*, February 18, 2000, 2B.

58. Shona McKay, "Willing and Able," *Report on Business Magazine*, October 1991, 58–63.

59. J. Southerst, "In Pursuit of Drugs," *Canadian Transportation*, November 1989, 58–65.

60. Steve Lambert, "Pushing Boundaries: Keeping an Eye on Employees," *The Globe and Mail*, August 20, 2011, B15.

61. Jerald Greenberg and Robert A. Baron, *Behavior in Organizations: Understanding and Managing the Human Side of Work*, 7th ed. (Upper Saddle River, NJ: Prentice Hall, 2000), 374–375.

62. Joshua Gallu and Dawn Kopecki, "Whistleblower Awarded Record US$5.1 Million; Firm Fined US$2.3 Billion; Former Salesman Was Appalled by Pfizer's Tactics," *National Post*, September 4, 2009, FP3.

63. Brent Jang and Patrick Brethour, "This WestJet Staffer Blew the Whistle on His Employer's Corporate Spying. He's Still Waiting for Someone to Say Thanks," *The Globe and Mail*, October 18, 2006, A1, A12.

64. Cora Daniels, "'It's a Living Hell,'" *Fortune*, April 15, 2002, 367–368.

65. Boyd Erman, "Whistleblower Hotline Opens," *The Globe and Mail*, May 26, 2009, B5.

66. Grant McCool and John Poirier, "Madoff Mess Manoeuvres," *National Post*, December 18, 2008, FP3.

67. Janet McFarland, "Five Grand Cache Executives Accused of Insider Trading," *The Globe and Mail*, December 9, 2011, B5.

68. David Glovin, Patricia Hurtado, and Bob Van Voris, "Galleon Boss Gets 11-Year Term; Rajaratnam Stays Silent in Facing Prison Time," *National Post*, October 14, 2011, FP1.

69. Daniel Stoffman, "Good Behaviour and the Bottom Line," *Canadian Business*, May 1991, 28–32.

70. "Looking Good in Green," *Maclean's*, May 9, 2011, 47.

71. "Giving's a Hit with CIBC Employees; CIBC," *National Post*, February 3, 2012, JV5.

72. Diana McLaren, "Spirit of Philanthropy Is Thriving," *The Globe and Mail*, December 10, 2008, B7.

73. "Survey Shows Canadian Businesses Engaged in Meeting Community Need," *Canada NewsWire*, February 7, 2008, 1.

74. Rita Trichur, "Strings Attached; Corporations Want More for Their Money," *The Globe and Mail*, October 29, 2011, B1.

75. Alan Muller and Gail Whiteman, "Exploring the Geography of Philanthropic Disaster Response: A Study of *Fortune* Global 500 Firms," *Journal of Business Ethics* 84 (2009): 589–603.

76. Diane McLaren, "Doing Their Part—With Goals in Mind," *The Globe and Mail*, December 10, 2008, B7.

77. Bruce Owen, "Camp Tim on Its Way," *Winnipeg Free Press*, May 28, 2010, A6.

78. Sandra Waddock and Neil Smith, "Corporate Responsibility Audits: Doing Well by Doing Good," *Sloan Management Review* (Winter 2000): 75–85.

79. Edward Waitzer, "Bottom Lines Benefit when Social Reporting is Embraced," *The Globe and Mail*, November 17, 2011, B2.

80. Marjo Johne, "Sustainabilty Performance a New Essential," *The Globe and Mail*, May 19, 2011, B8.

81. "Looking Good in Green," *Maclean's*, May 9, 2011, 47.

82. Alison Arnot, "The Triple Bottom Line," *CGA Magazine* (January–February 2004): 27–32.

83. Richard Blackwell, "Six Canadian Firms on Global Top 100 List," *The Globe and Mail*, January 25, 2012, B2.

84. www.corporateknights.ca/report/2011.

Chapter 4

1. Statistics Canada website, "Financial well-being of the Self Employed," www.statcan.gc.ca/daily-quotidien/110923/dq110923a-eng.htm [accessed September 26, 2011]; Tavia Grant, "Call It the Entrepreneurial Era," *The Globe and Mail*, March 30, 2010, B1.

2. Statistics Canada, Business Dynamics in Canada, Catalogue no. 61–534-XIE (Ottawa: Minister of Industry, 2006).

3. P. D. Reynolds, S. M. Camp, W. D. Bygrave, E. Autio, and M. Hay, Global Entrepreneurship Monitor: 2001 Executive Report (Kansas City, MO: Kauffman Center for Entrepreneurial Leadership, 2001); P. D. Reynolds, M. Hay, W. D. Bygrave, S. M. Camp, and E. Autio, Global Entrepreneurship Monitor: 2000 Executive Report (Kansas City, MO: Kauffman Center for Entrepreneurial Leadership, 2000).

4. Industry Canada, Key Small Business Statistics, 2011, www.ic.gc.ca/eic/site/sbrp-rppe.nsf/vwapj/KSBS-PSRPE_July-Juillet2011_eng.pdf/$FILE/KSBS-PSRPE_July-Juillet2011_eng.pdf [accessed September 26, 2011], p.7.

5. Industry Canada, Key Small Business Statistics, 2011, www.ic.gc.ca/eic/site/sbrp-rppe.nsf/vwapj/KSBS-PSRPE_July-Juillet2011_eng.pdf/$FILE/KSBS-PSRPE_July-Juillet2011_eng.pdf [accessed September 26, 2011].

6. Monica Diochon, Teresa Menzies, and Yvon Gasse, "Exploring the Relationship Between Start-up Activities and New Venture Emergence: A Longitudinal Study of Canadian Nascent Entrepreneurs," *International Journal of Management and Enterprise Development* 2, no. 3/4 (2005): 408–426.

7. Best Small and Medium Sized Employers in Canada, http://business.queensu.ca/centres/qcbv/bsme/bsme50.php [accessed September 11th 2011]; Queen's Releases List of Top Employers," *The Globe and Mail*, February 11, 2010.

8. Nancy M. Carter, William B. Gartner, and Paul D. Reynolds, "Firm Founding," in *Handbook of Entrepreneurial Dynamics: The Process of Business Creation*, ed. W. B. Gartner, K. G. Shaver, N. M. Carter, and P. D. Reynolds (Thousand Oaks, CA: Sage, 2004), 311–323.

9. William D. Bygrave and C. W. Hofer, "Theorizing About Entrepreneurship," *Entrepreneurship Theory and Practice* 16, no. 2 (Winter 1991): 14; Donald Sexton and Nancy Bowman-Upton, *Entrepreneurship: Creativity and Growth* (New York, NY: MacMillan Publishing Company, 1991), 7.

10. Facebook website, www.facebook.com/press/info.php?statistics [accessed 11 September 2011]; Fred Vogelstein, "How Mark Zuckerberg Turned Facebook Into the Web's Hottest Platform," *Wired*, September 6, 2007, www.wired.com/techbiz/startups/news/2007/09/ff_facebook?currentPage=3; Ellen McGirt, "Hacker, Dropout, CEO," *Fast Company*, May 2007, www.fastcompany.com/magazine/115/open_features-hacker-dropout-ceo.html.

11. Greg Keenan and Kevin Carmichael, "From the Ashes," *The Globe and Mail*, June 11, 2011, B9.

12. Heritage Foundation Index of Economic Freedom website, www.heritage.org/index/topten [accessed September 26, 2011].

13. Angela Dale, "Self-Employment and Entrepreneurship: Notes on Two Problematic Concepts," in *Deciphering the Enterprise Culture*, ed. Roger Burrows (London: Routledge, 1991), 45, 48.

14. Donald Sexton and Nancy Bowman-Upton, *Entrepreneurship: Creativity and Growth* (New York, NY: MacMillan Publishing Company, 1991), 11.

15. Allan A. Gibb, "The Enterprise Culture and Education: Understanding Enterprise Education and Its Links with Small Business, Entrepreneurship and Wider Educational Goals," *International Small Business Journal* 11 no. 3 (1993): 13–34; Donald Sexton and Nancy Bowman-Upton, *Entrepreneurship: Creativity and Growth*, (New York, NY: MacMillan Publishing Company, 1991).

16. Terrence Belford, "Intrapreneurs Combine Big-biz Clout with Entrepreneurial Style," *CanWest News*, March 23, retrieved from CBCA Current Events database. (Document ID: 1009719591).

17. Industry Canada, Small Business Research and Policy, *Key Small Business Statistics*, Table 1 (Ottawa: Public Works and Government Services Canada, July 2011), www.ic.gc.ca/eic/site/sbrp-rppe.nsf/vwapj/KSBS-PSRPE_July-Juillet2011_eng.pdf/$FILE/KSBS-PSRPE_July-Juillet2011_eng.pdf [accessed September 36 2011].

18. Industry Canada, Small Business Research and Policy, *Key Small Business Statistics*, Table 3 (Ottawa: Public Works and Government Services Canada, July 2011), www.ic.gc.ca/eic/site/sbrp-rppe.nsf/vwapj/KSBS-PSRPE_July-Juillet2011_eng.pdf/$FILE/KSBS-PSRPE_July-Juillet2011_eng.pdf [accessed September 26 2011].

19. Industry Canada, Small Business Research and Policy, *Key Small Business Statistics* (Ottawa: Public Works and Government Services Canada, July 2011), p.9, www.ic.gc.ca/eic/site/sbrp-rppe.nsf/vwapj/KSBS-PSRPE_July-Juillet2011_eng.pdf/$FILE/KSBS-PSRPE_July-Juillet2011_eng.pdf [accessed September 26 2011].

20. Industry Canada, Small Business Research and Policy, *Key Small Business Statistics* (Ottawa: Public Works and Government Services Canada, 2011), 20. .

21. William B. Gartner, Kelly G. Shaver, Nancy M. Carter, and Paul D. Reynolds, *Handbook of Entrepreneurial Dynamics* (Thousand Oaks, CA: Sage Publications, Inc., 2004), ix.

22. Industry Canada, Small Business Research and Policy, *Key Small Business Statistics* (Ottawa: Public Works and Government Services Canada, July 2011), p. 23.

23. Industry Canada, *Key Small Business Statistics* (Ottawa: Public Works and Government Services Canada, June 2011) p. 38.

24. Ibid., 40.

25. Richard Bloom, "Building a Future on Sweet Dreams," *The Globe and Mail*, October 21, 2004, B9.

26. Lauren McKeon, "Tied to Home," *Canadian Business*, April 14, 2008, 33.

27. RBC website, Female Entrepreneur Awards, www.theawards.ca/cwea/past-winners.cfm [accessed June 24, 2010].

28. Roma Luciw, "Stay-at-Home Moms Stay the Business Course," *The Globe and Mail*, March 3, 2007, B10.

29. BDC website, Young Entrepreneurs Award, www.bdc.ca [accessed June 24, 2010].

30. Dianne Rinehart, "Seed Money Gives Wing to Aboriginal Ventures," *The Globe and Mail*, October 17, 2007, E8.

31. Tell Us About Us website, www.tellusaboutus.com [accessed June 24, 2010]; Geoff Kirbyson, "Market-Research Firm Lands Major Contract," *The Winnipeg Free Press*, July 19, 2004, D7.

32. Donald F. Kuratko and Richard M. Hodgetts, *Entrepreneurship: Theory, Process, Practice*, 7th ed. (Mason, OH: Thomson South-Western, 2007), 118–125; John A. Hornday, "Research About Living Entrepreneurs," in *Encyclopedia of Entrepreneurship*, ed. Calvin Kent, Donald Sexton, and Karl Vesper (Englewood Cliffs, NJ: Prentice Hall,

1982), 26–27; Jeffry A. Timmons and Stephen Spinelli, *New Venture Creation: Entrepreneurship for the 21st Century*, 7th ed. (Boston, MA: McGraw-Hill Irwin, 2007), 9.

33. Jeffry A. Timmons and Stephen Spinelli, *New Venture Creation: Entrepreneurship for the 21st Century*, 7th ed. (Boston, MA: McGraw-Hill Irwin, 2007), 19.

34. J. D. Kyle, R. Blais, R. Blatt, and A. J. Szonyi, "The Culture of the Entrepreneur: Fact or Fiction," *Journal of Small Business and Entrepreneurship* (1991): 3–14.

35. R. H. Brockhaus and Pam S. Horwitz, "The Psychology of the Entrepreneur," in *The Art and Science of Entrepreneurship*, ed. D. L. Sexton and Raymond W. Smilor (Cambridge, MA: Ballinger Pub. Co., 1986); William B. Gartner, "What Are We Talking About When We Talk About Entrepreneurship?," *Journal of Business Venturing* 5 no. 1 (1990): 15–29; Allan A. Gibb, "The Enterprise Culture and Education: Understanding Enterprise Education and Its Links with Small Business, Entrepreneurship and Wider Educational Goals," *International Small Business Journal* 11 no. 3 (1993): 13–34; J. C. Mitchell, "Case and Situation Analysis," *Sociological Review* 31 no. 2 (1983): 187–211.

36. Donald Sexton and Nancy Bowman-Upton, *Entrepreneurship: Creativity and Growth* (New York, NY: MacMillan Publishing Company, 1991); Karl H. Vesper, *New Venture Strategies* (Englewood Cliffs, NJ: Prentice Hall, 1990); W. D. Bygrave and C. W. Hofer, "Theorizing About Entrepreneurship," *Entrepreneurship Theory and Practice* 16 no. 2 (Winter 1991): 14.

37. Walter Good, *Building a Dream* (Toronto: McGraw-Hill Ryerson, 1998), 40.

38. Ronald Ebert and Ricky Griffin, *Business Essentials* (Upper Saddle River, NJ: Prentice Hall, 2009), 137.

39. Wayne A. Long and W. Ed McMullan, *Developing New Ventures* (San Diego: Harcourt Brace Jovanovich, 1990), 374–375.

40. May Jeong, "Fast-Growing Apps Developer Polar Mobile Looks East," *The Globe and Mail*, August 24, 2011, B4; Omar El Akkad, "Nokia Picks Polar to Build 300 Mobile Apps," *The Globe and Mail*, August 27, 2011, B3.

41. Rasha Mourtada, "Tested to the Limit," *The Globe and Mail*, April 14, 2009, B4.

42. Michael E. Porter, "Know Your Place," *Inc.* 13 no. 9 (September 1992): 90–93.

43. Howard H. Stevenson, H. Irving Grousbeck, Michael J. Roberts, and Amarnath Bhide, *New Business Ventures and the Entrepreneur* (Boston: Irwin McGraw-Hill, 1999), 19.

44. Matt Braga, "The Fight for Shelf Space," *The Globe and Mail*, May 4, 2011, B10.

45. Ibid., 21.

46. Marc J. Dollinger, *Entrepreneurship: Strategies and Resources* (Upper Saddle River, NJ: Prentice Hall, 1999), 94–101.

47. Thomas W. Zimmerer and Norman M. Scarborough, *Essentials of Entrepreneurship and Small Business Management*, 4th ed. (Upper Saddle River, NJ: Pearson Prentice Hall, 2005), 359.

48. Michael E. Porter, "Know Your Place," *Inc.* 13 no. 9 (September 1992): 90–93.

49. Wallace Immen, "Co-Work Spaces Help Businesses Blossom," *The Globe and Mail*, June 18, 2011, B21.

50. Business Development Bank of Canada website, www.bdc.ca/EN/about/Pages/default.aspx [accessed September 26, 2011].

51. Dianne Rinehart, "It's Not Just Business, It's Personal," *The Globe and Mail*, October 10, 2007, B13.

52. Karl H. Vesper, *New Venture Mechanics* (Englewood Cliffs, NJ: Prentice Hall, 1993), 105.

53. Jeffry A. Timmons, *New Venture Creation* (Boston: Irwin McGraw-Hill, 1999), 277.

54. Lisa Stephens, "With Some Shape Shifting, This Company Has Legs," *The Globe and Mail*, October 5, 2005, B10.

55. George Anders, Carol Hymowitz, Joann Lublin, and Don Clark, "All in the Family," *The Wall Street Journal*, August 1, 2005, B1, B4.

56. Harvey Schacter, "Honey, You're Fired," *The Globe and Mail*, October 18, 2010, E5.

57. Anita Elash, "Frogbox Needs a Plan to Jump into the US Market," *The Globe and Mail*, June 15, 2011, B17.

58. Canadian Franchise Association, www.cfa.ca/Publications_Research/FastFacts.aspx [accessed September 26, 2011].

59. Tony Wilson, "Legal Advice on Starting a Franchise," *The Globe and Mail*, March 16, 2010.

60. Harvey's website, http://harveysfranchising.ca/eng/franchising_2.php [accessed June 24, 2010].

61. "Top 10 Corporations in Canada, 2010," *The Financial Post*, Special Edition, June 2010,

62. Quoted in Lowell B. Howard, *Business Law* (Woodbury, NY: Barron's Woodbury Press, 1965), 332.

63. "Rankings for Corporate Governance Practices," *The Globe and Mail*, June 18, 2010, B7.

64. Brent Jang, "Porter Again Puts off an IPO," *The Globe and Mail*, September 22, 2011, B5; Brent Jang, "Porter's IPO: Figuring the Flight Plan," *The Globe and Mail*, April 19, 2010, B9; Scott Deveau, "Porter's Aviation Grounds IPO," *Financial Post*, June 2, 2010.

65. Andrew Willis, "Market Survey Indicates Eager Demand for IPO's," *The Globe and Mail*, January 6, 2010, B9.

66. "Clearwater Foods Going Private," *National Post*, August 15, 2008, www. nationalpost.com/story-printer.html?id=725985.

67. Terry Pedwell, "Income Trusts Face Tough Rules," *Winnipeg Free Press*, November 1, 2006, B7.

68. Shirley Won, "Looking for Gems in 'Under-loved' Trust Sector," *The Globe and Mail*, June 18, 2010, B13.

69. "An Overview of Available Business Structures," www.umanitoba.ca/afs/agric_economics/MRAC/structures.html#Cooperatives.

70. Industry Canada, Key Small Business Statistics (Ottawa: Public Works and Government Services Canada, January 2011), 6.

71. Kevin Marron, "Want to Succeed? Read This," *The Globe and Mail*, October 19, 2005, E1, E5. Several excellent articles on starting and operating a small business are found in Section E, "Report on Small Business" in *The Globe and Mail*, October 19, 2005.

72. See Norman M. Scarborough and Thomas W. Zimmerer, *Effective Small Business Management: An Entrepreneurial Approach*, 7th ed. (Upper Saddle River, NJ: Prentice Hall, 2003).

Chapter 5

1. World Trade Organization website, www. wto.org/english/news_e/pres11_e/pr628_e.pdf [accessed August 28 2011], "Trade Growth to Ease in 2011, but Despite 2010 Record Surge, Crisis Hangover Persists" Press Release, April 7, 2011, p7.

2. Risha Gotlieb, "From Logs to Riches," *The Globe and Mail*, October 17, 2007, E10.

3. John W. Miller and Marcus Walker, "China Passes Germany as Top Exporter," *The Globe and Mail*, January 6, 2010, B8.

4. Peter Wonascott, "U.S. Takes Notice of China's Expanding Ties to Africa," *The Globe and Mail*, September 2, 2011, B9.

5. Jiri Maly, "Five Trends that Will Shape the Global Economy," *The Globe and Mail*, June 7, 2010, B5.

6. World Bank website [accessed 28 August 2011], http://data.worldbank.org/about/country-classifications; Ricky Griffin and Michael W. Pustay, *International Business: A Managerial Perspective*, 5th ed. (Upper Saddle River, NJ: Prentice Hall, 2007).

7. Thomas Friedman, *The World Is Flat* (New York: Farrar, Straus, and Giroux, 2005).

8. BBC News website, "China Overtakes Japan as World's Second-Biggest Economy," February 14 2011, www.bbc.co.uk/news/business-12427321 [accessed September 16, 2011].

9. Paul Brent, "A Few BRICS Short of a Load," *Canadian Business*, November 23 2009, p 21; Courtland L. Bovee, John V. Thill and George Dracopoulos, *Business In Action, 2nd Canadian edition*, (Pearson Education, 2008), Chapter 2; Shirley Won, "BRIC May Cure any Resource Sector Ills," *The Globe and Mail*, November 22, 2007, B17; Andrew Mills, "The Face of Brazil's Ascent," *The Globe and Mail*, March 12, 2010, B11.

10. Tom Krishner, "Indian Car Maker may Land Jaguar, Land Rover," *The Globe and Mail*, January 4, 2008, B3.

11. Jason Bush, "Ikea in Russia: Enough is Enough," *Business Week*, July 13, 2009, p.33.

12. Tavia Grant and Brian Milner, "Why Brazil Stands Out," *The Globe and Mail*, June 10, 2010, B1 & B6.

13. Steven Chase, "In Brazil, the Rise of the Mall," *The Globe and Mail*, Sept 2, 2011, B1.

14. The Guardian website [accessed 10 September 2011], www.guardian.co.uk/world/2011/apr/19/south-africa-joins-bric-club.

15. Eric Reguly, "BRICS Countries Plot European Bailout," *The Globe and Mail*, September 14, 2011, B1.

16. Ricky W. Griffin and Michael W. Pustay, *International Business: A Managerial Perspective*, 2nd ed. (Reading, MA: Addison-Wesley, 1999), Chapter 3; Dominick Salvatore, *International Economics*, 6th ed. (Upper Saddle River, NJ: Prentice Hall, 1998), 27–33; Karl E. Case and Ray C. Fair, *Principles of Economics*, 5th ed. (Upper Saddle River, NJ: Prentice Hall, 1999), 813–817.

17. John J Wild, Kenneth L.Wild, and Jerry C. Han, *International Business: The Challenges of Globalization*, 4th ed. (Upper Saddle River, NJ: Prentice Hall, 2008), 159–160.

18. This section is based on Michael Porter, *The Competitive Advantage of Nations* (Boston: Harvard Business School Press, 1990), Chapters 3 and 4; Warren J. Keegan, *Global Marketing Management*, 6th ed. (Upper Saddle River, NJ: Prentice Hall, 1999), 312–321; John J. Wild, Kenneth L. Wild, and Jerry C.Y. Han, *International Business: An Integrated Approach* (Upper Saddle River, NJ: Prentice Hall, 2000), 175–178.

19. World Economic Forum website, Global Competitiveness Report [accessed 11 September 2011], www.weforum.org/reports/global-competitiveness-report-2011-2012.

20. Bank of Canada, Banking and Financial Statistics, Series J4, Commodity Classification of Merchandise Exports, January 2011, S116–S117. Risha Gotlieb, "From Logs to Riches," *The Globe and Mail*, October 18, 2007.

21. Bank of Canada, Banking and Financial Statistics, Series J2, Canadian Balance of Payments, January 2011, S116–S117; Statistics Canada website [accessed Sept 11 2011], www40.statcan.gc.ca/l01/cst01/gblec02a-eng.htm.

22. Statistics Canada website [accessed Sept 11 2011], www40.statcan.gc.ca/l01/cst01/gblec02a-eng.htm.

23. Statistics Canada [accessed Sept 11 2011], www.statcan.gc.ca/tables-tableaux/sum-som/l01/cst01/gblec02a-eng.htm.

24. Karl E. Case and Ray C. Fair, *Principles of Economics*, 5th ed. (Upper Saddle River, NJ: Prentice Hall, 1999), 818–821.

25. Tavia Grant, "Strong Loonie Weakens Exports," *The Globe and Mail*, June 10, 2011, B1–B4.

26. Brian Parkin, "Germany Showing Strength as Unemployment Holds at Two-Decade Low: Economy." *Bloomberg Businessweek*, February 29, 2012.

27. Brian Milner, "Before New Downgrade, Decades of Economic Misery," *The Globe and Mail*, August 25, 2011, B1.

28. Mark MacKinnon, "China Sees Yuan Becoming Third Global Currency," *The Globe and Mail*, June 4, 2011, B8.

29. Geoffrey York, "McCain Laying Down its Chips on African strategy," *The Globe and Mail*, December, 22 2009, B3.

30. Carolyne Wheeler, "Yum Brands' Recipe for Fast-Food Success in China? Adapt to Local Tastes," *The Globe and Mail*, May 11, 2011, B5.

31. Mark MacKinnon, "Rim's Indonesian Bonanza," *The Globe and Mail*, March 25, 2010, B1.

32. Barrie McKenna, "China, India Crowd G7 in Driver's Seat," *The Globe and Mail*, July 19, 2006, B11; Andrew Batson, "China's Rise as Auto-Parts Power Reflects New Manufacturing Edge," *The Wall Street Journal*, August 1, 2006, A1, A6.

33. Diane Francis, "China Learns the Lingo," *The National Post*, January 16, 2010, p. FP2; Shirley Won, "Small Firms Beating a Path to the Middle Kingdom," *The Globe and Mail*, August 31, 2004, p. B7.

34. The Economist website, "Hollywood Goes Global," May 11, 2011, www.economist.com/node/18178291 [accessed September 13, 2011].

35. The Hershey Company website, www.thehersheycompany.com/about-hershey.aspx [accessed September 13, 2011].

36. Ray August, *International Business Law: Text, Cases, and Readings*, 3rd ed. (Upper Saddle River, NJ: Prentice Hall, 2000), 192–197.

37. *Fortune* 500 website, Global500 Rankings 2011 [accessed September 13, 2011], http://money.cnn.com/magazines/fortune/global500/2011/full_list/index.html.

38. Tom Krishner, "Indian Car Maker May Land Jaguar, Land Rover," *The Globe and Mail*, January 4, 2008, B3.

39. Ricky W. Griffin and Michael W. Pustay, *International Business: A Managerial Perspective*, 2nd ed. (Reading, MA: Addison-Wesley, 1999), 431–433; John J. Wild, Kenneth L. Wild, and Jerry C.Y. Han, *International Business: An Integrated Approach* (Upper Saddle River, NJ: Prentice Hall, 2000), 456–458.

40. Peter Wonacott, "Downturn Heightens China-India Tension on Trade," *The Wall Street Journal*, March 20, 2009, A8.

41. Gaurav Raghuvanshi and Eric Bellman, "Wal-Mart Tiptoes into India's Marketplace," *The Globe and Mail*, February 21 2010, p. B13.

42. Loretta Chao, "Groupon Shutters Offices as Chinese Venture Stumbles," *The Globe and Mail*, August 24, 2011, B11.

43. Makiko Kitamura, Yuki Hagiwara, Andreas Cremer, "VW-Suzuki Alliance Fizzles Amid Feud," *The Globe and Mail*, Sept 7, 2011, B11.

44. John J. Wild, Kenneth L. Wild, and Jerry C.Y. Han, *International Business: An Integrated Approach* (Upper Saddle River, NJ: Prentice Hall, 2000), Chapter 7; Ricky W. Griffin and Michael W. Pustay, *International Business: A Managerial Perspective*, 2nd ed. (Reading, MA: Addison-Wesley, 1999), 436–439.

45. Carolynne Wheeler, "Bombardier Laid Track Long Ago for Deal in China," *The Globe and Mail*, October 1, 2009, B1; Bertrand Marotte, "Bombardier Speeds Ahead in China," *The Globe and Mail*, September 29 2009, B1.

46. Ross Marowits, "Bombardier Looking to Morocco for Production," *The Globe and Mail*, May 7, 2011, B8.

47. Grant Robertson, "A Once-Cautious Bank Takes a Bold LeAP South," *The Globe and Mail*, August 20 2011, B6–B7.

48. Janet McFarland, "Corporate Canada Easy Prey for Foreign Buyers," *The Globe and Mail*, February 27, 2008, B1–B2.

49. Gordon Pitts, "Mixed Messages on Danger of Foreign Takeovers," *The Globe and Mail*, September 18, 2006, B1, B3. For an extensive analysis of the effect of foreign takeovers of Canadian business firms, see Roger Martin and Gordon Nixon, "Who, Canada," *The Globe and Mail*, July 2, 2007, B1–B3.

50. John Partridge, "Foreign Takeover Fears Played Down," *The Globe and Mail*, August 22, 2007, B3.

51. Anita Elash, "French Lingerie Firm's Pretty Babies Prompt Calls to Let Girls be Girls," *The Globe and Mail*, August 19, 2011, A3.

52. Marcus Gee, "Green Hats and Other Ways to Blow a Deal in China," *The Globe and Mail*, August 27, 2007, p. B1.

53. Rick Cash, "Dealing with the Dragon," *The Globe and Mail*, October 24, 2004, B3.

54. Elizabeth Holmes, "The Return of the Luxe Life," *The Globe and Mail*, May 4 2011, B17.

55. Karl E. Case and Ray C. Fair, *Principles of Economics*, 5th ed. (Upper Saddle River, NJ: Prentice Hall, 1999), 818–821.

56. Peter Kennedy, "Softwood Decision Gets Mixed Reviews," *The Globe and Mail*, December 8, 2005, B6.

57. Steve Merti, "Lumber Exporters Taste Sting of Softwood Deal," *Winnipeg Free Press*, September 22, 2006, B5.

58. "WTO Strikes Down U.S. Cotton Subsidy Appeal," *The Globe and Mail*, March 4, 2005, p. B10.

59. Scott Kilman and Roger Thurow, "To Soothe Anger Over Subsidies, U.S. Cotton Tries Wooing Africa," *The Wall Street Journal*, August 5, 2005, pp. A1, A6.

60. Simon Tuck, "Farmers to WTO: If It Ain't Broke…," *The Globe and Mail*, August 9, 2004, p. B1–B2.

61. Anthony DePalma, "Chiquita Sues Europeans, Citing Banana Quota Losses," *The New York Times*, January 26, 2001, C5; Brian Lavery, "Trade Feud on Bananas Not as Clear as It Looks," *The New York Times*, February 7, 2001, W1; David E. Sanger, "Miffed at Europe, U.S. Raises Tariffs for Luxury Goods," *The New York Times*, March 4, 1999, A1, A5.

62. Wendy Stueck, "Mining Firms Hit Again by Chavez Threat," *The Globe and Mail*, September 23, 2005, B4; also Barrie McKenna, "A Nation of Big Riches, Bigger Risks," *The Globe and Mail*, September 24, 2005, B4.

63. Iain Marlow, "Public Mobile Wants Top Court to Weigh in on Foreign Ownership," *The Globe and Mail*, June 10, 2011, B3.

64. Konrad Yakabuski, "Quebec Courts Margarine War," *The Globe and Mail*, October 14, 1997, B1, B4.

65. Kevin Doherty, "Yellow Margarine Ban to be Lifted in Quebec," *Montreal Gazette*, July 8, 2008, B1; Bertrand Marotte, "Ontario Calls for Dispute Panel in Quebec Margarine Battle," *The Globe and Mail*, March 26, 2002, p. B10.

66. Neville Nankivell, "Spilled Milk over Provincial Trade," *National Post*, April 24, 2000, C9.

67. Gerry Stobo, "Cross-Border Mobility," *CGA*, May–June 2005: 13–16.

68. Gary McWilliams, "Wal-Mart Era Wanes Amid Big Shifts in Retail," *The Wall Street Journal*, October 3, 2007, A1, A17.

69. The Star.com website, "UFC May Have Long Wait to Crack Ontario Market," www.thestar.com/sports/wrestling/ufc/article/783892--ufc-may-have-long-wait-to-crack-ontario-market [accessed July 9, 2010].

70. Brian Womack and Sara Forden, "Google to Pay $500 Million in Settlement Over Online Drug Ads," *The Globe and Mail*, August 25, 2011, B1.

71. Douglas Quan, "Billionaire Bodog Founder Calvin Ayre, Three Other Canadians Indicted on Illegal Gambling Charges," *National Post*, February 28, 2012.

72. Dawn Walton, "Builders Most Likely to Bribe, Report Finds," *The Globe and Mail*, January 21, 2000, p. B5.

73. Nicholas Bray, "OECD Ministers Agree to Ban Bribery as Means for Companies to Win Business," *The Wall Street Journal*, May 27, 1997, p. A2.

74. Elaine Kurtenbach, "Rio Workers Get Harsh Sentences," *The Globe and Mail*, March 29 2010, B1: Elaine Kurtenbach, "Rio Tinto Exec Admits to Some Bribery Charges," *The Globe and Mail*, March 23 2010, B12.

75. "Canada Ties for First in List of Countries Resistant to Corrupt Business," *National Post*, December 10, 2008, FP2; "Russian Firms Most Prone to Bribery, Survey Finds," *The Globe and Mail*, December 10, 2008, B14.

76. Transparency International website, www.transparency.org/policy_research/surveys_indices/cpi/2010/results [accessed September 16, 2011].

77. "EU Fines Banana Importers for Cartel Actions," *The Globe and Mail*, October 16, 2008, B11; "EU Imposes Highest Fine over Auto Glass Cartel," *The Globe and Mail*, November 13, 2008, B9; "Oil Companies Fined by EU over 'Paraffin Mafia' Cartel," *The Globe and Mail*, October 2, 2008, B7.

78. Toby Heaps, "Potash Politics," *Corporate Knights Magazine*, Winter, 2009, p 19–23.

79. Canadian Press, "China Decries U.S. Duties on Steel Pipes," *The Globe and Mail*, January 1, 2010. B4.

80. Peter Wonacott, "Downturn Heightens China-India Tension on Trade," *The Wall Street Journal*, March 20, 2009, A8.

81. "New Global Trade Regulator Starts Operations Tomorrow," *Winnipeg Free Press*, December 31, 1994, A5.

82. Barrie McKenna, "Boeing's WTO Win May Prove a Hollow Victory," *The Globe and Mail*, September 5, 2009, B5.

83. "US Hails WTO Victory over China," *The Globe and Mail*, December 22, 2009, B5.

84. Michelle MacAfee, "Trade Protest Turns Violent," *Winnipeg Free Press*, July 29, 2003, A9.

85. Europa website [accessed March 23 2010], http://europa.eu/index_en.htm.

86. Bruce Little, "Free-Trade Pact Gets Mixed Reviews," *The Globe and Mail*, June 7, 2004, B3.

87. Barrie McKenna, "Dead End for Free Trade," *The Globe and Mail*, May 17, 2008, B4–B5.

88. Rachel Pulfer, "NAFTA's Third Amigo," *Canadian Business*, June 15 2009, p 27.

89. Barrie McKenna, "Putting Canada-Mexico Trade in High Gear," *The Globe and Mail*, June 16, 2011, B12.

90. Peter Cook, "Free Trade-for-all Causes Confusion," *The Globe and Mail*, June 7, 2004, B7.

Chapter 6

1. Chris Knight, "McDonald's New Recipe for Success; The Golden Arches Has Fought Its Way Back, Not with the Burger, but with Coffee, Snack Wraps, and a Restaurant Facelift," *National Post*, September 5, 2009, FP1.

2. "McDonald's Canada Plans $1B Store Overhaul," *Reuters*, September 7, 2011, www.bnn.ca/News/2011/9/7.

3. "Maple Leaf rolls Out New Five-Year Plan; goal is to simplify; Part of Strategy is to Cut Product Portfolio by 60%," *National Post*, October 7, 2010, FP6.

4. Peter Burrows, "The Hottest Property in the Valley?" *Business Week*, August 30, 1999, 69–74.

5. Ben Worthen, "CEO Whitman Tells H-Ps Workers 'Everything is on Table' in Overhaul," *The Wall Street Journal*, March 22, 2012, B7; also "Hewlett Packard Reorganizes Under Onslaught from Mobile Devices," *National Post*, March 21, 2012, FP6.

6. Henry Mintzberg, *The Nature of Managerial Work*. New York: Harper and Row, 1973.

7. Alex Taylor III, "How a Top Boss Manages His Day," *Fortune*, June 19, 1989, 95–100.

8. Dan Ovsey, "Will Anyone Repair the C-Suite Brand?" *National Post*, March 13, 2012, FP7.

9. Virginia Galt, "Lousy People Skills Are Biggest Hurdle for Leaders," *The Globe and Mail*, October 15, 2005, B11.

10. Adam Bryant, "Quest to Build a Better Boss; Google Looks at What Makes a Good Manager," *National Post*, March 16, 2011, FP12.

11. "Hands-On From the Top Down; ING Direct," *National Post*, February 3, 2012, JV3.

12. The experiences of these and other bosses are depicted in the CBS television series *Undercover Boss*, which premiered in 2010. CEOs work with entry-level employees (who don't know they are working with the CEO). The program summarizes the lessons the CEOs learned. In 2012, a Canadian edition began on the W network. Another series, the "Big Switcheroo" on CBC, portrays situations where bosses trade jobs with lower-level workers.

13. Jason Buckland, "Canada's 10 Highest Paid CEOs," www.money.ca.msn.com/savings [accessed April 20, 2012].

14. Jerry Useem, "Boeing vs. Boeing," *Fortune*, October 2, 2000, 148–160; "Airbus Prepares

to 'Bet the Company' as It Builds a Huge New Jet," *The Wall Street Journal*, November 3, 1999, A1, A10.

15. Peter Tingling, "Fact or Fantasy?" *National Post*, April 21, 2009, FP12.

16. "Office Politics Seen As Key To Advancing," *The Globe and Mail*, March 2, 2012, B15.

17. Charles P. Wallace, "Adidas—Back in the Game," *Fortune*, August 18, 1997, 176–182.

18. Barry M. Staw and Jerry Ross, "Good Money After Bad," *Psychology Today*, February 1988, 30–33.

19. Gerry McNamara and Philip Bromiley, "Risk and Return in Organizational Decision Making," *Academy of Management Journal* 42 (1999): 330–339.

20. Brian O'Reilly, "What it Takes to Start a Startup," *Fortune*, June 7, 1999, 135–140.

21. Mary Bitti, "The Business Case for Sustainability; Green Strategy Can Lead to Competitive Advantage," *National Post*, November 22, 2011, FP6.

22. Greg Keenan, "Toyota Canada's New Head Lays Out Recovery Plan," *The Globe and Mail*, January 9, 2012, B1.

23. Brent Jang, "WestJet Sets Sights on Air Canada's Title," *The Globe and Mail*, January 2, 2012, B1.

24. Nick Rockel, "Keeping the Containers Moving," *The Globe and Mail*, November 15, 2011, B15.

25. Sue Shellenbarger, "Making Kids Work on Goals (And Not Just Soccer)," *The Wall Street Journal*, March 9, 2011, D1.

26. There is a lack of consensus regarding the definitions of the terms "vision" and "mission." Some authors define "mission" as the purpose of an organization (see Stephen Robbins, Mary Coulter, and Nancy Langton, *Management*. Toronto: Pearson, 2009, p. 175).

27. "Sony CEO Wields Ax, Sets Turnaround Targets," *BNN*, April 12, 2012.

28. Joanna Pachner, "A Perfect Predator," *Canadian Business*, July 20–August 16, 2010, 51.

29. Sinclair Stewart and Derek DeCloet, "It's Mr. Focus v. Mr. Diversification," *The Globe and Mail*, June 3, 2006, B4.

30. Joanna Pachner, "A Perfect Predator," *Canadian Business*, July 20–August 16, 2010, 51.

31. Martin Mittelstaedt, "A Conflicting Moment for Kodak," *The Globe and Mail*, May 24, 2011, B13.

32. Gordon Pitts, "Taking a Stand: How One CEO Gained Respect," *The Globe and Mail*, January 31, 2006, B8.

33. Bertrand Marotte, "Gildan Takes T-shirt Making to the Cutting-Edge of Casual Apparel," *The Globe and Mail*, July 3, 2004, B3.

34. Amy Hoffman, "Potash Strike Leaves Slippery Side Effects," *The Globe and Mail*, November 17, 2008, B1.

35. Steve Ladurantaye, "Maple Leaf Battered by Meat Recall Costs," *The Globe and Mail*, October 30, 2008, B3.

36. Kristine Owram, "Maple Leaf Claims 'Progress' After Recall," *The Globe and Mail*, February 25, 2009, B5.

37. "Hands-On from the Top Down; ING DIRECT," *National Post*, February 3, 2012, JV3.

38. Chrystia Freeland, "Americans Struggle to Adjust to New Culture of 'No,'" *The Globe and Mail*, November 26, 2010, B2.

39. Ric Dolphin, "Magna Force," *Canadian Business*, May 1988.

40. Isadore Sharp, "Quality for All Seasons," *Canadian Business Review* (Spring 1990): 21–23.

41. Derek Sankey, "Cult-Like Culture is Key," *Financial Post*, July 28, 2008, www. national-post.com/story-printer.html?id=684225.

42. "Canada's 10 Most Admired Corporate Cultures of 2011 Announced Today," Water-stone Human Capital, www.waterstonehc.com/news-events/news.

43. Calvin Leung, "Culture Club," *Canadian Business*, October 9–22, 2006, 115.

44. Christopher Swann, "You Can Trust Us Most: Survey," *National Post*, February 23, 2010, FP2.

45. Calvin Leung, "Culture Club," *Canadian Business*, October 9–22, 2006, 115, 116, 118, 120; "Golden Rule Is Measure of Success: 10 Most Admired Corporate Cultures," *National Post*, December 3, 2008, FP16.

46. Calvin Leung, "Culture Club," *Canadian Business*, October 9–22, 2006, 115, 116, 118, 120; "Golden Rule Is Measure of Success: 10 Most Admired Corporate Cultures," *National Post*, December 3, 2008, FP16.

47. Meagan Fitzpatrick, "RCMP 'Horribly Broken,' Need Fix Quickly: Report," *Winnipeg Free Press*, June 16, 2007, A9.

Chapter 7

1. Tim Kiladze and Iain Marlow, "RIM Shakeup Gets Chilly Welcome," *The Globe and Mail*, January 24, 2012, B1.

2. John A. Wagner and John R. Hollenbeck, *Management of Organizational Behavior* (Englewood Cliffs, NJ: Prentice Hall, 1992), 563–565.

3. Jay Diamond and Gerald Pintel, *Retailing*, 6th ed. (Upper Saddle River, NJ: Prentice Hall, 1996), 83–84.

4. "Lowe's Restructures Its Store and Merchandising Organizations," *National Post*, August 30, 2011, FP5.

5. "Lowe's Restructures Its Store and Merchandising Organizations," *National Post*, August 30, 2011, FP5.

6. "Nike Redefines Its Regions Amid Spending Pullback," *The Globe and Mail*, March 21, 2009, B7.

7. Roger Martin, "Don't Ask, Don't Tell," *The Globe and Mail*, July 22, 2012, A15.

8. Interview with Jamie Brown, CEO of Frantic Films.

9. Tom Randall, "Kindler Quits as Pfizer CEO Before Special Meeting; Veterans to Take Over; Executives Frustrated with Management Style, Source Says," *National Post*, December 7, 2010, FP2.

10. Rick Spence, "It Pays to Flatten the Pyramid; Eschewing Old Hierarchies Can Foster Innovation," *National Post*, June 6, 2011, FP4.

11. Michael E. Raynor and Joseph L. Bower, "Lead from the Center," *Harvard Business Review* (May 2001): 93–102.

12. Bruce Horovitz, "Restoring the Golden-Arch Shine," *USA Today*, June 16, 1999, 3B.

13. Lee Hawkins, "Reversing 80 Years of History, GM Is Reining in Global Fiefs," *The Wall Street Journal*, October 6, 2004, A1.

14. Julie Forster, "Sara Lee: Changing the Recipe—Again," *Business Week*, September 10, 2001, 87.

15. Donna Fenn, "The Buyers," *Inc.* (June 1996): 46–48.

16. Mitchell Osak, "Customers Always Know Best; Customer Innovation Centres are Designed to Break Down Organizational and Functional Silos," *National Post*, September 7, 2010, FP5.

17. Interviews with Jamie Brown, CEO of Frantic Films.

18. Nelson Wyatt, "Bell Canada Plan Creates 3 Divisions," *The Winnipeg Free Press*, May 8, 2003, B7.

19. "Yahoo Adopts New Structure in Search for Revival Following Layoffs," *National Post*, April 11, 2012, FP5.

20. J. Galbraith, "Matrix Organization Designs: How to Combine Functional and Project Forms," *Business Horizons* (1971): 29–40; H.F. Kolodny, "Evolution to a Matrix Organization," *Academy of Management Review* 4 (1979): 543–553.

21. Interview with Tom Ward, operations manager for Genstar Shipyards.

22. Lawton R. Burns, "Matrix Management in Hospitals: Testing Theories of Matrix Structure and Development," *Administrative Science Quarterly* 34 (1989): 48–50.

23. Diane Brady, "Martha Inc.," *Business Week*, January 17, 2000, 62–66.

24. Gail Edmondson, "Danone Hits Its Stride," *Business Week*, February 1, 1999, 52–53.

25. Frank Rose, "Think Globally, Script Locally," *Fortune*, November 8, 1999, 156–160.

26. Thomas A. Stewart, "See Jack. See Jack Run," *Fortune*, September 27, 1999, 124–127.

27. Wallace Immen, "The Power of Teamwork," *The Globe and Mail*, October 15, 2010, B15.

28. Jerald Greenberg and Robert A. Baron, *Behavior in Organizations: Understanding and Managing the Human Side of Work*, 7th ed. (Upper Saddle River, NJ: Prentice Hall, 2000), 308–309.

Chapter 8

1. See Angelo S. DeNisi and Ricky W. Griffin, *Human Resource Management* (Boston, MA: Houghton Mifflin, 2001) for a complete overview.

2. Susanna Kelly, "In RIM's Ravaged Heartland, Good Jobs Go Begging," *The Globe and Mail*, November 12, 2009, B4.

3. Barrie McKenna, "Labour Shortage Becoming 'Desperate,'" *The Globe and Mail*, February 8, 2012, B3; see also John Shmuel, "Labour Pains," *National Post*, February 14, 2011, FP1.

4. Patrick Brethour and Heather Scoffield, "Plenty of Work, Not Enough Bodies," *The Globe and Mail*, August 21, 2006, B4.

5. Heather Scoffield, "Amid Jobs Boom, Hundreds of Thousands Left Behind," *The Globe and Mail*, August 21, 2006, B5.

6. Elizabeth Church, "Store Owners Struggle with Staffing," *The Globe and Mail*, November 25, 1996, B6.

7. Wallace Immen, "The Rise of the Virtual Job Fair," *The Globe and Mail*, April 13, 2011, B16.

8. Diane Jermyn, "Internships Lead to Life-Changing Jobs," *The Globe and Mail*, March 14, 2012, B16.

9. Christine Dobby, "Intern Nation," *National Post*, June 11, 2011, FP7.

10. Lauren Weber, "Your Resume vs. Oblivion," *The Wall Street Journal*, January 24, 2012, B1.

11. Rachel Silverman, "No More Resumes, Say Some Firms," *The Wall Street Journal*, January 24, 2012, B6.

12. Katie Rook, "Curveball Job Questions: How Not to Strike Out," *The Globe and Mail*, September 3, 2005, B9.

13. Ogilvy Renault website, www.ogilvry-renault.com/en/;Emily Sternberg, Anouk Violette, William Hlibchuk, "Drug and Alcohol Testing by Employers in Canada—A Legal Issues Pulse Check," July 2, 2010; Canadian Human Rights Commission Policy on Alcohol and Drug Testing, June 2002, P1–16.

14. David Hutton, "Job Reference Chill Grows Icier," *The Globe and Mail*, June 18, 2008, B1

15. Wallace Immen, "Half of Workers Don't Fit In," *The Globe and Mail*, October 22, 2008, C2.

16. Kira Vermond, "Rolling Out the Welcome Mat," *The Globe and Mail*, April 26, 2008, B19.

17. Tony Wanless, "Picking Employees like a matchmaker," *National Post*, December 27, 2011, FP8

18. Bertrand Marotte, "From the Cockpit to the OR: CAE's Diversification," *The Globe and Mail*, May 25, 2010, B3

19. Jacqueline Nelson and Kasey Coholan, "Leaders in Leadership," *Canadian Business*, November 8, 2010, 61.

20. Wallace Immen, "Rookie Managers Left to Sink or Swim," *The Globe and Mail*, April 2, 2011, B17.

21. Fiona MacFarlane, "Key to C-Suite May Just be a Hero; Male Sponsors Help Women Attain Executive Jobs," *National Post*, November 30, 2011, FP8; see also Mary Bitti, "From Mentors to Sponsors; Promoting Women," *National Post*, September 27, 2011, FP10.

22. Tavia Grant, "Weekend Workout: Reverse Mentoring," *The Globe and Mail*, July 11, 2009, B14.

23. www.eaglesflight.com.

24. Kira Vermond, "Taking a Full-Circle Look at Work Reviews," *The Globe and Mail*, November 24, 2007, B18.

25. Iain Marlow, "Fixing the Dreaded Performance Review," *The Globe and Mail*, July 15, 2011, B13.

26. Rachel Silverman, "Work Reviews Losing Steam," *The Wall Street Journal*, December 19, 2011, B7.

27. Hugh Mackenzie, "Canada's CEO Elite 100," Canadian Centre for Policy Alternatives, January 2012.

28. Hugh Mackenzie, "Canada's CEO Elite 100," Canadian Centre for Policy Alternatives, January 2012.

29. www.ca.finance.yahoo.com/news/highest-paid-ceos-174613134.

30. Dana Flavelle, "Highest-Paid Canadian CEOs got 27 Percent Pay Hike," *thestar.com*, January 2, 2012.

31. Boyd Erman, "Shareholders Win Voice on CEO Pay at 3 Big Banks," *The Globe and Mail*, February 27, 2009, B1.

32. Joann Lublin, "Say on the Boss's Pay," *The Wall Street Journal*, March 7, 2008, B1–B2.

33. www.statcan.gc.ca.

34. "Plenty of Canadian Companies Offer Incentives but Few Track Their Effectiveness," *National Post*, November 10, 2010, FP14.

35. Elizabeth Church, "Nortel Workers Pick Tailor-Made Perks," *The Globe and Mail*, December 8, 2000, B11.

36. Vanessa O'Connell, "Retailers Reprogram Workers in Efficiency Push," *The Wall Street Journal*, September 10, 2008, A1, A11.

37. Cathryn Atkinson, "The Total Package: Anatomy of a Great Place to Work," *The Globe and Mail*, June 2, 2010, B11

38. David Roberts, "A Long Way from Cambodia," *The Globe and Mail*, July 5, 1994, B18.

39. Jennifer Myers, "The Right Way to Reward," *The Globe and Mail*, April 3, 2010, B13

40. http://actionplan.gc.ca/initiatives/eng/index.asp?mode=2&initiativeID=329.

41. www.cbc.ca.

42. Virginia Galt, "Companies, Unions, Expect Little Relief," *The Globe and Mail*, September 15, 2004, B4.

43. Virginia Galt, "Gift of Time Pays off for Savvy Employers," *The Globe and Mail*, December 28, 2004, B3.

44. Ibid.

45. Bruce McDougall, "The Thinking Man's Assembly Line," *Canadian Business*, November 1991, 40.

46. Kamal Dib, "Diversity Works," *Canadian Business*, March 29, 2004, 53–54.

47. Catalyst website, www.catalyst.org/publication [accessed July 1, 2010].

48. Vivian Smith, "Breaking Down the Barriers," *The Globe and Mail*, November 17, 1992, B24.

49. Richard Blackwell and Brent Jang, "Top Court Sides with Airline Attendants," *The Globe and Mail*, January 27, 2006, B1, B6.

50. Keith McArthur, "Criticism of Women's Fitness for Top Jobs Causes International Stir," *The Globe and Mail*, October 21, 2005, A1, A14.

51. Brent Jang, "Air Canada Plans to End forced Retirement at 60," *The Globe and Mail*, January 28, 2012, B8.

52. CBC website, "Mandatory Retirement Fades in Canada," www.cbc.ca/canada/story/2009/08/20/mandatory-retirement-explainer523.html, August 20,2009 [accessed July 1, 2010].

53. Omar El Akkad, "A Woman's Work May Never be Done," *The Globe and Mail*, March 28, 2006, B1, B4

54. Michael Moss, "For Older Employees, On-the-Job Injuries Are More Often Deadly," *The Wall Street Journal*, June 17, 1997, A1, A10.

55. Jill Mahoney, "Visible Majority by 2017," *The Globe and Mail*, March 23, 2005, A1, A7.

56. Virginia Galt, "P & G Leverages Its Cultural Diversity," *The Globe and Mail*, April 7, 2005, B1, B5.

57. Virginia Galt, "Western Union Remakes 'Canadian' Image," *The Globe and Mail*, November 23, 2004, B1, B24.

58. "Commitment to Diversity," *National Post*, February 3, 2012, JV10.

59. Max Boiset, *Knowledge Assets* (Oxford University Press, 1998)

60. Thomas Stewart, "In Search of Elusive Tech Workers," *Fortune*, February 16, 1998, 171–172.

61. www.statcan.ca.

62. Tavia Grant, "Financial Crisis Sparks More Demand for Temps at the Top," *The Globe and Mail*, November 14, 2008, B16.

63. Aaron Bernstein, "When Is a Temp Not a Temp?" *Business Week*, December 7, 1998, 90–92.

Chapter 9

1. David Lipsky and Clifford Donn, *Collective Bargaining in American Industry* (Lexington, MA: Lexington Books, 1981).

2. www.statcan.gc.ca/pub/75-001 [accessed May 3, 2012] (see Table 1).

3. www.statcan.gc.ca/pub/75-001 [accessed May 3, 2012] (see Table 1).

4. www.statcan.gc.ca/pub/75-001 [accessed May 3, 2012] (see Table 1).

5. www.ufcw.ca/index [accessed May 3, 2012].

6. Greg Keenan, "CAW Rewriting Playbook to Keep Factories Running," *The Globe and Mail*, September 5, 2006, B3.

7. Jeff Gray, "Rocky Times Loom for Labour," *The Globe and Mail*, January 7, 2012, B6.

8. Terence Corcoran, "Why the Public Sector Is Hanging On For All It's Worth," *National Post*, March 5, 2011, A1.

9. Tony Van Alphen, "CAW working on Biggest Union Merger Ever," the star.com, www.thestar.com/news/article/1103016 [accessed May 3, 2012].

10. Alexandra Posadzki, "Top Court Upholds Ag-Sector Ban," *Winnipeg Free Press*, April 30, 2011, A22.

11. Julius Meinitzer, "Farm Labour Ruling Boon to Employers; Bargaining Rights," *National Post*, May 4, 2011, FP12.

12. Joseph Szczesny, "UAW Targets Asian, German Auto Plants in U.S.," *National Post*, January 8, 2011, FP17.

13. "CAW Walks Away From Wal-Mart," *National Post*, April 20, 2000, C5.

14. Terence Corcoran, "Wal-Mart Wins big Union Battle," *National Post*, April 9, 2009, FP13; Bert Hill, "Another Wal-Mart Unionized; Second for Quebec," *National Post*, December 20, 2008, FP6; Jean-Francois Bertrand, "Union Contract Imposed on Quebec Wal-Mart Store a First," *Winnipeg Free Press*, August 16, 2008, B10.

15. Brent Jang, "CAW Eyes Union Drive at WestJet Airlines," *The Globe and Mail*, September 10, 2008, B3.

16. Sarah Binder, "McDonald's Store Closes, Union Wails," *The Globe and Mail*, February 14, 1998, B23.

17. Kris Maher, "Unions Forge Secret Pacts with Major Employers," *The Wall Street Journal*, May 10–11, 2008, A1.

18. Paul McKie, "Goldcorp Workers Accept Offer, Dismantle Union," *Winnipeg Free Press*, April 22, 2000, A6.

19. Murray McNeill, "Hotel Workers Sever Relationship with Union," *Winnipeg Free Press*, July 22, 2005, B14.

20. "Union Coverage in Canada, 2011, Appendix Table 3. *Statistics Canada*, www.hrsdc.gc.ca/eng/labour [accessed May 3, 2012].

21. Scott Deveau, "Pilots Reject Tentative Deal; Air Canada Vote," *National Post*, May 20, 2011, FP5.

22. Scott Deveau, "Pensions Next Big Issue for Companies; Air Canada vs. CAW," *National Post*, June 14, 2011, FP1.

23. Peter Brieger, "Court Rejects First Nation's Bid For Own Union Pact," *National Post*, November 29, 2007, www.nationalpost.com/story-printer.html?id=130625.

24. "Tembec Ends Three-Month Strike," *National Post*, August 19, 2011, p. FP4.

25. Brent Jang, "Rejected Deal Imposed on Air Canada Attendants," *The Globe and Mail*, November 8, 2011, B9.

26. Alison Auld, "N.S. Nurses Defy Strike Law," *The Globe and Mail*, June 28, 2001, B1.

27. Brent Jang, "Labour Board Calls Air Canada Stoppages Illegal," *The Globe and Mail*, April 14, 2012, B7.

28. Jeffrey Ball, Glenn Burkins, and Gregory White, "Why Labor Unions Have Grown Reluctant to Use the S-word," *The Wall Street Journal*, December 16, 1999, A1, A8.

29. Patrick Brethour, "Telus Gets Injunction Against Union," *The Globe and Mail*, July 25, 2005, B1, B4.

30. Brent Jang, "Labour Board Calls Air Canada Stoppages Illegal," *The Globe and Mail*, April 14, 2012, B7.

31. Greg Keenan, "U.S. Steel Workers Head Back to Work," *The Globe and Mail*, October 18, 2011, B12.

32. James Hagerty and Kate Linebaugh, "In U.S., a Cheaper Labor Pool," *The Wall Street Journal*, January 6, 2012, B1; also Rio Tinto Locks Out 800," *The Globe and Mail*, January 2, 2012, B3.

33. Scott Deveau, "Air Canada Readies Strike Back-Up; Plans to Use Non-Unionized Workers to Fill In," *National Post*, June 13, 2011, FP1.

34. Martin Cash, "Tractor Plant Workers Locked Out," *Winnipeg Free Press*, March 28, 2001, B3; Paul McKie, "A Bitter End at Versatile," *Winnipeg Free Press*, August 14, 2001, A1–A2.

35. "Staff Shuns Offer, Magna Plant to Close," *The Globe and Mail*, March 19, 2009, B4.

36. Simon Houpt, "Canadian Press Asks for Conciliator," *The Globe and Mail*, January 19, 2012, B10.

37. "CP Requests Conciliator in Pension Talks," *National Post*, February 18, 2012, FP7.

38. Scott Deveau, "Air Canada, Pilots Agree to Mediation," *National Post*, February 16, 2012, FP4.

39. Brent Jang, "Air Canada Moves to Appeal Arbitrator's Pension Ruling," *The Globe and Mail*, October 24, 2011, B3.

40. Brent Jang, "Union Buttons Cross the Line," *The Globe and Mail*, August 11, 2008, B3.

Chapter 10

1. "Time is Money: 1 in 5 Canadians Late for Work at Least Once a Week," *National Post*, February 24, 2011, FP5.

2. "Bosses: Killing Them with Kindness Pays Off," *The Globe and Mail*, October 8, 2008, C3.

3. Daniel Goleman, *Emotional Intelligence: Why It Can Matter More Than IQ* (New York: Bantam Books, 1995); also Kenneth Law, Chi-Sum Wong, and Lynda Song, "The Construct and Criterion Validity of Emotional Intelligence and Its Potential Utility for Management Studies," *Journal of Applied Psychology* 89 no. 3 (2004): 78–90.

4. Daniel Goleman, "Leadership That Gets Results," *Harvard Business Review*, March–April 2000, 78–90.

5. Wallace Immen, "Emotional Smarts Sway Hiring Choices," *The Globe and Mail*, August 24, 2011, B17.

6. "Half of Canadians Love Their Jobs," *The Globe and Mail*, February 17, 2010, B20.

7. "Canadians Ranked No. 3 in Satisfaction With Their Current Employer," *National Post*, April 14, 2010, FP5.

8. Doris Burke, Corey Hajim, John Elliott, Jenny Mero, and Christopher Tkaczyk, "The Top Ten Companies for Leaders," *Fortune*, October 1, 2007, http://money.cnn.com/galleries/2007/fortune/0709/ gallery.leaders_global_topten.fortune/ index.html.

9. Frederick W. Taylor, *Principles of Scientific Management* (New York: Harper and Brothers, 1911).

10. See Daniel Wren, *The History of Management Thought* (New York: John Wiley & Sons, 2004).

11. Douglas McGregor, *The Human Side of Enterprise* (New York: McGraw-Hill, 1960).

12. Abraham Maslow, "A Theory of Human Motivation," *Psychological Review* (July 1943): 370–396.

13. Frederick Herzberg, Bernard Mausner, and Barbara Bloch Snyderman, *The Motivation to Work* (New York: Wiley, 1959).

14. Victor Vroom, *Work and Motivation* (New York: Wiley, 1964); Craig Pinder, *Work Motivation* (Glenview, IL: Scott, Foresman, 1984).

15. J. Stacy Adams, "Toward an Under standing of Inequity," *Journal of Abnormal and Social Psychology* 75 no. 5 (1963): 422–436.

16. Jeff Buckstein, "In Praise of Praise in the Workplace," *The Globe and Mail*, June 15, 2005, C1, C5.

17. Deena Waisberg, "Tip of the Hat to Excellence; Employers get Creative with Rewards to Keep Top Performers," *National Post*, November 19, 2008, FP15.

18. Interviews with Sterling McLeod and Wayne Walker, senior vice-presidents of sales for Investors Group Financial Services.

19. Tavia Grant, "Workplace Democracy," *The Globe and Mail*, May 30, 2009, B14.

20. Harvey Schachter, "Managing Without Managers," *The Globe and Mail*, December 19, 2011, B5.

21. Tavia Grant, "Workplace Democracy," *The Globe and Mail*, May 30, 2009, B14.

22. Virginia Galt, "Change Is a Good Thing When Everyone Is Involved," *The Globe and Mail*, June 25, 2005, B11.

23. Robert Grant, "AES Corporation: Rewriting the Rules of Management," *Contemporary Strategy Analysis* (Hoboken, NJ: John Wiley & Sons, 2007), www. blackwellpublishing.com/grant/docs/17AES.pdf.

24. Patricia Kitchen, "TAP Your Employees," *Orlando Sentinel*, March 14, 2007, F1.

25. Mary Teresa Bitti, "The Power of Team-work," *National Post*, December 18, 2009, FP12.

26. "Looking Good in Green," *Maclean's*, May 9, 2011, 47.

27. Tom Peters, *Liberation Management*. New York: Alfred Knopf, 1992, 238–239.

28. Charles Snow, Scott Snell, Sue Canney Davison, and Donald Hambrick, "Use Transnational Teams to Globalize Your Company," *Organizational Dynamics*, Spring 1996, 61.

29. Gregory Moorhead and Ricky W. Griffin, *Organizational Behavior*, 6th ed. Boston: Houghton Mifflin, 2001, Chapter 7.

30. A. B. Drexler and R. Forrester, "Team-work—Not Necessarily the Answer," *HR Magazine*, January 1998, 55–58.

31. For a discussion of team effectiveness, see Nancy Langton and Stephen Robbins, *Organizational Behaviour*, 4th Canadian edition, Toronto: Pearson Canada, 2006, 217–230.

32. Gregory Moorhead and Ricky W. Griffin, *Organizational Behavior*, 6th ed. Boston: Houghton Mifflin, 2001, Chapter 7.

33. Ibid.

34. Ricky Griffin, *Task Design* (Glenview, IL: Scott, Foresman, 1982).

35. "Canadian Businesses World Leaders in Offering Work-From-Home Options," *National Post*, March 16, 2011, FP12.

36. Wallace Immen, "Most Firms Offer Flexible Work," *The Globe and Mail*, July 2, 2011, B11.

37. Diane Jermyn, "Canada's Best Places to Work," *The Globe and Mail*, October 7, 2011, E10; also Gail Johnson, "Companies Who Cut the Cost of Education," *The Globe and Mail*, December 8, 2011, B11.

38. Mary Gooderham, "Better Mom Becomes Better Manager," *The Globe and Mail*, October 15, 2010, E6.

39. Wallace Immen, "Flexible Work Policies Pay Off: Survey," *The Globe and Mail*, March 14, 2012, B18.

40. "Workers May Be in Office Less, But They're Still Plugged in and Stressed Out: Survey," *National Post*, March 21, 2012, FP11.

41. Diane Jermyn, "Canada's Best Places to Work," *The Globe and Mail*, October 7, 2011, E10; also Diane Jermyn, "Keeping Veteran Talent as Key Contributors," *The Globe and Mail*, June 7, 2011, B14; also Diane Jermyn, "The GTA's Top Employers for 2012," *The Globe and Mail*, November 16, 2011, E4.

42. Mary Gooderham, "Where It's Not All About the Money," *The Globe and Mail*, November 22, 2010, E2.

43. Jameson Berkow, "Workers of the World DISPERSE: Anything, Anywhere; Mobile Workers are Taking the Office With them in Greater Numbers," *National Post*, June 20, 2011, FP1.

44. "Looking Good in Green," *Maclean's*, May 9, 2011, 47.

45. Jameson Berkow, "Workers of the World DISPERSE: Anything, Anywhere; Mobile Workers are Taking the Office With them in Greater Numbers," *National Post*, June 20, 2011, FP1.

46. Joyce Rosenberg, "Out of Sight, On Your Mind: Learning to Trust Telecommuters," *The Globe and Mail*, September 20, 2008, B19.

47. Diane Jermyn, "The 10 Best to Work for," *The Globe and Mail*, September 30, 2010, B2; also Cam Cole, "Flyers' Goalie Carousel is Norm; Job Sharing in Post-Season More Prevalent," *National Post*, June 1, 2010, B9.

48. John Kotter, "What Leaders Really Do," *Harvard Business Review*, December 2001, 85–94.

49. Ronald Heifetz and Marty Linsky, "A Survival Guide for Leaders," *Harvard Business Review*, June 2002, 65–74.

50. Frederick Reichheld, "Lead for Loyalty," *Harvard Business Review*, July–August 2001, 76–83.

51. David Dorsey, "Andy Pearson Finds Love," *Fast Company*, August 2001, 78–86.

52. David A. Waldman and Francis J. Yammarino, "CEO Charismatic Leadership: Levels-of-Management and Levels-of-Analysis Effects," *Academy of Management Review* 24 no. 2 (1999): 266–285.

53. Ronald Ebert and Ricky Griffin, *Business Essentials* (Upper Saddle River, NJ: Prentice Hall, 2009), 129.

54. Jane Howell and Boas Shamir, "The Role of Followers in the Charismatic Leadership Process: Relationships and Their Consequences," *Academy of Management Review* 30 no. 1 (2005): 96–112.

55. J. Richard Hackman and Ruth Wageman, "A Theory of Team Coaching," *Academy of Management Review* 30 no. 2 (2005): 269–287.

56. "How Women Lead," *Newsweek*, October 24, 2005, 46–70.

57. Madelaine Drohan, "What Makes a Canadian Manager?" *The Globe and Mail*, Feburary 25, 1997, B18.

58. Rebecca Walbert, "Canada's Management Dividend," *National Post*, November 17, 2009, FP14.

59. Sinclair Stewart, "Passed by at TD, CEO Hits Stride in New York," *The Globe and Mail*, December 5, 2006, B1, B21; also Zena Olijnyk, Mark Brown, Andy Holloway, Calvin Leung, Alex Mlynek, Erin Pooley, Jeff Sanford, Andrew Wahl, and Thomas Watson, "Canada's Global Leaders," *Canadian Business*, March 28–April 10, 2005, 37–43.

60. Bryan Borzykowski, "Collaborating With a Far-Flung Team," *The Globe and Mail*, January 18, 2012, B7.

Chapter 11

1. *Our Time: GE Annual Report:* 2004 (Fairfield, CT: General Electric Co., 2005), 4–5.

2. Neil Reynolds, "Technology Spurring a New Manufacturing Revolution," *The Globe and Mail*, May 9, 2012, B2.

3. Andrew Nikiforuk, "Pure Profit," *Canadian Business*, April 3, 2000, 70–76.

4. Daniel Michaels and J. Lynn Lunsford, "Lack of Seats, Galleys Delays Boeing, Airbus," *The Wall Street Journal*, August 2008, B1.

5. Judy Strauss and Raymond Frost, *Marketing on the Internet* (Upper Saddle River, NJ: Prentice Hall, 1999), 266–271.

6. Eryn Brown, "America's Most Admired Companies," *Fortune*, March 1, 1999, 68, 70–73; http://walmartstores.com, April 24, 2000.

7. Susan Carey, "Airlines Lose the Winter Blahs," *The Wall Street Journal*, February 29, 2012, B1.

8. Judy Strauss and Raymond Frost, *Marketing on the Internet* (Upper Saddle River, NJ: Prentice Hall, 1999), 266–271.

9. Susan Carey, "The Case of the Vanishing Airport Lines," *The Wall Street Journal*, August 9, 2007, B1.

10. Mark Lander, "Slovakia No Longer a Laggard in Automaking," *nytimes.com*, April 13, 2004, www.nytimes.com/2004/04/13/business/worldbusiness.

11. John Letzing, "Amazon Adds That Robotic Touch," *The Wall Street Journal*, March 20, 2012, B1.

12. Rita Trichur, "Down on the Farm with Robo-Milker," *The Globe and Mail*, March 17, 2011, B4.

13. Timothy Hay, "The Robots are Coming to Hospitals," *The Wall Street Journal*, March 15, 2012, B12.

14. Hollie Shaw, "The Way Toyota Builds Cars," *National Post*, October 13, 2009, FP1.

15. Christina Passariello, "Louis Vuitton Tries Modern Methods on Factory Lines," *The Wall Street Journal*, October 9, 2006, A1, A15.

16. Neal Boudette, "Chrysler Gains Edge by Giving New Flexibility to Its Factories," *The Wall Street Journal*, April 11, 2006, A1, A15.

17. Greg Keenan, "Ford's New Maxim: Flex Manufacturing," *The Globe and Mail*, May 10, 2006, B3.

18. Lou Michel, "WNY's Trash, China's Treasure," *The Buffalo News*, July 20, 2008.

19. Don Marshall, "Time for Just in Time," *P&IM Review*, June 1991, 20–22. See also Gregg Stocker, "Quality Function Deployment: Listening to the Voice of the Customer," *APICS: The Performance Advantage*, September 1991, 44–48.

20. Lee J. Krajewski and Larry P. Ritzman, *Operations Management: Strategy and Analysis*, 6th ed. (Upper Saddle River, NJ: Prentice Hall, 2002), 153–154, 828–829; Robert S. Russell and Bernard W. Taylor III, *Operations Management*, 4th ed. (Upper Saddle River, NJ: Prentice Hall, 2003), 221–222, 593–595.

21. Robert S. Russell and Bernard W. Taylor III, *Operations Management*, 4th ed. (Upper Saddle River, NJ: Prentice Hall, 2003), 222–224.

22. Lee J. Krajewski and Larry P. Ritzman, *Operations Management: Strategy and Analysis*, 6th ed. (Upper Saddle River, NJ: Prentice Hall, 2002), 595.

23. Tom Murphy, "E Cyber Squeeze: The Pressure Is On," *Ward's Auto World* (December 2000): 44–47.

24. The Disney Institute, www. disneyinstitute.com/DisneyInstitute/ProfessionalPrograms/DisneyDifference/index.html.

25. Bruce Little, "Stock Answers," *The Globe and Mail*, June 6, 1995, B12.

26. Marina Strauss, "Low Fills/High Stakes," *The Globe and Mail*, May 12, 2010, B1.

27. Clare Ansberry, "A New Hazard for Recovery: Last-Minute Pace of Orders," *The Wall Street Journal*, June 25, 2002, A1, A12.

Chapter 12

1. Gordon Pitts, "Message for Manufacturers: Go Big, Don't Stay at Home," *The Globe and Mail*, December 6, 2005, B1, B7.

2. Julian Beltrame, "Canada's Productivity on the Rise," *The Globe and Mail*, March 14, 2012, B4.

3. Bart VanArk and Robert McGuckin, "International Comparisons of Labor Productivity

and per Capita Income," *Monthly Labor Review*, July 1999, 33–41.

4. Harvey Enchin, "Canada Urged to Stop Living Off Fat of the Land," *The Globe and Mail*, October 25, 1991, B1, B6.

5. Barrie McKenna and Tavia Grant, "Canada's Productivity Trap," *The Globe and Mail*, September 15, 2010, p. B1

6. Jon Hilsenrath, "Behind Surging Productivity: The Service Sector Delivers," *The Wall Street Journal*, November 7, 2003, A1, A8.

7. Alexandra Lopez-Pacheco, "Service Sector on Cusp of a Tech Revolution; Key Job Creator," *National Post*, November 16, 2010, FP14.

8. Peter Kennedy, "Canfor Goes High Tech to Cut Costs," *The Globe and Mail*, July 29, 2000, 3.

9. Wallace Immen, "Web Surfing a Boon to Productivity, Study Shows," *The Globe and Mail*, August 17, 2011, B17; see also Carly Weeks, "Compwwany Social Networks Could Spell the End of E-Mail," *The Globe and Mail*, September 15, 2011, B11; see also Wallace Immen, "Water Cooler Chats Can Raise Productivity," *The Globe and Mail*, November 3, 2010, B25.

10. "Canadian Auto Plant Takes Top Honours," *Winnipeg Free Press*, June 21, 2012, B7.

11. Lee J. Krajewski and Larry P. Ritzman, *Operations Management: Strategy and Analysis*, 5th ed. (Reading, MA: Addison-Wesley, 1999), 229–230.

12. Bruce McDougall, "The Thinking Man's Assembly Line," *Canadian Business*, November 1991, 40.

13. Thomas Foster Jr., *Managing Quality: An Integrative Approach* (Upper Saddle River, NJ: Prentice Hall, 2001), 22–23.

14. Ted Wakefield, "No Pain, No Gain," *Canadian Business*, January 1993, 50–54.

15. Scott McCartney, "Ranking Airlines by Lost Bags, Canceled Flights," *Wall Street Journal*, January 5, 2012, D3.

16. Ben Casselman and Russell Gold, "Unusual Decisions Set Stage for BP Disaster," *The Wall Street Journal*, May 27, 2010, A1.

17. Thomas Foster Jr., *Managing Quality: An Integrative Approach* (Upper Saddle River, NJ: Prentice Hall, 2001), 325–339.

18. Ibid.

19. James Evans and James Dean Jr., *Total Quality: Management, Organization, and Strategy*, 2nd ed. (Cincinnati, OH: South-Western, 2000), 230.

20. Margot Gibb-Clark, "Hospital Managers Gain Tool to Compare Notes," *The Globe and Mail*, September 9, 1996, B9.

21. "Quality Customer Care," *National Post*, February 3, 2012, JV6.

22. www.nist.gov/baldrige/award_recipients/concordia_profile.cfm.

23. Roberta S. Russell and Bernard W. Taylor III, *Operations Management*, 4th ed. (Upper Saddle River, NJ: Prentice Hall, 2003), 658–662; Thomas Foster Jr., *Managing Quality: An Integrative Approach* (Upper Saddle River, NJ: Prentice Hall, 2001), 85–86.

24. Roberta S. Russell and Bernard W. Taylor III, *Operations Management*, 4th ed. (Upper Saddle River, NJ: Prentice Hall, 2003), 137–140.

25. Sunil Chopra and Peter Meindl, *Supply Chain Management: Strategy, Planning, and Operation*, 6th ed. (Upper Saddle River, NJ: Prentice Hall, 2001), 3–6; Lee J. Krajewski and Larry P. Ritzman, *Operations Management: Strategy and Analysis*, 5th ed. (Reading, MA: Addison-Wesley, 1999), Chapter 11; Roberta S. Russell and Bernard W. Taylor III, *Operations Management*, 4th ed. (Upper Saddle River, NJ: Prentice Hall, 2003), Chapter 7; Thomas Foster Jr., *Managing Quality: An Integrative Approach* (Upper Saddle River, NJ: Prentice Hall, 2001), Chapter 9.

26. Sunil Chopra and Peter Meindl, *Supply Chain Management: Strategy, Planning, and Operation*, 6th ed. (Upper Saddle River, NJ: Prentice Hall, 2001), Chapter 20.

27. Ibid., 348–349.

28. Joseph Sternberg, "Now Comes the Global Revolution in Services," *The Wall Street Journal*, February 10, 2011, A17.

29. Christina Passariello, "Louis Vuitton Tries Modern Methods on Factory Lines," *The Wall Street Journal*, October 9, 2006, A1, A15.

30. Nick Rockel, "Keeping the Containers Moving," *The Globe and Mail*, November 15, 2011, p. B15.

31. Duncan Mavin, "Supply Chains Worry CEOs," *National Post*, September 11, 2008, FP3.

32. Richard Blackwell, "Factories Claim Their Place in the Global Supply Chain," *The Globe and Mail*, June 15, 2011, p. B5.

33. Catherine Greenman, "An Old Craft Learns New Tricks," *The New York Times*, June 10, 1999, G1, G7.

34. Gillian Babicz, "Six Sigma Software Generates Improvements," *Quality*, April 2002, 28.

35. Terrence Belford, "Real Estate Heaven Is No Mistake," *The Globe and Mail*, March 22, 2005, B9.

36. Neil Orkin, "Focus on China," *Training Magazine* 45 no. 6 (July–Aug. 2008), ABI/INFORM Global database, p.18.

37. "Evaluate the Value of Training," *Quality*, April 2002, 48.

38. Leonard L. Berry, A. Parasuraman, and Valarie A. Zeithaml, "Improving Service Quality in America: Lessons Learned," *Academy of Management Executive* 8 no. 2 (1994): 32–45.

Chapter 13

1. Kenneth C. Laudon and Jane P. Laudon, *Management Information Systems: Managing the Digital Firm*, 7th ed. (Upper Saddle River, NJ: Prentice Hall, 2002), 7–11.

2. www.communitechhub.ca/?page_id=134.

3. www.keylemon.com.

4. Kenneth C. Laudon and Jane P. Laudon, *Essentials of Management Information Systems*, 3rd ed. (Upper Saddle River, NJ: Prentice Hall, 1999), 383–388; E. Wainwright Martin et al., *Managing Information Technology: What Managers*

Need to Know, 3rd ed. (Upper Saddle River, NJ: Prentice Hall, 1999), 225–227.

5. Emily Smith, "Turning an Expert's Skills into Computer Software," *Business Week*, October 7, 1985, 104.

6. *Decision Support Systems and Intelligent Systems*, Efraim Turban and Jay E. Aronson 6th ed., Prentice Hall, Upper Saddle River, NJ. Sourced 2012.

7. www.soti.net/about.aspx.

8. www.scottishwater.co.uk/business/international/alberta-canada.

9. Steve Lambert, "Pushing Boundaries: Keeping an Eye on Employees" *The Globe and Mail*. August 20, 2011.

10. Emily Walzer, "Have it Your Way," *Sporting Goods Business* 38 no. 1 (2005): 42.

11. Joe Mullich, "Creativity in the Cloud: What Can Researchers do with 10,000 Computers for a Few Minutes?" *The Wall Street Journal. August 5*, 2011, B4.

12. "3D Systems Helps Walter Reed Army Medical Center Rebuild Lives," *3D Systems*, July 6, 2005, www.3Dsystems.com.

13. "Wireless Endoscopy—The Camera Is a Pill," *Three Rivers Endoscopy Center*, August 17, 2005, www.gihealth.com; "Expanding the Scope of GI," *Given Imaging*, July 6, 2005, www. givenimaging.com.

14. Steve Ladurantaye, "A Country of Clickers: Canada Tops in Web Usage," *The Globe and Mail*, March 2, 2012, B1.

15. Tavia Grant, "Canada Lags Peers in 'Internet Economy,'" *The Globe and Mail*, March 19, 2012, B3.

16. "An Intranet's Life Cycle," *morebusiness. com*, November 6, 2005, www.morebusiness. com/getting_started/website/d928247851.brc; "Calling All Workers," *CIO Magazine*, December 1, 2001, 222.cio.com/archive/120101/ ruke_ford.html.

17. www.gotomeeting.com.

18. Simon Avery, "Hunting Season for Computer Attackers," *The Globe and Mail*, July 6, 2005, B1, B4.

19. "Software Piracy Hits $1.1 Billion in 2011," *The Globe and Mail*, May16, 2012, B12.

20. "Canada's Software Piracy Rate Decreases," *Winnipeg Free Press*, May 24, 2006, B7.

21. "Hacker Sentenced to Prison for Breaking into Lowe's Companies Computers with Intent to Steal Credit Card Information," news release, Department of Justice, Western District of North Carolina, December 15, 2004.

22. www.riaa.com/phycialpiracy.php?content_selector=piracy_details_online.

23. For information on spyware, see www. webopedia.com/TERM/S/spyware.html.

24. www.webopedia.com.

25. Susan Krashinsky and Shane Dingman, "Networking Site Pinterest in Battle Against Spammers," *The Globe and Mail*, March 29, 2012, B6.

26. www.securelist.com/en/threats/spam?chapter=87.

27. Allison Jones, "Verification Revamp Urged vs. Net Fraud," *Winnipeg Free Press*, October 19, 2006, B10.

28. www.idtheftcenter.org/workplace_facts.html.

29. Jason Stein, "Madison, Wis., Company Offers Software that Protects Clients' Information," *The Wisconsin State Journal*, July 20, 2005, 1.

Chapter 14

1. Ronald Hilton, *Managerial Accounting*, 2nd ed. (New York: McGraw-Hill, 1994), 7.

2. David Milstead, "Accounting Issues Raise Big Red Flag Over Reborn GM," *The Globe and Mail*, November 27, 2010, B12.

3. Tim Leech, "Mend our SOX; It Cost Billions, but Hasn't Made Statements More Reliable," *National Post*, October 19, 2011, FP15.

4. www.cica.ca/about-cica-and-the-profession/what-do-cas-do/index.aspx.

5. www.cga-canada.org/en-ca/AboutCGACanada/CareerOpportunities/Pages/_ca_careers.aspx.

6. www.thebottomlinenews.ca/documents/Canadas_Accounting_Top_30.pdf.

7. Certified Management Accountants of Canada, www.cma-canada.org.

8. Bertrand Marotte, "Auditors Negligent in Collapse of Castor Holdings, Judge Rules," *The Globe and Mail*, April 15, 2011, B9; also Matthew McClearn, "Castor Oiled," *Canadian Business*, May 9, 2011, 18.

9. Huw Jones, "Deloitte Audit of RBS Under Scrutiny; Watchdog Probes; Should Auditor Have Been Tougher on Bank?" *National Post*, December 13, 2011, FP16; also "Auditors' Ethics Shoddy, British Regulator Says; Cites Pursuit of Non-Audit Revenues" *National Post*, September 15, 2010, FP7.

10. Sophia Pearson, "Deloitte Faces Suit for Failing to Detect U.S. $7 billion Loss; Alleged Negligence," *National Post*, September 27, 2011, FP2.

11. www.ifrs.org/Investor+resources/Investors+and+IFRS.htm.

12. Sunil Mistry, "Decide Your Accounting Framework; Options are Private Enterprise GAAP or IFRS," *National Post*, April 18, 2011, FP7.

13. Bruce Horovitz, "Restoring the Golden-Arch Shine," *USA Today*, June 16, 1999, 3B.

14. Charles T. Horngren, Walter J. Harrison Jr., and Linda Smith Bamber, *Accounting*, 5th ed. (Upper Saddle River, NJ: Prentice Hall, 2002), 17–20.

15. Brad Cherniak, "The Importance of Bridging the GAAP; Understanding your Accounting Guidelines," *National Post*, August 9, 2011, FP11.

16. John Greenwood, "Should Lifecos Just Leave?; Accounting Dispute" *National Post*, November 9, 2011, FP6.

17. David Milstead, "Cash Flow Follies: Groupon vs. Facebook," *The Globe and Mail*, February 16, 2012, B16.

18. Ronald Hilton, *Managerial Accounting*, 2nd ed. (New York: McGraw-Hill, 1994), 402–403.

19. Billie Cunningham, Loren Nikolai, and John Bazley, *Accounting: Information for Business Decisions* (Fort Worth, TX: Dryden, 2000), 133–134.

20. Charles T. Horngren, Walter J. Harrison Jr., and Linda Smith Bamber, *Accounting*, 4th ed. (Upper Saddle River, NJ: Prentice Hall, 1999), 562–563; Arthur J. Keown et al., *The Foundations of Finance: The Logic and Practice of Financial Management*, 2nd ed. (Upper Saddle River, NJ: Prentice Hall, 1998), 89–95.

21. Charles T. Horngren, Walter J. Harrison Jr., and Linda Smith Bamber, *Accounting*, 4th ed. (Upper Saddle River, NJ: Prentice Hall, 1999), 201–202.

22. www.xe.com/currencytables/?from=BRL&date=2012-01-01.

23. Alvin C. Burns and Ronald F. Bush, *Marketing Research*, 3rd ed. (Upper Saddle River, NJ: Prentice Hall, 2000), 70–84.

Chapter 15

1. American Marketing Association, "Marketing Services Guide," August 23, 2001, www.ama.org/about/ama/markdef.asp.

2. Philip Kotler, *Marketing Management*, 11th ed. (Upper Saddle River, NJ: Prentice Hall, 2003), 76–78.

3. Warren J. Keegan and Mark C. Green, *Global Marketing*, 3rd ed. (Upper Saddle River, NJ: Prentice Hall, 2003), 8–15.

4. Bank of Canada Banking and Financial Statistics, Series E1, Selected Monetary Aggregates, May 2010, S52

5. Rita Trichur, "Canadians Struggling to Dog Out of Debt," *Winnipeg Free Press*, December 12, 2009.

6. Tara Perkins, "Card Payment Players Clash over Code," *The Globe and Mail*, January 18, 2010, B5.

7. http://rbcroyalbank.shoppersdrugmart.ca/en/version=large&ProspectID=9CDF1728184145FDAC1003FC7BA150EE.

8. Philip Kotler and Peggy Cunningham, *Marketing Management* (Toronto: Prentice Hall, 2004), 18.

9. Peter Gumbel, "Mass vs. Class," *Fortune*, September 17, 2007, 82.

10. Chris Isidore, "Sweet Spot: Luxury SUV's are Hot," *CNNMoney*, January 7, 2004, http://money.cnn.com/2004/01/06/ news/companies/detroit_luxury_suv/ index.htm.

11. David Milstead, "As Tastes Change and Prices Rise, Campbell Soup Feels the Chill," *The Globe and Mail*, January 5, 2012, B12.

12. Christine Dobby, "Female Owned, Run and Played; Silicon Sisters Taps into Audience of Girl-Gamers," *National Post*, August 16, 2011, FP7.

13. Angus Whitley, "Tiny Power Shoppers; Children Aged Eight to 12 Wield Outsized Economic Clout when it Comes to Cellphones and the Virtual World of Video Games," *National Post*, August 28, 2010, FP7.

14. www.wikinvest.com/stock/Visa_(V) [accessed September 7, 2010].

15. Boyd Erman, "Visa's IPO Taps into the World's Love of Plastic," *The Globe and Mail*, February 26, 2008, B1, B6.

16. Tara Perkins, "Credit Card Perks Putting the Squeeze on Retailers," *The Globe and Mail*, June 24, 2008, B1, B5

17. Lauren Goldstein, "Dressing Up an Old Brand," *Fortune*, November 9, 1998, 154–156.

18. Peter Gumbel, "Mass vs. Class," *Fortune*, September 17, 2007, 82.

19. Tamara Audi, "Las Vegas Goes All Out to Attract Gay Travelers," *The Wall Street Journal*, November 2, 2007, B1.

20. Philip Kotler, *Marketing Management*, 11th ed. (Upper Saddle River, NJ: Prentice Hall, 2003), 292–294.

21. Naoufel Daghfous, John V. Petrof, and Frank Pons, "Values and Innovations: A Cross-cultural Study," *The Journal of Consumer Marketing* 16 no. 4 (2009): 314–331.

22. John Morton, "How to Spot the Really Important Prospects," *Business Marketing* (January 1990): 62–67.

23. www.businessweek.com/magazine/lego-is-for-girls-12142011.html.

24. Ellen Byron, "A Virtual View of the Store Aisle," *The Wall Street Journal*, October 3, 2007, B1.

25. Simon Houpt, "A Repentant Marketer Confesses His Sins," *The Globe and Mail*, September 23, 2011, B7.

26. Alvin C. Burns and Ronald F. Bush, *Marketing Research*, 3rd ed. (Upper Saddle River, NJ: Prentice Hall, 2000), 70–84.

27. Marina Strauss, "First You Have to Get Their Attention," *The Globe and Mail*, July 12, 1991, B1.

28. Tara Perkins, "They'll even Plan Your Funeral," *The Globe and Mail*, September 29, 2007, B4-B6

29. Tara Perkins, "A Piece of Drywall Away from Being Part of the Branch," *The Globe and Mail*, April 26, 2007, B6

30. Business News Network website, "Ottawa Bans Insurance Sales on Bank Websites," May 27, 2010, www.bnn.ca/news/17916.html.

31. Julie Jargon, "Kiwi Goes beyond Shine in Effort to Step Up Sales," *The Wall Street Journal*, December 20, 2007, B1.

32. Marina Strauss, "Mining Customer Feedback, Firms Go Undercover and Online," *The Globe and Mail*, May 13, 2004, B1, B25.

33. Deborah Ball, Sarah Ellison, and Janet Adamy, "Probing Shoppers' Psyche," *The Wall Street Journal*, October 28, 2004, B1, B8.

34. Oliver Bertin, "John Deere Reaps the Fruits of Its Labours," *The Globe and Mail*, September 2, 1991, B1, B3.

35. Peter Morton, "Marketing at Face Value," *National Post*, July 11, 2007, FP3.

36. John Grossman, "Focus Groups for the Internet Age; Software Company Collects

Customer Feedback in Real Time," *National Post*, October 3, 2011, FP4.

37. Steve Cunningham, "Focus Groups are Dead; New Strategies are Needed for the Internet Age," *National Post*, March 15, 2011, FP12.

38. Alvin C. Burns and Ronald F. Bush, *Marketing Research*, 3rd ed. (Upper Saddle River, NJ: Prentice Hall, 2000), 140–148.

39. Kenneth C. Laudon and Jane P. Laudon, *Management Information Systems: Managing the Digital Firm*, 7th ed. (Upper Saddle River, NJ: Prentice Hall, 2002), 221–222.

40. Ibid., 222–224.

41. Paul S. Foote and Malini Krishnamurthi, "Forecasting Using Data Warehousing Model: Wal-Mart's Experience," *The Journal of Business Forecasting Methods & Systems*, Fall 2001, 13–17.

42. *The Economist* website, Big Mac Index, March 18, 2010, www.economist.com/daily/chartgallery/displaystory.cfm?story_id=15715184.

43. Thomas Russell, Glenn Verrill, and W. Ronald Lane, *Kleppner's Advertising Procedure*, 11th ed. (Englewood Cliffs, NJ: Prentice Hall, 1990); James Engel, Martin Warshaw, and Thomas Kinnear, *Promotional Strategy*, 6th ed. (Homewood, IL: Richard D. Irwin, 1987).

44. David Parkinson, "The Lost Decade," *The Globe and Mail*, December 31, 2009, B1

45. *Canadian Business* website, Investor 500 Rankings, http://list.canadianbusiness.com/rankings/investor500/2009/q1/top-500/market-value/Default.aspx?sp2=1&d1=d&sc1=4.

Chapter 16

1. Ben Austen, "Rock N' Roll Will Never Die," *Bloomberg Businessweek*, January 23–29, 2012, p 74.

2. Black &Decker website, www.black-anddecker.com/Products-Accessories.aspx [accessed on February 20, 2012].

3. Brad Stone, "Nintendo Needs a Hit in a Hurry," *Bloomberg Businessweek*, Feb. 6–Feb 12, 2012.

4. Barrie McKenna and Matt Hartley, "Stringer Makes His Mark," *The Globe and Mail*, February 20, 2008, B1, B6.

5. Greg Keenan, "Electruc Roadster Approved in Canada," *The Globe and Mail*, January 26, 2010, B9; David Milstead, "Tesla Admits It Has a Rough Road Ahead," *The Globe and Mail*, February 5, 2010, B9; David Welch, "A Long Bet on Electric Cars," *Businessweek*, October 12, 2009, P32

6. CBC News website, Canadian Press, "Bombardier Says CSeries on Track for 2013 Launch," www.cbc.ca/news/business/story/2011/11/15/bombardier-cseries.html [accessed February 23, 2012].

7. Photo source http://e3.nintendo.com/hw/#/introduction.

8. James C. Anderson and James A. Narus, *Business Market Management: Understanding, Creating, and Delivering Value* (Upper Saddle River, NJ: Prentice Hall, 1999), 203–206.

9. Philip Kotler, *Marketing Management*,

11th ed. (Upper Saddle River, NJ: Prentice Hall, 2003), 328–339.

10. Julie Jargon, "The Iconic Oreo Squares Off in Kraft's Battle for Global Taste Buds," *The Globe and Mail*, May 1, 2008, B13.

11. "Kellogg to Swallow P&G's Pringles for $2.7- Billion," *The Globe and Mail*, February 16, 2012, B1.

12. Chris Sorensen and Jason Kirby, "Can Rim Recover?" *Canadian Business*, July 11, 2011, P 58-60.

13. Simon Houpt, "More Bad News for RM: Blackberry's Perceived Brand Value Takes a Beating," *The Globe and Mail*, September 16, 2011, B8.

14. Marina Strauss, "Shoppers Sees Gold in Private Labels," *The Globe and Mail*, January 3, 2005, B1–B2.

15. Courtland Bovee, John V. Thill, and George Dracopoulos, *Business in Action*, 2nd ed. (Don Mills, ON: Pearson Education, 2008), 332.

16. Marina Strauss, "(Re)Making a Name in No Name," *The Globe and Mail*, March 21, 2009, B3.

17. *Reader's Digest* website, Most Trusted Brands 2010, www.readersdigest.ca/trustedbrand/html/winners.html [accessed April 25, 2010].

18. Paul Glader, "Avid Boarders Bypass Branded Gear," *The Wall Street Journal*, July 27, 2007, B1–B2.

19. Keith McArthur, "Why Molson Is Crying in Its Beer," *The Globe and Mail*, July 10, 2004, B4.

20. Catherine McLean, "Why Canadian Brands Lose their Accents Abroad," *The Globe and Mail*, January, 12, 2012, B11;

21. Cyndee Miller, "Little Relief Seen for New Product Failure Rate," *Marketing News*, June 21, 1993, 1; Nancy J. Kim, "Back to the Drawing Board," *The Bergen [New Jersey] Record*, December 4, 1994, B1, B4.

22. MSN website, Steve Mertl, "Buick LaCrosse's French Slang Meaning Latest Example of Pitfalls of Car Names," http://autos.ca.msn.com/news/canadian-press-automotive-news/article.aspxcp-documentid=22011666 [accessed April 25, 2010].

23. Canadian Intellectual Property Office website, www.ic.gc.ca/eic/site/cipointernet-internetopic.nsf/eng/h_wr00002.html [accessed February 26, 2012].

24. Marina Strauss, "Canadian Gives Up Rights to Target Banner," *The Globe and Mail*, February, 2, 2012, B5; Chris Sorensen, "Multiple Targets," *Maclean's*, January 16, 2012, P48.

25. Marina Strauss, "Topshop vs. Top Shop," *The Globe and Mail*, October 13, 2011, B5.

26. Canadian Intellectual Patent Office (CIPO) website, www.cipo.ic.gc.ca/eic/site/cipointernet-internetopic.nsf/eng/Home [accessed April 25, 2010]; Canadian Western Diversification Canada website, www.wd.gc.ca/eng/7133.asp [accessed April 25, 2010].

27. Paul Waldie, "How RIM's Big Deal Was Done," *The Globe and Mail*, March 6, 2006, B1, B14.

28. Ashlee Vance, "When Patents Attack: Could Facebook Be Next?" *Newsweek*, September 5–11, 2011, p34.

29. "Google to Pay US$125 Million to Settle Copyright Lawsuits Over Book Project," *National Post*, October 29, 2008, FP6.

30. Deborah Ball, "The Perils of Packaging: Nestle Aims for Easier Openings," *The Wall Street Journal*, November 17, 2005, B1, B5.

31. Stuart Elliott, "Tropicana Discovers Some Buyers Are Passionate about Packaging," *The Wall Street Journal*, February 22, 2009.

32. William Pride and O. C. Ferrell, *Marketing*, 5th ed. (Boston: Houghton Mifflin, 1987).

33. Calvin Leung, "Marketing Ubiquity," *Canadian Business*, February 18, 2008, 28.

34. Kenneth E. Clow and Donald Baack, *Integrated Advertising, Promotion, and Marketing Communications* (Upper Saddle River, NJ: Prentice Hall, 2002), Chapter 5.

35. Canadian Media Directors Council, Media Digest, 2011–2012, Net Advertising Volume by Medium, P13 (Toronto: Marketing, 2012), 12.

36. Canadian Media Directors Council, Media Digest, 2009–2010, Daily Newspapers, P13 (Toronto: Marketing, 2009), 40, www.cmdc.ca/pdf/Media_Digest_2009.pdf.

37. Susan Krashinsky, "Papers Step Up in the Battle for Eyeballs," *The Globe and Mail*, April 29, 2011, B8.

38. Canadian Media Directors Council, Media Digest, 2011–2012, Net Advertising Volume by Medium, P13 (Toronto: Marketing, 2012), 15; Susan Krashinsky, "Reports of TV's Death Greatly Exaggerated," *The Globe and Mail*, April 13, 2010, B1.

39. Canadian Media Directors Council, Media Digest, 2009–2010, Canadian Market Data, P12 (Toronto: Marketing, 2009), 40, www.cmdc.ca/pdf/Media_Digest_2009.pdf.

40. Susan Krashinsky, "Why Most Super Bowl Ads Get Stopped at the Border," *The Globe and Mail*, February 3 2012, B8.

41. Marina Strauss, "Super Bowl Clobbers the Grey Cup," *The Globe and Mail*, January 26, 2008, B3.

42. Ronald Grover, "American Idol's Ads Infinitum," *Businessweek*, May 28, 2008, 38–39.

43. Canadian Media Directors Council, Media Digest, 2011–2012, Net Advertising Volume by Medium, P13 (Toronto: Marketing, 2012), 12.

44. Canadian Media Directors Council, Media Digest, 2011–2012, Net Advertising Volume by Medium, P13 (Toronto: Marketing, 2012), 29.

45. Canadian Media Directors Council, Media Digest, 2011–2012, Net Advertising Volume by Medium, P13 (Toronto: Marketing, 2012), 12.

46. Steve Ladurantaye, "Canadian Magazine Sales Slip in 2nd Half off 2011," *The Globe and Mail*, February 8, 2012, B11.

47. Canadian Media Directors Council, Media Digest, 2011–2012, Net Advertising Volume by Medium, P13 (Toronto: Marketing, 2012), 12.

48. Matt Hartley, "Tunnel Visionaries," *The Globe and Mail*, January 31, 2008, B18.

49. "30 Second Spot: Dispatches from the World of Media and Advertising," *The Globe and Mail*, October 31, 2008, B8.

50. Jason Madgder, "iGotcha Grabs Attention," *Montreal Gazette*, October 3, 2011, A18.

51. Aaron O. Patrick, "Technology Boosts Outdoor Ads as Competition Becomes Fiercer," *The Wall Street Journal*, August 23, 2006, A1, A10; Grant Robertson, "Growth in Internet Ads Outpaces All Others," *The Globe and Mail*, June 23, 2006, B4; Canadian Media Directors Council, Media Digest, 2009–2010, Net Advertising Volume by Medium, P13 (Toronto: Marketing, 2009), 28, www.cmdc.ca/pdf/Media_Digest_2009.pdf.

52. Mike Blaney, "Word of Mouth Advertising," blog, www.themarketingguy.wordpress.com/2007/10/09/word-of-mouth-advertising.

53. Sarah Scott, "Ready for Their Close-Up," *Financial Post Business*, September 2007, 40–45.

54. Simon Houpt, "Tell a Friend: Companies Flock to Word-of-Mouth Marketing," *The Globe and Mail*, April 16, 2010, B6.

55. Canadian Media Directors Council, Media Digest, 2011–2012, Net Advertising Volume by Medium, P13 (Toronto: Marketing, 2012), 12.

56. Simon Houpt, "Super Bowl Marketers Are Changing Their Game," *The Globe and Mail*, February 5, 2010, B5.

57. P. Kotler, G. Armstrong, and P. Cunningham, *Principles of Marketing, 6th Canadian ed.* (Toronto: Pearson, 2005), 89–91.

58. Ronald Ebert and Ricky Griffin, *Business Essentials* (Upper Saddle River, NJ: Prentice Hall, 2009), 161.

59. Stuart Elliott, "Real or Virtual? You Call It," *The New York Times*, October 1, 1999, C1, C6.

60. Canadian Media Directors Council, Media Digest, 2009–2010, Internet and Mobile Media, P74 (Toronto: Marketing, 2009), 40, www.cmdc.ca/pdf/Media_Digest_2009.pdf.

61. Omar El Akkad, "Why Facebook Paid $ 1 Billion for Instagram," *The Globe and Mail*, April 10, 2012, B18.

62. Canadian Media Directors Council, Media Digest, 2009–2010, In-Game Advertising, P76 (Toronto: Marketing, 2009), 40, www.cmdc.ca/pdf/Media_Digest_2009.pdf.

63. William Wells, John Burnett, and Sandra Moriarty, *Advertising: Principles and Practice*, 5th ed. (Upper Saddle River, NJ: Prentice Hall, 2000), 77–83.

64. Simon Houpt, "Real Beauty Duo Dives Into New Venture," *The Globe and Mail*, September 19, 2011, B1 & B4.

65. "Regulators Wary of Ads Rapping Rivals," *The Globe and Mail*, May 23, 1991, B4.

66. Simon Avery, "Do Not Call List Could Give Boost to Direct Mail," *The Globe and Mail*, September 29, 2008, B3.

67. Hollie Shaw, "Do Not Call List a Ringing Success," *National Post*, March 13, 2009, FP12.

68. Oliver Moore, "Clement Blasts Do-Not-Call Scammers," *The Globe and Mail*, January 26, 2009, A4.

69. John Heinzl, "Roll Up the Rim to Lose," *The Globe and Mail*, May 13, 2011, B3.

70. Grant Robertson, "Thanks, But No Thanks," *The Globe and Mail*, August 29, 2008, B5; Rebecca Dana, "When You're Here, You're Family—But What About a Playboy Model?" *The Wall Street Journal*, August 13, 2008, A1, A14.

71. www.prnewswire.com/news-releases/sean-diddy-combs-and-the-makers-of-ciroc-ultra-premium-vodka-launch-ciroc-peach-138901034.html.

72. Julie Jargon and Ilan Brat, "The Clown Stays, McDonald's CEO Says," *The Globe and Mail*, May 20, 2011, B11.

73. Tasmyn Burgmann, "Olympic Organizers on Lookout for Ambush Marketing," thestar.com, http://olympics.thestar.com/2010/article/753866-olympic-organizers-on-lookout-for-ambush-marketing [accessed May 11, 2010].

74. Warren J. Keegan, *Global Marketing Management*, 7th ed. (Upper Saddle River, NJ: Prentice Hall, 2002), Chapter 14.

75. *Reader's Digest* Facebook page, www.facebook.com/pages/Readers-Digest/103420776364574 [accessed February 27th, 2012].

76. Norman M. Scarborough and Thomas W. Zimmerer, *Effective Small Business Management: An Entrepreneurial Approach*, 6th ed. (Upper Saddle River, NJ: Prentice Hall, 2000), Chapter 11.

Chapter 17

1. Constance L. Hays, "Coke Tests Weather-Linked Pricing," *The Globe and Mail*, October 29, 1999, B11.

2. Harvey Schachter, "Dollars and Sense: The Science of Pricing," *The Globe and Mail*, January 18, 2012, B16.

3. Lawrence Solomon, "Revolution on the Road: Pay-Per-Mile Insurance," *National Post*, October 14, 2006, FP15.

4. Stephen Kindel, "Tortoise Gains on Hare," *Financial World*, February 23, 1988, 18–20.

5. Eric Lam, "Wal-Mart Stores Set to Reduce Prices to Win Back Customers From Rivals," *National Post*, March 16, 2010, FP8.

6. Greg Keenan, "Toyota's Discounts Ignite New Car War," *The Globe and Mail*, March 4, 2010, B3.

7. Jon Stoller, "Does Sustainability Boost the Bottom Line?" *The Globe and Mail*, May 24, 2012, B8.

8. Garry Marr, "Company Takes the Haggling—and Pricing Mystery—Out of Buying New Car," *National Post*, November 16, 2011, FP7.

9. Brent Jang, "Ottawa Forces Airlines to Advertise Full Ticket Prices," *The Globe and Mail*, December 17, 2011, B5.

10. For a discussion of the factors involved in setting prices for services, see Elizabeth Wasserman, "How to Price Business Services," *Inc.*, www.inc.com/guides/price-your-services.html.

11. Chester Zelasko, "Acesulfame-K," *Better Life Institute,* May 17, 2001, www.betterlifeunlimited.com/healthnews/health_az/display.aspx?id=69141141052.

12. Stewart A. Washburn, "Establishing Strategy and Determining Cost in the Pricing Decision," *Business Marketing*, July 1985, 64–78.

13. "About Carbonite," www.carbonite.com/about.

14. Judy Strauss and Raymond Frost, *E-Marketing*, 2nd ed. (Upper Saddle River, NJ: Prentice Hall, 2001), 166–167; Eloise Coupey, *Marketing and the Internet* (Upper Saddle River, NJ: Prentice Hall, 2001), 281–283.

15. George Stalk, "How 'Dynamic' Pricing Can Give Your Company an Edge," *The Globe and Mail*, September 7, 2009, B6.

16. "Wal-Mart Rounds Prices to Lure Shoppers," *The Globe and Mail*, April 15, 2009, B12.

17. Marina Strauss, "Taking 'e' Out of E-commerce: Meet the eBay Middleman," *The Globe and Mail*, October 6, 2004, B1, B19.

18. Tim Kiladze, "New Websites Help Muscle Out the Middlemen," *The Globe and Mail*, May 25, 2011, B7.

19. Ahmad Diba, "An Old-Line Agency Finds an Online Niche," *Fortune*, April 3, 2000, 258.

20. Fiscal 2001 In Review, Dell Annual Report, April 22, 2002, www.dell.com/downloads/global/corporate/annual/2001_DELL_Annual.pdf; Qiao Song, "Legend Outlines Role in China's Wireless Future," *ebn*, March 25, 2002, 3; Faith Hung, "Legend Looks to Defend Its Turf—WTO Entry Will Force China's Top PC Maker to Fend Off Unrestricted Rivals," *ebn*, December 17, 2001, 44; Neel Chowdhury, "Dell Cracks China," *Fortune*, June 21, 1999, 120–124.

21. Keith McArthur, "Para Paints' Bold Stroke," *The Globe and Mail*, October 18, 1999, M1.

22. Dale M. Lewison, *Retailing*, 5th ed. (New York: Macmillan, 1994), 454; Louis Stern and Adel I. El-Ansary, *Marketing Channels*, 4th ed. (Englewood Cliffs, NJ: Prentice Hall, 1992), 129–130.

23. Emily Senger, "Who Will Target Canada Next?" *Canadian Business*, February 15-28, 2011, 26; also Stuart Weinberg and Phred Dvorak, "Wal-Mart's New Hot Spot: Canada," *The Wall Street Journal*, January 27, 2011, B3.

24. Hollie Shaw, "Target to Open Pop-Up Store for One Day in Toronto to Introduce Brand," *National Post*, February 18, 2012, FP4.

25. Marina Strauss, "Virtual Shopping Gets Real in Toronto Subway Station," *The Globe and Mail*, April 3, 2012, B6.

26. Bertrand Marotte, "Contraband Killing Convenience Stores," *The Globe and Mail*, April 7, 2010, B9.

27. Direct Selling Association, www.dsa.org.

28. Gordon Pitts, "Tupperware Shows the World How to Party," *The Globe and Mail*, February 9, 2008, B3.

29. Christina Passariello, "To L'Oreal, Brazil's Women Need Fresh Style of Shopping," *The Wall Street Journal*, January 21, 2011, B1.

30. Stephanie Gleason, "Fuller Brush Goes Into Chapter 11," *The Wall Street Journal*, February 23, 2012, B8.

31. Expedia.com, www.expedia.com.

32. Ann Bednarz, "Acquisitions Tighten Supply-Chain Market," *Network World*, February 9, 2004, 21–22.

33. "Did You Know?" *Catalog News.com*, www.catalog-news.com, April 8, 2002; Judy Strauss and Raymond Frost, *E-Marketing* (Upper Saddle River, NJ: Prentice Hall, 2001), 140.

34. Matt Hartley, "Canadians Still Wary of Online Shopping," *National Post*, March 19, 2012, FP1.

35. Zena Olijnyk, "Dot-Com Wonder Boys," *Canadian Business*, April 14, 2003, 30–36.

36. Natalie Stechyson, "Online Shopping On The Rise," *National Post*, December 28, 2011, FP4;

37. Alistair Barr, "Shopping on the Run; Retailers Adapt as More Consumers Shop With Smartphones in Hand," *National Post*, November 21, 2011, FP3.

38. Peter Elkind, "Shhhhh! Amway's on the Web," *Fortune*, March 6, 2000, 76.

39. "LivePerson.com™," www.liveperson.com, April 19, 2000.

40. Bertrand Marotte, "Reeling in Fresh Customers," *The Globe and Mail*, April 20, 2010, B3.

41. David Milstead, "Coke Gets Back into the Bottling Business," *The Globe and Mail*, February 26, 2010, B10.

42. Walmart to Assume Product Shipping," *National Post*, May 2, 2010, FP4.

43. Kerry Capell, "Zara Thrives by Breaking All the Rules," *Bloomberg Businessweek*, April 26, 2010.

44. Claudia Cattaneo, "Oil Producers Jump on Oil Train," *National Post*, March 20, 2012, FP5.

45. Nathan Vanderklippe, "Arctic Seen As Possible Shipping Route for Massive Industrial Components," *The Globe and Mail*, November 15, 2010, B5.

46. Nicolas Van Praet, "Ship Glut to Sink Carriers' Revenue," *National Post*, July 29, 2011, FP1.

47. Nathan VanderKlippe, "Aging Pipes," *The Globe and Mail*, February 19, 2011, B6.

48. Sheldon Alberts, "Aftermath of a Spill; Enbridge Cleanup Grades Well, but Pipeline Fears Remain," *National Post*, July 23, 2011, FP3.

49. Anne T. Coughlan et al., *Marketing Channels*, 6th ed. (Upper Saddle River, NJ: Prentice Hall, 2001), 458–462.

50. Ronald J. Ebert and Ricky W. Griffin, *Business Essentials*, 9th edition. Boston, Mass.: Pearson, 2013, p. 314.

Chapter 18

1. Steve Mertl, "Durability of Canada's Plastic Money Being Questioned," http://ca.news.yahoo.com/blogs/dailybrew/durability-canada-plastic-currency-questioned-201813438.html [accessed May 22, 2012].

2. RCMP website, www.rcmp-grc.gc.ca/count-contre/cur-mon-2011-eng.htm [accessed May 12, 2012].

3. CBC News website, "Is Canada's New $20 Bill too 'Pornographic'?" [accessed May 12, 2012].

4. *Bank of Canada Banking and Financial Statistics*, Series E1, Selected Monetary Aggregates, April 2009, S50.

5. Martin Hutchinson and Christopher Swann, "Dollars Flowing Fast, But Inflation Stands Pat," *The Globe and Mail*, March 19, 2012, B9.

6. Canadian Bankers Association, Credit Card Statistics, www.cba.ca/contents/files/statistics/stat_cc_db038_en.pdf [accessed May 12, 2012].

7. Boyd Erman, "Visa's IPO Taps into the World's Love of Plastic," *The Globe and Mail*, February 26, 2008, B1, B6.

8. Canadian Bankers Association, Credit Card Statistics, www.cba.ca/contents/files/statistics/stat_cc_db038_en.pdf [accessed May 12, 2012].

9. Chris Sorensen, "Credit Card Tricks," *Maclean's*, July 11, 2011, P63.

10. Grant Robertson and Tim Kaladze, "Banks Warn Volcker Rule Could Violate NAFTA," *The Globe and Mail*, January 20, 2012, A1, B4.

11. Marina Strauss, "Need a Mortgage with Those Tools?" *The Globe and Mail*, February 6, 2010, A1, A9.

12. Tara Perkins, "They'll Even Plan Your Funeral," *The Globe and Mail*, September 29, 2007, B4–B6.

13. Tara Perkins, "A Piece of Drywall Away from Being Part of the Branch," *The Globe and Mail*, April 26, 2008, B6.

14. Business News Network website, "Ottawa Bans Insurance Sales on Bank Websites," May 27, 2010, www.bnn.ca/news/17916.?html [accessed July 10, 2010].

15. Karen Horcher, "Reconstruction Zone," *CGA Magazine*, June 1997, 19.

16. Barrie McKenna, "Envoy's Loonie Remarks Spark Krona Controversy," *The Globe and Mail*, March 3, 2012, B5.

17. *Bank of Canada Banking and Financial Statistics*, Series C1, Chartered Bank Assets, January 2012, S18.

18. Derek DeCloet, "As Canadian as.. Banking?" *Canadian Business*, December 2011, p20.

19. Grant Robertson, "CIBC Joins Big Banks Profit Parade," *The Globe and Mail*, March 9, 2012, B5.

20. Tara Perkins and Grant Robertson, "The Bank Machine with a Personal Touch," *The Globe and Mail*, June 3, 2010, B5.

21. Canadian Bankers Association, Debit Card Statistics, www.cba.ca/en/media-room/50-backgrounders-on-banking-issues/616-canadas-efficient-and-secure-payments-system [accessed May 15, 2012].

22. "Statistics for Smart Cards," *ePaynews.com*, June 14, 2004, www.epaynews.com/statistics/scardstats.html.

23. Grant Robertson and Rita Trichur, "Banks Plot Mobile Payment Future," *The Globe and Mail*, May 14, 2012, B1.

24. Rita Trichur and Grant Robertson, "CIBC, Rogers Launch Digital Wallet," *The Globe and Mail*, May 16, 2012, B7.

25. Grant Robertson, "Photo Chequing is on the Way," *The Globe and Mail*, March 27, 2012, B5.

26. Tavia Grant, "Yunus Sees Big Answers in Microcredit," *The Globe and Mail*, June 11, 2008, B8.

27. Special Feature on Cooperatives, "A Force in the Canadian Banking System," *The Globe and Mail*, May 15, 2012, CO 2.

28. "Credit Unions Continue to Lead in Customer Service," September 2, 2008, www.cucentral.ca/Synovate_2sept08.

29. Canadian Health Insurance association website, www.clhia.ca/domino/html/clhia/clhia_lp4w_lnd_webstation.nsf/page/F85B-39D8B2B428B185257824006528A4 [accessed May 23,2012].

30. "Google VC Fund Looking for 'Young Companies with Awesome Potential,'" *National Post*, April 1, 2009, FP2.

31. Canada's Venture Capital and Private Equity Association website, www.cvca.ca/files/Resources/2011_VC_Data_Deck.pdf [accessed May 24, 2012].

32. David George-Cosh, "Lean Times for Tech Startups: VC's Offer Ideas on How to Kickstart the Industry," *National Post*, January 16, 2009, FP4; Stephen Hurwitz, "Misadventure Capitalism: A Byzantine Cross-Border Investment Regime Is Killing the Canadian Venture-Capital and Technology Industries," *National Post*, May 1, 2009, FP11.

33. Brent Jang, "Air Canada Aces $1.6 Billion Bill for Pension Contributions by 2014," *The Globe and Mail*, May 31, 2011, B4.

34. Jeremy Torobin, "Dollar at Par: The New Normal," *The Globe and Mail*, March 18, 2010, pp. B1, B6; Bank of Canada website [accessed 27 March 2010], www.bankofcanada.ca/cgi-bin/famecgi_fdps.

35. LuAnn LaSalle, "Clearwater Eyes Productivity to Offset High Loonie," *The Globe and Mail*, March 24, 2010, B1.

36. Gordon Pitts, "How Captain High Liner Beat the Dollar Odds," *The Globe and Mail*, March 16, 2010, pp. B1–B4.

37. The Economist website, Big Mac Index, May 23, 2012, www.economist.com/blogs/graphicdetail/2012/01/daily-chart-3 [accessed May 26, 2012].

38. Robert J. Carbaugh, *International Economics*, 5th ed. (Cincinnati, OH: South-Western, 1995), Chapter 11.

39. "The IMF, Deficits, and Tighter Regulation," *The Globe and Mail*, October 22, 2008, B6.

40. International Monetary Fund website, www.imf.org/external/np/tre/activity/2012/010512.htm#tab1 [accessed May 23, 2012]. 43.

Chapter 19

1. John Heinzl, "Rogers: Nice Dividend Risky Stock Price," *The Globe and Mail*, May 2, 2012, B15.

2. Jeffrey Macintosh, "Unfair Trade: Alternative Trading Systems Make Stock Trading Cheaper and More Efficient, but There's a Downside," *National Post*, January 13, 2009, FP13.

3. Virtual Brokers website, www.virtualbrokers.com/contents.aspxpage_id=2 [accessed June 1, 2012].

4. Rob Carrick, "With Online Trading, It Pays to Shop Around," *The Globe and Mail*, June 2, 2008, B14.

5. Rob Carrick, "Qtrade Keeps its Lock on No. 1 in Globe's Annual survey," *The Globe and Mail*, November 14, 2011, E2.

6. Ben Levinsohn, "Beating a Path to Toronto's Exchanges," *Businessweek*, May 19, 2008, 52.

7. NYSE website, www.nyse.com/about/listed/lcddata.htmlticker=EL [accessed May 29, 2010].

8. David Berman, "After China Breaks," May 17, 2010, *The Globe and Mail* blog, www.theglobeandmail.com/globe-investor/markets/markets-blog/after-china-brakes/article1571458.

9. NASDAQ website, June 25, 2000, www.nasdaq.com/about/timeline.stm.

10. NASDAQ website, www.nasdaq.com [accessed June 1, 2012].

11. Simon Avery, "Why Apple Owns the Nasdaq," *The Globe and Mail*, March 1, 2012, B1.

12. Aaron Lucchetti, "As Housing Boomed, Moody's Opened Up," *The Wall Street Journal*, April 11, 2008, A1, A15.

13. Boyd Erman, "DBRS to Roll Out a New Road MAP on Risk," *The Globe and Mail*, February 8, 2008, B1, B6.

14. "Advantages and Disadvantages of Mutual Funds," *The Motley Fool*, www.fool.com.

15. "Why Exchange-Traded Funds?" Yahoo! Finance, Exchange-Traded Funds Center, http://finance.yahoo.com/etf/education/02 [accessed June 1 2012].

16. Rob Carrick, "Tread Carefully in the World of Hedge Funds," *The Globe and Mail*, May 27, 2006, B8.

17. Janet McFarland, "OSC Rules Norshield Hedge Fund Misled Investors," *The Globe and Mail*, March 9, 2010, B6.

18. Paul Waldie and Sinclair Stewart, "Hedge Funds in the Crosshairs," *The Globe and Mail*, May 30, 2005, B4; Sinclair Stewart and Paul Waldie, "The New Breed of 800-Pound Gorilla," *The Globe and Mail*, May 31, 2005, B7.

19. Boyd Erman and Derek DeCloet, "The Guys Who Had a Gut Feeling for Risk," *The Globe and Mail*, February 23, 2008, B4–B5.

20. Richard Blackwell, "TSE 300 Shift Will Shrink Index," *The Globe and Mail*, January 31, 2002, B17.

21. Richard Mackie, "Ontario Pursues Single Regulator," *The Globe and Mail*, December 22, 2003, B1, B4.

22. Janet McFarland, "Act's Police Powers Applauded," *The Globe and Mail*, May 28, 2010, B3.

23. John Doyle, "The Rich Get Robbed—And It's Delicious TV," *The Globe and Mail*, May 12, 2009, R3.

24. Gordon J. Alexander, William F. Sharpe, and Jeffery V. Bailey, *Fundamentals of Investments*, 3rd ed. (Upper Saddle River, NJ: Prentice Hall, 2001), 37–38.

Chapter 20

1. Stefan Stern," The Rise of the Bean Counters," *National Post*, August 23, 2006, WK5.

2. Derek Sankey, "CFO Positions Demand Ever-Expanding Skill Set; Decision Makers," *National Post*, April 11, 2012, FP10.

3. Brent Jang, "CP Unveils Strategic Spending Plan," *The Globe and Mail*, January 18, 2012, B9.

4. Hollie Shaw, "Walmart Canada to Invest $750 Million in Building Projects in 2012," *National Post*, February 8, 2012, FP4.

5. Denise Deveau, "No Garden Variety Insurance," *Financial Post*, October 20, 2008, www.nationalpost.com/story-printer.html?id=892400.

6. "RBC Tightens its Grip on Corporate Bond Sales," *Financial Post*, www.business.financialpost.com/2011/11/14/rbc.

7. Steve Ladurantaye, "Yellow Media Battles Debt Crunch," *The Globe and Mail*, February 10, 2012, B1.

8. Ashley Heher, "Hertz Agrees to Buy Rival Dollar Thrifty," *The Globe and Mail*, April 27, 2010, B8.

9. Industry Canada website, www.ic.gc.ca [accessed May 31, 2010].

10. Norman M. Scarborough and Thomas W. Zimmerer, *Effective Small Business Management: An Entrepreneurial Approach*, 6th ed. (Upper Saddle River, NJ: Prentice Hall, 2000), esp. 298–300.

11. Virginia Galt, "Hope for the Best, Prep for the Worst," *The Globe and Mail*, February 16, 2011, B19.

12. Harris Anwar, "Chief Risk Officer: A Valuable Addition to the C-Suite," *The Globe and Mail*, June 20, 2005, B13.

13. Gordon Pitts and Bertrand Marotte, "Has Sabia Jumped from the Frying Pan into the Fire?" *The Globe and Mail*, March 14, 2009, www.globeinvestor.com/ servlet/story/GAM.20090314.RSABIA14/GIStory.

14. Tara Perkins, "BMO Retreats to Its Low-Risk Roots," *The Globe and Mail*, March 5, 2008, B5.

15. Joe Castaldo, "Bay Street Hurt by Talent Deficit," *Canadian Business*, December 9, 2009, 15.

16. Thomas Fitch, *Dictionary of Banking Terms*, 2nd ed. (Hauppauge, NY: Barron's, 1993), 531.

17. Mark S. Dorfman, *Introduction to Risk Management and Insurance*, 6th ed. (Upper Saddle River, NJ: Prentice Hall, 2000), Chapter 1.

18. Denyse O'Leary, "The Scams That Drive Up Premiums," *The Globe and Mail*, May 2, 1995, B1; Denyse O'Leary, "Insurers United Against Fraud Face Serious Obstacles," *The Globe and Mail*, May 2, 1995, B1.

19. Sinclair Stewart, "Sun Life's Insurance Policy: The Great Indian Middle Class," *The Globe and Mail*, October 1, 2005, B1, B6.

20. Barbara Shecter, "Sun Life Limits Life Policies, Anuities; Poor Returns," *National Post*, December 13, 2011, FP1.

21. Yochi Dreazen, "As Iraq Terror Rises, Businessmen Find Niche in Life Insurance," *The Wall Street Journal*, August 19, 2005, A1, A16.

22. Mark S. Dorfman, *Introduction to Risk Management and Insurance*, 6th ed. (Upper Saddle River, NJ: Prentice Hall, 2000), 420–421.

Sources

Chapter 1

The Mobile Phone Market: It's the Wild West Iain Marlow, "Samsung Claims Top Spot in Smartphone Shipments," *The Globe and Mail*, April 28, 2012, B9; LuAnn LaSalle, "Blackberry Maker Dialing Down?" *Winnipeg Free Press*, March 31, 2012, B4; Hui Neo, "Asian Mobile Giants Race to Catch Apple, Samsung; Rapid Smartphones," *National Post*, February 27, 2012, FP3; Christopher Lawton, "Nokia Takes Aim at High-End U.S. Market," *Wall Street Journal*, January 10, 2012, B5; Iain Marlow, "Trade Group Takes RIM to Court over BBM Name," *The Globe and Mail*, December 23, 2011, B3; Iain Marlow, "RIM's Outlook Darkens with Delay of New Phone," *The Globe and Mail*, December 16, 2011, B1; Iain Marlow, RIM Shares Hit Seven-Year Low," *The Globe and Mail*, November 2, 2011, B3; Jameson Berkow, "Can Svelte Razr Recapture Sales for Motorola?; Aimed at Apple; Phonemaker Resurrects its Most Popular Brand," *National Post*, October 219, 2011, FP3; Carly Weeks, "The Dangers of a Smartphone Free-for-All," *The Globe and Mail*, September 1, 2011, B6; Iain Marlow, "Nokia Relinquishes Top Spot to Apple," *The Globe and Mail*, July 22, 2011, B8; Henry Blodget, "RIM is Dead," *Canadian Business*, June 13, 2011, 30; Christopher Lawton and Amir Efrati, "Nokia's Latest Headache: Android," *The Wall Street Journal*, June 2, 2011, p. B1; Eric Reguly, "New Crop of Rivals Hits Nokia Where It Hurts," *The Globe and Mail*, June 1, 2011, B1; Christine Dobby, "RIM Market Share Plummets as Users Opt for Android Over Blackberry," *National Post*, May 7, 2011, FP9; LuAnn LaSalle, "Consumers May Pass RIM Phones By, Analysts Say," *Winnipeg Free Press*, April 30, 2011, B10; Jacquie McNish, "Not a Great Week for RIM's Lazaridis," *The Globe and Mail*, April 14, 2011, B8; David Berman, "RIM Can't Seem to Buy a Break," *The Globe and Mail*, March 26, 2011, B7; "Android Dethrones Blackberry as Top U.S. Smartphone Platform," *National Post*, March 8, 2011, FP6; Matt Hartley, "After Huge Profits, Jobs Trashes RIM; CEO's Rant Overshadows Technology Giant's Record Revenue and Earnings," *National Post*, October 19, 2010, FP1; LuAnn LaSalle, "BlackBerrys Out of Touch with Consumers:

Analysts," *Winnipeg Free Press*, June 26, 2010, p. B8; "RIM Thumbs Its Way into the Top Five Mobile Handset Makers in First Quarter," *National Post*, May 1, 2010, p. FP5; "Research in Motion History," http://en.wikipedia.org/wiki/Research_In_Motion [accessed Jan. 23, 2010]; "Timeline: The History of Research in Motion," http://forums.crackberry.com/f2/timeline-history-research-motion-7162 [accessed January 23, 2010]; Grant Robertson, "Smart-Phone Application Scores Big," *The Globe and Mail*, January 15, 2010, p. B4; "Android Mobile Phone a Challenge to Apple, RIM," *National Post*, December 15, 2009, p. FP5; Bob Willis, "Patent Lawsuit Against RIM Could See BlackBerry Ban in U.S. Market," *National Post*, December 4, 2009, p. FP4; "Klausner Technologies Sues Motorola, RIM Over Visual Voicemail Patents," *National Post*, November 24, 2009, p. FP5; "Nokia Plays Defence With Launch of New Gadget," *The Globe and Mail*, August 25, 2009, p. B3.

Table 1.1 *Financial Post Magazine*, June 2012, p. 80.

Table 1.2 *The Competition Act*, Part VI, Offences in Relation to Competition, www.laws.justice.gc.ca/en/showdoc/cs/C-34/bo-ga:1_VI//en.

E-Business + Social Media Solutions Douglas McMillan and Brad Stone, "Zynga's Little Known Addiction: Whales," *Bloomberg Businessweek*, July 11–17, 2011; Douglas McMillan and Brad Stone, "That Listless Feeling Down on the Virtual Farm," *Bloomberg Businessweek*, Nov. 28–Dec. 4, 2011; Ari Levy and Joseph Galante, "Who Wants to Buy a Digital Elephant," *Bloomberg Businessweek*, March 8, 2010, 64–65; Ari Levy, Brian Womack, and Joseph Galante, "A Cash Crop for Facebook," *Bloomberg Businessweek*, March 8, 2010, 65; Douglas McMillan "Zynga and Facebook: It's Complicated," *Bloomberg Businessweek*, April 26–May 2, 2010, 50–51; BBC News website, "Sales of Virtual Goods Boom in the US" [accessed October 22, 2009]; CBC News website, "Bottled Water: Quenching a Planet's Thirst" [accessed August 20, 2009].

Managing in Turbulent Times Shirley Won, "Why Demand for Palladium is Looking White Hot," *The Globe and Mail*, March 7, 2011, p. B9; Carolyn Cui, "Chinese Cotton To Hoarding," *The Wall Street Journal*, January 29–30, 2011, p. B1; Peter Koven, "Rare-Earth Share Bonanza; Increased Sharp as U.S. Seeks Secure Supply," *National Post*, October 19, 2010, p. FP4; Paul Waldie, "A Bigger Piece of the Pie: China's Appetite Drives Up Pecan Prices," *The Globe and Mail*, October 19, 2010, p. B1.

Concluding Case 1-1 Neil Reynolds, "Methane Hydrate Technology Fuels a New Energy Regime," *The Globe and Mail*, May 16, 2012, B2; Gary Hunt, "The New Energy Order; Unconventional U.S. Oil and Gas Change Everything," *National Post*, February 17, 2012, FP13; Claudia Cattaneo, "All Eyes on Tight Oil's Future," *National Post*, February 16, 2012, FP5; Margot Habiby, "North American Oil Output Growth to Soar, IEA says; Behind Only OPEC," *National Post*, June 17, 2011, FP6; "ExxonMobil Makes Big Find of Oil Reserves in Gulf of Mexico," *National Post*, June 9, 2011, FP6; Brian Lee Crowley, "The Running Out of Resources Myth," *National Post*, May 27, 2011, FP11; Matt Ridley, "The Shale Revolution; Huge Supplies of Cheap Gas Shatter Peak Energy

Fears," *National Post*, May 6, 2011, p. FP11; Neil Reynolds, "The Fossil Fuel King of the World," *The Globe and Mail*, April 6, 2011, B2; Eric Reguly, "Nuclear's Loss Is Not a Worry," *The Globe and Mail*, March 17, 2011, B2; Claudia Cattaneo, "Peak Oil Demand Theory in Vogue," *National Post*, January 26, 2009, FP1; John Lyons and David Luhnow, "Brazil May Be The Globe's Next Big Spigot," *The Globe and Mail*, May 23, 2008, B8; "New Method To Extract Gas Hydrates," *Winnipeg Free Press*, April 17, 2008, A6; Neil King, "A Rosy View Of Oil Supply," *The Globe and Mail*, January 17, 2008, B7; Russell Gold and Ann Davis, "Oil Officials See Limit Looming on Production," *The Wall Street Journal*, November 19, 2007, A1; Shawn McCarthy, "Canada's Oil Boom Has Legs, IEA Says," *The Globe and Mail*, July 10, 2007, B1; Neil Reynolds, "Peak Oil Doomsayers Fall Silent As Reserves Grow Ever Larger," *The Globe and Mail*, April 11, 2007, B2; Robert Hirsch, "Peaking of World Oil Production: Recent Forecasts," *WorldOil*, April, 2007, Vol. 228; Patrick Brethour, "Peak Oil Theorists Don't Know Jack," *The Globe and Mail*, September 6, 2006, B1; Michael Lynch, "Oil Discovery Forecasts Doomed," *The Globe and Mail*, May 28, 2005, B6; Haris Anwar, "Supply: Are Saudi Reserves Drying Up?" *The Globe and Mail*, May 21, 2005, B19.

Concluding Case 1-2 Peter Foster, "Auto Bailouts in One Lesson," *National Post*, June 1, 2011, FP13; Greg Keenan, "Auto Bailouts Won't Be Repaid in Full, Flaherty Says," *The Globe and Mail*, May 31, 2011, B1; Derek DeCloet, "Why GM Survives but Nortel Doesn't," *The Globe and Mail*, June 23, 2009, p. B2; Tom Krisher, "Chrysler Factories Reopening," *Winnipeg Free Press*, June 18, 2009, p. B6; "Is Troubled Air Canada Next on Feds' Bailout List?" *Winnipeg Free Press*, June 17, 2009, p. B7; "Ottawa Gives Pulp Mills $1B Lifeline," *Business News Network*, www.bnn.ca/news/10177.html; "No Easy Road for Chrysler," *National Post*, June 11, 2009, p. FP1; Gwyn Morgan, "Apocalyptic Rhetoric Aside, GM Bailout is a Bad Idea," *The Globe and Mail*, June 8, 2009, p. B2; Terence Corcoran, "Still the Same Old Auto Game," *National Post*, June 4, 2009, p. FP13; Kristine Owram, "Bailout Keeps GM Alive," *Winnipeg Free Press*, June 2, p. B3; Philip Marchand, "Payback on Auto Bailouts Dubious; Little Debate," *National Post*, May 30, 2009, p. FP1; Shawn McCarthy and Greg Keenan, "Canada Set to Take Large Stake in GM," *The Globe and Mail*, May 29, 2009, p. B1; Konrad Yakabuski, "$1.4 Million for Every Job Saved," *The Globe and Mail*, May 29, 2009, p. A1; Shawn McCarthy and Karen Howlett, "GM-UAW Deal Puts Pressure on Canadian Counterparts," *The Globe and Mail*, May 22, 2009, p. B1; Roger More, "How GM Lost Its Way: Too Much Cost, Too Many Cars—Too Bad for the Big Three Automaker," *National Post*, May19, 2009, p. FP11; David Brooks, "Money for Fools," *National Post*, February 23, 2009, p. A12; Nicolas VanPraet, "Tories Reject Auto Bailouts; Liberals Critical," *National Post*, March 1, 2008, p. FP7.

Chapter 2

Video Content providers Must Evolve or Perish: Netflix and Beyond Jennifer Roberts, "Netflix Comes Roaring Back After Price-Hike Miscue," *The Globe and Mail*, January 26,

2012, B7; Susan Krashinsky, "Astral Taking HBO Over the Top to Fend Off Neflix Threat," *The Globe and Mail*, Dec. 14, 2011, B3; Marina Strauss and Iain Marlow, "Final Run For Blockbuster in Canada After Deals Rejected," *The Globe and Mail*, September 1, 2011, B1; Sara Tibken, "Netflix Cancels Plan to Split DVD, Streaming Sites," *The Globe and Mail*, October 11, 2011, B7; Susan Krashinsky, "A New Canadian Player on Hollywood TV Buying Spree," *The Globe and Mail*, May 30, 2011, B12; Susan Krashinsky, "Netflix's Higher Prices Leave it With Fewer Customers," *The Globe and Mail*, September 16, 2011, B3; Ronald Grover and Cliff Edwards, "Can Netflix Find Its Future by Abandoning the Past?" *Businessweek*, October 2, 2011, P32; David Milsted, "A Star is Reborn—As a value Stock," *The Globe and Mail*, November 3, 2011, B13; Susan Krashinsky, "Netflix Gets a Pass On Being Regulated—For Now," *The Globe and Mail*, October 6, 2011, B5; Susan Krashinsky, "Netflix Offers a Mea Culpa—and a Defense," *The Globe and Mail*, September 20, 2011, B4; Steve Laverdure, "For Blockbuster in Canada, The Closing Credits Roll," *The Globe and Mail*, May 6, 2011, B1

Figure 2.3 www.canadianeconomy.gc.ca/English/ economy/inflation.cfm.

Figure 2.4 *Bank of Canada Banking and Financial Statistics*, Series H5, April 2009, S101.

Managing in Turbulent Times Barrie McKenna, "Missing in Action: A Canadian R&D Ecosystem," *The Globe and Mail*, November 14, 2011, B1; Peter Foster, "Dim-Bulb R&D Policy," *National Post*, October 19, 2011, FP15; John Manley, "Centralize Ottawa's $5 B in R&D Funding," *National Post*, October 18, 2011, FP11; Barrie McKenna, "R&D Tax Scheme too Rich, Government Panel Finds," *The Globe and Mail*, October 18, 2011, B1; Barrie McKenna, "A Golden Opportunity to Fix Our Broken R&D Model," *The Globe and Mail*, October 17, 2011, B1.

Figure 2.5 Industrial Research and Development: *Intentions 2008*, Catalogue No. 88-202-XWE, Table 2, International Comparison of Business Enterprise Expenditures on Research and Development as a Percentage of Gross Domestic Product, by Selected OECD Countries (Ottawa: Minister of Industry, December 2010), http://publications.gc.ca/collections/collection_2011/statcan/88-202-X/88-202-x2010000-eng.pdf

Entrepreneurship and New Ventures "Nothing Shady about This Glen, Court Rules," *The Globe and Mail*, January 24, 2009, B7; "Cape Breton Distillery Toasts Scotch Shortage," CBC.ca, November 6, 2008, www.cbc.ca/canada/nova-scotia/story/2008/11/06/glenora-scotch.html; "Cape Breton Distiller Fighting to Defend Product's Name," CanWest News, April 7, 2008; "Scotch Whisky Association Filing Appeal in Dispute with N.S. Distiller," Canada NewsWire, March 9, 2007; Keith McArthur, "Could Name Dispute put N.S. Whisky on the Rocks?" *The Globe and Mail*, December 16, 2006, B7; Brian Flinn, "Battle of the Glen Shapes up over Nova Scotia Distiller," CanWest News, July 9, 2004, 1; Rod Currie, "Distillery Produces Single Malt Whisky in Cape Breton Highlands," Canada NewsWire, April 29, 2002; Corinne McLean, "Turning Liquid Silver into Gold: Glenora Captures the Spirit of Scotland," Plant 59 no. 15 (2000): 12; Allan Lynch, "Scotch on the Rocks," Profit 10 no. 8 (1991): 38, www.glenoradistillery.com/glen.html.

E-Business + Social Media Solutions Grant Robertson, "Corus Looks to iTunes to Boost Web Traffic," *The Globe and Mail*, May 12, 2009, B12; Susan Krashinsky, "New Bidders Make Play for Radio Stations," *The Globe and Mail*, June 9, 2010, B4; Corus Entertainment website, www.corusent.com/home/Radio/tabid/1663/Default.aspx [accessed June 11, 2010]; Corus Entertainment Annual Report 2011, www.corusent.com/home/CorusentFiles/files/Corporate%20-%20Annual%20Reports/CorusAR2011_LRS.pdf [accessed December 30, 2011].

Concluding Case 2-1 Air Canada's Challenging Environment: Competition, Economic Crisis, Fuel Prices, Volcanoes, and More; SkyTrax World Airline Awards, 2011 Results, www.worldairlineawards.com/Awards_2011/namerica.htm [accessed Dec 29, 2011]; Brent Jang, "Clouds Darken For Airlines," *The Globe and Mail*, October 6, 2011, B1; Brent Jang, "Air Canada Pushes for Greater Transatlantic Traffic," *The Globe and Mail*, December 18, 2009, B1; Slobodan Lekic, "Volcanic Ash Forces More Delays, Rerouting of Transatlantic Flights," *The Globe and Mail*, May 9, 2010, B1; Robin Millard, "Volcanic Ash Cancels, Delays More Flights," *National Post*, May 9, 2010; Brent Jang, "Air Canada's Problems Pile Up," *The Globe and Mail*, February 19, 2009, B1; CBC News website, "Volcanic Ash Costs Air Canada $20M over 5 Days," www.cbc.ca/world/story/2010/04/19/ash-cloud-airlines-cost.html, April 19, 2010; Air Canada Annual Report 2009, www.aircanada.com/en/about/investor/documents/2009_ar.pdf [accessed June 12, 2010].

Concluding Case 2-2 Inflation, Deflation, and the Validity of the CPI Allan Robinson, Bank of Canada, "CPI Statistics," www.bankofcanada.ca/rates/price-indexes/cpi [accessed 29 December 2011]; "Deflation Risk Helps Curb Interest Rates," *The Globe and Mail*, April 13, 2010, B1; Phil Green, "Hiding Inflation," *National Post*, April 29, 2010, FP11; Louise Egan, "Consumer Prices Decline," *Montreal Gazette*, September 18, 2009, B1; "Deflation Threat Persists Despite Signs of Revival," *National Post*, April 16, 2009, FP4; Allan Robinson, "Negative Inflation Rate Expected," *The Globe and Mail*, January 16, 2009, B10; Alia McMullen, "Japan Drawn Back into Vortex of Deflation," *National Post*, December 20, 2008, FP2; Eric Beauchesne, "Rising Food Prices Pack Punch," *Winnipeg Free Press*, July 24, 2008, B5; David Parkinson, "China Positioned to Unleash Global Deflation," *The Globe and Mail*, November 13, 2008, B12; George Athanassakos, "Confusion Reigns with Deflation-Inflation Conundrum," *The Globe and Mail*, November 6, 2008, B11; Heather Scoffield, "Now Canada Faces the Demons," *The Globe and Mail*, July 16, 2008, B5; Heather Scoffield, "Shock Move Sounds Inflation Alarm," *The Globe and Mail*, June 11, 2008, B1, B4; Andrew Batson, "Inflation, Spanning Globe, Is Set to Reach Decade High," *The Wall Street Journal*, April 10, 2008, A1, A12.

Chapter 3

Ethical Lapses Paul Sonne and Cassell Bryan-Low, "News Corp. Settles Phone-Hacking Cases," *The Wall Street Journal*, January 20, 2012, B4; Kit Cheliel, "Lawsuits Against News

Corp. Escalate," *National Post*, October 5, 2011, FP12; "Livent Founders Get Reduced Sentences as Court Upholds Fraud Convictions," *Winnipeg Free Press*, September 14, 2011, D2; Terence Corcoran, "Unfounded Attack on Murdoch," *National Post*, July 23, 2011, p. FP19; Mark Hosenball, "Coulson Tied to Payouts, Insider Says; Emails Suggest Ex-Editor Knew of Police Bribes," *National Post*, July 22, 2011, p. A10; James Kirkup, "'Lost Sight' of Paper: Murdoch; 'Clearly' Lied to," *National Post*, July 20, 2011, P. A10; Keith Weir, "Murdoch Apologizes, Top Aides Quit; 'Deeply Sad Day'; Rebekah Brooks, Dow Jones CEO Both Resign," *National Post*, July 16, 2011, p. A18; Steve Ladurantaye, "A Kingmaker in Damage Control Mode," *The Globe and Mail*, July 16, 2011, p. A3; Elizabeth Renzetti, "Who Will Mourn News of the World? The Taxi Drivers, Hairdressers and Café Owners," *The Globe and Mail*, July 9, 2011, p. F3; Eric Reguly, "Hacking Scandal Kills U.K. Tabloid," *The Globe and Mail*, July 8, 2011, p. A1; Susan Krashinsky, "Bad News for News of the World," *The Globe and Mail*, July 7, 2011, p. A11; Kate Holton and Jodie Ginsberg, "Murdoch Will Co-operate with Hacking Inquiry; Faces Boycotts," *National Post*, July 7, 2011, p. A13; "Cinar Corp. Reaches Agreement with Company founder to Settle Lawsuit," www.canada.com/story_print.html?id=8e57cda7-91f-48f2-aade-7574efc41d0b&sp [accessed May 18, 2011]; "Cookie Jar Group," www.en.wikipedia.org/wiki/Cookie_Jar_Group [accessed May 18, 2011]; "Ex-Cinar CEO Hasanain Panju Arrested," www.hollywoodreporter.com/news/cinar-ceo-hasanain-panju-arrested-163383 [accessed May 18, 2011]; Rheal Seguin, "Suspected Player in Alleged Cinar Fraud Arrested," *The Globe and Mail*, March 16, 2011, p. B9; Jacquie McNish, "Convictions Seen as Much-Needed Regulatory Win," *The Globe and Mail*, March 26, 2009, p. B4; Janet McFarland, "ICAO Appeal Panel Upholds Deloitte Decision," *The Globe and Mail*, February 19, 2009, p. B9; Janet McFarland, "Ex-Livent Official Tells of 'Absurd' Plan," *The Globe and Mail*, September 3, 2008, p. B5; Janet McFarland, "Livent Staff Dodged Drabinsky's Controls, Lawyer Says," *The Globe and Mail*, July 18, 2008, p. B2; Janet McFarland, "Ad Firms Helped Livent, Ex-Official Says," *The Globe and Mail*, July 16, 2008, p. B7; Janet McFarland, "All His Time Spent on Fraud: Ex-Livent Official," *The Globe and Mail*, July 15, 2008, p. B4; Allan Swift, "Cinar Chairman's Motives Questioned," *Winnipeg Free Press*, August 22, 2003, p. B6; also Bertrand Marotte, "New Cinar Head Planning an Encore for Company," *The Globe and Mail*, April 10, 2003, p. B4; also Bertrand Marotte, "Cinar Founders' Trustee Stages Coup," *The Globe and Mail*, April 30, 2002, pp. B1, B10; also Bertrand Marotte, "Cinar Settlement $2 Million," *The Globe and Mail*, March 16, 2002, pp. B1–B2; also Susanne Craig, John Partridge, and Bertrand Marotte, "Cinar Co-Founder Okayed Investment," *The Globe and Mail*, March 22, 2000, pp. B1, B4; also Susanne Craig, "Cinar Co-Founder Pushed Out," *The Globe and Mail*, March 15, 2000, pp. B1, B9; also Susanne Craig and Bertrand Marotte, "Cinar to Take Hit Following Probe," *The Globe and Mail*, February 21, 2000, pp. B1, B3.

E-Business + Social Media Solutions Ivor Tossell, "Legislation Threatens to Turn Internet into an All-You-Can-Sue Buffet," *The Globe and Mail*, December 28, 2011; Jeff Grey, "The Case Against isoHunt," *The Globe and Mail*, March 1, 2011; Erin Anderssen, "Daddy, What Are We Downloading Today?" *The Globe and Mail*, May 17, 2010, B1, B3; Robert Thompson, "A Crushing Blow for Web Pirates," *Canadian Business*, March 1, 2010, 17; YouTube website, www.youtube.com/t/howto_copyright [accessed June 1, 2010].

The Greening of Business Jeremy Cato, "It's Not Easy Buying Green," *The Globe and Mail*, July 15, 2011, D1; Peter Foster, "The Coming Green Car Pileup," *National Post*, January 14, 2011, FP11; Veronique Dupont, "Consumer Interest in Green Cars Lags; Still Niche Market," *National Post*, January 12, 2011, FP3; Garry Marr, "We'll Go Green If the Price is Right," *National Post*, November 17, 2010, FP10; Peter Foster, "Yellow Brick Road to Green Serfdom," *National Post*, November 10, 2010, FP17; Sarah Schmidt, "Public 'Greenwashed' by Eco-Friendly Claims: Study," *Winnipeg Free Press*, October 26, 2010, A2.

Managing in Turbulent Times David Gautheir-Villars, "Renault Security Held in Spy Case," *The Wall Street Journal*, March 12–13, 2011, B1; Edward Waitzer, "Should We Pay For Whistle-Blowing?" *National Post*, March 22, 2011, FP11; Dimitri Lascaris, "Speak Truth to Power," *National Post*, March 25, 2011, FP11; David Gauthier-Villars and Sebastian Moffett, "Renault to Yield in l'Affaire d'Espionnage," *The Wall Street Journal*, March 10, 2011, B1.

Concluding Case 3-1 Jeremy Cato, "It's Not Easy Buying Green," *The Globe and Mail*, July 15, 2011, p. D1; William Watson, "Green Except When It Costs," *National Post*, March 9, 2011, p. FP17; Lindsey Wiebe, "Logo La-La Land," *Winnipeg Free Press*, August 23, 2009, p. A7; Lindsey Wiebe, "Will Consumers Go For True 'Green' Products?" *Winnipeg Free Press*, August 2, 2009 (Books section), p. 6; Diane Katz, "The Grocery-Bag Dilemma: Is Paper or Plastic Greener?" *Winnipeg Free Press*, July 26, 2009, p. A11; Susan Krashninsky, "The Green Gap," *The Globe and Mail*, July 17, 2009, p. B4; "Beyond the Green Marketing Mirage; GoodGuide Supplies Instant Information on a Host of Products," *National Post*, June 22, 2009, p. FP5; Terrence Belford, "Developers Blue Over Green Roofs," *The Globe and Mail*, June 16, 2009, p. B10; David Ebner, "Coke Will Use The Olympics to Launch Its Latest Environmental Push, But Will a Generation That's Grown Wary of 'Greenwashing' Buy the PlantBottle?" *The Globe and Mail*, June 10, 2009, p. B1; William Watson, "The Uses of Eco-OCD," *National Post*, May 30, 2009, p. FP19; Jennifer Wells, "How Recession Changed the Green Marketplace," *The Globe and Mail*, April 20, 2009, p. B1; Konrad Yakabuski, "Green Dreams, Unplugged," *The Globe and Mail*, April 4, 2009, p. F1; Lawrence Solomon, "Green Economics: It Just Doesn't Add Up," *National Post*, March 31, 2009, p. FP11; Alia McMullen, "Will Green Agenda Fade? In Tough Times, Environmental Action May Lose Its Momentum," *National Post*, January 17, 2009, p. FP1; Joe Castaldo, "Green Counting," *Canadian Business*, October 13, 2008, p. 27.

Concluding Case 3-2 Lawrence Solomon, "Science Now Settled: New, Convincing

Evidence Indicates Global Warming is Caused by Cosmic rays and the Sun, Not Humans," *National Post*, August 27, 2011, FP17; David Evans, "Climate Models Go Cold; Carbon Warming Too Minor to be Worth Worrying About," *National Post*, April 8, 2011, FP15; Lawrence Solomon, "97% Cooked Stats; The 'Scientific Consensus' about Global Warming Turns out to have a Lot More to do with Manipulating the Numbers," *National Post*, January 4, 2011, FP7; Lawrence Solomon, "It's Official: There's No Consensus on Climate," *National Post*, July 10, 2010, FP19; Lawrence Solomon, "Catastrophism Collapses," *National Post*, July 3, 2010, FP19; Lawrence Solomon, "Junk Climate Poll Falls Apart," *National Post*, June 22, 2010, FP11; Rick Salutin, "Climategate's Not Evil, It's Just Unhinged," *The Globe and Mail*, December 11, 2009, A21; Ross McKitrick, "Contaminated Data," *The National Post*, December 5, 2007; Lawrence Solomon, "Open Mind Sees Climate Clearly," *The National Post*, June 29, 2007, p. FP15; Christopher Essex, "There is No Global Temperature," *The National Post*, June 23, 2007, p. FP15; Timothy Patterson, "Read the Sunspots," *The National Post*, June 20, 2007, p. FP17; Lauren Etter, "For Icy Greenland, Global Warming Has A Bright Side," *The Wall Street Journal*, July 18, 2006, pp. A1, A12; Jared Diamond, *Collapse*. Penguin Books, 2005, pp. 493–494; Robert Park, *Voodoo Science*. Oxford University Press, 2000, pp. 31–34, 43–45; James Trefil, *101 Things you Don't Know About Science and No One Else Does Either* (Boston: Houghton Mifflin, 1996), pp. 124–126, 142.

Chapter 4

Internet Entrepreneurs: Moving Products Beyond the Rack Becky Reuber, "Navigating the Shoals of Rapid Growth," *The Globe and Mail*, April 15, 2011, B8; Boyd Erman, "Beyond the Rack Lands $12-Million Financing," *The Globe and Mail*, July 12, 2010; "Flash Sale E-Tailer Beyond the Rack Expands Its Beauty Business by Adding Membership Base of BeautyStory.com," *Canadian Business*, July 5 2011, www.canadianbusiness.com/24772 [accessed September 27 2011]; Jameson Berkow, "Montreal's Beyond the Rack Named North America's Fastest-Growing Online Retailer," *Financial Post*, June 24, 2011; Sramana Mitra, "The Promise of e-Commerce," *Forbes Magazine*, September 4, 2010; Beyond the Rack website, www.beyondtherack.com [accessed September 27 2011]; Michael Krebs (CFO) provided statistics and information, [February 13, 2012].

Table 4.1 www.newswire.ca/en/story/918051.

Entrepreneurship and New Ventures http://www.tawsewinery.ca/.

The Greening of Business Jessica Leeder, "New Fund Has a Taste for Organic food," *The Globe and Mail*, September 5, 2011, B9; Mark Hume, "It All Depends on Which Way the Wind Blows," *The Globe and Mail*, July 26, 2011, S3; Sarah Elton, "A Bicycle Built for Food (and Other Goods)," *The Globe and Mail*, June 14, 2011, L3; Erin McPhee, "New Green Software a 'Quick Tax for Carbon,'" *National Post*, March 28, 2011, FP4; Deborah Cohen, "Rising Energy Costs Incentive to Go Greener; Entrepreneurs Finding New Ways to Cut Back," *National Post*, March 21, 2011, FP10; Todd Macintosh, "Small Firms Put Green

Focus on Energy; Eco-Survey," *National Post*, June 21, 2010, FP7; Green Enterprise Ontario website, http://greenenterprise.net/index.php [accessed June 18, 2010]; Laura Ramsay, "Small Firms Can Go Green Too: There's Lots of Help Out There," *The Globe and Mail*, October 14, 2008, p. E1; Burke Campbell, "Entrepreneur's Green Inspiration from the East," *National Post*, September 22, 2008, www.nationalpost.com/story-printer.html?id=812446.

Table 4.6 *Financial Post Magazine*, June 2012, p. 44.

E-Business + Social Media Solutions Susan Krashinski, "Making Money,140 Characters at a Time" *The Globe and Mail*, April 14, 2010, B1, B6; Amber MacArthur, "What Twitter Ads Mean to You" *The Globe and Mail*, April 13, 2010, B1; Lyndsie Bourgon, "Tweeting Them Where It Hurts," *Canadian Business*, November 23, 2009, P22; Lisan Jutras, "How Will the Twitterati Deal With the Ad Men?" *The Globe and Mail*, April 18, 2010, B1, B3; Twitter website, www.twitter.com [accessed June 14, 2010]; Hollie Shaw, "The Tweet Spot: Marketers Embrace Social Media," *Financial Post*, October 30, 2009, B1, B3; Spencer E. Ante, "The Real Value of Tweets," *Bloomberg Businessweek*, January 18, 2010, P31; Jon Fine, "Twitter Makes a Racket. But Revenues?" *Bloomberg Businessweek*, April 20, 2009, P89.

Concluding Case 4-1 Patricia Gajo, "Jean-Ius," *Nuvo* magazine, Spring 2010, P72-73; Parasuco website, www.parasuco.com [accessed June 23, 2010]; Kristin Laird, "Parasuco's New Ad Campaign Is in Ice," *Marketing* magazine, March 19, 2009; Eva Freide, "Flattery or Fakery," *Montreal Gazette*, July 22, 2008; Daniel Geiger, *Real Estate Weekly*, "Duane Reade Deal for Parasuco Space," www.rew-online.com/news/story.aspx?id=907, March 26, 2010.

Concluding Case 4-2 Burke Campbell, "Sisters Toast Family Roots as Business Bears Fruit," *National Post*, September 29, 2008, www.nationalpost.com/story-printer.html?id=846427; Gabriel Kahn, "A Vintage Strategy Faces Modernity," *The Wall Street Journal*, April 5–6, 2008, A6; Chris Morris, "Rumours of Irving Family Corporate Breakup Swirl," *Winnipeg Free Press*, November 23, 2007, B14; Gordon Pitts and Jacquie McNish, "Shaking the Family Tree," *The Globe and Mail*, November 22, 2007, B1, B9; Gordon Pitts and Jacquie McNish, "Irving Brothers Look to Break Up Empire," *The Globe and Mail*, November 21, 2007, B1, B6; Martin Peers, Matthew Karnitschnig, and Merissa Marr, "Shaken from the Family Tree," *The Globe and Mail*, July 20, 2007, B6; also Paul Waldie, "Mitchell's Feud Goes Public," *The Globe and Mail*, November 30, 2002, B3.

Chapter 5

Scotiabank: Canadian Bank or Global Player? Grant Robertson, "Shrinking Profit Margins Hit Scotiabank," *The Globe and Mail*, May 30, 2012, B3; Grant Robertson, "Scotiabank Takes Stake in Chinese Bank," *The Globe and Mail*, September 10, 2011, B9; Grant Robertson, "Scotiabank Finds a Pricier Merger Market," *The Globe and Mail*, May 11, 2011, B4; Grant Robertson, "Canada's Banks Make Grade in World Standings," *The Globe and Mail*, May 10, 2011, B4; Grant Robertson, "A Once Cautious Bank Takes a Bold LeAP South," *The Globe and Mail*, August 20, 2011, B6; Grant Robertson, "Scotiabank

Profits Jump," *The Globe and Mail*, August 30, 2011, B6; Steve Chase, "Scotiabank CEO Optimistic About Brazil Opportunities," *The Globe and Mail*, August 9, 2011, B4; Steven Chase, "In Brazil, the Rise of the Mall," *The Globe and Mail*, Sept 2, 2011, B1; Scotiabank website, http://scotiabank.com/cda/content/0,1608,CID821_LIDen,00.html [accessed September 19, 2011].

Figure 5.2 *Bank of Canada Banking and Financial Statistics*, Series J1, April 2009, S110.

Table 5.1 Bank of Canada, Banking and Financial Statistics, Series J4, Commodity Classification of Merchandise Exports, January 2011, S116-S117.

Entrepreneurship and New Ventures Interview with Lianne Foti.

Table 5.2 *Financial Post Magazine*, June 2012, p. 72.

Managing in Turbulent Times Craig Wong, "Feds Bury Potash Deal," *Winnipeg Free Press*, November 4, 2010, p. B5; Eric Reguly, "Potash Decision Surprised BHP," Business News Network, www.bnn.ca/News/2010/11/4/Potash-decision-surprised-BHP.aspx; Brenda Bouw, "Wall Warns of Huge Cost for BHP Deal," *The Globe and Mail*, October 1, 2010, p. B4; Boyd Erman, "BHP Win is a Paycheque-Hungry Miner's Dream," *The Globe and Mail*, September 28, 2010, p. B2; Brenda Bouw and Andy Hoffman, "A White Knight is on the Way, Potash CEO Insists," *The Globe and Mail*, September 8, 2010, p. B1; Richard Blackwell, "Explainer/Saskatchewan's Potash Royalty," *The Globe and Mail*, September 3, 2010, p. B3; Eric Reguly, "In the Battle for Potash Corp., Domestic Heroes are in Short Supply," *The Globe and Mail*, September 2, 2010, p. B2.

The Greening of Business Bruce Stanley, "Ships Draw Fire for Rising Role in Air Pollution," *The Wall Street Journal*, November 27, 2007, A1, A16; Bill McAllister, "Alaska Still Out Front on Environmental Monitoring," *The Juneau Empire*, May 29, 2004; Marilyn Adams, "Former Carnival Exec Says He Was Fired for Helping Federal Inquiry," *USA Today*, November 8–10, 2003; Marilyn Adams, "Cruise-Ship Dumping Poisons Seas, Frustrates U.S. Enforcers," *USA Today*, November 8–10, 2003; Michael Connor, "Norwegian Cruise Line Pleads Guilty in Pollution Case," Reuters, December 7, 2002; "What Is a Dead Zone?" *Oceana Interactive*, June 10, 2004, www.oceana.org/index.cfm?sectionID511&fuseaction59#25.

Concluding Case 5-1 Scott Anderson, "Tim Hortons to Go 'Upscale' in Expansion," *The Globe and Mail*, March 6, 2010, p. B2: Jasmine Budak, "The Donut Offensive," *Canadian Business*, March 1, 2010, p. 36–38; Sunny Freeman, "Tim Hortons Rides Out Price Increases," *The Globe and Mail*, February 26, 2010, p. B7; Simon Houpt, "Tim Hortons: At the Intersection of Commerce and Culture," *The Globe and Mail*, March 6, 2010, p. B1: Susan Ma, "Tims Takes Manhattan," *The Globe and Mail*, July 27, 2009, p. B3; Jason Kirby, "Tim's Takes on America," *Maclean's*, March 12, 2008, p. B3; Tim Hortons website, www.timhortons.com/us/en/about/investors.html [accessed Sept. 24, 2011]; Armina Ligaya, "What Fuels Tim Hortons Move into the Middle East," *The Globe and Mail*, May 19, 2011, p. B11; James Cowan, "Why Can't Tim Hortons Find a CEO?" *Canadian Business*, March 19, 2012, p. 11.

Concluding Case 5-2 Eric Reguly, "Beaudoin's Big, Bold Bet," *The Globe and Mail*, July 14, 2008, pp. B1, B10; Tu Thanh Ha, "A Power Plant That Is Quieter, Fuel Efficient But Still Years Away," *The Globe and Mail*, July 14, 2008, pp. B1, B10; Shawn McCarthy and Eric Reguly, "Canadian Hopes, Global Risks," *The Globe and Mail*, July 14, 2008, pp. A1, A6; Bertrand Marotte, "Bombardier Clinches Much Needed Order for C Series," *The Globe and Mail*, June 2, 2011, B3; Rhys Jones and Tim Jones, "Airbus Boosts Forecast for Deliveries" *The Globe and Mail*, September 20, 2011, B13; Greg Keenan, "C Series Airplane Chief Retiring From Bombardier," *The Globe and Mail*, August 25, 2011, B13; Greg Keenan, "Turkish Deal Boosts Bombardier's Middleast Presence," *The Globe and Mail*, November 16, 2011, B3.

Chapter 6

Crisis Management at BP "Transocean Report Pins Oil Spill Blame on BP," *Reuters*, June 22, 2011, www.bnn.ca/News/2011/6/22; Monica Langley, "U.S., BP Near Deal on Fund; Gulf of Mexico Oil Production Would Secure $20 Billion Damage-Claims Plan," *The Wall Street Journal*, August 10, 2010, p. A1; Shawn McCarthy, Kevin Van Paassen, and Cigdem Iltan, "Enbridge Shifts PR Campaign into High Gear," *The Globe and Mail*, July 31, 2010, p. B3; David Runk and Tim Martin, "Pipeline Oil Spill Firm's Latest," *Winnipeg Free Press*, July 30, 2010, p. A17; Lauren Krugel, "Response to Latest U.S. Oil Spill 'Inadequate,'" *Winnipeg Free Press*, July 29, 2010, p. A9; Paul Vieira, "Gulf Oil Spill 'Wake-Up Call' for Industry: New BP CEO; Safety a Priority," *National Post*, July 28, 2010, p. FP1; Guy Chazan, "BP Reveals Comeback Plan; Oil Giant Takes $32 Billion Charge on Spill, Taps New CEO; Investors Skeptical," *The Wall Street Journal*, July 28, 2010, p. A1; Russell Gold and Ben Casselman, "Alarm Was Disabled Before BP Blast," *The Wall Street Journal*, July 24, 2010, p. A1; Shawn McCarthy, "Gulf Residents Decry Drilling Ban," *The Globe and Mail*, July 14, 2010, p. B8; "Oil Leak From Grounded Cargo Ship Closes Section of St. Lawrence Seaway," *National Post*, July 14, 2010, p. FP4; Nathan VankerKlippe, "Devon Energy Blowout One of Several in Recent Years," *The Globe and Mail*, July 14, 2010, p. B7; "BP's Colossal PR Blunder," *National Post*, June 30, 2010, p. FP3; Carrie Tait, "BP Stock at 14-Year Low as Cleanup Costs Soar; Storm Worries," *National Post*, June 26, 2010, p. FP5; Shawn McCarthy and Paul Waldie, "In Deep Water Drilling, a Delicate Dance," *The Globe and Mail*, June 26, 2010, p. B1; "BP's Diplomat Unlikely to Repeat Gaffes; Changing of Guard; Bob Dudley Takes Control of Oil-Spill Daily Operation," *National Post*, June 23, 2010, p. FP3; David Ebner, "For BP's Lawyers, a High-Stakes Chess Match Begins," *The Globe and Mail*, June 17, 2010, p. B1; "Big Oil Blasted Over Safety; Hearing Heaps Scorn on Spending on Preparedness for Offshore Oil Spills," *National Post*, June 16, 2010, p. FP1; Peter Shawn Taylor, "BP's Credit Rating is Slashed Six Levels to Two Above Junk Over Clean-Up Costs," *National Post*, June 16, 2010, p. FP16; Andrew Willis, "As Slick Spreads, Oil Sands Beckon," *The Globe and Mail*, June 16, 2010, p. B1; "BP to Set up $20B Fund; Scraps Dividend," *Business News Network*, June 16,

2010, www.bnn.ca/newes/18322.html; Shawn McCarthy and Nathan VanderKlippe, "Spill Puts New Oil Frontiers at Risk," *The Globe and Mail*, June 11, 2010, p. B1; David Ebner, "BP Spill Causes Transatlantic Tensions," *The Globe and Mail*, June 11, 2010, p. B5; Nathan VanderKlippe, "Investors Flee BP as Spill Woes Mount," *The Globe and Mail*, June 10, 2010, p. B1; Eric Reguly, "Why BP Chief's Days are Numbered," *The Globe and Mail*, June 3, 2010, p. B2; Ben Casselman and Russell Gold, "Unusual Decisions Set Stage for BP Disaster," *The Wall Street Journal*, May 27, 2010, p. A1; Fabrice Taylor, "A Bullish Case for BP," *The Globe and Mail*, May 21, 2010, p. B12; Ben Casselman and Guy Chazan, "Disaster Plans Lacking at Deep Rigs," *The Wall Street Journal*, May 18, 2010, p. A1; Ben Casselman, "Rig Owner Had Rising Tally of Accidents," *The Wall Street Journal*, May 10, 2010, p. A1.

Entrepreneurship and New Ventures planetbeancoffee.com/earth/index.php.

The Greening of Business "Looking Good in Green," *Maclean's*, May 9, 2011, 47; Ford Aims for 25% of its Vehicles to be Electric or Hybrid by 2013," *National Post*, June 10, 2011, FP4; Alexandra Lopez-Pacheco, "Planet-Friendly Offices," *National Post*, October 2, 2009, FP12; "Rona Wins Kudos on Green Initiative," *The Globe and Mail*, November 22, 2008, B7; John Murphy, "Honda CEO Vies for Green Mantle," *The Wall Street Journal*, June 16, 2008, B1–B2; Sharda Prashad, "Good Green Goals," TheStar.com, April 22, 2007, www.thestar.com/ printArticle/205855.

E-Business + Social Media Solutions Audit Bureau of Circulations, "Publishers Continue Cross-Media Diversification, Begin to Monetize Mobile, www.accessabc.ca/press/press110711.htm [accessed January 2, 2012]; "Taiwan's AsusTek Unveils iPad Competitor," *The Globe and Mail*, June 1, 2010, B10; Yukuri Iwatini Kane and Geoffrey A. Fowler, "Apple Foes Have Head Start on E-Content," *The Globe and Mail*, April 3, 2010, B5; Rachel Metz, "iPad Could Be Kindle's First Big Threat," *The Globe and Mail*, March 30, 2010, B10; Jordan Timm, "Indigo 2.0," *The Globe and Mail Report on Business*, March 1, 2010, 29; Susan Krashinski, "Upstart Kobo Aims at Kindle," *The Globe and Mail*, February 9, 2010, B7; Susan Krashinski, "Magazine Sales Hit Hard at Newsstands," *The Globe and Mail*, February 9, 2010, B7; Simon Avery, "Amazon Slides after iPad Launch," *The Globe and Mail*, February 3, 2010, 16; John Barber, "Arrival of iPad Gives Publisher Clout in e-Book Pricing," *The Globe and Mail*, February 2, 2010, B5; John Barber, "Why Old Media Loves Apple's New Thing," *The Globe and Mail*, January 27, 2010, B7; Jason Kirby and Katie Engelhart, "Rupert Murdoch vs. the Internet," *Maclean's*, January 18, 2010, 40–42; Omar El Akkad, "E-Reader Rivals Jostle for Position," *The Globe and Mail*, January 7, 2010, B7; Jim Harris, "Newspapers Are Suffering," *Backbone*, November 2009, 10; Marina Strauss, "Turning a Page into the Digital Age," *The Globe and Mail*, June 27, 2009, B3.

Managing in Turbulent Times Eric Reguly, "Skies Getting Crowded in CSeries Niche," *The Globe and Mail*, June 21, 2011, B17; Greg Keenan, "Bombardier's Next Jet Faces New Hurdle: Cutthroat Prices," *The Globe and Mail*, December 7, 2010, p. B1; Scott Deveau,

"Build Larger CSeries, Bombardier Advised; Air Insight Report; Option of 150-Seat Version Could Steal Clients from Boeing," *National Post*, December 7, 2010, p. FP7; Bertrand Marotte, "Bombardier Sticks to Business-Jet Plan," *The Globe and Mail*, December 3, 2010, p. B3; Greg Keenan, "Airbus Turns Up the Heat on Bombardier, Boeing," *The Globe and Mail*, December 2, 2010, p. B3; Barry Critchley, "Bombardier Spices Up Orders for Indian Market; $390M Deal in Works," *National Post*, November 3, 2010, p. FP2; Bertrand Marotte, "Bombardier Plans Two New Business Jets," *The Globe and Mail*, October 30, 2010, p. B5; Laura Cameron, "For Bombardier, A Case of Déjà Vu," *Canadian Business*, September 13, 2010, p. 28.

Concluding Case 6-1 Jeff Gray, "Overtime Lawsuits Hit a Snag," *The Globe and Mail*, May 16, 2012, B9; Howard Levitt, "When Do Managers Punch the Clock?; How Employers Can Avoid Unwanted Overtime Payments," *National Post*, July 6, 2011, p. FP1; Jeff Gray, "Overtime Lawsuit Against Scotiabank Gets Green Light," *The Globe and Mail*, June 7, 2011, B6; Daryl-Lynn Carlson, "Overtime a Laborious Issue," *National Post*, October 27, 2010, LP4; Jim Middlemiss, "Hurdle for Overtime Class-Action Suits," *National Post*, September 15, 2010, FP8; Barry Critchley, "Managers at Centre of CN Class Action; Overtime at Issue; Judge to Rule on Whether Supervisors are Management," *National Post*, August 18, 2010, FP2; Peter Taylor, "Suing by the Hour; Out-of-Touch Labour Legislation is Making Life Difficult for Employers and Hard-Working Employees Alike," *National Post*, December 9, 2009, FP15; "CIBC Staffers Seek OK for Overtime Group Suit," *The Globe and Mail*, December 9, 2008, B10; Jim Middlemiss, "Lawsuit Seeks OT for Bankers; CIBC Targeted," *National Post*, October 29, 2008, FP1; Richard Blackwell, "KPMG to Pay workers Overtime," *The Globe and Mail*, February 20, 2008, B8; Virginia Galt, "Managers' Overtime Victory Short-Lived," *The Globe and Mail*, April 20, 2007, B3.

Concluding Case 6-2 Gordon Pitts, "Kraft CEO Still Digesting Cadbury Takeover," *The Globe and Mail*, June 7, 2010, p. B8; "Vale Resumes Negotiations with Striking Sudbury Nickel Workers," *National Post*, June 5, 2010, p. FP4; Heidi Ulrichsen, "Vale Inco Plans to Bring in a 'Couple Hundred' Replacement Workers," *Sudbury Northern Life*, April 19, 2010, www.northernlife.ca/news/local-News/2010/04/replacementworkers-190410. aspx; Stacey Lavaillie, "Date Set for USW, Vale Inco Bad Faith Bargaining Hearing," *Sudbury Northern Life*, April 9, 2010, www. northernlife.ca/newes/localNews/2010/04/ olrb-090410.aspx; Sharon Terlap, "GM's Plodding Culture Vexes Its Impatient CEO," *The Wall Street Journal*, April 7, 2010, p. B1; Kristine Owram, "Sudbury Strike Becomes Longest in Inco's History; Little Hope for Resolution," *The Canadian Press*, April 6, 2010, www.google.com/hostednews/canadi-anpress/article/ALeqM5j90NJ-uvH5ZhfZy08T; Steve Hamm, "IBM-Sun Merger Talks Off," *Bloomberg Businessweek*, April 5, 2009, www. businessweek.com/technology/content/ apr2009/tc2009045_914072.htm; Paul Waldie, "Culture Clash Pits Business School Dean Against Faculty," April 1, 2010, www.globe-campus.ca/in-the-news/aritcle/culture-clash;

Bernard Simon and Jonathan Wheatley, "Heading in Opposite Directions," *Financial Times*, March 11, 2010, p. 10; "Corporate Culture Clash Took Fizz Out Of Merger," Asia News Network, www.asianewsnet.net/print.php?id=10019; Michael de la Merced and Chris Nicholson, "Kraft to Acquire Cadbury in Deal Worth $19 Billion," *The New York Times*, January 20, 2010, www.mytimes.com/2010/01/20/business/global/20kraft.html?pagewanted=print; Simon Bowers, "Cadbury Warns of Culture Clash Under Kraft," www.guardian.co.uk/business/2009/oct/21/cadbury-kraft-sales-profits-job-losses; "James Gosling Warns of 'Culture Clash' if IBM Buys Sun," *Computer Business Review*, March 23, 2009, www.businessreviewonline.com/blog/archives/2009/03/james_gosling_w.html.

Chapter 7

The Organizational Structure of the "Occupy Wall Street" Movement Gordon Crovitz, "Occupy Astro Turf," *The Wall Street Journal*, January 30, 2012, A13; Omar El Akkad, "After the Campaign Put Out the Simple Twitter Hashtag #OccupyWallStreet, 'It Just Went Crazy,'" *The Globe and Mail*, December 22, 2011, A12; Kathryn Blaze Carlson, "Utopian Failure; Why The Occupy Movement is Doomed: Huan Brains Crave Hierarchy," *National Post*, November 26, 2011, A10; Gary Mason, "Founders of Leadnow Strive to Build a Progressive Voice with Real Focus," *The Globe and Mail*, November 26, 2011, A18; "Five Reasons Why Occupy Failed," *National Post*, November 19, 2011, A10; Gary Mason, "Sorry, Folks, But This Protest's in Danger of Fizzling Out," *The Globe and Mail*, November 3, 2011, A19; "Rogue Senate Page Lends Her Support to the 99ers; Occupation Peaceful; Protesters in Ottawa, Montreal Camping Out In Downtown Parks," *National Post*, October 18, 2011, A8; Kim Mackrael, "Occupy Wall Street: Who They Are, What They Want," *The Globe and Mail*, October 7, 2011, A23; Kelly McParland, "Confused Protesters March On; 'Movements' Don't Have Leaders or Clear Goals," *National Post*, October 4, 2011, A2;

Managing in Turbulent Times Gordon Pitts, "Immigrant, Engineer, Education Junkie: The Outsider at the Helm of Irving Oil," *The Globe and Mail*, November 3, 2011, B1; Dean Jobb, "Tough Times for the Irving Clan," *Canadian Business*, September 13, 2010, 14; Gordon Pitts, "Death, Departure Set Irving on New Path," *The Globe and Mail*, July 22, 2010, B1; Chris Morris, "Rumours of Irving Family Corporate Breakup Swirl," *Winnipeg Free Press*, November 23, 2007, B14; Gordon Pitts and Jacquie McNish, "Shaking the Family Tree," *The Globe and Mail*, November 22, 2007, B1, B9; Gordon Pitts and Jacquie McNish, "Irving Brothers Look to Break up Empire," *The Globe and Mail*, November 21, 2007, B1, B6.

Entrepreneurship and New Ventures *Hoover's Handbook of American Business 2011* (Austin, Texas: Hoover's Business Press, 2011); PBS.org, "Who Made America" (June 19, 2008), www.pbs.org/wgbh/theymadeamerica/whomade/fsmith_hi.html; http://www.Forbes.com/finance (February 16, 2006); Brian Dumaine, "How I Delivered the Goods," *Fortune Small Business*, October 2002; Charles Haddad, "FedEx: Gaining on the Ground,"

Businessweek, December 16, 2002, 126–128; Claudia H. Deutsch, "FedEx Has Hit the Ground Running, But Will Its Legs Tire?" *New York Times*, October 13, 2002, BU7.

The Greening of Business Erica Kelly, "Banking's New Shade of Green," *The Globe and Mail*, December 20, 2011, B8; Gail Johnson, "Easy To Be Green When Your Roof Saves You Money," *The Globe and Mail*, November 15, 2011, p. B11; Martin Cash, "Terminal Case of Energy Efficiency," *Winnipeg Free Press*, October 29, 2011, p. B6; Shelley White, "Part Office Building, Part Power Plant," *The Globe and Mail*, September 20, 2011, B10; "Green Buildings," *Canadian Business*, August 16–September 12, 2011, p. 55; Sarah Boesveld, "The Green Building Impact on Employees," *The Globe and Mail*, October 19, 2010, p. B12; Jay Somerset, "A Building with an Energy All Its Own," *The Globe and Mail*, November 11, 2008, B9.

Concluding Case 7-1 "The Business Picture/The End of An Era As Kodak Stops Making Cameras," *The Globe and Mail*, February 10, 2012, B2; Kana Inagaki and Juro Osawa, "Fujifilm Thrived By Changing Focus," *The Wall Street Journal*, January 20, 2012, B5; Mike Spector and Dana Mattioli, "Kodak: Tech Firms Hastened Slide," *The Wall Street Journal*, January 20, 2012, B1; Ben Dobbin, "Restructuring Halts Kodak Stock's Freefall," *The Globe and Mail*, January 11, 2012, B10; "Kodak Claims Apple Infringing on Four Patents Tied to Digital Images," *National Post*, January 11, 2012, FP12; Caroline Humer, "End of the Line for Film Group as Kodak Refocuses; Shares Jump 50%," *National Post*, January 11, 2012, FP12; Dana Mattioli, "Their Kodak Moments," *The Wall Street Journal*, January 6, 2012, B1; www.wikipedia.org/wiki/Eastman_Kodak; "Eastman Kodak Shares Jump After General Counsel Named Co-President," *National Post*, December 24, 2011, FP9; "Kodak Eases Fears; Shares Soar 72%," *The Globe and Mail*, October 24, 2011, B10.

Concluding Case 7-2 Paul Ziobro, "Kraft to Cut Jobs As Part of Split," *The Wall Street Journal*, January 18, 2012, B3; Mike Esterl, "PepsiCo Board Stands by Nooyi," *The Wall Street Journal*, January 13, 2012, B1; Julie Jargon and Paul Ziobro, "Corporate News: Kraft Picks Leaders for Split—Rosenfeld and Vernon Next Will Hash Out Details On Teams, Sort Smaller Brands," *The Wall Street Journal*, December 6, 2011, B3; Hollie Shaw, "Sobeys to Split Grocery Chain in Two," *National Post*, October 14, 2011, FP4; Joann Lublin and Bob Tita, "End of An Empire: Tyco Plans Split," *The Wall Street Journal*, September 20, 2011, B1; Paul Ziobro, "Kraft CEO Spent Billions Preparing to Dismantle," *The Wall Street Journal*, August 5, 2011, B1. Betsy Morris, "The Pepsi Challenge," *Fortune*, February 19, 2008, www.money.cnn.com/2008/02/18/news/companies/morris_nooyi.fortune/index.htm; Flex News, "PepsiCo Unveils New Organizations Structure, Names CEOs of Three Principal Operating Units," May 11, 2007, www.flex-news-foof.com/pages/12058/pepsi/pepsico-unveils-new-organizational-structure-names-ceos-three-principal-operating-units.html; Joann Lublin, "Place vs. Product: It's Tough to Choose a Management Model," *The Wall Street Journal*, June 27, 2001, pp. A1, A4; Richard Blackwell, "New CIBC Boss Promises Shakeup," *The Globe and Mail*, April 2, 1999, pp. B1, B4. Rekha Bach, "Heinz's Johnson to Divest Operations, ScrAP

Management of Firm by Region," *The Wall Street Journal*, December, 1997, pp. B10–B12; Jana Parker-Pope and Joann Lublin, "P&G Will Make Jager CEO Ahead of Schedule," *The Wall Street Journal*, September, 1998, pp. B1, B8.

Chapter 8

Millennials on the March http://humanresources.about.com/od/businessmanagement/a/top_ten_trends.htm; http://humanresources.about.com/od/managementtips/a/millennial_myth.htm; http://humanresources.about.com/od/managementtips/a/millenials.htm; Harvey Schachter, "Five Myths About Generation Y Workers," *The Globe and Mail*, April 2, 2012, B7.

Table 8.1 http://www.globeinvestor.com/series/top1000/tables/employers.

The Greening of Business "Looking Good in Green," *Maclean's*, May 9, 2011, 47; Katie Engelhart, "From the Bottom Up," *Canadian Business*, April 27–May 10, 2010, 60; Greg McMillan, "The Greening of the Jobscape," *The Globe and Mail*, November 14, 2008, p. B7; Marjo Johne, "Show Us the Green, Workers Say," *The Globe and Mail*, October 10, 2007, p. C1; "Creating Jobs by Going Green," www.premier.gov.on.ca/news/Product.asp?ProductID=1400.

E-Business + Social Media Solutions LinkedIN website, http://press.linkedin.com/about [accessed January 2, 2012]; Joe Light, "In the Hunt for Talent, Companies Polish Their 'Employee Brand,'" *The Globe and Mail*, May 21, 2011, B18; Wallace Immen, "Canadian Job Seekers Lag in Social Media," *The Globe and Mail*, April 16, 2011, B17; Wallace Immen, "Tweet Your Way to a Job" *The Globe and Mail*, May 19, 2010, B16; Tavia Grant, "LinkedIn Set to Open Shop in Canada," *The Globe and Mail*, March 29, 2010, B3; Tavia Grant, "Tweet-Tweet: Want Ads Singing a New Tune," *The Globe and Mail*, November 12, 2009, B1, B4; "LinkedIn: Balancing Friendships and Prospects," *The Globe and Mail*, February 4, 2009, C6; Matthew Boyle, "Enough to Make Monster Tremble," *Businessweek*, July 6, 2009, 43–45; Ijeoma Ross, "Online Recruiter Looks to Cast Wider Web," *The Globe and Mail*, May 12, 2008, B6; Susan Pinker, "Connecting Online: Small Investment, Big Return," *The Globe and Mail*, September 30, 2009, B20;

Managing in Turbulent Times Jonathan Chevreau, "PRPPs Will Do Nothing to Address Pension Crisis, Monica Townson Says," *National Post*, December 7, 2011, FP7; Jonathan Chevreau, "Jumping Into the Pension Pool: PRPPs Will Only Work if They are Mandatory," *National Post*, November 23, 2011, FP7; Jonathan Chevreau, "'Social Tragedy' in Pension Loss; Defined Benefit Plans a Great Value: Author," *National Post*, November 21, 2011, FP2; John Crocker, "Keep Defined-Benefit Pensions," *National Post*, November 15, 2011, FP17; R. Brown, "Air Canada Pioneers Pension Advance," *National Post*, November 4, 2011, FP11; Greg Keenan, "U.S. Steel Union Relents on Key Contract Demands," *The Globe and Mail*, October 13, 2011, p. B3; Barry Critchley, "Big Banks Face Benefit Shortfalls; Hit by Low Rates," *National Post*, September 28, 2011, FP1; "RBC Changing New-Hire Pensions," *The Globe and Mail*, September 24, 2011, p. B11.

Concluding Case 8-1 Geoff Cook, "A Question of Evidence: The Behaviour-Based Interview," *Training Journal*, 2006, 61; Sarah Hood, "Hire Echelon," *Canadian Business*, June 7–June 20, 2004, 71; Celene Adams, "Interview Style Probes Past to Predict Future," *The Globe and Mail*, April 29, 2002, B16; "Taking Questions to a Hire Level," *National Post*, March 23, 2001, C2; Barbara Simmons, "Be Ready for Tough 'Behaviour-Based' Interview," *Toronto Star*, December 16, 2000; Greg Crone, "The Right Questions Help Avoid Hiring Employees that are Clones of the Interviewer," *National Post*, October 27, 1999, C04; http://jobsearch.about.com/cs/interviews/a/behavioral.htm.

Concluding Case 8-2 http://humanresources.about.com/od/businessmanagement/a/top_ten_trends.htm; http://humanresources.about.com/od/recruiting/a/recruit_linked.htm; http://humanresources.about.com/od/careernetworking/a/social_media.htm; http://humanresources.about.com/od/careernetworking/a/social_media_2.htm.

Chapter 9

Hard Hits in Professional Sports Brian Mahoney, "Shorter Schedule Forces Brutal Stretches," *The Globe and Mail*, December 7, 2011, S5; Barry Wilner and Howard Fendrich, "NFL, Players Bang Out 10-Year Deal," *Winnipeg Free Press*, July 26, 2011, p. D1; Barry Wilner, "Players Prepare for Chaos," *Winnipeg Free Press*, July 26, 2011, p. D4; Howard Fenrich, "NFL Labour Dispute Enters Overtime," *Winnipeg Free Press*, July 23, 2011, C2; Barry Wilner, "Employees Hit Hardest If Players Don't Play," *Winnipeg Free Press*, June 14, 2011, p. C6; Dave Campbell, "No Indication of Significant Progress Toward New Agreement," *Winnipeg Free Press*, May 18, 2011, p. C2; "Business-Friendly Court Rules NFL Lockout Remains," *Winnipeg Free Press*, May 17, 2011, p. C2; Matthew Futterman, "NFL Owners Try Wedge," *The Wall Street Journal*, March 18, 2011, p. B8; Matthew Futterman, "NFL Girds for Fight, Says Loss Is Covered," *The Wall Street Journal*, March 14, 2011, p. B1; Eric Lam, "NFL Lockout Not Threat To Broadcasters," *National Post*, September 14, 2010, p. FP8.

Managing in Turbulent Times John Allemang, "Organized Labour is Fighting to Survive," *The Globe and Mail*, March 24, 2012, F1; Catherine Swift, "Fighting the Union Mentality," *National Post*, August 6, 2011, p. FP17; Kris Maher, "Unions Push to Undo Ohio Law," *The Wall Street Journal*, June 3, 2011, A5; Konrad Yakabuski, "Will Wisconsin's Chill on Labour Move North?" *The Globe and Mail*, March 12, 2011, p. F1; Paul Vieira, "Public Spat; The Battle Boiling Over in Wisconsin Simmers in Canada," *National Post*, March 5, 2011, p. FP1; Terence Corcoran, "Why the Public Sector Is Hanging On For All It's Worth," *National Post*, March 5, 2011, A1; Howard Levitt, "Are Unions Losing their Purpose? Law Affords More Protection to Employees," *National Post*, July 8, 2009, p. FP12.

Table 9.3 "Union Coverage in Canada, 2011," Appendix 2, *Statistics Canada*, www.hrsdc.gc.ca, accessed May 3, 2012.

E-Business + Social Media Solutions Charles Lewis, "Firing of Sportsnet Broadcaster After Gay Marriage Tweet Tests Religious Freedom, Free Speech," *National Post*, November 16, 2011; Jeff Gray, "Think Before You Tweet," *The Globe and Mail*, May 25, 2011, B9; Fox News website, "Twitter Feed F-Word Gets Chrysler Employee Fired," www.foxnews.com/us/2011/03/10/f-word-appears-chryslers-twitter-feed, March 11, 2011 [accessed January 4, 2012]; Scott Edmonds, "Car Dealership Employees Fired for Facebook Posts," *The Globe and Mail*, December 9, 2010, B9.

Concluding Case 9-1 Melanie Trottman, "Both Sides in Labor Fight Point to Oklahoma," *The Wall Street Journal*, January 27, 2012, A2; Jack Nicas and Kris Maher, "Right-to-Work Bill Advances," *The Wall Street Journal*, January 26, 2012, A2; Nicolas Van Praet, "Electrolux Idles Montreal Plant; Tennessee Gets Jobs After Months of Courting," *National Post*, December 15, 2010, FP1; Karen Selick, "Would You Like a Little Orwell With That?" *Winnipeg Free Press*, December 9, 2010, p. A15; Niels Veldhuis and Amela Karabegovic, "Reject Unions and Prosper," *National Post*, September 10, 2010, p. FP11.

Concluding Case 9-2 Matthew Dolan, "New Pay Pressure on UAW," *The Wall Street Journal*, January 13, 2011, p. B1; Diane Francis, "New Model Stuck in the Slow Lane; Labour Still Hoping for Wave of Unionization," *National Post*, October 30, 2010, p. FP3; Niels Veldhuis and Amela Karabegovic, "Reject Unions and Prosper," *National Post*, September 10, 2010, p. FP11; Kristine Owram, "GM to Invest $90 Million in Southwestern Ontario Plant," *Winnipeg Free Press*, November 10, 2009, p. B10; Greg Keenan, "Ford Confirms Plant Closing as GM Invests," *The Globe and Mail*, November 10, 2009, p. B3; Barry Critchley, "Ford, CAW Reach Deal to Keep 10% Footprint; St. Thomas to Close," *National Post*, October 31, 2009, p. FP2; "European Airlines Risk Labour Strikes in Slashing Jobs; Aer Lingus Latest," *National Post*, October 8, 2009, p. FP18; Greg Keenan, "Ford's Canadian Labour Costs Under Fire," *The Globe and Mail*, October 3, 2009, p. B6; "Ford Faces $1.76 Billion Pension Gap," *National Post*, September 24, 2009, p. FP5; "Ford and CAW in Cost-Cutting Negotiations; Match Chrysler, GM," *National Post*, September 9, 2009, p. FP5; Thomas Watson, "Why the Plan Won't Work," *Canadian Business*, July 20, 2009, p. 11; Tavia Grant, "Downturn Brings New Bargaining Tactic: Do Nothing," *The Globe and Mail*, July 8, 2009, p. B1; Barrie McKenna, "Anti-Union Lobby Fears 'Armageddon on Capitol Hill,'" *The Globe and Mail*, July 8, 2009, p. B4; Christiaan Hetzner and Angelica Gruber, "Air Canada Union Considers Next Move; Rejects Offer," *National Post*, July 3, 2009, p. FP5; "Benefits Leave Companies Weakened; Unionized Firms Fight to Compete, Economist Says," *National Post*, June 24, 2009, p. FP4; Sheldon Alberts, "Air Canada Unions Relent on Pensions; Grim Financials," *National Post*, June 10, 2009, p. FP1; Greg Keenan, "Being 'Blackmailed,' CAW Says," *The Globe and Mail*, May 20, 2009, p. B3; Jeff Sanford, "Kenny's Last Stand," *Canadian Business*, April 13, 2009, p. 26.

Chapter 10

Happiness and Satisfaction in the Workplace "One in Two U.S. Employees Looking to Leave or Checked out on the Job, Says *What's Working* Research," www.mercer.com/press-releases/1418665 [accessed January 3, 2012]; Derek Abma, "GenXers Least Happy At Work; Disappointment," *National Post*, November 30, 2011, FP10; Wallace Immen, "Study Highlights Generation GAP on Workplace Priorities," *The Globe and Mail*, November 2, 2011, B19; Rajeev Peshawaria, "To Motivate Your Employees, You Need to Know What They Want," *The Globe and Mail*, September 7, 2011, B19; "Not Happy At Work? You're Not Alone: One in Two Canadians Say They Would Leave," *National Post*, June 22, 2011, FP14; "Is Happiness Overrated?" *The Wall Street Journal*, March 15, 2011, D1; Phyllis Korkki, "Don't Take a Job for the Paycheque Alone; Benefits of High Salary Ambiguous," *National Post*, November 17, 2010, FP9; Wallace Immen, "Meaning Means More than Money at Work: Poll," *The Globe and Mail*, February 27, 2009, B14; Wallace Immen, "Boomers, Gen-Yers Agree: It's All About Respect," *The Globe and Mail*, January 24, 2007, C1.

Entrepreneurship and New Ventures Ronald J Ebert and Ricky W. Griffin, *Business Essentials* (Boston, MA: Pearson, 2013) p. 248.

Concluding Case 10-1 "One in Two U.S. Employees Looking to Leave or Checked out on the Job, Says *What's Working* Research," www.mercer.com/press-releases/1418665 [accessed January 3, 2012]; Marjo Johne, "Firing on All Cylinders with Social Media," *The Globe and Mail*, October 21, 2011, p. B15; Wallace Immen, "Canadian Companies Warm to Social Media," *The Globe and Mail*, June 10, 2011, p. B16; Darah Hansen, "New Age, New Problems; Social Media No. 1 Concern for Employers," *National Post*, June 8, 2011, p. FP11; Wallace Immen, "Feeling Unmotivated? HR Managers Say It's the Boss's Fault," *The Globe and Mail*, March 23, 2011, p. B21; Richard Branson, "Don't Leave Employees on the Outside Looking In," *Canadian Business*, July 20–August 16, 2010, p. 13; Joe Castaldo, "How To Coax Ideas Out of a Sheepish Staff," *Canadian Business*, April 27–May 10, 2010, p. 80; Katie Engelhart, "From the Bottom Up," *Canadian Business*, April 27–May 10, 2010, p. 60; Leena Rao, "I Love Rewards Raises $5.9 Million For Employee Rewards Program," TechCrunch website, retrieved May 7, 2009 from www.techcrunch.com/2009/05/07/i-love-rewards-raises-59-million-for-employee-rewards-program; Chris Atchison, "Masters of One," *Profit*, May 2009, Vol. 28, Issue 2, p. 18; Ari Weinzweig, "Ask Inc: Tough Questions, Smart Answers," *Inc.*, December 2007, Vol. 29, Issue 12, p. 84; Virginia Galt, "Ideas: Employees' Best-Kept Secrets," *The Globe and Mail*, June 18, 2005, p. B11; Frederick A. Starke, Bruno Dyck, and Michael Mauws, "Coping with the Sudden Loss of an Indispensable Worker," *Journal of Applied Behavioural Science*, 39(2), 2003, pp. 208–229; Timothy Aeppel, "On Factory Floors, Top Workers Hide Secrets to Success," *The Wall Street Journal*, July 1, 2002, pp. A1, A10; Timothy Aeppel, "Not All Workers Find Idea of Empowerment as Neat as it Sounds," *The Wall Street Journal*, September 8, 1997, pp. A1, A13.

Concluding Case 10-2 Wallace Immen, "Workplace IT: Mixed Marks for Canada," *The Globe and Mail*, January 4, 2012, B14; Mary Gooderham, "Steering Clear of the Morning Rush Hour," *The Globe and Mail*, November 16, 2011, E1; Jameson Berkow, "Workers of the World DISPERSE; Anything, Anywhere; Mobile Workers are

Taking the Office With Them in Greater Numbers," *National Post*, June 25, 2011, FP1; Howard Levitt, "Teleworking Need Not Be a Boondoggle; Guidelines for Approving Such an Arrangement," *National Post*, October 20, 2010, FP13; Joyce Rosenberg, "Out of Sight, on Your Mind; Learning to Trust Telecommuters," *The Globe and Mail*, September 20, 2008, B19; "Productivity Rises for Teleworkers: Survey," *The Globe and Mail*, October 15, 2008, C7; 37. Tavia Grant, "Lower Costs, Higher Morale Benefits of Four-Day Work Week," *The Globe and Mail*, August 18, 2008, B4; Randi Chapnik Myers, "The Back and Forth of Working from Home," *The Globe and Mail*, March 8, 2008, B16; Paul Lima, "With New Advances in Technology, Why Are We Still Jumping in the Car?" *The Globe and Mail*, October 20, 2008, E9; Kira Vermond, "In Support of Ditching the Commute," *The Globe and Mail*, November 17, 2007, B23.

Chapter 11

Options for Homes: a Unique Business Model www.optionsforhomes.ca; Jane Gadd, "A Toronto Condo for Under $100,000," *The Globe and Mail*, December 1, 2006.

Entrepreneurship and New Ventures "Hold on Tight! The World's First Unicycle Motorbike," MailOnline website, April 29, 2008, retrieved May 15, 2009 from www.dailymail.co.uk/news/article-562726/Hold-tight-The-worlds-unicycle-MOTORBIKE.html; James F. Quinn, "Uno and Only: Start with a Motorcycle, Add 'Star Wars' and Give the Segway a Run for its Futuristic Money," *Chicago Tribune* web edition, June 29, 2008, retrieved May 16, 2009 from www.motorcycleenhancements.com/uno_chicago_tribune/uno_chicago_tribune.htm#; Mary Teresa Bitti, "The Brett Wilson Show," *National Post* website, January 9, 2009, retrieved May 17, 2009 from www.nationalpost.com/related/topics/story.html id=1159190; Trish Crawford, "Star Power for the Uno: Milton Teen's 'Cool' Electric Bike Creates Buzz," *The Hamilton Spectator*, June 3, 2008, p. A01; Trish Crawford, "Teenager's Electric Unicycle Creates One Singular Sensation; Science Fair Project Getting World Attention," *Toronto Star*, June 3, 2008, p. A04; "Uno Inventory Lands $1.25 Million for Research Center," *Milton Canadian Champion*, November 21, 2008.

The Greening of Business Martin Hutchinson, "Solar Firm's Bankruptcy Shines Light on U.S. Policy," *The Globe and Mail*, September 15, 2011, p. B12; Peter Foster, "Scorched by Solar," *National Post*, September 3, 2011, p. FP17; Neil Reynolds, "The German Irony: Will It Have to Import Nuclear Energy?" *The Globe and Mail*, June 15, 2011, p. B2; Brian McKenna, "McGuinty's Green Energy 'Explosion' More of an Implosion," *The Globe and Mail*, June 13, 2011, p. B2; Claudia Cattaneo, "Consumers Will Opt for Lowest Cost: Report," *National Post*, April 28, 2011, p. FP8; Lawrence Solomon, "Nuclear Power Extremes; The Problems with Nuclear Support from Both Right and Left," *National Post*, April 9, 2011, p. FP19; "The New Impossible Energy No-Fly Zone," May 17, 2011, p. FP11; Richard Blackwell, "Activists Lose Court Challenge Over Wind Power Turbines," *Globe and Mail*, March 4, 2011, p. B5; Todd Woody, "Solar Power Plans Spark Lawsuit

Storm," *National Post*, February 25, 2011, p. FP3; Lawrence Solomon, "Green Collapse; Across the World, Unsustainable Subsidies for Wind and Solar are being Cut Back; Ontario is Next," *National Post*, December 4, 2010, p. FP19; Lawrence Solomon, "Profitin' in the Wind; Billionaire energy Tycoon T. Boone Pickens has a Two-Step Plan to Cash in on Climate Change. Today," *National Post*, July 18, 2009, p. FP19; "Fossil Fuel Dependency to Continue for Rest of Century, Expert Says," *National Post*, July 16, 2009, p. FP4; Sigurd Lauge Pedersen, "Wind Power Works," *National Post*, May 12, 2009, p. FP13; Michael J. Trebilcock, "Wind Power is a Complete Disaster," *National Post*, April 9, 2009, p. FP13; Diane Francis, "Canada's Nuclear Power Play," *National Post*, October 25, 2008, p. FP2; Neil Reynolds, "Wind Turbine Marketers are Full of Hot Air," *The Globe and Mail*, July 11, 2008, p. B2; Peter Moreira, "Irving Oil Looks to Make Waves With Tidal Power," *The Globe and Mail*, May 27, 2008, p. B7; Rebecca Smith, "New Wave of Nuclear Plants Faces High Costs," *The Wall Street Journal*, May 12, 2008, p. B1; Patrick Barta, "In Australia, a Wind-Powered Plant Makes Water from Ocean Fit to Drink," *The Wall Street Journal*, March 11, 2008, p. A1; Lauren Etter, "Ethanol Craze Cools As Doubts Multiply," *The Wall Street Journal*, November 28, 2007, p. A1; Patrick Barta, "Jatropha Plant Gains Steam in Global Race for Biofuels," *The Wall Street Journal*, August 24, 2007, p. A1; Patrick Barta and Jane Spencer, "As Alternative fuels Heat Up, Environmental Concerns Grow," *The Wall Street Journal*, December 5, 2006, p. A1; Richard Blackwell, "In Ontario and Alberta, How Much Wind Power is too Much?" *The Globe and Mail*, October 30, 2006 p. B1.

Managing in Turbulent Times Stephanie Nolan, "How the World's Cheapest Car Became India's Biggest Flop," *The Globe and Mail*, November 9, 2011, p. B1; Alex Nunez, "What $2500 Buys in India: Tata Nano Unveiled," *Autoblog*, January 10, 2008, www.autoblog.com/2008/01/10/what-2-500-buys-in-india-tata-nano-unveiled/4; Marcus Gee, "Game Changer," *The Globe and Mail*, April 11, 2008, B1.

Concluding Case 11-1 Greg Keenan, "GM to Slash Oshawa Line, Move Production to Tennessee," *The Globe and Mail*, June 2, 2012, B4; Greg Keenan, "Stage Set for Standoff with Unions, Auto Makers," *The Globe and Mail*, April 17, 2012, B1; Barrie McKenna, "Manufacturing Hard Hit, But It's Nowhere Near Dead," *The Globe and Mail*, March 19, 2012, B1; Gordon Pitts, "In Alberta, Oil Sands Fuel a Factory Boom," *The Globe and Mail*, March 6, 2012, B1; Greg Keenan, "Ten Years of High Loonie Takes Big Toll on Country's Factories," *The Globe and Mail*, March 2, 2012, B1; Greg Keenan, "Indiana Beckons Factories Squeezed by Higher Costs," *The Globe and Mail*, February 16, 2012, B1; Tavia Grant and Greg Keenan, "Factory Employment Hits a 35-Year Low as More Plants Close," *The Globe and Mail*, November 5, 2011, B1; Jacquie McNish, "Maple Leaf's Big Move," *The Globe and Mail*, October 20, 2011, B1; Kevin Carmichael, "From a Burst Bubble, a New Brand of Manufacturing Emerges in Ottawa," *The Globe and Mail*, June 11, 2011, B11.

Concluding Case 11-2 www.airtravel.about.com/od/basedinnorthamerica/top.top10na.htm [accessed July 10, 2012]; www.airtravel.about.com/od/airlines/tp/skytraxbest10.htm [accessed July 10, 2012]; Scott McCartney, "Ranking Airlines by Lost Bags, Canceled Flights," *The Wall Street Journal*, January 5, 2012, D3; Karen Howlett, "Ontario Launches Review of Travel Industry Watchdog Due to Conquest's Demise," *The Globe and Mail*, April 22, 2009; Keith Leslie, "Other Tour Operators 'Likely' Face Financial Problems: McGuinty," *The Globe and Mail*, April 21, 2009.

Chapter 12

Canada Goose: High Quality Outerwear www.canada-goose.com; Allison Jones, "Rival's Logo ruffles Canada Goose Feathers," *The Globe and Mail*, February 23, 2012, B9; http://business.financialpost.com/2011/11/24/dani-reiss-of-canada-goose-named-canadian-entrepreneur-of-the-year.

E-Business + Social Media Solutions "Be Open (Source)," *The Globe and Mail Report on Business*, November 2009, 62; Ian Harvey, "Outside Box, a Better Box," *Backbone*, January 2010, 11; Local Motors website, www.local-motors.com/about/mission, accessed January 2, 2011.

The Greening of Business Evan Ramstead, "Steelmakers Develop New Iron Recipes," *The Wall Street Journal*, August 29, 2008, B1; Kanako Tanaka, "Assessment of Energy Efficiency Performance Measures in Industry and Their Application for Policy," *Energy Policy*, 36, no. 8 (2008): 2877; POSCO Management Innovation for Customer Satisfaction, *Business Korea*, November 2001; "Tempering Profits with Green Logic," *Businessline*, June 25, 1998, 1.

E-Business + Social Media Solutions www.frabertsfreshfood.com.

Managing in Turbulent Times Noel Randewich, "Sales Hit Hard by Shortage of Hard Drives, Intel Says; Thai Flood Effect," *National Post*, December 13, 2011, p. FP11; "Honda Plants to return to Normal Levels Dec. 1," *National Post*, November 29, 2011, p. FP6; "Toyota Is Paralyzed by Thai Floods; Assembly Lines Halt," *National Post*, November 7, 2011, p. FP2; Scott Deveau, "Thailand Floods Hit Alliston Honda Plant; Parts Shortage," *National Post*, November 1, 2011, p. FP5; Barrie McKenna, "Supply Chain Disruptions from Japan Easing," *The Globe and Mail*, June 2, 2011, B6; Scott Deveau, "Toyota Could Fall to No. 3 in Sales; Earnings 77%," *National Post*, May 12, 2011, p. FP1; Greg Keenan, "Toyota Slashes Sales Outlook," *The Globe and Mail*, May 6, 2011, p. B1; Timothy Aeppel, "For Lean Factories, No Buffer," *The Wall Street Journal*, April 29, 2011, p. B1; Anita Elash, "Plant Shutdown Sends Small Production Firms Scrambling," *The Globe and Mail*, April 27, 2011, P. B7; "Ford to Idle Plants in Taiwan, China and South Africa in Wake of Parts Shortage," *National Post*, April 26,2011, p. FP3; Greg Keenan, "Toyota Extends Shutdowns at Plants in Canada, U.S.," *The Globe and Mail*, April 20, 2011, p. B3; James Hookway and Aries Poon, "Crisis Tests Supply Chain's Weak Links," *The Wall Street Journal*, March 18, 2011, p. A8; James

Hookway and Wilawan Watcharasakwet, "Worries Rise Over Disrupted Supplies," *The Wall Street Journal*, March 17, 2011, p. A15; Omar El Akkad and Iain Marlow, "Global Tech Supply Chain to Face Shortages, Delays," *The Globe and Mail*, March 16, 2011, p. B6.

Concluding Case 12-1 "2012 Vehicle Dependability Study," www.autos.jdpower.com [accessed June 22, 2012]; "2012 Initial Quality Study," www.autos.jdpower.com [accessed June 22, 2012]; Richard Russell, "An Inconvenient Truth," *The Globe and Mail*, July 22, 2011, D18; "U.S. Investigation of Toyota Finds No Electronic Flaws, Report Says," *National Post*, February 9, 2011, FP3; Chester Dawson and Hoshio Takahashi, "Toyota Set Push To Avoid Recalls," *The Wall Street Journal*, February 24, 2011, B1; Alexis Leondis, "Honda, Ford LeAP Over Toyota in U.S. Customer Loyalty Rankings," *National Post*, May 14, 2010, FP4; Greg Keenan and John Gray, "Toyota Faces Class-Action Suits," *Business News Network*, www.bnn.ca/news/15452.html [accessed February 1, 2010]; Greg Keenan, "Toyota Executives Plan Media Blitz," *The Globe and Mail*, February 1, 2010, B1; Greg Keenan, "Toyota Scrambles for Remedy as Recall Grows," *The Globe and Mail*, January 30, 2010, B3; Paul Vieira, "Toyota Finds a Fix; Pedal Maker Speeds Up Output as Recall Grows," *National Post*, January 29, 2010, FP1; Greg Keenan, "As Toyota Stumbles, Rivals Eye Gains," *The Globe and Mail*, January 29, 2010, B1; Greg Keenan, "Toyota Suspending Sales of Models Involved in Recall," *Globe and Mail*, January 27, 2010, B12; "Toyota Retains Quality Crown Over Ford, GM," *National Post*, June 23, 2009, FP12; John Lippert, Alan Ohnsman, and Kae Inoue, "Is Toyota the New GM? Founder's Grandson Thinks So," *The Globe and Mail*, June 23, 2009, B15.

Concluding Case 12-2 "U.S. Investigation of Toyota Finds No Electronic Flaws, Report Says," National Post, Feburary 9, 2011, p. FP3; Jamie Sturgeon, "Toyota Moves Fast on Recall," *National Post*, August 27, 2010, p. FP1; Rita Trichur and Tim Kiladze, "The Auto Shockwave," The Globe and Mail, March 16, 2011, p. B1 (Same); "Toyota is Paralyzed by Thai Floods," *National Post*, November 7, 2011, p. FP2. (supply chains); Greg Keenan, "Honda, Toyota Extend Production Cuts," The Globe and Mail, April 9, 2011, p. B8. (Same); Greg Keenan, "Toyota Extends Shutdowns at Plants in Canada, U.S.," The Globe and Mail, April 20, 2011, p. B3. (Same); "Ford to Idle Plants in Taiwan, China and South Africa in Wake of Parts Shortage," National Post, April 26, 2011, p. FP3.

Chapter 13

Skype: The Game Changer? "Is Skype a Game-Changer for Microsoft?" *The Washington Post*, May 14, 2011; www.nojitter.com/blog/229403109/microsoft-buys-skype-game-changer-or-hail-mary; http://www.brandchannel.com/home/post/2011/06/14/Skype-Video-Calling-on-TV-a-Game-Changer-for-Comcast.aspx; http://vicbrand.com/detail/microsofts+skype+deal+could+be+a+game+changer+for+mobile+say+agencies/4116.html; http://www.microsoft.com/en-us/news/press/2011/may11/05-10corpnewspr.aspx;

http://blogs.computerworld.com/20146/why_skype_might_help_not_hurt_windows_phone_and_nokia_with_carriers; http://channelnomics.com/2012/05/07/skype-stunting-microsoft-nokia-turnaround.

Table 13.1 http://www.branham300.com/index.php?year=2011&listing=1.

Managing in Turbulent Times Jameson Berkow, "Online Traffic Shifts from PCs; 60% Handled by Other Devices, Study Shows," *National Post*, October 27, 2011, FP12; Omar El Akkad, "Tablets Leading Charge into 'Post-PC' Age," *The Globe and Mail*, March 7, 2011, p. B5; Mike Malone and Tom Hayes, "Bye-Bye, PCs and Laptops," *The Wall Street Journal*, January 7, 2011, A13; Matt Hartley, "The End of the PC as We Know It," *National Post*, January 19, 2011, p. FP5; Joe Castaldo, "Death of the PC," *Canadian Business*, October 25, 2010, p. 44;

E-Business + Social Media Solutions Quentin Casey, "Measure of Success," *National Post*, April 4, 2011, p. FP1; Julie Jargon, Emily Steel, and Joann S. Lublin, "Taco Bell Makes Spicy Retort to Suit," *The Wall Street Journal*, January 31, 2011, p. B5; Steve Cunningham, "Social Media Will Transform Businesses into Learning Organizations," *National Post*, September 28, 2010, p. FE7; Jordan Timm, "Branding by the Masses," *Canadian Business*, April 27–May 10, 2010, p. 34.

Concluding Case 13-1 Jameson Berkow, "Lock Your Online Doors," *National Post*, January 19, 2012, FP12; Suzanne Kapner, "Adding Weapons for ATM Defenses," *The Wall Street Journal*, January 26, 2012, C1; Jameson Berkow, "The Next Target for Hackers: Your Car," *National Post*, December 28, 2011, FP1; Jameson Berkow, "Canadian Business Unprepared for Hackers," *National Post*, November 16, 2011, FP4; Jameson Berkow, "Cybercrime Cost US$388B in 2010: Report," *National Post*, September 8, 2011, FP14; Mat Hartley, "Breach Rattles Watchdogs; Sony's Privacy Policies Queried in Wake of Attack," *National Post*, April 28, 2011, FP1.

Concluding Case 13-2 Rita Trichur, "BCE Appealing CRTC Decision," *The Globe and Mail*, March 3, 2012, B10; Iain Marlow, "CRTC Unveils Compromise for Usage-Based Billing," *The Globe and Mail*, November 16, 2011, B3; Iain Marlow, "Activist Group, CRTC Panelists Spar at Web-Usage Hearing," *The Globe and Mail*, July 12, 2011; Iain Marlow, "BCE Put on Hot Seat at Hearing On Web Pricing," *The Globe and Mail*, July 12, 2011, B1; Steve Anderson, "Stop the Meter," *National Post*, March 29, 2011, FP15; Iain Marlow, "BCE Backtracks After Pressure Over Internet Usage Billing Plan," *The Globe and Mail*, March 29, 2011, B1; Mirko Bibic, "Pay for Usage; Busting the Myths Around Internet Prices," *National Post*, February 4, 2011, FP11; Terence Corcoran, "The 25-Gigabyte Internet Myth," *National Post*, February 3, 2011, FP11; Richard French, "Second-Guessing the CRTC Comes at a Price," *The Globe and Mail*, February 2, 2011, A17.

Chapter 14

Untangling An Accounting Mess at Bankrupt Nortel Janet McFarland, "Claims of Fraud 'Preposterous,'" *The Globe and Mail*,

January 20, 2012, B1; "Nortel Timeline: March 2004 to March 2006," *National Post*, January 14, 2012, FP5; "Nortel Timeline: April 2006 to January 2012," *National Post*, January 14, 2012, FP6; Theresa Tedesco, "Nortel Ghost Still Haunts Nation," *National Post*, January 14, 2012, FP4; Jamie Sturgeon, "Crown, Defence Square Off; Former CEO Dunn Accused of Fraud," *National Post*, January 13, 2012, FP1.

Table 14.1 http://www.thebottomlinenews.ca/documents/Canadas_Accounting_Top_30.pdf.

The Greening of Business Ken Garen, "Are You Ready to Prosper?" *The Practical Accountant*, June 2008, SR29; Jeff Sanford, "The Next Pension Crisis," *Canadian Business Journal*, 80, 14 (August 2007) 62–63; Dom Serafini, "Regulations Are the Consumers' Best Friends," *Intermedia*, July 2004, 32, 2, ABI/INFORM Global database, 23.

Concluding Case 14-1 Janet McFarland, "CGAs Abandon Merger Talks," *The Globe and Mail*, May 29, 2012, B4; Jeff Gray, "Canada's Bean Counters Get into a Brouhaha," *The Globe and Mail*, February 25, 2012, B4; Matthew McClearn, "The Settling of Accounts," *Canadian Business*, February 20, 2012, 62; Janet McFarland, "Accountants Mull New Designation," *The Globe and Mail*, October 29, 2011, B10; Matthew McClearn, "Canadian Accountants Attempt Merger, Confusion Ensues," January 19, 2012, http://cpacanada.ca/key-developments.

Concluding Case 14-2 Michael Rapoport, "U.S. Nears Accounting Shift," *The Wall Street Journal*, February 21, 2012, C3; Marjo Johne, "How Miners Met the Accounting Challenge," *The Globe and Mail*, January 19, 2012, B13; David Milstead, "Global Accounting Rules? Don't Tread on me, U.S. Says," *The Globe and Mail*, August 4, 2011, p. B11; Sunil Mistry, "Decide Your Accounting Framework; Options are Private Enterprise GAAP or IFRS," *National Post*, April 18, 2011, FP7; Joe Castaldo, "Accounting for Trouble?" *Canadian Business*, January 19–February 14, 2011, 15; Simon Avery, "New Accounting Standards Bring Warnings," *The Globe and Mail*, January 21, 2011, p. B11; Drew Hasselback, "We See the Problems, IFRS Chair Tells Insurers; New Rules Coming," *National Post*, November 24, 2010, FP2.

Chapter 15

Lululemon: A Clear Marketing Strategy, Even in Trying Times "Lululemon Shares Fall as Prospects Disappoint," CBC News, June 2, 2012; Marina Strauss, "Lululemon Stretches to Balance Expansion Against Profit," *The Globe and Mail*, June 7, 2012; "Lululemon to Open 25 New Stores by June as Profits Nearly Triple," *Canadian Business*, March 25, 2010; Marina Strauss, "Lululemon Rides out Recession in Quality Fashion," *The Globe and Mail*, March 29, 2010, B1; Marina Strauss, "Lululemon Ramps up Plans to Hit the Net," *The Globe and Mail*, March 27, 2009, B8; lululemon website, www.lululemon.com [accessed April 22, 2010]; Sunny Freeman, "Lululemon Targeting 45 Markets for Showroom Openings to Create Brand Buzz," *Canadian Business*, March 25, 2010; Sunny Freeman, "Ask the Legends: Chip Wilson," *Profit*, March 2010; *Canadian*

Business website [accessed April 22, 2010]; Marina Strauss, "New Mantra Pays Off for Lululemon," *The Globe and Mail*, December 10, 2009, B2; Marina Strauss, "Lululemon's Plan for Lean Times," *The Globe and Mail*, March 28, 2009, B3; Aili McConnon, "Lululemon's Next Workout," *Businessweek*, June 9, 2008, 42; Jennifer Wells, "Now Is Her Chance to Stretch," *The Globe and Mail*, April 3, 2008, B1; John Partridge, "Lululemon Shops for New Retailing Head at Starbucks," *The Globe and Mail*, January 5, 2008, B8; Paul Waldie and Marina Strauss, "Lululemon Supplier Navigates Rocky Shoals," *The Globe and Mail*, November 16, 2007, B3; http://investor.lululemon.com/releasedetail.cfm?ReleaseID=658839.

E-Business + Social Media Solutions David Berman, "Apple Girding for Big iPhone Sales," *The Globe and Mail*, September 8, 2011; John Lorinc, "The Age of the App," *The Globe and Mail Report on Business*, April 2010, 47–50; Peter Burrows, "Apps Trump Tunes at Apple," *Businessweek*, September 28, 2009, 34; Jim Harris, "Talking about a Revolution," *Backbone*, December 2008, 10; Brian X. Chen, Wired website, "Coder's Half-Million-Dollar Baby Proves iPhone Gold Rush Is Still On," www.wired.com/gadgetlab/2009/02/shoot-is-iphone [accessed April 22, 2010]; Matt Asay, CNET News website, "Apple Channels Google, Microsoft to Attract Developers," http://news.cnet.com/8301-13505_3-20003211-16.html [accessed April 22, 2010]; Omar El Akkad, "Apple Rides iPhone, Mac to Record Profit," *The Globe and Mail*, January 26, 2010, B1, B6; Chris Vandergaag, "The App Appeal," *Nuvo Magazine*, September, 2011, P 50; Peter Burrows, "How Apple Feeds its Army of App Makers," *Bloomberg Businessweek*, July 11, 2011, 39.

The Greening of Business "Coke Improves Green Credentials by Making Bottles from Plant-Based Plastics," *The Globe and Mail*, December 16, 2011, B7; Robert Matas, "B.C. Forecasts Boom Market for Clean-Energy Vehicles," *The Globe and Mail*, November 17, 2011, S3; Leslie Guevarra, "How Con-Way Delivers Greener Trucking; Sustainability," *National Post*, September 13, 2011, p. FP7; Richard Russell, "Rolling in the Green," *The Globe and Mail*, August 12, 2011, D20; "Ford Management Looks to Green Technology to Give Brand a Market Edge," *National Post*, June 14, 2011, p. FP9; Brent Jang, "CN Touts the Green Advantage of Rail Shipments," *The Globe and Mail*, April 28, 2011, p. B3; "PepsiCo to Begin Testing New Plant-Based Bottle Next Year," *National Post*, March 16, 2011, p. FP6; Bertrand Marotte, "A Green Twist on a Private Comfort," *The Globe and Mail*, March 4, 2011, p. B5.

Managing in Turbulent Times Patricia Lovett-Reid, "Boomers a Booming Investment; Industries for Aging Population Poised to Benefit," *National Post*, September 10, 2011, p. FP10; Gerry Marr, "Aging Boomers to Fuel Housing Needs by 2030; Study finds 80% of Demand to Arise from Seniors," *National Post*, September 9, 2011, p. FP3; Michael Dolan, "Baby Boomer Fears Cast Pall over Markets; Fewer Investors; Aging Population an Ominous Sign for Stocks," *National Post*, September 8, 2011, p. FP8; Ellen Byron, "How to Market to an Aging Boomer: Flattery, Subterfuge and Euphemism," *The Wall Street Journal*, February 5–6, 2011, p. A1.

Entrepreneurship and New Ventures www.modcloth.com/about_us.

Concluding Case 15-1 http://www.reuters.com/article/2011/01/13/us-target-canada-idUSTRE70C36E20110113 http://www.bizjournals.com/twincities/news/2011/01/13/target-entering-canada-paying-18b.html Colliers International, prepared by: Smerdon, James; Bell, David. (2011). The Retail Report Canada, Spring 2011 Edition.

Concluding Case 15-2 Batman Film Series (May 23, 2008), en.wikipedia.org/wiki/Batman_%28film_series%29; Claude Brodesser-Akner, "Hyping Joker-Without Exploiting Heath's Death," *Advertising Age*, May 12, 2008, adage.com/article.php?article_id=126981; Chungaiz, "New Batman Dark Knight Marketing Continues, Fantastic!" December 13, 2007, www.altogetherdigital.com/20071213/new-batman-dark-knight-marketing-continues-fantastic; Chris Lee, "The Dark Knight marketing blitz" March 24, 2008, articles.latimes.com/2008/mar/24/entertainment/et-batmanviral24. See also batman.wiki-bruce.com/Timeline; www.42entertainment.com; whysoserious.com.

Chapter 16

New Product Development Strategies & the Importance of Brand Equity Marc Hacking, "When Competitors Team Up," *The Globe and Mail*, January 24, 2012, B11; Ian Sherr, "Auto Makers Debut 'Intelligent' Car Systems," *The Globe and Mail*, January 13, 2012, B8; Magna Innternational Website, Vehicle Content, www.magna.com/about-magna/our-customers/vehicle-content [accessed April 28th, 2012]; Courtland Bovee, John Thill and George Dracopoulos, "Magna International," *Business in Action*, Pearson Education, 2009, p228.

Managing in Turbulent Times "Playing the Patent Game," BNN, www.bnn.ca/News/2011/7/27; Omar El Akkad, "The New Standard in Patent Law: i4i," *The Globe and Mail*, June 10, 2011, B1; "Microsoft Loses U.S. Top Court Case on Patent," *Business News Network*, www.bnn.ca/News/2011/6/9 [accessed June 9, 2011]; Omar El Akkad, "Microsoft, i4i Head to Top Court for Final Round in Legal Battle," *The Globe and Mail*, April 18, 2011, p. B1; Jameson Berkow, "Washington Backs i4i Against Microsoft; Patent Win Would Be Worth Hundreds of Millions," *National Post*, March 22, 2011, p. FP2; Jamie Sturgeon, "Wi-Lan Patent Case: Three Down, 15 to Go; Company Could Earn $600M in Settlements," *National Post*, January 21, 2011, p. FP5; Nathan Vanderklippe, "Patent Pending," *The Globe and Mail*, January 8, 2010, p. B4; Paul Waldie, "Dropping the Gloves Over a Hockey Bag," *The Globe and Mail*, December 16, 2010, p. B3.

The Greening of Business Jodi Lai, "Good Vibrations; Helping Clients Promote Social Change Allowed This Vancouver-Based Ad Agency to Succeed in a Down Economy," *National Post*, August 9, 2011, FP8; Mark Hume, "It All Depends on Which Way the Wind Blows," *The Globe and Mail*, July 26, 2011, S3; The Greening of Business: Promoting a Green Business Image Simon Haupt, "The Green GAP Is Wide Open: Survey Results Show That Canadian Companies Leave Public Perception Wanting," *The Globe and Mail*, June 1, 2010, B2; Hollie Shaw,

"Making the Case that Wearing Fur Can Be Eco-Friendly," *Winnipeg Free Press*, December 5, 2008, B6; Daryl-Lynn Carlson, "Advertising Guidelines Target 'Greenwashing,'" *Winnipeg Free Press*, November 21, 2008, B6; Marina Strauss, "Standing Out in a Sea of Green," *The Globe and Mail*, August 16, 2008, B3; Carly Weeks, "New Scrutiny for Green Claims," *The Globe and Mail*, March 11, 2008, B1, B6;

Table 16.1 *Financial Post Magazine*, June 2012, p. 88.

E-Business + Social Media Solutions Simon Houpt, "It's All Fun and Games—Until Someone Bonds with a Brand," *The Globe and Mail*, January 7, 2011, p. B1; Donna Hoffman and Marek Fodor, "Measuring ROI of Social Media Marketing; It Requires New Measurements That Begin with Tracking Customers' Investments," *National Post*, November 23, 2010, p. FP11; Jordan Timm, "Jerry Bears, Doobage and the Invention of Social Networking," *Canadian Business*, September 13, 2010, p. 74; Jordan Timm, "Amber Mac's New Rules of Engagement," *Canadian Business*, September 13, 2010, p. 55; "Social Media," http://en.wikipedia.org/wiki/Social_Media [accessed on April 27, 2011]; Lyndsie Bourgon, "Reaping Social Media Rewards," *Canadian Business*, July 20–August 16, 2010, p. 19.

Concluding Case 16-1 Susan Krashinsky, "In the War for Healthy Eating, Greek Yogurt Takes Palates by Storm," *The Globe and Mail*, March 16th, 2012, B5; Chris Nuttall-Smith, "Greek Yogurt Put to the Taste Test," *The Globe and Mail*, March 20, 2012; Leslie Beck, "Greek Yogurt Is All the Rage- But is it Good for Me?" *The Globe and Mail*, August 3 2011; Terence Corcoran, "Canada's Big Fat Chobani Greek Yogurt Drama," *Financial Post*, April 2, 2012; Dominique Vidalon and Noelle Mennella, "Danone Plays Catch-Up In Greek Yogurt Race," *The Edmonton Journal*, April 7, 2012.

Concluding Case 16-2 Harnessing the Power of Word-of-Mouth Advertising; VocalPoint website, www.vocalpoint.com//about.html [accessed April 29, 2012]; Jeff Kroeker, "Power of Digital Word of Mouth 'a gift' to Startup," *The Globe and Mail*, March 23, 2012, B3; Hollie Shaw, "Reaching Out via Web; Marketers Look for Creative Ways to Draw in Consumers," *National Post*, November 7, 2008, FP14; Nick Turner, "Cupcake Business Reaps Sweet Rewards; Location and Word of Mouth Key to Success," *National Post*, October 27, 2008, FP9; Sam Cage, "Word of Mouth Sells 'Remembrance' Gems," *National Post*, September 15, 2008; Sinclair Stewart, "Hey, Did You Hear about That Great New Toothpaste?" *The Globe and Mail*, November 20, 2007, B3; Erin White, "Word of Mouth Makes Nike Slip-On Sneakers Take Off," *The Globe and Mail*, June 7, 2001, B1, B4; Mike Blaney, "Word of Mouth Advertising," blog, www.themarketingguy.wordpress.com/2007/10/09/word-of-mouth-advertising; www.theinfluencers.ca/why_wom.php.

Chapter 17

Price-Conscious Consumers Marina Strauss, "Price Gap: Retailers, Suppliers Duck Blame," *The Globe and Mail*, September 8, 2011, B1; Jonathan Hutchison, "Price of Jersey Sets N.Z. Rugby Fans Against Adidas," *National Post*,

August 26, 2011, p. FP12; Marina Strauss, "J. Crew 'Fixing' Canadian Web Pricing," *The Globe and Mail*, August 25, 2011, p. B3; Marina Strauss, "J. Crew's Fashion-Pricing Faux Pas," *The Globe and Mail*, August 22, 2011, p. B1; Scott McCartney, "Whatever You Do, Don't Buy An Airline Ticket On …." *The Wall Street Journal*, January 27, 2011, p. D1; Paul Hunt, "Need a Pricing Strategy? Fire a Customer; Focus on Accounts that will Fuel Profitability," *National Post*, December 7, 2010, p. FP14; Paul Hunt, "Why Walmart Shoppers are Price Insensitive," *National Post*, November 9, 2010, p. FP8; Brent Jang, "An Ominous Flight Pattern," *The Globe and Mail*, November 27, 2010, p. B6; Alexandra Lopez-Pacheco, "Welcome the New Consumer; As More Consumers Embrace Mobile Technologies, Demands on Retailers Will Grow," *National Post*, September 21, 2010, p. FP10; Stuart Elliott, "Pizza by the Price: Pizza Hut Launches Two-Pronged Promotion in the U.S., Focusing Chiefly on Price Cuts and Stressing Consumer Loyalty," *National Post*, August 20, 2010, p. FP12; Marina Strauss, "Stores Aim to Convert 'Cherry Pickers,'" *The Globe and Mail*, November 19, 2008, p. B11; David Hutton, "Consumers Get Less Bang for Their Buck," *The Globe and Mail*, July 8, 2008, p. B2; Ann Zimmerman, "Behind the Dollar-Store Boom: A Nation of Bargain Hunters," *The Wall Street Journal*, December 13, 2004, pp. A1, A10; Timothy Aeppel, "After Cost Cutting, Companies Turn Toward Price Increases," *The Wall Street Journal*, September 18, 2002, A1, A12.

Managing in Turbulent Times Timothy Martin and Lauren Pollock, "American Ordered to Return to Orbitz," *The Wall Street Journal*, June 2, 2011, B1; "The Airlines Discover 'Content,'" *The Wall Street Journal*, January 21, 2011, p. A11; Mike Esterl, "Dogfight Erupts in Plane Ticket Sales," *The Wall Street Journal*, January 6, 2011, pp. A1, A14.

Table 17.1 *Financial Post Magazine*, June 2012, p. 85.

Entrepreneurship and New Ventures www.owfg.com; jimpattison.com/food/overwaitea-food-group.aspx.

E-Business + Social Media Solutions Marina Strauss and Omar El Akkad, "A Handheld Way Retailers Are Fighting Online Store Wars," *The Globe and Mail*, December 20, 2011, B1, B6; Marina Strauss, "Walmart's Endless Aisle Comes to a Computer Near You," *The Globe and Mail*, December 5, 2011, B1,B6; Matthew Boyle, "Walmart's Rocky Path From Bricks to Clicks," *Bloomberg Businessweek*, July 25, 2011, 30–32; "Turning to the Web or an Endless Aisle," *The Globe and Mail*, February 13, 2010, B3; "P&G Jumping into Online Retail with New Test Site," *The Globe and Mail*, January 15, 2010, B6; Geoffrey A. Fowler, "Amazon Aims to Become More than Books," *The Globe and Mail*, September 18, 2009, B9; Heather Green, "Amazon Aims to Keep You Clicking," *Businessweek*, March 2, 2009, 34.

The Greening of Business Shawn McCarthy, "New Keystone Route Skirts No-Go Zones," *The Globe and Mail*, April 20, 2012, B3; Lee-Anne Goodman, "Celebs Join Pipeline Battle," *Winnipeg Free Press*, November 7, 2011, p. A14; Tom Ford, "U.S. Environmental Politics Threaten Our

Prosperity," *Winnipeg Free Press*, November 7, 2011, p. A13; Shawn McCarthy, "State Department E-Mails Trigger Allegations of Bias," *The Globe and Mail*, September 23, 2011, p. B9; "Activists Plan 'Civil Disobedience' in Ottawa to Protest Keystone XL Pipeline," *National Post*, August 26, 2011, p. FP5; Sheldon Alberts, "Aftermath of a Spill; Enbridge Cleanup Grades Well, but Pipeline Fears Remain," *National Post*, July 23, 2011, p. FP3; Peter Foster, "Franken Pipeline," *National Post*, June 17, 2011, p. FP11; Nathan VanderKlippe, "Aging Pipes," *The Globe and Mail*, February 19, 2011, p. B6.

Table 17.2 *Financial Post Magazine*, June 2012, p. 90.

Concluding Case 17-1 Steve Ladurantaye, "Upstart Property Website Pries Open Industry Data Valut," *The Globe and Mail*, October 26, 2011, p. B1; Steve Ladurantaye, "Realtor Group Set to Open Online Trove of Real Estate Information," *The Globe and Mail*, July 21, 2011, B1; Sunny Freeman, "Real Estate Board Resists Mandated Fair-Competition Rules," *Winnipeg Free Press*, July 9, 2011, B9; Garry Marr, "New Toronto Real Estate Board Policy Will Let Consumers Browse MLS Data," *National Post*, June 25, 2011, FP17; Steve Ladurantaye, "Real Estate Industry, Competition Bureau Lock Horns Again," *The Globe and Mail*, May 28, 2011, B1; Steve Ladurantaye, "Competition Bureau Asked to Settle New Fight Over MLS Listings," *The Globe and Mail*, May 2, 2011, p. B1; Grant Robinson and Tara Perkins, "What Your Broker Doesn't Want You To Know," *The Globe and Mail*, December 22, 2010, p. B4; Michael McCullough, "Estate Sale," *Canadian Business*, November 9–22, 2010, p. 55; Peter Foster, CREA Cartel Not Broken Yet," *National Post*, October 26, 2010, p. FP11; Steve Ladurantaye, "The Deal That Ended a Year-Long Real Estate Battle," *The Globe and Mail*, October 26, 2010, p. B4; Jonathan Ratner, "New Deal May Alter Buying of Homes," *Winnipeg Free Press*, October 25, 2010, p. B6; Steve Ladurantaye, "Realtors Ratify Deal to Give Consumers Wider Choice on Services," *The Globe and Mail*, October 25, 2010, p. B4; "CREA Won Nothing in MLS Deal, Lawyer Says," *National Post*, October 19, 2010, p. FP6; Patricia Lovett-Reid, "Your Options in the Brave New Real Estate World; The Era of 5% Commissions May Soon Become a Distant Memory," *National Post*, October 16, 2010, p. FP10; Murray McNeill, "A Real Estate Revolution," *Winnipeg Free Press*, October 15, 2010, p. B6; Steve Ladurantaye, "Do-It-Yourselfers Are Shaking Up An Industry; Real Estate Agents Are Fighting Back," *The Globe and Mail*, May 20, 2010, p. B1; "How An Epic Battle Began," *National Post*, May 1, 2010, p. FP1; "Plans Shake Pillars of Real Estate; Proposals from Both Sides Would Overhaul Industry," *National Post*, February 12, 2010, p. FP1; Steve Ladurantaye, "The Battle to Unlock the Housing Market," *The Globe and Mail*, January 30, 2010, p. B1.

Concluding Case 17-2 Ben Sisario, "Spotify Arrives; New Online Music Service is Free—and Completely Legal," *National Post*, July 15, 2011, FP3; "Tiny Spanish Firm 24symbols Launches Digital Book-Reading and Sharing Site," *National Post*, July 5, 2011, FP13; Chris

Selley, "Post Offices: the New Vinyl Records," *National Post*, June 29, 2011, A16; Shawn Vuilliez, "On May 2, Vote for a Free Internet," *National Post*, April 16, 2011, A26; Stephen Baldwin, "How the Tables Have Turned; Internationla Record Store Day celebrates Music," *National Post*, April 15, 2011, PM9; Matt Hartley, "Music Alive and Well... Business Needs Work," *National Post*, March 31, 2011, FP12; Dave McGinn, "The Numbers Say..." *The Globe and Mail*, December 27, 2010, R11; "U.S. Court Fines Single Mother of Four $54,000 for Downloading Music," *National Post*, November 5, 2010, A16; L. Gordon Crovitz, "Phonograph, CD, MP3—What's Next?" *National Post*, November 23, 2010, A18; "Virgin-Universal World First; Unlimited Music Downloads by Subscription," *National Post*, July 16, 2009; Barrie McKenna, "The (Legal) Music Fades out for Canadians," *The Globe and Mail*, October 20, 2009, p. B14; "Woman Fined $1.92M in U.S. File Sharing Case; 'Kind of Ridiculous,'" *National Post*, June 20, 2009, A20; Matt Hartley, "From Pirate Bay, a Torpedo to Illegal File Sharing," *The Globe and Mail*, April 18, 2009, p. B3; Barry Hertz, "He's Been Downloading so Long, It Looks Like Up To Him," *National Post*, March 13, 2009, PM7; Grant Robertson, "Death Knell Sounds for CDs," *The Globe and Mail*, June 19, 2008, p. B3; Peter Shawn Taylor, "A Brief History of (c); Illegal MP3 File-Sharing? Pirate Movie Downloads? Contraband Cellphones? Mark Twain, Call Your Office," *National Post*, June 6, 2008, A17; Shawn McCarthy, "U.S. Court Shuts Door on Internet File-Sharing," *The Globe and Mail*, June 28, 2005, p. B3; Sarah McBride, "Stop the Music!" *The Wall Street Journal*, August 23, 2004, p. B1; Nick Wingfield, "The Day the Music Died," *The Wall Street Journal*, May 2, 2003, B8; Ted Birdis, "Music Industry Escalates Net Fight," *The Winnipeg Free Press*, June 26, 2003, A12; Anna Matthews and Charles Goldsmith, "Music Industry Faces New Threats on Web," *The Wall Street Journal*, February 21, 2003, B1, B4.

Chapter 18

Beware of the Credit Card Trap Roma Luciw, "Young and Prey to Debt," *The Globe and Mail*, November 8, 2011, L1; Rob Carrick, "Borrowing to Pay For Your Wedding," *The Globe and Mail*, May 1, 2012, B1; Canadian Bankers Association, www.cba.ca/en/media-room/50-backgrounders-on-banking-issues/467-fast-facts-the-canadian-banking-system [accessed May 27th, 2012]; Dianne Nice, "Credit Card Crackdown May Cost Consumers," *The Globe and Mail*, August 30, 2010, CBC website, "Card Costs: Who Pays What to Whom," Dec 17, 2010, www.cbc.ca/news/story/2009/04/16/f-cardfees.html [accessed May 27 2012].

E-Business and Social Media Solutions CRTC website, www.crtc.gc.ca/eng/publications/reports/rp1108.htm [accessed January 4th, 2011]; Michael Oliviera, "Canadians Slow to Join Mobile Web Browsing Trend," *The Globe and Mail*, December 14, 2011, B3; Tara Perkins and Ian Marlow, "Mobile Banking Makes Inroads," *The Globe and Mail*, February 8, 2010, B3; Rob Carrick, "Before You Hit 'Buy,'" *The Globe and Mail*, March 4, 2010, B7; Rob Carrick, "Ditching Your Adviser Has Never Been Easier," *The Globe and Mail*, August 27, 2009, B10; Valerie Bauman, "Video Game

Helps Students Score in Fiscal Skills," *The Globe and Mail*, December 14, 2009, B6; Lauren Young, "Big Banks Take a Hint from Mint.com," *Businessweek*, October 12, 2009, P62; Tara Perkins, "School's in and Banks Wake Up," *The Globe and Mail*, September 3, 2007, B3; Canadian Bankers Association website, www.cba.ca/en/media-room/50-backgrounders-on-banking-issues/125-technology-and-banking [accessed January 4, 2012].

Table 18.1 Financial Post Magazine, June 2012, p. 100.

Managing in Turbulent Times Terry Campbell, "Our Banks: Champions of Prudence," *National Post*, September 15, 2011, FP11; Konrad Yakabuski, "You May Love Canada's Banks Now, but ..." *The Globe and Mail*, April 30, 2009, B2; Janet Whitman, "Maybe Canadian Banks Are the New Swiss Watches: Stability Played up and Paying Off," *National Post*, April 4, 2009, FP4; Tara Perkins, "Why Canadian Banks Work," *The Globe and Mail*, March 7, 2009, B1; Theresa Tedesco, "The Great Solvent North," *The New York Times*, February 28, 2009, A19.

Table 18.2 Financial Post Magazine, June 2012, p. 104.

Concluding Case 18-1 Richard Blackwell and Grant Robertson, "Mortgage Wars May Prompt More People to Buy," *The Globe and Mail*, March 9, 2012, B3; Peter Shawn Taylor, "Mortgages for Free," *Canadian Business*, April 2, 2012, 28; Matthew McLearn, "Putting Out the Fire," *Canadian Business*, May 14, 2012, 38–42; Rob Carrick, "Ready to Be Bold? Sell the House and Rent," *The Globe and Mail*, May 1, 2012, B11; Rob Carrick, "Goodbye to Three Irritating Bank Practices," *The Globe and Mail*, March 6, 2012, B14; Richard Blackwell and Tara Perkins, "Mortgage Wars Combatants Losing Taste for Blood," *The Globe and Mail*, March 24, 2012, B1; Special Report, "The Housing Market Will Crash," *Canadian Business*, February 20, 2012, P 26–28.

Concluding Case 18-2 "Canada Penny Drops in Federal Budget as Jim Flaherty Signals End of One Cent Coin," *National Post*, March 30, 2012, http://news.nationalpost.com/2012/03/30/canada-penny-federal-budget-one-cent-coin [accessed May 27, 2012]; "SMEs Turn to Bartering, Saving Cash," *National Post*, January 5, 2009, FP8; Tom Hundley, "So Why Does the $1 Bill Still Exist?" *The Buffalo News*, July 20, 2008, D3; Yaroslav Trofimov, "Shrinking Dollar Meets Its Match in Dolphin Teeth," *The Wall Street Journal*, April 30, 2008, A1, A13; Roma Luciw, "Goodbye Penny, Hello $5 Coin?" *The Globe and Mail*, April 10, 2008, B5; Tara Perkins, "Lose the Loose Change? Bank Study Proposed Dropping Penny," *The Globe and Mail*, July 3, 2007, B3; "What Is Money?" Royal Canadian Mint website, www.mint.ca/store/dyn/PDFs/RCM_09AR_ENG_FA.pdf [accessed May 26, 2010]; Annual Report, P44, The British Museum, www.britishmuseum.org/explore/themes/money/what_is_money.aspx.

Chapter 19

Growing Up Social: Graduating to an IPO
Fabrice Taylor, "Facebook's Hidden Costs," *The Globe and Mail*, May 29, 2012, B9; Andrew Ackerman, "No Violations Found in Facebook IPO," *The Globe and Mail*, May 31, 2012, B8; Douglas MacMillan "How Mark Zuckerberg Jacked The Valley," *Canadian Business*, May 21–27, 2012,

61–67; "The Facebook Hype Meter," *Canadian Business*, June 11, 2012, 74; Lynn Cowan, "Groupon IPO Cheers Companies Waiting in the Wings," *The Globe and Mail*, November 5, 2011, B6; David Milstead, "As Groupon Shares Soar, it's Time to Discount the Frenzy," *The Globe and Mail*, November 8, 2011, B15; Fabrice Taylor, "Stop and Let it Pop," *Canadian Business*, June 2012, 20; Omar El Akkad and Paul Waldie, "Work Experience: LinkedIn Founder Net Worth: Billlions," *The Globe and Mail*, May 10, 2011, B1, B6; David Parkinson, "As As Facebook Falls Flat, LinkedIn Adds Friends," *The Globe and Mail*, May 30, 2012, B14.

Table 19.1 *Financial Post Magazine*, June 2012, p. 70.

E-Business + Social Media Solutions
Facilitating Financial Transactions: Protecting Electronic Funds Tara Perkins, "Trading (Slowly) Goes Mobile," *The Globe and Mail*, May 24, 2011, B17; Rob Carrick, "Have Your say on the Best Money Blogs," *The Globe and Mail*, May 3, 2011, B19; "Poll: How likely are you to conduct investing on a mobile device?" www.theglobeandmail.com/globe-investor/2011-online-broker-rankings/poll-how-likely-are-you-to-conduct-investing-on-a-mobile-device/article2236011 [accessed January 5, 2012]; Rob Carrick, Mathew Ingram, Howard Lindzon, Boyd Erman, David Berman, and Andrew Willis, "Best of Blogs," www.theglobeandmail.com/report-on-business/best-of-the-blogs/article683468/page2 [accessed January 5, 2012].

Table 19.3 *Financial Post Magazine*, June, 2009, 96. Material reprinted with the express permission of "The National Post Company," a Canwest Partnership.

The Greening of Business Peter Foster, "CAP and Tirade," *National Post*, February 16, 2011, FP13; Patricia Adams, "The Next Big Scam," *National Post*, January 13, 2010, FP15; Ronald Ebert and Ricky Griffin, "Green Trading," in *Business Essentials*, 7th ed. (Upper Saddle River, NJ: Prentice Hall, 2009), 227; Jeffrey Ball, "U.N. Effort to Curtail Emissions in Turmoil," *The Wall Street Journal*, April 12–13, 2008, A1, A5.

Managing in Turbulent Times Terence Corcoran, "Sino Kiss-Off Comes Too Late; Woes Take Down Forest of Global Reputations," *National Post*, June 22, 2011, FP1; Peter Koven, "Paulson Dumps Sino Stake; Shares Down 14.4% Before Hedge Fund's Sale Revealed," *National Post*, June 21, 2011, FP1; Peter Koven, "Block Questions Sino-Forest Documents; Shares Slip 4.5%; Did Related Firm Sell Sino-Forest Timber Rights?" *National Post*, June 18, 2011, FP4; Peter Koven and David Pett, "Sino Call Fails to Convince; Stock Plunges further 32% as CEO Tries to Explain Arcane Business Strategy," *National Post*, June 15, 2011, FP1; Jonathan Chevreau, "Investor ED Flags; Due Diligence is Critical, As Tale of Sino-Forest Shows," *National Post*, June 11, 2011, FP9; David Pett and John Shmuel, "Muddy Waters Research 'Craps'; Dundee Blasts Attacker of Sino-Forest," *National Post*, June 8, 2011, FP1; David Pett and John Shmuel, "Sino-Forest Falls 20.6% After Short Seller's Report; Muddy Waters," *National Post*, June 3, 2011, FP7.

Concluding Case 19-1 Stock Market Games and the Dark Side of Financial Advising-Sean Silcoff, "Victims of Fraudster Earl Jones Relieved by Settlement," *The Globe and Mail*,

March 7, 2012, B3; "Former Norbourg Execs Sentenced to Eight Years Each in Fraud Case," *The Globe and Mail*, September 3, 2011, B3; Ingrid Peritz, "Earl Jones Sentenced to 11 Years," *The Globe and Mail*, February 15, 2010, B1; Janet McFarland, "Former Agnico Executive Sentenced to Jail Time," *The Globe and Mail*, January 30, 2009, B3; Tara Perkins, "Former Trader Pleads Guilty in Fraud That Cost BMO $850 Million," *The Globe and Mail*, November 19, 2008, B1; Janet McFarland and Brent Jang, "Andrew Rankin: Barred from Trading Stocks, but Cleared of Criminal Charges," *The Globe and Mail*, February 22, 2008, B1, B4; Bertrand Marotte, "Mutual Fund Fraudster Gets 12 Years," *The Globe and Mail*, January 29, 2008, B1, B4; Richard Blackwell, "Firm, Ex-CEO Pay Millions in Penalties," *The Globe and Mail*, December 20, 2001, B1, B6; Richard Blackwell, "OSC Scores Trading Conviction," *The Globe and Mail*, July 22, 2000, B1–B2; Karen Howlett, Sinclair Stewart, and Paul Waldie, "Brokers Caught up in Police Probe," *The Globe and Mail*, June 20, 2003, B1, B20.

Concluding Case 19-2 Harvey Schachter, "Market Meltdown: The Buck Starts Here," *The Globe and Mail*, October 15, 2008, C2; Richard Blackwell, "From Subprime to Stock Swoon," *The Globe and Mail*, October 13, 2008, B3; "Wall Street's Rescue," *The Globe and Mail*, October 6, 2008, B4; "Contagion," Winnipeg Free Press, October 3, 2008, A15; "Investors Lost Billions, Large Banks and Brokerages Failed, Wall Street's Troubles Went Global," *The Globe and Mail*, October 1, 2008, B1; Kristine Owram, "Happy Days Here Again?," Winnipeg Free Press, September 20, 2008, B11; Justin Lahart, "The Crash of 2002," CNNMoney, July 19, 2002, ; "We All Got Burned, Now What?" CNNMoney, July 19, 2002, http://money.cnn.com; "Dow Plunges Below Its Post-Terrorist Attack Low," *USA Today*, July 19, 2002, www.usatoday.com.

Chapter 20

Hoarding Cash: Good or Bad Idea? Stephen
Fidler, "Firms' Cash Hoarding Stunts Europe," *The Wall Street Journal*, March 24–25, 2012, A10; David Parkinson, "The Myth of Canada's Cash Mountain," *The Globe and Mail*, March 24, 2012, B10; "U.S. Firms Hoarding Large Cash Stockpiles; $1.2T Saved After Bad Credit Crisis Memories," *National Post*, March 15, 2012, F6; Simon Avery, "Teck Keen to Put Its Cash to Work," *The Globe and Mail*, November 8, 2011, p. B16; Tim Kiladze, "Cash-Hoarding Firms Look Smart Now," *The Globe and Mail*, September 27, 2011, p. B15; Simon Avery, "Billions in the Vault, But Not Much Bang," *The Globe and Mail*, August 19, 2011, B10; Greg Keenan, "Fortress Balance Sheets' Breed a New Kind of Crisis," *The Globe and Mail*, August 10, 2011, p. B1; Paul Wiseman, "Strong Corporate Stats, Lingering U.S. Joblessness," Winnipeg Free Press, July 23, 2011, p. B16; David Parkinson, "Shareholders' Lament: Mountains of Cash, Miserly Payouts," *The Globe and Mail*, July 16, 2011, p. B15; Kevin Carmichael, "Caution Keeps Cash-Rich U.S. Employers from Hiring," *The Globe and Mail*, July 9, 2011, p. B1; Alan Reynolds, "The Myth of Corporate Cash Hoarding," *The Wall Street Journal*, February 23, 2011, p. A17.

Managing in Turbulent Times George Georgiopoulos, "Greece Dodges Debt Default as Bonds Swapped," *National Post*, March 9, 2012, FP1; Brian Blackstone, "ECB Sees No Losses on Athens Bond Buys," *The Wall Street Journal*, February 22, 2012, A9; Stephen Fidler, "Greece Gets a Stay, With Trouble on the Way," *The Wall Street Journal*, February 22, 2012, A8; Alkman Granitsas, Matina Stevis, and Nektaria Stamouli, "Greece Passes Sweeping Cuts," *The Wall Street Journal*, February 13, 2012, A1; Eric Reguly, "Time is Running Out for Greece," *The Globe and Mail*, February 7, 2012, B12; Grainne McCarthy and Gabriele Parussini, "IMF's Chief Warns on Debt Talks," *The Wall Street Journal*, January 26, 2012, A8; David Gauthier-Villars and Charles Forelle, "Europe Hit By Downgrades," *The Wall Street Journal*, January 14–15, 2012, A1; Tom Lauricella, Matt Wirz, and Alkman Granitsas, "Markets Bet on Greek Debt Deal," *The Wall Street Journal*, January 13, 2012, C1; Elena Becatoros, "Greek Bailout Vote Stuns World," *Winnipeg Free Press*, November 2, 2011, B5; "Analysis: Euro Zone Debt Deal Tackles Symptoms Not Cause," *BNN*, October 27, 2011, www.bnn.ca/News/2011/10/27; Tim Shufelt, "A Few Days Left to Solve Out-of-Reach Crisis; Analysis," *National Post*, October 22, 2011, p. FP5; Desmond Lachman, "When Greece Goes; Europe Must Firewall Spain, Italy before Athens Defaults," *National Post*, October 21, 2011, p. FP11; Kim Covert, "Postponement Talk Sparks Decline," *National Post*, October 21, 2011, p. FP8; Terence Corcoran, "Lessons from the Crisis," *National Post*, October 18, 2011, p. FP11; Madeline Chambers and Noah Barkin, "German Ire Sparks Talk of Greek Exit from EU; Ignores Targets," *National Post*, September 9, 2011, p. FP5; "Eurozone Leaders Grant Second Bailout to Greece," *Winnipeg Free Press*, July 22, 2011, p. B4; Eric Lascelles, "Bailouts Alone Won't Solve Euro Woes," *National Post*, May 7, 2011, p. FP19; Axel Bugge and Andrei Khalip, "Portugal Grabs for Financial Lifeline; Seeks EU Bailout," *National Post*, April 7, 2011, p. FP1.

Table 20.2 *Financial Post Magazine*, June 2012, p. 102.

Concluding Case 20-1 John Greenwood, "Court Approves $60M Payback in ABCP Ruling; Billions in Losses," *National Post*, March 14, 2012, FP2; John Greenwood, "Coventree To Pay $2.25M in Penalties; Fallout from ABCP Mess," *National Post*, November 10, 2011, FP2; Doug Alexander, "ABCP Holders to Get Back as Much as 81 Cents on Dollar; Nearly Double '09," *National Post*, May 21, 2011, FP4; Peter Koven, "Lessons of ABCP: Crisis Lost on Some Firms," *National Post*, September 1, 2010, FP6; Philip Ling, "$4.45 Billion Fund to Ensure ABCP Solution: Backstop in Place; Major Hurdle in Process Crossed, Purdy Says," *National Post*, December 27, 2008, p. FP4; Boyd Erman, "A Long, Tough Struggle Ends Finally, With a Deal," *The Globe and Mail*, December 26, 2008, p. B4; "Strategem Issues ABCP Warning," *The National Post*, www.nationalpost.com/story-printer.html?id=209530; John Greenwood, "Frustrated as Hell," *National Post*, October 21, 2008, www.nationalpost.com/story-printer.html?id=895020; Janet McFarland, Boyd Erman, Karen Howlett, and Tara Perkins, "Ordinary People, An Extraordinary Mess," *The Globe and Mail*, August 9, 2008, pp. B4–B6; David Friend,

"Investors in ABCP Approve Restructuring," *Winnipeg Free Press*, April 26, 2008, p. B13; Boyd Erman, "DBRS to Roll Out a New Road MAP on Risk," *The Globe and Mail*, February 8, 2008, pp. B1, B6; Gary Norris, "Financial Rescue Has Holes," *Winnipeg Free Press*, December 26, 2007, p.B17; Duncan Mavin, "Subprime Torpedoes CIBC," *Winnipeg Free Press*, December 7, 2007, p. B1; Matthew McClearn, "The Asset-Backed Commercial Paper Crunch has Burned Investors: Now Lawyer Purdy Crawford is Trying to Sort out the Mess," *Canadian Business*, November 5, 2007, pp. 130–139; Thomas Watson, "Issues of Trust," *Canadian Business*, November 5, 2007, pp. 141–147; Aaron Lucchetti and Kara Scannell, "Ratings Firms: A Dollar Short and Day Late?" *The Wall Street Journal*, September 26, 2007, pp. C1–C2; Karen Mazurkewich and John Greenwood, "Caisse Top ABCP Holder," *National Post*, September 18, 2007, pp. FP1, FP5; Peter Eavis, "Oh, the People You'll Blame," *Fortune*, September 17, 2007, pp. 118–124; John Greenwood, "Banks Left on Hook in Credit Market Freeze," *National Post*, September 15, 2007, p. FP7; John Greenwood and Duncan Mavin, "Credit Rout Far From Over," *National Post*, September 12, 2007, pp. FP1, FP13; Jeff Sanford "How This Happened," *Canadian Business*, September 10, 2007, pp. 87–88; Doug Alexander, "Banks Feel Heat of ABCP Meltdown," *National Post*, September 8, 2007, p. FP7; Tara Perkins, "Misguided, or Misunderstood?" *The Globe and Mail*, September 8, 2007, pp. B4–B5; John Greenwood, "ABCP Losses Could Hit 50%," *National Post*, September 5, 2007, pp. FP1, FP5; Kara Scannell and Deborah Solomon, "Unraveling the Subprime Mess," *The Wall Street Journal*, September 4, 2007, p. A6; "Mortgage Mayhem," *Fortune*, September 3, 2007, pp. 82–83; Jon Birger, "Markdown," *Fortune*, September 3, 2007, pp. 77–78; Shawn Tully, "Risk Returns with a Vengeance," *Fortune*, September 3, 2007, pp. 51–56; Boyd Erman, "Commercial Paper had Never Suffered for a Lack of Buyers and Sellers—Until Recent Liquidity Concerns Sent Investors Running for the Exits," *The Globe and Mail*, August 25, 2007, p. B2; John Greenwood, "Legal Actions Looming," *National Post*, August 24, 2007, pp. FP1, FP3; Barbara Shecter, "Greenspan's Rate Cuts Helped Create a Culture of Debt that Ignored Borders and was Ultimately Shunned as Too Risky," *National Post*, August 18, 2007, pp. FP1, FP4; Sean Silcoff, "Warnings were Issued Well Ahead of Crisis," *National Post*, August 18, 2007, pp. FP1, FP3; Andrew Willis and Boyd Erman, "Credit Crunch Claims Victim in Canada," *The Globe and Mail*, August 14, 2007, pp. B1, B4; David Wolf, "The Butterfly Market," *Canadian Business*, August 13/27, 2007, p. 15.

Concluding Case 20-2 Liam Vaughan, Elena Logutenkova, and Gavin Finch, "'Couldn't Come at Worse time for UBS'; Trader's Arrest May Revive Calls for Greater Risk Controls," *National Post*, September 17, 2011, FP3; "Insurer Seeks to Nullify Jackson Concert Cancellation Policy," *Winnipeg Free Press*, June 8, 2011, D2; Erik Holm and Serena NG, "Insurers Face Claims as Supply Chains Break," *The Wall Street Journal*, March 17, 2011, C3; Tara Perkins, "Insurance Industry Braces for Another Expensive Hit," *The Globe and Mail*,

March 12, 2011, p. B6; Erik Holm, "Jolie Takes Risk on 'Salt,'" *The Wall Street Journal*, February 12–13, 2011, p. B16; Grant Robinson and Tara Perkins, "What Your Broker Doesn't Want you to Know," *The Globe and Mail*, December 22, 2010, p. B4; Tara Perkins, "Former Trader Pleads Guilty in Fraud that Cost BMO $850 Million," *The Globe and Mail*, November 19, 2008, p. B1; Boyd Erman and Derek DeCloet, "The Guys Who Had a Gut Feeling for Risk," *The Globe and Mail*, February 23, 2008, pp. B4–B6; "Defiant Kerviel Refuses to Play 'Scapegoat,'" *The Globe and Mail*, February 6, 2008, p. B12; Paul Waldie, "Kerviel Made Millions from Mortgage Meltdown," *The Globe and Mail*, January 31, 2008, pp. 1, B13; Eric Reguly, "Exchange Says it Questioned Kerviel's Actions," *The Globe and Mail*, January 29, 2008, p. B7; Harris Anwar, "Chief Risk Officer: A Valuable Addition to the C-Suite," *The Globe and Mail*, June 20, 2005, p. B13; Oliver Bertin, "Sector Hit Hard by Sharp Increases in Premiums," *The Globe and Mail*, April 27, 2004, p. B14; Oliver Bertin, "Firms Face Major Hurdles En Route to U.S. Markets," *The Globe and Mail*, April 29, 2004, p. B16; Leslie Scism, "If Disaster Strikes this 'Titanic,' Chubb Could Lose Millions," *The Wall Street Journal*, April 9, 1997, p. A1; Leslie Scism, "Maybe Julie Andrews Could Offer Insurers a Spoonful of Sugar," *The Wall Street Journal*, April 4, 1997, p. A1; Patrick Reilly, "Insurers Are Downbeat on RAP Concert Tours," *The Wall Street Journal*, March 26, 1997, p. B1.

Image Credits

Part One

Name and Organization Index